D0208230

Argentina

Salta & the
Andean Northwest
p218

Iguazú Falls &
the Northeast
p150

Córdoba &
the Central
Sierras
p285

Mendoza &
the Central Andes
p318

Uruguay
p517

Buenos Aires p52

The Pampas &
the Atlantic Coast
p115

Bariloche &
the Lake District
p356

Patagonia
p400

Tierra del Fuego
p492

THIS EDITION WRITTEN AND RESEARCHED BY

Sandra Bao,
Gregor Clark, Bridget Gleeson, Carolyn McCarthy,
Andy Symington, Lucas Vidgen

PLAN YOUR TRIP

ON THE ROAD

SAN ANTONIO DE ARECO
P123

FARO JOSÉ IGNACIO P560

Contents

LA BOCA, BUENOS AIRES
P64

SAN TELMO,
BUENOS AIRES P63

SAN MARTÍN DE LOS
ANDES P378

Contents

Welcome to Argentina

It's apparent why Argentina has long held travelers in awe: tango, beef, gauchos, fútbol, Patagonia, the Andes. The classics alone make a formidable wanderlust cocktail.

City Life

Arriving in Buenos Aires is like jumping aboard a moving train. Outside the taxi window, a blurred mosaic of a modern metropolis whizzes by, and then the street life appears – the cafes, the purple jacaranda flowers draped over the sidewalks (in spring), and *porteños* (residents of Buenos Aires) in stylish clothing, walking purposefully past handsome early-20th-century stone facades. And it's not just Buenos Aires that's a stunner – Córdoba, Salta, Mendoza and Bariloche each have their unique personalities and unforgettable attractions.

Natural Wonders

From mighty Iguazú Falls in the subtropical north to the thunderous, crackling advance of Glaciar Perito Moreno in the south, Argentina is a vast natural wonderland. The country boasts rich wetlands, mountains painted in rustic colors – including some of the Andes' highest peaks, deserts dotted with cacti, massive ice fields and arid steppes, cool lichen-clad Valdivian forests, Andean salt flats and a spectacular Lake District. It also offers an abundance of wildlife, including penguins, flamingos, capybaras and more. All are stunning sights and adventures just waiting to be experienced.

Food & Drink

Satisfying that carnal craving for juicy steaks isn't hard to do in the land that has perfected grilling wonderfully flavorful sides of beef. *Parrillas* (steak restaurants) are everywhere and will offer up any cut you can imagine. And if you're a fan of pizza and pasta, these Italian staples are ubiquitous as well. But there's more – in Buenos Aires you can experience a huge variety of ethnic cuisine, from Southeast Asian and Middle Eastern to Scandinavian. Down it all with that famous Argentine wine, and you'll be struggling to maintain your waistline.

Argentine Culture

Tango is possibly Argentina's greatest contribution to the outside world, a steamy dance that's been described as 'making love in the vertical position.' And what about *fútbol* (soccer)? Argentines are passionately devoted to this sport and, if you're a fan, experiencing a live match should definitely be on your itinerary. Add a distinctive Argentine take on literature, cinema, music and arts, and you have a rich, edgy culture – part Latin American and part European – that you can't help but fall in love with.

Why I Love Argentina

By Sandra Bao, Writer

Argentina is my country – this is where I was born and raised, where I lived until my family emigrated to the USA. It's changed drastically since I was a little girl, but what I love most about Argentina is its people. They've nurtured their creativity, adaptability and perseverance, through good and very bad times, all while maintaining their traditions, humor and pride. I'm always happy to go back to this amazing place and its inhabitants – it's been a real privilege.

For more about our writers, see page 639

Above: Tango dancers, El Caminito (p65), Buenos Aires

Argentina & Uruguay

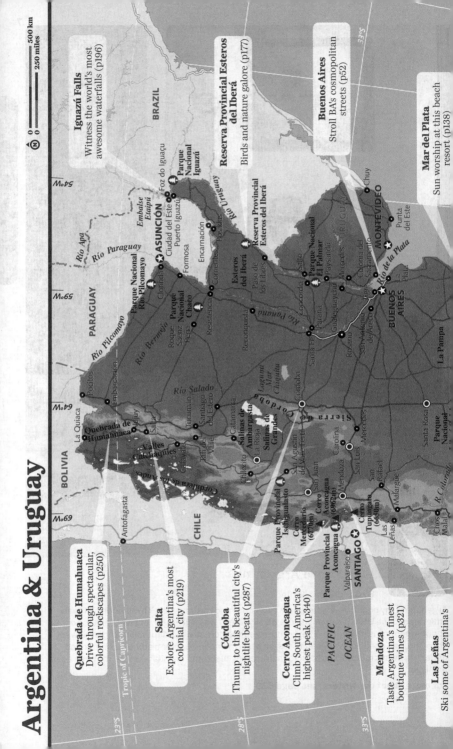

Iguazú Falls
Witness the world's most awesome waterfalls (p196)

Reserva Provincial Esteros del Iberá
Birds and nature galore (p177)

Buenos Aires
Stroll BA's cosmopolitan streets (p52)

Mar del Plata
Sun worship at this beach resort (p138)

Quebrada de Humahuaca
Drive through spectacular, colorful rockscapes (p250)

Salta
Explore Argentina's most colonial city (p219)

Córdoba
Thump to this beautiful city's nightlife beats (p287)

Cerro Aconcagua
Climb South America's highest peak (p340)

Mendoza
Taste Argentina's finest boutique wines (p321)

Las Leñas
Ski some of Argentina's

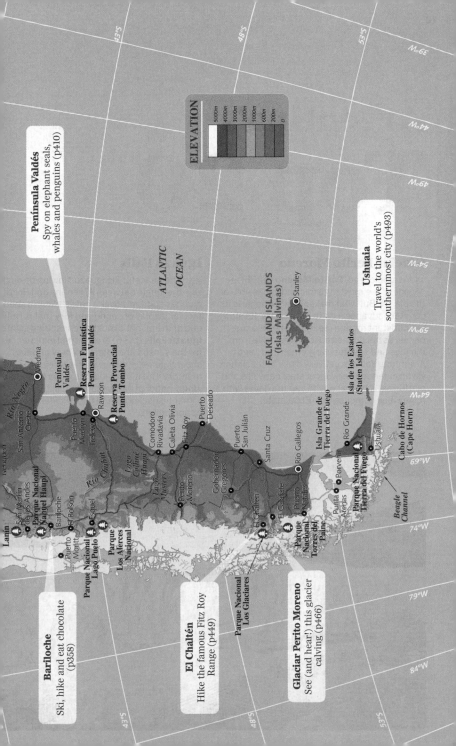

Bariloche
Ski, hike and eat chocolate (p358)

Península Valdés
Spy on elephant seals, whales and penguins (p410)

Ushuaia
Travel to the world's southernmost city (p493)

El Chaltén
Hike the famous Fitz Roy Range (p449)

Glaciar Perito Moreno
See (and hear!) this glacier calving (p466)

ELEVATION

	5000m
	4000m
	3000m
	2000m
	1000m
	600m
	200m
	0

ATLANTIC
OCEAN

FALKLAND ISLANDS
(Islas Malvinas)

Stanley

Reserva Faunística
Península Valdés

Península
Valdés

Reserva Provincial
Punta Tombo

Viedma

San Antonio
Oeste

Río Negro

Lanín

San Martín
de los Andes

Parque Nacional
Nahuel Huapi

Bariloche

El Bolsón

Esquel

Puerto
Montt

Parque Nacional
Lago Puelo

Parque
Los Alerces
Nacional

Rawson

Trelew

Puerto
Madryn

Río Chubut

Lago
Colhué
Huapí

Lago
Musters

Comodoro
Rivadavia

Caleta Olivia

Fitz Roy

Puerto
Deseado

Perito
Moreno

Gobernador
Gregores

Puerto
San Julián

Santa Cruz

Río Gallegos

El Chaltén

Parque Nacional
Los Glaciares

El Calafate

Puerto
Natales

Parque
Nacional
Torres del
Paine

Punta
Arenas

Porvenir

Isla Grande de
Tierra del Fuego

Río Grande

Parque Nacional
Tierra del Fuego

Ushuaia

Isla de los Estados
(Staten Island)

Cabo de Hornos
(Cape Horn)

Beagle
Channel

ATLANTIC
OCEAN

Argentina's
Top 20

Glaciar Perito Moreno

1 As glaciers go, **Perito Moreno** (p466) is one of the most dynamic and accessible on the planet. But what makes it exceptional is its constant advance – up to 2m per day. Its slow but constant motion creates incredible suspense, as building-sized icebergs calve from the face and spectacularly crash into Lago Argentino. You can get very close to the action via an extended network of steel catwalks and platforms. A typical way to cap the day is with a huge steak dinner back in El Calafate.

Iguazú Falls

2 The peaceful Río Iguazú, flowing through the jungle between Argentina and Brazil, plunges suddenly over a basalt cliff in a spectacular display of sound and fury that is truly one of the planet's most awe-inspiring sights. **Iguazú Falls** (p196) are a primal experience for the senses: the roar, the spray and the sheer volume of water will live forever in your memory. But it's not just the waterfalls – the jungly national parks that contain them offer romantic backdrop and fine wildlife-watching opportunities.

Wine Tasting around Mendoza

3 With so much fantastic **wine** (p328) on offer, it's tempting just to pull up a bar stool and work your way through a list – but getting out there and seeing how the grapes are grown and processed is almost as enjoyable as sampling the finished product. The best news is that wine tasting in Argentina isn't just for the wine snobs – there's a tour to meet every budget, from DIY bike tours for backpackers to tasting-and-accommodation packages at exclusive wineries.

Buenos Aires' Food Scene

4 Believe the hype: Argentine beef is some of the best in the world. Eat, drink and be merry at one of the country's thousands of *parrillas* (steak restaurants), where a leisurely meal can include waiters pouring malbec and serving up slabs of tasty steaks. But there's so much more in Buenos Aires (p86) – closed-door restaurants, pop-up restaurants and molecular gastronomy have all become buzzwords in Argentina's capital city, where you can also find nearly any kind of exotic ethnic cuisine. Above: A *parrillada* (mixed grill)

Cementerio de la Recoleta

5 A veritable city of the dead, Buenos Aires' top tourist attraction (p69) is not to be missed. Lined up along small streets' are hundreds of old crypts, each uniquely carved from marble, granite and concrete, and decorated with stained glass, stone angels and religious icons. Small plants and trees grow in fissures, while feral cats slink between tombs, some of which lie in various stages of decay. It's a photogenic wonderland, and if there's strange beauty in death you'll find it in spades here.

Hiking the Fitz Roy Range

6 With rugged wilderness and shark-tooth summits, **the Fitz Roy Range** (p455) is the trekking capital of Argentina. Experienced mountain climbers may suffer on its windswept and tough, world-class routes, but the beautiful hiking trails are surprisingly easy and accessible, and park rangers help orient every traveler who comes into the area. Once on the trail, the most stunning views are just a day hike from town. Not bad for those who want to reward themselves with a craft beer at El Chaltén's nearby La Cervecería brewpub.

Ruta de los Siete Lagos

7 A journey of extraordinary beauty, the **Ruta de los Siete Lagos** (Seven Lakes Route; p383) is a not-to-be-missed road trip. Your vehicular adventure winds through lush forests, past waterfalls and dramatic mountain scenery, and skirts the various crystal-blue lakes that give it its name. Stop for a picnic and go swimming, fishing and camping. You can also bus it in a couple of hours or bike it in a few days. Experiencing this gorgeous route is a decision you won't regret.

Below: Villa la Angostura (p375), on the shore of Lago Nahuel Huapi

Ushuaia, the End of the Earth

8 Shimmed between the Beagle Channel and the snow-capped Martial Range, this bustling port is the final scrap of civilization seen by Antarctica-bound boats. But more than the end of the earth, **Ushuaia** (p493) is a crossroads for big commerce and adventure. Snow sports brighten the frozen winters and long summer days mean hiking and biking until the wee hours. Happening restaurants, boisterous bars and welcoming B&Bs mean you'll want to tuck in and call this port home for a few days.

CHRISTIAN ASLUND / GETTY IMAGES ©

VERONICA GARBUTT / GETTY IMAGES ©

Colonial Salta

9 Argentina's northwest holds its most venerable colonial settlements, and none is more lovely than **Salta** (p219). This beautiful city is set in a fertile valley that acts as a gateway to the impressive Andean cordillera not far beyond. Postcard-pretty churches, a sociable plaza and a wealth of noble buildings give it a laid-back historical ambience that endears it to all who visit. Add in great museums, a lively folkloric music scene, some of the country's most appealing lodging options and a fistful of attractions within easy reach: that's one impressive place.

Above: Iglesia San Francisco (p219)

Skiing at Las Leñas

10 Hitting the slopes at **Las Leñas** (p345) isn't just about making the scene, although there is that; this mountain has the most varied terrain, the most days of powder per year and some of the fastest and most modern lift equipment in the country. Splash out for some on-mountain accommodations or choose from a variety of more reasonably priced options just down the road. Whatever you do, if you're a snow bunny and you're here in season, mark this one on your itinerary in big red letters.

San Telmo

11 One of Buenos Aires' most charming and interesting neighborhoods is **San Telmo** (p63), lined with cobblestone streets, colonial buildings and a classic atmosphere that will transport you back to the mid-19th century. Be sure to take in the Sunday *feria* (street fair), where dozens of booths sell handicrafts, antiques and knickknacks, while buskers perform for loose change. Tango is big here, and you can watch a fancy, spectacular show or catch a casual street performance – both will wow you with amazing feats of athleticism.

Above: Feria de San Telmo (p108)

MARCOS RADICELLA / GETTY IMAGES ©

Bariloche

12 A gorgeous lakeside setting, adjacent to one of the country's more spectacular and accessible national parks, makes **Bariloche** (p358) a winning destination year-round. During winter you can strap on the skis and take in the magnificent panoramas from on top of Cerro Catedral. Once the snow melts, get your hiking boots out and hit the trails in the Parque Nacional Nahuel Huapi, where a well-organized network of mountain refuges means you can keep walking as long as your legs will take it.

Above left: Hotel Llao Llao (p368)

Nightlife in Córdoba

13 Boasting seven universities (and counting) it's no surprise that Argentina's **second city** (p287) is one of the best places for night owls in the entire country. The wide variety of cute sidewalk bars, thumping megadiscos and live-music venues (all more or less within walking distance) could keep you occupied for months. While you're in town, try to catch a *cuarteto* show – popular all over the country, this music style was invented in Córdoba and all the best acts regularly play here.

Gaucho Culture

14 One of Argentina's most enduring icons is the intrepid gaucho, who came to life after Spaniards let loose their cattle on the grassy pampas so many centuries ago. These nomadic cowboys lived by taming wild horses (also left by the Spaniards), hunting cows and drinking *mate* (a bitter ritual tea). Today the best place to experience gaucho culture is during November's Día de la Tradición (p28) in San Antonio de Areco. Otherwise, check out folkloric shows at *estancias* (ranches) or at the Feria de Mataderos in Buenos Aires. Above: Día de la Tradición San Antonio de Areco (p123)

uebrada de Humahuaca

15 You're a long way from Buenos Aires up here in Argentina's north-estern corner, and it feels a whole world way. This **spectacular valley** (p250) of coured rock in Jujuy province impresses sually with its tortured formations and tist's palette of mineral colors, but is also of great cultural interest. The uebrada's settlements are traditional nd indigenous in character, with typical ndean dishes supplanting steaks on the staurant menus, and llamas, not herds of attle, grazing the sparse highland grass. elow: Purmamarca (p251)

Reserva Faunística Península Valdés

16 Once a dusty peninsula with remote sheep ranches, today **Península Valdés** (p410) is a hub for some of the best wildlife-watching on the continent. The main attraction is seeing endangered southern right whales up close. But the cast of wild characters also includes killer whales (orcas), Magellanic penguins, sea lions, elephant seals, rheas, guanaco and numerous sea birds. There's a ton to be seen on shore, but diving and kayak tours take you even deeper into the ambience.

Bottom: Magellanic penguins, Península Valdés

15

16

CAROL POLICH PHOTO WORKSHOPS / GETTY IMAGES ©

Jesuit Missions

17 The Jesuits brought some fine things to Argentina – wine making and universities to name just two. They also constructed some gorgeous missions. Many are wonderfully preserved, listed as Unesco World Heritage sites and open to the public, often featuring fascinating museums. In appropriately named Misiones province, **San Ignacio Miní** (p192) is the most impressive of the mission ruins. Nearby Santa Ana and Loreto are also very atmospheric. And if you can't get enough, day trip to nearby Paraguay for further amazing remnants of this intriguing social project. Above: San Ignacio Miní

Reserva Provincial Esteros del Iberá

18 These protected **wetlands** (p177) offer astonishing wildlife-watching opportunities around shallow vegetation-rich lagoons. Head out in a boat and you'll spot numerous alligators, exotic bird species, monkeys, swamp deer, and one of the world's cutest rodents, the capybara – but no, you can't take one home. It's an out-of-the-way location, and a wealth of stylish, comfortable lodges make this a top spot to book yourself in for a few days of relaxation amid an abundance of flora and fauna. Above right: Capybara (p598)

Cerro Aconcagua

19 The tallest peak in the western hemisphere, **Cerro Aconcagu** (p339) is an awe-inspiring sight, even if you're not planning on climbing it. People come from all over the world to do so, though it's not a task to be taken lightly. If you can take the time to train and acclimatize, and you're good enough to reach the top, you'll be granted bragging rights as one of a select group who have touched the 'roof of the Americas.' Otherwise, just get a peek at it from the nearest vantage point and save your energy for wine tasting in Mendoza.

Mar del Plata

20 Argentina's premier **beach resort** (p138) is a heaving zoo in summer but that's what makes it such fun. Compete with *porteños* (Buenos Aires residents) for a patch of open sand, then lie back and enjoy watching thousands of near-naked bodies worship the sun, play sand games or splash around in the surf. Outdoor activities such as surfing, fishing, horseback riding and even skydiving are also on deck. When the sun goes down it's time for steak or seafood dinners, followed by late-night entertainment from theater to nightclubs. Right: Cabo Corrientes and Playa Varese (p142)

SILVINA PARMA / GETTY IMAGES ©

Need to Know

For more information, see Survival Guide (p601)

Currency
Argentine peso (AR$)

Language
Spanish

Visas
Generally not required for stays of up to 90 days. Americans, Australians and Canadians must pay a 'reciprocity fee' before arriving.

Money
ATMs widely available. Credit cards accepted at most midrange to top-end hotels, and at some restaurants and shops.

Cell Phones
Local SIM cards (and top-up credits) are cheap and widely available, and can be used on unlocked GSM 850-/1900-compatible phones.

Time
Argentina Standard Time (GMT/UTC minus three hours).

When to Go

Salta
GO Apr–Oct

Iguazú Falls
GO Year-round

Buenos Aires
GO Year-round

Bariloche
GO Year-round

Ushuaia
GO Oct–Mar

Desert, arid climate
Dry, arid climate
Warm to hot summers, mild winters
Warm to hot summers, cold winters
Cold, Polar climate

High Season (Nov–Feb)

➡ Patagonia is best (and most expensive) December to February.

➡ Crowds throng to the beaches from late December through January.

Shoulder (Sep–Nov & Mar–May)

➡ Temperature-wise the best times to visit Buenos Aires.

➡ The Lake District is pleasant; leaves are spectacular in March.

➡ The Mendoza region has its grape harvests and wine festival.

Low Season (Jun–Aug)

➡ Good time to visit the North.

➡ Many services close at beach resorts, and mountain passes can be blocked by snow.

➡ July is a winter vacation month, so things can get busy at ski destinations.

Useful Websites

Argentina Independent (www.argentinaindependent.com) Current affairs and culture, plus much more.

Buenos Aires Herald (www.buenosairesherald.com) An international view of the country.

Ruta 0 (www.ruta0.com) Handy driving tips, like distance/duration between cities, gas consumption, road conditions and tariffs.

Lonely Planet (lonelyplanet.com/argentina) Destination info, hotel bookings, forums and more.

Important Numbers

Argentina country code	☏54
Directory assistance	☏110
International access code	☏00
National Tourist Information (in BA)	☏11-4312-2232
Police	☏101; ☏911 in some large cities

Exchange Rates

Australia	A$1	AR$10.88
Brazil	R$1	AR$4.02
Canada	C$1	AR$11.11
Chile	CH$100	AR$2.11
Euro	€1	AR$16.48
Japan	¥100	AR$13.40
NZ	NZ$1	AR$9.82
UK	UK£1	AR$20.39
Uruguay	UR$1	AR$0.46
USA	US$1	AR$14.44

For current exchange rates see www.xe.com

Rates on the Rise

Lonely Planet aims to give its readers as precise an idea as possible of what things cost. Rather than slapping hotels or restaurants into vague budget categories, we publish the actual rates and prices that businesses quote to us during research. The problem is that Argentina's inflation has been running at near 30%. But we've found that readers prefer to have real numbers in their hands and do compensatory calculations themselves.

Argentina remains a decent-value destination, but don't expect our quoted prices to necessarily reflect your own experience. Our advice: call or check a few hotel or tour-operator websites before budgeting for your trip, just to make sure you're savvy about current rates.

Daily Costs

Budget: Less than US$60

➡ Dorm bed: US$15–20

➡ Double room in good, budget hotel: US$50

➡ Cheap meal: less than US$11

Midrange: US$60–120

➡ Three-star hotel: US$80–150

➡ Average main dish: US$11–16

➡ Four-hour bus ticket: US$30

Top End: More than US$120

➡ Five-star hotel: US$150+

➡ Fine main dish: over US$16

➡ Taxi trip across town: US$10

Opening Hours

There are always exceptions, but the following are general opening hours. Note that some towns may take an afternoon siesta break.

Banks 8am–3pm or 4pm Monday to Friday; some open to 1pm Saturday

Bars 8pm or 9pm–4am or 6am nightly (downtown, some open and close earlier)

Cafes 6am–midnight or much later; open daily

Restaurants noon–3:30pm or 8pm–midnight or 1am (later on weekends)

Shops 9am or 10am–8pm or 9pm Monday to Saturday

Arriving in Argentina

Aeropuerto Internacional Ministro Pistarini ('Ezeiza'; Buenos Aires) Shuttle buses travel frequently to downtown BA in 40 to 60 minutes; local buses take two hours. Use official taxi services only; avoid touts.

Aeroparque Jorge Newbery ('Aeroparque', airport with mostly domestic flights; Buenos Aires) Shuttle buses travel frequently to downtown BA in 10 to 15 minutes; or take local bus 33 or 45. Taxis available.

Getting Around

Air Argentina is a huge country, so flights are good for saving time. Delays do happen occasionally.

Bus Generally the best way to get around Argentina; they're fast, frequent, comfortable, reasonably priced and cover the country extensively.

Car Renting a car is useful (but expensive) for those who want the most travel independence in remote regions such as Patagonia.

Train A few train lines can be useful for travelers, but generally this is not the most efficient method of transportation.

For much more on **getting around**, see p616

What's New

Centro Cultural Kirchner

Buenos Aires' newest cultural center is likely South America's biggest, boasting dozens of exhibition halls, event spaces, museums and auditoriums. (p57)

Espacio Memoria y Derechos Humanos

More popularly known as ESMA, this ex-naval campus played a key role during Argentina's Dirty War – it was once a large detainment and torture center, now converted into a memorial museum to help prevent such unimaginable occurrences from happening again. (p74)

Buenos Aires' Speakeasies

This bar trend is picking up speed in Argentina's capital – gorgeous, atmospheric and 'secret' bars that often require a special code to get in.

Burgers, Beer and Coffee

Small hamburger joints are a Buenos Aries mania, popping up in various neighborhoods and offering a few gourmet varieties of the popular American treat. Microbrew bars and modern, house-roastery coffee shops are another developing craze.

El Pedral

This new private nature reserve on a coastal *estancia* outside Puerto Madryn highlights Magellanic penguins, which are flocking here and offering a great wildlife experience for travelers. (p409)

Piattelli

A major project just outside Cafayate, this beautiful new winery is a state-of-the-art boutique affair with good tasting sessions and an excellent restaurant, offering lunch with picturesque vistas. (p240)

Salta's Paseo de la Familia

An enjoyable local eating scene can be found on this block of Catamarca, between San Luis and La Rioja. Street-food stalls dole out grilled chicken, pizza, tamales and *lomitos* (steak sandwiches) under a long awning, from breakfast to mid-afternoon.

El Shincal

These excellent Inca ruins, northwest of Catamarca, have been given a major facelift and now include a good introductory museum. (p276)

Hiking in Cachi

A new hike through private lands, southwest of Salta, is now offered by Urkupiña, and encompasses a scenic descent through the Valle Encantado and Cuesta del Obispo – with guaranteed condor-spotting. (p234)

Reintroductions of Wildlife, Esteros del Iberá

The late ecological philanthropist Doug Tompkins and his wife Kristine successfully reintroduced the giant anteater to the Esteros del Iberá area; current projects involve saving pampa deer, collared peccary, macaws and even jaguar. (p177)

Paseo Superior, Iguazú Falls

This walkway extension in Parque Nacional Iguazú leads along the top of the waterfalls on the Argentine side, offering up-close views of one of park's the biggest cascades, Salto San Martín. (p203)

For more recommendations and reviews, see lonelyplanet.com/argentina

If You Like...

Cities

Gourmet restaurants, world-class museums, fine shopping, cutting-edge music and rocking nightlife all contribute toward satisfying your needed dose of big-city culture.

Buenos Aires The mother of all Argentine cities. Plan to spend several days exploring the world-class offerings of this unique and astounding metropolis. (p52)

Córdoba From Jesuit ruins to art to *cuarteto* music (Córdoba's claim to fame), you'll experience it all in this historic city. (p287)

Salta Argentina's most colonial city offers plenty of culture, from exceptional museums to famous *peñas* (folk music clubs) where you can experience authentic folk music. (p219)

Bariloche Ski, hike or go whitewater rafting during the day, then munch on chocolate and Patagonian lamb at night. (p358)

Ushuaia The world's southernmost city, stunningly located, is one to mark off your destination list. (p493)

Beaches

Ah, those waves lapping on the shore, salty wind on your face and warm sand between your toes. What says 'vacation' more than a day at the beach? Whether you're looking for a party, adventure sports or isolation, Argentina has it.

Mar del Plata Popular with Argentina's middle class, 'Mardel' turns into the country's biggest summertime party. (p138)

Necochea Miles of beachcombing, decent surf breakers and even a pine forest to explore. (p146)

Pinamar Very popular destination with variety nearby, from affordable neighborhoods to one of Argentina's most exclusive beach resorts, Cariló. (p135)

Puerto Madryn Whether you like windsurfing, whale watching or diving, Puerto Madryn caters to your desires. (p401)

Punta del Este Sure, it's in Uruguay, but in summer this famous beach is full of wealthy Argentines, along with celebrities and models here to party. (p553)

Hiking & Mountaineering

Lining Argentina's western edge like a bumpy spine, the Andes rise to nearly 7000m at Aconcagua's peak and offer some of the continent's finest hiking and mountaineering.

Bariloche Set on the shores of Lago Nahuel Huapi, Bariloche is surrounded by snowy peaks that beckon climbers. (p358)

El Bolsón Drawing in hippies like patchouli, this laid-back town offers nearby hikes to forests, waterfalls and scenic ridges. (p371)

El Chaltén Argentina's ground zero for premier hiking, boasting gorgeous glaciers, pristine lakes and unparalleled mountain landscapes. (p449)

Mendoza Mountaineers flock here to summit Cerro Aconcagua, South America's highest peak. (p320)

Parque Nacional Torres del Paine This stupendous national park is in Chile, but very close to the Argentine border, and offers some of the world's best hiking. (p483)

Food

Argentina is known for its steak, but in Buenos Aires ethnic restaurants abound, and around the country there are tasty regional cuisines on offer.

Buenos Aires The mother of all Argentine cities. Plan to spend several days exploring the world-class offerings of this unique and astounding metropolis. (p86)

Andean Northwest If you make it up north, be sure to try *locro* (a spicy stew of maize, beans, beef, pork and sausage), *humitas* (sweet tamales) and empanadas. (p218)

Atlantic Coast Despite a huge coastline, Argentina isn't known for its seafood. If you're near the sea, however, there are places to sample fish, shrimp, oysters and king crab. (p115)

Lake District The area around Bariloche is known for its wild boar, venison and trout, plus locally made chocolates. (p356)

Patagonia If you like lamb, you'll be in heaven in Patagonia. Here, *cordero* is on every menu and sheep ranches reign supreme. (p400)

Memorable Landscapes

Argentina is made up of amazing landscapes, from cactus-filled deserts and lofty Andean peaks to deep-blue lakes and verdant forests. Throw in the wonders of Iguazú Falls and Patagonia, and the word 'unforgettable' comes to mind.

Andean Northwest Undulating desert landscapes are punctuated by sentinel-like cacti, alien rock formations and whole mountainsides sporting palettes of colors. (p218)

Iguazú Falls Spanning more than 2.5km, these are the most incredible waterfalls you will ever see. (p196)

Lake District Argentina's 'little Switzerland' is just that – snowdusted mountains looming over lakes edged by forest. (p356)

Andes Mountains Strung along the whole of South America, this spectacular mountain range is stunningly beautiful. (p339)

Top: *Locro* (corn and meat stew), tamales and empanadas
Bottom: Hiking in view of El Chaltén (p449), Patagonia

Patagonia Not many regions in the world can evoke the mysticism, wonderment and yearning of Argentina's last frontier – even if most of it is barren, windy nothingness. (p400)

Wildlife

Argentina's environments translate into homes for many creatures, including flightless, grasslands-loving ñandú (rheas); majestic Andean condors and pumas; and desert-dwelling camelids such as llamas, guanacos and vicuñas.

Península Valdés This bleak, oddly shaped peninsula attracts a plethora of wildlife, such as southern right whales, elephant seals, Magellanic penguins and orcas. (p410)

Reserva Provincial Esteros del Iberá Rich and amazing wetlands that harbor a wide range of interesting critters, from comical capybaras, black caimans and howler monkeys, to countless bird species. (p177)

Iguazú Falls These spectacular falls are located in tropical rainforest that is also home to several kinds of monkey, lizard and bird (including toucans). Also watch for coatis. (p196)

Ushuaia The southernmost city in the world has a few colonies of cormorants, sea lions and even penguins. It's also the stepping-off point to Antarctica, a fantastic wildlife wonderland. (p493)

Wine Tasting

Malbec is the dark, robust, plum-flavored wine that has solidly stamped the region of Mendoza on every oenophile's map. But Argentina has other worthy varietals: try a fresh torrontés, fruity bonarda or earthy pinot noir.

Mendoza Argentina's powerhouse wine region; produces the majority of the country's grapes and boasts countless wineries. (p321)

San Juan Much less famous than its Mendoza neighbor, but well known for its syrah and bonarda; it also boasts a winery located in a cave. (p347)

Cafayate Just south of Salta, this lovely town – second only to Mendoza for its quality wine production – is famed for the torrontés grape, among others. (p238)

Neuquén You don't think of wine when you think of this unremarkable city in the Lake District, but there are a few great wineries nearby. (p396)

Colonial Architecture

While Argentina isn't world-renowned for its unique buildings, its status as an ex-Spanish colony means there are some fine examples of colonial architecture to be found, especially to the north.

Córdoba Argentina's second-largest city boasts a beautiful center dotted with dozens of colonial buildings. (p287)

Salta Don't miss this city's most striking landmark, the colorful and intricate Iglesia San Francisco. (p219)

Buenos Aires It's mostly French- or Italian-styled buildings downtown, but head south to San Telmo for colonial buildings and cobblestone streets. (p52)

Colonia del Sacramento An easy boat ride away from BA lies Uruguay's architectural gem of a town, popularly called 'Colonia.' (p537)

Humahuaca Nestled in the Quebrada de Humahuaca valley, this picturesque town is the perfect base for exploring the region's other wonders. (p258)

Adventure Sports

The eighth-largest country in the world, Argentina covers a lot of ground and offers plenty of adventurous sports. Wild rivers, bare cliffs, snowy mountains and high thermals abound, so if you're looking for some adrenaline, you've found it.

Skiing and snowboarding The best ski resorts are Mendoza's Las Leñas & Los Penitentes, Bariloche's Cerro Catedral and San Martín de los Andes' Cerro Chapelco. (p36)

Rafting and kayaking Hit the pristine white waters rushing through the mountains around Mendoza, Bariloche and Esquel. (p38)

Mountain biking The mountains around Bariloche are great for adventurous trails, especially at Cerro Catedral in summer. (p38)

Rock climbing Try Cerro Catedral, the rocky walls around El Chaltén and the granite boulders of Los Gigantes, 80km west of Córdoba. Mendoza province also has some hot spots. (p35)

Paragliding Some of the loftiest spots are around La Cumbre, Bariloche and Tucumán. (p38)

Month by Month

January

January is peak summer in Argentina. *Porteños* (residents of Buenos Aires) who can afford it leave their sweltering city and head to the beach resorts, which are very crowded and expensive. It's also high season in Patagonia, so expect top prices there, too.

☆ Festival Nacional del Folklore

Near the city of Córdoba, the town of Cosquín hosts the National Festival of Folk Music during the last week of January. It's the country's largest and best known *folklórico* (folk music) festival. (p299)

🎊 Dakar Rally

Previously called the Paris–Dakar Rally, this 9000km all-terrain race (www.dakar.com) has now been run in South America since 2009. Both amateurs and professional racers complete in this endurance classic.

February

It's still summertime, but crowds at the beaches and in Patagonia start to thin later in the month. The Andean deserts and the Iguazú region continue to be very hot, but it's a great time to visit the Lake District. Mendoza's grape harvest begins.

🎊 Carnaval

Though not as rockin' as it is in Brazil, the celebration is very rowdy in the northeast, especially in Gualeguaychú (p183) and Corrientes (p173). Montevideo, the capital of Uruguay (p534), is another party spot. Dates vary depending on the city.

☆ Fiesta Nacional del Lúpulo

El Bolsón's hop festival honors the key ingredient for its artisanal craft beers. Expect musical performances, activities, food and plenty of beer tasting (of course). (p42)

March

Autumn is starting in Argentina and temperatures are more pleasant in Buenos Aires (though it's rainy). Prices fall at the beaches and in Patagonia, but the weather remains warm. The north starts to cool, and Iguazú Falls isn't quite so hot and humid.

🍷 Fiesta Nacional de la Vendimia

Mendoza city's week-long Fiesta Nacional de la Vendimia kicks off with parades, *folklórico* events and a royal coronation – all in honor of Mendoza's wines. (p325)

DÍA DE LA MEMORIA

Held on March 24 (the date a military coup took over the Argentine government in 1976), this public holiday commemorates the victims of Argentina's Dirty War. Over seven years, tens of thousands of people 'disappeared' and were never heard from again.

Top: Tango dancers, Festival y Mundial de Tango (p28)
Bottom: Fiesta Nacional de la Cerveza (Oktoberfest; p28)

April

The forests of the Lake District start changing from verdant green to fiery reds, yellows and oranges. Patagonia is clearing out but you might get lucky with decent hiking weather. Buenos Aires heads into low season, with still-pleasant temperatures.

✖ Festival Nacional del Chocolate

Happening during Easter week (dates vary annually), Bariloche's chocolate festival often highlights a 9m tall chocolate egg, cracked and consumed on Easter Sunday. Look for the world's longest chocolate bar, too.

☆ Festival Internacional de Cine Independiente

Independent film buffs shouldn't miss this festival in Buenos Aires, which screens more than 100 films from Argentina and Uruguay. (p76)

May

It's late autumn and Buenos Aires is cool as the rains die back. It's a good time to visit Iguazú Falls. The crowds also leave Mendoza, though vineyards are still a gorgeous red from autumn leaves.

✖ Día de Virgen de Luján

On May 8 thousands of devout believers make a 65km pilgrimage to the pampas town of Luján in honor of the Virgin Mary. Other pilgrimages take place in early October, early August, late September and on December 8.

June

Winter begins in Argentina. Services at the beach resorts and in Patagonia dwindle, but it's an ideal time to visit the deserts of the Andean Northwest and Iguazú Falls, which have less rain and heat at this time of year.

⭐ Fiesta de la Noche Más Larga

Ushuaia celebrates the longest night of the year with about 10 days' worth of music and shows. (p500)

⭐ Anniversary of Carlos Gardel's Death

On June 24, 1935, tango legend Carlos Gardel died in a plane crash in Colombia. Head to Buenos Aires' Chacarita cemetery to see fans pay their respects at his grave and statue.

July

Ski season is at its peak, so make sure your wallet is packed full and head off to the resorts around Bariloche, San Martín de los Andes and Mendoza. Whale watching season starts heating up in the Península Valdés area.

⭐ Día de la Independencia

Argentina's Independence Day is July 9, and celebrations are especially strong in Tucumán, where the country's independence was first declared.

August

Beach resort towns are dead and Patagonia is desolate and cold. Buenos Aires is still cool, but it's a great time to explore the theaters, museums and art galleries.

⭐ Festival y Mundial de Tango

World-class national and international tango dancers perform throughout Buenos Aires during this two-week festival. It's a great way to see some of the country's best tango dancers and musicians do their thing. (p76)

September

Spring has sprung, and it's peak season for whale watching (both southern right whales and orcas) around Península Valdés. Polo season begins in Buenos Aires and the ski slopes wind down.

🍷 Vinos y Bodegas

Lovers of the grape shouldn't miss this huge Buenos Aires event, which highlights vintages from bodegas (wineries) all over Argentina. (p76)

October

It's a fine time to visit Buenos Aires and central Argentina. The season is just starting in Patagonia, but the crowds haven't quite descended. Flowers are blooming in the Lake District.

🍺 Fiesta Nacional de la Cerveza/ Oktoberfest

Join the swillers and oompah bands at Argentina's national beer festival, Villa General Belgrano's Oktoberfest in the Central Sierras. (p308)

November

In Buenos Aires the weather is perfect and the jacaranda trees show off their gorgeous purple blooms. It's a good time to visit the beach resorts and Patagonia, since the crowds and high prices are still a month or so away.

⭐ Día de la Tradición

This festival salutes the gaucho and is especially significant in San Antonio de Areco (p123), the most classically gaucho of towns. However, it is also important (and much less touristy) in the mountain town of San José de Jáchal (p353).

December

Summer begins and it's excellent beach weather at the resorts (just before the January peak). It's also ideal weather for outdoor activities in the Lake District, and penguin and hiking seasons start in Patagonia.

☆ Buenos Aires Jazz

This big jazz festival takes place over five days in venues all over the city in either November or December, attracting tens of thousands of spectators.

Itineraries

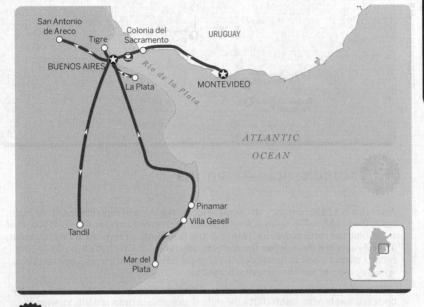

San Antonio de Areco
Tigre
Colonia del Sacramento
URUGUAY
BUENOS AIRES
La Plata
Río de la Plata
MONTEVIDEO
ATLANTIC
OCEAN
Pinamar
Villa Gesell
Tandil
Mar del Plata

1 WEEK A Week Around Buenos Aires

Seen Buenos Aires from top to bottom and wondering where else to visit? There's plenty of choice just outside Argentina's capital, from small and alluring cobblestoned towns to bigger, more exciting cities and bustling soft-sand beach resorts.

Tigre, with its hidden waterways and busy delta, is a popular *porteño* getaway for a day or two. Take a day-trip to peaceful **San Antonio de Areco**, which has a history of gaucho culture, or tidy **La Plata**, with its huge cathedral.

Perhaps you'd prefer a weekend at the beach? **Pinamar** and **Villa Gesell** make great summer escapes, as does **Mar del Plata**, the biggest Argentine beach destination of them all. Or head inland to **Tandil** for a couple of days; it's a pretty town near scenic hills and a large recreational reservoir.

And then there's Uruguay, just a (relatively) short boat ride away. **Colonia del Sacramento** is truly charming; filled with cobbled streets and atmospheric colonial buildings it makes a great day trip. Or stay overnight in **Montevideo**; kind of like BA's little sister, it's smaller and less frantic, but offers big-city delights such as a beautiful theater, an historic downtown and eclectic architecture.

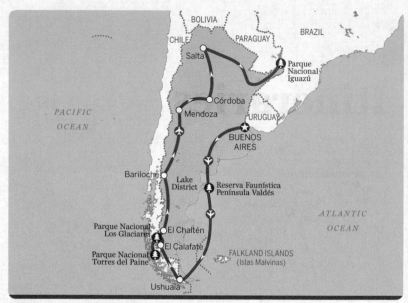

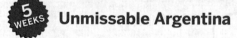

5 WEEKS Unmissable Argentina

Argentina is a huge country – the world's eighth largest – and experiencing all its highlights thoroughly will require at least a month, plus several airplane flights. If you want to see both the north and south, plan your trip accordingly: Patagonia is best in January and February, but this is when the northern deserts are at their hottest, so doing both regions might be best in spring or fall. Tailor the following destinations to your tastes, spending more or less time where you want to.

Take a few days to explore the wonders of **Buenos Aires**, with its fascinating neighborhoods and big-city sights. If it's the right season, fly south for wildlife viewing at **Reserva Faunística Península Valdés**; the whales, elephant seals and penguins here are especially popular. From here hop another flight to **Ushuaia**, the southernmost city in the world and a prime jumping-off point to Antarctica (add another two weeks and *minimum* US$5000 for this trip!).

Now you'll head north to **El Calafate**, where the stunning Glaciar Perito Moreno of **Parque Nacional Los Glaciares** is one of the world's most spectacular sights. If you love the outdoors, cross the border to Chile's **Parque Nacional Torres del Paine**, an awe-inspiring cluster of mountains boasting some of the earth's most beautiful landscapes. Back in Argentina, next stop **El Chaltén** is another world-class climbing, trekking and camping destination.

Further up the Andes is Argentina's Lake District, where a chocolate stop in **Bariloche** is a must. Gorgeous scenery, outdoor activities and lovely nearby towns can easily add days to your itinerary. Your next destination is **Mendoza**, Argentina's wine mecca, which also offers great outdoor adventures and mind-blowing Andean scenery. A 10-hour bus ride lands you in **Córdoba**, the country's second-largest city, with amazing colonial architecture and cutting-edge culture. From here go north to pretty **Salta**, where you can explore colorful canyons, charming villages and desert panoramas.

Pack your bags again and head east to **Parque Nacional Iguazú**, where the world's most massive falls will astound you. Fly back to BA and party till your plane leaves.

Top: Catedral de la Plata (p118)

Bottom: Ruta 40 (p438)

KAVRAM / SHUTTERSTOCK ©

30 DAYS Ruta Nacional 40

Argentina's quintessential road trip, RN 40 travels the length of the country. To do this adventure independently you'll need to rent a vehicle, ideally a 4WD as some sections are still unpaved.

Start near the amazingly colorful mountainsides of **Quebrada de Humahuaca** before hitting **Salta** and the wildly scenic villages of Valles Calchaquíes. Pause at lovely **Cafayate** and spectacularly located **Chilecito** before the long trip down to **Mendoza** to suss out the wine scene.

Continue south, stopping to check out the lagoons and hot springs around **Chos Malal**. Explore the lovely national parks of **Lanín** and **Nahuel Huapi** before hitting **San Martín de los Andes** and **Bariloche**, both of which offer fantastic outdoor opportunities. Further on, sidetrack to **Cueva de las Manos** for indigenous art.

Stop at **El Chaltén** for top-drawer hiking, then experience the **Glaciar Perito Moreno**. Cross the border to Chile and explore stunning **Parque Nacional Torres del Paine** before your last stop, **Ushuaia**; it's as far south as any highway in the world goes.

18 DAYS Patagonian Passage

Jaw-dropping Andean peaks, adorable mountain villages and exotic coastal wildlife – you'll hit them all on this spectacular Patagonian adventure.

Begin in **Ushuaia**, where you can hop on a boat to cruise around the Beagle Channel and hopefully see some penguins. Nearby **Parque Nacional Tierra del Fuego** offers a few end-of-the-world hikes (literally).

Now fly to **El Calafate** and lay your eyes on the spectacular and unforgettable **Glaciar Perito Moreno**. Outdoors lovers will want to cross the border and trek in Chile's famous **Parque Nacional Torres del Paine**. Head north again to **El Chaltén** for world-class hiking and camping.

Fly to **Bariloche**, where you can hike (or fish, or raft or bike) for days on end in the gorgeous national parks of **Nahuel Huapi** and **Lanín**. If you have an extra day or two, take a day trip to the hippie enclave of **El Bolsón** or the cute village of **Villa Traful**.

Finally, stop in **Puerto Madryn** to see the whales, elephant seals and penguins at **Reserva Faunística Península Valdés** – just make sure it's the right season.

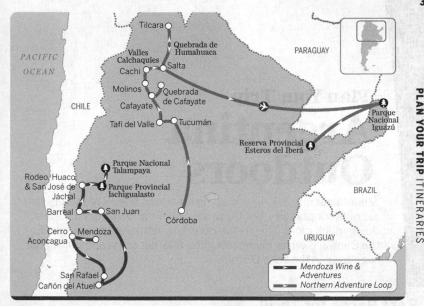

Mendoza Wine & Adventures
2 WEEKS

Uncork your trip in beautiful **Mendoza**, located on the flanks of the Andes. Not only are there world-class vineyards surrounding the city, but outdoor enthusiasts will be in heaven. White-water rafting and skiing are awesome in the area, and **Cerro Aconcagua** (the western hemisphere's highest peak) isn't too far away.

Now take a crack-of-dawn bus to **San Rafael**, where you can rent a bike and ride out to the city's wineries, some of which specialize in sparkling wine. The area is also home to scenic **Cañón del Atuel**, a colorful mini Grand Canyon. Then backtrack up north to **San Juan** to try the excellent syrah and regional whites. Rent a car and head west to ethereal **Barreal** for rafting, mountaineering and land sailing, then go further north to explore the remote and traditional villages of **Rodeo**, **Huaco** and **San José de Jáchal**.

Finally, be sure to visit the amazing landscapes of **Parque Provincial Ischigualasto** and **Parque Nacional Talampaya**; both boast spectacular rock formations, along with petroglyphs and dinosaur fossils.

Northern Adventure Loop
3 WEEKS

Start in **Córdoba**, Argentina's second-largest city, to explore one of the country's finest colonial centers.

Now head north to historic **Tucumán** to see where Argentina declared its independence from Spain. Over to the west is pretty **Tafí del Valle**; getting there via a gorgeous mountain road is half the fun. A bit further north is beautiful **Cafayate**, the place to knock back some aromatic torrontés wine. Sober up and day-trip to the epic **Quebrada de Cafayate**, then head to otherworldly **Valles Calchaquíes** and the adobe villages of **Molinos** and **Cachi**.

The central plaza of **Salta** is one of Argentina's best preserved; this city is also a great base for stellar excursions into the Andes. Now journey north through the magnificently eroded valley of **Quebrada de Humahuaca**, where you can overnight in lively little **Tilcara**.

Return to Salta and fly to the incredible **Parque Nacional Iguazú**, home to unbelievable waterfalls. With time, head to **Reserva Provincial Esteros del Iberá**, an amazing wetlands preserve full of capybaras, caimans and birds.

Plan Your Trip
Argentina Outdoors

Mountaineering, hiking and skiing have long been Argentina's classic outdoor pursuits, but these days locals and visitors alike are doing much more. They're kiteboarding in the Andes, paragliding in the Central Sierras, diving along the Atlantic coast and pulling out huge trout in the Lake District.

Best Bases for Thrill Seekers

Bariloche
One of Argentina's premier outdoor cities, with fine hiking, skiing, biking, fishing, rafting and even paragliding.

Mendoza
One word: Aconcagua. Plus great skiing, rafting, rock climbing and more.

El Chaltén
World-class hiking, trekking, rock climbing, kayaking and fishing.

Puerto Madryn
Dive with sea lions, or go windsurfing and kayaking.

Junín de los Andes
Gorgeous rivers offer some of the world's best fly-fishing (for huge trout!).

Córdoba
The closest city to Los Gigantes, Argentina's rock-climbing mecca (80km away).

Hiking & Trekking

Argentina is home to some superb stomping. The Lake District is probably the country's most popular hiking destination, with outstanding day and multiday hikes in several national parks, including Nahuel Huapi and Lanín. Bariloche is the best base for exploring the former, San Martín de los Andes the latter.

Patagonia, along the Andes, has out-of-this-world hiking. South of Bariloche, El Bolsón is an excellent base for hiking both in the forests outside of town and in nearby Parque Nacional Lago Puelo. Parque Nacional Los Glaciares offers wonderful hiking in and around the Fitz Roy Range; base yourself in El Chaltén and wait out the storms (in the brewery, of course).

Head to Parque Nacional Torres del Paine, in Chile but not far from El Calafate in Argentina, for epic hiking. Tierra del Fuego also has some good walks, conveniently in Parque Nacional Tierra del Fuego.

Then there are the high Andean peaks west of Mendoza. Although these areas are more popular for mountaineering, there's some great trekking here as well. The northern Andes around Quebrada de Humahuaca are also good.

Bariloche, Ushuaia, El Bolsón and Junín de los Andes have a hiking and mountaineering club called Club Andino, which is good for local information, maps and current conditions.

Lonely Planet's *Trekking in the Patagonian Andes* is a great resource if you're planning some serious trekking.

Mountaineering

The Andes are a mountaineer's dream, especially in the San Juan and Mendoza provinces, where some of the highest peaks in the western hemisphere are found. While the most famous climb is Aconcagua, the highest peak in the Americas, there are plenty of others in the Andes – many of them more interesting and far more technical. Near Barreal, the Cordón de la Ramada boasts five peaks more than 6000m, including the mammoth Cerro Mercedario, which tops out at 6770m. The region is less congested than Aconcagua, offers more technical climbs and is preferred by many climbers. Also near here is the majestic Cordillera de Ansilta, with seven peaks scraping the sky at between 5130m and 5885m.

The magnificent and challenging Fitz Roy Range, in southern Patagonia near El Chaltén, is one of the world's top mountaineering destinations, while the mountains of Parque Nacional Nahuel Huapi offer fun for all levels.

Rock Climbing

Patagonia's Parque Nacional Los Glaciares, home to Cerro Torre and Cerro Fitz Roy, is one of the world's most important rock-climbing destinations. Cerro Torre is considered one of the five toughest climbs on the planet. The nearby town of El Chaltén is a climber's haven, and several shops offer lessons and rent equipment. If you don't have the time or talent for climbs of the Cerro Torre magnitude, there are plenty of other options.

Los Gigantes, in the Central Sierras, is fast becoming the country's de facto rock-climbing capital and has lots of high-quality granite. There's also climbing around Carolina.

In Mendoza province, Los Molles is a small, friendly hub for rock climbing, and there's more nearby at Chigüido (near

SAILING...ON LAND?

In San Juan province's Parque Nacional El Leoncito, the lake bed of Pampa El Leoncito has become the epicenter of *carrovelismo* (land sailing). Here, people zip across the dry lake bed beneath Andean peaks in so-called sail cars. If you're interested, head straight to Barreal.

Malargüe). Around Mendoza city are the draws of Los Arenales and El Salto.

There's good climbing around Bariloche – Cerro Catedral especially has popular crags. There are also good routes in Torres del Paine, Chile. Finally, in the Pampas, there's some climbing in Tandil and Mar del Plata.

Fishing

Together, Patagonia and the Lake District constitute one of the world's premier fly-fishing destinations, where introduced trout species (brown, brook, lake and rainbow) and landlocked Atlantic salmon reach massive sizes in cold rivers surrounded by spectacular scenery. It's an angler's paradise.

In the Lake District, Junín de los Andes is the self-proclaimed trout capital of Argentina, and lining up a guide to take you to Parque Nacional Lanín's superb trout streams is easy. Nearby Aluminé sits on the banks of Río Aluminé, one of the country's most highly regarded trout streams. Bariloche and Villa la Angostura are other excellent bases.

Further south, Parque Nacional Los Alerces (near Esquel) has outstanding lakes and rivers. From El Chaltén, you can do day trips to Lago del Desierto or Laguna Larga. Río Gallegos is a superb fly-fishing destination. Other important Patagonian rivers include Río Negro and Río Santa Cruz.

The city of Río Grande, on Tierra del Fuego, is world famous for its fly-fishing. Its eponymous river holds some of the largest sea-run brown trout in the world.

Deep-sea fishing is possible in Camarones and Puerto Deseado; near Gobernador Gregores there's a lake with salmon and rainbow trout.

In subtropical northeast Argentina, the wide Río Paraná attracts fly-fishers, spin

MUSH, FIDO, MUSH!

You can't say you've done it all until you've tried dog sledding, and Argentina's a great place to start. Obviously, this activity is possible only when there's snow, during the winter months of June to October – though in Ushuaia the season might be longer. Here are a few places to check out:

Cavihue A village on the flanks of Volcán Copahue

San Martín de los Andes A picturesque town north of Bariloche

Ushuaia The southernmost city in the world!

fishers and trollers from around the world, who pull in massive river species, such as surubí (a huge catfish) and dorado (a trout-like freshwater game fish). The dorado, not to be confused with the saltwater mahi-mahi, is a powerful swimmer and one of the most exciting fish to catch on a fly.

Guides & Services

In smaller towns such as Junín de los Andes, you can usually go to the tourist office and request a list of local fishing guides or operators. Another good option for independent anglers heading to the Lake District is the Asociación de Guías Profesionales de Pesca Parque Nacional Nahuel Huapi y Patagonia Norte (www.guiaspatagonicos. com.ar), which maintains a list and contact details of licensed guides for northern Patagonia and the Lake District. For information about fly-fishing, contact **Asociación Argentina de Pesca con Mosca** (✆ in Buenos Aires 011-4773-0821; www.aapm.org.ar).

Many anglers use a tour agency based outside Argentina for guided excursions.

Rules & Regulations

In the Lake District and Patagonia, the season runs from November through April or May. In the northeast, the season runs from February to October. Lakes and streams on private land may stay open longer.

Trout fishing is almost always mandatory catch and release. Throughout Patagonia (including the Lake District), native species should *always* be thrown back. These are usually smaller than trout and include per-

ca (perch), puyen (common galaxias, a narrow fish native to the southern hemisphere), Patagonian pejerrey and the rare peladilla.

Fishing licenses are required and available at tackle shops, *clubs de caza y pesca* (hunting and fishing clubs), and sometimes at tourist offices and YPF gas stations.

Skiing & Snowboarding

Argentina's mountains have outstanding skiing, offering superb powder and plenty of sunny days. Many resorts have large ski schools with instructors from all over the world, so language is not a problem. At some of the older resorts, equipment can be a little antiquated, but in general the quality of skiing more than compensates.

There are three main snow-sport areas: Mendoza, the Lake District and Ushuaia. Mendoza is near Argentina's premier resort, Las Leñas, which has the best snow and longest runs; the resort Los Penitentes is also nearby. The Lake District is home to several low-key resorts, including Cerro Catedral, near Bariloche, and Cerro Chapelco, near San Martín de los Andes. Although the snow doesn't get as powdery here, the views are superior to Las Leñas. And Esquel, further south in Patagonia, has great powder at La Hoya.

The world's most southerly commercial skiing is near Ushuaia. The ski season everywhere generally runs from mid-June to mid-October.

Cycling

Cycling is a popular activity among Argentines, and spandex-clad cyclists are a common sight along many roads (despite a decided lack of bike lanes in the country). There are some outstanding paved routes, especially in the Lake District and, to a lesser extent, in the Andean northwest.

In the northwest, there are several excellent road routes, including the highway from Tucumán to Tafí del Valle, the direct road from Salta to Jujuy, and, arguably most spectacular of all, RN68, which takes you through the Quebrada de Cafayate. The Central Sierras are also great candidates for cycling, and the mostly paved network of roads rolls past a countryside

Top: Skiing, Cerro
Chapelco (p384)

Bottom: Kayaking,
Bariloche (p359)

BUENAVENTURAMARIANO / GETTY IMAGES ©

that is at times reminiscent of Scotland. Mendoza boasts some epic routes through the Andes, but most are doable only for the seasoned cyclist – those lacking thighs of glory can entertain themselves by pedaling between wineries in Maipú.

In the Lake District's Parque Nacional Nahuel Huapi, there are several excellent loops (including the Circuito Chico) that skirt gorgeous lakes and take in some of Patagonia's most spectacular scenery. Cyclists often take their bikes on the Cruce de Lagos, a famous two-day boat/bus journey across the Andes to Chile.

Patagonia is a popular and mythical destination, with its desolate, beautiful landscapes and wide-open skies. However, be ready for fierce, multidirectional winds and rough gravel roads. Take four-season gear, even in summer, when long days and relatively warm weather make for the best touring. The classic road down here is RN40, but cycling is tough because of the winds and lack of water; most cyclists alternate sections with Chile's Carretera Austral.

In recent years, Buenos Aires has become a more bike-friendly destination, with an expanding system of dedicated bike lanes, along with a free bike-share program. Mendoza and Córdoba also have some dedicated bike lanes.

Mountain Biking

Mountain biking is fairly undeveloped in Argentina and you'll find few places have true single tracks for mountain bikers. However, at most outdoor hubs (such as Bariloche) you can rent a mountain bike for a day of independent pedaling or for guided mountain-

bike rides – a fantastic way to see parts of an area you wouldn't otherwise explore.

Good places with mountain-bike rentals include San Martín de los Andes, Villa la Angostura, Bariloche and El Bolsón in the Lake District; Esquel in Patagonia; Mendoza and Uspallata in Mendoza province; Barreal in San Juan province; Tilcara in the Andean Northwest; and Tandil in La Pampa province.

White-Water Rafting & Kayaking

Currently, Río Mendoza and Río Diamante in Mendoza province are the reigning white-water destinations, while Río Juramento near Salta is an exciting alternative.

If you want great scenery, however, it's all about Patagonia. The Río Hua Hum and Río Meliquina, near San Martín de los Andes, and Río Limay and Río Manso, near Bariloche, are both spectacular. So is Río Aluminé, near wee Aluminé. From the Patagonian town of Esquel, you can join a rafting trip on the incredibly scenic, glacial-fed Río Corcovado. A relatively unknown rafting destination is Barreal, but it's more about the epic Andean scenery than the rapids. Scenic Class II to III floats are possible on most of these rivers, while Class IV runs are possible on the Ríos Mendoza, Diamante, Meliquina, Hua Hum and Corcovado. Experience is generally unnecessary for guided runs.

Kayaking is possible on many of the rivers mentioned, and also around Ushuaia, El Chaltén, Viedma, Puerto Madryn, Paraná, Rosario and Salta. Sea kayakers have options at Río Deseado and the *estancia* (ranch) at Bahía Bustamante.

Paragliding & Skydiving

Paragliding is popular in Argentina and it's a great place to take tandem flights or classes. Many agencies in Bariloche offer paragliding. Tucumán is especially big on this sport, but Salta, La Rioja and Merlo also have options in or near the Andean Northwest. Perhaps the best place is La Cumbre, in Córdoba's Central Sierras – it's also a thrilling place to try skydiving.

Plan Your Trip

Eat & Drink Like a Local

Argentines take barbecuing to heights you cannot imagine. Their best pizzas vie with those of New York and Naples. They make fabulous wines. Mate, that iconic tea, doubles as a social bond between family and friends. And your taste buds will sing as they sample Argentina's delectable ice cream.

Staples & Specialties

Beef

When the first Spaniards came to Argentina, they brought cattle. But efforts to establish a colony proved unfruitful, and the herds were abandoned in the pampas. Here the cows found the bovine equivalent of heaven: plenty of lush, fertile grasses on which to feed and few natural predators. After the Europeans recolonized, they bred these cattle with other bovine breeds.

Traditionally, free-range Argentine cows ate nutritious pampas grass and were raised without antibiotics and growth hormones. But this culture is being lost, and today most beef in restaurants comes from feedlots.

Average beef consumption in Argentina is around 59kg per person per year – though in the past, they ate much more.

Italian & Spanish

Thanks to Argentina's Italian heritage, the national cuisine has been highly influenced by Italian immigrants who entered the country during the late 19th century. Along with an animated set of speaking gestures, they brought their love of pasta, pizza, gelato and more.

Many restaurants make their own pasta – look for *pasta casera* (handmade

Tips for Eating Out

Reservations

Only necessary on weekends at better restaurants (or high season at Mar del Plata or Bariloche, for example).

Budgeting

To save a few bucks at lunch, opt for the *menú del día* or *menú ejecutivo*. These 'set menus' usually include a main dish, dessert and drink.

Large, modern supermarkets are common, and they'll have whatever you need for self-catering, including (usually) a takeout counter.

Paying the Bill

Ask for your bill by saying, *'la cuenta, por favor'* ('the bill, please') or making the 'writing in air' gesture. Some restaurants accept credit cards, but others (usually smaller ones) only take cash. This is especially true outside big cities.

At fancier restaurants, your final bill may arrive with a *cubierto* (small cover charge for bread and use of utensils). This is not a tip, which is usually around 10% and a separate charge.

Top: Empanadas

Bottom: A traditional *parrilla* grill

pasta). Some of the varieties of pasta you'll encounter are *ravioles*, *sorrentinos* (large, round pasta parcels similar to ravioli), *ñoquis* (gnocchi) and *tallarines* (fettuccine). Standard sauces include *tuco* (tomato sauce), *estofado* (beef stew, popular with ravioli) and *salsa blanca* (béchamel). Be aware that occasionally the sauce is *not* included in the price of the pasta – you choose and pay for it separately.

Pizza is sold at pizzerias throughout the country, though many regular restaurants offer it as well. It's generally excellent, so go ahead and order a slice or two.

Spanish cooking is less popular than Italian, but forms another bedrock of Argentine food. In Spanish restaurants here you'll find paella, as well as other typically Spanish seafood preparations. Most of the country's *guisos* and *pucheros* (types of stew) are descendants from Spain.

Local Specialties

Although *comidas típicas* can refer to any of Argentina's regional dishes, it often refers to food from the Andean Northwest. Food from this region, which has roots in pre-Columbian times, has more in common with the cuisines of Bolivia and Peru than with the Europeanized food of the rest of Argentina. It's frequently spicy and hard to find elsewhere (most Argentines can't tolerate anything spicy). Typical dishes can include everything from *locro* (a hearty corn or mixed-grain stew with meat) and tamales to *humitas* (sweet tamales) and fried empanadas.

In Patagonia, lamb is as common as beef. Along the coast, seafood is a popular choice and includes fish, oysters and king crab. In the Lake District, game meats such as venison, wild boar and trout are popular. In the west, the provinces of

THE BEEF ON BEEF

You walk into a traditional *parrilla* (steak restaurant), breeze past the sizzling grill at the entrance and sit down. You've never had to choose between more than two or three cuts of steak in your life, but the menu has at least 10 choices. What to do?

If you want to try a bit of everything, go for the *parrillada* (mixed grill). It often includes chorizo (beef or pork sausage), *costillas* (ribs) and *carne* (beef). It can also come with more exotic items such as *chinchulines* (small intestines), *molleja*s (sweetbreads) and *morcilla* (blood sausage). Order a *parrillada* for as many people as you want and the *parrilla* will adjust servings accordingly.

Prime beef cuts include the following:

Bife de chorizo Sirloin; a thick and juicy cut.

Bife de costilla T-bone or Porterhouse steak.

Bife de lomo Tenderloin; a tender though less flavorful piece.

Cuadril Rump steak; often a thin cut.

Ojo de bife Rib eye; a choice smaller morsel.

Tira de asado Short ribs; thin crispy strips of ribs.

Vacío Flank steak; textured, chewy and tasty.

If you don't specify, your steak will be cooked *a punto* (medium to well done). Getting a steak medium rare or rare is more difficult than you'd imagine. If you want a little pink in the center, order it *jugoso*; if you like it truly rare, try *vuelta y vuelta*. Often it comes overcooked, however; try showing your server a photo of a cut steak, cooked the way you want it.

Don't miss *chimichurri*, a tasty sauce often made of olive oil, garlic and parsley. Occasionally you can get *salsa criolla*, a condiment made of diced tomatoes, onion and parsley.

If you're lucky enough to be invited to an *asado* (family or friends' barbecue), do attend – here the art of grilling beef has been perfected, and the social bonding is priceless.

Mendoza, San Juan and La Rioja pride themselves on *chivito* (young goat). River fish, such as the dorado, pacú (a relative of the piranha) and surubí (a type of catfish), are staples in the northeast.

Snacks

Kioscos (kiosks) are all over town and provide sweets, cookies, ice cream and packaged sandwiches. On the streets, *pancho* (hot dog) and *garrapiñadas* (sugar-roasted peanuts) sellers prepare and sell their treats from carts.

Sandwiches de miga (thin, crustless sandwiches, usually with cheese and ham) are popular tea-time snacks. *Lomitos* (steak sandwiches) are the pinnacle of Argentine sandwiches, while the *choripán* is a classic barbecue sausage sandwich.

Empanadas – small, stuffed turnovers ubiquitous in Argentina – are prepared differently throughout the country (you'll find spicy ground-beef empanadas in the Andean Northwest, while in Patagonia lamb is a common filling). They make for a tasty, quick meal and are especially good for bus travel.

Desserts & Sweets

Two of Argentina's most definitive treats are *dulce de leche* (a creamy milk caramel) and *alfajores* (round, cookie-type sandwiches often covered in chocolate). Each region of Argentina has its own version of the *alfajor*.

Because of Argentina's Italian heritage, Argentine *helado* is comparable to the best ice cream anywhere in the world. There are *heladerías* (ice-cream stores) in every town, where the luscious concoctions will be swirled into a peaked mountain and handed over with a plastic spoon stuck in the side. Don't miss this special treat.

In restaurants, fruit salad and ice cream are often on the menu, while *flan* is a baked custard that comes with either cream or *dulce de leche* topping.

Drinks
Nonalcoholic Drinks

Argentines love their coffee, and you can order several versions. A *café con leche* is half coffee and half milk, while a *cortado* is an espresso with a little milk. A *café*

MATE & ITS RITUAL

The preparation and consumption of *mate* (pronounced *mah*-tay) is more than a simple drink. It's an elaborate ritual shared among family, friends and coworkers.

Yerba mate is the dried, chopped leaf of *Ilex paraguayensis*, a relative of the common holly. Argentina is one of the world's largest producers and consumers of the stuff, and its citizens down an average of 5kg per person per year.

Preparing and drinking *mate* is a ritual in itself. One person, the *cebador* (server), fills the *mate* gourd almost to the top with *yerba*, and then slowly pours hot water as he or she fills the gourd. The *cebador* then passes the *mate* to each drinker, who sips the liquid through the *bombilla*, a silver straw with a filter at the end. Each participant drinks the gourd dry each time. Remember it's bad form to touch the *bombilla*, and don't hold the *mate* too long before passing it on! A simple 'gracias' will tell the server to pass you by.

An invitation to partake in *mate* is a cultural treat and not to be missed, although the drink is an acquired taste and novices will find it very hot and bitter at first (adding sugar can be an option).

Mate is rarely served in restaurants or cafes, but you can buy a thermos, *mate* gourd, *bombilla* and a bag of herb at any large supermarket. Cure your gourd by filling it with hot water and *yerba* and letting it soak for 24 hours. Nearly all restaurants, cafes and hotels are used to filling thermoses, sometimes charging a small amount. Simply whip out your thermos and ask: '*¿Podía calentar agua para mate?*' ('Would you mind heating water for *mate*?'). And start making friends.

Top: *Mate*
Bottom: *Alfajores* filled with *dulce de leche*

AS FOOD STUDIO / GETTY IMAGES ©

chico is an espresso and a *lagrima* is mostly milk with a few drops of coffee.

Té negro or *té común* is black tea; herbal tea is usually *manzanilla* (chamomile). Chocolate lovers should try a *submarino*, a bar of chocolate melted in hot milk. Fresh-squeezed orange juice is *jugo de naranja exprimido*. A *licuado* is fruit blended with milk or water.

Even in big cities like Buenos Aires, the *agua de canilla* (tap water) is drinkable. In restaurants, however, most people order bottled mineral water – ask for *agua con gas* (with bubbles) or *agua sin gas* (without). In older, more traditional restaurants, carbonated water in a spritzer bottle (*un sifón de soda*) is a great for drinking. *Gaseosas* (soft drinks) are very popular in Argentina.

Alcoholic Drinks

Mendoza is Argentina's premier wine region and well known for its robust malbec, but other provinces also produce excellent wines. San Juan is famous for its succulent syrah and Cafayate for its torrontés, a crisp, dry white wine. Meanwhile, the Patagonia region is becoming a stronghouse for pinot noir.

If Argentina has a national beer, it's Quilmes. Order a *porrón* and you'll get bottled beer (a half-liter bottle in Buenos Aires; a big bottle up north); a *chopp* is a frosty mug of draft. Unless you order it with a meal, beer is usually served with a free snack.

Most fine restaurants have a wine list, called *la carta de vinos*. Sommeliers are scarce.

At the harder end of the spectrum, it's all about Fernet Branca, a bitter, herbed Italian digestif originally intended as medicine. Fernet con Coke is Argentina's favorite cocktail and, despite many claims that it won't give you hangover, it will (trust us).

Where to Eat & Drink

Restaurants are generally open from noon to 3pm for lunch and 8 or 9pm to midnight for dinner, though exact hours will vary depending on the restaurant.

For the best meats, head to a *parrilla* (steak restaurant). Pizzerias bake pizzas and *panaderías* are bakeries. *Confiterías* (cafes serving light meals) are open all day and into the night, and often have a long list of both food and drinks. Cafes, bars and pubs usually have a more limited range of snacks and meals available, though some can offer full meals. A *tenedor libre* (literally, 'free fork') is an all-you-can-eat restaurant; quality is usually decent, but a minimum-drink purchase is often mandatory and costs extra.

Argentines eat little for breakfast – usually just a coffee with *medialunas* (croissants – either *de manteca*, sweet, or *de grasa*, plain). *Tostadas* (toast) with *manteca* (butter) or *mermelada* (jam) is an alternative, as are *facturas* (pastries). Higher-end hotels and B&Bs tend to offer heartier breakfasts.

Vegetarians & Vegans

Health foods, organic products and vegetarian restaurants are available in Argentina's biggest cities, but outside of them you'll have to search harder.

Most restaurant menus include a few vegetarian choices, and pastas are a nearly ubiquitous option. Pizzerias and *empanaderías* (empanada shops) are good bets – look for empanadas made with *acelga* (chard) and *choclo (*corn). If you're stuck at a *parrilla*, your choices will be salads, omelets, pasta, baked potatoes, *provoleta* (a thick slice of grilled provolone cheese) and roasted vegetables. *Pescado* (fish) and *mariscos* (seafood) are sometimes available for pescatarians.

Sin carne means 'without meat,' and the words *soy vegetariano/a* ('I'm a vegetarian') will come in handy when explaining to an Argentine why you don't eat their nation's renowned steaks.

Vegans will have a much harder time in Argentina; the word for vegan is *vegano/a*. Make sure homemade pasta doesn't include egg, and that fried vegetables aren't cooked in lard (*grasa*; *manteca* means butter in Argentina). Some breads are made with milk or cheese. You'll need to be creative to survive here. One tip: look for accommodations with a kitchen, so you can shop for and cook your own food. Good luck.

Plan Your Trip
Travel with Children

While Argentina is best known for its steak, gauchos and tango – not your top kid-friendly themes – there is plenty this country has to offer your little ones. There are dinosaur museums to wow at, beach resorts to splash around in and plenty of outdoor activities to use up all that extra energy. You'll find Argentina makes a good, interesting and, yes, at times challenging but fun family destination.

Argentina for Kids

Argentina is remarkably child-friendly in terms of general travel safety and people's attitudes towards families. This is a country where family comes first.

Argentine parents will often send unaccompanied pre-adolescents on errands or neighborly visits. While you're not likely to do this, you can usually count on your children's safety in public.

Argentina's numerous plazas and public parks, many with playgrounds, are popular gathering spots for families. Argentine's frequently touch each other, so your children may be patted on the head by friendly strangers. Kids are a great ice-breaker and certainly make it easier for you to meet the locals.

And remember that families stay out very late in this country – it's common to see young kids and babies out past midnight with their parents. There's no early curfew and everyone's out having fun, so consider doing the same!

Best Regions for Kids

Buenos Aires
Argentina's capital provides plenty of museums, parks and shopping malls, many with fun areas for kids. For more details, see p72.

Atlantic Coast
Beaches and more beaches – bring swimsuits and sunscreen, and start building castles.

Iguazú
Waterfalls and wildlife galore, plus thrilling boat rides that guarantee a fun soaking.

Península Valdés
Rich with wildlife, such as splashy whales, smelly elephant seals and supercute penguins.

Bariloche
Outdoor activities are the draw here – go hiking, rock climbing, horseback riding and rafting.

Mendoza
Wine tasting is off-limits for the kids, but you can take them skiing and white-water rafting.

Children's Highlights

Watching Wildlife

➡ Visit **Güirá Oga** (p197) zoo in the Iguazú Falls area.

➡ **Esteros del Iberá** (p177) is full of marsh deer, black caimans and adorable capybaras.

➡ Check out whales, elephant seals and suit-wearing penguins on **Península Valdés** (p410).

➡ Rosario's **Jardín de los Niños** (p154), a fun discovery park, offers activities and puzzles for the little ones.

Energy Burners

➡ **Parque de la Costa** (p72), just outside BA in Tigre, has roller coasters and other theme-park fun.

➡ **Complejo Termal Cacheuta** (p336), outside Mendoza, is a thermal-baths complex with wave pool and waterslides.

➡ The Andes mountains offer great skiing around Bariloche and Mendoza.

Rainy Days

➡ Kids can overnight in their pajamas at Museo Paleontológico Egidio Feruglio (p415), Trelew's dinosaur museum.

➡ **Museo de La Plata** (p119) is Argentina's best natural history museum; the taxidermy and skeletons are especially awesome.

➡ **Glaciarium** (p458), El Calafate's slickest museum, highlights the wonders of glaciers.

➡ Bigger shopping centers often have playgrounds, video arcades, toy stores and ice-cream shops.

Outdoor Fun

➡ El Calafate's superactive Glaciar Perito Moreno is a wonder to behold for all ages.

➡ The beaches on Argentina's Atlantic coast are family-friendly, and offer up plenty of sand, surf and sun.

➡ Horseback rides and folkloric shows are highlights during your stay on an *estancia* (ranch).

Planning

Outdoor activities are best experienced outside the winter months of June through August (with the exception of skiing, of course). Small kids often get discounts on such things as motel stays, museum admissions and restaurant meals. Supermarkets offer a decent selection of baby food, infant formulas, disposable diapers, wet wipes and other necessities. Big pharmacies such as Farmacity also stock some of these items.

Strollers on crowded and uneven sidewalks can be a liability, so consider bringing a baby carrier. Public bathrooms are often poorly maintained, and baby changing tables are not common.

Sweet Dreams

The great majority of hotels accept children without any problems; the most upscale may even offer babysitting services. The only places with possible minimum age restrictions are small boutique hotels or guesthouses. Hostels are usually not the best environment for kids, but a few welcome them.

During summer, reserving a hotel with a pool can be a good idea. Also look for places with kitchenettes. Apartments are available, especially in BA; in less-urban holiday destinations you can look for *cabañas* (cabins) with full kitchens. Larger campgrounds often have *cabañas,* common cooking facilities and sometimes play structures.

Dining

Most restaurants offer a selection of food suitable for children, such as vegetables, pasta, pizza, chicken and *milanesas* (breaded meat cutlets). Empanadas make good, healthy snacks that are fun to eat, and don't forget to take the kids out for ice cream – it's a real Argentine treat!

Transportation

When it comes to public transportation, Argentines are usually very helpful. Taxis and *remises* (radio taxis) are common and affordable in most towns.

Regions at a Glance

As the eighth-largest country in the world, Argentina boasts nearly every kind of environment, from glaciated mountain peaks and cacti-dotted deserts, to animal-rich swamplands and shrubby, arid steppes. Outdoor fun-seekers will find their blissful adventures, beachcombers their warm stretches of sand and wine lovers their luscious vineyards.

The bigger cities, such as Buenos Aires and Córdoba, boast endless nightlife, entertainment, shopping and restaurants, along with a dose of culture, such as excellent museums, tango dance halls and colonial history. Argentina offers pretty much everything you might be looking for in a destination, so choose your desires, give yourself enough time to experience them all, and just take off!

Buenos Aires

Food
Nightlife
Tango

Steaks & More

There are plenty of fine steak houses in Buenos Aires. But you'll also find dozens of ethnic restaurants covering cuisines from Mexico, Brazil, India, China, Thailand, the Middle East...and practically anywhere else.

Burn the Midnight Oil

Buenos Aires is indeed the city that never sleeps. After dinner – which often ends after midnight on weekends – *porteños* (BA residents) head out for a drink, then hit the nightclubs after 2am. Other events happen at a more 'reasonable' hour, but you get the idea – this city loves staying up late.

Sultry Dancing

Ah, the tango. There's no denying the attraction of this sexy dance. And BA boasts countless dance venues and classes, along with world-class competitions. Put on your dancing shoes and get ready to fall in love – you're in the heart of tango land here.

p52

The Pampas & the Atlantic Coast

....

**Beaches
Gauchos
Hiking**

....

Life's a Beach

In January coastal cities such as Mar del Plata, Pinamar and Necochea become heaving hubs full of sun-bronzed Argentines lying on hot sands during the day and partying all night long.

Gaucho Culture

This quintessential icon's heyday was centuries ago, but today the culture is kept alive in San Antonio de Areco, where an annual festival celebrates the gaucho's life. You can also visit an *estancia* (ranch), where horseback riding, gaucho demonstrations and *asados* (barbecues) are highlights.

Hiking & Landscapes

The ancient, worn-down mountain ranges of the Pampas aren't as spectacular as the youthful Andes. But around Sierra de la Ventana are some hikes offering dramatic views of surrounding landscapes – including one where you peek through a rock 'window.'

p115

Iguazú Falls & the Northeast

....

**Water Features
Wildlife
Historic Missions**

....

Wide Rivers, Mighty Iguazú

Towns and cities along the region's two major rivers often boast great waterside strips for boating, strolling, eating and partying, while large fish attract anglers. Up north, Iguazú, the world's most impressive waterfalls, will leave you in awe.

Cute Capybaras

The Esteros del Iberá wetlands hold an astonishing wealth of creatures, including snapping caimans, colorful birdlife and roly-poly capybaras. A long hop north, Iguazú's national park and jungle ecosystem is equally rich in distinct wildlife species.

Jesuit Ruins

Built by Jesuits in the 17th and 18th centuries, remote *reducciones* (missions) were created to educate, evangelize and protect local Guaraní populations. They flourished for about 150 years before the Jesuits' expulsion left the missions exposed to slave raids and colonization.

p150

Salta & the Andean Northwest

....

**Indigenous Culture
Colonial Cities
Activities**

....

Before Columbus

The northwestern peoples witnessed the Inca; then the Spanish arrived. Centuries later, the ruins of cities remain, but the food, daily life and handicrafts speak of a persisting, living and changing culture.

Historical Towns

The northwestern cities are Argentina's oldest, and there's an unmistakable time-honored feel to them. Venerable churches, stately facades and handsome plazas planted with lofty trees – together with the relaxed pace of life – give these places an ambience unlike any other.

Out & About

The Andes dominate the geography here and boast excellent climbing, walking, and 4WD excursions. But there are also subtropical national parks replete with bird and animal life, and top-notch hang gliding and paragliding offer the opportunity to see how things look from above.

p218

Córdoba & the Central Sierras

Historic Buildings
Nightlife
Paragliding

Oldies but Goodies

The Jesuit legacy in Córdoba extends beyond wine making and higher education – they also constructed some fabulous buildings. Córdoba city boasts an entire block of well-preserved Jesuit architecture, and further examples are scattered around the province.

Bring on the Night

Catch an independent movie or a play, dance the night away or grab a few quiet drinks in a cozy bar – whatever you're looking for, Córdoba's young population and vibrant cultural scene make finding it a snap.

Take to the Skies

If you've ever even been vaguely tempted to try paragliding, this is the place to do it – the world-famous launch sites of La Cumbre and Merlo are home to scores of instructors offering tandem flights that will have you soaring with the condors.

p285

Mendoza & the Central Andes

Wine Tours
Mountains
Rafting

Hear It on the Grapevine

Get to the heart of Argentina's magnificent wine culture by visiting the vineyards, talking to the winemakers and seeing how it all comes together, from planting the vine to tasting the final, delicious product.

Lofty Ambitions

Snow-capped year-round and dominating the horizon, the Andes are one of Argentina's iconic images. Get up close and personal with them by climbing Aconcagua, the Americas' highest peak, or hitting the slopes in Mendoza's world-class ski resorts.

Wet & Wild

All that snowmelt from the Andes does more than just irrigate the grapevines. It also feeds a couple of rivers that gush down from the mountains, giving rafters the ride of their lives.

p318

Bariloche & the Lake District

Activities
Village Life
Paleontology

Get Out There

There's always something to do in the Lake District, a true year-round destination. Powder hounds hit the slopes in season at the province's top-notch ski resorts while the rest of the year the mountain trails, hikers' refuges and expansive vistas make it a trekker's paradise.

Kicking Back

One of the joys of traveling through this region is discovering small alpine villages nestled in the forest, surrounded by breathtaking mountain scenery – the perfect remedy for big-city blues.

Jurassic Parks

Some truly huge animals used to roam these parts – including the world's largest dinosaur and the world's largest carnivore. The sites where they were discovered are open to the public to teach a humbling lesson in size.

p356

Patagonia

Hiking
Wildlife-watching
Adventure

Wild Hiking

Iconic hikes around Fitz Roy and Torres del Paine bring deserved fame to the trails of Patagonia. But if you have time, check out the millennial forests of Parque Nacional Los Alerces and the electric turquoise lakes of ultra-remote Parque Nacional Perito Moreno.

Creature Feature

Abundant marine life makes the coast, and Península Valdés in particular, the hub for watching wildlife, but there's also the subtle allure of Patagonia's guanaco herds, soaring condors and ñandús that sprint across the steppe.

Real Adventure

Riding on an *estancia*, driving RN 40, glacier chasing or just getting deep into the Andean wilderness: Patagonia is all about unfettered freedom and the allure of the unexpected.

p400

Tierra del Fuego

Hiking
Sea Travel
Winter Sports

Hoof It

Austral summer's long days make for backpacking bliss. Dientes de Navarino is the iconic Fuegian trek, but the enchanted forests of Parque Nacional Tierra del Fuego also give a quick dose of big nature.

Set Sail

You don't have to round Cape Horn to find magic in these southern seas. Sail the Beagle Channel in search of marine life and indigenous ruins, boat through the Chilean fjords or paddle a sea kayak.

Winter Wonderland

Brave a winter journey to the frozen ends of the earth. From June to October, snow makes Ushuaia adventure central. Whoosh down the slopes of Cerro Castor, ski cross-country or zoom over the snowdrifts driven by sled dogs. Crackling bonfires, seafood banquets and comfy lodges cap the day.

p492

Uruguay

Beaches
Estancias
Food & Wine

A Beach for Every Taste

Beachside bliss wears many faces on Uruguay's Atlantic coast: chasing the perfect surf break at La Pedrera, getting friendly with sea lions at Cabo Polonio or scanning the sands for international celebrities at Punta del Este.

Wide Open Skies

Uruguay's gaucho soul lies in its vast interior land-scapes. For a taste of traditional ranch life, spend a few nights on an *estancia*, riding horseback into an endless horizon by day and savoring the warmth of the fire and the brilliance of the stars by night.

Carnivore Paradise

Something's always grilling in Uruguay. The classic *parrillada* (mixed grill) of steak, pork chops, chorizo and *morcilla* (blood sausage) is enough to make any carnivore swoon, especially when accompanied by a glass of tannat from one of the country's up-and-coming wineries.

p517

On the
Road

Buenos Aires

📱 011 / POP 3 MILLION / AREA 203 SQ KM

Why Go?

Whip together a beautiful metropolis with gourmet cuisine, awesome shopping and frenzied nightlife – and you get Buenos Aires. It's a rough-hewn mix of Paris' architecture, Rome's traffic and Madrid's late-night hours, all spiked with Latin American flavor. BA is cosmopolitan, seductive, emotional, frustrating and chock-full of attitude, and there's no other place like it in the world. Seek out classic BA: the old-world cafes, colonial architecture, curious markets and diverse communities. Visit with Evita at Recoleta's famous cemetery, fill your belly with luscious steaks, dance the sultry tango and take in a crazy *fútbol* (soccer) match. Unforgettable adventures? You'd better believe it.

Everyone knows someone who has been here and raved about it. You've put it off long enough. Come to BA and you'll understand why so many people have fallen in love with this amazing city. There's a good chance you'll be one of them.

Best Places to Eat

➡ i Latina (p92)
➡ Casa Saltshaker (p91)
➡ Chan Chan (p88)
➡ Sarkis (p91)
➡ Don Julio (p92)

Best Places to Stay

➡ Poetry Building (p82)
➡ Miravida Soho (p83)
➡ The 5th Floor (p83)
➡ Casa Calma (p79)
➡ Cabrera Garden (p83)

When to Go
Buenos Aires

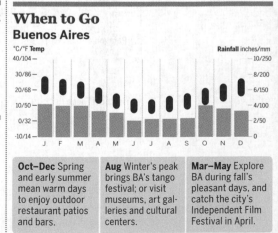

Oct–Dec Spring and early summer mean warm days to enjoy outdoor restaurant patios and bars.

Aug Winter's peak brings BA's tango festival; or visit museums, art galleries and cultural centers.

Mar–May Explore BA during fall's pleasant days, and catch the city's Independent Film Festival in April.

History

Buenos Aires was first settled in 1536 by Spaniard Pedro de Mendoza, but food shortages and attacks by indigenous groups prompted his hasty departure in 1537. Meanwhile, other expedition members left the settlement, sailed 1600km upriver and founded Asunción (now capital of Paraguay). Then in 1580 a new group of settlers moved back south and repopulated Mendoza's abandoned outpost.

For the next 196 years BA was a backwater and smuggler's paradise due to trade restrictions imposed by mother Spain. All the same, its population had grown to around 20,000 by 1776, the year Spain decreed the city as capital of the new viceroyalty of Río de la Plata.

BA's *cabildo* (town council) cut ties with its mother country on May 1810, but decades of power struggles between BA and the other former viceregal provinces ensued, escalating into civil war. Finally, in 1880 the city was declared the federal territory of Buenos Aires and the nation's capital forevermore.

Agricultural exports soared for the next few decades, which resulted in great wealth accumulating in the city. Well-heeled *porteños* (BA citizens) built opulent French-style mansions and the government spent lavishly on public works. But the boom times didn't last forever. The 1929 Wall Street crash dealt a big blow to the country's markets, and soon the first of many military coups took over. It was the end of Argentina's Golden Age.

Poverty, unemployment and decaying infrastructure became constant problems in the following decades. Extreme governments and a roller-coaster economy have also been recurring plagues, but despite this Argentina continues to bounce back every few years. Today BA remains a vibrant city with resilient and adaptable citizens – just like their ancestral settlers.

◉ Sights

◉ Microcentro

BA's Microcentro is where the big city hustles: here you'll see endless crowds of business suits and power skirts hastening about the narrow streets in the shadows of skyscrapers and old European buildings.

Florida, a long pedestrian street, is the main artery of this neighborhood. It's always

jammed during the day with businesspeople, shoppers and tourists seeking vehicle-free access from north to south. Buskers, beggars and street vendors thrive here as well, adding color and noise. Renovated old buildings, such as beautiful Galerías Pacífico, add elegance to the area.

Further south is BA's busy financial district, where there are several museums to investigate. After that comes Plaza de Mayo, often filled with people resting on benches or taking photos of the surrounding historic sites.

★ Plaza de Mayo
PLAZA

(Map p58; cnr Av de Mayo & San Martín) Planted between the Casa Rosada, the Cabildo and the city's main cathedral, grassy Plaza de Mayo is BA's ground zero for the city's most vehement protests. In the plaza's center is the **Pirámide de Mayo**, a white obelisk built to mark the first anniversary of BA's independence from Spain. If you happen to be here on Thursday at 3:30pm, you'll see the Madres de la Plaza de Mayo gather; these 'mothers of the disappeared' continue to march for social justice causes.

Casa Rosada
BUILDING

(Pink House; Map p58; ☎011-4344-3600; ⊙Free half-hour tours 10am-6pm Sat & Sun) On the eastern side of Plaza de Mayo stands the stately Casa Rosada. It's from the balconies here that Eva Perón famously preached to throngs of impassioned Argentines.

The building's color could have come from President Sarmiento's attempt at making peace during his 1868–74 term (by blending the red of the Federalists with the white of the Unitarists). Another theory, however, is that the color comes from painting the

Buenos Aires Highlights

1 Communing with BA's rich and famous dead at **Cementerio de la Recoleta** (p69).

2 Absorbing some history and seeing the presidential offices at **Plaza de Mayo** (p53).

3 Checking out the very popular Sunday **antiques fair** (p108) at Plaza Dorrego in San Telmo.

4 Eating and shopping at the gourmet restaurants and boutiques in **Palermo Viejo** (p91).

5 Marveling at amazingly high leg kicks and sexy moves at a tango show at a venue such as **Café de los Angelitos** (p99).

6 Partying all night long in Palermo's chic and super-happening nightclubs such as **Niceto Club** (p98).

7 Attending a loud, exciting and always passionate **fútbol game** (p66).

8 Strolling, shopping and people-watching on bustling **Florida** (p53).

9 Wandering **El Caminito** (p65) and watching weekend buskers in La Boca.

0 ━━━━━━━━━━ 2 km
0 ━━━━━━━━━━ 1 mile

Río de la Plata

Costanera R Obligado

Pier

Aliscafos
(Hydrofoils)

Estación
Marítima

Parque 3 de
Febrero

Estación
Saldías

PALERMO
CHICO

Av Figueroa Alcorta

del Libertador

General Las Heras

See Retiro, Recoleta & Barrio Norte Map (p70)

Dársena A

Austria

Av Pueyrredón

RECOLETA

❶ Cementerio
de la Recoleta

Av del Libertador

Retiro

Dársena
Norte

Gallo

BARRIO
NORTE

RETIRO

Av Callao

Av 9 de Julio

Florida

Av Eduardo Madero

Av Santa Fe

Av Córdoba

Av Córdoba

❽

Av Tristán Achával Rodríguez

Lago
de las
Gaviotas

TRIBUNALES

❺ Florida

ONCE

Av Corrientes

MICROCENTRO

Reserva Ecológica
Costanera Sur

ación Once

Pasco

Av de Mayo

Plaza de Mayo

❷

Lago
de los
Patos

Plaza
Miserere

Alberti

❺

CONGRESO

Café de los
Angelitos

Av Belgrano

Av 9 de Julio

Paseo Colón

Av Ing Huergo

Reserva Ecológica
Costanera Sur
(southern entrance)

BALVANERA

MONTSERRAT

Av Independencia

Club
Gricel

General
Urquiza

Jujuy

Av Juan de Garay

See The Center,
Congreso & San
Telmo Map (p58)

Plaza
Dorrego

❸

PUERTO
MADERO

See La Boca
Map (p65)

Pichincha

CONSTITUCIÓN

Av Brasil

Dársena Sur

Av Chiclana

Av Jujuy

Estación
Constitución

Av Entre Ríos

Bernardo de Irigoyen

Av Martín García

Av Almirante
Brown

Autopista La Plata
Buenos Aires

Av Caseros

Av Amancio Alcorta

BARRACAS

Av Patricios

LA BOCA

Brandsen

El Caminito ❾

palace with bovine blood, a common practice in the late 19th century.

The Casa Rosada now occupies a site where colonial riverbank fortifications once stood; today, however, after repeated landfills, the palace stands more than 1km inland. The side of the palace that faces Plaza de Mayo is actually the back of the building. The offices of the current Argentine president are here, but the presidential residence is in the calm suburbs of Olivos, north of the center.

Underneath the Casa Rosada, excavations have unearthed remains of the Fuerte Viejo, a ruin dating from the 18th century. These are accessible via entry to the Museo del Bicentenario.

Off-limits during the military dictatorship of 1976–83, the Casa Rosada is now reasonably accessible to the public. Free half-hour tours are offered.

Museo del Bicentenario MUSEUM

(Map p58; ☑ 011-4344-3802; www.museobicen tenario.gob.ar; cnr Av Paseo Colón & Hipólito Yrigoyen; ⊙10am-6pm Wed-Sun) FREE Behind the Casa Rosada you'll notice a glassy wedge marking this airy and sparkling underground museum, housed within the brick vaults of the old *aduana* (customs house). Head down into the open space, which has over a dozen side rooms – each dedicated to a different era of Argentina's tumultuous political history. There are mostly videos (in Spanish) and a few artifacts to see, along with temporary art exhibitions and an impressive restored mural by Mexican artist David Alfaro Siqueiros. Also check out Evita's gown.

Catedral Metropolitana CATHEDRAL

(Map p58; museum admission AR$40; ⊙7:30am-6:30pm Mon-Fri, 9am-7pm Sat & Sun, museum 10am-12:30pm Mon-Fri) This solemn cathedral was built on the site of the original colonial church and not finished until 1827. It's a significant religious and architectural landmark, and carved above its triangular facade and neoclassical columns are bas-reliefs of Jacob and Joseph. The spacious interior is equally impressive, with baroque details and an elegant rococo altar. There's a small museum dedicated to the cathedral's history inside. For Pope Francis souvenirs, visit the small gift shop near the entrance.

Cabildo MUSEUM

(Map p58 ☑ 011-4342-6729; www.cabildonacional. com.ar; Bolívar 65; admission AR$15; ⊙10:30am-5pm Tue-Wed & Fri, to 8pm Thu, to 6pm Sat & Sun) This mid-18th-century town hall building is now a museum. It used to have colonnades that spanned Plaza de Mayo, but the building of surrounding avenues unfortunately destroyed them. Inside you'll find a few mementos of the early 19th-century British invasions, some paintings in colonial and early independence style, and the occasional temporary exhibit. There are good views of Plaza de Mayo from the 2nd-floor balcony.

Galerías Pacífico LANDMARK

(Map p58; ☑ 011-5555-5110; cnr Florida & Av Córdoba; ⊙10am-9pm, food court to 10pm, tours 11:30am Mon-Fri) Covering an entire city block, this beautiful French-style building has fulfilled the commercial purpose that its designers envisioned when they constructed it in 1889. Galerías Pacífico is now a shopping center – dotted with lovely fairy lights at night – and boasts upscale stores along with a large food court. The excellent Centro Cultural Borges takes up the top floor. Tours are held in English and Spanish; go to the information kiosk near the food court.

Centro Cultural Borges CULTURAL CENTER

(Map p58; ☑ 011-5555-5359; www.ccborges.org. ar; cnr Viamonte & San Martín; ⊙exhibitions 10am-9pm Mon-Sat, noon-9pm Sun) One of the best cultural centers in BA, with inexpensive but high-quality art exhibitions and galleries, cinema, music, lectures, classes and workshops. Reasonably priced tango shows are also available.

Manzana de las Luces BUILDING

(Block of Enlightenment; Map p58; ☑ 011-4342-6973; www.manzanadelasluces.org; Perú 272; tours AR$35; ⊙tours 3pm Mon-Fri, 3pm, 4:30pm & 6pm Sat & Sun) In colonial times, the Manzana de las Luces was Buenos Aires' most important center of culture and learning. Even today, this collection of buildings still symbolizes high culture in the capital. On the northern side of the block are two of the five original buildings; Jesuit defensive tunnels were discovered in 1912. Tours (in Spanish) are available, and a cultural center on the premises offers classes, workshops and theater.

BUENOS AIRES IN...

Two Days

Start with a stroll in **San Telmo** and duck into some antiques stores. Walk north to **Plaza de Mayo** (p53) for a historical perspective, then wander the **Microcentro**, perhaps veering east to **Puerto Madero** – a great spot for a break.

Keep heading northward into **Retiro** and **Recoleta**, stopping off at the **Museo Nacional de Bellas Artes** (p71) to admire some impressionism. Be sure to visit the **Cementerio de la Recoleta** (p69) to commune with BA's bygone elite. For dinner and nightlife, **Palermo Viejo** is hard to beat.

On day two take in the **Congreso** neighborhood or head to **La Boca**. Shop in **Palermo Viejo** and at night catch a **tango show** or a performance at the **Teatro Colón** (p105).

Four Days

On your third day consider taking a day trip to **Tigre**, or **Colonia** in Uruguay. On the fourth day you can go on a unique **tour**, take a **tango lesson**, check out **Palermo's parks** or head to the **Feria de Mataderos** (p108), if it's a weekend. Be sure to find yourself a good steak restaurant for your last meal.

★**Centro Cultural Kirchner**   CULTURAL CENTER
(Map p58; ☑ 0800-333-9300; www.cultural kirchner.gob.ar; Sarmiento 151; ⊙ 5-9pm Thu & Fri, 2-9pm Sat & Sun, limited hrs outside summer) Néstor Kirchner just *had* to leave a physical legacy, and this breathtaking cultural center is possibly his best. It's located in Buenos Aires' ex-main post office, a massive beaux-arts structure eight stories tall and filling an entire city block. Dozens of rooms hold art galleries, theaters, event halls, auditoriums and even an Eva Perón room; there's also a rooftop terrace. The highlight, however, is La Ballena Azul, a giant concert hall that seats 1800 and is home to Argentina's national symphony orchestra.

Museo de la Ciudad   MUSEUM
(Map p58; ☑ 011-4331-9855; Defensa 219; ⊙ 11am-7pm) This upstairs museum was being remodeled at the time of research, but in the future you should expect exhibitions on *porteño* life and history. Downstairs is a large annex hall showcasing changing exhibits, while next door is an atmospheric restaurant with the Argentine art of *fileteado* (artistic drawing) on its walls.

Museo Etnográfico Juan B Ambrosetti   MUSEUM
(Map p58; ☑ 011-4331-7788; www.museoetno grafico.filo.uba.ar; Moreno 350; suggested donation AR$20; ⊙ 1-7pm Tue-Fri, 3-7pm Sat & Sun) This small but attractive anthropological museum was created by Juan B Ambrosetti not only as an institute for research and university training but also as an educational center for the public. On display are archaeological and anthropological collections from the Andean Northwest and Patagonia. Beautiful indigenous costumes are also featured, while an African and Asian room showcases some priceless pieces.

Museo de la Policía Federal   MUSEUM
(Map p58; ☑ 011-4394-6857; San Martín 353, 7th fl; ⊙ 2-7pm Tue-Fri) **FREE** This quirky and extensive police museum displays a whole slew of uniforms and medals, along with 'illegal activities' exhibits (cockfighting and gambling), drug paraphernalia (including an anal smuggling tube and a rubber arm stuck with a needle) and even a stuffed police dog. The fake Stradivarius violin and counterfeit bills are also entertaining. Look for it in an incongruous high-rise building; there's no sign for the museum.

Museo Mitre   MUSEUM
(Map p58; ☑ 011-4394-8240; San Martín 336; admission AR$20, Mon free; ⊙ 1-5pm Mon-Fri) This museum is located in the colonial house where Bartolomé Mitre – Argentina's first legitimate president elected under the constitution of 1853 – resided with his family from 1859 to 1906. Mitre's term ran from 1862 to 1868, and he spent much of it leading the country's armies against Paraguay. Two courtyards, salons, an office, a billiards room and Mitre's old bedroom are part of this complex. Since part of the museum

The Center, Congreso & San Telmo

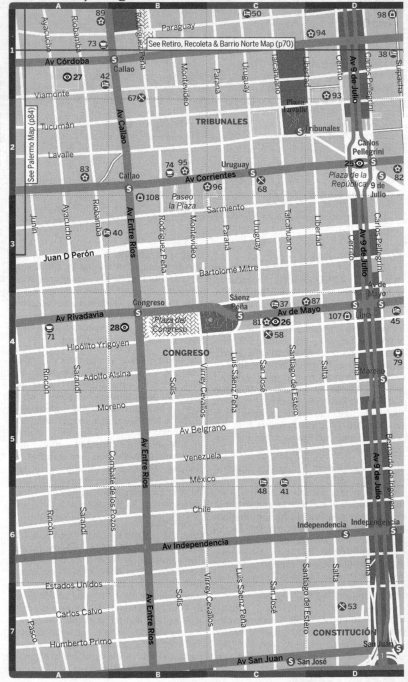

See Retiro, Recoleta & Barrio Norte Map (p70)

BUENOS AIRES

See Palermo Map (p84)

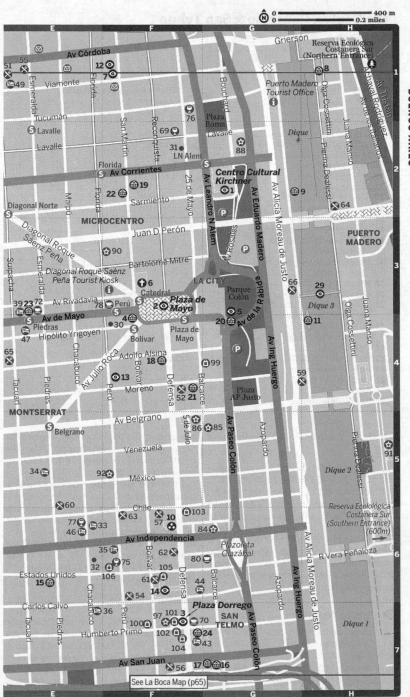

0   400 m
0   0.2 miles

Grierson

Reserva Ecológica
Costanera Sur
(Northern Entrance)

Av Córdoba

51
55
49

Viamonte

Esmeralda
Tucumán

Florida

12
7

Bouchard

Puerto Madero
Tourist Office

8

Av Tristán

Achával Rodríguez
Ayres Villanueva

Olga Cossettini

Juana Manso

Pierina Dealessi

San Martín

Reconquista

76
69
31 ● LN Alem

Plaza
Roma
Lavalle

Dique
4

Lavalle

Florida

Av Corrientes

19
22

Sarmiento

25 de Mayo

Av Leandro N Alem

Centro Cultural
Kirchner
1

Av Eduardo Madero

9

64

Diagonal Norte

Maipú

MICROCENTRO

Juan D Perón

Av Alicia Moreau de Justo

PUERTO
MADERO

Diagonal Roque
Saénz Peña

Suipacha
Esmeralda

90

Bartolomé Mitre

Diagonal Roqué Saénz
Peña Tourist Kiosk

6
Catedral

LA CITY

Parque
Colón

66
29

Dique 3

Juana Manso

Olga Cossettini

39 23 72

Av Rivadavia

Perú

78

Av de Mayo

Piedras

4
30

Plaza de
Mayo
2

5

20
11

Av de la Rábida

Av de la Rábida

47

Hipólito Yrigoyen

Bolívar

Plaza de
Mayo

Av Ing Huergo

65

Tacuarí
Piedras

Av Julio Roca

Chacabuco

Adolfo Alsina

18

99

59

13

Bolívar
Perú

Moreno

Defensa

Balcarce

52 21

Plaza
AP Justo

MONTSERRAT

Belgrano

Av Belgrano

5 de Julio

86 85

Av Paseo Colón

Azopardo

Pierina Dealessi

Venezuela

34

92

México

91

Dique 2

60

Chile

Reserva Ecológica
Costanera Sur
(Southern Entrance)
(600m)

77
46

33

63

10
57

103

84

Av Independencia

Plazoleta
Olazábal

R Vera Peñaloza

Estados Unidos
15

35
32

75
106

62

Bolívar

105

80

44

Defensa

Balcarce

Av Alicia Moreau de Justo

Av Ing Huergo

61
14

54

Carlos Calvo

36

Chacabuco

Perú

97 101 3
100

70

Plaza Dorrego
SAN
TELMO

Av Paseo Colón

Azopardo

Dique 1

Tacuarí
Piedras

Humberto Primo

102

104

24
43

Av San Juan

56

17 16

See La Boca Map (p65)

The Center, Congreso & San Telmo

is open air, you may find it closed during heavy rain.

Museo Mundial del Tango MUSEUM
(Map p58; ☎011-4345-6967; Av de Mayo 833, 1st fl; admission AR$20; ⊙2:30-7:30pm Mon-Fri) Located below the Academia Nacional del Tango is this tango museum. Just a couple of large rooms are filled with tango memorabilia, from old records and photos to historic literature and posters. Tango shoes are also featured, but the highlight has to be one of Carlos Gardel's famous fedora hats. Another entrance is at Rivadavia 830.

⊙ Puerto Madero

The newest and least conventional of the capital's 48 official barrios is Puerto Madero, located east of the Microcentro. Once an old waterfront, it's now a wonderful place to stroll, boasting cobbled paths and a long line of attractive brick warehouses that have been converted into ritzy lofts, business offices and upscale restaurants. Today this neighborhood holds some of BA's most expensive real estate.

In the mid-19th century the city's mudflats were transformed into a modernized port for Argentina's burgeoning international commerce. Puerto Madero was completed in 1898, but it had exceeded its budget – and by 1910 the amount of cargo was already too great for the new port. Only the 1926 completion of Retiro's Puerto Nuevo solved BA's shipping problems.

**Reserva Ecológica
Costanera Sur** NATURE RESERVE
(☎011-4893-1588; Av Tristán Achaval Rodríguez 1550; ⊙8am-7pm Tue-Sun Nov-Mar, to 6pm Apr-Oct) FREE The beautifully marshy land of this 350-hectare nature reserve has become a popular site for weekend picnics and walks. Bring binoculars if you're a birder – over 300 bird species can be spotted, along

BUENOS AIRES SIGHTS

with river turtles, iguanas and nutria. Further in at the eastern shoreline of the reserve you can get a close-up view of the Río de la Plata's muddy waters. On warm weekends and holidays you can rent bikes just outside either the **northern** (Map p58) or **southern** entrances.

Tours are given on weekends; monthly Friday night full-moon tours are also available (call for schedules).

Colección de Arte Amalia Lacroze de Fortabat MUSEUM

(Museo Fortabat; Map p58; ☎011-4310-6600; www.coleccionfortabat.org.ar; Olga Cossettini 141; admission AR$60; ☺noon-8pm Tue-Sun, tours in Spanish 3pm & 5pm Tue-Sun) Rivaling Palermo's Malba for cutting-edge looks is this stunning art museum, prominently located at the northern end of Puerto Madero. It shows off the collection of billionairess, philanthropist and socialite Amalia Lacroze de Fortabat, Argentina's wealthiest woman. There are galleries devoted to Antonio Berni and Raúl Soldi (both famous Argentine painters) and works by international stars like Dalí, Klimt, Rodin and Chagall; look for Warhol's colorful take on Fortabat herself in the family portrait gallery. Call ahead for group tours in English.

Fragata Sarmiento MUSEUM

(Map p58; ☎011-4334-9386; Dique 3; admission AR$5; ☺10am-7pm) Over 23,000 Argentine naval cadets and officers have trained aboard this 85m sailing vessel, which traveled around the world 37 times between 1899 and 1938. Onboard are detailed records of its lengthy voyages, a gallery of its commanding officers, plenty of nautical items including old uniforms, and even the stuffed remains of Lampazo (the ship's pet dog), serenely posed. Peek into the ship's holds, galley and engine room and note the hooks where sleeping hammocks were strung up.

Corbeta Uruguay
MUSEUM

(Map p58; ☑ 011-4314-1090; Dique 4; admission AR$5; ☺10am-7pm) This 46m-long military ship did surveys along Argentina's coast and supplied bases in Antarctica until it was decommissioned in 1926, after 52 years of service. Displayed below the main deck are interesting relics from Antarctica expeditions, such as crampons and snowshoes, along with historical photos and nautical items. Check out the tiny kitchen, complete with *mate* (tea-like beverage) supplies (of course).

Puente de la Mujer
BRIDGE

(Women's Bridge; Map p58; Dique 3) The striking Puente de la Mujer is Puerto Madero's signature monument. Unveiled in 2001, this gleaming-white structure spans Dique 3 and resembles a sharp fishhook or even a harp – it's supposed to represent a couple dancing the tango. Designed by acclaimed Spanish architect Santiago Calatrava and mostly built in Spain, this 160m-long pedestrian bridge cost AR$6 million and rotates 90 degrees to allow water traffic to pass.

◉ Congreso

Congreso is an interesting mix of old-time cinemas and theaters, bustling commerce and hard-core politics. The buildings still hold that European aura, but there's more grittiness here than in the Microcentro: it has a more local city feel, with an atmosphere of faded elegance and fewer fancy crowds.

Separating Congreso from the Microcentro is Av 9 de Julio, 'the widest street in the world!,' as proud *porteños* love to boast. While this may be true – it's 16 lanes at its widest – the nearby side streets Cerrito and Carlos Pellegrini make it look even broader.

Teatro Colón
BUILDING

(Map p58; ☑ 011-4378-7127; www.teatrocolon. org.ar; Tucumán 1171; tours AR$180; ☺tours 9am-5pm) This gorgeous and impressive seven-story building is one of BA's most prominent landmarks. It's the city's main performing-arts venue and the only facility of its kind in the country, a world-class forum for opera, ballet and classical music with astounding acoustics. Occupying an entire city block, the Colón can seat 2500 spectators and provide standing room for another 500. The theater's opening night was a presentation of Verdi's *Aïda,* and visitors have been wowed ever since. Worthwhile backstage tours run frequently.

Palacio del Congreso
BUILDING

(Congress Building; Map p58; Hipólito Yrigoyen 1849) Colossal and topped with a green dome, the Palacio del Congreso cost more than twice its projected budget and set a precedent for contemporary Argentine public-works projects. It was modeled on the Capitol Building in Washington, DC, and was completed in 1906. Across the way, the **Monumento a los Dos Congresos** honors the congresses of 1810 in BA and 1816 in Tucumán, both of which led to Argentine independence.

Senate tours are given at 12:30pm and 5pm on Monday, Tuesday, Thursday and Friday in English and Spanish; Chamber of Deputies tours are given at 11am, 1pm, 3pm and 5pm. Go to the entrance on Hipólito Yrigoyen and bring photo ID. All tours are free.

Palacio Barolo
BUILDING

(Map p58; ☑ 011-4381-1885; www.palaciobarolo tours.com; Av de Mayo 1370; tours 45min AR$175, 1½hr AR$340) One of the Congreso area's most striking buildings is this 22-story concrete edifice. The building's unique design was inspired by Dante's Divine Comedy; its height (100m) is a reference to each canto (or song), the number of its floors (22) to verses per song, and its divided structure to hell, purgatory and heaven. Finished in 1923, Palacio Barolo was BA's highest skyscraper until the construction of Edificio Kavanagh in Retiro. At the top is a lighthouse with an amazing 360-degree view of the city.

The only way to see Palacio Barolo is via tours; check ahead for times as they vary by the day.

Teatro Nacional Cervantes
BUILDING

(Map p58; ☑ 011-4815-8883; www.teatrocervan tes.gov.ar; Libertad 815) Six blocks southwest of Plaza San Martín is the lavishly ornamented Cervantes theater. From the grand tiled lobby to the main theater, you can smell the long history of this place. The Cervantes is definitely showing its age, with worn carpeting and rough edges, but improvement projects are planned. Until then, enjoy the faded elegance with a tour (call for current schedules). It presents theater, comedy, musicals and dance.

Palacio de las Aguas Corrientes   BUILDING, MUSEUM
(Map p58; cnr Av Córdoba & Riobamba) **FREE**
Swedish engineer Karl Nyströmer and Nor-
wegian architect Olaf Boye helped create
this gorgeous and eclectic waterworks building. On the 2nd floor is the small and quirky
Museo del Patrimonio (Map p58; ☑011-
6319-1104; ⊗9am-1pm Mon-Fri, tours in Spanish
11am Mon, Wed & Fri) **FREE**. The collection of
pretty tiles, faucets, handles, ceramic pipe
joints and plenty of old toilets and bidets
is well lit and displayed. Guided visits offer
a backstage glimpse of the building's inner
workings and huge water tanks. Bring photo
ID and enter via Riobamba.

Obelisco   LANDMARK
(Map p58; cnr Avs 9 de Julio & Corrientes) The
city's unmistakable landmark is the famous
Obelisco, which soars 67m above the oval
Plaza de la República and was dedicated in
1936, on the 400th anniversary of the first
Spanish settlement on the Río de la Plata.
Following major soccer victories, boisterous
fans circle the Obelisco in jubilant, honking
celebration.

◉ San Telmo

Full of charm and personality, San Telmo is
one of BA's most attractive and historically
rich barrios. Narrow cobbled streets and
low-story colonial housing retain an old-
time feel, though the tourist dollar continues to bring about changes.

Historically, San Telmo is famous for the
violent street fighting that took place when
British troops, at war with Spain, invaded
the city in 1806. British forces advanced up
narrow Defensa, but an impromptu militia
drove the British back to their ships. The victory gave *porteños* confidence in their ability to stand apart from Spain, even though
the city's independence had to wait another
three years.

After this San Telmo became a fashionable, classy neighborhood. In the late 19th
century, however, a yellow-fever epidemic
hit, driving the rich north into present-day
Recoleta. Many older mansions were subdivided and became *conventillos* (tenements)
to house poor families. Years ago these *conventillos* attracted artists and bohemians
looking for cheap rent, but these days they're
more likely to be filled with fancy shops.

BUENOS AIRES SIGHTS

BUENOS AIRES FOR FREE

Buenos Aires has a surprising range of free things to do. Many cultural centers offer free
or inexpensive events, and some museums have free or half-off days. Search www.bue.
gob.ar for upcoming festivals and events.

Centro Cultural Kirchner (p57) Has mostly free activities and concerts (check its
website), though you may have to reserve ahead.

Usina del Arte (p105) Offers several free concerts per week covering a wide range of
genres.

BA Free Tour (☑15-6395-3000; www.bafreetour.com; donation recommended) Actually a
'donation' group tour, but you can contribute only if you want to.

Museo Nacional de Bellas Artes (p71) World-class, classical art museum that's
worth a visit.

Reserva Ecológical Costanera Sur (p60) Marshy green space next to, but a
world away from, downtown BA.

Ferias Artesanales Usually held on weekends, these street markets are mostly craft
stalls, but there's often 'donation' entertainment as well (including tango shows at **Feria
de San Telmo**, p108).

Polo tournaments The Palermo Open's qualifying matches, held from September to
mid-October at Palermo's Campo Argentino de Polo, are free to attend.

Tango lessons Head to the bandstand at the **Barrancas de Belgrano** (p73), a grassy
park in Belgrano, at 7pm from Friday to Sunday in summer. A *milonga* (dance event)
follows. Cultural centers sometimes offer free tango classes too.

★ **Plaza Dorrego** PLAZA
(Map p58) After Plaza de Mayo, Plaza Dorrego is the city's oldest plaza. It dates to the 18th century and was originally a pit stop for caravans bringing supplies into BA from around Argentina. At the turn of the 19th century it became a public square surrounded by colonial buildings that survive to this day. There's still a wonderful old-time atmosphere here and cafe-restaurants that will definitely take you back in time – if you can ignore the nearby chain coffee shops.

Plaza Dorrego is the heart of San Telmo's famous Sunday *feria* (street market).

El Zanjón de Granados ARCHAEOLOGICAL SITE
(Map p58; ☑ 011-4361-3002; www.elzanjon.com.ar; Defensa 755; tours 1hr Mon-Fri AR$170, 40min Sun AR$150; ☺ tours noon, 2pm & 3pm Mon-Fri, every 20min 11am-6pm Sun) One of the more unique places in BA is this amazing urban architectural site. A series of old tunnels, sewers and cisterns (built from 1730 onwards) were constructed above a river tributary and provided the base for one of BA's oldest settlements, which later became a family mansion and then tenement housing and some shops. It's best to reserve ahead for tours.

Museo de Arte Moderno de Buenos Aires MUSEUM
(MAMBA; Map p58; ☑ 011-4300-9139; www.museodeartemoderno.buenosaires.gob.ar; Av San Juan 350; admission AR$20, Tue free; ☺ 11am-7pm Tue-Fri, to 8pm Sat & Sun) Housed in a recycled tobacco warehouse, this spacious, multistory museum shows off the works of (mostly) Argentine contemporary artists. Expect exhibitions showcasing everything from photography to industrial design, and from figurative to conceptual art. There's also an auditorium and gift shop.

Museo de Arte Contemporáneo Buenos Aires MUSEUM
(MACBA; Map p58; ☑ 011-5299-2010; www.macba.com.ar; Av San Juan 328; admission AR$50; ☺ noon-7pm Mon & Wed-Fri, 11am-7:30pm Sat & Sun) Art lovers shouldn't miss this fine museum, which specializes in geometric abstraction drawn from the technology-driven world that surrounds us today (think architecture, maps and computers). So rather than traditional paintings, you'll see large, colorful and minimalist pieces meant to inspire reflection.

Museo Penitenciario MUSEUM
(Map p58; ☑ 011-4361-0917; Humberto Primo 378; ☺ 2-6pm Thu, Fri & Sun) FREE Dating from 1760, this building was a convent and later a women's prison before it became a penal museum in 1980; reconstructed old jail cells give an idea of the prisoners' conditions. Don't miss the homemade playing cards and shivs, plus the tennis balls used to hide drugs.

Museo Histórico Nacional MUSEUM
(Map p65; ☑ 011-4307-1182; Defensa 1600; ☺ 11am-6pm Wed-Sun) FREE Located in Parque Lezama is the city's national historical museum. It's dedicated to Argentina's revolution on May 25, 1810, though it covers a bit of precolonial times too. There are several portraits of presidents and other major figures of the time, along with a beautifully lit generals' room. Peek into the re-created version of José de San Martín's bedroom – he was a military hero and liberator of Argentina (along with other South American countries).

Mercado de San Telmo MARKET
(Map p58; btwn Defensa & Bolívar, Carlos Calvo & Estados Unidos block; ☺ 9am-8pm) This market was built in 1897 by Juan Antonio Buschiazzo, the same Italian-born Argentine architect who designed Cementerio de la Recoleta. It occupies the inside of an entire city block, though you wouldn't be able to tell just by looking at the modest sidewalk entrances. The wrought-iron interior (note the amazing original ceiling) makes it one of BA's most atmospheric markets; locals shop here for fresh produce and meat. Peripheral antique stalls offer old treasures.

If you like coffee, look for the **Coffee Town** (Map p58; ☑ 011-4361-0019; www.coffeetownargentina.com; Bolivar 976, inside Mercado de San Telmo; ☺ 10am-8pm) kiosk.

☉ La Boca

Blue collar and raffish to the core, La Boca is very much a locals' neighborhood. In the mid-19th century La Boca became home to Spanish and Italian immigrants who settled along the Riachuelo, the sinuous river that divides the city from the surrounding province of Buenos Aires. Many came during the booming 1880s and ended up working in the many meat-packing plants and warehouses here, processing and shipping out much of Argentina's vital beef exports.

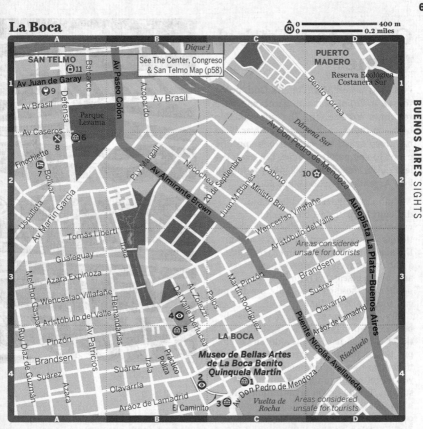

La Boca

BUENOS AIRES SIGHTS

La Boca

◎ **Top Sights**
  1 Museo de Bellas Artes de La Boca
     Benito Quinquela Martín...................C4

◎ **Sights**
  2 El Caminito..B4
  3 Fundación Proa..C4
  4 La Bombonera Stadium.........................B3
  5 Museo de la Pasión Boquense.............B4
  6 Museo Histórico Nacional A2

🛏 **Sleeping**
  7 Mundo Bolívar A2

🍴 **Eating**
  8 Hierbabuena A2
     Proa Cafe..(see 3)

🍷 **Drinking & Nightlife**
  9 Doppelgänger A1

🎭 **Entertainment**
  10 Usina del Arte.......................................D2

🛍 **Shopping**
  11 Moebius A1

After sprucing up the shipping barges, the port dwellers splashed leftover paint on the corrugated-metal sidings of their own houses – unwittingly giving La Boca what would become one of its claims to fame. Unfortunately, some of the neighborhood's color also comes from the rainbow slick of industrial waste on the river.

El Caminito (Map p65; Av Don Pedro de Mendoza, near Del Valle Iberlucea), near the southern edge of La Boca, is the barrio's most famous street – and has a reputation

Going to a Fútbol Game

In a land where Maradona is God, going to see a *fútbol* (soccer) game can be a religious experience. The *superclásico* between the Boca Juniors and River Plate has been called the number one sporting event to see before you die, but even the less-celebrated games will give you insight into Argentina's national passion.

Attending a regular match isn't too difficult. Keep an eye on the clubs' websites, which inform when and where tickets will be sold; often they're sold at the stadium before the game. You'll get a choice between *populares* (bleachers) and *plateas* (seats). Try to avoid the *populares;* these can get really rowdy and can sometimes be dangerous.

If you want to see a *clásico* – a match between two major teams – getting a ticket is much harder. Boca doesn't even put tickets for its key matches on sale; all tickets go to *socios* (members). Instead, you're better off going with an agency such as Tangol or via organizations like www.fcbafa.com or www.landingpadba.com. It won't be cheap, but it's much easier getting a ticket this way (and safer, with less chance of fake tickets).

However, if you do want to chance getting your own *clásico* or *superclásico* ticket, you can always look online at www.buenosaires.craigslist.org or www.mercadolibre.com.ar. If you're confident in your bargaining skills, scalpers exist, too.

Dress down, and try to look inconspicuous when you go. Take minimal cash and keep your camera close. You probably won't get in with water bottles, and food and drink in the stadium is meager and expensive. Arrive early to enjoy the insane build-up to the game. Most importantly – don't wear the opposing team's colors.

TEAMS

Buenos Aires has two dozen professional football teams – the most of any city in the world. Here are some of them:

Boca Juniors (☎011-5777-1200; www.bocajuniors.com.ar)

River Plate (☎011-4789-1200; www.cariverplate.com.ar)

Racing (☎011-4371-9995; www.racingclub.com)

Independiente (☎011-4229-7600; www.clubaindependiente.com/en)

San Lorenzo de Almagro (☎011-4016-2600; www.sanlorenzo.com.ar)

Clockwise from top left
1. River Plate supporters **2.** Boca Juniors player
3. La Bombonera Stadium

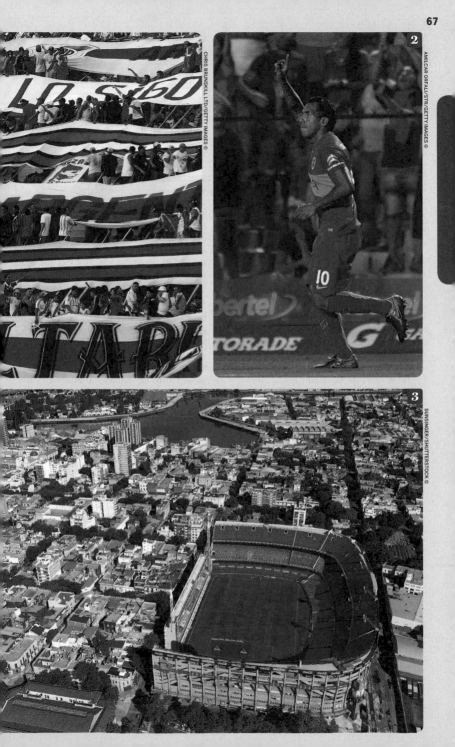

❶ BOCA WARNING

La Boca is a locals' neighborhood, and while kids and older folks safely walk the streets every day, visitors can stand out away from the touristy sights. It's best if you don't stray too far from the riverside walk, El Caminito or La Bombonera Stadium, especially while toting expensive cameras. And certainly don't cross the bridge over the Riachuelo. Buses 29, 64 and 152 go from Palermo or the city center to La Boca. Taxis are best after dark.

Some companies offer Boca day tours, which are a good way to see this neighborhood. Check out www.ba culturalconcierge.com and www.anda travel.com.

for being a tourist trap. Here, busloads of camera-laden tourists browse the small crafts fair, watch tango dancers perform for spare change and are prepositioned by touts to pose for photographs alongside tango props. A riverside pedestrian walkway offers a close-up sniff of the Riachuelo, while a few museums provide mental stimulation.

Fundación Proa MUSEUM
(Map p65; ☎011-4104-1000; www.proa.org; Av Don Pedro de Mendoza 1929; admission AR$40; ☺11am-7pm Tue-Sun) Only the most cutting-edge national and international artists are invited to show at this elegant art museum, which features high ceilings, white walls and large display halls. Stunning contemporary installations utilize a wide variety of media and themes, while the rooftop terrace is the stylish place in La Boca for relaxing with a drink or a snack – it boasts a view of the Riachuelo. Plenty of cultural offerings include talks, lectures, workshops, music concerts and cinema screenings.

★Museo de Bellas Artes de
La Boca Benito Quinquela Martín MUSEUM
(Map p65; ☎011-4301-1080; www.museoquin quela.gov.ar; Av Don Pedro de Mendoza 1835; suggested donation AR$20; ☺10am-6pm Tue-Fri, 11:15am-6pm Sat & Sun) Once the home and studio of surrealist painter Benito Quinquela Martín (1890–1977), this fine-arts museum exhibits his works and those of other classic Argentine artists. Martín used silhouettes of laboring men, smokestacks and water reflec-

tions as recurring themes, and painted with broad, rough brush strokes and dark colors. There are outdoor sculptures on the rooftop terraces, and the top tier has awesome views of the port.

Museo de la Pasión Boquense MUSEUM
(Map p65; ☎011-4362-1100; www.museobo quense.com; Brandsen 805; admission AR$115-130; ☺10am-6pm) High-tech and spiffy, this *fútbol* (soccer) museum chronicles the rough-and-tumble neighborhood of La Boca, La Bombonera Stadium, soccer idols' histories, video highlights, the championships, the trophies and, of course, the gooooals. There's a 360-degree theater in a giant soccer-ball auditorium, an old jersey collection and a gift shop. The museum is right under the stadium, a couple of blocks from the tourist part of El Caminito; get a tour of the pitch for a few extra pesos.

◉ Retiro

Well-located Retiro is one of the ritziest neighborhoods in BA, but it hasn't always been this way. The area was the site of a monastery during the 17th century and later became the *retiro* (country retreat) of Agustín de Robles, a Spanish governor. Since then, Retiro's current Plaza San Martín – which sits on a bluff – has played host to a slave market, a military fort and even a bullring. Things are more quiet and exclusive these days.

Plaza San Martín PLAZA
(Map p70) French landscape architect Carlos Thays designed the leafy Plaza San Martín, which is surrounded by some of Buenos Aires' most impressive public buildings. The park's most prominent monument is the obligatory equestrian **statue of José de San Martín**; important visiting dignitaries often come to honor the country's liberator by leaving wreaths at its base. On the downhill side of the park you'll see the **Monumento a los Caídos de Malvinas** (Map p70), a memorial to the young men who died in the Falklands War.

Palacio Paz BUILDING
(Círculo Militar; Map p70; ☎ext 147, 011-4311-1071; www.palaciopaz.com.ar; Av Santa Fe 750; tours in English/Spanish AR$100/70; ☺tours English 3:30pm Thu, Spanish 3pm Tue, 11am & 3pm Wed-Fri) Once the private residence of José C Paz – founder of the still-running news-

paper *La Prensa* – this opulent, French-style palace (1909) is the grandest in BA. Inside its 12,000 sq meters are ornate rooms with marble walls, salons gilded in real gold and halls boasting beautiful wood-tiled floors. The pièce de résistance is the circular grand hall with mosaic floors, marble details and stained-glass cupola. Nearly all materials came from Europe and were then assembled here.

Museo de Arte Hispanoamericano Isaac Fernández Blanco
MUSEUM

(Palacio Noel; Map p70; ☑011-4327-0228; www.museofernandezblanco.buenosaires.gob.ar; Suipacha 1422; admission AR$10, Wed free; ⊘1-7pm Tue-Fri, 11am-7pm Sat & Sun) Dating from 1921, this museum is in an old mansion of the neocolonial Peruvian style that developed as a reaction against French influences in turn-of-the-19th-century Argentine architecture. Its exceptional collection of colonial art includes silverwork from Alto Perú (present-day Bolivia), religious paintings and baroque instruments (including a Guarneri violin). The curved ceiling in the main salon is beautifully painted, and there's also a peaceful garden.

Museo de Armas
MUSEUM

(Weapons Museum; Map p70; ☑ext 179, 011-4311-1071; www.museodearmas.com.ar; Av Santa Fe 702; admission AR$40; ⊘1-7pm Mon-Fri) Even if you've spent time in the armed forces, you probably have never seen so many weapons of destruction. This maze-like museum exhibits a frighteningly large but excellent collection of over 3500 bazookas, grenade launchers, cannons, machine guns, muskets, pistols, armor, lances and swords; even the gas mask for a combat horse is on display. The evolution of rifles and handguns is especially thoroughly documented, and there's a small but impressive Japanese weapons room.

Torre Monumental
LANDMARK

(Map p70; ☑011-4311-0186; Plaza Fuerza Aérea Argentina; ⊘10am-6pm Mon-Fri, to 6:30pm Sat & Sun) **FREE** Standing prominently across from Plaza San Martín, this 76m-high miniature version of London's Big Ben was a donation from the city's British community in 1916 and built with materials shipped over from England. You can enter inside the base of the tower, where there are a few historical photos, but folks aren't allowed up the elevator.

⊙ Recoleta & Barrio Norte

BA's wealthiest citizens live and breathe in Recoleta, the city's most exclusive and fashionable neighborhood. In the 1870s many upper-class *porteños* relocated here from San Telmo during a yellow-fever epidemic. Today you can best see the wealth of this sumptuous quarter on Av Alvear, where many of the old mansions (and newer international boutiques) are located.

With parks, museums and French architecture, Recoleta is best known for its Cementerio de la Recoleta. On weekends, the **Plaza Intendente Alvear** hosts a popular crafts fair. A little further north is the 20m-high sculptural flower **Floralis Genérica**, whose giant metal petals 'close up' at night.

Barrio Norte is a subneighborhood southwest of Recoleta, but the lines are blurred.

★ Cementerio de la Recoleta
CEMETERY

(Map p70; ☑0800-444-2363; cnr Junín & Guido; AR$100; ⊘7am-5:30pm) This cemetery is arguably BA's number-one attraction, and a must on every tourist's list. You can wander for hours in this amazing city of the dead, where countless 'streets' are lined with impressive statues and marble mausoleums. Peek into the crypts and check out the dusty coffins and try to decipher the history of its inhabitants. Past presidents, military heroes, influential politicians and the just plain rich and famous have made it past the gates here.

Basílica de Nuestra Señora del Pilar
CHURCH

(Map p70; ☑011-4806-2209; www.basilicadelpilar.org.ar; Junín 1904; museum AR$6; ⊘museum 10:30am-6:10pm Mon-Sat, 2:30pm-6:10pm Sun)

EVITA'S GRAVE

She's Recoleta's biggest star, and everyone who visits **Cementerio de la Recoleta** wants to see her final resting place. Here's how to find it: go up to the first major 'intersection' from the entrance, where there's a statue. Turn left 90 degrees, continue until a mausoleum blocks your way, go around it to the right and turn right at the wide 'street.' After three blocks look to the left and you'll likely see people at her site, along with bunches of flowers. Don't expect anything grandiose; it's a pretty modest mausoleum.

Retiro, Recoleta & Barrio Norte

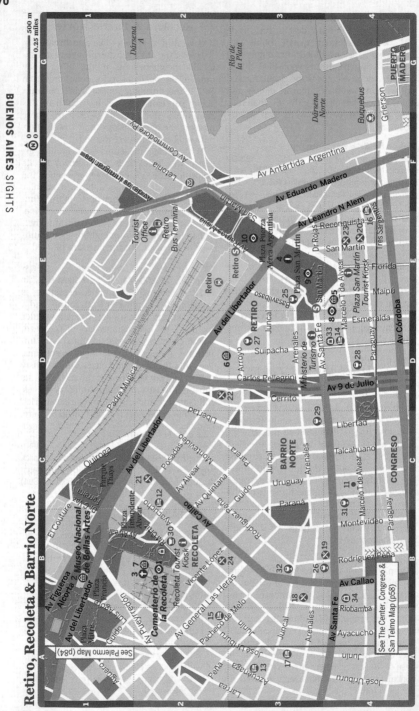

500 m
0.25 miles

Dársena A

Río de la Plata

Dársena Norte

PUERTO MADERO

Buquebus

Grierson

Av Antártida Argentina

Av Eduardo Madero

Av Los Inmigrantes

Letonia

Av Commodore PY

Tourist Office

Retiro

Bus Terminal

San Martín

Av Leandro N Alem

Reconquista

Av Dr Rojas

San Martín

Tres Sargentos

Retiro S

Plaza Fuerza Aérea Argentina

RETIRO

Av del Libertador

Basavilbaso

Juncal

Arroyo

Suipacha

Arenales

Ministerio de Turismo

Av Santa Fe

Carlos Pellegrini

Av 9 de Julio

Cerrito

Libertad

Talcahuano

BARRIO NORTE

Juncal

Uruguay

Arenales

Parana

CONGRESO

Montevideo

Marcelo T de Alvear

Rodríguez Peña

Av Callao

Riobamba

Paraguay

Ayacucho

See The Center, Congreso & San Telmo Map (p58)

Plaza San Martín

San Martín

Florida

Maipú

Esmeralda

Av Córdoba

Paraguay

Marcelo T de Alvear

Tourist Kiosk

Padre Mugica

El Couture

Quiroga

Av del Libertador

Av del Libertador

Montevideo

Posadas

Parera

Libertad

Av Alvear

Rodríguez Peña

Av Quintana

Guido

Av Callao

RECOLETA

Av Alvear

Ayacucho

Plaza Intendente Alvear

Cementerio de la Recoleta

Recoleta Tourist Kiosk

Vicente López

Av General Las Heras

Junín

Pacheco de Melo

José Urtubey

Museo Nacional de Bellas Artes

Av Figueroa Alcorta

Av del Libertador

Av del Libertador

Plaza Francia

Plaza Mitre

Luis Agote

See Palermo Map (p84)

Agüero

Guido

Larrea

Peña

Azcuénaga

Junín

Arenales

Av Santa Fe

Juncal

José Urtubey

Junín

Retiro, Recoleta & Barrio Norte

Top Sights
1 Cementerio de la Recoleta B2
2 Museo Nacional de Bellas Artes B1

Sights
3 Basílica de Nuestra Señora del Pilar B2
4 Monumento a los Caidos de Malvinas E3
5 Museo de Armas E4
6 Museo de Arte Hispanoamericano Isaac Fernández Blanco D2
7 Museo Participativo de Ciencias B2
8 Palacio Paz D4
9 Plaza San Martín E3
10 Torre Monumental E3

Activities, Courses & Tours
11 VOS C4

Sleeping
12 Alvear Palace Hotel C2
13 Art Suites A3
14 Casa Calma D4
15 Hotel Lion D'or A2
16 Hotel Tres Sargentos F4
17 Poetry Building A3

Eating
18 Como en Casa B3
19 Cumaná B4
20 Dadá E4
21 El Sanjuanino C2
22 Elena D2
23 Filo E4
24 Rodi Bar B2

Drinking & Nightlife
25 BASA Basement Bar E3
26 Casa Bar B4
27 Florería Atlántico D3
28 Flux D4
29 Gran Bar Danzón C3
30 La Biela B2
31 Milión C4
Pony Line Bar .... (see 22)
32 Shamrock Basement B3

Shopping
33 Autoría D4
34 El Ateneo B4
35 Feria Artesanal B2

The centerpiece of this gleaming white colonial church, built by Jesuits in 1716, is a Peruvian altar adorned with silver from Argentina's northwest. Inside, head to the left to visit the small but historic cloisters museum; it's home to religious vestments, paintings, writings and interesting artifacts, and there are good views of Recoleta cemetery.

★ Museo Nacional de Bellas Artes — MUSEUM

(Map p70; ☎011-5288-9900; www.mnba.gob.ar; Av del Libertador 1473; ⏲12:30-8:30pm Tue-Fri, 9:30am-8:30pm Sat & Sun) FREE This is Argentina's most important national arts museum and contains many key works by Benito Quinquela Martín, Xul Solar, Eduardo Sívori and other Argentine artists of the 19th and 20th centuries. There are also impressive international works by European masters such as Cézanne, Degas, Picasso, Rembrandt, Toulouse-Lautrec and Van Gogh. Everything is well displayed, and there's also a cinema, concerts and classes.

Museo Xul Solar — MUSEUM

(Map p84; ☎011-4824-3302; www.xulsolar.org.ar; Laprida 1212; admission AR$20; ⏲noon-8pm Tue-Fri, to 7pm Sat, closed Feb, tours in Spanish 4pm Tue & Thu, 3:30pm Sat) Xul Solar was a painter, inventor, poet and friend of Jorge Luis Borges. This museum (located in his old mansion) showcases over 80 of his unique and colorful yet subdued paintings. Solar's Klee-esque style includes fantastically themed, almost cartoonish figures placed in surreal cubist landscapes. It's great stuff, and bizarre enough to put him in a class of his own.

Palermo

Palermo is heaven on Earth for BA's middle class. Its large, grassy parks – regally punctuated with grand monuments – are popular destinations on weekends, when families fill the shady lanes, cycle the bike paths and paddle on the peaceful lakes. Many important museums and elegant embassies are also located here, and certain subneighborhoods of Palermo have become the city's hottest destinations for shopping and nightlife.

Palermo's green spaces haven't always been for the masses. The area around **Parque 3 de Febrero** was originally the 19th-century dictator Juan Manuel de Rosas' private retreat and became public parkland after his fall from power. Within these green spaces you'll now find a zoo, a planetarium and several gardens. Just south of the zoo is **Plaza Italia**, Palermo's main transport hub.

BUENOS AIRES FOR CHILDREN

Palermo's **Parque 3 de Febrero** (Map p84; cnr Avs del Libertador & de la Infanta Isabel; 🚲 10, 34, 130) is a huge park where on weekends traffic isn't allowed on the ring road (rent bikes, boats and in-line skates nearby). Other good stops here include a planetarium, a zoo and a Japanese garden. If you're downtown and need a nature break, there's **Reserva Ecológica Costanera Sur** (p60), a large nature preserve with good bird-watching.

Shopping malls make safe destinations for families – one of the best is **Mercado de Abasto** (p74), which boasts a full-blown children's 'museum' (ie fancy playground) and mini-amusement park.

In San Telmo, check out the puppet museum, **Museo Argentino del Títere** (Map p58; ☎ 011-4307-6917; www.museoargdeltitere.com.ar; Estados Unidos 802; ⊙ vary widely, call ahead) FREE, which has inexpensive weekend shows.

Recoleta's **Museo Participativo de Ciencias** (Map p70; ☎ 011-4806-3456; www.mpc.org.ar; Junín 1930; admission AR$65; ⊙ vary widely, check website) is a hands-on science museum with interactive learning displays. In Caballito is the good **Museo Argentino de Ciencias Naturales** (p74).

Christian parents might want to take the kids to **Tierra Santa** (p73), a unique and tacky (but fun) religious theme park. Not far away is **Parque Norte** (p75), a large water park that's perfect on a hot day.

Tigre, north of the city, makes a great day excursion. Get there via the Tren de la Costa; it ends right at **Parque de la Costa** (☎ 011-4002-6000; www.parquedelacosta.com.ar; Vivanco 1509; admission from AR$150), a typical amusement park with fun rides.

Outside the city is the exceptional zoo, **Parque Temaikén** (☎ 034-8843-6900; www.temaiken.org.ar; RP25, Km1, Escobar; adult/child AR$245/200; ⊙ 10am-7pm Wed-Sun Dec-Feb, to 6pm Tue-Sun Mar-Nov). Only the most charming animal species are on display (think meerkats, pygmy hippos and white tigers), roaming freely around natural enclosures. An excellent aquarium comes with touch pools, and plenty of interactive areas provide mental stimulation. Some Tuesdays are discounted.

To help calm down temper tantrums, visit one of BA's dozens of excellent ice-cream shops.

One of the capital's most trendsetting areas is **Palermo Viejo**, a scenic neighborhood with colonial buildings and plenty of fine shopping, dining and nightlife; it's further subdivided into Palermo Soho and Palermo Hollywood. The heart of this neighborhood is **Plaza Serrano** (Map p84), a small but very popular plaza surrounded by bars and restaurants, and host to a small weekend arts fair. Another popular but much smaller neighborhood to the north is **Las Cañitas**; many restaurants and other nightspots here attract hordes of hipsters at night, when Av Báez clogs with traffic.

★ **Museo de Arte Latinoamericano de Buenos Aires** MUSEUM
(Malba; Map p84; ☎ 011-4808-6500; www.malba.org.ar; Av Figueroa Alcorta 3415; admission AR$75, Wed AR$36; ⊙ noon-8pm Thu-Mon, to 9pm Wed) Sparkling inside its glass walls, this airy modern arts museum is one of BA's fanciest. Millionaire and philanthropist Eduardo Costantini displays his fine collection of Latin American art, which includes work by Argentines Xul Solar and Antonio Berni, plus some pieces by Mexicans Diego Rivera and Frida Kahlo. A cinema screens art-house films, and there's a gift shop and upscale cafe as well.

Museo Nacional de Arte Decorativo MUSEUM
(Map p84; ☎ 011-4802-6606; www.mnad.org; Av del Libertador 1902; admission AR$20, Tue free, tours AR$15; ⊙ 2-7pm Tue-Sun, closed Sun in Jan) This museum is housed in the stunning beaux-arts mansion called Residencia Errázuriz Alvear (1917), once the residence of Chilean aristocrat Matías Errázuriz and his wife, Josefina de Alvear. It now displays many of their very posh belongings, along with beautiful features such as Corinthian columns and a gorgeous marble staircase inspired by the Palace of Versailles. There's also an amazing hall which has a carved

wooden ceiling, stained-glass panels and a huge stone fireplace. There's also a lovely cafe outside.

Jardín Zoológico ZOO
(Map p84; ☑ 011-4011-9900; www.zoobuenos aires.com.ar; cnr Avs General Las Heras & Sarmiento; adult/child AR$180/free; ⊙ 10am-6pm Tue-Sun Oct-Mar, to 5pm Apr-Sep) Set on 18 hectares, Buenos Aires' Jardín Zoológico is a decent zoo, housing over 350 species – many in 'natural' and good-sized animal enclosures. On sunny weekends it's packed with families enjoying the large green spaces and artificial lakes. Some of the buildings housing the animals are impressive; check out the elephant house. An aquarium, a monkey island, reptile house and large aviary are other highlights; a few special exhibits (like the sea lion show or carousel) cost extra.

Jardín Japonés GARDENS
(Map p84; ☑ 011-4804-4922; www.jardinjapones. org.ar; cnr Avs Casares & Berro; adult/child AR$50/ free; ⊙ 10am-6pm) First opened in 1967 and then donated to the city of Buenos Aires in 1979 (on the centenary of the arrival of Argentina's first Japanese immigrants), Jardín Japonés makes a peaceful rest stop. Inside there's a Japanese restaurant along with lovely ponds filled with koi and spanned by pretty bridges. Japanese culture can be experienced through occasional exhibitions and workshops on ikebana, haiku, origami, taiko (Japanese drumming) and other events.

Museo Evita MUSEUM
(Map p84; ☑ 011-4807-0306; www.museoevita. org; Lafinur 2988; admission AR$40; ⊙ 11am-7pm Tue-Sun) Everybody who's anybody in Argentina has their own museum, and Eva Perón (1919–52) is no exception. Museo Evita immortalizes the Argentine heroine with plenty of videos, historical photos, books, old posters and newspaper headlines. However, the prize memorabilia has to be her wardrobe: dresses, shoes, handbags, hats and blouses lie proudly behind glass, forever pressed and pristine. Even Evita's old wallets and perfumes are on display. Our favorite is a picture of her kicking a soccer ball – in heels.

Tierra Santa THEME PARK
(☑ 011-4784-9551; www.tierrasanta.com.ar; Av Costanera R Obligado 5790; adult/child AR$100/40; ⊙ 9am-9pm Fri, noon-8pm Sat, Sun & holidays Apr-Nov, 4pm-10pm Fri-Sun & holidays Dec-Mar) Even respectful, devout Catholics will find this – the 'world's first religious theme park' – a very tacky place. It boasts animatronic dioramas of Adam and Eve and the Last Supper, but its pièce de résistance is a giant Jesus rising from a fake mountain – aka the resurrection – every half-hour. It's just north of Palermo, near the water.

Centro Islámico Rey Fahd MOSQUE
(Map p84; ☑ 011-4899-0201; www.ccislamico reyfahd.org.ar; Av Int Bullrich 55; ⊙ tours noon Tue, Thu & Sat) This landmark mosque, built by Saudis on land donated by former president Carlos Menem, is southeast of Las Cañitas. Free tours in Spanish are offered three-times weekly (bring your passport, dress conservatively and enter via Av Int Bullrich).

⊙ Belgrano

Bustling Av Cabildo, the racing heartbeat of Belgrano, is an overwhelming jumble of noise and neon; it's a two-way street of clothing, shoe and homeware shops that does its part to support the mass consumerism of *porteños*.

Only a block east of Av Cabildo, **Plaza Belgrano** is the site of a modest but fun weekend crafts fair.

Near the plaza stands the Italianate **Iglesia de la Inmaculada Concepción**, a church popularly known as 'La Redonda' because of its impressive dome. Four blocks northeast of Plaza Belgrano is **Barrancas de Belgrano**, an attractive park on one of the few natural hillocks in the city. And nearby, just across the train tracks, Belgrano's small **Chinatown** offers decent Chinese restaurants and cheap goods.

Museo de Arte Español Enrique Larreta MUSEUM
(☑ 011-4784-4040; Juramento 2291; admission AR$10; ⊙ 1-7pm Mon-Fri, 10am-8pm Sat & Sun) Hispanophile novelist Enrique Larreta (1875–1961) resided in this elegant colonial-style house across from Plaza Belgrano, which now displays his private art collection to the public. It's a grand and spacious old building, and contains classic Spanish art, period furniture, wood-carved religious items, and shields and armor. The wood and tiled floors are beautiful, and everything is richly lit. Tours in Spanish are given at 5pm Monday to Friday, and 4pm and 6pm on Saturday and Sunday. Be sure to stroll the lovely gardens out back.

Espacio Memoria y Derechos Humanos
MUSEUM

(ESMA; ☑011-4702-9920; www.espaciomemoria.ar; Av del Libertador 8151, Nuñez; ⊙noon-5pm Fri-Sun) FREE Argentina's Dirty War (1976–83) was the darkest chapter in its history. Human-rights groups estimate that up to 30,000 people were kidnapped, tortured and killed under the military dictatorship of Jorge Rafael Videla. Most of these atrocities happened right here at this old Naval campus called ESMA, described by some as Argentina's Auschwitz. Today these buildings have been turned into a museum as a memorial for the victims, and as a way to help prevent such an unimaginable occurrence from happening again.

◉ Once & Around

BA's most ethnically colorful neighborhood is Once, with sizable groups of Jews, Peruvians and Koreans. The cheap market around Once train station always bustles, with vendors selling their goods on sidewalks, and crowds everywhere.

Museo Argentino de Ciencias Naturales
MUSEUM

(Natural Science Museum; Map p84; ☑011-4982-6595; www.macn.gov.ar; Av Ángel Gallardo 490; admission AR$15; ⊙2-7pm) Way over to the west, the oval Parque del Centenario is a large open space containing this excellent natural-science museum. On display are large collections of meteorites, rocks and minerals, seashells, insects and dinosaur skeleton replicas. The taxidermy and skeleton rooms are especially good. Bring the kids; they can mingle with the hundreds of children who visit on school excursions.

Museo Casa Carlos Gardel
MUSEUM

(Map p84; ☑011-4964-2071; Jean Jaurés 735; admission AR$5, Wed free; ⊙11am-6pm Mon & Wed-Fri, 10am-6pm Sat & Sun) Small but noteworthy is this tribute to tango's most famous voice. Located in Gardel's old house, this museum traces his partnership with José Razzano and displays old memorabilia like photos, records and news clippings. There isn't a whole lot to see, so it's best for real fans or just the curious; look for the cluster of colorfully painted buildings.

Mercado de Abasto
BUILDING

(Map p84; ☑011-4959-3400; www.abasto-shopping.com.ar; Av Corrientes 3247; ⊙10am-10pm)

The historic Mercado de Abasto (1895) has been recycled by US-Hungarian financier George Soros into one of the most beautiful shopping centers in the city. The building, once a large vegetable market, received an architectural prize in 1937 for its Av Corrientes facade. It holds more than 200 stores, a large cinema, a large food court and the only kosher McDonald's outside Israel (the one upstairs and next to Burger King).

🏃 Activities

The extensive greenery in Palermo provides good areas for recreation, especially on weekends when the ring road around the rose garden is closed to motor vehicles. Recoleta has grassy parks also, if you can avoid the dog piles. Best of all is the Reserva Ecológica Costanera Sur, an ecological paradise just east of Puerto Madero; it's excellent for walks, runs, bike rides and even a bit of wildlife viewing.

Cycling

BA is not the greatest city for bicycles, but there are a few exceptions. It might be best to join a city bike tour, which includes bicycle and guide; tour companies usually offer bike rentals too. And if you're around on the first Sunday of each month, check out BA's version of **Critical Mass** (www.masacriticabsas.com.ar). For more info on cycling around BA, see the Getting Around section (p112).

Horseback Riding

Caballos a la Par HORSEBACK RIDING
(☑011-15-5248-3592; www.caballos-alapar.com) If you want to get out of town for a few hours and hop on a horse, forget those touristy *estancias* (ranches) and check out Caballos a la Par. Guided rides are given in a provincial park about an hour's drive from Buenos Aires. Even if you've never ridden before, you might be galloping by sundown.

Fútbol

Inspired by watching professional *fútbol* teams play the game? Well, you can partake yourself – just contact **FC Buenos Aires Fútbol Amigos** (www.fcbafa.com) to join fellow travelers, expats and locals for some pickup fun. The best part might be the *asados* (barbecues) that often happen after the games, plus of course the friends you make on the pitch.

Swimming

Finding a good swimming hole isn't easy in BA – unless you're lucky enough to be staying at a hotel with a decent pool (or are OK with splashing around indoors at the nearest gym).

Parque Norte SWIMMING
(☑ 011-4787-1382; www.parquenorte.com; Avs Cantilo & Guiraldes; admission Mon-Fri AR$80, Sat AR$100, Sun AR$110; ☺ pool 8:30am-8pm Mon-Fri, to 10pm Sat & Sun) When the temperatures and humidity skyrocket, head north to this large water park in Belgrano. It's great for families with huge shallow pools (perhaps 4ft at their deepest), plus a large water slide and lots of umbrellas and lounge chairs (both cost extra). There are plenty of grassy areas in which to enjoy a picnic or *mate* (tea-like beverage). Bring your own towels, and make sure you're clean – quick 'health' inspections are done to check for such unpleasantries as athlete's foot or lice.

Courses

Visitors have many opportunities to study almost anything in BA, from cooking to tango. Most cultural centers offer a wide variety of classes at affordable rates.

BA is a major destination for students of Spanish, and good institutes are common. Nearly all organize social activities and homestay programs, and all have private classes. When you're looking for an institute, it's always best to ask around for current recommendations.

Spanglish LANGUAGE COURSE
(www.spanglishexchange.com) For something different, try Spanglish. It's set up like speed dating; you'll speak five minutes in English and five in Spanish, then switch partners.

Academia Buenos Aires LANGUAGE COURSE
(Map p58; ☑ 011-4345-5954; www.academia buenosaires.com; Hipólito Yrigoyen 571, 4th fl, Microcentro)

Expanish LANGUAGE COURSE
(Map p58; ☑ 011-5252-3040; www.expanish. com; 25 de Mayo 457, 4th fl, Microcentro)

Rayuela LANGUAGE COURSE
(Map p58; ☑ 011-4300-2010; www.spanish-argentina.com.ar; Chacabuco 852, 1st fl, No 11, San Telmo)

Vamos LANGUAGE COURSE
(Map p84; ☑ 011-5984-2201; www.vamospanish. com; Av Coronel Díaz 1736, Palermo)

VOS LANGUAGE COURSE
(Map p70; ☑ 011-4812-1140; www.vosbuenos aires.com; Marcelo T de Alvear 1459, Recoleta)

Foto Ruta PHOTOGRAPHY
(☑ 011-6030-8881; www.foto-ruta.com) This workshop is run by two expat women who send folks out into neighborhoods with a few 'themes' to photograph – then everyone watches the slide show.

Tours

There are plenty of organized tours, from the large tourist-bus variety to guided bike rides to straight-up free (ie donation) walks. Some travel agencies also offer tours, including some very adventurous ones.

Companies offer tours in English and possibly other languages, and most have private tour options too.

BA Walking Tours WALKING TOUR
(☑ 15-5773-1001; www.ba-walking-tours.com) Day tours, night tours, historic tours and tango tours.

Biking Buenos Aires BICYCLE TOUR
(☑ 011-4300-5373; www.bikingbuenosaires.com) Friendly American and Argentine guides take you on various tours of Buenos Aires; tour themes include architecture and graffiti.

Buenos Aires Street Art WALKING TOUR
(www.buenosairesstreetart.com) Walking tour highlighting some of BA's most interesting street art. Supports local artists too.

Buenos Tours WALKING TOUR
(www.buenostours.com) Well-run private tours guided by friendly, knowledgeable and responsible local expats.

Graffitimundo TOUR
(☑ 15-3683-3219; www.graffitimundo.com) Excellent tours of some of BA's best graffiti. Learn artists' history and the local graffiti culture. Several tours available; stencil workshops too.

Urban Biking BICYCLE TOUR
(☑ 011-4314-2325; www.urbanbiking.com) One- and two-day cycling tours, along with bike and kayak excursions to Tigre.

Festivals & Events

Check with tourist offices for other happenings and for exact dates, as some can vary from year to year.

Festival Internacional de Cine Independiente
FILM

(http://festivales.buenosaires.gob.ar; ☺ mid-Apr) Highlights national and international independent films at venues all around Buenos Aires.

Arte BA
ART

(www.arteba.org; ☺ May) Popular event highlighting contemporary art, introducing exciting new young artists, and showing off top gallery works.

Festival y Mundial de Tango
TANGO FESTIVAL

(http://festivales.buenosaires.gob.ar; ☺ mid-Aug) Masterful tango performances, tango movies, classes, workshops, conferences and competitions in venues all over Buenos Aires.

Vinos y Bodegas
WINE

(www.expovinosybodegas.com.ar; ☺ Sep) A can't-miss event for wine aficionados, offering vintages from over 100 Argentine *bodegas* (wineries).

Noche de los Museos
ART

(www.lanochedelosmuseos.gob.ar; ☺ late Oct) Highly popular, one-night event where, from 8pm to 3am, hundreds of BA's museums, cultural centers and galleries open to the public for free exhibitions, concerts, performances and other events. Major lines offer free bus transport as well.

Creamfields
MUSIC

(www.creamfieldsba.com; ☺ Nov) BA's answer to the UK's outdoor, all-night, cutting-edge electronic-music and dance party, with dozens of international DJs and bands.

Campeonato Abierto de Polo
SPORTS

(www.aapolo.com; ☺ Dec) Watch the world's best polo players and their gorgeous horses thunder up and down Palermo's polo fields.

🛏 Sleeping

Over the last decade Buenos Aires has seen its accommodations options increase exponentially. Boutique hotels and guesthouses, especially, have mushroomed in neighborhoods such as San Telmo and Palermo, and hostels are a dime a dozen. You shouldn't have trouble finding the type of place you're looking for, but it's still a good idea to make a reservation beforehand – especially during holidays or the busy summer months of November through January.

Some places will help with transportation to and from the airport if you reserve ahead of time. The most expensive hotels will take credit cards but cheaper places might not. Some kind of breakfast is included nearly everywhere, often consisting of just a few *medialunas* (croissants) and coffee or tea – though many fancier places offer continental or buffet breakfasts.

Rates at top-end hotels often vary depending on occupancy levels. As a general rule, calling ahead or reserving via websites usually results in better pricing. At Hostelling International (HI) hostels, buying a membership card gives a discount off listed prices.

Prices listed here are for high season (roughly November to February) and include BA's whopping 21% accommodation tax. Rates can skyrocket during peak seasons (Christmas and Easter) or drop during slow seasons.

We've listed prices below in US dollars (at the official rate) to offset Argentina's high inflation rate. Many hotels quote their rates in US dollars and take US dollars as payment anyway.

🛏 Microcentro

As well as being very central, the Microcentro has the widest range and the largest number of accommodations in the city. Toward the north you'll be close to the popular pedestrian streets of Florida and Lavalle, as well as the neighborhoods of upmarket Retiro and Recoleta. The Plaza de Mayo area contains the bustling banking district and many historical buildings, and is within walking distance of San Telmo. During the day the whole area is very busy, but nights are much calmer as businesspeople flee the center after work. Don't expect a huge range of creative cuisine in this area – for that head to Palermo.

Gran Hotel Hispano
HOTEL $

(Map p58; ☏ 011-4345-2020; www.hhispano. com.ar; Av de Mayo 861; s/d US$55/72; ❋@🛜) The tiny stairway lobby here isn't an impressive start, but upstairs there's a sweet atrium area with covered patio. Most rooms are modern and carpeted; those in front are biggest, and those on the top floor are brightest. There's also a pleasant outside sun terrace. It's a popular, central and well-tended place, so reserve ahead. Pay in cash for a 10% discount.

SHORT- & LONG-TERM RENTALS

Many travelers visiting Buenos Aires love the city so much that they want to stay longer and find an apartment. But snagging a pad isn't as easy as it could be: renters often need to commit to two years and nearly always need a local's bond to guarantee monthly payments – almost impossible for most foreigners.

To cater to this demand, dozens of apartment websites have popped up in recent years. These sites charge significantly more than locals would pay, but they don't have those pesky requirements either. You can view pictures of rental properties, along with prices and amenities. Usually the photos match what you will get, but not always; if you'd like someone to check out an apartment before you rent it, Madi Lang at BA Cultural Concierge (p109) can make sure the place isn't on a busy street, in an outlying neighborhood or near a construction site.

➡ www.4rentargentina.com

➡ www.apartmentsche.com

➡ www.buenosaireshabitat.com

➡ www.oasiscollections.com/buenosaires

➡ www.santelmoloft.com

➡ www.stayinbuenosaires.com

If you're just looking for a room, check www.spareroomsba.com. Or look for longer-term guesthouses (where rooms usually share bathrooms) at www.casalosangelitos.com and www.lacasademarina.com.ar. Chill House Hostel (p82) has a long-term residence as well. And there's always the BA branch of Craigslist.

Portal del Sur
HOSTEL **$**

(Map p58; ☎ 011-4342-8788; www.portaldel surba.com.ar; Hipólito Yrigoyen 855; dm from US$16, s/d from US$40/50; ❄@🛜; Ⓢ Línea A Piedras) Located in a charming old building, this is one of the city's best hostels. Beautiful dorms and sumptuous, hotel-quality private rooms surround a central common area, which is rather dark but open. The highlight is the lovely rooftop deck with views and attached bar and lounge. Free tango and Spanish lessons, plus a walking tour; plenty of other activities available.

Milhouse Youth Hostel
HOSTEL **$**

(Map p58; ☎ 011-4345-9604; www.milhouse hostel.com; Hipólito Yrigoyen 959; dm from US$16, s/d from US$55/60; ❄@🛜; Ⓢ Línea A Av de Mayo) BA's premiere party hostel, this popular Hostelling International spot offers a plethora of activities and services. Dorms are good and private rooms can be very pleasant; most surround an appealing open patio. Common spaces include a bar-cafe (with pool table) on the ground floor, a TV lounge on the mezzanine and a rooftop terrace. A gorgeous annex building nearby offers similar services.

V & S Hostel Club
HOSTEL **$**

(Map p58; ☎ 011-4322-0994; www.hostelclub. com; Viamonte 887; dm from US$16, r from US$58; ❄@🛜; Ⓢ Línea C Lavalle) ✿ This attractive, central and ecofriendly hostel is located in a pleasant older building. The common space, which is also the dining and lobby area, is good for socializing. The spacious dorms are carpeted and the private rooms are excellent; all have their own bathroom. A nice touch is the tiny outdoor patio in back.

Goya Hotel
HOTEL **$$**

(Map p58; ☎ 011-4322-9269; www.goyahotel. com.ar; Suipacha 748; s US$60-70, d US$85-95; ❄@🛜) A good midrange choice with 42 modern, comfortable and carpeted rooms. Located on a pedestrian street, so little traffic noise. 'Classic' rooms are older and have open showers; 'superior' rooms are slicker and come with bathtubs. Pleasant breakfast room with patio; good breakfast too.

🛏 Congreso

Congreso contains many of the city's older theaters, cinemas and cultural centers. Lively Av Corrientes has many modest shops, services and bookstores. The Plaza del Congreso area is always moving, sometimes with mostly peaceful public demonstrations. Generally, this area is not quite as packed as the Microcentro and has a less business and touristy flavor, but still bustles day and night. Cutting-edge restaurants are limited.

Estoril Premium Hostel
HOSTEL $
(Map p58; ☎011-4382-9073; www.hostelestoril. com.ar; Av de Mayo 1385, 1st & 6th fl; dm from US$19, s/d from US$45/60; ✳@◐☞) A great hostel located across two floors in an old building. It's stylish and clean, with pleasant, good-sized dorms and hotel-quality doubles. There's a nice kitchen and internal patio, and the awesome rooftop terrace has amazing views of Av de Mayo. The same family also run a cheaper hostel on the 3rd floor.

Sabatico Hostel
HOSTEL $
(Map p58; ☎011-4381-1138; www.sabaticohostel. com.ar; México 1410; dm from US$15, r with shared/private bath from US$50/60; ✳@◐☞; ⒮Línea E Independencia) This *buena onda* (good vibes) hostel is located off the beaten tourist path in an atmospheric neighborhood. Rooms are small but pleasant and the good common areas include a nice kitchen, dining and living room, airy patio hallways and a pleasant rooftop terrace with hammocks, *asado* (barbecue grill) and soaking tub in summer. There's also a ping-pong table, foosball and bike rentals, plus Saturday *asados*.

Hotel Lyon
APARTMENT $$
(Map p58; ☎011-4372-0100; www.hotel-lyon. com.ar; Riobamba 251; d/tr/q US$85/105/120; ✳@◐☞; ⒮Línea B Callao) If you're a traveling family or group on a budget, consider this place. The two- and three- bedroom apartments available are basic and no-frills but very spacious, and all include large bathrooms and separate dining areas with fridges (but no kitchens). Reserve ahead; wi-fi in lobby only.

Imagine Hotel
HOTEL $$
(Map p58; ☎011-4383-2230; www.imagine hotelboutique.com; México 1330; r US$120-155; ✳@◐☞; ⒮Línea E Independencia) This beautiful 1850s guesthouse offers nine simple, colorful rooms, all decorated differently with rustic yet upscale furniture. The rooms surround three lovely outdoor patios accented with original tiles and leafy plants – the last one has a grassy garden. Breakfast includes fresh fruit, yogurt, and eggs to order. It's a quiet little paradise in a nontouristy neighborhood. Reserve ahead; dog on premises.

Livin' Residence
APARTMENT $$
(Map p58; ☎011-5258-0300; www.livin residence.com; Viamonte 1815; studio US$90, 1-bedroom apt US$109, 2-bedroom apt US$175; ✳◐; ⒮Línea D Callao) All of these studios and one- or two-bedroom apartments have a simple, contemporary feel, with tasteful furniture, flat-screen TVs, small kitchens and balconies. There's a tiny rooftop terrace with Jacuzzi, *asado* and nearby gym room. Security is good; reserve ahead.

🛏 San Telmo

South of the Microcentro, San Telmo has some of the most traditional atmosphere in Buenos Aires. Buildings are more charming and historical than those in the center, and tend to be only a few stories high. Many restaurants and fancy boutiques have opened here in recent years, and there are some good bars, tango venues and other nightspots for entertainment. Most accommodation options here are hostels, humble hotels or upscale guesthouses rather than five-star hotels.

América del Sur
HOSTEL $
(Map p58; ☎011-4300-5525; www.americahos tel.com.ar; Chacabuco 718; dm from US$18, d from US$70; ✳@◐; ⒮Línea C Independencia) This gorgeous boutique-like hostel is the fanciest of its kind in BA, and built especially to be a hostel. Beyond reception is a fine bar-bistro area with large, elegant wooden patio. Clean dorms with four beds all have amazingly well-designed bathrooms, while private rooms are tastefully decorated and better than those at many midrange hotels. A multitude of services are on offer.

Art Factory Hostel
HOSTEL $
(Map p58; ☎011-4343-1463; www.artfactoryba. com.ar; Piedras 545; dm from US$17, d from US$47; ✳@◐) Friendly and uniquely art-themed, this fine hostel offers more private rooms than most – and all feature huge murals, painted and decorated by different international artists. Even the hallways and water tanks have colorful cartoonish themes, and the 1850s rambling mansion adds some elegant atmosphere. Large rooftop terrace with hammocks and separate bar-lounge area with pool table.

Circus Hostel & Hotel
HOSTEL $
(Map p58; ☎011-4300-4983; www.hostelcircus. com; Chacabuco 1020; dm US$15, r from US$50; ✳@◐☞; ⒮Línea C Independencia) From the

trendy lounge in front to the wooden deck-surrounded wading pool in back, this hotel-hostel exudes hipness. Both dorms and private rooms, all small and simple, have basic furniture and their own bathrooms. There's a pool table and slick TV area too, but no kitchen.

Bohemia Buenos Aires HOTEL **$**
(Map p58; ☎011-4115-2561; www.bohemiabuenos aires.com.ar; Perú 845; r from US$60; ❖@🖵; ⓢLínea C Independencia) With its slight upscale-motel feel, this good-value San Telmo hotel offers 22 simple and neat rooms, most good-sized, if a bit antiseptic with their white-tiled floors. None of the rooms has a bathtub, so instead of taking a soak enjoy the peaceful grassy backyard and small interior patios. The breakfast buffet is a plus, and there's a restaurant. Cash discount.

★ **Mansión Vitraux** BOUTIQUE HOTEL **$$**
(Map p58; ☎011-4878-4292; www.mansion vitraux.com; Carlos Calvo 369; r from US$120; ❖@🖵🏊; ⓢLínea C Independencia) Almost too slick for San Telmo, this glass-fronted boutique hotel offers 12 beautiful rooms, all in different designs. All have either flat-screen or projection TV, and bathrooms boast very contemporary design. The breakfast buffet is in the basement wine bar, and a tasting might be included in your stay. There is also a large Jacuzzi, a dry sauna and a fancy rooftop terrace with small lap pool.

Mundo Bolívar BOUTIQUE HOTEL **$$**
(Map p65; ☎011-4300-3619; www.mundoboli var.com; Bolívar 1701; studio & apt US$85-110; ❖🖵; 🖵29) Fourteen spacious studios and loft apartments with kitchenettes have been renovated into attractive modern spaces – some with original details such as carved doorways or painted ceilings – at this amazing mansion. Separate entrances join with hallways connecting through the complex, and there are lovely garden patios in which to relax. English, Danish, German and Portuguese spoken. No breakfast; long-term stays available.

Patios de San Telmo BOUTIQUE HOTEL **$$$**
(Map p58; ☎011-4307-0480; www.patiosdesan telmo.com.ar; Chacabuco 752; r US$145-190; ❖@🖵) Located in an 1860 *conventillo* (tenement house) is this pleasant boutique hotel with 30 simple, elegant rooms surrounding several patios. There's a lovely 'library' room decorated with artwork, a back patio with hanging basket chairs and a tiny rooftop pool with wood deck. Buffet breakfast is served in the healthy restaurant downstairs.

🛏 Retiro

Retiro is a great, central place to be, *if* you can afford it – many of BA's most expensive hotels, along with some of its richest inhabitants, are settled here. Close by are leafy Plaza San Martín, the Retiro bus terminal and train station and many upscale stores and business services. Recoleta and the Microcentro are just a short stroll away.

Hotel Tres Sargentos HOTEL **$**
(Map p70; ☎011-4312-6082; www.hotel3 sargentos.com.ar; Tres Sargentos 345; s/d/tr US$50/65/80; ❖🖵; ⓢLínea C San Martín) A good deal for the location, this simple budget hotel has a decent lobby and is located on a pedestrian street. The carpets in the halls need changing, but the ones in the simple, comfortable rooms are clean enough. Some rooms higher up and facing out even offer a bit of a view. Five-person apartment available.

★ **Casa Calma** BOUTIQUE HOTEL **$$$**
(Map p70; ☎011-4312-5000; www.casacalma hotel.com.ar; Suipacha 1015; r from US$285; ❖@🖵; ⓢLínea C San Martín) ✔ Those with an ecoconscious mind now have their perfect hideaway in BA: this central, environmentally friendly and luxurious hotel. Rooms are beautifully pristine and relaxing (some even have sauna or Jacuzzi), with Zen-like baths and serene atmosphere. Yoga mats and bamboo bikes available; discount without breakfast.

🛏 Recoleta & Barrio Norte

Most of the accommodations in Recoleta are expensive, and what cheap hotels there are tend to be full much of the time. Buildings here are grand and beautiful, befitting the city's richest barrio, and you'll be close to Recoleta's famous cemetery, along with its lovely parks, museums and boutiques.

Yira Yira Guesthouse GUESTHOUSE **$**
(Map p58; ☎011-4812-4077; www.yirayiraba. com; Uruguay 911, No 1B; s/d/tr US$40/55/85; ❖@🖵; ⓢLínea D Callao) This casual, intimate apartment-home is run by the helpful Paz, who lives on-site. The floors are wooden and the ceilings high, and there are just four large rooms (all with shared bathrooms)

. El Caminito (p65)
a Boca's most famous street contains
uildings with colorful facades.

. Puerto Madero (p60)
uenos Aires' newest official barrio is a
vonderful place for a stroll. The floating
aval museum, Fragata Sarmiento (p61)
s pictured in the foreground.

. Parque 3 de Febrero (p71)
hese green gardens are home to a zoo and
planetarium.

. Teatro Colón (p62)
uenos Aires' much-loved theater regularly
osts performances by prominent figures.

facing the central living area with tiny patio. It's a good place to meet other travelers and is centrally located near downtown. Reserve ahead.

Hotel Lion D'or
HOTEL $

(Map p70; ☎ 011-4803-8992; www.hotel-liondor. com.ar; Pacheco de Melo 2019; s/d/tr from US$32/43/59; ✳️⚡; Ⓢ Línea D Pueyrredón) These digs have their charm (it's an old embassy), but rooms vary widely – some are small, basic and dark, while others are grand. Despite some rough edges, all are good value and most have been modernized for comfort. The old marble staircase and elevator are fabulous, and there's a nice rooftop area. The cheapest rooms share bathrooms; air-con costs extra.

Reina Madre Hostel
HOSTEL $

(Map p84; ☎ 011-4962-5553; www.rmhostel.com; Av Anchorena 1118; dm from US$16, s/d from US$40/44; ✳️@⚡; Ⓢ Línea D Pueyrredón) This wonderful hostel is clean, safe and well run. It's in an old building that has plenty of personality, with high ceilings and original tiles, and all rooms are comfortable and modern (and share bathrooms). There's a cozy living room with balcony and small kitchen plus lots of dining tables, but the highlight is the wooden-deck rooftop with *asado*. Pet cat on premises.

Art Suites
APARTMENT $$

(Map p70; ☎ 011-4821-6800; www.artsuites. com.ar; Azcuénaga 1465; 1- & 2-bedroom apt US$140-295; ✳️⚡; Ⓢ Línea D Pueyrredón) The 15 luxurious, modern and spacious apartments here are all bright and boast minimalist decor, full kitchens or kitchenettes, sunny balconies and slick, hip furniture. Windows are double-paned for quiet, staff speak English and security is excellent. Long-term discounts are available; reserve ahead. An annex offers more apartments.

★ Poetry Building
APARTMENT $$$

(Map p70; ☎ 011-4827-2772; www.poetrybuild ing.com; Junín 1280; apt US$215-285; ✳️⚡✉; Ⓢ Línea D Pueyrredón) These gorgeous studios and one- or two-bedroom apartments are perfect for families or small groups. Each one is different, eclectically decorated with reproduction antique furniture, and all come with fully stocked kitchens. Some boast an outdoor balcony or patio, but there's also a beautiful common terrace with soaking pool. Amenities include flat-screen TVs, plus iPod and cell-phone rentals.

Alvear Palace Hotel
HOTEL $$$

(Map p70; ☎ 011-4808-2100; www.alvearpalace. com; Av Alvear 1891; r from US$620; ✳️@⚡✉; ▢130) The classiest, most traditional hotel in BA. Old-world sophistication and excellent service will help erase the trials of your long flight into town, while the bathtub Jacuzzi, Hermès toiletries and Egyptian-cotton bed sheets aid your trip into dreamland. There's also an excellent restaurant, elegant tea room, champagne bar, fine spa, indoor swimming pool and – if you're in a deluxe suite – butler service.

🛏 Palermo

About a 10-minute taxi ride from the city center (and also well connected by bus and Subte lines), Palermo is the top choice for many travelers. Not only is it full of extensive parklands – which are great for weekend jaunts and sporting activities – but you'll have heaps of cutting-edge restaurants, happening bars, designer boutiques and hip dance clubs at your fingertips. Most of these places are located in the extensive subneighborhood of Palermo Viejo, which is further divided into Palermo Soho and Palermo Hollywood.

Mansilla 3935 B&B
B&B $

(Map p84; ☎ 011-4833-3821; www.mansilla3935. com; Mansilla 3935; s/d US$40/60; ✳️@⚡) Family-run B&B in a homey, darkish house, offering a great deal. Each of the six simple but lovely rooms comes with its own bathroom. Ceilings are high, and a few tiny patios add charm.

Chill House Hostel
HOSTEL $

(Map p84; ☎ 011-4861-6175; www.chillhouse. com.ar; Agüero 781; dm US$17, d US$49-67; @⚡; Ⓢ Línea B Carlos Gardel) One of the coolest-vibe hostels in BA is at this remodeled old house boasting high ceilings and a rustic artsy style. There are two dorms and eight private rooms with bathroom (No 6 is especially nice). There's also an awesome rooftop terrace where weekly *asados* take place, occasional live music and free bike rentals.

Eco Pampa Hostel
HOSTEL $

(Map p84; ☎ 011-4831-2435; www.hostelpampa. com.ar; Guatemala 4778; dm US$20, s/d US$70/85; @⚡; Ⓢ Línea D Plaza Italia) 🍃 Buenos Aires' first 'green' hostel is this casual spot sporting vintage furniture, low-energy light bulbs and a recycling system. The rooftop is home to a small veggie garden, compost pile and solar panels. Dorms are a good size and each of the eight private rooms comes with bathroom and flat-screen TV (most have air-con). There's another branch in Belgrano.

Art Factory Palermo
HOSTEL $

(Map p84; ☎ 2004-4958; www.artfactorypalermo.com.ar; Costa Rica 4353; dm from USD$15, r with shared/private bath from US$50/60; ✳ @ ☎) Decent and no-frills, this hostel sits just outside Palermo's border but is an easy walking distance to many of its restaurants and nightlife. Like its sister hostel in San Telmo, it's located in an old house and decorated with artsy murals and stencils. There's a small kitchen and living room area, and a limited number of bathrooms – so their use can get tight. A rooftop terrace is coming.

★ The 5th Floor
B&B $$

(Map p84; ☎ 011-4827-0366; www.the5thfloorba.com; near Vidt & Santa Fe; r US$90-170; ✳ @; S Línea D Scalabrini Ortíz) This upscale B&B offers seven elegant rooms, three with private balcony. All are tastefully decorated with art-deco furniture and modern amenities. The common living room is great for chatting with the English owner, a polo enthusiast, and there's also a pleasant back patio with lovely tile details. Excellent breakfast. Address given upon reservation; three-night minimum stay.

★ Cabrera Garden
B&B $$

(Map p84; ☎ 011-4777-7668; www.cabreragarden.com; José Antonio Cabrera 5855; r US$145-250; ✳ @ ☎ ❄; 🖵140) One of BA's loveliest stays is this gay-friendly three-room B&B. The remodelled 1920s building boasts a beautiful grassy garden with small patio and pool, and there's a wonderful living room in which to hang out. Rooms are very comfortable and all different, with modern conveniences like flat-screen TV and iPod docks. English, German and Polish spoken; reserve ahead.

Hotel Clasico
HOTEL $$

(Map p84; ☎ 011-4773-2353; www.hotelclasico.com; Costa Rica 5480; r US$120-170; ✳ ☎) Attractive hotel with 33 tastefully 'classic' rooms, some with tiny balconies but all with wood floors, modern conveniences and earthy color schemes. Go for the penthouse with terrace for something special. Creative elevator with one glass wall facing an artsy mural. Great breakfast served in the downstairs, rustic-hip restaurant.

Le Petit Palais
B&B $$

(Map p84; ☎ 011-4962-4834; www.lepetitpalais-buenosaires.com; Gorriti 3574; s/d from US$70/80; ✳ ☎) Small but charming, this French-run B&B offers just five simple but pleasant rooms, all with private bathroom. The highlight is the pretty little terrace on the 2nd floor, where possibly BA's best breakfast can be served in warm weather – fresh yogurt, jams and breads, all homemade, along with eggs, *medialunas* and cereals. Friendly cats on premises.

Infinito Hotel
BOUTIQUE HOTEL $$

(Map p84; ☎ 011-2070-2626; www.infinitohotel.com; Arenales 3689; r from US$105; ✳ @ ☎; S Línea D Scalabrini Ortíz) Starting at its small lobby cafe-reception, this hotel exudes a certain trendiness. Rooms are small but good, boasting flat-screen TVs, fridges and a purple color scheme, and there's a sauna and Jacuzzi. It tries to be ecologically conscious, mostly by recycling. Located near some parks but still within walking distance of Palermo's nightlife. Buffet breakfast included.

Rugantino Hotel
HOTEL $$

(Map p84; ☎ 011-6379-5113; www.rugantinohotelboutique.com; Uriarte 1844; r US$75-85; ✳ @ ☎; S Línea D Palermo) This small and intimate hotel is located in a 1920s building and run by an Italian family. Various tiny terraces and catwalks connect the seven simple but beautiful rooms, all decked out in hardwood floors and modern styling – combined with a few antiques. The climbing vine-greenery in the small central courtyard well is soothing, and you can expect espresso for breakfast.

Palermo Viejo B&B
GUESTHOUSE $$

(Map p84; ☎ 011-4773-6012; www.palermoviejobb.com; Niceto Vega 4629; s/d US$70/80; ✳ @ ☎; 🖵140) This small and intimate B&B is located in a remodeled casa chorizo – a long, narrow house. The six rooms all front a leafy outdoor patio hallway and are simple but quite comfortable; two have lofts. All come with fridge and a good breakfast. RSVP or call them ahead of time – they often leave on errands in the afternoon.

★ Miravida Soho
GUESTHOUSE $$$

(Map p84; ☎ 011-4774-6433; www.miravidasoho.com; Darregueyra 2050; r US$275-370; ✳ @ ☎; S Línea D Plaza Italia) Run by friendly owners, this gorgeous guesthouse comes with six beautiful and elegant rooms. All are very

Palermo

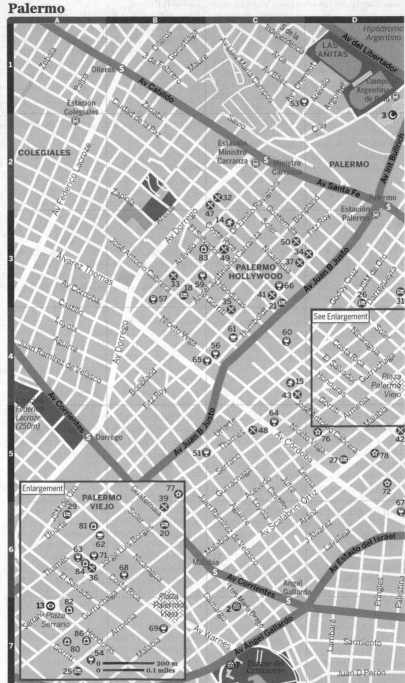

BUENOS AIRES

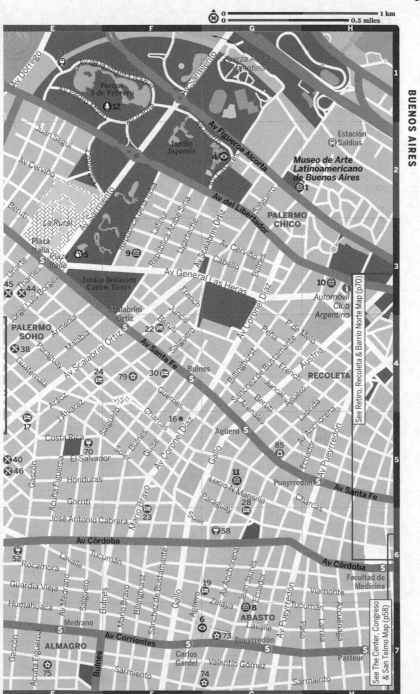

See Retiro, Recoleta & Barrio Norte Map (p70)

See The Center, Congreso & San Telmo Map (p58)

0 — 1 km
0 — 0.5 miles

Av Dorrego
35
Av de Libania Isabel
Av Pedro Monte
Parque
3 de Febrero
12
Juan Seguí
Av Cerviño
Beruti
La Rural
Av Sarmiento
Av Sarmiento
Av Sarmiento
Colonia
República de la India
Fuerza Aérea
Argentina
Av Figueroa Alcorta
Av Berro
Av Casares
Jardín
Japonés
4
Av del Libertador
Estación
Saldías
Museo de Arte
Latinoamericano
de Buenos Aires
1
PALERMO
CHICO

Plaza
Italia
Plaza
Italia
5
9
Lafinur
República Árabe Siria
Ugarteche
Av Scalabrini Ortiz
Av Cerviño
Cabello
Bulnes
Salguero
Av General Las Heras
10
Automóvil
Club
Argentino
Jardín Botánico
Carlos Thays
French
Juncal
Beruti
Salguero
Av Coronel Díaz
P de Melo
Peña
Austria
RECOLETA

45
44
Jorge Luis Borges
Uriarte
Thames
PALERMO
SOHO
38
Armenia
Paraguay
Malabia
Guatemala
Araóz
J Álvarez
17
Sinclair
Spalabrini
Ortiz
Av Scalabrini Ortiz
24
79
22
Av Santa Fe
Bulnes
30
Güemes
Charcas
16
Agüero
Billinghurst
Sánchez de Bustamante
Juncal
Arenales
Beruti
Sánchez de Bustamante
Láprida
85
Echeverría
Av Anchorena
Av Puyrredón
Pueyrredón
Av Santa Fe

Costa Rica
70
El Salvador
40
46
Gascón
Acuña Figueroa
Honduras
Gorriti
José Antonio Cabrera
Mario Bravo
23
58
Av Córdoba
Soler
Bulnes
Guise
Av Coronel Díaz
Gallo
11
Lucio N Mansilla
28
Paraguay
Soler

52
Rocamora
Lavalle
Tucumán
Av Medrano
Guardia Vieja
Salguero
Bulnes
Mario Bravo
Billinghurst
Sánchez de Bustamante
Gallo
Agüero
19
Zelaya
Av Anchorena
Jean Jaurès
Ecuador
Av Córdoba
Facultad de
Medicina
Viamonte
Azcuénaga

Humahuaca
Medrano
Av Corrientes
6
8
ABASTO
73
Lavalle
Pueyrredón
Av Puyrredón
Tucumán
Paso
Larrea
Pasteur

Gascón
Acuña Figueroa
ALMAGRO
75
Bulnes
Sarmiento
Carlos
Gardel
Valentín Gómez
74
Sarmiento

Palermo

comfortable and one has a private terrace. There's a wine cellar, bar-lounge area for evening wine tastings, a small and relaxing patio, and even an elevator. It serves good, full breakfasts; reserve ahead.

Mine Hotel   HOTEL **$$$**
(Map p84; ☎011-4832-1100; www.minehotel. com; Gorriti 4770; d US$320-430; ❄@☎❄; ☐55) 🏊 This hip boutique hotel offers 20 good-sized rooms; some come with Jacuzzi and balcony and all have a desk and natural decor touches. Get one overlooking the highlight of the hotel: the peaceful backyard, which boasts a small wading pool. There's a small bistro for the buffet breakfast, and Mine even attempts to be somewhat ecofriendly (re-using towels, low-energy bulbs, recycling).

Vain Boutique Hotel   BOUTIQUE HOTEL **$$$**
(Map p84; ☎011-4776-8246; www.vainuniverse. com; Thames 2226; r US$210-365; ❄@☎; ⑤Línea D Plaza Italia) Fifteen elegant rooms, most with high ceilings and wooden floors, live at this nicely renovated building. All are modern in that white, minimalist way, and boast sofas and small desks. The highlight, however, is the wonderfully airy, multilevel living room with attached wooden-decked terrace and Jacuzzi.

🍴 Eating

Eating out in Buenos Aires is a gastronomical highlight. Not only are the typical *parrillas* (steak restaurants) a dime a dozen, but the city's Palermo Viejo neighborhood boasts the most varied ethnic cuisine in the country. You can find Armenian, Brazilian, Mexican, Indian, Japanese, Southeast Asian and Middle Eastern cuisines – and even fusions of several. Most are acceptable and some are exceptional.

Microcentro eateries tend to cater to the business crowd, while nearby Puerto Madero is full of elegant and pricey restaurants. Congreso is pretty traditional cuisine-wise, including its 'Little Spain' neighborhood. Recoleta is another expensive neighborhood with touristy but fun dining options near the cemetery. San Telmo keeps attracting more and more worthwhile restaurants.

Reservations are usually unnecessary except at the most popular restaurants or perhaps on weekends. Except at five-star restaurants, wait staff provide simply adequate service – nothing fancy. Be warned that upscale restaurants charge a *cubierto*, a small cover charge for utensil use and bread. This doesn't include the tip, which should be at least 10% (15% at fancier places).

Many restaurants (especially outside the Microcentro) are closed on Monday and have limited hours on Sunday.

A good website for BA restaurants is www.guiaoleo.com (in Spanish); for good blogs in English there are www.saltshaker.net and www.pickupthefork.com.

✕ Microcentro

180 Burger Bar
BURGERS $

(Map p58; ☑ 011-4328-7189; Suipacha 749; burgers AR$60-75; ☺ noon-4pm Mon-Fri) Hankering for a hamburger? Then join the hip, young crowd that will likely be lined up at this small diner, and order up. Choose a 'salsa' (*mayochimi*, tzatziki, *barbacoa*) and add the cheese option if you wish. Chow down within the confines of concrete walls, clunky furniture and blasting music.

Latino Sandwich
SANDWICHES $

(Map p58; ☑ 4331-0859; www.latinosandwich.com; Tacuari 185; sandwiches AR$40-56; ☺ 8am-5pm Mon-Fri) Some of the best eateries in BA are holes-in-the-wall – and here's a case in point. This is the downtown place to grab sandwiches like an Argentine *milanesa* (breaded steaks; but with arugula and guacamole!), BBQ pork with cheddar cheese, or grilled zucchini and eggplant. There's only one communal table, as they cater to mostly to-go business clientele.

Vita
HEALTH FOOD $

(Map p58; ☑ 011-4342-0788; www.vitamarket.com.ar; Hipólito Yrigoyen 583; mains AR$60-65; ☺ 8am-8pm Mon-Wed, to 1am Thu & Fri, 10:30am-1am Sat, 11am-7pm Sun; ☑) Here's a hippie-ish, casual and health-oriented eatery offering tasty vegetarian dishes like organic seitan pizzas, lentil burgers and vegetable calzones. Various freshly mixed juices and *licuados* (fruit shakes) are available (with the option of adding a wheatgrass shot) and there are plenty of gourmet salads. Organic coffee is also served. Another branch is in Palermo.

Aldo's Vinoteca
ARGENTINE $$

(Map p58; ☑ 011-4334-2380; www.aldosvinoteca.com; Moreno 372; mains AR$120-180; ☺ noon-midnight Sun-Thu, to 1am Fri & Sat) This restaurant and wine shop is an upscale eatery serving a small but tasty menu of meat, seafood and pasta dishes, all amid walls lined with wine. What makes this place unique, however, is that the wine is sold at *retail* prices – thus making it easier to sample (and buy) the nearly 600 labels available.

✗ Puerto Madero

i Central Market   MODERN ARGENTINE **$$**
(Map p58; ☑ 011-5775-0330; Av Macacha Güemes 302; mains AR$140-250; ⊙8am-1am) Especially pleasant on sunny days is this modern restaurant on the waterfront – the tables on the promenade are great for people-watching. Order espresso and scones for breakfast, and panini (Italian-style sandwiches) or contemporary Argentine dishes for lunch. There's also more casual seating at the gourmet deli, plus a kitchenwares shop to poke around.

★Chila   MODERN ARGENTINE **$$$**
(Map p58; ☑ 011-4343-6067; www.chilaweb. com.ar; Alicia Moreau de Justo 876; 3-course menu AR$980, 7-course menu AR$1400, drinks not included; ⊙8pm-midnight Tue-Sun) Some of Buenos Aires' best and most original cuisine is created by award-winning chef Soledad Nardelli. Her three- and seven-course, haute cuisine dishes utilize only the best seasonal ingredients, and the restaurant also works closely with quality producers. Expect beautifully presented food, a professional staff and – if you're lucky – a table with a romantic view of the docks.

Le Grill   PARRILLA **$$$**
(Map p58; ☑ 011-4331-0454; www.legrill.com.ar; Alicia Moreau de Justo 876; mains AR$230-460; ⊙12:30-3pm & 7pm-midnight Mon-Fri, 7pm-midnight Sat, 12:30-3pm Sun) No surprise – grilled meat is the specialty at this highly sophisticated *parrilla*. Go for the rack of lamb, sucking pig or Kobe beef, though the dry-aged 'steak flight' (AR$480) is uniquely spectacular. There are a few seafood and pasta dishes for noncarnivores. Try to reserve a table in the atrium, with full view of Puente de la Mujer.

✗ Congreso

★Chan Chan   PERUVIAN **$**
(Map p58; ☑ 011-4382-8492; Hipólito Yrigoyen 1390; mains AR$60-90; ⊙noon-4pm & 8pm-12.30am Tue-Sat, to 11.30pm Sun) Thanks to fair prices and relatively quick service, this colorful Peruvian eatery is jam-packed at lunchtime with office workers devouring plates of *ceviche* (seafood cured in citrus) and *ajiaco de conejo* (rabbit and potato stew). There are also plenty of *arroz chaufa* (Peruvian-style fried rice) dishes, easily downed with a tangy pisco sour or a pitcher of *chicha morada* (a sweet fruity drink).

Pizzería Güerrín   PIZZA **$**
(Map p58; ☑ 011-4371-8141; Av Corrientes 1368; pizza slice AR$16; ⊙11am-1am Sun-Thu, to 2am Fri & Sat) A quick pit-stop on Av Corrientes is this cheap but classic old pizza joint. Just pay, then point at a prebaked slice behind the glass counter and eat standing up with the rest of the crowd. Or sit down and order one freshly baked – this way you can also choose from a greater variety of toppings for your pizza.

VEGETARIAN IN BUENOS AIRES

Argentine cuisine is internationally famous for its succulent grilled meats, but this doesn't mean vegetarians – or even vegans – are completely out of luck.

Most restaurants, including *parrillas*, serve a few items acceptable to most vegetarians, such as green salads, omelets, pizza and pasta. Key words to beware of include *carne* (beef), *pollo* (chicken), *cerdo* (pork) and *cordero* (lamb). *Sin carne* means 'without meat' and the phrase *'Soy vegetariano/a'* (I'm a vegetarian) can come in handy.

Close to the Microcentro there's the popular cafeteria **Granix** (Map p58; ☑011-4343-7546; Florida 165, 1st fl; per kilo AR$165; ⊙11am-3:30pm Mon-Fri; 🖉), located upstairs in a shopping mall, and hippie-ish but cool **Vita** (p87). **Broccolino** (Map p58; ☑011-4322-7754; www.broccolino.com; Esmeralda 776; mains AR$80-200; ⊙noon-11:30pm; 🖉) specializes in pasta – it's not meat-free, but there are many vegetarian choices. In San Telmo, try trendy **Hierbabuena** (Map p65; ☑011-4362-2542; Av Caseros 454; ⊙9am-midnight Tue-Sun, to 5pm Mon; 🖉).

The Palermo Viejo area has many more options, including:
Bio (p92)
Artemesia (Map p84; ☑4776-5484; Gorriti 5996; ⊙12:30-3pm & 9-11:30pm Tue-Sat, 10am-5pm Sun; 🖉)
Buenos Aires Verde (Map p84; ☑011-4775-9594; Gorriti 5657; ⊙9am-12:30am Mon-Sat)
El Rincón Orgánico (☑2062-9515; Bulnes 910; ⊙11am-8pm Mon-Sat), over in Almagro, focuses on organic dishes, which are mostly but not completely vegetarian.

Parrilla Peña

PARRILLA $$

(Map p58; ☑ 011-4371-5643; Rodríguez Peña 682; mains AR$80-160; ☺ noon-4pm & 8pm-midnight Mon-Sat, noon-4pm Sun) This simple, traditional and long-running *parrilla* is well known for its excellent-quality meats and generous portions. The service is fast and efficient and it's great value. Don't expect many tourists – this is a local's sort of place. Also on offer are homemade pastas, salads and *milanesas* (breaded steaks), along with several tasty desserts and a good wine list.

★ Aramburu

GOURMET $$$

(Map p58; ☑ 011-4305-0439; www.aramburu resto.com.ar; Salta 1050; prix fixe AR$1100, with wine pairing AR$1700; ☺ 8:30-11pm Tue-Sat) Chef Gonzalo Aramburu's 19-course 'molecular' meal is astounding; each artistically created plate is just a few bites of gastronomic delight. Expect enlightening tastes, textures and smells, plus unique presentations – all will translate into a highly memorable dining experience. Located in the edgy but upcoming neighborhood of Montserrat. Its sister restaurant, Aramburu Bis, is nearby.

✖ San Telmo

Bar El Federal

ARGENTINE $

(Map p58; ☑ 011-4361-7328; Carlos Calvo 599; mains AR$65-160; ☺ 8am-2am Sun-Thu, to 4am Fri & Sat; 🛜) Dating from 1864, this historic bar has a classic, somewhat rustic atmosphere accented with original wood, tiles, and an eye-catching antique bar. The specialties here are sandwiches (especially turkey) and *picadas* (shared appetizer plates), but there are also lots of pastas, salads, desserts and tall mugs of icy beer.

El Banco Rojo

INTERNATIONAL $

(Map p58; ☑ 011-4362-3177; Bolivar 914; mains AR$50-60; ☺ noon-12:30am Tue-Sat, to 11:30pm Sun) A San Telmo youth magnet, this small and trendy joint serves up sandwiches (Tandoori pork, lamb kofta), falafels, burgers, tacos and salads. Try the *empanada de cordero* (lamb turnover) if they have it. Very casual, with blasting rock music and counter seating only.

Gran Parrilla del Plata

PARRILLA $$

(Map p58; ☑ 011-4300-8858; www.parrilladel plata.com; Chile 594; mains AR$90-200; ☺ noon-4pm & 8pm-1am Mon-Sat, noon-1am Sun) There's nothing too fancy at this traditional corner *parrilla* (one of the best in San Telmo) – just old-time atmosphere and generous portions

> ### SUPPER CLUBS
>
> *Puertas cerradas* (closed-door restaurants), a phenomenon during the last decade, continue to be popular. These prix-fixe restaurants often have limited opening hours and days, and some won't tell you the address until you make reservations (usually mandatory). But if you want that feeling of being somewhere 'secret' – and eating very good, gourmet food – these places are highly appealing.

of tasty grilled meats at decent prices. There are also pastas for that unfortunate vegetarian that might get dragged along.

Chochán

ARGENTINE $$

(Map p58; ☑ 011-4307-3661; Piedras 672; mains AR$125-175; ☺ 8pm-midnight Mon-Fri, noon-4pm & 8pm-midnight Sat & Sun) This eatery is for pork-lovers only – ribs, braised shoulder, elbows and raviolis – everything is made from pork, or *chanchos* (Chochán being a play on words). Grab a sandwich – pork belly, pulled pork, pork tongue. Or white corn and smoked pork soup. Or a small plate like pork blood sausage. No guilt – pigging out here is totally allowed.

El Desnivel

PARRILLA $$

(Map p58; ☑ 011-4300-9081; Defensa 855; mains AR$100-180; ☺ noon-midnight Tue-Sun, 7pm-midnight Mon) This famous and long-running *parrilla* joint packs in both locals and tourists, serving them treats like chorizo sandwiches and *bife de lomo* (tenderloin steak). The sizzling grill out front is torturous while you wait for a table (which could be in the large back room) – get here early, especially on weekends.

★ Café San Juan

INTERNATIONAL $$$

(Map p58; ☑ 011-4300-1112; Av San Juan 452; mains AR$300-350; ☺ 12:30-4pm & 8pm-1am) Having studied in Milan, Paris and Barcelona, celebrity TV-chef Leandro Cristóbal now runs the kitchen at this renowned San Telmo bistro. Start with fabulous tapas, then delve into the grilled Spanish octopus, *molleja* (sweetbreads) cannelloni and the amazing pork *bondiola* (deliciously tender after nine hours' roasting). Most of the seafood is flown in daily from Patagonia. Reserve for lunch and dinner.

If you can't get a table here, try the **Café San Juan La Cantina** (Map p58; ⚡ 011-4300-9344; Chile 474; mains AR$200-250; ⏱ 12.30-4pm & 8pm-midnight Tue-Thu & Sun, to 1am Fri & Sat), located a few blocks away and with a different menu.

La Boca

Proa Cafe
CAFE $

(Map p65; ⚡ 011-4104-1003; www.proa.org/eng/cafe.php; Av Don Pedro de Mendoza 1929; mains AR$60-100; ⏱ 11am-7pm Tue-Sun) Chef Lucas Angelillo presides over this airy eatery, located on the top floor of Fundación Proa (free access). Stop in briefly for a fresh juice and gourmet sandwich, or stay longer and order a meat, seafood or pasta dish. Don't miss the rooftop terrace on a warm, sunny day – you'll get good views of the Riachuelo, hopefully without its corresponding scents.

Retiro

Filo
ITALIAN $$

(Map p70; ⚡ 011-4311-0312; www.filo-ristorante.com; San Martín 975; mains AR$120-190; ⏱ noon-1am) Popular with the business lunch crowd, this large, pop art–style Italian pizzeria tosses 30 kinds of thin-crust pies with fresh toppings – try a pie piled high with prosciutto and arugula. Other tasty choices include panini, gourmet salads, dozens of pastas and a whirlwind of drinks and desserts. The menu is extensive – there's something to please just about everyone here.

Dadá
INTERNATIONAL $$

(Map p70; ⚡ 011-4314-4787; San Martín 941; mains AR$130-200; ⏱ noon-2am Mon-Thu, to 5am Fri & Sat) The tiny bohemian Dadá, with walls painted red and a bar cluttered with wine bottles, feels like an unassuming neighborhood bar in Paris. Order something savory off the bistro menu during the day, like a stir-fry; at night you can dine on grilled salmon and down an expertly mixed cocktail.

★ Elena
MODERN ARGENTINE $$$

(Map p70; ⚡ 011-4321-1728; www.elenapony line.com; Four Seasons, Posadas 1086; mains AR$350-400; ⏱ 7-11am, 12:30-3:30pm & 7:30pm-12:30am) If you're looking for a splurge night out, Elena should be your destination. Located at the Four Seasons Hotel, this highly rated restaurant uses the best quality-sourced ingredients to create exquisite dishes. Order its specialty – the dry-aged meats – for something really special. Expect the cocktails, desserts and service to be five-star as well.

Recoleta & Barrio Norte

Cumaná
ARGENTINE $

(Map p70; ⚡ 011-4813-9207; Rodriguez Peña 1149; mains AR$75-125; ⏱ noon-4pm & 8pm-1am) To sample Argentina's regional cuisine, check out this colorful, budget-friendly eatery with huge picture windows and an old-fashioned adobe oven. Cumaná specializes in delicious *cazuela*, stick-to-your-ribs stews filled with squash, corn, eggplant, potatoes and meat. Also popular are the empanadas, *locro* and *humita* (corn, cheese and onion tamales). Come early to avoid a wait.

Como en Casa
ARGENTINE $

(Map p70; ⚡ 011-4816-5507; www.tortascomoen casa.com; Riobamba 1239; mains AR$80-130; ⏱ 8am-midnight Tue-Sat, to 8:30pm Sun & Mon) This gorgeous, upscale cafe-restaurant has a very elegant atmosphere and attracts Recoleta's wealthiest. Its best feature is the shady patio, complete with large fountain and surrounded by grand buildings, a must on a warm day. For lunch there are fancy sandwiches, salads, vegetable tarts and gourmet pizzas, while dinner options include goulash and homemade pastas. Plenty of luscious desserts, plus breakfast too.

El Sanjuanino
ARGENTINE $

(Map p70; ⚡ 011-4805-2683; Posadas 1515; empanadas AR$19, mains AR$80-150; ⏱ noon-4pm & 7pm-1am) This long-running, cozy little joint probably has the cheapest food in Recoleta, attracting both penny-pinching locals and thrifty tourists. Sit either upstairs or downstairs (in the basement) and order spicy empanadas, tamales or *locro* (corn and meat stew). The curved brick ceiling adds to the atmosphere, but many take their food to go – Recoleta's lovely parks are just a couple of blocks away.

Rodi Bar
ARGENTINE $$

(Map p70; ⚡ 011-4801-5230; Vicente López 1900; mains AR$100-200; ⏱ 7am-1am Mon-Sat) A great option for well-priced, unpretentious food in upscale Recoleta. This traditional corner restaurant with fine old-world atmosphere and extensive menu offers something for everyone, from inexpensive combo plates to relatively unusual dishes such as marinated beef tongue.

★**Casa Saltshaker** MEDITERRANEAN, ANDEAN $$$
(www.casasaltshaker.com; set menu incl wine pairings US$70; ⊙8:45pm Wed-Sat) Ex–New Yorker Dan Perlman is the chef behind this respected place, which is a *puerta cerrada* (closed-door restaurant) in his own home. You'll have to book ahead, arrive at an appointed hour and sit at a communal table, which can be a lot more fun than it sounds – especially for solo diners. Expect a five-course set menu focusing on creative Mediterranean- or Andean-inspired dishes. Address and telephone given upon reservation.

✖ Palermo

★**Sarkis** MIDDLE EASTERN $
(Map p84; ☑011-4772-4911; Thames 1101; mains AR$65-160; ⊙noon-3pm & 8pm-1am) The food is fabulous and well priced at this long-standing Middle Eastern restaurant – come with a group to sample many exotic dishes. Start with the roasted eggplant hummus, *boquerones* (marinated sardines), *keppe crudo* (raw meat) or *parras rellenas* (stuffed grape leaves), then follow up with kebabs or lamb in yogurt sauce. Less busy at lunchtime; expect a long wait for dinner.

Oui Oui INTERNATIONAL $
(Map p84; ☑011-4778-9614; www.ouioui.com.ar; Nicaragua 6068; mains AR$70-90; ⊙8am-8pm Mon-Sat; 🖥) *Pain au chocolat* and shabby chic? *Oui*. This charming and popular French-style cafe produces the goods – dark coffee, buttery croissants and jars of tangy lemonade – and boasts a small and cozy interior. Choose also from creative salads, gourmet sandwiches and luscious pastries. Its annex, **Almacén Oui Oui** (Map p84; cnr Dorrego & Nicaragua; ⊙8am-9pm Tue-Sun), is on the same block.

Fukuro Noodle Bar JAPANESE $
(Map p84; ☑15-3290-0912; www.fukuronoodlebar.com; Costa Rica 5514; noodle soup AR$110; ⊙8pm-midnight Tue-Thu, to 1am Fri & Sat) For a welcome change from all that meat consumption, check into this comfort-food eatery. Four kinds of ramen are on offer, along with a good selection of *bao* (steamed buns) and *gyoza* (potstickers). Gluten-free noodles available, plus sake and microbrew draft beer. Popular, with counter seating only.

NoLa CAJUN $
(Map p84; ☑15-6350-1704; www.nolabuenos aires.com; Gorriti 4389; mains AR$90-100; ⊙5pm-midnight Mon-Fri, 1pm-midnight Sat & Sun) The brainchild of American Lisa Puglia is this small, popular restaurant focusing on New Orleans Cajun cuisine. Everything is homemade, from the fried chicken sandwich (the hottest seller) to the chorizo gumbo to the spicy, vegetarian red beans and rice. The jalapeño cornbread and bourbon-coffee pecan pie are the bomb, as is the microbrewed beer.

El Preferido de Palermo ARGENTINE $
(Map p84; ☑011-4774-6585; Jorge Louis Borges 2108; mains AR$100-120; ⊙9am-11:30pm Mon-Sat) You can't get much more traditional than this atmospheric, family-run joint. Order tapas, meat platters, homemade pastas and seafood soups, or try one of its specialties – the tortillas, the *milanesas* and the Cuban rice with veal and polenta. Hanging hams, jars of olives and high tables with blocky wood stools add to the charm.

Burger Joint AMERICAN $
(Map p84; ☑011-4833-5151; Jorge Louis Borges 1766; burgers AR$60; ⊙noon-midnight) For some of the juiciest burgers in BA, head to this popular, graffiti-covered spot. NYC-trained chef Pierre Chacra offers just four kinds to choose from, but they're all stellar. Try the Mexican (jalapeños, guacamole and hot sauce) or Jamaican (pineapple, cheddar and bacon) with a side of hand-cut fries.

A DIFFERENT STEAK EXPERIENCE

Going to a *parrilla* is great, but there are other options for amazing steak experiences

Argentine Experience (www.theargentineexperience.com) Learn the story of Argentina's beef and how to make empanadas and *alfajores* (cookie sandwiches). Plus you'll eat a supremely tender steak.

Steaks by Luis (www.steakbuenosaires.net) An upscale *asado* (barbecue grill) experience where you'll nibble on cheese and sip boutique wine while watching large hunks of meat being grilled.

Parrilla Tour (www.parrillatour.com) Meet your knowledgeable guide at a restaurant for a *choripán* (traditional sausage sandwich), followed by an empanada. You'll finish at a local *parrilla*.

MUST-TRY FOODS

➔ *Bife de chorizo* – sirloin steak

➔ Empanadas – baked, savory turnovers

➔ *Helado* – arguably the best ice cream in the world

★Don Julio
PARRILLA $$

(Map p84; ☎011-4832-6058; Guatemala 4699; mains AR$115-230; ◷noon-4pm & 7:30pm-1am) Classy service and a great wine list add an upscale bent to this traditional, and very popular, corner steakhouse. The *bife de chorizo* (sirloin steak) is the main attraction here, but the baked goat cheese provolone, *bondiola de cerdo* (pork shoulder) and gourmet salads are a treat as well, and portions are large. Come early to avoid a wait.

Las Pizarras
INTERNATIONAL $$

(Map p84; ☎011-4775-0625; www.laspizarras bistro.com; Thames 2296; mains AR$140-215; ◷8pm-midnight Tue-Sun) At this simple and unpretentious yet excellent restaurant, Chef Rodrigo Castilla cooks up a changing rainbow of eclectic dishes such as grilled venison or rabbit stuffed with cherries and pistachios. Those with meeker stomachs can choose the asparagus and mushroom risotto or any of the homemade pastas. The chalkboard menu on the wall adds to the casual atmosphere.

Gran Dabbang
INTERNATIONAL, FUSION $$

(Map p84; ☎011-4832-1186; Scalabrini Ortiz 1543; small plates AR$80-95; ◷8pm-midnight Mon-Sat) Unique and creative would be the minimal words to describe the stunning cuisine at this unassuming restaurant on a busy avenue. About eight small plates are offered, a wild-eyed fusion of Indian, Thai, Paraguayan influences (among many), drawn from chef Mariano Ramón's world travels. Come early or late to avoid the inevitable wait.

Siamo nel Forno
PIZZA $$

(Map p84; ☎011-4775-0337; Costa Rica 5886; pizzas AR$120-160; ◷8pm-midnight Tue-Thu & Sun, to 1am Fri & Sat) Possibly the city's best Naples-style pizzas, made with quality ingredients and finished in a hot wood-fired oven so the thin crusts char beautifully. Try the Margherita, with tomatoes, fresh mozzarella, basil and olive oil; the Champignon & Prosciutto comes with mushrooms, ham and goat cheese. Also bakes up excellent calzone.

Bio
VEGETARIAN $$

(Map p84; ☎011-4774-3880; www.biorestaurant. com.ar; Humboldt 2192; mains AR$120-150; ◷11am-midnight Sun-Thu, to 1am Fri & Sat; 🖉) 🍃 Tired of meat? Then make a beeline for this casual family-run restaurant, which specializes in healthy, organic and vegetarian fare. Try the quinoa risotto, curry seitan, Mediterranean couscous or mushrooms a la Bahiana (Brazilian-style). Don't miss the refreshing ginger lemonade. Also caters to celiacs, vegans and raw foodists. Cooking class available.

El Tejano
BARBECUE $$

(Map p84; www.facebook.com/ElTejanoBA; Honduras 4416; mains AR$105-145; ◷12:30-4:30pm & 9pm-midnight Tue-Sat) Missing Texas barbecue from back home? Here's the place to scratch that itch. Authentic Texan Larry Rogers grills up the city's best beef and pork ribs, along with smoked brisket, pulled pork and chicken wings. The offerings may change by the day but you can always expect amazingly tender and delicious meats; the empanadas and fries are also amazing.

★i Latina
SOUTH AMERICAN $$$

(☎011-4857-9095; www.ilatinabuenosaires.com; Murillo 725; set menu AR$900, with wine pairing AR$1380; ◷set time 7pm or 9pm Tue-Sat) Located south of Palermo in Villa Crespo is one of BA's best restaurants: i Latina. The set menu consists of seven courses, all exquisitely prepared and presented. Flavors are incredibly stimulating and complex; this isn't a place to simply fill your tummy, but rather to savor a gustatory experience that will dazzle your taste buds. Reservation required.

Astor
MODERN ARGENTINE $$$

(Map p84; ☎011-4554-0802; www.facebook. com/Astorbistro; Humberto Primo 777, San Telmo; ◷12:30-3:30pm Mon-Wed, 12:30-3:30pm & 8:30pm-midnight Thu & Fri, 8:30pm-midnight Sat) French-trained Chef Antonio Soriano presides over the kitchen at this contemporary restaurant. The few main dishes change weekly but are always delicious, beautifully presented and accented with edible flowers. If you order the tasting menu (AR$370), bring your appetite.

La Carnicería
PARRILLA $$$

(Map p84; ☎011-2071-7199; Thames 2317; mains AR$180-190; ◷8pm-midnight Tue-Fri, 1-3pm & 8pm-midnight Sat & Sun) It took a while, but BA finally has its small, boutique *parrilla* – and it's very, very good. The menu is limited but everything on it is spectacular, from the baked cabbage appetizer to the crispy *provoleta* (barbecued cheese) to the tenderloin and rib cuts. Don't miss the *lengua* (tongue) if it's on the menu. Creativity runs rampant, and portions are huge. Reserve ahead.

Casa Coupage   INTERNATIONAL $$$
(Map p84; ☑ 011-4777 9295; www.casacoupage. com; Soler 5518; mains AR$200-220; tasting menu AR$560; ☺ 8:30-11pm Wed-Sat) Wine lovers will love this closed-door restaurant run by two friendly sommeliers, Santiago Mymicopulo and Inés Mendieta. Choose between their tasting menu or à la carte; the gourmet food is gorgeously presented and will be some of the best you'll experience in BA. The wine pairings are excellent and pours generous; expect to try some of Argentina's tastiest malbec, pinot, torrontés and chardonnay. Reserve ahead.

La Cabrera   PARRILLA $$$
(Map p84; ☑ 011-4831-7002; www.lacabrera. com.ar; José Antonio Cabrera 5099; mains AR$250-400; ☺ 12:30-4:30pm & 8:30pm-1am Sun-Thu, to 2am Fri & Sat) Hugely popular for grilling up BA's most sublime meats. Steaks weigh in at 400gm or 800gm and arrive with many little complimentary side dishes. Come at 7pm for happy hour, when everything is 40% off – just make sure you get here early enough to score a table. Three other locations, mostly nearby.

Sudestada   ASIAN $$$
(Map p84; ☑ 011-4776-3777; Guatemala 5602; set lunch AR$115-130, mains AR$210-235; ☺ noon-3:30pm & 8pm-midnight Mon-Thu, to 1am Fri & Sat) Sudestada's well-prepared curries, stir-fries and noodle dishes are inspired by the cuisines of Thailand, Vietnam, Malaysia and Singapore – and if you order them spicy, they're actually spicy. Don't forgot an exotic cocktail or delicious lychee *licuado* (fruit shake). The popular set-lunch special is great value.

🍷 Drinking & Nightlife

Cafes are an integral part of *porteño* life, and you shouldn't miss popping into one of these beloved hangouts to sip dainty cups of coffee and nibble biscuits with the locals. There are plenty of cafes in the city, and while you're walking around seeing the sights you're bound to run across one and find an excuse for a break. Some cafes are old classics and guaranteed to take you back in time.

Most cafes serve all meals and everything in between: breakfast, brunch, lunch, afternoon tea, dinner and late-night snacks. Generally they open early in the morning and late into the evening.

In a city that never sleeps, finding a good drink is as easy as walking down the street. Whether you're into trendy lounges, Irish pubs, traditional cafes or sports bars, you'll find them all within the borders of BA.

Argentines aren't huge drinkers and you'll be lucky to see one rip-roaring drunk. One thing they *do* do, however, is stay up late. Most bars and cafes are open until two or three in the morning, and often until 5am on weekends – or until the last customer stumbles out the door.

If you like to party with young, heavy-drinking crowds, check out **Buenos Aires Pub Crawl** (☑ 15-3894-0586; www.pubcrawl ba.com).

BA's *boliches* (nightclubs) are the throbbing heart of its world-famous nightlife. To be cool, don't arrive before 2am (or even 3am) and dress up. Payment for admission and drinks is nearly always in cash only.

For one of BA's biggest and most unique parties, check out the improvised percussion at **La Bomba de Tiempo** (Map p84; www. labombadetiempo.com; Sarmiento 3131; ☺ Mon 7pm); it's at 7pm every Monday at Ciudad Cultural Konex.

🍷 Microcentro

La Cigale   COCKTAIL BAR
(Map p58; ☑ 011-4893-2332; www.facebook.com/ lacigalebar; 25 de Mayo 597; ☺ noon-4pm & 6pm-close) This sensuous upstairs bar-restaurant is popular with both office workers (during the day) and music-industry folks (later in the evening). There's either live music or DJs most nights, but it's best known for its 'Minelek' night on Tuesday, when electronica and exotic cocktails draw heavy crowds. Fusion foods are served for both lunch and dinner.

Café Tortoni   CAFE
(Map p58; ☑ 011-4342-4328; www.cafetortoni. com.ar; Av de Mayo 829) BA's oldest and most famous cafe, the classic Tortoni has become so popular with foreigners that it's turned into a tourist trap. Still, it's practically an obligatory stop for any visitor to town: order a couple of *churros* (fried pastry dough) with your hot chocolate and forget about the inflated prices. There are also tango shows (p104) nightly – reserve ahead.

London City CAFE
(Map p58; 011-4342-9057; Av de Mayo 599; ⊙6am-2am) This classy and historic cafe has been serving java enthusiasts for over 50 years, and claims to have been the spot where Julio Cortázar wrote his first novel. Your hardest work here, however, will most likely be choosing which pastry to try with your fresh cup of coffee.

Bahrein CLUB
(Map p58; 011-6225-2731; www.bahreinba. com; Lavalle 345; ⊙Thu-Sun) Attracting a good share of BA's tattooed youth, Bahrein is a hugely popular downtown club housed in an old bank (check out the 'vault' in the basement). On the ground floor is the lounge-like Funky Room where resident DJs spin house music and electronica. Downstairs is the happening Xss discotheque, an impressive sound system and a dance floor for hundreds.

Congreso

Café de los Angelitos CAFE
(Map p58; 011-4952-2320; www.cafedelos angelitos.com; Av Rivadavia 2100; ⊙8am-midnight) Originally called Bar Rivadavia, this cafe was once the haunt of poets, musicians, even criminals, which is why a police commissioner jokingly called it 'los angelitos' (the angels) in the early 1900s. Restored to its former glory, this historic cafe is now an elegant hangout for coffee or tea; it also puts on tango shows (p99) in the evening.

Clásica y Moderna CAFE
(Map p58; 011-4811-3676; www.clasicay moderna.com; Av Callao 892; ⊙8am-9pm Mon-Fri, 9am-9pm Sat) Catering to the literary masses since 1938, this cozy and intimate bookstore-restaurant-cafe continues to ooze history from its atmospheric brick walls. It's nicely lit, serves fine, simple meals, and offers nightly live performances of folk music, jazz, bossa nova and tango (after 9pm). Mercedes Sosa (may she rest in peace), Susana Rinaldi and Liza Minnelli have all chirped here.

El Gato Negro TEAHOUSE
(Map p58; 011-4374-1730; Av Corrientes 1669; ⊙9am-10pm Mon, to 11pm Tue, to midnight Wed & Thu, to 2am Fri & Sat, 3-11pm Sun) Tea-lined wooden cabinets and a spicy aroma welcome you to this pleasant little sipping paradise. Enjoy imported cups of coffee or tea, along with breakfast and dainty *sandwiches de miga* (thin, crustless sandwiches, traditionally eaten at tea time). Imported teas and coffees are sold in bulk, and a range of exotic herbs and spices are also on offer.

San Telmo

★**Bar Plaza Dorrego** CAFE
(Map p58; 011-4361-0141; Defensa 1098; ⊙8am-midnight Sun-Thu, to 3:30am Fri & Sat) You can't beat the atmosphere at this traditional joint; sip your *submarino* (hot milk with chocolate) by a picturesque window and watch the world pass by, or grab a table on the busy plaza. Meanwhile, traditionally suited waiters, piped-in tango music, antique bottles and scribbled graffiti on walls and counters might take you back in time.

Doppelgänger COCKTAIL BAR
(Map p65; 011-4300-0201; www.doppelganger. com.ar; Av Juan de Garay 500; ⊙7pm-2:30am Tue-Thu, to 4am Fri, 8pm-4am Sat) This cool, emerald-hued corner bar is one of the only places in BA where you can count on a perfectly mixed martini. That's because Doppelgänger specializes in vermouth cocktails. The atmosphere is calm and the lengthy menu is fascinating: start with the journalist, a martini with a bitter orange twist, or channel Don Draper and go for the bar's bestseller – an old-fashioned.

La Puerta Roja BAR
(Map p58; 011-4362-5649; Chacabuco 733; ⊙5pm-late) There's no sign at this upstairs bar – just look for the red door. It has a cool, relaxed atmosphere with low lounge furniture in the main room and a pool table tucked behind. This is a traditional place, so you won't find fruity cocktails on the menu – but there is good international food like curries, tacos and chicken wings.

Gibraltar PUB
(Map p58; 011-4362-5310; Perú 895; ⊙noon-4am) One of BA's classic pubs, the Gibraltar has a cozy atmosphere and a good bar counter for those traveling alone. It's also a great place for fairly authentic foreign cuisine – try the Thai, Indian or English dishes. For a little friendly competition, head to the pool table in the back. There are sports on TV, and happy hour runs from noon to 8pm every day.

Retiro

★ Florería Atlántico
COCKTAIL BAR

(Map p70; ☑011-4313-6093; Arroyo 872; ⊙7pm-close Mon-Sat) One of BA's hottest bars, this basement speakeasy is located within a flower shop, adding an air of mystery and likely a main reason for its success. Hipsters, artists, chefs, businesspeople and expats all flock here for the excellent cocktails, whether classic or unique, and the lack of gas lines means all of the delicious tapas and main dishes are cooked on the *parrilla* grill.

BASA Basement Bar
BAR

(Map p70; ☑011-4893-9444; www.basabar. com.ar; Basavilbaso 1328) Also a fine restaurant, this trendy and high-class spot sets the mood right with open spaces, dim lighting and lounge-y sofas. Check out its cocktail list – the refreshing Moscow Mule is a pleasant surprise, especially on warm days. BASA isn't cheap, so consider dropping by during happy hour (starting at 7pm on weekdays, 8pm on weekends) for drink specials. Good food is also available, and DJs provide the sounds on weekends.

Milión
COCKTAIL BAR

(Map p70; ☑011-4815-9925; www.milion.com. ar; Paraná 1048; ⊙6pm-2am Sun-Wed, to 3am Thu, to 4am Fri & Sat) One of BA's most gorgeous and elegant bars, this sexy spot takes up three floors of a renovated old mansion. The garden out back is a leafy paradise, overlooked by a solid balcony that holds the best seats in the house. Nearby marble steps are also an appealing place to lounge with a frozen mojito or basil daiquiri, the tastiest cocktails on the menu. The downstairs restaurant serves international dishes.

Recoleta & Barrio Norte

★ Pony Line Bar
BAR

(Map p70; ☑011-4321-1200; www.elenapony line.com; Posadas 1086; ⊙11am-2am Mon-Thu, till 3am Fri, 6pm-3am Sat, 5pm-1am Sun) This sophisticated, upscale and polo-inspired bar is located in the five-star Four Seasons Hotel, so expect a very fine experience. Drinks are exceptional and high quality, from the artisanal beers to exotic cocktails to fine international liquors; the food is fantastic as well. Dress well, bring a fat wallet and come early if you'd like to avoid the crowds; otherwise reserve ahead.

WINE TASTING & MORE

Big on wine? There are a few ways in Buenos Aires to find out what Argentina's best grapes have to offer.

For private wine tastings, your best bet is with **Anuva Wines** (☑15-5768-8589; www. anuvawines.com). Try five boutique vintages with food pairings; it will also ship your wine purchases to the US. For informal tastings, inquire at **Pain et Vin** (Map p84; ☑011-4832-5654; Gorriti 5132), a casual wine and bread shop. **Bar du Marché** (Map p84; ☑011-4778-1050; www.bardumarchepalermo.com; Nicaragua 5946; ⊙12:30-4pm & 8pm-midnight Mon-Sat) is a low-key bistro offering 50 wines by the glass (plus a wine store next door), while **Gran Bar Danzón** (Map p70; ☑011-4811-1108; www.granbardanzon.com.ar; Libertad 1161) is an upscale lounge-restaurant that also has a good selection of wines by the glass.

Wine 'tours' are another good way to sample some of Argentina's best grapes. Try **Wine Tour BA** (www.winetourba.com), where you'll sip and nibble your way around the neighborhood of Palermo; another to try is **Urban Adventures** (www. urbanadventures.com).

Some *puertas cerradas* (closed-door restaurants) offer fine wines with their meals; **Casa Coupage** (p93), run by an Argentine sommelier couple, is especially wine oriented. Others to try include **Casa Saltshaker** (p91) and **i Latina** (p92).

For wine shops there's **Lo de Joaquín Alberdi** (p109) in Palermo – it offers tastings as well. In San Telmo, **Vinotango** (Map p58; ☑011-4361-1101; www.vinotango. com.ar; Estados Unidos 488; ⊙10:30am-9pm) is a good destination. **Aldo's Vinoteca** (p87) is a restaurant that sells wines at retail prices, and offers wine flights and weekly tastings too.

Finally, **Miravida Soho** (p83) is a boutique hotel that boasts a fine wine cellar and gives wine tastings for its guests.

La Biela
CAFE

(Map p70; ☎011-4804-0449; www.labiela. com; Av Quintana 600; ☺7am-2am Sun-Thu, to 3am Fri & Sat) A Recoleta institution, this classic landmark has been serving the *porteño* elite since the 1950s – when race-car champions used to frequent the place. The outdoor front terrace is unbeatable on a sunny afternoon, especially when the nearby weekend *feria* (street market) is in full swing. Just know that this privilege will cost 20% more.

Casa Bar
SPORTS BAR

(Map p70; ☎011-4816-2712; www.casabar argentina.com; Rodríguez Peña 1150; ☺6pm-5am Mon-Fri, 9pm-5am Sat, 7pm-5am Sun) This recycled antique house turned sports bar offers a large selection of spirits and microbrews, along with a wine list stocked with higher-end bottles. You'll also find nachos, pizzas and spicy hot wings on the menu, plus happy-hour specials from 7pm to 10pm. Casa Bar is stylish but casual – and a great spot to watch sports on TV, especially American football and baseball.

Shamrock Basement
CLUB

(Map p70; ☎011-4812-3584; Rodríguez Peña 1220; ☺Thu-Sat) This cool but unpretentious subterranean club is known for first-rate DJ lineups, pounding house music and a diverse young crowd. Thanks to the Shamrock, the ever-popular Irish pub upstairs, the place sees plenty of traffic throughout the night. Come at 3am to see the club in full swing, or just descend the stairs after enjoying a few pints at ground level.

🍷 Palermo

Many hotels and restaurants in Palermo have great bars, such as **Home Hotel** (Map p84; ☎011-4778-1008; www.homebuenosaires. com; Honduras 5860; ☺8am-midnight). For the hippest scene in town, head to Plaza Serrano (in Palermo Viejo) and settle in at one of the many trendy bars surrounding the plaza.

★LAB Training Center & Coffee Shop
CAFE, COFFEE

(Map p84; ☎011-4843-1790; www.labcafe.com. ar; Humbolt 1542; ☺8am-8pm Mon-Sat) High ceilings and industrial chic are hallmarks of this excellent coffee shop. Choose your house-roasted beans and have them run through a chemex, aeropress, V60, kalita, syphon or clever dripper. Mostly counter seating, though upstairs there's a communal table for those serious about work. Brewing and espresso classes also on offer.

★Victoria Brown
COCKTAIL BAR

(Map p84; ☎011-4831-0831; www.victoria brownbar.com; Costa Rica 4827; ☺9pm-4am Tue-Sat) Secreted behind a large draped door inside a cute coffee shop, this speakeasy lounge serves up excellent food and tasty, high-quality cocktails. It's a very popular place so dress up and come early to snag a sofa or curvy table-booth. Boasts a beautiful and sophisticated industrial-decor atmosphere; even the bathroom fittings are creative. Reserve ahead for dinner.

★878
COCKTAIL BAR

(Map p84; ☎011-4773-1098; www.878bar.com. ar; Thames 878; ☺7pm-3am Mon-Thu, to 4:30am Fri, 8pm-4:30am Sat & Sun) Hidden behind an unsigned door is this 'secret' bar, but it's hardly exclusive. Enter a wonderland of elegant, low lounge furniture and red-brick walls; for whiskey lovers there are over 80 kinds to try, but the cocktails are tasty too. If you're hungry, tapas are available (reserve for dinners).

★Verne
COCKTAIL BAR

(Map p84; ☎011-4822-0980; Av Medrano 1475; ☺8pm-3am Tue-Thu, to 4am Fri, 9pm-4am Sat, to 3am Sun) Upscale yet casual bar with slight Jules Verne theme. Cocktails are the specialties here, whipped up by one of BA's best bartenders, Fede Cuco. A few tables, some cushy sofas and an airy outdoor patio offer a variety of seating options, but plant yourself at the bar to see drinks being made; check out the French absinthe server. House-made Negroni available.

★Magdalena's Party
BAR

(Map p84; ☎011-4833-9127; www.magdalenas party.com; Thames 1795; ☺8pm-2am Mon, 11am-3am Thu, to 4am Fri & Sat, to 5pm Sun) Popular bar-restaurant with laid-back atmosphere and *buena onda* (good vibes). DJs spin from Thursday to Saturday nights, and with cheap drinks this is a good preclub spot; try the vodka lemonade by the pitcher. Happy hour runs from noon to midnight daily, and tasty expat-friendly food is served, such as freshly ground hamburgers, California-style burritos and organic coffee. Popular weekend brunch too.

Harrison Speakeasy
COCKTAIL BAR

(Map p84; ☎011-4831-0519; Malabia 1764; ☺9pm-12:30am Tue & Wed, to 2am Thu, to 4am Fri

& Sat) Enter through a wine cellar then vault door to one of BA's most exclusive and 'secret' bars. It's a time machine to 1920s New York, complete with candlelit atmosphere and fog-machine air. Head bartender Seba Garcia creates some of Argentina's best cocktails, but unless you eat beforehand at Nicky's sushi restaurant out front (ask to 'see the wine cellar' once you get the check) or charm your five-star hotel's concierge, it's unlikely you'll get in.

Frank's Bar
COCKTAIL BAR

(Map p84; 011-4777-6541; www.franks-bar. com; Arévalo 1445; 9pm-4am Wed-Sat) Very popular plush, elegant speakeasy bar that 'requires' a password (via telephone booth) to get in – request it at its Facebook or Twitter page. Inside it's a beautiful space with crystal chandeliers, billowy ceiling drapes and exclusive feel. Classic cocktails from before the 1930s are stirred – never blended – and served to a crowd of locals and foreigners.

Antares
BAR

(Map p84; 011-4833-9611; www.cerveza antares.com; Armenia 1447; 7pm-4am) Thirsty for a decent *cerveza*? Look no further than this modern but relaxed restaurant-bar with Argentine-brewed ales, porters, stout and barley wine. Order a beer flight, sample the brewmaster's special-edition selection or just enjoy the two-for-one pints during happy hour. Also in **Las Cañitas** (Map p84; Arévalo 2876).

El Carnal
BAR

(Map p84; 011-4772-7582; www.carnalbar. com.ar; Niceto Vega 5511; 7pm-5:30am Tue-Sat) See and be seen on the rooftop terrace at this ever-popular watering hole – preferably in the open air with an icy vodka tonic in hand. With its bamboo lounges and billowy curtains, the place can't be beat for a cool chill-out on a warm summer night. Early in the week reggae rocks, while Thursday to Saturday means pop and '80s tunes.

On Tap
BREWERY

(Map p84; 011-4771-5424; www.ontap.com.ar; Costa Rica 5527; 6pm-midnight Tue-Wed & Sun, to 1am Thu-Sat) This popular new brewery pours 20 Argentine microbrews on tap, including IPAs, pilsners, stouts, wheat porters and honey beers. It's more of a place to enjoy beers than to hang out – there's only counter seating and a communal table, though a few burgers and other pub food is available.

Bring a growler for refills; happy hour runs 6pm to 8:30pm.

Mundo Bizarro
COCKTAIL BAR

(Map p84; 011-4773-1967; Serrano 1222; 8pm-3am Mon-Thu, 9pm-4am Fri, to 5am Sat) This red-lit, futuristically retro and stylish lounge bar is open pretty much all through the night on weekends, when everything from old-time American music to hip DJs to jazz stirs up the air waves. If you're feeling peckish, check out the American-inspired bar food, which ranges from Tex-mex to burgers to hot apple pie with ice cream. Dance on the stripper pole after you've had a few drinks.

Sugar
SPORTS BAR

(Map p84; 011-4831-3276; www.sugarbuenos aires.com; Costa Rica 4619; 7pm-5:30am Tue-Fri, 11am-5:30am Sat, 11am-3am Sun) This lively expat watering hole brings in a youthful nightly crowd with well-priced drink specials and comfort food like chicken fingers and buffalo wings. Watch sports on the five large TV screens or come on Thursdays – also known as ladies' night – when things can get a little rowdy. On weekends, you can roll out of bed and arrive in time for eggs and mimosas.

Lattente Espresso & Brew Bar
CAFE, COFFEE

(Map p84; 011-4833-1676; www.cafelattente. com; Thames 1891; 9am-8pm Mon-Sat, 10am-8pm Sun) Riding on BA's java boom is this modern coffee shop serving house-roasted beans. Order your espresso, cappuccino, Americano or latte (via aeropress or V60) and have a seat at one of the tall communal tables along with other hipster caffeine junkies. A few cookies and an *alfajor* (cookie-type sandwich) or two are on offer.

Pachá
CLUB

(011-4788-4288; Av Rafael Obligado 6151; Sat) Popular, long-running electronica club well-known for attracting famous international DJs who spin tunes for the sometimes drug-addled crowds. Laser light shows and a great sound system makes the chic crowds happy through the early morning light – be sure to bring your shades and watch the sun come up from the terrace.

Kika
CLUB

(Map p84; www.kikaclub.com.ar; Honduras 5339; Tue-Sun) Being supremely well located near the heart of Palermo Viejo's bar scene makes Kika's Tuesday-night popular 'Hype' party easily accessible for the trendy crowds. It's a mix of electro, rock, hip-hop, drum and bass, and dubstep, all spun by both local and international DJs. Other nights see electronica, raggaeton, Latin beats and live bands ruling the roost.

Jet
CLUB

(☎ 011-4872-5599; www.jet.com.ar; Avenida Rafael Obligado 4801; ☺ Thu-Sat) Jet definitely has an exclusive vibe that attracts celebrities and fashionistas, so put on your best get-up or you won't make the dress code. Early on you can hang in the trendy cocktail lounge, nibble on tapas or sushi and enjoy the marina view. As the night progresses, however, the hip young clubbers start making their appearance – come after 3am for the best-looking crowd. Music runs toward house and electro.

Niceto Club
CLUB

(Map p84; ☎ 011-4779-9396; www.nicetoclub. com; Niceto Vega 5510; ☺ Thu-Sat) One of the city's biggest crowd-pullers, the can't-miss event at Niceto Club is Thursday night's Club 69, a subversive DJ extravaganza featuring gorgeously attired showgirls, dancing drag queens, futuristic video installations and off-the-wall performance art. On weekend nights, national and international spin masters take the booth to entertain lively crowds with blends of hip-hop, electronic beats, cumbia and reggae.

Crobar
CLUB

(Map p84; ☎ 011-4778-1500; www.crobar.com. ar; cnr Av de la Infanta Isabell & Freyre; ☺ Fri & Sat) Stylish and spacious Crobar remains one of BA's most popular nightlife spots. Friday usually features international DJs mashing up the latest techno selections, while Saturday is popular with the LGBT crowd and

---

GAY & LESBIAN BUENOS AIRES

In July 2010 Argentina became the first Latin American country to legalize same-sex marriage. Since then BA has become a huge gay destination, lending momentum to local events such as the **Marcha del Orgullo Gay** (Gay Pride Parade; www.marchadelorgullo. org.ar; ☺ Nov) and the **Queer Tango Festival** (www.festivaltangoqueer.com.ar).

To mix with local gays, check out popular bars like loud **Sitges** (Map p84; www.facebook.com/fiestaplop; cnr Federico Lacroze & Álvarez Thomas) and casual **Flux** (Map p70; ☎ 011-5252-0258; Marcelo T de Alvear 980; ☺ 7pm-3am Sun-Thu, to 4am Fri & Sat). The coffee shop **Pride Cafe** (Map p58; ☎ 011-4300-6435; Balcarce 869; ☺ 10am-8pm; 🖵) attracts mixed crowds in San Telmo. For a fun night of guided drinking and partying, there's **Out & About Pub Crawl** (www.outandaboutpubcrawl.com).

The best nightclubs are rough-and-tumble **Amerika** (Map p84; ☎ 011-4865-4416; www.ameri-k.com.ar; Gascón 1040; ☺ Fri-Sun) and sexy-beautiful **Glam** (Map p84; ☎ 011-4963-2521; www.glambsas.com.ar; José Antonio Cabrera 3046; ☺ Thu-Sat) and **Palacio Alsina** (Map p58; ☎ 011-4331-3231; www.palacioalsina.net; Adolfo Alsina 940; ☺ Sun, plus 1 Fri per month). Current hot gay parties include **Fiesta Plop** (www.facebook.com/fiesta plop), the monthly **Fiesta Dorothy!** (www.fiestadorothy.com) and **Rheo** (www.rheo. com.ar). **Niceto Club** (p98) has a raucous Thursday night cross-dressing event.

An especially gay-friendly accommodations is **Lugar Gay** (Map p58; ☎ 011-4300-4747; www.lugargay.com.ar; Defensa 1120; dm US$30, s US$50-70, d US$80-105), a casual guesthouse that also acts as an information center. **Casa Brandon** (Map p84; ☎ 011-4858-0610; www.brandongayday.com.ar; Luis Maria Drago 236; ☺ 8pm-3am Wed-Sun) is an art gallery–cultural center.

Good general websites are www.thegayguide.com.ar and www.nighttours.com/buenosaires. For free gay literature, look for *La Otra Guía*, **Circuitos Cortos** (www.circuitoscortos.com.ar/mapagay) and *Gay Maps* (www.gmaps360.com).

There aren't many places catering exclusively to lesbians. Try long-running and intimate **Bach Bar** (Map p84; ☎ 15-5184-0137; José Antonio Cabrera 4390; ☺ 11pm-6am Wed-Sun), but otherwise there are the gay spots listed above. **La Fulana** (www.lafulana.org. ar) is a lesbian cultural center.

Finally, gay classes and *milongas* (tango academies) are given at El Beso's **La Marshall Milonga** (p105), **Tango Queer** (Map p58; www.tangoqueer.com) in San Telmo, and Lugar Gay.

tends to feature electro-pop and Latin beats. The main levels are strewn with mezzanines and catwalks that allow views from above; bring a hefty wallet as this is a top-end spot.

☆ Entertainment

Nonstop Buenos Aires has endless possibilities for entertainment. Dozens of venues offer first-rate theatrical productions, independent or contemporary movies, sultry tango shows, raging dance parties and exciting sports matches.

Many newspapers publish entertainment supplements on Friday; the *Buenos Aires Herald* has a particularly handy one. Also check www.vuenosairez.com.

Major entertainment venues often require booking through **Ticketek** (☑ 011-5237-7200; www.ticketek.com.ar), which incurs a service charge. At *carteleras* (discount-ticket offices), you can buy tickets at 20% to 50% discount for many events like tango shows, theater performances, movies and concerts. There are offices inside **Galería Apolo** (☑ 011-4372-5058; www.cartelerabaires.com; Av Corrientes 1382, Galería Apolo); right on pedestrian **Lavalle** (☑ 011-4322-1559; www.123info. com.ar; Lavalle 742); and on **Av Corrientes** (☑ 011-6320-5319; www.veamasdigital.com.ar; Av Corrientes 1660, Local 2).

Tango Shows

Sensationalized tango shows aimed at tourists are common and impressive (though 'purists' don't consider them authentic). These usually include various tango couples, an orchestra and a couple of singers. They last about 1½ hours and come with a dinner option. Nearly all of them require reservations; some offer modest online discounts and optional pickup from your hotel.

Modest shows are more intimate and cost far less, but you won't get the theatrics, the costume changes or the overall visual punch (which could be a plus depending on your point of view). For discount tickets to some shows, check the *carteleras*. The website www.tangotix.com can help you choose the right show and sells discounted tickets.

Some *milongas* (tango academies) occasionally put on affordable tango shows; check out Confitería Ideal (p105), La Viruta (p105) or **Academia Nacional del Tango** (Map p58; ☑ 4345-6967; www.anacdel tango.org.ar; Av de Mayo 833).

For free (or rather, donation) tango, head to San Telmo on a weekend afternoon; dancers do their thing in the middle of Plaza Dorrego, though it can get crowded. Another good bet is weekends on El Caminito in La Boca, and often there's a couple dancing at the intersection of Florida and Lavalle.

Centro Cultural Borges TANGO
(☑ 011-5555-5359; www.ccborges.org.ar; cnr Viamonte & San Martín; shows US$22-28) This excellent cultural center has many quality offerings, including impressive, reasonably priced tango shows several times per week. Bien de Tango, on Friday and Saturday nights at 8pm, is especially good and comparable to other tango shows that are triple the cost. Check the cultural center's website or stop in beforehand to see what's on tap, and get an advance ticket.

Café de los Angelitos TANGO
(Map p58; ☑ 011-4952-2320; www.cafedelos angelitos.com; Av Rivadavia 2100; show from US$100, show & dinner from US$140) Angelitos puts on one of the best shows in Buenos Aires. It's tango – but also a bit more. The performers dress in top-notch costumes and use interesting props, like drapes and moving walls. They also dance to modern tunes such as those by local band Bajofondo, and despite a nightclub feel at times – especially due to the lighting – it's all very tastefully and creatively done.

Rojo Tango TANGO
(Map p58; ☑ 011-4952-4111; www.rojotango. com; Faena Hotel & Universe, Martha Salotti 445; show US$220, show & dinner from US$290) This sexy performance is the tango show to top all others – especially with its hefty price tag. Offering only 100 seats, the Faena's cabaret room is swathed in blood-red curtains and gilded furniture. The show itself loosely follows the history of the tango, starting from its cabaret roots to the modern fusions of Ástor Piazzolla.

Piazzolla Tango TANGO
(Map p58; ☑ 011-4344-8201; www.piazzollatango. com; Florida 165; show from US$90, show & dinner from US$135) This beautiful art-nouveau theater, just off pedestrian Florida street, used to be a red-light cabaret venue. The show here is based on the music of Ástor Piazzolla, a *bandoneón* (small type of accordion) player who revolutionized tango music by fusing in elements from jazz and classical music. Be aware most tables are communal and you'll be facing sideways to watch the show. Check its website for good discounts.

The Tango

A lone woman, dressed in slit skirt and high heels, sits at a small table. She glances around, in search of the subtle signal. Her gaze suddenly locks onto a stranger's eyes, and there it is: the *cabeceo*. She nods and rises to meet him, and the new pair head toward the dance floor.

History of Tango

The tango hasn't always been quite so mysterious, but it does have a long and somewhat complex history. Though the exact origins can't be pinpointed, some believe the dance started in Buenos Aires in the 1880s. Legions of European immigrants, mostly lower-class men, arrived in the great village of Buenos Aires to seek their fortunes. Missing their motherlands and the women they left behind, they sought out bars, cafes and bordellos to ease the loneliness. Here the men cavorted with waitresses and prostitutes, helping to evolve a dance blending machismo, passion and longing, with an almost fighting edge to it.

Small musical ensembles were soon brought in to accompany early tangos, playing tunes influenced by pampas *milonga* verse, Spanish and Italian melodies (dance hall) and African *candombe* drums. (The *bandoneón,* a small accordion, was brought into these sessions and has since become an inextricable part of the tango orchestra.) Here the tango song was also born. It summarized the new urban experience for the immigrants and was permeated with nostalgia for a disappearing way of life. Themes ranged from profound feelings about changing neighborhoods to the figure of the mother, male friendship

and betrayal by women. Sometimes raunchy lyrics were added.

The perceived vulgarity of the dance was deeply frowned upon by the reigning elites, but it did manage to influence some brash young members of the upper classes, who took the novelty to Paris and created a craze – a dance that became an acceptable outlet for human desires,

1–3. Tango dancers

expressed on the dance floors of elegant cabarets. The trend spread around Europe and even to the US, and 1913 was considered by some to be 'the year of the tango.' When the evolved dance returned to Buenos Aires, now refined and famous, the tango finally earned the respectability it deserved. The golden years of tango were just beginning.

Tango at a Milonga Today

Buenos Aires is full of *milongas* (tango dance events), from classic venues with old-time atmosphere to hip warehouse spaces where dancers wear jeans – in other words, there's something for everyone.

At an established *milonga,* finding a good, comparable partner involves many levels of hidden codes, rules and signals that dancers must follow. In fact, some men will only proposition an unknown woman after the second song, so as not to be stuck with a bad dancer. After all, it's considered polite to dance at least to the end of a set (four songs) with any partner; if you are given a curt *'gracias'* after just one song, consider yourself excused.

Your position in the area surrounding the dance floor can be critical. Ideally, you should sit where you have easy access to the floor and to other dancers' line of sight. You may notice singles sitting in front, while couples sit further back. Generally couples are considered 'untouchable' – for them to dance with others, they either enter the room separately, or the man may signal his intent by asking another woman to the floor. Now 'his' woman becomes available to others.

The *cabeceo* – the quick tilt of the head, eye contact and uplifted eyebrows – can happen from way across the room. The woman to whom the *cabeceo* is directed either nods yes and smiles, or pretends not to have noticed. If she says yes, the man gets up and escorts her to the floor. If she pretends not to have seen him, it's considered a rejection. When you're at a *milonga* and don't want

1. Tango class **2.** Musician playing the *bandoneón* (p100)

to dance with anyone, don't look around too much – you could be breaking some hearts.

Don't be surprised to see different *milongas* put on at a single venue, depending on the time or day. Each *milonga* can be run by a different promoter, so each will have its own vibe, style, music and table arrangement, as well as age levels and experiences.

For good information on Buenos Aires' tango scene and how to navigate it, get a copy of Sally Blake's practical guide *Happy Tango: Sallycat's Guide to Dancing in Buenos Aires, 2nd edition* (www.sallycatway.com/happytango). You can pick up free tango magazines at *milongas* and tango shoe shops (of which there are many in Buenos Aires).

Tango classes are often available in the same venue as *milongas,* in the hours before they start. But you can find them everywhere from youth hostels to cultural centers – some are even included free when you book a fancy tango show. Tourist-oriented classes are often taught in English.

So what is the appeal of the tango? Experienced dancers will say that the rush from a blissful tango connection with a stranger can lift you to exhilarating heights. But the dance can also become addictive – once you have fallen for the passion and beauty of the tango's movements, you can spend your life trying to attain a physical perfection that can never be fully realized. The true *tanguero* simply attempts to make the journey as graceful as possible.

TOP MILONGAS

➡ Salon Canning (p104)
➡ Club Gricel (p105)
➡ Confitería Ideal (p105)
➡ La Viruta (p105)
➡ La Catedral (p105)

El Viejo Almacén
TANGO

(Map p58; ☎011-4307-7388; www.viejoalmacen. com; cnr Balcarce & Av Independencia; show from US$90, show & dinner from US$140) One of Buenos Aires' longest-running shows (since 1969), this venue is a charming old building from the 1800s. A good dinner is served at a multistory restaurant in the main building, then everyone heads across the street to the small theater with intimate stage. The show starts with a quick movie about the tango show's history, then moves on to the highly athletic dancers with plenty of glitz. One highlight is the exceptionally good folklore segment.

La Ventana
TANGO

(Map p58; ☎011-4334-1314; www.laventanaweb. com; Balcarce 431; show from US$115, show & dinner from US$170) This long-running basement venue is located in an old converted building with rustic brick walls in San Telmo. The tango show includes a folkloric segment with Andean musicians and a display of *boleadores* (gaucho hunting weapons). There's also a patriotic tribute to Evita, and the dinner offers a wide variety of tasty main dishes – unusual for tango shows. Gala Tango is a more upscale experience and happens upstairs. Free tango lesson included.

Esquina Carlos Gardel
TANGO

(Map p84; ☎011-4867-6363; www.esquinacarlos gardel.com.ar; Carlos Gardel 3200; show from US$96, show & dinner from US$140) One of the fanciest tango shows in town plays at this impressive 430-seat theater, an old cantina right next to the lovely shopping mall Mercado de Abasto. This fine show highlights passionate, top-notch musicians and performers in period costumes, though a modern segment involving a skin suit is cutting-edge, athletic and memorable.

Café Tortoni
TANGO

(Map p58; ☎011-4342-4328; www.cafetortoni. com.ar; Av de Mayo 829) Nightly tango shows (reserve ahead) take place at this historic yet very touristy place. If you come earlier for the cafe, you may have to line up outside beforehand. Despite these downfalls, the Tortoni is BA's most famous cafe and still offers a beautiful atmosphere.

Los 36 Billares
TANGO

(Map p58; ☎011-4381-8909; www.los36billares. com.ar; Av de Mayo 1271; show US$10-12) Dating from 1894, this is one of the city's most historic cafe-bars. As its name implies, it's big on billiard tables (check out the basement). Tango shows happen a few times per week in the 60-seat back theater – just make sure, if you care, that the tango show highlights dancers, as sometimes it's only a tango music show. Tango classes offered Wednesdays at 7pm.

Todo Mundo
TANGO

(Map p58; ☎011-4362-2354; Pasaje Anselmo Aieta 1095) A pair of tango dancers entertain diners continuously from 12:30pm to 8pm during the day, working on tips, at this casual restaurant on Plaza Dorrego. Basic and mediocre-quality fare includes empanadas, pasta and *parrilla*. More complete tango shows happen for Thursday night dinners. Expect flamenco, rock, salsa, folk and jazz on other nights; all shows start around 10:30pm.

Milongas
Milongas are dance events where people strut their tango skills. The atmosphere at these events can be modern or historical, casual or traditional. Most have tango DJs that determine musical selections, but a few utilize live orchestras.

Milongas either start in the afternoon and run until 11pm, or start at around midnight and run until the early-morning light (arrive late for the best action). Classes are often offered beforehand.

To get the inside scoop on BA's tango scene while taking a 'tour' of *milongas*, check out www.narrativetangotours.com or www.tangotrips.com. For a current list of *milongas*, see www.hoy-milonga.com.

La Glorieta
MILONGA

(Barrancas de Belgrano; ⊙around 7pm Fri-Sun) For a unique outdoor experience, head to the bandstand at the Barrancas de Belgrano, where the casual *milonga* La Glorieta takes place. There's often a free tango lesson beforehand. Check the Facebook page for details.

Salon Canning
MILONGA

(Map p84; ☎15-5738-3850; www.parakultural. com.ar; Av Scalabrini Ortiz 1331) Some of BA's finest dancers (no wallflowers here) grace this traditional venue with its great dance floor. Well-known tango company Parakultural stages good events on Monday, Tuesday and Friday, involving live music, tango DJs, singers and dancers. Expect big crowds and plenty of tourists.

Club Gricel
MILONGA

(☑ 011-4957-7157; www.clubgriceltango.com.ar; La Rioja 1180) This old classic (far from the center; take a taxi) often has big crowds, especially on Thursday. It attracts an older, well-dressed clientele – along with plenty of tourists. There's a wonderful springy dance floor and occasionally live orchestras.

Confitería Ideal
MILONGA

(Map p58; ☑ 011-4328-7750; www.facebook.com/idealconfiteria; Suipacha 384, 1st fl) This institution (since 1912) is the mother of all historic tango halls, with classes and *milongas* offered daily (or nearly so). Live orchestras occasionally accompany dancers, and there are dinner-tango shows on Friday and Saturday. The actual cafe section could use a face lift, as it's a bit dim, stodgy and impersonal, but it remains a classic. Featured in the film *The Tango Lesson*.

La Catedral
MILONGA

(Map p84; ☑ 15-5325-1630; www.lacatedralclub.com; Sarmiento 4006) If tango can be youthful, trendy and hip, this is where you'll find it. The grungy warehouse space is very casual, with funky art on the walls, thrift-store furniture and dim atmospheric lighting. It's more like a bohemian nightclub than anything else, and there's no implied dress code – you'll see plenty of jeans. Great for cheap alcohol; the best-known *milongas* occur regularly on a Tuesday night.

La Viruta
MILONGA

(Map p84; ☑ 011-4774-6357; www.lavirutatango.com; Armenia 1366, basement) Popular basement venue. Good beginner tango classes are available before *milongas* – translating into many inexperienced dancers on the floor earlier on – so if you're an expert get here late (after 3:30am). Music can run the gamut from tango to rock to cumbia to salsa earlier in the evening, with more traditional tunes later. Tango shows also on offer.

El Beso
MILONGA

(Map p58; ☑ 011-4953-2794; Riobamba 416, 1st fl) A traditional and popular place, El Beso attracts some very good dancers – you should be very confident of your dancing skills if you come here. Located upstairs, it has good music and a cozy feel.

On Friday night, El Beso hosts the far less traditional but still well-known **La Marshall Milonga**, a gay *milonga*, for all who want to try a change of roles in their tango. There's a class at 10:30pm before the *milonga* at 11:30pm.

Live Music

Smaller venues showcase mostly local groups; international stars tend to play at large venues such as *fútbol* stadiums or **Luna Park** (Map p58; ☑ 011-5279-5279; www.lunapark.com.ar; cnr Bouchard & Av Corrientes). Clásica y Moderna (p94) occasionally hosts jazz groups.

With so many *porteños* boasting Spanish ancestry, it's not surprising that there are a few flamenco venues in town. Most are located in Congreso's Spanish neighborhood, near the intersection of Salta and Av de Mayo.

Música folklórica (folk music) also has its place in BA. There are several *peñas* (folk-music clubs) in the city, but other venues occasionally host *música folklórica* – keep your eyes peeled.

Centro Cultural Kirchner
CONCERT VENUE

(Map p58; ☑ 0800-333-9300; www.culturalkirchner.gob.ar; Sarmiento 151) Located in Buenos Aires' gorgeous ex-main post office, this gigantic building is home to dozens of event halls – including a concert venue that holds nearly 2000 and is home to Argentina's national symphony orchestra. Check the website for happenings and get there early for tickets. Most events are currently free, but may cost a nominal charge in the future.

Usina del Arte
CONCERT VENUE

(Map p65; www.usinadelarte.org; Agustín Caffarena 1) This restored old electricity factory is a valiant attempt to breathe new life into an edgy section of La Boca. It's a gorgeous red-brick building complete with scenic clock tower, and its concert hall – boasting top-notch acoustics – can seat 1200 spectators. Offers free or inexpensive art exhibitions, along with music, theater and dance performances. Check the website for current happenings.

Teatro Colón
CLASSICAL MUSIC

(Map p58; ☑ 011-4378-7100; www.teatrocolon.org.ar; Cerrito 628) BA's premier venue for the arts, with ballet, opera and classical music.

La Trastienda
ROCK, REGGAE

(Map p58; ☑ 011-5254-9100; www.latrastienda.com; Balcarce 460) This large, atmospheric theater in San Telmo welcomes over 700, features a well-stocked bar, and showcases national and international live-music acts almost nightly. Look for headers such as

Charlie García, Dividos, José González, Damien Rice and Conor Oberst. Check its website for the latest.

Notorious   JAZZ
(Map p58; ☑011-4813-6888; www.notorious. com.ar; Av Callao 966) This stylish, intimate joint is one of Buenos Aires' premier jazz venues. Up front you can buy CDs of various music genres, while in the back the restaurant-cafe (overlooking a verdant garden) hosts live shows nearly every night at 9:30pm. Log on to the website for schedules; most performances are jazz, but there's also Brazilian music.

Thelonious Bar   JAZZ
(Map p84; ☑011-4829-1562; www.thelonious. com.ar; Salguero 1884, 1st fl; ☺9pm-1am Thu, to 3am Fri & Sat) Upstairs in an old mansion lies this dimly lit jazz bar, with high brick ceilings and a good sound system. Come early to snag a seat (or reserve one ahead of time) and partake in the typically Argentine menu and good range of cocktails. Thelonious is known for its classic and contemporary Argentine jazz lineups, though international musicians sometimes entertain.

Ávila Bar   FLAMENCO
(Map p58; ☑011-4383-6974; Av de Mayo 1384; ☺Thu-Sat) Offering flamenco for many years now is this cozy little Spanish restaurant with good traditional food. Main dishes (or tapas) can include rabbit, paella and seafood stews. Flamenco shows start around 10:30pm and reservations are a must on weekends.

Los Cardones   FOLK MUSIC
(Map p84; ☑011-4777-1112; www.cardones.com. ar; Borges 2180; ☺from 9pm Wed-Sat) Come to this friendly, low-key *peña* for mellow guitar shows, audience-participatory jam sessions (and possible dancing), hearty regional cuisine from northern Argentina and free-flowing red wine. Shows start at 10pm on weekdays and 11pm weekends. Check out the website for details on the current lineup and reserve ahead for a good table.

Theater

Av Corrientes, between Avs 9 de Julio and Callao, has traditionally been the capital's center for theater, but there are now dozens of venues throughout the city.

Teatro Nacional Cervantes   THEATER
(Map p58; ☑011-5222-4109; www.teatrocervan tes.gov.ar; Libertad 815) This architecturally gorgeous theater featuring three halls, a grand lobby and red-velvet chairs has good productions at affordable prices.

Teatro San Martín   THEATER
(Map p58; ☑011-4371-0111; www.complejo teatral.gob.ar; Av Corrientes 1530) This major venue has several auditoriums (the largest seats over 1000 people) and showcases international cinema, theater, dance and classical music, covering conventional and more unusual events. It also has art galleries and often hosts impressive photography exhibitions.

Teatro Presidente Alvear   THEATER
(Map p58; ☑011-4371-0111; www.complejoteatral. gob.ar; Av Corrientes 1659) Inaugurated in 1942 and named after an Argentine president whose wife sang opera, this theater holds over 850 and shows many musical productions, including ballet. Occasional free shows are on offer.

Cinemas

BA is full of cinemas, both historical neon classics and slick modern multiplexes. The traditional cinema districts are along pedestrian Lavalle (west of Florida) and on Av Corrientes, but newer cineplexes are spread throughout the city; most large shopping malls have one.

Check out the *Buenos Aires Herald* for original titles of English-language films. Except for kids' films, most movies are in their original language (with Spanish subtitles).

🛒 Shopping

Shopping is practically a sport for many Buenos Aires' citizens who despite steeply rising inflation, continue to shop as if there's no tomorrow. As the saying goes, 'An Argentine will make one peso and spend two.'

In the Microcentro, Florida is a multipurpose pedestrian strip that buzzes with shoppers, while Av Santa Fe is a bit less pedestrian-friendly but equally prominent as the city's main shopping artery. San Telmo is ground zero for antiques, and Av Pueyrredón near Once train station is *the* place for cheap (and lower-quality) clothing. Jewelry shops are found on Libertad south of Av Corrientes. Leather jackets and bags are cheapest on Calle Murillo (500–600 block), in Villa Crespo.

For avant garde fashions, Palermo Viejo is the place to be. This neighborhood, split by railroad tracks into Palermo Soho and Palermo Hollywood, has the most concentrated number of clothing boutiques between Plaza Serrano and Plaza Palermo Viejo. You'll find housewares and plenty of knick-knack shops here too. Prices are high.

As in other Western countries, bargaining is not acceptable in most stores. Expensive items such as jewelry and leather jackets can be exceptions, especially if you buy several. At street markets you can try negotiating for better prices – just keep in mind you may be talking to the artists themselves, who generally don't make much money. San Telmo's antiques fair, Feria de San Telmo, is an exception: prices here are often inflated for tourists.

Microcentro & Congreso

Arte y Esperanza   CRAFTS
(Map p58; ☑ 011-4343-1455; www.arteyesperanza. com.ar; Balcarce 234; ⊙ 9am-6:30pm Mon-Fri) This store sells fair-trade, handmade products that include many from Argentina's indigenous craftspeople. Shop for silver jewelry, pottery, ceramics, textiles, *mate* gourds, baskets, woven bags, wood utensils and animal masks. There's another branch in **Retiro** (Map p58; ☑ 011-4393-3270; www.arteyesperanza. com.ar; Suipacha 892).

Zival's   MUSIC
(Map p58; www.zivals.com; Av Callao 395; ⊙ 9:30am-9:30pm Mon-Sat) This is one of the better music stores in town, especially when it comes to tango, folk, jazz and classical music. Listening stations are a big plus, and many books are also for sale.

Wildlife   OUTDOOR EQUIPMENT
(Map p58; ☑ 011-4381-1040; Hipólito Yrigoyen 1133; ⊙ 10am-8pm Mon-Fri, to 1pm Sat) If you're looking to buy all manner of outdoor and camping equipment, this is the place to do it. Crampons, knives, tents, backpacks, climbing gear, foul-weather clothing, skateboards, military gear and even the occasional mule saddle can be found at this somewhat offbeat and musty shop.

San Telmo

Walrus Books   BOOKS
(Map p58; ☑ 011-4300-7135; Estados Unidos 617; ⊙ noon-8pm Tue-Sun) Run by an American photographer, this tiny shop is probably the best English-language bookstore in BA. Thousands of new and used literature and nonfiction books line the shelves here, and there's a selection of Latin American classics translated into English. Bring your quality books to trade; literary workshops offered too.

Cualquier Verdura   CLOTHING, HOMEWARES
(Map p58; ☑ 011-4300-2474; Humberto Primo 517; ⊙ noon-8pm Thu-Sun) Located in a lovely, refurbished old house, this fun store sells eclectic items from vintage clothing to old books to recycled floppy-disc lamps to contemporary housewares and novelty toys. Wander through the outdoor patio and note the stained-glass windows on the wall and *mate*-drinking Buddha above the fountain.

Materia Urbana   ART, HOMEWARES
(Map p58; ☑ 011-4361-5265; www.materiaurbana. com; Defensa 702; ⊙ 11am-7pm Wed-Fri, 2-7pm Sat, 10:30am-7pm Sun) This innovative design shop shows the work of over 100 local artists; cool finds include leather animal organizers, retro tote bags, plastic *mate gourds* and jewelry made from metal, wood and leather.

Punto Sur   CLOTHING
(Map p58; ☑ 011-4300-9320; www.feriapunto sur.com.ar; Defensa 1135; ⊙ 11:30am-7:30pm) This is a great clothing store highlighting the works of nearly 70 Argentine designers. Creativity is rampant and it's a fun walkthrough for one-of-a-kind funky threads, including interesting knitwear, colorful skirts, printed T-shirts, jewelry and accessories, cool handbags and even kids' stuff.

Moebius   CLOTHING
(Map p65; ☑ 011-4361-2893; Defensa 1356; ⊙ 11am-8pm Tue-Sun) This funky little shop's racks are crowded with owner-designer Lilliana Zauberman's kaleidoscopic products: 1970s-style jersey dresses, whimsical ruffled bikinis, skirts printed with koi fish and frog patterns, cherry-red trench coats and handbags made from recycled materials. Around 60 designers sell their work here, so there's always something different, fun and new to keep an eye out for.

Gil Antiguedades   ANTIQUES
(Map p58; ☑ 15-6295-1079 annex; Humberto Primo 412; ⊙ 11am-1pm & 3-7pm Tue-Sun) Going on 45 years, this cluttered antique shop sells everything you can imagine – china tea sets, leather hatboxes, old toys, mirrors, vintage suitcases, lace tablecloths and crystal

glassware. Its annex (by appointment only) has wedding dresses and accessories.

Recoleta & Retiro

El Ateneo   BOOKS
(Map p70; Av Santa Fe 1860; ⊙9am-10pm Mon-Thu, to midnight Fri & Sat, noon-10pm Sun) Buenos Aires' landmark bookseller stocks a limited number of books in English, including Lonely Planet guides. There are several branches within the city, but this one – the Gran Splendid – is in a gorgeous old renovated cinema.

Autoría   ART, ACCESSORIES
(Map p70; ☑011-5252-2474; www.autoriabsas.com.ar; Suipacha 1025; ⊙9:30am-8pm Mon-Fri, 10am-6pm Sat) This cool designer's showcase – stocked with edgy art books, sculptural fashions, whimsical leather desk sculptures and unique jewelry of all materials (silk cocoons!) – strives to promote Argentine designers. Especially interesting are the recycled materials – check out the bags made of tyvek, inner tubes, firehoses or even old sails. Products are of high quality and prices are accessible.

Palermo

Rapsodia   CLOTHING
(Map p84; ☑011-4831-6333; www.rapsodia.com; Honduras 4872; ⊙10am-9pm) With fabrics from linen to leather and details like fringe and sequins, this large and popular boutique is a must for fashion mavens. Old and new are blended into creative, colorful styles with exotic and bohemian accents. Locals covet its dresses and jeans; over a dozen branches in the city.

Bolivia   CLOTHING
(Map p84; ☑011-4832-6284; Gurruchaga 1581; ⊙10:30am-8:30pm Mon-Sat, 3-8:30pm Sun) There's almost nothing here that your young, hip and possibly gay brother wouldn't love, from the stylish plaid shirts to the skin-tight jeans to the military-styled jackets. Metrosexual to the hilt, and paradise for the man who isn't afraid of patterns, plaid or pastels. Has a second **Palermo** (Map p84; ☑011-4832-6409; Nicaragua 4908; ⊙11:30am-8:30pm Mon-Sat) branch.

Calma Chicha   HOMEWARES
(Map p84; ☑011-4831-1818; www.calmachicha.com; Honduras 4909; ⊙10am-8pm) Calma Chicha specializes in creative housewares and

---

BUENOS AIRES STREET MARKETS

Some of BA's best crafts and souvenirs are sold at its many street markets, often by the artists themselves. You may have to sort through some tacky kitsch, but you'll also find creative and original art. Often there is also 'free' (ie donation) entertainment from casual performers.

Feria de San Telmo (Map p58; Defensa; ⊙10am-6pm Sun; ▣10, 22, 29, 45, 86) On Sundays, San Telmo's main drag is closed to traffic and the street is a sea of both locals and tourists browsing craft stalls, waiting at vendors' carts for freshly squeezed orange juice, poking through the antique glass ornaments on display on Plaza Dorrego, and listening to street performances by myriad music groups. Runs from Av San Juan to Plaza de Mayo.

Feria Artesanal (Map p70; Plaza Intendente Alvear; ⊙10am-7pm) Recoleta's hugely popular fair has dozens of booths and a range of creative, homemade goods. Hippies, mimes and tourists mingle. It's at its biggest on weekends; located just outside the Cementerio de la Recoleta.

Feria Plaza Serrano (Map p84; Plaza Serrano; ⊙10am-8pm Fri-Sun) Costume jewelry, hand-knit tops, *mate* gourds, leather accessories and a whole lot of junk fill the crafts booths at this small but lively fair on fashionable Plaza Serrano in Palermo.

Feria de Mataderos (☑011-4342-9629; www.feriademataderos.com.ar; cnr Avs Lisandro de la Torre & de los Corrales; ⊙11am-8pm Sun Apr–mid-Dec, 6pm-midnight Sat late Jan–mid-Mar) The unique Feria de Mataderos is far off in the working-class barrio of Mataderos, but it's worth hiking out here for the shows of horsemanship, folk dancing and cheap authentic treats. From downtown, take bus 126, 155 or 180 (one hour). Confirm hours beforehand; it closes for a couple weeks 'between' seasons.

accessories that are locally produced from leather, faux leather, sheepskin, cowhide, and brightly hued fabric. Look for butterfly chairs, throw rugs, leather place mats, bright pillows and cow-skin bags.

Patio del Liceo   MALL
(Map p84; ☑011-4822-9433; Av Santa Fe 2729) Eclectic little shopping mall with funky and casual vibe. In the past few years, young struggling artists have taken over and created an artistic hub here, filling it with various small boutiques, exhibition spaces and workshops. You'll find a couple of bookstores, a record store and some design stores. Hours vary depending on individual stores.

Hermanos Estebecorena   CLOTHING
(Map p84; ☑011-4772-2145; www.hermanos estebecorenashop.com; El Salvador 5960; ⊙11am-8pm Mon-Sat) The Estebecorena brothers apply their highly creative skills toward smartly designed tops, jackets that fold into bags, polo-collar work shirts and even seamless underwear. The focus is on original, highly stylish, very functional men's clothing that makes the artsy types swoon. Selection is limited, but what's there really counts.

Lo de Joaquín Alberdi   FOOD, WINE
(Map p84; ☑011-4832-5329; www.lodejoaquin alberdi.com; Jorge Luis Borges 1772; ⊙11am-9:30pm Mon-Sat, noon-9:30pm Sun) Nationally produced wines for every taste and budget line the racks and cellar of this attractive wine shop. Tastings happen Thursday and Friday at 7:30pm (double-check ahead of time) and include four wines and some cheeses.

❶ Orientation

BA is a huge metropolis, but most places of interest are in just a few easily accessible neighborhoods.

The heart of the city is **Microcentro**; it's small enough to walk around fairly easily. Just east is **Puerto Madero**, with scenic docklands and a large ecological park. Further south is **San Telmo**, known for its lovely colonial architecture and Sunday fair. South of here is **La Boca**, famed for colorful houses clad in corrugated metal.

West of the Microcentro sits **Congreso**, BA's seat of politics, boasting some stately buildings. To the north is upscale **Retiro**, home to the city's main train station and bus terminal. And just northwest lie **Recoleta** and **Barrio Norte**, boasting some of BA's most expensive real estate and dotted with art museums, fancy shops and luxurious mansions.

PESKY INFLATION

Be warned: while accurate at the time of research, prices quoted here are likely to rise rapidly. The unofficial inflation rate is over 30% (officially it's 15%).

Because of Argentina's high inflation, hotels and certain other businesses sometimes quote in US dollars. For accommodations we've published prices in dollars; for most other listings they are in pesos. Keep an attentive eye for AR$ and US$ as you look through the listings.

Further north is **Palermo**, an upper-middle-class suburb with spacious parks, plenty of shopping and heaps of restaurants; it's subdivided into the trendy neighborhoods of Palermo Soho, Palermo Hollywood and Las Cañitas, among others. And edging Palermo's borders are **Belgrano** and **Once**, both home to concentrations of ethnic Chinese, Korean, Peruvian and Jewish people.

BA's Ezeiza airport is about 35km south of the city center.

❶ Information

CONCIERGE SERVICES
BA Cultural Concierge (☑15-3876-5937; www.baculturalconcierge.com) Madi Lang's concierge service helps you plan itineraries, arrange airport transportation, run errands, get a cell phone, reserve theater tickets, scout out a potential apartment and do a thousand other things that'll help your trip to run smoothly.

EMERGENCY
Ambulance (☑107)
Police (☑911, 101)
Tourist Police (Comisaría del Turista; ☑011-4346-5748, 0800-999-5000; Av Corrientes 436; ⊙24hr) Provides interpreters for travel insurance reports.

INTERNET ACCESS & TELEPHONE
Internet cafes and *locutorios* (telephone offices) with internet access are relatively common in the center. Rates are cheap and connections are fast. Most cafes and restaurants have free wi-fi.

If you're in Buenos Aires for a long while, you can rent a desk, a cubicle, an office or a meeting room via **Areatres** (☑011-5353-0333; www.area tresworkplace.com; Malabia 1720; ⊙8:30am-8pm Mon-Fri). There are fax and copy services, complete internet connections, networking social events – even a Zen-like patio. Also has a second **Palermo** (☑011-5258-7600; Humboldt 2036) branch.

ℹ TRAVELING SAFELY IN BUENOS AIRES

While crime does exist in BA (as it does in any big city) and you'll notice that *porteños* are very security conscious, in general BA is fairly safe. In many places you can comfortably walk around at all hours of the night, even as a lone woman, as people generally stay out very late. However, be careful at night in some neighborhoods, including Constitución (around the train station), the eastern border of San Telmo, and La Boca (outside tourist streets).

Crime against tourists is almost always of the petty sort, such as pickpocketing in crowded markets, the Subte or buses, or bag snatches when you're not looking – things smart travelers can guard themselves against. Be wary of the old 'mustard trick' – someone pointing out 'bird droppings' or whatever on your clothing, placed there by an accomplice, and offering to clean it up (while your valuables go off with the accomplice).

Other things to watch out for are the occasional fake bill. Most people get them in dark environments like taxis or nightclubs.

Minor nuisances include the lack of respect shown by vehicles toward pedestrians, lax pollution controls and high noise levels.

If you've been robbed in some way, contact the **tourist police** (p109) to file a claim; they provide interpreters.

MEDIA

BA's most popular newspapers are the entertaining, tabloid-like *Clarín* and the more moderate and upper-class *La Nación*. *Página 12* provides a leftist perspective, while *Ámbito Financiero* is the voice of the business sector. For news in English there's the *Buenos Aires Herald*.

MEDICAL SERVICES

Dental Argentina (☎011-4828-0821; www.dental-argentina.com.ar; Laprida 1621, 2B) Dental services with English-speaking professionals.

Hospital Británico (☎4309-6400; www.hospitalbritanico.org.ar; Perdriel 74)

Hospital Italiano (☎4959-0200; www.hospitalitaliano.org.ar; Juan D Perón 4190)

MONEY

Banks and *cambios* (official money-exchange offices) are common in the city center; banks have longer lines and more limited opening hours but may offer better rates. *Cuevas* (clandestine money exchange offices) can come and go – ask around for one nearby. You're on your own if you use the ubiquitous *arbolitos* (ie unofficial money changers) on Florida, offering 'cambio, cambio, cambio' to passing pedestrians. Just remember there are quite a few fake bills floating about.

American Express (☎011-4310-3000; Arenales 707) in Retiro changes traveler's checks 10am to 4pm Monday to Friday.

POST

The post office has branches all over the city.

Correo Internacional (Map p70; ☎011-4891-9191; www.correoargentino.com.ar; Av Antártida Argentina; ◷9am-3:30pm Mon-Fri) For international parcels weighing 2kg to 20kg. Bring an open box or parcel as contents will be

checked; boxes are also sold here. Look for the building with the yellow facade.

DHL Internacional (Map p58; ☎0810-122-3345; www.dhl.com.ar; Av Córdoba 783) Many branches around town.

Federal Express (Map p58; ☎0810-333-3339; www.fedex.com; Maipú 753, Microcentro)

OCA (Map p58; ☎4311-5305; www.oca.com.ar; Viamonte 526, Microcentro) For domestic packages.

TOURIST INFORMATION

There are several small government tourist offices or kiosks in BA; hours vary throughout the year. The official tourism site of Buenos Aires is www.bue.gob.ar and the government site is www.buenosaires.gob.ar.

Diagonal Roque Saénz Peña Tourist Kiosk (Map p58; cnr Florida & Diagonal Roque Saénz Peña)

Plaza San Martín Tourist Kiosk (Map p70; cnr Florida & Marcelo T de Alvear, Retiro)

Puerto Madero Tourist Office (Map p58; Dique 4)

Recoleta Tourist Kiosk (Map p70; Av Quintana 596)

Ministerio de Turismo (Map p70; ☎011-4312-2232; www.turismo.gov.ar; Av Santa Fe 883, Retiro; ◷9am-7pm Mon-Fri) Mostly info on Argentina but helps with BA.

TRAVEL AGENCIES

Anda Responsible Travel (☎011-3221-0833; www.andatravel.com.ar; Billinghurst 1193, 3B) Most notable for its La Boca tour, which introduces travelers to local organizations working toward improving the lives of its citizens. Also does tours around Argentina that benefit local citizens, which are sometimes indigenous groups.

Say Hueque (☏ 011-5258-8740; www.say hueque.com; Thames 2062, Palermo) This independent travel agency specializes in customized adventure trips all around Argentina, and will also make air, bus and hotel reservations. It offers various BA tours as well. Also has a branch in San Telmo (☏ 011-4307-2614; Chile 557).

Tangol (☏ 011-4363-6000; www.tangol.com; Florida 971, Suite 31) Do-all agency that offers city tours, tango shows, guides to *fútbol* games, hotel reservations, Spanish classes, air tickets and country-wide packages. Also offers unusual activities including helicopter tours and skydiving. Has another branch in San Telmo (Defensa 831).

USEFUL WEBSITES

Argentina Independent (www.argentina independent.com) For current news.

Bubble (www.bubblear.com) For fun news.

LandingPadBA (www.landingpadba.com) For quirky articles.

Pick Up the Fork (www.pickupthefork.com) For foodie entertainment.

ⓘ Getting There & Away

AIR

Buenos Aires is Argentina's international gateway and easily accessible from North America, Europe and Australasia, as well as other capital cities in South America.

Almost all international flights arrive at BA's Ezeiza airport, about 35km south of the center. This modern airport has good services such as ATMs, restaurants and duty-free shops, an internet cafe, a pharmacy, a 24-hour post office and free but slow wi-fi.

Most domestic flights use Aeroparque Jorge Newbery airport, a short distance north of downtown BA.

Flight information for both airports, in English and Spanish, is available at 5480-6111 or www.aa2000.com.ar.

BOAT

BA has a regular ferry service to and from Colonia and Montevideo, both in Uruguay. Ferries leave from the **Buquebus** (Map p70; ☏ 011-4316-6500; www.buquebus.com; cnr Avs Antártida Argentina & Córdoba) terminal in Puerto Madero. There are many more launches in the warmer months of September to April.

BUS

BA's modern **Retiro bus terminal** (Map p70; www.tebasa.com.ar; Av Antártida Argentina) is 400m long, three floors high and has bays for 75 buses. The bottom floor is for cargo shipments and luggage storage, the top for purchasing tickets and the middle for everything else. The **information booth** (☏ 011-4310-0700; ⊙ 24hr) will help you find the right long-distance bus (or check the terminal's website); it's located near the escalators at the southern end of the terminal. Other services include a **tourist office** (Map p70; ⊙ 7:30am-2:30pm Mon-Fri, to 4:30pm Sat & Sun) on the same level as bus bay 36, ATMs, telephone offices (some with internet), cafes and many small stores.

You can buy a ticket to practically anywhere in Argentina and departures are fairly frequent to the most popular destinations. Prices vary widely according to bus company, class, season and inflation. Reservations are not necessary except during peak seasons (January, February and July). To get a current price on a destination, check www.omnilineas.com (certain long-distance destinations require connections).

Retiro bus terminal is connected to the local bus system, but it's a giant snarl and hard to figure out. There's a nearby Subte station and Retiro train station. Street taxis are numerous, though *remises* (call taxis) are generally more secure – there are several *remise* booths near the bus bays; the one near bus bay 54 is open 24 hours.

TRAIN

Privately run trains connect Buenos Aires' center to its suburbs and nearby provinces. The three main central stations are served by Subte.

TRAINS FROM BUENOS AIRES

DESTINATION(S)	STATION	CONTACT
Tigre, Rosario, Córdoba & Tucumán	Retiro	Línea Mitre (☏ 0800-222-8736; www.sofse.gob.ar)
Southern suburbs & La Plata	Constitución	Línea Roca (☏ 0800-222-8736; www.sofse.gob.ar)
Bahía Blanca, Tandil & Mar del Plata	Constitución	Ferrobaires (☏ 0810-666-8736; www.ferrobaires.gba. gov.ar)
Southwestern suburbs & Luján	Once	Línea Sarmiento (☏ 0800-222-8736; www.sofse.gob.ar)

ⓘ Getting Around

TO & FROM AIRPORTS

Chauffeur-Driven Car

For a special treat, reserve a luxury car from **Silver Star Transport** (☏ in Argentina 15-6826-8876, in the USA 214-502-1605; www.silverstarcar.com); you'll be driven by native English speakers from Ezeiza airport to the destination of your choice (US$160). There are car-rental booths at Ezeiza, but we do not recommend renting a car for your stay in Buenos Aires.

Bus

If you're really on a penny-pinching budget, take public bus 8 from Ezeiza airport, which costs AR$8, runs every 20 to 30 minutes and can take up to two hours to reach the Plaza de Mayo area. Catch it outside Terminal B, or outside Terminal A (turn to the right and walk a couple minutes to the bus stop across from the Petrobras gas station). You'll need an inexpensive SUBE card to pay for the bus; buy one at the kiosko across from check-in stand 25 (the sign says 'open 25 hours!').

A new service, **Arbus** (www.arbus.com. ar), offers inexpensive bus transport between Aeroparque Jorge Newbery and Ezeiza (only if you're an Aerolineas Argentinas passenger) and between Aeroparque and six locations around BA; you'll need a SUBE card. Check their website for details.

Shuttle

If you're alone, the best way to and from Ezeiza airport is taking a shuttle with a transfer company such as **Manuel Tienda León** (MTL; ☏ 011-4315-5115; www.tiendaleon.com; Av Eduardo Madero 1299, Ezeiza Airport). You'll see its stand immediately as you exit customs, in the transport 'lobby' area. Frequent shuttles cost AR$145 per person to the city center, run all day and night, and take 40 to 60 minutes, depending on traffic. They'll deposit you at their MTL office (from where you can take a taxi).

SUBE CARD

The **SUBE Card** (www.sube.gob.ar) is a handy and inexpensive rechargeable card that you use for the Subte, local buses and trains. It saves you money and means you don't have to keep a stash of coins on hand. Get it at some kiosks, lottery offices, post offices or any other business that displays the SUBE logo. Ezeiza airport and Retiro bus terminal also have Sube kiosks where you can buy this card. Charging the card itself is easy, and can be done at many kiosks or Subte stations.

Another shuttle service, directed at independent travelers, is **Hostel Shuttle** (☏ 011-4511-8723; www.hostelshuttle.com.ar). Check the website for prices, schedules and drop-off destinations (only at certain hostels), and try to book ahead. You can also try www.minibusezeiza.com.ar.

Shuttles between Ezeiza and Aeroparque Jorge Newbery airport (the domestic airport) cost AR$155; from Aeroparque to the center AR$60.

Taxi

If taking a taxi, avoid MTL's overpriced taxi service. Instead, go past the transport 'lobby' area outside customs, past the taxi drivers holding signs, and you'll see the freestanding city taxi stand with a blue sign saying **Taxi Ezeiza** (☏ 011-5480-0066; www.taxiezeiza.com.ar; ⏱24hr). At the time of writing it charged AR$450 to the center (for a discount reserve via their website). Note that if you pre-arrange your taxi back to Ezeiza after your stay in BA, the rate can be about 20% cheaper.

Taxis between Aeroparque and the city center cost around AR$130.

BICYCLE

Vehicular traffic in BA is dangerous and hardly respectful toward bicycles, but things are improving, with an expanding bike-lane system and a free bike-share program. The **Ecobici** (www.buenosaires.gob.ar/ecobici) bike-share program is mostly for residents but tourists can rent as well – have copies of your passport's main page and entry-stamp page. Rentals are for an hour on weekdays and two hours on weekends, with renewals possible.

Some areas call out for two-wheeled exploration, such as Palermo's parks and the Reserva Ecológica Costanera Sur. On weekends and some weekdays you can rent bikes at these places, or at private tours companies.

BUS

To understand BA's huge, complex bus system buy a *Guia T* (bus guide); they're sold at any newsstand, but try to find the handy pocket version or check www.omnilineas.com and click on 'City buses.' Most routes run 24 hours.

Colectivos (local buses) take either coins or a magnetic bus card called SUBE, but won't take bills. Bus ticket machines on board give small change from coins. Offer your seat to the elderly, pregnant women and women with young children.

CAR

Most local drivers are reckless, aggressive and even willfully dangerous. They ignore speed limits, signs, lines and signals, and will tailgate. Buses are a nightmare to reckon with, potholes are everywhere, and congestion and parking are a pain.

Public transportation is great and taxis are cheap and plentiful, but if you still insist on renting a car, you'll need to be at least 21 years of age and have a valid driver's license, credit card and passport; an international driver's license isn't necessary.

In Retiro, try **Avis** (☑011-4326-5542; www.avis.com.ar; Cerrito 1535); **Hertz** (☑011-4816-0899; www.hertz.com.ar; Paraguay 1138), which is also home to Thrifty Car Rental; or local, friendly and cheap **New Way** (☑011-4515-0331; www.new-wayrentacar.com; Marcelo T de Alvear 773).

SUBTE (SUBWAY)

BA's **Subte** (www.buenosaires.gob.ar/subte) is the quickest way to get around the city, though it can get mighty hot and crowded during rush hour and it's a haven for pickpockets. It consists of Líneas (Lines) A, B, C, D, E and H. Four parallel lines run from downtown to the capital's western and northern outskirts, while Línea C runs north–south and connects the two major train stations of Retiro and Constitución. Línea H runs from Once south to Av Caseros, with plans to expand it.

One ride on the Subte costs AR$4.50. To avoid queues buy several rides at once or get a SUBE card (p112).

Trains operate from 5am to around 10:30pm Monday to Saturday and 8am to around 10pm Sunday and holidays. Service is frequent on weekdays; on weekends you'll wait longer. At some stations platforms are on opposite sides, so be sure of your direction before passing through the turnstiles.

TAXI & REMISE

Buenos Aires' numerous and relatively inexpensive taxis are conspicuous by their black-and-yellow paint jobs. They click every 200m (or every minute of waiting time) and cost 20% more after 10pm. Make sure that the meter's set to the current price when you start your ride. Drivers do not expect a big tip, but it's customary to let them keep small change. Taxis looking for passengers will have a red light lit on the upper right corner of their windshield.

Most cab drivers are honest workers making a living, but there are a few bad apples. Try not to give them a 100 peso note for a small fare; sometimes they're short on change, but there have been cases where the driver quickly and deftly replaces a larger bill with a smaller (or fake) one. One solution is to state how much you are giving them and ask if they have change for it ('¿Tiene usted cambio de un cien?' – 'Do you have any change for a hundred?').

Be wary of receiving counterfeit bills. If you're suspicious this might happen, note aloud the last three numbers/letters on a bill as you're giving it to him.

At night the driver will turn on the light *(luz)* so you can carefully check your change (look for a watermark on bills). They'll do the same with your bills. And make sure you get the right change.

Pretend to have an idea of where you're going; a few taxis offer the 'scenic' route (though also be aware there are many one-way streets in BA). A good way to do this is to give the taxi driver an intersection rather than a specific address. Also, if you are obviously a tourist going to or from a touristy spot, don't ask how much the fare is beforehand; this makes it tempting to quote a higher price rather than using the meter.

Try to snag an 'official' taxi, usually marked by a roof light and license number printed on the doors. Official drivers must display their license on the back of their seat or dashboard; write down the details in case of problems or forgotten items.

You can also call a *remise* (call taxi) instead of hailing street cabs. *Remises* look like regular cars and don't have meters. They cost a bit more than street taxis but are more secure, since an established company sends them out. Any hotel or restaurant will call a *remise* for you.

Tigre & the Delta

The city of Tigre (35km north of BA) and the surrounding delta region is a popular weekend getaway for weary *porteños*. Latte-colored waters – rich with iron from the jungle streams flowing from inland South America – offer hidden gems in this marshy region. Glimpse how locals live along peaceful canals, with boats as their only transportation. All along the shorelines are signs of water-related activity, from kayaking to canoeing to sculling.

◉ Sights

Museo de Arte Tigre   MUSEUM
(☑4512-4528; www.mat.gov.ar; Paseo Victorica 972; admission AR$30; ◷9am-7pm Wed-Fri, noon-7pm Sat & Sun) Tigre's fanciest museum is located in a 1912 social club. This beautiful art museum showcases famous Argentine artists from the 19th and 20th centuries. The building itself is worth a visit.

Puerto de Frutos   MARKET
(Sarmiento 160; ◷10am-6pm) At this popular market, vendors sell homewares, furniture, wicker baskets, souvenirs and knick-knacks; there are restaurants too. Weekends are busiest.

Museo Naval   MUSEUM
(Naval Museum; ☑4749-0608; Paseo Victorica 602; admission AR$20; ◷8:30am-5:30pm Mon-Fri,

10:30am-6:30pm Sat & Sun) This worthwhile museum traces the history of the Argentine navy with an eclectic mix of historical photos, model boats and airplanes, artillery displays and pickled sea critters.

Museo del Mate   MUSEUM
(☑ 4506-9594; www.elmuseodelmate.com; Lavalle 289; admission AR$30; ☺ 11am-6pm Wed-Sun) For something special, visit this museum with over 2000 items dedicated to the national drink. There's a small outdoor *mate* 'bar' as well.

☞ Tours

Frequent, reasonably priced commuter launches depart from Estación Fluvial (behind the tourist office) for various destinations in the delta. A popular destination is the Tres Bocas neighborhood, a half-hour boat ride from Tigre, where you can take residential walks on thin paths connected by bridges over narrow channels. There are several restaurants and accommodations here. The Rama Negra area has a quieter and more natural setting with fewer services, but it's an hour's boat ride away.

Several companies offer inexpensive, one- to two-hour boat tours, but commuter launches give you flexibility if you want to go for a stroll or stop for lunch at one of the delta's restaurants.

Bonanza Deltaventura   ADVENTURE TOUR
(☑ 4409-6967; www.deltaventura.com) Adventures include canoe trips, bike rides and horseback rides.

El Dorado Kayak   KAYAKING
(☑ 15-4039-5858; www.eldoradokayak.com) Kayaking tours deep inside the delta; all equipment and lunch included.

🛏 Sleeping & Eating

Tigre's huge delta region is dotted with dozens of accommodations, including camping, B&Bs, *cabañas* (cabins) and beach resorts. Since many are reached only by boat, most provide meals. Tigre's tourist office has photos and information on all accommodations and many are listed on its website. Book on weekends and holidays, when prices can rise significantly.

Tigre's cuisine is not cutting-edge, but dining can be atmospheric. Ask the tourist office about the various restaurants in the delta. The following accommodations are in the city of Tigre itself.

Casona La Ruchi   GUESTHOUSE $
(☑ 4749-2499; www.casonalaruchi.com.ar; Lavalle 557; r without bathroom US$60; @ 🛜 🞉) This family-run guesthouse is in a beautiful old 1893 mansion. Most of the four romantic bedrooms have balconies; all have shared bathrooms with original tiled floors. There's a pool and large garden out back.

Hotel Villa Victoria   GUESTHOUSE $$
(☑ 4731-2281; www.hotelvillavictoria.com; Liniers 566; r Sun-Fri from US$100, Sat from US$140; 🞉 @ 🛜 🞉) Run by an Argentine-Swedish family, this boutique hotel is more like a fancy guesthouse. Only six simple yet elegant rooms are available, and there's a pool in the large grassy garden. Swedish, French and English are spoken.

Maria Luján   ARGENTINE $$
(☑ 4731-9613; Paseo Victorica 611; mains AR$110-220; ☺ 8:30am-midnight) For an upscale meal on Paseo Victorica, the city's pleasant riverside avenue, try María Luján, which has a great patio.

Almacén de Flores   CAFE $$
(☑ 011-5197-4009; Boulevard Saenz Peña 1336; mains AR$95-150; ☺ 9:30am-7pm Sun-Wed, to 2am Thu-Sat) A good eatery is bohemian Almacén de Flores, offering healthy, gourmet fare.

ℹ Information

Tourist Office (☑ 4512-4497; www.vivitigre. gov.ar; Mitre 305; ☺ 9am-6pm Mon-Fri) Located behind McDonald's.

ℹ Getting There & Away

BOAT

Sturla Viajes (www.sturlaviajes.com.ar) has limited transport boats to Tigre that leave from Grierson 400 in Puerto Madero, along with tours that include boat transport and a trip around the Delta. Check its website for schedules.

BUS

Take bus 60 (marked 'Panam') straight to Tigre (1½ hours).

TRAIN

From Retiro train station you can take a 'Tigre' train straight to Tigre (one hour). The best way to reach Tigre, however, is via the **Tren de la Costa** (tickets AR$40) – a pleasant light-rail train with attractive stations and views. This train line starts in the suburb of Olivos: to get there, take a train from Retiro train station and get off at Mitre station, then cross the bridge to the Tren de la Costa. Buses 59, 60 and 152 also go to the Tren de la Costa.

The Pampas & the Atlantic Coast

Best Places to Eat

Best Places to Stay

Why Go?

There's Buenos Aires, and then there's the province of Buenos Aires. Home to more than a third of the country's population, this is the nation's economic powerhouse: these fertile grasslands financed Argentina's turn-of-the-century golden age and still produce most of the country's famous beef.

While the region isn't exactly packed with tourist attractions, simple pleasures and traditional gaucho culture are waiting to be discovered. Charming San Antonio de Areco offers a glimpse of Argentina's real-life cowboys in action, while the picturesque hills around Tandil are lovely for hiking and feasting on locally produced *picadas* (shared appetizer plates). Beach towns on the Atlantic coast provide a breezy escape from the summer heat.

If you have a few days to spare, check into one of the region's historic *estancias* (ranches), where you can ride a criollo horse under the huge sky – and experience the faded elegance of Argentina's past for yourself.

When to Go
Mar del Plata

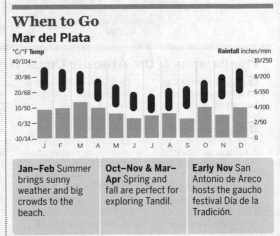

Jan–Feb Summer brings sunny weather and big crowds to the beach.

Oct–Nov & Mar–Apr Spring and fall are perfect for exploring Tandil.

Early Nov San Antonio de Areco hosts the gaucho festival Día de la Tradición.

NORTHERN PAMPAS

The pampas is both a general term for a large geographic region of fertile plains and the name of the province that lies to the west of Buenos Aires (La Pampa). The pampas grasslands roll southwards from the Río de la Plata to the banks of the Río Negro, stretching west toward the Andes and all the way up to the southern parts of Córdoba and Santa Fe provinces, taking in the entire Buenos Aires and La Pampa provinces.

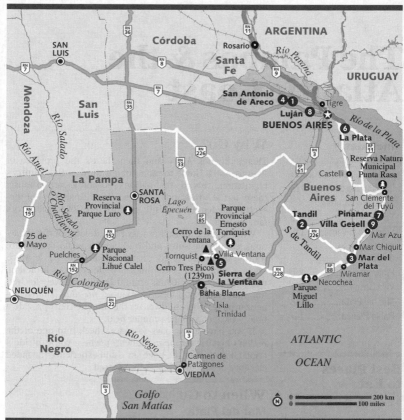

The Pampas & the Atlantic Coast Highlights

1 Going gaucho in **San Antonio de Areco** (p123), the prettiest town in the pampas.

2 Packing a picnic of locally produced prosciutto and cheese and going for a hike in the hills of **Tandil** (p125).

3 Soaking up the sun and a vibrant cultural scene in **Mar del Plata** (p138), the 'Pearl of the Atlantic.'

4 Spending the weekend riding horses and relaxing at one of the region's traditional Argentine **estancias** (p117).

5 Peeking through a natural rock 'window' after hiking up the mountain in laid-back **Sierra de la Ventana** (p128).

6 Wandering the streets of **La Plata** (p117), South America's first fully planned city.

7 Going windsurfing, swimming or cycling in the stylish beach resort of **Pinamar** (p135).

8 Following the footsteps of generations of Catholic pilgrims to the cathedral in **Luján** (p121).

9 Walking the quaint wooden boardwalk along the coast in **Villa Gesell** (p137).

WORTH A TRIP

HOME ON THE RANGE

One of the best ways to spend a few days in the region – and soak up a bit of traditional gaucho culture while remaining within easy reach of Buenos Aires – is to check in to an *estancia* (ranch). Once the private homes of wealthy landowners, many of the province's grandest mansions are now open to the public. Choose between a *día de campo* (country day; an access pass to the ranch that typically includes an elaborate lunch and afternoon tea, plus horseback riding and other outdoor activities) or stay for a night or two.

Upscale **Estancia El Ombú de Areco** (📞492080; www.estanciaelombu.com; RP31, Cuartel VI, Villa Lía; día de campo US$100, s/d incl full board US$325/410; ✸🛜✸) is a 300-hectare ranch with a gorgeous colonial mansion that dates from 1880. It's named after the massive *ombú* (Phytolacca dioica) tree casting shade over the gardens. At El Ombú, it's old-fashioned hospitality all the way. In addition to horseback riding, you can watch (and even take part in) rounding up cattle herds. The *estancia* also provides complimentary bicycles, or you can just relax in the gardens or linger over an alfresco lunch or tea. It's located about 20km outside of San Antonio de Areco.

A slightly more affordable option – and one that's also, conveniently, closer to town – is **Estancia La Cinacina** (📞452045; www.lacinacina.com.ar; Zerboni s/n; d from US$117; ✸✸). With thematic gaucho shows, the *estancia* is on the touristy side, but it's popular with travelers. Stay overnight or come on a weekend for the *día de campo* (fill out the website form for the latest prices and availability).

Several other *estancias* in the area offer similar experiences. Check www.sanantonio deareco.com/donde-dormir/estancias for a full list, and make sure you do your homework before checking in anywhere: travelers regularly complain about overpriced and logistically challenging experiences at some *estancias*.

Private transfers directly from Buenos Aires to most *estancias* are available for an extra charge – see the properties' individual websites for details. Another option is **Areco Bus** (p125), a shuttle that offers transportation from Buenos Aires.

The rich soil and lush natural grasses of the northern pampas make it Argentina's best cattle-raising country. The region yields plentiful hides, beef, wool and wheat for global markets, stamping Argentina on the world's economic map.

From the mid-19th century, the province of Buenos Aires was the undisputed political and economic center of the country. When the city of Buenos Aires became Argentina's capital, the province submitted to national authority, but didn't lose its influence. By the 1880s, after a brief but contentious civil war, the province responded by creating its own provincial capital in the model city of La Plata.

La Plata

📞 0221 / POP 654,000

Just over an hour from Buenos Aires, La Plata enjoys a few interesting distinctions: the bustling university city is considered South America's first planned city, and the first in Latin America to have electric street lighting.

It all started when Buenos Aires became Argentina's new capital in 1880. Governor Dardo Rocha founded La Plata to give the province of Buenos Aires its own capital – and decided he wouldn't leave its design up to chance. He chose engineer Pedro Benoit's elaborate city plan, based upon balance and logic, with diagonal avenues crossing the regular 5km-square grid pattern to connect the major plazas, creating a distinctive star design. Elegant on paper, this blueprint creates confusion at many intersections, with up to eight streets going off in all directions. (Fascinating aerial photos of the city plan, including photographs taken from space, are easily viewable online.)

Today, La Plata has the same belle epoque architecture, gracious municipal buildings and leafy parks as Buenos Aires, but on a smaller scale. The big draws are its imposing neo-Gothic cathedral – the largest in Argentina – and a famous building designed by Le Corbusier, his only completed work in Latin America.

◉ Sights

La Plata's main sights are all within walking distance of each other.

La Plata

★ **Catedral de la Plata**   CHURCH
(☏ 423-3931; www.catedraldelaplata.com; Plaza Moreno, calle 51 & 15; museum admission weekday/weekend $55/48; ◷ 10am-7pm, museum from 11am Tue-Sun) Construction began on La Plata's spectacular neo-Gothic cathedral in 1885, but the church wasn't inaugurated until 1932, and tower construction was only completed in 1999. The cathedral was inspired by medieval predecessors in Cologne and Amiens, and has fine stained-glass windows and polished granite floors; 90-minute tours (11am, 2:30pm and 4pm Monday to Friday, reservations necessary) include the museum and an elevator ride to the top. There's also a gift shop and cafe on-site.

★ **Casa Curutchet**   ARCHITECTURE
(☏ 421-8032; www.capbacs.com; Av 53, No 320; admission AR$40; ◷ 9am-1pm Mon & Tue, 9am-5pm Wed-Fri, 1-5pm Sat) The famed French-Swiss architect Le Corbusier only built two structures in the Americas: Carpenter Center for the Visual Arts at Harvard, and Casa Curutchet. The strikingly modern house, commissioned by the Argentine surgeon Pedro Curutchet in 1948, is a prime example of Le Corbusier's five points of

architecture. The house was featured in the award-winning film *El hombre de al lado* (The Man Next Door; 2009). Though tours are supposed to run every half-hour, it's best to email in advance.

Paseo del Bosque PARK

Plantations of eucalyptus, gingko, palm and subtropical hardwoods cover Paseo del Bosque, parkland expropriated from an *estancia* at the time of the city's founding. It attracts a collection of strolling families, smooching lovers and sweaty joggers, and contains various interesting sights: a small lake with paddleboats for rent, an observatory, the modest **Jardín Zoológico** (☎427-3925; admission AR$15; ⊙10am-6pm Tue-Sun), the open-air **Teatro Martín Fierro**, which hosts music and drama performances; and the star attraction, Museo de La Plata (p119).

Museo de La Plata MUSEUM

(☎425-7744; www.museo.fcnym.unlp.edu.ar; Paseo del Bosque s/n; admission AR$20, children under 12yr free, Tue free; ⊙10am-6pm Tue-Sun; ♿) This excellent museum features the paleontological, zoological, archaeological and anthropological finds of famous Patagonian explorer Francisco P Moreno. The eclectic collection includes Egyptian tomb relics, Jesuit art, amusing taxidermy, amazing skeletons, mummies, fossils, rocks and minerals, scary insects and reconstructed dinosaurs. There's also a cafe. Arrange English tours in advance.

🛏 Sleeping

Único Ecohostel HOSTEL $

(☎423-2626; www.hostelunico.com; Calle 4, No 565; dm/d/tr from US$19/66/91; ❋🛜) 🌿 A traveler's favorite, this gleaming modern hostel is conveniently located only a block from the bus station. Highlights include a pair of common kitchens, a lovely outdoor patio and garden, and ecofriendly amenities, including solar hot water. Note that the neighborhood can feel a little rough around the edges after dark.

Hotel Catedral HOTEL $

(☎483-0091; www.hcatedral.com.ar; Calle 49, No 965; s/d/tr US$42/64/73; 🛜) Simple, small and well-run, Hotel Catedral, two blocks west of the cathedral plaza, is a top pick for budget travelers.

★Benevento Hotel HOTEL $$

(☎423-7721; www.hotelbenevento.com.ar; Calle 2, No 645; d US$83; ❋@🛜) This charmingly renovated hotel, housed inside an elegant French-inspired building that dates from 1915, offers pretty rooms with high ceilings and cable TV. Most have wood floors, plus balconies overlooking the busy street; top-floor rooms are the most modern and offer great views over the city. It's a few blocks from the bus station.

San Marco Hotel HOTEL $$

(☎422-9322; www.sanmarcohotel.com.ar; Calle 54, No 523; d from US$97; ❋🛜) This comfortable three-star enjoys a prime location in the

ARCHITECTURE OF LA PLATA

Architecture fans plan trips to La Plata just to see Le Corbusier's **Casa Curutchet** (p118). But the city skyline has several other highlights you'll spot on a quick stroll around the center.

Opposite the cathedral is the **Palacio Municipal** (cnr Av 51 & Calle 11), designed in German Renaissance style by Hanoverian architect Hubert Stiers. On the west side of the plaza, the **Museo y Archivo Dardo Rocha** (☎427-5591; www.amigosmuseorocha.com.ar; Calle 50, No 935; ⊙9am-5pm Mon-Fri, 3-6pm Sat & Sun) FREE was the vacation house of the city's creator and contains period furniture and many of his personal knickknacks.

Two blocks northeast, the **Teatro Argentino** (www.teatroargentino.gba.gov.ar; Av 51 btwn Calles 9 & 10) is a concrete monolith, but boasts great acoustics – ideal for the line-up of ballet, symphony orchestras and opera. Two blocks further northeast, in front of Plaza San Martín, is the ornate **Palacio de la Legislatura** (Plaza San Martín), also in German Renaissance style. Nearby, catch the French Classic **Pasaje Dardo Rocha** (cnr Av 6 & Calle 50), once La Plata's main railroad station and now the city's major cultural center, containing two museums. Also close by is the Flemish Renaissance **Casa de Gobierno** (Plaza San Martín), housing the provincial governor and his retinue.

heart of town, between Plaza San Martín and Paseo del Bosque. Travelers particularly like the breakfast buffet.

🍴 Eating & Drinking

At the time of research, a buzzed-about Argentinian chef, Mauro Colagreco, was about to open **Carne**, an organic burger bar, at Calle 50, No 452. Let us know how it turns out.

Further afield, a 10-minute taxi ride from the center in the historic bohemian neighborhood Meridiano V, you'll find several bars and live-music venues, plus theater, cinema and cultural centers catering to university students Thursday through Sunday evenings.

★ Cervecería Modelo   PUB FOOD $
(www.cerveceriamodelo.com.ar; cnr Calles 5 & 54; mains AR$52-89; ⊘8am-1am Sun-Thu, to 3am Fri & Sat; 🕿) Dating from 1894, its ceiling hung with hams and its floors strewn with peanut shells, this classic place serves snacks, meals and ice-cold ales to a happy crowd. There are great sidewalk tables, and it's not too old to boast a big-screen TV and wi-fi.

Market Café   CAFE $
(🖉483-5631; www.marketcafeargentina.com.ar; Calle 48, No 640; mains AR$50-75; ⊘8am-9pm Mon-Sat; 🖉) This sleek cafe and eatery is a breath of fresh air in La Plata. Come in the morning for an artfully prepared latte and freshly baked pastries, or later for fresh salads, wraps, smoothies, burgers and cocktails.

Lo de Antonio Parrilla Fonda   PARRILLA $$
(🖉482-6104; Calle 54, No 654; mains AR$80-150; ⊘noon-3pm & 8pm-midnight Mon-Sat; 🖻) A corner *parrilla* with an elegant edge – spacious wooden booths, fine cutlery – and a full menu of steaks and pastas, plus a succinct children's menu. It's a convenient stop if you're walking between the cathedral and the park.

Molly's Beer House   BEER GARDEN
(🖉482-1648; Calle 53, No 538; ⊘7pm-2am) A welcome new addition to La Plata, this stylish bar occupies a beautifully restored old house. There's a lovely open-air courtyard, adding to the modern beer-garden atmosphere, and a menu of 35 different varieties of craft beer.

THE BEEF ON BEEF

Juicy, grass-fed steaks have always been one of Argentina's biggest tourist attractions. But these days, this type of beef has nearly disappeared. Stuffing cattle into pens and feeding them grain is becoming a standard way of raising cattle for market. Today, over 80% of Argentina's cows slaughtered each year experience their last few months in a feedlot.

Factory-farmed meat is a fairly recent phenomenon in Argentina. The country's agriculturally rich and vast pampas plains were ideal grounds for raising free-range beef, and up until 2001, around 90% of cattle ate only their natural food: grass. But in the last decade, several developments have changed this. The price of agricultural crops such as soybeans, of which Argentina is one of the world's top producers, has skyrocketed, making it more lucrative to grow the legume than dedicate space to cattle. A severe drought in recent years dealt another blow to the beef industry – there just wasn't enough grass to feed the herds.

But perhaps the biggest factor detrimental to the grass-fed cattle has been government subsidies for feedlot development, with the intention of producing beef more quickly than before. It's less profitable to raise a fully grass-fed cow – which takes much longer to reach maturity – than a grain-fed one. And the Argentine government also passed legislation keeping beef prices artificially low within its borders, while at the same time using taxes to discourage cattle ranchers from making profits by exporting beef. So even more ranchers have turned pastureland into soy or corn rows to stay alive.

At this rate, practically all Argentine cattle will soon live out their last few months in dirt-floor corrals, with their movements restricted, eating an un-cowlike diet of grains. They'll be shot full of immunizations and antibiotics, which are crucial to treating ailments brought on by these unnatural conditions. Their beef will be slightly less flavorful and nutritious, yet more tender – due to the lower percentage of muscle, plus higher level of fat. And the modern world of commercial beef production will finally have caught up to Argentina, wiping away a part of its history, reputation...and perhaps some of that famous Argentine pride.

ℹ Information

Municipal Tourist Office (📞 427-1535; www.laciudad.laplata.gov.ar/turismo; cnr Calles 7 & 50, Pasaje Dardo Rocha; ⏰10am-8pm) Just off Plaza San Martín.

ℹ Getting There & Away

La Plata's **bus terminal** (www.laplataterminal.com) has plenty of connections to other parts of Argentina, plus a helpful website with links and information.

Grupo Plaza (www.grupoplaza.com.ar) runs frequent buses (AR$21 to 26, 1½ to two hours) between Buenos Aires and La Plata's bus station. Though the buses stop at many locations in Buenos Aires, the easiest place to get on and off is at Retiro, the start/end of the line. Buses leave from the side street Martínez Zuvería, adjacent to Plaza Canadá in front of Buenos Aires' Retiro train station. You can also board or disembark along Ave 9 Julio or at Constitución train station. Check www.laplataterminal.com for a full list of stops along the journey. Buses leave approximately every 20 to 30 minutes until 10pm, with fewer departures on weekends. Another bus line, Costera Metropolitana, makes the same trip – the company doesn't have a website, but La Plata's bus station website has more details.

La Plata is also served by Buenos Aires' **Línea Roca** (p111) suburban train line, with half-hourly services from the Constitución station (AR$5.75, 1½ hours). At the time of research, new train cars and a faster 'express' service were about to be implemented.

Buses from La Plata

DESTINATION	COST (AR$)	TIME (HR)
Bahía Blanca	658-868	8-11
Bariloche	1671-1905	24
Córdoba	655-770	10-13
Mar del Plata	375-428	5
Mendoza	900	17

Luján

📞 02323 / POP 106.000

Luján is a small riverside town that famously overflows several times per year as pilgrims make their way here to visit Argentina's most important shrine. It boasts a huge Spanish-style plaza with an imposing neo-Gothic cathedral, as well as a couple of interesting museums. The riverside area is lined with restaurants and barbecue stands selling *choripán* (a spicy pork sausage in

WORTH A TRIP

L'EAU VIVE

It's not every day you have the chance to dine on French cuisine – prepared by Carmelite nuns from around the world – in small-town Argentina. **L'Eau Vive** (📞 421774; www.leauvivedeargentina.com.ar; Constitución 2112; mains around AR$150; ⏰noon-2:15pm & 8:30-10pm Tue-Sat, noon-2:15pm Sun) is on the outskirts of Luján, but plenty of foodies consider the friendly restaurant worth a detour. The menu features expertly prepared fish, cheese plates and a range of gourmet desserts. Reservations recommended. Take bus 501 from the center, or catch a taxi.

a crunchy roll). You can rent boats for a paddle, while a chairlift carries sightseers over the grubby river – an oddly charming touch.

⊙ Sights

★ Basílica Nuestra Señora de Luján
CHURCH

(📞 02323-42-0058; www.basilicadelujan.org.ar; San Martín 51; crypt admission AR$15; ⏰basilica 8am-7pm, crypt 10:15am-5pm Mon-Fri, 10am-6pm Sat & Sun) Luján's undisputed focal point is this imposing neo-Gothic basilica, built from 1887 to 1935 and made from a lovely rose-colored stone that glows in the setting sun. The venerated statue of the Virgin sits in the high chamber behind the main altar. Under the basilica you can tour a crypt that's inhabited by Virgin statues from all over the world. Masses take place in the basilica several times a day.

Complejo Museográfico Enrique Udaondo
MUSEUM

(📞 02323-420245; Torrezuri 917; admission AR$5; ⏰11:30am-5pm Mon-Fri & 10:30am-6pm Sat & Sun) On the west side of Luján's gargantuan basilica plaza, this gorgeous colonial-era museum complex rambles with several display rooms, pretty patios and gardens. The Sala General José de San Martín showcases Argentina's battles for independence, while the Sala de Gaucho contains some beautiful *mate* (a bitter ritual tea) ware, horse gear and other gaucho paraphernalia. Also part of the complex is the fascinating Museo del Transporte (p122).

LA VIRGENCITA

Argentina's patron saint is a ubiquitous presence – you can spot her poster on butcher-shop walls, her statue in churches throughout the country and her image on the dashboards of taxis. She wears a triangular blue dress, stands on a half-moon and radiates streams of glory from her crowned head.

In 1630 a Portuguese settler in Tucumán asked a friend in Brazil to send him an image of the Virgin for his new chapel. Unsure what style of Virgin was required, the friend sent two – including one of the Immaculate Conception. After setting out from the port of Buenos Aires, the cart bearing the statues got bogged down near the river of Luján and only moved when the Immaculate Conception was taken off. Its owner took this as a sign, and left the statue in Luján so that a shrine could be built there. The other statue continued its journey to the northwest.

Since then the Virgin of Luján has been credited with a number of miracles – from curing tumors and sending a fog to hide early settlers from warring Indians, to protecting the province from a cholera epidemic. She was rewarded for her trouble in 1886 when Pope Leo XIII crowned her with a golden coronet set with almost 500 pearls and gems.

Every year millions of pilgrims from throughout Argentina visit Luján's basilica, where the original 17th-century statue is still displayed, to honor the Virgin for her intercession in affairs of peace, health, forgiveness and consolation. If you arrive here during the massive pilgrimage on the first Sunday in October, you'll spot families of exhausted pilgrims snoozing in the square, enjoying barbecues by the river and filling plastic bottles with holy water from the fountain.

Museo del Transporte   MUSEUM
(Torrezuri 917, Complejo Museográfico Enrique Udaondo; admission AR$5; ☉ 11:30am-5pm Mon-Fri & 10:30am-6pm Sat & Sun) Luján's transportation museum displays a remarkable collection of horse-drawn carriages from the late 1800s, the first steam locomotive to serve the city from Buenos Aires and a monster of a hydroplane that crossed the Atlantic in 1926. The most offbeat exhibits, however, are the stuffed and scruffy remains of Gato and Mancha, the hardy Argentine criollo horses ridden by adventurer AF Tschiffely from Buenos Aires to New York. This trip took 2½ years, from 1925 to 1928.

★ Festivals & Events

On **Día de la Virgen de Luján**, the first Saturday in October, throngs of the faithful walk the 65km from the Buenos Aires neighborhood of Liniers to Luján – a journey of up to 18 hours. Other large gatherings occur on May 8 (Virgin's Day), the first weekend in August for the colorful **Peregrinación Boliviana**, the last weekend in September for the 'gaucho' pilgrimage (watch for horses) and December 8 for **Immaculate Conception Day**.

🛏 Sleeping & Eating

Luján can easily be seen on a day trip from Buenos Aires. If you decide to overnight on a weekend, however, be sure to reserve ahead. The central parts of San Martín, 9 de Julio and the riverfront are all lined with restaurants.

Hotel Hoxón   HOTEL $$
(☎ 0810-333-1070; www.hotelhoxon.com; 9 de Julio 760; s/d/tr from US$70/114/135; ✳ @ 🛜 🏊) The best and biggest in town, this place two blocks north of the basilica has modern, clean and comfortable rooms. Superiors are carpeted and come with fridge and air-con. There's also a swimming pool with raised sundeck.

ⓘ Information

Tourist Office (☎ 02323-427082; www.lujan.tur.ar; San Martin 550; ☉ 9am-6pm)

ⓘ Getting There & Away

Lujan's **bus terminal** (Av de Nuestra Señora de Luján & Almirante Brown) is three blocks north of the basilica. From Buenos Aires, take bus 57 (AR$29, two hours), operated by **Transportes Atlántida** (☎ 434957). It leaves every half-hour from Plaza Italia (in Palermo) and Plaza Miserere (outside the Once train station, with a bus stop on Av Rivadavia).

San Antonio de Areco

☑ 02326 / POP 20,000

San Antonio de Areco is the prettiest town in the pampas. About 115km northwest of Buenos Aires, it welcomes many day-tripping *porteños* (residents of Buenos Aires) who come for the peaceful atmosphere and picturesque colonial streets. The town dates from the early 18th century and preserves many traditions of the gaucho and criollo (people of pure Spanish descent born in the New World), especially among its artisans, who produce fine silverwork and saddlery. Gauchos from all over the pampas show up for November's Día de la Tradición, where you can catch them, and their horses, strutting the cobbled streets in all their finery.

San Antonio de Areco's compact town center and quiet streets are very walkable. Around the Plaza Ruiz de Arellano, named in honor of the town's founding *estanciero* (ranch owner), are several historic buildings, including the **iglesia parroquial** (parish church).

Like many other small towns in this part of Argentina, Areco shuts down during the afternoon siesta.

◉ Sights

★ Museo Gauchesco Ricardo Güiraldes   MUSEUM

(☑ 455839; Camino Ricardo Güiraldes s/n; ⊘ 11am-5pm Wed-Mon) **FREE** Recently reinaugurated after major restorations – the building, like many others in town, sustained serious flood damage in 2009 – this sprawling museum in Parque Criollo dates to 1938 and includes an old flour mill, a re-created *pulpería* (tavern), a colonial-style chapel and a 20th-century reproduction of an 18th-century *casco* (ranch house). Displays include horse gear, *gauchesco* artwork and rooms dedicated to Ricardo Güiraldes, author of the novel *Don Segundo Sombra*.

Puente Viejo   BRIDGE

(Old Bridge) The *puente viejo* (old bridge), spanning the Río Areco, dates from 1857 and follows the original cart road to northern Argentina. Once a toll crossing, it's now a pedestrian bridge leading to San Antonio de Areco's main attraction, the Museo Gauchesco Ricardo Güiraldes.

Museo Las Lilas de Areco   MUSEUM

(☑ 456425; www.museolaslilas.org; Moreno 279; adult/student AR$100/50; ⊘ 10am-8pm Thu-Sun mid-Sep–mid-Mar, to 6pm rest of year) Florencio Molina Campos is to Argentines what Norman Rockwell is to Americans – a folk artist whose themes are based on comical caricatures. This pretty courtyard museum displays his famous works. There are separate admission fees to access the gallery and the adjacent Sala de Carruajes (carriage room); the prices quoted here get you into both. Stop for a *café con leche* or a slice of homemade cake at the museum's cafe.

✲ Festivals & Events

Día de la Tradición   CULTURAL

(⊘ Nov) Areco is the symbolic center of Argentina's vestigial cowboy culture, and on Día de la Tradición the town puts on the country's biggest gaucho celebration. If you're in the area, don't miss it. The weekend event is held in early to mid-November, and includes displays of equestrian skill, folk dancing and craft exhibitions; see www.sanantoniodeareco.com for exact dates.

⌂ Sleeping

While San Antonio is a popular destination for day trips out of Buenos Aires, it's worth hanging around as there are some lovely places to stay (and great places to eat and drink, too – you'll need more than a day to try them all). Book on weekends, when prices go up.

Areco Hostel   HOSTEL $

(☑ 453120; www.arecohostel.com.ar; Arellano 121; dm/s/d/tr without bathroom from US$32/45/75/110; ☎) In an atmospheric old building

---

THE ARTISANS OF SAN ANTONIO DE ARECO

Even on the shortest stroll around town you can't miss the silversmith shops and artisan studios lining the streets of San Antonio de Areco. Local artisans are known throughout the country – *mate* (herbal tea) paraphernalia, *rastras* (silver-studded belts), knives and leather goods are the most traditional items to buy.

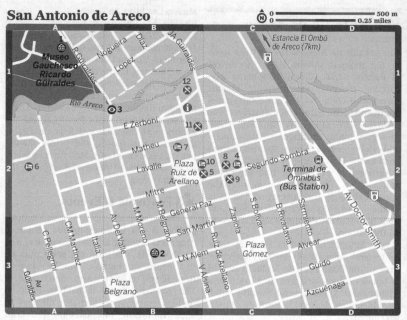

San Antonio de Areco

Estancia El Ombú
de Areco (7km)

Terminal de
Ómnibus
(Bus Station)

San Antonio de Areco

facing the central square, San Antonio's nicest hostel offers a small range of dormitory-style accommodations as well as private rooms with shared baths. The clean, tiled guest kitchen, narrow but grassy backyard, included continental breakfast and friendly management add to the appeal.

★ **Paradores Draghi** GUESTHOUSE $$
(☎455583; www.paradoresdraghi.com.ar; Matheu 380; s/d from US$105/120; ❄@🖳⛵) It's worth staying over in Areco just so you can check in here. Lovingly run by a mother-daughter team and conveniently located near the main plaza, this nine-room boutique guesthouse has spacious rooms, breezy patios, a grassy garden with a beautiful pool, a lovely continental breakfast, and a private silver workshop and museum where you can learn about silverware-making.

Antigua Casona GUESTHOUSE $$
(☎456600; www.antiguacasona.com; Segundo Sombra 495; d from US$145; ❄🖳⛵) Another wonderful place to stay in Areco, this restored traditional home offers five high-ceilinged rooms with wooden floors; all are set around covered tile hallways and leafy patios. There's a communal *parrilla* (grill), should you be tempted to grill your own steak, and a small but picturesque swimming pool set in a brick-lined courtyard.

✗ Eating

★ **La Esquina de Merti** ARGENTINE $
(www.esquinademerti.com.ar; cnr Arellano & Segundo Sombra; mains AR$45-90; ⊙9am-midnight) Housed inside an old *pulpería* right on the

plaza, this antique corner cafe is one of San Antonio de Areco's most traditional and atmospheric. Stop in for coffee, empanadas, sandwiches, a glass of wine, or a steak grilled on the *parrilla*. When the weather's nice the outdoor tables are a prime spot for gaucho-watching.

★ **Boliche de Bessonart**   ARGENTINE $
(cnr Zapiola & Segundo Sombra; picadas AR$25-80; ⊙11am-3pm & 6pm-late Tue-Sun) A local landmark. This weather-beaten corner building, originally a general store, is more than 200 years old – for the past several decades, it's been a family-run bar popular with gauchos and young people alike. Small crowds pour in most nights for *picadas*, washed down with free-flowing beer, red wine, or *fernet* (a bitter aromatic spirit).

Puesto La Lechuza   PARRILLA $
(⌨ 470136; Victorino Althaparro 423; mains AR$45-85; ⊙noon-3pm & 8pm-midnight Sat, noon-3pm Sun) Open weekends only, this charming riverside spot is ideal on a warm day, when you can savor a lunch of empanadas or grilled steak under the trees. There's live guitar music on Saturday nights starting around 9:30pm.

La Olla de Cobre   CAFE $
(⌨ 453105; www.laolladecobre.com.ar; Matheu 433; snacks AR$20-55; ⊙10am-1pm & 2:30-7:30pm Wed-Sun, 10am-1pm Mon) This cozy cafe specializes in artisanal chocolates and *alfajores* (traditional Argentinian cookie sandwiches) to go with coffee, tea, and hot chocolate. It's also a great place to pick up an edible gift.

Almacén Ramos Generales   ARGENTINE $$
(www.ramosgeneralesareco.com.ar; Zapiola 143; mains AR$65-160; ⊙noon-3pm & 8pm-midnight) Another of San Antonio's historic dining venues, this elegantly restored space was once a general store. Today, it offers a quaintly rustic setting and a traditionally Argentinian culinary experience that's slightly more upscale than many options in town.

❶ Information

There are a few banks with ATMs along Alsina.
Tourist Office (⌨ 453165; www.sanantonio deareco.com; cnr Zerboni & Arellano; ⊙10am-7pm Mon-Fri, 8am-8pm Sat & Sun)

❶ Getting There & Away

Areco's **bus terminal** (Av Smith s/n) is five blocks east of the central square. **Chevallier** (⌨ 453904; www.nuevachevallier.com) runs frequent buses to/from Buenos Aires (AR$105, two hours).

A more expensive option, but a useful one if you're trying to connect to one of the area's *estancias* (ranches) is the shuttle service operated by an independent company like **Areco Bus** (www.arecobus.com.ar; roundtrip AR$300-500). On weekends, the service offers roundtrip transportation between Buenos Aires and San Antonio de Areco (AR$300) and roundtrip transportation between Buenos Aires and certain *estancias*, including El Ombú de Areco (AR$500). Check the website for the latest itineraries and to make reservations.

SOUTHERN PAMPAS

Spreading out from the capital, the pampas region extends south beyond the borders of Buenos Aires province and west into the province of La Pampa.

In the southern part of Buenos Aires province, the endlessly flat plain is punctuated by sierras (hills). The Sierras de Tandil are ancient mountain ranges, worn to soft, low summits with heights that barely reach 500m. A little to the west, Sierra de la Ventana's jagged peaks rise to 1300m, attracting hikers and climbers.

Further west again, in the province of La Pampa, are the modest granite boulders of Parque Nacional Lihué Calel.

The hillside towns of Tandil and Sierra de la Ventana offer outdoor activities and a relaxing country atmosphere, while La Pampa's provincial capital of Santa Rosa is a decent resting point for overland travelers on their way west or south.

Tandil

⌨ 0249 / POP 124,000

Pretty Tandil sits at the northern edge of the Sierras de Tandil, a 2.5-million-year-old mountain range worn down to gentle, grassy peaks and rocky outcroppings – perfect for rock climbing and mountain biking. It exudes a rare combination of laid-back country charm with the energy of a thriving regional city. The town center is leafy and relaxed, with many places observing the afternoon siesta. Later in the evening,

THE PAMPAS & THE ATLANTIC COAST TANDIL

however, locals crowd the squares and streets, shopping and partaking in the city's cultural offerings. Going out for *picadas* – wooden boards piled high with locally produced cheeses and cured meats – is a local tradition, and Tandil is known throughout Argentina for its excellent salamis. Something else Tandil is known for? Nurturing a disproportionate number of Argentina's tennis stars, the latest of whom is Juan Martín del Potro.

The town arose from Fuerte Independencia, a military outpost established in 1823. In the early 1870s, it was the scene of one of the province's most remarkable battles, when renegade gauchos gathered in the hills before going on a murderous rampage against landowners and recent immigrants. Eventually the immigrants prevailed, and the culinary skills they brought from Europe have made the area an important producer of specialty foods.

⊙ Sights

The walk to **Parque Independencia** from the southwestern edge of downtown offers good views of the city, particularly at night, while the central **Plaza de Independencia**, surrounded by the typical municipal buildings and a church, is where the locals go for a stroll in the evenings.

Cerro El Centinela   PARK

(www.cerrocentinela.com.ar) For great views over Tandil and a relaxing afternoon hike, head 6km west of town to this hilltop park. There's a bakery, a restaurant with outdoor tables, and a chairlift that can whisk you further up the ridgeline (only open on weekends outside warm months). Take a taxi.

Cerro La Movediza   HILL

(www.lapiedramovediza.com.ar; Av Campos s/n) At the north edge of town, the Piedra Movediza, a 300-ton stone, teetered precariously atop Cerro La Movediza for many years before finally falling in 1912. A 'replica' (non-moving) stone was built in 2007; like

---

THE GLORIOUS GAUCHO

If the melancholy *tanguero* (tango dancer) is the essence of the *porteño* (resident of Buenos Aires), then the gaucho represents the pampas: a lone cowboy-like figure, pitted against the elements, with only his horse for a friend.

In the early years of the colony, the fringe-dwelling gauchos lived entirely beyond the laws and customs of Buenos Aires, eking out an independent and often violent existence in the countryside. They slaughtered cattle roaming free and unsupervised on the fertile pampas and drank *mate,* the caffeine-rich herbal tea.

As the colony grew, cattle became too valuable to leave unprotected. Foreign demand for hides increased and investors moved into the pampas to take control of the market, establishing the *estancia* (ranch) system in which large landholdings were handed out to a privileged few. Many freewheeling gauchos became exploited farmhands, while those who resisted domestication were threatened with prison or the draft.

By the late 19th century, those in charge felt the gaucho had no place in modern Argentina. President Sarmiento (governed 1868–74) declared that 'fertilizing the soil with their blood is the only thing gauchos are good for' – and already much gaucho blood had been spilled, their horsemanship making them excellent infantrymen for Argentina's civil war and the brutal campaigns against the Indians.

Like so many heroes, the gaucho only won love and admiration after his demise. His physical bravery, honor and lust for freedom are celebrated in José Hernández's 1872 epic poem *Martín Fierro* and Ricardo Güiraldes' novel *Don Segundo Sombra*. His rustic traditions form part of Argentina's sophisticated folk art, with skilled craftspeople producing intricate silver gaucho knives and woven ponchos, while his image is endlessly reproduced – most amusingly in Florencio Molina Campos' caricatures.

These days, the gaucho-for-export is much easier to spot than the real deal, especially in folkloric shows at many *estancias*. But the gaucho's descendants can be found on cattle farms throughout the pampas, riding over the plains in their dusty *boinas* (a kind of beret) and *bombachas* (riding pants). And on special occasions, such as the Día de la Tradición, they sport their best horse gear and show off their riding skills.

it's predecessor, it's still a major tourist draw (and a fun photo op). Take a taxi or bus 503.

Museo Tradicionalista Fuerte Independencia
MUSEUM

(☑ 443-5573; 4 de Abril 845; admission AR$20; ☺ 2:30-6:30pm Tue-Sun Mar-Nov, 4-8pm Tue-Sun Dec-Feb) This historical museum, worth a walk-through for context, exhibits a large and varied collection on Tandil's history. Photographs commemorate major events, and the place is filled with relics – from carriages to ladies' gloves – donated by local families.

🏃 Activities

The **Lago del Fuerte**, only 12 blocks south of Plaza de Independencia, is a huge reservoir that you can easily walk around in a couple of hours. In summer, you can rent **canoes** and **kayaks** and hang around for lunch or *merienda* (afternoon snack with tea, coffee or *mate*) at one of the restaurants along the shoreline.

For details on the plentiful outdoor activities around town, including bike rentals, trekking, canoeing, rappelling, mountain biking and rock climbing, ask the tourist office for its comprehensive list of tour operators and rental agencies.

🛌 Sleeping

Reservations are a must during summer, Easter week and holiday weekends. Many Argentines come here specifically for the experience of staying in one of the many *cabaña* (cabin) complexes in the area – many have terraces, fireplaces and/or swimming pools, so they're great places to unwind. But they're only convenient if you have a car. The following options are in town.

Gran Hotel Roma
HOTEL $

(☑ 442-5217; www.hotelromatandil.com.ar; Alem 452; d from US$62; 🖥) The top budget pick in town, Gran Hotel Roma is bare-bones basic and showing its age. But it's tough to top the convenient location only a block from Tandil's main plaza, and there's free wi-fi and a bar downstairs.

Casa Chango
HOSTEL $

(☑ 442-2260; www.casa-chango.com.ar; 25 de Mayo 451; dm/d/tr from US$17/58/88; 🖥🖥) The best parts of this hostel are the bright and attractive common areas, including the communal dining room and kitchen, with colorful tiles, high ceilings and historical charm. Dorms are just so-so, and travelers

have been complaining of poor service and declining standards of cleanliness, so unless you're on a tight budget, it's best to consider other options first.

You & Me Apartment
BUNGALOW $$

(☑ 444-8669; www.tandiltravel.com/you-me-apartment.htm; cnr Pinto y Buzón; d from US$80; 🖥🖥) This adorable two-person bungalow, if you can manage to snag it, is like having your own private home in Tandil, complete with a small garden where you can enjoy a leisurely breakfast under the trees. Located a few blocks from the bus station on the way into town, it's lovingly operated and well-equipped with a small kitchen and wi-fi.

Plaza Hotel
HOTEL $$

(☑ 442-7160; www.plazahoteldetandil.com.ar; Pinto 438; s/d from US$84/103; 🖥🖥) Location, location, location: Tandil's Plaza Hotel might not win any awards for cutting-edge design, but it's comfortable, and prominently situated right on the main plaza.

Belgrano 39 B&B
B&B $$

(☑ 0249-15-460-7076, 0249-442-6989; hutton@speedy.com.ar; Belgrano 39; r US$80; 🖥🖥) There's only room for four people, but this peaceful B&B, run by a one-of-a-kind British woman with an encyclopedic knowledge of Tandil, is well worth seeking out. It features two rooms flanked by a large lovely garden and pool, with off-street parking available. Advance reservations required.

🍴 Eating & Drinking

Your best bet for a memorable meal in Tandil is to go out for *picadas*, pack a picnic and go hiking, or relax at one of several restaurants lining the shores of the Lago del Fuerte.

Grill Argentino
ARGENTINE $
(Gral Rodríguez 552; mains AR$58-120; ☺noon-3pm & 8:30pm-midnight) This centrally located, cavernous dining hall, half a block off the plaza, is popular for its efficient service and its reasonably priced, abundant servings of Argentine classics such as *milanesas* with fries, pasta and steaks.

★Época de Quesos
ARGENTINE $$
(www.epocadequesos.com/tandil; cnr San Martín & 14 de Julio; picadas for 1/2 people from AR$160/370, mains from AR$59; ☺9am-midnight) This adorably rustic landmark is an essential stop. The shop in the front sells a wide variety of local cheeses and cured meats, perfect for a picnic. It's wonderfully cozy and atmospheric at night, when candlelight casts a warm glow over the wooden furniture and mismatched cutlery. It's the place to be for *picadas* and wine on a weekend evening.

Tierra de Azafranes
INTERNATIONAL $$
(☑443-6800; www.tierradeazafranes.com.ar; cnr San Martín & Av Santamarina; mains AR$88-140; ☺noon-3pm & 8:30pm-midnight Wed-Mon) This popular and smartly decorated restaurant is known for its fish, steaks, pastas, risottos and paella, plus special seafood stews in colder weather. There's a good wine list, too. It's located between the main plaza and the bus station.

Parrilla El Trébol
PARRILLA $$
(☑444-2333; cnr Mitre & 14 de Julio; mains AR$75-145; ☺8pm-midnight Tue-Fri, noon-midnight Sat, noon-3pm Sun) This simple *parrilla*, specializing in perfectly grilled steaks and top-notch salads, is a locals' favorite.

Antares
BAR
(www.cervezaantares.com; 9 de Julio 758; ☺7:30pm-2am) Belly up to the bar with the locals at the Tandil branch of this popular chain of modern breweries. Sample the goods from the copper tap cylinders behind the bar, and come for live music on weekend nights. It's also a great place to grab a bite to eat (mains AR$60 to AR$120).

🛍 Shopping

Syquet
FOOD
(www.syquet.com.ar; cnr Gral Rodríguez & Mitre; ☺9am-1pm & 5-9pm Mon-Fri, 9am-9pm Sat, 10am-9pm Sun) This charming corner emporium sells a tantalizing array of local cheeses,

salamis and hams, along with other gourmet regional products. You'll spot several other businesses offering similarly tempting spreads around town, and most are happy to offer free samples.

❶ Information

There are plenty of banks with ATMs in the center.

Tourist Office (☑444-8698; www.tandil.gov.ar; Rodríguez 445; ☺9am-8pm Mon-Sat, 9am-1pm Sun) Opposite Tandil's central plaza. There's another branch at the bus terminal.

❶ Getting There & Away

Tandil's **bus terminal** (☑432092; Av Buzón 400) is located 12 blocks east of the main plaza. Walk or take a taxi (about AR$35) from in front of the terminal.

Trains from Buenos Aires' Constitución station (*primera*/Pullman class AR$120/145, seven hours) arrive at Tandil's train station, **Estación Tandil** (☑423002; www.ferrobaires.gba.gov.ar), on Tuesday and Friday nights and head back on Wednesday and Sunday nights, but double check the schedule online, as service can be suspended.

Buses from Tandil

DESTINATION	COST (AR$)	TIME (HR)
Buenos Aires	320-380	5½
Córdoba	930-1065	14-15
Mar del Plata	231	3
Mendoza	1050-1200	17
Necochea	146-160	3

❶ Getting Around

Tandil's excellent public transportation system (rides AR$7.20) reaches every important sight. Bus 500 (yellow) goes to Lago del Fuerte, buses 501 (red) and 505 (brown) go to the bus terminal, and bus 503 (blue) goes to Cerro La Movediza, the university and the bus terminal.

Sierra de la Ventana
☑0291 / POP 5000

Sierra de la Ventana is quiet and peaceful, a getaway for busy *bahienses* (residents of Bahía Blanca) who roll into town on weekends with cars full of kids, dogs and the fixings for a killer *asado* (barbecue). The main attractions are the picturesque hills and the wealth of outdoor activities in the region: hiking up nearby peaks, trout fishing and bathing in the streams and pools, riding on horse or bicycle through the hills, and climbing or rappelling among the rocks.

🏃 Activities

Lots of outdoor pursuits are on offer in this region. You can tackle many on your own. For hiking guides, rappelling, horseback riding and other tours, stop into the offices of the agencies listed we've listed, conveniently located on Av San Martin.

Several small outfitters offer bike rentals. One to try is **Rodados El Montañes** (☑ 0291-648-0142; cnr Fortín Mercedes & Iguazú ; ☺ 9am-1pm & 5-8:30pm Mon-Sat).

On a hot day, the river area behind Alihuen Hotel is popular for splashing about. Find a quieter stretch of stream by hiking down to the edge of Arroyo San Bernardo, located south of Av San Martin, past Hotel Provincial, in the area known as Barrio Parque Delfino.

👉 Tours

Tierra Ventana   ADVENTURE TOUR
(☑ 509-4696; www.tierraventana.com; Av San Martín s/n; ☺ 10am-6pm Mon-Sat) Guided excursions on offer include a half-day trek to Cerro Ventana, a photo safari to Cerro Tigre, a visit to Parque Provincial Tornquist, and a nighttime astronomy tour.

Silver Viajes y Turismo   HORSEBACK RIDING
(Av San Martín 156; ☺ 9am-6pm Mon-Sat) Specializes in horseback riding, but also arranges hiking trips and 4WD excursions.

🛏 Sleeping

Book ahead in summer and during long weekends. The tourist office has an extensive list of *cabañas,* some of which are only convenient if you're arriving in your own rental car.

Alihuen Hotel   HOTEL $$
(☑ 0291-491-5074; www.lasierradelaventana. ar/alihuen; cnr Tornquist & Frontini; d/tr from US$81/108; 🔞🖥) About four blocks from the main drag and strategically positioned on the banks of the river is this charmingly antique hotel. It's not exactly luxurious, with creaky wood floors and simple furnishings, but there's plenty of atmosphere – and plenty of outdoor space for relaxing, including a swimming pool for when the weather's warm.

Cabañas Bodensee   CABAÑAS $$
(☑ 0291-491-5356; www.sierrasdelaventana.com. ar/bodensee; Rayces 455, Villa La Arcadia; cabaña for 2/4 people from US$78/97; 🔞🖥) This peaceful complex of cabins, situated around an appealing swimming pool, is a lovely respite within easy walking distance of the town center. Each cabin features a small kitchen and a porch with a large *parrilla*. It's located in the neighborhood of Villa La Arcadia, just across the river from most of Sierra de la Ventana's attractions.

Hotel Provincial   HOTEL $$
(☑ 0291-491-5024; www.hotelprovincialsierra. com; Drago 130; d/tr from US$139/157; 🔞🔞🖥) A grand old place that's been recently remodeled. Guest rooms feel fresh and relatively luxurious, but the real draw are the public spaces: two swimming pools, a living room with a soaring fireplace and views of the mountains, a modern restaurant, and a spa. It's a favorite pick for families and couples alike.

🍴 Eating

Some restaurants close one or more days per week outside the December to March summer months. Self-caterers will find several supermarkets and artisanal food shops on the main street.

❶ Orientation

The town is divided into two sections by Río Sauce Grande. The main street, Av San Martín, lies south of the river, as do the bus and train stops and most other services.

❶ Information

A good resource for information about activities, accommodations, activities and transportation in the region is www.sierrasdelaventana.tur.ar (in Spanish).

Banco Provincia (San Martín 260) Has ATMs.
Tourist Office (☑ 0291-491-5303; www.sierra delaventana.org.ar; Av del Golf s/n; ☺ 8am-8pm) Across the tracks from the train station.

❶ Getting There & Around

Condor Estrella (☑ 0291-491-5091; www. condorestrella.com.ar) has buses to Buenos Aires (AR$550, nine hours, six times weekly) and Bahía Blanca (AR$110, 2½ hours, twice daily), leaving from a small office on Av San Martín, a block from the YPF gas station. Condor Estrella also runs a daily bus between Sierra de la Ventana and Villa Ventana (AR$30, 20 minutes).

130

1. Traditional gaucho ornaments and dagger 2. Horseback riding at La Candelaria 3. La Candelaria 4. Gaucho preparing *mate* (a bitter, tea-like beverage)

LA CANDELARIA / WOW FACTOR ©

Staying on an Estancia

One of the best ways to enjoy the open spaces of the pampas is to visit an *estancia* (ranch). Argentina's late-19th-century belle epoque saw wealthy families adorn their ranches with lavish homes and gardens.

Those glorious days being long gone, many of these establishments are open to tourists. The *día de campo* (day in the country) usually includes a huge *asado* (barbecue) with drinks, a tour of the historic home and use of the property's horses, bicycles and swimming pool. Some places offer a *show gauchesco,* featuring folk dances and feats of horsemanship, while others host polo matches. *Estancias* are a sustainable tourism option, helping to preserve part of the country's past while providing an impressive guest-to-tree ratio. Most offer overnight stays, which include meals and activities.

Estancia Options

These are all within a few hours' drive of Buenos Aires.

Los Dos Hermanos (✆011-4723-2880; www.estancialosdoshermanos.com; día de campo US$100) This down-to-earth ranch is best for day trips and horseback riding.

La Candelaria (✆02227-494132; www.estanciacandelaria.com; día de campo from US$94, d with full board from US$217) At sunset, this extravagant French-style castle is the ultimate photo op.

Estancia Ave María (p127) A refined rural getaway outside of Tandil.

Candelaria del Monte (✆02271-442-431; www.candelariadelmonte.com.ar; Ruta 41, San Miguel del Monte; r with full board per person US$220; ▣) Laid-back and elegant, with a beautiful swimming pool.

Puesto Viejo Estancia (✆11 5279-6893; www.puestoviejoestancia.com.ar; RP 6, Km83, Cañuelas; día de campo adult/child US$85/43, r with full board per person US$225; ▣) Learn to play polo at this chic ranch and polo club.

WORTH A TRIP

VILLA VENTANA

Just 17km northwest of Sierra de la Ventana is the peaceful village of Villa Ventana. There's nothing much to do here except wander the dusty streets, which meander through pretty residential neighborhoods full of pine trees, and investigate the ruins of South America's first casino (by guided tour only; see the **tourist office** (☑0291-491-0095; ⊗8am-6pm Mon-Thu, to 7pm Fri-Sun, to 8pm daily Jan & Feb), located at the town's entrance). Villa Ventana is also a closer base than Sierra de la Ventana from which to visit Parque Provincial Ernesto Tornquist.

There are several places to stay, though none are particularly budget-friendly. A convenient option is **Cabañas La Ponderosa** (☑0291-491-5491; www.villalaponderosa.com. ar; cnr Cruz del Sur & Hornero; cabañas for 1/2/3/4/5 US$85/100/110/130/140; ☎), diagonally across from the minibus stop. The complex features well-sized, homey and comfortable wood *cabañas* (cabins), some with a loft and all with a kitchenette. Prices drop on weekdays and from April to mid-December.

Condor Estrella runs a daily bus between Sierra de la Ventana and Villa Ventana (AR$30, 20 minutes); you can catch a ride to Parque Provincial Ernesto Tornquist by catching the same bus (AR$35, 30 minutes) to Tornquist. If the schedule isn't convenient for your travel plans, you can always take a cab to the park, and arrange a *remise* (private taxi) to Sierra de la Ventana. The latter ride costs around AR$150 to AR$200 for up to three passengers.

Ferrobaires (www.ferrobaires.gba.gov.ar) operates a twice-weekly train service to Sierra de la Ventana on the train line that runs between Bahía Blanca and Buenos Aires (AR$115 to AR$205).

If you're headed to Bahía Blanca, it's quicker (and often more convenient) to reserve a ride with **Norte Bus** (☑0291-15-468-5101) (AR$120, one hour), a long-distance-van company offering door-to-door service. The shuttle leaves Sierra de la Ventana two or three times a day; call to reserve.

Parque Provincial Ernesto Tornquist

This 67-sq-km **park** (☑491-0039; www.torn quist.gov.ar; adult/child AR$10/4; ⊗8am-5pm Dec-Mar, 9am-5pm Apr-Nov), 22km from Sierra de la Ventana, draws visitors from throughout the province. There are two entrances. The first is 5km west of Villa Ventana and home to the **Centro de Visitantes**, which has a small display on local ecology. The main hike here is **Cerro Bahía Blanca** (two hours roundtrip), offering great views. There are also **Cuevas con Pinturas Repustres**, or cave paintings, but you can only visit these with a guided tour, available from various agencies around Sierra de la Ventana, such as Tierra Ventana (p129).

The park's highlight, however, is at its other entrance, 3km further west. The five-hour (roundtrip) hike to 1150m **Cerro de la Ventana** leads to a window-shaped rock formation near its peak. The climb offers dramatic views of surrounding hills and the distant pampas. Register with rangers before 11am at the trailhead, and take plenty of water and sun protection.

Less demanding destinations accessible from the Cerro de la Ventana trailhead include **Piletones** (2½ hours roundtrip) and **Garganta Olvidada** (one hour roundtrip). To visit the gorge and waterfall pool at **Garganta del Diablo** (six hours roundtrip), you must go with a tour company.

Condor Estrella (p129) serves Tornquist from Sierra de la Ventana (AR$40, one hour) twice daily – tell the driver you want to get off at the park entrance. For better timing, to catch the park opening, arrange a *remise* (taxi) to the park from Sierra de la Ventana or Villa Ventana.

Santa Rosa

☑02954 / POP 103,000

About 600km from Buenos Aires – and a long way from pretty much anywhere else – Santa Rosa is unlikely to be of interest unless you find yourself traveling overland, in which case it's a convenient stopping point and transportation hub. It's a pleasant enough place, however, with a small-town feel, friendly people and busy plaza area.

⊙ Sights & Activities

Laguna Don Tomás, surrounded by a park of the same name, is 1km west of the city center. This is the place for locals to sail, swim, cycle or stroll through an appealing network of wooded paths.

La Malvina HISTORIC BUILDING
(☑436-555; Parque Don Tomás; ⏰hours vary) FREE On the edge of the *laguna*, La Malvina – the elegant original *estancia* of Santa Rosa's founder – has been restored and reopened to the public. Now a mini-museum displaying old photographs of the settlement's early days, it's worth a walk-through. If you're interested in architecture you'll enjoy the side-by-side photos showing Santa Rosa's primary buildings, then and now.

🛏 Sleeping & Eating

Residencial Atuel HOTEL $
(☑422597; www.atuel.aehglp.org.ar; Luro 356; s/d/tr US$30/48/60; ❄🛜) Just steps from the bus terminal, this friendly place has worn but tidy rooms with cable TV. It's certainly convenient, and good enough for one night.

Hotel Calfucurá HOTEL $$
(☑433303; www.hotelcalfucura.com; Av San Martín 695; s/d from AR$85/97; ❄🛜🏊) Once Santa Rosa's best hotel, Hotel Calfucurá is fraying around the edges. Though the place could use an update, guest rooms are comfortable (the showers in particular are excellent), the pool is a nice perk in hot weather, and the location between the bus terminal and the main plaza is handy.

La Capital CAFE $
(cnr 9 de Julio & Avellaneda; mains AR$35-105; ⏰7:30am-midnight Mon-Sat, 5:30pm-late Sun) Santa Rosa's oldest cafe, located in a cool modernist corner building on the main plaza, is basic but classic. It's open all day, busy at breakfast, and again at lunch, when the menu includes empanadas, pizza, salads and sandwiches. When the weather's nice pull up a chair at one of the sidewalk tables for a cold beer.

ⓘ Information

You'll find several ATMs in the city center.
Provincial Tourist Office (☑424404; www. turismolapampa.gov.ar; cnr Luro & San Martín; ⏰7am-9pm Mon-Fri, 9am-1pm & 4-9pm Sat & Sun) Across from the bus terminal; longer hours in January and February.

ⓘ Getting There & Away

Aerolíneas (☑427588; www.aerolineas.com. ar; Pico 267) flies to Buenos Aires. The airport is 3km from downtown. A taxi between the airport and the center costs approximately AR$35.

The **bus terminal** (Luro 365) is seven blocks east of the plaza. Buses go to Buenos Aires (AR$565 to AR$656, eight to 11 hours), but at the time of research the only way to get to Bahía Blanca was to drive yourself or to take the daily door-to-door minibus service (four hours) offered by **Vivian Tours** (☑421200; cnr Luro & Rosas; shuttle service AR$330 one-way). Call to reserve; the shuttle leaves Santa Rosa for Bahía Blanca in the afternoon or early evening.

For car rentals try **Sixt** (☑414600; www.sixt. com.ar; Lisandro de la Torre 96), with downtown and airport locations and good online rates.

Reserva Provincial Parque Luro
☑02954

Home to a mix of introduced and native species, as well as over 150 species of birds, this 76-sq-km **reserve** (☑452600; www.parqueluro. tur.ar; Ruta Nacional 35, Km292; admission AR$4, guided visits at Museo El Caserío & Museo El Castillo AR$8; ⏰9am-7pm) near Santa Rosa is a peaceful place to spend time away from the city. It's quiet during the week, but gets busy on weekends when local families bring all the fixings for an afternoon *asado* (barbecue) and spend the day here. Avoid Sundays if you're hoping to beat the crowds, and be sure to bring water and sun protection in the baking summer.

At the turn of the 20th century, Pedro Luro, a French-Basque immigrant who fashioned himself into one of Argentina's more important landowners, created the country's first hunting preserve here. He imported exotic game species, such as red deer and European boar, and built an enormous French-style mansion to accommodate his European guests. He later abandoned it as sport hunting fell out of vogue and the European aristocracy suffered the upheavals of WWI and the Great Depression. The reserve was sold, then neglected, its animals escaping through the fence or falling victim to poachers.

Since its acquisition by the province in 1965, Parque Luro has served as a refuge for native species such as puma and wild fox, along with exotic migratory birds including flamingo. One of the park's biggest draws, however, is during the fall mating season of the red deer. In March and April the males bellow loudly (called 'la Brama') to attract female harems, while scuffling among themselves.

Hourly tours of the **Museo El Castillo** (AR$8), Luro's opulent château-style mansion, offer insight into the luxurious eccentricities that Argentine landowners could indulge. As the story goes, Luro was only able to obtain the gorgeous walnut fireplace by purchasing an entire Parisian restaurant. Besides the museum, there's the **Museo San Huberto** FREE with its interesting collection of early-20th-century horse-drawn carriages and **Museo El Caserío** (AR$8), where the French painter Tristán Lacroix lived and worked in 1911.

The park's sights are all located around a 6km ring road; nature walks veer off it, so pull over whenever the mood strikes. Reach the visitors center by following the main road about 2km from the entrance. Bring your own food, though there's a small store and a basic restaurant (the latter closed for renovations at the time of research) – and feel free to use the public *parrillas*, as all the Argentine families do. Campsites and a few nicely outfitted *cabañas* (sleeping up to five) are also available; make contact through the park's official website.

Parque Luro is 35km south of Santa Rosa. From the bus terminal, catch the **Dumascat** (437090; www.dumascat.com.ar) bus bound for General Acha and ask to be dropped off at the park entrance (AR$12, 30 to 40 minutes, several daily), then find out when a bus returns to Santa Rosa. Alternatively, rent a car in Santa Rosa, or take a taxi, though you'll want to be sure you arrange a pickup as well.

Parque Nacional Lihué Calel

02952

In the local indigenous language of Pehuenche, Lihué Calel means Sierra de la Vida (Range of Life), and describes a series of small, isolated mountain ranges and valleys that create unique microclimates in a nearly featureless pampean landscape.

This desert-like **park** (436595; www.parquesnacionales.gob.ar; 8am-7pm) FREE is a haven for native cats such as puma and yagouaroundi. You can spot armadillo, guanaco, mara (Patagonian hare) and vizcacha,

while birdlife includes the rhea-like ñandú and many birds of prey such as the carancho (crested caracara).

Lihué Calel receives only about 400mm of rainfall per year, but sudden storms can create brief waterfalls over granite boulders near the visitors center. Even when the sky is cloudless, the subterranean streams in the valleys nourish the *monte* (a scrub forest with a surprising variety of plant species). Within the park's 10 sq km exist 345 species of plants, nearly half the total found in the entire province.

The most rewarding hike in the area is the hour-long climb to the 589m peak **Cerro de la Sociedad Científica Argentina**; watch for flowering cacti such as *Trichocereus candicans* between boulders. From the summit there are outstanding views of the entire sierra and surrounding marshes and salt lakes.

About 10km by car from the visitors center is the **Casona**, the ruins of the old house of former Estancia Santa María. Another 2km further along, the road peters out at the parking lot for the **Valle de las Pinturas**, where a 600m trail leads down a rock-strewn valley to some petroglyphs. These same two attractions are accessible to walkers via a 9km footpath from the visitors center.

More information is available at the visitors center (open 8am to 6pm). Spring, when flowers are blooming and the temperatures aren't too hot, is the best time to visit the park.

🛏 Sleeping

Near the visitors center is a comfortable and free campground with shade trees, firepits (bring wood or carbon), picnic tables, flush toilets and showers. Stock up on food before arriving; the nearest decent supplies are at the town of Puelches, 32km south.

❶ Getting There & Away

Parque Nacional Lihué Calel is 228km southwest of Santa Rosa, and there are no direct buses to the park. Long-distance buses leaving Santa Rosa, and for Neuquén or Bariloche, pass by the entrance; if you arrange ahead of time with the driver, it shouldn't be a problem to get dropped off here (though getting picked up again would be trickier). But generally speaking, driving yourself – you can rent a car in Santa Rosa – is the best way to visit the park.

ATLANTIC COAST

Argentines can justly claim Latin America's highest peak (Cerro Aconcagua), its widest avenue (Buenos Aires' 9 de Julio) and perhaps its coolest capital – among many other attributes – but its beaches aren't exactly something to write home about. Forget the tropical paradises fringed with palm trees on Brazil's Atlantic coast: there's no white sand here, the winds can be fierce, and the water is cloudy rather than turquoise. So it's no tropical paradise, although Argentina's beaches are still pleasant enough in summer. Each January and February they reliably attract tens of thousands of people from all over the country. In fact, so many people flock to the shore that at times you might have a hard time finding a free spot to spread your towel.

If you want to avoid the crush of summertime crowds, simply visit in the shoulder months of December and March, when the weather is still warm enough to enjoy the beaches and their activities. In the dead of winter, however, coastal towns here take on an abandoned feel and the gray weather can be depressing. Mar del Plata is an exception – the coast's largest city is a cultural capital, with plenty to do year-round.

Accommodation prices along the coast vary widely, depending on the season. They rise sharply from mid-December through February, when reservations are crucial (and some places require minimum stays). Prices then start declining in March but rise again during Easter, after which most places close down until November. At the places that do stay open, bargains can be found during these cooler months. From March to December, opening hours (especially at tourist offices and restaurants) are much shorter than what we've listed here.

San Clemente del Tuyú

📱 02252 / POP 12,000

With absolutely none of the glitz or glamour of the resorts down the coast, family-oriented San Clemente attracts low-key beachgoers. There are reasonably priced accommodations near the waterfront, including **Hotel Brisas Marinas** (📞522219; www.brisas-marinas. com.ar; Calle 13, No 50; d from US$63; 🌐), and plenty of restaurants on the main drag, Calle 1. The **tourist information office** (📞423249; www.sanclementedeltuyu.com.ar; Av Costanera btwn Calles 2 & 63; ⏰8am-midnight Jan & Feb, 9am-8pm Mar-Dec) is across from the beach.

A few kilometers north of San Clemente del Tuyú are several protected areas, including **Reserva Natural Municipal Punta Rasa** (whose beach is popular with kiteboarders) and **Parque Nacional Campos del Tuyú** (home of the rare pampas deer).

For tamer wildlife (or entertainment for kids on a rainy day), there's **Mundo Marino** (www.mundomarino.com.ar; Av Décima 157; adult/child under 11yr AR$329/219; ⏰10am-8pm Jan & Feb, 10am-6pm Mar-Dec, weekends only Apr-Nov), South America's largest marine park (although note that it has seal and dolphin shows, which may concern some visitors – animal welfare groups claim keeping sea mammals in enclosed tanks is harmful for these complex animals). Argentines also come to the area to visit the spa-like recreation center called **Termas Marinas** (www. termasmarinas.com.ar; Faro San Antonio CC No 9; adult/child under 10yr AR$235/160; ⏰10am-8pm Jan & Feb, 10am-6pm Mar-Dec), featuring mineral-rich thermal baths where you can float and soak all day.

From San Clemente's **bus terminal** (cnr Avs Naval & Talas del Tuyú), about 25 blocks from the town center, frequent buses run to Buenos Aires (AR$319 to AR$364, 4½ hours) and Pinamar (AR$300, three hours).

Pinamar

📱 02254 / POP 25,000

Located about 120km up the coast from Mar del Plata, Pinamar is a very popular destination for style-conscious *porteños* who'd rather not make the trip to the beaches of Uruguay. The city was founded and designed in 1944 by architect Jorge Bunge, who figured out how to stabilize the shifting dunes by planting pines, acacias and pampas grass. It was once the refuge for the country's upper echelons, but is now somewhat less exclusive and more laid-back.

🏃 Activities

The main activity in Pinamar is simply relaxing and socializing on the beach, which stretches all the way from north of the town down to Cariló. But the area also offers a wealth of outdoor activities, from windsurfing and waterskiing to horseback riding and fishing. You can also ride bicycles in the wooded areas near the golf course, or through the leafy streets of nearby Cariló.

For bike rentals, try **Leo** (📞488855; Av Bunge 1111; bike rental per hr AR$50; ⏰9am-9pm),

ALONG THE COAST

The destinations we list here are only a sampling of what's available along this stretch of Argentina's Atlantic coast. If you have a rental car, excursions to the following beach enclaves – particularly popular with Argentine families who have some extra money to spend – are a snap.

Starting in the north, just south of Pinamar, there are the tranquil and largely residential villages of **Ostende** and **Valeria**. Further down the coast is woodsy **Cariló**, a favorite of well-off Argentines. It's a worthwhile detour at night for its fashionable restaurants or for a stroll under the trees, ice-cream cone in hand.

On the other side of Villa Gesell, continuing down the coast, are **Mar de las Pampas** and **Mar Azul**, exclusive beach neighborhoods with expensive lodging (rented only by the week in summer) and upscale services, all dropped into a pine forest. The beach here is less crowded, too, making the area a good day-trip destination, even if you're staying in busier Villa Gesell.

on the main street near the tourist office. If you want to learn how to kiteboard, go to Sport Beach, the last *balneario* (river beach) located about 5km north of Av Bunge. There are many more options for activities – ask at the tourist office.

★ Festivals & Events

Pinamar's film festival, **Pantalla Pinamar** (www.pantallapinamar.gov.ar), takes place in March, and there are concerts and parties on the beach around New Year.

🛌 Sleeping

Reservations are a must in January, when some places have a one-week minimum stay. Best options for the budget-minded are near the southern beaches of Ostende and Valeria, though you'll also find some cheaper hotels and *hospedajes* (family homes) along Calle del Cangrejo, north of the tourist office.

Cabañas Pinaforet CABAÑAS $$
(☑02254-409277; www.pinaforet.com.ar; cnr Apolo & Jason; per week Jan & Feb from US$1290; ❀🕾) This sweet cluster of five spacious log cabins set among piney grounds is only a few paces from the bus terminal, within a few minutes' walk of the town center and beach. Each sleeps up to four people, making this a great budget option in low season (despite the high weekly prices quoted in summer). Contact them for the low-season rates.

Hotel Mojomar HOTEL $$
(☑02254-407300; www.hotelmojomar.com.ar; De las Burriquetas 247; d from US$107; ❀🕾) The Mojomar is upscale, if not luxurious, with a great location three blocks off Av Bunge, and only a block from the beach. The look

is modern but warm; guest rooms are small but comfortable, and some have sea views.

La Vieja Hostería BOUTIQUE HOTEL $$$
(☑482804; www.laviejahosteria.com.ar; Del Tuyú 169; d from US$132; ❀🕾❀) In a beautifully remodeled 1940s house, Pinamar's nicest boutique hotel has elegantly appointed rooms, inviting common areas (including a poolside deck and a patio with massage tents) and a perfect location, just south of the main street and two blocks in from the beach.

🍴 Eating

Countless restaurants and food stands line the beachfront and Av Bunge; wander onto the side streets to find better deals (and fewer crowds).

★ Tante INTERNATIONAL $$
(De las Artes 35; mains AR$55-175; ☺noon-midnight) This elegant tearoom, restaurant and bar – a few blocks in from the beach, just off Av Bunge – was once the home of a well-known 1950s soprano. Nowadays it serves up German, French and alpine specialties such as fondue, crepes, goulash, wurst and sauerkraut. Afternoon teas are a delight. There's a second location in Cariló.

Los Troncos ARGENTINE $$
(cnr Eneas & Lenguado; mains AR$45-130; ☺noon-3pm & 8pm-midnight Thu-Tue) In business for four decades, this beloved backstreet eatery is often packed with locals even in low season. There's a casual but convivial old-school ambience, and the menu includes everything from roast meats to seafood stews to homemade pastas, all done to perfection.

Jalisco MEXICAN $$
(www.jalisco.com.ar; Bunge 456; mains AR$120-150; ⊙1-3:30pm & 7:30pm-1:30am) At this popular Tex-Mex eatery on Pinamar's main street, the fun begins at the entryway, adorned with cactus-shaped lamps and *papel picado* (colorful Mexican-style paper cutouts). Menu choices range from fajitas and quesadillas to pasta and seafood dishes. There's a second location in Cariló.

Cantina Tulumei SEAFOOD $$
(Bunge 64; mains AR$60-160; ⊙noon-4pm & 8pm-1am) Hit the outdoor deck at this main-street eatery, one block in from the waterfront, for reasonably priced, quality seafood. Fish is prepared in at least a dozen different sauces; homemade pastas are also a good choice.

❶ Information

Municipal Tourist Office (☑491680; www.pinamar.tur.ar; cnr Av Bunge & Shaw; ⊙8am-8pm Mon-Fri, 10am-8pm Sat, 10am-5pm Sun)

❶ Getting There & Away

Pinamar's **bus terminal** (☑403500; Jason 2250) is about eight blocks north of the town center, just off Av Bunge. Destinations include Buenos Aires (AR$350, five hours) and Mar del Plata (AR$152, 2½ hours).

There are frequent buses to nearby Villa Gesell (AR$45, 30 minutes). For the southern beaches of Ostende, Valeria del Mar and Cariló, catch a Montemar local bus just outside the long-distance terminal.

Villa Gesell

☑02255 / POP 30,000

Smaller and less flashy than its neighbors Pinamar and Mar del Plata, laid-back Villa Gesell is still a hit with the younger crowd. Uniquely for the coastal towns, it offers a wood-planked beach boardwalk, making walks along the sands much easier. It's also known for summer choral performances and rock and folk concerts, and there are plenty of outdoor activities to enjoy. The town is compact, with most services located on its main drag, Av 3, three blocks in from the beach.

In the 1930s, merchant, inventor and nature lover Carlos Gesell designed this resort of zigzag streets, planting acacias, poplars, oaks and pines to stabilize the shifting dunes. Though he envisioned a town merging with the forest he had created, it wasn't long before high-rise vacation shares began their malignant growth and the trees started to disappear.

◉ Sights & Activities

Feria Artesanal MARKET
(Crafts Fair; Av 3 btwn Paseos 112 & 113) There's a nightly handicrafts fair from mid-December to mid-March. Expect lots of handmade jewelry, carved wood, paintings and souvenirs. The rest of the year it's a weekend-only event.

Muelle de Pesca FISHING
(Playa & Paseo 129) Gesell's 15m fishing pier offers year-round fishing for mackerel, rays, shark and other marine species. It's located south of the town center.

Windy Playa Bar SURFING
(www.windyplayabar.com.ar; cnr Paseo 104 & beach; ⊙8am-dusk in summer) You can't miss it: just look for the faux pirate ship parked on the sand. At Windy, you can rent surf gear or sign up for lessons; the beach bar is also one-stop shopping for renting beach equipment or just grabbing some cold drinks and sandwiches with a view.

Casa Macca BICYCLE RENTAL
(Av Buenos Aires 449; per hr AR$50) For bicycle rentals, try Casa Macca. It's located between Paseo 101 and Av 5.

🛏 Sleeping

La Deseada Hostel HOSTEL $
(☑02255-473276; www.ladeseadahostel.com.ar; cnr Av 6 & Paseo 119; dm/d from US$35/75; @ ﹫) Teeming with young Argentines in January, but tranquil in the off season, this ultra-homey hostel sits atop a sloping, evergreen-fringed lawn in a residential area between the bus terminal and the center, six blocks from the beach. Eight-bed dorms, plus private rooms (only available outside high season), are complemented by spacious common areas and a nice guest kitchen. Breakfast is served till 1pm.

Medamar Playa Hotel HOTEL $$
(☑02255-463106; www.medamarplaya.com; cnr Costanera & Paseo 111; s/d from US$79/92; ﹫ 🐾) This boxy green-and-white beachfront hotel is dated, but service is friendly and the location can't be beat. Outside of busy summertime it's worth trying for one of the rooms with a private balcony facing the ocean and the tiny swimming pool.

Hotel de la Plaza   HOTEL $$

(📞 02255-468793; www.delaplazahotel.com; Av 2, No 375; d/tr from US$100/140) Centrally located between the beach and Villa Gesell's commercial center, this tidy hotel is professionally run and open 365 days of the year – a great pick if you happen to be passing through out of season. Several restaurants are located less than a block away.

✖ Eating & Drinking

Rancho Hambre   EMPANADAS $

(Av 3, No 871; empanadas AR$15, pizzas AR$90-180; ⏰ noon-3pm & 7:30pm-late, closed Sun lunch & all day Wed) This main street hot-spot features 36 varieties of empanadas, from the humble (minced beef) to the more elaborate (arugula, parmesan and walnuts, or bacon with mozzarella and muscat-infused prunes). Pick up a dozen to go, or stick around and order a pizza. There's a second location on the corner of Av 3 and Paseo 125.

El Viejo Hobbit   PUB FOOD $$

(Av 8 btwn Paseos 11 & 12; snacks AR$60-110, fondue AR$200-340; ⏰ 6pm-late Fri & Sat Apr-Nov, daily Dec-Mar) An obligatory stop for beer lovers and Tolkien fans, this whimsical backstreet bar plunges you straight into Hobbit-land from the minute you pass through the round front door. Several beers brewed on-site complement a menu focused on fondue. There's a cozy 2nd floor, plus a backyard with a miniature Hobbit house for kids to play in.

La Delfina   PARRILLA $$

(cnr Paseo 104 & Av 2; mains AR$80-125; ⏰ noon-3pm & 8pm-midnight) A huge menu means there's something for everyone at this popular *parrilla,* from steaks, pastas, and salads to desserts and a lengthy wine list. Right on the main drag, it's easy to find.

Sutton 212   INTERNATIONAL $$

(📞 460674; cnr Paseo 105 & Av 2; mains AR$70-140; ⏰ 5pm-dawn) This lively restaurant, with ample outdoor deck seating, serves dishes ranging from Mediterranean to Asian fusion, along with gourmet crepes, sushi and sandwiches. DJs and live music keep things buzzing later in the evening, when the place becomes a happening bar.

ℹ Information

Tourist Office (📞 478042; www.turismo.gesell. gob.ar; Paseo 107 btwn Avs 2 & 3; ⏰ 8am-8pm Mar-Dec, to midnight Jan & Feb) Conveniently located in the center. There's another branch at the bus terminal (corner of Av 3 and Paseo 140; open from 5am to midnight mid-December to Easter, 8am to 8pm during the rest of the year).

ℹ Getting There & Away

The **bus terminal** (cnr Av 3 & Paseo 140) is 30 blocks south of the town center. Destinations include Buenos Aires (AR$424, 5½ hours) and Mar del Plata (AR$125, two hours). You can buy bus tickets in the town center at **Central de Pasajes** (📞 472480; cnr Av 3 & Paseo 107), saving you a trip to the terminal. You'll have to buy tickets for more local destinations, such as Pinamar (AR$45, 30 minutes), at the station.

During summer only, **Sol** (p145) flies to Buenos Aires.

Local buses into town (AR$6, 15 minutes) leave regularly from a shelter just across Av 3 from the long-distance terminal, or you can grab a taxi.

Mar del Plata

📞 0223 / POP 614,000

Turn on the TV, anywhere in Argentina, on a summer morning: you'll see the sun-drenched shores of Mar del Plata and hear the newscasters' latest reports on the temperatures of air and ocean. 'Mardel' is the classic Argentine beach destination, 400km down the coast from the capital city. It's popular with people from all over the country – a little too popular, in fact. If you end up here on a summer weekend, you'll be guaranteed to say 'Wow, this beach is crowded.' There might be a couple of places where you could get in a few swimming strokes without taking somebody's eye out, but mostly it's shoulder-to-shoulder bodies: not exactly a relaxing getaway.

After spending a few days on its comically packed sands, watching street performers on the beachside Plaza Colón or exploring the wonders of the port, however, you might get the sense of adoration that the country feels for this place. Mar del Plata has historic charm: it used to be a glamorous seaside resort in the 1920s and '30s, a fact you'll notice in the elegant architecture and the antique photos displayed everywhere in town, from hotel lobbies to cafes to postcards.

If you're here during the week, and especially outside of summer, you'll really start to get the appeal of the place. The crowds disperse, hotel prices drop and the place takes on a more relaxed feel. Out-of-season visitors will find that Mardel is a large and interesting city with plenty of cultural attractions, many of them connected by the pedestrian thoroughfares of downtown or the oceanfront promenade that winds along the high cliffs of the city's curving coastline.

History

Europeans were slow to occupy this stretch of the coast, so Mardel was a late bloomer. Not until 1747 did Jesuit missionaries try to evangelize the indigenous people of the southern pampas; the only reminder of their efforts is a chapel replica near Laguna de los Padres.

More than a century later, Portuguese investors established El Puerto de Laguna de los Padres. Beset by economic problems in the 1860s, they sold out to Patricio Peralta Ramos, who founded Mar del Plata proper in 1874. Peralta Ramos helped develop the area as a commercial and industrial center, and later as a beach resort. By the turn of the 20th century, many wealthy *porteño* families owned summer houses, some of which still grace Barrio Los Troncos.

Since the 1960s the 'Pearl of the Atlantic' has lost some of its exclusivity, with the Argentine elite seeking refuge in resorts such as nearby Pinamar or Punta del Este (Uruguay). Still, Mar del Plata remains a thriving Argentine beach town. As a local taxi driver recently explained to us, 'there's enough hotel rooms for everyone, and if it rains, there's a lot to see and do aside from the beach.'

⊙ Sights

For a look at Mar del Plata's golden age, go for a stroll down Avenida Alvear: you'll see some of the city's finest old mansions, some of which now house museums and cultural spaces. About 10 blocks inland, you'll find **Barrio Los Troncos**, a fashionable neighborhood for shopping, dining and bar-hopping.

★ Puerto Mar del Plata   PORT

(www.puertomardelplata.net) Mar del Plata is one of Argentina's most important fishing centers. Its port area, 8km south of the city center, is worth a visit, though public access to the jetty – and its graveyard of ruined ships, half-sunken and rusting in the sun – is now restricted. You can still watch the fishing boats come and go from the **Banquina de Pescadores**, the port's scenic and slightly touristy wharf. Grab some calamari and a beer here while you're at it.

To get to the port from downtown, you have two options. You can take local bus 511 (which stops at various points downtown and along the oceanfront road) all the way to the wharf (AR$6). You'll need a magnetic card to board. A taxi from downtown costs between AR$80 and AR$120. If you're going by taxi, consider arranging your return, as it's not easy to flag a taxi heading the other way. Note that the wharf mentioned here is not to be confused with the **Centro Comercial de Mar del Plata**, a cluster of high-end restaurants located near the entrance to the larger port complex.

★ Torreón del Monje   HISTORIC BUILDING

(☑ 0223-486-4000; www.torreondelmonje.com.ar; cnr Viamonte & Paseo Jesús de Galindez) Grand and castle-like, positioned on a cliff over the ocean, Torreón del Monje is hard to miss –

LITERARY LADY OF LA PLATA

She was 'the most beautiful cow in the pampas' according to French novelist Pierre Drieu, and Jorge Luis Borges called her 'the most Argentine of women.' In the 1920s and 1930s, Victoria Ocampo gathered writers and intellectuals from around the globe to her home, Villa Victoria, creating a formidable literary and artistic salon.

Ocampo never went to university, but her voracious appetite for knowledge and love of literature led her to become Argentina's leading lady of letters. She founded the literary magazine *Sur,* which introduced writers such as Virginia Woolf and TS Eliot to Argentine readers. She was also an inexhaustible traveler and a pioneering feminist, and was loathed for her lack of convention. A ferocious opponent of Peronism, chiefly because of Perón's interference with intellectual freedom, Ocampo was arrested at Villa Victoria at the age of 63. She entertained her fellow inmates by reading aloud and acting out scenes from novels and cinema.

If Victoria is remembered as a lively essayist and great patron of writers, her younger sister, Silvina, was the literary talent, writing both short stories and poetry. Silvina won several literary prizes for her works, and in 1940 married Adolfo Bioy Casares, a famous Argentine writer and friend of Jorge Luis Borges.

Mar del Plata

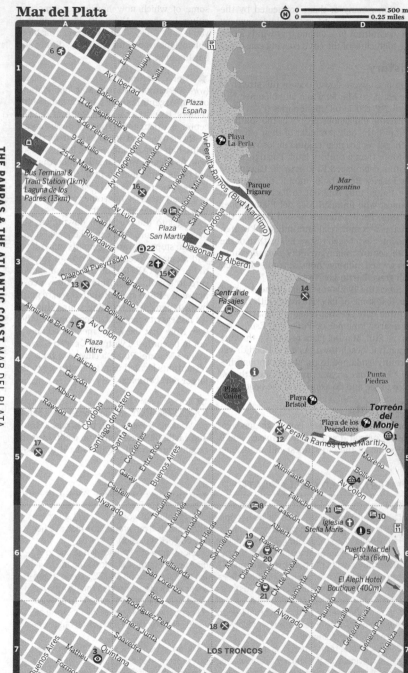

Mar del Plata

THE PAMPAS & THE ATLANTIC COAST MAR DEL PLATA

look for the red domes and the stone footbridge straddling the oceanfront road. This classic landmark is a throwback to Mar del Plata's glamorous heyday. The Argentine businessman Ernestro Tornquist, intent on beautifying the area around his own summer getaway, had the medieval-style lookout tower built in 1904. Stop for the view, and perhaps a coffee break on the terrace.

Though the on-site cafe and restaurant only gets mixed reviews, it's a good place to stop for a drink.

Museo Municipal de Arte Juan Carlos Castagnino
MUSEUM
(☎486-1636; www.mardelplata.gob.ar; Av Colón 1189; admission AR$10; ☺2-8pm Mon & Wed-Fri, 3-8pm Sat & Sun) Built in 1909 as the summer residence of a prominent Argentine family, the turreted Villa Ortiz Basualdo now houses this fine arts museum; its interior exhib-its paintings, photographs and sculptures by Argentine artists.

Centro Cultural Villa Victoria
CULTURAL CENTER
(☎492-0569; www.mardelplata.gob.ar; Matheu 1851; admission AR$20; ☺2-8pm Wed-Mon) Victoria Ocampo (p139), founder of the literary journal *Sur,* hosted literary salons with prominent intellectuals from around the world – Borges, Le Corbusier, and Rabindranath Tagore were among more distinguished guests – here at her summer chalet. It's now a cultural center that features changing art and cultural exhibitions, plus live music, poetry readings and yoga classes.

Catedral de los Santos Pedro y Cecilia
CHURCH
(www.catedralmardelplata.org.ar; Plaza San Martín; ☺8am-8pm) Facing the leafy Plaza San Martín, this neo-Gothic building features gorgeous stained glass, an impressive central chandelier from France, English tiled floors and occasional choral concerts.

Torre Tanque
TOWER
(☎451-4681; Falucho 995; ☺8am-5pm Mon-Fri, 2-5pm holiday weekends) FREE This interesting medieval-style water-storage tower, atop Stella Maris hill, was finished in 1943 and is still functioning. It offers spectacular views over Mar del Plata and further out to sea. Free guided tours (in Spanish) are available at 2:30pm, 3:30pm and 4:30pm.

Aquarium Mar del Plata
AQUARIUM
(☎0223-467-0700; www.aquarium.com.ar; Av Martínez de Hoz 5600; adult/3-10yr AR$299/225; ☺10am-8:30pm daily Jan & Feb, to 7pm daily Dec & Mar, to 6pm Sat & Sun only Apr-Nov) Located 14km south of the center, near the lighthouse, is Mar del Plata's aquarium. Animals on display include penguins, flamingos, crocodiles and lots of fish. There are sea-lion, dolphin and waterskiing shows, along with a cinema. Those concerned with the welfare of sea mammals should be aware that keeping them in enclosed tanks or swimming with them in the wild is considered by some to be disruptive to the behavior of the animals and their habitats.

You can also swim with sharks and other watery creatures and sit on the beach.

🏖 Beaches

Mar del Plata's beaches are mostly safe and swimmable. Downtown faces onto the most central beach, **Playa Bristol**, with its wharf and restaurant; the boardwalk here, next to the casino area, is always packed with activity. The next beach to the north is **Playa La Perla**, favored by a younger crowd and filled with *balnearios* (bathing resorts, or sections of beach with services such as beach chairs and parasols). To the south of Punta Piedras are **Playa Varese** and **Cabo Corrientes**, a pair of small beaches that are protected by small rocky headlands.

South of these beaches, at the more fashionable end of town, lies Playa Grande, also crowded with *balnearios*. About 11km south of the center, just past the port, you'll find the huge **Punta Mogotes** complex – slightly more relaxed and favored by families, who fill the *balnearios* to overflowing in January. This is also the location of **Playa Waikiki**, a popular spot for surfing.

Beyond the lighthouse is a less urbanized area. Though the beaches here are still filled with yet more *balnearios* in the summer, they're a quieter option. And for the adventurous, there's **Playa Escondida**, some 25km south of Mardel, which claims to be Argentina's only legal nude beach. Bus 221 gets you there.

Activities

Mar del Plata and its surrounds offer plenty of opportunities to enjoy outdoor activities and adventure sports.

Biking is a good way to get around town – just remember that the city is hilly! The streets of Los Troncos are relatively calm and pleasant for cycling. Rent bicycles at a classic stand: **Bicicletería Madrid** (0223-494-1932; Yrigoyen 2249; per hr from AR$45; 9am-7pm Mon-Fri, 10am-7pm Sat & Sun) has been in operation on Plaza Mitre for more than six decades.

Surf is best in March or April. **Kikiwai Surf School** (0223-485-0669; www.clubde surfkikiwai.wix.com/kikiwaisurfclub; Av Martínez de Hoz 4100, Playa Kikiwai; 1-day class per person AR$450), run by surf pioneer Daniel Gil, offers surfing classes and rents boards; find it at Waikiki beach (about 11km south of center). You can also rent boards (AR$100/260 per hour/day) and gear and arrange lessons at other surf outfitters around town. Visit www.mardelplata.com/tour/surf.html for more information in English on surf breaks and conditions.

As the sea lions attest, Mar del Plata is one of the best spots for fishing in Argentina. The rocky outcrop at **Cabo Corrientes**, just north of Playa Grande, is a good spot to try, as are the two breakwaters – **Escollera Norte** and **Escollera Sur** – at the port. Freshwater fishing is popular at Laguna de los Padres, while **Mako Team** (493-5338; www.makoteam.com.ar) offers ocean fishing excursions.

The rocky cliffs by the sea and the hills of Sierra de los Padres make for excellent climbing and rappelling. **Acción Directa** (0223-474-4520; www.acciondirecta.com.ar; Av Libertad 3902; 10am-1pm & 5-9pm Mon-Fri, 10am-1pm Sat) runs a school – it also offers mountain biking, canoeing and overnight active camping trips.

Tours

Crucero Anamora BOAT TOUR
(489-0310; www.cruceroanamora.com.ar; adult/child under 10yr AR$220/150) This 30m boat offers harbor tours four times daily in summer and twice daily on weekends in winter from Dársena B at the port – just past the Banquina Pescadores at the Puerto Mar del Plata (p139).

Festivals & Events

The city's **International Film Festival** (www.mardelplatafilmfest.com) takes place in November. Launched in 1950, it's considered South America's most important film festival.

In January Mar del Plata also celebrates **Fiesta Nacional de los Pescadores** (Fisherman's Festival; www.patronespescadores.com.ar), which sees locals cooking up seafood feasts, along with a traditional procession.

Another large celebration is February's **Fiesta Nacional del Mar** (National Sea Festival; www.mardelplata.com/fiesta-nacional-del-mar.html), which includes the election and coronation of a 'Sea Queen.'

Sleeping

Prices start climbing in November and December, peak in January and February, then drop off in March. Reserve ahead in summer. In the off-season some accommodations close their door's.

Mar del Plata's crowded campgrounds are mostly south of town; the tourist office provides information about their facilities.

Che Lagarto Hostel HOSTEL $
(0223-451-3704; www.chelagarto.com; Alberti 1565; dm/d from US$19/65;) This popular branch of the Che Lagarto chain pretty much has it all: friendly staff, a central lo-

MAR CHIQUITA

A humble and windy little gem, the beach village of Mar Chiquita is home to **Albúfera Mar Chiquita** (www.reservamarchiquita.com.ar), a 35km-long lagoon with an impressive range of wildlife. The word *albúfera* comes from the Arabic phrase 'al-buhayra,' or 'the small sea' – which is, of course, also the meaning of the name 'Mar Chiquita.'

The lagoon is a special body of water. Fed by creeks from the Sierras de Tandil and sheltered by a chain of sand dunes, the lagoon alternately drains into the ocean or absorbs seawater, depending on the tides. This creates a unique ecosystem boasting huge biodiversity, and is the only lagoon of its kind in Argentina.

The spot is a paradise for bird-watchers, with over 220 species of birds, 86 of which are migratory, including flamingos. There are also over 55 fish species in the lagoon, making it a popular spot to cast a line into the water. The beach is popular for windsurfing and kiteboarding – or just hanging out for a while.

The **visitors center** (☏ 0223-469-1288; saladeinterpretacion@hotmail.com; cnr Belgrano & Rivera del Sol; ⊙ 9am-8pm Dec-Easter, 9am-4pm Mon-Fri & 10am-6pm Sat & Sun rest of year) is beside the lagoon, a few blocks inland from the beach. Between December and March they can help arrange accommodations – there are several basic *hosterías* in town – and tours of the lagoon. Bring cash, as the closest ATM is 4km away in Mar de Cabo.

Mar Chiquita is 34km north of Mar del Plata. It's easiest to visit in a car, but if you're willing to try the public transport system, **Rápido del Sud** (☏ 0223-494-2507; www.el-rapido.com.ar) runs frequent buses that can drop you at the highway roundabout 2.5km outside Mar Chiquita (AR$30, 45 minutes). For transport into town, your best bet is a taxi or local bus 221 from Mar del Plata (AR$8 to AR$12, 1½ hours, every two hours in summer, every four hours the rest of the year); it goes all the way to the beach and the lagoon's edge.

THE PAMPAS & THE ATLANTIC COAST MAR DEL PLATA

cation close to Mardel's best nightlife and shopping, and squeaky clean (fan-cooled) private rooms and dorms. There's also a guest kitchen and a pleasant living area and cocktail bar. There's free wi-fi in the public areas.

★ **Villa Nuccia** GUESTHOUSE $$
(☏ 0223-451-6593; www.villanuccia.com.ar; Almirante Brown 1134; d from US$134; ❋@☞≋) This beautiful guesthouse offers a small range of elegant and spacious rooms. Some are in a renovated house, others are in a modern annex; all are individually decorated. There's a rear garden with a swimming pool and Jacuzzi, and guests rave about the breakfast and afternoon tea, both featuring homemade cakes.

Hotel 15 de Mayo HOTEL $$
(☏ 0223-495-1388; www.hotel15demayo.com; Mitre 1457; s/d from US$68/98; ❋☞) Conveniently located between Plaza San Martín and La Perla beach, this modern hotel is great value for its guest rooms (on the small side, but spotless, with flat-screen TVs), professional service, breakfast buffet and fast wi-fi.

Hotel Sirenuse HOTEL $$
(☏ 0223-451-9580; www.hotelsirenuse.com.ar; Mendoza 2240; d from US$82; ❋@☞) Friendly, family-run and wonderfully cozy, this small hotel on Stella Maris hill, just a few blocks from Playa Varese, is one of Mardel's best-value choices. With dark wood furnishings and a hearty breakfast, the place feels more like a mountain lodge than a beach getaway. Travelers rave about the kind owners; you'll need to book well ahead.

El Aleph Hotel Boutique GUESTHOUSE $$$
(☏ 451-4380; www.elalephmdq.com.ar; LN Alem 2542; d from US$155; ❋@☞≋) Located on a residential street a couple of blocks south of Playa Varese, this upscale guesthouse considers itself Mar del Plata's first boutique hotel. El Aleph features decorated rooms set around a grassy yard with small pool. Amenities include spacious bathrooms, plasma TVs, afternoon tea and a great breakfast buffet. The atmosphere is exclusive but relaxed.

✕ Eating

Mar del Plata's numerous restaurants, pizzerias and snack bars often struggle to keep up with impatient crowds between December and March; there are always long lines.

For fresh seafood, head south of town to the port. At the entrance, just off the busy oceanfront road, you'll see a large cluster of seafood restaurants surrounding a parking lot. This area is known as the **Centro Comercial del Puerto**.

And for a glimpse at one of the city's more stylish neighborhoods, head inland along Avenida Alvear to **Barrio Los Troncos**. The upscale barrio is filled with adorable cafes, bars and restaurants.

La Fonte D'Oro
CAFE $

(cnr Córdoba & San Martín; snacks AR$15-45; ☺8am-late) This stylish cafe has several locations in town; one of the nicest is on the pedestrian promenade of San Martín, near the cathedral. Have a quick *cortado* at the curving coffee bar, or grab an outdoor table and order a freshly baked pastry or a slice of chocolate cake while you watch the world go by.

Montecatini
ARGENTINE $

(cnr La Rioja & 25 de Mayo; mains AR$52-120; ☺noon-3pm & 8pm-midnight; ☷) For solid, good-value dishes, make like the locals and head to this large, modern and popular restaurant – one of four branches in town. There's something for everyone on the menu (meat, fish, pasta, *milanesas,* sandwiches) and portions are generous. The weekday lunch special (AR$110, including dessert and a drink) is a steal. Good for families and large groups.

El Bodegón
ARGENTINE $

(La Rioja 2068; mains AR$75-150) Thanks to a recent change in ownership, there's a youthful crowd and free-flowing *cerveza* at this stylish pub and *parrilla*. On weekdays, there are great-value set menus at both lunch and dinner (AR$120 to AR$150). It's conveniently located in the center, a quick walk from either Plaza Mitre or Plaza San Martin.

★Sur
SEAFOOD $$

(☑0223-493-6260; Alvarado 2763; mains AR$95-250; ☺8pm-midnight) The hype around Sur creates high expectations: many locals consider it the best seafood restaurant in town. Brick walls hung with nautical-themed prints form a cozy backdrop; specials all revolve around fresh fish and shellfish. There's also an extensive wine list and famously delicious desserts.

Tisiano
ITALIAN $$

(☑486-3473; San Lorenzo 1332; mains AR$90-160; ☺8pm-late Mon-Fri, noon-3pm & 8pm-late Sat

& Sun) Tucked into a back patio off a busy street in trendy Barrio Los Troncos, Tisiano is one of the locals' top picks for fresh pasta. Dishes prepared with seafood, like shrimp linguine, are particularly good, as is the range of gourmet salads. After dinner, wander around the neighborhood; it's filled with bars and pubs.

Taberna Baska
SPANISH $$

(☑480-0209; www.tabernabaska.wix.com/mardel plata; 12 de Octubre 3301; mains AR$85-210; ☺noon-3pm Tue-Sun, 8:30pm-midnight Tue-Sat) A few blocks inland from the port, this renowned Basque restaurant is a local classic. Checkered tablecloths and dignified waiters give it an old-school atmosphere that complements traditional dishes like garlic shrimp, mixed seafood stews, paella, *pulpo* (octopus), *bacalao* (cod) and fish in seven different sauces.

La Marina
SEAFOOD $$

(☑489-9216; 12 de Octubre 3147; mains AR$75-180; ☺noon-4pm & 8pm-midnight Thu-Mon, noon-4pm Tue) You won't find seafood any fresher or more affordable than at this down-to-earth place a few blocks inland from the entrance to the port. In business since 1957, its specialties range from crispy *rabas* (fried squid rings) to the delicious *cazuela especial La Marina,* a seafood stew packed with fish, shrimp, squid and mussels simmered in white wine, cream and saffron.

Alito
ARGENTINE $$

(☑492-1741; www.alitomdp.com.ar; Blvd Marítimo, cnr Las Heras & La Costa; mains AR$83-199; ☺noon-3:30pm & 7:30pm-midnight; ☷) With indoor and outdoor seating across from the waterfront near Plaza Colón, Alito is popular for its central location, wide-ranging menu and well-priced daily specials. Salads, grilled fish, seafood pastas, wok-style stir-fries and steaks are all popular options; there's also a full wine list and a special list of *postres helados* (ice-cream desserts.) Reserve online.

Espigón de Pescadores
SEAFOOD $$

(☑493-1713; www.espigondepescadores.com.ar; Blvd Marítimo & Av Luro; mains AR$55-168; ☺noon-3pm & 8pm-midnight) Located out on the fishing pier, this seafood restaurant offers great water views – especially from its 2nd floor (open in summer only). The menu runs through typical Mardel offerings of meat, pasta and seafood, but the food is nothing remarkable; you're here for the experience of dining on the pier.

🍷 Drinking & Nightlife

The following venues are located in chic Barrio Los Troncos and the area along Irigoyen and LN Alem, between Almafuerte and Rodríguez Peña, a section of the city that's thick with cocktail bars and nightlife. Consider these recommendations as just a place to begin: the best thing to do is wander around the neighborhood for yourself and see what appeals.

★ Almacén Estación Central   BAR

(cnr Alsina & Garay; ⊙ 7pm-late) This hip bar in a quaint and thoughtfully restored antique building – an old corner store where the former president of Argentina, Marcelo Torcuato de Alvear, reportedly did his shopping – gets packed with locals every night. Gourmet pub food and frequent happy hour deals, even on weekends, only add to the appeal.

Antares   BAR

(Olavarría 2724; ⊙ 7pm-4am) The cool microbrewery mini-chain has several locations in Mar del Plata; this one, in Barrio Los Troncos is arguably the most popular. Come for a variety of craft beers on tap, plus excellent pub food and a lively local crowd. Come early if you want to actually have a conversation with someone – Antares gets louder as the night rolls on. There's also a tasting room, known as **Bar de la Fábrica** (12 de Octubre 7749) at the factory itself.

La Bodeguita del Medio   BAR

(Castelli 1252; ⊙ 6pm-4am) Come for the famously delicious mojitos, the Cuban-inspired food and the live music at this atmospheric and art-filled cocktail bar, named after one of Hemingway's favorite haunts in Havana.

🛍 Shopping

Forgot your swimsuit? Calle Güemes, in Barrio Los Troncos, is lined with upscale shops and boutiques, while downtown has more mainstream chains and department stores.

Diagonal de los Artesanos   CRAFTS, MARKET

(Plaza San Martín; ⊙ 6pm-1am mid-Dec–late Feb, 3-8pm Sat & Sun Mar-Nov) This long-running craft fair features nearly 200 vendors: they set up their stalls on Plaza San Martín and along Diagonal Pueyrredon to sell everything from *mate* gourds and knives to sweaters and silverwork. The fair happens daily (and starts in the evening) during the summer; outside the peak season, it only runs on Saturday and Sunday.

Mercado de Pulgas   MARKET

(Plaza Rocha; ⊙ 11am-7pm Thu-Sun mid-Dec–late Feb, 11am-6pm Sat & Sun Mar-Nov) This relaxed flea market, selling everything including the kitchen sink, is at 20 de Septiembre between San Martín and Av Luro, seven blocks northwest of Plaza San Martín.

ℹ Information

There are several money exchanges and *locutorios* (internet cafes) along San Martín and Rivadavia. There are also several branches of the city's official tourist information office around town.

Tourist Office (📞 495-1777; www.turismo mardelplata.gov.ar; Blvd Marítimo 2270; ⊙ 10am-8pm Mar-Dec, to 10pm Jan & Feb) Centrally located and exceptionally helpful.

ℹ Getting There & Away

AIR

From Mardel's Ástor Piazzolla International Airport, 10km north of town, **Aerolíneas Argentinas** (📞 496-0101; www.aerolineas.com.ar; Moreno 2442; ⊙ 10am-6pm Mon-Fri) and **Sol** (www.sol.com.ar) have several daily flights to Buenos Aires.

BUS

Mar del Plata's sparkling bus terminal is next to its train station, about 2km northwest of the beach. To reach the center, cross Av Luro in front of the terminal and take local bus 511, 512 or 513 heading southeast; taxis to downtown cost around AR$35.

In the city center, the ticket agency **Central de Pasajes** (📞 493-7843; cnr San Martín & Corrientes; ⊙ 10am-8pm) sells long-distance bus tickets for most companies, saving you a trip to the terminal.

Buses from Mar del Plata

DESTINATION	COST (AR$)	TIME (HR)
Bahía Blanca	505	8
Bariloche	1504	19
Buenos Aires	394-520	5½
Córdoba	1096-1248	16-18
Mendoza	1215-1550	18-21
Necochea	139	2¼
Pinamar	152	2½
Puerto Madryn	1035	16
Tandil	201	4
Villa Gesell	138	1½

WORTH A TRIP

MIRAMAR

If you've read *The Motorcycle Diaries*, or saw the film based on Ernesto 'Che' Guevara's memoir, you might remember Miramar. The beach resort was the first stop that the future revolutionary and his traveling companion, Alberto Granado, made on their epic trip around South America – Guevara's girlfriend, Chichina, was vacationing here with her family at the time.

Today, it's still a family-friendly destination with a long, wide beach and gentle waves. Compared to Mar del Plata, 45km to the north, Miramar is fairly low-key, but like any other Argentine resort it does get crowded in summer.

The **tourist office** (☑ 02291-420190; www.miramar.tur.ar; cnr Calle 21 & Costanera; ☉ 8am-9pm), located at the beach, has details about various activities around town, including horseback riding, golfing and fishing. Miramar is known for its surf, more easily accessible at the north end of town where there are a few surf schools. For accommodations, try **Hotel Danieli** (☑ 02291-432366; www.hoteldanielimiramar.com.ar; Calle 24, No 1114; d from US$120; ☜) or one of the other basic but comfortable hotels around the beach and pedestrian zone.

From Mar del Plata, buses (AR$22, one hour) run regularly to Miramar's bus terminal at Av 40 and Calle 15, within six blocks of the center.

Travelers looking for downright isolation can head to **Mar del Sud**, a small town 16km south of Miramar. It's known for its rustic atmosphere, black-rock beach and fishing waters, and claims some hotel ruins as a main tourist attraction. There are no tall buildings here and much fewer services than its neighbor, so if you're looking to get away from the crowds this should be your stop.

TRAIN

The **train station** (☑ 475-6076; www.sofse.gob.ar; Av Luro 4700 at Italia; ☉ 6am-midnight) is adjacent to the bus terminal, 2km from the beach. Trains with *primera* (AR$200) and Pullman (AR$240) class service run between Mar del Plata and Buenos Aires' Constitución station (six hours) three times weekly (on Monday, Wednesday, and Friday) in each direction. The fancier *Marplatense* service (AR$250, 5¾ hours) runs only once weekly, leaving Buenos Aires on Thursday and returning from Mar del Plata on Saturday. Visit www.ferrobaires.gba.gov.ar for more information, and be sure to reserve tickets well ahead in summer.

ⓘ Getting Around

The **airport** (☑ 478-0744) is 10km north of the city. Take bus 542, marked 'aeropuerto' (AR$4.80, 30 minutes) from the corner of Blvd Marítimo and Belgrano. Taxis cost from around AR$100, depending on where you're going.

Despite Mar del Plata's sprawl, frequent buses reach just about every place in town. However, most buses (including the airport bus) require *tarjetas de aproximación* (magnetic cards) that must be bought ahead of time at *kiosco* (newsstands) and charged up.

The webpage www.cualbondi.com.ar/mar-del-plata provides useful maps of all local bus routes. The tourist office can also help with transportation details.

Car rentals are available downtown at **Alamo** (☑ 495-2935; Córdoba 2270).

Necochea

☑ 02262 / POP 85,000

Totally pumping in summer and near dead in winter, Necochea has a beach-town feel and remains relatively undisturbed by the high-rises that keep springing up. It's not the most charming of the towns along Argentina's central Atlantic coast, but with such a long and wide beach, it's fairly certain that you'll find a spot to lay your towel – and Necochea has some of the best-value lodging on the coast.

⦿ Sights & Activities

The dense pine woods of **Parque Miguel Lillo**, a large greenbelt along the beach, are popular for cycling, horseback riding, walking and picnicking. Horses and bikes can be rented inside the park.

The Río Quequén Grande, rich in rainbow trout and mackerel, also allows for easy rafting and kayaking, particularly around the falls at **Saltos del Quequén**. Local outfitters organize both river and ocean kayak trips in summertime; just take a stroll downtown to see what's on.

At the village of **Quequén** at the river's mouth, a lighthouse and several stranded shipwrecks offer good opportunities for exploration and photography below sculpted cliffs.

With some of the best waves along the Atlantic coast, Necochea is a hit with surfers; it also attracts windsurfers year-round.

🛌 Sleeping

Note that some accommodations are only open December to March.

Dyd Hotel
HOTEL $

(📞 425-560; www.dydnecochea.com.ar; Calle 77, No 314; s/d from US$54/63; 📶) Simple but colorfully decorated, this friendly hotel has small but well-equipped rooms. The best part is the location, two long blocks from the beach and a few blocks north of the main plaza – it's relatively quiet here in high season. Note that rooms are fan-cooled, not air-conditioned.

Hostería del Bosque
HOTEL $$

(📞 420002; www.hosteria-delbosque.com.ar; Calle 89, No 350; d/tr from US$120/187; 🅿️@📶) Four blocks in from the beach, this homey yet elegant family-run *hostería* is by far the most atmospheric place to stay in town. Rooms are large and comfortable, and some have views of Parque Miguel Lillo across the street. There's a lovely garden and a good buffet breakfast; it's popular, so reserve ahead.

Hotel Mirasol
HOTEL $$

(📞 525158; www.mirasolhotel.com.ar; Calle 4bis, No 4133; s/d from US$66/78; 🅿️📶) Enjoying a prime location on Plaza San Martín, half a block from the pedestrian zone and two blocks from the beach, this friendly place offers comfortable budget rooms year-round. Best value are the three upstairs units with air-con and windows overlooking the square.

🍴 Eating & Drinking

There are several casual dining options around Plaza San Martín. Many of the *balnearios* have eateries where you can grab a bite beachside. In low season many restaurants are only open on weekends.

Ernnan's
CAFE $

(📞 521427; Calle 83, No 284; mains AR$45-90; 🕗8am-late; 📶) Sitting on the edge of Necochea's main square, this high-ceilinged cafe with sidewalk seating and free wi-fi makes a great place for a snack any time of day, serving everything from *medialunas* (croissants) and gourmet sandwiches to pizza and paella.

Taberna Española
SPANISH $$

(📞 520-539; cnr Calles 83 & 8; mains AR$85-200; 🕗noon-3pm & 8pm-midnight) Head to this vintage corner restaurant for fine seafood, Spanish-style. Deals include the *plato del día* (daily special), served with coffee or dessert for AR$69.

Antares
BAR

(📞 421976; www.cervezaantares.com; Calle 4, No 4266; 🕗7pm-late Wed-Sun Apr-Nov, daily Dec-Mar) One block in from the beach, this is the Necochea branch of the popular bar-restaurant chain. Along with several craft-style beers, there's a good selection of pub-style food (mains AR$80 to AR$125). Look for several other bars nearby, on Calle 87 between Calles 4 and 6.

ℹ️ Information

Tourist Office (📞 438333; www.necochea.tur.ar; cnr Avs 2 & 79; 🕗8am-9pm Dec-Mar, 10am-4pm Apr-Nov) On the beach.

ℹ️ Getting There & Away

The **bus terminal** (Av 58, btw Calle 47 & Av 45) is 3.5km from the beach; taxis to the center cost AR$30 to AR$35, or take a local bus marked 'playa.' Destinations include Buenos Aires (AR$557, 7½ hours), Mar del Plata (AR$139, two hours) and Tandil (AR$146, three hours).

Bahía Blanca

📞 0291 / POP 291,000

Grandiose buildings, an attractive plaza and boulevards lined with shade trees lend oft-overlooked Bahía Blanca the feel of a cosmopolitan city in miniature. It is useful as a resting point during overland trips from Buenos Aires to Patagonia, but it's not entirely without interest.

The hordes of sailors who dock here, at what is now South America's largest naval base, attest to Bahía Blanca's militaristic beginnings. In an early effort to establish military control on the periphery of the pampas, Colonel Ramón Estomba situated the pompously named Fortaleza Protectora Argentina at the natural harbor of Bahía Blanca in 1828.

ℹ️ GETTING TO THE PORT

Unless you have a rental car, you have two options for getting to Ingeniero White (the port neighborhood) from downtown Bahía Blanca. Option one is to take bus 500 (30 to 40 minutes) from the south side of Plaza Rivadavia. Note that cash is not allowed for payment: you'll need to purchase a bus card from a nearby kiosk, which can be a challenge when the shops close in the afternoon. Option two is to take a 20-minute taxi ride (AR$150 one-way). Coming back, there are also taxis available, parked at the stand near Museo del Puerto.

👁️ Sights

Contrary to popular expectation, the city center is not close to the port itself – to get to the port neighborhood, known as Ingeniero White, you'll need to take a taxi ride, or bus trip from Plaza Rivadavia. To get a good sense of Bahía Blanca, you'll want to see both sections.

Downtown, attractions are mostly of the architectural variety, thanks to the wave of construction by European immigrants in the early 20th century. Go for a stroll past the city's neoclassical performing arts center, **Teatro Municipal** (Alsina 425), and the **Museo de Arte Contemporáneo** (☑459-4006; Sarmiento 450; ⊙9am-8pm Tue-Fri, 4-8pm Sat & Sun) FREE, showcasing local and national artists.

Near the port, you can't get very close to the water – it's still very much in commercial use – but you can get a taste of the port's colorful history at the pair of museums. Bring your camera: full of rustic metal houses, abandoned trains and rusted old ship hulls, Ingeniero White is a photographer's delight.

⭐ Museo Taller
Ferrowhite   HISTORIC BUILDING
(☑457-0335; www.ferrowhite.bahiablanca.gov.ar; Juan B Justo 3883; admission by donation; ⊙9am-noon Mon-Fri, 4-8pm Sat & Sun Jun-Aug & Dec-Feb, 3-7pm Sep-Nov & Mar-May,) Grandiose and ghostly, Ferrowhite is the kind of landmark you see from far away and think 'what in the world is that?' The castle-like power plant, built by Italians in the 1930s, sits beside massive grain elevators on the edge of the bay. Now it holds a small museum and cafe. But half the fun is just walking around outside the abandoned structure with its elegant architecture and shattered windows: paranormal activity has been reported here many times over.

Museo del Puerto   MUSEUM
(☑0291-457-3006; www.museodelpuerto.blogspot.com; cnr Guillermo Torres & Cárrega; donation requested; ⊙9am-noon Mon-Fri, 4-8pm Sat & Sun) Housed in a colorfully painted former customs building, this small but engaging museum is a tribute to the region's immigrants. The rooms include archives and photographs, and mock-ups of an old *peluquería* (barber shop) and bar. The historical collection starts in the yard outside, where a wooden fishing boat and other antique artifacts hearken back to the port's intriguing past.

🛏️ Sleeping

The most pleasant place to stay is around central Plaza Rivadavia, where you'll also find a range of restaurants and cafes.

⭐ Hotel Muñiz   HOTEL $$
(☑0291-456-0060; www.hotelmuniz.com.ar; O'Higgins 23; s/d from US$48/73; ❄@🛜) A downtown landmark, the Muñiz is located in a beautiful old building. Note the vintage charm on the lobby level: black-and-white tiled floors, polished woodwork, an antique phone booth. Upstairs, four levels of guest rooms are linked by long hallways. It's a great (and affordable) choice only steps away from the central plaza.

Apart Hotel Patagonia Sur   HOTEL $$
(☑0291-455-2110; www.apartpatagoniasur.com.ar; Italia 64; s/d from US$72/85; 🛜♿) A popular pick for families and budget travelers, this friendly aparthotel has dated but perfectly functional apartment-style rooms with kitchenettes. An added bonus: the included continental breakfast features fresh fruits and a surprising variety of homemade cakes and pastries. It's a short walk south of the plaza, near the intersection of O'Higgins and Italia.

🍴 Eating

If you find yourself in Ingeniero White at night, look for the trio of corrugated metal buildings on the plaza near the Museo del Puerto. After dark they open as food stands selling sandwiches and beer to a local crowd.

⭐**El Mundo de la Parrilla**   PARRILLA **$$**
(Av Colón 379; mains AR$60-150; ⊘8pm-late Mon,
noon-3pm & 8pm-late Tue-Sun) Locals agree that
this busy and casually elegant *parrilla* is
one of the best dining options in town. In
addition to gourmet empanadas, succulent
lechón (roasted suckling pig) and practically
every cut of steak imaginable, the restau-
rant offers 20 varieties of salads and a range
of excellent and traditionally Argentinian
desserts.

Gambrinus   ARGENTINE **$$**
(www.gambrinus1890.com; Arribeños 174; mains
AR$55-130; ⊘noon-3pm & 8pm-1am) This tradi-
tional restaurant, located in a lovely corner
building on a side street a few blocks south
of the main plaza, dates from the 19th century. The menu features Spanish- and Italian-
inspired Argentinian classics. There's a good
wine list and a number of beers on tap; the
vivacious local crowd and walls plastered
with vintage ads contribute to the welcoming atmosphere.

Bamboo   BUFFET **$$**
(Chiclana 298; buffet lunch/dinner AR$150/165,
half-price for children; ⊘noon-3pm & 8:30pm-
midnight) This *tenedor libre* (all-you-can-eat
restaurant), efficiently run by a Chinese
family, is a good choice if you're famished
after a marathon bus ride. Choose from a
range of Asian-inspired dishes and Argen-
tinian classics, including a wide array of
grilled meats.

ℹ️ **Information**

Tourist Kiosk (☎0291-459-4000; www.
turismo.bahiablanca.gov.ar; Alsina 65, Munici-
palidad de Bahía Blanca; ⊘9am-6pm Mon-Fri,
9:30am-1pm & 2:30-6pm Sat) The bus terminal
also has a tourist office.

ℹ️ **Getting There & Away**

AIR
Aerolíneas Argentinas (☎0291-456-0561;
www.aerolineas.com.ar; San Martín 298;
⊘10am-6pm Mon-Fri) and **LAN** (☎0810-999-

9526; www.lan.com; Chiclana 344; ⊘9am-6pm
Mon-Fri) offer flights from Bahía Blanca's
airport, 15km east of town (AR$180 by taxi;
there are no buses).

BUS
Bahía Blanca's **bus terminal** (Brown 1700) is
about 2km southeast of Plaza Rivadavia. Taxis to
the city center cost around AR$50; local buses
514 and 517 run to the bus station from Plaza
Rivadavia, but you'll have to buy a magnetic
card at a newsstand to use them (and there's no
kiosco selling them at the terminal).

There are several businesses – including
kioscos and *locutorios* (private telephone offic-
es) – around the south end of Plaza Rivadavia
that sell bus tickets, saving you a trip to the bus
terminal to do so. These businesses sell different
bus company's tickets, so ask around if you want
a particular schedule, company or price.

Travelers to Sierra de la Ventana have two
options: **Condor Estrella** (p129) runs two
daily buses (AR$110, 2½ hours) and **Norte
Bus** (p132) operates a door-to-door shuttle
(AR$120, one hour) with two or three departures
per day. Call ahead to reserve a spot.

Buses from Bahía Blanca

DESTINATION	COST (AR$)	TIME (HR)
Bariloche	1031-1175	12-14
Buenos Aires	658-750	9
Córdoba	915-1075	13-15
Mar del Plata	505	7
Mendoza	863-1166	15-17
Neuquén	551-629	7½
Sierra de la Ventana	110-120	2½
Trelew	750-868	10-12

TRAIN
Ferrobaires (www.ferrobaires.gba.gov.ar) runs
trains from the **Estación Ferrocarril Roca**
(☎0291-452-9196; Cerri 750) to Buenos Aires'
Constitución station several days of the week
(AR$115 to AR$205, 14 hours). Check the web-
site for more details on routes and fare options,
and to make reservations.

Iguazú Falls & the Northeast

Best Parks & Reserves

➡ Parque Nacional Iguazú (p203)

➡ Reserva Provincial Esteros del Iberá (p177)

➡ Parque Nacional El Palmar (p185)

➡ Bañado la Estrella (p210)

Best Places to Stay

➡ La Alondra (p173)

➡ Rancho de los Esteros (p179)

➡ Boutique Hotel de la Fonte (p200)

➡ Casa de China (p176)

Why Go?

Northeast Argentina is defined by water. Muscular rivers roll through plains that they flood at will, while fragile wetlands support myriad birdlife, snapping caimans and cuddly capybaras. The peaceful Río Iguazú, meandering through jungle between Brazil and Argentina, dissolves in fury and power in the planet's most awe-inspiring waterfalls.

The river then flows into the Paraná, one of the world's mightiest watercourses, which surges southward, eventually forming the Río de la Plata near Buenos Aires. Along it are some of the country's most interesting cities: elegant Corrientes, colonial Santa Fe and booming Rosario, as well as Posadas, gateway to the ruined splendor of the Jesuit missions.

Dotted throughout are excellent parks that represent the region's biological diversity. The Esteros del Iberá harbor a particularly astonishing richness of wildlife.

When to Go
Puerto Iguazú

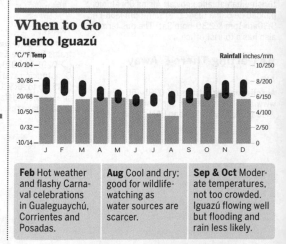

Feb Hot weather and flashy Carnaval celebrations in Gualeguaychú, Corrientes and Posadas.

Aug Cool and dry; good for wildlife-watching as water sources are scarcer.

Sep & Oct Moderate temperatures, not too crowded. Iguazú flowing well but flooding and rain less likely.

ALONG THE RÍO PARANÁ

The mighty Paraná, the continent's second-longest river at 4000km, dominates the geography of Northeast Argentina. The cities along it have their town centers a sensible distance above the shorelines of this flood-prone monster, but have a *costanera* (riverbank) that's the focus of much social life. The river is still important for trade, and large oceangoing vessels ply it to and beyond Rosario, the region's top urban destination.

The Paraná is the demesne of enormous river fish – surubí, dorado and pacú among others – that attract sports fishers from around the world. Their distinctive flavors enliven the menus of the region's restaurants; make sure you try them.

Rosario

📍0341 / POP 1.19 MILLION

Birthplace of both the Argentine flag and Che Guevara, Rosario is still an important river port but has done a great job of regenerating its center. The derelict buildings of the long *costanera* (riverbank) have been converted into galleries, restaurants and skate parks, and river beaches and islands buzz with life in summer. The center – a curious mishmash of stunning early-20th-century buildings overshadowed by ugly apartments – has a comfortable, lived-in feel, and the down-to-earth *rosarinos* (people from Rosario) are a delight. All are very proud of Rosario-born-and-bred Lionel Messi, soccer's number-one player.

History

Rosario's first European inhabitants settled here around 1720. After independence Rosario quickly superseded Santa Fe as the province's economic powerhouse, though, to the irritation of *rosarinos*, the provincial capital retained political primacy.

Rosario was a port of entry for European agricultural colonists and from 1869 to 1914 its population grew nearly tenfold, though a decline of economic and shipping activity during the 1960s hit hard.

Nationalistic Argentines cherish Rosario, home to Cuna de la Bandera (Cradle of the Flag), a monument to the nation's flag.

👁 Sights

Though you can't enter, you may want to check out the apartment building at **Entre Ríos 480** (Entre Ríos 480), where the newborn Ernesto 'Che' Guevara had his first home.

★Costanera   WATERFRONT

Rosario's most attractive feature is its waterfront, where what was once derelict warehouses and train tracks has been reclaimed for the fun of the people. It stretches some 15km from its southern end at Parque Urquiza to the city's northern edge, just short of the suspension bridge crossing into Entre Ríos province. It's an appealing place to wander and watch what's going on, from the plentiful birdlife and impromptu *fútbol* games to massive cargo ships surging past on the river.

➡ Costanera Sur

The grassy zone below downtown includes plenty of space for jogging and courting, as well as the **Estación Fluvial** (La Fluvial; 📞0341-447-3838; www.estacionfluvial.com; ⊗noon-5pm Mar-Oct, 10am-6pm Nov-Feb) building, offering boat trips and eating and drinking options. Heading further north, you pass various cultural venues before reaching **Parque de España** (Paraná riverbank) and its mausoleum-like edifice. Beyond here is a zone of bars and restaurants that gets lively at weekends, and then the city's contemporary art museum.

➡ Costanera Norte

In summer this strip beginning 5km north of downtown attracts crowds for its beaches. The mediocre public beach of Rambla Catalunya is backed by a promenade and bar-restaurants; beyond, the best beach is **Balneario La Florida** (admission AR$25; ⊗9am-8pm Oct-Apr), with services and a safe bathing area. Picturesque stalls behind it sell river fish. The summer-only 'Linea de la Costa' bus heads here from Rioja/Roca. Otherwise take bus 102N/103N/143N and walk a few blocks east from Blvd Rondeau.

★Monumento Nacional a La Bandera   MONUMENT

(www.monumentoalabandera.gob.ar; Santa Fe 581; elevator AR$10; ⊗9am-6pm Tue-Sun, 2-6pm Mon) Manuel Belgrano, who designed the Argentine flag, rests in a crypt beneath this colossal stone obelisk built where the blue-and-white stripes were first raised. If rampant nationalism isn't your thing, it's nevertheless worth taking the elevator to the top for great views over the waterfront, Paraná and islands. The attractive colonnade houses an eternal flame commemorating those who died for the fatherland.

★Paraná Delta   ISLAND

Rosario sits on the banks of the Río Paraná upper delta, a 60km-wide area of mostly

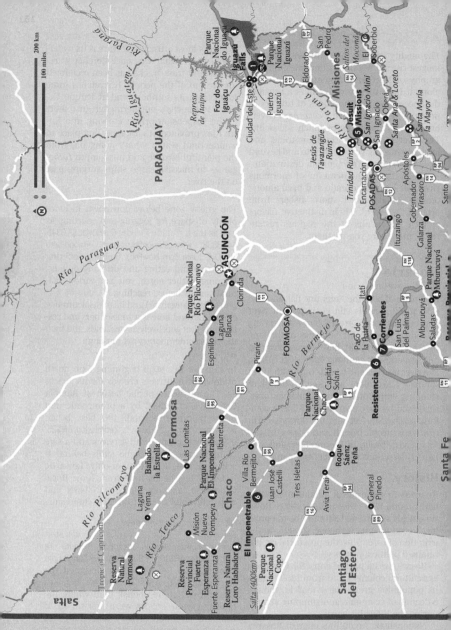

Iguazú Falls & the Northeast Highlights

1 Dropping your jaw in stunned amazement at the beauty and power of the **Iguazú Falls** (p196).

2 Getting personal with the mighty Paraná in livable, lovable **Rosario** (p151).

3 Cooing at the cute capybaras of the **Reserva Provincial Esteros del Iberá** (p177).

4 Munching delicious freshwater fish by the Río Uruguay in pretty **Colón** (p183).

5 Pondering a unique experiment in humanity at the ruined **Jesuit missions** (p192).

6 Admiring the sculptures

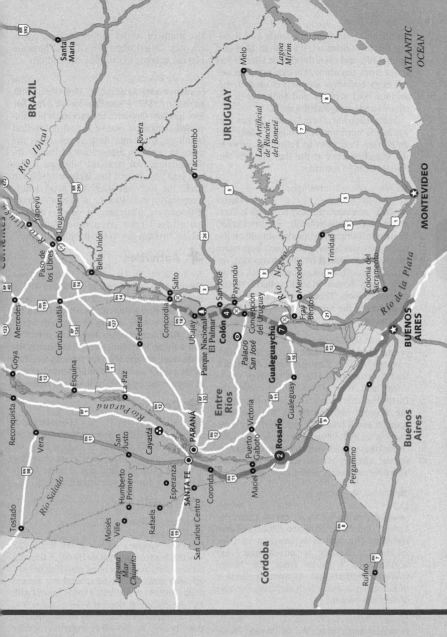

in **Resistencia** (p205) then hitting **'El Impenetrable'** (p209) in the Chaco, a bastion of traditional indigenous culture.

7 Living it up at one of the region's classic Carnaval celebrations in **Gualeguaychú** (p183) or **Corrientes** (p173).

uninhabited, subtropical islands and winding *riachos* (streams). It's rich in bird and animal life, and even the closest islands feel miles from anywhere, though you can see the city's buildings looming close at hand. Various boat services and tours reach the islands and/or explore the delta.

From Estación Fluvial (p151), boats run weekends from mid-September to May and daily from December to February across to the island beaches at the Banquito de San Andrés (AR$85 return).

Museo de Arte Contemporáneo de Rosario
GALLERY

(MACRO; www.macromuseo.org.ar; Av de la Costa at Blvd Oroño; admission AR$10; ⊙2-8pm Thu-Tue) Housed in a brightly painted grain silo on the waterfront, this is part of Rosario's impressive riverbank renewal. It features temporary exhibitions, mostly by young local artists, of varying quality, housed in small galleries spread over eight floors. There's a good view of river islands from the *mirador* (viewpoint) at the top and an attractive cafe-bar by the river.

Museo de la Memoria
MUSEUM

(www.museodelamemoria.gob.ar; Córdoba 2019; admission AR$10; ⊙10am-6pm Tue-Fri, 4-7pm Sat & Sun) A former army HQ, not far from where police held, tortured and killed during the Dirty War, this museum seeks to remember the violence and victims. If you can read Spanish, you'll find it's a small but very moving display, with witness descriptions, photos of the 'disappeared' and an attempt to look at the wider history of man's inhumanity to man. There are temporary exhibitions upstairs.

★ Museo Municipal de Bellas Artes
GALLERY

(www.museocastagnino.org.ar; cnr Av Carlos Pellegrini & Blvd Oroño; admission AR$10; ⊙2-8pm Wed-Mon) This gallery is worth a visit for its inventive displays of contemporary and 20th-century artworks from the Macro (p154) collection, and its small collection of European works, which contains a couple of very fine pieces.

Museo Histórico Provincial
MUSEUM

(www.museomarc.gob.ar; Av del Museo, Parque Independencia; admission AR$10; ⊙9am-6pm Tue-Fri, 2-7pm Sat & Sun, 3-8pm Sat & Sun Dec-Mar) The well-presented collection features plenty of post-independence exhibits plus excellent displays on indigenous cultures from all over Latin America. Particularly interesting is the collection of baroque religious art from

the southern Andes. Information in Spanish only. Closed when Newell's Old Boys are playing at home in the adjacent stadium.

Museo de la Ciudad
MUSEUM

(www.museodelaciudad.gob.ar; Blvd Oroño 2300; admission AR$10; ⊙9am-3pm Tue-Fri, 2-7pm Sat, 9am-1pm Sun) Opposite the racetrack in a tin-roofed bungalow, one of Rosario's loveliest buildings, this enthusiastic museum is the place to begin an exploration of Parque Independencia. An excellent bilingual leaflet will lead you around this large, centenarian park; the museum itself has good-quality temporary exhibitions, a reconstructed 19th-century pharmacy, a cute exhibition space in a former greenhouse, and an involved, bring-it-out-to-the-people attitude.

🏃 Activities

Jardín de los Niños
AMUSEMENT PARK

(Parque de la Independencia; admission AR$10; ⊙2-7pm Fri-Sun) This former zoo has been converted into a marvelous activity park for kids, with a wide variety of innovative puzzles, climbing frames, hands-on activities and a flying machine. Helpful assistants explain it all; it's good fun for parents too. Two other (also excellent) child-oriented places in town make up the 'Tríptico de la Infancia'.

🎓 Courses

Spanish in Rosario
LANGUAGE COURSE

(☑0341-15-560-3789; www.spanishinrosario.com; Catamarca 3095) Rosario is a great base for learning Spanish; this place offers enjoyable language programs and can arrange family stays and volunteer work placements.

👉 Tours

★ Rosario Kayak & Motor Boat Tours
TOUR

(Paseos en Lancha y Kayak; ☑0341-15-571-3812; www.boattours.com.ar; Estación Fluvial) A friendly, professional, recommended multilingual set-up with great boat trips around the Paraná delta (AR$180 to AR$250, 1 to 1½ hours) with an optional lunch stop on a delta island. You can also explore the islands by kayak (AR$350, three hours). It also offers water-taxi service to the delta islands (from AR$70 return) and rents bikes for AR$150 per day. Book by phone, email or at the Estación Fluvial.

Rosario Free Tour
WALKING TOUR

(☑0341-560-3789; www.rosariofreetour.com; Maipú & Urquiza; ⊙tours at 11:30am Sat) Two-hour walking tours in Spanish and English.

Meet on the steps of the old customs building at the end of Maipú. Though it's technically free, a donation is appropriate.

✨ Festivals & Events

Rosario packs out for the October 12 long weekend. Many hotels and hostels double their prices and fill up well ahead of time.

Semana de la Bandera FIESTA
Climaxing in ceremonies on June 20, the anniversary of the death of Belgrano, Flag Week is Rosario's major fiesta.

🛏 Sleeping

There are dozens of hostels, but they're often block-booked by groups of police or other government workers. There's also a herd of average midrange hotels. Prices generally drop midweek.

Residence Boutique Hostel HOTEL, HOSTEL $
(☎0341-421-8148; www.residenceboutique.com. ar; Buenos Aires 1145; dm/d/tr US$23/60/80; ❄@🛜) Rather a special place, this lovely early-20th-century building houses a serene, beautiful hotel and hostel. Public spaces are full of art nouveau flourishes, and the compact, stylish private rooms offer great value for this level of comfort. Dorms are similarly upmarket, and the little garden patio and breakfast area are lovely places to relax. Original and striking.

La Casa de Arriba HOSTEL $
(☎0341-430-0012; www.lacasadearriba.com.ar; Córdoba 2889; dm weekend/weekday US$19/15; @🛜) A designer's flair has made a fabulous hostel from this old house. Exposed brick, creative use of space, modern shelf-style bunks and a welcoming attitude makes this a comfortable, stylish Rosario base. Its distance from the center is offset by its relative proximity to bars and nightlife.

Hotel La Paz HOTEL $
(☎0341-421-0905; www.hotellapazrosario.com.ar; Barón de Maua 36; s/d US$35/42; ❄@🛜) Well positioned on Plaza Montenegro, and still looking good after 70 years in operation, this welcoming budget hotel offers value for money. Family rooms at the front have balconies overlooking Plaza Montenegro.

La Casa de Pandora HOSTEL $
(☎0341-679-9314; www.lacasadepandora.com.ar; Entre Ríos 583; dm US$14-15; @🛜) Small, arty and welcoming, this is one of many Rosario hostels but it does some basics – cleaning, for example – better than many competitors. It's a cute spot with attractive dorms, kitchen and a petite courtyard. Various workshops – yoga, dance, folk music – are held, and it hires bikes.

Esplendor Savoy Rosario HOTEL $$
(☎0341-429-6000; www.esplendorsavoyrosario. com; San Lorenzo 1022; standard/superior r US$110/120, ste US$180; ❄@🛜🏊) Even among Rosario's many elegant early-20th-century buildings, this art nouveau gem is a standout. It's a flawless contemporary conversion; rooms feature modern conveniences that blend well with the centenarian features. An indoor pool, elegant cafe-bar and roof garden are among the attractions. It's popular during events, so don't expect a peaceful stay.

1412 HOTEL $$
(☎0341-448-7755; www.1412.com.ar; Zeballos 1412; r US$84; ❄🛜) Comfortably stylish, this decent-value modern hotel is perfectly located for sorties to the busy restaurant strip on Avenida Carlos Pellegrini. The handsome lobby offers free tea, coffee and cakes all day, while rooms are pleasingly, flawlessly modern.

Plaza Real HOTEL $$
(☎0341-440-8800; www.plazarealhotel.com; Santa Fe 1632; standard/superior r US$118/140; ❄@🛜🏊) Luxurious rooms, apartments and suites are to be had in this business hotel with rooftop pool. Fine facilities – gym, sauna, pool, open-air Jacuzzi – a cracking breakfast and polite friendly service make it a reliable choice.

**Roberta Rosa de
Fontana Suites** APARTMENT $$
(☎0341-449-6767; www.rrdfsuites.com.ar; Entre Ríos 914; s/d US$79/88; ❄🛜🏠) Situated very centrally above a colorful cafe, these rooms are modern and commodious, with brushed concrete ceilings, black floors and a small kitchenette. They come in various sizes, making it a good family option.

Catamarca Suites Land HOTEL $$
(☎0341-440-0020; www.catamarcasuitesland. com.ar; Catamarca 1219; r US$75; ❄🛜) Spacious apartment-style doubles with breakfast bar, microwave and minibar have plenty of style, while big comfy beds and powerful showers add value. Rooms have a balcony looking down the street to the Paraná and there's a small roof terrace with a Jacuzzi. Breakfast is brought up to your room. Cash only.

Rosario

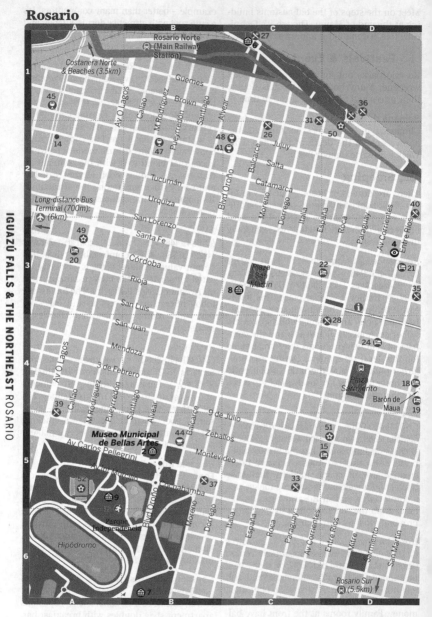

Hotel Plaza del Sol
HOTEL $$

(☏0341-426-4448; www.hotelesplaza.com; San Juan 1055; s/d US$111/122; ❋@🛜🏊) Despite a tired facade, renovated rooms here look good; most are very spacious, all have balconies and hydromassage tub, and beds are comfortable. It's the best of the clutch of hotels on Plaza Montenegro; there's a gym, sauna, sundeck and heated indoor pool on the 11th floor, plus helpful service. It's decent value if you get an online deal or cash discount.

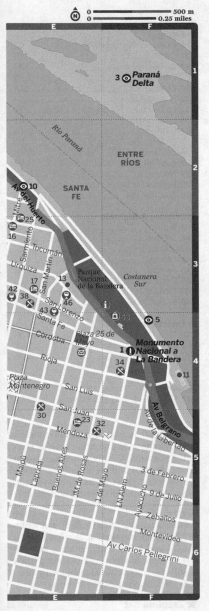

many rooms. The deluxe-plus rooms are somewhat bigger than the first-category deluxe rooms, and feature a bathtub. Executive suites have a Jacuzzi.

Puerto Norte Hotel HOTEL $$$

(☏0341-436-2700; www.puertonortehotel.com; Carballo 148; city/executive/premium r US$176/200/236; ✱@🖥🛎) In a new riverside development north of the center, this flashy hotel is built atop 14 former grain silos, the circular spaces of which house the reception and bar. Rooms are handsome and well-equipped, with coffee-pod machines and beds backed by whole-wall photos of old Rosario. The restaurant and rooftop spa complex, including outdoor and indoor pools, have spectacular panoramas.

Cheapest-category city views are more interesting than those from executive rooms. For brilliant river views, you'll need to upgrade to a premium room or suite.

✗ Eating

Central Rosario seems empty come suppertime. That's because half the city is out on Av Carlos Pellegrini. Between Buenos Aires and Moreno there's a vast number of family-friendly eateries, including barnlike *parrillas* (steak restaurants), dozens of pizza places, buffets, bars and excellent ice-creameries. Just stroll along and take your pick. Most places have street terraces.

★ La Marina SPANISH, SEAFOOD $

(1 de Mayo 890; mains AR$40-95; ⏱noon-4pm & 8pm-midnight Mon-Sat) Just above the flag monument, this basement place decorated with faded Spanish tourism posters is a top spot for inexpensive and really delicious seafood, like *rabas* (calamari) or succulent river fish on the grill. No bookings, so be prepared to wait, as it's deservedly popular. Don't confuse with the restaurant above.

Lo Mejor del Centro PARRILLA $

(Santa Fe 1166; mains AR$65-160; ⏱noon-3pm & 8pm-midnight; 🖥) When this *parrilla* went bust, the staff managed to reopen it as a cooperative, and what a great job they've done. The meat's as good as you'll taste in Rosario, but you can also enjoy homemade pasta, paella, creative salads and a warm, convivial buzz at the tightly packed, ageing tables. There are various midweek set menus that are great value.

El Ancla ARGENTINE $

(Maipú 1101; mains AR$50-100; ⏱7am-1am Mon-Fri, 8am-4pm & 7pm-1am Sat, 10am-4pm &

Ros Tower HOTEL $$$

(☏0341-529-9000; www.rostower.com.ar; Mitre 295; deluxe/deluxe-plus r US$176/200, junior/executive ste US$230/272; ✱@🖥🛎) Offering great service and facilities, this sleek business-spa hotel offers top river views from

Rosario

7pm-1am Sun) One of Rosario's many beloved corner restaurants, this much-frequented local has an appealingly venerable interior and an authentic feel. The food – with lots of inexpensive single-plate meals – is reliably good and you always seem to get a friendly welcome. A good budget choice.

De Buen Humor ICE CREAM $
(www.debuenhumorhelados.com.ar; Rioja 1560; cones AR$24-42; ⏰10am-11pm; 🛜🖉🏠) Ice cream here comes from happy cows, they say. We can't vouch for that, but anyone with a sweet tooth will be mooing contentedly at the optimism-filled decor, patio seating, and tasty cones, concoctions and fruit salads. *Rosarinos* eat 7kg of ice-cream each per year, so you've got some catching-up to do.

Comedor Balcarce ARGENTINE $
(cnr Balcarce & Brown; mains AR$50-120; ⏰noon-3pm & 8:15pm-midnight Mon-Sat) In business for decades, this typical corner *bodegón* (tradi-

tional diner) is one of a fast-disappearing breed. Home-style Argentine cooking comes in big portions. Quality is average to good, prices are great and it's an authentic, friendly experience. Don't let its affectionate nickname, *El Vómito* (the Vomit), put you off.

Nuria BAKERY $
(www.nuria.com.ar; Santa Fe 1026; pastries from AR$15; ⏰7am-9pm Mon-Sat, 7am-7pm Sun) This much-loved Rosario institution – now with several more modern outlets around town – is still a seductively old-fashioned place to pick up delicious pastries and cakes.

★ Zazpirak Bat BASQUE $$
(www.zazpirakbat.com; Entre Ríos 261; mains AR$80-150; ⏰8pm-12:30am Tue-Sat, 12:30-4pm Sun) From outside, this Basque cultural center gives few clues that there's a restaurant inside, and the menu seems a little humdrum at first glance. But what a place this is. Fish and seafood are prepared to give

maximum expression to the natural flavors; it's all delicious, quantities are enormous, and the salads are particularly praiseworthy.

Escauriza
SEAFOOD $$
([J] 0341-454-1777; cnr Bajada Escauriza & Paseo Ribereño; mains AR$110-195; ⊗noon-3:30pm & 8pm-midnight) Backing Florida beach, this legendary place is one of Rosario's best spots for fish. The enormous indoor-outdoor dining area is redolent with the aromas of chargrilling river catch like surubí; start with some delicious seafood empanadas. Service, quality and quantity are all highly impressive. Book, get there at noon, or wait and wait at summer weekend lunchtimes. No credit cards. Awful coffee.

Don Ferro
PARRILLA $$
(www.puertoespana.com.ar; riverbank nr España; mains AR$100-220; ⊗7:30am-1am; 🐾) The handsomest restaurant in town, Don Ferro is exquisitely set in an old brick railroad shed, with a delightful terrace on the platform, excellent service and seriously delicious meat. The menu is wide-ranging, though, and has mixed-grilled vegetables and more meaty options than most. Wines are very overpriced. It's on the riverbank near España.

El Viejo Balcón
PARRILLA $$
(cnr Italia & Wheelwright; mains AR$90-190; ⊗noon-3pm & 8pm-midnight) Be prepared to wait for a table at this long-time Rosario favorite in a parrilla-rich zone by the river. The meat is generously proportioned and of excellent quality: staff even listen to how you want it cooked. But there's enough on the menu here – crepes, pastas – to cater for all tastes.

La Estancia
PARRILLA $$
(www.parrillalaestancia.com.ar; Av Carlos Pellegrini 1501; mains AR$100-220; ⊗noon-3:30pm & 8pm-1am, to 2am Fri & Sat; 🐾) A sound choice on the Pellegrini strip, this typical upmarket grillhouse has really excellent cuts of meat – the vacío (flank steak) is special – allied with enough waiters that you'll never have to, er, wait. The only downsides are closely spaced tables and a mediocre wine list.

Restaurant Bruno
ITALIAN $$
(Montevideo 2798; pasta AR$125-185; ⊗8pm-midnight Tue-Sat, noon-3:30pm & 8-11pm Sun) An elegant villa a block from Pellegrini, is decorated with dark wood and tasteful gondolier prints. Well-heeled locals flock here for homemade pasta, which has a huge reputation. Go for gnocchi, lasagna or canelloni over fettucini, but the combination of stylish interior with trattoria-style comfort works. Portions are large.

Los Potrillos
PARRILLA $$
([J] 0341-482-4027; www.lospotrillos.com.ar; cnr Av Carlos Pellegrini & Moreno; mains AR$140-210; ⊗noon-3:30pm & 8pm-1am; 🐾) Decorated with warm colors and a sweeping horse mural, this parrilla offers plenty more than just grilled meat, with a fine selection of river fish and other seafood dishes, tasty homemade pasta and a decent wine list. It's high on quality and quantity and the menu is reasonably translated for once.

Los Jardines
ARGENTINE $$
(www.losjardinesenrosario.com; Paraná riverbank near España; mains AR$80-190; ⊗8am-midnight) With a stepped terrace right down by the river (access by lift or stairs right behind the Don Ferro restaurant), this has a lovely setting, though rusty piping and a fishing pier obscure some of the view. A wide-ranging menu includes a decent weekday lunch deal, large salads, cocktails, grilled river fish and more. Quality is up and down, but it's a fine hideaway.

La Chernia, El Chucho y La Cholga
SEAFOOD $$
(www.rubenmolinengo.com; cnr JM de Rosas & Mendoza; mains AR$100-205; ⊗11:30am-3pm & 8:30pm-midnight) Step back a century in time as you walk into this beautifully decorated romantic corner restaurant. The long menu is all fish, from local river varieties to stews and soups bursting with tasty seafood. Shared platters for two are an enjoyable and good-value way to go here.

Davis
ARGENTINE $$$
([J] 0341-435-7142; www.complejodavis.com; Av de la Costa 2550; mains AR$155-235, bar snacks AR$65-150; ⊗9am-1am Tue-Thu & Sun, 9am-2am Fri & Sat, 12:30pm-1am Mon; 🐾) Occupying Rosario's most charming position, right on the river below the contemporary art museum with 180-degree views, Davis offers a smart restaurant inside a glass cube, and outdoor riverside seating with an overpriced bar menu of sandwiches and similar. The eats are much better inside – try the riverfish platter for two – but have a beer on the deck first to make the most of the location.

🍷 Drinking & Nightlife

Rosario has a great number of restobares, which function as hybrid cafes and bars and generally serve a fairly standard selection of snacks and plates. Many are good for a

IGUAZÚ FALLS & THE NORTHEAST ROSARIO

PICHINCHA
....

Between Oroño and Francia, and north of Urquiza, the barrio of Pichincha is the city's most interesting for nightlife. The leafy streets and wide pavements make it seem a sleepy suburb by day, but at night every corner seems to have a quirky bar or hipster restaurant. The city's best *boliches* (nightclubs) are also found here.

morning coffee, an evening glass of wine – or anything in between.

Espiria   CAFE
(www.facebook.com/culturaespiria; Montevideo 2124; ⊙8am-1am Mon-Thu, 9am-2am Fri & Sat, 10am-1am Sun; 🛜) Perfect for combining with a visit to the nearby art gallery, this enchanting cafe-bookshop-gallery occupies a beautiful house with stained glass and an enticing patio. Tasty sandwiches, snacks and breakfasts (light meals AR$70 to AR$140), coffees and delicious juices make this one of Rosario's most relaxing spots, and it's a cocktail venue later, too.

El Diablito   PUB
(Maipú 622; ⊙9pm-3:30am Tue-Sat) With a red-lit interior true to its origins as a brothel, this place has an atmosphere all of its own. The soundtrack is 70s and 80s rock, and the decor is sumptuous with stained-glass panels and age-spotted mirrors. A classic place to drink.

Pichangú   BAR
(cnr Salta & Rodríguez; ⊙6pm-1am Mon-Wed, 6pm-2am Thu, 7pm-3am Fri & Sat) Brightly lit and cheerful, this inviting corner space is a co-operative that puts on regular music and other cultural events. It's a social, slightly chaotic scene and a good place to meet locals. It does a reasonable line in pizzas and the like, with several vegan options.

El Cairo   BAR
(www.barelcairo.com; cnr Sarmiento & Santa Fe; ⊙8am-1am Mon-Thu, 8am-2am Fri & Sat, 10am-1am Sun; 🛜) High-ceilinged and elegant, with huge panes of glass for people-watching (and vice versa), this classic Rosario cafe is good at any time of day, but especially in the evening, when it mixes a decent cocktail and puts on good Argentine pub grub. This is also one of the rare places that serve *mate*.

Pasaporte   BAR
(cnr Maipú & Urquiza; ⊙7am-late Mon-Fri, 8am-late Sat & Sun; 🛜) Sublimely cozy with a pretty terrace and timeworn wooden furniture, the Pasaporte is a favorite for morning coffee with workers from the government building opposite. But it also has a low-key but enjoyable evening atmosphere, particularly when it's raining outside.

Fenicia   BREWERY
(www.feniciabrewing.com.ar; Francia 168; ⊙noon-late Tue-Fri, 6pm-late Sat & Sun; 🛜) You can smell the malt at this brewpub, where the delicious ales are produced right beneath your feet. It's a fine place to start exploring this bar-rich nightlife zone, and it also does a handy line in quesadillas, burgers and salads. The roof terrace is good on a warm evening. It's northwest of the city center, near the train station.

Rock & Feller's   BAR
(www.rockandfellers.com.ar; cnr Blvd Oroño & Jujuy; ⊙10am-3am; 🛜) This enormous bar is a striking sight with its wall-to-wall guitar-hero decoration, good-looking bar and terrace area, and comfy padded stools emblazoned with rock icons. Based on the much-imitated Hard Rock Café template, this is very popular locally for its menu of pizzas, sandwiches and the like. At night it's fairly dressy, though most of the bands featured wouldn't get in.

Bound   CLUB
(Blvd Oroño 198; ⊙9pm-late Fri & Sat) Rosario's best *boliche* at the time of writing, this stylish spot is in the heart of the liveliest nightlife zone. It operates a pretty fascist door policy, so think twice if the queue's long.

☆ Entertainment

There are lots of tango places in Rosario; grab the monthly listings booklet from the tourist office and check www.rosario turismo.com.

Rosario has two rival *fútbol* teams with several league titles between them. **Newell's Old Boys** (☎0341-425-4422; www.newellsold boys.com.ar; Parque Independencia) plays in red and black at Estadio Marcelo Bielsa and has a long, proud history of producing great Argentine players. **Rosario Central** (☎0341-421-0000; www.rosariocentral.com; cnr Blvd Avellaneda & Génova) plays in blue and yellow stripes at Estadio 'El Gigante de Arroyito'. Buy tickets from the stadiums from two hours before the match.

La Casa del Tango
TANGO

(www.facebook.com/casadeltangorosario; Av Illia 1750; ⊙9am-noon Mon-Fri) This tango center has info on performances and classes around town, often offers fun, very cheap evening lessons, and stages various events. Regular 9pm Saturday concerts are a great deal at AR$50. There's also a good cafe and restaurant. It's on the riverbank road near the junction with España.

Distrito Siete
LIVE MUSIC

(www.facebook.com/distritosie7e; Av Lagos 790; ⊙9am-1am Mon-Thu, 9am-4:30am Fri & Sat, 6pm-1am Sun; 🕿) This warehouse-like industrial space is run by the Giros local social movement and sees plenty of live acts as well as classes, activities, a cheap daily meal, and a bar where you can stop for a coffee or beer and see what's going on.

La Chamuyera
TANGO

(Av Corrientes 1380; ⊙Mon-Sun) With an underground feel reminiscent of its semi-illegal past, this atmospheric venue is one of Rosario's best tango spots. The Thursday *milonga* kicks off at 10:30pm and there's a practice session on Monday nights. Other events include language nights, poetry readings and a variety of concerts: it's always worth stopping by for a beer and a look.

🛍 Shopping

Mercado de Pulgas del Bajo
MARKET

(Av Belgrano; ⊙2-8pm Sat, noon-8pm Sun) A small handicrafts market by the tourist office, where dealers sell everything from silverwork to leather goods. There are several other weekend markets along the riverbank, including an excellent Sunday retro market near where Oroño meets the 'coast.'

ℹ Information

All-night pharmacies include one on the corner of San Lorenzo and Entre Ríos.

Bus Terminal Tourist Information (www.rosarioturismo.com; Terminal de Ómnibus; ⊙9am-7pm) Opposite platform 32.

Hospital Clemente Álvarez (☑0341-480-8111; Av Carlos Pellegrini 3205) Southwest of the city center.

Tourist Kiosk (Córdoba, nr Av Corrientes; ⊙8am-7pm Mon-Fri, 9am-7pm Sat, 10am-6pm Sun) On the main pedestrian street.

Tourist Office (☑0341-480-2230; www.rosarioturismo.com; Av del Huerto; ⊙8am-7pm Mon-Fri, 9am-7pm Sat, 9am-6pm Sun) On the riverbank in the city center. Very helpful, and the website is excellent.

ℹ Getting There & Away

AIR

Aerolíneas Argentinas (☑0810-222-86527; www.aerolineas.com.ar; España 840; ⊙10am-6pm Mon-Fri, 9am-noon Sat) Flies daily to Buenos Aires. Also serves Mendoza, Córdoba, El Calafate and Puerto Iguazú.

Gol (www.voegol.com.br) Serves São Paulo and Rio de Janeiro in Brazil.

Sol (☑0810-444-4765; www.sol.com.ar) Flies daily to Buenos Aires and also services Córdoba and, seasonally, Punta del Este.

TAM (www.tam.com.br) Flies to São Paulo in Brazil.

BUS

The modernized **long-distance bus terminal** (☑0341-437-3030; www.terminalrosario.gob.ar; Cafferata & Santa Fe) is 25 blocks west of downtown. To get there, any bus along Santa Fe will do the trick. From there, take a bus marked 'Centro' or 'Plaza Sarmiento.' It's about AR$40 to AR$70 in a taxi.

There are direct daily services to nearly all major destinations, including international services.

Buses from Rosario

DESTINATION	COST (ARS)	TIME (HR)
Buenos Aires	250-285	4
Córdoba	360	5½-7
Corrientes	641	9-11
Mendoza	750-820	12-15
Paraná	150-170	3-3½
Posadas	879	14-15
Salta	1220	14-17
Santa Fe	117-128	2½-3½
Tucumán	812	11-13

TRAIN

From **Rosario Sur train station** (www.trenesargentinos.gob.ar; cnr San Martín & Battle y Ordóñez; ⊙ticket office 6pm-1am), 7.5km south of the center down Avenida San Martín, new trains run an improved service daily to Buenos Aires (second/first class AR$175/225, 6½ hours), leaving Rosario at 12:26am and leaving Retiro at 4:07pm.

Other trains stopping at **Rosario Norte train station** (www.trenesargentinos.gob.ar; Av del Valle 2750) en route between Buenos Aires and Córdoba, and Buenos Aires and Tucumán, are slow, downmarket and cheap. They book out well in advance.

Bus 140 runs south down Sarmiento to the Rosario Sur station. Take bus 134 north up Mitre to a block from the Rosario Norte train station.

AWAKENNING/GETTY IMAGES ©

Monumento Nacional a La ...ndera (p151)

...ilt where the Argentine blue-and-white ...g was first raised, this obelisk also marks ...e resting place of the flag's designer, ...nuel Belgrano.

...Gualeguaychú Carnaval (p183)

...gentina's longest and flashiest Carnaval ...ebration kicks off in summer.

...Reserva Provincial Esteros del ...erá (p177)

...ese wetlands are full of wildlife, including ...autiful orange-colored marsh deer.

...San Ignacio Miní (p192)

...e best-preserved mission ruins in all of ...gentina.

LEANDRO HERRANZ/GETTY IMAGES ©

ℹ Getting Around

TO/FROM THE AIRPORT

For the **airport** (Fisherton; ☑ 0341-451-3220; www.aeropuertorosario.com; Av Jorge Newbery s/n), 8km west, bus 115 runs west along Santa Fe. A taxi will charge around AR$130.

BICYCLE

To rent a bike, **Rosario Kayak & Motor Boat Tours** (p154) at the Estación Fluvial, has well-equipped town bikes for AR$150 per day. You'll need your passport and an AR$300 deposit.

BUS

Local buses run from the terminal on Plaza Sarmiento (see www.rosario.gov.ar). You can pay the AR$6.50 fare in coins, but unless you've broken a piggy bank, it's much easier to buy a rechargeable AR$25 card from little booths at many major central bus stops. Trips then cost AR$5.75.

Santa Fe

☑ 0342 / POP 526,100

There's quite a contrast between Santa Fe's relaxed center, where colonial buildings age gracefully in the humid heat and nobody seems to get beyond an amble, and a Friday evening in the Recoleta district, where university students in dozens of bars show the night no mercy. Capital of its province, but with a small-town feel, Santa Fe is an excellent place to visit for a day or two.

Santa Fe (de la Veracruz) moved here in 1651 from its original location at Cayastá, 75km to the north. In 1853, Argentina's first constitution was ratified by an assembly meeting here; these days ambitious riverfront rehabilitation has added extra appeal to this historic city.

Santa Fe's remaining colonial buildings are within a short walk of Plaza 25 de Mayo. Av San Martín, north of the plaza, is the major commercial street and part of it forms an attractive *peatonal* (pedestrian street) with palms and terraces.

To the east, a bridge crosses the river, then a tunnel beneath the Paraná connects Santa Fe with its twin city of Paraná in Entre Ríos.

◉ Sights

★ Convento y Museo de San Francisco   MONASTERY

(Amenábar 2257; admission AR$15; ⊙ 8am-12:30pm & 3:30-7pm Tue-Fri, 8am-noon & 4-7pm Sat) Santa Fe's principal historical landmark is this Franciscan monastery and museum, built in 1680. While the museum is mediocre, the church is beautiful, with an exquisite wooden ceiling. The lovely cloister has a real colonial feel and is full of birdsong and the perfume of flowers. The monastery is still home to a handful of monks.

On your left as you enter the church is a fine polychrome Christ by grumpy Spanish master Alonso Cano, sent as a sympathy gift by the Queen of Spain when the town moved in 1649. By the altar, a stone marks the tomb of a priest killed by a jaguar taking refuge in the church during 1825 flooding.

★ Museo Histórico Provincial   MUSEUM

(www.museobrigadierlopez.gob.ar; Av San Martín 1490; admission AR$10; ⊙ 8:30am-12:30pm & 2:30-8:30pm Tue-Fri, 5:30-8:30pm Sat & Sun) In a lovable 17th-century building, this museum has a variety of possessions and mementos of various provincial governors and *caudillos* (provincial strongmen), as well as religious art and fine period furnishings, including a sedan chair once used to carry around the Viceroy of Río de la Plata. Opening hours are for summer: it doesn't close mid-afternoon the rest of the year.

Museo Etnográfico y Colonial Provincial   MUSEUM

(www.museojuandegaray.gob.ar; 25 de Mayo 1470; donation AR$4; ⊙ 8:30am-12:30pm & 3-7pm Tue-Fri, 8:30am-12:30pm & 4-7pm Sat & Sun) Run with heartwarming enthusiasm by local teachers, this museum has a chronological display of stone tools, Guaraní ceramics, jewelry, carved bricks and colonial objects. Highlights include a set of *tablas* – a colonial game similar to backgammon – and a scale model of both original Santa Fe settlements. Afternoon opening hours vary.

Plaza 25 de Mayo   SQUARE

The center of colonial Santa Fe is a peaceful square framed by fine buildings. The vast **Casa de Gobierno** (Government House; Pl 25 de Mayo) was built in 1909 and replaced the demolished *cabildo* (town council building), seat of the 1852 constitutional assembly. On the square's east side, the exterior simplicity of the Jesuit **Iglesia de la Compañía** (Pl 25 de Mayo) masks an ornate interior. The **cathedral** (Pl 25 de Mayo) is a little underwhelming by comparison, and dates from the mid-18th century.

Cervecería Santa Fe   BREWERY

(☑ 0342-450-2237; www.cervezasantafe.com. ar; Calchines 1401) This is the brewery that produces Santa Fe lager as well as brewing Budweiser and Heineken under license. Free tours run at 5pm Tuesday to Saturday; you'll need to wear sturdy footwear and long pants for safety reasons. Numbers are limited: you can reserve online.

Tours

Costa Litoral BOAT TOUR
(☑ 0342-456-4381; www.costalitoral.info; Dique 1) From the redeveloped harbor area, a large catamaran runs weekend trips around the river islands (adult/child AR$160/100, two hours, 11am Saturday and Sunday) or to Paraná (adult/child AR$260/160, 5½ hours, 2pm Saturday and Sunday) with a couple of hours to explore the city. Book tickets in the cafe opposite the dock.

Sleeping

The area around the bus terminal is the budget-hotel zone. Nearly all hotels offer a discount for cash payment.

Hotel Constituyentes HOTEL $
(☑ 0342-452-1586; www.hotelconstituyentes.com. ar; San Luis 2862; s/d US$35/45, without bathroom US$25/35; ❈ @ ☞) Spacious rooms, low prices and proximity to the bus terminal are the main drawcards of this relaxed place. It's not luxury, but the owners are always looking to improve things and it makes a pleasant budget base. Rooms at the front suffer from street noise. Breakfast is extra.

Hotel Galeón HOTEL $
(☑ 0342-454-1788; www.hotelgaleon.com.ar; Belgrano 2759; s/d US$52/64; ❈ @ ☞) Handy for the bus, this unusual hotel is all curved surfaces and weird angles. There's a variety of room types, none of which is a conventional shape; the place is in need of a refit but the beds are comfortable enough and wi-fi is decent. Substantial discounts offered for cash.

Hostal Santa Fe de la Veracruz HOTEL $
(☑ 0342-455-1740; www.hostalsf.com; Av San Martín 2954; standard s/d US$46/63, superior US$66/80; ❈ @ ☞) Decorated with indigenous motifs, this retro hotel on the pedestrian street offers polite service, spacious superior rooms and slightly downbeat standards. It's time for repainting though – those dozen shades of beige are looking very dated. Siesta fans will love the 6pm checkout.

★ Ámbit Boulevard BOUTIQUE HOTEL $$
(☑ 0342-455-7179; www.ambithotel.com.ar; Blvd Gálvez 1408; superior/premium r US$100/112; ❈ ☞ ☯) An early 20th-century flour magnate's mansion has been converted into this compact, rather lovely hotel. Exquisitely decorated rooms were each designed as a charity project by different architects; all are charming. Premium category rooms have high ceilings and venerable floorboards, while 'superior' rooms are in the modern upstairs annex but don't lack charm. A little spa-style plunge pool sits between floors.

Los Silos HOTEL $$
(☑ 0342-450-2800; www.hotellossilos.com.ar; Dique 1; s/d US$120/134; ❈ @ ☞ ☯ ♠) Santa Fe's decaying waterfront has been smartened, and this creatively designed hotel is a centerpiece. Brilliantly converted from grain silos, it features original, rounded rooms with marvelous views and plenty of modern comfort, though some are looking in need of a touch-up. Vistas from the rooftop pool, spa and sundeck are super, and service is excellent throughout.

A handsome cafe and a play area for kids are other highlights; there's also an attached casino.

Eating

The best zones for cheap eats are across from the bus terminal, and the nightlife zone of La Recoleta.

El Quincho de Chiquito ARGENTINE $
(cnr Brown & Obispo Vieytes; set menu AR$150; ⊙ 11:30am-3pm & 8pm-midnight) This legendary local institution is *the* place for river fish, on the *costanera* 6km north of downtown. There are few frills and no choice: four or five courses of delicious surubí, sábalo or pacú are brought out; you can repeat as often as you want. Drinks are extra but cheap.

It's around AR$50 each way in a taxi (staff will call you one to take you back) or catch bus 16 from any point on the waterfront road.

Club Social Sirio Libanés MIDDLE EASTERN $
(25 de Mayo 2740; mains AR$50-130; ⊙ 11:30am-2:30pm & 7-11:30pm Tue-Sun; ☞) Hidden down a passageway leading to a gym, this offers tasty, well-prepared Middle Eastern–style dishes as well as river fish, pasta and *parrilla* options; it's a pleasingly unusual place to eat. There's outdoor seating in the interior patio. Kitchen closes at 2pm at lunch.

Merengo BAKERY $
(Av General López 2632; alfajores from AR$5; ⊙ 9am-12:30pm & 3-8pm) In 1851, Merengo stuck two biscuits together with *dulce de*

Santa Fe

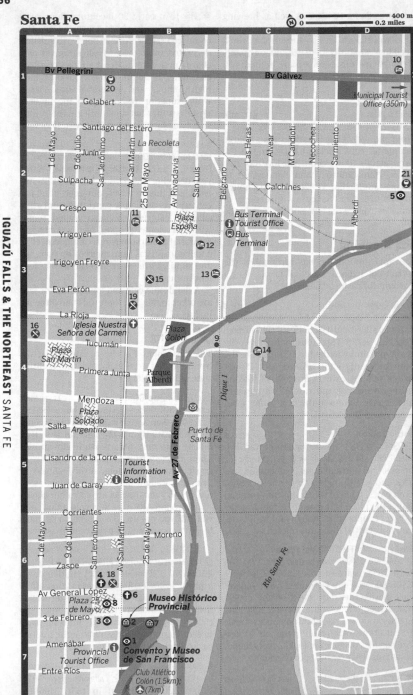

N

0 — 400 m
0 — 0.2 miles

Bv Pellegrini

Bv Gálvez

10

Municipal Tourist
Office (350m)

Gelabert

20

Santiago del Estero

La Recoleta

Las Heras

Alvear

M Candioti

Necochea

Sarmiento

1 de Mayo

9 de Julio

Junín

San Jerónimo

Av San Martín

25 de Mayo

Av Rivadavia

San Luis

Belgrano

Calchines

Alberdi

21

Suipacha

5

Crespo

11

Plaza
España

Bus Terminal
Tourist Office

Yrigoyen

17

12

Bus
Terminal

Irigoyen Freyre

13

Eva Perón

15

19

La Rioja

Iglesia Nuestra
Señora del Carmen

Plaza
Colón

9

14

16

Tucumán

Plaza
San Martín

Primera Junta

Parque
Alberdi

Dique 1

Mendoza

Plaza
Soldado
Argentino

Salta

Puerto de
Santa Fe

Lisandro de la Torre

Tourist
Information
Booth

Juan de Garay

Av 27 de Febrero

Corrientes

1 de Mayo

9 de Julio

San Jerónimo

Av San Martín

25 de Mayo

Moreno

Río Santa Fe

Zaspe

4 18

Av General López

Plaza 25
de Mayo

6

Museo Histórico
Provincial

8

3 de Febrero

3

2

Amenábar

Provincial
Tourist Office

1

Convento y Museo
de San Francisco

Entre Ríos

Club Atlético
Colón (1.5km);
(7km)

Santa Fe

leche (milk caramel) and invented the *alfajor*, now Argentina's favorite snack. It's still going strong: this cute little shop on the plaza is one of several branches.

⭐ La Boutique del Cocinero   INTERNATIONAL $$

(☎0342-456-3864; www.laboutiquedelcocinero. com; Yrigoyen 2443; mains AR$130-170, workshops AR$325; ⊙dinner 8:30pm-1am Sat, shop 5-8:30pm Mon-Fri) This innovative, welcoming shop has an open kitchen that hosts sociable weekly workshops (normally Thursday or Friday: check the page) where you cook a meal – perhaps French, sushi or Lebanese – then sit down to eat it together. On Saturday evenings it's a restaurant, with a short menu of high-quality dishes from various international cuisines. Great vibes; great spot.

Restaurante España   ARGENTINE $$

(www.lineaverdehoteles.com; Av San Martín 2644; mains AR$120-210; ⊙11:30am-3pm & 8pm-midnight; 🐾) This hotel restaurant on the pe-destrian street is a lovely space, with high ceilings, attentive waistcoat-and-tie staff and an old-fashioned feel. There's a huge menu that covers the range of fish (both locally caught and from the sea), steaks, pasta, chicken and crepes, with a few Spanish dishes thrown in to justify the name. The wine list is a winner, too.

El Aljibe   ITALIAN $$

(☎0342-456-2162; Tucumán 2950; mains AR$80-160; ⊙noon-2:30pm & 9pm-12:30am Tue-Sat, noon-2:30pm Sun & Mon; 🐾) Warmly lit and cordial, this appealing neighborhood Italian uses great ingredients to create flavor-filled salads, pasta and meat dishes.

🍸 Drinking & Nightlife

Santa Fe's nightlife centers on the intersection of 25 de Mayo and Santiago del Estero, the heart of the area known as La Recoleta, which goes wild on weekend nights – a crazy contrast to the sedate pace of life downtown. Places change name and popularity rapidly, so just take a look around the dozens of bars and clubs.

Chopería Santa Fe   BAR

(San Jerónimo 3498; ⊙8am-2am; 🐾) A great place to try the local lager is this historic corner pub. It's a huge affair, with streetside tables, a cypress-shaded terrace and an immense interior. A wide range of Argentine bar food – *picadas* (shared appetizer plates), sandwiches, pizzas and the like – is available to soak it up.

Patio de la Cerveza   BREWERY

(cnr Calchines & Lavalle; ⊙2pm-1am) Part of the Santa Fe brewery opposite, this picturesque beer garden has its lager piped across the road via a 'beerduct' bridge. It's a great outdoor setting for a *liso*, as draft beers, traditionally served in 8oz cylindrical glasses, are known hereabouts, and there's a menu of deli plates, sandwiches, salads, etc to accompany it.

☆ Entertainment

The city's best *fútbol* team, **Colón** (www.club colon.com.ar), is a regular in the top division. It plays at the Brigadier Estanislao López stadium, where you can pick up tickets.

❶ Information

Bus Terminal Tourist Office (☎0342-457-4124; www.santafeturismo.gov.ar; Belgrano 2910; ⊙8am-8pm)

Hospital Provincial José María Cullen (☎0342-457-3340; Av Freyre 2150)

Municipal Tourist Office (☑ 0342-457-4123; www.santafeturismo.gov.ar; cnr Blvd Gálvez & Avellaneda; ☺ 7am-8pm Mon-Fri, 10am-4pm Sat & Sun) In the monumental Belgrano train station building (turn right as you enter). Hires bikes for free, but you'll theoretically need photo ID and a business card or receipt from the hotel you're staying in.

ℹ Getting There & Away

Aerolíneas Argentinas (www.aerolineas.com. ar; 25 de Mayo 2287; ☺ 9:30am-5:30pm Mon-Fri, 9am-noon Sat) and **Sol** (☑ 0810-444-4765; www.sol.com.ar) fly to Buenos Aires. The airport is 7km south of town on RN 11. A remise costs about AR$80.

From the **bus terminal** (☑ 0342-457-4124; www.terminalsantafe.com; Belgrano 2910) there are services throughout the country. Buses to nearby Paraná are frequent but often oversubscribed: prepare for long queues. It's AR$350 in a remise.

Buses from Santa Fe

DESTINATION	COST (AR$)	TIME
Buenos Aires	410-440	6-7½hr
Córdoba	270-370	5hr
Corrientes	507	6½-8hr
Paraná	16.25	40min
Posadas	750	12hr
Resistencia	539	6½-8hr
Rosario	128	2hr
Tucumán	774	11½hr

Cayastá

An interesting day trip from Santa Fe takes you to that city's original location, the **Cayastá ruins** (Santa Fe la Vieja; ☑ 03405-493056; www.santafe-conicet.gov.ar/santafelavieja; RP1, Km78, Cayastá; admission AR$9; ☺ 9am-1pm & 3-7pm Tue-Fri, 10am-1pm & 4-7pm Sat & Sun Oct-Mar, 9am-1pm & 2-6pm Tue-Fri, 10am-1pm & 3-6pm Sat & Sun Apr-Sep), picturesquely set beside the Río San Javier, which has eroded away a good portion of them.

There's ongoing archaeological investigation, but the most fascinating find by far has been the **Iglesia de San Francisco**. The Spanish and mestizo inhabitants of old Santa Fe were buried directly beneath the earth-floored church, and nearly 100 graves have been excavated, including those of Hernando Arias de Saavedra ('Hernandarias'), the first locally born governor of Río de la Plata province, and his wife, Jerónima,

daughter of Juan de Garay, who founded Santa Fe and Buenos Aires. The skeletons have now been replaced by replicas, but it's still a spooky, atmospheric place.

You can also see remains of two other churches, the *cabildo* (town council) and a handsome reconstructed period house. Near the entrance an attractive **museum** displays finds, including quality indigenous pottery with parrot and human motifs.

Last entry is strictly one hour before closing. If you want to visit in the morning, get the 9am bus from Santa Fe.

There's a mediocre on-site restaurant and a couple of decent *parrillas* in town. Several spots in Cayastá and along the RP1 offer cabin-type lodgings and boat trips on the river.

Cayastá is 76km northeast of Santa Fe on RP1 and served regularly from Santa Fe's bus terminal (AR$58, 1½ hours) by Paraná Medio. Ask the driver to drop you at *las ruinas*, 1km short of Cayastá itself.

Paraná

☑ 0343 / POP 247,700

Unpretentious Paraná, capital of Entre Ríos province, is a sleepy, slow-paced city perched on the hilly banks of its eponymous river. There's a lovely riverbank for strolling and a few minor attractions. Paraná was the capital of the Argentine Confederation (which didn't include Buenos Aires) from 1853 to 1861.

A tunnel beneath the main channel of the Paraná connects the city to Santa Fe.

◉ Sights

★ **Museo Histórico de Entre Ríos**   MUSEUM
(cnr Buenos Aires & Laprida; donation AR$5; ☺ 8am-12:30pm & 3-8pm Tue-Fri, 9am-noon & 4-7pm Sat, 9am-noon Sun) Flaunting local pride, this modern museum on Plaza Alvear contains information on the short-lived Republic of Entre Ríos and the battle of Monte Camperos, as well as *mate* paraphernalia and numerous solid wooden desks and portraits of Urquiza. Much of it was the collection of a local poet.

★ **Museo y Mercado
Provincial de Artesanías**   HANDICRAFTS
(Av Urquiza 1239; ☺ 7am-1pm & 4-8pm Mon-Fri, 9am-noon Sat) 🆓 Promoting handicrafts from throughout the province, this is a likable little place. Ask the curator to explain things to you; you'll be amazed at the intricacy of some of the work, like the hats made from tightly woven palm fibers.

Costanera WATERFRONT

From the northern edge of downtown, Parque Urquiza slopes steeply downward to the banks of the Río Paraná. During summer, the waterfront fills with people strolling, fishing and swimming. There's a public beach, **Playa El Parque**, west of the Paraná Rowing Club's private strand, but a better strip of sand, **Playas de Thompson**, is 1km further east, beyond the port.

👉 Tours

Regular small-boat trips leave at weekends (daily in summer) from behind the tourist office on the *costanera*, but safety doesn't seem a high priority.

Costa Litoral BOAT TOUR

(☑0343-423-4385; www.costalitoral.info; Buenos Aires 212) This outfit runs weekend afternoon one-way trips to Santa Fe (adult/child AR\$160/100) and one-hour cruises on the river (adult/child AR\$100/60) in a large catamaran. Trips leave from near the tourist office on the *costanera*.

Paraná en Kayak KAYAKING

(☑0343-422-7143; www.paranaenkayak.com.ar) Easy kayak trips on the river as well as longer routes.

🛏 Sleeping

⭐**Las Mañanitas** HOTEL \$

(☑0343-407-4753; www.lasmanianitas.com.ar; Carbó 62; s/d US\$40/65; 🅿@🛜🏊) There's a summer-house feel about this delightfully relaxed little budget place, which has nine rooms alongside a courtyard and garden with pool. The rooms are colorful and comfortable; they differ widely from darkish duplexes to simpler, lighter chambers – but it's the grace and friendliness of the whole ensemble that makes this a winner.

Paraná Hostel HOSTEL \$

(☑0343-422-8233; www.paranahostel.com.ar; Pazos 159; dm/d US\$14/32; 🅿@🛜) Right in the mix in central Paraná, this tranquil traveler-focused hostel has good security, a tree-shaded back patio and garden, as well as smart furnishings, decent facilities and comfy single-sex dorms. Upstairs are attractive, airy private rooms that share a bathroom. Rooms with air-con cost US\$2 more.

Entre Ríos Apart Hotel APARTMENT \$

(☑0343-484-0906; www.aparthotel-entrerios. com; Montevideo 55; s/d US\$44/68; 🅿🛜🍳) Spotless, spacious apartments here have

stove, microwave and fridge, as well as a fold-out sofa, decent bathroom and attractive bedroom. In a clean-lined modernized building, rates include breakfast and parking, making this a great deal.

Hotel Bristol HOTEL \$

(☑0343-431-3961; hotelbristolparana@hotmail. com; Alsina 221; s/d US\$33/49, without bathroom US\$21/35; 🅿🛜) Right by the bus terminal, this budget hotel is well kept and quiet. It's all very clean, correct, and hospitable. Simple rooms with small bathrooms offer great value.

Maran Suites HOTEL \$\$

(☑0343-423-5444; www.maran.com.ar; cnr Alameda de la Federación & Mitre; s US\$110-120, d US\$135-145; 🅿@🛜🏊) Towering over the western end of Parque Urquiza, this sleek modern hotel has a rare combination of style and personal service. Try for a room as high as possible, for city or river views. All are very spacious and decorated with flair; 'presidential' suites (US\$280) are big enough to get lost in and boast a Jacuzzi with memorable water vistas.

Howard Johnson Mayorazgo HOTEL \$\$\$

(☑0343-420-6800; www.hjmayorazgo.com.ar; Etchevehere; r from US\$177; 🅿🛜🏊) The long curved facade of this remodeled five-star dominates the waterfront from above. All rooms face the river, are very spacious, and offer great views from large windows. A little extra gets you a balcony, but these are lower down. There's indoor and outdoor pool, spa, gym and a large casino. You'll find better rates online. Parking included.

🍴 Eating

Giovani ARGENTINE \$

(Av Urquiza 1045; mains AR\$60-110; ⊙noon-3pm & 8pm-midnight Mon-Fri, to 1am Sat, to 11pm Sun; 🛜) With as-it-should-be service and thoughtful touches such as free coffee, this stylish restaurant in the center of town serves excellent meats from the *parrilla* and delectable pasta. There's a good line in river fish and a rather refined, romantic atmosphere.

Flamingo Grand Bar CAFE \$

(cnr Av Urquiza & José de San Martín; light meals AR\$55-80, mains AR\$70-155; ⊙8am-midnight; 🛜) Smart seats and a plaza-side location make this a favorite throughout the day, from morning croissants and juices through to *lomitos* (steak sandwiches) and lunch specials, to decent à la carte dishes and *picadas*.

IGUAZÚ FALLS & THE NORTHEAST PARANÁ

Paraná

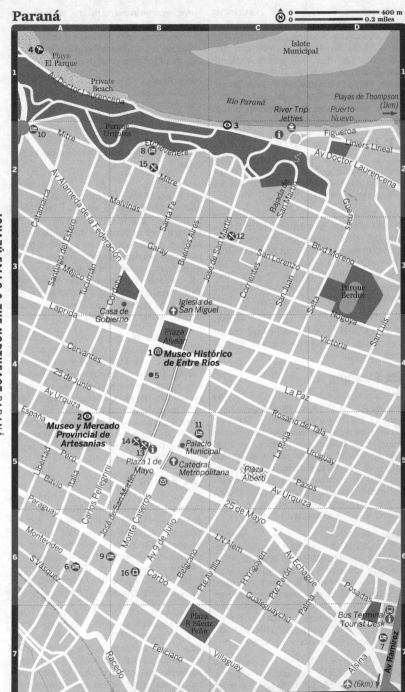

Paraná

Don Charras   PARRILLA **$$**
(☎ 0343-422-5972; cnr José de San Martín & San Lorenzo; mains AR$80-130; ☺ 11:30am-3pm & 8:30pm-midnight Tue-Thu, 11:30am-3pm & 8:30pm-1am Fri-Sun, ; 🛜) Thatched and atmospheric, this *parrilla* is a popular Paraná choice. Fridays and Saturdays see special fire-roasted options, otherwise just enjoy the usual chargrilled selection and solicitous service. Deep-pan stews are designed to share between three or more. Starters, drinks and the salad bar are scandalously overpriced, but the meat comes out in most generous portions.

Lola Valentina   ARGENTINE **$$**
(☎ 0343-423-5234; Mitre 310; mains AR$80-150; ☺ noon-4pm & 8pm-midnight; 🛜) Blending the cheerful vibe of a favorite corner eatery with formal service, this place offers great value for a long menu of Argentine classics, delicious homemade pastas, *parrilla* options and plenty of river fish choice. It fills fast, so get there early or book.

🍷 **Drinking & Nightlife**

Paraná is quiet midweek, but gets busy at weekends. Most of the action is at the eastern end of the riverfront around Liniers Lineal.

🛍 **Shopping**

A recommended place to buy quality handicrafts is the Museo y Mercado Provincial de Artesanías (p168).

Centro de Artesanos   HANDICRAFTS
(☎ 0343-422-4493; www.facebook.com/centrode artesanosparana; cnr Av 9 de Julio & Carbó; ☺ 9am-1pm & 4-8pm Mon-Sat Apr-Oct, 9am-1pm & 5-9pm Mon-Sat Nov-Mar) 🌿 Traditional *artesanías* (handicrafts) are on display and for sale here. There's some very high-quality ware, and prices are fair.

ℹ **Information**

Hospital San Martín (☎ 0343-423-4545; www.hospitalsanmartin.org.ar; Presidente Perón 450)
Tourist Office (☎ 0343-423-0183; www. turismoparana.gov.ar; Plaza 1 de Mayo s/n; ☺ 8am-8pm) Helpful, with good brochures. There's another branch by the Río Paraná (☎ 0343-420-1837; Laurencena & San Martín; ☺ 8am-8pm), and in the bus terminal (☎ 0343-420-1862; ☺ 8am-8pm).

ℹ **Getting There & Around**

The airport is 6km south, accessible only by *remise* (AR$60). Aerolineas Argentinas serves Buenos Aires.

The **bus terminal** (☎ 0343-422-1282) is eight blocks southeast of the central square. Buses 1, 4, 5 and 9 run downtown. Buses leave every 30 minutes for Santa Fe (AR$16.25, 40 minutes); you may have to queue as commuter-card holders have priority.

Buses from Paraná

DESTINATION	COST (AR$)	TIME (HR)
Buenos Aires	425	7-8
Colón	132	4-5
Concordia	144	4-5
Córdoba	320-360	6
Paso de los Libres	426-474	6-7
Rosario	150-170	3-3½

Corrientes

☎ 0379 / POP 356,300

Stately Corrientes sits below the confluence of the Paraná and Paraguay rivers, just across the water from its twin city, Resistencia. One of the nation's most venerable cities, it has elegant balconied buildings dating

Corrientes

Corrientes

from the turn of the 20th century that lend a timeworn appeal to its colorful streets. The *costanera* is everybody's destination of choice for strolling, licking ice creams or sipping *mate* with friends.

Corrientes is a magnet for regional indigenous crafts; Guaraní culture has a strong presence. The city is famous for its Carnaval. Graham Greene's novel *The Honorary Consul* was set here.

◉ Sights & Activities

Various operators run boat trips on the Paraná; the tourist office has a list.

★ Museo de Artesanías Tradicionales Folclóricas   MUSEUM

(Quintana 905; ☉8am-noon & 3-7pm Mon-Fri, 9am-noon & 4-7pm Sat) **FREE** This intriguing museum in a converted colonial house has small displays of fine traditional *artesanía* (handicrafts) plus a good shop, but the highlight is watching students being taught to work leather, silver, bone and wood by master craftspeople. Other rooms around the courtyard are occupied by working artisans who will sell to you directly. Museum guides are enthusiastic, knowledgeable and friendly.

Museo Histórico de Corrientes   MUSEUM

(9 de Julio 1044; ☉8am-noon & 4-8pm Tue-Fri) **FREE** This museum is set around an attractive patio and exhibits weapons, antique furniture, coins, and items dealing with religious and civil history. It's a little bit higgledy-piggledy, but staff are proud of the exhibition and keen to chat. The room on the War of the Triple Alliance is the most interesting.

Playa Arazaty   BEACH

(Costanera Sur; ☉late Nov-Mar) **FREE** This wide stretch of sand south of the Resistencia bridge is the city's best river beach. Don't dip until it's officially open – currents are dangerous. A bit of terraforming is done each season to make it safer for bathing, and there are lifeguards.

Turistas Con Ruedas   CYCLING

(Costanera at 9 de Julio; ☉8am-noon & 3-7pm) **FREE** Head down to the riverside tourist office with your passport, and grab a free bike to explore the city for a couple of hours.

🎊 Festivals & Events

★ Carnaval Correntino   CARNIVAL

Corrientes' traditionally riotous Carnaval competes with Gualeguaychú's as the country's showiest. Celebrated over four consecutive weekends starting nine weeks before Easter, parades along the *costanera* attract participants from neighboring provinces and countries, with huge crowds.

🛏 Sleeping

Bienvenida Golondrina   HOSTEL $

(☏0379-443-5316; www.hostelbienvenidagolondrina.com; La Rioja 455; dm US$21-23, s/d US$41/57; ✹@🛜) Occupying a marvelous centenarian building, all high ceilings, stained glass and artistic flourishes, this hostel makes a great base a few steps from the *costanera*. Comfortable wide-berthed dorm beds have headroom, facilities (including free bikes) are great, and the warmly-welcoming management couldn't be more helpful. Prices drop midweek.

Orly Hotel   HOTEL $

(☏0379-442-0280; www.hotelorlycorrientes.com.ar; San Juan 867; s/d US$50/60, superior r US$130; ✹@🛜⊠) This professional, central three-star is divided in two; older standard rooms are fine but smallish. They're gradually being renovated, so ask for a newer one. Superior 'suites' however, are much better, with huge beds, modish couches and good bathrooms, though we'd change the carpet. A sunlit breakfast room overlooks the pool deck. A sauna, Jacuzzi and gym add value.

La Rozada   BOUTIQUE HOTEL $$

(☏0379-443-3001; www.larozada.com; Plácido Martínez 1223; s/d US$78/88; ✹🛜) An excellent option near the riverfront, this hotel has commodious apartments and suites unusually set in a tower in the courtyard of an appealing 19th-century, battleship-gray historic building. Fine views are on offer from most rooms. A balcony room is slightly more expensive. There's an attractive bar area; guests can use the pool at the nearby rowing club.

Astro Apart Hotel   HOTEL $$

(☏0379-446-6112; www.astroapart.com; Bolívar 1285; s/d US$60/75; ✹@🛜) Top value is to be had at this modern place, featuring sizable, handsome white rooms with great beds and large windows. They come with simple kitchen and offer plenty of handy facilities as reasonably-priced extras. Parking included; breakfast is brought to the room.

Don Suites   HOTEL $$

(☏0379-442-3433; www.donsuites.com.ar; La Rioja 442; s/d US$77/83, superior s/d US$89/99; ✹@🛜⊠) Paces from the *costanera*, the Don offers pleasingly modern rooms with fridge and microwave. Rooms higher up are better, with river views, more natural light and a fresher feel – those on the ground floor can feel a bit musty. Pleasant pool area and helpful staff.

★ La Alondra   BOUTIQUE HOTEL $$$

(☏0379-443-5537; www.laalondra.com.ar; Av 3 de Abril 827; r/apt/ste US$199/232/315; ✹@🛜⊠)

Sumptuously furnished with dark-wood antiques, this wonderfully renovated house is an oasis of relaxation from the unappealing main road. Most rooms surrounding the small finger-shaped pool are suites boasting plush king-sized beds and characterful bathrooms with claw-foot tubs. A second area is characterfully created from a former industrial butchery. Strikingly handsome public spaces, excellent food and classy service complete a most impressive package.

Turismo Hotel Casino HOTEL $$$

(☑ 0379-446-2244; www.turismohotelcasino.com.ar; Entre Ríos 650; r US$190-210, ste from US$231; ✳ @ 🎧 🏊 ♿) By the riverfront casino, what was a stately old hotel is now dominated by a slick modern tower. It's excellent, with huge rooms that are elegantly and artistically furnished but cozy and quiet. River views cost a little extra; other drawcards include an enclosed playground for kids, a big pool with plenty of loungers, and spa facilities.

These are rack rates: you can usually expect to pay 30% less.

✗ Eating

El Quincho PARRILLA $

(cnr Av Juan Pujol & Calle Roca; parrillada for two AR$200-260; ⊙ 11:30am-3pm & 9pm-2am Mon-Sat, 11:30am-3pm Sun) Rustic and welcoming, this Corrientes classic sits on a roundabout a short walk from the center. It's more about Argentine grill staples such as chorizo and *morcilla* (blood sausage) than fancy cuts of steak; there's always a great-value *parrilla* deal on, plus regular regional specials and live *chamamé* music at weekends. Quality good; quantity enormous

Martha de Bianchetti CAFE, BAKERY $

(cnr 9 de Julio & Mendoza; pastries from AR$15; ⊙ 7am-1pm & 4-10pm Mon-Sat; 🎧) This old-fashioned Italian-style bakery and cafe serves mind-altering pastries and excellent coffee accompanied by *chipacitos* (little cheese scones). It's all warm when the doors open and the lovely smell wafts halfway down the block. Ice cream too.

★ El Mirador del Paraná ARGENTINE $$

(☑ 0379-442-9953; www.facebook.com/elmiradordelparana; Costanera at Edison; mains AR$80-160; ⊙ noon-3pm & 8:30pm-1am Wed-Mon; 🎧) Perched right above a river beach, the lovely bow-shaped deck here makes a great lunchtime destination. There's a fairly unsophisticated menu of *parrilla* and Argentine

staples, but quality is good. Speciality surubí dishes go a step beyond: '*al paquete*' is very succulent, cooked in foil with walnuts. Service is enthusiastic; the setting is memorable. Edison is a continuation of Bolívar.

Enófilos ARGENTINE $$

(Junín 1260; mains AR$110-205; ⊙ 11:30am-3:30pm & 8pm-12:30am Mon-Sat; 🎧) An *enófilo* is a wine lover, so the cellar gets plenty of attention at this attentive upstairs restaurant on the *peatonal*. The wine 'list' is a small temple at the room's center; traditional *correntino* ingredients like succulent surubí, are given creative flair, and fine cuts of meat are showcased to advantage with sauces and fresh vegetables. The international menu is more hit-and-miss.

Típico ARGENTINE $$

(☑ 0379-454-8666; San Juan 455; mains AR$100-180; ⊙ 11:45am-3:30pm & 7:45pm-1:45am) Finding this pleasant patio, once part of San Francisco monastery, behind a chain cafe is a surprise. Enthusiastically run by the chatty chef-owner, this specializes in typical *correntino* dishes, from clay-stewed meat to tasty river fish creations. It's a likable spot, and flavors are intriguing. Check the price on starter portions offered.

🍷 Drinking & Nightlife

The *costanera* has plenty of action, with several bars and *boliches* (nightclubs) in the Costanera Sur zone south of the Resistencia bridge and bars strung out north of it. Near the intersection of Junín and Buenos Aires, several bars and clubs pump along at weekends.

Sherwood BAR

(www.sherwoodrestobar.com; Quevedo 11; ⊙ 7pm-2am; 🎧) This massive complex on the *costanera* does a bit of everything – food, DJs, etc – but is best for a mojito or negroni on its spacious front deck or upstairs for better river views. It tries for the upmarket image with front-of-house staff in suits, but is actually very relaxed once you're in. Quevedo is an extension of Belgrano.

☆ Entertainment

El Calderón TRADITIONAL MUSIC

(☑ 0379-440-0755; Pellegrini 1509) With concerts most weekend nights, this central spot is an excellent place to encounter *chamamé*, the roots music of Corrientes province. Check its Facebook page for upcoming events.

CHAMAMÉ

Tango? What's that? Up here it's all about *chamamé*, one of the country's most intoxicating musical forms. Rooted in the polka, introduced by European immigrants, it's also heavily influenced by Guaraní culture. Its definitive sound is the accordion, traditionally accompanied by the guitar, *guitarrón* (an oversized guitar used for playing bass lines), the larger *bandoneón* (accordion) and the *contrabajo* (double bass). Of course, a *conjunto* (band) is hardly complete without a singer or two.

Chamamé is a lively dance for a couple, except when the man takes his solo *zapateo* (tap dance). Corrientes province is the heart of *chamamé* and therefore the easiest place to find a live performance. Check out Spanish-only website www.corrientes chamame.com.ar for upcoming performances and online tunes to introduce you to the genre. Corrientes holds a fortnight-long *chamamé* festival in early January.

Parrilla Puente Pexoa   TRADITIONAL MUSIC
(☑ 0379-445-1687; RN 12 at Virgen de Itatí roundabout; ⊙ from 8:30pm Fri & Sat) This relaxed restaurant features *chamamé* dances every weekend and is outrageous fun when the dancing starts. Men and women show up in full gaucho regalia, and up to four *conjuntos* (bands) may play each night, starting around 11pm.

It's around AR$60 in a taxi; make sure you specify it's the *parrilla* you're going to, as Puente Pexoa itself is a place further away.

🛍 Shopping

**Museo de Artesanías
Tradicionales Folclóricas**   HANDICRAFTS
(Quintana 905; ⊙ 8am-noon & 3-7pm Mon-Fri, 9am-noon & 4-7pm Sat) ✐ This museum shop sells a wide variety of traditional artisanal handicrafts at fair prices. Your purchase here helps to fund the continued teaching of traditional skills.

Super Disco   MUSIC
(9 de Julio 1781; ⊙ 8:30am-12:30pm & 5-9pm Mon-Sat) This CD shop specializes in Corrientes *chamamé*. You can listen before you buy.

ℹ Information

There are various irregularly open information offices around town, including at the airport and bus terminal.

Municipal Tourist Office (☑ 0379-447-4733; www.ciudaddecorrientes.gov.ar; cnr Av Costanera & 9 de Julio; ⊙ 7am-8pm) The main municipal tourist office, though opening can be patchy.

Municipal Tourist Kiosk (Plaza JB Cabral; ⊙ 7am-8pm) This helpful little kiosk on the plaza is theoretically open daily.

Provincial Tourist Office (☑ 0379-442-7200; http://turismo.corrientes.gob.ar; 25 de Mayo 1330; ⊙ 7:30am-2pm & 3:30-8:30pm Mon-Fri) Helpful for information about the province.

ℹ Getting There & Away

Aerolíneas Argentinas (☑ 0379-442-3918; www.aerolineas.com.ar; Junín 1301; ⊙ 8am-12:30pm & 4:30-8pm Mon-Fri, 9am-noon Sat) flies to Buenos Aires daily. It also flies there from nearby Resistencia.

The **long-distance bus terminal** (☑ 0379-447-7600; Av Maipú 2400) is 3km southeast of the town center. Resistencia has better long-distance bus connections to the west and northwest. Buses to Resistencia (AR$7, 40 minutes) leave frequently from the **local bus terminal** (cnr Av Costanera General San Martín & La Rioja). Shared taxis that zip you into Resistencia for AR$25 are faster. They leave from two locations: **Martínez 1016** by the river, and **Av 3 de Abril 953** (Av 3 de Abril 953).

Buses from Corrientes

DESTINATION	COST (AR$)	TIME (HR)
Buenos Aires	864	12-14
Córdoba	833	11-14
Mercedes	146	3-4
Paso de los Libres	220	5
Posadas	270	4-4½
Puerto Iguazú	527	9-10
Rosario	641	9-11
Salta	827	13
Santa Fe	507	6½-8

ℹ Getting Around

Local bus 109 goes to the **airport** (RN 12), 12km east of town on the Posadas road. Bus 103 runs between the local bus terminal and the long-distance bus terminal via downtown. Buses cost AR$5.25, payable only in coins or a charge card, available from some kiosks.

A taxi to/from the long-distance bus terminal will cost AR$50 to AR$70.

Mercedes

📞 03773 / POP 40,700

The main access point for the spectacular Esteros del Iberá wetlands, Mercedes is a rather handsome gaucho town with a mighty easy pace to life. Its claim to fame is the nearby – and completely surreal – roadside shrine to gaucho Antonio Gil, an enormously popular religious phenomenon. Prices are low here, and there are appealing places to stay.

🛏 Sleeping

⭐ Casa de China
B&B $

(📞 03773-15-627269; lacasadechina@hotmail.com; Beltrán 599; r per person US$30; 🛜) This 19th-century mansion offers magnificently characterful rooms with miles-high ceilings, large beds and antique furniture. Gardens, original artworks, gorgeous veranda spaces and a generous breakfast add enchantment. Best, though, is China herself, a warm-hearted, cultured and interesting host with a fund of stories and a lovably informal style. If you're not looking for hotel-style amenities, you won't want to leave.

Hostel Gitanes
HOSTEL $

(📞 03773-421558; hostelgitanes@gmail.com; Av San Martín 224; r per person with/without bathroom US$17/13; ❄🛜) Out the back of a family home, this self-contained hostel has decent basic rooms with air-conditioning, a small kitchen, and a yard. Rooms are private: a great deal for solo travelers. The owners couldn't be more helpful or welcoming.

El Viejo Hostel
HOSTEL $

(📞 03773-15-405206; www.corrientes.com.ar/elviejohostel; Rivas 688; dm US$15; 🛜) Set along a courtyard with a grassy garden out back, this venerable building offers simple, high-ceilinged dorms, a decent kitchen and a pleasant front room. Best is the tranquil vibe and genuinely cordial hospitality. You can also camp here. No breakfast, but free tea and coffee.

Hotel Horizontes
HOTEL $

(📞 03773-420489; Gómez 734; s/d US$20/40; ❄🛜) A block from the bus terminal, this bare but very clean hotel offers good value, spotless rooms with compact bathrooms. Streetside rooms suffer from some traffic noise.

GAUCHITO GIL

Spend time on the road anywhere in Argentina and you're bound to see roadside shrines surrounded by red flags and votive offerings. These pay homage to Antonio Gil, a Robin Hood–like figure whose burial place 9km west of Mercedes attracts hundreds of thousands of pilgrims yearly.

Little is certain about 'El Gauchito,' as he is affectionately called, but romantic tales have sprung up to fill the gaps. What is known is that he was born in 1847 and joined the army – some versions say to escape the wrath of a local policeman whose fiancée had fallen in love with him – to fight in the War of the Triple Alliance.

Once the war ended, Gil was called up to join the Federalist Army, but went on the run with a couple of other deserters. The trio roamed the countryside, stealing cattle from rich landowners and sharing it with poor villagers, who in turn gave them shelter and protection. The law finally caught up with them, and Gil was hung by the feet from the espinillo tree that still stands near his grave, and beheaded.

So how did this freeloading, cattle-rustling deserter attain saintlike status? Moments before his death, Gil informed his executioner that the executioner's son was gravely ill. He told the soldier that if he were buried – not the custom with deserters – the man's son would recover.

After lopping off Gil's head, the executioner carried it back to the town of Goya where – of course – a judicial pardon awaited Gil. On finding that his son was indeed seriously ill, the soldier returned to the site and buried the body. His son recovered quickly, word spread and a legend was born.

'Gauchito' Gil's last resting place is now the site of numerous chapels and storehouses holding thousands of votive offerings – including T-shirts, bicycles, pistols, knives, license plates, photographs, cigarettes, hair clippings and entire racks of wedding gowns – brought by those who believe in the gaucho's miracles. January 8, the date of Gil's death, attracts the most pilgrims.

Hotel Manantiales Mercedes HOTEL $$
(☑ 03773-421700; www.manantialeshoteles.com; cnr Pujol & Sarmiento; s/d/tr US$55/97/143; ❄❂☎) Right on the plaza, this modern hotel is Mercedes' most upmarket, with well-equipped rooms sporting contemporary color schemes, a restaurant, a casino, a spa and a gym. Service is polite and helpful. Rates are reasonable value and include parking.

Ivyra Pyta HOTEL $$
(☑ 03773-422105; www.ivyrapyta.com.ar; España 440; s/d US$44/77; ❄☎) Spacious public areas and long corridors give way to slightly more compact rooms at this modern establishment. Boutique bedheads and modish colours add a touch of class, and bathrooms are well above average. Value and amiability are high. Cash discount.

✕ Eating

Che Rhoga ARGENTINE $
(Av San Martín 2296; mains AR$50-120; ☺8:30pm-midnight Tue, 11:30am-2:30pm & 8:30pm-midnight Wed-Sun; ☎) It's a bit of a hike out to this homey restaurant on the roundabout at the entrance, but it's worth it for toothsome homemade pasta, steaks in tasty sauces and low prices. Service tries hard to be formal. A great place.

Sal y Pimienta ARGENTINE $
(Gómez 665; mains AR$45-98; ☺11:30am-3pm & 7:30-11:30pm; ☎) A local favorite, this uncomplicated joint near the bus terminal has a wide-ranging menu and unbeatable prices for tasty meats, river fish, pastas and pizzas. *Lengua* (tongue) makes a fine starter, and service is smart.

🛍 Shopping

Manos Correntinas HANDICRAFTS
(San Martín 499; ☺9am-noon & 5-8pm Mon-Fri, 9am-noon Sat) ✐ A friendly gallery and shop that displays the work of a cooperative of local craftspeople. There's some excellent basketwork and leatherwork. English spoken.

ℹ Information

Most services are along San Martín, which links bus terminal with plaza.

Tourist Information (☑ 03733-15-438769; www.guiadigitalmercedes.com.ar; Estación de Ómnibus; ☺6am-midnight Mon-Fri, 7am-noon and 3-7pm or 4-8pm Sat & Sun) The handiest of the tourist information places, this is at the bus terminal. The best for info on transport to Colonia Pellegrini.

ℹ Getting There & Away

The **bus terminal** (☑ 03773-420165; cnr San Martín & Perreyra) is six blocks west of the plaza. Destinations include Buenos Aires (AR$610 to AR$650, eight to 10 hours), Paso de los Libres (AR$71, two hours) and Corrientes (AR$146, three to four hours).

Reserva Provincial Esteros del Iberá

This stunning wetland reserve is home to an abundance of bird and animal life, and is among South America's finest places to see wildlife. Although tourism has increased substantially in recent years, Los Esteros del Iberá remains comparatively unspoiled. The main base for visiting the park is the sleepy village of Colonia Pellegrini, 120km northeast of Mercedes; it offers a variety of excellent accommodations. Rural *estancias* in the larger area also make enticing bases.

The lakes and *esteros* (lagoons) are shallow, fed only by rainwater, and thick with vegetation, which accumulates to form *embalsados* (floating islands); this fertile habitat is home to a stunning array of life. Sinister black caimans bask in the sun while capybaras feed around them. Other mammals include the beautiful orange-colored marsh deer, howler monkeys (officially the world's noisiest animal), the rare maned wolf, coypu, otters and several species of bat.

The birdlife is simply extraordinary; there are some 350 species present in the reserve, including colorful kingfishers, delicate hummingbirds, parrots, spoonbills, kites, vultures, several species of egret and heron, cormorants, ducks, cardinals and the plump southern screamer, which would really light up Big Uncle Bob's eyes at a Christmas roast.

Ibera: Vida y Color, on sale at various places around Colonia Pellegrini, is a useful wildlife guide with beautiful photos of most of the birds, plants and animals you may see.

The area around Pellegrini is only a small part of the 13,000-sq-km expanse of the Esteros, which can be accessed from several places, including 80km north, at Galarza.

☞ Tours

Lodges can organize these activities; they are usually included in the accommodation price. Otherwise, the best place to organize boat trips and other excursions is the campsite (from where most trips leave). Note that few guides speak English; if you want

ECOLOGICAL ISSUES IN THE IBERÁ

The Iberá ecosystem is delicate. The ecological foundation set up by US entrepreneurs-turned-conservationists Douglas and Kristine Tompkins has bought large tracts of private land and proposes to donate them to the Corrientes government, if it puts them and the existing Iberá reserve under the control of the Argentine government as a national park.

What seemed a straightforward act of ecological philanthropy became a hot potato, pitting landowners, agribusiness and politicians against each other. But locals seem to be slowly coming around to the idea as they see the potential benefits.

Check out www.theconservationlandtrust.org and www.proyectoibera.org for more information. The late Douglas Tompkins had this to say:

Why was there so much opposition to begin with?

Conservation encounters opposition wherever it is. Not one national park was created in the US without drawn-out battles with locals. Conservation is a political act and when it has to do with what one does with land then you are treading in hot political territory. A local cultural shift takes time and you also have to do your part well.

And now?

The opposition has virtually disappeared today. In fact, there is a conservation/tourism fever seizing the province from the political leadership and all through the entire profile of society. It is like suddenly everyone woke up.

What's the deal with the Guaraní aquifer?

The Guaraní aquifer is a nonissue. It's massive, somewhere around 1.2 million sq km. Iberá is a mere 1.3 million hectares of that. One percent. A shallow surface wetland with little to do with the deep aquifer. The Iberá's importance as a water source is also over-estimated. The Paraná passes more water than the whole Iberá under the Corrientes–Resistencia bridge every 18 hours.

Dangers to the ecosystem

The industrial rice plantations and the big industrial tree plantations of even-aged exotic monocultures. Then on top of that you have arrogant fools who flout laws and build dike-like roads for dozens of kilometers disrupting the hydrology. Those are the big three threats to the wetlands. Some bad grazing practices exist, but they are mild in comparison.

What's your message to Iberá's people?

The formation of a national park would bring benefits to the entire area and province, help biodiversity conservation and be a point of pride for locals. And of course a big economic development component with the advent of lots of tourism. It would be the largest national park in Argentina, the province would benefit by the tourism and the nation would pay the costs for operating the park, a kind of double win for the province and its citizens.

Life goes on as usual for everyone, it is only the 560,000 hectares of provincial land, coupled with 175,000 hectares of foundation land that would constitute a national park. Beyond that all landowners just continue on. Zero change for them. The only thing that will change is the value of their land will go up.

The reintroduction of giant anteaters?

This project is already an unqualified success. We have two established populations with lots of animals in the wild, reproducing nicely and healthily. One of the most successful things we have ever done in conservation. We are very happy about it. The pampa deer has been really successful too, with an established population growing at 25% annually. We have also started reintroducing peccaries and macaws, the latter extinct for more than a century. Our biggest and most exciting challenge is jaguars; we've started breeding them too.

Thanks also to Carolina Morgado and Ignacio Jiménez Pérez.

IGUAZÚ FALLS & THE NORTHEAST RESERVA PROVINCIAL ESTEROS DEL IBERÁ

an English-speaking guide, it's best to go through one of the lodges.

★ Boat Trips
BOAT TOUR
(per person AR$150-180) The best way to appreciate the area. The classic trip is a two- to three-hour excursion in a *lancha* (boat) around the Laguna Iberá and its *embalsados*. You'll see myriad bird and animal life, elegant lilies, water hyacinths and other aquatic plants. The guide will punt you remarkably close to the creatures. You can also take night trips; take plenty of insect repellent.

Walks & Horseback Rides
WALKING TOUR
Day walks (AR$60) are simple affairs: if you don't speak Spanish, you might as well do it yourself. Much better are night walks (AR$120 for two hours), but cover up with repellent. Longer guided walks are also available, as are horseback rides (AR$200), although these are more for the ride's sake than for wildlife-spotting.

⌷ Sleeping

⌷ Colonia Pellegrini

Colonia Pellegrini's numerous accommodations are divided between *hospedajes*, usually simple rooms behind a family home, and *posadas* or *hosterías*, comfortable lodges that offer full-board rates and excursions. Multiday packages are offered by most lodges, who can also book transfers from Mercedes or Posadas.

Posada Rancho Jabirú
GUESTHOUSE $
(📞03773-15-443569; www.posadaranchojabiru.com.ar; Yaguareté s/n; s/d/tr US$30/44/66; ❄🅿) The best of the budget options. Set in a carefully-tended flowery garden, it has spotless rooms sleeping up to five in a pretty bungalow. It's run by the friendly folk of Yacarú Porá restaurant next door.

Hospedaje Los Amigos
GUESTHOUSE $
(📞03773-15-493753; hospedajelosamigos@gmail.com; cnr Guazú Virá & Aguapé; r per person US$15; ❄) An excellent budget choice, with a kindly owner, this place offers spotless rooms with big beds and decent bathrooms for a pittance. You can also eat simply but well here: full-board rates (add US$8) are available.

Hospedaje San Cayetano
GUESTHOUSE $
(📞03773-15-400929; www.argentinaparamirar.com.ar; cnr Guazú Virá & Aguapé; s/d US$30/60; ❄🅿🅿) This friendly choice with plunge pool, kitchen and *parrilla* is constantly improving, and offers appealing twins, doubles and family rooms with good beds and showers. Rooms can be shared if others want to, and prices are a little negotiable. Runs good boat trips. Beethoven, the parrot, covers front-of-house.

El Paso Cabañas
CABAÑAS $
(📞03773-15-400274; www.elpasoibera.com.ar; cnr Timbó & Yaguareté; d US$60, 4-person cabins US$100; ❄🅿🅿) Dotted across a sizable grassy garden, this is especially good for families. Cabins are comfortable and sleep up to six, while simpler rooms share a stove and fridge. It's run by helpful people who run excursions, and there's an on-site restaurant. English and German spoken.

Hospedaje Iberá
GUESTHOUSE $
(📞03773-15-627261; www.hospedajeibera.com.ar; cnr Guazú Virá & Ysypó; r per person US$15) Set behind a shop, this has a range of clean and spacious rooms with fan and hot-water bathroom.

Camping Iberá
CAMPGROUND $
(📞03773-15-629656; www.ibera.gov.ar; Mbiguá s/n; per person 1st/subsequent days AR$70/50, per vehicle 1st day only AR$40) This municipal campground by the lake is a great place with grassy pitches, nearly all with their own covered barbecue/eating area. Boat trips leave from here, and it's worth checking out the view as the sun sets. Book ahead as it's not huge. Also rents canoes.

Rancho Inambú
GUESTHOUSE $$
(📞03773-15-401362; www.ranchoinambu.com.ar; Yerutí s/n; r per person US$45; ❄) On the northern side of town near the soccer pitch, this is one of few midrange choices. Rooms are simple, rustic and comfortable and are set in a pleasant jungly garden. The cordial owner is a keen bird-watcher so his excursions are particularly good for that.

★ Rancho de los Esteros
LODGE $$$
(📞03773-15-493041; www.ranchodelosesteros.com.ar; cnr Ñangapiry & Capivára; s US$318, d standard/superior US$407/424, incl full-board & activities; ❄🅿🅿🅿) This exquisitely peaceful lakeside retreat is run with traditional Argentine country hospitality by its owners. Four gorgeous, super-spacious rooms (they can fit a family) surround a beautifully maintained wetland garden full of birdsong. Traditional architecture, attentive hosts, tasty meals and lakeside shelter to watch the

spectacular sunsets make this a very special place. Minimum two-night stay.

Ecoposada del Estero   LODGE $$$
(☏03773-15-443602; www.ecoposadadelestero.com.ar; Yaguareté s/n; s/d incl full-board & activities US$210/350; ☎☀) ✐ Best in town for bird-watching, this place is warmly run by a couple who know the area intimately. Ecological design has resulted in comfortable adobe buildings with wide verandas, hammocks and attractive homemade recycled wooden furnishings. Excursions are great but you'll see plenty from here: the lodge sits right on the edge of an *estero*, has abundant birdlife and a high observation platform.

Ñandé Retá   LODGE $$$
(☏03773-499411; www.nandereta.com; Guazú Virá s/n; s/d for 2 nights incl full-board & activities US$520/803; ☀@☎☀☷) This place has been around longer than most, and is still one of the most pleasing. Surrounded by pines and eucalypts, it has a peaceful, hidden-away feel that is highly seductive. It's very family friendly, the rooms are colorful and rustic in feel, service is excellent and the pool decent-sized. There are usually good-value bed-and-breakfast-only rates available too.

Aguapé Lodge   LODGE $$$
(☏03773-499412, reservations 011-4742-3015; www.iberaesteros.com.ar; Yacaré s/n; s/d incl full-board & activities US$340/540, incl full-board US$160/230; ☎☀) This luxurious, long-established colonial-style posada is in a beautiful setting above the lake. It has attractive, high-ceilinged rooms, all-white walls and dark wood, along a veranda looking over the lawn to the water, and a wide variety of excursions. Cheaper 'rustic' rooms in another building are smaller, but also have plenty of character. Service is excellent.

Posada de La Laguna   LODGE $$$
(☏03773-499413; www.posadadelalaguna.com; Guazú Virá s/n; d incl full board & activities US$400; ☀☎☀) Simple and elegant, in wide lakeside grounds, this lodge has bright white rooms with great beds and paintings by the owner. The emphasis is on relaxation (no TV), and staff pull it off, with friendly service, guided trips and good meals. Rooms in the building closer to the lake are slightly more charming, those in the other building are more private.

Irupé Lodge   LODGE $$$
(☏0376-443-8312; www.ibera-argentina.com; Yacaré s/n; standard s/d US$165/220, superior US$220/275; ☀☎☀) On the lake near the causeway, this rustic lodge makes you feel very welcome. While standard rooms are satisfactory, artistic wooden furniture, a pool and views across the water are the highlights. Superiors are a lot better, more attractive and sizable with greater privacy and verandas. Excursions are extra. Argentines pay 25% less.

Rancho Iberá   LODGE $$$
(☏03773-15-412661; www.posadaranchoibera.com.ar; cnr Caraguatá & Aguará; d for 2 nights incl full-board & activities US$537; ☀☎) Attractively decorated rooms with narrow beds surround a tranquil veranda and garden at this friendly, central place. There are kayaks for guests to use and a self-contained *cabaña*.

🛏 Around the Region

★Estancia Rincón del Socorro   LODGE $$$
(☏03782-15-475114; www.rincondelsocorro.com; RP40, Km83; s/d incl full-board & activities US$480/640; ☎☀☷) This ranch, 31km south of Pellegrini, is a place in which to come to terms with the big sky and abundant wildlife. It's substantial country comfort rather than luxury; the pretty rooms interconnect, making them great for family stays, while freestanding cabins sleep two. Beyond, vast lawns blend into pastureland and contemplation.

There's one cheaper room (single/double US$390/520). Excursions from here are great, with chances of seeing the reintroduced giant anteater. If Socorro isn't remote enough, San Alonso, its sister estancia, is only reachable by plane.

Hotel Puerto Valle   LODGE $$$
(☏03786-425700; www.puertovalle.com.ar; RN12, Km1282; s/d incl full-board, transfers & activities from US$590/850; ☀@☎☀) This luxurious secluded option is on the bank of the Paraná – huge here, above the Yacyreta dam – near the Esteros' northeastern tip. Rooms, some in the historic original building, others in annexes, are impeccable, with great river views. Meals and service are excellent. Excursions to the Iberá, their cayman farm, monkey path and along the river are included. B&B rates available.

Iberá Lodge   LODGE $$$
(☏0379-423-0228; www.iberalodge.com; RP29; s/d incl full-board, transfers & activities US$450/620; ☎☀☷) This handsome complex has a totally rural location by the lake shore, 55km north of Mercedes via RP29. Rooms are

furnished in elegant country style; riding and boat trips are included. Grassy grounds and a plethora of facilities, including games room, spa and excellent food, make this a fine retreat. Cheaper for Argentines.

✗ Eating

Lodges provide meals for their guests; many allow nonguests if you ask in advance. There are other simple options in town. Eating hours are early for Argentina.

Yacarú Porá   ARGENTINE $
(cnr Caraguatá & Yaguareté; mains AR$55-100; ⊙noon-2:30pm & 7:30-10:30pm; ☎) Run with charm and enthusiasm, this bungalow guarantees a warm welcome. Food is prepared to order and features generous portions of meat, chicken dishes, pasta, salads, omelets and *milanesas* (breaded cutlets).

Los Carros   ARGENTINE $
(cnr Mburucuyá & Yaguareté; mains AR$40-70; ⊙11:30am-2pm & 7-9pm) Likable and family-run, this simple place, with the picturesque horse carts it's named for in the yard, does tasty home-cooked food adorned with herbs from the garden and fresh vegetables. There's no menu and a limited selection: if you fancy local specialties, order in advance.

Restaurante El Paso   ARGENTINE $$
(www.elpasoibera.com.ar; cnr Timbó & Yaguareté; mains AR$80-200; ⊙11am-3pm & 7-10pm) With a range of fish, beef and chicken dishes, as well as some regional specialties, this makes a decent meal stop. Its speciality is farmed caiman, which comes stir-fried, as a *milanesa* (breaded fillet) or in empanadas.

ℹ Information

There is no bank or ATM, so take cash. Wi-fi is widespread but unreliable. **Kiosco El Paso** (cnr Ruta 40 & Yacaré; ⊙8am-8pm; ☎) on the main road at the town entrance will let you use their wi-fi if you buy something.

Municipal Tourist Office (www.ibera.gov.ar; RP40; ⊙8am-noon & 2-7pm) At the Mercedes entrance to the village, just after crossing the causeway.

Visitor Center (RP40; ⊙8am-6pm) The reserve's visitor center, on the Mercedes side of the causeway, has a good exhibition on local wildlife (Spanish) and an audiovisual presentation. The short path opposite gives you a sporting chance of seeing howler monkeys; and other paths and boardwalks introduce you to the area's different plants and habitats.

ℹ Getting There & Away

Transport options change regularly: check at Mercedes bus terminal tourist information.

The road from Mercedes to Colonia Pellegrini (120km) is driveable in a normal car except after rain.

At the time of research, there were no buses. The cheapest way to get here were two scheduled minibus/4WD services. Chartered transfers (from these or other operators) cost AR$1400 from Mercedes for up to four people. If it hasn't been raining, you could also get a *remise*.

The road from Posadas is worse (take the turning between Gobernador Virasoro and Santo Tomé in a normal car). Drivers charge AR$3000 for a charter to Posadas, or AR$2500 to Gobernador Virasoro, from where frequent buses travel the 80km on to Posadas.

There's no gas station in Pellegrini; the closest are in Mercedes and the main road junction near Santo Tomé. Fill up before you head in. A couple of places in Pellegrini can sell you gas and diesel if necessary.

Be aware that car-rental companies may refuse you service if you mention that the Iberá is one of your destinations.

Daniel Ortiz (☎03773-15-431469; AR$250-300) Runs daily from Mercedes at 7:30am to 8:30am, stopping outside the bus terminal but also doing hotel pick-ups. Returns from Pellegrini at around 4pm to 5pm. Price a little variable.

Iberá Bus (Mario Azcona; ☎03773-15-462836; AR$200) Leaves from the market on Pujol between Gómez and Alvear in Mercedes at midday to 12:30pm Monday to Friday and 9:30am Saturdays. Returns from Pellegrini 4am Monday to Saturday.

Martín Sandoval (☎03773-15-466072) Reliable for private transfers to Posadas and Mercedes.

Maxi Ojeda (☎03773-15-450486) Based in Pellegrini; runs transfers to Mercedes and Posadas.

ALONG THE RÍO URUGUAY

The lesser of the two great rivers that converge to form the Río de la Plata, the Uruguay divides the country of the same name from Argentina, and also forms part of the border with Brazil. Bridges provide access to these neighbors, whose influences have blended with those of indigenous and immigrant groups in the area. The Argentine riverside towns have lots to offer and are popular summer and weekend destinations.

IGUAZÚ FALLS & THE NORTHEAST RESERVA PROVINCIAL ESTEROS DEL IBERÁ

Concepción del Uruguay

☎ 03442 / POP 89.300

Set around a stately plaza, Concepción is a typical riverside town, wondering what to do with itself now that trade on the Río Uruguay has died off. It makes a decent stopover, has good sleeping and eating choices, and boasts the Palacio San José outside town.

◉ Sights

The principal sights in the town itself are around the noble main plaza, where the earthy-pink-colored basilica holds the remains of Justo José de Urquiza.

Palacio San José PALACE
(www.palaciosanjose.com; RP39, Km30; adult/child AR$25/5; ☺8am-7pm Mon-Fri, 9am-6pm Sat & Sun) Topped by twin towers and surrounded by elegant gardens, Justo José de Urquiza's ostentatious pink palace is 33km west of Concepción. Set around an arched patio, with a walled garden out back, it was built partly to show up Urquiza's arch rival in Buenos Aires, Juan Manuel de Rosas, and partly to show the power and wealth of Entre Ríos province. Local *caudillo* (provincial strongman) Urquiza was largely responsible for Rosas' 1852 downfall and the eventual adoption of Argentina's modern constitution.

Sometime allies such as Domingo Sarmiento and Bartolomé Mitre supped at Urquiza's 8.5m dining-room table and slept in the palatial bedrooms. The bedroom in which Urquiza was murdered by a mob sent by Ricardo López Jordán is a permanent shrine, created by Urquiza's wife.

From Concepción, **Sarbimas** (☎03442-427777) or other *remise* companies will take up to four people there and back, including a two-hour wait, for AR$320. Another option is a tour – **Turismo Pioneros** (☎03442-433914; www.facebook.com/pionerosturismo; Mitre 908) will take two people for AR$180, including a guided visit. You could also jump off a Caseros-bound bus and walk 3km to

the palace. There's a mediocre restaurant and picturesque grounds for picnicking.

⌕ Sleeping

★**Antigua Fonda** HOTEL $
(☎03442-433734; www.antiguafonda.com.ar; España 172; s/d US$39/49; ❀ ☎) Though you wouldn't know, this has been created from part of what was once a historic Concepción hotel. Pleasing, spacious rooms in shades of cream surround a small grassy garden, with artistic touches and a relaxing vibe. It's a block west and three south of the plaza. Great value.

Residencial Centro GUESTHOUSE $
(☎03442-427429; www.nuevorescentro.com.ar; Moreno 130; r US$32; ❀ ☎) The best budget hotel in town has a variety of rooms around a courtyard near the plaza. They vary slightly in price depending on size and if they have air-con; there's more light in the ones upstairs.

Antigua Posta del Torreón BOUTIQUE HOTEL $$
(☎03442-432618; www.postadeltorreon.com.ar; Almafuerte 799; s/d/superior d US$59/76/89; ❀ ☎ ☲) This intimate hotel a block west and four south of the plaza offers a real haven for a relaxing stay. It's an elegantly refurbished 19th-century mansion with original features and rooms surrounding a postcard-pretty courtyard complete with fountain and small pool. Superiors are worth the upgrade: much more spacious, with lovely furniture.

✕ Eating

Sumeria MICROBREWERY $$
(www.sumeriabar.com.ar; Eva Perón 207; mains AR$100-210; ☺7pm-2am Thu-Sun, opens extra days in summer; ☎) In an historic corner house, this is a new concept for Concepción. Tasty microbrewed beers (including a honey one) accompany a varied menu that takes in salmon *chivitos* (Uruguayan steak sandwich), innovative salads and deli plates that include a vegetarian one. On Thursdays it does sushi. There's a pleasant patio: in all, a great place to hang out.

Head north three blocks from the northeast corner of the plaza.

El Conventillo de Baco ARGENTINE $$
(☎03442-433809; http://erbiodiaz.wix.com/el-nuevo-conventillo; España 193; mains AR$105-150; ☺11am-3pm & 8pm-midnight Wed-Mon, 11am-3pm Tue) This handsome and totally recommendable spot has both indoor and

---

ℹ **ENTERING URUGUAY**

Three main crossings link Argentina with its eastern neighbor Uruguay. From south to north these are Gualeguaychú–Fray Bentos, Colón–Paysandú (cars pay an AR$100 toll on these two bridges) and Concordia–Salto. All three are open 24 hours.

GUALEGUAYCHÚ CARNAVAL

A mellow riverside town, Gualeguaychú is quiet out of season but kicks off in summer with the country's longest and flashiest Carnaval celebration (www.carnavaldelpais.com. ar). Any weekend from mid-January to late February you'll find things in full swing. The main venue is the Corsódromo, where admission is AR$150 to AR$220 most nights.

There's a string of decent budget hotels along Bolívar between Bartolomé Mitre and Monseñor Chalup, and several hostels in town.

Gualeguaychú is easily reached by bus from Buenos Aires (3½ hours), Paraná and other Río Uruguay towns. Gualeguaychú is also a crossing point to Uruguay: Fray Bentos lies just across the bridge.

outdoor dining in an attractive patio space and specializes in well-prepared river fish and seafood. Good value.

ⓘ Information

Tourist Office (☎ 03442-425820; www.concep cionentrerios.tur.ar; cnr Galarza & Supremo Entrerriano; ⊗7am-1pm & 2-8pm) The handiest tourist office is a block east of the plaza.

ⓘ Getting There & Around

The **bus terminal** (☎ 03442-422352; cnr Galarza & Chiloteguy) is 10 blocks west of the plaza. Bus 1 runs between them; a *remise* costs AR$20.

A train arrives in Concepción from Paraná on Fridays and returns on Sundays (AR$24, seven hours).

Buses from Concepción

DESTINATION	COST (AR$)	TIME (HR)
Buenos Aires	260	4
Colón	24	¾
Concordia	73	2¾
Gualeguaychú	40	1
Paraná	133	5

Colón

☑ 03447 / POP 24,800

The most appealing destination for riverside relaxation in Entre Ríos, Colón's population almost doubles with Argentine holidaymakers in January, but the pretty town takes it all in its stride. With numerous places to stay, a thriving handicrafts scene and worthwhile, out-of-the-ordinary restaurants, it's a great place to be. It's also a base for visiting Parque Nacional El Palmar.

Colón is connected to Paysandú in Uruguay by bridge. The center of the action is

Plaza San Martín, a block back from the river, and the street 12 de Abril running up to it.

◉ Sights & Activities

Strolling around the riverbank, the beach and quiet leafy streets is the highlight here. Numerous *artesanía* shops sell everything from *mate* gourds to pickled coypu.

☞ Tours

Ita i Cora Aventura BOAT TOUR
(☎ 03447-423360; itaicora@gmail.com; San Martín 97; 2hr tour AR$280) The best option for getting out on the river. Its standard tour is a charismatic two-hour affair taking in sand flats and a forest trail in the middle of the Río Uruguay. Excellent English spoken.

Naturaleza Yatay BUS TOUR
(☎ 03447-15-465528; www.naturalezayatay.com. ar; El Palmar tour AR$280) Runs good guided trips to the El Palmar national park. Can organize tailored bird-watching excursions. English spoken.

✦ Festivals & Events

Fiesta Nacional de la Artesanía HANDICRAFTS
(www.fiestadelaartesania.com.ar) This crafts fair in February in Parque Quirós features high-standard live folkloric entertainment.

⊨ Sleeping

There are numerous summer campgrounds, cabins, bungalows and apartments available for rent. Look for signs saying '*Alquilo a turistas*.' The tourist office can supply you with a list of official accommodations: there are several hundred.

Hostería El Viejo Almacén GUESTHOUSE $
(☎ 03447-422216; Av Urquiza 108; s/d US$30/58; ❄ⓢ) In the restaurant of the same name, this is ultra-friendly and has simple, neat yellow-painted rooms with both fan and

IGUAZÚ FALLS & THE NORTHEAST COLÓN

YAPEYÚ

This delightfully peaceful place is no one-horse town: there are many horses, and the sound of their hooves thumping the reddish earth in the evening is one of the nicest things about it. Yapeyú is a great spot to relax: the sort of place where locals will greet you on the street.

An hour north of Paso de los Libres by bus, Yapeyú was founded in 1626 as the southernmost of the Jesuit missions. It's also famous for being the birthplace of the great Argentine 'Liberator', José de San Martín.

You can examine the Jesuit ruins – the **museum** (Sargento Cabral s/n; ⊙ 8am-noon & 3-6pm Tue-Sun) **FREE** here has a comprehensive overview of all the missions – and admire the ornate **Casa de San Martín** (⊙ 8am-noon & 2-6pm) **FREE**, a pavilion that now shelters the ruins of the house where San Martín was born in 1778.

On the plaza between these, **Hotel San Martín** (☑ 03772-493120; Sargento Cabral 712; s/d US$25/40; ❇ 🛜) is a simple, welcoming place set around an echoey inner courtyard. Up a notch, **El Paraíso Yapeyú** (☑ 03772-493056; www.paraisoyapeyu.com.ar; cnr Paso de los Patos & San Martín; bungalows for 2/4 people US$60/95; ❇ 🛜 🏊 🅿) is a faded complex of bungalows with a nice riverside position. More upmarket options are on the highway west of town. **Comedor del Paraíso** (Matorras s/n; mains AR$40-60; ⊙ 7am-3pm & 8-10:30pm) is a likably simple central spot to eat with no menu, just a limited choice of what's available that day.

Four daily buses (AR$36, one hour) run to/from Paso de los Libres and to Posadas (AR$181, 4½ hours) in the other direction. More buses stop on the highway at the edge of the town.

air-con plus plenty of space. Go for one near the front if in-room wi-fi is important. An excellent deal: the only problem is a rumbling stomach from the aromas of grilling meat. You can book online.

La Casona de Susana   HOSTEL, GUESTHOUSE $
(☑ 03447-425349; www.lacasonadesusana.com.ar; cnr 3 de Febrero & Paysandú; dm US$20, d US$40-70; ❇ 🛜 🏊) This is a quirky but welcoming spot between the bus terminal and river. Shared or private accommodation is available in three different room grades – simple but serviceable en-suite dorms to plush, colorful modern rooms. All have fridges, there's a pretty pool out back and kitchen use. Air-con extra in summer.

★ **Hostería 'Restaurant del Puerto'**   HOTEL $$
(☑ 03447-422698; www.hosteriadecolon.com.ar; Alejo Peyret 158; r US$85-90; ❇ @ 🛜 🏊 🅿) In what has a strong claim to be Colón's loveliest house, this has characterful rooms decorated faithfully in the style of the 1880 building, with enormous windows, plenty of wood and noble rustic furniture. Family duplexes (US$110) are a good deal, as are midweek discounts. The restaurant serves good dinners, and there's an outdoor heated pool and Jacuzzi out back. No cards.

Hotel Plaza   HOTEL $$
(☑ 03447-421043; www.hotel-plaza.com.ar; cnr 12 de Abril & Belgrano; standard/superior d US$118/148; ❇ @ 🛜 🏊 🅿) This Colón staple has been around for a century, but now looks modern and glistening. The rooms, all exterior, aren't quite as posh; the superiors (Neo) have more space and quality bathrooms. But the combination of plaza-side location (some rooms have balconies) and decent-sized heated pool out the back make it a winner. Four-night minimum stay in high summer.

Hotel Costarenas   HOTEL $$$
(☑ 03447-425050; www.hotelcostarenas.com.ar; cnr Av Quirós & 12 de Abril; s/d US$103/150, with view US$124/177, superior d US$187-229; ❇ @ 🛜 🏊 🅿) A favorite of weekending *porteños,* this offers smart, very well-kept riverside accommodation. The handsome downstairs spa/pool complex is included; there's also an outdoor pool and a good restaurant. Rooms are bland cream but well-equipped; those with views are lighter and larger, while superior rooms add a few more square meters. Family rooms have kitchenette. Service is personable.

🍴 Eating & Drinking

El Sótano de los Quesos   DELI $
(www.elsotanodelosquesos.com.ar; cnr Chacabuco & Av Costanera; mixed plates for 1/2 people

AR$90/150; ⊗5-11:30pm Wed-Mon; 🚗) This intriguing spot serves artisanal cheeses and other delicacies at pretty thatched tables on a lawn overlooking the port. There's also locally made wine and beer, and a cellar shop whose aromas will almost compel you to buy. Opening hours extend in summer. Flooding sometimes drives it across the street.

El Viejo Almacén
ARGENTINE $

(🚗03447-422216; cnr Urquiza & Paso; mains AR$55-140; ⊗11:30am-3pm & 8pm-midnight; 🛜) A block from the plaza and offering a quiet, brick-walled interior decorated with old-time photos, this has a wide-ranging menu including great homemade pasta, delicious empanadas, river fish and *parrilla* options. Portions aren't as big as in some places – probably a good thing – but prices are low and vegetables come from their organic garden.

La Cantina
ARGENTINE $

(Peyret 79; mains AR$50-110; ⊗11am-2:30pm & 8:30pm-midnight Tue-Sun) Just off the plaza, this likable family-run restaurant does a nice line in uncomplicated and filling fare, with sizable chicken and beef dishes alongside tasty homemade pasta and river-fish options, including surubí empanadas.

★La Cosquilla del Ángel
ARGENTINE $$

(🚗03447-423711; cnr San Martín & Balcarce; mains AR$110-160; ⊗noon-4pm Mon, noon-4pm & 8pm-midnight Wed-Sun; 🛜) Colón's best restaurant combines elegant, romantic decor and service with a whimsical and unpretentious approach, particularly in the curiously named dishes and the intriguing restaurant name: The Angel's Tickle. Many dishes combine sweet and savory flavors; try the *mollejitas* (sweetbreads). The pasta is recommended and the wine list is above average.

Restaurant del Puerto
ARGENTINE $$

(www.hosteriadecolon.com.ar; Peyret 158; mains AR$100-170; ⊗8pm-midnight Thu-Tue; 🛜) In a lovely old building near the river, this restaurant does tasty evening meals with good service and plenty of imaginative river-fish dishes. It's good for a lighter dinner, with plenty of salad vegetables and fruit used. No cards.

🛍 Shopping

La Casona
HANDICRAFTS

(12 de Abril 106; ⊗9:30am-12:30pm & 6-9pm) 🚗 On the corner of the plaza, this cooperative sells a wide range of handmade goods.

ℹ️ Information

Tourist Office (📠03447-423000; www.colonturismo.tur.ar; cnr Gouchón & Av Costanera; ⊗8am-9pm) Occupies the former customs building, built by Urquiza. There is also an office in the bus terminal (8am to 7pm).

ℹ️ Getting There & Around

Colón's **bus terminal** (📠03447-421716; cnr Rocamora & 9 de Julio) is eight blocks north of the main shopping and entertainment street, 12 de Abril. A *remise* downtown costs around AR$35.

Destinations include Buenos Aires (AR$305, 4½ to six hours), Gualeguaychú (AR$53, two hours) via Concepción (AR$24, 40 minutes), Concordia (AR$61, two hours) via Ubajay (AR$32, one hour) and Paysandú, Uruguay (AR$61 to AR$75, 45 minutes, three to five Monday to Saturday, one Sunday).

Parque Nacional El Palmar

On the Uruguay's bank, midway between Colón and Concordia, 8500-sq-km **Parque Nacional El Palmar** (📠03447-493049; www.parquesnacionales.gob.ar; RN 14, Km199; Argentines/Mercosur/foreigners AR$70/100/120) preserves the last extensive stands of yatay palm on the Argentine littoral. In the 19th century, the native yatay covered large parts of Entre Ríos, Uruguay and southern Brazil, but intensive agriculture, ranching and forestry destroyed much of the palm savanna.

Reaching a maximum height of about 18m, the larger specimens clustered throughout the park create a striking and soothing subtropical landscape that lends itself to photography. Grasslands and gallery forests along the watercourses shelter much wildlife.

Park admission (valid for 48 hours) is collected at the entrance from 7am to 7pm, but the gate is open 24 hours.

👁 Sights & Activities

Facilities are 12km from the highway entrance down a good dirt road. Here, the **visitor center** (⊗8am-6pm) has displays on natural history; you can organize canoeing, cycling and horseback-riding trips. Roads lead off the main access road to three viewpoints. **Arroyo Los Loros**, a short distance north of the campground, is a good place to observe wildlife. South of the visitor center is Arroyo El Palmar, a pleasant stream accessed at two viewpoints, **La Glorieta** and **El Palmar**. These have short marked trails;

the latter has a bird-watching hide. There are three other short trails near the visitor center, and another hide by the river. Guided walks are available by prior arrangement.

There is river access for swimming and boating from the campground.

🛏 Sleeping & Eating

Ubajay has basic rooms at the bus terminal, plus other cheap lodgings.

Camping El Palmar   CAMPGROUND $
(☑ 03447-423378; campsites per adult/child/tent US$8/4/5) This sociable campground by the visitor center is the park's only place to stay, with shady, level campsites, hot showers and electricity. The shop sells snacks and food, including slabs of beef for the barbecues; opposite, there's a restaurant.

La Aurora del Palmar   LODGE, CAMPGROUND $$
(☑ 03447-15-431689; www.auroradelpalmar.com.ar; RN14, Km202; campsites per adult/child/tent US$11/5/11, d/q from US$120/180; ❉ 🛜 🛏 🚻) Near the park entrance, this cattle ranch and citrus farm has a protected palm forest as spectacular as the national park itself. It's an original, well-run place with shady campsites, family duplexes in a pretty bungalow, and attractive rooms in renovated railway carriages. There's a good swimming pool and a restaurant. Canoeing, horseback riding and palm safaris are available.

❶ Getting There & Away

El Palmar is on RN14, a major national highway, with frequent north–south bus services. Any bus will drop you at the park entrance, 12km from the visitors center. You could walk or hitchhike from here or else get off 6km north at Ubajay (check out the Model T Ford in the bus terminal), from where a remise will cost you around AR$180 to the visitors center. Call ☑ 03447-15-520-1941.

The easiest way to get here is by tour from Colón. You can also charter a remise from Colón: a return trip plus two hours at the park, covering all the trails, costs AR$540 (up to four people). **Remis Colón** (☑ 03447-422221; Alem 13) is recommended.

Concordia

☑ 0345 / POP 149,500

This pleasant agricultural service town on the Río Uruguay won't keep you spellbound for weeks, but it makes a convenient stop for a night. It's a citrus town – you can smell the tang in the air at times – and has a fine central plaza, riverside beaches and fishing. It also offers a border crossing, across a hydroelectric dam, to the Uruguayan city of Salto.

◉ Sights & Activities

Museo Judío de Entre Ríos   MUSEUM
(☑ 0345-421-4088; www.museojudioer.org.ar; Entre Ríos 476; donation AR$30; ⊗ 8:30am-12:30pm Sun-Tue, Thu & Fri) Three rooms detailing the arrival and struggles of the Jewish gauchos, their way of life and the Holocaust seen through the eyes of those who experienced it. Also temporary exhibitions. One block west and 2½ south of the plaza.

Castillo San Carlos   RUIN
(admission AR$25; ⊗ 9am-noon & 2-5pm, 3-6pm from Nov-Feb) In riverside Parque Rivadavia, northeast of town, this ruined mansion was built in 1888 by a French industrialist who

---

THE GAUCHO JUDÍO

The gaucho is an archetypal Argentine image, but it's little-known that many were of Jewish origin. The first known mass Jewish immigration was in the late 19th century, when 800 Russian Jews arrived fleeing persecution from Czar Alexander III.

The Jewish Colonization Association, funded by a German philanthropist, began distributing 100-hectare parcels of land to immigrant families; the first major colony was Moisés Ville in Santa Fe province, which became known at the time as Jerusalem Argentina. Today there are only about 300 Jewish residents left in town (15% of the population), but many traditions prevail: the tiny town boasts four synagogues, the bakery sells Sabbath bread, and kids in the street use Yiddish slang words like 'schlep' and 'schlock.'

These rural Jews readily assimilated into Argentine society, mixing their own traditions with those of their adopted country, so it was not unusual to see a figure on horseback in baggy pants, canvas shoes and skullcap on his way to throw a hunk of cow on the asado (barbecue). Many descendants have since left the land in search of education and opportunities in the cities. Argentina's Jews number about 200,000, making them Latin America's largest Jewish community.

To learn more about the gauchos judíos, visit Concordia's **Museo Judío de Entre Ríos**.

mysteriously abandoned the property years later. Writer Antoine de Saint-Exupéry briefly lived here; there's a monument to *The Little Prince* nearby.

Sleeping

Hotel Pellegrini
HOTEL $

(📞 0345-422-7137; www.turismoentrerios.com/hotelpellegrini; Pellegrini 443; s/d US$30/42; 🌡🐕) By far the best budget choice, three blocks south of the plaza, this friendly family-run spot offers simple, clean rooms with TV and bathroom. You'll usually need to book ahead, as it's deservedly popular.

Hotel Salto Grande
HOTEL $$

(📞 0345-421-0034; www.hotelsaltogrande.net; Urquiza 581; turista s/d US$66/83, standard US$88/110, especial US$110/138; 🌡@🐕🏊) Just south of the main plaza, this hotel offers excellent service and fair prices. It's showing its age but is gradually being renovated. There are several grades of room; the 'especial' ones are remodeled, but 'standards' aren't much better than regular 'turista' ones. Above-average breakfast and parking included.

✖ Eating

El Reloj
PIZZA $

(Pellegrini 580; pizza AR$70-100; ⏱11am-3:30pm & 7pm-1am Mon-Sat; 🐕) This spacious brick-walled pizzeria has good ambience and a staggering selection of options. Half-and-half? No problem. It also does *parrilla*. Look out for special deals operating almost nightly.

Malaika
ARGENTINE $$

(📞 0345-422-4867; www.facebook.com/malaikaconcordia; 1 de Mayo 59; mains AR$100-160; ⏱11am-4pm & 6pm-2am Tue-Sun; 🐕🍴) Relaxed and handsome, this cafe-bar serves a variety of tasty meals, with salads, pizzas, pasta, snacks and more elaborate fare, including vegetarian options and daily specials. Decent wines, accessible prices, homemade bread, caring service and a romantic mood seal the deal.

ⓘ Information

Tourist Office (📞 0345-421-3905; www.concordia.tur.ar; cnr Pellegrini & Mitre; ⏱8am-9pm) On the plaza. The bus terminal info desk can also help.

ⓘ Getting There & Away

The **bus terminal** (📞 0345-421-7235; cnr Justo & Hipólito Yrigoyen) is 13 blocks north of Plaza 25 de Mayo. Four daily buses (none Sundays) go to Salto, Uruguay (AR$80 to AR$88, 1¼ hours).

THERMAL SPAS

Many towns along the Río Uruguay – Gualeguaychú, Colón and Concordia for starters – have tapped the region's abundant geothermal aquifers to create appealing thermal spa complexes: a major focus of domestic tourism in these parts. They are well-equipped places with several indoor and outdoor pools of various temperatures. Entry to most of them is around AR$70 to AR$150. Check www.termasdeentrerios.com for a complete list.

From the port beyond the east end of Carriego, launches cross the river to Salto (AR$70, 15 minutes, four daily Monday to Saturday).

Buses from Concordia

DESTINATION	COST (AR$)	TIME (HR)
Buenos Aires	400	5½-6
Colón	61	2
Concepción	73	2¾
Corrientes	335	7-8
Paraná	128	4½
Paso de los Libres	160	4
Posadas	460-560	8½

ⓘ Getting Around

Bus 2 takes Yrigoyen south from the bus terminal to the town center. On its northward run catch it on Pellegrini in front of Banco de la Nación. A taxi should cost about AR$35.

Paso de los Libres
📞 03772 / POP 40,500

The name ('Crossing of the Free') is the most romantic thing about this border town on the Río Uruguay. It faces the larger Brazilian city of Uruguaiana opposite, and is connected to it by a well-used bridge. There's little to detain the traveler, but the town has plenty of cross-border life, a picturesque central plaza, and acceptable sleeping and eating options.

🛏 Sleeping & Eating

Hotel Alejandro Primero
HOTEL $

(📞 03772-424100; www.alejandroprimero.com.ar; Coronel López 502; s/d US$50/70; 🌡@🐕🏊) Ageing but reliable, this has an elegant and old-fashioned lobby and restaurant and less impressive but very spacious rooms. Ask for one with views over the river and Uruguaiana. There's also a pleasant outdoor pool and garden area. Card payments cost extra.

Hotel Las Vegas
HOTEL $
(☑ 03772-423490; hotellasvegas2000@hotmail.com; Sarmiento 554; s/d US$30/50; ❄ ✿) Despite the burgundy carpets and '70s feel, this isn't so old and is a well-kept budget place in the town center. Rooms are dark but comfortable with adequate bathrooms. Rooms up the back have more light and space. Ask for air-con if you want it: you do.

El Nuevo Mesón
ARGENTINE $
(Colón 587; mains AR$65-110; ⏱11:30am-3pm & 8pm-midnight; ✿) Still the best place to eat in Libres, with waiters smartly turned out in black-and-white and a wide range of decent dishes. There's pizza, *parrilla*, the river fish *pacú* and more elaborate creations, but it's all fairly priced – unlike a couple of tourist traps in town – and tasty. Grab a table outside in fine weather.

ⓘ Information

There's no tourist office, but there are maps of town all over the town center. You can change money on the international bridge.

ⓘ Getting There & Away

The **bus terminal** (☑ 425600) is 1km from downtown. There are services to Buenos Aires (AR$570, eight to nine hours), Posadas (AR$219 to AR$275, five to six hours) and Corrientes (AR$220, five hours) via Mercedes (AR$71, three hours).

Buses to Uruguaiana (AR$15), Brazil, leave frequently, stopping on Av San Martín at Colón and opposite the bus terminal (by the castlelike building).

The frontier is open 24 hours. Travelers report that you can transit to Uruguay without requiring a Brazilian visa here, but don't bank on it.

ⓘ Getting Around

Buses and minibuses (AR$5) run from the corner below the bus terminal into town. A taxi downtown is AR$30.

MISIONES

The narrow northeastern province of Misiones juts out like an Argentine finger between Brazilian and Paraguayan territory and is named for the Jesuit missions whose ruins are now a major attraction. Buses churn through Misiones en route to the Iguazú Falls in the north of the province, but a detour will take you to another stunning cascade – the Saltos del Moconá on the Río Uruguay.

The landscape here is striking; you will see a change to gently rolling low hills, stands of bamboo, and fields of papaya and manioc. Plantations grow from the region's trademark red-brown soil – the province is the main producer of *mate,* Argentina's national drink.

Posadas

☑ 0376 / POP 324,800

Capital of Misiones, and a base for visiting the Jesuit ruins after which the province is named, Posadas is a modern city that gazes across the wide Río Paraná to Encarnación in Paraguay. It's a stopover on the way north, and though offers few in-town sights, has a pleasant riverbank and an enjoyable vibe.

⊙ Sights

The Jesuit missions are the area's big attraction.

★ Costanera
WATERFRONT
In the afternoon, the *costanera* comes alive with joggers, cyclists, dog walkers, *mate* sippers, hot-dog vendors and young couples staring at Paraguay across the water. Pride of place goes to 'Andresito,' a huge stainless-steel **sculpture** of Guaraní provincial strongman Andrés Guacarurí (Guazurary), looking like the Tin Man in search of a heart.

Fundación Artesanías Misioneras
GALLERY
(www.famercosur.com.ar; cnr Alvarez & Arrechea; ⏱8:30am-12:30pm & 5-8:30pm Mon-Fri, 9:30am-12:30pm & 5-8pm Sat) 🆓 Guaraní culture is strong in this part of Argentina; particularly fine pieces are displayed and sold here. There's another branch on the *costanera*.

☞ Tours

Many operators offer tours to Iguazú Falls, the Jesuit missions and the Esteros del Iberá.

Guayrá
TOUR
(☑ 0376-443-3415; www.guayra.com.ar; La Rioja 1481) Very helpful agency (on the 3rd floor) offering half-day tours to the Jesuit missions, Paraguayan missions, Saltos del Moconá and more.

Yacaré Tours
TOUR
(☑ 0376-442-1829; www.yacaretours.com.ar; Bolívar 1419) Offers half-day trips to Argentine

Posadas

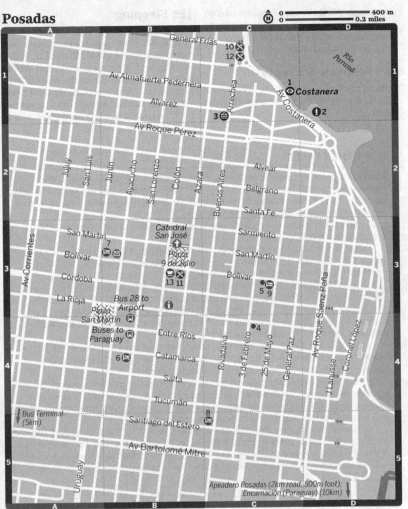

Posadas

◎ Top Sights
1 Costanera C1

◎ Sights
2 Andresito statue D1
3 Fundación Artesanías Misioneras C1

✦ Activities, Courses & Tours
4 Guayrá C4
5 Yacaré Tours C3

🛏 Sleeping
6 Grand Crucero Posadas Express B4

7 Hotel Posadas Urbano B3
8 Le Petit Hotel C5
9 Posadeña Linda C3

✕ Eating
10 Astillero C1
11 La Querencia B3
12 La Tradicional Rueda C1

🍷 Drinking & Nightlife
13 La Nouvelle Vitrage B3

(two people AR$1650) and Paraguayan (two people AR$1250) missions. Also has trips to *mate* plantations, the Saltos del Moconá, Esteros del Iberá and more.

★ Festivals & Events

Posadas celebrates Carnaval (in February or March, depending on the year) with great gusto.

🛏 Sleeping

Posadeña Linda　　　　　　HOSTEL $

(☎ 0376-443-9238; www.hostelposadasmisiones. com; Bolívar 1439; dm US$13-15, d US$32; ❋ @ 🛜 🛋) Run with a caring attitude, this narrow hostel a short walk from the plaza offers a genuine welcome, comfortable bunkrooms with bathroom and a patio with a tiny plunge pool. En suite private rooms are a little mus-

---

THE OTHER FALLS

Apart from Iguazú, the remote and unusual Saltos del Moconá also live long in the memory. A geological fault in the bed of the Río Uruguay divides the river lengthwise and water spills over the shelf between the two sections, creating a waterfall some 3km long and up to 15m high, depending on the water level.

The falls aren't always visible; if the river is high, you're out of luck. January to March is normally the best time to visit.

The falls are at Misiones' eastern edge, roughly equidistant from Posadas and Puerto Iguazú. From Posadas, several daily buses leave for El Soberbio (AR$123, four hours); from here it's 63km to the falls: there are three daily bus services.

At the end of the road, you cross the Río Yabotí (or not, if it's high) and arrive in **Parque Provincial Moconá** (http://saltosdelmocona.tur.ar; RP 2; foreigners AR$30; ⊙ 9am-5pm). Here there's a visitor center, walking trails with views of the falls, boat excursions to get you up close (AR$250), and a restaurant. The park website tells you the visible height of the falls; it's crucial to check before coming.

Various operators, including most accommodations in the area, run boat trips to the falls from points further away: these are recommended, as you get to see Brazilian and Argentine jungle reserves on each side, an attraction in itself.

El Soberbio is an interesting service center for a lush agricultural area growing tobacco, citronella and manioc. There's a ferry crossing to Brazil, and blond heads are everywhere, a legacy of German and Eastern European immigrants joining the native Guaraní population. Oxcarts are still commonly used for transport.

The several places to stay include spotless motel-style **Hostal Del Centro** (☎ 03755-495133; cnr Rivadavia & San Martín; s/d US$17.50/35; ❋ 🛜), right in the center of town but built around a grassy courtyard; rooms are good for the price and there's a kitchen you can use.

Several upmarket jungly lodges, simple cabins and campsites are closer to the falls, including:

Posada Guatambú (☎ 011-4729-6820; www.posadaguatambu.com; RP2, Km35; cabins US$71) Two sweet, roomy cabins make for a romantic retreat at this spot 3km off the road midway between El Soberbio and the falls. It's a spectacular property, with ample forested grounds and a river to bathe in. Hosts are engaged and welcoming, and provide tasty homestyle meals.

Posada La Misión (☎ 011-15-3415-0500; www.lodgelamision.com.ar; RP2, Km36; s/d incl dinner US$107/130, master suite US$191/227; ❋ 🛜 🛋 🐾) This superbly-situated spot sits on the riverbank 35km from El Soberbio. There are two types of room – rustic with fan and beautiful 'master suites' with air-con, veranda with view and modern bathroom with Jacuzzi. Rates are half-board and include excursions if you stay two nights or more.

Don Enrique Lodge (☎ 011-15-5932-6262; www.donenriquelodge.com.ar; Colonia La Flor; s/d incl full-board & activities US$150/260; 🛜) Beautiful wooden bungalows in a very remote location with the river below make for a romantic getaway. Delicious food and welcoming hosts seal the deal. Rate is full board, with guided walks and other activities included. The turnoff is 16km from El Soberbio, then another 16km up a rough road. A pickup will take you the last stretch.

ty but a decent deal. It's colorful and relaxing with a compact but OK kitchen. Despite the address, it's between 1411 and 1419.

Le Petit Hotel
HOTEL $

(☎0376-443-6031; www.hotellepetit.com.ar; Santiago del Estero 1630; s/d US$50/60; ❊@☎) Not so *petit* after a recent expansion, but peaceful and simple, this hotel is run by kindly people. It features dark, clean, adequate rooms that are spotlessly clean and surround a leafy patio or central atrium. It feels a little overpriced but has a nice location in a quiet, safe residential zone seven blocks from the heart of things. Cards 20% extra.

★ Hotel Posadas Urbano
HOTEL $$

(☎0376-444-3800; www.hahoteles.com; Bolívar 2176; s/d/ste US$96/111/157; ❊@☎❊) This smartly renovated hotel has rapidly become top dog with its wide array of facilities and great central location. Bright, very large carpeted chambers all have gleaming bathrooms, balconies and big windows with views over town. Suites add space but little else. The atrium pool area, art exhibitions, gym and spa facilities, and appealing lounge add points.

Grand Crucero Posadas Express
HOTEL $$

(☎0376-443-6901; www.grandcrucero.com; San Lorenzo 2208; s/d/ste US$100/114/193; ❊@☎) Owned by a bus company, this smart reconversion of an older hotel has resulted in crisp modern rooms with local art on the walls and a fresh feel. All come with safe, minifridge and good-looking bathrooms, while suites are large, have two flatscreens, laptop and coffee machine. Staff are professional and friendly and there's a bar-restaurant.

✗ Eating

A delicious speciality is *galeto* (chargrilled chicken pieces stuffed with bacon, red peppers and butter). A string of popular places along Bolívar west of the plaza do *lomitos*, sandwiches and other cheap eats.

★ La Tradicional Rueda
PARRILLA $$

(La Ruedita; Arrechea & Av Costanera; mains AR$85-150; ⊗11am-3:30pm & 7:30pm-midnight or later; ☎) Stylish and traditional in feel, with uniformed waiters and sturdy wooden seats, this two-level grillhouse has a prime riverside position: look for the wooden wheel outside. There's excellent service; quality meats and nice lines in salads and river fish put this a class above most *parrilla* places.

La Querencia
PARRILLA $$

(Bolívar 1867; mains AR$90-130; ⊗noon-2:30pm & 8pm-12:30am Mon-Sat, noon-2:30pm Sun; ☎) On the plaza, this upmarket *parrilla* specializes in delicious *galeto*. Also memorable are the brochettes (giant spikes with various delicious meats impaled upon them). Salads are also unusually well prepared. Service is great and the atmosphere a highlight.

Astillero
ARGENTINE $$

(Av Costanera s/n; mains AR$110-170; ⊗noon-3pm & 8pm-midnight; ☎) Tucked away behind foliage on the riverbank strip, this has a treehouse feel with three levels and a balcony with limited Paraná vistas. The food was a bit up-and-down when we visited, but the setting is romantic and the menu has potential. The wine list is full of good things, but lacks budget options.

🍷 Drinking & Nightlife

Most weekend action is down at the *costanera*, where a knot of eateries, bars and clubs go loud and late.

La Nouvelle Vitrage
CAFE

(Bolívar 1899; ⊗6am-1am; ☎) This traditional, amiable cafe on the plaza has a comfy interior and a terrace perfect for watching everyday life in Posadas go by. It serves an excellent Fernet and cola: you know you want one.

ℹ Information

Misiones Tourist Office (☎0376-444-7539; www.misiones.tur.ar; Colón 1985; ⊗7am-8pm) There are other tourist kiosks around town, but this is the most reliably open.

ℹ Getting There & Away

AIR

Aerolíneas Argentinas (☎0810-222-86527; Sarmiento 2280; ⊗8am-noon & 4-8pm Mon-Fri, 8am-noon Sat) flies daily to Buenos Aires.

BUS

Buses to Encarnación (AR$18), Paraguay, leave every 20 minutes, stopping at the corner of San Lorenzo and Entre Ríos. With queues and border formalities, the trip can take more than an hour.

Everyone gets out to clear Argentine emigration. If the bus leaves without you, keep your ticket and catch the next one. The same happens on the Paraguayan side. There's a tourist office by Paraguayan immigration, and official moneychangers hanging around. Get small denominations: a 100,000 guaraní note is hell to change.

Buses from Posadas

DESTINATION	COST (ARS)	TIME (HR)
Buenos Aires	957	12-14
Corrientes	270	4-4½
Paso de los Libres	219-275	5-6
Puerto Iguazú	258	4½-5½
Resistencia	287	4½-5
Rosario	879	14-15
San Ignacio	46	1
Tucumán	980	15

TRAIN

A shiny new rail service connects Posadas and Encarnación in Paraguay, leaving Posadas every 30 minutes from 7:15am to 6:15pm (AR$18, six minutes). You clear both Argentine and Paraguayan authorities at the **Apeadero Posadas station** (www.sofse.gob.ar).

⊕ Getting Around

Posadas' bus terminal can be reached from downtown by bus 8, 15 (from Junín), 21 or 24 (AR$8). It costs about AR$90 in a taxi. From the bus terminal, catch buses from the adjacent local terminal.

Bus 28 (AR$8) goes to the airport from San Lorenzo (between La Rioja and Entre Ríos). A remise costs around AR$100.

Buses 7 and 12 (AR$8) go to the Apeadero Posadas station.

San Ignacio

✔ 0376 / POP 6800

The best preserved of the Argentine missions, San Ignacio Miní is the central attraction of this small town north of Posadas. You could visit from Posadas or on your way to Iguazú, but making this a stopover appeals: there are good places to stay, and you'll have a chance to check out the excellent sound-and-light show at the ruins. San Ignacio is a good base for visiting other mission ruins, both in Argentina and Paraguay.

San Ignacio is 56km northeast of Posadas via RN12. From the highway junction, Av Sarmiento leads 1km to the town center, where Rivadavia leads six blocks north to the ruins.

◉ Sights

★**San Ignacio Miní**   RUIN
(www.misiones.tur.ar; entrance Calle Alberdi s/n; combined missions ticket foreigners/Mercosur/Argentines AR$150/130/100; ⊙ 7am-5:30pm Apr-Oct, 7am-7pm Nov-Mar) These mission ruins are the most complete of those in Argentina: at-mospheric and impressive for the quantity of carved ornamentation still visible and for the amount of restoration. The interpretation center provides good background information, and the ruins themselves feature interactive panels providing multilingual audio.

Admission includes entry to the nearby ruins at Santa Ana and Loreto and to Santa María la Mayor, a little further afield.

There is a worthwhile sound-and-light show (foreigners AR$150) at the ruins every non-rainy night.

Founded in 1610 in Brazil, but abandoned after repeated slaver attacks, San Ignacio was established here in 1696 and functioned until the Jesuit expulsion. The ruins, rediscovered in 1897 and restored between 1940 and 1948, are a great example of 'Guaraní baroque.' At its peak, the settlement had a Guaraní population of nearly 4000.

The interpretation center includes an audiovisual and unbiased information (in Spanish and English) about the missions from both Jesuit and Guaraní perspectives. You can listen to Guaraní music, including some religious pieces composed at the missions, and inspect a virtual model of San Ignacio as it would have been.

There are free guided tours (multilingual) of the ruins. You pass between rows of Guaraní houses before arriving at the plaza, on one side of which is the enormous red sandstone church. Impressive in its dimensions, it is the focal point of the settlement. While the red-brown stone picturesquely contrasts with the green grass, the buildings were originally white. Before lime was available, it was obtained by burning snail shells.

Times for the nightly show vary according to the number of groups. It's a touching, at times haunting, experience played out in various locations using projections onto a mist of water spray, giving a ghostlike quality. Headsets offer a variety of languages.

Casa de Horacio Quiroga   MUSEUM
(Av Quiroga s/n; admission AR$50; ⊙ 7am-5:30pm) Uruguayan writer Horacio Quiroga was a get-back-to-nature type who found his muse in the rough-and-ready Misiones backwoods lifestyle. His simple stone house at the southern end of town (a 30-minute walk) was built by himself. An adjacent wooden house is a reconstruction made for a biopic. To reach them, a trail through sugarcane lets you learn via panels and audioguide about Quiroga's deeply tragic life, so full of shotgun accidents and doses of cyanide it's almost funny.

🏃 Activities

Parque Provincial Teyú Cuaré   OUTDOORS

Head down to this protected peninsula on the Río Paraná for forest walking – there are four marked interpretive trails – and cycling, views from riverside clifftops and beaches. There are several small Guaraní settlements here which welcome visitors and sell handcrafts. A local will show you around for a fee or tip.

A TRIUMPH OF HUMANITY

For a century and a half from 1609, a great social experiment was carried out in the jungles of South America by the Society of Jesus (the Jesuits). Locating themselves in incredibly remote areas, priests set up *reducciones* (missions), where they established communities of Guaraní whom they evangelized and educated, while at the same time protecting them from slavery and the evil influences of colonial society. It was a utopian ideal that flourished and led Voltaire to describe it as 'a triumph of humanity which seems to expiate the cruelties of the first conquerors.'

For the Guaraní who were invited to begin a new life in the missions, there were tangible benefits, including security, nourishment and prosperity. Mortality declined immediately and mission populations grew rapidly. At their peak the 30 Jesuit *reducciones* that were spread across what's now Argentina, Brazil and Paraguay were populated by more than 100,000 Guaraní. Each mission had a minimum of Europeans: two priests was the norm, and the Guaraní governed themselves under the Jesuits' spiritual authority. The Jesuits made no attempt to force the Guaraní to speak Spanish and only sought to change those aspects of Guaraní culture – polygamy and occasional cannibalism – that clashed with Catholic teaching. Each Guaraní family was given a house and children were schooled.

The typical *reducción* consisted of a large central plaza, dominated by the church and *colegio*, which housed the priests and also contained art workshops and storerooms. The houses of the Guaraní occupied the rest of the settlement in neat rows; other buildings might include a hospital, a *cotiguazú* that housed widows and abandoned wives, and a *cabildo* where the Guaraní's chosen leader lived.

Settlements were self-sufficient; the Guaraní were taught agriculture and food was distributed equally. As time went on and the missions grew, wooden buildings were replaced by stone ones and the churches, designed by master architects with grandiose dreams, were stunning edifices with intricate baroque stonework and sculpture comparable with the finest churches being built in Europe.

Indeed, the missions' most enduring achievement was perhaps artistic. The Guaraní embraced the art and music they were introduced to and, interweaving European styles with their own, produced beautiful music, sculpture, dance and painting in 'Guaraní baroque' style. The Jesuits' religious music strongly attracted the Guaraní to Catholicism.

However, mission life necessarily had a martial side. Raiding parties of *bandeirantes* (armed bands) from Brazil regularly sought slaves for sugar plantations, and the Jesuits were resented by both Spanish and Portuguese colonial authorities. There were regular skirmishes and battles until a notable victory over an army of 3000 slavers at Mbororó in 1641 ushered in a period of comparative security.

The mission period came to an abrupt end. Various factors, including envy from the colonial authority and settlers, and a feeling that the Jesuits were more loyal to their own ideas than those of the Crown, prompted Carlos III of Spain to ban them from his dominions in 1767, following the lead of Portugal and France. With the priests gone, the communities were vulnerable and the Guaraní gradually dispersed. The decaying missions were then ruined in the wars of the early 19th century.

The 1986 film *The Mission* is about the last days of the Jesuit missions and intriguingly cast a Colombian tribe, the Waunana, who had had almost no contact with white people, as the Guaraní.

Almost nothing remains of several of Argentina's 15 missions, but those well worth visiting include San Ignacio Miní in San Ignacio, Loreto and Santa Ana; Yapeyú; and Santa María la Mayor. The fabulous Paraguayan missions at Jesús de Tavarangüe and Trinidad can be easily visited on a day trip too. Others are not too far away in southern Brazil.

☞ Tours

★ Tierra Colorada
TOUR

(☎ 0376-437-3448; tierracoloradaturismo@gmail.com; RN12) This all-round helpful operator just below the bus terminal runs tours to the Paraguayan missions (US$40 per person) and Moconá falls (AR$2500 for up to four people), plus good-value transfers and packages to Los Esteros del Iberá. It also hires bikes (per day AR$120), can arrange kayaking on the river and visits to Guaraní settlements, securely stores baggage, books buses and gives impartial tourist information.

🛏 Sleeping & Eating

Various daytime-only eating options – serving burgers, pizzas and *milanesas* – crowd the streets around the ruins.

★ Adventure Hostel
HOSTEL $

(☎ 0376-447-0955; www.sihostel.com.ar; Independencia 469; dm US$12-16, d US$50, campsites per person US$10; ❄ @ ☎ ☕ 🐕) This well-run, motivated place has comfortable dorms with either three beds or four bunk-berths, decent private rooms with renovated bathrooms, and excellent facilities. There's everything from a climbing wall to pool (both kinds), ping-pong and seesaws in the spacious grounds. Tasty homemade breakfasts are included. The restaurant does decent pasta-pizza-type meals; there's also bike hire (AR$120 per day) and powered campsites. HI discount. It's next to the plaza, two blocks south of the church

Hotel La Toscana
HOTEL $

(☎ 0376-447-0777; www.hotellatoscana.com.ar; cnr H Irigoyen & Uruguay; s/d/tr/q US$30/40/45/50; ❄ ☎ ☕) In a peaceful part of town half a block from the highway, this simple, welcoming Italian-run place is a relaxing retreat indeed. Cool, spacious basic rooms surround a great pool, deck and garden area. It's a top spot to unwind and offers top value.

Hotel San Ignacio
HOTEL $

(☎ 0376-447-0047; www.hotelsanignacio.com.ar; cnr Sarmiento & San Martín; s/d US$25/44, 4-person cabañas US$62; ❄ @ ☎) Located bang in the center, this is an excellent budget choice for clean, quiet, comfortable rooms, great bathrooms, benevolent owners, and an attached bar and internet cafe. A-frame cabins out back are good value for groups. The bar does simple food. You may never find it easier to be the best pool player in town, but the foosball is a different story. No breakfast.

La Misionerita
ARGENTINE $

(RN12; mains AR$65-110; ☺ 4am-midnight; ☎) On the highway opposite the town entrance, this has impressive opening hours, friendly service and a decent range of burgers, *milanesas* and the like, along with grill options and river fish. One of the few evening options.

ℹ Information

Tourist Office (☺ 7am-9pm) At the highway junction. Not very useful.

ℹ Getting There & Away

The bus terminal is on the main road near the town entrance. Services between Posadas (AR$45, one hour) and Puerto Iguazú (AR$140 to AR$180, four to five hours) are frequent.

Santa Ana & Loreto

Atmospherically decaying in the humid forest, these two Jesuit missions are both off RN12, between Posadas and San Ignacio.

Admission for both is via a combined missions ticket that includes San Ignacio Miní and Santa María la Mayor. Guided tours are included in the admission price.

◉ Sights

Santa Ana
RUIN

(www.misiones.tur.ar; combined missions ticket foreigners/Mercosur/Argentines AR$150/130/100; ☺ 7am-5:30pm Apr-Oct, 7am-7pm Nov-Mar) At Santa Ana, which was founded in 1633 but moved here in 1660, dense forest has been partially removed to reveal a settlement that had over 7000 Guaraní inhabitants at its peak. The enormous 140-sq-meter plaza attests to its importance. The muscular church's thick walls and photogenic strangler figs lend a dramatic effect to what must have been a magnificent building, though none of its decorative embellishments remain. The cemetery, used into the later half of the 20th century, is now neglected.

Behind the church, a channel and reservoir remain from what was a sophisticated irrigation system.

Nuestra Señora de Loreto
RUIN

(www.misiones.tur.ar; combined missions ticket foreigners/Mercosur/Argentines AR$150/130/100; ☺ 7am-5:30pm Apr-Oct, 7am-7pm Nov-Mar) Loreto, founded in 1632, has few visible remains but is atmospheric. There's ongoing restoration, but the jungle is king here again and it's difficult to interpret the tumbled mossy stones

WORTH A TRIP

VISITING THE PARAGUAYAN MISSIONS

From Posadas (or San Ignacio) there's a very rewarding day trip to two Jesuit missions in Paraguay. The ruined but majestic churches at Trinidad and Jesús de Tavarangüe have been carefully restored and preserve fabulous stonework.

From Posadas, bus or train it to Encarnación. From the bus terminal (buses stop here, or bus here from the Encarnación train station; G2500), buses (most marked Ciudad del Este) run roughly half-hourly to Trinidad (G7000, 50 to 60 minutes). Get the driver to let you off at the turnoff to the ruins; it's then a 700m walk.

The **Trinidad ruins** (Trinidad, Paraguay; combined mission ticket G35,000; ⊘ 7am-7pm Apr-Sep, 7am-5:30pm Oct-Mar) are spectacular, with the church's red-brown stone contrasting strongly with the flower-studded green grass and surrounding hillscapes. There is much decoration preserved: scalloped niches still hold timeworn sculptures, and the font and elaborate baroque pulpit are impressive. Doorways are capped with fine carved decoration. You can climb to the top of one of the walls; an earlier church and bell tower have also been restored. There's a hotel and restaurant by the ruins.

Walk back to the main road and turn right. At the gas station 200m along is the turnoff to **Jesús de Tavarangüe**, 12km away. Shared taxis (G7500) wait here to fill, and buses pass every two hours. You can get a taxi to take you, wait for you and bring you back to the turnoff for about G30,000.

The restored church at **Jesús** (Jesús de Tavarangüe, Paraguay; combined mission ticket G35,000; ⊘ 7am-7pm Apr-Sep, 7am-5:30pm Oct-Mar) was never finished. Spectacular trefoil arches (a nod to Spain's Moorish past) and carved motifs of crossed swords and keys make it perhaps the most picturesque of all the Jesuit ruins. The treble-naved church, with green grass underfoot, is on a similarly monumental scale as Trinidad. Climb the tower for views of the surrounding countryside.

Back on the main road, Encarnación-bound buses stop by the gas station. From Encarnación, Posadas-bound buses stop outside the bus terminal, opposite the school.

A joint ticket for the ruins at Trinidad, Jesús and San Cosme (southwest of Encarnación) is G35,000; it's valid for three days.

Though some nationalities need a visa to enter Paraguay (check before you go), officially you can get a 24-hour transit stamp on the bridge (so bus not train). This is sometimes free and sometimes charged.

A single-entry visa (US$65, but US$135 for Australians) from the **Paraguayan consulate** (☑ 0376-442-3858; http://paraguay.int.ar; San Lorenzo 1561; ⊘ 7am-2pm Mon-Fri) in Posadas can be ready in about an hour. You'll need two passport photos, a copy of your credit card or similar proof of funds. You can try going through without stamping in, but you risk a fine if caught.

You can also visit the ruins from San Ignacio: get the bus to Corpus, then cross to Paraguay on the ferry (8am to 5pm Monday to Friday). The 24-hour stamps are available here too.

Tour operators in both Posadas and San Ignacio offer day trips to the Paraguayan ruins.

among the trees, so the free guided tour is worthwhile. It was one of the more important missions; a printing press was built here, the first in the southern part of the continent.

ℹ Getting There & Away

Buses heading north from Posadas stop at the turnoffs on RN12 for both sites. Santa Ana's is at Km1382.5, from where it's a 700m walk to the ruins. Loreto's is at Km1389, with a 2.5km walk. It can be intensely hot, so take plenty of water.

From San Ignacio, an hourly bus (AR$13 to Loreto, AR$18 to Santa Ana) leaves from the center to the turnoffs for both missions – some actually drop off at the Loreto ruins themselves. This makes it easy to see both in a day trip from San Ignacio. You can get a *remise* from San Ignacio to take you to both, including waiting time, for about AR$500.

Santa María la Mayor

Further afield, **Santa María la Mayor** (RP2, Km43; combined missions ticket foreigners/ Mercosur/Argentines AR$150/130/100; ⊘ 7am-5:30pm Apr-Oct, 7am-7pm Nov-Mar) is the fourth mission on the joint admission ticket. A sizable plaza is the main feature, with the church very ruinous. The settlement was large, with printing press and prison; the chapel is a 20th-century addition. It's a relaxing place surrounded by jungle that's great for bird-watching, with toucans and trogons easily spotted.

The ruins are on the RP2 between Concepción de la Sierra and San Javier, 110km southeast of Posadas.

To get there, take a bus from Posadas to Concepción. There, change to a San Javier-bound service and ask the driver to let you off at the ruins, 25km down the road. You can get a San Javier–bound bus direct from Posadas, but not all run via the ruins: check.

IGUAZÚ FALLS

One of the planet's most awe-inspiring sights, the Iguazú Falls are simply astounding. A visit is a jaw-dropping, visceral experience, and the power and noise of the cascades – a chain of hundreds of waterfalls nearly 3km in extension – live forever in the memory. An added benefit is the setting: the falls lie split between Brazil and Argentina in a large expanse of national park, much of it rainforest teeming with unique flora and fauna.

The falls are easily reached from either side of the Argentine–Brazilian border, as well as from nearby Paraguay. Both Argentina's Puerto Iguazú and Foz do Iguaçu, on the Brazilian side, have a wide choice of accommodations.

History & Environment

According to Guaraní tradition, the falls originated when a warrior named Caroba incurred the wrath of a forest god by escaping downriver in a canoe with a young girl, Naipur, with whom the god was infatuated. Enraged, the god caused the riverbed to collapse in front of the lovers, producing a line of precipitous falls over which Naipur fell and, at their base, turned into a rock. Caroba survived as a tree overlooking it.

Geologists have a more prosaic version. The Río Iguazú's course takes it over a basaltic plateau that ends abruptly just short of the confluence with the Paraná. Where the lava flow stopped, thousands of cubic meters of water per second now plunge down as much as 80m into sedimentary terrain below. Before reaching the falls, the river divides into many channels with rocks and islands separating the many distinct cascades that together form the famous 2.7km-long *cataratas* (waterfalls).

Seeing the Falls

The Brazilian and Argentine sides offer different views and experiences. Go to both (perhaps to the Brazilian first) and hope for sun. The difference between a clear and an overcast day at the falls is vast: ideally plan a multiple-day stay to have a better shot at optimal conditions.

While the Argentine side, with its variety of trails and boat rides, offers many more opportunities to see individual falls close up, the Brazilian side yields the more panoramic views. You can easily make day trips to both sides of the falls, no matter which side of the border you base yourself on. Some choose to see both sides in one day, but it's a rush and not recommended.

National Parks

Both the Argentine and Brazilian sides of the falls are national parks: Parque Nacional Iguazú and Parque Nacional do Iguaçu, respectively. High temperatures, humidity and rainfall encourage a diverse habitat: the parks' rainforest contains more than 2000 identified plant species, countless insects, 400 species of birds, and many mammals and reptiles.

The Iguazú forests consist of multiple levels, the highest a 30m canopy. Beneath are several additional levels of trees, plus a dense ground-level growth of shrubs and herbaceous plants.

Pumas, jaguars and tapirs all reside in the parks, but you won't see them. Most common is the coati, a relative of the raccoon, and capuchin monkeys. Iguanas are common, and watch out for snakes.

Tropical bird species add color, with toucans and various parrot species easily seen. The best time to see birds is early morning along the forest trails.

Despite regular official denials, the heavy impact of so many visitors to the area has clearly driven much of the wildlife further into the parks, so the more you explore the region away from the falls themselves, the more you'll see.

❶ Dangers & Annoyances

River currents are strong and swift; tourists have been swept downriver and drowned. Of course, don't get too close to the falls proper.

Heat and humidity are often intense and there's plenty of hungry insect life, so pack sunscreen and repellent. Take your own water.

On both sides, you'll encounter coatis. Keep food well away from them; though these clown-

Iguazú Falls

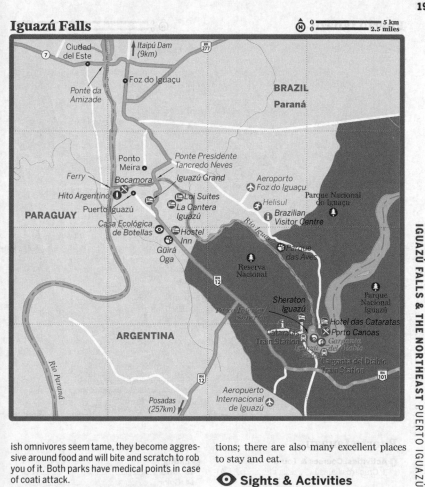

ish omnivores seem tame, they become aggressive around food and will bite and scratch to rob you of it. Both parks have medical points in case of coati attack.

You are likely to get soaked, or at least very damp, from the spray at the falls, so keep documents and cameras protected in plastic bags. You can buy plastic ponchos on both sides.

Stamps on sale at the Argentine side of the park cannot be posted anywhere but in the park itself or large cities.

Puerto Iguazú

☏ 03757 / POP 42,000

Booming Puerto Iguazú sits at the confluence of the Ríos Paraná and Iguazú and looks across to Brazil and Paraguay. There's little feeling of community: everyone is here to see the falls or to make a buck out of them, and planning laws seem nonexistent as hotels go up on every street. Still, it's quiet, safe and has good transportation connec-

tions; there are also many excellent places to stay and eat.

👁 Sights & Activities

There's little to see in the town itself.

Hito Argentino   VIEWPOINT
(Av Tres Fronteras) A kilometer west of the center, this is a great viewpoint with a small obelisk painted in Argentine colors at the impressive confluence of the Ríos Paraná and Iguazú. From here you can see Brazil and Paraguay, with similar markers on their sides. A desultory *artesanía* market is also here.

Güirá Oga   ZOO
(www.guiraoga.com.ar; RN12, Km5; admission AR$100; ⊙9am-6pm, last entry 5pm) 🌿 On the way to the falls, this is an animal hospital and center for rehabilitation of injured wildlife. It also carries out valuable research into the Iguazú forest environment and has a breeding program for endangered species.

Puerto Iguazú

Puerto Iguazú

You get walked around the jungly park by one of the staff, who explains about the birds and animals and the sad stories of how they got there. The visit takes about 80 minutes.

Tours leave roughly every half hour. Guides who can speak English, will do so, but there are dedicated English tours at 10am and 2pm too.

Casa Ecológica de Botellas ARCHITECTURE
(http://lacasadebotellas.googlepages.com; RN12, Km5; adult/child AR$70/40; ⊙9am-6:30pm) 🖋

About 300m off the falls road, this fascinating place is well worth a visit. The owners have taken used packaging materials – plastic bottles, juice cartons and the like – to build not only an impressive house, but furnishings and a bunch of original handicrafts that make unusual gifts. The guided visit talks you through their techniques.

🖝 Tours

Numerous local operators offer day tours to the Brazilian side of the Iguazú falls, some taking in the Itaipu dam and Paraguay shopping as well. Many have offices at the bus terminal. At the port, there are various options for boat trips around the junction of the Paraná and Iguazú rivers.

Cruceros Iguazú   BOAT TOUR
(📞 03757-421111; www.crucerosiguazu.com; Zona Puerto; 2-hour cruise AR$290) Daily two-hour late-afternoon cruises on the Paraná and Iguazú rivers in a large catamaran.

Iguazú Bike Tours   BICYCLE TOUR
(📞 03757-15-678220; www.iguazubiketours.com. ar) These guys run anything from gentle jaunts through the nearby forest to long vehicle-supported rides through the lesser-visited corners of Parque Nacional Iguazú.

🛌 Sleeping

There are numerous sleeping options for all budgets, including a string of resort-type hotels between town and Parque Nacional Iguazú and lots of cabin accommodation south of this road. In the streets around the bus terminal are many hostels. Many places don't accept credit cards or add a hefty surcharge.

Garden Stone   HOSTEL $
(📞 03757-420425; www.gardenstonehostel.com; Av Córdoba 441; dm US$14, d with/without bathroom US$55/45; 🌐🖥🏊) The best feature about this amiably-run hostel is its perfectly relaxing garden area, where there's a pool, common area and simple kitchen. Other good things include handiness for the bus terminal, the tasty breakfast (included), darkish but OK dorms, and its general peaceful vibe. Private en-suite rooms are attractive and good value.

Porämbá Hostel   HOSTEL $
(📞 03757-423041; www.porambahostel.com; El Urú 120; dm US$13-14, r US$38-68; 🌐@🖥🏊) In a very peaceful location but an easy walk from the bus terminal, this is a welcoming family-run hostel with a variety of non-crowded

dorms, private rooms with or without bathroom, and a small pool. It's a chilled place with a kitchen and a calming atmosphere.

Hospedaje Lola   GUESTHOUSE $
(📞 03757-423954;   residenciallola@hotmail.com; Av Córdoba 255; r US$25-30; 🌐@🏊) Plenty of price gouging goes on in Puerto Iguazú, but it stops at Lola's front door. This cheap, cheerily-run spot is very close to the bus terminal and features compact, clean rooms with bathroom for a great price. Wi-fi is good if you're close to the family part of the house.

Hotel Lilian   HOTEL $
(📞 03757-420968;   hotellilian@yahoo.com.ar; Beltrán 183; s US$42, standard/superior d US$55/65, q US$79; 🌐@🏊) Run by a hospitable family who isn't out to rip tourists off, this friendly place offers plenty of value, with bright and cheerful rooms around a plant-filled patio. Most superiors – worth the small extra outlay – have a balcony and heaps of natural light. All bathrooms are spacious and spotless. Things get done the way they should here.

Irupé Mini   GUESTHOUSE $
(Hostel Irupe; 📞 03757-423618; Av Misiones 82; s US$10, d with/without air-con US$25/20; 🌐🏊) This is very basic but offers friendliness, location and decent value for cheap private rooms, which are tight, with tiny bathrooms. Go for rooms at the back, which have more light. Sometimes offers dorm rates.

Hospedaje Familiar   GUESTHOUSE $
(📞 03757-420810; Beltrán 137; s/tw/d US$20/ 25/30) Quiet with a genuinely cordial welcome, this home offers simple, slightly musty rooms with clean en-suite bathrooms at a great price. There's a basic guest kitchen and tranquil atmosphere.

Hostel Inn   HOSTEL $
(📞 03757-421823;   www.hostel-inn.com;   RN12, Km5; dm/d US$19/57; 🌐@🏊) More back-packer resort than hostel, set in expansive grounds between town and the falls, with a party atmosphere, bar and huge pool (expect music thumping) out front. The dorms in separate buildings are quiet enough, though it's time for a bit of upkeep. Private rooms are quite a bit better. Buses stop right outside. HI discount.

★ Jasy Hotel   HOTEL $$
(📞 03757-424337; www.jasyhotel.com; San Lorenzo 154; d/q US$110/136; 🌐🏊🏊) Original and peaceful, these 10 two-level rooms, with a great design for family sleeping, climb a hill

like a forest staircase and are all equipped with a balcony gazing over plentiful greenery. Artful use of wood is the signature; you'll fall in love with the bar and deck area. Prepare to stay longer than planned. There's a decent restaurant open evenings.

Secret Garden Iguazú
B&B $$

(☎ 03757-423099; www.secretgardeniguazu.com; Los Lapachos 623; s/d US$90/125; ❋ 🛜) Down the back of a garden full of birds and greenery is a bungalow with three spacious, enchanting rooms at this welcoming off-track B&B. Crosscut timber furniture and well-selected nature prints make for a relaxing environment. Breakfast and afternoon tea are standout moments, featuring homemade jams, chutneys and banana bread. Both host and staff are helpful, making this a fabulously personalized stay.

Posada del Jacarandá
HOTEL $$

(☎ 03757-423737; www.posadadeljacaranda.com; cnr Andresito & Caraguatá; r US$105; ❋ @ 🛜 ❄ 🐾) Harmonious rooms, a terrific attitude to guests, gleaming polished floors and a peaceful ambience make this a worthwhile midrange choice in the quiet streets to the southeast of town. There's a pretty pool area, above-average breakfast and attractive use of wood throughout. More than the sum of its parts.

Jardín de Iguazú
HOTEL $$

(☎ 03757-424171; www.jardindeiguazu.com.ar; Bompland 274; s/d US$120/133; ❋ 🛜 ❄) Appealing for its handy central location, competent staff, pleasant pool and Jacuzzi, and comfortably bland modern rooms. The standards aren't super-spacious, so if that's important to you, upgrade to a superior, which costs very little extra. Reliable and well-run.

Guest House Puerto Iguazú
GUESTHOUSE $$

(☎ 03757-423346; www.guesthousepuertoiguazu.com; Lindstron 14; r with/without bathroom US$92/72, ste US$133; ❋ 🛜 ❄) In a hidden-away plot overlooking the Río Iguazú, this is something of a haven, run by a nearby hotel. There are just a handful of rooms, elegant and comfortable; two share a good bathroom. You can use the spacious kitchen, watch birds in the garden, or kick back on the poolside terrace with river views.

Hotel La Sorgente
HOTEL $$

(☎ 03757-424252; www.lasorgentehotel.com; Av Córdoba 454; s/d US$97/133; ❋ @ 🛜 ❄) Life couldn't be easier at this hotel, set around a verdant garden – if you can't face the long walk around the pool, take the bridge across it. Attractively remodeled, if dark, rooms surround it. Breakfast, served in the authentic Italian restaurant, gets the seal of approval, too. Cheaper if you pay cash. Staff are a little distant, but that's life.

★ Boutique Hotel de la Fonte
HOTEL $$$

(☎ 03757-420625; www.bhfboutiquehotel.com; cnr Corrientes & 1 de Mayo; r US$190-260; ❋ @ 🛜 ❄) The mark of a good hotel is constant improvement, and this place adds great features so fast we can barely keep up. It's a secluded, enchanting spot, featuring characterful individually decorated rooms and suites around a tree-filled courtyard garden that is romantically lit at night. One of the welcoming owners is an architect, and it shows in the numerous small decorative touches and artistic design.

Outdoor hot tubs, a saltwater pool, and all-over style and elegance are other great features. The other owner is a chef who runs the town's best restaurant on-site, so you're in luck there too. A standout.

La Cantera Iguazú
LODGE $$$

(☎ 03757-493016; www.hotellacanteraiguazu.com; Selva Iryapú s/n; r US$164-272; ❋ @ 🛜 ❄ 🐾) Nestled in forest 1.5km off the falls road, this intimate lodge has appealing 'tierra' rooms with mosquito-proof balcony in wooden buildings, some with trees growing through them. Upper-level 'jungle' rooms offer better views and have a hammock. Cheaper 'forest' rooms are less rustic, while harmonious wooden 'villa' rooms sleep four and have balcony Jacuzzis. Good pool area and excellent service.

A forest walk with a Guaraní guide is included and it has its own transport service to both sides of the falls.

Loi Suites
RESORT $$$

(☎ 03757-498300; www.loisuites.com.ar; Selva Iryapú s/n; r US$384-769; ❋ @ 🛜 ❄ 🐾) Spectacularly set in the jungle, yet just a few kilometers from town, this giant complex has several buildings connected by walkways. It's decorated in a relaxed country style and features a huge tree-surrounded triple pool area as its highlight. Rooms are spacious and comfortable; upgrade to a balcony for bird-watching opportunities. There's a spa complex too. Online prices are usually lower.

Iguazú Jungle Lodge
HOTEL $$$

(☎ 03757-420600; www.iguazujunglelodge.com; cnr Yrigoyen & San Lorenzo; r/f US$270/355; ❋ 🛜 ❄ 🐾) A little corporate in feel, but with a secluded ambience, considering its comparatively central location, this hotel offers spacious, well-equipped accommodations with quality beds and jungle balconies in a resort-style complex surrounding a large pool. Some come with lounge and kitchen. Staff are multilingual and very helpful. It's a great option for families, with a games room and suites. Good on-site restaurant.

✗ Eating

Restaurants in Puerto Iguazú are pricey but generally of good quality, and open early for dinner to cater for tourists. Credit cards aren't widely accepted: ask first.

★ Feria   MARKET $
(Feirinha; cnr Av Brasil & Félix de Azara; picadas for 2 AR$100-150; ⏰8am-midnight) A really nice place to eat or have a beer is this market in the north of town. It's full of stalls selling Argentine wines, sausages, olives and cheese to visiting Brazilians, and several of them put out *picadas*, grilled meats, other simple regional dishes and cold beer. There's folk music some nights and a good evening atmosphere.

La Misionera   EMPANADAS $
(P Moreno 210; empanadas AR$12; ⏰11am-midnight Mon-Sat) Excellent empanadas with a big variety of fillings, as well as delivery option.

Lemongrass   CAFE $
(Bompland 231; snacks AR$30-75; ⏰8:30am-2:30pm & 5-9:30pm Mon-Sat; 🖉) One of few decent cafes in Puerto Iguazú, this offers good fresh juices, decent coffee, delicious sweet temptations, sandwiches, burgers and tasty savory tarts. Beers, mint-dependent mojitos and caipirinhas are also available.

★ María Preta   ARGENTINE $$
(Av Brasil 39; mains AR$85-165; ⏰7pm-12:30am; 🖉🖉) The indoor-outdoor eating area and live music make this a popular dinner choice, whether it's for steaks that are actually cooked the way you want them, for a wide range of typical Argentine-Spanish dishes, or for something a little snappier: caiman fillet. It stays open as a bar and venue until 2am or later.

Bocamora   ARGENTINE $$
(☎03757-420550; www.bocamora.com; Av Costanera s/n; mains AR$110-160; ⏰kitchen noon-3:30pm & 7-11:30pm Wed-Mon; 🖉) A romantic location overlooking two rivers and three

nations is reason enough to come to this place just down the hill from the Argentine border marker. It specializes in grilled meats and well-prepared plates of river fish; the food is competent and tasty, service is very hospitable and the view is just breathtaking.

Though the kitchen closes, the place is open all afternoon.

Color   PARRILLA, PIZZA $$
(☎03757-420206; www.parrillapizzacolor.com; Av Córdoba 135; mains AR$120-205; ⏰11:30am-midnight; 🖉) This popular indoor-outdoor pizza 'n' *parrilla* packs them into its tightly spaced tables, so don't discuss state secrets. Prices are OK for this strip, and the meat comes out redolent of wood smoke; the wood-oven pizzas and empanadas are also very toothsome.

La Dama Juana   ARGENTINE $$
(☎03757-424051; www.facebook.com/ladama juanaiguazu; Av Córdoba 42; mains AR$110-170; ⏰11:30am-midnight; 🖉) Offering a compact interior and pleasant balcony terrace, this is more informal than most of this strip and offers significant value. Service comes with a smile; abundant meat or fish plates with innovative sauces, and colorful salads, make for pleasant dining. Given that the place is named after a wine bottle (demijohn), the wine list is mediocre.

Terra   ASIAN $$
(☎03757-421931; Av Misiones 125; mains AR$85-160; ⏰4pm-midnight; 🖉🖉) Chalked signatures of myriad satisfied customers mark the walls of this chilled bar-restaurant that specializes in well-prepared, good-value wok dishes, with teriyaki salmon, pasta and salads as other options. The streetside terrace fills fast.

La Vitrina   PARRILLA $$
(http://lavitrina-puertoiguazu.com; Av Victoria Aguirre 773; mains AR$90-160; ⏰noon-midnight; 🖉) This homey barn of a place is where you should come for great *asado de tira* (ribs) among other *parrilla* choices (including grilled vegetables). It's less touristy than some – you may even spot locals – and has enticing outdoor seating. There's live music at weekends.

★ De La Fonte   GASTRONOMY, ITALIAN $$$
(www.bhfboutiquehotel.com; cnr Corrientes & 1 de Mayo; mains AR$170-330; ⏰7pm-midnight Mon-Sat; 🖉) This exquisite hotel restaurant, domain of a maverick creative talent, is super-strong on presentation, whether

homemade pasta or inventive creations with a touch of molecular gastronomy. The imagination on display presents local tropical flavors seamlessly intertwined with prime cuts of carefully sourced fish or meat. The homemade bread is a delight. Degustation menus (AR$680 to AR$900) showcase great culinary ability: leave room for dessert.

La Rueda ARGENTINE $$$
(☑ 03757-422531; www.larueda1975.com; Av Córdoba 28; mains AR$135-205; ⊗ 5:30pm-midnight Mon-Tue, noon-midnight Wed-Sun; ☎) A mainstay of upmarket eating in Puerto Iguazú, this culinary heavyweight still packs a punch. The salads are imaginative and delicious, as are the imaginative river-fish (mostly pacú and surubí) creations. Meat with a variety of sauce options is reliably good; the homemade pasta is cheaper but doesn't disappoint. Service is good but slow. The wine list has a high flagfall.

Aqva ARGENTINE $$$
(☑ 03757-422064; www.aqvarestaurant.com; cnr Av Córdoba & Thays; mains AR$165-230; ⊗ noon-11:30pm; ☎) Solicitous service and plenty of flavor keep this split-level corner bungalow filled with the buzz of contented diners. The quality of the meat is excellent, and there's also an ample river fish selection, though the salmon is better. Starters offer plenty of variety, from lamb carpaccio to a tasty sampler plate of local specialties.

🍷 Drinking & Nightlife

Tourism and Brazilians from Foz make Puerto Iguazú's nightlife lively. Action centers on Avenida Brasil, where a string of bars attract evening drinkers.

★Vinosophie WINE BAR
(Av Brasil 136; ⊗ 5pm-1am; ☎) Attentive service and a prime position right in the middle of the short Iguazú 'strip' make this a great place to kick off the evening. Wine by the glass isn't cheap, but is well served in the elegant interior or at spacious outdoor tables. A thoughtful menu of snacks and inventive fuller meals (AR$120 to AR$170) make it a sound all-round choice.

Cuba Libre CLUB
(www.facebook.com/cuba.megadisco; cnr Av Brasil & Paraguay; ⊗ 11pm-late Wed-Sun) This unsubtle but fun nightclub just off the Avenida Brasil strip fills up with Brazilians looking for a big night out on the weak peso. The dance floor fills late but fast.

ℹ️ Information

Currency exchange places are along Av Victoria Aguirre downtown. If you've got Brazilian reais, you're much better off changing them in Brazil or buying services with them here rather than changing at official rates. There are various free wi-fi zones around town.

Hospital (☑ 03757-420288; cnr Av Victoria Aguirre & Ushuaia)

Municipal Tourist Office (☑ 03757-423951; www.iguazuturismo.gob.ar; Av Victoria Aguirre 337; ⊗ 8am-2pm & 4-9pm)

Paraguayan Consulate (☑ 03757-424-230; http://paraguay.int.ar; P Moreno 236; ⊗ 7am-3pm) Paraguayan visas cost US$65 for most but US$135 for Australians at the time of research. Visa processing takes three hours, and you'll need your passport, two photos and a copy of your credit card.

Provincial Tourist Office (☑ 03757-420800; www.turismo.misiones.gov.ar; Av Victoria Aguirre 311; ⊗ 8am-9pm) The most helpful office.

ℹ️ Getting There & Away

Aerolíneas Argentinas (☑ 03757-420168; www.aerolineas.com.ar; Av Victoria Aguirre 295; ⊗ 8am-noon & 3-7pm Mon-Fri, 8am-1pm Sat) flies from Iguazú to both Buenos Aires airports, Mendoza via Córdoba or Rosario, Salta and El Calafate (via BA). LAN (www.lan.com) also flies the Buenos Aires route.

The **bus terminal** (cnr Avs Córdoba & Misiones) has departures for all over the country.

There are Brazilian domestic services across the border in Foz do Iguaçu. Some Brazilian buses leave from Puerto Iguazú or offer a free taxi to connect.

Buses from Puerto Iguazú

DESTINATION	COST (AR$)	TIME (HR)
Buenos Aires	1212	17-19
Córdoba	1306	22
Corrientes	527	9-10
Posadas	258	4½-6
Resistencia	542	10-11
San Ignacio	140-180	4-5

ℹ️ Getting Around

Four Tourist Travel (☑ 03757-420681, 03757-422962) runs an airport shuttle for AR$90 per person that meets most flights; from town, it needs to be booked in advance. A *remise* costs AR$250 from the airport, AR$200 to the airport, which is 25km from town.

Frequent buses cross to Foz do Iguaçu, Brazil (AR$20 or R$4, 35 minutes, hourly 6:30am to 6:30pm), and to Ciudad del Este, Paraguay

(AR$30, one hour, seven daily 6:50am to 5:45pm), from the local side of the bus terminal. There are also buses direct to the Brazilian side of the Iguazú falls (AR$80 return, hourly 8:30am to 2:30pm, last return 5pm).

A taxi to Foz costs around AR$200; to the Brazilian side of the Iguazú falls it's AR$450 return. Avoid the *remise* office at the bus terminal: it's more expensive than others. Always negotiate. We particularly like the taxi stop on Córdoba opposite El Mensú, which has some knowledgeable multilingual drivers and metered cabs.

Local buses cost AR$7 and are useful for reaching hotels located along the falls road, or the triple frontier marker.

Jungle Bike (🖉03757-423720; www.jungle bike.com.ar; Av Misiones 44; bike hire per hr/day AR$40/150; ⊗8am-8:30pm) Near the bus terminal; offers bikes for hire, as well as guided excursions. Mountain bikes available for AR$250 per day.

Parque Nacional Iguazú

🖉 03757

On the Argentine side of the marvelous Iguazú Falls, this **park** (🖉03757-491469; www. iguazuargentina.com; adult foreigners/Mercosur/Argentines A$260/200/160, child A$65/50/40, parking AR$70; ⊗8am-6pm) has plenty to offer, and involves a fair amount of walking.

The spread-out complex at the entrance has various amenities, including lockers (AR$50), an ATM – you have to pay in cash in pesos – and a restaurant. There's also an exhibition, Yvyrá-retã, with a display on the park and Guaraní life essentially aimed at school groups. The complex ends at a train station, from which a train runs every half-hour to the Cataratas train station, where the waterfall walks begin, and to the Garganta del Diablo. You may prefer to walk: it's only 650m along the Sendero Verde path to the Cataratas station, and a further 2.3km to the Garganta, and you may well see capuchin monkeys along the way.

There's enough at the park to detain you for a couple of days; admission is reduced by 50% if you visit the park again the following day. Get your ticket stamped when leaving on the first day to get the discount.

⊙ Sights

It really is worth getting here by 9am: the gangways are narrow and getting stuck in a conga line of tour groups in searing heat and humidity takes the edge off the experience. Three circuits provide the viewing via a series of trails, bridges and *pasarelas* (catwalks).

★ Paseo Inferior   WATERFALL

This circuit (1400m) descends to the river (most is wheelchair accessible), passing delightfully close to falls on the way. At the end of the path prepare for a drenching at the hands of Salto Bossetti if you're game. Just short of here, a free launch makes the short crossing to Isla San Martín. At the same junction you can buy tickets for the popular boat rides under the falls.

Isla San Martín   ISLAND

From the end of the Paseo Inferior, a free launch takes you across to this island with a trail of its own that gives the closest look at several falls, including Salto San Martín, a huge, furious cauldron of water. It's possible to picnic and swim on the lee side of the island, but don't venture too far off the beach. When the water is high – and this is the case more often than not – island access is shut off.

★ Paseo Superior   WATERFALL

The Paseo Superior (1750m) is entirely level (and wheelchair accessible) and gives good views of the tops of several cascades and across to more. A recently constructed final section crosses a large swathe of the Iguazú river, ending above the powerful Salto San Martín before wending its way back across river islands.

★ Garganta del Diablo   WATERFALL

A 1.1km walkway across the placid Río Iguazú leads to one of the planet's most spectacular sights, the 'Devil's Throat.' The lookout platform is perched right over this amazingly powerful, concentrated torrent of water, a deafening cascade plunging to an invisible destination; vapors soaking the viewer blur the base of the falls and rise in a smoke-like plume that can be seen several kilometers away. It's a place of majesty and awe, and should be left until the end of your visit.

From Cataratas train station, train it or walk the 2.3km to the Garganta del Diablo stop. The last train to the Garganta leaves at 4pm, and we recommend taking it, as it'll be a somewhat less crowded experience. If you walk, you'll see quite a lot of wildlife around this time of day, too. Another option is to visit at lunchtime, as most organized tours stop to eat for an hour around 1:30pm.

🏃 Activities

Relatively few visitors venture beyond the immediate falls area to appreciate the park's forest scenery and wildlife, but it's well

MISIONES JUNGLE WITHOUT THE CROWDS

The Iguazú jungle is a fabulous habitat of birds, plants, insects and mammals, but mass tourism at the falls means you're unlikely to see as much wildlife as you might wish. One option for seeing more is to head east to the other end of the park. Around the *mate*-growing town of Andresito are several lodges, including excellent **Surucuá** (☑ 0376-15-437-1046; www.surucua.com; Andresito; s/d incl transfers & full board US$172/276, 2-days US$310/496; ☏ ☀) ✔ . Run by a welcoming young Misiones couple, this is right in the jungle. Comfortable rustic accommodations and delicious home-cooked meals featuring local ingredients are supplemented by activities including jungle walks and memorable kayak trips among river islands. It's a bird-watcher's paradise, with over 200 species recorded including trogons, toucans, hummingbirds and manakins. Relaxation is guaranteed with a swimming pool and no mobile coverage, though there is wi-fi. Multinight stays are cheaper. You will be picked up from Andresito, served by four daily buses from Puerto Iguazú (AR$100, 2½ hours).

worth doing. On the falls trails you'll see large lizards, coatis, monkeys and birds, but you'll see much more on one of the few trails through the dense forest.

Sendero Macuco
FISHING

This jungle trail leads through dense forest to a nearly hidden waterfall, Salto Arrechea. The first 3km to the top of the waterfall is almost completely level, but there is a steep, muddy drop to the base of the falls and beyond to the Río Iguaçu, about 650m in all. Figure on about 1¼ hours each way from the trailhead.

You can swim at the waterfall. Early morning is best, with better opportunities to see wildlife. Last entry is at 3pm. There's a map-guide available at the information desks.

⚲ Tours

Safaris Rainforest
JUNGLE TOUR

(☑ 03757-491074; www.rainforest.iguazuargentina. com) Using knowledgeable guides, this is the best option for appreciating Parque Nacional Iguazú's flora and fauna. It offers combined driving-walking excursions: the Safari a la Cascada takes you to the Arrechea waterfall (AR$380, 90 minutes); better is the Safari en la Selva (AR$450, two hours), a trip in a less-touristed part of the park that includes explanations of Guaraní culture.

Groups are small and you don't need the falls admission ticket; morning departures can include hotel pickup, and afternoon departure includes a transfer back to Puerto Iguazú. Best to book in advance by phone, online or at information booths at the falls.

Iguazú Jungle Explorer
BOAT TOUR

(☑ 03757-421696; www.iguazujungle.com) Offers three combinable tours: most popular is the short boat trip leaving from the Paseo Inferior

that takes you right under one of the waterfalls for a high-adrenalin soaking (AR$350). The Gran Aventura combines this with a jungle drive (AR$650), while the Paseo Ecológico (AR$200) is a wildlife-oriented tour in inflatable boats upstream from the falls.

Full Moon Walks
WALKING TOUR

(☑ 03757-491469; www.iguazuargentina.com/en/ luna-llena) For five consecutive nights per month, these guided walks visit the Garganta del Diablo. There are three departures nightly. The first, at 8pm, offers the spectacle of the inflated rising moon; the last, at 9:30pm, sees the falls better illuminated. Don't expect wildlife. The price (AR$500) includes admission and a drink; dinner is extra (AR$200). Book in advance as numbers are limited. Extra buses from Puerto Iguazú cater for moonwalkers.

🛏 Sleeping & Eating

There's one hotel within Parque Nacional Iguazú. Numerous snack bars offer predictably overpriced fare. The food is really awful; bring a (coati-proof) picnic, eat at one of two buffet restaurants or lunch at the Sheraton.

Sheraton Iguazú
HOTEL $$$

(☑ 03757-491800; www.sheraton.com/iguazu; standard r with forest/falls view from US$330/390; ☀ @ ☏ ☀) With a privileged position within Parque Nacional Iguazú itself and looking right upriver to the Garganta del Diablo, this hotel has spacious rooms with balconies, all recently renovated. The jungle-side view is pretty too. There's a good outdoor pool area, as well as an indoor pool and spa. These rates reflect online reality: rack tariffs are double.

The restaurant has a limited selection (mains AR$320 to AR$390). In-room wi-fi costs extra. There's no legal park access after hours. You have to pay one park entrance fee per stay.

La Selva
BUFFET $$

(www.iguazuargentina.com; buffet AR$260; ☺11am-3:30pm) During your visit, this restaurant, close to the Parque Nacional Iguazú's main entrance, will get talked up so much you'll fear the worst, but it's actually OK, with a buffet of hot and cold dishes, and extra-cost *parrillada*. It's well overpriced but information kiosks give out vouchers offering a substantial (think 40%) discount, so head there first.

Fortín
BUFFET $$

(www.fortincataratas.com; all-you-can-eat meals AR$250; ☺10am-4pm) Well located near the Paseos Inferior and Superior falls walkways, this offers a mediocre and overpriced buffet spread with *parrilla* choices. Bargain hard for a better deal. A beer on the deck is a decent alternative.

❶ Getting There & Away

Parque Nacional Iguazú is 20km southeast of Puerto Iguazú. From Puerto Iguazú's bus terminal, buses leave every 20 minutes for the park (AR$50, 40 minutes) between 7:20am and 7:20pm, with return trips between 7:50am and 8pm. The buses make flag stops along the road. A taxi from town to the park entrance is AR$250 (AR$400 return).

Gran Chaco

The Gran Chaco is a vast alluvial lowland, stretching north from Santa Fe and Córdoba provinces, across the entirety of Chaco and Formosa, and into Paraguay, Bolivia and Brazil. The western side, known as the Chaco Seco (Dry Chaco), has been dubbed the Impenetrable, due to its severe lack of water across an endless plain of thorn scrub. The eastern side is attractively fertile, and an important wildlife habitat.

Deforestation continues apace here, with vast areas being cleared to plant soya, of which Argentina is now one of the world's major producers. This has seriously affected Toba tribes, whose traditional environment is being destroyed.

Crossing the Gran Chaco from Formosa to Salta along the northern RN81 is an interesting option on mostly decent paved road.

Protests from indigenous and other community groups often temporarily close roads in the Chaco – be patient and chat to the protesters while you wait.

Resistencia

☑ 0362 / POP 385,700

This baking-hot provincial capital is perched on the edge of the barely populated Chaco, northern Argentina's 'outback'. It isn't the most likely candidate for the garland of artistic center of the north, yet its streets are studded with several hundred sculptures and there's a strong boho-cultural streak that represents a complete contrast to the tough cattle-and-scrub solitudes that characterize the province.

◉ Sights

At last count, more than 600 **sculptures** graced the city, a number that increases with every Bienal. The streets are packed with them, especially around the plaza and north up Avenida Sarmiento. Every Bienal, a brochure is printed with a sculpture walking tour around the city. Locals can buy pieces at a symbolic cost, but they have to display them streetside.

★ MusEUM
GALLERY

(www.bienaldelchaco.com; Av de los Inmigrantes 1001; ☺9:30am-1:30pm & 4-8pm Mon-Sat) FREE The headquarters of the sculpture Bienal and the venue for it, this exhibition room and grounds house many of the most impressive pieces from past festivals. It's well worth a visit. It also distributes brochures in English and Spanish of sculptural walking tours in town. The avenue is a northward continuation of Wilde. If going by taxi, mention the adjacent Domo del Centenario.

Museo del Hombre Chaqueño
MUSEUM

(http://museohombrechaco.blogspot.com; JB Justo 280; ☺8am-1pm & 3-8:30pm Mon-Fri) FREE This small but excellent museum is run by enthusiastic staff (some English spoken) who talk you through displays covering the three main pillars of Chaco population: indigenous inhabitants (there are some excellent ceramics and Toba musical instruments here); criollos who resulted from interbreeding between the European arrivals and the local populations; and 'gringos', the wave of mostly European immigration from the late 19th century onwards. Best is the mythology room upstairs, where you'll get to meet various quirky characters from Chaco popular religion.

El Fogón de los Arrieros
CULTURAL CENTER

(www.fogondelosarrieros.com.ar; Brown 350; admission AR$10; ☺8am-noon & 4-7pm Mon-Fri)

Founded in 1943, this is a cultural center and gallery that for decades has been the driving force behind Resistencia's artistic commitment. It's famous for its eclectic collection of objets d'art from around the Chaco and Argentina. The museum also features the wood carvings of local artist and cultural activist Juan de Dios Mena. Check out the irreverent epitaphs to dead patrons in the memorial garden; it's called 'Colonia Sálsipuedes' (leave if you can).

✨ Festivals & Events

Bienal de Escultura SCULPTURE
(www.bienaldelchaco.com) During the third week of July in even years, this brings 10 renowned Argentine and international sculptors to Resistencia. Arranging themselves around the fountain at MusEUM, they have seven days to complete a sculpture under the public gaze. The medium changes every time.

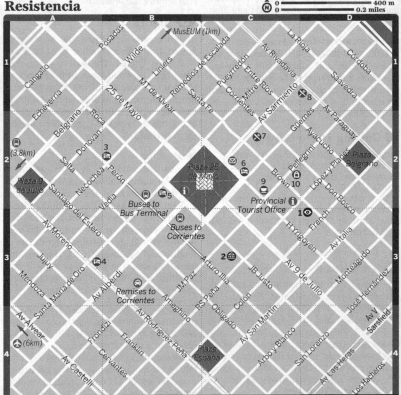

Resistencia

Resistencia

⊙ Sights
1 El Fogón de los Arrieros.......................D3
2 Museo del Hombre Chaqueño.............C3

🛏 Sleeping
3 Amerian Hotel Casino Gala.................B2
4 Hotel Alfil..A3
5 Hotel Colón...B2
6 Niyat Urban Hotel...............................C2

✗ Eating
7 Coco's Resto.......................................C2
8 Juan Segundo......................................D1

⊖ Drinking & Nightlife
9 El Viejo Café..C2

🛍 Shopping
10 Fundación Chaco Artesanal................C2

IGUAZÚ FALLS & THE NORTHEAST GRAN CHACO

🛏 Sleeping

Hotel Colón   HOTEL $
(📞0362-442-2861; www.colonhotelyapart.com; Santa María de Oro 143; s/d/apt US$44/60/68; ❄ @🛜) Art deco fans mustn't miss this 1920s classic, just south of the plaza. It's an amazingly large and characterful building with enticingly curious period features. Refurbished rooms are great; make sure you get one, as there are some far sketchier chambers with foam mattresses and dilapidated bathrooms. Good-value apartments are available.

Hotel Alfil   HOTEL $
(📞0362-442-0882; Santa María de Oro 495; s/d US$25/35; ❄🛜) A few blocks south of Plaza 25 de Mayo, the old-fashioned Alfil is a reasonable budget choice. Interior rooms are dark but worthwhile if the significant street noise in the exterior rooms (with their strangely inaccessible balconies) will bother you. Air-con is US$2 extra, but it's a decent deal despite the lack of breakfast.

★ Amerian Hotel Casino Gala   HOTEL $$
(📞0362-445-2400; www.hotelcasinogala.com.ar; Perón 330; s/d US$113/125; ❄@🛜🏊) The city's smartest choice, with various grades of room and slick service. Rooms are excellent for these rates: very spacious, attractively stepped and with a dark, elegant, vaguely Asian feel to the decor. As well as slot machines, there's a sauna, gym and self-contained spa complex. The huge outdoor pool with bar is a highlight.

Niyat Urban Hotel   HOTEL $$
(📞0362-444-8451; www.niyaturban.com.ar; Yrigoyen 83; s/d US$73/82; ❄@🛜) Shiny and confident, this plaza-side hotel offers excellent service and plenty of value for gleaming but very small modern rooms, which boast great bathrooms, comfy beds and big flatscreens. Some overlook the plaza. There's also a gym with vistas and a small spa complex with saunas and outdoor Jacuzzi.

🍴 Eating

Juan Segundo   ARGENTINE $$
(Av Paraguay 24; mains AR$105-180; ⊙noon-2pm daily, plus 9pm-12:30am Tue-Sat; 🛜) With a casually elegant chessboard-tiled interior and appealing outdoor tables in an upmarket zone of the city, Juan Segundo offers decent *parrilla* choices and salads, and even better fish and meat dishes with well-prepared sauces. There's a play area

for kids but not many cheap choices on the short wine list.

No Me Olvides   ARGENTINE, BAR $$
(Laprida 198; mains AR$90-175; ⊙6am-3am; 🛜) Huge windows and a high-ceilinged interior make this popular corner spot feel much larger than it is. Verve and color are added by vibrant paintings, paper lampshades and arty touches. As the heroic opening hours suggest, it does everything from breakfasts to late-night cocktails. The menu is a touch overpriced but the pasta, ciabattas and *lomitos* are really excellent.

Coco's Resto   ARGENTINE $$
(Av Sarmiento 266; mains AR$110-160; ⊙noon-2:30pm & 8:30pm-midnight Mon-Sat, noon-2:30pm Sun; 🛜) Stylishly occupying two front rooms of a house, this intimate, well-decorated restaurant is popular with suited diners from the nearby state parliament. A wide-ranging menu of pastas, meats soused in various sauces, river fish and a long wine list make this a pleasant Chaco choice.

🍷 Drinking & Nightlife

El Viejo Café   CAFE
(Pellegrini 109; ⊙6am-3am; 🛜) In an elegant old edifice, with an eclectically decorated interior, this is a fine choice any time of day. Its terrace is sweet for a sundowner, and it gets lively later on weekends, when there's usually live music. Solid if unspectacular meals (mains AR$65 to AR$110) are also available

🛍 Shopping

There's a selection of *artesanía* stalls on the southern side of Plaza 25 de Mayo.

Fundación Chaco Artesanal   HANDICRAFTS
(fundacionchacoartesanal@gmail.com; Pellegrini 272; ⊙9am-12:30pm & 4:30-7:30pm Mon-Fri) ✐ Selection of indigenous crafts as well as CDs from the Toba choir. Head upstairs in the Centro Cultural Leopoldo Marechal.

ℹ Information

Hospital Perrando (📞0362-444-2399; Av 9 de Julio 1100)

Provincial Tourist Office (📞0362-445-3098; www.chaco.travel; López y Planes 185; ⊙7:30am-8pm) This regional tourist office has reasonably up-to-date information on the further-flung parts of the Chaco.

Terminal Tourist Office (www.chaco.travel; ⊙7am-8pm Mon-Fri Sat, 7am-9:30am &

6-8:30pm Sat & Sun) In the bus terminal. There's a municipal office opposite it.

Tourist Office (☑ 0362-445-8289; Roca 20; ☺ 7am-noon & 2:30-8pm) On the southern side of Plaza 25 de Mayo.

❶ Getting There & Away

Aerolíneas Argentinas (☑ 0362-444-5551; www.aerolineas.com.ar; Justo 184; ☺ 8am-12:30pm & 4:30-8pm Mon-Fri, 8am-noon Sat) flies to Buenos Aires daily.

Resistencia's **bus terminal** (☑ 0362-446-1098; cnr MacLean & Islas Malvinas), 4km southwest of the center, serves destinations in all directions. Buses zip between Corrientes and Resistencia (from AR$25, 40 minutes) frequently. You can also catch a bus (AR$7) to Corrientes from the city center, on Av Alberdi just south of Plaza 25 de Mayo. Faster are **shared taxis** (Frondizi 416; ☺ 24hr) (AR$25, 30 minutes).

Buses from Resistencia

DESTINATION	COST (AR$)	TIME (HR)
Asunción (Paraguay)	203	6
Buenos Aires	864	13-14
Córdoba	833	10-14
Posadas	287	4½-5
Puerto Iguazú	542	10-11
Salta	719	12-13
Santiago del Estero	586	8½-9½
Tucumán	675-735	11-12

❶ Getting Around

Aeropuerto San Martín is 6km south of town on RN11; a *remise* costs around AR$80.

The bus terminal is a AR$80 taxi from the center, or you can take bus 3, 9 or 110 from

INDIGENOUS GROUPS OF THE GRAN CHACO

With some 50,000 members, the **Toba** of the Gran Chaco are one of Argentina's largest indigenous groups, but protests highlight the stark reality that many communities suffer from abandoned government facilities and desperate poverty. Few Argentines have much idea about the struggles of this *pueblo olvidado* (forgotten people).

In Resistencia, the Toba live in barrios (neighborhoods) that are separated from the rest of the city. But venturing further into the Chaco, it's easy to find Toba *asentamientos* (settlements). Except for the occasional government-built health center, nearly all buildings are made of adobe, with dirt floors and thatched or corrugated metal roofs.

The Toba refer to themselves as Komlek (Qom-lik) and speak a dialect of the Guaycurú linguistic group, known locally as Qom. They have a rich musical tradition (the Coro Toba Chelaalapi, a Toba choir, had World Heritage designation). Along with basketry and ceramics, the Toba are known for the *n'viké*, their version of the fiddle, which they make out of a gas can. Though its name signifies the noise of a jaguar sharpening its claws on tree bark, it sounds very melodic.

The region's most numerous indigenous group (over 60,000) is the **Wichí**, who remain extremely isolated (they live nearly 700km from Resistencia, in the far northwest of Chaco province and in Formosa and Salta provinces) and are the most traditional. They still obtain much of their food through hunting, gathering and fishing. The Wichí are known for their wild honey and their beautiful *yica* bags, which they weave with fibers from the chaguar plant, a bromeliad native to the dry Chaco.

The **Mocoví** are the Gran Chaco's third-largest indigenous group, with a population of 17,000, concentrated primarily in southern Chaco province and northern Santa Fe. Until the arrival of Europeans, the Mocoví sustained themselves primarily through hunting and gathering, but today they rely mostly on farming and seasonal work. They are famous for their burnished pottery, the most developed of indigenous Chaco ceramics.

For more information, stop by Resistencia's **Centro Cultural Leopoldo Marechal** (☑ 0362-445-2738; Pellegrini 272; ☺ 9am-2pm & 4:30-7:30pm Mon-Fri), which has crafts exhibits and a shop sponsored by the Fundación Chaco Artesanal, and the same city's Museo del Hombre Chaqueño. You can also journey into the Impenetrable to visit the Toba or Wichí. Their communities are welcoming; a visit in late afternoon, when often the whole village joins in a communal game of volleyball or soccer, is a great time to meet folk.

PENETRATING 'EL IMPENETRABLE'

If you have a yen to get off the beaten track, the more remote areas of the Chaco are for you. From Castelli, you can head west along *ripio* (gravel) roads to remote Fuerte Esperanza (buses and shared *remises* run this route), which has two nature reserves in its vicinity – **Reserva Provincial Fuerte Esperanza** and **Reserva Natural Loro Hablador**. Both conserve typical dry Chaco environments, with algarrobo and quebracho trees, armadillos, peccaries and many bird species. **Loro Hablador**, 40km from Fuerte Esperanza, has more vegetation, a good campground and short walking trails. It adjoins similar **Parque Nacional Copo** in Santiago del Estero province. Fuerte Esperanza has simple *hospedajes* (guesthouses). Further north, **Misión Nueva Pompeya** was founded in 1899 by Franciscans who established a mission station for Matacos in tough conditions. The main building, with its square-towered church, is a surprising sight in such a remote location. There are cheap lodgings in town.

One of the best ways to visit is via a tour from Castelli. Be warned, summer temperatures can be uncomfortably warm out here.

Santa María de Oro near Perón. Don't walk it: travelers have reported muggings.

A two-ride city bus ticket costs AR$15 from the main shop in the terminal, or at Roca 35 on the plaza.

Parque Nacional Chaco

Preserving several diverse ecosystems that reflect subtle differences in relief, soils and rainfall, this very accessible **park** (☑03725-499161; www.parquesnacionales.gob.ar) FREE protects 150 sq km of the humid eastern Chaco. It is 115km northwest of Resistencia via RN16 and RP9. The access town is Capitán Solari.

🏃 Activities

Hiking and bird-watching are the principal activities here. From the main campground, where there's a small exhibition, an easy 2km circular trail takes you across a rickety bridge and through the forest for good bird-watching. A 5km walk, cycle or drive takes you to a short trail leading to viewpoints over lakes. A longer 12km road, suitable for cars, bikes and horses, heads south to the Panza de Cabra lake.

Pack plenty of repellent for the voracious mosquitoes.

🛌 Sleeping & Eating

The campground has power, toilets, drinking water and rental bikes. Vendors sometimes appear at weekends, but best bring your own food.

Hospedaje Los Quebrachos GUESTHOUSE $
(José Luis Ávalos; ☑03725-15-454532; s/d US$15/23; ❈❉) On the way to the park, and less than a kilometer from its entrance, this is a typical little Chaco ranch with a double and quadruple room with a kitchen. There's also a small pool.

ℹ Getting There & Away

La Estrella runs five buses daily from Resistencia (AR$57, 2½ hours) to Capitán Solari, from where the park is 5.5km away. It's a pleasant walk, but the **park office** (www.parquesnacionales.gob. ar; cnr Fernández & Galarza; ⊙9am-3pm) may help. Failing that, take a *remise* (AR$100): a list of phone numbers is on the door of the **tourist office** (Fernández & plaza; ⊙8:30am-noon & 2:30-6pm Mon-Fri, 9am-noon & 3-6pm Sat & Sun) on the square.

The road may be impassable after rain.

Roque Sáenz Peña

☑0364 / POP 96,900

Something of a frontier town, thriving Presidencia Roque Sáenz Peña is well out in the Chaco, and a gateway to the 'Impenetrable' beyond. It's known for its thermal baths, fortuitously discovered by drillers seeking potable water in 1937, and makes an appealing stop, with a rugged, friendly feel.

◉ Sights & Activities

Complejo Ecológico Municipal ZOO
(adult/child AR$20/8, vehicles AR$20; ⊙7:30am-6pm) At the junction of RN16 and RN95, 4km east of downtown, the town's spacious zoo and botanical garden emphasizes birds and mammals found in the Chaco region, alongside a few lions, tigers, bears and a bafflingly large chicken pen.

NORTH TO FORMOSA AND PARAGUAY

Buses run from Resistencia to Asunción, Paraguay's capital, crossing in Argentina's far north at **Clorinda**, a chaotic border town with little of interest beyond bustling markets.

A better stop is baking-hot **Formosa**, a medium-sized provincial capital two hours' bus ride north of Resistencia. Hotels, restaurants and services can be found along Av 25 de Mayo, which links the sleepy plaza with the Río Paraguay waterfront – the best place to stroll once the temperatures drop.

Laguna Oca offers good bird-watching 6km from town, but the rest of the province has even more.

One good spot is **Parque Nacional Río Pilcomayo** (☎03718-470-045; www.parques nacionales.gob.ar; RN86; ☺8am-6pm), 126km northwest of Formosa and 55km west of Clorinda. Daily buses connect these with **Laguna Blanca**, an easy-paced citrus town where you'll find inexpensive lodgings – **Residencial Guaraní** (☎03718-470024; cnr San Martín & Sargento Cabral; r per person US$18; ✺) is the standout – and *remises* (taxis) to the national park. The park's main feature is also called **Laguna Blanca**, where rangers can take you out in boats to spot caiman.

Formosa province's standout attraction is **Bañado la Estrella** (www.banadolaestrella. org.ar). This stunning wetland area, a floodplain of the Río Pilcomayo, harbors an astonishing range of birdlife, as well as alligators, capybaras, sizable serpents and beautiful water plants. From the roads that cross this 200km-long finger-shaped area, it's easy to spot a huge variety of wildlife: pack binoculars.

The handiest town is Las Lomitas, 300 km west of Formosa on RN81 with regular bus service (AR$197, 5½ to six hours). From here, paved RP28 heads north, cutting across the wetlands via a causeway, starting 37km north of Las Lomitas and extending for some 15km. Las Lomitas has accommodations, including **Hotel Eva** (☎03715-432092; hotel_ eva@hotmail.com; Av San Martín 250; r US$28-43; ✺@☎), a friendly place whose dark rooms don't live up to the elegant stone-faced exterior. Upgrade to an intermediate room for a better bed.

Complejo Termal Municipal   SPA
(☎0364-443-3177; www.facebook.com/complejo termalsp; Brown 545; ☺7:30am-10pm) Roque's famous thermal baths draw their saline water from 150m below ground. The complex, around since the 1930s, is now a top-class facility, offering thermal baths (AR$81) in individual rooms, saunas and Turkish baths (AR$54), and a big pool with water jets and a retractable roof (AR$81). Treatments on offer include kinesiology, massage and aromatherapy.

🛏 Sleeping

Hotel Presidente   HOTEL $
(☎0364-442-4498; San Martín 771; s/d US$27/40; ✺@☎) Well-run and inexpensive, this is a pleasing budget place right in the heart of town, with friendly staff and rooms with comfortable beds, fridge and hairdryer.

★ Atrium Gualok   HOTEL $$
(☎0364-442-0500; www.atriumgualok.com.ar; San Martín 1198; s/d US$72/86; ✺@☎✺) Right next to the spa complex, this fine modern hotel gives a feeling of space throughout.

Rooms are indeed set around a lofty central atrium and are sleek, minimalist and great value for its standard. There's an enticing pool area and the hotel has its own spa complex and casino. Substantial discount for paying cash.

🍴 Eating

★ Raices   PARRILLA $
(Parera 560; mains AR$60-105; ☺10:30am-3pm & 7:30pm-1am Mon-Sat, 10:30am-3pm Sun) Convivial and welcoming, this neighborhood restaurant a few blocks north of the center is worth the stroll. Check out its huge barbecue before entering to enjoy really tasty *vacío* (flank steak), delicious chicken and other staples.

Ama'nalec   ICE CREAM $
(Moreno 601; ice creams AR$20-60; ☺8am-11:45pm; ☎) This busy corner place does tempting little pastries and very tasty ice cream, a godsend in Roque's paralyzing heat. It has some unusual flavors: figs in cognac is worth a lick.

❶ Getting There & Away

The **bus terminal** (☑0364-420280; Petris, btwn Avellaneda & López) is seven blocks east of downtown. There are regular buses to Resistencia (AR$102, two hours), and services running west to Salta, Tucumán, Santiago del Estero and Mendoza.

Juan José Castelli

☑0364 / POPULATION 27,200

A fairly prosperous agricultural service center, Castelli is a green, fertile looking place but gateway to the more arid Impenetrable wilderness to the west. With several excellent accommodation choices, it makes a great base for exploring the Chaco.

☞ Tours

★EcoTur Chaco
DRIVING TOUR

(Carlos Aníbal Schumann; ☑0364-447-1073; www. ecoturchaco.com.ar; Av San Martín 500) Personable Carlos is an enthusiastic Chaco expert and offers memorable 4WD tours that get right into the heart of the Impenetrable region, both geographically and culturally. The standout trip is a two-day affair that eschews roads in favor of tracks and visits indigenous communities, remote settlements, reserves and national parks. Day-trips and excursions camping on ranches are also possible.

⛺ Sleeping & Eating

There are four good hotels in and around town, two out on or near the highway.

Portal del Impenetrable
HOTEL $

(☑0364-15-470-8848; www.hotelportaldelimpenetrable.com; Ruta 9; s/d US$30/41; ✴@☎) At the entrance to town, this spacious – almost too spacious – modern hotel offers interesting artworks, efficient service and capacious rooms. It's a commodious Chaco base at half the price of many Argentine hotels of this standard. An extra few pesos gets you a superior room, with plasma screen and minibar.

Nuevo Hotel Florencia
HOTEL $

(☑0364-447-1426; http://hotelflorencia.com. ar; Av San Martín 870; s/d US$25/38; ✴@☎) Clean and welcoming, this is a value-for-pesos budget hotel on the main road in the heart of town. Rooms are simple but well-equipped, and have the sort of useful features, like plenty of electrical sockets, that many more illustrious places lack. There's a bit of echoing noise.

Diony's
ARGENTINE $

(Vázquez 543; mains AR$50-90; ☺8am-3pm & 8:30pm-1am; ☎) Alongside the square, this spacious restaurant is set in the Club del Progreso and is the town's most reliable option for standard but well-prepared Argentine fare. Prices are low and value is high, with a nice line in omelets as starters, followed by chicken, beef, pork or fish with a wide variety of sauces.

❶ Getting There & Away

Castelli is served by four daily buses from Resistencia (AR$171, five hours), and more regular services from Roque Sáenz Peña (AR$68, two hours).

Parque Nacional do Iguaçu (Brazil)

This Brazilian **park** (☑3521-4400; www.cata ratasdoiguacu.com.br; adult foreigners/Mercosul/ Brazilians R$52.30/41.30/31.30, child R$8; ☺9am-5pm) is entered via an enormous visitor center, with snack bar, ATMs and rip-off lockers (R$30), among other amenities. Parking here costs R$19.

Tickets can be purchased by card or a variety of currencies. All catering outlets take cards, so day-trippers won't need to obtain Brazilian currency. There are ATMs at the visitor center. Double-decker buses await to take you into the park proper. Keep your eyes peeled for animals. The last bus back from the falls is at 6:30pm.

◎ Sights & Activities

The double-decker bus into Parque Nacional do Iguaçu makes two stops before the main falls stop. These are trailheads for excursions that cost extra. If you plan to do any of these, chat with one of the agents touting them around the park visitor center; they can get you a discount. There are several other combinations and boat trips available. Some of these excursions need to be booked a day before.

★Cataratas do Iguaçu
WATERFALL

The main waterfall observation trail provides unforgettable vistas. It is the third, and principal, bus stop on the route that takes you into the national park. From here you walk 1.5km down a paved trail with brilliant views of the falls on the Argentine side, the jungle and the river below. Every twist reveals a more splendid vista until the path

The Iguazú Falls

There are few more impressive sights on the planet than this majestic array of cascades on the border of Argentina and Brazil. Set in luxurious tropical jungle, the falls are accessible, and provide a primal thrill that will never be forgotten.

Brazilian Side

Hit the Brazilian side (p211) first to appreciate the wide panorama from its short viewing path within a birdlife-rich national park. Cascade after cascade is revealed, picturesquely framed by tropical vegetation before you end up below the impressive Salto Floriano (p214).

Garganta del Diablo

The highlight of the falls is the 'Devil's Throat.' Stroll out over the placid Iguazú river before gazing in awe as it drops away beneath you in a display of primitive sound and fury that leaves you breathless (p203).

Argentine Side

Two spectacular walkways, one high, one low, get you in close to torrents of water of extraordinary power. Expect awesome photos, expect to get wet, and expect to be exhilarated (p203).

Boat Trips

Not wet enough yet? Then prepare to be absolutely drenched. Zippy motorboats take thrillseekers right in under one of the biggest waterfalls on the Argentine side (p204). More sedate kayaking and rafting excursions are also available on the Brazilian side (p214).

Jungle Trails

The waterfalls aren't the only thing on offer. National parks on both sides of the river offer various easy-to-medium trails through the jungle that give great wildlife-watching opportunities (p204 and p214).

Clockwise from top left
1. Foz do Iguaçu (p215). Brazilian side **2.** Rainforest walkway, Iguazú Falls **3.** Coatis

ENTERING BRAZIL

Many nationalities require visas to enter Brazil. At the time of writing, these included citizens of the USA, Australia, Canada and Japan. EU citizens did not. Download the application form at https://scedv.serpro.gov.br and take it to a Brazilian consulate. The one in **Puerto Iguazú** (☎03757-420192; Córdoba 278 ; visa fee Australia/Canada/Japan/USA/other R$35/65/25/160/20; ☺visas 8am-1:30pm Mon-Fri) will likely be cheaper than in your home country. You'll need a return ticket (from Argentina will do), photo and a bank or credit card statement. If you get there early, it can usually be ready by the next working day and same day may be possible.

That said, it is usually – but not always – possible to take a day trip by bus to the Brazilian falls without a visa. You'll have to catch the Foz do Iguaçu–bound bus, not the one that goes direct to the Brazilian falls. Argentine officials will stamp you out; stay on the bus when it passes Brazilian immigration and don't blame us if you're out of luck that day. Taxi drivers can usually get you through without immigration formalities too. Bear in mind that this isn't officially sanctioned, so if you get caught, you may be fined.

ends right under majestic Salto Floriano, which will give you a healthy sprinkling via the wind it generates.

A catwalk leads out to a platform with majestic views, with the Garganta del Diablo close at hand, and a perspective down the river in the other direction. If the water's high, it's unforgettable.

From here, an elevator heads up to a viewing platform at the top of the falls at Porto Canoas, the last bus stop. Porto Canoas has boat excursions, a gift shop, a couple of snack bars and a buffet restaurant.

Trilha do Poço Preto   HIKING, BOAT
(☎045-3529-9665; www.macucosafari.com.br; adult/child R$278/139) This easy 9km trail takes you on a guided journey through the jungle on foot, by bike or vehicle. It ends above the falls, where you can kayak then take a boat cruise around river islands to Porto Canoas. You can also return via the Bananeiras Trail. First stop on park bus route.

Bananeiras Trail   WALKING TOUR
(☎045-3529-9665; www.macucosafari.com.br; adult/child incl boat ride R$/216/108) This is a 1.6km walk passing lagoons and observing aquatic wildlife, which ends at a jetty where you can take boat rides or silent 'floating' excursions in kayaks down to Porto Canoas. Second stop on the park bus route.

Macuco Safari   BOAT TOUR
(☎045-3574-4244; www.macucosafari.com.br; adult/child R$179/89.50) This two-hour safari includes a 3km trailer ride through the jungle, a 600m walk to a small waterfall and then a boat ride (half-price without this) to the falls for a soaking. Don't confuse with the

Macuco trail on the Argentine side. Second stop on the park bus route.

Helisul   SCENIC FLIGHTS
(☎045-3529-7474; www.helisul.com; Rodovia das Cataratas, Km 16.5; flights R$308; ☺9am-5:30pm) By the park visitor center, this set-up runs 10-minute chopper jaunts over the Brazilian side of the falls. Environmental impact is questionable, but it's undeniably exhilarating. There are open panels in the windows for photography.

🛏 Sleeping & Eating

★Hotel das Cataratas   HOTEL $$$
(☎045-2102-7000; www.belmond.com; BR469, Km32; r without/with view from R$1966/2317, ste from R$2136; ✱@🛜🅿🐶) In the Parque Nacional do Iguaçu near the falls, the location of this excellent hotel appeals enormously, though only a few rooms have falls views, and those only partial. It's decorated throughout in understated, elegant Portuguese colonial style, with tiling in the bathrooms and dark wood in the bedrooms. Public areas have cozy appeal, and the fine pool area is surrounded by birdsong. Service is excellent.

After-hours falls access is a major perk. Make sure you climb the belvedere for the view. Online rates are much better.

Restaurante Porto Canoas   BUFFET $$
(www.cataratasdoiguacu.com.br; buffet R$58; ☺noon-4pm) Situated at the end of the main trail at the Parque Nacional do Iguaçu, this restaurant has a long pleasant terrace overlooking the river just before it descends into maelstrom – a great spot for a beer or

caipirinha – and an OK buffet lunch with plenty of salads and hot dishes.

ℹ️ Getting There & Around

From Foz, catch the 120 bus from the urban bus terminal or stops along Av Juscelino Kubitschek; the trip takes 30 to 40 minutes, stops at the airport and costs R$3, paid as you enter the terminal.

Taxis from Foz to the park entrance cost R$40 to R$50. Haggle.

From Puerto Iguazú, there's a direct bus to the Brazilian falls hourly (AR$80 return, 40 minutes), with departures from 8:30am to 2:30pm and returns from 10am to 5pm (Brazilian time). This stops at Brazilian **immigration** (p214) and collects passports. You can also take the regular bus to Foz do Iguaçu (AR$20, hourly 6:30am to 6:30pm) and get off a couple of stops after crossing the international bridge. Cross the road, and wait for the Parque Nacional bus. Repeat at the same stop on the way back.

Foz do Iguaçu (Brazil)

📱 045 / POP 263.500

Hilly Foz is basecamp for the Brazilian side of the Iguazú falls, and gives you a chance to get a feel for a Brazilian town. It's much bigger and more cosmopolitan than Puerto Iguazú, and has a keep-it-real feel that its Argentine counterpart lacks.

ℹ️ Orientation

Foz is at the confluence of the rivers Iguaçu (Iguazú) and Paraná; international bridges connect it to Puerto Iguazú, Argentina and Ciudad del Este, Paraguay. Av das Cataratas leads 20km to the Brazilian side of the Iguazú falls, passing the Argentina bridge on the way.

◉ Sights

Itaipu DAM
(📱 0800-645-4643; www.turismoitaipu.com.br; Tancredo Neves 6702; panoramic/special tour R$27/68; ⊙ regular tour hourly 8am-4pm) This bi-national dam is the world's second-largest hydroelectric power station and, at some 8km long and 200m high, is a memorable sight, especially when a vast torrent of overflow water cascades down the spillway.

The visitor center, 12km north of Foz, has regular tours and the more detailed *circuito especial* (minimum age 14), taking you into the power plant itself.

Buses (R$3, 30 minutes) head here quarter-hourly from the urban bus terminal.

The project was controversial: it plunged Brazil into debt and necessitated large-scale destruction of rainforest and the displacement of 10,000 people. But it cleanly supplies most of Paraguay's energy needs, and 20% of Brazil's.

A variety of other attractions within the complex include a museum, wildlife park and river beaches.

Parque das Aves ZOO
(www.parquedasaves.com.br; Av das Cataratas, Km 17.1; admission R$34; ⊙ 8:30am-5pm) Near the Parque Nacional do Iguaçu entrance is this large bird park. It has a huge assortment of our feathered friends, mostly Brazilian, with good information in English and Spanish. Walk-through aviaries get you up close and personal with toucans, macaws and hummingbirds.

🛏️ Sleeping

Normally you'll get a rate up to 50% lower than rack rates. Don't be afraid to ask for a discount: it's expected.

Pousada Sonho Meu GUESTHOUSE $
(📱 045-3573-5764; www.pousadasonhomeufoz.com.br; Mem de Sá 267; s/d R$160/210; ✳️@🐾🛜⊠) This is a delightful oasis barely 50m from the urban bus terminal. Rooms are simply decorated with bamboo; there's a standout pool (complete with a mini *catarata!*), breakfast area and outdoor guest kitchen, and a warm welcome throughout. Cash only. Prices can be half those indicated.

★ **Tetris Container Hostel** HOSTEL $
(📱 045-3132-0019; www.tetrishostel.com.br; Av das Cataratas 639; dm R$35-40, d from R$160; ✳️@🐾🛜⊠) 🖋️ Brazil's coolest hostel is crafted from 15 shipping containers – even the pool is a water-filled shipping container! – and makes full use of other industrial byproducts as well, like sinks made from oil drums. Colorful bathrooms brighten the dorms (a four-bed female plus 10- and 12-bed mixed) and the patio/bar area is tops. From 7pm to 10pm there's music and a great local scene.

ℹ️ CHANGING THE CLOCKS

From mid-October to mid-February, southern Brazil changes the clocks for summer, putting it an hour ahead of Argentina, which doesn't observe daylight saving time.

Foz do Iguaçu (Brazil)

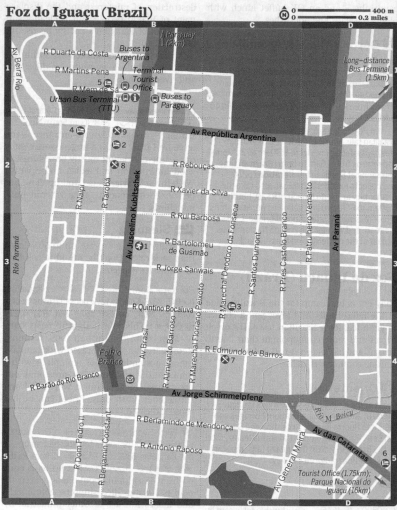

Foz do Iguaçu (Brazil)

Iguassu Guest House HOSTEL $
(☏ 045-3029-0242; www.iguassuguesthouse.com.
br; R Naipi 1019; dm/d R$40/130; ✳@🛜🏊)
Great facilities and welcoming management
mark this out from the Foz hostel herd.
There's a small pool out the back, it's spotless, and there's a really good open kitchen
and lounge area. Dorms vary in size; private
rooms are very compact. The urban bus terminal is just around the corner.

Hotel Rafain Centro HOTEL $$
(☏ 045-3521-3500; www.rafaincentro.com.br;
Marechal Deodoro da Fonseca 984; s/d rack
R$347/435, discounted R$170/215; ✳@🛜🏊)

Much more appealing than the hulking megahotels around town, the Rafain is a four-star place with plenty of facilities, style, artistic detail and friendly staff. Rooms are simple with large balconies and there's a cracking pool and terrace. Regular discounting makes for superb value.

Hotel Del Rey   HOTEL **$$**
(☑ 045-2105-7500; www.hoteldelreyfoz.com.br; Tarobá 1020; s/d R$255/270; ❋ @ ❷ ❊) Friendly, spotless and convenient. Rooms are spacious and comfortable, facilities excellent and the breakfast buffet huge. Book it ahead as its qualities are no secret.

✖ Eating

It's easy to eat cheaply. Many places will serve you a soft drink and *salgado* (baked or fried snack) for as little as R$4, and cheap locals offer buffet lunch for R$10 to R$20. The Lebanese community ensures dozens of shawarma (kebab) places.

Churrascaria do Gaúcho   STEAK **$**
(www.facebook.com/churrasdogaucho; Av República Argentina 632; all-you-can-eat buffet R$28.50; ☺11am-11pm; ☏) Near the local bus terminal, this isn't a refined spot, but offers excellent value for its tasty cuts of meat and reasonable salad options.

Armazém   BRAZILIAN **$$**
(☑ 045-3572-0007; www.armazemrestaurante. com.br; Edmundo de Barros 446; mains R$30-75; ☺7pm-midnight daily, plus 11:30am-3:30pm Sat & Sun; ☏) This well-frequented high-ceilinged restaurant serves top-shelf Brazilian food. From starters like cheese-laden carpaccio to delicious chicken, cod and beef mains, all just about enough for two, it delivers on taste. The wine list covers the whole Southern Cone. Free hotel pickups and drop-offs.

Búfalo Branco   CHURRASCARIA **$$**
(☑ 045-3523-9744; www.bufalobranco.com.br; Rebouças 530; all-you-can-eat grill R$80; ☺noon-11pm; ☏✐) This spacious Foz classic draws locals and tourists alike for its classy but overpriced *rodízio* (all-you-can-eat mixed grill), which features delicious beef as well as more unusual choices like chicken hearts and turkey balls. The salad bar is great, and

includes tasty Lebanese morsels and sushi rolls. Look diffident outside the door and you might get a cheaper deal.

☕ Drinking & Nightlife

Brazil is all about an ice-cold bottle of beer in a plastic insulator served in a no-frills local bar with red plastic seats. Unbeatable. For a healthier tipple, juice bars give you the chance to try exotic fruits such as *acerola, açaí* or *cupuaçu*.

Nightlife centers on Av Jorge Schimmelpfeng. A row of big indoor-outdoor bars here all specialize in *chopp* (draft beer) and do decent food designed to share.

ℹ Information

Other currencies are widely accepted, but it's cheaper to pay in Brazilian reais. The closest ATM to the urban bus terminal is a block beyond, under the Muffato supermarket.

P.I.T (☑ 0800-45-1516; www.pmfi.pr.gov.br/ turismo; Av das Cataratas 2330, Vila Yolanda; ☺7am-11pm) Between town and the falls. There's a handier office in the urban bus terminal (☑ 0800-45-1516; www.pmfi.pr.gov.br/ turismo; Kubitschek 1310; ☺7:30am-6pm).

ℹ Getting There & Away

There are daily flights to Rio de Janeiro, Porto Alegre, Curitiba and São Paulo among other Brazilian cities.

Long-distance buses include Curitiba (10 hours), São Paulo (16 hours) and Rio de Janeiro (22 hours). Buy tickets at downtown **Central de Passagens** (☑ 045-3528-8284; www.centralde passagens.com; Av Juscelino Kubitschek 526).

ℹ Getting Around

The **long-distance bus terminal** (☑ 045-3522-3336; Av Costa e Silva 1601) is 5km northeast of downtown. To get downtown, get a taxi for R$25 or catch bus 105 or 115 (R$3).

For the airport, catch the **falls bus** (p205).

Buses to Puerto Iguazú (R$4/AR$20) run along Rua Mem de Sá alongside the urban bus terminal half-hourly from 8am until 8pm; they stop along Av Juscelino Kubitschek. Buses for Ciudad del Este, Paraguay (R$5), run every 15 minutes (half-hourly on Sundays); catch them on Av Juscelino Kubitschek opposite the urban bus terminal.

Salta & the Andean Northwest

Why Go?

Argentina's northwest sits lofty, dry and tough beneath the mighty Andes. Nature works magic here with stone: weird, wonderful, tortured rockscapes are visible throughout.

There's a definite Andean feel characterizing the area's indigenous communities, traditional handicrafts, llamas and Inca ruins, and the high, arid puna (Andean highlands) stretching into Chile and Bolivia. This region's cities were Argentina's first colonial settlements and have special appeal.

Several popular routes await. From travelers' favorite Salta, head through a national park studded with cactus sentinels to gorgeous Cachi, then down through traditional weaving communities in the Valles Calchaquíes to Cafayate, home of some of Argentina's best wines. Another route from Salta soars upward to the puna mining settlement of San Antonio de los Cobres, heads north to the spectacular salt plains of the Salinas Grandes, and then down to the visually wondrous and history-filled Quebrada de Humahuaca.

Best National Parks

➜ Calilegua (p250)

➜ Talampaya (p283)

➜ El Rey (p232)

➜ Los Cardones (p233)

Best Places to Stay

➜ Estancia las Carreras (p267)

➜ Killa (p241)

➜ Kkala (p229)

➜ Posada El Arribo (p248)

➜ Miraluna (p235)

When to Go

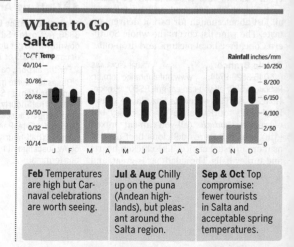

Salta

Feb Temperatures are high but Carnaval celebrations are worth seeing.

Jul & Aug Chilly up on the puna (Andean highlands), but pleasant around the Salta region.

Sep & Oct Top compromise: fewer tourists in Salta and acceptable spring temperatures.

SALTA & JUJUY PROVINCES

Intertwined like yin and yang, Argentina's northwestern provinces harbor an inspiring wealth of natural beauty and traditional culture. Bounded by Bolivia to the north and Chile to the west, the zone climbs from sweaty cloud forests westward to the puna highlands and some of the most majestic peaks of the Andes cordillera.

The two capitals, especially colonial Salta, which is beloved by travelers, are launchpads for exploring the jagged chromatic ravines of the Quebrada de Cafayate and Quebrada de Humahuaca; the villages of the Valles Calchaquíes, rich in artisanal handicrafts; the stark puna scenery; the national parks of Calilegua and El Rey; and for nosing aromatic Cafayate torrontés (dry white wine).

Salta

☑ 0387 / POP 655,600 / ELEV 1187M

Sophisticated Salta is a favorite, engaging active minds with its outstanding museums and lighting romantic candles with its plaza-side cafes and the live *música folklórica* of its vibrant *peñas* (folk music clubs). It offers the facilities (and the traffic and noise) of a large town, retains the comfortable pace of a smaller place and preserves more colonial architecture than most Argentine cities.

Founded in 1582, it's now the most touristed spot in northwest Argentina, and offers numerous accommodation options. The center bristles with tour agents: this is the place to get things organized for onward travel. A popular option is to hire a car here to explore the surrounding area.

◉ Sights

★ Museo de Arqueología de Alta Montaña   MUSEUM
(MAAM; www.maam.gob.ar; Mitre 77; foreigner/Argentine AR$70/50; ☺11am-7:30pm Tue-Sun) One of northern Argentina's premier museums, this has a serious and informative exhibition focusing on Inca culture and, in particular, the child sacrifices left on some of the Andes' most imposing peaks.

The centerpiece is the mummified body of one of three children (rotated every six months) discovered at the peak of Llullaillaco (p222) in 1999. It was a controversial decision to display the bodies and it is a powerful experience to come face-to-face with them.

Intricately plaited hair and clothes are perfectly preserved, and their faces reflect – you decide – a distant past or a typical 21st-century Salta face; a peaceful passing or a tortured death.

The grave goods impress by their immediacy, with colors as fresh as the day they were produced. The *illas* (small votive figurines of animals and humans) are of silver, gold, shell and onyx, and many are clothed in textiles. It's difficult to imagine that a more privileged look at pre-Columbian South American culture will ever be offered us. Also exhibited is the 'Reina del Cerro,' a tomb-robbed mummy that ended up here after a turbulent history. Good videos give background on the sacrifices and on the Qhapaq Ñan, the Inca road system given Unesco status in 2014. There's a shop and library as well as a cafe-bar with terrace.

Museo Histórico del Norte   MUSEUM
(Caseros 549; admission AR$20; ☺9am-6pm Tue-Fri, 9am-1:30pm & 2:30-7pm Sat, 9am-1:30pm Sun) Set on the plaza in the lovely *cabildo* (town hall), this collection ranges from pre-Columbian ceramics through colonial-era religious art (admire the fine pulpit from Salta's Jesuit church) and displays on Salta in the 19th and 20th centuries. The endless portraits of Salta's governors wouldn't be out of place in a beard-and-mustache museum, while the transportation collection includes an enormous 1911 Renault that puts Hummers to shame.

Iglesia San Francisco   CHURCH
(www.conventosanfranciscosalta.com; cnr Caseros & Córdoba; ☺8am-1pm & 2-9pm Mon-Sat, 8am-1pm & 5-9pm Sun) This magenta-and-yellow church is Salta's most striking. The exuberant facade is topped by a slender tower; inside are several much-venerated images, including the Niño Jesús de Aracoeli, a rather spooky crowned figure. There's a lovely garden cloister, accessed via tours (English available, AR$40; from 10am to 1pm and 2pm to 6:30pm Tuesday to Saturday) that include a mediocre museum of religious art and treasures.

★ Pajcha – Museo de Arte Étnico Americano   MUSEUM
(www.museopajchasalta.com.ar; 20 de Febrero 831; foreigner/Argentine AR$40/20; ☺10am-1pm & 4-8pm Mon-Sat) This eye-opening private museum is a must-see if you're interested in indigenous art and culture. Juxtaposing archaeological finds with contemporary and recent artisanal work from all over Latin America, it takes an encouragingly broad

Salta & the Andean Northwest Highlights

❶ Wondering at nature's palette in the memorable **Quebrada de Humahuaca** (p250).

❷ Observing weavers at work in the memorable **Valles Calchaquíes** (p233).

❸ Cleansing your lungs in the crisp mountain air of **Tafí del Valle** (p266).

❹ Hitting Wild West **Chilecito** (p281), the base for uplifting mountain excursions.

❺ Soaking up the colonial ambience and enticing boutique hotels of sophisticated **Salta** (p219).

❻ Quaffing torrontés at northern Argentina's wine

capital of **Cafayate** (p238).

7 Trying the northwest's regional cuisine, where llama meat and quinoa replace beef and pasta in places such as **San Antonio de los Cobres** (p245).

8 Experiencing subtropical forest while ascending through steamy **Parque Nacional Calilegua** (p250).

9 Gazing over crater lakes, 6000m volcanoes and awesome Andean scenery in **western Catamarca** (p277).

Santa Fe

Córdoba

San Juan

MENDOZA

SAN JUAN

CÓRDOBA

Río Segundo

Río San Juan

Río Barmejo

Río Blanco

Laguna Mar Chiquita

Merlo

Chepes

Villa Santa Rita

Chamical

Salinas Grandes

Patquía

LA RIOJA

La Rioja

Anillaco

Sierra de Velasco

Parque Nacional Talampaya

Parque Provincial Ischigualasto

Villa Unión

Chilecito

Tinogasta

Sierra de Famatina

Laguna Brava

Cerro Bonito Chico (6850m)

Cerro Pissis (6779m)

Fiambalá

El Shincal

Belén

Londres

Villa Las Pirquitas

CATAMARCA

Campo de los Alisos

Concepción

Western Catamarca

Termas de Río Hondo

SANTIAGO DEL ESTERO

La Banda

Colonia Dara

Añatuya

Villa Ojo de Agua

Río Dulce

RP 116

RN 89

RP 98

RN 34

RN 5

RN 9

RN 34

RN 157

RN 64

RN 9

RN 38

RN 42

RP 46

RN 38

RN 60

RN 40

RN 45

RN 60

RN 74

RN 40

RP 26

RP 5

RP 9

RN 38

RP 27

RP 28

RP 29

RN 79

RN 150

RP 510

RN 79

RN 38

RN 157

RN 9

RN 60

RN 36

view of Andean culture and beyond. It's an exquisite dose of color and beauty run with great enthusiasm by the English-speaking management.

The quality of the pieces (amazing macaw-feather creations, religious sculpture from the Cuzco school, tools of the trade of Bolivian Kallawaya healers and finely crafted Mapuche silver jewelry) is extraordinarily high, testament to decades of study and collection by the anthropologist founder.

Convento de San Bernardo   CONVENT
(Caseros s/n; ⊙pastries 9am-noon & 4-6pm Mon-Sat) Only Carmelite nuns may enter this 16th-century convent, but visitors can approach the handsome adobe building to admire its carved, 18th-century algarrobo-wood door and buy nun-made pastries. The church can be visited before Mass (from 7am to 8:30am weekday and Sunday mornings, 7pm to 8pm Saturday evenings).

Cerro San Bernardo   HILL
For outstanding views of Salta, take the **teleférico** (☎0387-431-0641; one way/roundtrip AR$55/110; ⊙10am-7pm) from Parque San Martín to the top of this hill, a kilometer's ride that takes eight minutes. Alternatively, take the trail starting at the **Güemes monument**. Atop is a cafe (whose terrace has the best views), a watercourse and *artesanía* (handicraft) shops.

Courses

Salta appeals as a spot for a taking a Spanish course, and there are several organizations. Search online for recent recommendations.

Tours

Salta is the base for a range of tours, offered by numerous agencies, with a high concentration on Buenos Aires and Caseros near the plaza. Popular trips head to Cafayate (AR$530), Cachi (AR$600), San Antonio de los Cobres (the Tren a las Nubes route; AR$700), Salinas Grandes and Purmamarca (AR$1050) and more.

Operators such as **Altro Turismo** (Marina Turismo; ☎0387-431-9769; www.altroturismo.com. ar; Caseros 489) and **Tastil** (☎0387-431-1223;

THE CHILDREN GIVEN TO THE MOUNTAIN

The phrase 'human sacrifice' is sensationalist, but it is a fact that the Inca culture sometimes sacrificed the lives of high-born children to please or appease their gods. The Inca saw this as an offering to ensure the continuing fertility of their people and the land. The high peaks of the Andes were always considered sacred, and were chosen as sacrifice sites; the Inca felt that the children would be reunited with their forefathers, who watched over the communities from the loftiest summits.

Carefully selected for the role, the children were taken to the ceremonial capital Cuzco, Peru, where they were central to a large celebration – the *capacocha*. Ceremonial marriages between the children helped cement diplomatic links between tribes across the empire. At the end of the fiesta, they were paraded around the plaza, then were required to return home in a straight line – an arduous journey that could take months. Once home, they were feted and welcomed, then taken into the mountains. There they were fed, and given quantities of *chicha* (maize alcohol). When they passed out, they were taken up to the peak of the mountain and entombed, sometimes alive, presumably never to awaken, and sometimes having been strangled or killed with a blow to the head.

Three such children were found in 1999 near the peak of **Llullaillaco**, a 6739m volcano 480km west of Salta, on the Chilean border. It's the highest known archaeological site in the world. The cold, the low pressure and a lack of oxygen and bacteria help preserve the bodies almost perfectly. The Doncella (Maiden) was about 15 years old at the time of death, and was perhaps an *acila* (a 'virgin of the sun'), a prestigious role in Inca society. The other two, a boy and girl both aged from six to seven (the girl damaged by a later lightning strike), had cranial deformations that indicated they came from high-ranking families. Each was accompanied by a selection of grave goods which included textiles and small figurines of humanoids and camelids.

The mummies' transfer to Salta was controversial. Many felt they should have been left where they were discovered; but once their location was known, this was impossible. Whatever your feelings about the children, and the role of archaeology, they offer an undeniably fascinating glimpse of Inca religion and culture.

TREN A LAS NUBES

Argentina's most famous rail trip, **Tren a las Nubes** (Train to the Clouds; www.trenalas nubes.com.ar; cnr Ameghino & Balcarce; roundtrip US$182; ⊘ Sat Apr–mid-Dec), heads from Salta down the Lerma Valley before ascending multicolored Quebrada del Toro, continuing past Tastil ruins and San Antonio de los Cobres, before reaching a stunning viaduct spanning a desert canyon at La Polvorilla (altitude 4220m).

It's an incredible feat of engineering but a notoriously unreliable service. The trip, way overpriced, is a touristy one (a tourist trap, in many ways) with piped music, and Spanish and English commentary. It's a long day – leaving Salta at 7am and getting back into town (the return is by bus) at 9pm. The train stops twice, at the viaduct and at San Antonio. The return bus trip stops at the Tastil museum (no ruins visit).

The price includes mediocre snacks; there's a buffet car and dining car for fuller meals. You're not encouraged to take food on board. Medical staff are on hand for altitude sickness.

The train runs Saturdays from April to mid-December. Book tickets online, at the office (☎ 0387-422-8021; www.trenalasnubes.com.ar; Alberdi 53, shop 33; ⊘ 8am-8pm Mon-Fri, 9am-3pm Sat) or at travel agents. Look out for discount vouchers around town.

Salta tour operators run trips along the road paralleling the tracks: also a spectacular ascent. Only some include the viaduct. You could also get the bus to San Antonio de los Cobres, explore the town and get a cab to La Polvorilla from there.

www.turismotastil.com.ar; Caseros 468) are reliable. We recommend operators for interesting trips beyond the standard excursions.

Alternativa Salta DRIVING TOUR
(☎ 0387-15-502-5588; www.alternativasalta.com) Runs brilliant multiday 4WD trips into the spectacular, remote highlands of northwestern Argentina.

Clark Expediciones BIRD-WATCHING
(☎ 0387-492-7280; www.clarkexpediciones.com) Professional agency offering trips with English-speaking guides to national parks and remote uplands. This outfit is serious about bird-watching; trips include a half-/full day in the Reserva del Huaico, a 60-hectare cloud-forest reserve 8km west of Salta, two days to Parque Nacional El Rey and multiday tailored itineraries.

MTB Salta MOUNTAIN BIKING
(☎ 0387-15-527-1499; www.mtbsalta.com; Güemes 569) Arranges a variety of excellent mountain-biking and hiking tours around the province, ranging from half-days in the nearby forests to multiday excursions in the Valles Calchaquíes.

Norte Trekking HIKING
(☎ 0387-431-6616; www.nortetrekking.com; Güemes 265) Trips to Parque Nacional El Rey, multiday hikes and mountain climbing, with some guaranteed departure dates listed on its website. Also runs excellent 4WD excursions into the mountainous west of the province.

Salta Rafting RAFTING
(☎ 0387-421-3216; www.saltarafting.com; Caseros 177) This well-managed setup runs two-hour white-water rafting trips on the Class III Río Juramento, 100km from Salta (US$59 including barbecue lunch; transportation US$30 extra). You can also take spectacular 400m ziplines across a canyon (four-line trip US$40). A combo with lunch is US$94.

Sayta HORSEBACK RIDING
(☎ 0387-15-683-6565; www.saltacabalgatas.com. ar; Chicoana) This *estancia* (ranch) near Chicoana, 41km south of Salta, runs excellent horseback-riding days, with gaucho culture and optional *asado* (barbecue grill). A half-day with/without lunch costs US$85/60; a full day US$120 to US$140 (with overnight accommodation US$150). A two-day/one-night package is US$250. Prices include transfers from Salta.

★ Socompa TOUR
(☎ 0387-431-5974; www.socompa.com; Balcarce 998) This professional setup runs highly recommended tours into the Andean highlands. Its flagship five-day Puna Experience takes in the best of the highland scenery of Catamarca and Salta provinces using comfortable accommodations and multilingual guides. Another tour covers highlights of the northwest, including a sally into Chile. Book well ahead. Tours are private: you can't join a group.

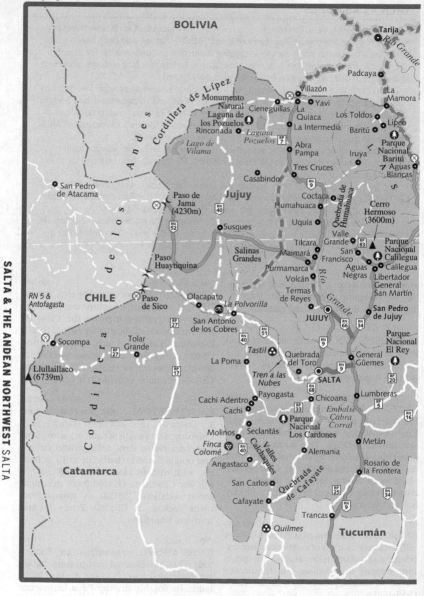

🛏 Sleeping

Salta has dozens of hostels, some cleaner than others, and competition keeps prices low. Boutique hotels and apartments pop up like mushrooms.

★ **Espacio Mundano** B&B **$**
(☎0387-572-2244; www.espaciomundano.com.
ar; Güemes 780; r US$58-82; ❋🐾🖥) There's absolutely nothing mundane about this artistic oasis in the heart of Salta. The place is a riot of color, lovely ceramic beasts and all manner of craft creations. It's highly original,

center, some of which look onto tiny garden patios. It's run by kindly, courteous people, is spotless and is a pleasingly reliable choice. A few extras such as big fluffy towels and hair-dryers put it above most in its price band.

Residencial El Hogar
GUESTHOUSE $

(📞0387-431-6158; www.residencialelhogar.com.ar; Saravia 239; d US$51; 🌢🛜) Run with genuine warmth, this pleasing little place is on a quiet residential street with the San Bernardo hill looming over the end of it. It's still an easy stroll into the center, though. Attractive rooms with nice little touches, helpful owners and a tasty breakfast make this a recommendable base at a fair price.

Coloria Hostel
HOSTEL $

(📞0387-431-3058; www.coloriahostel.com; Güemes 333; dm US$10-12, d US$35; 🌢🛜🏊) Upbeat, engaged staff and a glorious open-plan common area that looks over the garden and small pool are the major highlights of this enjoyable central hostel. It's colorful and quite upmarket by Salta standards; cleanliness is good; and dorms, though there's not a huge amount of space, are comfortable. Private rooms are very tight.

La Posta
GUESTHOUSE, HOSTEL $

(📞0387-422-1985; hostallaposta@gmail.com; Córdoba 368; dm/s/d US$15/28/45; 🛜) This simple but enchanting guesthouse makes a great budget choice for those looking for a quiet, peaceful central stay. Caring owners keep it spotless, and the en suite rooms are excellent. Dorms have breathing room and lockers, and breakfast is tasty with decent coffee. An appealingly relaxing place.

Munay Hotel
HOTEL $

(📞0387-422-4936; www.munayhotel.com.ar; Av San Martín 656; s/d US$44/68; 🌢🛜) Though it's on a busy, chaotic street (lots of local character, though), we still think this is a worthwhile budget hotel. A handy location, a staff that's pleased to see you, well-furnished and clean bedrooms, shower curtains and breakfast – a fine choice. Some rooms are small, but management is happy to give you a bigger one if it can.

Las Rejas
HOSTEL $

(📞0387-422-7959; www.lasrejashostel.com; Güemes 569; dm U$10-12, d with/without bathroom US$40/30; 🛜) Occupying rather a characterful building, this hostel has trendy exposed brick in the common areas thanks to a stylish recent renovation. Two levels of rooms and dorms out the back offer good space

friendly and likably chaotic. The three rooms are individually decorated and appealing, with either en suite or exterior bathroom.

Posada de las Farolas
HOTEL $

(📞0387-421-3463; www.posadalasfarolas.com.ar; Córdoba 246; s/d US$45/65; 🌢🛜) Good value for neat, clean air-conditioned rooms in the

Salta

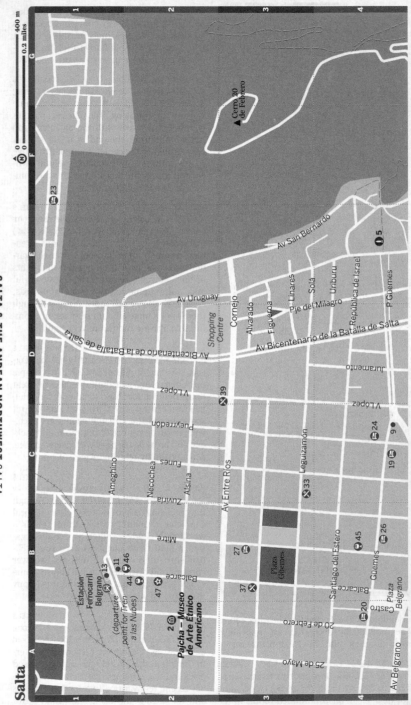

400 m
0.2 miles

Estación Ferrocarril Belgrano

(departure point for Tren a las Nubes)

Paícha – Museo de Arte Étnico Americano

Plaza Güemes

Plaza Belgrano

Cerro 20 de Febrero

Av San Bernardo

Av Uruguay

Shopping Centre

Av Bicentenario de la Batalla de Salta

Av Entre Ríos

25 de Mayo

20 de Febrero

Av Belgrano

Balcarce

Mitre

Alsina

Funes

Necochea

Zuviría

Ameghino

Pueyrredón

V López

V López

Juramento

Cornejo

Alvarado

Figueroa

Pje Linares

Pje del Milagro

Solá

Uriburu

República de Israel

P Güemes

Santiago del Estero

Güemes

Leguizamón

Castro

Balcarce

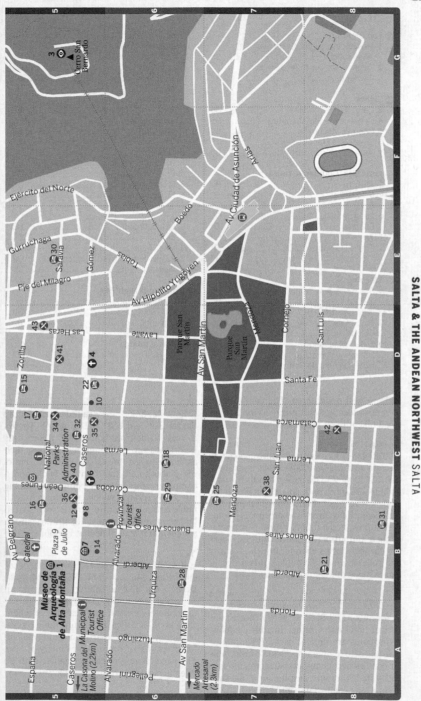

Salta

and are well maintained. The combination of central location and relaxed vibe is tops. Good bike hire on premises.

Salta por Siempre
HOSTEL **$**

(☎ 0387-423-3230; www.saltaporsiempre.com.ar; Tucumán 464; dm/s/d US$18/30/42, d with bathroom US$50; @ 🛜) This superfriendly hostel is eight blocks south of the plaza, but worth the trudge. The quiet, handsome building has clean, colorful rooms with bathrooms – some dorms have beds, others bunks – a proper kitchen and attractive shared spaces. There are cheaper dorms around, but the security and reliable operation makes this a decent choice. Look online for best rates.

Hotel Andalucía
HOTEL **$**

(☎ 0387-431-3259; www.hotelandaluciasalta.com. ar; Alberdi 651; s/d US$30/42; ❋ 🛜) Though this budget hotel has a rather lugubrious lobby area, rooms are much crisper. It's a family-run place that offers spotless, comfortable air-conditioned chambers that are modern with OK bathrooms despite some old-time decor. Good comfort at a good price.

★ Carpe Diem
B&B **$$**

(☎ 0387-421-8736; www.carpediemsalta.com.ar; Urquiza 329; s/d US$100/110; @ 🛜) There's a real home-from-home feel about this B&B that's full of thoughtful touches, such as home-baked bread at breakfast, enticing places to sit about with a book, and a computer with internet connection in the attractive rooms, which are stocked with noble antique furniture. Singles with shared bathroom in the appealing grassy garden are small but a good deal at US$56.

★ La Candela
HOTEL **$$**

(☎ 0387-422-4473; www.hotellacandela.com.ar; Pueyrredón 346; d US$130-192; ❋@🛜❋) Decked out like a country villa with an L-shaped pool and a grassy garden, this is nevertheless central and features excellent staff, good facilities and comfortable rooms, including a duplex apartment out back. Different grades of room differ chiefly by size. The decor is one of easy elegance, with an eclectic range of art on the walls.

There are also a couple of simpler, cheaper rooms (US$109).

⭐ Ankara Suites
APARTMENT $$

(☏ 0387-421-3969; www.ankarasuites.com; Zorrilla 145; apt US$125-146; ❄@🛜) These very inviting apartments offer great flexibility in the center of Salta. They come with polished floors, breakfast bar (brought to your room), fully equipped kitchens and very comfortable double bedrooms. Bathrooms are attractively modern, with spacious showers. Service is excellent and the place seems exceptionally well run. There's a top-floor Jacuzzi and sauna, as well as free laundry facilities.

Bloomers B&B
B&B $$

(☏ 0387-422-7449; www.bloomers-salta.com.ar; Vicente López 129; d US$110-140; ❄@🛜) Book ahead to grab one of the five rooms at this exquisitely stylish yet comfortable guesthouse. The second B here stands for brunch, served until noon. The color-themed rooms are all different and all delightful. It's like staying at a friend's – you can use the kitchen – but few of our friends have a place this pretty.

Hotel del Antiguo Convento
HOTEL $$

(☏ 0387-422-7267; www.hoteldelconvento.com.ar; Caseros 113; s/d US$70/88, d superior US$105-120; ❄@🛜🏊) Rooms are modern and sunny at this central hotel, and there's a great little pool area out the back. A duplex apartment next to it sleeps four. Superiors on the top floor are excellent, with extra facilities.

⭐ Kkala
BOUTIQUE HOTEL $$$

(☏ 0387-439-6590; www.hotelkkala.com.ar; cnr Las Higueras & Las Papayas; r US$260-390; ❄@🛜🏊) Tucked away in the upmarket residential barrio of Tres Cerritos, this peaceful place makes relaxation easy. Exquisite rooms, suites and public areas surround a small garden with a heated pool; the higher grades come with views and their own Jacuzzi. Decks with city vistas make perfect spots for a sundowner from the honesty bar. Service is top-notch.

⭐ Legado Mítico
BOUTIQUE HOTEL $$$

(☏ 0387-422-8786; www.legadomitico.com; Mitre 647; r standard/superior/deluxe US$255/275/295; ❄@🛜) The elegant rooms, some faithful to the style of this noble old Salta house, some with a subtle indigenous theme, are reason enough to book in at this tranquil central retreat, particularly if you grab one of the downstairs ones that have their own secluded bamboo-strewn patio. Courteous service

and an atmosphere of refined relaxation are other high points. No under 12s.

⭐ Villa Vicuña
BOUTIQUE HOTEL $$$

(☏ 0387-432-1579; www.villavicuna.com.ar; Caseros 266; r US$154-174; ❄🛜🏊) Beautifully realized in modern antique style in a central location, this hotel boasts luminous, easy-on-the-eye rooms with old-style floor tiles along a finger-shaped patio in a typically elegant Salta house. There's a feeling of light and space throughout; the back garden with pool is a highlight, as are numerous decorative details and the pleasant service.

Finca Valentina
ESTANCIA $$$

(☏ 0387-15-415-3490; www.finca-valentina.com. ar; RN 51, Km6; s/d standard US$125/155, superior US$150/185; 🛜🏊) Only the chirping of birds and cicadas breaks the silence at this fabulously peaceful ranch 6km beyond the airport and a 20-minute drive from the center. The comfortable, homey elegance focuses on cool white spaces and abundant lounging potential on verandas. An excellent breakfast is included and other meals are available.

Balcón de la Plaza
BOUTIQUE HOTEL $$$

(☏ 0387-421-4792; www.balcondelaplaza.com.ar; España 444; r US$180-204; ❄@🛜) Polite and genuinely helpful service, an appealingly genteel ambience, and 10 understated and elegant rooms with handsome bathrooms and king-sized beds are all points in favor of this recently opened boutique. Another is its excellent location, half a block from the plaza. It occupies a lovely building dwarfed by ugly brethren on either side. Rates are usually substantially lower than rack prices.

🍴 Eating

It's a toss-up between Salta and Tucumán for Argentina's best empanadas, but they're wickedly toothsome in both places. Locals debate the merits of fried (in an iron skillet – juicier) or baked (in a clay oven – tastier).

⭐ Chirimoya
VEGETARIAN $

(España 211; mains AR$50-90; ⏱9am-4pm & 8:30pm-12:30am Mon-Sat; 🛜🍴) Colorful and upbeat, this vegan (some honey is used) cafe-restaurant makes an enticing stop. Delicious blended juices and organic wines wash down daily changing specials served in generous portions. It's all delicious. Does deliveries, too.

LOCAL KNOWLEDGE

PASEO DE LA FAMILIA

A simple and enjoyable local eating scene can be found on the **Paseo de la Familia** (Catamarca btwn San Luis & La Rioja; meals AR$30-100; ⊘ most stalls 8am-3pm) occupying a block of Catamarca south of San Luis. Street-food stalls dole out grilled chicken, pizza, tamales and *lomitos* (steak sandwiches) to plastic tables under a long awning. Most open from breakfast time to 3pm or so, but some plan to open in the evenings, too.

Jovi II
ARGENTINE $

(Balcarce 601; mains AR$70-110; ⊘ noon-4pm & 8pm-1am) A long terrace overlooking the palms of Plaza Güemes is just one reason to like this popular local restaurant. It does a huge range of dishes well, without frills and in generous portions. Several rabbit dishes, tasty fish and a succulent plate of the day are backed up by excellent service.

La Tacita
EMPANADAS $

(Caseros 396; empanadas AR$8; ⊘ 8am-11pm Mon-Sat, 10am-11pm Sun) This very basic little eatery offers some of the city's best empanadas in a welcoming no-frills setting. Great for a quick stop while sightseeing.

La Monumental
PARRILLA $

(Entre Ríos 202; mains AR$105-155; ⊘ noon-3pm & 8pm-1am) The fluorescent lighting and phalanx of fans mark this out as a classic neighborhood grill. Generous quantities, including an impressive array of free nibbles, cheap house wine and decent meat seal the deal. Half-portions (70% of the full-portion price) are more than enough for one. Don't confuse it with the more upmarket restaurant with the same name diagonally opposite.

Viejo Jack
PARRILLA $

(Av Bicentenario de la Batalla de Salta 145; mains AR$70-130; ⊘ 12:30-3:30pm & 8pm-1am or later) Far enough out of the tourist zone to be authentic, but not so far it's a pain to get to, this is a down-to-earth spot very popular with locals for its *parrillada* (mixed grill) and pasta. The serves are huge – designed for two to four – but you'll get a single portion (still enough for two!) for 70% of the price.

Ma Cuisine
FUSION $$

(España 83; mains AR$90-150; ⊘ 8pm-midnight Tue-Sat; ☏) The refreshingly crisp interior of this likable little place sees a variety of changing dishes – pasta, fish and meat, all well prepared and served with things such as noodles or stir-fried vegetables – chalked up on the board. The friendly young couple that runs it lived in France, so there's a certain Gallic influence at work.

La Céfira
ARGENTINE $$

(☑ 0387-421-4922; www.lacefira.com; Córdoba 481; mains AR$65-150; ⊘ 7pm-midnight Mon-Sat, noon-3pm Sun; ☏ ☑) This handsome pasta-driven dining room a few blocks south of the center is a cut far above the usual gnocchi-with-four-cheese-sauce joints. Inventive, flavorsome temptations (think ingredients such as squid ink, dressed crab, curried pumpkin and poppyseeds) made with excellent homemade pastas always include lots of vegetarian options. There are some meat and fish dishes, too.

El Charrúa
ARGENTINE, PARRILLA $$

(www.parrillaelcharrua.com.ar; Caseros 221; mains AR$120-200; ⊘ noon-3:30pm & 7pm-12:30am Mon-Fri, to late Sat & Sun; ☏) Bright and homey, this popular restaurant goes way beyond the normal *parrilla* (steak restaurant) focus and includes some regional dishes, specials and decent pasta. Service and quality are generally reliable, and the price is fair for this standard.

Bartz
TAPAS $$

(☑ 0387-461-0160; www.bartzsalta.com; Leguizamón 465; tapas AR$40-95; ⊘ 11:30am-1am Mon-Sat; ☏) Some extremely tasty flavor combinations are available on the eclectic tapas list at this friendly cafe-restaurant north of the center. Influences include Spanish, Greek, Japanese and more. The talented chef puts together attractive but unpretentious combinations that include delicious salmon and tuna options. Dishes are generously proportioned – think three to four of them to comfortably feed two.

El Solar del Convento
ARGENTINE $$

(☑ 0387-421-5124; Caseros 444; mains AR$110-165; ⊘ 8am-midnight; ☏) Warmly decorated and popular, this reliable touristy choice offers solicitous service – the free aperitif wins points – and a varied menu. It specializes in *lomo* (sirloin) with tasty sauces, and also has fish dishes and *parrillada* options. Try the tender *bondiola* (pork shoulder) as a change from steak. The meat here is decent value for central Salta; the wine list could offer more, for less.

🍷 Drinking & Nightlife

Peñas are the classic Salta nighttime experience. The two blocks of Balcarce north of Alsina, and the surrounding streets, are the main zone for these and other nightlife. Bars and clubs around here follow the typical boom-bust-reopen-with-new-name pattern, so just follow your nose.

Cafe Mitre   BAR
(Mitre 368; ☺8:30am-1am Mon-Fri, 6pm-3am Sat; 🛜) Chunky, colorful chairs and tables, a stylish interior, and a great little people-watching terrace out front make this visually easy on the eye. Friendly service, decent coffee and good cocktails make it a spot to linger.

Café del Tiempo   BAR
(www.cafedeltiempo.com.ar; Balcarce 901; ☺6pm-3am Mon-Sat, 8am-2am Sun; 🛜) Decked out to resemble a Buenos Aires cafe, this has prices to match and offers a stylish terrace in the heart of the Balcarce zone; it's a top spot for a drink. Expect some sort of performance or live music every night. The menu includes llama dishes and international offerings such as chop suey; *picadas* (shared appetizer plates) are great for groups.

Macondo   BAR
(www.facebook.com/macondo.barensalta; Balcarce 980; ☺8pm-late Wed-Sun; 🛜) With all the *folklórica* music on this street, the mostly indie mix in this trendy bar might come as a relief. Popular with locals and tourists, it keeps it lively until late and has a good streetside terrace. There's live music most nights.

🛍 Shopping

An artisan's market sets up every Sunday along Balcarce, stretching a couple of blocks south from the station.

Mercado Artesanal   HANDICRAFTS
(Av San Martín 2555; ☺9am-9pm) 🌿 For souvenirs, this provincially sponsored market is noteworthy. Articles include native handicrafts, such as hammocks, string bags, ceramics, basketry, leatherwork and the region's distinctive ponchos. Take bus 5A from downtown.

ℹ Information

Calle España, just west of the plaza, was the money changers' hangout when we last visited.
Hospital San Bernardo (☏0387-431-7472; www.hospitalsanbernardo.gob.ar; Tobías 69)
Municipal Tourist Office (☏0387-437-3340; www.saltalalinda.gov.ar; Caseros 711; ☺8am-9pm Mon-Fri, 9am-9pm Sat & Sun) Gives out maps. Also runs desks in the bus terminal and at the airport, open roughly 9am to 9pm, depending on staffing.

PEÑAS

Salta is famous Argentina-wide for its *folklórica* (folk music), which is far more national in scope than tango. A *peña* is a bar or social club where people eat, drink and gather to play and listen, traditionally in the form of an impromptu jam session.

These days, the Salta *peña* is quite a touristy experience, incorporating a dinner-show with CD sales and tour groups; nevertheless, it's a great deal of fun. Traditional fare such as empanadas and red wine are served but most places offer a wider menu of meat and regional dishes.

Peña heartland is Calle Balcarce, between Alsina and the train station. There are several here, along with other restaurants, bars and *boliches* (nightclubs) – it's Salta's main nightlife zone.

Some are a lot better and more traditional than others.

La Casona del Molino (☏0387-434-2835; www.facebook.com/lacasonadelmolino; Burela 1; ☺9pm-4am Tue-Sun) This former mansion, about 20 blocks west of Plaza 9 de Julio, is a Salta classic. Several spacious rooms feature performers who work around the tables rather than on a stage, as well as spontaneous jams and lots of dancing. The food is of very good quality (mains AR$40 to AR$70). Get there early-ish to guarantee a table. There's a cover on weekend nights.

La Vieja Estación (☏0387-421-7727; www.la-viejaestacion.com.ar; Balcarce 885; cover charge AR$20; ☺7pm-3am) The best established of the Balcarce *peñas*, with a stage, wooden tables and a good atmosphere. Music starts at 10pm. Top empanadas and other regional food is served, including some interesting Andean fusion options (mains from AR$100 to AR$190).

PARQUE NACIONAL EL REY

East of Salta, this **national park** (elrey@apn.gov.ar) **FREE** lies at the southern end of the Yungas subtropical corridor and protects a gloriously biologically diverse habitat.

It's a beautiful, varied landscape ranging from meadowlands and low scrub forest to subtropical cloud forest. There are various well-marked trails, some accessible by vehicle. There's abundant birdlife, and mammals such as peccaries and brown brocket deer are often spotted. **Laguna Los Patitos**, 2km from park headquarters, offers waterbird observation. Longer trails lead to moss-covered **Pozo Verde**, a three- to four-hour climb to an area teeming with birdlife. Other trails are of similar day-trip length and involve multiple river crossings. Shorter 2km **Sendero La Chuña** heads out from the campsite and is a good introduction to this ecosystem.

There is free camping with a huge grassy area for tents; facilities include toilets, drinkable water, cold showers and evening power but there's no shop. Contact **APN in Salta** (APN; ☏ 0387-431-2683; www.parquesnacionales.gov.ar; España 366; ⊙ 8am-2pm Mon-Fri) for up-to-date info. The closest noncamping accommodations is at a curious ecological community 4km down the park road from the turnoff.

From the access road on RP 5 it's 37km on gravel to the park entrance and a further 10km to the trailheads/campsite. Several streams are impassable in a regular (non-4WD) car after rain (likely from December to March). Tours from Salta also come here. Last fuel is at the General Güemes–Salta junction, 160km from the park, so fill up there.

Provincial Tourist Office (☏ 0387-431-0950; www.turismosalta.gov.ar; Buenos Aires 93; ⊙ 8am-9pm Mon-Fri, 9am-8pm Sat & Sun) Top marks – friendly, efficient and multilingual. Ask staff about provincial road conditions.

❶ Getting There & Away

AIR

Salta's **airport** (SLA; ☏ 0387-424-3115) is 9.5km southwest of town on RP 51.

Aerolíneas Argentinas (☏ 0810-222-86527; www.aerolineas.com; Caseros 475; ⊙ 8am-12:45pm & 4-6:45pm Mon-Fri, 9am-12:45pm Sat) Flies several times daily to Buenos Aires; also serves Córdoba, Mendoza and Puerto Iguazú.

Andes (☏ 0810-777-26337; www.andesonline.com; Caseros 459; ⊙ 8am-1pm & 4:30-7pm Mon-Fri, 9:30am-1pm Sat) Thrice weekly flights to Buenos Aires with connection to Puerto Madryn.

BoA (☏ 0387-471-1558; www.boa.bo; Mitre 37, shop 24) In a shopping arcade off the plaza. Flies to Santa Cruz (Bolivia).

LAN (☏ 0810-999-9526; www.lan.com; Caseros 476; ⊙ 9am-1pm & 5-8pm Mon-Fri) Flies to Buenos Aires; also Santiago via Iquique (Chile).

BUS

Salta's **bus terminal** (☏ 0387-431-5022; Av Hipólito Yrigoyen; ⊙ information 6am-10pm) has ATMs, tourist information and left-luggage services.

Three companies run to San Pedro de Atacama, Chile (AR$810, nine to 10 hours), with daily departures at 7am via Jujuy and Purmamarca.

They continue to Calama, Antofagasta, Iquique and Arica (AR$1283).

Ale Hermanos runs two to three times daily to San Antonio de los Cobres (AR$115, 5½ hours) and Cachi (AR$120, 4½ hours).

For Puerto Iguazú, change in Resistencia. For Bariloche, change in Mendoza. Companies sell through-tickets.

Buses from Salta

DESTINATION	COST (AR$)	TIME (HR)
Buenos Aires	1300-1500	18-22
Cafayate	159	4
Córdoba	918	11-14
Jujuy	75	2
La Quiaca	240	7½
La Rioja	616	10
Mendoza	1275-1350	18-20
Resistencia	719	10-12
Salvador Mazza	411	6½
Santiago del Estero	445	7
Tucumán	290	4¼

CAR

There are dozens of agencies: get several quotes. Typically, it's AR$800 to AR$1000 per day, and triple that for a 4WD.

There are often advance booking specials online. Most offer discounts for paying cash.

Companies, including international names, are mostly slipshod operations. Mechanical problems are common, and don't expect state-of-the-art roadside assistance: you're often better sorting minor problems yourself. Complaints are frequent.

A list of providers is available at http://turismo.salta.gov.ar. We've found **Alto Valle** (📞 0387-15-683-6231; www.altovallerentacar.com.ar; Zuviria 524) pleasingly well priced and professional.

Always check with the **provincial tourist office** (p232) for current conditions. Punctures are common, so check the kit before leaving Salta.

You can't take rental cars into Bolivia, but it's possible to head into Chile by paying a bit extra and giving a few days' notice.

ℹ Getting Around

Grab a rechargeable *tarjeta magnética* bus card (AR$10) from certain kiosks. Fares cost AR$3.75.

Bus 8A from San Martín by Córdoba runs to the airport, otherwise it's AR$100 in a taxi from downtown.

Several local buses connect downtown with the bus terminal; it's not a long walk if you prefer.

Valles Calchaquíes

One of Argentina's most seductive rural zones is a winning combination of rugged landscapes, traditional weavers' workshops, strikingly attractive adobe villages and some top wines. Small but sophisticated Cafayate, with its wineries and paved highway, presents quite a contrast to more remote settlements such as Angastaco or Molinos, while Cachi, accessible from Salta via a spectacular road that crosses the Parque Nacional Los Cardones, is a peaceful, popular base. Vernacular architecture merits special attention: even modest adobe houses sport neoclassical columns or neo-Moorish arches.

The indigenous Diaguita (Calchaquí) here put up some of the stiffest resistance to Spanish rule.

Chicoana

📞 0387 / POP 5800

Tucked away near the junction of the Cafayate and Cachi roads, just 41km south of Salta, the likeable town of Chicoana is surrounded by lush vegetation and makes a fine stop for lunch, for the night (a tempting final stop if you're flying out of Salta the next morning) or for a spot of horseback riding.

◉ Sights & Activities

Several operators offer horseback riding. The tourist office will provide you with a list. Head west of town up the road (Adolfo) toward Finca Los Los for excellent perspectives over the subtropical greenery of the zone.

🛏 Sleeping & Eating

There are several places to stay, including a hostel behind (and run out of) the *parrilla* restaurant on the square, and a eucalypt-shaded campground just beyond.

Bo Hotel   BOUTIQUE HOTEL **$$**
(📞 0387-490-7068; www.bo-chicoana.com.ar; 25 de Mayo 25; s/d US$103/127; ❋ @ 🛜 ⛲) On the left as you enter town, this smart place in substantial grassy grounds offers eight spacious rooms decorated in an upbeat style with modern fabrics and colors. Enjoy a range of facilities, including free bikes, a spa and helpful service.

Finca Las Margaritas   ESTANCIA **$$$**
(📞 0387-15-592-9194; www.fincalasmargaritas.com.ar; RP 49, Paraje Bella Vista; d/f US$161/181; 🛜 ⛲) Eight kilometers from Chicoana, signposted off the RN 33, this divine *estancia* has the lot: elegant rooms themed on the different crops produced by the farm, wide verandas, a classic rural Argentine ambience and good food. Can arrange excursions in the area.

Bocha   ARGENTINE **$**
(Güemes s/n; mains AR$50; ⏱ 10:30am-3pm) This very simple family-run *comedor* (basic cafeteria) is the town's favorite eating place. Big round tables are parked across a concrete floor. Choose from three or four daily specials, all delicious. Soup is offered after the mains.

ℹ Information

Tourist Office (www.chicoanasalta.org; cnr Córdoba & El Carmen; ⏱ 8am-8pm) On a corner of the square; very helpful.

ℹ Getting There & Away

Chicoana is connected to Salta via local buses (interurban route 5, AR$9, 60 minutes), which run east along Belgrano and west along San Martín. You'll need a Salta bus card.

Parque Nacional Los Cardones

Flanking the winding RP 33 from Salta to Cachi across the Cuesta del Obispo, **Parque Nacional Los Cardones** (www.parquesnacionales.gob.ar; RP 33) takes its name from the cardón (candelabra cactus), the park's most striking plant species. The most picturesque part is the Valle Encantado, accessed via a 4km track (driveable) at Km61. A few further *miradores* (viewpoints) are signposted along the road, and a couple of short interpretative trails from along the straight stretch Recta de Tin-Tin. There's a modern **park office** (☑ 03868-15-452879; loscardones@apn.gov.ar; Payogasta; ◷ 8am-3pm Mon-Fri) in Payogasta, 11km north of Cachi.

Take plenty of water and protect yourself from the sun. Buses between Salta and Cachi will stop for you, but verify times in advance.

In the treeless Andean foothills and puna, the cardón has long been an important source of timber for rafters, doors, windows and more. You see it often in the region's traditional buildings.

Cachi

☑ 03868 / POP 2600 / ELEV 2280M

The biggest place by some distance hereabouts – you'll hear locals refer to it as 'the city' – enchanting Cachi is nevertheless little more than a village surrounded by stunning scenery. Overlooked by noble mountains, it boasts fresh highland air, sunny days and crisp nights. The cobblestones, adobe houses, tranquil plaza and the opportunities on hand to explore the surrounds mean that it's the sort of place that can easily eat extra days out of your carefully planned itinerary.

⊙ Sights

Museo Arqueológico　　　　　MUSEUM
(admission by donation; ◷ 9am-6pm Tue-Sun) This well-presented and professionally arranged museum on the plaza gives an account of the surrounding area's cultural evolution, with good background information (in Spanish) on archaeological methods. Don't miss the wall in the secondary patio, composed of stones with petroglyphs.

Iglesia San José　　　　　　　CHURCH
(Plaza 9 de Julio s/n; ◷ 9am-9pm) This church (1796) has graceful arches and a barrel-vaulted ceiling of cardón wood. The confessional and other features are also cardón, while holy water lives in a large *tinaja* (oil jar).

🏃 Activities

A short walk from Cachi's plaza brings you to a **viewpoint** and then the picturesque hilltop **cemetery**; nearby is an unlikely airstrip.

There's a handful of rather unremarkable **archaeological sites** dotted around the valley; these make destinations for picturesque hikes or drives. There's a winery in town, and others within easy driving distance.

Many locals rent horses for **horseback riding**; look for signs or ask in the tourist office.

Valley Walking　　　　　　　　WALKING
Six kilometers from Cachi, Cachi Adentro is a tiny village where not a lot happens: ride the see-saws in the demi-plaza or sip a soda from the store. It's a particularly lovely walk from Cachi in summer, when streams and cascades are alive with water.

From here, you could return a longer way (20km total): bear left past the church and then take a left down the road signposted Las Trancas. This winds around the valley and eventually crosses the river; 400m afterwards, turn left (heading right leads 2km up to the lovely Algarrobal campground). This will lead you back to Cachi via the hamlet of La Aguada. This section is spectacular in the late afternoon.

🎯 Tours

★**Urkupiña**　　　　　　　　　　OUTDOORS
(☑ 03868-491317; www.urkupinatur.wix.com/cachi; Zorrilla s/n) Excellent agency offering a wide range of activities. Trips to nearby archaeological sites cost US$25 to US$35; longer jaunts along RN 40 in both directions make entertaining ways to reach Cafayate (US$60) or San Antonio (US$76). Great hiking tours include a descent through the Valle Encantado and Cuesta del Obispo (US$89) or the red sandstone cave formations of Acsibi (US$85).

Cycling, caving and quad-bike tours are also available, as well as climbing.

Chiwanku　　　　　　　　　　OUTDOORS
(☑ 0387-15-561-6854; www.chiwanku.com.ar; Suárez s/n) Offers a range of activities, including enjoyable downhill biking through the Parque Nacional Los Cardones (US$40); hikes around the Acsibi red sandstone caves (US$88) and Inca archaeological sites (US$43); wine routes; and excursions to the remote west of the province.

🛏 Sleeping

Nevado de Cachi　　　　　　GUESTHOUSE $
(☑ 03868-491912; Ruiz de los Llanos s/n; s/d US$20/35; ☎) Just off the plaza, this decent budget choice has rooms around a grapevine-

draped patio. Beds are comfortable, and bathrooms – there's one cheaper room with exterior bathroom – work well enough. Prices are slightly negotiable and vary by room; upstairs ones are hotter but quieter. Overall, a bargain. Breakfast not included.

Viracocha HOSTEL $

(☑ 03868-15-491713; www.hostelcachi.com.ar; Ruiz de los Llanos s/n; dm US$19, d with/without bathroom US$60/40; 🛜) Central and relaxed, this likable hostel has good dorms featuring sturdy bunk beds with plenty of headroom. Private rooms are colorful and comfortable; mattresses throughout are decent. There's no kitchen, but there's courtyard space and tea- and coffee-making facilities. A romantically lit restaurant serving OK regional specialties and Andean cuisine is attached.

Hospedaje Don Arturo GUESTHOUSE $

(☑ 03868-491087; www.hospedajedonarturo.blogspot.com; Bustamante s/n; s/d US$20/30, without bathroom US$25/40; 🛜) Very solid budget choice: rooms are cramped but spotless. The best features are the lounge area and back deck overlooking the riverbed.

La Mamama HOSTEL $

(☑ 03868-491305; Suárez 590; dm/r without bathroom US$9/18) A welcoming spot at the quiet end of a central street, with kitchen use (a tiny fee once only), simple rooms with saggy mattresses and a Cachi-casual feel.

Camping Municipal CAMPGROUND, HOSTEL $

(☑ 03868-491902; oficinadeturismo.cachi@gmail.com; campsites per 2 people plus tent US$5, with power US$8, cabins US$32; ☀) On a hill southwest of the plaza, this offers grassy, tree-shaded pitches, plus hedge-bordered sites with barbecues. The municipal pool is here, plus a hostel – normally for groups but may open for you – with dorms (US$2.50, including sheets US$4) and a couple of cabins.

★ Miraluna CABAÑAS $$

(☑ 0387-432-0888; www.miraluna.com.ar; La Aguada; 2-person apt US$135, 4-person US$185-195; 🛜☀♨) 🍃 Seven kilometers from town in the hamlet of La Aguada, these beautifully romantic, rustic cabins come in three sizes and have a spectacular, fabulously peaceful setting in a working vineyard surrounded by breathtaking mountain and valley views. Breakfast features tasty home-baked bread, and other light meals are available. You can also help yourself to vegetables from the organic garden. Winery visit included.

★ El Cortijo BOUTIQUE HOTEL $$

(☑ 03868-491034; www.elcortijohotel.com; Av ACA s/n; s US$100, d standard/superior US$125/145; ❄🛜☀) This stylish small hotel – boutique in the true sense of the word – offers recently renovated rooms that include spacious superiors decorated with finesse, and some lovely master suites, particularly one with its own private terrace with loungers. Some have fabulous views of the sierra. There's also a decent on-site restaurant and helpful staff. A pool is pending. Good value.

Hostería Villa Cardón GUESTHOUSE $$

(☑ 03868-491701; www.facebook.com/hosteria villacardon; Aranda s/n; d standard/superior US$87/98; 🛜) Friendly young owners bend over backward here to make your stay a pleasant one, and the four white, minimalist, comfortable rooms opening off a courtyard on a quiet backstreet are perfect for relaxation. Breakfast is a highlight, and the overall package is faultless. The teahouse out front is great, too. Single rates available off-season.

Sala de Payogasta BOUTIQUE HOTEL $$

(☑ 03868-496754; www.saladepayogasta.com; RN 40, Km4509, Payogasta; s/d/ste US$59/79/109, ste with views US$129; 🛜) This historic ranch has rooms set around an achingly beautiful courtyard. They are rustic and in harmony with the environment, though not luxurious. Suites have hydromassage tubs and a cute fireplace; the best has a fine outlook over fields and mountains. The breakfast and dining room shares the same vista. There's a small spa complex, and a working winery opposite, where lunches are served.

It's 10km from Cachi on the Salta road, just outside of Payogasta.

La Merced del Alto HOTEL $$$

(☑ 0387-490020; www.lamerceddelalto.com; s/d US$190/220; @🛜☀) Built of traditional whitewashed adobe, with ceramic floors and cane ceilings, this hotel across the river (2.5km) is designed to resemble an historic monastery. It offers excellent facilities and great peace, with cool, restrained rooms looking over either the hills beyond (slightly dearer) or the interior patio. Public areas include an inviting lounge, good restaurant and rustic spa (extra charge).

Service is excellent. Substantially cheaper for Argentines.

✖️ Eating

Local eateries in the streets near the plaza do no-frills traditional plates.

Ashpamanta
VEGETARIAN $

(Bustamante s/n; dishes AR$60-105; ☺ noon-3pm & 7-10pm; ⚡) Offering reliably tasty vegetarian cuisine, this has a snug candlelit interior and simple seating around a pretty patio. The menu covers pasta, salads and a couple of more elaborate mains – quinoa risotto, veggie lasagna – prepared in an open kitchen behind the bar.

Oliver
PIZZA $

(Ruíz de los Llanos 160; mains AR$50-105; ☺ 7am-midnight; 🛜⚡) This homey, multilevel, wooden-tabled restaurant on the plaza is a reliable choice for tasty pizza, bruschetta and a couple of creative meaty mains. The setting is a fine place for a sundowner.

El Molle de Maiz Pérez
NORTHWEST ARGENTINE $

(Suárez s/n; mains US$50-85; ☺ noon-3pm & 7-11pm; ⚡) This little one-man show has an attractive interior, with cardón tables on upturned logs, including a couple outdoors on the pretty street. There are a few quirks – just go with the flow – but the food – roast chicken, *locro* (a spicy stew of maize, beans, beef, pork and sausage), pizzas and great *milanesas* (breaded cutlets) – is delicious. Owner-chef Carlos is kindly and keen to chat. Evening opening is unreliable.

ℹ️ Information

Tourist Office (☎ 03868-491902; oficinade turismo.cachi@gmail.com; Güemes s/n; ☺ 9am-9pm) On the plaza.

ℹ️ Getting There & Away

Two to three daily buses run between Salta (AR$120, four hours) and Cachi: a spectacular ride.

From Cachi, Seclantás is serviced daily at 7am (AR$28), with the service continuing four times weekly to Molinos (AR$40) and Angastaco (AR$95).

Buses run north as far as La Poma, the end of the line. The road beyond, to San Antonio de los Cobres, is an arduous, spectacular ascent crisscrossing a river via lonely goat farms to a 4895m pass. It's only passable in a non-4WD at certain times (normally September to December); phone the **police** (☎ 0387-490-9051) for advice. Otherwise, approach San Antonio the long way round.

For Cafayate, bus to Angastaco, and connect there. At the time of research, this was possible Mondays, Fridays and Sundays. A tour from Cachi is also an option.

Seclantás

📞 03868 / POP 300 / ELEV 2100M

Charmingly peaceful Seclantás is the spiritual home of the Salta poncho. There are many weavers' workshops in town and along the eastern branch of the road to Cachi (dubbed the 'Ruta de los Artesanos'). Drop by these homes and browse the wares.

Places to stay cluster around the lovely tree-shaded plaza. **El Capricho** (☎ 03868-498064; www.elcaprichosalta.com.ar; Cornejo s/n; d US$42, tw without bathroom US$26) has rustic rooms set around a pretty garden courtyard. The nearby campground has cabins and a public pool.

There's a daily 7am bus from Cachi to Seclantás; it continues to Molinos and Angastaco four days a week.

Molinos

📞 03868 / POP 900 / ELEV 2020M

If you think the nearby town of Cachi is laid-back, wait until you see Molinos, a lovely backwater with a collection of striking colonial buildings and beautiful adobe houses; a stroll through the streets will reveal some real gems. Molinos takes its name from the still-operational flour mill on the Río Calchaquí; its picturesque appeal is augmented by shady streets and good accommodations. There's a plaza-side ATM.

◉ Sights

Centro de Interpretación Molinos
MUSEUM, WORKSHOP

(☎ 0387-15-459-2666; casaindaleciogomez@yahoo. com.ar; Cornejo s/n; donation AR$15; ☺ 8am-1:30pm & 2-7:30pm) 🖋 This restored historic house has a good English and Spanish display on the region's culture and history, and tourist information. It's also a space for artisans – especially weavers – to work and sell their crafts, one of a number of inspiring sustainable projects around the area.

Iglesia San Pedro Nolasco
CHURCH

(☺ 8am-8pm) The town's lovely church in the Cuzco style dates from the 17th and 18th centuries, and features twin bell towers and a cactus-wood ceiling. The Stations of the Cross are tapestries by local artisans.

WORTH A TRIP

COLOMÉ BODEGA

Fine wines are produced at this ecological **bodega** (03868-494200; www.bodegacolome.com; standard/old-vines tastings AR$50/300; 10am-6pm), which is set (as they say hereabouts) 'where the devil lost his poncho,' 18km down a spectacular gravel road west from Molinos. The vineyards enjoy a stunning natural setting, surrounded by hills and mountains that seem to change color hourly. Forward-thinking on several fronts is also in evidence: the complex is electrically self-sufficient, has funded substantial infrastructural improvements in the local community and boasts a stunning **museum** (museo@colomeargentina.com; Colomé; visits 3pm & 5pm Tue-Sun) FREE designed by artist James Turrell, with a permanent exhibition of nine of his works. These are utterly memorable installations involving light and the strange frontiers of our own perception; it's a remarkable place.

Both bodega and museum visits should be booked ahead by phone or email, though it can be fine to simply turn up. As well as tastings, the bodega serves delicious salads and sandwiches (AR$90 to AR$100) and a meat option.

Some 9km beyond Colomé, Bodega El Humanao is also worth a visit for its beautifully balanced cabernet-malbec blend, among others wines.

Criadero Coquera & Casa Entre Ríos FARM
(8am-12:30pm & 3:30-7pm Mon-Sat) FREE
A kilometer west of Molinos, this is where the government's agricultural research arm raises vicuñas. You can take a tour and feed these beautiful camelid creatures; if there's nobody there, they don't really mind you just heading on up the side to see the animals. Here also is the Casa de Entre Ríos, where there's a fine artisans' market selling spectacular ponchos and wall hangings woven from sheep, llama and vicuña wool.

Sleeping & Eating

A couple of down-home places do decent, cheap meals.

Los Cardones de Molinos GUESTHOUSE $
(0387-15-408-1724; cardonesmolinos@hotmail.com; cnr Sarmiento & San Martín; s/d US$30/60, without bathroom US$20/40;) This is an excellent sleeping choice, with comfortable rooms featuring cactus furniture. You're treated as one of the family and can use the kitchen; breakfast is included, there's a washing machine, and the exceptionally welcoming and accommodating owner is a great source of local advice.

★**Hacienda de Molinos** HOTEL $$
(03868-494094; www.haciendademolinos.com.ar; Cornejo s/n; r standard/superior US$125/151;) Across from the church, this gloriously colonial adobe hacienda is also known as Casa de Isasmendi, after Salta's last colonial governor, who lived and died here. It's been picturesquely restored: sober, handsome rooms with inviting beds, antique furniture, cane ceilings and great bathrooms, set around lovely patio spaces. It's on the edge of the village and utterly peaceful.

There's an overpriced but reasonable on-site restaurant (open from noon to 3pm and 7:30pm to 10:30pm).

Getting There & Away

There's a bus to Molinos from Salta (AR$145, six hours) via Cachi (AR$40, two hours) on Monday, Wednesday, Friday and Sunday. It continues to Angastaco (AR$40, two hours). Return services run on Monday, Tuesday, Thursday and Saturday. Shared *remises* (taxis) run thrice daily to Salta (AR$200) via Cachi.

Local *remise* operators such as recommended **Sergio Rueda** (0387-15-447-8446) run to Angastaco (around AR$500) on demand and can also take you to Colomé (AR$300 including waiting time) and other wineries.

Angastaco

03868 / POP 900 / ELEV 1955M

Tiny Angastaco sits among some of the most dramatically tortuous rockscapes of the valley route. Forty kilometers south of Molinos and 54km north of San Carlos, it's an oasis with vineyards, fields of anise and cumin, and the ruins of an ancient *pucará* (walled city).

Angastaco has an ATM and gas station (with internet access).

◎ Sights

Museo Arqueológico   MUSEUM
(◎ 7am-1pm Mon-Fri Oct-Apr, 7:30am-1:30pm May-Sep) FREE This little archaeological museum is in the smart municipal building behind the church. If it's shut, ask in the offices and someone may open it up for you.

🛏 Sleeping & Eating

Hospedaje El Cardón   GUESTHOUSE $
(✆ 03868-15-459-0021; Martínez s/n; r per person with/without bathroom US$12/10) A decent budget choice run by a staunch older lady. Rooms are basic but a bargain. It's 50m to your right if you're standing facing the village church.

★ Finca El Carmen   ESTANCIA $$
(✆ 0387-15-412-5900; www.vallesdelcarmen.com.ar; RN 40, Km4420; s/d US$66/104; ☎) Seven kilometers north of the Angastaco turnoff, this is an intriguing place to stay. It's set on a fabulously atmospheric historic ranch whose adobe buildings include an 18th-century Jesuit church, and is run by a friendly family offering excellent hospitality. The six rooms are all different, and there are *cabañas* (cabins) sleeping five. Just passing by? Drop in: visit the church, eat or browse the handicrafts.

Rincón Florido   NORTHWEST ARGENTINE $
(dishes AR$35-45; ◎ 11:30am-3pm) A curious and heartwarming lunch stop just beyond the municipal building. Three courtyard tables in a family home are vine-shaded and watched over by a talking parrot and myriad curious objects, from farm implements to armadillo shells. There's no menu. Food is simple and good, with delicious empanadas, vegetables from the garden and their own sweetish red wine.

❶ Getting There & Away

Buses head south to San Carlos and Cafayate at 5:35am Monday to Saturday and 5pm Monday, Friday and Sunday (AR$60, two hours).

Buses arrive here from Salta (AR$187, eight hours) via Cachi, Seclantás and Molinos four days a week (Monday, Wednesday, Friday and Sunday; return journeys the next morning). On Monday, Friday and Sunday, you can connect to the Cafayate service.

Otherwise, for Molinos, 40km north, transports (ask around) run the route for AR$450 to AR$500 total. They'll often meet the Cafayate bus, where you can share the fare with other passengers. Otherwise, it's a hitchhike; best done from the main road (there's shade and a cafe).

San Carlos
✆ 03868 / POP 1900 / ELEV 1624M

A sizable village, San Carlos lies 22km north of Cafayate and is connected to the town by a paved road – a pleasant shock if you're arriving from the north. There's a special place to stay here in La Casa de los Vientos (✆ 03868-495075; www.casadelosvientos.com.ar; Barrio Los Vientos; d/q US$50/70; ◎ 🛜 ☎ 🐾) 🐾, signposted off the main road at the Cachi end of town. Built in the traditional manner of adobe, with terracotta tiles and cane ceilings, it incorporates some ingenious environmental innovations. The well-traveled owner is a potter, and the rooms (all different) are decorated with rustic flair and beauty. There's a heated indoor pool and a very genuine welcome.

One to four daily buses run from Cafayate (AR$17, 45 minutes).

Cafayate
✆ 03868 / POP 13,300 / ELEV 1683M

Argentina's second center for quality wine production, Cafayate is a popular tourist destination but still has a tranquil small-town feel. It's spectacularly scenic, with the green of the vines backed by soaring mountains beyond, and is one of northwest Argentina's most seductive destinations. It's easily reached from Salta via the tortured rockscapes of the Quebrada de Cafayate; it's also a major stop on RN 40 and the Valles Calchaquíes route. With a selection of excellent accommodations for every budget, and several wineries to visit in and around town, it invites an extended stay. Also, check out the excellent *artesanías* (handicrafts).

Cafayate is famous for its torrontés, a grape producing aromatic dry and sweet white wines, but bodegas hereabouts also produce fine reds from cabernet sauvignon, malbec and tannat.

◎ Sights & Activities

Museo de la Vid y El Vino   MUSEUM
(www.museodelavidyelvino.gov.ar; Av General Güemes; foreigners/Argentines AR$30/10; ◎ 9am-7pm Tue-Sun) This impressive museum gives a good introduction to the area's wine industry. The atmospheric first section, which deals with the viticultural side – the life of the vines – through a series of poems and images, is particularly appeal-

Cafayate

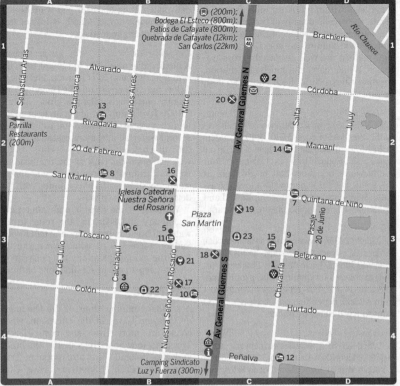

Cafayate

◎ Sights
1 Bodega Nanni	C3
2 El Porvenir	C1
3 Museo Arqueológico	B3
4 Museo de la Vid y El Vino	C4

✈ Activities, Courses & Tours
5 Majo Viajes	B3

🛏 Sleeping
6 Casa Árbol	B3
7 El Hospedaje	C3
8 Hostal del Valle	B2
9 Hotel Munay	C3
10 Killa	B4
11 Lo de Peñalba	B3
12 Portal del Santo	C4

13 Rusty-K Hostal	B2
14 Vieja Posada	C2
15 Villa Vicuña	C3

✖ Eating
16 Casa de las Empanadas	B2
17 Casa de las Empanadas II	B3
18 El Rancho	C3
19 El Terruño	C3
20 Heladería Miranda	C2

🍷 Drinking & Nightlife
21 Chato's Wine Bar	B3

🛍 Shopping
22 Jorge Barraco	B4
23 Mercado Artesanal	C3

ing. The second part covers the winemaking side, and there's a cafe where you can try and buy. English translations are good throughout.

Museo Arqueológico MUSEUM
(cnr Colón & Calchaquí; admission by donation; ☺10:30am-9pm Mon-Fri, to 6pm Sat) This private museum's collection was left by

enthusiastic archaeologist Rodolfo Bravo and merits a visit. Sourced mostly from grave sites within a 30km radius from Cafayate, the excellent array of ceramics, from the black and gray wares of the Candelaria and Aguada cultures to late Diaguita and Inca pottery, are well displayed across two rooms. While there's not much explanation, the material speaks for itself. Closes an hour for lunch in summer.

Bodega Nanni
WINERY

(☑ 03868-421527; www.bodegananni.com; Chavarría 151; tours free, tastings AR$30; ☺ 10:30am-1pm & 2:30-6:30pm Mon-Sat, 11am-1pm & 2:30-6pm Sun) The half-hourly tour and tastings of four young wines are short and bright here at this small, central winery with a lovely grass patio. Wines are organic, uncomplicated and drinkable. There's a good on-site restaurant.

El Porvenir
WINERY

(☑ 03868-422007; www.elporvenirdecafayate.com; Córdoba 32; tours free, tastings from AR$60; ☺ 9am-12:30pm & 3-6pm Wed-Sat) This well-run bodega focuses on quality wine production. The tour is free, but generous tastings cost from AR$60, depending on which wines you want to try. Reserve by phone.

Bodega El Esteco
WINERY

(☑ 03868-421283; www.elesteco.com.ar; tours AR$70; ☺ tours 10am, 11am, noon, 3:30pm, 4:30pm & 5:30pm Mon-Fri, 10am, 11am & noon Sat & Sun) This corporate affair on the northern edge of town is a smart and attractive winery producing some of the region's best wines.

Piattelli
WINERY

(☑ 03868-15-418214; www.piattelli.com.ar; RP 2; standard tours AR$80, with premium wines AR$150; ☺ 9:30am-6pm, tours 10am, 11am, noon, 1pm, 3pm & 4pm) Built as if money and space were no object, this elegant US-owned, slightly over-the-top winery is 3km from town. Tours show you three levels of relatively small-scale but state-of-the-art winemaking equipment and culminate in a long tasting of seven wines. There's an on-site restaurant that does delicious lunches. Despite scheduled English-speaking tours, most tours are bilingual if needed.

Bodega de las Nubes
WINERY

(☑ 03868-422129; www.bodegamounier.com.ar; tours incl tasting AR$15; ☺ 9:30am-5pm Mon-Fri, to 1:30pm Sat) Five kilometers west of Cafayate along the road to Río Colorado (it's signposted 'Mounier'), this small, organic and

friendly winery has a fabulous position at the foot of the jagged hills. It also does tasty deli plates. Ring ahead if you want to eat. Grape-picking day in March is lots of fun, with volunteers welcomed.

Río Colorado
WALKING, SWIMMING

A picturesque walk 6km southwest from the center leads you to Río Colorado. From here, follow the river upstream (the Diaguita community encourages taking a guide, around AR$200 per group) for about an hour to get to a 10m **waterfall**, where you can swim. A second waterfall and more cascades lie further up. Look out for **rock paintings** on the way. There's a car park at the trailhead, as well as a campsite and a drinks and snacks stand. A visit here can be combined with Bodega de las Nubes (p240).

Warning: if the river is high after rains in January and February, the route to the waterfall becomes strenuous and dangerous. Sudden torrents can come down quickly from the mountains at any time of year, so always keep an eye upstream while bathing.

☞ Tours

A standard minibus tour of the Quebrada de Cafayate leaves in the afternoon, when colors are more vivid, and costs US$20. Three- to four-hour treks in the Quebrada and Río Colorado are also popular. Daylong trips to Cachi (US$90) are tiring, while Quilmes (US$25) is cheaper in a taxi if you're two or more. Horseback rides start at two hours (US$70). Places around the plaza hire out bikes (US$20 for a full day) but thorns mean that the likelihood of punctures is skyhigh, so it's not such a great option.

Tour operators have offices on the plaza. Most are mediocre but the Quebrada scenery speaks for itself. **Majo Viajes** (☑ 03868-422038; majoviajes@gmail.com; Nuestra Señora del Rosario 77) is straight-talking and reliable.

✯ Festivals & Events

The **Serenata a Cafayate** (www.serenata.todowebsalta.com.ar; admission Thu/weekend AR$150/300; ☺ Feb) is a very worthwhile three-day *folklórico* festival. **Fiesta de la Virgen del Rosario** (October 4) is the town fiesta and gets lively.

🛏 Sleeping

Cafayate has numerous places to stay, with boutique hotels and simple *hospedajes* (family homes) on every street.

★ Rusty-K Hostal
HOSTEL $

(☏ 03868-422031; rustykhostal@hotmail.com; Rivadavia 281; dm US$18; d with/without bathroom US$50/45; @ ☎) The peace of the vine-filled patio garden here is a real highlight, as is the spotlessness of the rooms and dorms, and the friendliness. Cute doubles and an excellent attitude make this Cafayate's budget gem. These prices are for high summer and drop substantially out of season. Book ahead.

Casa Árbol
GUESTHOUSE, HOSTEL $

(☏ 03868-422238; www.facebook.com/casaarbol cafayate; Calchaquí 84; dm/d US$12/35; ☎) ✈ There's something really pleasant about this casual spot which has airy, beautiful decor and a genuine welcome. Pretty, spotless rooms and a four-bed dorm share two bathrooms. There's lounging room to spare in the patio, breakfast area and garden.

El Hospedaje
GUESTHOUSE $

(☏ 03868-421680; elhospedaje@gmail.com; Salta 13; d US$70; ✳ ☎ ☲) On a corner just a block from the plaza, this easygoing guesthouse dotted with antique cash registers is nonetheless peaceful. Rooms vary in layout but are mostly on the compact side. They surround a pretty patio fragrant with the smell of lavender.

Lo de Peñalba
HOSTEL, GUESTHOUSE $

(☏ 03868-422213; www.lodepenalba.com.ar; Nuestra Señora del Rosario 79; dm/s/d/tr US$18/45/60/75; ☎) Right on the plaza, this is a welcoming spot behind a tour agency. It offers simple but comfortable en suite rooms around a pretty patio, and dorm beds with key lockers and plenty of room to move. There's a kitchen too, and a good vibe.

Hostal del Valle
GUESTHOUSE $

(☏ 03868-421039; www.welcomeargentina.com/ hostaldelvalle; San Martín 243; s/d US$54/60; ✳ ☎) This enticing place offers myriad pot plants, and pretty rooms with large, inviting beds and excellent bathrooms. Smaller, darker rooms downstairs are a little cheaper and still worthwhile. The staff is friendly and a simple breakfast is served in a rooftop conservatory with privileged views.

Camping Sindicato Luz y Fuerza
CAMPGROUND $

(☏ 03868-421568; www.facebook.com/campinglyf cafayate; Av General Güemes S s/n; campsites per person/tent/car US$2/2.50/1.50; ☎ ☲) Very handy for town, this campsite gets busy and its sandy pitches don't offer much shade. Facilities are good, though, and a lively social atmosphere is guaranteed. It packs out in February, when prices double.

★ Portal del Santo
HOTEL $$

(☏ 03868-422400; www.portaldelsanto.com.ar; Chavarría 250; d downstairs/upstairs US$135/154; ✳ @ ☎ ☲) Cool white elegance is the stock-in-trade of this hospitable family-run hotel resembling a colonial palace with arched arcades. Lower rooms open onto both the front porch and the inviting garden-pool-Jacuzzi area; top-floor chambers have mountain views and even more space. All have fridge and microwave; suites sleep four. The owners are helpful and put on a great homemade breakfast.

Vieja Posada
HOTEL $$

(☏ 03868-422251; www.viejaposada.com.ar; Mamaní 87; s/d US$50/75; ☎ ☲) This hotel has real character in its patio and garden spaces. A reformed historic building, it offers compact rooms and an historic ambience of adobe, antiques and solid wooden benches, perfect for contemplation. There's secure parking and a tiny plunge pool. Breakfast features homemade chayote jam.

Hotel Munay
HOTEL $$

(☏ 03868-422189; www.munayhotel.com.ar; Chavarría 64; s/d US$55/85; ✳ ☎ ☲) The elegant simplicity and clean uncluttered lines of this hotel seem to reflect the surrounding sierra. Rooms are unadorned, attractive and spotless, with good bathrooms. Excellent value, helpful service and a hospitable atmosphere make this a sound choice.

★ Killa
BOUTIQUE HOTEL $$$

(☏ 0387-422254; www.killacafayate.com.ar; Colón 47; d/junior ste/ste US$150/190/240; ✳ ☎ ☲) Classy, comfortable and well run, this handsome and recommendable hotel has colonial style given warmth by its creative use of natural wood, stone and local *artesanía*. The gorgeous rooms – not a TV in sight – have color and great bathrooms, and the upstairs suites – worth the extra investment – have cracking views and private balcony spaces. There's a pretty pool area and impeccable hospitality.

★ Villa Vicuña
BOUTIQUE HOTEL $$$

(☏ 03868-422145; www.villavicuna.com.ar; Belgrano 76; d standard/superior US$154/174; ✳ @ ☎) Peacefully set around twin patios, Villa Vicuña offers an intimate retreat, with

MATTHEW WILLIAMS-ELLIS/GETTY IMAGES ©

Bodega El Esteco (p240)
me of Cafayate's best wines
e produced in this picturesque
tting.

**Museo de Arqueología de
lta Montaña (p219)**
ese artefacts were found
ongside mummified Inca children
the peak of Llullaillaco.

Tren a las Nubes (p223)
e 'Train to the Clouds',
gentina's most famous rail trip,
osses the stunning La Polvorilla
aduct.

**Parque Nacional
alampaya (p283)**
ock formations abound in this
sert national park.

JUAN MABROMATA/AFP/GETTY IMAGES ©

beautiful, spotless rooms with French doors, big beds and reproduction antique furniture. Rooms are in two styles: one more colonial in feel, with dark wood and religious icons. There are numerous helpful little details; service and breakfast are good; and you can relax in the courtyard, contemplating the offbeat mural sculpture.

Patios de Cafayate
ESTANCIA $$$

(☑ 03868-422229; www.patiosdecafayate.com; RN 40; r US$273-371, ste US$418-484; ✦ @ 🛜 ✖) A short walk north of town, this secluded place is a seductive getaway. Set in a beautiful centenarian *estancia*, it's a classy, elegant spot with helpful professional service. Rooms are classically colonial, with noble dark-wood furniture, local *artesanía*, and perspectives over either the surrounding vineyards or the garden area, which includes a great swimming pool and Jacuzzi. Enter via El Esteco winery.

Grace Cafayate
RESORT $$$

(La Estancia de Cafayate; ☑ 03868-427000; www.gracehotels.com; RN 40, Km4340; d/villa US$280/500; ✦ @ 🛜 ✖ 🐾) This huge gated development covers 7km of golf course, vines, scrubland and residential lots. Rooms are spacious and well equipped, and the surrounding villas are great for family stays, with kitchens, barbecue areas and private patios. Bathrooms are particularly impressive, with huge shower space and double bathtubs. Golf carts and manicured lawns, though, give it all a retirement-village feel: suburban banality surrounded by scenic splendor.

The turnoff is 1.5km south of central Cafayate, from where it's another 3.5km to reception.

🍴 Eating

There are many options around the plaza, most offering adequate local dishes backed by live *folklórica* music at weekends.

★ Casa de las Empanadas
EMPANADAS $

(Mitre 24; dozen empanadas AR$90; ⊙ 11am-3pm & 8pm-midnight Tue-Sun) Decorated with the scrawls of contented customers, this no-frills place has a wide selection of empanadas that are all absolutely delicious. Local wine in ceramic jugs, and *humitas* (stuffed corn dough, resembling Mexican tamales) and tamales can round out the meal. If it's closed, head to its other **branch** (Nuestra Señora del Rosario 156; ⊙ 11am-3pm & 7-11pm).

Parrilla Restaurants
PARRILLA $

(Rivadavia, btwn San Lorenzo & 12 de Octubre; steaks AR$60-110; ⊙ 7pm-midnight Mon-Sat, 11am-3pm Sun) A long way from the slightly mannered tourist scene around the plaza, this string of no-frills grillhouses makes a worthwhile dinner escape. The Gallito is locally renowned, but adjacent Parrilla Santos – just a concrete floor, a barbecue and a corrugated-metal roof – has equally tasty meat. Uncomplicated and great value.

Heladería Miranda
ICE CREAM $

(Av General Güemes N s/n; cones AR$25-40; ⊙ 1:30pm-midnight) A frequent dilemma in Argentina is whether to go for a rich red cabernet or a dry white torrontés, but it doesn't usually occur in ice-cream parlors. It does here: the Miranda's wine sorbets are Cafayate's pride and joy, but other fresh fruit flavors, including *tuna* (cactus-fruit), are also delicious.

★ Piattelli
ARGENTINE $$

(☑ 03868-15-405491; RP 2; mains AR$110-190; ⊙ 12:30-4pm; 🕿) A lovely indoor-outdoor setting overlooking picture-perfect vineyards at this upmarket winery 5km from Cafayate makes a fine lunch stop. The sophisticated food doesn't disappoint. A range of international influences spice up the menu, and at weekends (when booking is advisable) they fire up the outdoor grill with some of the finest parrilla offerings in this part of the nation.

El Terruño
ARGENTINE $$

(☑ 03868-422460; www.teruno.todowebsalta.com.ar; Av General Güemes N 30; mains AR$110-200; ⊙ noon-3:30pm & 7:30pm-midnight; 🕿) Plazaside seating and polite if scatty service presents, strangely, two menus here. One is less traditional, with dishes such as inventive seafood-based salads, and well-prepared mains, including plenty of fish dishes. Overpriced, but friendly and reliable enough.

El Rancho
NORTHWEST ARGENTINE $$

(Toscano 4; mains AR$70-160; ⊙ noon-3pm & 7:30pm-midnight or 1am; 🕿) A cut above the string of hit-and-miss places around the plaza, this has a short, simple menu of local dishes, including *locro,* plus decent meat and chicken plates. The house specialty is rabbit. It appeals on winter nights, with a crackling fire.

🍷 Drinking

★ Chato's Wine Bar   WINE BAR
(Nuestra Señora del Rosario 132; ⊘7-11pm) Run by a cordial English-speaker, the only proper wine bar in Cafayate serves a long list of wines by the glass and is great for a tasting session (five-wine flights from AR$100), a drink in friendly surroundings or a chat. Munch on a *picada* (shared appetizer plate) so it doesn't go to your head. A move of location to San Martín 223 was planned when we visited.

🛍 Shopping

There are numerous *artesanía* shops and market complexes around the central plaza.

Mercado Artesanal   HANDICRAFTS
(Av General Güemes; ⊘9am-10:30pm) 🖉 The Mercado Artesanal cooperative features high-quality local work at more-than-fair prices.

Jorge Barraco   GIFTS
(Colón 157; ⊘8am-10pm) For fine silver, check out the workshop of Jorge Barraco.

ⓘ Information

Tourist Office (☑03868-422442; Av General Güemes s/n; ⊘9am-7pm Tue-Sun) Attached to the wine museum. Offers an invaluable printout of winery opening times.

ⓘ Getting There & Away

The new **bus terminal** (RN40) is at the northern entrance to town.

Flechabus (www.flechabus.com.ar) runs five to six daily services to Salta (AR$159, four hours) and one or two to Angastaco (AR$60, two hours) via San Carlos (AR$17, one to four daily, 30 minutes).

El Aconquija (☑03868-421052; http://transportesaconquija.com.ar) leaves two to four times daily for Tucumán (AR$240 to AR$270, five to 6½ hours) via Amaicha and Tafí del Valle (AR$140 to AR$170, 2½ to four hours); some go via Santa María (AR$75, two hours). Counterintuitively, quicker buses are cheaper.

El Indio (☑0387-431439) runs once daily to Salta (AR$160) and Santa María (AR$80).

ⓘ Getting Around

Taxis (☑03868-422128) congregate opposite the cathedral – call if there are none – and are useful for reaching bodegas and other destinations. To Quilmes with waiting time costs around AR$450; to San Carlos one way it's AR$120.

Quebrada de Cafayate

North of Cafayate, the Salta road heads through barren, spectacular Quebrada de Cafayate, a wild landscape of richly colored sandstone and unearthly rock formations. Carved out by the Río de las Conchas, the canyon's twisted sedimentary strata exhibit a stunning array of tones, from rich red ocher to ethereal green. While you get a visual feast from the road itself – it's one of the country's more memorable drives or rides – it's worth taking time to explore parts of the canyon. The best time to appreciate the Quebrada is in the late afternoon; low sun brings out the most vivid colors.

A short way north of Cafayate, Los Médanos is an extensive dune field that gives way to the canyon proper, where a series of distinctive landforms are named and signposted from the road. Some, such as El Sapo (the Toad) are underwhelming, but around the Km46–47 mark, the adjacent Garganta del Diablo (Devil's Throat) and Anfiteatro (Amphitheater) are much more impressive. Gashes in the rock wall let you enter and appreciate the tortured stone, whose clearly visible layers have been twisted by tectonic upheavals into extraordinary configurations.

These landmarks are heavily visited, and you may be followed by locals hoping for some pesos for a bit of 'guiding.' *Artesanía* sellers and musicians hover, too. Though drinks are sometimes on sale, don't rely on it.

ⓘ Getting There & Away

There are several ways to see and explore the canyon. Tours from Salta are brief; it's better to take a tour or taxi from closer Cafayate. Minibus tours stop at major sights; other longer tours add some hiking away from the road. Biking it from Cafayate is possible, but regular punctures make this an unreliable option.

You could also combine buses with some walking and/or hitchhiking. Carry food and plenty of water in this hot, dry environment. A good place to start exploration is the Garganta del Diablo; several other attractions are within easy walking distance of there.

San Antonio de los Cobres

☑0387 / POP 4300 / ELEV 3775M

This dusty mining town is on the puna 168km west of Salta, and sits more than 2600m above it. It's suffered since the deterioration of the region's mining and associated railway, but is an example of a typical highland settlement, with adobe houses, near-deserted streets and a serious temperature drop after sundown. It's worth stopping in to experience this facet of Andean life. You can head north from here to the Quebrada de Humahuaca via the Salinas Grandes and Purmamarca, and, some of the year, south to Cachi.

◉ Sights

There's little to see in town (though sunsets are spectacular!) but 16km to the west is the impressive viaduct at **La Polvorilla**, the last stop of the Tren a las Nubes (p223) rail trip. You can climb up a zigzag path to the top and walk across it. *Remises* in San Antonio charge about AR$200 for the return journey.

🛏 Sleeping & Eating

Simple restaurants dot Belgrano, and are good bets for empanadas, *milanesas* and other local staples.

Hostería El Palenque   GUESTHOUSE $
(☎0387-490-9019; hostalelpalenque@hotmail.com; Belgrano s/n; r per person US$17) Welcoming and tidy, this fine choice is a few blocks from the center, past the church. It looks closed from outside, but it's not. Superclean rooms are insulated and (comparatively) warm; there's hot water and sound family ownership. Two rooms share a bathroom; two others are en suite. Breakfast is extra. Wi-fi is planned.

El Portal de los Andes   GUESTHOUSE $
(☎0387-490-9282; Las Vicuñitas s/n; s/d US$27/40; ☎) This likeable little setup is in a pretty building on the Salta side of the river. Rooms are spotless, with comfortable beds; the interesting boss is welcoming; and the restaurant does a nice line in local dishes.

Hotel de las Nubes   HOTEL $$
(☎0387-490-9059; www.hoteldelasnubes.com; RN 51; s/d US$69/86; ☎) The town's best hotel has simple decoration in its comfortable-enough rooms, which are sparsely furnished but boast double glazing and heating. Book ahead. The restaurant (open noon to 2pm and 7pm to 9:30pm) serves a short menu of local dishes; it's overpriced (mains from AR$125 to AR$200) but tasty enough. The long-serving barman is good for a chat.

★**Quinoa Real**   NORTHWEST ARGENTINE $$
(☎0387-490-9270; Belgrano s/n; mains AR$60-130; ☎9am-3:30pm & 7:30-11:30pm) On the refurbished central block, this is aimed at tourists, with traditional fabrics on tables and a menu of local ingredients. Llama features heavily, such as in tasty empanadas, carpaccio and fillets, but roast lamb with a chili-and-garlic kick is also recommendable. Vegetarians will be cheered by a range of savory filled tarts and quinoa options. There's also quinoa-flavored craft beer.

❶ Information

Tourist Office (☎0387-15-578-7877; culturayturismoandino@gmail.com; RN 51; ☎9am-9pm Mon-Sat, to 3pm Sun) Just by the bridge in the center of town, this complex includes a decent artisanal market and a cafe.

❶ Getting There & Away

Two to three daily buses run from Salta (AR$115, 5½ hours) and **Tren a las Nubes** (p223) stops here. Precious little transportation crosses the Paso de Sico to Chile; ask around town for trucks. From San Antonio, a good *ripio* (gravel) road runs 97km north, skirting the Salinas Grandes to intersect with paved RP 52.

Salinas Grandes

Bring sunglasses for this spectacular **salt plain** in a remote part of the puna, some 3350m above sea level. A lake that dried up in the Holocene, this is now a 525-sq-km crust of salt up to half-a-meter thick. On a clear day, the blinding contrast between bright blue sky and the cracked and crusty expanse of white is spellbinding. Over the year, wind strips much of the salt away; it's most spectacular after summer rains replenish it.

The *salinas* are in Salta province, but most easily reached by heading west along spectacular, paved RP 52 from Purmamarca. About 5km west of the intersection of RP 52 and the good *ripio* road that heads 97km to San Antonio de los Cobres, there's a salt-mining building; opposite, you can head out onto the salt pan to check out the rectangular basins from which the salt is periodically dug out. Artisans sell stone carvings and llamas made from salt. Limited drinks and snacks are available.

The only way of reaching the *salinas* by public transportation is to jump off a Chile- or Susques-bound bus from Jujuy or Purmamarca. Check timetables carefully before doing this; on some days it's possible to catch a bus back to Purmamarca a couple of hours later, but on other days it's not. This road has enough traffic to hitchhike.

Otherwise, grab a *remise* from Purmamarca, or take a tour from Purmamarca, Tilcara, Jujuy or Salta. From the latter, it's a long day, unless you opt to overnight.

The *salinas* are impressive, but the otherworldly *salares* of southwestern Bolivia are even more so; if you're heading that way (or have already been), you might prioritize other attractions.

Jujuy

📞 0388 / POP 265,300 / ELEV 1201M

Of the trinity of northwestern cities, (San Salvador de) Jujuy lacks Salta's colonial sophistication or Tucuman's urban vibe and is often bypassed by travelers. Nevertheless, it has a livable feel, enticing restaurants and is the most culturally indigenous of any of Argentina's cities.

The city was founded in 1593, after two previous incarnations were razed by angry indigenous groups who hadn't given planning permission.The province bore the brunt of conflict during the independence wars, with Spain launching repeated invasions down the Quebrada de Humahuaca from Bolivia; Jujuy was famously evacuated in what is known as the *éxodo jujeño*.

The city's name is roughly pronounced *hoo-hooey;* if it sounds like an arch exclamation of surprise, you're doing well.

◉ Sights

★ Culturarte
GALLERY

(www.facebook.com/culturarte.ccultural; cnr San Martín & Sarmiento; ⊗8am-11pm Mon-Sat) FREE
An attractive modern space, this showcases exhibitions by well-established Argentine contemporary artists. There's often work of excellent quality here, and it makes a fun place to check out the Jujuy scene. The cafe has a nice little balcony terrace overlooking the center of town.

Museo Temático de Maquetas Tupac Amaru
MUSEUM

(Alvear 1152; ⊗8am-11pm) 🖉 FREE Set up by and housed in the headquarters of an indigenous political organization, this unexpectedly charming museum tells the history, traditions and mythology of indigenous Argentina in a series of entertaining dioramas.

COCA CHEWING

In the northwest, you'll see signs outside shops advertising *coca* and *bica*. The former refers to the leaves, mainly grown in Peru and Bolivia, which are traditionally chewed by Andean peoples. They have a mild stimulant effect and combat fatigue, altitude sickness and hunger (and are also used to produce cocaine). *Bica* refers to bicarbonate of soda, an alkaline that, when chewed along with the leaves, increases the effect. Chewing coca and possessing small amounts for personal use are legal, but only in the northwest. Taking them back down south or into Chile is illegal, and there are regular searches.

If you read Spanish, you'll find copious information here on these subjects.

☞ Tours

Numerous Jujuy operators offer trips to the Quebrada de Humahuaca, Salinas Grandes, Parque Nacional Calilegua and other provincial destinations. The Provincial Tourist Office (p249) can give you a full listing.

✯ Festivals & Events

Semana de Jujuy
FIESTA

(⊗Aug) Jujuy's biggest event, the weeklong Semana de Jujuy, commemorates Belgrano's evacuation of the city during the wars of independence.

🛏 Sleeping

There are several central hostels, mostly acceptable but mediocre.

Munay Hotel
HOTEL $

(📞0388-422-8435; www.munayhotel.com.ar; Alvear 1230; s/d US$44/68; 🖂) This good-value budget hotel offers small but comfortable and spotless rooms in a nice little package a couple of blocks away from the action. Service is friendly, and limited parking is available for an extra charge. Interior rooms suffer from some ambient noise.

D-Gira Hostel
HOSTEL $

(📞0388-15-408-0386; www.facebook.com/dgira. hosteljujuy; JM Gorriti 427; dm US$10-11, d US$33; @🖂) Located in an unfashionable but relatively central zone of the city, this beats the downtown hostels on several points. Number

Jujuy

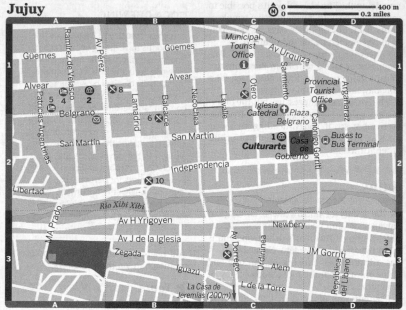

Map legend:

Güemes · Ramírez de Velasco · Av Pérez · Güemes · Municipal Tourist Office · Av Urquiza · Alvear · Alvear · Otero · Sarmiento · Provincial Tourist Office · Argañaraz · Patricias Argentinas · Belgrano · Lamadrid · Balcarce · Necochea · Lavalle · Iglesia Catedral · Plaza Belgrano · Canónigo Gorriti · San Martín · San Martín · San Martín · Culturarte · Casa de Gobierno · Buses to Bus Terminal · Independencia · Río Xibi Xibi · MA Prado · Libertad · Av H Yrigoyen · Newbery · Av J de la Iglesia · Av Dorrego · Urdininea · JM Gorriti · Zegada · Iguazú · Alem · República del Líbano · La Casa de Jeremías (200m) · L de la Torre

one is the genuine welcome, then you can add the purple walls and seriously comfortable blond-timber bunks with their plump mattresses and decent bedding. Dorms all have en suite bathrooms and plenty of room. Ongoing improvements and a can-do attitude make this a worthwhile stop.

★ Posada El Arribo
BOUTIQUE HOTEL $$
(🖰 0388-422-2539; www.elarribo.com; Belgrano 1263; s/d US$70/109; 🌬@📶🏊) An oasis in

the heart of Jujuy, this highly impressive family-run place is a real visual feast. The renovated 19th-century mansion is wonderful, with original floor tiles, high ceilings and wooden floors; there's patio space galore and a huge garden. The modern annex behind doesn't lose much by comparison, but go for an older room if you can.

✗ Eating

Jujuy's lively **Mercado del Sur** is a genuine trading post where indigenous Argentines swig *mazamorra* (cold maize soup) and peddle coca leaves. Simple eateries around here serve hearty regional specialties; try *chicharrón con mote* (stir-fried pork with boiled maize) or spicy *sopa de maní* (peanut soup).

Manos Jujeñas
NORTHWEST ARGENTINE $
(Av Pérez 381; mains AR$60-110; ⊙11am-3pm & 7-11pm Tue-Sun) 🌱 One of Jujuy's best addresses for no-frills traditional slow-food cooking, this fills up with a contented buzz on weekend evenings. There are several classic northeastern dishes to choose from, but it's the *picante* – marinated chicken or tongue (or both) with onion, tomato, rice and Andean potatoes – that's the pride of the house. Take-out also available.

Madre Tierra BAKERY, CAFE **$**
(Belgrano 619; mains AR$50; ⊙6:30am-3pm
& 4-10:30pm Mon-Sat; 🛜🖋) This place is a
standout. The vegetarian food (there's a
daily set menu) is excellent and the sandwiches and pizzas can be washed down with
fresh juice or organic beer. There's lovely
garden-patio seating and the bakery out the
front does wholesome breads.

Viracocha NORTHWEST ARGENTINE **$**
(cnr Independencia & Lamadrid; mains AR$70-110;
⊙11:30am-3pm & 8:15pm-12:30am, closed Sun
Oct-Mar, closed Tue Apr-Sep; 🛜) 🖋 Atmospheric
vaulted restaurant serving excellent traditional dishes such as *picantes* of any meat
you can think of, pickled llama and warming
peanut soup.

⭐**Krysys** ARGENTINE **$$**
(Balcarce 272; mains AR$80-140; ⊙12:30-3pm
& 8:30pm-12:30am Mon-Sat, 12:30-3:30pm Sun;
🛜) The best *parrilla* option is this central,
upscale place offering all your barbecued fa-
vorites in a relaxed atmosphere. But there's
plenty more on the menu, with a range of
tasty sauces to go with the chicken, pork or
beef, and various appetizing starters. Prices
are fair, and you'll get the meat the way you
want it cooked.

🍷 **Drinking & Nightlife**

The big *boliches* (nightclubs) are out on RN
9 south of town.

☆ **Entertainment**

Jujuy's several folkloric *peñas* have live mu-
sic at weekends.

La Casa de Jeremías TRADITIONAL MUSIC
(www.facebook.com/lacasa.dejeremias; Guzmán
306) Friday and Saturday nights are the
best times to head over to this popular
spot, which has live Jujuy folkloric bands
at weekends. It does decent traditional food
also. Check the Facebook page for upcoming
events.

ℹ️ **Information**

Municipal Tourist Office (📞0388-402-0246;
www.sansalvadordejujuy.gob.ar; cnr Alvear
& Otero; ⊙7am-10pm) Friendly and central.
Hours vary depending on staffing.
Provincial Tourist Office (📞0388-422-1343;
www.turismo.jujuy.gov.ar; Canónigo Gorriti
295; ⊙7am-10pm Mon-Fri, 8am-9pm Sat &
Sun) Excellent office on the plaza, with good
brochures and staff.

ℹ️ **Getting There & Away**

AIR
Aerolíneas (📞0388-422-2575; www.aero
lineas.com.ar; San Martín 96; ⊙8:30am-
12:30pm & 4:30-8:30pm Mon-Fri, 8:30am-
12:30pm Sat) services Buenos Aires and also
Mendoza via Córdoba.

BUS
The new **bus terminal** is 6km southeast of the
center. It's got great facilities, including showers
and a **tourist office** (Bus Terminal; ⊙7:30am-
9:30pm Mon-Fri, 8am-1pm & 3:30-9:30pm Sat
& Sun).

Daily buses going from Salta to Chile stop here.

Buses from Jujuy

DESTINATION	COST (ARS)	TIME (HR)
Buenos Aires	1400	20-23
Córdoba	835	12-16
Humahuaca	66	2
La Quiaca	115	4-5
Mendoza	1207	21
Purmamarca	42	1¼
Salta	75	2
Salvador Mazza	322	7
Tilcara	45	1¾
Tucumán	325	5

ℹ️ **Getting Around**

El Cadillal airport is 33km east. A **shuttle ser-
vice** (📞15-432-2482; AR$100) leaves three
times daily from the corner of Canónigo Gorriti
and Belgrano to coincide with flights; alterna-
tively it's AR$340 in a *remise*.

Several local buses head to the bus station
(AR$5.50), including 8A and 9A from Canónigo
Gorriti between San Martín and Independencia.
From the bus terminal, several lines run very
regularly to the center.
Hertz (📞0388-422-9582; www.hertz.com;
Balcarce 578; ⊙9am-noon & 5-9pm Mon-Sat)
is central for car rental; there are also airport
operators.

Las Yungas

Eastern Jujuy province is a humid, fertile
subtropical zone where arid, treeless alti-
plano gives way to montane forest and, in
places, dense cloud forest. It's a spectacular,
vibrantly green area.

Parque Nacional Calilegua

This accessible, beautiful, biodiverse park stretches up the Serranía de Calilegua range to peaks offering boundless views above the forest and across the Chaco to the east.

The spectacular 22km road through the park ascends from 550m to 1700m, taking you through the three types of forest that characterize the park's different altitude layers and offering spectacular vistas.

Along this road are trailheads for 10 marked hikes, from 10-minute strolls to tough descents down to river level. The best places for bird- and mammal-watching are near the stream courses in the early morning or late afternoon. Most trailheads are within easy walking distance of the park entrance. Rangers offer guiding services on the longer trails.

From Valle Grande, work is underway to finalize the road connection to the Quebrada de Humahuaca. You can hike to Humahuaca or Tilcara from here.

The ranger station at Aguas Negras, the **park entrance** (calilegua@apn.gov.ar; ⊙9am-1pm & 2-6pm) FREE, is the best source of information about trails and conditions. There's another ranger station at Mesada de las Colmenas, halfway along the road through the park.

The free **campground** is at the entrance. It has bathrooms and shower, but no power, drinking water or shop.

Libertador General San Martín is a sizable sugarcane town with little charm but several places to stay. Little Calilegua is more appealing, with a tumbledown tropical feel and a deafening chorus of cicadas around the historic Sala de Calilegua estate. **Jardín Colonial** (☑03886-430334; eljardin colonial@hotmail.com; San Lorenzo s/n, Calilegua; s/d/tr US$20/27/38; ❀🐾🐕) is a characterful, haphazardly run centenarian bungalow with attractive rooms and a verdant, sculpture-filled garden. It's cheap and very casual: there are no locks on the rooms and you're left to your own devices. Toucans roost in the trees opposite. Breakfast is US$3 extra. On the park-like plaza in the heart of town, **Hostería Benítez** (☑03886-433119; benitezhosteria@gmail.com; 19 de Abril s/n, Calilegua; s/d US$45/60; ❀🐾) offers a warm family welcome and clean, comfortable, well-kept rooms of hotel standard. Good breakfasts and dinners are served in the appealing dining area.

Very regular buses between Jujuy or Salta and Salvador Mazza stop at Libertador General San Martín and Calilegua, and may let you off at the park junction, 3km north of Libertador's center and 2km south of Calilegua. It's 8km from here to Aguas Negras ranger station; there's enough traffic to hitchhike. It's also easy to taxi it from either town.

Quebrada de Humahuaca

North of Jujuy, the memorable Quebrada de Humahuaca snakes its way upward toward Bolivia. It's a harsh but vivid landscape, a dry yet river-scoured canyon overlooked by mountainsides whose sedimentary strata have been eroded into spectacular scalloped formations revealing a spectrum of colors in undulating waves. The palette of this World Heritage–listed valley changes constantly, from shades of creamy white to rich, deep reds; the rock formations in places recall a necklace of sharks' teeth, in others the knobbly backbone of some unspeakable beast.

ℹ BOLIVIA VIA SALVADOR MAZZA OR AGUAS BLANCAS

RN 34 continues past Calilegua to Argentina's northernmost settlement, Salvador Mazza (aka Pocitos), a major frontier with Bolivia. Cross the **border** (⊙24hr), and take a shared taxi 5km to Yacuiba in Bolivia, which has buses to Tarija and Santa Cruz. There's no Bolivian consulate, so get your visa in Jujuy or Salta if you need one. Salvador Mazza is served by numerous buses from Jujuy, Salta and beyond.

Another crossing in this area is the international bridge between Aguas Blancas and Bermejo, from where there are good onward bus connections to Tarija. Aguas Blancas is served by bus from Salta, but there are more frequent connections to Orán, from where shared taxis leave for Aguas Blancas from opposite the bus station. Direct services with Juarez are available between Salta and Tarija (AR$700, eight hours, twice weekly).

Pirate shared taxis outside Salta's bus terminal head direct for the Bolivian border and cost little more than the bus.

Dotting the valley are dusty, picturesque, indigenous towns offering a fine variety of places to stay, plus historic adobe churches, handicrafts and homey restaurants serving warming *locro* and llama fillets. The region has experienced a tourism boom in recent years and gets very full in summer, when accommodation prices soar.

Buses run along this old colonial post route regularly; it's easy to jump off and on as required. Closest car hire is Jujuy. The Quebrada shows its best side early in the morning, when colors are more vivid and the wind hasn't got up.

Purmamarca

🗐 0388 / POP 500 / ELEV 2192M

Little Purmamarca, 3km west of the highway, sits under celebrated Cerro de los Siete Colores (Hill of Seven Colors), a spectacular, jagged formation resembling the marzipan fantasy of a megalomaniac pastry chef. The village is postcard-pretty, with adobe houses and ancient algarrobo trees by the bijou 17th-century church. This, and its proximity to Jujuy, has made it very touristy; if you're looking for an authentic Andean village, move on. Nevertheless, Purmamarca is a gloriously beautiful spot and an excellent place to shop for woven goods; a flourishing market sets up on the plaza every day.

Make sure you take the easy but spectacular 3km walk around the *cerro* (hill), whose striking colors are best appreciated in the morning or evening sunlight.

🛏 Sleeping

El Pequeño Inti
GUESTHOUSE $

(🗐 0388-490-8089; Florida s/n; s/d US$40/45) Small and enticing, this fine little choice is just off the plaza. Offering value (for two), it has unadorned rooms with comfortable beds and marine-schemed bathrooms. Wi-fi woud be a nice touch, though.

Mama Coca
HOSTEL $

(🗐 0388-490-8434; mamacocapurma@hotmail. com; Rivadavia s/n; dm/d US$10/25; 🖎) Close to the bus station and behind a restaurant, this casual hostel is a simple – very simple – place to hole up. It's friendly and family-run, with a small vine-shaded patio. Dorms have a decent amount of space. It's cheaper if you don't want breakfast. No kitchen.

⭐ Huaira Huasi
HOTEL $$

(🗐 0388-423-7134; www.huairahuasi.com.ar; RN 52, Km5; d US$134-155, q US$225; ❄@🛜🐾) One of a handful of characterful hotels on the main road above town, this stands out for its majestic valley views and handsome terracotta-colored adobe buildings. There are two apartments that sleep five, and are just beautifully decorated with local fabrics and cardón wood; rooms are obviously smaller but still lovely. Good value and charming hosts.

⭐ Los Colorados
APARTMENTS $$$

(🗐 0388-490-8182; www.loscoloradosjujuy.com.ar; Chapacal s/n; s/d/q US$120/160/250; ❄🛜🐾) Looking straight out of a science-fiction movie, these strange but inviting apartments are tucked right into the *cerro*, and blend in with it. They are stylish, spacious and cozy; fine places to hole up for a while and a great option for families.

La Comarca
BOUTIQUE HOTEL $$$

(🗐 0388-490-8001; www.lacomarcahotel.com.ar; RN 52, Km3.8; s/d US$142/180; ❄@🛜🏊🐾) On the main road but an easy stroll into town, this well-run place offers a variety of sweet mauve-colored accommodations surrounding a carefully tended lawn and garden. Rooms open onto this and the main building, which offers a great lounge area, a sauna, a pretty little pool and more. Houses and cabins sleep up to six. Staff is polite, friendly and helpful. Views are just fabulous.

Terrazas de la Posta
HOTEL $$$

(🗐 0388-490-8053; www.terrazasdelaposta.com. ar; s US$145, d standard/superior US$157/182; ❄🛜) Located at the edge of the center, these

CHILE VIA SUSQUES

The paved road climbs doggedly from Purmamarca through spectacular bleak highland scenery to a 4150m pass, then crosses a plateau partly occupied by the Salinas Grandes. You hit civilization at **Susques**, 130km from Purmamarca, which has gas and an ATM.

Susques is well worth a stop for its terrific village **church** (admission by donation; ⊙ 8am-6pm). Dating from 1598, it has a thatched roof, cactus-wood ceiling and beaten-earth floor, as well as charismatic, naïve paintings of saints on the whitewashed adobe walls. There's an occasionally open tourist office on the main road, and basic places to stay.

Beyond Susques, the road continues 154km to the Paso de Jama (4230m), a spectacular journey. This is the Chilean border, although Argentine immigration (8am to midnight) is some way before it. There's gas here. No fruit, vegetables or coca leaves are allowed into Chile – there are checks. The paved road continues toward San Pedro de Atacama.

Daily buses run from Jujuy to Susques (AR$115, four to five hours) via Purmamarca (AR$90). Services from Salta and Jujuy to Chile stop here.

---

handsome rooms with spacious bathrooms share a veranda with great sierra views. Service is good, and it's a peaceful place to stay. Superior rooms are larger, with air-con, minibar and eye-catching modern styling. Reliable, relaxing and comfortable. You get a discount at the restaurant on the plaza.

✖ Eating

Purmamarca's best food is cooked by a charismatic chef called Gabriel, who was due to open a new place on Lavalle, half a block uphill from the plaza: ask around.

Bramasole　　　　NORTHWEST ARGENTINE **$**
(Libertad s/n; mains AR$80-120; ⊙ noon-4pm & 7-11pm; 🛜) With a pleasantly modern interior, this spot run by a helpful local couple is worth stopping at. Delicious hand-cut empanadas, *locro* that's given a boost for the eyes and tastebuds with the addition of spring onion, and various llama dishes are all very toothsome.

Tierra de Colores　　　NORTHWEST ARGENTINE **$**
(Libertad s/n; mains AR$60-110; ⊙ noon-4:30pm & 7-11:30pm) A likeably rustic dining area with cane ceiling is a venue for delicious traditional food, served in generous portions. Juicy tamales, tasty *locro* and sizable llama brochettes are the go. Service is pleasant, and there's touristy but enjoyable live music.

El Churqui de Altura　　NORTHWEST ARGENTINE **$$**
(Salta s/n; mains AR$100-160; ⊙ noon-3:30pm & 7:30-10:30pm; 🛜) At the top of town, this place has dishes of local trout, goat or llama stews and oven-cooked empanadas that are pretty tasty, though the wines are a bit

overpriced. Llama fillet in malbec sauce is a popular choice.

ⓘ Information

There's an ATM plaza-side.

Tourist Office (⌨ 0388-490-8443; Florida s/n; ⊙ 7am-noon & 2-7pm, extended hours Jan & Feb) Just off the plaza. Opening unreliable.

ⓘ Getting There & Away

Buses run to Jujuy (AR$45, 1¼ hours) or Tilcara (from AR$10.50, 30 minutes) and Humahuaca (from AR$33, 1¼ hours). You can walk or get a cab (AR$20) to the main road junction where more buses pass.

Purmamarca has no **gas station**; the closest can be found 25km north, at Tilcara. Westward, the nearest is in Susques, a 130km climb away. South, the closest at time of research was Jujuy (62km).

Tilcara

📞 0388 / POP 4400 / ELEV 2461M

Picturesque Tilcara is many people's choice as their Quebrada de Humahuaca base. The mixture of local farmers getting on with a centuries-old way of life and arty urban refugees looking for a quieter existence has created an interesting balance on the town's dusty streets. A forest of boutique hotels and lots of hostels mean accommodations are plentiful.

◉ Sights

Pucará　　　　　　　　　　　　　RUIN
(admission incl Museo Arqueológico foreigner/Argentine AR$50/25, Mon free; ⊙ 9am-6pm) This

reconstructed pre-Columbian fortification is 1km south of the center across an iron bridge. Its situation is strategic, commanding the river valley both ways and, though the site was undoubtedly used earlier, the ruins date from the 11th to 15th centuries. There are great views and, seemingly, a cardón cactus for every soul that lived and died here. For further succulent stimulation, there's a botanic garden by the entrance.

The 1950s reconstruction has taken liberties; worse yet is the earlier, ridiculous monument to pioneering archaeologists bang where the plaza would have been. Nevertheless, you can get a feel of what would have been a sizable fortified community. Most interesting is the 'church,' a building with a short paved walkway to an altar; note the niche in the wall alongside.

Museo Arqueológico   MUSEUM
(Belgrano 445; admission incl Pucará foreigner/Argentine AR$50/25, Mon free; ◷ 9am-6pm) This well-presented collection of regional artifacts in a striking colonial house has some pieces from the *pucará* fortification just south of the center, and exhibits give an insight into the life of people living around that time (from the 11th to 15th centuries). The room dedicated to ceremonial masks is particularly impressive.

🏃 Activities

You'll see phone numbers for *cabalgatas* (horseback rides) everywhere; most accommodations can arrange these. Guides for walks around the area congregate at the tourist office.

Garganta del Diablo   HIKING
(admission AR$15) Of several interesting Tilcara walks, most popular is the 4km hike to Garganta del Diablo, a pretty canyon leading to a waterfall. Walk toward the *pucará*, 1km south of the center across an iron bridge, but turn left along the river before crossing the bridge. Swimming is best in the morning, when the sun is on the pool. You can also reach it by road.

Bicicletería Carlitos   BICYCLE RENTAL
(Tilcara Mountain Bike; ☏ 0388-15-500-8570; tilcarabikes@hotmail.com; Belgrano s/n; per hr/day US$3.50/15; ◷ 9am-7pm) A friendly setup about 100m past the bus terminal that hires out well-maintained mountain bikes and provides a helpful map of trips in the area.

👉 Tours

Operators around town run trips around the Quebrada and Salinas Grandes. A recommended guide for the spectacular multiday trek to Parque Nacional Calilegua is **Juan Pablo Maldonado** (☏ 0388-15-504-5322).

★ Caravana de Llamas   TREKKING
(☏ 0388-15-408-8000; www.caravanadellamas.com; Belgrano s/n) 🌿 A highly recommended llama-trekking operator running 90-minute (US$25), half-day (US$50 to US$70) and full- or multiday (US$100 per day) excursions of varying difficulty around Tilcara, Purmamarca and Salinas Grandes. The guide is personable and well informed about the area. Llamas are pack animals: you walk; they carry the bags. Drop by to meet the llamas (US$8) opposite the tourist office.

Runa Tour   CULTURAL TOUR
(☏ 0388-495-5388; www.runatour.tur.ar; Belgrano 481; 1-/2-/3-day excursions US$200/350/400) 🌿 Locally run, this operator offers interesting excursions to indigenous communities, where you learn about corn and quinoa cultivation and visit archaeological sites. You can combine this with a horse-ride or drive to the spectacular Serranía de Hornocal (p258), a jagged row of rock 'teeth.' Another option takes you over the mountains and down to the Yungas, combining riding and driving, or just riding.

🎊 Festivals & Events

Tilcara celebrates several festivals during the year, the most notable of which, apart from Carnaval, is January's **Enero Tilcareño**, which features sports, music and cultural activities. August's indigenous **Pachamama** (Mother Earth) festival is also worthwhile.

🛏 Sleeping

There's a huge variety of accommodations, with numerous upmarket boutique hotels and dozens of simple hostels, guesthouses and good-value rooms in private homes (the tourist office keeps a list of these).

★ La Casa del Indio   GUESTHOUSE $
(☏ 0388-15-862526; www.argentinaturismo.com.ar/casadelindio; Ambrosetti s/n; d/tr US$50/65; 🐾) It would be difficult to find more charming hosts than the young couple that run this appealing place, which consists of two rooms off a sweet little courtyard beside the family home. Simple and traditional in style, with some attractive stonework, it offers

tranquillity, independence and comfort, as well as a relaxingly wild garden.

Can be tricky to find: go straight up the hill from the bus terminal and turn third right.

Albahaca Hostel HOSTEL $
(☑ 0388-15-585-5994; www.albahacahostel.com.ar; Padilla s/n; dm/d US$9/25; ☎) Simple but well priced and very friendly, with decent dorms, comfortable private rooms and a sociable roof terrace. A place to make friends.

La Calabaza CABAÑAS $
(☑ 0388-495-5169; www.calabazatilcara.com.ar; Sarahuaico s/n; d/q US$65/135; ☎👐) Set above an orchard-garden across the main road from the center, this cute spot has a casual hippy vibe and very friendly welcome. The view: just spectacular. There's a cabin with kitchen sleeping four, perfect for a family, and an adorable little double with views from the bed and tea/coffee facilities. Three-night minimum stay in summer. Breakfast extra.

Malka GUESTHOUSE, HOSTEL $
(☑ 0388-495-5197; www.malkahostel.com.ar; San Martín 129; dm/s/d US$25/45/80, 4-person cabin US$190; @☎) ✈ This rustic complex is both guesthouse and hostel. The secluded, shady situation, thoughtfully different dorms, and smart stone-clad rooms with hammocks and deck chairs make it the sort of retreat where you end up staying longer than expected. A yoga and meditation room and courses are further reasons to linger. Good breakfast included and HI discount.

Dorms have key lockers and a spacious kitchen. Facing the church, head left for a block, then turn right and follow this road.

★ Posada de Luz LODGE $$
(☑ 0388-495-5017; www.posadadeluz.com.ar; Ambrosetti 661; r US$105-143; @☎🏊👐) With a nouveau-rustic charm, this little place is a fantastic spot to unwind for a few days. The pricier rooms have sitting areas, but all feature adobe walls, cane ceilings, pot-bellied stoves and individual terraces with deck chairs and views out over the valley. Pretty grounds include a barbecue area and children's playground; excellent personal service is a real highlight.

★ Cerro Chico CABAÑAS $$
(☑ 0388-495-5744; www.cerrochico.com; d/q US$100/120; ☎🏊) Two kilometers from town down a dirt road, this attractively rustic complex climbs a hill, with gorgeous Que-

brada views and a remote, relaxing feel. The standard cabins are compact but handsome, set amid a lovely hillside garden, and the pool area is a great little spot. Turn left after the bridge into Tilcara and follow the signs. Three-night minimum stay usually applies.

★ Patio Alto HOTEL, HOSTEL $$
(☑ 0388-495-5792; www.patioalto.com.ar; Torrico 675; dm/s/d US$34/124/143; @☎👐) Great vistas from the coziness of your large bed are the highlight of the handsome modern rooms at this top-of-the-town hotel. A good breakfast, afternoon tea and other thoughtful details are included. There's also an upmarket dorm that is every bit as nice as the rooms, with four single beds, cane lockers and kitchen use; the only thing missing is the view.

Antigua Tilcara GUESTHOUSE, HOSTEL $$
(☑ 0388-527-3805; www.antiguatilcara.com.ar; Sorpresa 484; dm US$25, d standard US$81, d superior US$88-92; @☎) ✈ Run with real enthusiasm and offering a genuine welcome, this excellent place has a spacious dorm with single beds and two grades of room, both handsome. Superiors are worth the small investment for extra space and views. There's a great cafe-bar area with vistas, cracking breakfasts, a small kitchen, and various sustainable practices are in place.

Con los Ángeles LODGE $$
(☑ 0388-495-5153; www.posadaconlosangeles.com.ar; Gorriti 156; d standard/superior US$98/118; @☎👐) The lovely, extensive grassy garden, complete with sun loungers, comes as a surprise after the street. Warmly run by a friendly young family, this lodge features stylish common areas and thoughtfully decorated king-bedded rooms arrayed along the lawn. Dinners are available for guests.

Gaia Habitaciones Boutique BOUTIQUE HOTEL $$
(☑ 0388-15-414-0833; www.gaiatilcara.com.ar; Belgrano 472; s/d/q US$60/83/140; ☎) Right in the center, this nevertheless offers seclusion in its upstairs rooms that overlook a courtyard dominated by a lovely peppercorn tree. It's run by a friendly young family and sweet adobe-style chambers offer stylishly rustic decor, sizable showers and free tea and coffee (and no TV, for better relaxation).

Aguacanto LODGE $$
(☑ 0388-495-5817; www.aguacanto.com.ar; Corte 333; d/4-person apt US$88/170; ☎) Spruce

rooms and apartments surround a lawn featuring hammocks and one of Tilcara's most amazing views. Service is very friendly. Prices drop off-season.

✗ Eating

★ Ma'koka
CAFE $

(Belgrano s/n; sandwiches AR$45-65; ⊙8:30am-9pm; 🛜📶) 🍃 With a gloriously eclectic music mix and interesting texts on the area and the Andes in general, this excellent bookstore-cafe has the best coffee in town, tasty cakes and top sandwiches on bread made from coca or local corn varieties. Great choices for celiacs too, with manioc bread and other treats. The owner is knowledgeable about indigenous Argentina.

Peña de Carlitos
NORTHWEST ARGENTINE $

(Lavalle 397; dishes AR$55-80; ⊙10am-midnight; 🛜) This cheery, long-standing local restaurant where the scrawls of happy customers adorn the walls offers live folkloric music with no cover charge from 9:30pm every night. There's more of a mix of locals and visitors than in most places, and low-priced OK-quality regional dishes. Try the llama empanadas.

★ El Nuevo Progreso
ARGENTINE $$

(📲0388-495-5237; Lavalle 351; mains AR$105-160; ⊙6-11:30pm Mon-Sat; 📶) An engaging atmosphere and delicious tourist-oriented cuisine features imaginatively prepared llama dishes, excellent meat plates, interesting veggie options and great salads. Service can be a bit stand-offish but it's well worthwhile. Book at weekends.

El Patio
ARGENTINE $$

(📲0388-495-5044; Lavalle 352; mains AR$100-170; ⊙11:30am-3:30pm & 7-11:30pm Wed-Mon; 📶) Tucked away between plaza and church, this has a lovely shaded patio, garden seating and a cozy interior. It offers a wide range of tasty salads, inventive llama dishes and a far-from-the-madding-crowd atmosphere. Presentation and quantity could be better, but quality is good. The llama brochettes are great.

Arumi
NORTHWEST ARGENTINE $$

(Lavalle 660; mains AR$85-170; ⊙7pm-midnight Tue-Sun; 🛜) Art on the walls, regular live events and a comfortably attractive evening ambience are allied with highland ingredients of good quality here. Delicious tamales and pleasingly honest stews take their place alongside tasty llama and beef with sauces

and homemade pastas and pizzas. Service is caring.

❶ Information

Tourist Office (Belgrano 366; ⊙8am-9pm Mon-Fri, 9am-1pm & 2-9pm Sat, 9am-1pm Sun) Has information on walks. Often open Sunday afternoons despite official hours. Conversely, often not open when it's supposed to be.

❶ Getting There & Away

The bus terminal is on the main street, Belgrano; further services stop on the main road nearby. There are buses roughly every 45 minutes to Jujuy (AR$45, 1½ hours) and north to Humahuaca (AR$20, 45 minutes) and La Quiaca (AR$90, three hours). Several daily buses hit Purmamarca (AR$10.50, 30 minutes) and Salta (AR$122, 3½ hours).

Around Tilcara

Maimará, 8km south of Tilcara, is a typical adobe valley settlement set beneath the spectacular and aptly named Paleta del Pintor (Painter's Palette) hill. Its hillside cemetery is a surprising sight with a picturesque backdrop, but the friendly village has more to offer, with decent accommodations and a winery.

Part of a chain that ran from Lima to Buenos Aires during viceregal times, **Posta de Hornillos** (admission AR$10; ⊙9am-6pm) is a beautifully restored staging post 11km south of Tilcara. The interesting exhibits include leather suitcases, some impressively fierce swords and a fine 19th-century carriage.

Uquía

📲03887 / POP 500 / ELEV 2818M

It's not often that you imagine the heavenly host armed with muzzle-loading weapons, but in this roadside village's picturesque 17th-century **church** (admission by donation; ⊙10am-noon & 2-4pm) that's just what you see. A restored collection of Cuzco-school paintings – the *ángeles arcabuceros* (arquebus-wielding angels) – features Gabriel, Uriel et al putting their trust in God but keeping their powder dry. There's also a gilt altarpiece with fine painted panels. Follow the road uphill past the church, keep going past the cemetery, and you'll reach the Quebrada de las Señoritas and beautiful orange rock formations.

To eat, head three blocks uphill and turn left. **Cerro La Señorita** (Viltipoco s/n; mains

Quebrada de Humahuaca

The tortured rockscapes and palette of mineral colors that changes through the day make this arid valley a highlight of the northwest. Exploring the indigenous villages and towns strung along it is a delight.

Iruya

A long, rickety drive over a spectacular mountain pass, this remote village preserves a traditional and indigenous feel. Surrounded by imposing cliffs and mountains, it's a place whose slow pace obliges you to step off the frenzied wheel for a day or three (p259).

Purmamarca

This small town is dominated by its surrounding crags, which feature some of the valley's most vibrant mineral colorings. The focus of things here is the great artisan market on the square (p251).

Tilcara

A range of excellent small hotels, stunning landscapes, excursions and the cactus-studded ruins of an indigenous fortress make this a favorite base in the Quebrada (p252).

Humahuaca

The valley's largest town has an authentic feel and makes a good base for the region. Picturesque cobbled streets, fair-trade handcrafts and typical northwestern dishes, such as *locro* or llama stew are highlights (p258).

Uquía

This village has the region's standout church, a beautiful 17th-century structure whose interior famously features paintings of the main angels packing muzzle-loading weaponry (p255).

Clockwise from top left
1. Iruya 2. Market, Purmamarca
3. Pucará (p252), Tilcara 4. Local fabrics

2

3

AR$85-140; ⊙8am-9pm) ✎ is a bastion of delicious home cooking and baking, all using fresh produce from the garden, which the small dining area overlooks.

Humahuaca

📞 03887 / POP 8000 / ELEV 2989M

The Quebrada de Humahuaca's largest settlement is also its most handsome, with atmospheric cobblestoned streets, adobe houses and quaint plazas. You can feel the nearby puna here, with chilly nights, sparse air and a quiet indigenous population. Humahuaca is less altered by tourism than the towns further south, though there are good handicrafts shops, and folk musicians strum and sing in the restaurants.

◉ Sights & Activities

Built in 1641, Humahuaca's **Iglesia de la Candelaria** faces Plaza Gómez. Nearby, the lovably knobbly **cabildo** (Plaza Gómez) is famous for its clock tower, where a life-size figure of San Francisco Solano emerges at noon to deliver a benediction. From the plaza, a staircase climbs to the rather vulgar **Monumento a la Independencia**.

★**Serranía de Hornocal**　　　MOUNTAIN
Twenty-five kilometers east of Humahuaca, this jagged row of rock 'teeth' offers utterly spectacular colors. Tours run here but it's driveable in a normal car with care. It's prettiest from 4pm onward, when the western sun brings out vivid hues. Turn left straight after crossing the bridge and follow this spectacular road (veer left 3km along for a short stretch of better road), which climbs to a 4000m pass. Here, head right for 1.7km to the viewpoint, near a phone mast.

🎊 Festivals & Events

Humahuaca observes February 2 as the day of its patron, the **Virgen de Candelaria**.

🛏 Sleeping

The boutique hotel boom hasn't yet hit Humahuaca, which keeps it real with cheap family-run accommodations and budget hotels. Prices rise for Carnaval and drop outside of summer.

★**La Humahuacasa**　　　HOSTEL $
(📞0388-15-412-0868; www.humahuacasa.com.ar; Buenos Aires 740; dm/d US$15/50; 🖂) Artistic, superwelcoming and personable, this is

central and offers appealingly cozy dorms around a small patio. It's an involved, social place with a decent kitchen and a good vibe. Everything is very clean and well run. There's one private room – an en suite double.

★**Hostal La Soñada**　　　GUESTHOUSE $
(📞03887-421228; www.hostallasoniada.com; San Martín s/n; d/q US$50/70; @🖂) Just across the tracks from the center, this is run by a kindly local couple and features eight spotless rooms with colorful bedspreads and good bathrooms. Rooms surround a pretty courtyard. Breakfast is served in the attractive common area, and guests are made to feel very welcome.

Hostal El Coquena　　　HOTEL $
(📞0388-15-480-0384; hostalelcoquena@hotmail.com; Tres Sargentos s/n; r US$60; 🖂) Just across the bridge from the center, this is quiet and cordially run by a welcoming couple. It's attractively spacious, with plenty of room to move in the common area, wide covered gallery, sizable rooms and very ample bathrooms. Breakfast is tasty, and there's a kitchen guests can use. A good deal and, though not luxurious, Humahuaca's best hotel.

El Sol　　　HOSTEL $
(📞03887-421466; www.elsolhosteldehumahuaca.com; Barrio Milagrosa s/n; dm US$15, d with/without bathroom US$65/40; @🖂) In a peaceful location, signposted 800m across the river bridge, this appealing adobe hostel has a variety of quirky dorm rooms with lockers, and really pretty doubles (size varies substantially) under traditional cane ceilings. Some dorms are cramped, but the tranquillity makes up for it. Kitchen use and breakfast are included, and there are HI discounts.

Posada La Churita　　　GUESTHOUSE $
(📞03887-421055; Buenos Aires 456; r per person US$15) Run by warm-hearted and motherly Olga, this is one of a few unheated cheapies on this street. In theory the rooms – spick and span, with individual beds – are dorms, but you may well get one to yourself. Shared bathrooms are clean and the hot water's reliable. Guests have use of the kitchen and a common area.

　　Also runs a sister establishment that offers OK rooms with bathroom and parking.

Hostería Naty　　　GUESTHOUSE $
(📞03887-421022; www.hosterianaty.com.ar; Buenos Aires 488; s/d US$33/39; 🖂) In the heart

of town, this has friendly management and dark, simple but comfortable rooms of varying shapes and sizes at a fair price. The ones around the outside patio are quieter. Breakfast is included and there's parking round the back. The owners are good sources of information on what to see and do around town.

Eating & Drinking

Most places offer a very competitive lunchtime set meal for AR$60 to AR$90.

Aisito NORTHWEST ARGENTINE $
(Buenos Aires 435; mains AR$50-90; ⊙11am-3pm & 7-11pm) Warmly decorated and blessed with caring service, this is a pleasing option for well-priced local cuisine. Tasty baked empanadas take their place alongside well-blended stir-fries and succulent llama. There's excellent live music at weekends, and nightly in summer.

Mikunayoc NORTHWEST ARGENTINE $
(cnr Corrientes & Tucumán; mains AR$50-110; ⊙11am-3:30pm) The wide-ranging menu here includes several interesting llama dishes, cordial service and a range of empanadas with intriguing fillings. The salads are also a good bet. It's a pleasant, colorful place so you can forgive the odd lapses.

Pacha Manka NORTHWEST ARGENTINE $$
(Buenos Aires 457; mains AR$80-160; ⊙11:30am-3pm & 7pm-midnight; ✎) One of the town's better restaurants, this has a cozy atmosphere and a range of traditional cuisine pepped up with a few innovations. There are some very appealing flavors here – the llama pickled in wine and onion is excellent, and several mains come with an pleasing medley of stir-fried vegetables.

Shopping

The handicrafts market, near the defunct train station, has woolen goods, souvenirs and atmosphere. Near the plaza, **Manos Andinas** (Buenos Aires 401; ⊙8am-noon & 3:30-8pm) ✎ sells fair-trade *artesanía*.

Information

The **tourist office** (Plaza Gómez s/n; ⊙7am-9pm Mon-Fri, 9am-9pm Sat & Sun) is in the *cabildo* (municipal building); there's an ATM also on Plaza Gómez. The tourist office on the highway is shut, but young rascals outside sell pamphlets that the other office gives out for free.

Getting There & Away

The **bus terminal** (cnr Belgrano & Entre Ríos) is three blocks south of the plaza. There are regular buses to Salta (AR$148, 4½ hours), Jujuy (AR$66, 2¼ hours) and La Quiaca (AR$60, two to three hours). There are three to four daily buses to Iruya (AR$60, three hours).

Iruya

☎03887 / POP 1100 / ELEV 2780M

There's something magical about Iruya, a remote village just 46km from the main road but a world away in other respects. It makes a great destination for a few days for proper appreciation of the Quebrada de Humahuaca region away from the highway. There's some epic hiking around the town.

The journey is worthwhile in itself. Turning off RN 9, 26km north of Humahuaca, the *ripio* road ascends to a spectacular 4000m pass at the Jujuy–Salta provincial boundary. Here, there's a massive *apacheta* (travelers' cairn). Plastic bottles are from liquid offerings to Pachamama.

You then wind down a spectacular valley and eventually reach Iruya, home to a pretty yellow-and-blue church, steep streets, adobe houses and breathtaking mountainscapes (with soaring condors). It's an indigenous community with fairly traditional values, so respect is called for.

There's a bank with ATM, gas station and internet places.

Activities

Hiking and learning about local culture are two major attractions, and it's easy to combine them with walks to indigenous communities such as San Isidro (two hours) or San Juan (four hours). Both have appealing overnighting possibilities with local families. Guides are available in Iruya for these and longer treks.

Sleeping

There are many cheap accommodations in people's homes, costing around US$5 per person in a private room.

Milmahuasi HOSTEL $
(☎0387-15-445-7994; www.milmahuasi.com; Salta s/n; dm/s/d US$16/42/72; @☎) ✎ This hostel and guesthouse is brilliantly run by people with a real passion for Iruya. Well-traveled Víctor can explain anything from the best hikes to the local geology: ask about the wi-fi project. Both dorms and private rooms are

spotless and rustically attractive, with great, comfortable mattresses. Good breakfast is included, and evening vegetarian specials are offered, along with chats on the cultural background. HI discount.

Hostería Iruya　　　　　　　　HOTEL **$$**
(📞 03887-482002; www.hoteliruya.com; San Martín 641; s/d US$82/109, with view US$100/117; 🛜) At the top of the town, this place has simple, light white rooms with wide beds, a spacious common area and a picturesque stone terrace with memorable views. It's worth the extra cash for the big-windowed rooms with valley vistas. There's a decent restaurant.

✕ Eating

Several simple eateries serve local cuisine.

★ Comedor Iruya　　NORTHWEST ARGENTINE **$**
(Comedor Tina; 📞 0388-15-404-3606; mains AR$50-60; ⏱ 11am-4pm & 8pm-midnight Mon, Tue, Thu & Fri, 11am-4pm & 10:15pm-midnight Wed, Sat & Sun) By far the best place to eat in town is this local favorite on the road into town just before the gas station. Genial Juan and Tina serve delicious home-style meat and salad dishes in a cozy atmosphere. It's an absolute bargain. If they've just baked empanadas, grab as many as you can eat.

🛈 BOLIVIA VIA LA QUIACA

From La Quiaca to Villazón, Bolivia, walk or take a taxi to the bridge, then clear immigration (open 24 hours). Bolivia is much nicer than Villazón promises, so head past the cut-price stalls and straight to the bus terminal or train station. Cheap but reliable accommodations are near the bus terminal and plaza if you need. Buses and minibuses head to Tupiza (1½ hours), La Paz (20 hours) and elsewhere. The train station (see www.fca.com.bo for timetables) is 1.5km north of the border, and serves Tupiza (three hours), Uyuni (six hours) and beyond. Bolivia is one hour behind northern Argentina. For a quick Villazón visit, clear Argentine immigration but don't get stamped into Bolivia (technically illegal but nobody minds). La Quiaca has a **Bolivian consulate** (📞 03885-422283; www.consuladoboliviano.com.ar; 9 de Julio 100; ⏱ 7am-6:30pm Mon-Fri).

🛈 Getting There & Away

Buses from Humahuaca (AR$60, three hours) leave three to four times daily; there is also service from Tilcara (AR$80, four hours) and Jujuy (AR$100, five hours).

The *ripio* road is often impassable in summer due to rain. You'll regularly see villagers hitchhiking – a good way to meet locals.

La Quiaca

🔁 03885 / POP 13,800 / ELEV 3442M

Truly the end of the line, La Quiaca is 5171km north of Ushuaia, and a major crossing point to Bolivia. It's a cold, windy place that has decent places to stay, but little to detain you.

After leaving the Quebrada de Humahuaca, paved RN 9 passes through **Abra Pampa**, a windy town 90km north of Humahuaca, and climbs through picturesque and typical altiplano landscapes. Look for vicuñas off main routes.

La Quiaca is divided by its defunct train tracks; most services are west of them. North of town, a bridge crosses the river to Villazón, Bolivia.

🛏 Sleeping & Eating

Hostel El Apolillo　　　　　　HOSTEL **$**
(📞 03885-422388; http://elapolillohostel.blogspot.com; Árabe Siria 146; dm/d US$15/45; 🖥🛜) ✦ This traveler's rest is conscientiously run by a cordial couple, and has a colorful patio, comfortable dorms, a good kitchen area and a very cozy en suite private room. It makes an ecological effort, with solar heating and other sustainable practices, and there's a pool table.

Copacabana Hostel　　　　GUESTHOUSE **$**
(📞 03885-423875; www.hostelcopacabana.com.ar; Pellegrini 141; r per person without bathroom US$15; 🖥🛜) Across the tracks and a block up the street with Banco de la Nación on the corner, this place decked out in pinks, reds and ochers offers small, rather sweet heated rooms with shared bathrooms and amiable staff. Ongoing renovations are constantly improving this attractive place. Handily, the staff can reserve Bolivian trains for you. HI discount.

Hostería Munay　　　　　　　HOTEL **$**
(📞 03885-423924; www.munayhotel.com.ar; Belgrano 51; s/d US$44/68; 🛜) Set back from the pedestrian street (you can still drive in), this is a decent option, with heated rooms decorated with *artesanía*. You can often negotiate a discount. It's not wonderful but has about the best hotel rooms in town.

Hotel de Turismo HOTEL $
(☎0388-423390; laquiacahotel@gmail.com; cnr Árabe Siria & San Martín; s/d US$35/50; @🛜) Long in decline but acceptable (and there are rumors of renovation), this hotel offers adequate heated rooms with parquet floors and decent bathrooms. The restaurant (mains AR$90 to AR$130) is the town's most reliable option, amid scant competition.

ⓘ Information

Change money on the Bolivian side of the border or at the bus terminal.

Information Kiosk (Av España s/n; ⊗10am-1pm & 4-8pm) Run by a hostel, this offers decent information opposite the bus terminal.

ⓘ Getting There & Away

The chaotic **bus terminal** (cnr Belgrano & España) has frequent connections to Jujuy (AR$110, four to five hours), Salta (AR$240, 7½ hours) and (good-value) Buenos Aires (AR$1200, 24 to 28 hours). There is no transportation to Bolivia, but a few Argentine long-distance buses leave directly from the bus station over the border in Villazón.

Yavi

☎03885 / POP 200 / ELEV 3440M

Picturesque, indigenous Yavi, 16km east of La Quiaca on a good road, is a great detour and a lazy little hideaway, with the tumble-down romanticism of its adobe-lined streets and two fascinating colonial-era buildings. There's no phone signal so relaxation is easy.

◉ Sights & Activities

Local walks can take you to even smaller, rural Yavi Chico or along the river to see cave paintings. A longer excursion heads to pretty Laguna Colorada.

★**Iglesia de San Francisco de Asís** CHURCH
(Marqués Campero s/n; admission by donation; ⊗9am-1pm & 2-6pm) Built by the local marquis in the late 17th century, Yavi's intriguing church – one of northern Argentina's most fascinating – preserves stunning altarpieces in sober baroque style, covered in gold leaf and adorned with excellent paintings and sculptures, mostly from the Cuzco school. The translucent onyx windows also stand out.

Casa del Marqués Campero MUSEUM
(Museo Histórico Provincial; Marqués Campero s/n; admission AR$10; ⊗8am-1pm & 2-6:30pm) Alongside the house of the marquis who

built Yavi's church in the late 17th century is a museum. It displays beautifully restored furniture, exhibits on puna life and has a charming library.

🛏 Sleeping & Eating

As well as a decent campground by the museum, Yavi has several simple accommodations.

La Casona HOSTEL, GUESTHOUSE $
(☎03885-425148; mccalizaya@hotmail.com; cnr Pérez & San Martín; dm US$9, d with/without bathroom US$35/25; 🛜) Simple but likable, this traveler favorite has rustic rooms (with stoves for winter nights) around the back courtyard, and offers a friendly welcome. A bar and handicrafts store with gnarled wooden floors is out front. This is the most reliable spot for information.

Hostería Pachamá GUESTHOUSE $
(☎03885-423235; www.pachamahosteria.net; cnr Pérez & RN 5; s/d US$15/30; 🛜) At the entrance to town, with rather charming rooms set around an adobe courtyard, and a pretty eating area. Should have wi-fi by the time you read this.

ⓘ Getting There & Away

Five buses run Monday to Saturday from La Quiaca (AR$10, 20 minutes), leaving from the school on Av Hipólito Yrigoyen. Shared *remises* (AR$15, 20 minutes) leave from the nearby Mercado Municipal once full.

TUCUMÁN & AROUND

Though the country's second-smallest province, Tucumán has played a significant role in Argentina's story. It was here that independence was first declared, and the massive sugar industry is of great economic importance.

Tucumán city is full of heat and energy, in complete contrast to the lung-cleansing air of Tafí del Valle, up in the hills. Beyond, Argentina's most important pre-Columbian site is Quilmes, on the Cafayate road. South of Tucumán province, Santiago del Estero is a backwater with an enjoyably sleepy feel.

Tucumán

☎0381 / POP 864,700 (URBAN AREA) / ELEV 420M

Baking hot, energetic and brash, (San Miguel de) Tucumán, the cradle of Argentine independence, is the nation's fifth-largest city

Tucumán

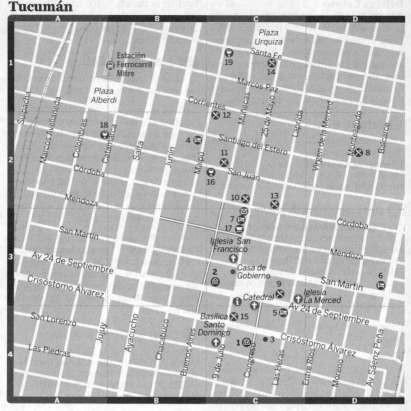

and feels like it; the metropolitan bustle can come as quite a shock compared with other more genteel northwestern capitals. You may prefer it at night, when the fumes and heat of the day have lulled, and cafes and bars come to life.

Tucumán's blue-collar feel and down-to-earthness is complemented by a lively cultural scene. There's world-class paragliding and hang gliding, too, in the hills west of town.

History

Founded in 1565 Tucumán hosted the congress that declared Argentine independence in 1816. Unlike other northwestern colonial cities, it successfully reoriented its economy after independence. At the southern end of the sugarcane zone, it was close enough to Buenos Aires to take advantage of the capital's growing market. From 1874 the railway facilitated transportation and rapid growth.

Economic crises have hit hard in the past, but sugarcane's increasing use as a fuel source keeps locals optimistic.

⊙ Sights

Casa de la Independencia   MUSEUM
(Casa Histórica; Congreso 151; adult/child AR$30/ free; ⊙10am-6pm) Unitarist lawyers and clerics declared Argentina's independence from Spain on July 9, 1816, in this late-colonial mansion. Portraits of the signatories line the walls of the original room. There's plenty of information in Spanish on the lead-up to this seismic event, and English guided tours (free) are available. There's a sound-and-light show nightly except Thursdays; entry is AR$10/5 per adult/child. Get tickets at the tourist office.

Alongside the building are areas with handicrafts stalls and stands selling traditional foods.

Tucumán

Museo Folclórico Manuel Belgrano MUSEUM
(Av 24 de Septiembre 565; ⊙9am-1pm & 5-9pm Tue-Fri, 5-9pm Sat & Sun) FREE Occupying a colonial house, this pleasant museum features a good collection of traditional gaucho gear, indigenous musical instruments (check out the armadillo *charangos*) and weavings, as well as some pottery.

☞ Tours

Tour operators offer excursions ranging from sedate city strolls to canoeing, challenging hikes and paragliding; the city has hosted the Paragliding World Cup. Most paragliding operators are based in San Javier in the hills to the west. The tourist office can supply a fuller list. One worthwhile hike is the beautiful 72km trek from Tucumán to Tafí del Valle. Many do it in three days, but it's mostly uphill, so four is more relaxed. Find waypoints on www.wikiloc.com (search for Yerba Buena-Tafí).

Montañas Tucumanas OUTDOORS
(☎0381-15-467-1860; www.montanastucumanas.com) A cordial, professional setup offering hiking, climbing, canyoning, rappelling and more.

Tucumán Parapente PARAGLIDING
(☎0381-15-444-7508; www.tucumanparapente.com.ar) Excellent tandem paragliding flights over the Yungas forests, as well as instruction. One of many operators.

Turismo del Tucumán TOUR
(☎0381-422-7636; www.turismodeltucuman.com; Crisóstomo Álvarez 360) Guided trips to spots of interest around the province, including the Yungas circuit (AR$360), Tafí del Valle (AR$450) and Quilmes (AR$690).

Carlos Castro HANG GLIDING
(☎0381-15-500-5273; pacoflight@hotmail.com) Recommended hang-gliding instructor offering tandem flights (AR$1000 including instruction, flight and hotel transfers). Best to book two or more days ahead.

✸ Festivals & Events

Celebrations of the **Día de la Independencia** (Argentina's Independence Day) on

July 9 are vigorous. *Tucumanos* also celebrate the **Batalla de Tucumán** (Battle of Tucumán) on September 24.

🛏 Sleeping

A La Gurda
HOSTEL $

(☏ 0381-497-6275; www.lagurdahostel.com.ar; Maipú 490; dm/s/d US$12/25/36, tw without bathroom US$32; ❋ @ ?) Upstairs in a lovely old house, this very pleasant hostel does lots right. It offers eight-bed dorms with lockers and OK-value private bunk rooms with aircon. There's a pool table and excellent bathroom facilities, bar service and a kitchen; everything's spotless. Management is helpful and friendly.

Casa Calchaquí
GUESTHOUSE $

(☏ 0381-425-6974; www.casacalchaqui.com; Lola Mora 92, Yerba Buena; d/q US$53/80, s/d without bathroom US$35/40; ☺ Mar-Jan; ❋ @ ? ≋ ⋔) Eight kilometers west of the center in upmarket Yerba Buena barrio, this is a welcome retreat. Comfortably rustic rooms surround a relaxing garden space with hammocks, bar service and a mini-pool. Yerba Buena has good restaurants and nightlife. Grab a taxi (AR$75) or bus 102 or 118 from opposite the bus terminal.

The street is off Av Aconquija (at 1100): Banco Galicia is on the corner. Bikes are available for hire. Ask about the guesthouse's rustic accommodations in a spectacular off-piste setting near Amaicha del Valle.

Hotel Colonial
HOTEL $

(☏ 0381-422-2738; www.hotelcolonialweb.com.ar; San Martín 36; s/d US$35/56; ❋ ? ≋) If you can handle a few dated color schemes – the milk-chocolate-brown toilets aren't looking as slick as they no doubt used to – this is a reliable and comfortable budget base. There is a touch of colonial to the decor of the public areas, and service is taken seriously. There's a pool in an annex across the street.

★ Tucumán Center
HOTEL $$

(☏ 0381-452-5555; www.tucumancenterhotel.com. ar; 25 de Mayo 230; s/d US$109/125; ❋ @ ? ≋) It's hard to fault this upmarket business-class hotel that's bang in the center. Service and facilities – including an outdoor pool and access to a proper gym just down the road – are first-rate, and the huge beds are mighty comfortable. Suites come with space to spare and a bathtub with bubbles. Excellent value.

Hotel Bicentenario
HOTEL $$

(☏ 0381-431-9119; www.hotelbicentenario.com.ar; Las Heras 21; s/d US$85/95; ❋ @ ? ≋) Sometimes you're happy to give character a miss and just want a sparklingly clean, modern hotel where the showers work, the beds are comfortable, and there's a rooftop pool, a sundeck and a gym. This is that place: it's got all the facilities in an excellent central location. Rooms are bland but good looking, and service is genuinely helpful. The price is right, too.

🍴 Eating

Tucumán is famous for its excellent eggy empanadas. The best are hand-cut: ask the tourist office for a 'Ruta de la Empanada' leaflet to track down the tastiest.

★ Mi Nueva Estancia
PARRILLA $

(Córdoba 401; mains AR$70-110; ☺ 11am-3pm & 8pm-12:30am Mon-Thu, 11am-4pm & 8pm-1:30am Fri-Sun; ?) Delicious! That's the verdict on the cuts of meat at this popular grill restaurant, but the salad bar and other menu choices also win points. Value is great here for both quality and quantity, and service is friendly and efficient.

El Portal
NORTHWEST ARGENTINE $

(Av 24 de Septiembre 351; empanadas AR$9, mains AR$60-90; ☺ noon-4pm & 8pm-midnight) Half a block east of Plaza Independencia, this rustic indoor-outdoor eatery has a tiny but perfectly formed menu, based around empanadas, *locro* and the like, supplemented by some *milanesas* and pizzas. Delicious and authentic.

Il Postino
ITALIAN $

(cnr 25 de Mayo & Córdoba; pizza & pasta AR$55-100; ☺ 7am-2am; ? ✍) Pizza and pasta are served with panache in this atmospheric brick warehouse eatery. It's popular with everyone, and you often have to wait for a table. It's worth it: the standard (of the pizza especially) is sky-high. It also serves tapas-sized snacks. There's another branch nearby at Junín 86.

Shitake
VEGETARIAN $

(9 de Julio 94; all-you-can-eat AR$70; ☺ 11:30am-3:30pm & 7:30pm-1am Mon-Sat; ? ✍) With a tasty array of vegetarian dishes in its buffet, this small, well-run spot gives value for money. Pizzas, empanadas, soy *milanesas* and much more are on offer. Drinks are extra. You can also take out, paying by weight.

La Sirio-Libanesa MIDDLE EASTERN $
(www.facebook.com/lasiriolibanesa.comidasara
bes; Maipú 575; set menu for 1/2 people AR$90/
150; ⊘11am-3pm & 8pm-midnight Mon-Sat,
11am-3:30pm Sun; 🞠) The restaurant at the
Syrian-Lebanese society offers tasty Levan-
tine cuisine that makes a welcome change
of scene. Mashed eggplant, tasty *kipe naye*
(marinated raw mincemeat) and tabbouleh
salad all feature; there are several set menus,
as well as à la carte.

★**Setimio** ARGENTINE $$
(Santa Fe 512; mains AR$120-210, tapas AR$60-
100; ⊘food 10am-4pm & 7:30pm-1:30am; 🞠)
Wall-to-wall bottles decorate this smart wine
shop and restaurant, whose menu features
Spanish-style tapas, fine salads and well-
prepared fish dishes among other tooth-
some gourmet delights. Several wines are
available by the glass, and you can pick any
of the hundreds of bottles from the shelves
for a small corkage fee.

La Leñita PARRILLA $$
(🞠0381-422-9196; San Juan 633; mains AR$105-
165; ⊘coffee & snacks 7am-1am, mains 11am-
3:30pm & 7:30pm-1am; 🞠) One of the better
parrilla restaurants in this part of the
world, this stands out for service and the
good quality of the meat. Try *picana* (rump
steak) or the delicious *mollejitas* (sweetbreads). The empanadas – you'll get one as a
welcome bite – are delicious. The staff often
sings *folklórica* music halfway through the
night.

Cilantro ARGENTINE $$
(🞠0381-430-6041; Monteagudo 541; mains
AR$110-180; ⊘noon-4pm & 8pm-2am Mon-Sat,
noon-4pm Sun; 🞠) With an understated but
handsome interior, this offers professional
service and a considered selection of pork,
fish and beef dishes with interesting sauces,
as well as a decent choice of Asian-style
stir-fries. The list of changing specials is
well worth considering: go for the delicious
tamales if they're on.

🍷 Drinking & Nightlife

From Thursday to Saturday nights, the ac-
tion is in the Abasto region, on Calle Lillo.
Follow San Lorenzo west from the town
center, and you'll hit the middle of the zone.
There are dozens of bars and nightclubs –
take your pick. Other *boliches* can be found
in Yerba Buena, 6km west of the town center.

★**Filipo** CAFE
(Mendoza 501; licuados AR$37; ⊘7am-1am Mon-
Thu, to 3am Fri & Sat, 8am-1am Sun; 🞠) Glasses
gleaming on the gantry, outdoor tables and
bow-tied waiters make this a great cafe.
Top espresso, prize-worthy apple *licuados*
(blended fruit drinks) and beer served as if
it were Bollinger are the highlights.

Plaza de Almas BAR
(www.facebook.com/catorcealmas.argentina; Maipú
791; ⊘12:30pm-3am Mon-Sat, 8pm-3am Sun; 🞠)
This intimate and engaging multilevel place
is popular with under-40 *tucumanos* and
is one of the best of the city's many combi-
nation cafe-bar-restaurant-cultural centers.
The short but interesting menu (mains
AR$40 to AR$70) offers a range of kebabs
and salads, among other international-style
choices. There's a knot of bars around it,
making it an appealing nighttime destina-
tion.

Managua BAR
(www.facebook.com/casamanagua; San Juan 1015;
⊘9pm-late Tue-Sun) There's loads of character
at this lovably bohemian bar set in a high-
ceilinged historic house, with indoor-outdoor
space and lots of comfortable places to be.
There's a separate area for concerts, where
you'll find something going on most nights of
the week. Well worth some time.

Costumbres Argentinas BAR
(www.facebook.com/costumbresargentinas.bar;
San Juan 666; ⊘9pm-2am or later) Though the
saintly devilish address seems like a con-
tradiction in terms, this unusual, popular
and welcoming bar has an arty bohemian
vibe and sometimes puts on live music. The
big two-level beer garden is the place to
be on summer nights. Simple food is also
available.

☆ Entertainment

There are several places around the center
that put on live *folklórica* music, generally
at weekends. The tourist office has a full list.

ⓘ Information

Tourist Office (🞠0381-430-3644; www.
tucumanturismo.gob.ar; Av 24 de Septiembre
484; ⊘8am-9pm Mon-Fri, 9am-9pm Sat &
Sun) On the plaza; very helpful and knowledge-
able. There's another office in the shopping
center at the bus terminal, open the same
hours.

WORTH A TRIP

DAY-TRIPPING FROM TUCUMÁN

The fertile, hilly area northwest of Tucumán is known as **Las Yungas**. It offers plenty of appealing day trips to get you out of the hot, busy city. The **tourist office** (p265) provides good information on destinations such as the reservoir of **El Cadillal**, offering camping, swimming, windsurfing and a 'ski-lift,' and the **Parque Sierra de San Javier**, a university-operated reserve offering guided walks.

To the south of Tucumán, the **Parque Nacional Campo de los Alisos** makes a tempting destination, particularly if you have your own transportation. A hilly park at the zone where the montane forest and cloud forest meets the Andes proper, it offers good walking and climbing. There's free camping and a climbers' *refugio*. The park entrance is 12km beyond Alpachiri, reachable by bus from Tucumán. The park office in Concepción, 18km before Alpachiri, might be able to help with transportation.

ⓘ Getting There & Away

AIR

Aerolíneas (☑ 0381-431-1030; www.aerolineas.com.ar; 9 de Julio 110; ⊗ 8:30am-1pm & 5-8pm Mon-Fri, 9am-12:30pm Sat) and **LAN** (☑ 0381-422-0606; www.lan.com; San Juan 426; ⊗ 9am-1pm & 5-8pm Mon-Fri) fly several times daily to Buenos Aires; Aerolíneas also flies to Córdoba.

BUS

Tucumán's **bus terminal** (☑ 0381-430-0352; Brígido Terán 350; 🛜) is a major affair, with 60 platforms and plenty of shops and services. The bus information booth is outside, by the supermarket.

Buses from Tucumán

DESTINATION	COST (AR$)	TIME (HR)
Buenos Aires	1107	15-18
Cafayate	240-270	6½
Catamarca	205	3¼-3¾
Córdoba	561	7-9
Jujuy	325	4½-5½
La Quiaca	508	9-11
La Rioja	300-345	5½
Mendoza	906	13-15
Puerto Iguazú	1395	21
Resistencia	726	11-12
Salta	290	4¼
Salvador Mazza	596	10-13
Santiago del Estero	125	2
Tafí del Valle	80	2-3

TRAIN

Tucumán is connected to Buenos Aires (via La Banda/Santiago del Estero and Rosario) twice weekly from beautiful **Estación Mitre** (☑ 0381-430-9220; www.sofse.gob.ar; Plaza Alberdi s/n). Expect long delays, poor visibility, ordinary food and questionable cleanliness. Because the trip is so cheap, it books up well in advance: think months.

At time of research, trains were leaving Buenos Aires' Retiro station at 8:47am on Monday and Friday for the 26-hour journey. From Tucumán, trains left at 4:16pm on Wednesday and 9:01pm on Saturday. The trip costs AR$70/130 in 1st class/Pullman (reclinable seats) or AR$800 for two in a sleeper. There's a bar/restaurant on board.

ⓘ Getting Around

Aeropuerto Benjamín Matienzo is 8km east of downtown. A *remise* costs around AR$100 from the town center.

Around the city, local buses clearly mark major destinations on the front. Fares cost AR$4, using coins or prepurchased card; there's a sales point near the bus terminal tourist office. Schedules at www.tucubondi.com.ar.

There are several car-rental places.

Tafí del Valle

☑ 03867 / POP 3400 / ELEV 2100M

This lovely hill town, set in a green valley with fabulous vistas of the surrounding mountains, is where Tucumán folk traditionally head to take refuge from the summer heat. Tafí makes a fine spot to hang out for a few days; it offers crisp mountain air, hiking options, many budget accommodations and a laid-back scene. There are also memorable historic ranches to stay at.

The journey from Tucumán is a spectacular one: a narrow river gorge with dense subtropical forest on all sides opens onto the reservoir-filled valley beneath the snowy peaks of the Sierra del Aconquija.

The precipitous mountain road merits a window seat.

◉ Sights & Activities

Several people around town hire out horses (look for *'alquilo caballos'* or *'cabalgatas'*) for rides in the valley. The tourist office can give you details of the **Ruta del Artesano**, which features a number of visitable handicraft workshops in and around town. Download the PDF from www.tucumanturismo.gov.ar.

Hiking in the mountains around Tafí is an attractive prospect. An easy, well-marked hike climbs **Cerro El Pelao** for views over the town. The path starts on the left as soon as you've crossed the bridge. From the same road you can walk a pleasant 10km to **El Mollar**, following the river and the reservoir, visit the menhir park (p269) and bus back.

Other hills include 3000m **Matadero**, a four- to five-hour climb; 3600m **Pabellón** (six hours); and 4500m **El Negrito**, reached from the statue of Cristo Redentor on RN 307 to Acheral. Trails are badly marked, and no maps are available; you can hire guides: ask at the tourist office.

You can walk between here and Tucumán.

Capilla La Banda   CHURCH, MUSEUM
(Av José Silva; admission AR$15; ⊙8am-6pm) This 18th-century Jesuit chapel, acquired by the Frías Silva family of Tucumán after the Jesuits' expulsion and then expanded in the 1830s, was restored to its original configuration in the 1970s. Note the escape tunnel under the altar. A small collection of funerary urns, Cuzco-school religious art, ecclesiastical vestments and period furniture is displayed.

The chapel is a short walk from downtown. Cross the river bridge and you'll see it on your left after 750m.

🛏 Sleeping

There are many choices, including a string of cabin complexes on and near the main road. Tafí packs out for January high season. Prices drop substantially the rest of the year. Unheated rooms can get distinctly chilly any time.

★Nomade Hostel   HOSTEL $
(☑0381-307-5922; www.nomadehostel.com.ar; Los Castaños s/n; dm US$18, d with/without bathroom US$48/60; @🖘) 🍃 Relaxed, colorful, enthusiastic and welcoming, this hostel is an easy 10-minute walk from the bus ter-

minal (turn right, go round the bend, veer right). It's got a lovely location with great views from the spacious garden. Rates include breakfast and tasty home-cooked dinners; the atmosphere here is excellent. It's best to book ahead in summer. Prices drop substantially off-season. HI discount.

From August to November volunteers can tend the organic garden in exchange for bed and board.

Hotel Virgen del Valle   HOTEL $
(☑03867-421016; virgendelvalle@tafidelvalle.com; Los Menhires s/n; d US$48; ❋@🖘) Just off the main drag in the heart of town, this features spacious, comfortable but darkish rooms around a small courtyard. It's not luxury, and there are a few inconveniences but it's a good deal for two at this price.

Hospedaje Celia   GUESTHOUSE $
(☑03867-421170; Belgrano 443; r per person US$15) Set back from the road 100m uphill from the church, Celia offers bright, white and comfortable rooms in a tranquil, friendly setting, with heating and private bathrooms. There are inconveniences – no in-room sockets, for example – but staff will give you an extension lead and the price is right.

★Estancia Las Carreras   ESTANCIA $$
(☑03867-421473; www.estancialascarreras.com; RP 325, Km13, Las Carreras; d US$130; 🖘) This visually striking estancia 13km from Tafí, surrounded by hills great for hiking and horseback riding, has only the lowing of cattle to disturb the tranquillity. A historic Jesuit ranch, working farm and cheese factory, it offers superb accommodations in a characterful 18th-century complex. Public areas are wonderful; there are few better bases for relaxation hereabouts.

★Estancia Los Cuartos   ESTANCIA $$
(☑0381-15-587-4230; www.estancialoscuartos.com; Critto s/n; d US$65-90; @🖘) 🍃 Oozing with character, this lovely spot with grazing llamas lies between the bus terminal and the center. Two centuries old, it feels like a museum, with venerable books lining antique shelves, and authentic rooms redolent with aged wood and woolen blankets but with great modern bathrooms. Newer rooms offer less history but remain true to the feel of the place.

Traditional cheeses are also made here. Don't confuse this with nearby Hostería Los Cuartos.

Las Tacanas
ESTANCIA $$

(☏03867-421821; www.estancialastacanas.com; Perón 372; d/q US$129/169; @☂) Impeccably preserved and decorated, this fabulous historic complex in the center of town feels like a rural retreat. It was once a Jesuit *estancia* and is a memorable place to stay. Adobe buildings, more than three centuries old, house a variety of tasteful, rustic rooms (one is especially historic) with noble furniture and beamed ceilings. Don't expect modern luxury: it's the character and history you're paying for.

Hostería Lunahuana
HOTEL $$

(☏03867-421330; www.lunahuana.com.ar; Av Miguel Critto 540; s/d US$75/124; @☂) This stylish and popular central hotel has rooms decorated with flair; some have mezzanines accessed by spiral staircases. The whole place is decked out with interesting and tasteful decorations, and service is professional and friendly.

Descanso de las Piedras
CABAÑAS $$

(☏0381-15-570-1266; www.descansodelaspiedras.com; Madre Teresa de Calcuta s/n; d/q US$95/180; ☂❄♨) ✿ Welcoming and social, these cute orange cabins and rooms surround a grassy area with solar-heated pool, vegetable garden, ducks and llamas, and a burbling stream. It's a relaxing retreat 20 minutes' walk from the center and a great option for families; cabins sleeping up to seven are available. Cross the bridge and follow the signs. It's up to 50% cheaper off-season.

Waynay Killa
HOTEL $$$

(☏0381-413-1280; www.waynaykilla.com; Ubaldini s/n; d/tr US$161/184; ✳@☂❄♨) ✿ Unobtrusively set on a hillside 2km from the center, this new hotel takes sustainability to excellent levels, generating power, treating its own sewage, and carbon filtering its kitchen. Handsome public areas make good use of natural light and local art, while rooms face the valley or the hills, either of which guarantees a great vista. Half have balconies (same rate).

Staff is excellent, as are the facilities, which include an indoor pool and spa area, and a bar-restaurant with great views from its outdoor deck. Suites with kitchenettes and further amenities were in development at last visit.

✖ Eating & Drinking

Eating options dot the central streets; other choices are out on the main road. Try the tasty local Kkechuwa artisanal beers.

Restaurante El Museo
NORTHWEST ARGENTINE $

(Av José Silva s/n; dishes AR$30-90; ☺noon-4pm) Set in the venerable adobe Jesuit chapel a kilometer from the center, this makes a very atmospheric venue to lunch on traditional home-cooked local specialties, such as *humitas,* tamales and empanadas. Just turn up and see what's cooking that day.

Rancho de Félix
NORTHWEST ARGENTINE $

(cnr Belgrano & Perón; mains AR$75-130; ☺11:30am-3pm & 8pm-midnight; ☂) This warm, thatched barn of a place is incredibly popular for lunch. Regional specialties such as *locro* and *humitas* feature heavily on the menu, but *parrilla* and pasta are also on offer. Quality is reasonably good, and prices are fair. It sometimes doesn't open evenings if things are quiet.

Flor de Sauco
CAFE $

(Av Miguel Critto s/n; cakes AR$20-50; ☺8:30am-10:30pm; ☂) This sociable and pleasant bungalow is a popular all-day spot for a coffee, snack or cake. It bills itself as a teahouse, but, though there's quite a selection, it's all teabags. Nice terrace and views. Service is willing but slow.

ⓘ Orientation

Tafí's center is a triangle of three streets. Critto is the main drag. If you turn left out of the bus terminal, you're following it into the center. Off it, Perón is the center of activity, and Belgrano climbs from Perón past the church.

ⓘ Information

Casa del Turista (☏0381-15-594-1039; www.tafidelvalle.gob.ar; Los Faroles s/n; ☺8am-10pm) On the pedestrian street.

ⓘ Getting There & Away

Tafí's **bus terminal** (☏03867-421025; Av Critto) is 400m east of the center.

Aconquija has six to nine buses a day to Tucumán (AR$80, two to three hours), Santa María (AR$95, two hours, four to five daily) and Cafayate (AR$140, 3½ hours, two to five daily) via Amaicha del Valle (AR$75) and the Quilmes ruins turnoff (AR$130).

The road from Tucumán is beautiful, and the road to Santa María, Quilmes and Cafayate is scenic, crossing the 3050m pass known as Abra del Infiernillo (Little Hell Pass).

Around Tafí del Valle

The circuit of the valley makes a beautiful drive or cycle (47km). Highlights include standout views, and the Jesuit *estancia*, hotel and cheese factory of Las Carreras (p267); guided visits are from 9am to 6pm for AR$15 including coffee; visit at 5pm to see the milking. At pretty **El Mollar**, at the other end of the valley from Tafí, you can visit the **Parque de los Menhires** (Plaza s/n, El Mollar; admission AR$15; ☺9am-7pm Tue-Fri, 2-7pm Sat & Sun) FREE on the plaza, a collection of more than 100 carved standing stones found in the surrounding area. They were produced by the Tafí culture some 2000 years ago.

Tour companies in Tafí run mediocre excursions round this circuit (costing from AR$200 to AR$300). If there's more than one of you, a *remise* will do it for less. Aconquija buses head to El Mollar (AR$10), and also to Las Carreras (AR$12). The final stop on the Las Carreras route is El Rincón, from where a 4km downhill walk will take you to El Mollar, allowing you to do the full valley circuit. Three daily buses also do the whole circuit (AR$40), but you can't get off.

Santa María

☑03838 / POP 10,800 / ELEV 1900M

Actually within Catamarca province, this fine stopover sits between Tafí del Valle and Cafayate, and is a handy base for the Quilmes ruins.

◉ Sights

The attractive plaza, nine blocks north of the bus terminal, is the center of town.

Museo Arqueológico Eric Boman
MUSEUM

(cnr Belgrano & Sarmiento; ☺9am-1pm & 6-8pm Mon-Fri, 10am-1pm & 6-8pm Sat) FREE On one corner of the plaza, Museo Arqueológico Eric Boman has a worthwhile collection of ceramics plus gold and silver grave jewelry from this important archaeological zone. Ask to see the back room, where elaborately decorated funerary urns are stored. An *artesanía* cooperative next door sells woven goods and other handicrafts at more-than-fair prices.

🛏 Sleeping

There are many places to stay in town.

Residencial Pérez GUESTHOUSE $
(☑03838-420257; hotelperez@hotmail.com; San Martín 94; s/d US$20/30) The welcoming Residencial Pérez has spotless rooms set around a viney courtyard behind a cafe near the plaza (no sign).

ℹ Information

Tourist Office (☑03838-421083; www.santamariadeyokavil.com.ar; Plaza General Belgrano s/n; ☺7am-11pm Mon-Fri, 8am-11pm Sat & Sun) A helpful tourist office located under the trees in the square.

ℹ Getting There & Away

There are several buses daily to Tucumán (AR$160, five hours) via Tafí del Valle (AR$95, two hours) and two daily to Cafayate (AR$75, two hours) via Quilmes. Several buses and minibuses a week go to Belén (AR$114, four hours). *Remises* from the terminal to the center cost AR$12.

Amaicha del Valle

☑03892 / POP 3200 / ELEV 2000M

On the main road between Tafí del Valle and Cafayate, this dusty settlement has an indigenous feel and, indeed, is famous for its **Pachamama festival** in February, which includes music, dancing and a llama sacrifice to bless the harvest. Ornate and unusual **Museo de Pachamama** (www.museopachamama.com; admission AR$50; ☺8:30am-6:30pm) combines a picturesque collection of indigenous art and artifacts with the sculpture and tapestries of the artist who designed the striking indoor-outdoor building.

Amaicha is useful for getting to the ruins at Quilmes, and has several places to stay, including hostels and campgrounds. Buses between Tafí (AR$75, 1½ hours) and Cafayate (AR$60, 1½ to 2½ hours) stop here.

Quilmes

Dating from about AD 1000, **Quilmes** (adult/child AR$30/free; ☺8am-6pm) was a complex indigenous urban settlement that occupied about 30 hectares and housed as many as 5000 people. The inhabitants survived contact with the Inca, which occurred from about AD 1480 onward, but could not outlast the siege of the Spaniards, who in 1667 deported the remaining 2000 to Buenos Aires.

Quilmes' thick walls underscore its defensive purpose, but clearly this was more than just a *pucará* (walled city). Dense construction radiates from the central nucleus. For revealing views of the extent of the ruins, climb as high as you can; there are trails on either side up to the remains of watchtowers that also offer great perspectives. Be prepared for intense sun with no shade, and a large fly population keen on exploring your facial orifices. Guides at the entrance will offer an explanation and/or tour for a tip. Don't expect accurate archaeological analysis.

Legal battles between the Diaguita community and the government mean the hotel and restaurant are long closed. In theory, the museum at the site may one day reopen: here's hoping, for it's difficult to interpret the ruins without it. Friendly folk selling local ceramics also sell cold drinks and will look after your bags; there's also a place at the main road junction that will do it, saving you lugging them.

ⓘ Getting There & Away

Buses between Cafayate and Santa María or Tafí drop off at the junction; from there it's a 5km walk or hitchhike to the ruins. Alternatively, get off at Amaicha del Valle, where a *remise* will charge around AR$160 one way to the ruins: bargain to get a decent price including waiting time. Often a few people want to go, so you can share costs.

Sebastián Pastrana (☏ 0381-15-443-6805) runs good four-hour tours from Amaicha (AR$120), departing 10:30am and 3:30pm.

A *remise* from Cafayate or Santa María is also an option and tours run from Cafayate and Tafí.

Santiago del Estero

☏ 0385 / POP 360,900 INCL LA BANDA

Placid, hot Santiago enjoys the distinction of the title 'Madre de Ciudades' (Mother of Cities), for this, founded in 1553, was the first Spanish urban settlement in what is now Argentina. Sadly, it boasts no architectural heritage from that period; nevertheless it makes a pleasant stop.

Santiagueños enjoy a nationwide reputation for folk music and, to put it politely, valuing rest and relaxation over work. Nevertheless, there's plenty of bustle around the town center, particularly in the evenings when life orbits around the pretty plaza and adjoining pedestrian streets.

◉ Sights

★ Centro Cultural del Bicentenario   MUSEUM, GALLERY

(CCB; www.ccbsantiago.com; Pellegrini 149 & Libertad s/n; adult/child 9-14yr AR$10/5; ⊗ 9am-2pm & 4-9pm Tue-Fri, 10am-1pm & 6-9pm Sat, 6-9pm Sun) This excellent cultural center is an airy, modern space housing three museums, all imaginatively displayed; the highlight is the **anthropological collection**, with a stunning array of indigenous ceramics, jewelry and flutes. Fossils of mastodons and glyptodonts, extinct creatures that somewhat resembled large armadillos, also impress. The sparsely labeled **historical museum** is attractively set around the patio of Santiago's noblest building and touches on slavery, 19th-century strife and the role of women. The top-floor **art gallery** features good temporary exhibitions.

All info is in Spanish. The downstairs cafe is a popular meeting place, does good coffee and is a pleasant air-conditioned retreat from the Santiago heat.

Parque Aguirre   PARK

This enormous eucalypt- and casuarina-filled riverside area has campgrounds, a swimming pool and a *costanera* (riverside road). It's a fine place for a wander, with plenty to keep the kids entertained, and has a few *confiterías* (cafes offering light meals) and bars. Avoid the disgracefully neglected zoo, scheduled for closure but dragging on. Those poor tigers will have someone's hand off one day.

✦ Festivals & Events

Marcha de los Bombos   PARADE

(www.marchadelosbombos.com.ar) During the last week of July, *santiagueños* celebrate the founding of the city. The centerpiece is this boisterous procession into the center by thousands of locals banging all manner of drums.

⌫ Sleeping

Hotel Avenida   HOTEL $

(☏ 0386-421-5887; www.havenida.com.ar; Pedro León Gallo 403; s/d US$27/50; ❈ ☏) You have to feel for these people: they set up a welcoming little hotel, beautifully decorated with indigenous art and right opposite the bus terminal. Then the city moved the bus terminal to the other side of town. Nevertheless, it's well worth the short walk from the center. Spotless, renovated, friendly and always improving: a great little place.

Santiago del Estero

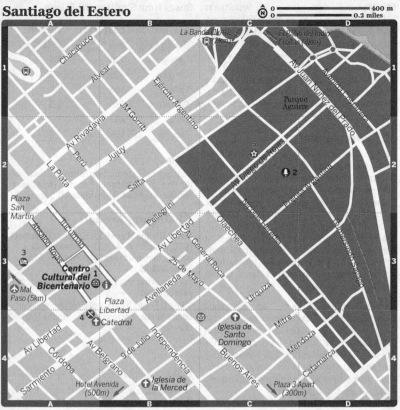

★ **Altos del Estero** HOTEL **$$**
(☎0385-422-7718; www.hotelaltosdelestero.com;
Salta 40; s/d US$60/80; ✹@🛜➤) Converted
from a car park, ensuring plenty of space
in a central location, this modern offering
is cool and pleasant, with helpful service.
Its inviting rooms offer significant value;
many have street-side or pool-side balco-
nies, decked out in soft contemporary beiges
and browns. The pool is decent, and price
includes parking.

Plaza 3 Apart APARTMENT **$$**
(www.plaza3apart.com.ar; Buenos Aires 778; apt
d/f US$100/148; ✹@🛜🛁) An excellent op-
tion for families, this large apartment hotel
offers suites with fully equipped kitchens,
dining-living areas and two bedrooms.
There are often over-the-counter discounts
offered. Facilities include spa and gym.

🍴 Eating & Drinking

Head to Roca between Salta and Libertad
for a selection of popular cafes, bars and
modish salon restaurants. This is the main
eating and drinking area.

Mía Mamma ARGENTINE $$
(24 de Septiembre 15; mains AR$75-130; ⊙noon-3pm & 9pm-12:15am; 🐟) Tucked away but on the plaza, this is a discreet and reliable restaurant with well-dressed waiters who see to your every need. There's a salad bar with plenty of vegetables and a wide choice of food that includes enormous *parrilla* options as well as tasty *arroz a la valenciana* (paella).

☆ Entertainment

El Patio del Indio Froilán TRADITIONAL MUSIC
(www.elindiofroilan.com.ar; Av Libertador Norte s/n, Barrio Boca del Tigre; ⊙Sun) For more than 40 years now, indigenous local hero Froilán González has been making drums from the trunks of the ceibo tree. They are used by some of the biggest names in Latin music. On Sundays, locals and visitors gather at this open space and workshop from early afternoon to eat empanadas, investigate drum-making and listen and dance to live music. Great scenes.

La Casa del Folclorista TRADITIONAL MUSIC
(www.facebook.com/lacasadelfolcloristasde; Av Diego de Rojas s/n; ⊙9pm-1am daily, noon-3pm Sat & Sun) On the way to the riverfront, this big barn of a *peña* has live folk bands Friday and Saturday (AR$50 cover) and cheap *parrilla* and empanadas any time. The music kicks off around 11pm.

ⓘ Information

Tourist Office (☑0385-421-3253; www.turismosantiago.gob.ar; Libertad 417; ⊙7am-9pm Mon-Fri, 10am-1pm & 5-8pm Sat, 10am-1pm Sun) On the plaza. Also opens Sunday afternoons from June to August.

ⓘ Getting There & Away

AIR

Aerolíneas (☑0385-422-4333; www.aerolineas.com.ar; 24 de Septiembre 547; ⊙8:30am-noon & 5-8pm Mon-Fri, 9am-noon Sat) flies daily to Buenos Aires.

BUS

Santiago's swish **bus terminal** (☑0385-422-7091; www.tosde.com.ar; Chacabuco 550) is six blocks northwest of Plaza Libertad. For Salta and Catamarca, there are better connections via Tucumán. Bus 20 (AR$3.50) heads into town, but it's only AR$16 in a taxi.

Buses from Santiago del Estero

DESTINATION	COST (AR$)	TIME (HR)
Buenos Aires	960	12-15
Catamarca	220	4½
Córdoba	409	5-6
La Rioja	505	7-8
Resistencia	586	8-9
Salta	445	7
Tucumán	125	2

TRAIN

Santiago del Estero's twin town La Banda is on the **line** (p266) between Tucumán (four hours) and Buenos Aires' Retiro station (23 hours).

ⓘ Getting Around

Buses 115 and 119 (AR$3.50) go to the **airport** (SDE; ☑0385-434-3651; Av Madre de Ciudades), 6km northwest of downtown. A taxi costs AR$40.

A new urban train links Santiago's bus terminal with La Banda.

Bus 117 does a circuit of Santiago's center before heading across the river to the train station.

CATAMARCA & LA RIOJA

Comparatively little-visited by travelers, these provinces are wonderful fun to explore, and are rich in scenery and tradition. Both were home to important pre-Columbian cultures and consequently the region contains many important archaeological sites. The provinces rise westward into the Andes, with some of the country's most spectacular highland scenery accessible by tour or 4WD: it's an utterly memorable landscape.

Catamarca

☑0383 / POP 200,100 / ELEV 530M

Vibrant Catamarca has a completely different feel to the other towns of this size within the region. San Fernando del Valle de Catamarca, to give the city its full name, has a lovely central plaza filled with robust jacaranda, araucaria, citrus and palm trees, and streets dotted with fine buildings. A few blocks west, Parque Navarro's huge eucalypts scent the air and are backed by the spectacular sierra beyond.

Catamarca

SALTA & THE ANDEAN NORTHWEST CATAMARCA

◉ Sights

Sights outside of town easily accessible by bus include the grotto where the town's Virgin was found, a reservoir, indigenous ruins and the picturesque foothills around Villa Las Pirquitas. The tourist office will explain them all and show you where to get the bus.

★ Museo Arqueológico Adán
Quiroga   MUSEUM
(Sarmiento 450; ⊙7:30am-1pm & 3:30-9pm Mon-Fri, 10am-7pm Sat & Sun) FREE This fine archaeological museum displays a superb collection of pre-Columbian ceramics from several different cultures and eras. Some pieces – particularly the black Aguada ceramics with their incised, stylized animal decoration – are of truly remarkable quality. Also present are a couple of mummies found at 5000m, a spooky shrunken head from the Amazon, and trays used to snort lines of ground

tobacco. There's also a colonial and religious section. Closed weekends in January.

Catedral Basílica de Nuestra Señora del Valle
CATHEDRAL

(Plaza 25 de Mayo; ⊘6am-9:30pm) This 19th-century cathedral shelters the Virgen del Valle, patron of Catamarca and one of northern Argentina's most venerated images. Her back is to the church: you can get a look at her face by ascending to the Camarín, a chapel accessed down the side of the building, decorated with stained-glass panels telling her story. On Av República round the corner, a slick new museum is only of interest to serious devotees of the Virgin.

👉 Tours

Alta Catamarca
DRIVING TOUR

(☑0383-443-0333; www.altacatamarca.tur.ar; Esquiú 433) A well-run agency offering tours of the sights close to the city (AR$315), as well as longer excursions to the attractions in the west of the province, including Belén, the Ruta de Adobe, the Seismiles, Antofagasta de la Sierra and the surrounding puna. A five-day, four-night excursion costs AR$9900 per person for two, or AR$7800 for four.

🎊 Festivals & Events

Fiesta de Nuestra Señora del Valle
RELIGIOUS

The Fiesta de Nuestra Señora del Valle takes place for two weeks after Easter, as hordes of pilgrims come to honor the Virgen del Valle. On her saint's day, December 8, she is similarly feted.

Fiesta Nacional del Poncho
CULTURAL

(www.facebook.com/fiestadelponcho; ⊘mid-Jul) This celebration of handicrafts and traditional Catamarca culture brings a huge artisanal market, plenty of folkloric performers and an excellent atmosphere.

🛏 Sleeping

There's a wide selection of reliable but rather mediocre midrange hotels on Sarmiento just north of the plaza.

Residencial Tucumán
GUESTHOUSE $

(☑0383-442-2209; Tucumán 1040; s/d US$30/40; ❄🅗) This well-run, immaculately presented *residencial* (budget hotel) has comfortable, spotless rooms, is excellent value and is about a one-minute walk from the bus terminal. There are other options nearby if it's full.

Puna Hostel
HOSTEL $

(☑0383-442-5296; www.facebook.com/punahostal; San Martín 152; dm/tw US$10/25; 🅗) It's a cheap sleep at this simple central hostel, but they sardine 'em into the dorms, with not much room to move between bunks: stuffy on hot days. It's a friendly place, though, with a back garden and kitchen.

★ Hotel Casino Catamarca
HOTEL $$

(☑0383-443-2928; www.hotelcasinocatamarca.com; Esquiú 151; r studio/standard/superior US$97/114/151; ❄@🅗☲) There's space to spare at this peaceful but central hotel, which features handsome modern design and bags of facilities. Rooms are more than ample. Some have balconies; superiors add minibar, king-size beds and hydromassage tubs. White sheets contrast with wooden floors. There's a restaurant, decent gym, small spa complex, and a cracking long pool and lawn. And a casino, of course.

🍴 Eating & Drinking

The main nighttime action is in a zone about 2km west of the center on and around Av Galindez.

Caravati
CAFE $

(Sarmiento 683; dishes AR$70-120; ⊘8am-3pm & 6pm-2am; 🅗) The most inviting of the plaza's terraces, this is named after the Italian architect who designed much of central Catamarca, including the cathedral alongside. The handsome interior is popular for a good line in pizzas, sandwiches and more substantial dishes, including a worthwhile weekday lunch. Service can be very poor.

La Cueva del Santo
TAPAS, SPANISH $$

(☑0383-422-6249; www.facebook.com/lacueva.delsanto; Av República 1162; pintxos AR$16-50, dishes AR$60-110; ⊘9pm-1am Tue-Sat, coffee 8:30-11:30am Mon-Fri; 🅗) The patchy Catamarca dining scene is given a real boost by this sweet spot opposite the striking 19th-century hospital. It deals in authentic Spanish fare: the highlight are delicious Basque-style cold and hot *pintxos* (canapetype tapas). It's a sociable, fun experience. Operates reduced hours in summer.

Sopra Tutto
ITALIAN $$

(☑0383-445-2114; Rivadavia 404; mains AR$70-140; ⊘9pm-midnight Tue-Sat) Really excellent homemade pasta, beautifully presented and flavorsome, is produced in this warmly run, cozy corner trattoria that doubles as a pasta shop during the day. Service by the owners

THE WILD NORTHWEST

If you like getting off the beaten track, you're sure to appreciate out-of-the-way Antofagasta de la Sierra in the far northwest of Catamarca province, 300km beyond Belén. This puna (Andean highlands) village sits at 3320m amid spectacular landscape.

Driving yourself or by tour from Belén or Catamarca you can take in other sights in the area: the spectacular pumice fields of Campo de Piedra Pomez, remote volcanoes, the salt flats and hamlet of Antofalla, and flamingo-stocked lakes.

It's particularly worth visiting in early March for the livestock- and traditional culture-based Fiesta de la Puna. There are accommodations in family homes and a couple of guesthouses, including **Hostería de Antofagasta** (☑03835-410679; Principal s/n, Antofagasta de la Sierra; s/d US$18/33). It's freezing in winter. Buses run here from Catamarca via Belén at 6:15am Wednesdays and Fridays (AR$150, 12 to 15 hours), returning at 10am on Mondays and Fridays.

is attentive, and there's an authentic feel of Italian family cooking, pepped up with some modern flair.

🛍 Shopping

Catamarca enthusiastically promotes its fine natural products; the region is well known for wines, olive oil, walnuts, jams and conserves. There are several shops stocking these along Sarmiento and Rivadavia near the plaza.

Mercado Artesanal y Fábrica de Alfombras HANDICRAFTS
(www.artesaniascatamarca.gob.ar; Av Virgen del Valle 945; ☺7am-1pm & 3-9pm Mon-Fri, 8am-8pm Sat, 8am-2pm Sun) For Catamarca's characteristic hand-tied rugs, visit this artisans market, which also sells ponchos, blankets, jewelry, red onyx sculptures, musical instruments and basketry. Adjacent is a carpet-weaving workshop, where they'll happily show you around for free. It's only open Monday to Friday morning but is scheduled for a refit, aimed at making it a major attraction.

ℹ Information

Municipal Tourist Office (Sarmiento 620; ☺8am-9:30pm) By the cathedral.
Provincial Tourist Office (☑0383-443-7791; www.turismocatamarca.gob.ar; cnr Rivadavia & República; ☺9am-9pm) Desk in a shopping arcade on a corner of the plaza.

ℹ Getting There & Around

AIR
Aerolíneas (☑0383-442-4460; www.aerolineas.com.ar; Sarmiento 589; ☺8am-1pm & 6-9pm Mon-Fri, 9am-1pm Sat) has six weekly flights from Buenos Aires to **Aeropuerto Felipe**

Varela (☑0383-443-0080), 17km east of town on RP 33. It's AR$160 in a *remise* to the center.

BUS
Catamarca's spruce **bus terminal** (☑0383-442-3415; Av Güemes 850) includes a shopping complex and cinema. There are services around the province and across the country, including to Tucumán (AR$185, 3¾ hours), La Rioja (AR$138, two hours) and Buenos Aires (AR$980, 14 to 16 hours).

Belén

☑03835 / POP 12,300 / ELEV 1250M

Slow-paced Belén, a stop on RN 40, feels like, and is, a long way from anywhere, and will appeal to travelers who like things small-scale and friendly. It's one of the best places to buy woven goods, particularly ponchos. There are many *teleras* (textile workshops) around town, turning out their handwoven wares made from llama, sheep and alpaca wool. The intriguing nearby ruins of El Shincal are another reason to visit.

👁 Sights

Museo Cóndor Huasi MUSEUM
(cnr Belgrano & San Martín; admission AR$5; ☺8am-1pm & 4-7pm Mon-Fri) Upstairs at the end of a shopping arcade at a corner of the plaza, this museum has a good archaeological collection, with a range of ceramics from different eras of settlement in the region.

Arañitas Hilanderas TEXTILE WORKSHOP
(Av Virgen de Belén s/n; ☺9am-7pm Mon-Fri, 9am-6pm Sat) FREE This cooperative is a good place to see weavers at work and buy their goods. Follow Belgrano past the Hotel Belén to find it.

Rua Chaky TEXTILE WORKSHOP

(☑ 03835-461068; ruachaky@hotmail.com; Casa 28, Barrio 17 de Agosto; ☺ 7am-10pm) 🏷 FREE Drop by any time to this family home in a pretty barrio to watch shawls and ponchos being made in the traditional manner on the loom. They've been weaving for five generations and will explain about the natural dyes they use. It's on the other side of the main road from town, a kilometer and a bit from the center.

👉 Tours

★ Chaku Aventuras TOUR

(☑ 03835-463976; www.chakuaventuras.com.ar; Belgrano 607; 2-/3-day tours US$280/430) This well-run setup does excellent, memorable excursions into the west and northwestern highlands of the province. A two-day trip takes in the Ruta del Adobe, the Termas de Fiambalá and the mighty mountains near the Chilean border; a three-day trip heads northwest to Antofagasta and the spectacular puna scenery in that region. Other options and tailored trips are available.

🛏 Sleeping & Eating

Look out for local specialties *jigote* (reminiscent of moussaka or lasagna) and *mote* (stewed corn paste with pork bits).

★ Hotel Belén HOTEL $

(☑ 03835-461501; www.belencat.com.ar; cnr Belgrano & Cubas; s/d US$45/51, s/d superior US$62/70; ❄ @ 🛜 🏊) A surprising presence in town, this stylish hotel has dark, comfortable rooms featuring exposed rock bathrooms, indigenous art, an archaeological collection and very comfortable beds. If you can ignore a few creaks and quirks – sound travels way too easily between bathrooms, service is patchy and not everything works all the time – it's a very characterful stay at a decent price.

Freddy Hostal GUESTHOUSE $

(☑ 03835-461230; justi05@hotmail.com.ar; Av Calchaquí 461; s/d/tr/q US$20/28/35/45; ❄ 🛜) One of a handful of cheap places on the main road through town, this is run by an hospitable couple and features simple but appealing rustic rooms around a patio with a cactus garden. Air-con costs a little extra.

1900 ARGENTINE $

(☑ 03835-461100; Belgrano 391; mains AR$60-120; ☺ 12:30-3pm & 9pm-1:30am Tue-Sat) Beyond-the-call service is the key to this highly enjoyable restaurant a block down from the plaza. It's very popular, but it hates to turn people away, so a Tetris-like reshuffling of tables is a constant feature. Prices are more than fair, and there are a number of large platters designed to be shared. Well-mixed salads and juicy brochettes are highlights.

🛍 Shopping

A marquee off the plaza is home to a number of *artesanía* stalls selling ponchos, camelid-wool clothing and foot-trodden local wine. For more upmarket woven goods, head to the workshops around town or shops around the center. **Familia Avar Saracho** (☑ 03835-461091; avarsaracho@hotmail.com; Roca 144; ☺ 10am-11pm) has reasonable prices and arranges shipping.

ℹ Information

There's a bank at the corner of General Paz and Lavalle, near the tourist office.

Tourist Office (☑ 03835-461304; turismo belencat@gmail.com; General Paz 168; ☺ 6am-1pm & 2-8pm) Also has a small mineral exhibition. There's a booth on the plaza, too.

ℹ Getting There & Away

Belén's **bus terminal** (cnr Sarmiento & Rivadavia) is one block south and one west of the plaza. Catamarca (AR$200, four to five hours) is served several times daily. Night services run to La Rioja and Córdoba, and several weekly buses and minibuses go to Santa María (AR$110, four hours), which is a scenic journey. Five buses a week go to Tinogasta (AR$65, 3½ hours).

Londres & El Shincal

Lying 15km southwest of Belén, sleepy Londres dates from 1558, though it moved several times before returning here in 1612, and the inhabitants again fled during the Diaguita uprising of 1632. Its name (London) celebrated the marriage of the prince of Spain (later Philip II) to Mary Tudor, Queen of England, in 1554.

Seven kilometers west of Londres are the Inca ruins of **El Shincal** (admission AR$30; ☺ 8am-6:30pm). Founded in 1471, the town occupied a commanding position in the foothills of the mountains, surveying the vast valley to the south. The setting is spectacular, with fantastic views and great atmosphere. The *ushnu* (ceremonial platform) is set in the middle of a central square and is flanked by two partially restored *kallankas* (buildings of multiple or unknown function). Two hilltop platforms aligned to the rising and setting sun probably served as both lookouts and altars to the sun. The renovated museum at the entrance gives a scale model and good background in Inca and pre-Inca culture, while signboards along the way explain local plants. All information is in Spanish, though guides that congregate in the mornings may speak some English. There's a cafe-restaurant on-site.

Five to six buses Monday to Saturday run from Belén to Londres (AR$35) and the ruins. Further buses just reach Londres. A *remise* from Belén with waiting time is around AR$250.

Beyond Londres, Chilecito is 200km south in La Rioja province along RN 40, if you have transportation. The drive is a spectacular one, with the imposing Sierra Famatina to the west and Sierra de Velasco to the east. The road is excellent.

Western Catamarca

✍ 03837

Western Catamarca province is well worth exploring. The area is home to historic adobe churches; vineyards; and stunning views from the hot springs above Fiambalá, an oasis town set in an arid valley among dunes. Its spectacular mountainscapes have been favorite terrain for the Dakar rally since it moved from Africa. In the far west, a cluster of awe-inspiring 6000m-plus peaks form the planet's second-loftiest ensemble after the Everest region. The main settlements are Tinogasta and Fiambalá, 50km apart. If you don't have transportation, tours from Belén or Catamarca are the best ways to see the area.

◉ Sights & Activities

★ Ruta del Adobe   HISTORIC BUILDING
FREE The road between Tinogasta and Fiambalá is designated the 'adobe route' for its ensemble of fantastic historic buildings. These are built with thick walls of mud, straw and dung and have cane roofs supported by algarrobo beams. Buildings are signposted off the road and include former inns and little museums. This was an important trade route to Bolivia and Peru. On public transportation you can check out the Iglesia de San Pedro, at the southern entrance to Fiambalá, and the adjacent Comandancia de Armas.

Museo del Hombre   MUSEUM
(Azarelli s/n, Fiambalá; admission AR$10; ⊙ 7:30am-1:30pm & 3:30-8pm Mon-Fri, 8am-1pm & 3-8pm Sat & Sun) This interesting local museum has sections on geology and archaeology, including high-quality ceramics and two haunting Inca mummies with well-preserved funerary goods. Another room is dedicated to mountaineering, giving details of famous expeditions to the province's 14 peaks that stand above 6000m.

Termas de Fiambalá   SPRING
(Fiambalá; admission AR$50; ⊙ 7am-10pm) Lying 15km east into the mountains from Fiambalá, these thermal springs emerge from rock and cascade down the mountainside in a series of pools: the highest is around 40ºC; the cooler ones are below. The views over the desert valley are epic. It's best after 5pm when there's more shade. Weekends are rowdy. There's a campsite and various simple accommodations options here. It's AR$170 in a *remise* from Fiambalá.

★ Los Seismiles   MOUNTAIN
West of Fiambalá, the paved road winds its way up into some serious mountains, topping out at the Chilean border. It's a stunning drive, with no services apart from a white-elephant hotel halfway between Fiambalá and the frontier. Los Seismiles are the peaks above 6000m, and you'll see several of them, including Ojos del Salado (6879m), the world's highest volcano.

Even more awe-inspiring scenery is accessed via a lonely mining road that leads 90km to Monte Pissis (6793m), the Americas' third-highest peak. It's about five hours return (50km) to a viewpoint over this imposing mountain, with hauntingly beautiful blue, black and turquoise lakes in the foreground. Due to its isolation, this is best by tour – operators in Belén and Catamarca can arrange it.

⌇ Sleeping & Eating

Fiambalá has lots of simple lodgings and a hostel. Camping is possible, but beware of frequent high winds and sandstorms.

Hostería Municipal   HOTEL $
(✍ 03837-496291; Almagro s/n, Fiambalá; s/d US$25/40; ❊ 🛈) The heart of Fiambalá is this place built around an unattractive shaded courtyard. Rooms are decent, and there's a restaurant serving simple meals.

★ **Casagrande** BOUTIQUE HOTEL $$
(☎ 03837-421140; www.casagrandetour.com; Moreno 801, Tinogasta; d US$122; ❈❂☷) This standout option in Tinogasta occupies an historic adobe building that has been added to and given sublime original decorative touches by the welcoming owners. Cozy rustic rooms are traditionally built with cane ceilings; there's a beautiful Jacuzzi room and outdoor pool; and inventive meals, including excellent salads, are available. It rents sandboards and bikes.

❶ Information

Fiambalá Tourist Office (☎ 03837-496250; www.fiambala.gov.ar; Plaza Principal s/n, Fiambalá; ☺7am-9pm Mon-Fri, 8am-9pm Sat & Sun) On the plaza.

❶ Getting There & Away

There are three or more daily buses from Catamarca to Tinogasta and Fiambalá (5¾ hours, AR$125). A few weekly reach La Rioja and Córdoba. Five weekly buses link Belén and Tinogasta (AR$65, 3½ hours).

La Rioja

☎ 0380 / POP 181,000 / ELEV 500M

Encircled by the Sierra de Velasco's graceful peaks, La Rioja is quite a sight on a sunny day. And there are plenty of those: summer temperatures rise sky-high in this quiet, out-of-the-way provincial capital. It's an understated but quite charming place; even if you're on a short highlights tour, you might consider stopping off (it's halfway between Mendoza and Salta) to take a tour to Parque Nacional Talampaya and Parque Provincial Ischigualasto.

◉ Sights

La Rioja is a major devotional center, so many landmarks are ecclesiastical.

★ **Museo Folklórico** MUSEUM
(Pelagio Luna 811; admission by donation; ☺9am-1pm & 5-9pm Tue-Fri, 9am-1pm Sat & Sun) This hugely worthwhile museum is set in a wonderful early-17th-century adobe building, and has fine displays on various aspects of the region's culture. Themes include *chaya* (local La Rioja music), the Tinkunaco festival, weaving and winemaking. The informative guided tour is excellent if your Spanish is up to it.

Convento de Santo Domingo CHURCH
(cnr Pelagio Luna & Lamadrid; ☺9:30am-12:30pm & 6-8pm Mon-Fri) Built in 1623 by the Diaguita under the direction of Dominican friars, this is Argentina's oldest monastery. The date appears in the carved algarrobo door frame, also the work of Diaguita artists. There's a museum of religious art alongside.

☞ Tours

Corona del Inca TOUR
(☎ 0380-442-2142; www.coronadelinca.com.ar; Pelagio Luna 914) Offers various excursions to provincial highlights.

Runacay TOUR
(☎ 03825-470368; www.runacay.com) Offer tours around Parque Nacional Talampaya and Parque Provincial Ischigualasto, as well

---

EL TINKUNACO – CONFLICT RESOLUTION IN THE 16TH CENTURY

The fascinating and moving **El Tinkunaco** (☺noon 31 Dec) ceremony is a symbolic representation of the resolution of clashing cultures that occurred at the birth of La Rioja. When Juan Ramírez de Velasco founded the city in 1591, he blithely ignored the fact that the land was owned and farmed by the Diaguita, who naturally took exception to their territory being carved up among Spanish settlers. They rebelled in 1593, and a bloody conflict was averted by the mediation of the friar Francisco Solano, later canonized for his efforts. The Diaguita trusted the cleric and listened to his message. They agreed to down their arms on two conditions: that the Spanish *alcalde* (mayor) resign; and that his replacement be the Christ child. The Spaniards agreed and peace was made. The new mayor became known as Niño Jesús Alcalde.

The Tinkunaco (the word means 'meeting' in Quechua) commemoration commenced not long afterwards. Every year at noon on December 31, two processions – one representing the Spaniards, one the Diaguita – cross town to the Casa de Gobierno. The processions meet, and solemnly all fall to their knees before the image of the Niño Jesús Alcalde, then embrace. It's a powerful moment with its message about cultural differences and compromises.

La Rioja

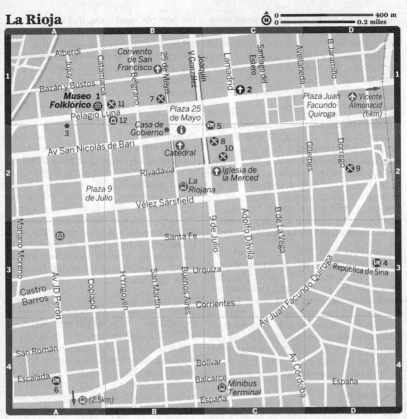

as good trips to Laguna Brava and other lofty destinations.

✱ Festivals & Events

El Tinkunaco (p278) is one of Argentina's most interesting ceremonies.

La Chaya CARNAVAL

The local variant of Carnaval. Its name, derived from a Quechua word meaning 'to get someone wet,' should give you an idea of what to expect. The musical style associated with the festival is also called *chaya*.

🛏 Sleeping

La Rioja's hotels are, with a couple of exceptions, a very mediocre bunch. Discounts are offered for cash.

Wayra Hostel HOSTEL $

(📞 0380-15-435-4140; www.wayrahostel.com.ar; Escalada 1008; dm US$11-15, d US$25-35; ❄ 🤖) Pleasant, clean and friendly, this is a well-run place with a peaceful feel despite some main-road noise. Pay the extra pesos for the downstairs dorm, which has plenty of space and is a little quieter. Private rooms are neat and decent value. The hostel picks you up for free from the bus terminal, rents out bikes and can organize paragliding and tours.

★Hotel Pucara HOTEL **$$**
(☎0380-443-7789; www.hotelpucaralarioja.com.ar; República de Siria 79; s/d US$50/77; ❄@📶) Cool and tranquil, this modern hotel has attractive, comfortable lodgings in a quiet barrio. The friendly young owners have made it a welcoming place, with stonework and traditional art decorating public areas and the five clean, dark rooms, which have decent mattresses. Though not a luxury establishment, in many ways it's La Rioja's best hotel.

Naindo Park Hotel HOTEL **$$$**
(☎0380-447-0700; www.naindoparkhotel.com; Av San Nicolás de Bari 475; s/d US$151/168; ❄@📶🏊) Just off the plaza, and dominating it assertively, what is on paper La Rioja's top hotel has good service, a fistful of facilities and prices to match. The rooms are commodious and good sized, but at last visit were in need of a refit. Still, they have original art on the walls and decent views. Hard to say it offers value though.

Eating

Regional dishes include *locro,* juicy empanadas, *chivito asado* (barbecued goat), *humitas, quesillo* (a cheese specialty) and olives. Cheap local wines are a good bargain in restaurants.

Café del Paseo CAFE **$**
(cnr Pelagio Luna & 25 de Mayo; light meals AR$60-100; ⏲7:30am-3pm & 5:30pm-1am; 📶) This is your spot on the corner of the plaza to observe local life. Executives with i-gadgets mingle with families, and tables of older men chew the fat over another slow-paced La Rioja day.

El Marqués ARGENTINE **$**
(Av San Nicolás de Bari 484; meals AR$50-80; ⏲8am-1am Mon-Sat) This simple local eatery just off the plaza puts many pricier restaurants to shame. Sandwiches, traditional local dishes, pasta, pizza, omelets and grilled meats are well prepared and fairly priced. It's something of a bargain and the fruit *licuados* are delicious, too.

★La Stanza ITALIAN **$$**
(Dorrego 164; mains AR$100-180; ⏲12:30-3pm & 8:30pm-midnight Tue-Sat, 12:30-3pm Sun) One of the best places in town, this stylish, attractive restaurant has an upbeat, surprisingly urban vibe and serves imaginative pasta dishes that are a cut above most places. Better still are the main dishes, which feature delicious and inventive portions of meat, accompanied by tasty medleys of baked vegetables. Service is helpful and there's an appealingly cheery ambience.

Orígenes ARGENTINE **$$**
(☎0380-442-8036; www.origeneslarioja.com.ar; cnr Catamarca & Pelagio Luna; mains AR$90-180; ⏲11:30am-3:30pm & 8pm-midnight; 📶) Smart and enthusiastic, this occupies a corner of an enormous, handsome 19th-century school, now turned cultural center. It draws on local traditions but brings a modern chef's expertise to bear on them. The result is excellent in many ways, including the inspiring salads, a meal in themselves, and the pretty presentation of the dishes. Prices are more than fair.

La Vieja Casona ARGENTINE **$$**
(☎0380-442-5996; www.lacasonalunch.com.ar; Rivadavia 457; mains AR$80-180; ⏲11:30am-3:30pm & 8:30pm-12:30am; 📶) Cheerfully lit and decorated, this is a cracking place with a great range of regional specialties, creative house choices and a menu of standard Argentine dishes – the *parrillada* (mixed grill including steak) here is redolent of wood smoke and of excellent standard. There's a fair selection of La Rioja wines, too, and wonderful smells from the busy kitchen.

Shopping

La Rioja is famous for weaving and silverwork that combine indigenous techniques with Spanish designs and color combinations.

Fittingly for a place named after Spain's most famous wine region, La Rioja wine has a national reputation.

Mercado Artesanal de La Rioja HANDICRAFTS
(Pelagio Luna 792; ⏲9am-12:50pm & 6-10pm Tue-Sat, 9am-12:50pm Sun) 🍃 La Rioja crafts are exhibited and sold here, as are other popular artworks at prices lower than most souvenir shops. Afternoon closing is earlier in winter.

Information

Municipal Tourist Office (Plaza 25 de Mayo; ⏲8am-1pm & 4-9pm Mon-Fri, 8am-9pm Sat & Sun) In a kiosk on the plaza.

ⓘ Getting There & Away

AIR

Aerolíneas Argentinas (☑0380-442-6307; www.aerolineas.com.ar; Belgrano 63; ☺8am-1pm & 5:30-8:30pm Mon-Fri, 8:30am-12:30pm Sat) Flies six times weekly to and from Buenos Aires.

BUS

La Rioja's **bus terminal** (Av Circunvalación s/n) is picturesquely backed by the sierra. It's 3km south from downtown.

For Chilecito, **La Riojana** (☑0380-443-5279; Buenos Aires 154; AR$150; ☺9:15am-1:15pm & 6:15-9:15pm Mon-Fri, 9:30am-1pm & 7-9pm Sat, 9:30am-12:30pm & 6-9pm Sun) minibuses run three times daily (AR$150, 2½ hours, twice Sundays), and are a little quicker than the bus. Minibuses leave from the **minibus terminal** (☑0380-446-8562; Artigas 750) seven blocks south of the plaza, though they may let you board at the office beforehand.

Buses from La Rioja

DESTINATION	COST (AR$)	TIME (HR)
Belén	162	5
Buenos Aires	985	14-17
Catamarca	138	2
Chilecito	120	3
Córdoba	400	6
Mendoza	563	8-9½
Salta	616	10
San Juan	405-429	6
Santiago del Estero	535	7-8
Tucumán	343	5½-6½

ⓘ Getting Around

Aeropuerto Vicente Almonacid (IRJ; ☑0380-446-2160) is 7km east of town on RP 5. A taxi costs around AR$120.

A cab from the bus terminal to downtown costs about AR$50. Local buses (AR$6) run between the terminal and center, including numbers 2, 6, 7 and 8.

Chilecito

☑03825 / POP 33,700 / ELEV 1080M

With a gorgeous situation among low rocky hills and sizable snowcapped peaks, Chilecito, a stop on spectacular RN 40, has several interesting things to see, including an amazing abandoned cableway leading to a mine high in the sierra. With the intense heat, its mining heritage and the slopes around town dotted with cardón cactus, Chilecito has a Wild West feel and is definitely the most appealing place to spend a few quiet days in this part of the country. It's also a base for spectacular excursions into the sierra.

◉ Sights

★**Museo del Cablecarril** MUSEUM, CABLE CAR (Av Presidente Perón s/n; admission AR$15; ☺8:30am-noon & 1-6pm) This old cable-car station documents the extraordinary engineering and mining project that created modern Chilecito at the beginning of the 20th century. The simple, picturesque museum preserves photos, tools and documents, as well as communications equipment, including an early cellphone. You'll be shown (in Spanish) the museum, then you can examine the cable-car terminus itself, where ore carts now wait silently in line. It's best in late afternoon when sun bathes the rusted metal and snowy sierras.

With a car, you can investigate the second and third cable-car stations, too. Guided tours visit the ninth and final stop of La Mejicana, high in the sierra.

The museum is on the main road at the southern entrance to town, a block south of the bus terminal.

Cristo del Portezuelo MONUMENT (Maestro s/n; ☺8am-10pm Mon-Fri, 8:30am-10pm Sat & Sun) FREE Head down Maestro from the plaza to reach this recent addition: a huge statue of Christ on a platform accessed by a 203-step ascent flanked by terraced cactus gardens. Views from the top give super perspectives over town, and local couples canoodle, secure at the savior's feet. There's a cafe, and a painfully slow funicular (AR$10) for weary legs.

Molino de San Francisco MUSEUM (Ocampo 63; admission AR$20; ☺8:30am-12:30pm & 2-6pm) Chilecito founder Don Domingo de Castro y Bazán owned this colonial flour mill, which houses an eclectic assemblage of archaeological tools, antique arms, early colonial documents, minerals, traditional wood and leather crafts, banknotes, stuffed birds, woodcuts, cellphones and paintings. It's four blocks west of the plaza.

La Riojana WINERY (☑03825-423150; www.lariojana.com.ar; La Plata 646; ☺tours 11am, noon, 1pm, 3pm & 4pm Mon-Fri,

10am, 11am & noon Sat) FREE La Riojana co-operative is the area's main wine producer, and a sizable concern; some 30 million liters a year are produced here. A good free tour shows you through the bodega – think large concrete fermentation tanks rather than rows of musty barrels – and culminates in a generous tasting. It's a block north and five west of the plaza.

Tours

Cuesta Vieja   TOURS
(📞03825-424874; www.cuestavieja.com.ar; González 467) This friendly, reliable Chilecito tour operator is an excellent choice for excursions into the sierra, to Parque Nacional Talampaya and Parque Provincial Ischigualasto, or for heading up in the air for a scenic flight.

Salir del Cráter   TOUR
(📞03825-15-679620; www.salirdelcrater.com.ar) A recommended Chilecito operator running excursions around western La Rioja province, including Parque Nacional Talampaya. Competent booking procedures and excellent guides.

Sleeping

★**Posada Nocenta Pisetta**   GUESTHOUSE $
(📞03825-498108; claudiapisetta@hotmail.com; Finca la Cuadra, off RP 12; d US$60-70, q US$95; ❄️🛜🏊) This historic country ranch makes a great place to stay, 4km from central Chilecito. It belonged to the owner's grandfather, and the fine, thick-walled adobe house offers sparely decorated chambers with antique wooden furnishings and original floorboards and tiles. All are different: there's a particularly good family suite, though only kids over 12 are admitted. The welcome is genuine: a wonderful place.

El Viejo Molino   GUESTHOUSE $
(📞03825-429445; nicorody@hotmail.com; Jamín Ocampo 64; s/d/q US$46/61/91; ❄️🛜🍴) Run with a warmly personal touch, this attractive spot overlooks a small garden next to the Molino de San Francisco museum. Modern rooms are comfortable, stylish and well equipped. There's an appealing restaurant serving pizzas and regional specialties, sierra views and a beautifully peaceful atmosphere.

Hotel Ruta 40   HOTEL $
(📞03825-422804; Libertad 68; s/d US$25/40, without bathroom US$20/35; ❄️🛜) A laid-back budget hotel a couple of blocks from the plaza, this comfortable spot offers a variety of rooms with decent enough beds and clean, spacious bathrooms. Check out a few – some look over a vine-covered patio to the hills beyond.

Hotel El Caudillo   GUESTHOUSE $
(Hostal Mary Pérez; 📞03825-423156; hostal_mp@hotmail.com; Florencio Dávila 280; s/d US$25/50; ❄️🛜) The enterprising owner is gradually remodelling and modernizing this former guesthouse, and doing rather a good job of it. Rooms are darkish and have excellent mattresses; there's also a good split-level room for groups, with kitchen access. A decent deal on a quiet street.

MAC Royal Suites   HOTEL $$$
(📞03825-422002; www.macroyalsuites.com; 19 de Febrero 361; s/d/ste US$242/363/545; ❄️@ 🛜🍴) Mimicking the color of the surrounding hills but out of place in low-rise Chilecito, this modern hotel bears the initials of the casino magnate owner. Facilities, which include indoor and outdoor pools, saunas, a cactus garden and a modern gym, are great. Rooms are stylish and spacious, with hydromassage bathtubs and elegant furniture. Still, it seems overpriced, and wifi is charged. Service, though, is warm and enthusiastic.

Eating & Drinking

★**El Rancho de Ferrito**   ARGENTINE $
(Av Pelagio Luna 647; mains AR$60-110; ⊙11am-3pm & 7-11pm Tue-Sat, 11am-3pm Sun) A block west and seven north of the plaza, this inviting local restaurant is worth every step. You've seen the menu before – except for house specialties such as *cazuela de gallina* (chicken stew: yum) and local wines – but the quality, price and authentic atmosphere make it truly excellent.

Yops   BAR
(AE Dávila 70; ⊙9:15am-2pm & 8:30pm-2am Mon-Sat) Simple but atmospheric, this bohemian spot is comfortably Chilecito's best cafe, serving fine coffee, cold beer and decent mixed drinks. Watch the locals' epic chess battles.

🛈 Information

The plaza has banks with ATMs.
Tourist Office (📞03825-429665; www.emutur.com.ar; Castro y Bazán 52; ⊙9am-10pm; 🛜) Half a block off the plaza. There's also a booth at the bus terminal.

ⓘ Getting There & Away

The **bus terminal** (Av Presidente Perón s/n; 🕾) is 1.5km south of the center. It's a spectacular trip from La Rioja (AR$120, three hours), passing the red rock formations of Los Colorados en route, with the snowcapped Sierra de Famatina in the background. There are direct services from Chilecito to further-flung destinations such as Buenos Aires. **La Riojana** (✆ 03825-424710; Maestro 61; AR$150) minibuses also do the La Rioja run a little quicker (2½ hours).

There are no buses north to Belén; to avoid the lengthy backtrack you could join a tour to El Shincal. Otherwise, there's an Andesmar bus twice a week to Tinogasta at 4am. Better connections north are envisaged.

Parque Nacional Talampaya

The spectacular rock formations and canyons of this dusty desert **national park** (✆ 03825-470356; www.parquesnacionales.gob.ar; admission foreigner/Mercosur/Argentine/car AR$120/100/70/15; ⏰ excursions 8am-5pm Oct-Feb, 8:30am-4:30pm Mar-Sep) are evidence of the erosive action of water; these days it's hard to believe that ever existed here. The sandstone cliffs are amazing, as are the distant surrounding mountainscapes. Talampaya is relatively close to fossil-rich **Parque Provincial Ischigualasto** in San Juan province, and it's easy to combine the two if you have transportation or visit with a tour.

◉ Sights & Activities

You must enter by guided visit, arranged at the visitor center. The standard 2½-hour (AR$360) trip is in a comfortable minibus and there's little walking involved; nevertheless, take water and protection from the fierce sun. For a little extra, you can extend the visit to another canyon or do the route on the roof of a truck. Other visits include further-flung valleys and other parts of the park.

Guided walks (AR$300 to AR$400) and trips on bicycles (AR$400) are also available; a more appealing way of exploring if the heat's not too intense, though you'll still likely have to pay for transportation into the park if you're on foot. There are night excursions (AR$350) when there's a full moon. Be aware that different excursions are operated by different companies, so it can be difficult to get the full information on what's available.

Cañón de Talampaya   CANYON

The focus of a visit to the park is this spectacular dry (usually) watercourse bounded by sheer sandstone cliffs. Condors soar on thermals, and guanacos, rheas and maras can be seen in the shade of algarrobo trees along the sandy canyon floor. A series of enigmatic petroglyphs carved into oxidized sandstone slabs are the first stop on the standard visit, followed by in-canyon highlights such as the Chimenea, whose impressive echo is a guaranteed hit; the Catedral formation and the clerical figure of El Monje.

Ciudad Perdida &
Cañón Arco Iris   ROCK FORMATION

In another part of the park, accessed from the road 14km before reaching the main park entrance, these impressive formations are accessed via guided 4WD tours, which wait to fill (AR$250 to AR$300; three to four hours).

SALTA & THE ANDEAN NORTHWEST PARQUE NACIONAL TALAMPAYA

WESTERN RIOJA TRIPS

The western portion of La Rioja province is fascinating, with plenty of intriguing destinations in the sierras. The towns of Chilecito and Villa Unión are launchpads for a range of excellent excursions. **Parque Nacional Talampaya** (p283) is one appealing trip, which also takes in the **Parque Provincial Ischigualasto** and (from Chilecito) crosses the picturesque Miranda pass. For some serious 4WD mountain action, head up to the abandoned mine at **La Mejicana** (4603m), an ascent that takes in some amazing scenery and a broad palette of colors, including a striking yellow river. Deeper into the sierras by the Chilean border is sizable **Laguna Brava**, a flamingo-filled lake surrounded by awesomely bleak and beautiful Andean scenery. Higher still, at 5600m, is the remote sapphire-blue crater lake of Corona del Inca, only accessible in summer.

Operators in Chilecito such as **Salir del Cráter** (p282) and **Cuesta Vieja** (p282) run these trips, which cost around US$100 to US$400 for up to four people. In Villa Unión, a good operator is **Runacay** (p278). Companies collaborate to try and put a group together.

Sendero Triásico
MUSEUM

This 'Triassic' path takes you past life-size replicas of dinosaurs whose fossilized remains have been found in the Talampaya area.

🛌 Sleeping & Eating

There's shadeless camping at the visitor center, which has decent toilets and showers. A cafe there serves meals and cold drinks.

Simple accommodations are available in Pagancillo, 29km north. A further 29km up the road, larger Villa Unión has several cabin and hotel options, some quite stylish.

❶ Information

The visitor center is just off the RP 26. Here you pay the admission and arrange guided visits. Entry is valid for two days and includes a free jaunt that introduces biological and cultural aspects of the park. Don't sweat if you miss it: you get most of this info on park tours, too.

❶ Getting There & Away

Buses from La Rioja to Pagancillo and Villa Unión (AR$110, 3½ hours) will leave you at the park entrance, from where it's only a 500m walk to the visitor center. The earliest bus (Facundo) leaves La Rioja at 7am, giving you plenty of time to make a day trip. There's a **bus** (☑ 03825-527178) between Villa Unión, 58km up the road, and Chilecito (AR$125, three hours) over the spectacular Miranda Pass. It leaves Villa Unión at 3pm on Mondays, Thursdays and Sundays; you can make it if you cadge a lift off someone in your tour group. A Friday bus also leaves nearby Guandacol at 5pm. From Chilecito, departures are 1:30pm Monday, Wednesday and Saturday, and 1pm Friday.

If you want to see Talampaya and Ischigualasto in one day, tour operators in **La Rioja** (p278) or **Chilecito** (p283) will do it. It can be cheaper taking a *remise* from either of those or from closer Villa Unión.

Córdoba & the Central Sierras

Best Places to Eat

➡ El Bistro del Alquimista (p305)

➡ La Nieta 'e la Pancha (p294)

➡ Tono (p312)

➡ Kasbah (p302)

➡ El Paseo (p309)

Best Places to Stay

➡ 279 Boutique B&B (p305)

➡ Hotel Azur Real (p293)

➡ Hostel Rupestre (p293)

➡ Estancia La Estanzuela (p316)

➡ Hospedaje Casa Rosita (p309)

Why Go?

Argentina's second city is bursting with life. Home to not one but seven major universities, Córdoba has a young population that ensures an excellent nightlife and a healthy cultural scene. Córdoba also boasts a fascinating history, owing its architectural and cultural heritage to the Jesuits, who set up shop here when they first arrived in Argentina.

The rolling hill country out of town is dotted with places that could grab your attention for a day or a month, including five Jesuit missions that make for an easy day trip from the capital.

Adventure buffs also head to the hills where the paragliding is excellent, or to a couple of national parks that offer excellent trekking opportunities.

Further to the southwest, the Valle de Conlara and Sierras Puntanas offer a real chance to get away from the crowds and into the heart of the countryside.

When to Go
Córdoba

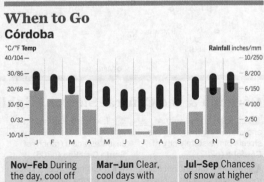

Nov–Feb During the day, cool off riverside in the Sierras. At night, hit Córdoba's bars.

Mar–Jun Clear, cool days with occasional rain – ideal for outdoor activities.

Jul–Sep Chances of snow at higher altitudes. Low rainfall makes for good trekking weather.

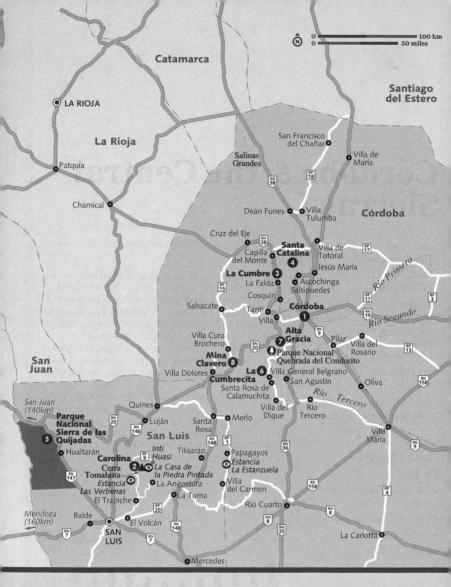

Córdoba & the Central Sierras Highlights

1 Lapping up the culture and wandering the gorgeous streets of the stately city of **Córdoba** (p287).

2 Checking out ancient caves, rock art and stunning scenery around **Carolina** (p315).

3 Getting high with the paragliding fanatics at **La Cumbre** (p301).

4 Taking a breather at the atmospheric 17th-century Jesuit *estancia* (ranch) of **Santa Catalina** (p305).

5 Breaking in your hiking boots among the surreal rock formations of **Parque Nacional Sierra de las Quijadas** (p315).

6 Mellowing out in the pedestrian-only mountain village of **La Cumbrecita** (p309).

7 Visiting Che's house in **Alta Gracia** (p304).

8 Cooling off riverside in the quaint resort town of **Mina Clavero** (p310).

National Parks

In San Luis province, the rarely visited Parque Nacional Sierra de las Quijadas is an excellent alternative to the better-known Parque Provincial Ischigualasto in San Juan province: getting there is far easier, and you'll often have the desert canyons and rock formations all to yourself. Parque Nacional Quebrada del Condorito is well worth a day trip from Córdoba to see the impressive Andean condors the park protects.

ⓘ Getting There & Around

Córdoba makes an excellent stop if you're heading south or southwest toward Mendoza. The city has bus connections throughout the country.

The towns throughout the sierras are all easily accessible by public transportation, but many tiny, remote towns and Jesuit *estancias* (ranches) can only be reached with your own wheels. The sierras' dense network of roads, many well paved but others only gravel, make them good candidates for bicycle touring; Argentine drivers here seem a bit less ruthless than elsewhere in the country. A mountain bike is still the best choice.

CÓRDOBA

📞 0351 / POP 1.317 MILLION / ELEV 400M

It's an old guidebook cliché, but Córdoba really *is* a fascinating mix of old and new. Where else will you find DJs spinning electro-tango in crowded student bars next to 17th-century Jesuit ruins?

Despite being a whopping 715km away from Buenos Aires, Córdoba is anything but a provincial backwater – in 2006 the city was awarded the hefty title of Cultural Capital of the Americas, and the title fitted like a glove. Four excellent municipal galleries – dedicated to emerging, contemporary, classical and fine art respectively – are within easy walking distance of each other and the city center.

◎ Sights

There's plenty to see, so allow yourself at least a couple of days for wandering around. Most churches are open roughly from 9am to noon and from 5pm to 8pm. Museum opening hours change regularly depending on the season and the administration.

Most colonial sites lie within a few blocks of Plaza San Martín, the city's urban nucleus. The commercial center is just northwest of the plaza, where the main pedestrian malls – 25 de Mayo and Rivera Indarte – intersect. Obispo Trejo, just west of the plaza, has the finest concentration of colonial buildings. Just south of downtown, Parque Sarmiento offers relief from the bustling, densely built downtown.

East–west streets change names at San Martín/Independencia and north–south streets change at Deán Funes/Rosario de Santa Fe.

◎ Centro

Downtown Córdoba is a treasure of colonial buildings and other historical monuments.

Iglesia Catedral CATHEDRAL
(cnr Independencia & 27 de Abril; ⊗ 8am-8pm Mon-Fri, 8am-noon & 5-8pm Sat & Sun) The construction of Córdoba's cathedral began in 1577 and dragged on for more than two centuries under several architects, including Jesuits and Franciscans, and though it lacks any sense of architectural unity, it's a beautiful structure. Crowned by a Romanesque dome, it overlooks Plaza San Martín. The lavish interior was painted by renowned *cordobés* (Córdoban) painter Emilio Caraffa.

Museo de la Memoria MUSEUM
(www.apm.gov.ar; San Jerónimo s/n; ⊗10am-5pm Tue-Fri) FREE A chilling testament to the excesses of Argentina's military dictatorship, this museum occupies a space formerly used as a clandestine center for detention and torture. It was operated by the dreaded Department of Intelligence (D2), a special division created in Córdoba, dedicated to the kidnap and torture of suspected political agitators and the 'reassignment' of their children to less politically suspect families.

The space itself is stark and unembellished, and the walls are covered with enlarged photographs of people who are still 'missing' after 30 years. There's not much joy here, but the museum stands as a vital reminder of an era that human-rights groups hope will never be forgotten.

Museo Histórico Provincial Marqués de Sobremonte MUSEUM
(📞0351-433-1661; Rosario de Santa Fe 218; admission AR$15; ⊗9:30am-2:30pm Mon-Fri) It's worth dropping into this museum, one of the most important historical museums in the country, if only to see the colonial house it occupies: an 18th-century home that once

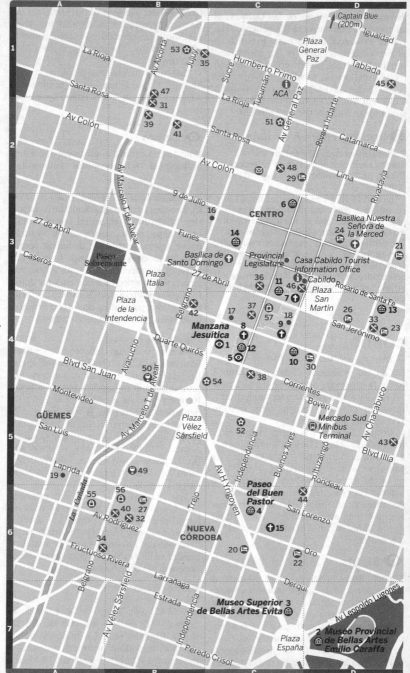

Captain Blue
(200m)

Igualdad

Plaza
General
Paz

Tablada

45

La Rioja

Av Alcorta

53

Jujuy

35

Sucre

Humberto Primo

Tucumán

ACA

45

Santa Rosa

47

31

39

41

La Rioja

Santa Rosa

51

Av General Paz

Rivera Indarte

Catamarca

Av Colón

Av Marcelo T de Alvear

Av Colón

48

29

Lima

Rivadavia

9 de Julio

16

CENTRO

6

27 de Abril

Caseros

Paseo
Sobremonte

Funes

14

Basílica Nuestra
Señora de
la Merced

24

Plaza
Italia

Basílica de
Santo Domingo

27 de Abril

Provincial
Legislature

Casa Cabildo Tourist
Information Office

21

Plaza
de la
Intendencia

Belgrano

42

36

11

46

7

Cabildo

Rosario de Santa Fe

13

Duarte Quirós

17

37

57

8

1

12

5

Manzana
Jesuítica

18

9

Plaza
San
Martín

26

33

23

San Jerónimo

Blvd San Juan

Avacucho

50

54

10

30

38

Corrientes

Boveri

Montevideo

GÜEMES

San Luis

Plaza
Vélez
Sársfield

52

Mercado Sud
Minibus
Terminal

Av Chacabuco

43

Blvd Illia

Laprida

19

49

Av Marcelo T de Alvear

Av H Yrigoyen

Independencia

Buenos Aires

Ituzaingó

Rondeau

55

56

40

27

32

Av Rodríguez

Paseo
del Buen
Pastor

4

44

San Lorenzo

Oro

34

Fructuoso Rivera

Belgrano

NUEVA
CÓRDOBA

15

20

22

La Cañada

Av Vélez Sársfield

Larrañaga

Estrada

Independencia

Trejo

Museo Superior
de Bellas Artes Evita

3

Peredo Crisol

Plaza
España

Av Leopoldo Lugones

Museo Provincial
de Bellas Artes
Emilio Caraffa

2

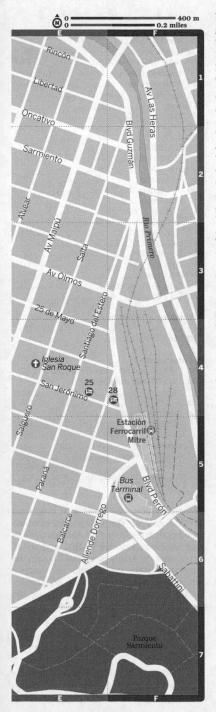

belonged to Rafael Núñez, the colonial governor of Córdoba and later viceroy of the Río de la Plata. It has 26 rooms, seven interior patios, meter-thick walls and an impressive wrought-iron balcony supported by carved wooden brackets.

Cripta Jesuítica   MUSEUM
(cnr Rivera Indarte & Av Colón; admission AR$5; ⊘10am-4pm Mon-Fri) Built at the beginning of the 18th century by the Jesuits, the Cripta Jesuítica was originally designed as a novitiate and later converted to a crypt and crematorium. Abandoned after the Jesuit expulsion, it was demolished and buried around 1829 when the city, while expanding Av Colón, knocked the roof into the subterranean naves and built over the entire structure. It remained all but forgotten until Telecom, while laying underground telephone cable in 1989, accidentally ran into it.

The city, with a new outlook on such treasures, exquisitely restored the crypt and uses it regularly for musical and theatrical performances and art exhibits. Entrances lie on either side of Av Colón in the middle of the Rivera Indarte pedestrian mall.

Museo Municipal de Bellas Artes Dr Genaro Pérez   GALLERY
(Av General Paz 33; ⊘10am-8pm Tue-Sun) FREE This art gallery is prized for its collection of paintings from the 19th and 20th centuries. Works, including those by Emilio Caraffa, Lucio Fontana, Lino Spilimbergo, Antonio Berni and Antonio Seguí, chronologically display the history of the *cordobés* school of painting, at the front of which stands Genaro Pérez himself. The museum is housed in Palacio Garzón, an unusual late-19th-century building named for its original owner; it also has outstanding changing contemporary art exhibits.

Plaza San Martín & Around   PLAZA
Córdoba's lovely and lively central plaza dates from 1577. Its western side is dominated by the white arcade of the restored **Cabildo** (colonial town-council building), completed in 1785 and containing three interior patios, as well as basement cells. All are open to the public as part of the **Museo de la Ciudad** (Independencia 30; admission AR$7; ⊘9:30am-12:30pm & 3-5pm Mon-Fri, 9.30am-1pm & 3-7pm Sat & Sun), a block to the south.

Occupying nearly half a city block, the **Iglesia de Santa Teresa y Convento de Carmelitas Descalzas de San José**

Córdoba

(cnr Caseros & Independencia; ⊙6-8pm) was completed in 1628 and has functioned ever since as a closed-order convent for Carmelite nuns. Only the church itself is open to visitors.

★ **Manzana Jesuítica**   BUILDING
Córdoba's beautiful Manzana Jesuítica (Jesuit Block), like that in Buenos Aires, is also known as the Manzana de las Luces (Block of Enlightenment), and was initially associated with the influential Jesuit order. The Colegio Nacional de Monserrat is next door. In 2000 Unesco declared the Manzana Jesuítica a World Heritage site, along with five Jesuit *estancias* throughout the province.

Colegio Nacional de Monserrat   BUILDING
(Obispo Trejo 294) The Colegio Nacional de Monserrat dates from 1782, though the college itself was founded in 1687 and transferred after the Jesuit expulsion. Though the interior cloisters are original, the exterior was considerably modified in 1927 by restoring architect Jaime Roca, who gave the building its present baroque flare.

Museo Histórico de la Universidad Nacional de Córdoba   MUSEUM
(Obispo Trejo 242; guided visits per person AR$15; ⊙tours Mon-Sat 10am & 5pm in English, 11am & 3pm in Spanish) In 1613 Fray Fernando de Trejo y Sanabria founded the Seminario Convictorio de San Javier, which, after being

elevated to university status in 1622, became the Universidad Nacional de Córdoba. The university is the country's oldest and contains, among other national treasures, part of the Jesuits' Grand Library and the Museo Histórico de la Universidad Nacional de Córdoba.

Guided visits are the only way to see the inside and are well worth taking. The guides let you wander through the Colegio and peek into the classrooms while students run around.

Iglesia de la Compañía de Jesús   CHURCH
(cnr Obispo Trejo & Caseros; ⊘7am-1pm & 5-8pm) FREE Designed by the Flemish Padre Philippe Lemaire, this church dates from 1645 but was not completed until 1671, with the successful execution of Lemaire's plan for a cedar roof in the form of an inverted ship's hull. Lemaire, unsurprisingly, was once a boat builder. Inside, the church's baroque altarpiece is made from carved Paraguayan cedar from Misiones province.

The Capilla Doméstica, completed in 1644, sits on Caseros, directly behind the church. Its ornate ceiling was made with cowhide stretched over a skeleton of thick taguaro cane and painted with pigments composed partially of boiled bones.

⊙ Nueva Córdoba & Güemes

Before the northwestern neighborhoods of Chateau Carreras and Cerro de las Rosas lured the city's elite to their peaceful hillsides, Nueva Córdoba was the neighborhood of the *cordobés* aristocracy. It's now popular with students, which explains the proliferation of brick high-rise apartment buildings. Still, a stroll past the stately old residences that line the wide Av H Yrigoyen reveals the area's aristocratic past.

Once a strictly working-class neighborhood, Güemes is now known for the eclectic antique stores and artisan shops that line the main drag of Belgrano, between Rodríguez and Laprida. Its weekend *feria artisanal,* one of the country's best, teems with antique vendors, arts and crafts and a healthy dose of Córdoba's hippies. It's within the same block as the **Museo Iberoamericano de Artesanías** (cnr Belgrano & Laprida; ⊘10am-3pm Mon-Fri, 10am-9pm Sat & Sun) FREE, which houses beautiful crafts from throughout South America. A good way back to the city center is along La Cañada, an acacia-lined stone canal with arched bridges.

★**Paseo del Buen Pastor**   GALLERY
(Av H Yrigoyen 325; ⊘10am-9pm) FREE This cultural center and performance space was built in 1901 as a combined chapel, monastery and women's prison. In mid-2007 it was re-inaugurated to showcase work by Córdoba's young and emerging artists. There are a couple of hip cafe-bars in the central patio area where you can kick back with an Appletini or two. The attached chapel (which has been desanctified) hosts regular live-music performances – stop by for a program, or check Thursday's edition of the local newspaper *La Voz del Interior* for details.

★**Museo Superior de Bellas Artes Evita**   GALLERY
(Av H Yrigoyen 551; admission AR$15; free Wed; ⊘10am-8pm Tue-Sun) The Palacio Ferreyra – Nueva Córdoba's landmark building – was built in 1914 and designed by Ernest Sanson in the Louis XVI style. The building itself is amazing, and has recently been converted into this fine-arts museum, featuring more than 400 works in 12 rooms spread over three floors. If you're into art or architecture, this place is a don't-miss.

★**Museo Provincial de Bellas Artes Emilio Caraffa**   GALLERY
(www.museocaraffa.org; Av H Yrigoyen 651; admission AR$15; ⊘10am-8pm Tue-Sun) One of the city's best contemporary art museums stands ostentatiously on the eastern side of Plaza España. Architect Juan Kronfuss designed the neoclassical building as a museum and it was inaugurated in 1916. Exhibits change monthly. South of the museum the city unfolds into its largest open-space area, the **Parque Sarmiento**, designed by Charles Thays, the architect who designed Mendoza's Parque General San Martín.

Parroquia Sagrado Corazón de Jesús de los Capuchinos   CHURCH
(cnr Buenos Aires & Obispo Oro) If you're in the neighborhood, it's worth stopping by to check out this marvelous neo-Gothic church built between 1928 and 1934, whose glaring oddity is its missing steeple (omitted on purpose to symbolize human imperfection). Among the numerous sculptures that cover the church's facade are those of Atlases symbolically struggling to bare the spiritual weight of the religious figures above them (and the sins and guilt of the rest of us).

⚓ Courses

Córdoba is an excellent place to study Spanish; in many ways, being a student is what Córdoba is all about. Lessons cost about AR$70 per hour for one-on-one tuition or AR$800 per week in small classes.

Facultad de Lenguas   LANGUAGE COURSE
(☎ 0351-433-1074; www.lenguas.unc.edu.ar; Av Vélez Sársfield 187; ⊙ 9am-3pm Mon-Fri) Spanish school; part of the Universidad Nacional de Córdoba.

Able Spanish School   LANGUAGE COURSE
(☎ 0351-422-4692; www.ablespanish.com; Tucumán 76; ⊙ 9am-8pm Mon-Sat) Offers accommodation and afternoon activities at extra cost and discounts for extended study.

Tsunami Tango   DANCE
(Laprida 453) Tango classes and *milongas* (tango halls) from Tuesday to Sunday. Check www.tangoencordoba.com.ar for their schedule and other tango-related information for Córdoba in general.

☞ Tours

All of the city's hostels and most of the hotels can arrange tours within the city and around the province.

City Tours   WALKING TOUR
(tours in Spanish/English AR$50/80) Absorb Córdoba's rich history by taking one of the guided walking tours that depart at 9:30am and 11:30am Monday to Friday from Casa Cabildo. Reserve a day in advance if you want a tour in English. There are also free thematic tours on an irregular basis – ask at the tourist office to see the schedule.

✯✯ Festivals & Events

During the first three weeks of April, the city puts on a large **crafts market** (locally called 'FICO') at the city fairgrounds, in the north near Chateau Carreras stadium. Bus 31 from Plaza San Martín goes there. Mid-September's **Feria del Libro** is a regional book fair.

🛏 Sleeping

Hotels on and around Plaza San Martín make exploring the center a cinch, but you'll have to walk several blocks for dinner and nightlife. Hotels along La Cañada and in Nueva Córdoba, on the other hand, mean going out to dinner and hitting the bars is a simple matter of walking down the street.

🛏 Centro

Hostel Alvear   HOSTEL $
(☎ 0351-421-6502; www.alvearhostel.com.ar; Alvear 158; dm/d from US$11/38; @🛜) An excellent location and spacious dorms set in an atmospheric old building make this one of the better hostels in the downtown area.

Hotel Quetzal   HOTEL $
(☎ 0351-426-5117; www.hotelquetzal.com.ar; San Jerónimo 579; s/d US$43/64; ❄@🛜) Spacious, minimalistic, modern rooms are on offer here. A surprisingly tranquil option in a busy neighborhood.

Sacha Mistol   HOTEL $$
(☎ 0351-424-2646; www.sachamistol.com; Rivera Indarte 237; r from US$98; ❄🛜🏊) Another of Córdoba's new breed of stylish and original hotels. Rooms are spacious and comfortable, decorated with eclectic art and well-chosen furnishings. It's set in a carefully renovated classic house and features art exhibitions and a small lap pool all in a quiet, central location on the pedestrian mall.

Hotel Garden   HOTEL $$
(☎ 0351-421-4729; www.garden-hotel.com.ar; 25 de Mayo 35; s/d US$60/78; ❄🛜) About as central as it gets. The large, modern rooms here are probably the best deal in this price range and certainly the best deal in the downtown area. Breakfast is served in a cafe around the corner. Staff can also hook you up with some very good value apartments in various locations around the downtown area.

Hotel Viña de Italia   HOTEL $$
(☎ 0351-425-1678; www.hotelvinadeitalia.com.ar; San Jerónimo 611; s/d US$50/62, apt US$80-92; ❄🛜) There's a bit of elegance left in this 150-room hotel, and the midsize rooms include TV, phone, air-con and heating. The rooms aren't nearly as graceful as the lobby, but they're still a good deal, especially the apartments, which sleep four to six.

Windsor Hotel   HOTEL $$
(☎ 0351-422-4012; www.windsortower.com; Buenos Aires 214; r/ste US$112/130; ❄🛜🏊) In a great downtown location, the Windsor is one of the few classic hotels in town with any real style. The lobby's all dark wood and brass, and the rooms have been tastefully renovated with modern fittings.

Hotel Sussex   HOTEL $$
(☎ 0351-422-9070; www.hotelsussexcba.com.ar; San Jerónimo 125; s/d US$76/85; ❄🛜🏊)

LOS GIGANTES

This spectacular group of rock formations, 80km west of Córdoba, is fast becoming Argentina's rock-climbing capital. The two highest peaks are the granite giants of Cerro de La Cruz (2185m) and El Mogote (2374m). There are numerous Andean condors – the park is only 30km from Parque Nacional Quebrada del Condorito, and the birds have slowly taken to this area as well. The area is home to the tabaquillo tree, with its papery peeling bark, which is endangered in Argentina and only found here and in Bolivia and Peru.

Getting here is complicated. **Sarmiento** (☑0351-433-2161) buses leave Córdoba's main bus terminal at 8am Wednesday to Monday and 6am on Tuesday (AR$92, two hours). The bus pretty much turns around and comes back again, meaning you have to spend the night. Schedules change frequently, so be sure to check.

Get off at El Crucero (tell the driver you're going to Los Gigantes). From there it's a 3km walk to La Rotonda, where there is a super-basic **hospedaje** (☑03541-449-8370; campsites per person AR$60, dm AR$120, kitchen use per person AR$50) and a small store (beer, soft drinks and snacks only), which is open on weekends.

At La Rotonda you can hire guides (AR$85) to show you around the cave complexes and take you to the top of Cerro de La Cruz. It's not a long hike, but there is some tricky rock scrambling involved. Guides are recommended because the maze of trails through the rocks can be hard to follow and if the fog comes down you can easily get lost.

Córdoba hostels such as **Hostel Rupestre** (p293) and tour operators such as **Nativo Viajes** (☑0351-424-5341; Independencia 174; ☺9am-6pm Mon-Fri, 10am-3pm Sun) offer trekking excursions and day trips to Los Gigantes. Córdoba's tourist office maintains a list of rock-climbing guides.

Another wonderful lobby (this one sporting vaulted ceilings, grand piano and fine art) leads on to more workaday rooms. At this price, you'd want to be getting plaza views.

★**Hotel Azur Real**　　BOUTIQUE HOTEL **$$$**
(☑0351-424-7133; www.azurrealhotel.com; San Jerónimo 243; r US$130-180; ❋@☞☀) Surprisingly one of a kind here in Córdoba, the Azur mixes minimal chic with eclectic local and international furnishings to pull off a very stylish little boutique hotel. Rooms are all they should be and the common areas (including rooftop deck and pool area) are extremely inviting.

🛏 Nueva Córdoba & La Cañada

★**Hostel Rupestre**　　HOSTEL **$**
(☑0351-15-226-7412; www.rupestrehostel.com.ar; Obispo Oro 242; dm US$11-14, s/d without bathroom US$24/30; ☞☀) A very well-appointed, stylish hostel just on the edge of Nueva Córdoba's party zone. The location's great and the whole setup is very well thought out, with a small wading pool on the rooftop, an indoor climbing gym, spacious dorms and friendly, enthusiastic staff.

Gaiadhon Hostel　　HOSTEL **$**
(☑0351-15-800-5923; www.gaiadhonhostel.com. ar; Buenos Aires 768; dm US$11-13, s/d without bathroom US$26/39; ☞) A cozy little hostel tucked away in a good location. If it ever fills up there wouldn't be much elbow room, but it's got a good atmosphere, and spotless if slightly cramped dorms and private rooms.

Hotel Viena　　HOTEL **$$**
(☑0351-460-0909; www.hotelviena.com.ar; Laprida 235; s/d US$59/75; ❋@☞) This modern hotel in the heart of Nueva Córdoba offers bright, clean rooms and an excellent breakfast buffet. There are lots of nooks for sitting in the lobby area, and there's a restaurant on the premises. Good choice.

🍴 **Eating**

Mercado Norte　　MARKET **$**
(cnr Rivadavia & Oncativo; set meals from AR$60; ☺8am-3pm Mon-Sat) Córdoba's indoor market has delicious and inexpensive food, such as pizza, empanadas (baked savory turnovers) and seafood. Browsing the clean stalls selling every imaginable cut of meat, including whole *chivitos* (goat) and pigs, is a must.

Sol y Luna
VEGETARIAN $

(General Paz 278; mains from AR$45; ⊘noon-3:30pm Mon-Sat; 🎅🖊) A fantastic selection of vegetarian offerings. Pay by the kilo or choose from the limited selection of set meals.

Bruncheria
CAFE $

(Rodriguez 244; mains AR$60-100; ⊘9:30am-1:30am Mon-Thu, 10am-3am Fri-Sun; 🎅) Down in the hipster sector of Güemes, the Bruncheria offers a great mix of fresh decor, yummy food and cool music. It's a good spot for that second breakfast (in case the coffee and croissant didn't fill you up), but the sandwiches are winners, too.

Bursatil
CAFE $

(San Jerónimo & Ituzaingó; mains AR$60-90; ⊘8am-6pm Mon-Sat; 🎅) Stylish, modern cafes are starting to pop up in the old part of town, and Bursatil is one of the finest. There's a cool modern interior, good coffee and a small, Asian-inspired menu.

La Zete
MIDDLE EASTERN $

(cnr Corrientes & Salguero; mains AR$70-110; ⊘10am-11pm) Excellent Middle Eastern food (with a couple of Mediterranean faves thrown in) provides a welcome dash of variety. There's not much to be said for the decor, but the flavors more than make up for that.

La Parrilla de Raul
PARRILLA $

(cnr Jujuy & Santa Rosa; mains from AR$60; ⊘noon-3pm & 8:30pm-12:30am; 🎅) Of Córdoba's *parrillas* (steakhouses), this is probably one of the most famous. *Parrillada* (mixed grill) for two costs only AR$120, not including extras such as drinks or salad.

Mega Doner
MIDDLE EASTERN $

(Ituzaingó 528; set meals AR$90-120; ⊘8am-midnight) Conveniently located in Nueva Córdoba's bar district, this place specializes in real giro *doner kebabs*. Daily lunch specials are an excellent deal and there's outdoor seating.

El Ruedo
CAFE $

(cnr Obispo Trejo & 27 de Abril; mains around AR$90; ⊘7am-3am; 🎅) It doesn't stray too far from the steak, sandwich and pizza formula here, but the plaza-side spot under big shady trees is a winner, as are the *limonadas con soda* (lemon juice with soda water) on a hot day.

★La Nieta 'e la Pancha
FUSION $$

(Belgrano 783; mains AR$120-170; ⊘7pm-12:30am Mon-Fri, 11:30am-1am Sat & Sun; 🎅) The wonderful staff prepares and serves a changing menu of delectable regional specialties, creative pastas and house recipes. Be sure to save room for dessert. Check out the lovely upstairs terrace, which catches breezes and gives ample people-watching ops on the street below.

El Gran Vidrio
ARGENTINE $$

(Humberto Primo 497; mains AR$110-160; ⊘7:30am-7:30pm Mon-Fri, 9am-5pm Sat; 🎅) Fine dining in stylish surrounds. The menu doesn't wander too far from your standard Argentine pasta and meat fare, but there's an enjoyable mix of ingredients (duck, goat, couscous and seafood) and a superb wine list. The on-site contemporary art gallery adds to the appeal.

El Arrabal
ARGENTINE $$

(📋0351-460-2990; Belgrano 899; mains AR$100-150; ⊘11:30am-1am Tue-Sun; 🎅) One of the few old-style restaurants in Nueva Córdoba (OK, so it may be a reconstruction...), this place serves slightly pricey but imaginative regional and house specialties. It packs out for the dinner tango show (AR$220, dinner included) at 11pm Thursday to Saturday. Make a reservation.

LOCAL FLAVOR

Looking to chow down with Córdoba's student crowd? Pull up a stool at any of the following, where the empanadas, beer and *locro* (spicy corn-and-meat stew) flow freely.

La Alameda (Obispo Trejo 170; empanadas AR$10, locro AR$50; ⊘noon-11:30pm) Pull up a bench and wash down your homemade empanadas with some ice-cold beer. Then write some graffiti on the wall.

La Candela (Duarte Quirós 67; empanadas AR$10, locro AR$45; ⊘11am-1am) Rustic and wonderfully atmospheric, run by three cranky but adorable *señoras*.

La Vieja Esquina (cnr Belgrano & Caseros; empanadas AR$8, locro AR$45; ⊘11am-6pm Mon-Sat) A cozy little lunch spot with stools and window seating. Order at the bar.

Patio de la Cañada
PARRILLA **$$**

(☑ 0351-427-0628; Alcorta 360; mains AR$120-180; ☉ noon-4pm & 8.30pm-1am; ☎) One of the better-value *parrillas* around, offering top-quality meats at reasonable prices. The all-you-can-eat *parrilla* (mixed grill; AR$95) is especially good value.

La Mamma
ITALIAN **$$**

(cnr Santa Rosa & Alcorta; mains AR$110-160; ☉ noon-3pm & 8pm-1am Tue-Sat; ☎) Probably Córdoba's most famous pasta restaurant, with an excellent selection that goes far beyond the standard Argentine offerings. The Grande Mamma sauce (featuring caramelized onions, cream cheese, mushrooms and greens) comes highly recommended.

Novecento
INTERNATIONAL **$$**

(☑ 0351-423-0660; cnr Rosario de Santa Fe & Independencia; mains AR$90-130; ☉ 9am-4pm Mon-Fri; ☎) There are few more atmospheric options for dining downtown than this cute little cafe-restaurant, set in the courtyard of the historic Cabildo building. The menu ticks all the 'classic' boxes and throws in a few welcome surprises.

Alcorta
PARRILLA **$$**

(☑ 0351-424-7452; Av Alcorta 330; mains AR$120-170; ☉ noon-3:30pm & 7pm-12:30am; ☎) This upmarket *parrilla,* esteemed for its grilled meats (many say they're the best in town), also serves delicious pasta and fish. Try the *mollejitas al sauvignon blanc* (sweetbreads in a white wine sauce).

🍷 Drinking & Nightlife

Córdoba's drink of choice is fernet (a strong, medicinal-tasting herbed liquor from Italy), almost always mixed with Coke. If you don't mind a rough morning, get into the stuff.

Nightlife in Córdoba basically divides itself into three areas. All the bright young things barhop in Nueva Córdoba – a walk along Rondeau between Avs H Yrigoyen and Chacabuco after midnight gives you a choice of dozens of bars, mostly playing laid-back (or ribcage-rattling) electronic music. For a slightly older crowd and a more laid-back scene, check out the bar scene on Belgrano, in the blocks around the artisans market.

Across the river to the north on Av Las Heras between Roque Sáenz Peña and Juan B Justo (the area known locally as Abasto) are the discos and nightclubs. Go for a walk along here and you'll probably pick up free passes to some, if not all, of them.

Los Infernales
BAR

(Belgrano 631; ☉ 8pm-5am Tue-Sun) A laid-back bar playing an eclectic range of music. Live music Thursday to Sundays and a big *patio cervecero* (beer garden) make this a standout.

Maria Maria
CLUB

(cnr San Juan & Alvear; ☉ 9pm-late Thu-Sun) An ever-popular spot for drinks and dancing, attracting a good range of locals, travelers and expats.

Captain Blue
CLUB

(Las Heras 124; ☉ 8pm-late Wed-Sat) One of the best spots in town to catch Latin dance grooves such as salsa and bachata. Weekends it often has live bands.

☆ Entertainment

La Voz del Interior, Córdoba's main newspaper, has a reasonably comprehensive entertainment section every Thursday with show times and the like.

Cuarteto music (a Córdoba invention) is big here and played live in many venues. Unfortunately, it's also the gangsta rap of Argentine folk music and tends to attract undesirable crowds. **La Sala del Rey** (Humberto Primero 439; ☉ 9pm-late Thu-Sat) is a respectable venue and the best place to catch a *cuarteto* show.

Centro Cultural Casona Municipal
CONCERT VENUE

(www.casonamunicipal.com.ar; cnr Av General Paz & La Rioja; ☉ 9am-9pm Mon-Fri) Shows contemporary and avant-garde art, hosts concerts and offers month-long art and music courses.

Teatro del Libertador General San Martín
THEATER

(☑ 0351-433-2319; Av Vélez Sársfield 365; admission AR$60-250; ☉ box office 9am-9pm) It's well worth going to a performance here, if only to see the opulence of the country's most historic theater. It was completed in 1891, and the floor was designed to be mechanically raised and leveled to the stage, so seats could be removed, allowing for grand parties for the aristocracy in the early 1900s.

Cineclub Municipal Hugo del Carril
CINEMA

(☑ 0351-433-2463; www.cineclubmunicipal.org.ar; Blvd San Juan 49; admission AR$2.50 Mon-Wed, AR$4 Thu-Sun; ☉ box office 9am-late) For a great night (or day) at the movies, pop into

CHRISTIAN KOBER/SHUTTERSTOCK ©

LUIS DAVILLA/COVER/GETTY IMAGES ©

rque Nacional Sierra de
uijadas (p315)
worldly rock formations make
eat hiking opportunities.

2. Iglesia Catedral (p287)
Córdoba's beautiful church is
crowned by a Romanesque dome.

3. Museo Jesuítico Nacional de
Jesús María (p304)
This Unesco-listed Jesuit *estancia* has
superbly landscaped grounds and an
informative museum.

this municipal film house, which screens everything from art flicks to Latin American award winners and local films. Stop by for a program. There's also live music and theatrical performances here.

🛍 Shopping

Antique stores line Calle Belgrano in Güemes, where there is also a **feria artisanal** (Artisans Market; cnr Rodriguez & Belgrano; ⊙5-10pm Sat & Sun), one of the country's best. You'll find Argentine handicrafts at several stores downtown.

Paseo Colonial   ACCESSORIES
(Belgrano 795; ⊙10am-9pm Mon-Sat, 5-10pm Sun) To find out what the city's hip young designers have been working on, slip into this little arcade, featuring a variety of small shops selling clothes, homewares and jewelry.

Talabartería Crespo   SOUVENIRS
(☑0351-421-5447; Obispo Trejo 141; ⊙8am-6pm Mon-Sat) Leather goods made from *carpincho* (a large rodent that makes a beautifully spotted leather) are the specialty here. Sweaters, knives and *mate* (a bitter ritual tea) paraphernalia grace the shelves as well.

ℹ Information

Cambios (money-exchange offices) and ATMs are on Rivadavia north of the plaza; both are also at the main bus terminal and airport.

ACA (Automóvil Club Argentino; ☑0351-421-4713; cnr Av General Paz & Humberto Primo; ⊙24hr) Argentina's auto club; good source for provincial road maps.

Almundo (☑0351-422-9453; www.asatej.com; Av Vélez Sársfield 361; ⊙10am-10pm Mon-Sat, 4-10pm Sun) On the 3rd floor of Patio Olmos shopping center. Nonprofit student travel agency with great staff. Open to all ages and nonstudents.

Cambio Barujel (cnr Rivadavia & 25 de Mayo; ⊙9am-6pm Mon-Fri, 9am-2pm Sat) High commissions.

Casa Cabildo Tourist Information Office
(☑0351-434-1200; Independencia 30; ⊙8am-8pm) The provincial and municipal tourist boards occupy the same office in the historic Casa Cabildo. There are also branches located at the airport and the bus terminal.

Emergency Hospital (☑0351-427-6200; cnr Catamarca & Blvd Guzmán)

Maguitur (25 de Mayo 122; ⊙9am-6pm Mon-Fri, 9am-2pm Sat) Charges 3% on traveler's checks.

Main Post Office (Av General Paz 201; ⊙8am-6pm Mon-Fri, 9am-1pm Sat)

ℹ Getting There & Away

AIR

Córdoba's international airport, **Ingeniero Ambrosio Taravella** (☑0351-475-0877), is about 15km northwest of the city center.

Aerolíneas Argentinas/Austral (☑0351-410-7600; Av Colón 520) has offices downtown and flies several times daily to Buenos Aires, Salta and Puerto Iguazú. **Sol** (☑0810-122-7765; www.sol.com.ar) flies to Rosario and Neuquén.

BUS

Córdoba's **bus terminal** (NETOC; ☑0351-434-1692; Blvd Perón 300) is about a 15-minute walk from downtown.

In the new terminal (across the road, accessed by tunnel), several bus companies offer services to the same destinations as those offered by the minibus terminal. Be aware that those leaving from the terminal stop everywhere, often adding an hour to the journey time.

Several companies offer service to Chilean destinations, including Santiago (AR$1273, 16 hours), although some involve changing buses in Mendoza.

Buses from Córdoba

DESTINATION	COST (AR$)	TIME (HR)
Bahía Blanca	950	12
Bariloche	1697	22
Buenos Aires	850	10
Catamarca	445	5-6
Corrientes	940	12
Esquel	1872	25
Jujuy	1226	12
La Rioja	460	7
Mendoza	725	10
Montevideo (Uruguay)	1230	15
Neuquén	1238	17
Paraná	428	6
Puerto Iguazú	1726	22
Puerto Madryn	1695	18-20
Resistencia	940	13
Río Gallegos	3237	40
Rosario	410	6
Salta	1181	12
San Juan	675	14
San Luis	515	6
San Martín de los Andes	1516	21
Santiago del Estero	589	6
Tucumán	670	8

MINIBUS

Frequent minibuses leave from **Mercado Sud minibus terminal** (Blvd Illía nr Buenos Aires). Most go direct, while some stop at every little town along the way. It's worth asking, as this can make an hour's difference to your travel time.

In summer there may be direct buses to La Cumbrecita, but it will probably be quicker to go first to Villa General Belgrano.

Minibuses from Córdoba

DESTINATION	COST (ARS)	TIME (HR)
Alta Gracia	17	1
Capilla del Monte	58	3
Cosquín	34	1¼
Jesús María	19	1
La Cumbre	48	3
Mina Clavero	55	3
Villa Carlos Paz	18	1
Villa General Belgrano	71	2

TRAIN

Trains leave Córdoba's **Estación Ferrocarril Mitre** (☑ 0351-426-3565; Blvd Perón s/n) for Rosario (AR$34/69 in *primera*/Pullman class, nine hours) and Buenos Aires' Retiro station (AR$50/90/300 in *primera*/Pullman/*camarote*, 17 hours) at 4:40pm on Wednesday and Saturday. There is a dining car and bar on board. Tickets often sell out weeks in advance, especially in the *camarote* (two-person sleeping cabin), so book as soon as possible.

Trains to Cosquín (AR$6.50, two hours) leave from **Estación Rodriguez del Busto** (☑ 0351-477-6195; Cardeñosa 3500) on the northwest outskirts of town at 8:44am and 10:55am daily, with an extra noon service on weekends. The R4 bus stops at 27 de Abril 160 en route to the station or it's an AR$55 taxi ride.

ⓘ Getting Around

The airport is 15km north of town via Av Monseñor Pablo Cabrera. Intercórdoba goes to/from the airport from the main bus station (AR$12). A taxi into town should cost around AR$140.

Buses require rechargeable magnetic cards or *cospeles* (tokens), both of which are available from nearly every kiosk in town. Rides cost AR$9.15.

A car is very useful for visiting some of the nearby Jesuit *estancias* that cannot be reached by bus. Depending on seasonal demand, economy cars cost around AR$750 with 200km. Try **Europcar** (☑ 0351-429-9640; Av Colón 396; ⊙ 9am-7pm Mon-Fri, 9am-2pm Sat).

THE CENTRAL SIERRAS

Nowhere near as visually spectacular as the nearby Andes, the Central Sierras more than make up for it by being way more hospitable. The area is dotted with little towns that are worth a quick visit or a longer stay, and is connected by an excellent road network with frequent bus services.

From the hippie chic of paragliding capital La Cumbre to the over-the-top kitsch of Villa Carlos Paz, you'd have to be one jaded traveler not to find something to your liking here. Kicking back is easily done – the riverside village of Mina Clavero is a favorite, as are the ex-Jesuit centers of Alta Gracia and Jesús María. Things get decidedly Germanic down south, and the pedestrian-only La Cumbrecita is not to be missed for *spaetzle* (German egg noodles), bush walks and swimming holes.

Cosquín

☑ 03541 / POP 19,500 / ELEV 720M

Cosquín is known throughout the country for its **Festival Nacional del Folklore** (www.aquicosquin.org), a nine-day national folk-music festival that's been held in the last week of January since 1961. The town gets packed for the festival, stays busy all summer and goes pleasantly dead the rest of the year. The slightly more hardcore **Cosquín Rock Festival** used to be held here, until the neighbors decided that teenagers with wallet chains, studded wristbands and piercings weren't really the tourist trade they were looking for. The festival relocated a few years ago to the banks of the nearby (and aptly named) Lago San Roque.

East of town, 1260m **Cerro Pan de Azúcar** offers good views of the sierras and, on a clear day, the city of Córdoba. An **aerosilla** (chairlift; return AR$85; ⊙ 9am-6pm) runs to the summit regularly in summer – check with the tourist office in the off season. A taxi to the base should cost about AR$120/160 one way/return with a half-hour wait.

Across the river from the center of town (turn left after the bridge), Av Belgrano forms 4km of waterfront promenade – a great place for a stroll on a summer's day, dotted with swimming holes that pack out when the temperature rises.

The **municipal tourist office** (☑ 0351-454644; www.cosquin.gov.ar; San Martín 560; ⊙ 7am-2pm Mon-Fri, 9am-6pm Sat & Sun) has a good map of the town.

Central Sierras

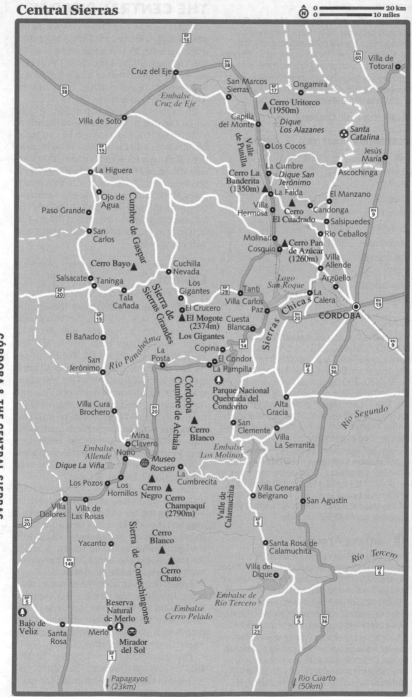

🛏 Sleeping & Eating

San Martín, between the plaza and the stadium, is lined with cafes, restaurants and *parrillas*.

Hospedaje Petit   HOTEL $
(☑ 0351-451311; petitcosquin@hotmail.com; A Sabattini 739; s/d US$45/60) Steepled roofs and lovely antique floor tiles in the lobby give way to some fairly ordinary, modern rooms in the interior. It's decent value, though – clean, spacious and central.

Hostería Siempreverde   HOTEL $$
(☑ 0351-450093; www.hosteriasiempreverde.com; Santa Fe 525; s/d US$60/80; 🛜) This lovely old house has good-sized, modern rooms out back. There's a big, shady garden and the breakfast and lounge area is comfortable and stylish.

La Casona   PARRILLA $
(cnr San Martín & Corrientes; mains AR$80-120; ⏱ 11:30am-11pm) A frequently recommended *parrilla* set in an atmospheric old building and specializing in grilled *chivito* (goat) and locally caught trout.

🛈 Getting There & Away

There are many daily departures north to La Cumbre (AR$34, 1¼ hours); and south every 20 minutes to Villa Carlos Paz (AR$25, 40 minutes) and Córdoba (AR$34, 1¼ hours). There are a few departures daily for Buenos Aires (AR$745, 11 hours).

Trains depart for Córdoba's Estación Rodriguez del Busto (AR$6.50, 2½ hours) at 8am and 3:30pm daily, with an extra 4:30pm service on weekends.

La Cumbre

☑ 03548 / POP 7540 / ELEV 1141M

A favorite getaway for Córdoba dwellers and foreigners alike, La Cumbre packs a lot of character into a small space. It's an agreeable little town due to its wide streets and mild mountain climate, and there are plenty of adventures to be had in the surrounding hills. The town gained worldwide fame among paragliders when it hosted the 1994 World Paragliding Cup, and enthusiasts of the sport have made La Cumbre their home, giving the town an international feel. The launch site, 380m above the Río Pinto, provides a spectacular introduction to the sport and there are plenty of experienced instructors around, offering classes and tandem flights.

🔘 Sights & Activities

A few places around town rent bikes (around AR$50 per day) – the tourist office should be able to tell you who can hook you up.

Head to the south side of town to the 12km stretch of road known as **Camino de los Artesanos**, where more than two dozen homes sell homemade goodies, from jams and chutneys to wool, leather and silver crafts. Most homes open from 11am to sunset.

There are excellent views from the **Cristo Redentor**, a 7m statue of Christ on a 300m hilltop east of town; from the Plaza 25 de Mayo, cross the river and walk east on Córdoba toward the mountains – the trail begins after a quick jut to the left after crossing Cabrera.

Flying from the launch at Cuchi Corral (and hanging out by the Río Pinto afterward) is truly a memorable experience. The launch site (La Rampa) is about 10km west of town via a signed dirt road off the highway. **Pablo Jaraba** (☑ 03548-15-570951; www.cuchicorral.com) offers tandem flights and lessons. Check in the tourist office for current operators and recommendations. Everyone charges about the same. Tandem flights cost around AR$1000 for a half-hour; full courses cost AR$12,000.

At the **Aeroclub La Cumbre** (☑ 03548-452544; Camino a los Troncos s/n; ⏱ 9am-8pm) you can arrange everything from tandem flights to ultralights and parachute jumps. Ask for Andy Hediger (former paragliding world champion).

🛏 Sleeping

The proprietors of most places can arrange any activities available in La Cumbre.

Hostel La Cumbre   HOSTEL $
(☑ 03548-451368; www.hostellacumbre.com; San Martín 186; dm US$15, r with/without bathroom US$42/38; 🖩🛜🏊) A couple of blocks behind the bus terminal, this converted English mansion is one of the most impressive hostels in the Sierras. Views from the front balcony are superb.

Camping El Paso   CAMPGROUND $
(☑ 03548-452-2545; Monseñor P Cabrera s/n; campsites US$5) Below the Cristo Redentor east of town, La Cumbre's exceptional campgrounds are only a short tramp from the center.

Posada de la Montaña LODGE $$
(☏ 03548-451867; www.posadadelamontaña.com.
ar; 9 de Julio 753; s/d US$80/110; ✼🐕❄) A
short walk from downtown, this very com-
fortable hotel offers spacious, quaintly dec-
orated rooms with great views and a leafy
garden with a small pool. Breakfast is ample
and it's run by a friendly bunch of young
locals.

✖ Eating & Drinking

★ Kasbah ASIAN $
(Alberdi & Sarmiento; mains AR$70-120; ⊙12:30pm-
12:30am; 🛜) You may not be expecting a good
Thai curry out here, but this cute little trian-
gular restaurant comes up with the goods.
Also on offer is a range of Chinese and Indian
dishes.

Casa Caraffa ARGENTINE $$
(cnr Caraffa & Rivadavia; mains AR$90-160;
⊙noon-3:30pm & 8pm-midnight) La Cumbre's
best-established restaurant is still going
strong, with some good *parrilla* offerings
alongside a fine selection of fish dishes. The
salmon with orange sauce and grilled vegetables is bound to satisfy.

El Pungo PUB
(www.elpungopub.com.ar; Camino de los Artesanos
s/n; cover from AR$40; ⊙noon-late Sat & Sun)
This somewhat legendary watering hole attracts musicians from all over the country
(Argentine folk musicians Charly García and
Fito Páez have played here).

❶ Information

Banco de la Provincia de Córdoba (cnr López
y Planes & 25 de Mayo; ⊙9am-1pm Mon-Fri)
Has an ATM.

Tourist Office (☏ 03548-452966; www.
lacumbre.gov.ar; Av Caraffa 300; ⊙8am-9pm
Apr-Jun & Aug-Nov, to midnight Dec-Mar & Jul)
Across from the bus terminal in the old train
station. Friendly staff will supply a handy map
of the town and surroundings.

❶ Getting There & Away

Buses depart regularly from La Cumbre's
convenient **bus terminal** (General Paz, near
Caraffa), heading northward to Capilla del Monte
(AR$22, 30 minutes) and San Marcos Sierras
(AR$30, one hour) or south to Cosquín (AR$34,
1¼ hours), Villa Carlos Paz (AR$52, 1½ hours)
and Córdoba (AR$48, 2½ hours). Minibuses
(which take about half an hour less) are the fastest way to Córdoba. There is also a direct service
to Buenos Aires (AR$758, 12½ hours).

San Marcos Sierras

☏ 03549 / POP 930 / ELEV 625M

Once a moribund hill town, San Marcos got
an injection of life in the late sixties when
the hippies discovered its mild climate, way-
off-the-grid isolation and good farmland
and began flocking here. Over the decades,
curious tourists began appearing, having
heard about the hippie town in the Sierras,
and eventually the town's emphasis shifted
from agriculture and handicraft manufacture to tourism.

Taken aback by the swing toward capitalism, many of the old crew moved out
but traces of San Marcos' hippie heritage
remain – the community has successfully
campaigned against the use of genetically
modified crops in the valley as well as sealed
roads and even a gas station in town. These
days the town makes for a pleasant getaway
and the creekside location in a pretty valley
is as enticing as ever.

There's no bus terminal, but buses arrive
and depart from a stop near the main plaza.
The **tourist office** (☏ 03549-496452; www.
sanmarcossierras.gov.ar; cnr Libertad & Sarmiento;
⊙9am-6pm) has a good map of the town and
surrounds and decent info on walks and upcoming events. There's an ATM in the Municipal building on Sarmiento, but bring
cash in case it isn't working.

◉ Sights & Activities

San Marcos enjoys a fabulous natural setting, and there are some excellent walks just
out of town, including the riverside walk
to **El Viejo Molino** (admission AR$10; ⊙9am-
3pm), a 17th-century flour mill that was used
to grind the town's cereals until the 1950s.

Museo Hippie MUSEUM
(AR$30; ⊙11am-6pm Thu-Mon) 🌿 Far more
interesting for the stream-of-consciousness
commentary on the evolution of the hippie
movement in Argentina (dating back to the
Greek Philosophers) than the actual artifacts it holds, this small museum on the
northern outskirts of town is worth a visit –
if nothing else, it's a pleasant walk out there.

🛏 Sleeping & Eating

Restaurants and cafes surround the main
plaza. Most accommodations are within a
kilometer of here.

Hostel Agrimon HOSTEL **$**
(☎ 03549-496397; posadaargimon@infovia.com.
ar; Sarmiento 341; dm/d US$14/40; @ 🛜) A
sweet little hostel right in front of the main
plaza. Dorms are spacious, sleep four and
come with private bathrooms, and doubles
are good value, too. A shady garden out back
and an OK kitchen and living area round out
the deal.

Camping Kachay Kukuy CAMPGROUND **$**
(☎ 03549-15-448178; www.kachaykukuy.com; Libertad s/n; camping per person US$5, dm US$10,
cabins for 2/3 people US$45/60) The best set-
up campground is at the entrance to town.
There are lots of shady sites, good amenities

and some fine cabins if you don't feel like
roughing it. Tents can be hired for AR$50
to AR$80.

Madre Tierra HOTEL **$**
(☎ 03549-496394; secretosdemadretierra@
hotmail.com; San Martín 650; s/d US$50/60;
❄ 🛜 ❋) Probably the most formal setup
in town, with stylish, modern rooms (a bit
on the small side) arranged around a good-
sized swimming pool. It's about 500m over
the bridge north of the plaza.

Piano Resto Bar INTERNATIONAL **$**
(Córdoba 145; mains AR$70-120; ⊙10am-2am)
A great little coffee spot on the plaza that
serves up some decent food, too. Don't miss

CLOSE ENCOUNTERS

It's not just the freaks and hippies. Even normal-looking people in Capilla del Monte have
stories about strange lights appearing in formation in the night skies over nearby Cerro
Uritorco. The stories go way back, too. In 1935 Manuel Reina reported seeing a strange
being dressed in a tight-fitting suit while he was out walking on a country road. In 1986
Gabriel and Esperanza Gómez apparently saw a spaceship so big that its lights illuminated the surrounding countryside. The next day a burn mark measuring 122m by 64m was
found at the point where it had reportedly landed.

A couple of years later, 300 people were said to have witnessed another ship, which left
a burn mark 42m in diameter. And in 1991, another burn mark was found. This one measured 12m in diameter, with an estimated temperature of 340°C. Geologists were called in
and they claimed that nearby rocks had recently been heated to a temperature of 3000°C.

Why all this activity around Capilla del Monte? This is where it gets really weird. One
theory is that *Ovnis* (UFOs) visit the area because Cerro Uritorco is where the knight
Parsifal brought the Holy Grail and the Templar Cross at the end of the 12th century. He
did this to lay them beside the Cane of Order, which had been made 8000 years before
by Lord Voltán of the Comechingones, the indigenous tribe that inhabited this region.

Another theory is that they are drawn here because underneath Uritorco lies Erks, a
subterranean city in which, according to 'hermetic scientists', the future regeneration of
the human species will take place. Inside you'll find the Esfera Temple and the three mirrors used to exchange data with other galaxies, and where you can see the details of the
life of every human being.

The official explanation? Good ol' meteorological phenomena, caused by super-
charged ion particles in the atmosphere, mixed in with a healthy touch of mass hysteria.

Whatever you believe, one thing's for sure – all this hype isn't hurting little Capilla del
Monte's tourist industry one bit. Until recently, the only people climbing Uritorco were
goatherds and a few interested townsfolk. These days, numbers can approach 1000 per
day, all hoping to catch a glimpse of the mysterious lights.

If you want to climb Uritorco (1950m), you must start the climb before noon, and
begin your descent by 3pm. The 5km hike to the top affords spectacular views. From
Capilla del Monte, catch a taxi or walk the 3km to the base of the mountain.

Capilla del Monte is a comfortable enough place to base yourself – the town has plenty of restaurants and lodging – the **tourist office** (☎03548-481903; www.capilladelmonte.
gov.ar; cnr Av Pueyrredón & Buenos Aires; ⊙8am-8pm) in the old train station has mounds of
information. For more info on UFOs reported in the area, drop in to the **Centro de Informes Ovni** (☎03548-482485; www.ciouritorco.org; Juan Cabus 397; ⊙10am-4pm). There
is a frequent bus service south to Córdoba (AR$58, three hours), stopping at all towns
on the RN 38, and long-distance service to Buenos Aires.

the local beer 'Quilpo', which gets flowing when the impromptu jam sessions strike up later at night.

ⓘ Getting There & Away

There are five buses daily from La Cumbre (AR$30, one hour). Buses also pass through here en route from Cruz del Eje to Córdoba (AR$300, four hours).

Jesús María

📞 03525 / POP 31,600

Sleepy little Jesús María earns its place on the map by being home to one of the most atmospheric Jesuit *estancias* in the region – the Unesco-listed **Museo Jesuítico Nacional de Jesús María** (📞 03525-420126; admission AR$20; ⊙ 8am-7pm Tue-Fri, 10am-noon & 3-7pm Sat & Sun). The church and convent were built in 1618 and are set on superbly landscaped grounds. The Jesuits, after losing their operating capital to pirates off the Brazilian coast, sold wine they made here to support their university in colonial Córdoba. The museum has good archaeological pieces from indigenous groups throughout Argentina, informative maps of the missionary trajectory and well-restored (though dubiously authentic) rooms.

Jesús María is also home to the annual **Fiesta Nacional de Doma y Folklore** (www.festival.org.ar), a 10-day celebration of gaucho horsemanship and customs beginning the first weekend of January. The festival draws crowds from all over the country, and accusations of animal cruelty from animal-rights groups, who argue that whipping horses and making them perform acrobatics in front of noisy crowds under bright lights is tantamount to torture.

Most people visit Jesús María as a day trip from Córdoba. Frequent minibuses (AR$19, one hour) leave Córdoba's Mercado Sud terminal and the bus terminal daily.

Alta Gracia

📞 03547 / POP 48,100 / ELEV 550M

Set around a 17th-century Jesuit reservoir, Alta Gracia is a tranquil little mountain town of winding streets and shady parks. The star attraction here is the 17th-century Jesuit *estancia*, whose exquisite church, nighttime lighting and lovely location between a tiny reservoir and the central plaza make it one of the most impressive of Córdoba province's World Heritage sites. Revolutionary Che Guevara spent his adolescence in Alta Gracia and his former home is now a museum. Many people come on day trips from Córdoba, but the city is emerging as a destination in its own right and as a base for exploring the southern sierras.

The **tourist office** (📞 03547-428128; www.altagracia.gov.ar; Reloj Público, cnr Av del Tajamar & Calle del Molino; ⊙ 7am-10:30pm Nov-Feb, to 7pm Mar-Oct) occupies an office in the clock tower.

◉ Sights & Activities

Jesuit Estancia
BUILDING

From 1643 to 1762, Jesuit fathers built the **Iglesia Parroquial Nuestra Señora de la Merced** (west side of Plaza Manuel Solares) **FREE**, the *estancia's* most impressive building. Directly south of the church, the colonial Jesuit workshops of **El Obraje** (1643) are now a public school. Beside the church is the **Museo Histórico Nacional del Virrey Liniers** (📞 03547-421303; www.museoliniers.org.ar; admission AR$20, free Wed; ⊙ 9am-7pm Tue-Fri, 9:30am-6:30pm Sat, Sun & holidays), named after former resident Virrey Liniers, one of the last officials to occupy the post of Viceroy of the River Plate.

If you want to know every last historical detail, guided tours in English (AR$40 per person; held at 10am, 11:30am, 3:30pm and 5pm) are available and recommended – call to reserve one day in advance. If you just have a passing interest, each room has an information sheet in English, which gives you a fair understanding of what's going on.

Directly north of the museum, across Av Belgrano, the **Tajamar** (1659) is one of the city's several 17th-century dams, which together made up the complex system of field irrigation created by the Jesuits.

Museo Casa de Ernesto Che Guevara
MUSEUM

(Avellaneda 501; admission AR$75; ⊙ 2-7pm Mon, 9am-7pm Tue-Sun) In the 1930s, the family of youthful Ernesto Guevara moved here because a doctor recommended the dry climate for his asthma. Though Che lived in several houses – including the house in Rosario, where he was born – the family's primary residence was Villa Beatriz, which was purchased by the city and restored as this museum.

ESTANCIA SANTA CATALINA

One of the most beautiful of the Sierra's Unesco World Heritage sites, the Jesuit *estancia* (ranch) of **Santa Catalina** (☎03525-421600; www.santacatalina.info; admission AR$20; ⏰10am-1pm & 2-6pm Tue-Sun, closed Jan, Feb, Jul & Semana Santa), some 20km northwest of Jesús María, is a quiet, tiny place, where the village store occupies part of the *estancia*, and old-timers sit on the benches outside and watch the occasional gaucho ride past on a horse. Much of the *estancia* is off-limits to visitors, but **guided tours** (each site AR$30) are available, taking in the chapel, cloisters and novitiate, where unmarried slave girls were housed.

The grounds, although a fraction of their former selves, are lovely and well maintained and you can easily while away an hour or two wandering around. Outside the *estancia*, around the back, is the original reservoir built by the Jesuits, now slowly being overtaken by tall-stemmed lilies.

Santa Catalina is the only Unesco World Heritage *estancia* still under private ownership. Part of the family owns and operates **La Ranchería de Santa Catalina** (☎03525-424467; d with bathroom US$105, s without bathroom US$45; ☎), a lovely inn, restaurant (meals from AR$100) and crafts store in the *ranchería*. It has only two rooms, which occupy the former slave quarters and, though small, are carefully decorated and retain their original stone walls. Three more rooms with bathrooms are being constructed, using traditional techniques. The place is run by a friendly couple who are more than willing to fill you in on the illustrious story of the *estancia*, from Jesuit times to the present.

A taxi out here from Jesús María costs about AR$190.

Its cozy interior is now adorned with a photographic display of Che's life, and a couple of huge photographs commemorating a recent visit from Fidel Castro and Hugo Chávez. If you think you've been on the road for a while, check out the map detailing Che's travels through Latin America – whatever you think of the man's politics, you have to admit he was well traveled. A small selection of Che paraphernalia (including cigars, of course) is on sale.

🛏 Sleeping & Eating

A number of cafe-bar-restaurants with sidewalk seating are scattered along Av Belgrano, in the three blocks downhill from the Jesuit museum.

Alta Gracia Hostel   HOSTEL $
(☎03547-428810; www.altagraciahostel.com.ar; Paraguay 218; dm US$12, r US$35) Five short blocks downhill from the Jesuit museum, Alta Gracia's hostel offers a fair deal. Dorms are roomy enough and the kitchen should meet your needs.

★ 279 Boutique B&B   BOUTIQUE HOTEL $$
(☎03547-424177; www.279altagracia.com; Giorello 279; r US$65; ☎) 🅿 Alta Gracia's best accommodation by far only offers two rooms,

but that just adds to the charm. Run by an ex-New York photographer, it's a stylish, intimate place with just the right blend of old features rescued from the original house and slick modern styling.

Breakfast is fantastic, the location's great and attention to detail is superb. More like this, please.

★ El Bistro del Alquimista   FUSION $$
(Castellanos 351; meals AR$130-250; ⏰Mon-Sat 4pm-midnight; ☎) This is the way the gourmet scene in Argentina *should* be heading – an open kitchen with chefs doubling as waitstaff and well-presented, innovative dishes served up in a casual atmosphere with super-attentive service. The four-course menu changes daily and the wines all come from boutique winemakers.

ℹ Getting There & Away

Minibuses depart regularly for Córdoba (AR$17, one hour) a block uphill from the *estancia*. The **bus terminal** (Tacuarí at Perón) near the river also has departures for Córdoba and Buenos Aires (AR$950, 13 hours). Buses to Villa General Belgrano stop every hour on RP 5, about 20 blocks along Av San Martín from the center.

The Legend of Che

One of Cuba's greatest revolutionary heroes, in some ways even eclipsing Fidel Castro himself, was an Argentine. Ernesto Guevara, known by the common Argentine interjection 'che,' was born in Rosario in 1928 and spent his first years in Buenos Aires. In 1932, after Guevara's doctor recommended a drier climate for his severe asthma, Guevara's parents moved to the mountain resort of Alta Gracia.

He later studied medicine in the capital and, in 1952, spent six months riding a motorcycle around South America, a journey that opened Guevara's eyes to the plight of South America's poor.

After his journey, Guevara traveled to Central America, finally landing in Mexico, where he met Fidel Castro and other exiles. The small group sailed to Cuba on a rickety old yacht and began the revolution that overthrew Cuban dictator Fulgencio Batista in 1959. Unfulfilled by the bureaucratic task of building Cuban socialism, Guevara tried, unsuccessfully, to spread revolution in the Congo, Argentina and finally Bolivia, where he was killed in 1967.

Today Che is known less for his eloquent writings and speeches than for the striking black-and-white portrait as the beret-wearing rebel – an image gracing everything from T-shirts to CD covers – taken by photojournalist Alberto Korda in 1960.

In 1997, on the 30th anniversary of Che's death, the Argentine government issued a postage stamp honoring Che's Argentine roots. You can take a look at the stamps and other Che memorabilia by visiting Alta Gracia's modest Museo Casa de Ernesto Che Guevara (p304).

Clockwise from top left
1. A family photo on display at the Museo Casa de Ernesto Che Guevara (p304) **2.** Che's childhood home in Alta Gracia (p304) **3.** Che's image adorns a wall in Buenos Aires

Villa General Belgrano

📞 03546 / POP 7800 / ELEV 720M

More a cultural oddity than a full-blown tourist attraction, Villa General Belgrano flaunts its origins as a settlement of unrepatriated survivors from the German battleship *Graf Spee,* which sank near Montevideo during WWII.

The annual Oktoberfest held during the first two weeks of October draws beer lovers from all over the world. In summertime, the village slowly fills with holidaymakers enjoying the tranquil streets and evergreen-dotted countryside. Unless you're really excited about microbrew beer, *torta selva negra* (Black Forest cake) and goulash, Villa General Belgrano makes a fine day trip from Córdoba or nearby La Cumbrecita. Despite its decidedly Germanic flavor, you'd be lucky to hear any of the modern-day inhabitants speaking the language of the old country.

◉ Sights & Activities

If you're up for a stroll, a lovely path runs between Corrientes and El Quebracho, alongside the Arroyo La Toma, a creek one block back from the main street.

Lookout Tower   TOWER
(Roca 168; admission AR$10; ⊘ 9am-8pm) For an overview of the town and surrounds, make your way up to the lookout tower attached to the tourist office.

OKTOBERFEST IN VILLA GENERAL BELGRANO

If you're in the Sierras around the start of October, consider hitting Villa General Belgrano, which celebrates its German heritage with a 10-day, nationally recognized Oktoberfest. While the beer runs as freely as it does at Oktoberfests all over the world, there are also parades, endless concerts and other cultural presentations. The festival also features so much delicious street food that you'll be loosening a couple of buttons on your lederhosen, even if you're not a drinker.

For more info on the festival, have a look at www.elsitiodelavilla.com/oktoberfest.

Friedrich   BICYCLE RENTAL
(📞 03546-461451; Roca 224; ⊘ 9am-6pm Mon-Sat) Friedrich rents mountain bikes for AR$30/150 per hour/day.

🛏 Sleeping & Eating

In the December-to-March high season, hotel prices rise and rooms book out quickly. Unless you book weeks before Oktoberfest, plan on hitting the festival as a day trip from Córdoba. There are numerous restaurants along the main strip of Roca and San Martín.

Albergue El Rincón   HOSTEL $
(📞 03546-461323;   www.hostelelrincon.com.ar; Fleming 347; campsite per person US$10, dm/d without bathroom US$14/45, s/d with bathroom US$42/52; ☀) ✿ This beautiful Dutch-owned hostel, surrounded by forest, has excellent, spacious dorm rooms, outdoor and indoor kitchens, a *parrilla* and its own biodynamic farm. Outstanding breakfasts cost AR$40. It's a good 900m walk from behind the bus terminal to the entrance gate; follow the signs.

Berna Hotel   HOTEL $$
(📞 03546-461097;   www.bernahotel.com.ar; Sarfield 86; r from US$82; ❄🉐☀) Set on sprawling grounds in a great location between the bus terminal and town, the Berna offers spacious rooms with all the comforts. Some of the goodies here include an on-site spa, a children's play area and a huge pool.

Blumen   INTERNATIONAL $$
(Roca 373; mains AR$100-150; ⊘ noon-11pm Tue-Sun) With one of the widest menus in town, Blumen serves up tasty, if slightly expensive, dishes. It's a great spot for a few drinks – the huge shady beer garden is all wooden tables and pagodas, with plenty of space in between and the microbrew beer flowing readily.

ℹ Information

The **tourist office** (📞 03546-461215; www.elsitiodelavilla.com; Roca 168; ⊘ 8:30am-8pm) is on the main street, as are banks with ATMs.

ℹ Getting There & Away

The bus terminal is a few blocks uphill from the main street. Buses leave every hour for Córdoba (AR$71, two hours), and daily for Buenos Aires (AR$923, 11 hours). There are seven departures daily for La Cumbrecita (AR$48, one hour).

La Cumbrecita

03546 / POP 550 / ELEV 1300M

The pace of life slows waaaay down in this alpine-styled village, nestled in the forest in the Valle de Calamuchita. The tranquility is largely thanks to the town's pedestrian-only policy. It's a great place to kick back for a few days and wander the forest trails leading to swimming holes, waterfalls and scenic lookouts.

Visitors must park their cars in the dirt parking lot (AR$50) before crossing the bridge over Río del Medio by foot.

The helpful **tourist office** (03546-481088; www.lacumbrecita.gov.ar; 8:30am-9pm Nov-Feb, 10am-6pm Mar-Oct) is on the left, just after you cross the bridge into town.

Sights & Activities

Hiking is the best reason to visit La Cumbrecita. Short trails are well marked and the tourist office can provide a crude but useful map of the area. A 25-minute stroll will take you to **La Cascada**, a waterfall tucked into the mountainside. **La Olla** is the closest swimming hole, surrounded by granite rocks (people jump where it's deep enough). **Cerro La Cumbrecita** (1400m) is the highest point in town, about a 20-minute walk from the bridge. Outside town, the highest mountain is the poetically named **Cerro Wank** (1715m); a hike to the top takes about 40 minutes.

For guided hikes further into the mountains, as well as horseback riding (AR$360 for four hours), trout fishing and mountain biking, contact **Viviendo Montañas** (03546-481172; Las Truchas s/n; 9am-1pm & 3-8pm), which has an office on the main road in town. The company can also take you trekking to the top of **Cerro Champaquí** (2790m), the highest peak in the Sierras (a two-day trek).

Sleeping & Eating

La Cumbrecita has more than 20 hotels and *cabañas* in the surrounding hills; the tourist office is a good resource. Make reservations in summer (January and February), during Easter and during Villa General Belgrano's Oktoberfest.

★**Hospedaje Casa Rosita** HOTEL $
(03546-481003; Calle Principal s/n; s/d without bathroom US$25/40) A humble little *hospe-*

daje (family home) set in a charming house by the river at the entrance to the village. If you can, go for room 1, which has a bay window overlooking the river.

Hostel Planeta HOSTEL $
(03546-404847; planetacumbrecitahostel@gmail.com; dm/r per person US$16/22;) The best hostel in town is reached via a steep path next to the Hotel Las Verbenas tennis court. It's set in a lovely traditional house and has a good dining area and kitchen, reasonable dorms and killer views.

Hotel La Cumbrecita HOTEL $$
(03546-481052; www.hotelcumbrecita.com.ar; s/d US$50/80;) Built on the site of the first house in La Cumbrecita, this rambling hotel has some excellent views out over the valley. Rooms aren't huge, but most have fantastic balconies. The extensive grounds include a gym and tennis courts.

Restaurante Bar Suizo EUROPEAN $
(Calle Pública s/n; mains AR$70-100; 8am-10pm;) Pull up a wooden bench under the pine tree and try some of the excellent Swiss German options such as *spaetzle* with wild mushroom sauce.

★**El Paseo** PARRILLA $$
(mains AR$100-150; noon-midnight Thu-Sun) Out by the La Olla swimming hole, this place serves up a good *parrilla,* plus all the Germanic standards. It's great for afternoon beer.

ESTANCIAS IN THE CENTRAL SIERRAS

From rustic little getaways to sprawling, atmospheric ranches, the Central Sierras offer a small but excellent selection of *estancias* (ranches).

Estancia La Estanzuela (p316) Wonderfully preserved, set on lush grounds.

Estancia Las Verbenas (p315) Set in a beautiful glade, it's a truly rustic experience.

La Ranchería de Santa Catalina (p305) Spend the night in the old slave quarters.

CÓRDOBA & THE CENTRAL SIERRAS LA CUMBRECITA

❶ Getting There & Away

From Villa General Belgrano, **Transportes Pajaro Blanco** (☎ 03546-461709; ☺ 8am-8pm) has seven departures to La Cumbrecita (AR$48, one hour) from 7am to 7:30pm. The last bus back from La Cumbrecita leaves at 8:40pm. In summer there may be occasional minibuses from Córdoba's Mercado Sud terminal.

Parque Nacional Quebrada del Condorito

ELEV 1900-2300M

This national park protects 370 sq km of stunning rocky grasslands across the Pampa de Achala in the Sierras Grandes. The area, particularly the *quebrada* (gorge) itself, is an important condor nesting site and flight training ground for fledgling condors. A 9km, two- to three-hour hike from the park entrance at **La Pampilla** leads to the Balcón Norte (North Balcony), a clifftop over the gorge where you can view the massive birds circling on the thermals rising up the gorge. You can easily visit as a day trip from Córdoba or on your way to Mina Clavero.

Any bus from Córdoba to Mina Clavero will drop you at La Pampilla (AR$52, 1½ hours), where a trailhead leads to the gorge. To return to Córdoba (or on to Mina Clavero), flag a bus from the turnoff. Hostels in Córdoba arrange day tours to the park.

For more information on the park, contact **Intendencia del PN Quebrada del Condorito** (☎ 03541-433371; Resistencia 30; ☺ 9am-6pm Mon-Fri) in Villa Carlos Paz.

Mina Clavero

☎ 03544 / POP 8500 / ELEV 915M

Really jumping in summertime, Mina Clavero pretty much empties out for the rest of the year, leaving visitors to explore the limpid streams, rocky waterfalls, numerous swimming holes and idyllic mountain landscapes at their own pace.

Mina Clavero is 170km southwest of Córdoba via RN 20, the splendid Nuevo Camino de las Altas Cumbres (Highway of the High Peaks). It sits at the confluence of Río de Los Sauces and Río Panaholma, in the Valle de Traslasierra.

The **tourist office** (☎ 03544-470171; www.mina clavero.gov.ar; Av San Martín 1464; ☺ 7am-midnight Dec-Mar, 9am-9pm Apr-Nov) has standard brochures and a useful map of town.

◎ Sights & Activities

Mina Clavero's *balnearios* (swimming areas) get mobbed in summer, but are often empty the rest of the year. The boulder-strewn gorges of the Río Mina Clavero are easily explored. A lovely *costanera* (riverside road) has been constructed, running from the pedestrian bridge all the way to the **Nido de Aguila**, the best swimming hole around – this makes for a great afternoon stroll. From there head west along the Río de Los Sauces and you'll hit **Los Elefantes**, a *balneario* named for its elephant-like rock formations. A 3km walk south along the river will take you to **Villa Cura Brochero**, where you'll find black pottery that is characteristic of this region.

🛏 Sleeping

Many accommodations close around the end of March, when the town almost rolls up the sidewalks.

★**Andamundos Hostel**   HOSTEL $
(☎ 03544-470249; www.andamundoshostel.com.ar; San Martín 554; dm/s/d US$15/28/45; @ ☎) A rustic little setup a couple of blocks from the center of town. The big yard backing onto the river is a bonus.

Costa Serrana   HOTEL $$
(☎ 03544-471802; www.costaserrana.com.ar; Olmos 1303; 1/2 bedroom apt US$89/111; ❄ ☎ ☎) With a fantastic, central location these apartments represent some of the best value for money in this price range. Furnishings are rustic chic, the breakfast buffet is expansive and the grounds are lovely, featuring a generously sized swimming pool overlooking the river.

✕ Eating

Most of Mina Clavero's restaurants are along San Martín. Head south over the river for more upscale *parrillas* and restaurants.

---

❶ MINA CLAVERO SHORTCUT

The Río Mina Clavero splits the town in two. If you arrive at the bus terminal, take the pedestrian bridge across the river – it takes you straight into the downtown area. Otherwise you have to go the long way around.

THERE'S SOMETHING WEIRD IN THEM THAR HILLS

For some reason, Córdoba's Sierras region is one of the quirkiest in Argentina, and the great thing about traveling in the region is that every once in a while you stumble upon something truly wonderful and unexpected. Here are a few of our favorites:

Capilla del Monte (p303) This otherwise sleepy little hill town is world-famous among UFO watchers who come here in the hope of communing with extraterrestrials from on top of the mystical Cerro Uritorco.

Villa General Belgrano (www.elsitiodelavilla.com/oktoberfest) The town's strong German heritage gives it a very European flavor, which really takes off as the beer starts flowing in Oktoberfest.

Villa Carlos Paz (www.villacarlospaz.gov.ar/turismo) Like a mix between Vegas and Disneyland, this lakeside getaway is dotted with theme hotels (the Great Pyramids, the Kremlin) and centered on a massive cuckoo clock.

Museo Rocsen (www.museorocsen.org; admission AR$55; ⊗9am-sunset) Near the tiny town of Nono, outside of Mina Clavero, the 27,000-plus pieces on display here form probably the most eclectic collection of trash 'n' treasure you're ever likely to see.

Hotel Eden (www.edenhotellafalda.com; admission by tour AR$45; ⊗10am-6pm) Take a guided tour of this extravagant hotel, built in 1897, and where the guest list included Albert Einstein, the duke of Savoy and several Argentine presidents.

Rincón Suizo
CAFE $

(Champaqui 1200; mains AR$70-100; ⊗11am-10pm) This comfy teahouse on the river prides itself on its homemade ice creams, delicious Swiss food (including fondue, raclette and ratatouille) and *torta selva negra*.

Palenque
INTERNATIONAL $

(San Martín 1191; mains AR$60-110; ⊗11am-1am; 🛜) Funky works of art on the walls and live music on the weekends make this a popular spot. It's a great place for drinks and the snacks and meals are a good deal, too.

Don Jorge
ARGENTINE $$

(Mitre 1198; mains AR$80-150; ⊗8am-midnight; 🛜) Excellent *parrilla*, reasonable pizza and a bunch of other Argentine staples, served up in a large, casual dining room. It's across the road from the bus station.

❶ Getting There & Away

The **bus terminal** (Mitre 1191) is across the Río Mina Clavero from the town center. There are several daily buses to Córdoba (AR$62, three hours) and at least three a day to Merlo (AR$44, 2½ to three hours). Minibuses to Córdoba are faster (AR$55, 2½ hours). A couple of buses per day depart for Buenos Aires (AR$979, 13 hours). For destinations in San Juan and Mendoza provinces, go to nearby Villa Dolores (AR$28, one hour).

SAN LUIS & AROUND

The little-visited province of San Luis holds a surprising number of attractions, made all the better by the fact that you'll probably have them all to yourself.

The province is popularly known as La Puerta de Cuyo (the door to Cuyo), referring to the combined provinces of Mendoza, San Luis, La Rioja and San Juan.

The regional superstar is without doubt the Parque Nacional Sierra de las Quijadas, but the mountain towns along the Valle de Conlara and Sierras Puntanas are well worth a visit if you're looking to get off the tourist trail.

Merlo

📞 02652 / POP 17,000 / ELEV 890M

At the top of the Valle de Conlara, the mountain town of Merlo is a growing resort known for its gentle microclimate (the local tourist industry buzzword) in a relatively dry area. The town is located 200km northeast of San Luis, tucked into the northeast corner of San Luis province.

The **municipal tourist office** (📞02652-476078; www.villademerlo.gov.ar; Coronel Mercau 605; ⊗8am-8pm) has maps and information on hotels and campgrounds.

◉ Sights & Activities

For a sweeping view of the town and valley, head up to the miradores (lookouts) overlooking town. Taxis charge around AR$480 to take you to the **Mirador del Sol**, halfway up the mountain and then another 12km to the **Mirador de los Condores**, which is on top of the mountain ridge, and gives views in both directions. There's a **confitería** (mains AR$80-120; ⊙8am-7pm) at Mirador del Sol and if the wind is right, you can watch the parasailing maniacs taking off from the nearby launchpad.

In Rincón del Este, 2km from the center, on the road to the miradores, the **Reserva Natural de Merlo** (⊙daylight hours) `FREE` is a lovely spot for creekside walks up to a couple of swimming holes. Tour operators in the park offer a range of activities including guided walks, ziplines and rock climbing. **El Rincón del Paraiso** (set meals around AR$100; ⊙8am-6pm), about 400m from the park entrance, is a beautiful, shady restaurant in the middle of the park – a great place for lunch or a couple of drinks.

Serranias Tour (☏02652-474737; www.serraniastour.com.ar; Av del Sol 186; ⊙9am-1pm & 3-8pm Mon-Fri, 9am-1pm Sat) is one of the many established tour operators in town. It offers tours to the nearby archaeological and paleontological park at Bajo de Veliz (half-day AR$450), and a trip combining the nature reserve and Miradors del Sol and de los Condores (half-day AR$350). They can hook you up with parasailing operators – flights cost around AR$1000 and last 20 to 30 minutes, depending on wind conditions.

⌱ Sleeping

Casa Grande Hostel   HOSTEL $
(☏02656-474579; www.casagrandehostelmerlo.com; Dos Venados 740; dm/d US$15/45) A short walk from the downtown action, this is Merlo's hippest hostel by far. Plenty of party action, decent rooms and sprawling grounds.

Hostería Cerro Azul   HOTEL $
(☏02652-478648; www.hosteriacerroazul.com.ar; cnr Saturno & Jupiter; r US$70; ☏☒) This bright, modern hotel just off the main drag offers big rooms with spacious bathrooms. The lounge-dining area is gorgeous, with high cathedral ceilings.

✗ Eating & Drinking

★Tono   ARGENTINE $$
(Av del Sol 690; mains AR$100-150; ⊙noon-1am; ☏) Specializing in regional foods and using lots of local ingredients, this place is a good bet anytime, but Thursday to Saturday nights feature live *trova* (folk) bands, making it even better.

Basta Lola   ARGENTINE $$
(Av del Sol 599; mains AR$100-160; ⊙10am-midnight Tue-Sat) Excellent home-style cooking in a cute corner location. The homemade pastas are the standouts, but make sure you leave room for dessert.

La Cerveceria   BAR
(Av del Sol 515; ⊙2pm-late; ☏) If you're looking for a beer, this is your spot – there are eight different types of microbrew on offer, plus the national and imported standbys, sidewalk seating and snacks.

❶ Getting There & Away

Long-distance buses leave from the **new bus terminal** (RN 1 at Calle de las Ovejas), about eight blocks south of the town center.

Buses from Merlo

DESTINATION	COST (AR$)	TIME (HR)
Buenos Aires	864	12
Córdoba	268	6
Mendoza	595	8
Mina Clavero	44	3
San Luis	97	4

❶ Getting Around

Local buses leave from the **old bus terminal** (☏02652-492858; cnr Pringles & Los Almendres) in the center of town. There are departures for Piedra Blanca (AR$10, 20 minutes), Bajo de Veliz (AR$28, one hour), Papagayos (AR$28, one hour) and the nearby artisan village of Cerro de Oro (AR$12, 30 minutes).

San Luis

☏0266 / POP 170,000 / ELEV 700M

Even people from San Luis will tell you that the best the province has to offer lies outside of the capital. That said, it's not a bad little town – there are a few historic sights here and the central Plaza Pringles is one of the prettiest in the country. The town's main

EL VOLCÁN

A small village nestled in the hills east of San Luis, El Volcán (there is no volcano here, by the way) is a laid-back summer getaway spot. The star attraction is the river that runs through the middle of town, where Balneario La Hoya, a series of natural rock pools, offers shady swimming spots and picnic areas.

El Volcán is close enough to San Luis to make it an easy day trip, but there are plenty of cabins for rent, especially during summer.

Hotel El Volcán (☑0266-449-4044; www.hotelelvolcan.com; Banda Norte s/n; s/d US$35/50; ❋ 🅿 🛇) is the only real hotel in the village. It's a sprawling complex set on shady grounds that run down to the river. The hotel closes off-season – call to make sure it's open. **El Mantial** (Balneario La Hoya; mains AR$70-90; ⊙8am-9pm) has decent food and great views out over the river. Portions are big and service is quick, if somewhat impersonal.

Regular buses run to and from San Luis' main bus terminal (AR$12, 30 minutes).

---

nightlife strip, Av Illia, with its concentration of bars, cafes and restaurants, makes for a fun night out.

The commercial center is along the parallel streets of San Martín and Rivadavia between Plaza Pringles in the north and Plaza Independencia in the south. Most services for travelers are within a few blocks of the plaza, with the exception of the bus terminal.

On the north bank of the Río Chorrillos, San Luis is 260km from Mendoza via RN 7 and 456km from Córdoba via RN 148.

◉ Sights

The center of town is the beautiful tree-filled Plaza Pringles, anchored on its eastern side by San Luis' handsome 19th-century **cathedral** (Rivadavia). Provincial hardwoods such as algarobo (carob tree) were used for the cathedral's windows and frames, and local white marble for its steps and columns.

On the north side of Plaza Independencia is the provincial **Casa de Gobierno** (Government House). On the south side of the plaza, the **Iglesia de Santo Domingo** (cnr 25 de Mayo & San Martín) and its convent date from the 1930s, but reproduce the Moorish style of the 17th-century building they replaced. Take a peek at the striking algarobo doors of the attached **Archivo Histórico Provincial** around the corner on San Martín.

Dominican friars at the **mercado artesanal** (cnr 25 de Mayo & Rivadavia; ⊙8am-1pm Mon-Fri), next to Iglesia de Santo Domingo, sell gorgeous handmade wool rugs as well as ceramics, onyx crafts and weavings from elsewhere in the province.

Also stroll over to the lovely former **train station** (Avs Illia & Lafinur) for a look at its green corrugated-metal roofs and decorative ironwork dating from 1884.

☞ Tours

Las Quijadas Turismo TOUR
(☑0266-443-1683; San Martín 874; ⊙9am-1pm & 4-8pm Mon-Sat) Tours to Parque Nacional Sierra de las Quijadas, La Angostura and Inti Huasi.

🛏 Sleeping

San Luis' better hotels cater to a business crowd, filling up quickly on weekdays and offering discounts on weekends.

San Luis Hostel HOSTEL $
(☑0266-442-4188; www.sanluishostel.com.ar; Falucho 646; dm/tw US$12/28; @ 🖥 🛇) San Luis' best and most central hostel has it all, from pool table to DVD library, excellent kitchen and shady backyard with barbecue. The 16-person dorms (segregated for male and female) could be a bit more atmospheric, but apart from that it's pure gold.

Hotel Castelmonte HOTEL $
(☑0266-442-4963; Chacabuco 769; s/d US$42/56; ❋🛇) An excellent-value hotel. Its spacious rooms have wooden parquetry floors and good firm beds. While central, it's set back from the road, keeping things nice and quiet.

Hotel Regidor HOTEL $$
(☑0266-442-4756; www.hotelregidorsanluis.com.ar; San Martín 848; s/d/apt US$58/88/110; ❋ 🛇 🖥) Don't let the shabby exterior fool you –

the rooms here are lovingly cared for, the staff is great and the big garden and pool area out back is a welcome sight in summer months.

✗ Eating & Drinking

Traditional San Luis dishes include *empanadas de horno* (baked empanadas) and *cazuela de gallina* (chicken soup).

There are numerous laid-back bars along Av Illia. As is the deal all over the country, they start late and end late. Go for a stroll and see which one you like.

Aranjuez   CAFE $

(cnr Pringles & Rivadavia; mains AR$60-100; ⊙8am-11:30pm; 🔊) A fairly standard cafe-bar-restaurant on the plaza, this one gets a mention for the sidewalk tables out on the pedestrian thoroughfare that make it a great spot for drinks, snacks and people-watching.

Los Robles   PARRILLA $$

(Colón 684; mains AR$100-160; ⊙12:30-3pm & 9pm-midnight Mon-Sat; 🔊) This upmarket *parrilla* has great atmosphere, attentive service and a menu that goes way beyond the usual offerings.

ℹ Information

Several banks, mostly around Plaza Pringles, have ATMs.

ACA (Automóvil Club Argentino; ☑0266-442-3188; Av Illia 401; ⊙24hr) Auto club; good source for provincial road maps.

Post Office (cnr Av Illia & San Martín; ⊙8am-6pm Mon-Fri & 9am-1pm Sat)

Regional Hospital (☑0266-442-2627; Av República Oriental del Uruguay 150) On the eastward extension of Bolívar.

Tourist Office (☑0266-442-3957; www.turismo.sanluis.gov.ar; cnr Av Illia & Junín; ⊙9am-9pm) The helpful staff can supply a good map of the town and its attractions plus offer good advice on regional attractions.

ℹ Getting There & Around

AIR

San Luis Airport (☑0266-442-2427) is 3km northwest of the center; taxis cost around AR$40.

Aerolíneas Argentinas (☑0266-442-5671; Av Illia 472; ⊙9am-6pm Mon-Fri, 9am-1pm Sat) flies daily to Buenos Aires.

BUS & CAR

San Luis' new **bus terminal** is on the eastern edge of town. For provincial destinations, including El Volcán (AR$12, 30 minutes), Carolina (AR$22, two hours), Inti Huasi (AR$24, 2½ hours) and Balde (AR$16, 45 minutes), you can get a bus from here or the **downtown stop**, which saves you a trek out to the terminal.

Buses to the center (AR$3.50) leave from in front of the Toyota dealership across the road from the terminal.

There are long-distance departures daily to most tourist destinations. For destinations such as Neuquén and Bariloche, you might have to head first to Mendoza or San Rafael.

Hertz (☑0266-15-4549002; Av Illia 305; ⊙9am-1pm & 3:30-5:30pm Mon-Fri, Sat 9am-1:30pm) is the local car-rental agency.

Buses from San Luis

DESTINATION	COST (AR$)	TIME (HR)
Buenos Aires	1150	11
Córdoba	515	7
Mendoza	335	5
Rosario	725	9
San Juan	425	5
San Rafael	260	5
Santa Fe	757	12

Balde

☑0266

This small village, 35km west of San Luis, is remarkable only for its thermal baths. The municipal complex is a decidedly down-at-heel affair, while a new spa resort offers oodles of comfort in gorgeous surrounds.

Centro Termal Municipal (☑0266-449-9319; Av Esteban Agüero s/n; 1hr bath per person AR$25, campsites US$5, cabin for 2 people US$45; ⊙baths 8am-6pm) offers small rooms with a bath and a bed to relax on, rented by the hour. They're clean enough and decent value for a quick dip. Cabins (located across the road) are spacious for two.

Los Tamarindos (☑0266-444-2220; www.jardinesdetamarindos.com; Av Esteban Agüero s/n; s/d US$55/70, cabin s/d US$63/80; ⊙baths 8am-6pm; 🔊🏊) is a wonderful thermal baths complex featuring a couple of public pools for day use – an outdoor one at 26°C (AR$30 per person) and a lovely, clean indoor one (AR$45 for both). The rooms here are standard, with small baths fed by hot spring water, but the cabins are a real treat – they're much more spacious and have a separate tub where you can get neck deep in the water.

Regular buses run to and from San Luis' bus terminal to the bus terminal at Balde (AR$16, 45 minutes), which is a short walk to either of the complexes.

Parque Nacional Sierra de las Quijadas

Fans of the Road Runner cartoons will feel oddly at home among the red sandstone rock formations in this rarely visited **national park** (📞02652-490182; usopublicoquijadas@apn.gov.ar; admission AR$80). The park comprises 1500 sq km of canyons and dry lake beds among the Sierra de las Quijadas, whose peaks reach 1200m at Cerro Portillo. Recent paleontological excavations by the Universidad Nacional de San Luis and New York's Museum of Natural History unearthed dinosaur tracks and fossils from the Lower Cretaceous, 120 million years ago.

Despite the shortage of visitors here, access to the park is excellent: buses from San Luis to San Juan will drop visitors at the park entrance and ranger station just beyond the village of Hualtarán, about 110km northwest of San Luis via RN 147 (San Juan is 210km to the northwest). At this point, a 6km dirt road leads west to a viewpoint overlooking the **Potrero de la Aguada**, a scenic depression beneath the peaks of the sierra that collects the runoff from much of the park and is a prime wildlife area. At the ranger station you can hire guides; two-hour, 3km treks to see the famous dinosaur footprints leave hourly between 9am and 4pm and cost AR$120 per person. Four-hour treks to a 150m-deep canyon in the park leave at 1:30pm and cost AR$220. A minimum group size of two people applies to both treks.

Other **hiking** possibilities in the park are excellent, but the complex canyons require a tremendous sense of direction or, preferably, the assistance of a local guide. Even experienced hikers should beware of summer rains and flash floods, which make the canyons extremely dangerous.

There's a shady **campground** FREE near the overlook, and a small store with groceries and drinks, including very welcome ice-cold beer.

Buses from San Juan to San Luis pass every hour or so, but they don't always stop. It's sometimes possible to catch a lift from the park entrance to the overlook.

Valle de las Sierras Puntanas

From San Luis the RP 9 snakes its way northwards, following the course of the Río Grande. Along the way, small villages are slowly developing as tourist destinations while still retaining much of their original character. The picturesque mining town of Carolina and nearby Inti Huasi cave are highlights of the region, and the landscapes higher up in the valley, with their rolling meadows and stone fences, probably resemble the Scottish highlands more than anything you've seen in Argentina so far.

Estancia Las Verbenas

Set in a gorgeous glade in the Valle de Pancanta, this **estancia** (📞0266-429-6151; www.lasverbenas.com.ar; RP 9, Km68; per person incl full board US$45; 📶) does rustic to the hilt, with plenty of hearty food served up among animal-skin decoration and rough-hewn furniture. Rooms are basic but comfortable. Three-hour horseback-riding tours (AR$220 per person) to a nearby waterfall are bound to be a highlight of your stay here. The signposted entrance to the property is just after the bridge on the highway, from where it's another 4km to the farmhouse. If you're coming by bus, call and staff will pick you up from the highway.

Carolina

📞02651 / POP 250 / ELEV 1610M

Nestled between the banks of the Río Grande and the foothills of Cerro Tomalasta (2020m), Carolina is a photogenic little village of stone houses and dirt roads. Take away the power lines and you could be stepping back in time 100 years. The region boomed in 1785 when the Spanish moved in to exploit local gold mines that had first been used by the Inca. Nobody uses street addresses in Carolina – the town is small enough to navigate without them.

⊙ Sights & Activities

One of the quirkier museums in the country, **Museo de Poesia** (⊙10am-6pm Tue-Sat) FREE honors San Luis' favorite son, poet Juan Crisóstomo Lafinur. The museum has a few artifacts from the poet's life, plus handwritten homages to the man by some of Argentina's leading poets.

Across the creek and up the hill from the poetry museum is a small stone labyrinth, set on the hilltop. It should provide an hour or so of entertainment (or, if your sense of direction is really bad, days of frustration).

Huellas Turismo (www.huellasturismo. com.ar; ⊗9am-1pm & 3-7pm) is the local tour operator – it can set you up with tours of the local gold mine, rock-climbing and rappelling trips on Cerro Tomalasta, and tours of Inti Huasi, La Casa de la Piedra Pintada and La Angostura.

🛏 Sleeping & Eating

Accommodation is improving in Carolina, but if you can't find a place, ask in the restaurants for a *casa de familia* (room in a private house with shared bathroom), which rent for around AR$100 per person.

Rincón del Oro Hostel   HOSTEL $
(☑02651-490212; Pringles s/n; dm/d without bathroom US$11/22; ☎) Set on a hilltop overlooking town, this great little hostel has a rustic, intimate feel despite its 57-bed capacity.

La Tomalasta   CAFETERIA $
(mains AR$50-80; ⊗8am-11pm) Good-value home-cooked meals. If it looks like it's closed, go around the back to the general store and ask them to open up.

ℹ Getting There & Away

Regular buses run from Carolina to San Luis (AR$22, two hours), passing through El Volcán. Some continue on to Inti Huasi (AR$10, 30 minutes).

Inti Huasi

This wide, shallow **cave** (⊗daylight hours) 𝗙𝗥𝗘𝗘, whose name means 'house of the sun' in Quechua, makes an interesting stop, as much for the gorgeous surrounding countryside as the cave itself. Radiocarbon dating suggests that the cave was first inhabited by the Ayampitín some 8000 years ago. There are regular buses here from San Luis (AR$24, 2½ hours), passing through Carolina (AR$10, 30 minutes).

La Casa de la Piedra Pintada

Coming from Carolina, 3km before the Inti Huasi cave, a dirt track turns off to Paso de los Reyes. From the turnoff, it's an easy walk to **La Casa de la Piedra Pintada** 𝗙𝗥𝗘𝗘, where more than 50 rock carvings are easily visible in the rock face. Follow the road until you reach an open meadow at the base of Cerro Sololasta and you see the new cable-and-wood walkway up the cliff face that gives you access to the site. Once you're finished looking at the rock art, continue up the hill for spectacular views out over the Sierras Puntanas.

The road used to be signposted, but isn't any more, which makes finding this place a little tricky – you can ask directions at Inti Huasi, or pay someone to guide you for a nominal fee.

Valle de Conlara

Heading northeast to Merlo from San Luis, the landscape changes dramatically as the road climbs into the hills. Leaving San Luis, the land is arid and desertlike; Papagayos has its own unique vistas, punctuated by palm trees, while Merlo is a lush mountain town.

Estancia La Estanzuela

Set on a Jesuit mission dating from 1750, this gorgeous **estancia** (☑02656-420559; www.estanzuela.com.ar; 1 or 2 people incl full board US$180; ☎) 𝄞 has been left in near-original condition from the days when it was a working farm. Floors are wood or stone, walls are meter-thick adobe and many ceilings are constructed in the traditional gaucho style. The house is decorated like a museum, with antique furniture, paintings and family heirlooms galore. A small pond that the Jesuits built for irrigation serves for romantic rowboating outings and there is plenty of horseback riding and nature walking to be done. This is a very special – near-magical – place and the minimum three-night stay should not be hard to adhere to. Prices include meals, drinks and activities.

The property is located 2km off RP 1, between Villa del Carmen and Papagayos. The closest public transportation is to Papagayos from Merlo. Reservations for rooms are essential and must be made at least two days in advance. If you don't have your own transportation, ask about getting picked up in Papagayos or San Luis.

Papagayos

🖉 02656 / POP 430

Possibly the last thing you're expecting to see in this part of the world is a valley full of palm trees, but that's exactly where this small town is situated. The town is located on the banks of the Arroyo Papagayos and has huge Caranday palms surrounding it, giving the area a certain notoriety for handicrafts made from their trunks and branches.

Small stores (mostly attached to workshops) selling these *artesanias en palma* are scattered around town. **Rosa López** (in front of plaza) has the best range. The tourist office can provide a map showing all the store locations, along with other local attractions.

The arroyo (creek) is a good place to cool off – its length is dotted with swimming holes. For a more formal swimming environment, the Balneario Municipal offers swimming pools, picnic and barbecue areas.

For horseback riding and trekking to local waterfalls and swimming spots out of town, ask at the tourist office or Hostería Los Leños.

The **Oficina de Turismo** (🖉 02656-481868; RP 1 s/n; ☺ 8am-8pm) is useful for contacting guides and arranging tours, and has decent maps of the town.

Hostería Los Leños (🖉 02656-481812; www.hosterialoslenios.blogspot.com; Av Comechingones 555; r US$58; ❋ 🛜 ☎) **FREE** is the best-looking hotel in town, featuring fresh new rooms with spacious bathrooms and a good-sized swimming pool. Also on offer are excellent home-cooked meals (mains AR$70 to AR$100), and staff can set you up with a picnic lunch if you're off on a day trip.

From Papagayos' main plaza there are regular buses to Merlo (AR$28, one hour).

Mendoza & the Central Andes

Best Wineries

➜ Di Tomasso (p334)

➜ Posada Salentein (p336)

➜ Viñas de Segisa (p351)

➜ Pulenta Estate (p336)

➜ Bianchi Champañera (p341)

Best Parks

➜ Parque Provincial Aconcagua (p339)

➜ Parque Provincial Volcán Tupungato (p341)

➜ Parque Provincial Payunia (p345)

➜ Parque Provincial Ischigualasto (p355)

Why Go?

A long, narrow sliver of desert landscape, the Mendoza region is home to two of Argentina's claims to fame – the Andes and **wine** (p328). The city itself is lively and cosmopolitan and the surrounding area boasts hundreds of wineries offering tours – an educational (and occasionally intoxicating) way to spend an afternoon or a month.

If you can put your glass down for a minute, there's plenty more to keep you busy. Just down the road is Aconcagua, the Americas' highest peak and a favorite for mountain climbers the world over. A couple of ski resorts give you the chance to drop into fresh powder while Mendoza's tour operators offer up a bewildering array of rafting, mountain biking and paragliding options.

To the north, often-overlooked San Juan province is well worth a visit, as much for its small but important selection of wineries as for the surreal desert landscape of the Parque Provincial Ischigualasto.

When to Go
Mendoza

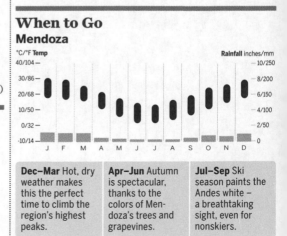

Dec–Mar Hot, dry weather makes this the perfect time to climb the region's highest peaks.

Apr–Jun Autumn is spectacular, thanks to the colors of Mendoza's trees and grapevines.

Jul–Sep Ski season paints the Andes white – a breathtaking sight, even for nonskiers.

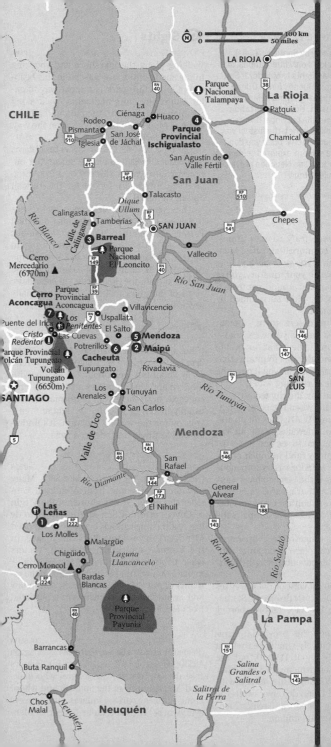

Mendoza & the Central Andes Highlights

1 Carving tracks in fresh powder on the world-class slopes of **Las Leñas** (p345).

2 Grabbing some wheels and treating yourself to a tour of the wineries in **Maipú** (p334).

3 Getting away from the crowds and into the stunning Valle de Calingasta in **Barreal** (p351).

4 Discovering dinosaur fossils embedded in bizarre rock formations in **Parque Provincial Ischigualasto** (p355).

5 Making the scene in any number of hip bars on Av Arístides in **Mendoza** (p332).

6 Soaking those aching traveling bones in the thermal complex at **Cacheuta** (p336).

7 Touching the roof of the Americas on **Cerro Aconcagua** (p340), the highest peak in the Western Hemisphere.

ⓘ Getting There & Away

With flights to/from nearby Santiago (Chile), Mendoza has the region's only international airport. There are regular flights to Mendoza, San Juan and San Luis from Buenos Aires. During ski season there are usually flights to Malargüe, near Las Leñas ski resort. Bus transportation is excellent throughout the province. If you're going south to the Lake District, the fastest way can be to head to Neuquén city, but if you don't mind taking it slow, a seldom-explored section of RN 40 between Mendoza and Neuquén provinces can be a worthwhile detour.

Mendoza

☑ 0261 / POP 1.1 MILLION / ELEV 703M

A bustling city of wide, leafy avenues, atmospheric plazas and cosmopolitan cafes, Mendoza is a trap. Even if you've (foolishly) only given it a day or two on your itinerary, you're bound to end up hanging around, captivated by the laid-back pace, while surrounded by every possible comfort.

Ostensibly it's a desert town, though you wouldn't know unless you were told – *acequias* (irrigation ditches) that run beside every main road and glorious fountains that adorn every main plaza mean you'll never be far from the burble of running water.

Lively during the day, the city really comes into its own at night, when the bars, restaurants and cafes along Av Arístides fill up and overflow onto the sidewalks, with all the bright young things, out to see and be seen.

All over the country (and in much of the world), the name Mendoza is synonymous with wine, and this is the place to base yourself if you're up for touring the vineyards, taking a few dozen bottles home or just looking for a good vintage to accompany the evening's pizza.

The city's wide range of tour operators also makes it a great place to organize rafting, skiing and other adventures in the nearby Andes.

Mendoza is 1050km west of Buenos Aires via RN 7 and 340km northwest of Santiago (Chile) via the Los Libertadores border complex.

Strictly speaking, the provincial capital proper is a relatively small area with a population of only about 115,000, but the inclusion of the departments of Las Heras, Guaymallén and Godoy Cruz, along with nearby Maipú and Luján de Cuyo, swells the population of Gran Mendoza (Greater Mendoza) to a little over one million.

◉ Sights

Parque General San Martín
PARK

Walking along the lakeshore and snoozing in the shade of the rose garden in this beautiful 420-hectare park is a great way to enjoy one of the city's highlights. Walk along Sarmiento/Civit out to the park and admire some of Mendoza's finest houses on the way. Pick up a park map at the **Centro de Información** (☑ 0261-420-5052; cnr Avs Los Platanos & Libertador; ⊙9am-5pm), just inside the impressive entry gates, shipped over from England and originally forged for the Turkish Sultan Hamid II.

The park was designed by Carlos (Charles) Thays in 1897, who also designed Parque Sarmiento in Córdoba. Its famous **Cerro de la Gloria** has a monument to San Martín's Ejército de los Andes (Army of the Andes) for its liberation of Argentina, Chile and Peru from the Spaniards. On clear days, views of the valley make the climb especially rewarding.

★ Museo Municipal de Arte Moderno
GALLERY

(Plaza Independencia; admission AR$23; ⊙9am-8pm Tue-Fri, from 2pm Sat & Sun) This is a relatively small but well-organized facility with modern and contemporary art exhibits. Free concerts and theatrical performances are usually held here on Sunday night at 8pm – stop by for the weekly program. It's underground at the Plaza Independencia.

Iglesia, Convento y Basílica de San Francisco
CHURCH

(Necochea 201; ⊙9am-1pm Mon-Sat) Many *mendocinos* (people from Mendoza) consider the image at this church of the Virgin of Cuyo, patron of San Martín's Ejército de los Andes, miraculous because it survived Mendoza's devastating 1968 earthquake. In the Virgin's semicircular chamber, visitors leave tributes to her and to San Martín. A mausoleum within the building holds the remains of San Martín's daughter, son-in-law and granddaughter, which were repatriated from France in 1951.

Museo Histórico General San Martín
MUSEUM

(Remedios Escalada de San Martín 1843; admission AR$10; ⊙9am-1pm & 3-8pm Mon-Fri) Honors José de San Martín, the general who liberated Argentina from the Spanish and whose name graces parks, squares and streets everywhere; the Libertador is dear to Men-

DON'T MISS

WINERIES NEAR MENDOZA

Thanks to a complex and very old system of river-fed aqueducts, land that was once desert now supports 70% of the country's wine production. Mendoza province is wine country, and many wineries near the capital offer tours and tasting. Countless tourist agencies offer day tours, hitting two or more wineries in a precisely planned day, but it's also easy enough to visit on your own. Hiring a *remise* (taxi) is also feasible. Some winery tours and tastings are free, though some push hard for sales at the end, and you never taste the *good* stuff without paying. Malbec, of course, is the definitive Argentine wine.

With a full day it's easy to hop on buses and hit several of the Mendoza area's most appealing wineries in the outskirts of neighboring **Maipú** (p334), only 16km away. For a look at what the cutting-edge wineries are doing, consider renting a car or going on a tour of the **Valle de Uco** (p336). Another option is the area of **Luján de Cuyo**, 19km south of Mendoza, which also has many important wineries. Buses to Maipú leave from La Rioja, between Garibaldi and Catamarca in central Mendoza; buses to wineries in Luján de Cuyo leave from Mendoza's **bus terminal** (p335).

Mendoza's **tourist office** (p335) on Garibaldi near Av San Martín provides a basic but helpful map of the area and its wineries. Also look for the useful three-map set *Wine Map: Wine and Tasting Tours*.

Luigi Bosca (☑0261-498-1974; www.luigibosca.com.ar; San Martín 2044, Luján de Cuyo; guided visits AR$200; ☉by reservation Mon-Sat) Luigi Bosca, which also produces Finca La Linda, is one of Mendoza's premier wineries. If you're into wine, don't miss it. Tours are available in Spanish and English. Take bus 380 (AR$5.50, one hour) from platform 53 in Mendoza's bus terminal.

Bodegas Chandon (☑0261-490-9968; www.bodegaschandon.com.ar; RN 40, Km29, Agrelo, Luján de Cuyo; guided visits AR$160; ☉by reservation Mon-Sat) The modern Bodegas Chandon is popular with tour groups and known for its sparkling wines (champagne). Tours are available in Spanish and English. Take bus 380 (AR$4.50, one hour) from platform 53 in Mendoza's bus terminal.

Catena Zapata (☑0261-413-1100; www.catenawines.com; Calle Cobos 5519, Agrelo, Luján de Cuyo; tours AR$200; ☉by appointment 9am-6pm Mon-Fri) Catena Zapata is one of Argentina's most esteemed wineries. Tours are fairly mundane but are conducted in English, German or Spanish. Tasting – if you put down the cash – can be educational indeed. Get there by taxi (cheaper if you catch a bus to Luján de Cuyo and grab one from there).

doza, where he resided with his family and recruited and trained his army to cross into Chile. The museum is in a small arcade off Av San Martín.

★ **Museo Fundacional**   MUSEUM
(cnr Alberdi & Videla Castillo; admission AR$27; ☉8am-8pm Tue-Sat, from 2pm Sun) Mendoza's Museo Fundacional protects excavations of the colonial *cabildo* (town council), destroyed by an earthquake in 1861. At that time, the city's geographical focus shifted west and south to its present location. A series of small dioramas depicts Mendoza's history, working through all of human evolution as if the city of Mendoza were the climax (maybe it was).

🏃 Activities

Once you've sucked down enough fine wine and tramped around the city, get into the Andes, Mendoza's other claim to fame, for some of the most spectacular mountain scenery you'll ever see.

Climbing & Mountaineering

Mendoza is famous for Cerro Aconcagua (p340), the highest mountain in the Americas, but the majestic peak is only the tip of the iceberg when it comes to climbing and mountaineering here. The nearby Cordón del Plata boasts several peaks topping out between 5000m and 6000m, and there are three important rock-climbing areas in the province: Los Arenales (near Tunuyán), El Salto (near Mendoza) and Chigüido (near Malargüe).

Mendoza

Pick up a copy of Maricio Fernandez' full-color route guide (Spanish only), *Escaladas en Mendoza,* at Inka Expediciones (p340). For up-to-date information and a list of recommended guides, contact the **Asociación Argentina de Guías de Montaña** (www.aagm.com.ar).

For climbing and hiking equipment, both rental and purchase, visit **Chamonix** (☏ 0261-425-7572; www.chamonix-outdoor.com.ar; Barcala 267; ⊙ 9am-1pm & 3-6pm Mon-Sat).

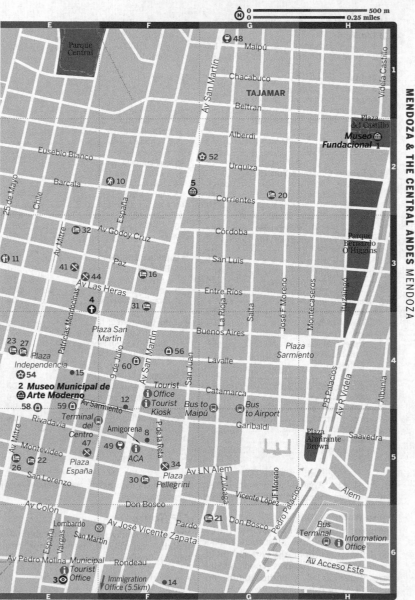

Skiing & Snowboarding

Los Penitentes has the best skiing near Mendoza, although further south, Las Leñas has arguably the best skiing in South America. For standard ski and snowboard equipment rental, try **Esquí Mendoza Competición** (☏0261-429-7944; Av Las Heras 583; ◷9am-8pm) or any of the shops along Av Las Heras. In high season, all charge around AR$230 per day for a skis-boots-poles package and about AR$280 per day for a snowboard with boots. Most rent gloves, jackets and tire chains, as well. If you're an intermediate or

Mendoza

advanced skier, Argentina Ski Tours (p324) can set you up with much better equipment.

White-Water Rafting

The major rivers are the Mendoza and the Diamante, near San Rafael. Most agencies offer half-day descents (from AR$420) and multiday expeditions. Transport costs AR$180 extra. Well-regarded Argentina Rafting operates a base in Potrerillos but you can book trips at its Mendoza office.

🍃 Courses

Intercultural   LANGUAGE COURSE
(☎0261-429-0269; www.spanishcourses.com.ar; República de Siria 241; ◎9am-8pm Mon-Sat) Offers group and private Spanish classes and internationally recognized exams. Can also

help find longer-term accommodation in Mendoza.

☞ Tours

Numerous agencies organize climbing and trekking expeditions, rafting trips, mule trips and cycling trips.

Argentina Rafting   ADVENTURE TOUR
(☎0261-429-6325; www.argentinarafting.com; Amigorena 86; ◎9am-6pm Mon-Sat) Rafting, mountain biking, kayaking, paragliding and rock climbing, among other activities.

Argentina Ski Tours   SKI TOUR
(☎0261-423-6958; www.argentinaskitours.com; Av Belgrano 1194B; ◎11am-8:30pm Mon-Fri, from 5:30pm Sat) Full-service ski tours and lessons in Spanish or English. Best quality ski-

equipment rental in town. Also brokers a range of on-mountain accommodations.

Huentata
GUIDED TOUR

(📞 0261-420-3863; www.huentata.com.ar; Sarmiento 45, Local 15; ⊙9am-8pm) Conventional travel agency that organizes trips in and around town. Possibilities include half-day tours of the city (AR$180), and day tours of the Cañón del Atuel (AR$570), Villavicencio (AR$280) or the high cordillera around Potrerillos, Vallecito and Uspallata (AR$480).

Wine Tours

For the casual sipper, a self-guided tour of Maipú or any of the bodega tours offered by various travel agencies around town will likely satisfy. There are also a few companies operating out of Mendoza offering deluxe wine tours. They're not cheap, but small group sizes, English-speaking guides and access to exclusive vineyards are among the benefits. Most also offer tours of the Valle de Uco, an important new wine-growing region 150km south of Mendoza that's near-impossible to explore by public transportation and is only just starting to appear on tour-agency itineraries.

All of the operators listed below can set you up with horseback tours of the vineyards, too, usually a full-day affair with gourmet lunch included (US$190).

Trout & Wine
TOUR

(📞 0261-425-5613; www.troutandwine.com; Espejo 266; ⊙9am-1pm & 3-8pm Mon-Sat) Organizes custom-designed, full-day tours of Luján de Cuyo (US$195) and the Uco Valley (US$205) with a maximum group size of eight. From November to March it runs fly-fishing tours in the Valle de Uco for US$260, including all gear and a barbecue lunch out in the highlands accompanied by – you guessed it – some very fine wines.

Mendoza Wine Camp
TOUR

(📞 0261-423-6958; www.mendozawinecamp.com; Av Belgrano 1194B; ⊙11am-8:30pm Mon-Fri, from 5:30pm Sat) 🍃 A young company whose tours tend more towards interaction and education. Also offers a great *asado* (barbecue grill) cooking-class day trip. Prices run to about US$200 per day.

Ampora Wine Tours
TOUR

(📞 0261-429-2931; www.mendozawinetours.com; Av Sarmiento 647; ⊙9am-9pm Mon-Sat, from 5pm Sat & Sun) A well-established operation

that concentrates on midrange and top-end wines. It has tours leaving every day to Luján de Cuyo (US$195) and the Uco Valley (US$210). Tours focus more on tasting than winemaking techniques.

🎊 Festivals & Events

Mendoza's biggest annual event, the **Fiesta Nacional de la Vendimia** (National Wine Harvest Festival), lasts about a week, from late February to early March. It features a parade on Av San Martín, with floats from each department of the province, numerous concerts and *folklórico* (folk music) events, and it all culminates in the coronation of the festival's queen in the Parque General San Martín amphitheater.

🛏 Sleeping

Note that hotel prices rise from January to March, most notably during the Fiesta Nacional de la Vendimia in early March. Some hostels in Mendoza will only rent you a bed if you buy one of their tours.

★ Hostel Alamo
HOSTEL $

(📞 0261-429-5565; www.hostelalamo.com.ar; Necochea 740; dm US$14-17, d US$37-58; @🛜🏊) An impeccable hostel in a great location, the Alamo offers roomy four-bed dorms, great hangout areas and a wonderful backyard with a small swimming pool.

Hostel Lagares
HOTEL $

(📞 0261-423-4727; www.hostellagares.com.ar; Corrientes 213; dm/d US$17/65; ❇🛜) This 'deluxe' hostel may charge a bit more than some of the competition, but you get a whole lot in return – it's spotlessly clean, the dorms are spacious and the breakfast generous. Some charming indoor and outdoor common areas add to the appeal.

Hostel Lao
HOSTEL $

(📞 0261-438-0454; www.laohostel.com.ar; Rioja 771; dm US$20, r with/without bathroom US$58-65/40; ❇🛜🏊) More like a cool B&B than a hostel, there are only four dorm beds here. The rest of the accommodations are in spacious private rooms set in a converted family home. More expensive rooms front straight onto the pretty backyard area.

Mendoza Inn
HOSTEL $

(📞 0261-438-0818; www.mendozahostel.com; Av Arístides Villanueva 470; dm US$12-15, d with/without bathroom US$45/39; @🛜🏊) With a great location and friendly, bilingual staff, this is one of the city's better hostels. Common areas are spacious and the big shady backyard and pool are definite pluses.

Hotel Casino
HOTEL $

(☎0261-425-6666; www.nuevohotelcasino.com.ar; Gutiérrez 668; s/d US$40/56; ✳☎) Facing on to Plaza Chile, the Hotel Casino offers some good, spacious rooms and some smallish, ordinary ones. They're all clean and comfortable, but have a look at a few before deciding.

Punto Urbano Hostel
HOSTEL $

(☎0261-429-5281; www.puntourbanohostel.com; Av Godoy Cruz 332; dm US$12-15, d with/without bathroom US$56/51; @☎) Just north of the city center, this hostel maintains an air of intimacy despite its grand proportions. The dorms are regular, but the doubles are extremely good value – spacious, with wide-screen TVs and tastefully decorated bathrooms. The large backyard – good for smoking, drinking, barbecuing and generally hanging out – is an added bonus.

Banana Hostel
HOSTEL $

(☎0261-423-3354; www.bananahostel.com.ar; Julio A Roca 344; dm US$16-30, d with/without bathroom US$76/65; ✳@☎≋) A spacious hostel set in the quiet residential neighborhood known as La Quinta. The common areas are great, as is the big backyard and huge swimming pool.

Hotel Zamora
HOTEL $

(☎0261-425-7537; Perú 1156; s/d US$37/48; ✳☎) With a lot more style than most in this price range, this sweet little family-run hotel offers comfortable rooms, a buffet breakfast and a charming courtyard, with tinkling fountain and Spanish tilework.

Alcor Hotel
HOTEL $$

(☎0261-438-1000; www.alcorhotel.com.ar; Paz 86; s/d US$52/65; ✳☎) One block from busy Av Las Heras, this is a recently renovated hotel that has maintained a few of its original charms. Rooms are big, light and well proportioned, with some comfy touches. Discounts apply for stays longer than three days.

Hotel Nutibara
HOTEL $$

(☎0261-429-5428; www.nutibara.com.ar; Mitre 867; s/d US$94/113; ✳☎≋) A short hop from the main plaza, the Nutibara offers a good deal in this price range. Rooms vary in size (some singles are quite cramped) and there's some serious beige-and-cream color scheming going on, but the pool area is fantastic

and the whole setup is very well run and maintained.

Hotel Abril
HOTEL $$

(☎0261-429-0027; www.hotel-abril.com; Patricias Mendocinas 866; s/d from US$64/78; ✳@☎) A modern hotel with touches of class, the Abril never really lives up to its 'boutique' claims, but is a pretty good deal for the price, amenities and location.

Hotel San Martín
HOTEL $$

(☎0261-438-0677; www.hsm-mza.com.ar; Espejo 435; s/d US$70/85; ✳@☎) Fronting the plaza, this three-story brick hotel offers solid value. There's plenty of tasteful tile work and rooms are spacious and comfortable, with modern bathrooms and big windows.

Hotel Argentino
HOTEL $$

(☎0261-405-6300; www.argentino-hotel.com; Espejo 455; s/d from US$88/108; ✳@☎≋) Right on the central plaza, this business-class hotel has some fine features, including large rooms and a decent-sized swimming pool. Pay extra for a balcony overlooking the plaza.

Palace Hotel
HOTEL $$

(☎0261-423-4200; www.hotelpalace.com.ar; Av Las Heras 70; s/d US$52/75; ✳☎) The fading '70s charm of this large hotel is compensated for by its great, central location and a few classy decorations left over from the good ol' days. Rooms are generously sized and those at the front boast views out over the busy avenue.

B&B Plaza Italia
B&B $$

(☎0261-423-4219; www.plazaitalia.net; Montevideo 685; r US$110; ✳☎) This five-room B&B is hard to beat when it comes to friendliness and delicious breakfasts. The house is lovely, the owners (who speak English) are divine, and the living room is just right for reading. It's like being at home.

★ Modigliani Suites
APARTMENT $$$

(☎0261-429-9222; www.modiglianisuites.com; Av LN Alem 41; apt US$141-304; ✳☎) Good-value furnished apartments are extremely hard to come by in Mendoza, but these ones are fantastic. The owner-architect has a keen eye for detail and the charming suites have just that right mix of minimalist cool and pleasing decoration. The on-site art gallery is an added bonus, as are the contemporary works that grace each apartment.

Hotel Bohemia BOUTIQUE HOTEL **$$$**
(0261-420-0575; www.bohemiahotelboutique.com; Granaderos 954; s/d US$125/155; ❄@ ☎✉) Somewhat out of place in Mendoza's otherwise workaday hotel scene, this repurposed family home features slick design, comfortable common areas and small but well-appointed rooms featuring minimalist decoration. It's about eight blocks west of the Plaza Independencia.

✕ Eating

Some of Mendoza's best restaurants, often with outdoor seating and lively young crowds, are along Av Arístides Villanueva, the western extension of Av Colón. West of Plaza Independencia, Av Sarmiento is lined with the city's most traditional, albeit touristy, *parrillas* (steak restaurants), while east of the plaza along the Sarmiento *peatonal* (pedestrian street), you'll find numerous sidewalk cafes with outdoor seating. The Sarmiento cafes are required visiting for coffee.

El Palenque ARGENTINE **$**
(Av Arístides Villanueva 287; mains AR$80-140; ⊕noon-2am Mon-Sat; ☎) Don't miss this superb, extremely popular restaurant styled after an old-time *pulpería* (tavern), where the house wine is served in traditional *pinguinos* (white ceramic penguin-shaped pitchers). The food and appetizers are outstanding, and the outside tables are always full and fun.

La Flor de la Canela PERUVIAN **$**
(Av Juan B Justo 426; mains AR$65-100; ⊕noon-3pm & 9pm-1am, closed Wed) Need something spicy? Check out this authentic, bare-bones Peruvian eatery a few blocks from the center. What it lacks in atmosphere it makes up for in flavor.

Cocina Poblana MIDDLE EASTERN **$**
(Av Arístides Villanueva 217; dishes from AR$70; ⊕noon-3pm & 7pm-midnight Mon-Sat) The very tasty, inexpensive Middle Eastern food here (hummus, falafel, dolmas) comes as a welcome break from all that steak. The shish kebab served with tabouleh salad is a definite winner.

Arrope VEGETARIAN **$**
(Primitiva de la Reta 927; per 100g AR$18; ⊕8am-3pm; ✎) Feeling a little meat-heavy? Slip into this cozy vegetarian cafe-restaurant and choose from a wide range of animal-free goodies on the buffet table.

La Mira FUSION **$**
(Av Belgrano 1191; mains AR$85-140; ⊕9am-midnight) Delicious, innovative dishes in a relaxed environment. Each dish comes as a full meal (some with side orders of vegetables) and there's a small but respectable wine list.

Mercado Central MARKET **$**
(cnr Av Las Heras & Patricias Mendocinas; mains from AR$70; ⊕8:30am-11pm) The renovated Mercado Central is a good hunting ground for cheap pizza, empanadas and sandwiches.

★ Anna Bistro FUSION **$$**
(Av Juan B Justo 161; mains from AR$120; ⊕noon-2am; ☎) One of Mendoza's best-looking restaurants offers a wonderful garden area, cool music and carefully prepared dishes.

Fuente y Fonda ARGENTINE **$$**
(Montevideo 675; mains AR$150; ⊕noon-3pm & 8pm-midnight) Good, honest, home-style cooking. The concept is traditional family dining, so expect big portions of hearty food in the middle of the table for everyone to share. A decent wine list and yummy free desserts round out the picture.

El Patio de Jesús María PARRILLA **$$**
(cnr Villanueva & Boulogne Sur Mer; mains AR$100-180; ⊕noon-4pm & 7:30pm-1am) One of Mendoza's favorite *parrillas* now has a convenient downtown location, at the end of the Arístedes bar strip. Portions are huge – beef is the obvious choice here, but the goat isn't to be overlooked either.

Patancha INTERNATIONAL **$$**
(Perú 778; mains AR$90-150; ⊕10am-2am Mon-Sat) A cute little place serving up some great tapas alongside traditional favorites such as *humitas* (stuffed corn dough resembling Mexican tamales) and the occasional surprise such as seafood stirfry. The AR$55 set lunch is a bargain.

Tasca de la Plaza SPANISH **$$**
(0261-423-3466; Montevideo 117; mains AR$120-150; ⊕noon-3pm & 7:30pm-1am Mon-Fri, 7:30pm-1am Sat) With excellent Mediterranean and Spanish tapas (mostly seafood), great wines, intimate atmosphere, good art and friendly service, La Tasca is one of Mendoza's best.

Maria Antioneta INTERNATIONAL **$$**
(Av Belgrano 1069; mains AR$100-160; ⊕8am-midnight Mon-Sat, 10am-5pm Sun; ☎) The wonderful, fresh blend of flavors on the menu

Mendoza's Wine

Since the Jesuits first planted vines in northern Argentina more than 500 years ago, Argentine wine has gone from strength to strength, and the country is now recognized as one of the leading international wine producers. If you're at all interested in wine, make sure the Mendoza area is firmly on your itinerary.

From Humble Beginnings...

The first major improvement in Argentine wine came with the arrival of European immigrants in the 19th century. These folks brought varieties from their home countries, replacing the Jesuit's criollo vines with 'noble' varieties such as merlot and cabernet sauvignon. The new grapes brought a minimal increase in quality, but even so, Argentine wine remained a very domestic product, often to be enjoyed with a big blast of soda to take the edge off.

Then, as if from nowhere, Argentine wines hit the world stage with a vengeance, and these days a Mendoza merlot has just as much (if not more) cachet than a comparably priced Chilean red.

Terroir & Technique

While the wineries have definitely improved their marketing, in the end it all comes down to quality – Argentine wines are good and they just keep getting better. One of the keys to successful wine making is controlled irrigation. A big rain before a harvest can spoil an entire crop, something winemakers in the desert-like Mendoza region don't have to worry about. Nearly every drop of water is piped in, and comes as beautiful fresh snowmelt from the Andes.

Desert vineyards have another advantage – the huge variation between daytime and nighttime temperatures. Warm days encourage sugar production and help the grapes grow a nice thick skin. Cool nights ensure good acidity levels and low humidity means bugs and fungus aren't a problem.

The techniques are improving, too – better hygiene standards; the further replacement of old criollo vines with noble varieties such as malbec, cabernet sauvignon, merlot and syrah; and the practice of aging wines in smaller oak barrels (with a lifespan of a few years) rather than large barrels (which would

---

MENDOZA SHOPPING LIST

Looking for the *really* good stuff? Here are the top picks in the malbec category from the 2015 Argentine Wine Awards:

➤ Septima Obra Malbec 2012, Bodega Septima – Codorniu Argentina SA

➤ Riglos Quinto Malbec 2013, Finca Las Divas SA – Bodega Riglos

➤ Casarena Malbec Jamilla's Single Vineyard 2012, Perdriel – Casarena Bodegas & Vineyards

➤ Zuccardi Aluvional Vista Flores Malbec 2012, Familia Zuccardi

---

1. Vineyard, Luján de Cuyo (p321)
2. Winery restaurant, Luján de Cuyo (p321)

be used for up to 70 years) have all had positive effects.

And you can't talk about Argentine wines without talking price-to-quality ratio. The country's economic crash in 2001 was a boon for exporters as prices plummeted and overnight Argentine wine became a highly competitive product. Land here is (relatively) cheap and labor so inexpensive that nearly every grape in the country is handpicked, a claim that only top-end wines in other countries can make.

Touring the Vineyards

As Mendoza's wine industry grows, so does its sister industry of wine tourism. These days it's not whether you can do a wine tour, but really which one and how.

There are options for every budget. If you're watching your pesos, biking around the **Maipú region** (p334) is an excellent-value option. Wineries here are close together and their tour prices are low, so you can visit several in a day

and taste some decent wines without breaking the bank. Be aware that this is a very popular way to spend the day, and some wineries will herd you through like cattle to make space for the next group.

If you're not a cyclist but not ready to commit to a full-on wine tour either, a good middle option is the satellite town of **Luján de Cuyo** (p321), 19km south of Mendoza. You can bus and taxi around the area with a minimum of planning, hit three or four wineries and be back in Mendoza before nightfall.

Those who can afford a little more and are interested in learning about techniques in a relaxed setting should consider a **tour** (p325). You'll avoid the crowds and sometimes get to meet the winemakers. The gourmet lunch at one of the wineries and top-shelf tastings that come with these tours may tip the scales, too. Tour companies can organize custom tours for the serious connoisseur, designed to take in the specific wineries, regions or even wines that you are particularly interested in.

1. Cycling on a wine tour 2. Wine grapes

But if you have the time and money, the best way to tour the region is strictly DIY. Rent a car in Mendoza, buy one of the winery maps on sale at every newsstand and create your own itinerary. Make the most of your freedom by visiting the **Valle de Uco** (p336) – home to some of the Mendoza region's most cutting-edge wineries. It's about 150km south of the city, but there are plenty of wineries offering accommodations and even specialty Wine Lodges – you can stay out there and tootle around to your heart's content. Be warned, though – Argentina has a zero-tolerance law for driving under the influence. If you get pulled over after a heavy day in the tasting room, you could be in big trouble.

SHIPPING WINE

While it's illegal to post wine from Argentina, countries such as the USA and Canada have no restriction on how much you can bring home in your luggage, provided you pay duty. And duty can be as low as US$5 for 40 bottles for the US.

If you are planning on transporting wine, it's best to stop in at a specialty wine store where they can pack bottles to avoid breakage (remember that many airlines have restrictions on bottles in hand luggage).

here are echoed in the design of the dining room – a pleasing mix of retro and modern styling. Everything's good – well presented and flavorful – and accompanied by an excellent selection of wines and desserts.

La Marchigiana   ITALIAN $$
(Patricias Mendocinas 1550; mains AR$110-160; ⊙noon-3pm & 7pm-1am) Mendoza's most frequently recommended Italian restaurant. The decor may seem stark, but the service is warm and a few Argentine twists to the classic Italian menu keep things interesting.

Azafrán   FUSION $$$
(⊘0261-429-4200; Av Sarmiento 765; mains AR$150-230; ⊙noon-3pm & 7pm-1am Mon-Sat) It's hard to figure out what's the bigger draw here – the rustic-chic decor, the small but creative menu or the extensive wine list. Who cares? Enjoy them all.

Siete Cocinas   ARGENTINE $$$
(⊘0261-423-8823; cnr San Lorenzo & Mitre; mains AR$160-220; ⊙8:30pm-1am Mon-Sat) Promising a gastronomical tour of Argentina's seven regional cuisines, this place delivers handsomely with delicacies such as goat-cheese ravioli, slow-cooked pork and Patagonian lamb-and-mushroom pie.

🍸 Drinking & Nightlife

For a great night on the town, walk down Av Arístides Villanueva, where it's bar after bar; in summer, entire blocks fill with tables and people enjoying the night. On the other side of town is the Tajamar, which is similar, but more laid-back and bohemian. This area is your best bet to hear live music.

Wine is available pretty much everywhere in Mendoza (right down to gas stations), but there are a few places that specialize.

Finding a dance floor generally means abandoning downtown for one of two areas: the northwest suburb of El Challao, or Chacras de Coria, along the RP 82 in the southern outskirts. The former is reached by bus 115 from Av Sarmiento. Chacras de Coria is reached from the stop on La Rioja between Catamarca and Garibaldi by taking bus 10, *interno* (internal route number) 19, or from the corner of 25 de Mayo and Rivadavia by taking bus 10, *interno* 15. In both cases simply asking the driver for *los boliches* (the nightclubs) is enough to find the right stop. The nightclubs in both El Challao and Chacras de Coria are all right

next to each other, and you can walk along to take your pick from the ever-changing array. **La Guanaca** (Ruta Panamericana s/n, Chacras de Coria; ⊙10pm-5:30am Fri & Sat) is the long-time favorite out here – with a bit of luck it may still be going by the time you arrive.

Many visitors to Mendoza (and *mendocinos* for that matter) find the effort involved getting to these places far outweighs the fun they have there, often opting for the smaller bars along Av Arístides Villanueva and the Tajamar.

Por Acá   BAR
(Av Arístides Villanueva 557; ⊙8pm-late Wed-Sat) Purple and yellow outside and polka-dotted upstairs, this bar-lounge gets packed after 2am, and by the end of the night, dancing on the tables is not uncommon. Good retro dance music.

La Reserva   GAY
(Rivadavia 34; admission free-AR$75; ⊙from 9pm Tue-Sat) This small, nominally gay bar packs in a mixed crowd and has outrageous drag shows at midnight every night, with hardcore techno later.

Blah Blah Bar   BAR
(Escalada 2307; ⊙from 6pm) A Tajamar favorite, Mendoza's version of a dive bar is hip but restrained, with a casual atmosphere and plenty of outdoor seating.

Uvas Lounge & Bar   WINE BAR
(Chile 1124; ⊙11am-midnight) In the super-formal surrounds of Mendoza's best-looking hotel, the Park Hyatt, this is a relaxed and intimate wine bar offering wine by the glass, cheese platters and tapas.

☆ Entertainment

Check the tourist offices or museums for a copy of *La Guía*, a monthly publication with comprehensive entertainment listings. *Los Andes*, the daily rag, also has a good entertainment section.

For everything from live music to avante-garde theater, check the program at the **Centro Cultural Tajamar** (⊘0261-425-5503; Escalada 1921; admission free-AR$35; ⊙from 8pm) in the Tajamar district.

The main theaters in town are **Teatro Quintanilla** (⊘0261-423-2310; Plaza Independencia) and the nearby **Teatro Independencia** (⊘0261-438-0644; cnr Espejo & Chile).

🔒 Shopping

Av Las Heras is lined with souvenir shops, leather shops, chocolate stores and all sorts of places to pick up cheap Argentine trinkets. Items made of *carpincho* (spotted tanned hide of the capybara, a large rodent) are uniquely Argentine and sold in many of the stores.

Specialty wine stores stock fine wines, have staff who speak at least a little English and can pack your bottles for shipping.

Carrefour   SUPERMARKET, WINE
(cnr Avs Las Heras & Belgrano; ⊘ 8am-10pm) Unless you are looking for a very obscure top-of-the-range bottle (or a sales assistant who knows what they're talking about), the best place to buy wine in town, in terms of price and variety, is the supermarket Carrefour.

Plaza de las Artes   MARKET
(Plaza Independencia; ⊘ 5-11pm Fri-Sun) Outdoor crafts market.

Raices   HANDICRAFTS
(Av España 1092; ⊘ 8am-7pm Mon-Fri, to 1pm Sat) High-quality weavings, jewelry and more. There is another location nearby on Av Sarmiento 162.

Juan Cedrón   WINE
(Av Sarmiento 278; ⊘ 9am-1pm & 4-9pm Mon-Sat) A small but well-chosen wine selection lines the walls. Doubles as a wine bar. Occasional tastings and sidewalk tables.

Centro Internacional del Libro   BOOKS
(☑ 0261-420-1266; Lavalle 14; ⊘ 9am-6pm Mon-Fri, to 2pm Sat) Small selection of classics and best-sellers in English.

SBS   BOOKS
(Gutiérrez 54; ⊘ 9am-6pm Mon-Sat) A large range of novels in English, Lonely Planet guidebooks, maps and wine-related literature. Also Test of English as a Foreign Language (TOEFL) resources and textbooks for Spanish students.

ℹ Orientation

The city's five central plazas are arranged like the five-roll on a die, with Plaza Independencia in the middle and four smaller plazas lying two blocks from each of its corners. Be sure to see the beautifully tiled Plaza España.

Av San Martín is the main thoroughfare, crossing the city from north to south, and Av Las Heras is the principal commercial street.

A good place to orient yourself is the **Terraza Mirador** (free; ⊘ 9am-1pm), which is the rooftop terrace at **City Hall** (9 de Julio 500), offering panoramic views of the city and the surrounding area.

ℹ Information

DANGERS & ANNOYANCES

Mendoza has long been one of Argentina's safer destinations, but economic woes have caught up here, too, resulting in an increased number of street crimes. Tourists are rarely the target here and the city is still a safe place, but there are a few things to watch out for. Bag snatching and pickpocketing are on the rise.

The areas around the bus terminal and on Cerro de la Gloria (in Parque General San Martín) now have an increased police presence, but are still considered dangerous at night. Increased caution is recommended during the early afternoon, too, as police tend to take the siesta along with everybody else. There have been several reports of people picking locks on hostel lockers – if you have something really valuable, leave it at your hostel's reception or, better yet, in its safe.

EMERGENCY

Servicio Coordinado de Emergencia (☑ 0261-428-0000) Call for an ambulance.

IMMIGRATION

Immigration Office (☑ 0261-424-3512; Av San Martín 1859; ⊘ 9am-4pm Mon-Fri) In Godoy Cruz, south of the city center.

MEDIA

La Guía This free monthly events magazine is a must-have if you plan on keeping up with Mendoza's hectic cultural scene. Pick up a copy at any tourist office.

Wine Republic (www.wine-republic.com) An excellent English-language magazine focusing on wine but also featuring good reviews of up-and-coming restaurants, Mendoza gossip and a couple of entertaining articles. Pick up a copy at your hotel, one of the tourist offices or **Trout & Wine** (p325).

CUYO

The provinces of Mendoza, San Juan, San Luis and La Rioja are traditionally known as the Cuyo, a term derived from the indigenous Huarpe word *cuyum*, meaning 'sandy earth.' The Huarpes were the original practitioners of irrigated agriculture in the region, a legacy still highly visible throughout the region today. The term is one you'll encounter often, whether in the names of local bus companies, businesses and newspapers, or in everyday conversation.

MAIPÚ: A GOURMET EXPERIENCE

The small town of Maipú, just out of Mendoza, is so packed with wineries, olive-oil farms and other gourmet businesses that it's easy to hit five or six in a day. All offer tours and most finish proceedings with at least a small sampling of their produce.

Accordingly, a few companies in Maipú rent bikes, making a day tour of the area an excellent outing, and a lot more fun than the often rushed half-day wine tours on offer from Mendoza tour agencies.

To get to Maipú, catch the 173 bus from the bus stop on La Rioja in Mendoza and get off at the triangular roundabout. Bike-hire competition here is serious business (there have been fistfights in the street between operators) and the main companies are all within walking distance of each other. Go for a stroll and see who has the best wheels. Among operators are **Mr Hugo Bikes** (0261-497-4067; www.mrhugobikes.com; Urquiza 2228; bikes per day AR$80; 9am-7pm Mon-Sat) and **Coco Bikes** (0261-481-0862; Urquiza 1781; bike hire AR$70; 9am-6pm Mon-Sat). All will supply you with a (basic) map of the area and may throw in goodies like a bottle of water and discount vouchers for tastings.

Reservations are not necessary at most of the places on this route.

Carinae (0261-499-0470; www.carinaevinos.com; Aranda 2899; tours AR$50; 10am-6pm) is the furthest south you really want to go – it's a small, French-owned winery producing a lovely rosé and some good reds. Tour fees are deducted from any wine purchases you make.

Across the road is **LAUR** (www.laursa.com.ar; Aranda 2850; tours AR$20; 10am-6pm Mon-Sat), a 100-year-old olive farm. The 15-minute tour tells you everything you need to know about olive-oil production and is followed by a yummy tasting session.

Heading back to Urquiza, go past the big roundabout and venture north. The first winery you come to is **Di Tomasso** (0261-587-8900; www.familiaditommaso.com; Urquiza 8136; tours AR$40; 10am-6pm Mon-Sat), a beautiful, historical vineyard dating back to the 1830s. The tour includes a quick pass through the original cellar section.

Heading north again, take a right on Moreno to get to **Viña del Cerno** (0261-481-1567; www.elcerno-wines.com.ar; Moreno 631; tours AR$40, full tasting AR$90; 10am-6pm Mon-Sat), a small, old-fashioned winery supervised by its two winemaker owners. The underground cellar complex is atmospheric, but tastings can be a little rushed.

Making your way back to Urquiza, drop in at **Tempus Alba** (0261-4813501; www.tempusalba.com; Moreno 572), a large, modern winery that offers a quick, self-guided tour of the and a tasty lunch menu (mains AR$80–120) in its restaurant overlooking the vines.

Back on Urquiza, continue north until you get to the big roundabout. Turn right and follow the signs to **Historia y Sabores** (Carril Gómez 3064; tastings AR$40; 10am-6pm Mon-Fri, 9am-1pm Sat). Seven families run this little chocolate- and liqueur-making operation. Tours are brief, but the lovely, rustic surrounds and comfy bar (where you're offered a free shot of liqueur) make it a worthwhile stop.

Along Urquiza, keep heading north until you get to where you got off the bus, take a right on Montecaseros and continue for 500m to reach **Bodega La Rural** (0261-497-2013; www.bodegalarural.com.ar; Montecaseros 2625; tours AR$90; 9am-1pm & 2-5pm Mon-Fri). Winery tours here are fairly standard (and you probably have the idea by now) but the museum is fascinating – displaying a huge range of winemaking equipment from over the years, including a grape press made from an entire cowskin. Tours in Spanish leave on the hour. If you want one in English, call ahead, or you can simply walk around on your own.

MEDICAL SERVICES

Hospital (0261-420-0600, 0261-420-0063; cnr José F Moreno & Alem)

MONEY

There are many ATMs downtown. Banco de la Nación and Banco Menoza are architectural landmarks; the latter is massive.

Banco de la Nación (cnr Necochea & 9 de Julio; 9am-1pm Mon-Fri)

Banco Mendoza (cnr Gutiérrez & España; 9am-1pm Mon-Fri)

Cambio Santiago (Av San Martín 1199; 8am-6pm Mon-Fri, 9am-1pm Sat & Sun) Charges 2% commission on traveler's checks.

POST

Post Office (cnr Av San Martín & Colón; ⊙8am-6pm Mon-Fri, 9am-1pm Sat)

TOURIST INFORMATION

ACA (Automóvil Club Argentina; ☑0261-420-2900; cnr Av San Martín & Amigorena; ⊙24hr) Argentina's auto club; good source for provincial road maps.

Municipal Tourist Offices (www.turismo.men doza.gov.ar) The municipality has information offices at the bus terminal (☑0261-431-5000; ⊙8am-8pm) and city hall (☑0261-413-2101; 9 de Julio 500; ⊙9am-9pm).

Tourist Kiosk (☑0261-420-1333; Garibaldi; ⊙8am-6pm) This helpful kiosk near Av San Martín is the most convenient information source.

Tourist Office (☑0261-420-2800; www. turismo.mendoza.gov.ar; Av San Martín 1143; ⊙8am-10pm Mon-Fri) Good maps and plenty of brochures.

TRAVEL AGENCIES

Almundo (☑0261-429-0029; Av Sarmiento 223; ⊙9am-1pm & 4:30pm-8:30pm Mon-Fri, 10am-1pm Sat) Recommended student and discount travel agency.

❶ Getting There & Away

AIR

Aerolíneas Argentinas/Austral (☑0261-420-4185; Av Sarmiento 82; ⊙10am-6pm Mon-Fri, to 1pm Sat) These airlines share offices; Aerolíneas flies several times daily to Buenos Aires.

LANChile (☑0261-425-7900; Rivadavia 256; ⊙10am-7pm Mon-Fri) LANChile flies twice daily to Santiago de Chile.

BUS

Mendoza is a major transport hub, so you can travel to just about anywhere in the country. Mendoza's **bus terminal** (☑0261-431-3001; cnr Avs de Acceso Este & Costanera) has domestic and international departures. You can book tickets at no extra cost downtown at the **Terminal del Centro** (9 de Julio 1042; ⊙9am-1pm & 5-9pm).

Domestic

Several companies send buses daily to Uspallata (AR$68, two hours) and Los Penitentes (AR$82, four hours), the latter for Aconcagua.

During the ski season several companies go directly to Las Leñas (about AR$200, seven hours).

A number of companies offer a morning bus service to the Difunta Correa Shrine (AR$160 return, departs 7:30am) in San Juan province; the journey is three hours each way and the bus waits three hours before returning. Buses to Maipú leave from the stop on La Rioja between Garibaldi and Catamarca.

There are daily departures from Mendoza's bus terminal to most destinations in the following table, and sometimes upwards of 10 to 20 per day to major cities. Prices reflect midseason fares.

DESTINATION	COST (ARS)	TIME (HR)
Bariloche	1375	20
Buenos Aires	1375	13-17
Catamarca	874	10
Córdoba	805	10
Jujuy	1376	22
Malargüe	201	5
Mar del Plata	1550	19
Neuquén	1025	10-12
Resistencia	1493	24
Río Gallegos	2849	41
Rosario	1025	12
Salta	1142	18
San Juan	224	2½
San Luis	335	3½
San Rafael	72	3
Tucumán	1127	14
Vallecito	260	3

International

Numerous companies cross the Andes every day via RN 7 (Paso de Los Libertadores) to Santiago, Chile (AR$595, seven hours), Viña del Mar (AR$500, seven hours) and Valparaíso (AR$500, eight hours). The pass sometimes closes due to bad winter weather; be prepared to wait (sometimes days) if weather gets extreme.

Several carriers have connections to Lima, Perú (AR$4296, 60 to 70 hours), via Santiago, Chile.

International buses depart from the main bus terminal. Companies are at the eastern end of the terminal.

❶ Getting Around

TO/FROM THE AIRPORT

Plumerillo International Airport (☑0261-520-6000; Acceso Norte s/n) is 6km north of downtown on RN 40. Bus 68 ('Aeropuerto') from Calle Salta goes straight to the terminal.

Mendoza's bus terminal is really just across the street from downtown. After arriving, walk under the Videla underpass and you'll be heading toward the center, about 15 minutes away. Otherwise, the 'Villa Nueva' trolley (actually a bus) connects the terminal with downtown.

BUS

Local buses cost AR$3.50 – more for longer distances – and require a magnetic Redbus card, which can be bought at most kiosks in denominations of AR$5 and AR$10. Most *lineas* (bus lines) also have *internos* (internal route numbers) posted in the window; for example, *linea* 200 might post *interno* 204 or 206; watch for both numbers. *Internos* indicate more precisely where the bus will take you.

CAR

Car-rental agencies are at the airport and along Primitivo de la Reta.

Avis (☑ 0261-447-0150; Primitivo de la Reta 914; ☺ 8:30am-8:30pm Mon-Fri, 8:30am-1pm & 5:30-8pm Sat & Sun)

Localiza (☑ 0261-429-6800; Primitivo de la Reta 936, Local 4; ☺ 8am-8pm Mon-Fri, 9am-1pm & 5-8pm Sat & Sun)

National/Alamo (☑ 0261-429-3111; Primitivo de la Reta 928; ☺ 8am-8pm Mon-Fri, 8:30am-1pm & 4-8pm Sat & Sun)

Cacheuta

☑ 02624 / POP 640 / ELEV 1237M

About 40km southwest of Mendoza, in the department of Luján de Cuyo, Cacheuta is renowned for its medicinal thermal waters and agreeable microclimate.

The excellent, open-air thermal-baths complex **Complejo Termal Cacheuta** (☑ 02624-490139; www.termascacheuta.com; RP 82, Km41; weekday/weekend AR$110/130; ☺ 10am-6pm) is one of the best in the country due to its variety of pools and dramatic setting on the side of a valley. Midweek is the best time to come, as weekends get crowded with kids splashing around on the waterslide and in the wave pool, and the air runs thick with the smoke from a thousand *parrillas*.

Expreso Uspallata (☑ in Mendoza 0261-438-1092) runs daily buses to Cacheuta (AR$68, 1½ hours) from Mendoza.

TOURING THE VALLE DE UCO

Seriously remote and woefully signposted, the Valle de Uco – home to some of Mendoza's top wineries – is best visited on a guided tour. If you've got the time and patience, though, you can easily rent a car in Mendoza to make the trip.

The valley is an easy day trip from Mendoza, but there are some wonderfully atmospheric places to stay out here, including **Tupungato Divino** (☑ 02622-448948; www.tupungatodivino.com.ar; cnr RP 89 & Calle los Europeos; r from US$145; ❄ @), **Posada Salentein** (☑ 02622-429000; www.bodegasalentein.com; RP 89 s/n; r with full board from US$265; ❄ @ 🛜 ☀) and **Casa Antucura** (☑ 0261-15-339-0491; www.casaantucura.com; Barandica s/n, Tunuyán; r from US$320; ❄ @ ☀).

If you're looking for a lunch stop, most of the wineries offer gourmet meals. Otherwise, **Ilo** (☑ 02622-488323; cnr Cabral & Belgrano, Tupungato; mains AR$110-180; ☺ noon-3pm & 8pm-midnight Mon-Sat) is generally considered the best in Tupungato – the good range of seafood dishes makes it a winemakers' favorite.

Reservations are essential for touring any of the 'must see' wineries in the region.

Pulenta Estate (☑ 0261-507-6426; www.pulentaestate.com; RP 86; ☺ 9am-5pm Mon-Fri, to 1pm Sat) A boutique winery started by the ex-owners of the Trapiche label. Tours of the beautiful modern facility focus on tasting, not production.

Andeluna Estate (☑ 0261-15-508-9525; www.andeluna.com.ar; RP 89, Km11; ☺ 10am-5pm) Tastings of the wonderful wines produced here take place in a charming old-world style tasting room. There are also great mountain views from the patio.

La Azul (☑ 02622-423593; www.bodegalaazul.com.ar; RP 89 s/n; ☺ 10am-5pm Mon-Sat) A small winery producing excellent malbecs. Tours are in Spanish only, but focus mainly on tasting – you're in and out in 20 minutes.

Salentein (☑ 02622-429000; www.bodegasalentein.com; RP 89 s/n; ☺ 9am-5pm Mon-Sat) A state-of-the-art, Dutch-owned winery that's distinctive for its on-site, contemporary-art gallery and its method of moving grapes and juice by hand and gravity, rather than by machine. English-language tours take place at 11am and 3pm.

Francois Lurton (☑ 0261-441-1100; www.francoislurton.com; RP 94, Km21) An ultramodern facility run by two French brothers from a famous winemaking family, producing one of the best Mendoza torrontés on the market. Excellent tours with impressive tasting areas and barrel room.

🛏 Sleeping

Camping Termas de Cacheuta
CAMPGROUND **$**

(☑ 02624-482082; RN 7, Km39; campsite per person US$5) Campers can pitch a tent at Camping Termas de Cacheuta.

Hotel & Spa Cacheuta
HOTEL **$$$**

(☑ 02624-490153; www.termascacheuta.com; RP 82, Km38; s/d with full board from US$157/234; ☒) There is lodging at the lovely Hotel & Spa Cacheuta, where prices include a swimming pool, hot tubs, massage, in addition to optional recreation programs. Nonguests may use the baths for around AR$480 per person.

Potrerillos

☑ 02624 / ELEV 1351M

Set above the newly built Potrerillos reservoir in beautiful Andean *precordillera* (foothills), Potrerillos is one of Mendoza's white-water hot spots, usually visited during a day's rafting trip from the capital.

Located about 1km uphill from the ACA campground, **Argentina Rafting** (☑ 02624-482037; www.argentinarafting.com; Ruta Perilago s/n) offers rafting and kayaking on the Río Mendoza. Trips range from a 5km, one-hour Class II float to a 50km, five-hour Class III–IV descent over two days. Organize trips at the Mendoza office (p324) or at the base here in Potrerillos.

🛏 Sleeping

Camping del ACA
CAMPGROUND **$**

(☑ 02624-482013; RN 7, Km50; campsites members/nonmembers US$8/9) Camping del ACA offers shady sites near the reservoir just below the new town.

Villavicencio

☑ 0261 / ELEV 1800M

If you've ordered mineral water from any restaurant or cafe in Argentina, odds are you've ended up with a bottle of Villavicencio on your table. These springs are the source, and their spectacular mountain setting once hosted the prestigious thermal baths resort of the **Gran Hotel de Villavicencio** (☉ 8am-8pm) FREE. Popular with the Argentine elite during the middle of the 20th century, the resort has been closed for more than a decade; promises have floated around for years that it will 'soon' reopen.

Panoramic views from the hair-raising winding turns leading to Villavicencio make the journey an attraction in itself. There is free camping alongside the attractive **Hostería Villavicencio** (☑ 0261-439-6487; meals AR$110-150; ☉ 10:30am-6pm), which has no accommodations but serves gourmet meals in charming surrounds.

There is no public transportation to the valley. Nearly every tour operator in Mendoza (p324) offers half-day tours (AR$280) that take in the hotel grounds, the bottling plant and short walks in the surrounding countryside.

Uspallata

☑ 02624 / POP 3800 / ELEV 1751M

A humble little crossroads town on the way to the Chilean border, Uspallata is an oasis of poplar trees set in a desolate desert valley. The polychrome mountains surrounding the town so resemble highland Central Asia that director Jean-Jacques Annaud used it as the location for the epic film *Seven Years in Tibet*.

The town first gained fame as a low-budget base for the nearby ski fields at Los Penitentes, but has recently been coming into its own, with a few companies offering treks, horseback riding and fishing expeditions in the surrounding countryside.

There's a post office and a Banco de la Nación, which has an ATM. The **tourist office** (☑ 02624-420009; RN 7 s/n; ☉ 8am-9pm) is across from the YPF gas station. It has good information on local sights and activities and some very basic (but still useful) area maps.

👁 Sights

A kilometer north of the highway junction in Uspallata, a signed lateral leads to ruins and a museum at the **Museo Las Bóvedas** (☉ 11am-5pm) FREE, a smelting site since pre-Columbian times. An easy 8km walk north of town brings you to **Cerro Tunduqueral** (☉ 11am-6:30pm) FREE, where you'll find sweeping views and Inca rock carvings.

👉 Tours

Desnivel Aventura
OUTDOORS

(☑ 0261-15-589-2935; www.desnivelaventura.com) Desnivel Aventura offers a range of outdoor activities, including horseback riding, mountain-bike tours, rock climbing, trekking and 4WD off-roading. It also rents mountain bikes for AR$30/90 per hour/day.

Fototravesías 4x4 GUIDED TOUR

(☑ 0261-15-511-9502; www.fototravesias4x4.com) 🏷 Fototravesías 4x4, near the main intersection, offers exciting 4WD tours in the surrounding mountains. The owner is a photographer and is especially amenable to ensuring travelers get good shots.

🛏 Sleeping & Eating

In the summer high season (when climbers from around the world descend on the area), reservations are wise.

Hostel International Uspallata HOSTEL $

(☑ 0261-15-466-7240; www.hosteluspallata.com. ar; RN 7 s/n; dm/d US$11/45, cabin US$60-80) Friendly hostel 7km east of town, with plain but comfortable rooms and a couple of sweet little cabins. Dinner (AR$85 to AR$120) is available. There's good hiking from the hostel and you can rent bikes and horses here. Ask the bus driver to drop you at the front before you hit Uspallata.

Hotel Portico del Valle HOTEL $$

(☑ 02624-420103; Las Heras s/n; dm/s/d US$18/780/920) A recently constructed, vaguely modern hotel right on the crossroads. It's nothing fancy, but fine for a few days. The hostel is in a separate building a few blocks away. Enquire at reception.

Hostería Los Cóndores HOTEL $$

(☑ 02624-420002; www.loscondoreshotel.com.ar; Las Heras s/n; s/d US$84/110; ❄ ♨) Close to the junction, this is the finest hotel in the center of town. There's plenty of space, modern furnishings, and a gut-busting breakfast buffet is included in the price.

★ Café Tibet CAFE $

(cnr RN 7 & Las Heras; mains AR$65-100; ☺ 8am-11pm) No visit to Uspallata would be complete without at least a coffee in this little oddity. The food is nothing spectacular, but the decor, comprising leftover props from *Seven Years in Tibet*, is a must for fans of the surreal.

El Rancho PARRILLA $$

(cnr RN 7 & Cerro Chacay; mains AR$100-150; ☺ noon-3pm & 7pm-1am Tue-Sun) This is the coziest and most reliable *parrilla* in town, serving all the usual, plus a good roasted *chivo* (goat).

ℹ Getting There & Away

Expreso Uspallata (☑ 0261-432-5055) runs several buses daily to and from Mendoza (AR$68, 2½ hours). Buses continue from Uspallata to Las Cuevas (AR$75, two hours), near the Chilean border, and stop en route at Los Penitentes, Puente del Inca and the turnoff to Laguna Los Horcones for Parque Provincial Aconcagua. They can be flagged from all of these locations on their return to Uspallata from Las Cuevas.

Andesmar has daily morning departures to Santiago (AR$500, six hours) and Valparaíso (AR$500, seven hours) in Chile.

There's been talk for years of a new bus service to connect Uspallata with Barreal in San Juan province – the road has now been paved, so it may well be operating by the time you read this.

All buses leave from the Expreso Uspallata office in the little strip mall near the junction.

Los Penitentes

☑ 02624 / ELEV 2581M

So named because the pinnacles resemble a line of monks, **Los Penitentes** (☑ 0261-429-9953; www.lospenitentes.com; lifts per day AR$360-490) has both excellent scenery and snow cover (in winter). It's 165km west of Mendoza via RN 7, and offers downhill and cross-country skiing at an altitude of 2580m. Lifts (AR$360 to AR$490 per day) and accommodations are modern, and the vertical drop on some of its 21 runs is more than 700m. Services include a ski school (private lessons start around AR$340), equipment rentals (skis AR$195 per day, snowboards AR$260) and several restaurants and cafeterias.

In high ski season (July and August) and during peak climbing season (December through to March), it's recommended to make reservations up to a month in advance.

🛏 Sleeping

Hostel Los Penitentes HOSTEL $

(☑ in Mendoza 0261-425-5511; www.penitentes.com. ar; dm US$24-31) A cozy converted cabin, owned by Mendoza's HI Campo Base, it accommodates 38 people in extremely close quarters, and has a kitchen, wood-burning stove and three shared bathrooms. It's all good fun with the right crowd. Lunch and dinners are available for AR$70 to AR$100 each.

Hostería Los Penitentes HOTEL $$

(☑ in Mendoza 0261-524-4708; www.hosteria-penitentes.com; d from US$135) This modest *hostería* with plain, comfortable rooms has a restaurant and bar, and offers full board with ski passes.

Refugio Aconcagua HOTEL $$

(☑ in Mendoza 0261-424-1565; www.refugioaconcagua.com.ar; r with half-board per person US$110)

There's nothing fancy about the rooms at this place, but they're an OK size, and considering you're in the middle of the resort, with a private bathroom and two meals a day, they're a good deal. The restaurant here serves up big, hearty set meals (AR$80 to AR$200) and is open year-round.

Hotel Ayelén   HOTEL $$$
(☑in Mendoza 0261-428-4343; s/d from US$129/193) This recently renovated hotel is one of the class acts on the mountain. The restaurant is fantastic, and consistently gets rave reviews. Both are only open weekends off-season.

Puente del Inca
☑0261 / ELEV 2270M

One of Argentina's most striking natural wonders, this stone bridge over the Río de las Cuevas glows a dazzling orange from the sediment deposited by the warm sulfuric waters. The brick ruins of an old spa, built as part of a resort and later destroyed by flood, sit beneath the bridge, slowly yielding their form to the sulfuric buildup from the thermal water that trickles over, around and through it. Due to the unstable nature of the structure, the area has been closed off and you can't cross the bridge or enter the hot baths any more, but you can still get some fairly wild photos.

Puente del Inca enjoys a spectacular setting, and whether or not you climb, it's a good base for exploring the area. Trekkers and climbers can head north to the base of Aconcagua, south to the pinnacles of Los Penitentes, or even further south to 6650m Tupungato.

About 1km before Puente del Inca (directly across from Los Puquios), the small **Cementerio Andinista** is a cemetery for climbers who died on Aconcagua.

🛏 Sleeping & Eating

A string of restaurants by the roadside offer filling but unexciting meals from around AR$100.

Los Puquios   CAMPGROUND
(☑0261-15-688-6190; www.lospuquios.com.ar; camping free) FREE In summer, free camping is possible at the mini ski resort of Los Puquios.

Hostel El Nico   HOSTEL $
(☑0261-592-0736; elnicohostel@gmail.com; dm/d US$22/44) A cozy little hostel sleeping 14

people. Can organize treks in summer and snowshoe/skiing expeditions in winter.

❶ Getting There & Away

A few buses a day leave from Mendoza's bus terminal for Puente del Inca (AR$93, four hours), passing through Uspallata. If you're on a day trip, check return times with the driver – you don't want to get stuck up here. Buses from Chile pass through but are often full and won't stop to pick you up.

Nearly every Mendoza tour operator offers day tours to Puente del Inca, often combined with Las Cuevas.

Parque Provincial Aconcagua

North of RN 7, nearly hugging the Chilean border, Parque Provincial Aconcagua protects 710 sq km of the wild high country surrounding the western hemisphere's highest summit, 6962m Cerro Aconcagua. Passing motorists (and those who can time their buses correctly) can stop to enjoy the view of the peak from **Laguna Los Horcones**, a 2km walk from the parking lot just north of the highway.

Only highly experienced climbers should consider climbing Aconcagua (p340) without the relative safety of an organized tour – even then, it's a serious climb that requires training and preparation.

☞ Tours

Many of the adventure-travel agencies in and around Mendoza arrange excursions into the high mountains. It is also possible to arrange trips with some overseas-based operators.

Several guides from the Asociación Argentina de Guías de Montaña (www.aagm.com. ar) lead two-week trips to Aconcagua, including **Pablo Reguera** (www.pabloreguera.com. ar) and **Mauricio Fernández** (www.summit -mza.com.ar).

All guides and organized trips are best set up online or by telephone *at least* a month in advance. Everything – guides, mules, hotels etc – must be booked far in advance during peak climbing months. There are also some great experienced guides in the region.

Prices vary between operators and depend very much on what is included in the expedition, but US$3500 is a ballpark figure for the basic Aconcagua ascent.

CLIMBING CERRO ACONCAGUA

Often called the 'roof of the Americas,' the volcanic summit of Aconcagua covers a base of uplifted marine sediments. The origin of the name is unclear; one possibility is the Quechua term Ackon-Cahuac, meaning 'stone sentinel,' while another is the Mapuche phrase Acon-Hue, signifying 'that which comes from the other side.'

Italian-Swiss climber Mathias Zurbriggen made the first recorded ascent in 1897. Since then, the peak has become a favorite destination for climbers from around the world, even though it is technically less challenging than other nearby peaks. In 1985 the Club Andinista Mendoza's discovery of an Incan mummy at 5300m on the mountain's southwest face proved that the high peaks were a pre-Columbian funerary site.

Reaching the summit requires a commitment of at least 13 to 15 days, including acclimatization time; some climbers prefer the longer but more scenic, less crowded and more technical Polish Glacier Route.

Potential climbers should acquire RJ Secor's climbing guide *Aconcagua* (Seattle, The Mountaineers, 1999). The website www.aconcagua.com.ar and Mendoza government's website, www.aconcagua.mendoza.gov.ar, are also helpful.

Nonclimbers can trek to **base camps** and **refugios** (rustic shelters) beneath the permanent snow line. On the Northwest Route there is also the relatively luxurious Hotel Refugio Plaza de Mulas, which has been plagued by ownership troubles over the years – if you'd like to stay there, check with trekking operators about whether it's operating.

Permits

From December to March permits are obligatory for both trekking and climbing in Parque Provincial Aconcagua; **park rangers** (p340) at Laguna Los Horcones will not permit visitors to proceed up the Quebrada de los Horcones without one. Fees vary according

---

Fernando Grajale HIKING
(www.grajales.net) A well-established operator with experience on the main- and less-traveled routes. Contact online.

Inka Expediciones HIKING
(☏ 0261-425-0871; www.inka.com.ar; Av Juan B Justo 345, Mendoza; ⊙9am-6pm Mon-Fri, to 1pm Sat) Fixed and tailor-made expeditions.

Rudy Parra's Aconcagua Trek HIKING
(☏ 0261-15-466-5825; www.rudyparra.com; Barcala 484) Popular company with guaranteed departures. Also offer helicopter descents. Contact online.

ⓘ Information

During trekking season there are rangers stationed at Laguna Los Horcones; the junction to Plaza Francia, about 5km north of Los Horcones; at Plaza de Mulas on the main route to the peak; at Refugio Las Leñas, on the Polish Glacier Route up the Río de las Vacas to the east; and at Plaza Argentina, the last major camping area along the Polish Glacier Route.

ⓘ Getting There & Away

The two park entrances – Punta de Vacas and Laguna Los Horcones – are directly off RN 7 and are well signed. The Los Horcones turnoff

is only 4km past Puente del Inca. If you're part of an organized tour, transport will be provided. To get here by bus, take an early morning Expreso Uspallata bus from Mendoza. Buses bound for Chile will stop at Puente del Inca, but often fill up with passengers going all the way through.

From Los Horcones, you can walk back along the RN 7 to Puente del Inca or time your buses and catch a Mendoza-bound bus back down.

Las Cuevas & Cristo Redentor

☏ 02624 / ELEV 3200M

Pounded by chilly but exhilarating winds, the rugged high Andes make a fitting backdrop for Cristo Redentor, the famous monument erected after a territorial dispute between Argentina and Chile was settled in 1902. The view is a must-see, either with a tour or by private car (a tunnel has replaced the hairpin road to the top as the border crossing into Chile), but the first autumn snowfall closes the route. You can hike the 8km up to El Cristo via trails from the roadside if you don't have a car.

to the complex park-use seasons – check www.aconcagua.mendoza.gov.ar for the latest information.

Organized tours rarely, if ever, include the park entrance fee. Fees should be paid in Argentine pesos but can be paid in US dollars, and you must bring your original passport with you when you pay the fee. The permit start-date takes effect when you enter the park.

All permits are available only in Mendoza at the **municipal tourist office** (p335).

Routes

There are three main routes up Cerro Aconcagua. The most popular one, approached by a 40km trail from Los Horcones, is the **Northwest Route** (Ruta Noroeste) from Plaza de Mulas, 4230m above sea level. The **South Face** (Pared Sur), approached from the base camp at Plaza Francia via a 36km trail from Los Horcones, is a demanding technical climb.

From Punta de Vacas, 15km southeast of Puente del Inca, the longer but more scenic **Polish Glacier Route** (Ruta Glaciar de los Polacos) first ascends the Río de las Vacas to the base camp at Plaza Argentina, a distance of 76km. Climbers on this route must carry ropes, screws and ice axes, in addition to the usual tent, warm sleeping bag and clothing, and plastic boots. This route is more expensive because it requires the use of mules for a longer period.

Mules

The cost of renting cargo mules, which can carry about 60kg each, has gone through the roof: the standard fee among outfitters is AR$1340 for the first mule from Puente del Inca to Plaza de Mulas, though two mules cost only AR$1870.

For mules, contact **Rudy Parra'st Aconcagua Trek** (p340) or **Fernando Grajale** (p340). If you're going up on an organized tour, the mule situation is, of course, covered.

Parque Provincial Volcán Tupungato

Tupungato (6650m) is an impressive volcano, partly covered by snowfields and glaciers, and serious climbers consider the mountain a far more challenging, interesting and technical climb than Aconcagua. The main approach is from the town of **Tunuyán**, 82km south of Mendoza via RN 40, where the **tourist office** (☑02622-488097, 02622-422193; cnr República de Siria & Alem; ☺8am-8pm) can provide info. Many of the outfitters who arrange Parque Provincial **Aconcagua treks** (p339) can also deal with Tupungato.

San Rafael

☑0260 / POP 118,000 / ELEV 690M

A busy, modern town whose streets are lined with majestic old sycamores and open irrigation channels, San Rafael reveals its charms slowly – if you have a few days, it's worth giving it a chance. It's not exactly Mendoza, but it's getting there.

There is nothing to do in town – part of its allure, really – except wander its shady streets and plazas or while the day away in a cafe. There are, however, several esteemed wineries within biking distance that are well worth a visit.

◉ Sights & Activities

San Rafael is flat (hence the proliferation of bike riders here), and when in Rome...get a bike.

There are a few wineries within walking or cycling distance of town offering free tours and tasting. Head west on RN 143, which has a welcome bike path along its side. For info, contact the tourist office (p342).

Bianchi Champañera　　　　WINERY
(☑0260-443-5600; www.vbianchi.com; cnr RN 143 & Valentín Bianchi; tours AR$35; ☺9am-noon & 2-5pm Mon-Sat) The modern and highly regarded Bianchi Champañera is 6km from San Rafael. Tours are friendly, offering visitors a glimpse into the making of sparkling wine, and English is spoken.

Suter　　　　WINERY
(☑0260-442-1076; www.sutersa.com.ar; Av H Yrigoyen 2850; short tours free; ☺9:30am-12:30pm & 2-5pm Mon-Fri) Halfway between Fincas Andinas and San Rafael, Suter is a rather

unromantic, modern affair, but a worth-while stop for some discounted wine. You can set up a half-day tour, visiting the vineyards with an agronomist, tasting specialty wines and eating a big lunch in the vineyard.

Ciclos Adelcor BICYCLE RENTAL
(cnr Av H Yrigoyen & Los Franceses; per hr AR$20; ⊙9am-1pm & 4-8pm Mon-Sat) Several places around town rent out clunkers, but if you're looking for a smooth ride, try Ciclos Adelcor.

⌂ Sleeping

Hotel España HOTEL $
(☑0260-442-1192; www.hotelespanasrl.com.ar; Av San Martín 270; s/d from US$47/66; ❀♠☼) It may not scream 'Spain,' but the mod 1960s-ish interior is definitely unique. Rooms in the 'colonial' sector open onto a delightful pool area, making them more attractive (and a better deal) than the spacious rooms in the pricier 'celeste' sector.

Hostel Tierrasoles HOSTEL $
(☑0260-443-3449; www.tierrasoles.com.ar; Alsina 245; dm from US$15, d with/without bathroom US$58/51; @♠) Simply the best-looking hostel in town, Hostel Tierrasoles has OK-sized dorms and a couple of good sitting areas. The inviting backyard (with barbecue for guest use) rounds out the picture.

Camping El Parador CAMPGROUND $
(☑0260-442-7983; Isla Río Diamante; campsites US$7.50) Located about 6km south of downtown.

★San Martín Hotel & Spa HOTEL $$
(☑0260-442-0400; www.sanmartinhotelspa.com; San Martín 435; r from US$85; ❀@♠☼) San Rafael's snazziest hotel is a surprisingly good deal, with large, bright rooms, spacious and modern bathrooms and a full-service on-site day spa.

Hotel Francia HOTEL $$
(☑0260-442-9351; www.alojamientofrancia.com.ar; Francia 248; s/d US$76/93; ❀♠) Lovely, spacious rooms set around a leafy garden a couple of blocks from the main drag. The young couple who run the place are charming and have loads of info on things to do in town and around.

✕ Eating & Drinking

San Rafael's eating and nightlife zone is spread out along eight blocks west of the casino at the corner of Yrigoyen and Pueyrredón. Go for a wander and see what grabs your fancy.

Nina PIZZA $
(cnr Av San Martín & Olascoaga; mains AR$90-140; ⊙8am-1am; ♠) The menu doesn't stretch much beyond pizzas and sandwiches, but this is a good coffee spot and becomes a happening bar with live music later.

La Pagoda BUFFET $
(Av Bartolomé Mitre 188; tenedor libre AR$90; ⊙noon-3pm & 8-11:30pm) Anybody familiar with the *tenedor libre* (all-you-can-eat) scene in Argentina won't find too many surprises here, but the food (Argentine and Chinese) is fresh enough – get there early – and there's certainly plenty of it.

Diablo's SEAFOOD $$
(cnr Av H Yrigoyen & Castelli; mains AR$75-160; ⊙noon-1am Tue-Sun) This cozy little corner eatery features a great range of tapas, surprisingly fresh seafood dishes, some good local wines and an impressive range of imported and microbrew beers.

Las Duelas INTERNATIONAL $$
(Paseo Pelligrini 190; mains AR$80-160; ⊙9am-late) This fine little sidewalk cafe on a semi-pedestrian strip, specializes in salads and good sandwiches and a couple of innovative main courses.

La Gringa ARGENTINE $$
(Chile 26; mains AR$80-150; ⊙11am-1am; ♠) A solid menu offering all the Argentine standards – pizza, pasta, *parrilla* – with a couple of inventive mains to keep things interesting.

❶ Orientation

Most areas of interest in town are northwest of the Av H Yrigoyen and Av San Martín intersection. The bus terminal is a couple of kilometers to the north.

❶ Information

Banco de Galicia (Av H Yrigoyen 28; ⊙9am-1pm Mon-Fri) Several banks along Av H Yrigoyen have ATMs, including Banco de Galicia.

Cambio Santiago (Almafuerte 64; ⊙9am-1pm & 4-9pm Mon-Fri, 9am-1pm Sat) Charges 2.5% on traveler's checks.

Hospital Teodoro J Schestakow (☑0260-442-4490; Emilio Civit 151)

Municipal Tourist Office (☑0260-442-4217; www.sanrafaelturismo.gov.ar; Av H Yrigoyen 745; ⊙8am-8pm) Helpful staff and useful brochures and maps.

Post Office (cnr San Lorenzo & Barcala; ⊙8am-6pm Mon-Fri, 9am-1pm Sat)

ℹ Getting There & Around

San Rafael is 230km southeast of the city of Mendoza via RN 40 and RN 143, and 189km northeast of Malargüe via RN 40.

Aerolíneas Argentinas/Austral (☎0260-443-8808; Av H Yrigoyen 395; ⊙10am-6pm Mon-Fri, to 1pm Sat) flies daily except on Sunday to and from Buenos Aires.

Renta Autos (☎0260-442-4623; www.rentadeautos.com.ar; Av H Yrigoyen 797; ⊙9am-6pm Mon-Fri, 9am-1pm & 5-8pm Sat & Sun) Renta Autos offers the town's best deals on car rentals.

BUS

San Rafael's new **bus terminal** (☎0260-442-7720; General Paz 800) is an AR$35 taxi ride from downtown.

If you're headed to Patagonia, there's one minibus per day that leaves from the bus terminal for Buta Ranquil (AR$336, eight hours) in Neuquén province via Malargüe. It leaves at 7:30pm daily except on Saturday and seats sell out very quickly. Book (and pay) a couple of days in advance to ensure a seat.

There are regular daily departures to the following destinations.

DESTINATION	COST (AR$)	TIME (HR)
Bariloche	1133	16
Buenos Aires	1021	14
Córdoba	600	11
Las Leñas	116	3
Malargüe	71	3
Mendoza	72	3
Neuquén	795	9
San Luis	260	4

Cañón del Atuel & Valle Grande

South of San Rafael along the Río Atuel, RP 173 passes through a multicolored ravine that locals compare to Arizona's Grand Canyon, though much of the 67km Cañón del Atuel has been submerged by four hydroelectric dams. Nevertheless, there is white-water rafting on its lower reaches, and several operators at the tourist complex of Valle Grande, midway down the canyon, do short but scenic floats down the river, and other trips.

RP 173 turns inot a dirt road past the dam at Valle Grande, and continues through the scenic Cañón del Atuel to the Podunk village of El Nihuil, 79km from San Rafael – you'll need a private vehicle or tour group if you want to see this stretch.

🏃 Activities

Sport Star OUTDOORS

(☎0260-15-458-1068; www.sportstar.com.ar; RP 173, Km35; ⊙10am-5pm) Offers the widest range of activities, including trekking, horseback riding, kayaking, mountain-bike tours, canoes and rappelling.

🛏 Sleeping & Eating

Cabañas Río Azul CABIN $$

(☎0260-442-3663; www.complejorioazul.com.ar; RP 173 Km33; 2-/4-person cabin US$111/120; 🛜❄) Most places to stay in the canyon cater to large groups and are rather unpleasant, but this place offers comfortable *cabañas* (cabins) with a lovely grassy area over the river – a great spot to while away a day or two in the sun, especially in the off-season.

Hotel Valle Grande HOTEL $$

(☎0260-15-458-0660; RP 173 Km35; s/d US$97/140; ❄🛜❄) In the 'town' of Valle Grande, this three-star hotel offers the best accommodations around, in a lovely setting by the river, and a good restaurant, too.

ℹ Getting There & Away

Numerous San Rafael tour companies run day trips to Valle Grande, starting at AR$220. Regular buses run from San Rafael's bus terminal to Valle Grande (AR$26, one hour). Buses to El Nihuil take the alternative RP 144, which doesn't go through the canyon.

Malargüe

☑0260 / POP 21,600 / ELEV 1400M

Despite serving as a base for Las Leñas, one of Argentina's snazzier ski resorts, Malargüe is a mellow little town and popular as a cheaper alternative to the luxury hotels on the mountain. The dry *precordillera* that surrounds the town is geologically distinct from the Andes proper, and two fauna reserves, Payén and Laguna Llancancelo, are close by. Caving is possible at Caverna de Las Brujas and Pozo de las Animas. The nearby Parque Provincial Payunia is a 4500-sq-km reserve with the highest concentration of volcanic cones in the world.

⊙ Sights

Planetarium PLANETARIUM

(☎0260-447-2116; cnr Villegas & Aldeo; tours AR$30; ⊙5-9pm) Due to Malargüe's remote location, it's a great spot for stargazing, and the newly opened Planetarium is an excellent, state-of-the-art complex featuring some freaky architecture and some reasonably entertaining audiovisual presentations.

☞ Tours

Several companies offer excellent 4WD and horseback-riding excursions, and if you don't have a car, these are generally the best way to get into the surrounding mountains. Possible **day trips around Malargüe** (p345) include Caverna de Las Brujas (AR$430 per person, which includes AR$60 park entrance fee and obligatory guide), Los Molles and Las Leñas (AR$400) and the marvelous Laguna Llancancelo and Malacara volcano (AR$430 plus AR$65 entry fee). One of the most exciting drives you may ever undertake is the 12-hour 4WD tour through Parque Provincial Payunia (AR$550); be sure your tour stops at all the sites – those that combine the visit with Laguna Llancancelo only visit half the sites in Payunia.

Karen Travel   TOUR
(☑0260-447-2226; www.karentravel.com.ar; Av San Martín 54) The owner of Karen Travel speaks English – this company has received rave reviews.

Payunia Travel   TOUR
(☑0260-447-2701; www.payuniatravel.com; Av San Martín 13) Well-established agency in town offering tours.

🛏 Sleeping

Malargüe has abundant, reasonably priced accommodations. Prices drop by up to 40% outside the ski season (June 15 to September 15). Singles are nonexistent during ski season, when you'll likely be charged for however many beds are in the room.

Eco Hostel Malargüe   HOSTEL $
(☑0260-447-0391; www.hostelmalargue.com; Finca 65, Colonia Pehuenche; dm US$13, d with/without bathroom US$72/56; �*) Six kilometers south of town, this hostel/B&B is set on an organic farm and built using sustainable practices. Rooms are simple but comfortable, the surrounds are beautiful and breakfast (featuring farm produce) is a winner, too.

Camping Municipal Malargüe   CAMPGROUND $
(☑0260-447-0691; Alfonso Capdevila s/n; campsites US$8) At the northern end of town, 300m west of Av San Martín, this is the closest place to camp.

Hosteria Keoken   HOTEL $
(☑0260-447-2468; Puebla 252; s/d US$45/55; ☎) A cute little no-frills option right off the main street. Rooms are cozy and comfortable enough for the price and the place is run by a doting señora.

El Nevado   APARTMENT $$
(☑0260-15-440-0712; www.aparthotelnevado.com.ar; Puebla 343; apt from US$65; ☎) Excellent value apartments available by the day or for longer stays. They come with fully-equipped kitchens, separate sleeping areas and a cute little garden out back.

Hotel de Turismo   HOTEL $$
(☑0260-447-1042; Av San Martín 224; s/d US$45/85) The Turismo's a good standby – there are plenty of rooms (which are nothing special) so it rarely fills up. Downstairs, the restaurant-cafe lifts the tone with a few charming touches.

★Hotel Malargüe   BOUTIQUE HOTEL $$$
(☑0260-447-2300; www.hotelmalarguesuite.com; RN 40 s/n; s/d from US$120/160; ✳@☎☀) At the northern edge of town, the most luxurious hotel for miles around lays it all on – buffet breakfast, art gallery, indoor pool... Rooms are spacious and modern and come with hydromassage tubs, which are a welcome sight after a hard day on the slopes.

🍴 Eating

★El Quincho de María   ARGENTINE $
(Av San Martín 440; mains AR$80-130; ☺noon-11pm) The finest dining in the center is at this cozy little *parrilla*, where everything from the gnocchi to the empanadas is handmade. Don't miss the mouth-watering shish kebabs for AR$60.

Los Olivos   ARGENTINE $$
(San Martín 409; mains AR$110-170; ☺noon-11:30pm) A good range of well-prepared food here – the menu's split into 'gourmet' (offering regional faves like goat and trout) and 'classic', with inventive twists on Argentine standards.

ℹ Information

Banco de la Nación (cnr Av San Martín & Inalicán; ☺9am-1pm Mon-Fri) One of several banks downtown with ATMs.

Post Office (cnr Adolfo Puebla & Saturnino Torres; ☺8am-6pm Mon-Fri, 9am-1pm Sat)

Tourist Office (☑0260-447-1659; www.malargue.gov.ar; RN 40, Parque del Ayer; ☺8am-

8pm) Helpful tourist office with facilities at the northern end of town, on the highway. A small kiosk (⊙9am-9pm) operates out of the bus terminal.

❶ Getting There & Around

From Malargüe's **bus terminal** (cnr Av General Roca & Aldao) there are several direct buses to Mendoza daily (AR$201, five hours), plus others requiring a change in San Rafael (AR$72, three hours). Outside of winter, there's one bus per day to Los Molles and Las Leñas (AR$45, 1½ hours), leaving at 8:30am and returning from Las Leñas at 5:30pm.

Transportes Leader (☑0260-447-0519; San Martín 775), operating out of the Club Los Amigos pool hall, has one minibus leaving for Buta Ranquil (AR$271, five hours) in Neuquén at 9pm Sunday to Friday. Seats sell out fast – it's recommended that you book (and pay) at least two days in advance.

For winter transportation to Los Molles and Las Leñas ski resorts, travel agencies offer a roundtrip shuttle service, including ski rentals, from AR$450 to AR$600 per person.

Around Malargüe

☑0260

Geologically distinct from the Andean mountains to the west, the volcanically formed landscapes surrounding Malargüe are some of the most mind-altering in Argentina, and have only recently begun to receive tourist attention. Visiting these places is impossible without your own transportation, though Malargüe's excellent travel agencies can arrange excursions to all of them.

Just over 200km south of Malargüe on the RN 40, the spectacular **Parque Provincial Payunia** is a 4500-sq-km reserve, with a higher concentration of volcanic cones (over 800 of them) than anywhere else in the world. The scenery is breathtaking and shouldn't be missed. The 12-hour 4WD tours or three-day horseback trips offered by most of the agencies in Malargüe are well worth taking.

Lying within its namesake fauna reserve about 60km southeast of Malargüe, **Laguna Llancancelo** is a high mountain lake visited by more than 100 species of birds, including flamingos.

Caverna de Las Brujas (tours AR$100; ⊙sunrise-sunset) is a magical limestone cave on **Cerro Moncol**, 72km south of Malargüe and 8km north of Bardas Blancas along RN 40. Its name means 'Cave of the Witches.' The cave complex stretches for 5km. Guided tours (admission and flashlights included in the price) take two to three hours. Tours depart with a minimum group size of two, although getting more people together will bring down the per-person cost. Check with tour operators in Malargüe (p344) for details.

Los Molles

Before Las Leñas took over as the prime ski resort in the area, Los Molles was the only place around where you could grab a *poma* (ski lift). These days it's a dusty, windswept village that would be slowly sinking into obscurity if not for its reasonably priced accommodations alternatives for those wishing to be near, but not in, Las Leñas, and its favored status for rock climbers, hikers and other rugged outdoor types. The village straddles RP 222, 55km northwest of Malargüe. Karen Travel in Malargüe (p344) offers a range of activities in the dramatic countryside that surrounds the village.

Buses heading between Malargüe (AR$35, one hour) and Las Leñas (AR$15, 30 minutes) pass through the village.

🛏 Sleeping

Hostel Pehuenche　　　　HOSTEL **$**
(☑in Buenos Aires 011-4776-6476; www.pehuenchehostel.com; dm US$18-20, s/d US$55/75; 🛜) Hostel Pehuenche is one of the best set-up hostels in the country, offering a bar, 'digital playroom,' transfers to Las Leñas and extra-snuggly duck down duvets.

Hotel Los Molles　　　　HOTEL **$$**
(☑0261-423-4848; www.losmolleshotel.com.ar; RP222, Km30; s/d US$104/138 to 160/214) The most modern and best equipped of the hotels in town, it features big rooms with balconies facing out over the valley. A decent restaurant serves good-value set meals (AR$110).

Las Leñas

☑0260

Designed primarily to attract wealthy foreigners, **Las Leñas** (☑0260-447-1281; www.laslenas.com; 1-day ticket high/low season from AR$795/495, week passes AR$2635-3875; ⊙mid-Jun–late-Sep) is Argentina's most self-consciously prestigious ski resort. Since its opening in 1983 it has attracted an international clientele who spend their days on the slopes and nights partying until the sun comes up. Because of the dry climate, Las Leñas has incredibly dry powder.

Its 33 runs cover 33 sq km; the area has a base altitude of 2200m, but slopes reach 3430m for a maximum drop of 1230m. Outside the ski season Las Leñas is also attempting to attract summer visitors who enjoy week-long packages, offering activities such as mountain biking, horseback riding and hiking.

Prices for lift tickets vary considerably throughout the ski season. Children's tickets are discounted about 30%. One-day, three-day, four-day, one-week two-week and season passes are available. Rental equipment is readily available and will set you back about AR$300 per day for skis or snowboards.

Las Leñas is 445km south of Mendoza and 70km from Malargüe, all via RN 40 and RP 222.

🛏 Sleeping & Eating

Las Leñas has a small village with five luxury hotels and a group of 'apart hotels,' all under the same management. They are generally booked as part of a week-long package, which includes lodging, unlimited skiing and two meals per day. Despite the country's economic troubles, rates for foreigners staying in Las Leñas have changed little. All bookings are either online at www.laslenas.com or centrally through **Ski Leñas** (📞 011-4819-6060, in Buenos Aires 011-4819-6000; ventas@laslenas.com; Cerrito 1186, 8th fl, Buenos Aires).

Apart Hotel Gemenis (weekly per person from US$680) and **Apart Hotel Delphos** (weekly per person from US$710) offer similar packages without meals, but do have well-equipped kitchenettes.

There are also small apartments with two to six beds and shared bathrooms, equipped for travelers to cook for themselves. Budget travelers can stay more economically at Los Molles, 20km down the road, or at Malargüe, 70km away.

Restaurants in the village run the comestible gamut, from cafes, sandwich shops and pizzerias to upscale hotel dining rooms. The finest restaurant of all is Las Cuatro Estaciones, in Hotel Piscis.

Hostel Las Leñas   HOSTEL $
(dm with/without bathroom per week US$433/288) Hostelling has finally made it to Las Leñas. It's nothing special, but it is (relatively) cheap sleeps on the mountain.

Hotel Acuario   HOTEL $$$
(s/d per week from US$1400/2800; ⊛) The most humble of the hotels here is still very comfortable, and, with 'only' 40 rooms, cozier than other options.

Hotel Escorpio   HOTEL $$$
(s/d per week from US$1440/1800; 🛜) This 47-room hotel is nominally three stars, but still top-notch, with an excellent restaurant. Guests can use facilities at the Hotel Piscis.

Hotel Aries   HOTEL $$$
(s/d per week from US$2016/2620; 🛜⊛) Aries is a four-star hotel with a sauna, gym facilities, a restaurant and luxuriously comfortable rooms.

Virgo Hotel & Spa   HOTEL $$$
(s/d per week from US$1400/2800; 🛜⊛) The newest hotel in the village, this one goes all out, with a heated outdoor swimming pool, sushi bar, whirlpool bath and cinema.

Hotel Piscis   HOTEL $$$
(s/d per week from US$3864/4300; 🛜⊛) The most extravagant of Las Leñas' lodgings is the five-star, 99-room Hotel Piscis. This prestigious hotel has wood-burning stoves, a gymnasium, sauna, an indoor swimming pool, the elegant **Las Cuatro Estaciones** restaurant, a bar, a casino and shops. Rates depend on time of the season, and are based on double occupancy.

❶ Getting There & Away

There is a bus service operating in season from Mendoza (AR$150, 6½ hours), San Rafael (AR$60, three hours) and Malargüe (AR$45, 1½ hours).

Ruta Nacional 40

From Malargüe the RN 40 winds its way south through rugged desert landscapes and into Neuquén province. Despite what many will tell you, there *is* public transportation along this route. **Transportes Leader** (📞 442-1851; Perú 65) runs minibuses between San Rafael and Buta Ranquil Sunday to Friday, stopping in Malargüe. From Buta Ranquil there are connections to Neuquén and Chos Malal, but you may get stuck for the night. There's no real reason to be here, but there are a couple of cheap hotels, one nice accommodations option, and enough restaurants and cafes to keep you from starving.

San Juan

📱 0264 / POP 109,100 / ELEV 650M

Living in the shadow of a world-class destination like Mendoza can't be easy and, to its credit, San Juan doesn't even try to compete. Life in this provincial capital moves at its own pace, and the locals are both proud of and humble about their little town.

No slouch on the wine-production front, San Juan's wineries are refreshingly low-key compared to the Mendoza bustle, and the province's other attractions are all within easy reach of the capital. Most come here en route to Parque Provincial Ischigualasto.

In 1944 a massive earthquake destroyed the city center, and Juan Perón's subsequent relief efforts are what first made him a national figure. The city goes dead in summer, especially on Sunday, when all of San Juan heads to the nearby shores of Dique Ullum for relief from the sun.

◉ Sights

Museum hours change often, so check with the tourist office for updated information.

Lookout Tower　　　　　　　LOOKOUT
(cnr Mendoza & Rivadavia; admission AR$15; ⊘9am-1pm & 5-9pm) If you need a little per-spective on things, make your way up the Lookout Tower for a sweeping view out over the town and surrounding countryside.

Casa Natal de Sarmiento　　　MUSEUM
(Sarmiento 21 Sur; admission AR$25; ⊘9am-7pm Mon-Fri, to 2pm Sat, 11am-6pm Sun) Casa Natal de Sarmiento is named for Domingo Faustino Sarmiento, whose prolific writing as a politician, diplomat, educator and journalist made him a public figure within and beyond Argentina. Sarmiento's *Recuerdos de Provincia* recounted his childhood in this house and his memories of his mother. It's now a museum.

Museo de Vino Santiago Graffigna MUSEUM
(📱0264-421-4227; www.graffignawines.com; Colón 1342 Norte; ⊘10am-7pm Mon-Sat, to 4pm Sun) **FREE** Museo de Vino Santiago Graffigna is a wine museum well worth a visit. It also has a wine bar where you can taste many of San Juan's best wines. Take bus 12A from in front of the tourist office on Sarmiento (AR$3, 15 minutes) and ask the driver to tell you when to get off.

⚑ Tours

Tour operators in San Juan provide lots of options for taking in the sights.

DIFUNTA CORREA

Legend has it that during the civil wars of the 1840s Deolinda Correa followed the movements of her sickly conscript husband's battalion on foot through the deserts of San Juan, carrying food, water and their baby son in her arms. When her meager supplies ran out, thirst, hunger and exhaustion killed her. But when passing muleteers found them, the infant was still nursing at the dead woman's breast. Commemorating this apparent miracle, her shrine at Vallecito is widely believed to be the site of her death.

Difunta literally means 'defunct,' and Correa is her surname. Technically she is not a saint but rather a 'soul,' a dead person who performs miracles and intercedes for people; the child's survival was the first of a series of miracles attributed to her. Since the 1940s her shrine, originally a simple hilltop cross, has grown into a small village with its own gas station, school, post office, police station and church. Devotees leave gifts at 17 chapels or exhibit rooms in exchange for supernatural favors. In addition, there are two hotels, several restaurants, a commercial gallery with souvenir shops, and offices for the nonprofit organization that administers the site.

Interestingly, truckers are especially devoted. From La Quiaca, on the Bolivian border, to Ushuaia in Tierra del Fuego, you will see roadside shrines with images of the Difunta Correa and the unmistakable bottles of water left to quench her thirst. At some sites there appear to be enough parts lying around to build a car from scratch!

Despite lack of government support and the Catholic Church's open antagonism, the shrine of Difunta Correa has grown, as belief in her miraculous powers has become more widespread. People visit the shrine year-round, but at Easter, May 1 and Christmas, up to 200,000 pilgrims descend on Vallecito. Weekends are busier and more interesting than weekdays.

There are regular departures to Vallecito from San Juan and Mendoza.

San Juan

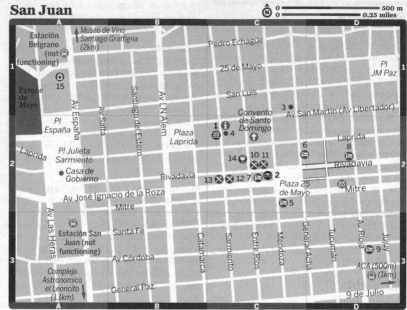

San Juan

Mario Agüero Turismo   TOUR

(📞 0264-422-5320; General Acha 17 Norte; ⊙9am-1pm & 4-8pm Mon-Fri, 9am-1pm Sat) Offers organized tours, including Parque Provincial Ischigualasto.

Triasico Turismo   TOUR

(📞 0264-422-8566; www.triasico.com.ar; Sarmiento 42 Sur; ⊙9am-1pm & 4-8pm Mon-Sat) Specializes in Ischigualasto tours (AR$640, minimum two people) – come here if you're struggling to get a group together.

🛏 Sleeping

San Juan Hostel   HOSTEL $

(📞 0264-420-1835; www.sanjuanhostel.com; Av Córdoba 317 Este; dm US$11-12, s/d US$25/32, without bathroom US$16/21; ❄@🛜) An excellent little hostel with a variety of rooms placed conveniently between the bus terminal and downtown. Good info on tours and local attractions, and a rooftop Jacuzzi rounds out the picture.

Hotel Selby   HOTEL $

(📞 0264-422-4766; www.hotelselby.com.ar; Rioja 183 Sur; s/d US$45/50) There's nothing really flash going on here, but the rooms are a decent size and the downtown location can't be beat. Good value for the price.

Hotel Alhambra
HOTEL $

(☑0264-421-4780; www.alhambrahotel.com.ar; General Acha 180 Sur; s/d US$30/40; ✻ 🛜) Smallish, carpeted rooms with splashes of dark-wood paneling, giving them a classy edge. Little touches such as leather chairs and gold ashtray stands in the hallways give it a kitschy appeal and the central location seals the deal.

Hotel del Bono Suite
HOTEL $$

(☑0264-421-7600; www.hoteldelbono.com.ar; Mitre 75 Oeste; d/ste US$96/110; ✻🛜≋) With some slick design features taking the edge off the corporate blandness, this is a good deal for the price, and the well-stocked kitchenettes and rooftop pool are added bonuses.

Albertina Hotel
HOTEL $$

(☑0264-421-4222; www.hotelalbertina.com; Mitre 31 Este; s/d from US$78/85; ✻@🛜) A slick, business-class hotel on the plaza. The tiny rooms are a bit of a letdown, but the bathrooms are big.

✗ Eating & Drinking

Most restaurants are right downtown, and many of the city's hippest eateries are around the intersection of Rivadavia and Entre Ríos.

Baró
INTERNATIONAL $

(Rivadavia 55 Oeste; mains AR$80-120; ⊙8am-11:30pm) This popular, main-street cafe-restaurant has the best variety of pasta dishes in town and a relaxed atmosphere that make it a good stop for coffee or drinks at any time.

Soychú
VEGETARIAN $

(Av José Ignacio de la Roza 223 Oeste; buffet AR$60; ⊙noon-9pm Mon-Sat, 11am-3pm Sun; 🖉) Excellent vegetarian buffet attached to a health-food store selling all sorts of groceries and a range of teas. Arrive early for the best selection.

★ de Sánchez
FUSION $$

(Rivadavia 61 Oeste; mains AR$130-200; ⊙noon-3pm & 8pm-midnight Tue-Sun) San Juan's snootiest downtown restaurant is actually pretty good. It has a creative menu with a smattering of seafood dishes, an adequate wine list (featuring all the San Juan heavy hitters) and a hushed, tranquil atmosphere.

Remolacha
PARRILLA $$

(cnr Av José Ignacio de la Roza & Sarmiento; mains AR$90-150; ⊙noon-3pm & 8pm-1am) One of the biggest parrillas in town, the dining room is a bit ordinary, but eating in the garden is a lush experience. Get a table by the picture windows looking into the kitchen and you'll be able to see your meal being hacked off the carcass before getting thrown on the flames. Excellent salads, too.

Flores Art Bar
BAR

(Entre Rios 145; ⊙7pm-3am) There are some OK bar snacks on offer here, but the place works best as a bar – cool music, great atmosphere and an excellent cocktail list.

🛍 Shopping

Mercado Artesanal Tradicional
MARKET

(Traditional Artisans Market; Centro de Difusión Cultural Eva Perón; ⊙10am-7pm Mon-Sat) The Mercado Artesanal Tradicional is an excellent local handicrafts market with an assortment of items for sale including ponchos and the brightly colored mantas (shawls) of Jáchal.

❶ Orientation

San Juan is 170km north of Mendoza via RN 40 and 1140km from Buenos Aires. Like most Argentine cities, San Juan's grid pattern makes orientation very easy; the addition of cardinal points – norte (north), sur (south), este (east) and oeste (west) – to street addresses helps even more. East–west Av San Martín and north–south Calle Mendoza divide the city into these quadrants. The functional center of town is south of Av San Martín, often referred to as Av Libertador.

JUST A LOAD OF HOT AIR

While traveling through San Juan, especially in autumn and winter, you may become acquainted – through hearsay if not through experience – with one of the region's meteorological marvels: el zonda. Much like the chinook of the Rockies or the foehn of the European Alps, the zonda is a dry, warm wind that can raise a cold day's temperature from freezing to nearly 20°C (68°F). The zonda originates with storms in the Pacific that blow eastward, hit the Andes, dump their moisture and come whipping down the eastern slopes, picking up heat as they go. The wind, which varies from mild to howling, can last several days; sanjuaninos (people from San Juan) can step outside and tell you when it will end – and that it will be cold when it does. It's a regular occurrence, giving the region – and the sanjuaninos – severe seasonal schizophrenia, especially during winter.

ℹ Information

ACA (Automóvil Club Argentina; ☑ 0264-422-3781; 9 de Julio 802) Argentina's auto club; good source for provincial road maps.

Banco de San Juan (cnr Rivadavia & Entre Ríos; ☺ 9am-1pm Mon-Fri) Has an ATM.

Cambio Santiago (General Acha 52 Sur; ☺ 8am-6pm Mon-Fri, 9am-1pm Sat & Sun) Money exchange.

Hospital Rawson (☑ 0264-422-2272; cnr General Paz & Estados Unidos)

Post Office (Av José Ignacio de la Roza 259 Este; ☺ 8am-6pm Mon-Fri, 9am-1pm Sat)

Tourist Office (☑ 0264-422-2431; www.turismo.sanjuan.gov.ar; Sarmiento 24 Sur; ☺ 8am-7pm) Has a good map of the city and its surroundings, plus useful information on the rest of the province, particularly Parque Provincial Ischigualasto.

ℹ Getting There & Away

AIR

Aerolíneas Argentinas/Austral (☑ 0264-421-4158; Av San Martín 215 Oeste; ☺ 10am-6pm Mon-Fri, to 1pm Sat) flies twice daily to Buenos Aires except Sunday (once only).

BUS

From San Juan's **bus terminal** (☑ 0264-422-1604; Estados Unidos 492 Sur) you can book tickets to Santiago, Viña del Mar and Valparaíso in Chile but you'll have to change buses in Mendoza.

Except in summer, when there may be direct buses, service to Patagonian destinations south of Neuquén requires a change of bus in Mendoza; through-tickets can be purchased in San Juan.

Various companies serve the following destinations daily.

DESTINATION	COST (AR$)	TIME (HR)
Barreal	95	4
Buenos Aires	1460	14
Calingasta	80	3½
Catamarca	673	8
Córdoba	675	11
Huaco	75	3
La Rioja	506	7
Mendoza	225	3
Rodeo	105	3½
San Agustín de Valle Fértil	130	4½
San José de Jáchal	105	3
San Luis	425	5
Tucumán	932	13
Vallecito	46	1

ℹ Getting Around

Las Chacritas Airport (☑ 0264-425-4133) is located 13km southeast of town on RN 20. A taxi or *remise* (radio taxi) costs AR$90.

If there's two or more of you, hiring a car to get to Ischigualasto can work out a better deal than taking a tour. One caveat being that many rental outfits try to steer you away from one-day rentals. The tourist office keeps a list of rental operators, including **Classic** (☑ 0264-422-4622; Av San Martín 163 Oeste; ☺ 9am-7pm), across from the tourist office and **Trebol** (☑ 0264-422-5935; Laprida 82 Este; ☺ 9am-8pm), inside the Alkazar Hotel.

Around San Juan

Only 18km west of San Juan, the 32km sq **Dique Ullum** is a center for nautical sports: swimming, fishing, kayaking, waterskiing and windsurfing (though no rental equipment is available). *Balnearios* (beach clubs) line its shores, and hanging out for a day in the sun is part of being in San Juan. At night, many of the *balnearios* function as dance clubs. Bus 23 from Av Salta or Bus 29 from the San Juan bus terminal via Av Córdoba both go hourly to the dam outlet.

Valle de Calingasta

The Calingasta Valley is a vast smear of scenic butter cradled between the Andes and the rumpled, multicolored *precordillera*, and is one of the most beautiful regions in both San Juan and Mendoza provinces.

With the completion of two new reservoirs, the spectacular cliffside RP 12 is now closed. Most maps will show the old road, but drivers have to take RP 5 north to Talacasto, then the RP 149, which snakes around west and then south to Calingasta.

Calingasta

☑ 02648 / POP 2200 / ELEV 1430M

Calingasta is a small agricultural town shaded by álamos (poplars) on the shores of Río de los Patos. There's little to do, though a visit to the 17th-century adobe chapel **Capilla de Nuestra Señora del Carmen** makes a nice stop on the way to Barreal. Looming on the horizon 7km out of town is **Cerro El Calvario**, the site of an indigenous cemetery where several mummies have been found. One example can be seen in Calingasta's small **archaeological museum** (admission AR$10; ☺ 10am-1pm & 4-8pm Tue-Sat), just off the main plaza.

OFF THE BEATEN TRACK

RUTA DEL VINO DE SAN JUAN

San Juan's winery tourism industry isn't quite as developed as that of Mendoza, but in a lot of ways that's a good thing. There are no crowds for a start, and tours are occasionally conducted by the winemakers themselves. A few wineries have gotten together to promote the Ruta del Vino de San Juan (the San Juan Wine Route). The best way to do it, if you want to hit them all in one day, is to **hire a car** (p350). Starting from downtown San Juan, it's about a 40km return stopping at all the places listed here. It is feasible to do it by public transportation and taxi, too. None of the wineries listed below require reservations.

The first stop on the route should be **Las Marianas** (☑0264-423-1191; www.bodegalas marianas.com.ar; Calle Nuevo s/n; ☺10am-1pm & 5-8pm Tue-Sat) FREE. One of the prettiest wineries in the region, this one was built in 1922, abandoned in 1950 and reinstated in 1999. The main building is gorgeous, with thick adobe walls and a few examples of the original winemaking equipment lying around. The mountain views out over the vineyard are superb. If you're coming by bus, catch the 16 (AR$4.10, 40 minutes) near the corner of Santa Fe and Mendoza in San Juan. Get off at the corner of Calle Aberastain and Calle Nuevo, where you'll see a signpost to the winery (an 800m walk).

Making your way back to Calle Aberastain, turn right and follow the road south for 500m to **Viñas de Segisa** (☑0264-492-2000; www.saxsegisa.com.ar; cnr Aberastain & Calle 15; ☺9am-7pm Mon-Sat) FREE. This stately old winery has more of a museum feel than others. The tour of the underground cellar complex is excellent and tastings are generous.

If you're not up for a walk, now's the time to call a *remise* (shared taxi). If you are, make your way back north to Calle 14, turn right and continue for 5km until you hit RN 40. Turning left, after about 1km you'll come to **Fabril Alto Verde** (☑0264-421-2683; www.fabril-altoverde.com.ar; RN40, btwn Calle 13 & 14; ☺9am-1pm & 2:30-6:30pm Mon-Fri) FREE, a big, state-of-the-art winery that sells 90% of its wine for export; tours here are in English or Spanish and come accompanied by a rather dreary promotional video. The award-winning organic brands Buenas Hondas and Touchstone are produced here.

Next, catch a 24 bus heading north on RN 40 up to Calle 11. Turning right down Calle 11 for 300m brings you to **Miguel Mas** (☑0264-422-5807; miguelmas@infovia.com.ar; Calle 11 s/n; ☺9am-5pm Mon-Fri) ✔ FREE This small winery makes some of the country's only organic sparkling wine and other wine. The whole process – apart from inserting the cork in bottles – is done by hand. Tours (in Spanish only) take you through every step of the process.

Making your way back out to RN 40, flag down a 24 bus, which will take you back to the bus terminal in San Juan.

The folks at Calingasta's **tourist office** (☑02648-441066; www.calingastaturismo.gov.ar; RP 12; ☺8am-8pm), at the entrance to town from San Juan, are helpful for sights and lodging in the area.

If you wish to spend the night, lay your head at the modest **Hospedaje Nora** (☑02648-421027; cnr Cantoni & Sarmiento; r per person US$21), featuring simple but spacious rooms in a family house. Those in the building out the back are a better deal. There's a **municipal campground** (campsites US$6) down by the river. The meals at **La Morocha** (mains from AR$65; ☺noon-3pm & 6-11pm) will stave off your hunger – on offer are tasty empanadas and good-value set meals.

Two buses a day roll through town, heading for San Juan (AR$80, 3½ hours) and Barreal (AR$16, 30 minutes).

Barreal

☑02648 / POP 3460 / ELEV 1650M

Barreal's divine location makes it one of the most beautifully situated towns you'll likely ever come across. Sauces (weeping willows), álamos and eucalyptus trees drape lazily over the dirt roads that meander through town, and views of the Cordillera de Ansilta – a stretch of the Andes with seven majestic peaks ranging from 5130m to 5885m – are simply astonishing. Wandering along Barreal's back roads is an exercise in dreamy laziness.

Presidente Roca is the main drag through town, a continuation of RP 149 that leads from Calingasta to Barreal and on to Parque Nacional El Leoncito. Only a few streets have names; businesses listed without them simply require asking directions.

◉ Sights & Activities

Wander down to the **Río de los Patos** and take in the sweeping views of the valley and the **Cordillera de Ansilta**, whose highest peak, **Ansilta**, tops out at 5885m. To the south, **Aconcagua** and **Tupungato** are both visible, as is the peak of **Cerro Mercedario** (6770m).

At the south end of Presidente Roca is a sort of triangular roundabout. Follow the road east (away from the Andes) until it leads into the hills; you'll see a small shrine and you can **hike** into the foothills for more stunning views. Follow this road for 3km and you'll come to a mining site (the gate should be open). Enter and continue for 1km to reach a **petrified forest**.

White-water rafting is excellent – more for the scenery than for the rapids themselves – and most trips start 50km upriver at **Las Hornillas**. Contact **Barreal Rafting** (☑0264-15-530-7764), the best-established rafting operator in town.

Las Hornillas (site of two *refugios* – rustic shelters – and a military outpost) also provides **climbing** access to the Cordón de la Rameda, which boasts five peaks over 6000m, including Cerro Mercedario. Climbing here is more technical than Aconcagua and many mountaineers prefer the area. Ramon Ossa, a Barreal native, is a highly recommended mountain guide and excursion operator who knows the cordillera intimately; contact him at **Cabañas Doña Pipa** (☑02648-441004; www.fortunaviajes.com.ar). He can arrange trips to Cerro Mercedario and expeditions across the Andes in the footsteps of San Martín, including mules and equipment.

Barreal is best known for *carrovelismo* (land sailing), an exhilarating sport practiced on a small cart with a sail attached. Fanatics come from miles away to whizz around out on the gusty, cracked lake bed at Pampa El Leoncito, about 20km from town and adjacent to the national park. **Rogelio Toro** (☑0264-15-671-7196; dontoro.barreal@gmail.com) hires the necessary equipment and also gives classes.

For access to the *refugio* at Las Hornillas, climbing information, guide services and **mountain-bike** rental, visit Maxi at **Cabañas Kummel** (☑02648-441206; Presidente Roca s/n).

🛏 Sleeping & Eating

Posada Don Lisandro HOSTEL $
(☑0264-15-505-9122; www.donlisandro.com.ar; Av San Martín s/n; dm US$11, d with/without bathroom US$350/280) This newish posada (inn) is actually a 100-year-old house. The original cane-and-mud ceilings remain, as do a few sticks of room furniture. There's a kitchen for guest use and lovely, shady grounds to lounge around in.

★ El Alemán HOTEL $$
(☑0264-15-411-9913; www.elalemanbarreal.com; d/q US$92/121) 🕭 Down by the river, with sweeping views of the Andes, this German/Argentine-owned complex has some of the best-looking rooms in town. Rooms are cute and cozy, and the lack of TVs adds to the overall tranquility of the place. There's an excellent restaurant on the premises, serving hearty dishes and superb breakfasts made from the freshest ingredients. Call ahead to get picked up from the town center.

Restaurante Isidro ARGENTINE $
(Presidente Roca s/n; mains AR$70-100; ⊙8am-3pm & 8-11:30pm) Offers a fairly standard range of meats and pastas, and some delicious meat empanadas. Also a good selection of wines from the San Juan region.

ℹ Information

Banco de la Nación (Presidente Roca s/n; ⊙9am-1pm Mon-Fri) Has an ATM.
Tourist Office (☑02648-441066; turismo@calingasta.gov.ar; Presidente Roca s/n; ⊙8am-8pm) Located beside the main plaza; offers a list of excursion operators and accommodations.

ℹ Getting There & Away

Barreal's right at the end of the line, but there are two departures per day for San Juan (AR$80, four hours), which pass through Calingasta (AR$16, 30 minutes).

There's been talk for years about a bus service that will connect Barreal with Uspallata in Mendoza province – it may well be operating by the time you read this.

Parque Nacional El Leoncito

The 76-sq-km Parque Nacional El Leoncito occupies a former *estancia* (ranch) 22km south of Barreal. The landscape is typical of the Andean *precordillera*, though it's drier than the valley north of Barreal. Lately, its primary attraction is the **Pampa de Leoncito**, where a dry lake bed makes for superb *carrovelismo* (land sailing). The high, dry and wide-open valley rarely sees a cloud, also making for superb stargazing. Hence, the park is home to the Complejo Astronomico el Leoncito (www.casleo.gov.ar), which contains two important observatories, the Observatorio El Leoncito and Observatorio Cesco. Night visits are also possible, but must be scheduled ahead of time by contacting the Complejo's **San Juan office** (☑ 0264-421-3653; www.casleo.gov.ar; Av España 1512 sur, San Juan; ⊙ 9am-1pm & 3-6pm Mon-Fri).

Camping is not permitted here, but in the northwest corner of the park, Cascada El Rincon is a lovely, small waterfall set in a shallow canyon. If you're looking for somewhere to picnic and splash around on a hot day, this is your spot.

There is no public transportation to the park, and with 17km of entrance road added to the 22km to get here from Barreal, it's certainly too far to walk and probably too far to ride. If you don't have your own transportation, contact Ramon Ossa at Cabañas Doña Pipa (p352) in Barreal – his informative tours of the park have been heartily recommended.

San José de Jáchal

☑ 02647 / POP 10,900 / ELEV 1170M

Founded in 1751 and surrounded by vineyards and olive groves, Jáchal is a charming village with a mix of older adobes and contemporary brick houses. *Jachalleros* (the local residents) are renowned for their fidelity to indigenous and gaucho craft traditions; in fact, Jáchal's reputation as the Cuna de la Tradición (Cradle of Tradition) is celebrated during November's **Fiesta de la Tradición**. Except during festival season, finding these crafts is easier in San Juan.

Across from the main plaza the **Iglesia San José**, a national monument, houses the **Cristo Negro** (Black Christ), or Señor de la Agonía (Lord of Agony), a grisly leather image with articulated head and limbs, brought from Potosí in colonial times.

Jáchal's accommodations scene isn't what you'd call thriving, but the **Hotel San Martín** (☑ 02647-420431; www.hotelsanmartinjachal.com.ar; Echegaray 387; s/d US$24/35; ❋ @ �), a few blocks from the plaza, does the job. It's not quite as contemporary as it looks from the

OFF THE BEATEN TRACK

HUACO

Heading north from San José de Jáchal on RN 40, visitors pass through a beautiful landscape that is rich with folkloric traditions and rarely seen by foreigners. East of Jáchal, RN 40 climbs the precipitous **Cuesta de Huaco**, with a view of Los Cauquenes dam, before arriving at **Huaco**, a sleepy village 36km from Jáchal, whose 200-year-old **Viejo Molino** (Old Mill) justifies the trip. Some visitors get captivated by Huaco's eerie landscape and middle-of-nowhere atmosphere. If you're one of them, you can stay at **Hostería Huaco** (☑ 0264-423-9590; www.hosteriahuaco.com.ar; Calle La Paz s/n; s/d US$32/38; ⃰❋), a beautifully set up little hotel with great mountain views from the backyard pool. One bus daily from Huaco heads to San Juan (AR$75, four hours), passing though Jáchal (AR$32, one hour) on the way.

outside, but rooms are big and comfortable and the bathrooms are modern.

La Taberna de Juan (San Martín s/n; mains AR$80-120; ⊙ noon-11pm) is a bright and cheery *parrilla* facing the plaza. Meat is the go here, but there's a range of pasta dishes and salads, too. Set lunches are particularly good value.

There are several daily buses to San Juan (AR$105, three hours) from Jáchal's **bus terminal** (cnr San Juan & Obispo Zapata).

Rodeo

☑ 02647 / POP 2600 / ELEV 2010M

Rodeo is a small, ramshackle town with picturesque adobe houses typical of the region, 42km west of San José de Jáchal.

Rodeo has recently become famous – world famous – for **windsurfing** and **kitesurfing**. The town is only 3km away from one of the best windsurfing sites on the planet: **Dique Cuesta del Viento**, a reservoir where, between mid-October and early May, wind speeds reach 120km/h nearly every afternoon, drawing surfers from around the globe. Even if you don't take to the wind, it's worth spending a day or two wandering around Rodeo and hanging out on the beach, absorbing the spectacular views and watching the insanity of airborne windsurfers.

West of town on RN 510 is the department of Iglesia, home of the *precordillera* thermal baths of **Pismanta**. RN 510 continues west to Chile via the lung-busting 4765m **Paso del Agua Negra** (open summer only).

Inside the town hall, the **tourist office** (municipalidad_iglesia@yahoo.com.ar; ☺ 8am-8pm) provides a list of places to stay and information on local attractions.

From San Juan's bus terminal, there are several departures daily for Rodeo (AR$30, 5½ hours).

🛏 Sleeping & Eating

Rancho Lamaral   HOSTEL $
(☑ 0264-15-660-1197;   www.rancholamaral.com; campsite per person US$12, dm/d US$20/50) On Playa Lamaral, on the shore of the reservoir, HI-affiliate Rancho Lamaral offers simple rooms in a refurbished adobe house. It also offers windsurfing classes and kitesurfing courses, and rents all equipment.

Posta Huayra   HOTEL $$
(☑ 0264-15-451-6179;   www.postahuayra.com.ar; Zeballos s/n; s/d US$45/75) Nestled amongst the poplars below town, this atmospheric little option offers supremely comfortable rooms in a hippy-chic style with plenty of indigenous motifs. The recommended on-site restaurant is open to non-guests.

La Surfera   INTERNATIONAL $
(Santo Domingo s/n; mains AR$80-120; ☺ noon-1am; 🍴) La Surfera is on the main street in the center of town. This laid-back restaurant-cafe-reggae bar is HQ for Rodeo's surprisingly large hippy community. Vegetarian meals are predictably good; meat dishes could be better.

San Agustín de Valle Fértil
☑ 02646 / POP 4400

Reached via comically undulating highways that cut through the desert landscape, San Agustín de Valle Fértil makes an excellent base for trips to the nearby Parque Provincial Ischigualasto. It's a measure of just how dry the countryside is that this semi-arid valley gets called 'fertile.'

Apart from visiting the park, there's not much to do around these parts, but the ponderous pace of life here, where people sit on the sidewalks on summer evenings greeting passersby, has mesmerized more than one visitor.

🛏 Sleeping & Eating

Hostel Campo Base   HOSTEL $
(☑ 02646-420063;   www.hosteldelvalledelaluna. com.ar; Tucumán, btwn San Luís & Libertador; dm from US$12; 🐾) The best set-up hostel in town has good-sized dorms and all the standard hostel amenities. This is a good place to come if you're looking to put a group together for an Ischigualasto tour – you might find the hostel has one already organized.

Cabañas de Valle Pintado   CABIN $$
(☑ 0264-434-5737; www.vallepintado.com.ar; cnr Tucumán & Mitre; r/cabin US$45/78; 🐾🏊) Some of the best-value rooms and cabins in town, a block from the plaza. Rooms are spacious and spotless with little kitchenettes and cabins sleep four comfortably. The lovely garden and good-sized pool are the cream on the pudding.

La Florencia   PARRILLA $
(cnr Mitre & Acha; mains AR$70-120; ☺ noon-3pm & 8pm-midnight) Has a good range of *parrilla* offerings, including *chivito* (baby goat – order two hours in advance) and a delicious *lomo al roquefort* (beef with roquefort cheese sauce; AR$32).

ⓘ Orientation

San Agustín lies among the Sierra Pampeanas, gentle sedimentary mountains cut by impressive canyons, 247km northeast of San Juan via RN 141 and RP 510, which continues to Ischigualasto and La Rioja. San Agustín is small enough that locals pay little attention to street names, so you may need to ask for directions.

ⓘ Information

Municipal Tourist Office (General Acha; ☺ 7am-1pm & 5-10pm Mon-Fri, 8am-1pm Sat) Across from the plaza. Can help arrange car or mule excursions into the mountain canyons and backcountry.

Post Office (cnr Laprida & Mendoza; ☺ 8am-6pm Mon-Fri, 9am-1pm Sat)

Turismo Vesa (☑ 02646-420143; www.turismovesa.com; Mitre s/n) For tours to Parque Provincial Ischigualasto, Talampaya, El Chiflón and horseback riding.

ⓘ Getting There & Away

From San Agustín's **bus terminal** (Mitre, btwn Entre Ríos & Mendoza) daily buses head to San Juan (AR$130, 4½ hours).

Parque Provincial Ischigualasto

Also known fittingly as **Valle de la Luna** (Valley of the Moon; admission AR$160; ⊙8am-6pm), this park takes its name from the Diaguita word for 'land without life'. Visits here are a spectacular step – or drive, as the case may be – into a world of surreal rock formations, dinosaur remains and glowing red sunsets. The park is in some ways comparable to North American national parks such as Bryce Canyon or Zion, except that here, time and water have exposed a wealth of fossils (some 180 million years old, from the Triassic period).

The park's **museum** displays a variety of fossils, including the carnivorous dinosaur Herrerasaurus (not unlike *Tyrannosaurus rex*), the *Eoraptor lunensis* (the oldest-known predatory dinosaur) and good dioramas of the park's paleoenvironments.

The 630-sq-km park is a desert valley between two sedimentary mountain ranges, the Cerros Colorados in the east and Cerro Los Rastros in the west. Over millennia, at every meander in the canyon, the waters of the nearly dry Río Ischigualasto have carved distinctive shapes in the malleable red sandstone, monochrome clay and volcanic ash. Predictably, some of these forms have acquired popular names, including **Cancha de Bochas** (the ball court), **El Submarino** (the submarine) and **El Gusano** (the worm), among others. The desert flora of algarrobo trees, shrubs and cacti complement the eerie landforms.

From the visitor center, isolated 1748m **Cerro Morado** is a three- to four-hour walk, gaining nearly 800m in elevation and yielding outstanding views of the surrounding area. Take plenty of drinking water and high-energy snacks.

⌖ Tours

All visitors to the park must go accompanied by a ranger. The most popular tours run for three hours and leave on the hour (more or less), with cars forming a convoy and stopping at noteworthy points along the way, where the ranger explains (in Spanish only) exactly what it is you're looking at.

If you have no private vehicle, an organized tour is the only feasible way to visit the park. These are easily organized in San Agustín. Otherwise ask the tourist office there about hiring a car and driver. Tour rates (not including entry fees) are about AR$800 per person from San Juan (through any travel agency in town), or about AR$300 per person from San Agustín. Tours from San Juan generally depart at 5am and return well after dark.

A variety of other tours (around AR$100 per person) are available from the visitor center here. Options include spectacular full-moon tours (2½ hours) in the five days around the full moon, treks to the summit of Cerro Morado (three to four hours), and a 12km circuit of the park on mountain bikes.

🛏 Sleeping & Eating

Visitor Center   CAMPGROUND **$**
(campsites per person AR$45) There is camping at the visitor center, which has a *confitería* (cafe) serving simple meals (breakfast and lunch) and cold drinks; dried fruits and bottled olives from the province are available. There are toilets and showers, but because water is trucked in, don't count on it. There's no shade.

❶ Getting There & Away

Ischigualasto is about 80km north of San Agustín via RP 510 and a paved lateral road to the northwest. Given its size and isolation, the only practical way to visit the park is by private vehicle or organized tour. Note that the park roads are unpaved and some can be impassable after rain, necessitating an abbreviated trip.

Bariloche & the Lake District

Why Go?

Home to some of the country's most spectacular scenery, the Lake District is one of Argentina's prime tourist destinations. People come to ski, fish, climb, trek and generally bask in the cool, fresh landscapes created by the huge forests and glacier-fed lakes.

The paleontological sites and outstanding wineries just out of the city of Neuquén are well worth stopping off for en route; and way, way south is the resort town of Bariloche, with its picture-postcard location on the banks of the Lago Nahuel Huapi.

Getting away from the crowds is easily done. The lakeside villages of Villa Traful and San Martín de los Andes fill up for a short time in summer and are blissfully quiet the rest of the year. To the north, Chos Malal makes an excellent base for exploring nearby volcanoes, lagoons and hot springs.

Best Places to Eat

➡ Tres Catorce (p398)

➡ La Gorda (p372)

➡ La Trattoria de la Famiglia Bianchi (p363)

➡ Corazón Contento (p381)

➡ Ñancú Lahuén (p378)

Best Places to Stay

➡ La Casona de Odile Hostel (p372)

➡ Hostel Bajo Cero (p376)

➡ El Hostal del Río (p390)

➡ Hostería Chimehuín (p388)

➡ Hostería La Masía (p380)

When to Go
Bariloche

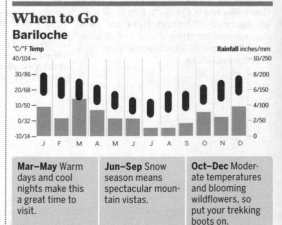

°C/°F Temp — Rainfall inches/mm

Mar–May Warm days and cool nights make this a great time to visit.

Jun–Sep Snow season means spectacular mountain vistas.

Oct–Dec Moderate temperatures and blooming wildflowers, so put your trekking boots on.

Bariloche & the Lake District Highlights

1 Driving the **Ruta de los Siete Lagos** (p379), aka RN 40, a breathtaking road winding between alpine lakes and pehuén forests.

2 Soaking your worries away in a bubbling mud bath in the thermal resort town of **Copahue** (p392).

3 Basing yourself in **Bariloche** (p358) for some fun mountain adventures.

4 Getting off the tourist trail in **Chos Malal** (p394) and out into its spectacular surrounds.

5 Following in the footsteps of dinosaurs at **Lago Barreales** (p397).

6 Hitting the hippie market in **El Bolsón** (p371) for fresh fruits and other yummies.

7 Winding down for a few days surrounded by the gorgeous scenery of **Villa Traful** (p377).

National Parks

The spectacular but often crowded Parque Nacional Nahuel Huapi is the cornerstone of the Lake District's parks. Bordering it to the north, Parque Nacional Lanín gets fewer trail trampers and has equally spectacular sights, including Volcán Lanín and humbling pehuén forests. The tiny Parque Nacional Los Arrayanes is worth a day trip from Villa la Angostura to check out its beautiful cinnamon-colored arrayán trees.

ℹ Getting There & Away

The region's two primary ground transport hubs are Neuquén and Bariloche, where buses arrive from throughout the country. The main airports are in these cities, plus San Martín de los Andes, while smaller ones are in Zapala, Chos Malal and El Bolsón. All have flights to/from Buenos Aires.

Bariloche

☑ 0294 / POP 109,300 / ELEV 770M

Strung out along the shoreline of Lago Nahuel Huapi, in the middle of the national park of the same name, Bariloche (formally San Carlos de Bariloche) has one of the most gorgeous settings imaginable. This, combined with a wealth of summer and winter activities in the surrounding countryside, has helped it become, for better or worse, the Lake District's principal destination.

The soaring peaks of Cerros Catedral, López, Nireco and Shaihuenque (to name just a few) – all well over 2000m high – ring the town, giving picture-postcard views in nearly every direction.

These mountains aren't just for gazing, though – excellent snow coverage (sometimes exceeding 2m at the *end* of the season) makes this a winter wonderland, and a magnet for skiers and snowboarders.

In summertime the nature buffs take over, hitting the hills to climb, hike trails, fish for trout and ride mountain bikes and horses.

There's so much fun to be had that this has become the destination for Argentine high school students' end of year celebrations. And if all this wasn't enough, Bariloche is also Argentina's chocolate capital and the only thing that approaches the amount of storefront window space dedicated to fresh chocolate is the infinite number of peculiar gnomes of all sizes and demeanors sold in nearly every shop downtown.

Officially founded in 1902, the city really began to attract visitors after the southern branch of the Ferrocarril Roca train line arrived in 1934 and architect Ezequiel Bustillo adapted Central European styles into a tasteful urban plan. Bariloche is now known for its alpine architecture, which is given a Patagonian twist through the use of local hardwoods and unique stone construction, as seen in the buildings of Bustillo's *centro cívico* (civic center).

The flip side of Bariloche's gain in popularity is uncontrolled growth: in the last two decades the town has suffered, as its quaint neighborhoods have given way to high-rise apartments and time-shares. The silver lining is that many accommodations have remained reasonably priced.

◎ Sights

Centro Cívico   AREA

A stroll through Bariloche's center, with its beautiful log-and-stone buildings designed by architect Ezequiel Bustillo, is a must. Besides, posing for a photo with one of the barrel-toting Saint Bernards makes for a classic Argentine snapshot, and views over the lake are superb. The buildings house the municipal tourist office and the museum.

Museo de la Patagonia   MUSEUM

(☑ 0294-442-2309; Centro Cívico; entry by donation; ⊙ 10am-12:30pm & 2-5pm Tue-Fri, 10am-5pm Sat) The museum is filled with archaeological and ethnographic materials, life-like stuffed animals and enlightening historical evaluations on such topics as Mapuche resistance to the Conquest of the Desert.

🏃 Activities

Bariloche and the Nahuel Huapi region are among Argentina's most important outdoor recreation areas, and numerous operators offer a variety of activities, particularly horseback riding, mountain biking and white-water rafting.

Mountaineering & Trekking

The park office distributes a brochure with a simple map, adequate for initial planning, that rates hikes as easy, medium or difficult and suggests possible loops. Many of these hikes are detailed in Lonely Planet's *Trekking in the Patagonian Andes*.

Club Andino Bariloche   HIKING

(☑ 0294-442-2266; www.clubandino.org; 20 de Febrero 30; ⊙ 9am-1:30pm & 3-7pm) Provides loads of information (including on camping), and issues obligatory permits for trekking in Parque Nacional Nahuel Huapi. It also sells trekking maps, all of which include mountain-bike trails. Gives information on hikers' refuges in the park.

Skiing

Nahuel Huapi's ski resort, Cerro Catedral (p370), was once South America's trendiest, and has been superseded only by Las Leñas (near Mendoza) and resorts in Chile. Las Leñas has far superior snow (dry powder), but it lacks Catedral's strong point: views. There's nothing like looking over the shimmering lakes of Nahuel Huapi from its snowy slopes.

Day passes run between AR$550 and AR$790, depending on the season. If you need lessons, stop into the ski schools at Cerro Catedral or Club Andino Bariloche. Two-hour private lessons run at about AR$1600. For rental equipment, try **Baruzzi Deportes** ([☑]0294-442-4922; www.barilochefishing.com; Urquiza 250; ⊘9am-1pm & 3-6pm Mon-Fri, 9am-1pm Sat) or **Martín Pescador** ([☑]0294-442-2275; martinpescador@speedy.com.ar; Rolando 257; ⊘9am-1pm & 4:30-9pm Mon-Fri, 10am-1pm & 6-9pm Sat). Equipment is also available on-site. Sets of skis, boots and poles rent for around AR$300, and snowboarding gear about AR$340 per day.

Mountain Biking

Bicycles are ideal for the Circuito Chico (though this 60km loop demands endurance) and other trips near Bariloche; most roads are paved and even the gravel roads are good.

Bikeway   BICYCLE RENTAL
([☑]0294-461-7686; www.bikeway.com.ar; Av Bustillo Km12.5) Mountain-bike rental, including gloves and helmet, costs around AR$120 per day at a number of places like Bikeway.

Fishing

Fly-fishing draws visitors from around the world to Argentina's accessible Andean-Patagonian parks, from Lago Puelo and Los Alerces in the south to Lanín in the north.

On larger lakes, such as Nahuel Huapi, trolling is the preferred method, while fly-fishing is the rule on most rivers. The season runs mid-November to mid-April. For more information, contact the **Asociación de Pesca y Caza Nahuel Huapi** (Hunting & Fishing Club; [☑]0294-442-1515; apcnh@speedy.com.ar; cnr Av 12 de Octubre & Onelli; ⊘9am-6pm Mon-Sat). For rental equipment and guide

hire, try Baruzzi Deportes or Martín Pescador. Both offer guided fishing trips for about AR$6750 per day for one or two people (price is the same either way and includes all equipment, lunch, transportation and guide). Fishing licenses (AR$360/1080/1440 per day/week/season) are required and are available at these shops.

Horseback Riding

Most travel agencies along Av Bartolomé Mitre offer horseback-riding trips.

Cabalgatas Carol Jones   HORSEBACK RIDING
([☑]0294-442-6508; www.caroljones.com.ar) For something special, contact the amiable Carol Jones, who offers half-day horseback riding from her family *estancia* (ranch) outside of town for AR$1100 per person. The price includes transportation to/from town and an excellent *asado* (barbecue grill) outside. She also offers multiday pack trips by horse for AR$3000 per person per day.

Cabalgatas Tom Wesley   OUTDOORS
([☑]0294-444-8193; Av Bustillo, Km15.5) This horseback riding specialist has been long in the business and has an excellent reputation.

Rafting & Kayaking

Rafting and kayaking on the Río Limay and the Río Manso have become increasingly popular in recent years. The best time to be on the rivers is November through February, though you can raft October through Easter.

EXtremo Sur   RAFTING
([☑]0294-442-7301; www.extremosur.com; Morales 765; ⊘9am-6pm) In business since 1991, this outfit offers several trips on the Río Manso: the Manso Inferior (Class II to III, AR$1290 per person) is suitable for all ages; the Manso a la Frontera (Class III to IV, AR$1690 per person, ages 14 and up) is a fun and beautiful stretch of the river before the Chilean border.

There's also a three-day Expedición Río Manso (Class III to IV), in which you camp riverside at excellent facilities.

Aguas Blancas   RAFTING
([☑]0294-443-2799; www.aguasblancas.com.ar; Morales 564; ⊘9am-1pm & 3-7pm) This business has an excellent reputation and offers trips on the Río Manso.

Pura Vida Patagonia   KAYAKING
([☑]0294-15-441-4053; www.puravidapatagonia.com.ar) Offers kayaking trips on the Lago Nahuel Huapi, ranging from half-day stints

Bariloche

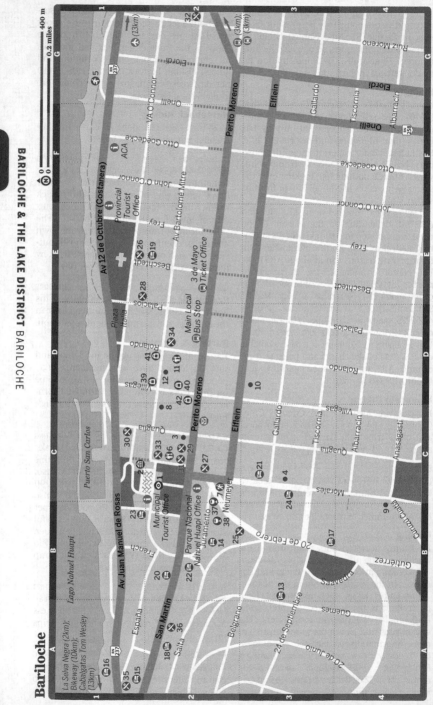

400 m
0.2 miles

Lago Nahuel Huapi

Puerto San Carlos

La Selva Negra (2km);
Bikeway (10km);
Cabalgatas Tom Wesley
(13km)

(13km)

(3km);
(3km)

Provincial Tourist Office

ACA

Plaza Italia

Main Local Bus Stop
3 de Mayo Ticket Office

Municipal Tourist Office

Parque Nacional Nahuel Huapi Office

Neumeyer

Elflein
Perito Moreno

Ruiz Moreno
Elordi
Gallardo
Tiscornia
Albarracín
Onelli
Otto Goedecke
John O'Connor
Frey
Beschtedt
Palacios
Rolando
Villegas
Quaglia
Morales
Anasagasti
Curuzú Cuatiá
Gutiérrez
Saavedra
Güemes
Belgrano
24 de Septiembre
20 de Junio
20 de Febrero

Av Juan Manuel de Rosas
Av 12 de Octubre (Costanera)
Av Bartolomé Mitre
VA O'Connor
España
French
Salta
San Martín

Bariloche

to overnight camp-'n'-kayak trips, custom-designed to match your skill level.

Paragliding

Parapente Bariloche PARAGLIDING
(☎0294-15-455-2403; Cerro Otto base) The mountains around Bariloche make for spectacular paragliding. If you wish to take to the sky, it will cost you around AR$1400 for a 20-minute to half-hour tandem flight with, among others, Parapente Bariloche.

📖 Courses

La Montaña LANGUAGE COURSE
(☎0294-452-4212; www.lamontana.com; Elflein 251, 2nd fl; ⊙9am-4pm Mon-Fri) This is a recommended Spanish school.

🧭 Tours

Countless tourist agencies along and near Av Bartolomé Mitre, such as Turisur, run minibus tours to the national park and as far south as El Bolsón. Prices range from AR$115 for a half-day trip along the Circuito Chico to AR$280 to San Martín de los Andes via the scenic Ruta de los Siete Lagos (p379).

Adventure Center DRIVING TOUR
(☎0294-442-8368; www.adventurecenter.com.ar; Perito Moreno 30; ⊙9am-6pm) Three-day trips down the fabled RN 40 as far as El Calafate. Trips run from the end of October to April.

Bariloche Moto Tours MOTORBIKE TOUR
(☎0294-446-2687; www.barilochemototours.com) Organizes custom motorbike tours to everywhere between southern Patagonia and northern Chile, and beyond.

Espacio BOAT TOUR
(☎0294-443-1372; www.islavictoriayarrayanes.com; Av Bartolomé Mitre 139) Espacio offers cruises on Nahuel Huapi lake in its 40ft catamaran *Cau Cau* during summer. Reserve your place two days in advance.

🎉 Festivals & Events

In January and February the **Festival de Música de Verano** (Summer Music Festival) puts on several different events, including the **Festival de Música de Cámara** (Chamber Music Festival), the **Festival de Bronces** (Brass Festival) and the **Festival de Música Antigua** (Ancient Music Festival).

At Easter, the **Festival Nacional del Chocolate** features live music and parades, not to mention a 9m-high Easter egg and 150m-long chocolate bar, among other sweet, sugary attractions.

On May 3 the **Fiesta Nacional de la Rosa Mosqueta** celebrates the fruit of the wild shrub used in many regional delicacies.

For 10 days in August, Bariloche holds its **Fiesta Nacional de la Nieve** (National Snow Festival).

🛏 Sleeping

From camping and private houses to five-star hotels, Bariloche's abundant accommodations make it possible to find good value even in high season, when reservations are a good idea. Prices peak during ski season (July and August), drop slightly during high season (January and February) and are lowest the rest of the year.

Hostel Los Troncos
HOSTEL $

(☎0294-443-1188; www.hostellostroncos.com.ar; San Martín 571; dm/d from US$26/63; 🛜) A step above most other hostels in town, the Troncos offers modern rooms with private bathrooms and cozy touches such as private reading lamps. There's also a range of super comfy hangout areas, an industrial-sized kitchen and a cute little courtyard garden.

Hostel 41 Below
HOSTEL $

(☎0294-443-6433; www.hostel41below.com; Juramento 94; dm US$16-19, d without bathroom US$50; @🛜) An intimate hostel with clean dorms, fine doubles (with good views) and a mellow vibe. The kitchen and common room are excellent.

Periko's
HOSTEL $

(☎0294-452-2326; www.perikos.com; Morales 555; dm US$180, d with/without bathroom US$54/45; @🛜) An atmospheric little hostel set up on the hill overlooking town. There's a good variety of rooms on offer, excellent common areas and kitchen and you can get some good-quality info from the on-site travel agency.

Hospedaje Wikter
HOTEL $

(☎0294-442-3248; www.hospedajewikter.com.ar; Güemes 566; s/d US$35/60; 🛜) Up the hill away from the center, this friendly little *hospedaje* offers spacious rooms in a bright, modern building. Bathrooms are bigger than most in this price range and some rooms have good views.

La Selva Negra
CAMPGROUND $

(☎0294-444-1013; www.campingselvanegra.com.ar; Av Bustillo, Km2.950; campsites per person US$12) Located 3km west of town on the road to Llao Llao, this is the nearest organized camping area. It has good facilities and, in the fall, you can step outside your tent to pick apples.

Hostel Patanuk
HOSTEL $

(☎0294-443-4991; www.patanuk.com; Av Juan Manuel de Rosas 585; dm/d AR$90/260; 🛜) Bariloche's only lakefront hostel is a definite winner. Big picture windows put you right in front of the water and mountains. Hardwood floors, a spacious kitchen and comfy lounge round out the picture.

Hotel Tirol
HOTEL $$

(☎0294-442-6152; www.hosteriatirol.com.ar; Libertad 175; r with city/lake view US$128/148; @🛜) Right in the middle of town, this charming little lodge offers comfortable, spacious rooms. Those out the back have spectacular views out over the lake and to the mountain range beyond, as does the bright sitting/breakfast area.

Hostería La Paleta del Pintor
HOTEL $$

(☎0294-442-2220; www.lapaletadelpintor.com.ar; 20 de Febrero 630; s/d US$73/90; 🛜) Everything about this place screams 'cute,' but the rooms are big and airy, with small but spotless bathrooms and big-screen TVs.

Hotel Aconcagua
HOTEL $$

(☎0294-442-4718; www.hotelaconcaguabariloche.com; San Martín 289; s/d US$67/79; ✱🛜) You can't beat the central location here, right on the main drag and the lake/mountain views out the back windows are pretty stunning as well. The rooms themselves are aging a bit, but the whole place is neat as a pin and very well run.

Hotel Carlos V
HOTEL $$

(☎0294-442-5474; www.carlosvpatagonia.com.ar; Morales 420; s/d US$110/133; @🛜) At first glance a fairly standard business hotel, the Carlos V has plenty of hidden charm. That, the central location and the good-sized rooms make it hard to beat.

Hostería Piuke
HOTEL $$

(☎0294-442-3044; res.piuke@gmail.com; F Beschtedt 136; s/d US$69/87; 🛜) One of the better-value hotels down near the lakefront, this one has good-sized, comfortable rooms and some very hip retro '70s furnishings.

Hostería La Sureña
HOTEL $$

(☎0294-442-2013; www.hosterialasurena.com.ar; San Martín 432; s/d US$68/79; 🛜) A cozy, hectically decorated lobby leads on to a wide variety of rooms – some are spacious and well-appointed, others are workaday and cramped. Have a look at a few if you can.

Hotel Edelweiss
HOTEL $$$

(☑0294-444-5500; www.edelweiss.com.ar; San Martín 202; s/d from US$164/248; @♠☎) One of the better business-class hotels in town, the Edelweiss manages to retain a warmth despite its size. All the facilities are here, including a fantastic 7th-floor day spa and swimming pool.

🍴 Eating

Bariloche has some of Argentina's best food, and it would take several wallet-breaking, belt-bursting and intestinally challenging weeks to sample all of the worthwhile restaurants. Regional specialties, including *cordero* (lamb, cooked over an open flame), *jabalí* (wild boar), *ciervo* (venison) and *trucha* (trout), are especially worth trying.

Covita
VEGETARIAN $

(☑0294-442-1708; VA O'Connor 511; mains AR$30-60; ⊙noon-3pm Mon-Sat, 8-11pm Fri & Sat; 🍴) Wonderfully healthy cafe that caters to macrobiotic, vegan and even raw-food diets. Choose from salads, stirfries, curries, and sushi, among others. Fresh organic juices, too.

La Fonda del Tio
ARGENTINE $

(Av Bartolomé Mitre 1130; mains AR$60-120; ⊙noon-3:30 & 8pm-midnight) No tourist nonsense here – just big servings of straight-up Argentine classics. It's a short menu, which changes daily, so it's always worth popping in to see what's on offer.

La Marca
INTERNATIONAL $

(Urquiza 240; mains AR$100-160; ⊙noon-midnight; 🕾) Upscale *parrilla* (steak restaurant) with reasonable (for Bariloche) prices. Choose from the impressive range of *brochettes* (shasliks) – beef, chicken, venison, lamb and salmon. On a sunny day, grab a garden table at the side.

Helados Jauja
ICE CREAM $

(Perito Moreno 48; ice cream from AR$35; ⊙9am-11:30pm) Ask anyone in town who serves the best ice cream in Bariloche and they'll reply with one word: 'Jauja.' Many say it's the best in the country.

Rock Chicken
FAST FOOD $

(San Martín 234; mains AR$75-120; ⊙10am-late) Late night munchies? Midday junkfood cravings? The beef, burgers and fried chicken here won't be winning any culinary awards, but they get the job done.

★La Trattoria de la Famiglia Bianchi
ITALIAN $$

(☑0294-442-1596; España 590; mains AR$120-180; ⊙noon-11:30pm; 🕾) Finally, an Italian restaurant that offers something different. Excellent, creative pastas, a good range of meat dishes and some wonderful risottos, with ingredients such as seafood and wild mushrooms.

Alto El Fuego
PARRILLA $$

(☑0294-443-7015; 20 de Febrero 445; mains AR$130-250; ⊙noon-3pm & 8pm-midnight; 🕾) The most frequently recommended *parrilla* in town, featuring the killer combination of great cuts of meat and a well-chosen wine list. It's a small place – if you're coming for dinner, make a reservation. Or (if weather permits) go for lunch and take advantage of the breezy deck area.

La Esquina
CAFE $$

(cnr Urquiza & Perito Moreno; mains AR$140-220; ⊙9am-midnight; 🕾) The most atmospheric *confitería* (cafe offering light meals) in town has good coffee, reasonably priced sandwiches and burgers, and some good regional specialties.

Familia Weiss
ARGENTINE $$

(Palacios 167; mains AR$120-180; ⊙noon-4pm & 8pm-midnight Mon-Thu, noon-midnight Fri-Sun; 🕾) A popular family restaurant offering good-value regional specialties such as venison, trout and goulash. The picture menu is handy for the Spanish-challenged, there's a good atmosphere and nightly live music.

Días de Zapata
MEXICAN $$

(☑0294-442-3128; Morales 362; mains AR$120-160; ⊙noon-3:30pm & 7pm-midnight; 🕾) A warm and inviting little Mexican restaurant. Dishes tend more toward the Tex Mex than you would think (the owners hail from Mexico City), but the flavors are good and the servings generous.

Kostelo
INTERNATIONAL $$

(☑0294-443-9697; Quaglia 111; mains AR$130-220; ⊙noon-3pm & 8pm-midnight Tue-Sun; 🕾) Modern and upscale bar-restaurant best for its location right near the lake. The food isn't bad, however – creative, well-presented and with decent portions. Try to get a table with water view.

CHOCOLATE SURTIDO

ELENAMIRAGE/GETTY IMAGES ©

ALFREDO MAIQUEZ/GETTY IMAGES ©

ALEXANDRE CAPPY/GETTY IMAGES ©

3

1. Bariloche (p358)
The Lake District's principal destination is also Argentina's chocolate capital.

2. Parque Nacional Los Arrayanes (p375)
Hike among cinnamon-colored arrayán trees at this small but diverse national park.

3. San Martín de los Andes (p378)
Cerro Chapelco attracts snowboarders and skiiers.

4. Laguna Frias (p370)
This peaceful lake is in Parque Nacional Nahuel Huapi (p368), one of Argentina's most popular national parks.

La Marmite
ARGENTINE $$

(☎0294-442-3685; Av Bartolomé Mitre 329; mains AR$130-200; ⊗noon-1am; 🛜) A trusty choice for Patagonian standards such as trout and venison. Also the place to come for chocolate fondue (AR$300 for two), in case you haven't eaten enough of the stuff cold.

🍷 Drinking & Nightlife

Los Vikingos
BAR

(cnr Juramento & 20 de Febrero; ⊗7pm-3am Mon-Sat) A laid-back little corner bar serving a good range of local microbrewery beers at excellent prices. The music's cool and the decor eclectic. DJs play on weekends.

South Bar
BAR

(Juramento s/n; ⊗8pm-4am) Mellow local pub where you can actually have a conversation while you drink your beer. Darts, too.

🛍 Shopping

Bariloche is renowned for its chocolates, and dozens of stores downtown, from national chains to mom-and-pop shops, sell chocolates of every style imaginable. Quality, of course, varies: don't get sick on the cheap stuff.

★Mamuschka
FOOD

(☎0294-442-3294; Av Bartolomé Mitre 298; ⊗9:15am-10pm) Quite simply, the best chocolate in town. Don't skip it. Seriously.

Abuela Goye
FOOD

(☎0294-443-3861; Av Bartolomé Mitre 258; ⊗9:30am-7:30pm) Another of Bariloche's long-time chocolate makers. Still small and still worth trying.

Huitral-Hue
CLOTHING

(☎0294-442-6760; Villegas 250; ⊗9:30am-1pm & 4:30-9:30pm Mon-Sat) Good selection of traditional ponchos, textiles and wool sweaters.

Paseo de los Artesanos
HANDICRAFTS

(cnr Villegas & Perito Moreno; ⊗sunrise-sunset) Local craftspeople display wares of wool, wood, leather, silver and other media here.

ℹ️ Orientation

The principal commercial area is along Av Bartolomé Mitre. Do not confuse VA O'Connor (also known as Vicealmirante O'Connor or Eduardo O'Connor) with similarly named John O'Connor, which cross each other near the lakefront. Similarly, Perito Moreno and Ruiz Moreno intersect near Diagonal Capraro, at the east end of the downtown area.

THE CRUCE DE LAGOS

One of Argentina's classic journeys is the Cruce de Lagos, a scenic 12-hour bus-and-boat trip over the Andes to Puerto Montt, Chile. Operated exclusively by **Turisur** (☎0294-442-6109; www.cruceandino.com; Mitre 219, Bariloche; per person AR$1650), the trip begins around 8am in Bariloche (departure times vary) with a shuttle from Turisur's office to Puerto Pañuelo near Hotel Llao Llao. The passenger ferry from Puerto Pañuelo leaves immediately after the shuttle arrives so, if you want to have tea at Llao Llao, get there ahead of time on your own (but make sure you bought your ticket in advance). Service is daily in the summer, Monday to Friday the rest of the year. In winter (mid-April to September) the trip takes two days and passengers are required to stay the night in Peulla, Chile, where you have the choice of **Hotel Natura Patagonica** (☎in Chile 65-297-2289; www.hotelnatura.cl; s/d US$211/220; @🛜) or the **Hotel Peulla** (☎in Chile 65-297-2288; www.hotelpeulla.cl; s/d US$138/146; @🛜). There used to be a more economical option at Puerto Blest, but it was closed at time of research. Ask about this option at Turisur.

Bicycles are allowed on the boats, and sometimes on the buses (provided you dismantle them), so cyclists may end up having to ride the stretches between Bariloche and Pañuelo (25km), Puerto Blest and Puerto Alegre (15km), Puerto Frías and Peulla (27km), and Petrohué and Puerto Montt (76km); the **tourist office in Bariloche** (p367) may have info about alternative transportation between Petrohué and Puerto Montt for cyclists hoping to avoid the ride.

In winter it's not possible to purchase tickets only for segments of the trip (except between Puerto Pañuelo and Puerto Blest; AR$750). In summer (December to April) it's possible to buy just the boat sections (AR$900). Either way, if you're cycling Turisur will cut your rate slightly since you won't be riding the buses. Though the trip rarely sells out, it's best to book it at least a day or two in advance.

ℹ Information

Banks with ATMs are ubiquitous in the downtown area.

ACA (Automóvil Club Argentino; ☑ 0294-442-3001; Av 12 de Octubre 785) Argentina's auto club has provincial road maps.

Cambio Sudamérica (Av Bartolomé Mitre 63; ⊙ 9am-8pm Mon-Fri, to 1pm Sat) Change foreign cash and traveler's checks here.

Hospital (☑ 0294-442-6100; Perito Moreno 601) *Long* waits, no charge.

Municipal Tourist Office (☑ 0294-442-3022; Centro Cívico; ⊙ 8am-9pm) It has many giveaways, including useful maps and the blatantly commercial but still useful *Guía Busch*, updated biannually and loaded with basic tourist information about Bariloche and the Lake District.

Parque Nacional Nahuel Huapi Office (☑ 0294-442-3111; San Martín 24; ⊙ 8am-4pm Mon-Fri, 9am-3pm Sat & Sun) Office for the nearby **national park** (p368).

Post Office (Moreno 175; ⊙ 8am-6pm Mon-Fri, 9am-1pm Sat)

Provincial Tourist Office (☑ 0294-442-3188, 0294-442-3189; secturrn@bariloche.com.ar; cnr Av 12 de Octubre & Emilio Frey; ⊙ 9am-7pm) Has information on the province, including an excellent provincial map and useful brochures in English and Spanish.

ℹ Getting There & Away

AIR

Aerolíneas Argentinas (☑ 0294-443-3304; Av Bartolomé Mitre 185; ⊙ 9am-7pm Mon-Fri, to 1pm Sat) has flights to Buenos Aires twice daily Monday through Wednesday and three times daily the rest of the week. In high season there are direct weekly flights to Córdoba and El Calafate and possibly Ushuaia.

LAN (☑ 0810-999-9526; www.lan.com; Av Bartolomé Mitre 534; ⊙ 9am-2pm & 3-6pm Mon-Sat) flies to Chile and Buenos Aires, and **LADE** (☑ 0294-442-3562; www.lade.com.ar; John O'Connor 214; ⊙ 9am-3pm Mon-Sat) covers southern destinations.

BOAT

It's possible to travel by boat and bus to Chile aboard the **Cruce de Lagos** (p366) tour.

BUS

Bariloche's **bus terminal** (☑ 0294-443-2860) and train station are east of town across the Río Ñireco on RN 237. Shop around for the best deals, since fares vary and there are frequent promotions. During high season it's wise to buy tickets at least a day in advance. The bus terminal tourist office is helpful.

The principal route to Chile is over the Cardenal A Samoré (Puyehue) pass to Osorno

(AR$350, five hours) and Puerto Montt (AR$375, six hours), which has onward connections to northern and southern Chilean destinations. Several companies make the run.

To San Martín de los Andes and Junín de los Andes, Albus, Transportes Ko-Ko and **Turismo Algarrobal** (☑ 0294-442-7698) take the scenic (though possibly chokingly dusty) Ruta de los Siete Lagos (RN 40) during summer, and the longer, paved La Rinconada (RN 237) route during the rest of the year.

Buses from Bariloche

DESTINATION	COST (AR$)	TIME (HR)
Bahía Blanca	1100	12-14
Buenos Aires	1784	20-23
Córdoba	1619	22
El Bolsón	123	2
Esquel	290	4½
Junín de los Andes	145	3
Mendoza	1375	19
Neuquén	512	7
Río Gallegos	1483	28
San Martín de los Andes	177	4
San Rafael	1133	15
Viedma	950	12
Villa la Angostura	60	1½

Train

As troubled as any of the intercity train lines, when it's running the **Tren Patagonico** (☑ 02944-423172; www.trenpatagonico-sa.com.ar) leaves the **train station** (☑ 02944-423172), across the Río Ñireco next to the bus terminal. If it is operating, it generally leaves Bariloche for Viedma (16 hours) at 5pm on most Sundays (and the occasional Monday); fares will probably range from AR$562 in *primera* (first class seated) to AR$1123 in *camarote* (1st-class sleeper). All this information is incredibly fluid – it's best to check with the tourist office beforehand.

ℹ Getting Around

TO/FROM THE AIRPORT

Bariloche's airport is 15km east of town via RN 237 and RP 80. A *remise* (taxi) costs about AR$140. Bus 72 (AR$15) leaves from the main bus stop on Perito Moreno.

BUS

At the **main local bus stop** (Perito Moreno, btwn Rolando & Palacios), Codao del Sur and Ómnibus 3 de Mayo run hourly buses to Cerro Catedral.

Codao uses Av de los Pioneros, while 3 de Mayo takes Av Bustillo.

From 6am to midnight, municipal bus 20 leaves the main bus stop every 20 minutes for the attractive lakeside settlements of Llao Llao and Puerto Pañuelo. Bus 10 goes to Colonia Suiza 14 times daily. During summer three of these, at 8:05am, noon and 5:40pm, continue to Puerto Pañuelo, allowing you to do most of the Circuito Chico using public transport. Departure times from Puerto Pañuelo back to Bariloche via Colonia Suiza are 9:40am, 1:40pm and 6:40pm. You can also walk any section and flag down buses en route.

Ómnibus 3 de Mayo buses 50 and 51 go to Lago Gutiérrez every 30 minutes, while in summer the company's Línea Mascardi goes to Villa Mascardi/Los Rápidos three times daily. Ómnibus 3 de Mayo's Línea El Manso goes twice on Friday to Río Villegas and El Manso, on the southwestern border of Parque Nacional Nahuel Huapi.

Buses 70, 71 and 83 stop at the main bus stop, connecting downtown with the bus terminal.

CAR

Bariloche is loaded with the standard car-rental agencies and is one of the cheapest places to rent in the country. Prices vary greatly depending on season and demand, but usually come in around AR$400 per day, with 200km.

Andes (✆0294-443-1648; www.andesrenta car.com.ar; San Martín 162; ◷9am-6pm)

Budget (✆0294-444-2482; www.budget bariloche.com; Av Bartolomé Mitre 717; ◷9am-7pm)

Hertz (✆0294-442-3457; www.hertz.com.ar; Elflein 190; ◷9am-9pm)

TAXI

A taxi from the bus terminal to the center of town costs around AR$40. Taxis within town generally don't go over the AR$25 mark.

---

❶ BARILOCHE BUS CARDS

Bariloche's local buses work with magnetic cards that can be purchased at the **3 de Mayo ticket office** (✆0294-442-5648; Perito Moreno 480), downtown or at the bus terminal. You can also pick up handy *horarios* (schedules) for all destinations from these offices. Cards cost AR$20 (recharged with however er much credit you want). For most routes a ride will cost AR$9, with AR$15 being the highest fare. Some hostels loan cards to guests on payment of a deposit.

Parque Nacional Nahuel Huapi

⌖ 02944

One of Argentina's most-visited national parks, **Nahuel Huapi** (✆0294-442-3111; admission AR$120) occupies 7500 sq km in mountainous southwestern Neuquén and western Río Negro provinces. The park's centerpiece is Lago Nahuel Huapi, a glacial remnant over 100km long that covers more than 500 sq km. To the west, a ridge of high peaks separates Argentina from Chile; the tallest is 3554m Monte Tronador, an extinct volcano that still lives up to its name (meaning 'Thunderer') when blocks of ice tumble from its glaciers. During the summer months, wildflowers blanket the alpine meadows.

Nahuel Huapi was created to preserve local flora and fauna, including its Andean-Patagonian forests and rare animals. The important animal species include the huemul (Andean deer) and the miniature deer known as pudú. Most visitors are unlikely to see either of these, but several species of introduced deer are common, as are native birds.

Circuito Chico

One of the area's most popular and scenic driving excursions, the Circuito Chico begins on Av Bustillo, on Bariloche's outskirts, and continues to the tranquil resort of **Llao Llao**. At Cerro Campanario the **Aerosilla Campanario** (✆0294-442-7274; return AR$150; ◷9am-5:30pm) lifts passengers to a panoramic view of Lago Nahuel Huapi.

Llao Llao's **Puerto Pañuelo** is the point of departure for the boat and bus excursion across the Andes to Chile, as well as to Parque Nacional Los Arrayanes on Península Quetrihué.

Even if you don't plan to spend a night in **Hotel Llao Llao** (✆0294-444-8530; www.llao llao.com.ar; d from US$374; ✳@🛜🏊), arguably Argentina's most famous hotel, take a stroll around the grounds. It was once featured on the one-peso banknote, when such a thing existed. From Llao Llao you can head across to **Colonia Suiza**, named for its early Swiss colonists. A modest *confitería* has excellent pastries, and there are several campgrounds and even a hostel.

The road passes the trailhead to 2076m **Cerro López**, a three-hour climb, before returning to Bariloche. At the top of Cerro

Parque Nacional Nahuel Huapi

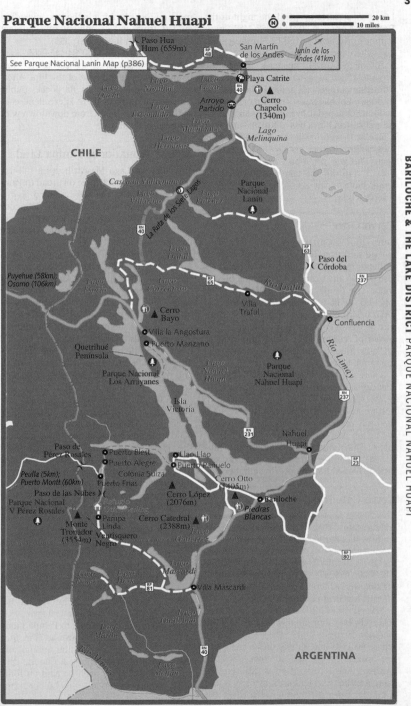

López it's possible to spend the night at the **Refugio López** (📞0294-15-458-4459; www.cerrolopez.com; dm about US$25; ☉mid-Dec–mid-Apr), where meals are also available.

Although travel agencies offer the Circuito Chico as a half-day tour (AR$115 through most agencies in Bariloche), it's easily done on public transportation or, if you're up for a 60km pedal, by bike. Less enthusiastic cyclists can hop a bus to Km18.6 and rent a bike at **Bike Cordillera** (📞0294-452-4828; www.cordillerabike.com; per day AR$300; ☉9am-6pm). This way you'll bike much less, avoid busy Av Bustillo and take advantage of the loop's more scenic sections. Call ahead to reserve a bike.

Cerro Otto

Cerro Otto (1405m) is an 8km hike on a gravel road west from Bariloche. There's enough traffic to make hitchhiking feasible, and it's also a steep and tiring but rewarding bicycle route. The **Teleférico Cerro Otto** (📞0294-444-1035; Av de Los Pioneros, Km5; adult/child AR$200/140) carries passengers to the summit; a free bus leaves Bariloche from the corner of Av Bartolomé Mitre and Villegas or Perito Moreno and Independencia to the mountain base.

There's a trail from the small Piedras Blancas ski resort to Club Andino's **Refugio Berghof** (dm US$19), at an elevation of 1240m. At the time of research this *refugio* was only operating as a day shelter – check with Club Andino Bariloche (p358) for the latest. The *refugio* also contains the **Museo de Montaña Otto Meiling** (guided visit AR$30), named for a pioneering climber.

Cerro Catedral

This 2388m **peak** (📞0294-440-9000; www.catedralaltapatagonia.com; ☉mid-Jun–mid-Oct), 20km southwest of Bariloche, is the area's most important snow-sports center. Several chairlifts and the **Aerosilla Cerro Bellavista** (📞0294-440-9000; AR$260) carry passengers up to 2000m, where there's a restaurant-*confitería* offering excellent panoramas.

Several **trekking** trails begin here: one relatively easy four-hour walk goes to Club Andino's **Refugio Emilio Frey** (dm AR$180), where 40 beds and simple meals (AR$130) are available, as are kitchen facilities (AR$45). This *refugio* itself is exposed, but there are sheltered tent sites in what is also Argentina's prime **rock-climbing** area. For more on rock climbing in the area, including guided trips and equipment hire, contact Club Andino in Bariloche (p358).

Hostería Knapp (📞0294-446-0460; www.knappcerrocatedral.com.ar; r per person from US$108; ☎) is at the base of the lifts. Alternatively you can stay in Bariloche; public transportation from there is excellent, consisting of hourly buses from downtown with Ómnibus 3 de Mayo.

Monte Tronador & Pampa Linda

Traveling via Lago Mascardi, it's a full-day trip up a dusty, single-lane dirt road to Pampa Linda to visit the **Ventisquero Negro** (Black Glacier) and the base of Tronador (3554m). Visitors are rewarded with views of dozens of waterfalls plunging over the flanks of extinct volcanoes.

From Pampa Linda – the starting point for several excellent **hikes** – hikers can approach the snow-line Club Andino **Refugio Otto Meiling** (dm US$30) on foot (about four to six hours' hiking time) and continue to **Laguna Frías** via the **Paso de las Nubes**; it's a five- to seven-hour walk to an elevation of 2000m. It's also possible to complete the trip in the opposite direction by taking Turisur's ferry from Puerto Pañuelo to Puerto Blest, and then hiking up the Río Frías to Paso de las Nubes, before descending to Pampa Linda via the Río Alerce. The *refugio* itself prepares delicious meals (around AR$220-300, kitchen use AR$100) and is well stocked with good wine and beer. You can hire a guide at the *refugio* to take you on a number of excursions, which range from a three-hour hike to a nearby glacier to the multiday ascent of Cumbre Argentina on Tronador.

Climbers intending to scale Tronador should anticipate a three- to four-day technical climb requiring experience on rock, snow and ice.

The road to **Pampa Linda** passes **Los Rápidos**, after which it becomes extremely narrow. Traffic is therefore allowed up to Pampa Linda until 2pm. At 4pm cars are allowed to leave Pampa Linda for the return trip. For AR$130 one way, Club Andino Bariloche (p358) has summer transportation (end of November to April) to Pampa Linda at 8:30am daily, returning around 5pm. Buses depart from in front of Club Andino, and the 90km ride takes about 2½ hours. Park entry fees (AR$120) must be paid en route at the ranger station at **Villa Mascardi** (the bus stops so you can do this).

📖 Sleeping

In addition to the campgrounds in the Bariloche area, there are sites at Lago Gutiérrez, Lago Mascardi, Lago Guillelmo, Lago Los Moscos, Lago Roca and Pampa Linda. *Refugios* are mostly open from December to the end of April. Reservations are not accepted – beds are allocated on a first come, first served basis, but a space will always be found (maybe on the floor) for whoever arrives.

Within the park are a number of hotels tending to the luxurious, though there is also the moderately priced **Hostería Pampa Linda** (📞0294-449-0517; www.hosteriapampa linda.com.ar; s/d with half board US$160/220) in the southern foothills of Cerro Tronador. For a real treat, stay at the secluded **Hotel Tronador** (📞0294-449-0556; www.hoteltrona dor.com; s/d from US$106/123; ⊙Nov–mid-Apr), at the northwest end of Lago Mascardi on the Pampa Linda road.

ℹ️ Information

A good source of information about the park is the **Nahuel Huapi national park office** (p367) in Bariloche.

For trekking maps and information about hiking in the region, see Lonely Planet's *Trekking in the Patagonian Andes* by Carolyn McCarthy or, if you read Spanish, the locally published *Las Montañas de Bariloche* by Toncek Arko and Raúl Izaguirre.

ℹ️ Getting There & Around

Parque Nacional Estado de Rutas (📞105) For road conditions in and around the national parks, call the toll-free number.

El Bolsón

📞0294 / POP 17,000 / ELEV 300M

It's not hard to see why the hippies started flocking to El Bolsón back in the '70s. It's a mellow little village for most of the year, nestled in between two mountain ranges. When summer comes, it packs out with Argentine tourists who drop big wads of cash and disappear quietly to whence they came.

In the last 30-odd years El Bolsón has been declared both a non-nuclear zone and an 'ecological municipality' (are you getting the picture yet?). What's indisputable is that just out of town are some excellent, easily accessible hikes that take in some of the country's (if possibly not the world's) most gorgeous landscapes.

The town welcomes backpackers, who often find it a relief from Bariloche's commercialism and find themselves stuffing their bellies with natural and vegetarian foods, and the excellent beer, sweets, jams and honey made from the local harvest.

Rows of poplars lend a Mediterranean appearance to the local *chacras* (farms), most of which are devoted to hops (El Bolsón produces nearly three-quarters of the country's hops) and fruits.

Motorists should note that El Bolsón is the northernmost spot to purchase gasoline at Patagonian discount prices (although recent decreases in subsidies have seen the difference drop to around AR$1 per liter).

⊙ Sights & Activities

The principal landmark in town is the ovoid Plaza Pagano. Most services are nearby.

★ Feria Artesanal   MARKET
(⊙10am-4pm Tue, Thu, Sat & Sun) 🖉 Local craftspeople sell their wares at this market, along the eastern edge of Plaza Pagano, which boasts over 300 artists, who make and sell everything from wooden cutting boards and handcrafted *mate* (a bitter ritual tea) gourds to jewelry, flutes and marionettes. With numerous food vendors (adhering to the regulation that everything sold in the market must be handmade), it's also a chance to sample local delicacies. On sunny Sundays the *feria* (market) operates about half-tilt.

Grado 42   RAFTING
(📞0294-449-3124; www.grado42.com; Av Belgrano 406; ⊙8:30am-8:30pm Mon-Sat, 10:30am-1pm & 5-7pm Sun) For adventures in the surrounding countryside, this company offers extensive trekking, mountain biking and other tours around El Bolsón, and rafting on the Río Manso. Trips on the Manso Inferior (Class II to III) cost AR$960 per person (including snack); on the Manso a la Frontera (Class II to IV) trips cost AR$1490 (including breakfast).

El Tabano   BICYCLE RENTAL
(📞0294-449-3093; Perito Moreno 2871; ⊙9am-6pm Mon-Sat) Rents bikes for AR$60/200 per hour/day.

🎊 Festivals & Events

Local beer gets headlines during the **Festival Nacional del Lúpulo** (National Hops Festival), over four days in mid-February. El Bolsón also hosts a weekend **jazz festival** (www.elbolsonjazz.com.ar) in December.

🛏 Sleeping

Budget travelers are more than welcome in El Bolsón, where reasonable prices are the rule rather than the exception.

★ La Casona de Odile Hostel   HOSTEL $
(📞 0294-449-2753; www.odile.com.ar; dm/d US$18/55; @🛜) 🍴 Five kilometers north of the center is one of the best hostels in the country. Set on two hectares of park-like riverside land, this is one of those places you come to for a couple of days and find yourself there two weeks later.

Traveler-run, it's got all you could possibly want – good amenities, comfy dorms and rooms, an on-site microbrewery, yoga classes, massage, cheap, hearty dinners and bike hire.

La Casa del Arbol   HOSTEL $
(📞 0294-472-0176; www.hostelelbolson.com; Perito Moreno 3038; dm from US$16, d with/without bathroom from US$47/40; @🛜) A great little hostel, with a couple of good private rooms, spacious dorms and excellent kitchen, living and outdoor areas.

Hostería Luz de Luna   HOTEL $
(📞 0294-449-1908; www.luzdeluna.guiapatagonia. net; Dorrego 150; s/d US$55/75; 🛜) Although spacious, the rooms here manage to retain a pleasant, homelike feel. Individual decoration and spotless bathrooms add to the appeal. Go for one upstairs for better light and views.

Camping Refugio Patagónico   CAMPGROUND $
(📞 0294-448-3888; www.refugiopatagonico.com. ar; Islas Malvinas s/n; campsites per person US$7, dm/d US$14/100; 🛜) Not bad as far as campgrounds go – basically a bare field, but a pleasant stream burbles alongside it. Services are good, including *asados* and a modern toilet block. If you're looking for a room, there are much better deals elsewhere.

La Posada de Hamelin   GUESTHOUSE $$
(📞 0294-449-2030; www.posadadehamelin.com. ar; Granollers 2179; s/d US$70/90; 🛜) A beautiful little rustic getaway. There are only four rooms, but they're all gorgeous, with exposed beams and rough-hewn walls. The sunny upstairs dining area is a great place to munch on an empanada (baked savory turnover).

Hostería La Escampada   HOTEL $$
(📞 0294-448-3905; www.laescampada.com.ar; Azcuénaga 561; s/d US$60/100; 🛜) A refreshing break from El Bolsón's stale accommodation scene, the Escampada is all modern design, with light, airy rooms and a relaxed atmosphere.

Hostería San Jorge   HOSTEL $$
(📞 0294-449-1313; www.sanjorgepatagonico.com; Perito Moreno & Azcuénaga; s/d US$65/90; 🛜) Big, spotless rooms set around a cute little garden in a great central location. The breakfast buffet featuring home-made yummies adds to the appeal.

🍴 Eating

El Bolsón's restaurants lack Bariloche's variety, but food is consistently good value and often outstanding, thanks to fresh local ingredients and careful preparation. *Trucha arco iris* (rainbow trout) is the local specialty.

Feria Artesanal   MARKET $
(Plaza Pagano; ⏰10am-4pm Tue, Thu, Sat & Sun) 🍴 The market is the best and most economical place to eat. Goodies here include fresh fruit, Belgian waffles with berries and cream, huge empanadas for AR$10, sandwiches, fritatas, *milanesa de soja* (soy patties), locally brewed beer and regional desserts.

La Salteñita   FAST FOOD $
(Av Belgrano 515; empanadas AR$10; ⏰10am-9pm) For spicy northern empanadas, try this cheap rotisserie.

Jauja   ICE CREAM $
(Av San Martín 2867; cones from AR$35; ⏰8am-11pm; 🛜) The most dependable *confitería* (cafe offering light meals) in town serves up all your faves with some El Bolsón touches (such as homemade bread and strawberry juice) thrown in. The daily specials are always worth checking out – the risotto with lamb and wild mushrooms is divine. The attached ice-creamery is legendary – make sure you leave room for a kilo or two.

★ La Gorda   INTERNATIONAL $$
(📞 0294-472-0559; 25 de Mayo 2709; mains AR$130-190; ⏰7-11:30pm Tue-Sun) This is El Bolsón's don't-miss eating spot. Huge portions of delicious, well-prepared food in relaxed, stylish surrounds. Good vegetarian options, a couple of Asian dishes, fine cuts of meat and some interesting sides. If it's a warm night, try for a garden table. Bookings highly recommended either way.

El Bolsón

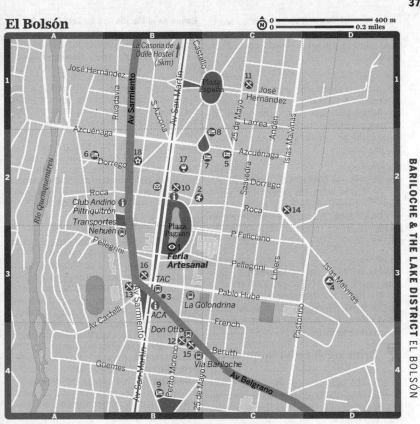

El Bolsón

◎ Top Sights
1 Feria Artesanal	B3

◈ Activities, Courses & Tours
2 El Tabano	B2
3 Grado 42	B3

⬢ Sleeping
4 Camping Refugio Patagónico	D3
5 Hostería La Escampada	C2
6 Hostería Luz de Luna	A2
7 Hostería San Jorge	C2
8 La Casa del Arbol	C2
9 La Posada de Hamelin	B4

⊗ Eating
Feria Artesanal	(see 1)

10 Jauja	B2
11 La Gorda	C1
12 La Salteñita	B4
13 Las Brasas	B3
14 Otto Tipp	C2
15 Pasiones	B4
16 Patio Venzano	B3

⊙ Drinking & Nightlife
17 Barr 442	B2

⊙ Entertainment
18 Centro Cultural Eduardo Galeano	B2

⊙ Shopping
Monte Viejo	(see 3)

Otto Tipp   ARGENTINE $$
(☎0294-449-3700; cnr Roca & Islas Malvinas; mains AR$120-200; ☺noon-1am Dec-Feb, from 8pm Wed-Sat Mar-Jan; �🛜) After a hard day of doing anything (or nothing) there are few better ways to unwind than by working your way through Mr Tipp's selection of microbrews. Guests are invited to a free sampling

of the six varieties and there's a good selection of regional specialties, such as smoked trout and Patagonian lamb cooked in black beer.

Pasiones ARGENTINE $$
(cnr Belgrano & Berutti; mains AR$100-150; ☺noon-4pm & 8-11:30pm; 🖥) Specializing in excellent, homemade pastas, this sunny little spot has huge picture windows featuring some of the best views in town. Occasionally has live music.

Patio Venzano ARGENTINE $$
(cnr Av Sarmiento & Pablo Hube; mains AR$120-190; ☺noon-midnight) On sunny days you'll want to arrive a little early to guarantee an outside table. No surprises on the menu (pasta, *parrilla*), but the atmosphere's a winner.

Las Brasas PARRILLA $$$
(☎0294-449-2923; cnr Av Sarmiento & Pablo Hube; mains AR$130-220; ☺11:30am-midnight; 🖥) The finest *parrilla* option in town. Las Brasas' signature dish is Patagonian lamb, but it offers other *parrilla* favorites, plus a variety of trout dishes.

🍸 Drinking & Entertainment

Barr 442 BAR
(☎0294-449-2313; Dorrego 442; ☺from 8pm Wed-Sat) This venue doubles as a disco on Friday nights and often has live music on Saturday nights.

Centro Cultural Eduardo Galeano THEATER
(☎0294-445-5657; centrogaleano@gmail.com; cnr Dorrego & Onelli) Small performance space featuring local (sometimes international) theater, music and dance. Stop by for a program or ask around town.

🛍 Shopping

El Bolsón is a craft-hunter's paradise. Besides the regular feria artesanal (p371) there are several other outlets for local arts and crafts.

Monte Viejo HANDICRAFTS
(cnr Pablo Hube & Av San Martín; ☺9am-6pm) Quality ceramics, woodcrafts, silver and Mapuche textiles.

ℹ Information

ACA (Automóvil Club Argentino; ☎0294-449-2260; cnr Avs Belgrano & San Martín) Auto club; has provincial road maps.

Banco de la Nación (cnr Av San Martín & Pellegrini; ☺9am-1pm) Has an ATM.

Club Andino Piltriquitrón (☎0294-449-2600; Sarmiento, btwn Roca & Feliciano; ☺6-8pm) Visitors interested in exploring the surrounding mountains can contact this office for information on hiking conditions, which refuges are open and general trail queries. Keeps a desk in the tourist office during hiking season.

Post Office (Av San Martín 2806; ☺8am-6pm Mon-Fri, 9am-1pm Sat)

Tourist Office (☎0294-449-2604; www.elbolson.gov.ar) At the north end of Plaza Pagano. It has a good town map and brochures, plus thorough information on accommodations, food, tours and services. Maps of the surrounding area are crude but helpful. Superb staff.

ℹ Getting There & Away

El Bolsón has no central bus terminal, but most companies are on or near Av San Martín.

Via Bariloche (☎0294-445-5554; cnr Av Belgrano & Berutti) goes to Bariloche (AR$115, two hours) and Esquel (AR$170, two to three hours), and to points north of there, usually with a change in Neuquén (AR$554, eight hours).

TAC (☎0294-449-3124; cnr Av Belgrano & Av San Martín) also goes to Bariloche and Neuquén; the company sells tickets to Mendoza, Córdoba and other northern destinations, though you'll have to change buses in Neuquén.

Don Otto (☎0294-449-3910; Av Belgrano 406) goes to Bariloche and Comodoro Rivadavia (AR$750, 11 hours), with connections in Esquel for Trelew and Puerto Madryn.

ℹ Getting Around

BUS

Local bus service to nearby sights is extensive during the busy summer months, but sporadic in fall and winter, when you'll have to hire a taxi or take a tour. The tourist office provides up-to-date information. Local buses cost AR$4.50.

Transportes Nehuén (☎0294-449-1831; cnr Sarmiento & Padre Feliciano) has summer bus services to many local destinations.

La Golondrina (☎0294-449-2557; cnr Pablo Hube & Perito Moreno) goes to Cascada Mallín Ahogado, leaving from the south end of Plaza Pagano; and to Lago Puelo, leaving from the corner of Av San Martín and Dorrego.

TAXI

Remises (taxis) are a reasonable mode of transportation to nearby trailheads and campgrounds. Companies include **Remises Buen Viaje** (☎0294-449-3103) and **La Unión** (☎0294-449-2858); call for rides.

Around El Bolsón

The outskirts of El Bolsón offer numerous ridges, waterfalls and forests for hikers to explore. With lots of time, and food and water, some of the following places can be reached by foot from town, though buses and *remises* to trailheads are reasonable. Mountain biking is an excellent way to get out on your own; for rentals try **Maputur** (☎0294-449-1440; Perito Moreno 2331) in El Bolsón.

Popular destinations include **Cabeza del Indio**, a lookout 7km from town and **Cascada Mallín Ahogado**, a small waterfall 10km north of town that provides access to the Club Andino Piltriquitrón's **Refugio Perito Moreno** (☎El Bolsón 0294-448-3433; per night with/without sheets US$10/7), a great base for several outstanding hikes. From here it's 2½ hours to the 2206m summit of **Cerro Perito Moreno** (☎0294-449-3912; lift pass AR$250-380, ski/snowboard rental AR$170/220) a small ski resort with a base elevation of 1000m.

Serious hikers head for the 2260m **Cerro Piltriquitrón**, a granite ridge yielding panoramic views across the valley of the Río Azul to the Andean crest along the Chilean border. Midway up is the **Bosque Tallado** (Sculpture Forest) and the Club Andino's **Refugio Piltriquitrón** (dm US$8, camping free). Beds here are outstanding value, but bring your own sleeping bag. Moderately priced meals are available. From the *refugio* it's another two hours to the summit. Water is abundant along most of the summit route, but hikers should carry a canteen and bring lunch to enjoy at the top.

For more information on these and other hikes in the area and the various hikers' *refugios* operating, contact the Club Andino Piltriquitrón in El Bolsón (p374).

In Chubut province, 15km south of El Bolsón, the **Parque Nacional Lago Puelo** protects a windy, azure lake suitable for swimming, fishing, boating, hiking and camping. By the waterfront the launch **Juana de Arco** (☎0294-449-8946; www.interpatagonia.com/juanadearco) takes passengers across the lake to Argentina's Pacific Ocean outlet at the Chilean border (AR$300, three hours). Hardcore hikers can walk into Chile from here – a small tourist office at the dock has details.

Peuma Hue (☎0294-449-9372; www.peuma-hue.com.ar; s/d from US$70/110) 🏊 is a comfortable lakeside resort complex nestled between two rivers, with great views of the mighty Piltriquitrón mountain range. There are both free and fee campsites at the park entrance, including **Camping La Pasarela** (☎0294-449-9061; www.lpuelo.com.ar; campsites per person US$10, dm/cabin US$17/75).

Regular buses go to Lago Puelo from El Bolsón in summer, but there's reduced service on Sunday and off-season.

Villa la Angostura

☎0294 / POP 11,100 / ELEV 850M

An upmarket resort town on the northwestern shore of Lago Nahuel Huapi, Villa la Angostura provides accommodations and services for nearby Cerro Bayo, a small but popular winter-sports center.

It's worthwhile stopping by in summer, too, for lake cruises and walks in the small but incredibly diverse Parque Nacional Los Arrayanes (a small peninsula dangling some 12km into the lake), and because this is the southern starting point for the breathtaking trip along the Ruta de los Siete Lagos.

The village consists of two distinct areas: El Cruce, which is the commercial center along the highway, and La Villa, nestled against the lakeshore, 3km to the south. Though La Villa is more residential, it still has hotels, shops, services and, unlike El Cruce, lake access. Puerto Manzano, in La Villa, is where boats leave for tours to the Parque Nacional Los Arrayanes.

◉ Sights & Activities

Several outfitters in town offer trekking, horseback riding and guided mountain-bike rides, and the tourist office provides information on each. Mountain biking is a great way to explore the surrounding area.

Parque Nacional Los Arrayanes   PARK
(admission AR$120) 🏞 This inconspicuous, often overlooked park, encompassing the entire Quetrihué Peninsula, protects remaining stands of the cinnamon-barked arrayán, a member of the myrtle family. In Mapudungun (language of the Mapuche) the peninsula's name means 'place of the arrayánes.' Regulations require hikers to enter the park before midday and leave it by 4pm in winter, and around 6pm to 7pm in summer.

The park headquarters is at the southern end of the peninsula, near the largest concentration of arrayánes, in an area known as **El Bosque**. It's a three-hour, 12km hike to the tip of the peninsula, on an excellent interpretive nature trail. You can also hike out and get the ferry back from the point, or vice versa. There are two small lakes along the trail.

From the park's northern entrance at La Villa, a very steep 20-minute hike leads to two panoramic overlooks of Lago Nahuel Huapi.

Cabalgatas Correntoso
HORSEBACK RIDING

(☎0294-15-451-0559; www.cabalgatacorrentoso.com.ar; Cacique Antriao 1850) For horseback riding (half-day to multiday trips). Contact Tero Bogani, who brings the gaucho side of things to his trips. Prices start at AR$450 for a three-hour outing.

Centro de Ski Cerro Bayo
SKIING

(☎0294-449-4189; www.cerrobayoweb.com; full-day pass AR$455-760) From June to September, lifts carry skiers from the 1050m base up to 1700m at this 'boutique' (read: small but expensive) winter resort, 9km northeast of El Cruce via RP 66. All facilities, including rental equipment (AR$250 to AR$350), are available on-site.

Cerro Belvedere
HIKING

A 4km hiking trail starts from Av Siete Lagos, northwest of the tourist office, and leads to an overlook with good views of Lago Correntoso, Nahuel Huapi and the surrounding mountains. It then continues another 3km to the 1992m summit. After visiting the overlook, retrace your steps to a nearby junction that leads to Cascada Inayacal, a 50m waterfall. If you're coming out here, get a map at the tourist office, as the trails can be confusing.

Aquiles
BICYCLE RENTAL

(Arrayanes 150; ◷9am-1pm & 4-8pm) Rents quality mountain bikes for AR$70 per day.

🛏 Sleeping

Except for camping and Angostura's growing hostel scene, accommodations are pricey; in summer, single rooms are almost impossible to find – expect to pay for two people.

★Hostel Bajo Cero
HOSTEL $

(☎0294-449-5454; www.bajocerohostel.com; Río Caleufu 88; dm/d US$25/63; @🛜) A little over a kilometer west of the bus terminal is this gorgeous hostel, with large, well-designed dorms and lovely doubles. It has a nice garden and kitchen, plus airy common spaces.

Residencial Río Bonito
GUESTHOUSE $

(☎0294-449-4110; www.riobonitopatagonia.com.ar; Topa Topa 260; d/tr US$50/65; @🛜) Bright and cheery rooms in a converted family home a few blocks from the bus terminal. The big, comfortable dining-lounge area is a bonus, as are the friendly hosts and kitchen use for guests.

Camping Cullumche
CAMPGROUND $

(☎0294-449-4160; moyano@uncu.edu.ar; Blvd Quetrihué s/n; campsites per person US$8) Well signed from Blvd Nahuel Huapi, this secluded but large lakeside campground can get very busy in summer, but when it's quiet, it's lovely.

La Roca de la Patagonia
HOTEL $$

(☎0294-449-4497; www.larocadelapatagonia.com.ar; Pascotto 155; s/d US$82/94; ❄🛜) A cute little place just off the main drag, with just six rooms. It's set in a large converted house, so there are some great dimensions here. Decor is very Patagonia – lots of wood and stone, and there are fantastic mountain views from the deck.

Verena's Haus
HOTEL $$

(☎0294-449-4467; www.verenas-haus.com.ar; Los Taiques 268, El Cruce; s/d US$82/93; 🛜) With all the heart-shaped motifs and floral wallpaper, this one probably doesn't qualify as a hunting lodge, but it is a good deal for couples looking for a quiet, romantic spot. Rooms are big, spotless and packed with comfy features.

Hotel Angostura
HOTEL $$

(☎0294-449-4224; www.hotelangostura.com; Blvd Nahuel Huapi 1911, La Villa; s/d from US$80/97, bungalow US$122-200; 🛜) Ignore the squishy rooms and the deer-antler light fittings – this is an awesome location. It's perched up on a clifftop overlooking the bay and the national park; your biggest problem here is going to be neck crick from checking out the view – no matter which way you're walking.

Encanto del Rio
HOTEL $$$

(☎0294-447-5357; www.encantodelrio.com.ar; RN 40, Km1110; r/cabin/apt US$186/256/312; ❄🛜🏊) Located halfway between downtown and Puerto Manzano, this supremely comfortable setup has a great range of options. The rooms are well equipped and spacious, with views of the mountains or river. The cabins add a touch of privacy and include a full kitchen. The apartments are good, too, although a little overpriced.

✖ Eating

There are several restaurants and *confiterías* in El Cruce along Los Arrayanes and its cross streets.

Gran Nevada
ARGENTINE $

(Av Arrayanes 106; mains AR$90-130; ☺noon-11:30pm) With its big-screen TV (quite possibly showing a football game) and big, cheap set meals, this is a local favorite. Come hungry, leave happy.

Nicoletto
ITALIAN $$

(Pascotto 165; mains AR$100-180; ☺noon-3pm, 8-11:30pm) The best pasta for miles around is to be found at this unassuming family-run joint just off the main street. It's all good – freshly made and with a fine selection of sauces, but the trout *sorrentino* (large, round filled pasta) with leek sauce come highly recommended.

La Encantada
ARGENTINE $$

(☑0294-449-5515; Cerro Belvedere 69, El Cruce; mains AR$120-170; ☺noon-midnight; ☏) A cute little cottage offering all of your Patagonian and Argentine favorites. The food is carefully prepared and beautifully presented, and the atmosphere is warm and inviting. The pizza is some of the best in town and there's a good selection of local beers and wines.

Los Troncos
ARGENTINE $$

(Av Arrayanes 67, El Cruce; mains AR$130-190; ☺8am-11pm; ☏) Specializing in 'mountain food,' this lovely little place serves up a range of tempting dishes, such as deer stew, trout with almond sauce and wild mushroom stew.

Lancomilla
PARRILLA $$

(Av Arrayanes 176; mains AR$110-200; ☺noon-midnight; ☏) The most popular *parrilla* on the main drag, this one does some good lamb dishes, along with the standard offerings.

Tinto Bistro
INTERNATIONAL $$$

(Av Arrayanes 256; mains AR$180-260; ☺8:30pm-1am Mon-Sat) Besides the fact that the food (regional cuisine prepared with European flair) is excellent, the owner, Martín Zorreguieta, is the brother of Máxima, Queen of the Netherlands. Feast on that.

ⓘ Information

Banco de la Provincia (Calle Las Frambuesas, btwn Cerro Belvedere & Nahuel Huapi, El Cruce; ☺9am-1pm Mon-Fri) Has an ATM.

Post Office (Las Fuschias 121; ☺8am-6pm Mon-Fri, 9am-1pm Sat) In a shopping gallery behind the bus terminal.

Tourist Office (☑0294-449-4124; Av Arrayanes 9; ☺8am-9pm)

ⓘ Getting There & Away

Villa la Angostura's **bus terminal** (cnr Av Siete Lagos & Av Arrayanes, El Cruce) is across the street from the tourist office. Some buses stop in El Cruce on runs between Bariloche and San Martín de los Andes.

For Chile, **Andesmar** (☑0294-449-5217) goes over Paso Cardenal Samoré to Osorno (AR$300, 3½ hours).

There are numerous daily departures to Bariloche (AR$60, one hour) and two daily departures to Neuquén (AR$837, seven hours). Albus goes several times daily in summer to San Martín de los Andes (AR$121, four hours) by the scenic Ruta de los Siete Lagos. La Araucana has daily services to Villa Traful (AR$82, two hours).

ⓘ Getting Around

BOAT

Two companies run daily ferries from the dock (next to Hotel Angostura in La Villa) to the tip of Quetrihué Peninsula in Parque Nacional Los Arrayanes (AR$280/350 one way/return, plus AR$120 national park entrance). Purchase tickets at the dock before hiking out, to secure a space on the return. The ride takes 45 minutes and you can put a bicycle on the boat.

BUS

Local buses cost AR$5.50 to go anywhere in town. Transportes 15 de Mayo runs hourly buses from the terminal to La Villa (15 minutes), up Av Siete Lagos to Lago Correntoso (15 minutes), and south down Av Arrayanes to Puerto Manzano on Lago Nahuel Huapi (15 minutes). From July through September, and December through March, 15 de Mayo runs six or seven daily buses to the ski resort at Cerro Bayo (AR$60, one hour).

TAXI

Taxis are the best means of getting to the trailheads, although some are served by local buses. Both leave from the local bus terminal on Av Siete Lagos, just north of Av Arrayanes.

Villa Traful

☑0294 / POP 360 / ELEV 720M

This little village enjoys an almost achingly beautiful location surrounded by mountains on the southern banks of Lago Traful. The place really packs out in January, February and Easter, when booking accommodations three months in advance is advised. The rest of the year, you may just have it to yourself.

Depending on what you're into, November, December, March and April are great times to be here.

Getting here is half the fun – Villa Traful is 80km north of Bariloche via unpaved RP 65.

◉ Sights

Cascadas de Arroyo Blanco & Coa Có
WATERFALL

These two waterfalls are a moderately easy, two-hour round-trip walk from town that can be done without a guide. Walk uphill on the street running beside the *guardaparque* (park ranger) office and follow the signs. From where the path forks at the open field it's 500m on the left to the 30m-high Coa Có. Return and take the other fork for 1km to the smaller Cascadas de los Arroyos Blanco.

Far more spectacular than the actual waterfalls are the lookouts along the way, which give you a bird's-eye view of the forest, lake and mountains beyond.

Lagunas las Mellizas
LAKE

Starting with a boat ride across the lake, this trek of moderate difficulty begins with a 2½-hour climb through cypress forests, before reaching a lookout with views of the Lagunas Azul and Verde (Blue and Green Lagoons). If you've still got the legs for it, fording a stream gets you to an area with a variety of well-preserved **Tehuelche rock paintings**, dated at around 600 years old.

☞ Tours

Eco Traful
TOUR

(☎0294-447-9139; ◷10am-1pm & 4-7pm) A recommended agency that leads trips to Lagunas Las Mellizas (AR$450/560 per person walking/horseback) and Cerro Negro (AR$300 per person), and organizes boat rides and fishing trips.

⌷ Sleeping & Eating

There are only a few places to stay unless you rent a *cabaña* (cabin; the tourist office has a complete listing). There are also a couple of restaurants tucked into the trees and a general store.

Albergue & Camping Vulcanche
HOSTEL $

(☎0294-447-9028; www.vulcanche.com; campsites per person US$5, dm $12; ☏) In a beautiful wooded area on the eastern edge of the village, this grassy campground and hostel has decent dorms and a good kitchen.

Hostería Villa Traful
HOTEL $$

(☎0294-447-9005; www.hosteriavillatraful.com; s/d from US$86/110) A pleasant little mom-and-pop-run operation on the western edge of town. Rooms are aging but comfortable, there's a good restaurant on the premises, and the owners organize boating and fishing trips.

★Ñancú Lahuén
ARGENTINE $$

(mains AR$110-150; ◷11:30am-11pm; ☏) A cute little log cabin set up in the center of the village. Trout dishes are the specialty (try 'em with the almond sauce), but the menu stretches to *parrilla* and a good range of salads as well.

❶ Information

Banco de la Provincia de Neuquén, in the middle of the village, has an ATM that accepts Visa and MasterCard.

Tourist Office (☎0294-447-9099; www.villatraful.gov.ar; ◷daily Dec-Feb, Sat-Wed Mar-Jan) Shares an office with the *guardapaque* in the middle of the village.

❶ Getting There & Away

Villa Traful has better bus connections in summertime (December to February). La Araucana has daily services to Villa la Angostura (AR$82, two hours) and summer services to San Martín de los Andes (AR$115, 2½ hours). There are services from Bariloche (AR$62, two hours) daily in summer.

San Martín de los Andes

☎02972 / POP 28,000 / ELEV 645M

Like a mellower version of Bariloche, San Martín has two peak periods: winter for skiing at Cerro Chapelco and summer for trekking, climbing, etc, in nearby Parque Nacional Lanín. Brave souls also swim in the chilly waters of Lago Lácar on the western edge of town. Between these times it's a quiet little town with a spectacular setting that retains much of the charm and architectural unity that once attracted people to Bariloche. A boat ride on the lake is pretty much a must if you're passing through, and if the snow's cleared (anytime from November onward) and you're heading south, you should seriously think about leaving town via the scenically neck-straining Ruta de los Siete Lagos (RN 40), which runs south to Villa la Angostura, Lago Nahuel Huapi and Bariloche.

Sights

Almost everything in San Martín de los Andes is within walking distance of the *centro cívico*, and the shady lakefront park and pier are a delightful place to spend an afternoon.

★ **Museo Primeros Pobladores**   MUSEUM
(M Rosas; admission AR$10; ☺8:30am-3:30pm Tue, 9am-1pm Wed-Fri) Regional archaeological and ethnographic items such as arrowheads, spear points, pottery and musical instruments are the focus of this museum,

located two doors north of the tourist office, near Av Roca.

Activities

Ruta de los Siete Lagos   DRIVING
(Seven Lakes Route) From San Martín, RN 40 follows an eminently scenic but rough, narrow and sometimes dusty route past numerous alpine lakes to Villa la Angostura. It's known as **La Ruta de los Siete Lagos** (p383) and its spectacular scenery has made the drive famous. Sections of the 110km route close every year due to heavy

San Martín de Los Andes

snowfalls – December to May is the best time to schedule this trip, but ask around for current conditions.

Full-day tours from San Martín, Villa la Angostura and Bariloche regularly do this route, but there's also a scheduled bus service and, with a little forward planning, it's possible to drive/cycle it yourself.

HG Rodados BICYCLE RENTAL
(☑ 02972-427345; Av San Martín 1061; ⊙ 9am-1pm & 4-8pm Mon-Fri, 9am-1pm Sat) Mountain biking is an excellent way to explore the surrounding area and a good way to travel the Ruta de los Siete Lagos. Rent bikes here for around AR$30/110 per hour/day.

Mirador Bandurrias VIEWPOINT
(admission AR$10) A 2.5km steep, dusty hike ends with awesome views of Lago Lácar; be sure to take a snack or lunch. Tough cyclists can reach the mirador (viewing point) in about an hour via dirt roads.

Playa Catrite BEACH
Walk, bike or hitch to this protected rocky beach, 4km away down RN 40 (there's a bus three times daily in summer). It has a laid-back restaurant with a nice deck.

Lanín Turismo RAFTING
(☑ 02972-425808; www.laninturismo.com; Av San Martín 431; ⊙ 9am-8pm Mon-Sat) With this outfit, rafting on the Río Chimehuin or the Río Aluminé costs about AR$520 for the day trip, including transfers. The rivers are spectacular and suitable for kids.

Andestrack OUTDOORS
(☑ 02972-420588; www.andestrack.com.ar; Coronel Rhode 782; ⊙ 9am-1pm & 3-8pm Mon-Sat) There are excellent opportunities for trekking and climbing in Parque Nacional Lanín. This is a young, enthusiastic company that has been highly recommended for mountain biking, canoeing, snowshoeing and dog sledding in the park.

Bumps SKIING
(☑ 02972-428491; www.skibumps.com.ar; Villegas 459; ⊙ 9am-6pm Mon-Sat) Skiing and snowboarding at nearby Cerro Chapelco attracts enthusiastic winter crowds. In San Martín, rental equipment is available here and at many other places along Av San Martín. Ski gear and snowboards rent for AR$205 to AR$390 per day. You can also rent equipment on the mountain.

🎉 Festivals & Events

San Martín celebrates its founding on February 4, with speeches, parades and other festivities; the parade itself is an entertainingly incongruous mix of military folks, firefighters, gauchos, polo players and fox hunters.

🛏 Sleeping

As a tourist center, San Martín is loaded with accommodations, but they're relatively costly in all categories, especially in summer high season (January to March) and peak ski season (mid-July and August), when reservations are a must. Quality, however, is mostly high. In low season, prices can drop by 40%.

El Oso Andaluz Hostel HOSTEL $
(☑ 02972-427232; www.elosoandaluz.com.ar; Elordi 569; dm/d from US$11/35; ❈ @ 🛜) San Martín's coziest little downtown hostel has a good bed-to-bathroom ratio, atmospheric common areas and good-value private rooms.

Camping ACA CAMPGROUND $
(☑ 02972-427332; Av Koessler 2175; campsites per person US$9) This is a spacious campground on the eastern outskirts of town. However, you should try to avoid sites near the highway. There's a two-person minimum per site.

Hostería Hueney Ruca HOTEL $
(☑ 02972-421499; www.hosteriahueneyruca.com.ar; cnr Obeid & Coronel Pérez; s/d US$63/74; 🛜) The big terracotta-tiled rooms here look onto a cute, well-kept little backyard. Beds are big and firm and bathrooms spacious, with glass-walled shower stalls.

★ Hostería La Masía HOTEL $$
(☑ 02972-427688; www.hosterialamasia.com.ar; Obeid 811; s/d AR$560/890; 🛜) Taking the whole Edelweiss thing to the next level, La Masía offers plenty of dark-wood paneling, arched doorways and cast-iron light fittings. Rooms are big and comfortable and most have mountain views. Fireplaces warm the lobby, and the owners are usually around to make sure everyone feels at home. Superb.

Rotui HOTEL $$
(☑ 02972-429539; www.rotui.com.ar; Perito Moreno 1378; s/d from US$60/120; ❈ 🛜) A lovely wood-and-stone lodge set on immaculately manicured grounds overlooking the Arroyo Pochulla creek. Rooms are sumptuously

appointed, with king-sized beds, polished floorboards and duck-down quilts. The apartments and cabins on offer are a good deal for groups.

Hotel Antiguos
HOTEL $$

(☑ 02972-411876; www.hotelantiguos.com.ar; Diaz 751; r from US$115; ❋ 🐾) Set just off the main drag, the Antiguos indulges in San Martín's heavy-wood-and-stone fetish, and does it well. Some rooms have sweeping garden/ mountain views, all are spacious and luxuriously appointed. The roaring fireplace in the lounge area makes for a welcome sight in winter.

La Raclette
HOTEL $$

(☑ 02972-427664; www.hosterialaraclette.com; Coronel Pérez; s/d from US$71/112; @ 🐾) Not suitable for claustrophobes, the narrow, low-ceilinged hallways here lead on to spacious, comfortable rooms. What really tips the scales are the downstairs common areas – a lounge-bar area and cozy little conversation pit centered on a big open fireplace.

✗ Eating

★ Corazón Contento
CAFE $

(Av San Martín 467; mains AR$85; ⏱ 9am-11pm; 🐾) A cute little bakery-cafe serving up an excellent range of fresh and healthy snacks and meals. The salads are great and the freshly baked scones and muffins hit the spot.

Pizza Cala
PIZZA $

(Av San Martín 1129; mains AR$60-130; ⏱ noon-1am; 🐾) The local's choice for pizza is this ever-expanding place near the plaza. All the classics are here, plus some 'gourmet' options such as smoked trout, spinach and eggplant.

Bamboo
PARRILLA $$

(cnr Belgrano & Villegas; mains from AR$140; ⏱ noon-4pm & 9pm-1am; 🐾) One reader claims this upmarket *parrilla* serves 'the best meat in all of Argentina.' We haven't tried all the meat in Argentina (yet), so you be the judge.

Torino
ARGENTINE $$

(cnr Elordi & Villegas; mains from AR$120; ⏱ noon-3pm & 8pm-midnight; 🐾) One of the widest menus in town, with each dish done nearly to perfection. There's a good range of seafood on offer, alongside the requisite pasta and meat dishes, and they take a decent stab at sushi if you're game.

El Regional
ARGENTINE $$

(Villegas 953; mains AR$120-180; ⏱ 11:30am-4pm & 6-11:30pm) A big atmospheric barn of a place, El Regional serves up some good trout dishes, but the specialty here are the *tablas* (sampler platters), featuring Patagonian classics such as boar, venison and trout in a variety of styles. There's an impressive craft beer selection on offer, too.

La Casona
ARGENTINE $$

(Villegas 744; mains AR$100-160; ⏱ noon-3pm & 8pm-midnight; 🐾) The cozy atmosphere belies the wide menu, with some good twists on regional favorites. Try the boar stew in blackberry sauce or the lamb and wild mushroom risotto.

El Mesón
INTERNATIONAL $$$

(☑ 02972-424970; Rivadavia 885; mains AR$140-200; ⏱ noon-3pm & 8-11:30pm) This cute little place has one of the most creative menus in town, with plenty of trout dishes, paella and a couple of vegetarian options.

🔒 Shopping

Many local shops sell regional products and handicrafts.

Artesanías Neuquinas
HANDICRAFTS

(☑ 02972-428396; M Rosas 790; ⏱ 9am-6pm Mon-Sat) A Mapuche cooperative with high-quality weavings and wood crafts on offer.

El Carpincho
ACCESSORIES

(Capitán Drury 814; ⏱ 9am-1pm & 3-6pm Mon-Sat) Gaucho regalia.

Patalibro
BOOKS

(☑ 02972-421532; Av San Martín 866; ⏱ 9am-8pm) Good selection of books on Patagonia in Spanish; some Lonely Planet titles and novels in English. Carries the excellent *Sendas y Bosques* park trail maps (AR$160).

ℹ Information

There are many travel agencies along Av San Martín, Belgrano and Elordi, which offer standard services as well as excursions.

ACA (Automóvil Club Argentino; ☑ 02972-429194; Av Koessler 2175; ⏱ 24hr) Good source for provincial road maps.

Andina Internacional (☑ 02972-427871; Capitán Drury 876; ⏱ 9am-6pm) Money exchange, including traveler's checks.

Banco de la Nación (Av San Martín 687; ⏱ 9am-1pm Mon-Fri) Has an ATM.

Lanín National Park Office (Intendencia del Parque Nacional Lanín; ☑ 02972-427233;

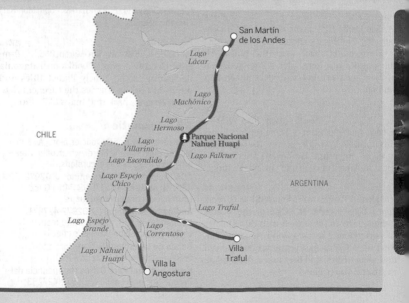

CHILE

San Martín
de los Andes

*Lago
Lácar*

*Lago
Machónico*

*Lago
Hermoso*

**Parque Nacional
Nahuel Huapi**

*Lago
Villarino*

Lago Escondido

Lago Falkner

*Lago Espejo
Chico*

ARGENTINA

*Lago Espejo
Grande*

Lago Traful

*Lago
Correntoso*

*Lago Nahuel
Huapi*

Villa
Traful

Villa la
Angostura

Top: Lakeshore near Villa La Angostura
Bottom: Lago Falkner

1 DAY La Ruta de los Siete Lagos

A spectacular road between towering, snow-capped mountains, crystal-clear lakes and dense pine forests, this is a 110km Lake District classic. Bike it in a few days, drive it in one, tour it or bus it – just don't miss it.

Starting at **San Martín de los Andes** (p378), head out of town on the RN 40, skirting the banks of **Lago Lácar** (p385) and passing the Mapuche town of Curruhuinca. After 20km you'll come to the lookout at Arroyo Partido.

From here it's a 5km downhill coast to a bridge over the Río Hermoso. Two short climbs and 5km later, you'll reach the dark-blue Lago Machónico. A further 5km brings you to a turnoff to the right, where it's 2km of dirt road to Lago Hermoso, surrounded by mixed ñire and radale forests. Colored deer are common in this area, as are hunters, so be on the lookout (for both) when walking in the woods.

Entering the Parque Nacional Nahuel Huapi (p368), it's 15km to the Cascada Vullignanco, a 20m waterfall made by the Río Filuco. Two kilometers on, the road runs between Lago Villarino and Lago Falkner, which has a wide sandy beach.

Two kilometers further on is Lago Escondido, from where it's 8km of downhill zigzag to a turnoff to the left. Follow this side (dirt) road for 2km to get to the north end of Lago Traful.

After 30km look for the **Villa Traful** (p377) turnoff – it's 27km from here to the villa, down a good dirt road, passing scenic lakeside bush campgrounds.

Sticking to the main road, though, you'll skirt the banks of Lago Correntoso and after 20km you'll come to a bridge and a disused *hostería* (lodging house). If you're looking for a side trip, just before the bridge, turn right and take the uphill road that ends at Lago Espejo Chico after 2km.

Continuing south, you'll catch glimpses of Lago Espejo Grande on the right through the trees. There are several lookouts along the road.

From here it's another 15km to a crossroads where you turn left, and 10km on asphalt to **Villa la Angostura** (p375).

www.parquenacionallanin.gov.ar; cnr Elordi & Perito Moreno; ◷8am-2pm Mon-Fri) The office provides limited maps as well as brochures and information on road conditions on the Ruta de los Siete Lagos.

Post Office (cnr Pérez & Roca; ◷8am-6pm Mon-Fri, 9am-1pm Sat)

Ramón Carrillo Hospital (☑02972-427211; cnr Coronel Rohde & Av San Martín)

Tourist Office (☑02972-427347; www.sanmartindelosandes.gov.ar; cnr Av San Martín & M Rosas; ◷8am-9pm) Provides surprisingly candid information on hotels and restaurants, plus excellent brochures and maps.

ⓘ Getting There & Away

AIR

There are regular flights from **Chapelco airport** (☑02972-428388; RN 40) to Buenos Aires with **Aerolíneas Argentinas** (☑02972-410588; Mariano Moreno 859; ◷8am-10pm Mon-Sat, 9am-9pm Sun).

BOAT

Naviera (☑02972-427380; naviera@smandes.com.ar; ◷9:30am-7:30pm Mon-Sat, 10:30am-7:30pm Sun) sails from the **passenger pier** (Muelle de Pasajeros; Costanera MA Camino) at midday on a sightseeing trip of Lago Lácar's lakeside villages. Eventually it reaches Paso Hua Hum on the Chilean border, where Chile-bound passengers can disembark and continue on foot. Departure times change; call the ferry company or check with the tourist office. The seven-hour return trip costs AR$750.

BUS

The **bus terminal** (☑02972-427044; cnr Villegas & Juez del Valle) is a block south of the highway and 3½ blocks southwest of Plaza San Martín.

La Araucana (☑02972-420285) goes to Villa Traful daily during summer (AR$115, 2½ hours). If you're heading to Villa la Angostura or Bariloche in summer, Albus regularly takes the scenic Ruta de los Siete Lagos (RN 40) instead of the longer but smoother Rinconada route.

To get to Aluminé you must first change buses in Zapala or Junín de los Andes (where there are three departures per week).

Igi-Llaima (☑02972-428878) takes RP 60 over Paso Tromen (also known as Mamuil Malal) to Temuco, Chile (AR$720, six hours), passing the majestic Volcán Lanín en route; sit on the left for views.

From San Martín there is direct service in summer via RN 231 over Paso Cardenal A Samoré (Puyehue) to Osorno and Puerto Montt in Chile.

There are frequent daily departures to these destinations.

DESTINATION	COST (AR$)	TIME (HR)
Bariloche	177	4½
Buenos Aires	1956	20-23
Junín de los Andes	55	1
Neuquén	692	6
Villa la Angostura	121	4
Zapala	343	3½

ⓘ Getting Around

Chapelco airport (p384) is midway between San Martín and Junín. Any bus heading north out of San Martín can drop you at the entrance.

Transportation options slim down during low season. In summer Transportes Airen goes twice daily to Puerto Canoa on Lago Huechulafquen (AR$55) and will stop at campgrounds en route. **Albus** (☑02972-428100) goes to the beach at Playa Catrite on Lago Lácar (AR$32) several times daily, while **Transportes Ko-Ko** (☑02972-427422) runs four buses daily to Lago Lolog (AR$28) in summer only.

San Martín has no lack of car-rental agencies.

Alamo (☑02972-410811; Av San Martín 836, 2nd fl; ◷9am-6pm)

Sur (☑02972-429028; Villegas 830; ◷9am-6pm Mon-Fri, to 2pm Sat & Sun)

Cerro Chapelco

Located 20km southeast of San Martín, **Cerro Chapelco** (☑02972-427845; www.chapelco.com) is one of Argentina's principal winter-sports centers, with a mix of runs for beginners and experts, and a maximum elevation of 1920m. The **Fiesta Nacional del Montañés**, the annual ski festival, is held during the first half of August.

Lift-ticket prices vary, depending on when you go; full-day passes run from AR$555 to AR$790 for adults, AR$445 to AR$630 for children. The slopes are open from mid-June to early October. The low season is mid-June to early July and from August 28 to mid-October; high season is around the last two weeks of July. Rental equipment is available on-site as well as in San Martín.

Transportes Ko-Ko runs two buses each day (three in summer; AR$60 return) to the park from San Martín's bus terminal. Travel agencies in San Martín also offer packages with shuttle service, or shuttle service alone (AR$80); they pick you up at your hotel.

Parque Nacional Lanín

Dominating the view in all directions along the Chilean border, the snowcapped cone of 3776m Volcán Lanín is the centerpiece of this **national park** (www.parquenacional lanin.gov.ar; admission AR$80), which extends 150km from Parque Nacional Nahuel Huapi in the south to Lago Ñorquinco in the north.

Protecting 3790 sq km of native Patagonian forest, Parque Nacional Lanín is home to many of the same species that characterize more southerly Patagonian forests, such as the southern beeches – lenga, ñire and coihue. The area does host some unique specimens, though, such as the extensive stands of the broadleaf, deciduous southern beech, raulí, and the curious pehuén (monkey puzzle tree; *Araucaria araucana*), a pinelike conifer whose nuts have long been a dietary staple for the Pehuenches and Mapuches. Note, though, that only indigenous people may gather *piñones* (pine nuts) from the pehuénes.

The towns of San Martín de los Andes, Junín de los Andes and Aluminé are the best bases for exploring Lanín, its glacial lakes and the backcountry. The Lanín national park office in San Martín (p381) produces brochures on camping, hiking and climbing in the park. Scattered throughout the park proper are several ranger stations, but they usually lack printed materials. The national park's website is full of useful information. At the time of writing admission was charged to enter the park only if you were heading towards Puerta Canoa.

ⓘ Getting There & Away

Although the park is close to San Martín and Junín, public transportation is not extensive. With some patience, hitchhiking is feasible in high season. Buses over the Hua Hum and Tromen passes, from San Martín and Junín to Chile, will carry passengers to intermediate destinations, but are often full.

Lago Lácar & Lago Lolog

From San Martín, at the east end of Lago Lácar, there is bus service on RP 48, which runs along the lake to the Chilean border at Paso Hua Hum. You can get off the bus anywhere along the lake or get off at Hua Hum and hike to **Cascada Chachín**; bus drivers know the stop. From the highway, it's 3km down a dirt road and then another 20 minutes' walk along a trail to the waterfall. It's a great spot for a picnic.

About 15km north of San Martín de los Andes, Lago Lolog offers good fishing in a

---

EXCURSIONS TO PARQUE NACIONAL LANÍN

In summer, buses leave the terminal in Junín several times a day for destinations within the national park, allowing you to hit the trails and camp in some beautiful areas. The buses run three 'circuits' and charge AR$55 one way.

Circuito Curruhué (via RP 62)

Buses depart Junín de los Andes once or twice daily for **Lago Curruhué** and **Lago Epulafquen**; near the latter is a trailhead that leads to the **Termas de Lahuen-Có** (☏02972-424709; www.lahuenco.com; s/d from US$325/490) spa, about one hour's walking from the head. Package tours out here – including lunch and spa treatments – cost around US$100 and can be organized through the center or through tour operators in town (note that transportation costs extra). Luxurious rooms are available, should you want to spend the night. You can also hike from here to the crater of **Volcán Achen Niyeu**.

Lago Huechulafquen (via RP 61)

From Puerto Canoa, on the north shore of Lago Huechulafquen, there are worthwhile hikes (p386). Buses depart Junín's terminal twice in the morning (usually around 8am and 11am) and once in the afternoon (around 4pm). Be sure to catch the last bus back unless you plan to camp.

Circuito Tromen (via RP 60)

Buses depart Junín de los Andes twice daily for **Lago Tromen** (p387). Lago Tromen can also be reached by taking any bus that goes to Chile and getting off at Tromen.

Parque Nacional Lanín

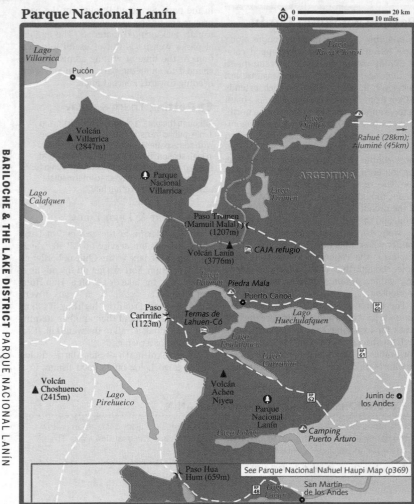

largely undeveloped area. You'll find free camping at **Camping Puerto Arturo**. Transportes Ko-Ko runs four buses daily in summer to Lago Lolog from San Martín (AR$40).

Lago Huechulafquen

The park's largest lake is also one of its most central and accessible areas. Despite limited public transportation, it can be reached from San Martín and – more easily – Junín de los Andes (p385). RP 61 climbs from a junction just north of Junín, west to Huechulafquen and the smaller Lago Paimún,

offering outstanding views of Volcán Lanín and access to trailheads of several excellent hikes.

Activities

From the ranger station at **Puerto Canoa** there's a seven-hour roundtrip hike to **Cara Sur de Lanín** (south face of Volcán Lanín). Park rangers require you set out by 11am. Ranger stations are at the entrance to Huechulafquen and at Puerto Canoa. From Puerto Canoa, the boat **Jose Julian** (☑ 02972-428029; www.catamaranjosejulian.com. ar; trips AR$350) offers boat trips on the lake.

It's also possible to hike across to Paso Tromen or continue climbing to either of two *refugios:* the **RIM refugio** belongs to the army's Regimiento de Infantería de Montaña, while the **CAJA refugio** belongs to the Club Andino Junín de los Andes (p389). Both are fairly rustic but well kept and can be bases for attempts on the summit. The initial segment follows an abandoned road, but after about 40 minutes it becomes a pleasant woodsy trail along the **Arroyo Rucu Leufu**, an attractive mountain stream. Halfway to the *refugio* is an extensive **pehuén forest**, the southernmost in the park, which makes the walk worthwhile if you lack time for the entire route. The route to RIM's *refugio*, about 2450m above sea level, takes about seven hours one way, while the trail to CAJA's *refugio* takes a bit longer.

Another good backcountry hike circles **Lago Paimún**. This requires about two days from Puerto Canoa; you return to the north side of the lake by crossing a cable platform strung across the narrows between Huechulafquen and Paimún. A shorter alternative hike goes from the very attractive campground at **Piedra Mala** to **Cascada El Saltillo**, a nearby forest waterfall. If your car lacks 4WD, leave it at the logjam 'bridge' that crosses the creek and walk to Piedra Mala – the road, passable by any ordinary vehicle to this point, quickly worsens after a harsh winter. Horses are available for rent at Piedra Mala. Transportes Ko-Ko runs buses to Piedra Mala daily in summer from the San Martín bus terminal.

🛏 Sleeping

Campsites are abundant along the highway; travelers camping in the free sites in the narrow area between the lakes and the highway must dig a latrine and remove their own trash. If you camp at the organized sites (which, though not luxurious, are maintained), you'll support Mapuche concessionaires who at least derive some income from lands that were theirs before the state usurped them a century ago. Good campsites include **Camping Raquithue** (per person US$5) and **Bahía Cañicul** (☎0297-249-0211; per person US$5).

Noncampers should treat themselves to a stay at **Hostería Refugio Pescador** (☎0294-15-425-5837; www.refugiodelpescador.com; r per person incl full board US$82) or the three-star **Hostería Paimún** (☎02972-491758; www.hos teriapaimun.com.ar; r per person incl full board US$126); both cater to fishing parties.

Lago Tromen & Volcán Lanín

The northern approach to **Volcán Lanín** (3776m), which straddles the Argentina–Chile border, is the shortest and usually the earliest in the season to open for hikers and climbers. Before climbing Lanín, ask permission at the Lanín national park office (p381) in San Martín or, if necessary, of the *gendarmería* (border guards) in Junín, from where there are **buses** (p385). To prove that you are adequately equipped, it's obligatory to show equipment, such as plastic tools, crampons, ice axe and clothing – including sunglasses, sunblock, gloves, hats and padded jackets.

From the trailhead at the Argentine border station, it's five to seven hours to the **CAJA refugio** (capacity 20 people), at 2600m on the Camino de Mulas route; above that point, snow equipment is necessary. There's a shorter but steeper route along the ridge known as the **Espina del Pescado**. Trekkers can cross the Sierra Mamuil Malal to Lago Huechulafquen via Arroyo Rucu Leufu.

Contact Andestrack (p380) or the park office in San Martín to organize guides for climbing Lanín. The hike usually takes two days: you leave early the first and stay at the RIM *refugio* (rustic shelter), rise before dawn the following day, hike to the summit and walk down. If you want to go up in winter, Andestrack can set you up with guides to hike up and board or ski down.

If you're more interested in short walks, from Lago Tromen there is a **1½-hour roundtrip walk** along the river, passing a fine araucaria forest and a lookout with fabulous views of the lake. You can also do the 45-minute walk to the base of **Volcán Lanín's Cara Norte** (north face).

Northern Lakes

Situated in the park's densest pehuén forests, isolated Lago Quillén is accessible by dirt road from Rahué, 17km south of Aluminé, and has many good **campsites**. Other nearby lakes include **Lago Ruca Choroi**, directly west of Aluminé, and **Lago Ñorquinco** on the park's northern border. There are Mapuche reservations at Ruca Choroi and Quillén.

Junín de los Andes

⚡ 02972 / POP 12,600 / ELEV 800M

A much more humble affair than other Lake District towns, Junín's a favorite for fly fishers – the town deems itself the trout capital of Neuquén province and, to drive the point home, uses trout-shaped street signs. A couple of circuits leading out of town take in the scenic banks of the Lago Huechulafquen, where Mapuche settlements welcome visitors. Outside of peak season, these circuits are best done by private vehicle (or incredibly enthusiastic cyclists), but travel agents based here offer reasonably priced tours.

◎ Sights & Activities

Junín's surroundings are more appealing than the town itself, but the museum is well worth seeing.

Museo Mapuche   MUSEUM
(Padre Milanesio 751; entry by donation; ☉9am-12:30pm & 2-7pm Mon-Fri, 9am-12:30pm Sat) The collection here includes Mapuche weavings and archaeological pieces.

Vía Cristi   LANDMARK
Situated about 2km from the center of town, near the end of Av Antardida Argentina, Vía Cristi contains a collection of 22 sculptures, bas reliefs and mosaics winding its way up Cerro de la Cruz and vividly depicting the Conquest of the Desert, Mapuche Legends, Christian themes and indigenous history.

Trout Fishing   FISHING
(per day/week/season AR$360/1080/1440) The area around Junín is prime country for trout fishing, and the Río Aluminé, north of Junín, is an especially choice area. Catch-and-release is obligatory. Fishing permits are available through the tourist office.

Ciclismo Mavi   BICYCLE RENTAL
(Felix San Martín 415; ☉9am-1pm & 3-6pm) Rents mountain bikes for AR$30/160 per hour/day.

⛵ Tours

Picurú Turismo   TOUR
(⚡02792-492829; www.picuruturismo.tur.ar; Coronel Suárez 371; ☉9am-6pm Mon-Fri, 9am-1pm & 4-7pm Sat) Recommended tour operator for trips into Parque Nacional Lanín and tours of Mapuche communities.

✯ Festivals & Events

In January the **Feria y Exposición Ganadera** displays the best of local cattle, horses, sheep, poultry and rabbits. There are also exhibitions of horsemanship, as well as local crafts exhibits, but this is the *estanciero's* (ranch owner's) show.

In July, the Mapuche celebrate their crafts skills in the **Semana de Artesanía Aborígen**.

The **National Trout Festival** takes place in November.

🛌 Sleeping

High season coincides with fishing season (November through April); during low season prices drop.

Reencuentro Hostel   HOSTEL $
(⚡02972-492220; www.elreencuentrohostel.blogspot.com; Pedro Illera 189; dm/s/d/tr US$9/10/19/29; @🛜) Homey small house with two five-bed dorms and rickety wood floors.

Camping Laura Vicuña   CAMPGROUND $
(Ginés Ponte s/n; campsites per person US$6; 🛜) You won't find a much more sublime location for an urban campground: perched on an island in between two burbling creeks, with all the facilities, plus fully equipped cabins (three-night minimum).

★Hostería Chimehuín   HOTEL $$
(⚡02972-491132; www.interpatagonia.com/hosteriachimehuin; cnr Coronel Suárez & 25 de Mayo; s/d US$67/95; 🛜) This is a beautiful spot a few minutes from the center of town. Book early and you'll have a good chance of snagging a room with a balcony overlooking the creek. Either way, rooms are big, warm and comfortable and the whole place has a tranquil air to it.

Rüpü Calel   HOTEL $$
(⚡02972-491569; Coronel Suárez 560; s/d US$42/60; 🛜) While they may look big and bare to some, the rooms here have a pleasing simplicity and are sparkling clean, as are the spacious bathrooms.

🍴 Eating

Junín's dining scene is slowly improving. Local specialties such as trout, wild boar and venison may be available.

Sigmund   ARGENTINE $
(Juan M de Rosas 690; mains AR$80-140; ☉noon-midnight; 🛜) Fabulous trendy eatery

with colorful artsy decor, healthy food and great *onda* (vibe). Choose from dozens of pizzas, pastas, sandwiches and salads, all delivered with friendly service.

Lespos   PIZZA **$$**
(Domingo Milanesio 520; mains AR$100-150; ☺noon-1am) An inviting little pizza and burger bar, with a better atmosphere than most. There's a wide range of pizzas on offer and a good music selection seals the deal.

Ruca Hueney   PARRILLA **$$**
(☑02792-491113; cnr Colonel Suárez & Domingo Milanesio; mains AR$110-160; ☺noon-midnight; ☜) Ruca Hueney, Junín's oldest restaurant, is reliable and has the most extensive menu in town. Portions are large; service is abrupt. There's a cheaper takeout counter next door in case you were thinking about a picnic in the park across the street.

ℹ Orientation

The center is between the highway and the river. Don't confuse Av San Martín, which runs on the west side of Plaza San Martín, with Félix San Martín, two blocks west.

ℹ Information

Banco de la Provincia de Neuquén (Av San Martín, btwn Coronel Suárez & General Lamadrid; ☺9am-1pm Mon-Fri) Opposite the plaza.
Club Andino Junín de los Andes (Milanesio 362; ☺4-6pm Tue-Fri, 11am-1pm Sat) This mountaineering club provides information on the Volcán Tromen climb, as well as other excursions within Parque Nacional Lanín.
Lanín National Park Office (☑02972-491160; cnr Domingo Milanesio & Coronel Suárez; ☺8am-9pm) Inside the tourist office. Has information on Parque Nacional Lanín.
Post Office (cnr Coronel Suárez & Don Bosco; ☺8am-6pm Mon-Fri, 9am-1pm Sat)
Tourist Office (☑02792-491160; junindelos andes.gov.ar; cnr Domingo Milanesio & Coronel Suárez; ☺8am-9pm) Enthusiastically helpful staff. Fishing permits and a list of licensed fishing guides available.

ℹ Getting There & Away

Junín and San Martín de los Andes share Chapelco airport, which lies midway between the two towns. There are regularly scheduled flights to Buenos Aires and Neuquén. A *remise* into town should run you about AR$90. Another option is walking the 1km out to the highway and flagging down a passing bus (AR$23, 25 minutes).

The **bus terminal** (☑02792-492038; cnr Olavarría & Félix San Martín) is three blocks from the main plaza. El Petróleo goes three times a week to Aluminé (AR$159, three hours).

Buses from Junín de Los Andes

DESTINATION	COST (AR$)	TIME (HR)
Buenos Aires	1906	22
Neuquén	645	6
San Martín de los Andes	55	1
Zapala	293	3

Aluminé
☑02942 / POP 4600 / ELEV 400M

Time seems to have stopped for Aluminé and, although it's an important tourist destination, it is less visited than destinations to the south. Situated 103km north of Junín de los Andes via RP 23, it's a popular fly-fishing destination and offers access to the less-visited northern sector of Parque Nacional Lanín. The Río Aluminé also offers excellent white-water rafting and kayaking.

⊙ Sights & Activities

The tourist office keeps a list of available **fishing** guides and sells licenses (AR$360/1080/1440 per day/week/season). **Mali Viajes** (☑02942-496310) offers scenic back-road tours along the Circuito Pehuenia (p390) in summer.

Aigo & Salazar   VILLAGES
The nearby Mapuche communities of Aigo and Salazar, on the 26km dirt road to **Lago Ruca Choroi** (in Parque Nacional Lanín), sell traditional weavings, araucaria pine nuts and, in summer, *comidas típicas* (traditional dishes). Salazar is an easy, signposted 12km walk or bike ride out of town – just follow the river. Aigo is another 14km along.

Aluminé Rafting   OUTDOORS
(☑02942-496322; www.interpatagonia.com/alu minerafting; Conrado Villegas 610; ☺9am-6pm Mon-Sat) For rafting on the Río Aluminé (best in November), as well as kayaking, fly-fishing, trekking and rock climbing.

🛏 Sleeping & Eating

If you're traveling in a group, ask the tourist office about its list of self-catering cabins – some just out of town – that offer good value for three or more people. High season coincides with the November-through-April fishing season.

Nid Car HOTEL $
(☎02942-496131; nidcaralumine@yahoo.com.ar; cnr Christian Joubert & Benigar; s/d US$28/34) Very standard and slightly spacious rooms just uphill from the plaza. Cheapest in town and not a bad deal as long as you're not fussy.

★ El Hostal del Río HOTEL $$
(☎02942-15-696808; www.elhostaldelrio.com.ar; RP 23 s/n; s/d US$65/95; ☏) A couple of kilometers north of town, this charming stone-and-wood fishing lodge offers supreme comforts with fantastic views of the Río Aluminé from the deck. Rooms are spacious and spotless and the shady grounds and other common areas are lovingly maintained.

La Posta del Rey ARGENTINE $$
(Christian Joubert 336; mains AR$110-160; ⊗8am-11pm; ☏) Inside the Hostería Aluminé, this is the best eating option in town, serving up all the Argentine standards, plus some good Patagonian favorites such as lamb, venison and trout.

ℹ Information

Banco del Provincia del Neuquén (cnr Conrado Villegas & Torcuato Mordarelli; ⊗Mon-Fri 9am-1pm) Bank and ATM.
Tourist Office (☎02942-496001; info@ alumine.gov.ar; Christian Joubert, Plaza San Martín; ⊗8am-8pm mid-Mar–Nov, 9am-9pm Dec–mid-Mar) For local info and maps, fishing permits, road conditions, etc.

ℹ Getting There & Away

Aluminé's **bus terminal** (☎02941-496048) is just downhill from the plaza, an easy walk to any of the hotels listed here. Aluminé Viajes and Albus go daily to/from Neuquén (AR$352, six hours), Zapala (AR$221, three to 3½ hours) and San Martín de los Andes (AR$159, 4½ hours). There's one bus a day to Villa Pehuenia (AR$112, one hour) at 7:30pm.

Villa Pehuenia

☎02942 / POP 700 / ELEV 1200M

Villa Pehuenia is an idyllic little lakeside village situated on the shores of Lago Aluminé, 102km north of Junín de los Andes (via RP 23 and Aluminé) and 120km west of Zapala (via RP 13). There are several Mapuche communities nearby, including Puel, located between Lago Aluminé and Lago Moquehue.

The village lies at the heart of the Pehuen region, named of course after the pehuén (araucaria) trees that are so marvelously present. If you have a car, the **Circuito Pehuenia** is a great drive; it's a four- to six-hour loop from Villa Pehuenia past Lago Moquehue, Lago Ñorquinco, Lago Pulmarí and back around Lago Aluminé.

🏃 Activities

Volcán Batea Mahuida HIKING
From the top of this volcano you can see eight others (from Lanín to the south to Copahue to the north) in both Argentina and Chile. Inside Batea Mahuida is a small crater lake. You drive nearly to the top (summer only) and then it's an easy two-hour walk to the summit at 2010m.

Batea Mahuida SKIING
(☎02942-467711; www.cerrobateamahuida.com.ar; day pass AR$300-400) ⚑ Volcán Batea Mahuida is the location of this small Mapuche-operated ski park, which is little more than a few snowy slopes with a T-bar and a poma. If you're a Nordic skier, you're in better luck – a circuit goes around the park, taking in awesome views of the volcano and lakes.

Los Pehuenes ADVENTURE SPORTS
(☎02942-498029; www.pehuenes.com.ar; Centro Comercial; ⊗9am-1pm & 4-8pm) The local adventure-tourism operator offers rafting, trekking, horseback riding and 4WD off-roading trips.

🛏 Sleeping & Eating

Many businesses in Villa Pehuenia close down off season. *Hosterías* and *cabañas* are spread around the Peninsula de los Coihues.

Hostería de las Cumbres HOTEL $$
(☎02942-498097; www.posadalascumbre.com.ar; d US$70; ⊗year-round; ☏) Right down by the waterfront in the main part of town, this cozy little *hostería* has smallish rooms coming off way-narrow corridors. Lake views

THE MAPUCHE

The Lake District's most prevalent indigenous group, the Mapuche, originally came from Chilean territory. They resisted several attempts at subjugation by the Inca and fought against Spanish domination for nearly 300 years. Their move into Argentina began slowly. Chilean Mapuche were making frequent voyages across the Andes in search of trade as far back as the 17th century. Some chose to stay. In the 1880s the exodus became more pronounced as the Chilean government moved into Mapuche land, forcing them out.

Another theory for the widespread move is that, for the Mapuche, the *puelmapu* (eastern land) holds a special meaning, as it is believed that all good things (such as the sun) come from the east.

Apart from trade, the Mapuche (whose name means 'people of the land' in Mapudungun, their language) have traditionally survived as small-scale farmers and hunter-gatherers. There is no central government – each extended family has a *lonko* (chief) and in times of war families would unite to elect a *toqui* (axe-bearer) to lead them.

The role of the *machi* (shaman) was and still is an important one in Mapuche society. It is usually filled by a woman, whose responsibilities included performing ceremonies for curing diseases, warding off evil, dreamwork, and influencing weather, harvests and social interactions. The *machi* was also well schooled in the use of medicinal herbs but, as Mapuche access to land and general biodiversity in the region has decreased, this knowledge is being lost.

Estimates of how many Mapuche live in Argentina vary according to the source. The official census puts the number at around 300,000, while the Mapuche claim that the real figure is closer to 500,000.

Both in Chile and Argentina, the Mapuche live in humble circumstances in rural settings, or leave the land to find work in big cities. It is estimated that there are still 200,000 fluent Mapudungun speakers in Chile, where nominal efforts are made to revive the language in the education system. No such official program has been instituted in Argentina and, while exact numbers are not known, it is feared that the language here may soon become extinct.

Apart from loss of language, the greatest threat to Mapuche culture is the loss of land, a process that has been under way ever since their lands were 'redistributed' after the Conquest of the Desert and many Mapuche were relocated to reserves – often the lowest-quality land, without any spiritual significance to them. As with many indigenous peoples, the Mapuche have a special spiritual relationship with the land, believing that certain rocks, mountains, lakes and so on have a particular spiritual meaning.

Despite a relatively well-organized land-rights campaign, the relocation continues today, as Mapuche lands are routinely reassigned to large commercial interests in the oil, cattle and forestry industries. Defiant to the end, the Mapuche don't look like fading away any time soon. They see their cultural survival as intrinsically linked to economic independence and Mapuche-owned and -operated businesses are scattered throughout the Lake District.

---

from the front rooms, however, make this one a winner.

★ **La Escondida**   HOTEL $$$
(☎02942-15-691166; www.posadalaescondida.com; r from US$185; ⊗year-round; ☏) A small posada (inn) tucked away down by the lakefront. There are just six rooms, all fitted out in fine detail and with decks overlooking the water. Sitting areas are sumptuous, the restaurant is one of the best in the village, and there are good-value cabins (without water views) on offer if you're traveling in a group.

La Moquehuina   ARGENTINE $$
(mains AR$120-200; ⊗noon-3pm & 9pm-midnight Tue-Sat year-round) With just three tables, it's a good idea to drop by here at some point to make a reservation. You'll be glad you did, for the gourmet versions of Patagonian classics and excellent selection of craft beers and local wines on offer.

ⓘ Information

Banco de la Provincia del Neuquén (RP 13 s/n; ⊗9am-1pm Mon-Fri) Next to the police station; has an ATM.

Oficina de Turismo (☎02942-498044; www.villapehuenia.gov.ar; RP 13 s/n; ☺9am-8pm) At the entrance to town. Extremely helpful and provides good maps of the region.

ℹ Getting There & Around

Exploring the area is tough without a car, though hitchhiking is definitely feasible in summer. **Destinos Patagonicos** (☎02942-498067; Centro Comercial) is the representative for Albus, the only bus company currently serving the village. There are daily buses to Zapala (AR$286, 4½ hours), Neuquén (AR$458, seven hours) and Aluminé (AR$112, one hour).

Caviahue

☎02948 / POP 610 / ELEV 1600M

On the western shore of Lago Caviahue, the ski village of Caviahue lies at the southeast foot of Volcán Copahue. A better-looking village than Copahue to the north, this one is growing rapidly, too – construction noise fills the air during summer.

🏃 Activities

There are some good short walks from the village, including a popular day trek that goes up past **Cascada Escondida** to **Laguna Escondida**. Another walk to the four waterfalls known as **Cascadas Agrio** starts from across the bridge at the entrance to town. The tourist office has an excellent map showing these and other walks around the area.

Hotel Caviahue   SPA
(☎02948-495044; hotelcaviahue@issn.gov.ar; 8 de Abril s/n; treatments from AR$150) If you fancy some pampering, this hotel has a day spa where you can enjoy a thermal bath and treatments.

Centro de Ski Cerro Caviahue   SKIING
(☎02948-495043; www.caviahue.com) A little under 2km west of Caviahue, this ski resort has seven chairlifts, and four pomas, which take skiers all the way up to the peak of Volcán Copahue (2953m). Equipment hire (skis or snowboard AR$195–280 per day) is also available on the mountain or in the village. Adult day passes range from AR$440 to AR$680, depending on the season.

⌂ Tours

Caviahue Tours   HIKING, OUTDOORS
(☎02948-495138; www.caviahuetours.com; Av Bialous Centro Comercial local 11; ☺9am-1pm

& 4-8pm) If you have a taste for adventure, this company organizes treks, including to Laguna Termal and Volcán Copahue, rents mountain bikes in summer and offers dog-sledding trips in winter.

🛏 Sleeping

Hebe's House   HOSTEL $
(☎02948-495138; www.hebeshouse.com.ar; Mapuche & Puesta del Sol; dm/d US$20/60; ☺Dec-Sep; 🛜) Hebe crams them in to cozy but cramped dorms. It's set in a cute alpine building and offers kitchen access, laundry facilities and plenty of tourist information. If you're coming in winter, book well ahead.

Hotel Caviahue   HOTEL $$
(☎02948-495044; hotelcaviahue@issn.gov.ar; 8 de Abril s/n; s/d US$57/77; 🛜) A rambling, older-style hotel set up the hill, with views out over the village, lake and mountains. It's the only hotel open in the village year-round. Rates drop around 30% off-season. Also on the premises is the only **restaurant** (mains AR$60 to AR$100) in town to stay open year-round.

ℹ Information

Oficina de Turismo (☎02948-495036; www.caviahue-copahue.gov.ar; ☺9am-8pm) is at the entrance to town. It has good maps and up-to-date info on local accommodations. There's another office in the *municipalidad* (city hall).

ℹ Getting There & Away

One bus daily runs to Neuquén (AR$270, 6½ hours) via Zapala (AR$156, 3½ hours). If you're headed for Chos Malal, you can shave a couple of hours off your travel time by getting off in Las Lajas (AR$122, 2½ hours) and waiting for a bus there. Check your connection times with the bus company **Cono Sur** (☎02942-432607), though – if you're going to get stranded, Zapala is the place to do it.

Copahue

☎02948 / ELEV 2030M

This small thermal-springs resort stands on the northeastern side of its namesake volcano among steaming, sulfurous pools, including a bubbling hot-mud pool, the popular **Laguna del Chancho** (admission AR$50; ☺8am-6pm). The setting, in a natural amphitheater formed by the mountain range, is spectacular, but the town isn't much to look at.

LAGUNA TERMAL TREK

This day trip, which should be possible in around eight hours, is easy enough to do on your own, leaving from Copahue. Due to snow conditions, it's only possible from December to April unless you bring special equipment. If you'd like to take the side route to the peak of Volcán Copahue, it's recommended that you go with an experienced guide. **Caviahue Tours** (p392) is among the many tour operators offering guides on this route.

From the **Hotel Valle del Volcán** at the upper (southwest) edge of the village, cross the little footbridge and climb briefly past a life-size **statue of the Virgin**. The well-worn foot track leads across a sparsely vegetated plain towards the exploded cone of **Volcán Copahue**, dipping down to lush, green lawns by the northern shore of the **Lagunas Las Mellizas**' western 'twin.' Follow a path along the lake's north side past little black-sand beaches and gushing springs on its opposite shore, to reach the start of a **steam pipeline**, one to 1¼ hours from the village. The roaring of steam from the subterranean **Copahue Geothermal Field** entering the *vapoducto* and irregular explosive blasts of discharging steam can be heard along much of the trek. Cross the lake outlet – further downstream is a wide, easy ford – then cut up southwest over snowdrifts past a tarn to meet a 4WD track at the edge of a small waterlogged **meadow**. Turn right and follow this rough road up around left (or take a vague trail marked with white paint splashes to its right until you come back to the road on a rocky ridge below a wooden cross). The 4WD track continues westward up through a barren volcanic moonscape to end under a tiny **glacier** on the east flank of Volcán Copahue, 1¼ to 1½ hours from the pipeline.

Ascend southwest over bouldery ridges, crossing several small mineral-and-meltwater streams. To the northwest, in Chile, the ice-smothered **Sierra Velluda** and the near-perfect snowy cone of **Volcán Antuco** rise up majestically. From the third streamlet (with yellowy, sulfur-encrusted sides), cut along the slope below a hot spring, then climb to the top of a prominent gray-pumice spur that lies on the international border. Ascend the spur until it becomes impossibly steep, then traverse up rightward over loose slopes into a gap to reach **Laguna Termal**, 1¼ to 1½ hours from the end of the 4WD track (3½ to 4¼ hours from Copahue).

Filling Volcán Copahue's eastern crater, this steaming hot lake feeds itself by melting the snout of a glacier that forms a massive rim of ice above its back wall. Sulfurous fumes often force trekkers to retreat from the lake, but these high slopes also grant a wonderful vista across the vast basin (where both villages are visible) between the horseshoe-shaped **Lago Caviahue** (Lago Agrio) and the elongated **Lago Trolope** to the northeast. From here, more experienced trekkers can continue up to the summit of Volcán Copahue.

To get back to Copahue, retrace your ascent route. If you have a decent map of the area, you can follow the Arroyo Caviahue (Río Agrio) and RN 26 back to town.

Warning

Particularly on windy days, acrid fumes rising from Laguna Termal can be overpowering due to sulfur dioxide gas (which attacks your airways). Approach the lake cautiously – don't even consider swimming in it. Less experienced trekkers are advised to go with an organized tour.

Copahue has been gaining in popularity, mainly with Argentine tourists, as the growth in tourist infrastructure shows. Due to snow cover, the village is only open from the start of December to the end of April.

The village centers on the large, modern **Complejo Termal Copahue** (☎0299-442-4140; www.termasdecopahue.com; Ortiz Velez; baths AR$80, spa treatments from AR$150), which offers a wide range of curative bathing programs.

In summer, one bus daily runs to Neuquén (AR$300, seven hours) via Zapala (AR$176, four hours). There are no scheduled departures for the rest of the year.

🛏 Sleeping & Eating

Residencial Codihue
HOTEL $

(☑ 02948-495543; www.codihue.wix.com; Velez s/n; s/d US$45/80) Residencial Codihue is the best budget option in town, with simple rooms just down the road from the thermal baths complex. Full board is available.

Hotel Termas
HOTEL $$

(☑ 02948-495525; www.hoteltermascopahue.com. ar; Doucloux s/n; s/d from US$76/112; 🛜) The best hotel in the village, Hotel Termas, features modern rooms, atmospheric common areas and an excellent restaurant serving traditional Argentine and regional foods.

Parrillada Nito
PARRILLA $$

(Zambo Jara s/n; mains AR$110-160; ⊙noon-11:30pm) Parrillada Nito is the most reliable *parrilla* (steak house) in town.

Chos Malal

☑ 02948 / POP 13,100 / ELEV 862M

Cruising through the stark, desertlike landscape north of Zapala doesn't really prepare you for arrival at this pretty little oasis town. Set at the convergence of Río Neuquén and Río Curi Leuvú, the town boasts two main plazas, bearing the names of the two superheroes of Argentina – San Martín and Sarmiento. Around the former is the majority of the historic buildings, including the Fuerte IV Division fort (go around the back for sweeping views out over the river valley). Five blocks south is Plaza Sarmiento, where you'll find banks and businesses.

🛏 Sleeping & Eating

Most accommodations are located between the two plazas. People in Chos Malal eat a lot of goat, and you may find yourself doing the same while you're here.

Baalback
HOTEL $

(☑ 02948-421495; 25 de Mayo 920; s/d US$18/35) A no-frills *residencial* (budget hotel) a few blocks from the plaza, the Baalback is about as good as it gets for budget digs in this town.

Hosteria La Farfalla
HOTEL $$

(☑ 02948-421349; www.farfalla.com.ar; cnr Salta & Islas Malvinas; s/d US$65/90; ❇🛜) Chos Malal's most comfortable lodgings by far can be found at this charming little lodge a few blocks south of the plaza. Rooms are spacious and comfortable, but it's the expansive grounds and lovely garden that make the place.

Las Delicias de L'Traful
BAKERY $

(Roca 80; pastries from AR$15; ⊙7:30am-1:30pm & 4:30-9:30pm) A small bakery-cafe serving up yummy, super-fresh baked goods and excellent coffee.

El Viejo Caicallén
PARRILLA $$

(General Paz 345; mains AR$100-140; ⊙noon-11pm Mon-Sat) The best *parrilla* in town is at this happy place, offering all sorts of meat dishes, pastas, salads and sandwiches. There are usually a couple of regional faves, such as black-butter trout and grilled goat, to choose from, too.

ℹ Information

Banco de la Nación (cnr Sarmiento & Urquiza; ⊙9am-1pm Mon-Fri) Has an ATM.

Hospital Zonal Gregorio Avárez (☑ 02948-421400; cnr Entre Ríos & Flores) English speaker usually on-site.

Tourist Information (☑ 02948-421425; turnorte@neuquen.gov.ar; 25 de Mayo 89; ⊙8am-9pm) Has good maps of the town and surrounds.

ℹ Getting There & Away

Regular buses depart for Zapala (AR$232, three hours) and Neuquén (AR$404, six hours). There's one bus per day to Varvarco (AR$195, three hours) at 2pm. Two minibuses a day leave for Buta Ranquil (AR$94, two hours) – if you want to connect to the bus for Mendoza catch the 4:30pm one.

North along the Ruta Nacional 40

Following the RN 40 north from Chos Malal towards San Rafael gives you more wild desert scenery, tiny windswept towns and expansive, empty vistas. Despite what many will tell you, there *is* public transportation along this route. **Transportes Leader** (☑ in Buta Ranquil 02948-493268; cnr Malvinas & Jadull) runs minibuses between Buta Ranquil and San Rafael, Monday to Saturday (AR$336). There's regular bus service from Neuquén and Chos Malal to Buta Ranquil, where you may get stuck for the night. There's no real reason to be here, but there are a couple of cheap hotels, one nice one, and enough restaurant-cafes to keep you from starving.

NORTH OF CHOS MALAL

Heading north from Chos Malal brings you to a couple of wonderful, rarely visited attractions. Public transportation is rare and often nonexistent, but if you have the time and patience you'll be well rewarded.

Parque Archaeologico Colo Michi-Co

This small archaeological site features one of the most important collections of **Pehuenche rock art** in Patagonia. There are over 600 examples here, carved with symbolic figures and abstract designs. Getting to the site without a private vehicle is tricky. Buses leave Chos Malal at 2pm daily for the village of Varvarco (AR$195, three hours). From there, it's 9km south on the RP 39 to the Escuela Colo Michi-Co (buses will drop you off), where you'll see a signpost leading to the park, an 8km walk away. Bring everything – there's nothing out here.

If all that walking doesn't excite you, contact **Señora La Gallega** (☏02948-421329) in Varvarco – there aren't any *remises* (taxis) there, but the señora should be able to hook you up with a car and driver, charging around AR$25 per kilometer, plus waiting time. Hitchhiking is common practice in the area, but be prepared for long waits.

Aguas Calientes

These excellent natural outdoor **hot springs** located at the foot of the **Volcán Domuyo** are spread over 20 sq km and feature three main sites. The main one at **Villa Aguas Calientes** is suitable for swimming; **Las Olletas** is a collection of bubbling mud pits and **Los Tachos** are geysers, spurting up to heights of 2m. The site is 40km north of Varvarco, where the last public transportation terminates. If you don't have your own wheels and can get to Varvarco on your own, you can ask about hiring a driver with **Señora La Gallega**.

Zapala

☏02942 / POP 32,100 / ELEV 1200M

Taking its name as an adaptation of the Mapuche word *chapadla* (dead swamp), Zapala got off to a bad start, image-wise. Not much has changed. This is a humble little place where the locals amuse themselves with walks up and down the main street, punctuated by lengthy pauses on street corners.

⊙ Sights & Activities

The main excuse for rolling through town is to visit the nearby Parque Nacional Laguna Blanca, with its awesome array of birdlife, or to take advantage of the town's bus connections for the rarely visited northern reaches of the Lake District.

Centro Cultural　　　ARTS CENTER
(San Martín & Chaneton; ⊙5-10pm) In front of the plaza, this center hosts concerts, and shows work by local artists and recently released Hollywood blockbusters.

✤ Festivals

Zapala's **Feria de la Tradición**, held in the second week in November, showcases regional culture, with plenty of folk music, gaucho horse skill demonstrations, handicraft exhibits and regional food on sale.

⊫ Sleeping & Eating

Zapala has very limited accommodations.

Hotel Pehuén　　　HOTEL $
(☏02942-423135; cnr Etcheluz & Elena de la Vega; s/d US$45/59; ☎) Despite its (rather mysterious) two-star status, this is the best budget deal in town, conveniently near the bus terminal, with clean rooms, an attractive (classy, even) lobby and a good restaurant below.

Hotel Hue Melén　　　HOTEL $$
(☏02942-432109; www.hotelhuemelen.com; Almirante Brown 929; s/d US$78/90; ✳☎) You may be faintly surprised by the quiet stylishness of this hotel-casino complex. King-sized beds, full bathtubs, contemporary art on the walls...it's wonderful what gambling money can buy you.

El Chancho Rengo
CAFE $

(cnr Av San Martín & Etcheluz; sandwiches AR$50-80; ⊙8am-11:30pm) It's likely half the town saunters in here for an espresso each day. Outdoor tables, and good coffee and sandwiches, make it great for a light bite.

Detente
ARGENTINE $$

(Italia 87; mains AR$80-160; ⊙12:30-3pm & 9pm-2am Mon-Fri, 9pm-2am Sat) A laidback place serving some of Zapala's best food (the competition isn't fierce, by the way). The menu doesn't stray far from meat, pizza and pasta, but they do it well, and with friendly service.

ℹ Information

Banco de la Provincia del Neuquén (cnr Av San Martín & Etcheluz; ⊙9am-1pm Mon-Fri) Bank with ATM.

Laguna Blanca National Park Office (📞02942-431982; lagunablanca@apn.gov. ar; 12 de Julio 686; ⊙8am-3pm Mon-Fri) For information on Parque Nacional Laguna Blanca.

Tourist Office (📞02942-424296; RN 22, Km1398; ⊙7am-9pm) Located on the highway, 2km west of town center.

ℹ Getting There & Away

The **bus terminal** (📞02942-421370; cnr Etcheluz & Uriburu) is about four blocks from Av San Martín. During summer there are frequent departures for Copahue (AR$176, four hours).

Buses from Zapala

DESTINATION	COST (AR$)	TIME (HR)
Aluminé	180	3½
Buenos Aires	1430	18
Caviahue	156	3
Chos Malal	232	3
Junín de los Andes	293	3
Laguna Blanca	76	½
Neuquén	220	3
San Martín de los Andes	343	3½
Villa Pehuenia	286	4½

Parque Nacional Laguna Blanca

At 1275m above sea level and surrounded by striking volcanic deserts, Laguna Blanca is only 10m deep, an interior drainage lake that formed when lava flows dammed two small streams. Only 30km southwest of Zapala, the lake is too alkaline for fish, but hosts many bird species, including coots, ducks, grebes, upland geese, gulls and even a few flamingos. The 112.5-sq-km park primarily protects the habitat of the black-necked swan, a permanent resident.

Starting 10km south of Zapala, paved and well-marked RP 46 leads through the park toward the town of Aluminé. If you're catching a bus, ask the driver to drop you off at the information center. If you don't have your own transport, ask at the National Parks office in Zapala if you can get a ride out with the rangers in the morning. A taxi to the park should charge around AR$450, including two hours' waiting time.

There is a small improved campground with windbreaks, but bring all your own food. There's a **visitor center** (⊙9am-6pm Fri-Sun) with information displays and maps of walking trails, but no place to eat.

Neuquén

📞0299 / POP 231,200 / ELEV 265M

There are only two reasons to stop in Neuquén – the wealth of paleontological sites in the surrounding area, and the excellent wineries just out of town. That said, the town has a strangely hypnotic effect, with its wide, tree-lined boulevards and liberal smattering of plazas.

At the confluence of the Río Neuquén and the Río Limay, Neuquén is the province's easternmost city. Most travelers hit Neuquén en route to more glamorous destinations in Patagonia and the Lake District – the town is the area's principal transport hub, with good connections to Bariloche and other Lake District destinations, to the far south and to Chile. Paved highways go east to the Río Negro valley, west toward Zapala and southwest toward Bariloche.

◉ Sights

Just outside of town are three of the most important Patagonian wineries – **NQN** (📞0299-489-7500; www.bodeganqn.com.ar; RP 7, Picada 15; ⊙10am-4:30pm), **Fin del Mundo** (📞0299-555-5330; www.bodegadelfindelmundo. com; RP 8, Km9, San Patricio Del Chañar; ⊙10am-4pm Mon-Fri, to 5pm Sat) and **Schroeder** (📞0299-489-9600; www.familiaschroeder.com; Calle 7 Nte, San Patricio del Chañar; admission AR$50; ⊙10am-5pm). Access to the vineyards

BIG, BIG BONES

Neuquén is one of the earth's dinosaur hot spots, along with Parque Provincial Ischigualasto in San Juan province. Here, three important paleontology sites – Plaza Huincul, Villa El Chocón and Centro Paleontológico Lago Barreales – lie within a couple of hours' drive from Neuquén city and will delight anyone even slightly interested in dinosaurs.

In 1989 a local Neuquenian named Guillermo Heredia discovered a dinosaur bone on his property 7km east of the town of **Plaza Huincul**. Paleontologists investigated the site and later unearthed a dozen bones belonging to what they named *Argentinosaurus huinculensis* – the largest known dinosaur in the world. The gargantuan herbivore, dating from the mid-Cretaceous period, measured an incredible 40m long and 18m high. The sheer size of the *Argentinosaurus huinculensis* is difficult to fathom, which is why stopping to gawk at the replica skeleton at Plaza Huincul's **Museo Municipal Carmen Funes** (☎0299-496-5486; Córdoba 55; AR$18; ⏰9am-7pm Mon-Fri, 10:30am-8:30pm Sat & Sun) is a humbling lesson in size.

About 80km southwest of Neuquén city, **Villa El Chocón** boasts the remains of the 100-million-year-old, 14m, 8-ton, meat-eating *Giganotosaurus Carolinii*, the world's largest known carnivore. Discovered in 1993 by fossil hunter Rubén Carolini, the dinosaur is even bigger than North America's better known *Tyrannosaurus rex*. El Chocón is also home to giant dinosaur footprints along the shore of Ezequiel Ramos Mexía reservoir. (One local confessed how families used to fire up *asados* (barbecues) in the footprints before they knew what they were!)

For true dino-freaks, the best place to satiate the hunger for bones is the **Centro Paleontológico Lago Barreales** (☎0299-15-418-2295; www.proyectodino.com.ar; Costa Dinosaurio; admission AR$40; ⏰9am-7pm), located 90km northwest of Neuquén. It was closed at the time of research, but if you're at all interested in dinosaurs, you should check the website for latest developments. When it's operating, you can actually work – as in get your hands dirty digging – on-site with paleontologists in one of the world's only fully functioning dinosaur excavation sites open to the public. Quickie visits include a cruise through the on-site museum and a guided tour of the site – about 1½ hours worth. But the real pleasure comes from the unique opportunity offered by sticking around. Bear in mind that this is a working archaeological site, and visits (even day trips) should be organized well in advance. Under the supervision of renowned paleontologist and project director Jorge Calvo, volunteers spend their days dusting off Cretaceous-period bones and picking at fossils, and nights in the silence of the desert. As Calvo says, 'when you set to work picking at the soft rock, uncovering fossilized leaves and bones that are 90 million years old, you forget about the rest of the world – some people even forget to eat.'

From Neuquén's bus terminal, there are regular buses to Plaza Huincul (AR$55, 1¾ hours), and all buses between Neuquén and Zapala stop there. There are also regular buses to Villa El Chocón from Neuquén (AR$42, 1¼ hours). Centro Paleontológico Lago Barreales is a bit more difficult to reach; contact the site for driving directions or possible transportation options (there are no buses to the site). If you drive, take RP 51, not RN 7.

is almost impossible without your own vehicle, but Turismo Arauquen (p397) can get you out there, often in combination with a paleontological tour.

Museo Nacional de Bellas Artes MUSEUM
(cnr Bartolomé Mitre & Santa Cruz; ⏰10am-8pm Mon-Sat, 4-8pm Sun) FREE Showcases fine arts from the region and often features traveling exhibitions.

👉 Tours

Turismo Arauquen TOUR
(☎0299-442-6476; www.arauquen.com; H Yrigoyen 720; ⏰9am-7pm Mon-Fri, to 1pm Sat) Offers guided visits to paleontology sites for

about AR$620 per person (minimum four), which can be combined with winery visits (AR$380 per person). If you have less than four people in your group, winery tours happen every Saturday guaranteed.

🛏 Sleeping

Neuquén's hotels mainly cater to the business set. They are fairly unexciting in all ranges and less than great value for budget travelers.

Punto Patagonico Hostel HOSTEL $
(📞0299-447-9940; www.puntopatagonico.com; Periodistas Neuquinas 94; dm US$25, d with/without bathroom US$70/50; @ 🛜) Neuquén's best hostel is a good deal – it's well set up with comfy dorms, a spacious lounge and a good garden area.

Parque Hotel HOTEL $
(📞0299-442-5806; www.parquehotelnqn.com.ar; Av Olascoaga 271; s/d US$40/56; 🛜) There are a few charming touches in the spacious, tile-floored rooms here. Some are showing their age these days, but most have good views out over the busy street below.

Hotel Neu HOTEL $$$
(📞0299-443-0084; www.hotelneu354.com; Rivadavia 354; s/d US$135/178; ❄🛜) One of the better business-class hotels in town, the Neu keeps it simple with fresh, modern decor in medium-sized but uncramped rooms. The location is super-central and there's an on-site gym.

🍴 Eating & Drinking

The many *confiterías* along Av Argentina are all pleasant spots for breakfast and morning coffee. There are numerous bars and *confiterías* in the area north of Parque Central and around the meeting of the diagonals.

La Nonna Francesa INTERNATIONAL $
(📞0299-430-0930; 9 de Julio 56; mains AR$90-150; ⊙11am-3pm & 8pm-midnight Mon-Sat) Some of Neuquén's finest dining can be found at this French-Italian trattoria – the pastas are all extremely good, but the trout dishes are the absolute standouts.

Confitería Donato CAFE $
(cnr Juan B Alberdi & Santa Fe; mains AR$60-90; ⊙8am-11pm; 🛜) Plenty of dark-wood paneling and brass fittings give this place an old-time feel and the wraparound seats

may have you lounging around for hours. The menu runs the usual *confitería* gamut, with plenty of sandwiches, cakes and coffee on offer. There's live music Friday to Sunday nights and the occasional tango show – drop in for the schedule.

★Tres Catorce INTERNATIONAL $$
(9 de Julio 63; mains AR$100-160; ⊙8pm-2am Tue-Sun; 🛜) Neuquén's dining scene has improved considerably over the years, with this casually stylish eatery at the forefront. On offer are carefully prepared dishes, thoughtful garnishes and a small but well-selected range of boutique wines.

🛍 Shopping

Paseo de los Artesanos HANDICRAFTS
(Av Independencia, Parque Central; ⊙10am-9pm Wed-Sun) Neuquén's largest selection of regional handicrafts is at this outlet, north of the old train station.

Artesanías Neuquinas HANDICRAFTS
(Brown 280; ⊙8am-1pm & 5-9pm Mon-Fri, 9am-1pm Sat) 🖊 This provincially sponsored store offers a wide variety of high-quality Mapuche textiles and wood crafts.

ℹ Orientation

Known as Félix San Martín in town, the east–west RN 22 is the main thoroughfare, lying a few blocks south of downtown. Don't confuse it with Av San Martín (ie sans the 'Félix'), the obligatory homage to Argentina's national icon. The principal north–south street is Av Argentina, which becomes Av Olascoaga south of the old train station. Street names change on each side of Av Argentina and the old train station. Several diagonal streets bisect the conventional grid.

ℹ Information

Neuquén's dozens of travel agencies are almost all located near downtown. Several banks around the corner of Av Argentina and Juan B Justo have ATMs.

ACA (Automóvil Club Argentino; 📞0299-442-2325; cnr Diagonal 25 de Mayo & Rivadavia) Argentina's auto club; good source for provincial road maps.

Cambio Pullman (Ministro Alcorta 144; ⊙9am-7pm Mon-Sat) Money exchange.

Post Office (cnr Rivadavia & Santa Fe; ⊙8am-6pm Mon-Fri, 9am-1pm Sat)

Provincial Tourist Office (📞0299-442-4089; www.neuquentur.gov.ar; Félix San Martín 182; ⊙7am-9pm) Great maps and brochures. There's a more centrally located kiosk (Olascoaga s/n; ⊘8am-8pm) in the Central Park.

Regional Hospital (📞0299-443-1474; Buenos Aires 421)

❶ Getting There & Away

AIR

Neuquén's **airport** (📞0299-444-0525) is west of town on RN 22. **Aerolíneas Argentina/Austral** (📞0299-442-2411, 0299-442-2410, 0299-442-2409; Santa Fe 52) flies to Buenos Aires four times daily Monday to Friday, and twice daily on weekends.

BUS

Neuquén is a major hub for domestic and international bus services. Accordingly, its **bus terminal** (📞0299-445-2300; cnr Solalique & RN 22), about 3.5km west of Parque Central, is well decked out, with restaurants, gift stores and even a luggage carousel! To get downtown take either a Pehueche bus (AR$5.50; buy a ticket at local 41) or a taxi (AR$50).

Several carriers offer service to Chile: Via Bariloche goes to Temuco (AR$400, nine hours).

Neuquén is a jumping-off point for deep-south Patagonian destinations. Northern destinations such as Catamarca, San Juan, Tucumán, Salta and Jujuy may require a bus change in Mendoza, though the entire ticket can be purchased in Neuquén.

Provincial destinations are served numerous times daily; the following table lists daily departures to nearly all long-distance destinations.

DESTINATION	COST (AR$)	TIME (HR)
Aluminé	352	6
Bahía Blanca	589	7½
Buenos Aires	1324	17
Chos Malal	404	6
Córdoba	1181	16
El Bolsón	554	7
Esquel	722	10
Junín de los Andes	645	6
Mendoza	1025	13
Puerto Madryn	750	11
Río Gallegos	1995	29
San Martín de los Andes	692	6
San Rafael	795	10
Viedma	605	8
Villa la Angostura	837	7
Zapala	220	3

❶ Getting Around

Neuquén is a good province to explore by automobile, but drivers should be aware that RN 22, both east along the Río Negro valley and west toward Zapala, is a rough road with heavy truck traffic. If you're looking for a rental car, **Turismo Arauquen** (p397) has the best rates in town.

Patagonia

Best National Parks & Reserves

➜ Parque Nacional Los Glaciares (p455)

➜ Reserva Faunística Península Valdés (p410)

➜ Parque Nacional Torres del Paine (p483)

➜ Parque Nacional Los Alerces (p440)

Best Places to Stay

➜ Aguas Arriba (p464)

➜ El Cabo (p421)

➜ Estancia El Cóndor (p459)

➜ Bahía Bustamante (p425)

Why Go?

On South America's southern frontier, nature grows wild, barren and beautiful. Spaces are large, as are the silences that fill them. For the newly arrived, such emptiness can be as impressive as the sight of Patagonia's jagged peaks, pristine rivers and dusty backwater oases. In its enormous scale, Patagonia offers an innumerable wealth of potential experiences and landscapes.

Though no longer a dirt road, lonely RN 40 remains the iconic highway that stirred affection in personalities as disparate as Butch Cassidy and Bruce Chatwin. On the eastern seaboard, paved RN 3 shoots south, connecting oil boomtowns with ancient petrified forests, Welsh settlements and the incredible Península Valdés. Then there is the other, trendy Patagonia where faux-fur hoodies outnumber the guanacos. Don't miss the spectacular sights of El Calafate and El Chaltén, but remember that they're a world apart from the solitude of the steppe.

When to Go
El Calafate

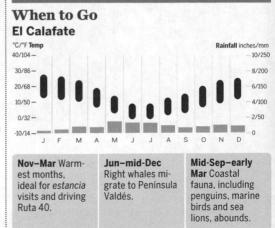

| | Nov–Mar Warmest months, ideal for *estancia* visits and driving Ruta 40. | Jun–mid-Dec Right whales migrate to Península Valdés. | Mid-Sep–early Mar Coastal fauna, including penguins, marine birds and sea lions, abounds. |

❶ Getting There & Around

Patagonia is synonymous with unmaintained *ripio* (gravel) roads, missing transport links and interminable bus rides. Flights, though expensive, connect the highlights. Before skimping on your transport budget, bear in mind that the region comprises a third of the world's eighth-largest country.

If you're busing it along the eastern seaboard, note that schedules are based on the demands of Buenos Aires, with arrivals and departures frequently occurring in the dead of night. Low-season transport options are greatly reduced. In high season demand is high – buy tickets as far in advance as possible.

COASTAL PATAGONIA

Patagonia's cavorting right whales, penguin colonies and traditional Welsh settlements are all accessed by Argentina's coastal RN 3. While this paved road takes in some fascinating maritime history, it also travels long yawning stretches of landscape that blur the horizon like a never-ending blank slate. It's also a favored travel route for oversized trucks on long-haul trips.

Wildlife enthusiasts shouldn't miss the world-renowned Península Valdés, the continent's largest Magellanic penguin colonies at Área Natural Protegida Punta Tombo, and Reserva Natural Ría Deseado's diverse seabird population. The quiet villages of Puerto San Julián and Camarones make for quiet seaside retreats, while Gaiman tells the story of Welsh settlement through a lazy afternoon of tea and cakes.

Puerto Madryn

🄹 0280 / POP 73,600

The gateway to Península Valdés, Puerto Madryn bustles with tourism and industry. It retains a few small-town touches: the radio announces lost dogs, and locals are welcoming and unhurried. With summer temperatures matching those of Buenos Aires, Madryn holds its own as a modest beach destination, but from June to mid-December the visiting right whales take center stage. From July to September, these migrating whales come so close they can be viewed without taking a tour – either from the coast 20km north of town or from the town pier.

The city is the second-largest fishing port in the country and home to Aluar, Argentina's first aluminum plant, built in 1974. A sheltered port facing Golfo Nuevo, Puerto Madryn was founded by Welsh settlers in 1886. Statues of immigrants and Teheulche along the shoreline pay tribute to its history. The Universidad de la Patagonia is known for its marine biology department, and ecological centers promote conservation and education.

◉ Sights

Puerto Madryn is just east of RN 3, 1371km south of Buenos Aires and about 65km north of Trelew. The action in town centers on the *costanera* (seaside road) and two main parallel avenues, Av Roca and 25 de Mayo. Bulevar Brown is the main drag alongside the beaches to the south. Most hostels rent bikes, which is a convenient way to get around and see area beaches.

★ **EcoCentro**   MUSEUM
(🄹 445-7470; www.ecocentro.org.ar; J Verne 3784; admission AR$125; ⊗ 5-9pm Wed-Mon, cruiseship days 10am-1pm) Celebrating the area's unique marine ecosystem, this masterpiece brings an artistic sensitivity to extensive scientific research. There are exhibits on the breeding habits of right whales, dolphin sounds and southern elephant-seal harems, a touch-friendly tide pool and more. The building includes a three-story tower and library, the top features glass walls and comfy couches for reading.

Bring your binoculars: whales may be spotted from here. It's an enjoyable 40-minute walk or 15-minute bike ride along the *costanera* to the EcoCentro. Shuttles run three times daily from the tourist office on Av Roca, or you can catch a Línea 2 bus to the last stop and walk 1km.

Observatorio Punta Flecha   WILDLIFE RESERVE
(⊗ high tide) FREE Run by Fundación Patagonia Natural, this whale-watching observatory sits 17km north of Puerto Madryn on Playa el Doradillo. Offers tourist information and opens at high tide, when there are more whales and visitors to the beach.

Museo Provincial de Ciencias Naturales y Oceanográfico   MUSEUM
(🄹 445-1139; cnr Domecq García & Menéndez; admission AR$10, free Tue; ⊗ 9am-7pm Mon-Fri, 3-7pm Sat) Feeling strands of seaweed and ogling a preserved octopus give a hands-on museum experience. The 1917 Chalet Pujol features marine and land mammal exhibits, preserved specimens, plus collections of Welsh wares. Explanations in Spanish are geared to youth science classes, but it's visually

Patagonia Highlights

1 Gazing upon the blue-hued **Glaciar Perito Moreno** (p466) as icebergs fall in thunderous booms.

2 Getting immersed in the millennial forests and clear lakes of lush **Parque Nacional Los Alerces** (p440).

3 Hiking under the toothy **Cerro Fitz Roy** (p455) near El Chaltén, Argentina's trekking capital.

4 Seeing southern right whales cavort in the waters of **Reserva Faunística Península Valdés** (p410).

5 Riding the wide-open range and feasting on slow-roasted lamb at an **estancia** (p452).

6 Blazing your own trail on the legendary **Ruta 40** (p438).

7 Detouring to Chile to imbibe the raw beauty of **Parque Nacional Torres del Paine** (p483).

ATLANTIC OCEAN

FALKLAND ISLANDS (Islas Malvinas)

Puerto Deseado

Reserva Natural Ría Deseado

RN 281

Parque Interjurisdiccional Marino Isla Pingüino

RN 3

RP 49

La Paloma

Monumento Natural Bosques Petrificados

Puerto San Julián

Santa Cruz

Parque Nacional Monte León

RN 3

Hostería Cueva de las Manos

Cueva de las Manos

Santa Cruz

RP 12

Gobernador Gregores

Río Chico

RP 25

Lago Pueyrredón

Bajo Caracoles

Estancia La Oriental

Las Horquetas

RN 40

RP 29

RN 40

Lago Cardiel

Río Santa Cruz

RP 9

RÍO GALLEGOS

RN 3

RN 1

Punta Delgada

Cabo Vírgenes

Cerro Sombrero

Strait of Magellan

Cabo Espíritu Santo

Cerro San Lorenzo (3706m)

Parque Nacional Perito Moreno

Villa O'Higgins

Candelario Mansilla

Aguas Arriba

Estancia El Cóndor

6 **Ruta 40**

Tres Lagos

RN 288

Esperanza

RP 5

Bella Vista

RN 40

Parque Nacional Pali Aike

Río Gallegos

Río Rubens

Río Rubens

Cerro Fitz Roy (3405m) **3**

El Chaltén

RP 23

Hostería Viedma

Lago Viedma

Parque Nacional Los Glaciares

Estancia Helsingfors

Lago Argentino

El Calafate

RP 7

Cerro Castillo

Río Turbio

Puerto Natales

Villa Tehuelches

Río Verde

PUNTA ARENAS

Cueva del Milodón

Region XII

Glaciar **1** **Perito Moreno**

Cerro Cristal (1286m)

Parque Nacional Torres del Paine **7**

2

0 200 km
0 120 miles

informative and creatively presented. Twist up to the cupola for views of the port.

🏃 Activities

With interesting shipwrecks and sea life nearby, Madryn and the Península Valdés have become Argentina's diving capitals. Newcomer 'baptism' dives run around AR$800; some agencies also offer courses, night dives and multiday excursions.

In high season, a hut next to Bistro de Mar Nautico offers windsurfing lessons and rents out regular and wide boards and kayaks by the hour. South of Muelle Piedra Buena, **Playa Tomás Curti** is a popular windsurfing spot.

Some of the following diving outfitters also offer the popular option of snorkeling with sea lions (per person AR$1400) in Punto Lomas. All of these outfitters are PADI-affiliated.

Lobo Larsen   DIVING
(☑447-0277, 15-451-6314; www.lobolarsen.com; Av Roca 885, Local 2) Reputable local outfitter; offers multilingual service and special 'baptism' excursions for first-timers.

Scuba Duba   DIVING
(☑445-2699; www.scubaduba.com.ar; Blvr Brown 893) Quality scuba-diving operator.

Madryn Buceo   DIVING
(☑0280-15-456-4422; www.madrynbuceo.com; Blvr Brown 1900) Offers dive 'baptisms,' snorkeling with sea lions and regular outings, with hostel pickup service.

Regina Australe   CRUISE
(☑445-6447; www.reginaaustrale.com.ar; Muelle Piedra Buena; adult/child aged 4-12 AR$350/250; ⊙ticket office 10am-1pm & 2-7pm) This 300-passenger ship cruises the Golfo Nuevo to Punta Lobo, departing conveniently from the town pier, where tickets are sold. The three-hour tour leaves at 1pm on Saturday, Sunday, Wednesday and holidays. The ship has three decks, a bar and fast food.

In season, whales may be glimpsed, although it's pointedly not a whale-watching excursion. However, the closed cabins are helpful for families who want to get on the water without braving the elements.

Costas de Patagonia   ADVENTURE SPORTS
(☑15-472-1142; www.costasdepatagonia.com) Offers trekking and kayaking with sea lions year-round. There are also multiday expeditions to the Golfo San José, a good spot for wildlife-watching.

Napra Club   WATER SPORTS
(☑445-5633; www.napraclub.com; Blvr Brown 860; ⊙9am-8pm) This rental shack offers bicycles (per day AR$210), stand-up paddle boards (per hour AR$200) and guided sea kayaking (per two hours AR$250) in sit-on-tops. If need be, you can also rent a wet suit. Located next to Bistro de Mar Nautico.

👉 Tours

Countless agencies sell tours to Península Valdés for around AR$800; prices do not include the AR$260 park admission fee or whale watching (AR$890). Most hotels and hostels also offer tours; get recommendations from fellow travelers before choosing. You can also take a tour to visit the elephant seals and penguins at Punta Ninfas (AR$650).

Ask agencies about the size of the tour group, if tours include an English-speaking guide, meals and stops – different tour companies often visit different locations. Bringing your own binoculars is a good idea.

Tours to Punta Tombo from Puerto Madryn cost about the same as those offered from Trelew (AR$800), but they require more driving time and thus less time with the penguins.

Tides and weather can be important to planning tour dates; check aanppv_nueva.peninsulavaldes.org.ar for information.

Argentina Vision   ECOTOUR
(☑0280-445-5888; http://argentinavision.com; Av Roca 536; ⊙8am-8:30pm Mon-Fri, 9am-12:30pm & 5-8:30pm Sat) The only tour agency in Puerto Madryn that handles visits to Estancia San Lorenzo and its penguin colony on Península Valdés.

Flamenco Tour   TOUR
(☑445-5505; www.flamencotour.com; Belgrano 25) Offerings range from the standard whale-watching and snorkeling trips to stargazing 4WD journeys along the coast (telescopes and bilingual instruction included).

Nievemar   TOUR
(☑445-5544; www.nievemartours.com.ar; Av Roca 493) Excursions include whale watching and visits to sea-lion colonies and Bosque Petrificado Sarmiento. Also an Amex representative.

🛏 Sleeping

Book ahead, especially if you want a double room. Tourist offices offer a comprehensive lodging list with prices that include nearby *estancias* (ranches) and rental apartments.

Puerto Madryn

Puerto Madryn

◎ Sights

1 Museo Provincial de Ciencias
   Naturales y Oceanográfico................A1

✦ Activities, Courses & Tours

2 Argentina Vision.....................................C3
3 Flamenco Tour B2
4 Lobo Larsen...C4
   Napra Club..................................(see 20)
5 Nievemar..C3
6 Regina Australe.....................................B1
7 Scuba Duba D4

⊜ Sleeping

8 Chepatagonia Hostel...........................C3
9 Dazzler C3
10 El Gualicho B3
11 El Patio B&B B3
12 El Retorno C4
13 Hostería Las Maras..............................A2
14 Hotel Bahía Nueva B1

15 Hotel Piren...C2
16 La Casa de Tounens..............................A2
17 La Loica...B3
18 La Tosca B3

⊗ Eating

19 Ambigú B1
20 Bistro de Mar Nautico..........................D4
21 Bodegón C3
22 El Almendro...A3
23 Guiseppe..C2
24 La Taska..B3
25 Lupita..B3
26 Mr Jones...B3
27 Olinda...C2
28 Plácido..C3
29 Una Mesa..B3

⊙ Drinking & Nightlife

30 Margarita Bar...B1

All hostels have kitchens and many offer pickup from the bus terminal, but most are a short, flat walk away.

⭐ La Tosca
HOSTEL $

(☑ 445-6133; www.latoscahostel.com; Sarmiento 437; dm US$26, with bathroom d/tr/q US$104/117/130, without bathroom s/d/tr US$65/78/98; @ 🛜) A cozy guesthouse where the staff greet you by name. The creation of a well-traveled couple, La Tosca is modern and comfy, with a grassy courtyard, good mattresses, and varied breakfasts with homemade cakes, yogurt and fruit. Double suites and a post-checkout bathroom with showers are wonderful additions. There's also bike rental.

La Casa de Tounens
HOSTEL $

(☑ 447-2681; www.lacasadetounens.com; Passaje 1 de Marzo 432; s/d with bathroom US$45/55, dm/s/d without bathroom US$18/40/45; @ 🛜) A congenial nook near the bus station, run by a friendly Parisian-Argentine couple. With few rooms, personal attention is assured. There's a cozy stone patio strewn with hammocks, a barbecue grill for guests and homemade bread for breakfast.

Chepatagonia Hostel
HOSTEL $

(☑ 445-5783; www.chepatagoniahostel.com.ar; Storni 16; dm/d US$19/60; @ 🛜) This stylish and cheerful hostel is owned by a friendly couple who book tours for guests and fire up the grill for barbecues twice a week. Adding to the appeal are comfortable beds and the possibility of glimpsing whales from the hostel balcony. Guests can wash clothes and cook. Bikes are available for rent (AR$150 per day).

El Retorno
HOSTEL $

(☑ 445-6044; www.elretornohostel.com.ar; Mitre 798; dm/s/tw US$14/30/40; @ 🛜) Run by the indefatigable Gladys, a den mother to travelers from all over. Besides dorms and snug doubles, there's a solarium, barbecue area and bike rental.

La Loica
HOSTEL $

(☑ 494-6426; www.loicahostel.com; Mitre 416; dm/d without bathroom US$22/55; 🛜) New on the scene, this partially renovated hostel features good mattresses and one bathroom for every two rooms. In terms of decor it's somewhat of a bachelor pad, but its staff has plenty of experience in the hospitality industry. Work in progress: a roof deck.

Camping ACA
CAMPGROUND $

(☑ 445-2952; info@acamadryn.com.ar; Camino al Indio; s/d campsites US$9/12; ⊗ closed May-Aug) These 800 gravel campsites are sheltered by trees to break the incessant wind. Although there are no cooking facilities, some snacks (and sometimes prepared meals) are available. From downtown, city bus 2 goes within 500m of the campground; get off at the last stop (La Universidad).

El Gualicho
HOSTEL $

(☑ 445-4163; www.elgualicho.com.ar; Marcos A Zar 480; dm/d/tr US$15/55/63; @ 🛜) This contempo hostel provides very stylish digs, though mattresses are mysteriously cheap quality. We love its ample common spaces, with billiards and hammocks, but being truly massive (with 120 beds) makes it somewhat impersonal. Doubles have TVs. Bikes are for rent and a massive activity board keeps you posted.

La Posada Hotel
INN $

(☑ 447-4087; www.la-posada.com.ar; Mathews 2951; s/d US$62/72; @ 🛜 🐾) This modern inn amid rolling green lawns offers a quiet alternative to lodging in town. Its tidy, light-filled rooms with bright accents come with cable TV; in the garden there's a pool and barbecue grill. It's 2km south of the town center.

⭐ Casa de Piedra
B&B $$

(☑ 447-3521; www.lapiedrahosteria.com; Arenales 82; d/tr US$96/120; @ 🛜) 🏄 This wonderful B&B shines with warm and attentive service. The artisan owners have thoughtfully crafted every detail, from stone patterns in the walkway to wood details and an oversized rocking horse. Immaculate rooms with private entrances off a cement courtyard feature coffee and tea service, flat-screen TVs, lock boxes and mini-fridges.

⭐ El Patio B&B
B&B $$

(☑ 15-440-8887, 447-5224; www.elpatiohostalpatagonia.com; Mitre 46; d with/without bathroom US$90/75; @) Guests get a warm welcome at this rustic B&B located in an old-fashioned building with quotes from songs adorning the walls. There are seven whitewashed rooms around a pleasant sunny courtyard. Breakfast includes whole wheat bread, yogurt, fruit and cereal. The owner Carla has also worked as a naturalist guide and has helpful tips.

Casa Patagonica
B&B $$

(☑ 445-1540; www.casa-patagonica.com.ar; Av Roca 2210; d/tr US$77/86; @ 🛜) Warm and relaxed, with homemade cakes for breakfast and a *quincho* (thatched-roof building) for cooking or barbecues. Lodgings are in a brick home with vaulted ceilings and impeccably kept rooms, five blocks from the beach and 1km south of the town center.

Hostería Las Maras INN $$
(☑ 445-3215; www.hosterialasmaras.com.ar; Marcos A Zar 64; s/d US$105/120, superior US$125/140; @ 🖐) Brick walls, exposed beams and wicker furniture create an intimate setting for couples – in the lobby anyway. Guest rooms are just small, prim and serviceable – if design matters to you, upgrade to a superior room.

Hotel Bahía Nueva HOTEL $$
(☑ 445-0045, 445-0145; www.bahianueva.com.ar; Av Roca 67; s/d/tr US$74/89/107; @ 🖐) Stretching to resemble an English countryside retreat, the Bahía Nueva includes a foyer library and flouncy touches. Its 40 rooms are well groomed, but only a few have ocean views. Highlights include a bar with billiards and a TV (mostly to view movies and documentaries), and tour information.

★ Hotel Territorio BOUTIQUE HOTEL $$$
(☑ 447-1496; www.hotelterritorio.com.ar; Av Roca 33; ste incl spa US$219; @ 🖐🖐) Set behind beautiful dunes with ocean views, this 36-room hotel is minimal chic, with polished concrete, plush modern furniture and an entire whale vertebrae gracing a yawning hall. Kids can use a spacious play room. The Punta Cuevas location is a trek from the town center, but there's a cool cocktail bar and a contemporary spa.

Dazzler HOTEL $$$
(☑ 447-5758; Blvr Brown 637; d with city/sea views US$180/200) This upscale newcomer sports 95 oversized rooms with great ocean views, king-sized beds and all the amenities in a modern, minimalist style. The rooftop solarium, Jacuzzi and spa are welcome extras. The on-site restobar has had some acclaim, but its lobby location lacks privacy.

Hotel Piren HOTEL $$$
(Av Roca 439; d US$120-170) This decent-value high-rise on the waterfront shares space with timeshare condominum apartments. Staff could not be prouder of the *Charlie and the Chocolate Factory*–style glass elevator, which climbs 10 floors to dizzying views. Public spaces sport sleek design, though there's considerable difference in quality between the old and new sections.

✖ Eating

La Taska CAFE $
(☑ 15-499-4870, 445-7200; 9 de Julio 461; mains AR$80-150; ⊙ noon-11:45pm) Locals laud the abundant portions and affordable prices at this small neighborhood eatery run by an effervescent chef.

Panacea BISTRO $
(☑ 419-5886; cnr Roca & Apeleg; mains AR$65-135; ⊙ 8am-1am; 🖐🖐) On the quiet side of Roca, this relaxed cafe features daily specials and good vegetarian/vegan options in addition to pasta, stuffed pizza, seafood and some Middle Eastern and Indian fare, with bread baked on-site. It's popular with locals who want to escape the tourist spots.

Mr Jones INTERNATIONAL $
(9 de Julio 116; mains AR$80-150; ⊙ 8pm-late) Serving a wealth of yummy stouts and reds, homemade pot pie, and fish and chips, this favorite local pub always delivers. Service is friendly but tends to be slow.

Lupita MEXICAN $
(☑ 15-472-2454; Av Gales 195; mains AR$80-120; ⊙ 8pm-1am) This tiny, colorful eatery serves up nachos and fajitas to travelers yearning for something spicy. While it's not straight out of Guadalajara, a valiant effort is made with homemade whole wheat tortillas and house salsas.

★ Plácido ARGENTINE $$
(☑ 445-5991; www.placido.com.ar; Av Roca 506; mains AR$75-200; ⊙ noon-3pm & 8pm-late) Chic and waterfront, this white-linen restaurant serves consistently great food. Beautifully presented versions of traditional dishes include shrimp in garlic and *cordero patagónico* (Patagonian lamb) in a minimalist setting. Try the shellfish sampler paired with a white from Bodega del Fin del Mundo.

Olinda ARGENTINE $$
(☑ 447-0304; Av Roca 385; mains AR$70-235; ⊙ noon-4pm & 7:30pm-1am) With deck seating and a cool candlelit atmosphere, this contemporary cafe serves a range of tasty blackboard specials that go down easy with pitchers of lemonade or gin and tonic. Dishes like Patagonian lamb, local shrimp grilled with sea salt and homemade bread come fresh. Set menus are a good deal and the elaborate desserts easily serve two.

Bistro de Mar Nautico SEAFOOD $$
(⌨447-4289; Blvr Brown 860; mains AR$75-280; ☺8am-midnight) With unbeatable beachfront atmosphere and bustling old-school waiters, this busy cafe does the job. Seafood lovers can get grilled fish or crisp calamari. There's also burgers, pizzas and even breakfast with gorgeous water views that few Madryn restaurants can boast. After 8pm there's a limited menu.

El Almendro INTERNATIONAL $$
(⌨470525; Alvear 409; mains AR$110-165; ☺8pm-late Tue-Sun) With guests often treated to an aperitif, it isn't hard to love this family-run restaurant with its tantalizing menu, attentive service and serviceable wine list. Dine on gnocchi with pumpkin seeds or balsamic glazed steaks in a cozy and elegant house.

Ambigú ARGENTINE $$
(⌨472541; www.ambiguresto.com.ar; cnr Av Roca & Roque Sáenz Peña; mains AR$105-165; ☺noon-2:30pm & 7:30pm-midnight) Locals gravitate toward this corner cafe offering the full gamut of dishes. The setting is an elegant renovation of a historic bank building, backlit by warm colors.

Guiseppe ITALIAN $$
(⌨445-6891; 25 de Mayo 381; mains AR$80-150; ☺noon-4pm & 8pm-1am) This Italian bistro hits just the right note with fresh pastas, gnocchi and pizza *a la piedra,* served up on classic red-checkered tablecloths. If you want something a little more exotic, go for the *risotto de langostinos* (with crawfish).

Bodegón CAFE $$
(⌨447-2547; Blvr Brown s/n; mains AR$118-150; ☺noon-3pm & 8pm-midnight) With its tiny tables and brick walls, this intimate cafe wouldn't be out of place in Buenos Aires. As expected it serves the classics: steak with fries, *cazuelas* (meat stews) and *milanesas,* with wine named for famous *fútbol* (soccer) teams. The ideal boy's night out.

★Una Mesa ARGENTINE $$$
(⌨447-4479; Belgrano 346; mains AR$200-400; ☺8pm-midnight Fri & Sat) An original and wholly worthwhile option run by a young chef couple, this petite home offers an intimate dining experience, with fresh plates of seafood, risotto and meats in artful presentations. Don't skip the exquisite desserts. They also offer cooking classes with chef Juan or pastry chef Julia. See their Facebook page, Unamesa.

▼ Drinking & Nightlife

Bars and dance clubs come and go, so ask locals what's *de moda* (in) now.

Margarita Bar PUB
(Roque Sáenz Peña; ☺11am-4am) With a trendy edge, this low-lit brick haunt has a laundry list of cocktails, a friendly bar staff and decent food (mains AR$60 to AR$175). On weekends there's dancing after 1:30am.

❶ Information

Banco de la Nación (9 de Julio 127) Has an ATM and changes traveler's checks.

Boutique del Libro (⌨445-7987; cnr 28 de Julio & Av Roca, Portal de Madryn 208; ☺9:30am-1:30pm & 3:30-9pm Mon-Fri, 9:30am-9:30pm Sat, 11am-9pm Sun) Stocks a good selection of regional Patagonia books, maps, and a few English-language novels and guidebooks. It's on the 2nd floor of a mall next to the tourist information center.

Hospital Subzonal (⌨445-1999; R Gómez 383)

Post Office (cnr Belgrano & Gobernador Maíz)

Tourist Office (⌨445-3504; www.madryn.gov.ar/turismo; Av Roca 223; ☺8am-9pm Dec-Feb, limited hours Apr-Nov) Helpful and efficient staff, and there's usually an English or French speaker on duty. Check the *libro de reclamos* (complaint book) for traveler tips. There's another helpful desk at the bus terminal (open 7am to 9pm in high season).

❶ Getting There & Away

Due to limited connections, it pays to book in advance, especially for travel to the Andes.

AIR
Though Puerto Madryn has its own modern airport, **Aeropuerto El Tehuelche**, 5km west of town, most commercial flights still arrive in Trelew, 65km south.

Regional airline **Andes** (⌨445-2355; www.andesonline.com; Belgrano 41) has flights to Buenos Aires' Aeroparque (AR$2757) several times a week. **Aerolíneas Argentinas** (⌨445-1998; Av Roca 427) flies from Trelew but has a ticketing representative here.

BUS
Puerto Madryn's full-service **bus terminal** (www.terminalmadryn.com; cnr Ciudad de Nefyn & Dr Ávila), behind the historic 1889 Estación del Ferrocarril Patagónico, has an ATM machine, cafe and a helpful tourist information desk. Bus timetables are clearly posted and luggage storage is available.

Bus companies include **Andesmar** (⌨447-3764), **Don Otto** (⌨445-1675), **Mar y Valle** (⌨447-2056), **Que Bus** (⌨445-5805), **TAC** (⌨445-5805) and **TUS** (⌨445-1962). **Chaltén**

Travel (☑ 445-4906; Av Roca 115) has buses to Esquel and offers connecting service north on RN 40 (to Bariloche) or south (to Perito Moreno and El Chaltén).

The bus to Puerto Pirámides, operated by Mar y Valle (AR$75, 1½ hours), leaves at 8:55am and 5pm, returning to Madryn at 11am and 7pm. Wednesday and Friday there are 6:30am departures. Times may change seasonally, so consult ahead.

Buses from Puerto Madryn

DESTINATION	COST (AR$)	TIME (HR)
Bariloche	814	15
Buenos Aires	1350	18-20
Comodoro Rivadavia	438	6-8
Córdoba	1300	18
Esquel	644	9
Mendoza	1475	23-24
Neuquén	710	12
Río Gallegos	1312	15-20
Trelew	47	1
Viedma	416	5-6

❶ Getting Around

Rent a bicycle for travel in and around town. Taxis can be hired to Puerto Pirámides (AR$1170) and Punta Loma/Doradillo (AR$445).

TO/FROM THE AIRPORT

Southbound 28 de Julio buses to Trelew, which run hourly Monday through Saturday between 6am and 10pm, will stop at Trelew's airport on request.

Radio taxis, including **La Nueva Patagonia** (☑ 447-6000), take travelers to and from Madryn's airport for about AR$80, while **Eben-Ezer** (☑ 447-2474) runs shuttle services to the Trelew airport.

CAR

A roundtrip to Península Valdés is a little over 300km. A group sharing expenses can make car rental a relatively reasonable and more flexible alternative to taking a bus tour if you don't have to pay for extra kilometers – rent under clear terms.

Rates vary, depending on the mileage allowance and age and condition of the vehicle. The best bet for competitive rates and friendly and comprehensive service is **Hi Patagonia Rent-a-Car** (☑ 445-0155; www.hipatagonia.com; Rawson 419). The family-owned agency **Centauro** (☑ 0280-15-340400; www.centaurorentacar.com.ar; Av Roca 733) also gets high marks. Basic vehicles run AR$1350 per day, with insurance and 200km included.

Around Puerto Madryn

Home to a permanent sea-lion colony and cormorant rookery, the **Reserva Faunística Punta Loma** (admission AR$50) is 17km southwest of Puerto Madryn via a good but winding gravel road. The overlook is about 15m from the animals, best seen during low tides. Many travel agencies organize two-hour tours according to the tide schedules; otherwise, check tide tables and hire a car or taxi, or make the trek via bicycle.

Continue on the same road for **Punta Ninfas**, a cliffside marked by a lighthouse, to see elephant seals on the beach. There's also a penguin colony forming here. Please exercise self-restraint and snap photos at a nonthreatening distance. It's 78km from Puerto Madryn on a dusty dirt road.

On the way, **El Pedral** (☑ 0280-447-3043; reservaelpedral.com; camino a Punta Ninfas; s/d incl meals & transfer US$375/500; ⊗ mid-Sep–mid-April) is a private *estancia* and nature reserve with a growing Magellanic penguin colony and beautiful coastal digs in a historic home.

Punta Flecha observatory is a recommended whale-watching spot 20km north of Puerto Madryn via RP 1.

Coastal Río Negro

At the gateway to Patagonia, Viedma shares the lush Río Negro with sister city Carmen de Patagones. With stylish riverfront cafes, Viedma, capital of Río Negro province, exudes prosperity. Historic Carmen de Patagones is worth touring for its steep cobblestone streets and colonial stylings.

Heading south, La Ruta de los Acantilados is a beautiful stretch of Atlantic coastline. Repeated wave action has worn the ancient cliff faces (three million to 13 million years old) to reveal a wealth of fossils. While the area teems with activity in summer, it shuts down in the low season.

Balneario El Cóndor, 31km southeast of Viedma at the mouth of the Río Negro, has the largest parrot colony in the world, with 35,000 nests in its cliff faces. Its century-old lighthouse is Patagonia's oldest.

Some 30km further south, there's a permanent southern sea-lion colony at **La Lobería** (Reserva Faunística de Punta Bermeja), on the north coast of Golfo San Matías. The population peaks during spring, when males come ashore to fight other males and establish harems of up to 10 females. The females give birth from December onward. An observation balcony sits directly above the mating beaches, safe and unobtrusive. Buses from Viedma pass within 3km of the colony.

At the northwest edge of Golfo San Matías, 179km west of Viedma along RN 3, the crowded resort of Las Grutas owes its name to its eroded sea caves. Thanks to an exceptional tidal range, the beaches can expand for hundreds of meters. The **tourism office** (☑ 02934-497470; www.lasgrutasturismo. com.ar; Galería Antares, Primera Bajada) has tide schedules. Buses leave hourly to San Antonio Oeste, 16km northeast, with more lodging.

Reserva Faunística Península Valdés

Home to sea lions, elephant seals, guanacos, rheas, Magellanic penguins and numerous seabirds, Unesco World Heritage site Península Valdés is one of South America's finest wildlife reserves. More than 80,000 visitors per year come to this sanctuary, which has a total area of 3600 sq km and more than 400km of coastline.

The wildlife viewing is truly exceptional, though the undisputed main attraction is the endangered *ballena franca austral*

(southern right whale). The warmer, more enclosed waters along the Golfo Nuevo, Golfo San José and the coastline near Caleta Valdés from Punta Norte to Punta Hércules become prime breeding zones for right whales between June and mid-December.

One doesn't expect lambs alongside penguins, but sheep *estancias* occupy most of the peninsula's interior, which includes one of the world's lowest continental depressions, the salt flats of Salina Grande and Salina Chica, 42m below sea level. At the turn of the 20th century, Puerto Pirámides, the peninsula's only village, was the shipping port for the salt extracted from Salina Grande.

About 17km north of Puerto Madryn, paved RP 2 branches off RN 3 across the Istmo Carlos Ameghino to the entrance of the **reserve** (admission adult/child aged 5-12 AR$260/130; ☉ 8am-8pm). The **Centro de Interpretación** (☉ 8am-8pm), 22km beyond the entrance, focuses on natural history, displays a full right whale skeleton and has material on the peninsula's colonization, from the area's first Spanish settlement at Fuerte San José to later mineral exploration. Don't miss the panoramic view from the observation tower.

If you are sleeping in Puerto Madryn but plan to visit the park on two consecutive days, ask a ranger to validate your pass so you can reenter without charges.

Reserva Faunística Península Valdés

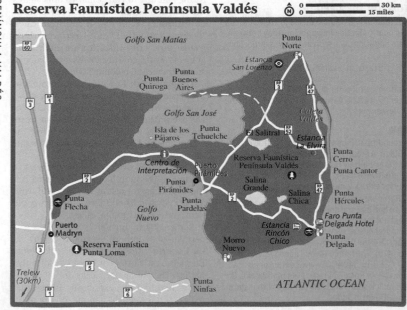

WHALE TROUBLES

Southern right whale populations are growing around the world. However, many threats affect their present and future. Newborn calves have been dying in unprecedented numbers in the Península Valdés nursery ground, according to the International Whaling Commission. Long-term research from the **Instituto de Conservación de Ballenas** (ICB; www.icb.org.ar), a nonprofit that studies the whales and has photo-identified over 3000 individuals since 1971, has found that the whales have fewer calves than expected following diminished krill in feeding grounds near the South Georgia Islands. The scarcity is the direct consequence of a warming climate. The institute is also studying a vexing local problem on Península Valdés: gulls feeding off live whales, which produces lesions and affects their normal behavior. Members of the local whale-watching community have joined with the ICB, contributing data and photographs to help better understand the problems. For those who want to help, you can Adopt a Whale via the ICB website, which also has links to scientific publications.

Puerto Pirámides

📞 0280 / POP HUMANS 565, WHALES 400–2700

Set amid sandy cliffs on a bright blue sea, this sleepy old salt port now bustles with tour buses and visitors clad in orange life jackets. Whales mean whopping and ever-growing tourism here, but at the end of the day the tour buses split and life in this two-street town regains its cherished snail's pace.

Av de las Ballenas is the main drag, which runs perpendicular to Primera (1era) Bajada, the first road to the beach, stuffed with tour outfitters.

🏃 Activities

While most visitors focus on whale watching, adventure offerings continue to grow.

Bicycles or kayaks can be rented and area *estancias* offer **horseback riding**. There's also **mountain biking** aplenty. Or visitors can walk to the **sea-lion colony** less than 5km from town (though mostly uphill). It is a magnificent spot to catch the sunset, occasional whale sightings and views across the Golfo Nuevo toward Puerto Madryn. Time your visit with the tides; high tide finds all the sea lions swimming out to sea.

👉 Tours

This is the place to glimpse spy-hopping, breaching and tailing cetaceans on a **whale-watching excursion** (adult/child AR$890/450), arranged in Puerto Madryn or Puerto Pirámides. The standard trip lasts 1½ hours, but longer excursions are available.

When choosing a tour, check what kind of boat will be used: smaller, Zodiac-style inflatable rafts offer more intimacy but may be less comfortable. By law, outfitters are not allowed within 100m of whales without cutting the motor, nor allowed to pursue them.

Check your outfitter's policies. When the port is closed due to bad weather, tour bookings are usually honored the following day (although these days are more crowded). Outside of whale-watching season (June to December), boat trips aren't worthwhile unless you adore sea lions and shorebirds.

⭐ **Patagonia Explorers** KAYAKING
(📞 0280-15-434-0618; www.patagoniaexplorers. com; Av de las Ballenas; 2hr kayak US$70) This band of brothers (and sister) offer top-notch guided hikes and sea-kayaking trips. A three-day excursion on the Golfo San José includes paddling with sea lions and lots of wildlife-watching and wilderness camping. There's also full moon and sunset options. Check the website or visit the office for details.

Bottazzi WHALE WATCHING
(📞 449-5050; www.titobottazzi.com; 1era Bajada) A recommended family business in its second generation and the only company with its own agency in Puerto Madryn. Popular and more personalized sunset cruises feature a smaller boat; it's a great option for wildlife photography.

Southern Spirit WHALE WATCHING
(📞 449-5094; www.southernspirit.com.ar; 1era Bajada; sub adult/child AR$1780/890) This reputable outfitter offers both conventional and underwater viewing via the semi-submergible, custom-built *Yellow Submarine*. Though not an actual sub, its narrow underwater chamber lined with stools and windows provides full views of cavorting whales when there's good visibility. The boat holds 35 to

40 passengers. Also offers a coastal overnight trek to spend an evening with whale-song.

Hydrosport
WHALE WATCHING

(☑449-5065; www.hydrosport.com.ar; 1era Bajada) In addition to whale watching, runs dolphin-watching tours and has naturalists and submarine audio systems on board.

Whales Argentina
WHALE WATCHING

(☑449-5015; www.whalesargentina.com.ar; 1era Bajada) Offers quality trips with a bilingual guide; also runs personalized excursions on a four-seater semi-rigid boat.

Patagonia Scuba
DIVING

(☑0280-15-457-8779; www.patagonia-scuba.com.ar; Av de las Ballenas s/n; diving baptism AR$800) A reputable PADI-certified outfitter offering diving trips and snorkeling with sea lions (AR$1400); the best water visibility is in August. It rents kayaks too. Also check its Facebook page.

Traccion a Sangre
MOUNTAIN BIKING

(☑0296-549-5047; www.traccionasangre.com.ar; Av de las Ballenas s/n; guided half-day AR$800) Rents mountain bikes and offers guided mountain-biking tours on the peninsula. The office is shared with Patagonia Scuba.

🛏 Sleeping

Staying over helps pack in more watching wildlife, though it's worth noting that there are few good-value lodgings here and little happening at night. Still, campers gloat about hearing whales' eerie cries and huffing blowholes in the night – an extraordinary experience.

You will have to get a voucher from your hotel if you plan to exit and reenter the Reserva Faunística Península Valdés, so as to not pay the park entry fee twice. Watch for signs advertising rooms, cabins and apartments for rent along the main drag. Wi-fi is notoriously slow, something that's uniform no matter how much you pay for lodgings.

Hostel Bahía Ballenas
HOSTEL $

(☑15-456-7104; www.bahiaballenas.com.ar; Av de las Ballenas s/n; dm US$20; ❇@🛜) A welcoming brick hostel with two enormous dorms; the 'Backpackers' sign will catch your eye. Guests get discounts on area tours. Rates include kitchen use; breakfast is extra (AR$40).

Camping Municipal
CAMPGROUND $

(☑15-420-2760; per person US$12) Convenient, sheltered gravel campsites with clean toilets, a store and hot pay showers, down the road behind the gas station. Come early in summer to stake your spot. Avoid camping on the beach: high tide is very high.

Hidden House
GUESTHOUSE $

(☑449-5078, 15-464-4380; hiddenhouse@gmail.com; Segunda Bajada; per person US$65; ❇🛜) Lovely and partially tucked behind the dunes, this airy home is a fun destination, with flower boxes, friendly dogs and chair loungers in the dunes. Very personal service is provided by chef host Mumo, who can cook up meals and put on a great barbecue. The street is unmarked; it's the second sea-access road. They're on Facebook.

La Casa de la Tía Alicia
GUESTHOUSE $$

(☑449-5046; Av de las Ballenas s/n; d US$83; 🛜) A cozy spot for couples, this petal-pink house has just three cabin-style rooms in bright crayon-box colors around a cute garden area. There's in-room tea service, and the management has a conscientious approach to recycling water and composting.

Motel ACA
MOTEL $$

(☑449-5004; www.motelacapiramides.com; Av Roca s/n; d US$130; ❇🛜) One of the better bets in town, though it can be noisy. Shared spaces offer bay views through huge glass windows. AAA members get a 30% discount with their membership card.

Cabañas en el Mar
CABIN $$

(☑15-466-1629; www.cabañasenelmar.com; Av de las Ballenas; 4-/5-person cabin US$150/160; ❇🛜) Smack in the center of all the action (where the road splits to the waterfront), these comfortable new cabins are spotless, cool and well equipped. Bedrooms have a TV, and kitchens have full-sized refrigerators and stoves.

⭐Del Nomade Hostería Ecologica
LODGE $$$

(☑449-5044; www.ecohosteria.com.ar; Av de las Ballenas s/n; d US$165; @🛜) 🍃 Owned by a renowned Argentine nature photographer, these eight stylish ecolodge rooms have a homey, minimalist style and homemade breakfasts. Maximum effort has been put into making it green – using wood from fallen trees, enzymatic water treatment, solar panels, composting and natural cleaning agents. You can get in the wildlife mood browsing the photo displays and stacks of *National Geographic* magazines.

Excursion lunch boxes are available (AR$60) as well as long-stay discounts.

Restingas Hotel　　　　　HOTEL **$$$**

(☑ 449-5101; www.lasrestingas.com; 1era Bajada; d garden/ocean view US$231/271; @ 🛜 🞿) A beach-front luxury hotel and spa with spacious rooms and an attractive glass-walled living room. While service appears lax, watching whales from your bedroom is a big plus. Guests praise the abundant buffet breakfast; its gourmet restaurant is open to the public.

De Luna　　　　GUESTHOUSE **$$$**

(☑ 449-5083; www.deluna.com.ar; Av de las Ballenas s/n; d/cabin US$195/120) A bright and cheerful option. Choose from spacious and inviting rooms in the main house, or a crunched but lovely guest cabin, perched above the house with excellent views. There's no sign and check-in is at Del Nomade next door.

✖ Eating & Drinking

Restaurants flank the beachfront, down the first street to the right as you enter town. Note that water here is desalinated: sensitive stomachs should stick to the bottled stuff. If self-catering, it's best to haul your groceries from Puerto Madryn.

El Viento Viene　　　　CAFE **$**

(1era Bajada; mains AR$40-95; ☉ 9am-8pm) This little nook is a charming spot for coffee, sandwiches and homemade pie, and also sells innovative arts and crafts.

La Estación　　　　SEAFOOD **$**

(Av de las Ballenas s/n; mains AR$100; ☉ noon-4:30pm & 7-11pm Fri-Wed) This funky, fresh eatery is the ideal spot to crack open a bottle of wine and savor it. Though the vibe is casual, dishes like *langostinos a la plancha* (grilled prawns), fresh scallops and lamb *sorrentinos* (large, round filled pastas) are fit for royalty. Reserve a table ahead, as there are precious few.

★ Guanaco　　　　PUB FOOD **$$**

(☑ 449-5046; Av de las Ballenas s/n; mains AR$142-180; ☉ 7-11:30pm Mon, Tue, Thu & Fri, noon-3:30pm & 7-11:30pm Sat & Sun) Art installations on a covered porch announce this funky *cervecería* serving Hernan's artisan brews and other regional brews. Dishes like lamb ravioli, fish with butter and herbs and huge salads are satisfying. Service might be slow; it's a small operation. A sure sign things are going well is it has been known to close for lack of inventory.

❶ Information

A small **tourist office** (☑ 449-5048; www.puerto piramides.gov.ar; 1era Bajada; ☉ 8am-8pm)

helps with travelers' needs. Visitors can access the internet at **India** (Av de las Ballenas; per hr AR$500; ☉ 10:30am-8pm; 🛜) and take out cash from the ATM at **Banco del Chubut** (Av de las Ballenas).

❶ Getting There & Around

Buses stop behind the YPF gas station, the site of the future bus station. The Mar y Valle bus service travels from Puerto Pirámides to Puerto Madryn (AR$75, 1½ hours) Monday through Friday at 8:10am, 1pm and 6pm. On weekends there are 6pm departures. Bus tours from Puerto Madryn may allow passengers to get off here.

Around Puerto Pirámides

If you're driving around the peninsula, take it easy. Roads are *ripio* and washboard, with sandy spots that grab the wheels. If you're in a rental car, make sure you get all the details of the insurance policy. Hitchhiking here is nearly impossible and bike travel is long and unnervingly windy.

A private *estancia* on Península Valdés, **Estancia San Lorenzo** (www.pinguinospuntanorte.com.ar; Punta Norte; adult/child aged 5-12 AR$620/310) offers excellent wildlife-watching opportunities. Book visits through Argentina Vision (p404) in Puerto Madryn.

ISLA DE LOS PÁJAROS

In Golfo San José, 800m north of the isthmus, this bird sanctuary is off-limits to humans, but visible through a powerful telescope. It contains a replica of a chapel built at Fuerte San José.

PUNTA DELGADA

In the peninsula's southeast corner, 76km southeast of Puerto Pirámides, sea lions and, in spring, a huge colony of elephant seals, are visible from the cliffs. Entry is AR$150 as viewing is only accessed via the property of Faro Punta Delgada Hotel. However, guests of the hotel and those having lunch there can enter without extra charge.

With a prime location for wildlife-watching, **Estancia Rincón Chico** (☑ 0280-447-1733; www.rinconchico.com.ar; per person d occupancy incl full board US$376; ☉ mid-Sep–Mar) hosts university marine biologists, student researchers and tourists. Lodging is in a modern, corrugated-tin ranch house with eight well-appointed doubles and a *quincho* for barbecues. In addition to guided excursions there are paths for cycling and walking on your own. There's a two-night minimum.

Faro Punta Delgada Hotel (☎02965-15-406304, 445-8444; www.puntadelgada.com; s/d incl excursion US$263/308, lunch adult/child aged 12-18 AR$200/100) is a luxury hotel in a lighthouse complex that once belonged to the Argentine postal service. Horseback riding, 4WD tours and other activities are available. Nonguests can dine at the upscale restaurant serving *estancia* fare. Guided naturalist walks down to the beach leave frequently in high season.

PUNTA CANTOR & CALETA VALDÉS

In spring, elephant seals haul themselves onto the long gravel spit at the sheltered bay 43km north of Punta Delgada. September sees females giving birth to pups, while males fight it out defending their harem – a dramatic sight from the trails that wind down the hill. You may even see guanacos strolling the beach.

A few kilometers north of the private Estancia La Elvira, there's a sizable colony of burrowing Magellanic penguins.

PUNTA NORTE

At the far end of the peninsula, solitary Punta Norte boasts an enormous mixed colony of sea lions and elephant seals. Its distance means it is rarely visited by tour groups. But the real thrill here is the orcas: from mid-February through mid-April these killer whales come to feast on the unsuspecting colonies of sea lions. The chances are you won't see a high-tide attack, but watching their dorsal fins carving through the water is enough to raise goose bumps.

There's a small but good **museum** that focuses on marine mammals, and has details on the Tehuelche and the area's sealing history. There's also a **cafe** with basic snacks, open only if it's busy enough to warrant it.

Trelew

☎0290 / POP 98,600

Though steeped in Welsh heritage, Trelew isn't a postcard city. In fact, this uneventful midsized hub may be convenient to many attractions, but it's home to few. The region's commercial center, it's a handy base for visiting the Welsh villages of Gaiman and Dolavon. Also worthwhile is the top-notch dinosaur museum.

Founded in 1886 as a railway junction, Trelew (tre-*ley*-ooh) owes its easily mispronounced name to the Welsh contraction of *tre* (town) and *lew* (after Lewis Jones, who promoted railway expansion). During the following 30 years, the railway reached Gaiman, the Welsh built their Salón San David (a replica of St David's Cathedral, Pembrokeshire), and Spanish and Italian immigrants settled in the area. In 1956 the federal government promoted Patagonian industrial development and Trelew's population skyrocketed.

Trelew is situated 65km south of Puerto Madryn via RN 3.

The city center surrounds Plaza Independencia, with most services located on Calles 25 de Mayo and San Martín, and along recently renovated Av Fontana. East–

THE LITTLE PRINCE

From an apartment in Manhattan in 1941, a French pilot and writer, in exile from the battlefields of Europe, scripted what would become one of the most-read children's fables, *The Little Prince*. Antoine de Saint-Exupéry, then 40 years old, had spent the previous 20 years flying in the Sahara, the Pyrenees, Egypt and Patagonia – where he was director of Aeropostal Argentina from 1929 to 1931. Intertwined in the lines of *The Little Prince* and Asteroid B612 are images of Patagonia ingrained from flights over the windy, barren landscape.

Legend has it that the shape of Isla de los Pájaros (p413), off the coast of Península Valdés, inspired the elephant-eating boa constrictor (or hat, as you may see it), while the perfectly conical volcanoes on the asteroid are modeled on those seen en route to Punta Arenas, Chile. The author's illustrations show the little prince on mountain peaks resembling the Fitz Roy Range (one such peak now bears his name). And, possibly, meeting two young daughters of a French immigrant after an emergency landing in Concordia, near Buenos Aires, helped mold the character of the prince.

Antoine de Saint-Exupéry never witnessed the influence his young character would enjoy. In 1944, just after the first publication of *The Little Prince*, he disappeared during a flight to join French forces-in-exile stationed in Algiers. His Patagonia years also figure in two critically acclaimed novels, *Night Flight* and *Wind, Sand and Stars*, both worthwhile reads on long Patagonia trips.

west streets change names on either side of Av Fontana.

◉ Sights

The tourist office sometimes has an informative walking tour brochure, in Spanish and English, describing most of the city's historic buildings.

★ Museo Paleontológico Egidio Feruglio
MUSEUM

(☏442-0012; www.mef.org.ar; Av Fontana 140; adult/child AR$95/65; ⊗9am-6pm Mon-Fri, 10am-7pm Sat & Sun) Showcasing Patagonia's most important fossil finds, this natural-history museum offers outstanding life-sized dinosaur exhibits and more than 1700 fossil remains of plant and marine life. Nature sounds and a video accent the informative plaques, and tours are available in a number of languages. The collection includes local dinosaurs, such as the tehuelchesaurus, patagosaurus and titanosaurus.

With an international team, museum researchers helped discover a new and unusual species called *Brachytrachelopan mesai*, a short-necked sauropod. Egidio Feruglio, after whom the museum is named, was an Italian paleontologist who came to Argentina in 1925 as a petroleum geologist for YPF.

Kids aged eight to 12 can check out the 'Explorers in Pyjamas' program, which invites kids to sleep over and explore the museum by flashlight. The museum also sponsors interesting group tours to Geoparque Paleontológico Bryn Gwyn, in the badlands along the Río Chubut (25km from Trelew, or 8km south of Gaiman via RP 5). The three-hour guided visits are a walk through time, visiting exposed fossils dating as far back as the Tertiary period, some 40 million years ago.

Museo de Artes Visuales
MUSEUM

(☏443-3774; Mitre 351; admission AR$10; ⊗9am-7pm Mon-Fri, 2-8pm Sat & Sun) Adjoined to the tourist office, this small visual-arts museum features works on loan from the Museo Nacional de Bellas Artes in Buenos Aires, as well as polished relics from Welsh colonization.

Museo Regional Pueblo de Luis
MUSEUM

(☏442-4062; cnr Av Fontana & Lewis Jones; admission AR$30; ⊗8am-8pm) In a former train station, this small museum displays historical photographs, clothing and period furnishings of Welsh settlers, along with relics from the area's indigenous peoples.

☞ Tours

Several travel agencies run excursions to Área Natural Protegida Punta Tombo (AR$700, plus AR$180 admission), some passing by Puerto Rawson on the way back to see *toninas overas* (Commerson's dolphins) when conditions are agreeable. The actual time at Punta Tombo is only about 1½ hours. Full-day trips to Península Valdés (AR$1800, plus AR$260 admission) are also on offer, but going to Puerto Madryn first is a better bet: there are more options, prices are similar and there's less driving time.

Local agencies worth checking out are Amex representative **Nievemar** (☏443-4114; www.nievemartours.com.ar; Italia 20), which accepts traveler's checks, and **Explore Patagonia** (☏443-7860; Roca 84).

☆ Festivals & Events

Gwyl y Glaniad
CULTURAL

(⊗28 Jul) The landing of the first Welsh is celebrated by taking tea in one of the many chapels.

Eisteddfod de Chubut
CULTURAL

(⊗late Oct) A Welsh literary and musical festival, the tradition of which started in 1875.

Trelew

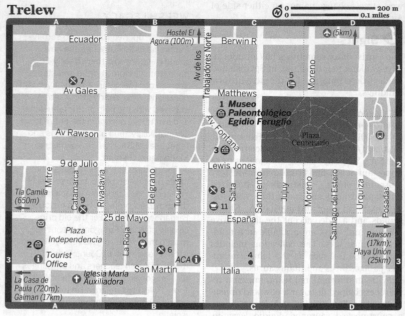

Aniversario de la Ciudad   CULTURAL
(⊙20 Oct) Commemorates the city's founding in 1886.

🛌 Sleeping

Trelew's accommodations are largely dated and geared toward the business traveler; in addition, spots fill up fast. Travelers can find more variety in nearby Puerto Madryn or Gaiman.

Hostel El Agora   HOSTEL $
(🗹442-6899; www.hostelagora.com.ar; Edwin Roberts 33; dm US$19; ❋@🛜) A backpacker haven, this cute brick house is sparkling and ship-shape. Features include a tiny patio, book exchange and laundry. It also does guided bicycle tours. It's two blocks from Plaza Centenario and four blocks from the bus terminal.

★La Casa de Paula   B&B $$
(🗹15-435-2240; www.casadepaula.com.ar; Marconi 573; s/d/tr/q US$100/120/130/140; ❋🛜) A haven after a day of sun and wind, artist Paula's house beckons with huge king beds covered in down duvets and woven throws. An eclectic and warm decor fills this modern home, with jazz on the radio and cozy living areas stacked with fashion mags. There's also a lush garden and an outstanding breakfast with homemade jam.

The new suites with balcony or patio are ideal for families.

La Casona del Río   B&B $$
(🗹443-8343; www.lacasonadelrio.com.ar; Chacra 105; s/d/tr US$110/125/165; @) Located 5km outside the city center, on the bank of the Río Chubut, this English-style B&B is a thoroughly charming refuge. Guest rooms are smart and bright; other features include a library, tennis court, gazebo and rental bikes.

Patagonia Suites Apart   APARTMENT $$
(🗹442-1345, 0280-453-7399; www.patagonian suites.com; Matthews 186; d from US$115; 🛜) A foxy addition to town, these 13 modern apartments (from studios to multiple bedrooms) feature wood details, hairdryers and corduroy bedspreads. They also come with fully equipped kitchens and cable TV. The complex faces Plaza Centenario.

🍴 Eating

Tía Camila   ARGENTINE $
(🗹443-2950; 25 de Mayo 951; mains AR$50-120; ⊙12:30-3pm & 8:30-11:45pm Thu-Mon) A humble neighborhood restaurant, Tía Camila does a brisk business in simple and filling fare, ranging from homemade pastas to delectable *costellitas* (ribs) served with mashed potatoes and salad. There's also takeout.

Trelew

La Bodeguita   ARGENTINE $
(Belgrano 374; mains AR$80-120; ⊘noon-3pm &
8pm-midnight Tue-Sun) A popular stop for meats,
pasta and seafood, this restaurant boasts attentive service and a family atmosphere.

Miguel Angel   ITALIAN $$
(✐443-0403; Av Fontana 246; mains AR$110-180;
⊘noon-3pm & 8pm-midnight Tue-Sun) This chic
eatery, outfitted with sleek white booths, de-
parts from the everyday with savory dishes
such as gnocchi and wild mushrooms, and
pizza with bacon and basil on crisp, thin crust.

Sugar   MODERN ARGENTINE $$
(25 de Mayo 247; mains AR$90-190; ⊘7am-1am;
✐) Facing Plaza Independencia, this modern restaurant spices up a basic menu of
classic Argentine fare with options like
quinoa *milanesas*, stir-fried beef, grilled
vegetables and herbed fish. There are salads
and fresh juice on offer too. While it isn't
gourmet, it's still a welcome change from
Argentine same-old, same-old.

Majadero   ARGENTINE $$$
(✐443-0548; Av Gales 250; mains AR$110-240;
⊘8pm-midnight Mon-Sat, noon-6pm Sun) Iron
lamps and brickwork restore the romance to
this 1914 flour mill – undoubtedly the nicest
restaurant setting in town. On weekends it's
busy, with the wood-fired *parrilla*, grilling
steaks and even vegetables.

🍷 Drinking & Nightlife

★ **Touring Club**   CAFE
(Av Fontana 240; ⊘6:30am-2am) Old lore ex-
udes from the pores of this historic *con-
fitería* (cafe offering light meals; snacks
AR$60), from the Butch Cassidy 'Wanted'
poster to the embossed tile ceiling and an-
tique bar back. Even the tuxedoed waitstaff
appear to be plucked from another era. Ser-
vice is weak and the sandwiches are only
so-so, but the ambience is one of a kind.

Boru Irish Pub & Restobar   PUB
(Belgrano 341; ⊘8pm-4am) Hip and attractive,
featuring a beautiful wood bar and a row of
cozy red booths, Boru serves up icy beer and
plates piled high with french fries.

ℹ️ Information

ATMs and *locutorios* (private telephone offices)
with internet are plentiful downtown and around
Plaza Independencia.

ACA (Automóvil Club Argentino; ✐435197; cnr
Av Fontana & San Martín) Argentina's auto club;
good source for provincial road maps.

Post Office (cnr 25 de Mayo & Mitre)

Tourist Office (✐442-0139; www.trelewturismo.
wordpress.com; cnr San Martín & Mitre; ⊘8am-
8pm Mon-Fri, 9am-9pm Sat & Sun) Helpful, with
some English-speaking staff.

ℹ️ Getting There & Away

AIR
Trelew's airport is 5km north of town off RN 3.

The following are one-way base fares.
Aerolíneas Argentinas (✐442-0222; Ri-
vadavia 548) flies direct daily to Buenos Aires
(AR$2050), and several times a week to Ushuaia
(AR$3090) and El Calafate (AR$3990).

LADE (✐443-5740), found at the bus termi-
nal, flies to Comodoro Rivadavia weekly.

BUS
Trelew's full-service bus terminal is six blocks
northeast of downtown.

For Gaiman (AR$15), **28 de Julio** (✐443-
2429) has 18 services daily between 7am and
11pm (reduced weekend services), with most
continuing to Dolavon (AR$20, 30 minutes).
Buses to Playa Unión (AR$18) leave hourly.

Mar y Valle (✐443-2429) and 28 de Julio run
hourly buses to Puerto Madryn. Mar y Valle goes
to Puerto Pirámides (AR$99, 2½ hours) daily
at 8:15am, with additional service in summer.
El Ñandú (✐442-7499) goes to Camarones
(AR$125 to AR$220, four hours) at 8am on Mon-
day, Wednesday and Friday.

Long-distance bus companies include **El
Cóndor** (✐443-1675), **Que Bus** (✐442-2760),

Andesmar (☑443-3535), **TAC** (☑443-9207), **TUS** (☑442-1343) and **Don Otto/Transportes Patagonia** (☑442-9496).

Of several departures daily for Buenos Aires, Don Otto has the most comfortable and most direct service. Only Don Otto goes to Mar del Plata, while TAC goes to La Plata. TAC and Andesmar service the most towns. For Comodoro Rivadavia there are a few daily departures with TAC, Don Otto or Andesmar, all of which also continue to Río Gallegos.

Buses from Trelew

DESTINATION	COST (AR$)	TIME (HR)
Bahía Blanca	472	12
Bariloche	577	13-16
Buenos Aires	935	18-21
Comodoro Rivadavia	294	5-6
Córdoba	1063	19
Esquel	601	8-9
Mar del Plata	847	17-21
Mendoza	1200	24
Neuquén	516	10
Puerto Madryn	45	1
Río Gallegos	860	14-17
Viedma	375	8

ⓘ Getting Around

From the airport, taxis charge AR$90 to downtown and AR$600 to Puerto Madryn. Car-rental agencies at the airport include **Hertz** (☑447-5247) and **Rent a Car Patagonia** (☑442-0898; www.rentacarpatagonia.com.ar; Rivadavia 86).

Around Trelew

Rawson, 17km east of Trelew, is Chubut's provincial capital, but nearby **Playa Unión**, the region's principal playground, has the capital attraction: *toninas overas* (Commerson's dolphins). Playa Unión is a long stretch of white-sand beach with blocks of summer homes and restaurants serving crisp, fresh *rabas* (calamari). Dolphin tours depart **Puerto Rawson** from April to December. For reservations, contact **Estacion Maritima** (estacionmaritima@gmail.com; adult/child AR$650/325) or **Toninas Adventure** (☑0280-15-467-5741, 449-8372; www.facebook.com/ToninasAdventure).

To reach the beach, get off at Rawson's plaza or bus terminal and hop on a green 'Bahía' bus, which heads to Puerto Rawson before turning around.

Gaiman

☑0280 / POP 9600

Cream pie, dainty tea cakes, *torta negra* (a rich, dense fruit cake) and a hot pot of black tea – most visitors eat their dose of culture when visiting this quintessential Welsh river-valley village. Locals proudly recount the day in 1995 when the late Diana, Princess of Wales, visited Gaiman to take tea (her teacup is displayed at Ty Te Caerdydd). Today about one-third of the residents claim Welsh ancestry and teahouse traditions persist, even though their overselling sometimes rubs the charm a little thin.

The town's name, meaning Stony Point or Arrow Point, originated from the Tehuelche who once wintered in this valley. After the Welsh constructed their first house in 1874, the two groups peacefully coexisted for a time. Later immigrant groups of criollos, Germans and Anglos joined. Gaiman's homey digs provide good value, but the town offers little diversion beyond quiet strolls past stone houses with rose gardens after a filling teahouse visit.

Tiny Gaiman is 17km west of Trelew via RN 25. Av Eugenio Tello is the main road, connecting the main town entrance to leafy Plaza Roca. Most of the teahouses and historic sites are near the plaza. Across the river are fast-growing residential and industrial areas.

◉ Sights

Gaiman is ideal for an informal walking tour, past homes with ivy trellises and drooping, oversized roses. Architecturally distinctive churches and chapels dot the town. **Primera Casa** (cnr Av Eugenio Tello & Evans; admission AR$15; ⊙11am-6pm) was its first house, built in 1874 by David Roberts. Dating from 1906, the **Colegio Camwy** (cnr MD Jones & Rivadavia) is considered the first secondary school in Patagonia.

Museo Histórico Regional Gales   MUSEUM
(cnr Sarmiento & 28 de Julio; admission AR$10; ⊙3-8pm daily Dec-Mar, 3-7pm Tue-Sun Apr-Nov) The old train station houses this fine small museum holding the belongings and photographs of Gaiman pioneers.

Museo Antropológico   MUSEUM
(cnr Bouchard & Jones; admission AR$15; ⊙11am-6pm) The Museo Antropológico offers humble homage to indigenous cultures and history. Ask the tourist office for access.

Nearby is the 300m **Túnel del Ferrocarril**, a brick tunnel through which the first trains to Dolavon passed in 1914.

🛏 Sleeping

★ Yr Hen Ffordd
B&B $

(☎449-1394; www.yrhenffordd.com.ar; Jones 342; s/d/tr US$40/50/60; 🛜) This charming B&B is run by a young couple who give you a set of keys to the front door so you can come and go as you please. Rooms are simple but cozy, with cable TV and private bathrooms with great showers. In the morning, work up an appetite for the divine homemade scones.

Hostería Gwesty Tywi
B&B $

(☎449-1292; www.hosteria-gwestytywi.com.ar; Chacra 202; s/d/tr US$55/70/85; @🛜) Diego and Brenda run this wonderful Welsh B&B with large gardens and snug, frilly rooms. They are glad to help with travel planning and occasionally fire up the barbecue, to the delight of guests. Breakfast includes a selection of jams, cold meats and bread. The location is a bit far from the town center.

Dyffryn Gwyrdd
GUESTHOUSE $

(☎449-1777; patagongales@yahoo.com.ar; Av Eugenio Tello 103; s/d US$30/45; 🛜) Open when the rest are not, this canary-yellow place features bright and simple carpeted rooms with fans and throw pillows. The bathrooms are dated but spotless, and there's a quiet bar and TV area.

Camping Bomberos Voluntarios
CAMPGROUND $

(☎449-1117; cnr Av Yrigoyen & Moreno; adult/child US$3/1) An agreeable campground with hot-water showers and fire pits.

🍴 Eating & Drinking

Tarten afal, tarten gwstard, cacen ffrwythau, spwnj jam and *bara brith* and a bottomless pot of tea – hungry yet? Afternoon tea is taken as a sacrament in Gaiman – though busloads of tourists get dump-trucked in teahouses without warning. The best bet is to look for places without buses in front, or wait for their departure. Tea services usually run from 2pm to 7pm.

Siop Bara
BAKERY $

(Av Eugenio Tello 505; snacks AR$50; ⊘8am-1pm & 3-9pm) This Welsh bakery is the perfect quick, no-fuss stop for pastries, gelato and excellent sandwiches.

Gwalia Lan
ARGENTINE $$$

(cnr Av Eugenio Tello & Jones; set lunch AR$250; ⊘12:30-3pm & 7:30pm-midnight Tue-Sat, 12:30-3pm Sun) Considered Gaiman's best restaurant, Gwalia Lan serves homemade pasta and well-seasoned meat dishes that are consistently good. Service is attentive.

★ Ty Gwyn
TEAHOUSE

(☎499-1009; 9 de Julio 111; ⊘2-7:30pm) A favorite of locals, this white house serves cakes, jams and breads that are all homemade and fresh, *always* (tea AR$200). In business for 30 years.

Ty Nain
TEAHOUSE

(Yrigoyen 283; ⊘2-7pm Jun-Apr) It's been years since Ty Nain was written up in the *Washington Post* and *Los Angeles Times,* but the endorsements are still plastered on the front lawn. Inside an ivy-clad 1890 home, Ty Nain persists as one of the country's most traditional teahouses (tea AR$170). The adjoining museum has some interesting Welsh artifacts.

Ty Cymraeg
TEAHOUSE

(☎449-1010; www.gaimantea.com; Matthews 74; ⊘2-7:30pm Tue-Sun) Teatime in this riverside house includes sumptuous pies and jams (tea AR$150). The youngest member of the Welsh family that owns the place, an energetic twentysomething named Miguel, is happy to explain Welsh traditions from poetry competitions to the significance of carved wooden 'love spoons' – his knowledge adds significantly to the experience.

Plas y Coed
TEAHOUSE

(☎449-1133; www.plasycoed.com.ar; Jones 123; ⊘2-7:30pm) Run by the original owner's great-granddaughter in a gorgeous brick mansion, Plas y Coed pleases the palette and senses, with friendly service, fresh cakes and serious crochet cozies for that steaming-hot pot (tea AR$180). Rooms are also available for rent (doubles US$70).

ℹ Information

There's one ATM on Plaza Roca at Banco del Chubut, but it does not always work, so bring cash. *Locutorios* and internet can be found along the main drag.

Post Office (cnr Evans & Yrigoyen) Just north of the river bridge.

Tourist Office (☎449-1571; www.gaiman. gov.ar; cnr Rivadavia & Belgrano; ⊘9am-8pm Dec-Mar, 9am-6pm Apr-Nov) Ask for a map and guided tours of historic houses. Has more information on its Facebook page: Gaiman Turismo.

ℹ Getting There & Away

During the week, 28 de Julio buses depart for Trelew frequently from Plaza Roca (AR$15, from 7am to 11pm, fewer services on weekends). Most buses to Dolavon (AR$15) use the highway, but some take the much longer gravel 'valley' route. *Remise* (taxi) services are cheaper in Gaiman than in Trelew; the trip to Trelew costs around AR$160 for up to four passengers.

Around Gaiman

To experience an authentic historic Welsh agricultural town, head to the distinctly nontouristy **Dolavon** (population 2800; www.dolavon.com.ar), 19km west of Gaiman via paved RN 25. Welsh for 'river meadow,' the town offers pastoral appeal, with wooden waterwheels lining the irrigation canal framed by rows of swaying poplars. The historic center is full of brick buildings, including the 1880 **Molino Harinero** (☑0280-449-2290; romanogi@infovia.com.ar; Maipú 61), with still-functioning flour mill machinery. Its restaurant **La Molienda** (☑0280-449-2290; mains AR$150) serves handmade breads and pasta with local wines and cheeses. Call owner Romano Giallatini for opening hours.

Área Natural Protegida Punta Tombo

Continental South America's largest penguin nesting ground, **Área Natural Protegida Punta Tombo** (admission AR$180; ⊗8am-6pm Sep-Apr) has a colony of more than half a million Magellanic penguins and attracts many other birds, most notably king and rock cormorants, giant petrels, kelp gulls, flightless steamer ducks and black oystercatchers. A new management plan requires rangers to accompany visitors on rookery visits.

Trelew-based travel agencies run daylong tours but may cancel if bad weather makes the unpaved roads impassable. If possible, come in the early morning to beat the crowds. Most of the nesting areas in the 200-hectare reserve are fenced off: respect the limits and remember that penguins can inflict serious bites.

The **Centro Tombo** (⊗8am-6pm) is an interpretive visitor center. Guests and tours park here and take a shuttle to the rookery. Shuttle frequency depends on demand, but it's greater in the morning. There's a bar and *confitería* on-site, but it's best to bring a picnic lunch.

Punta Tombo is 110km south of Trelew and 180km south of Puerto Madryn via well-maintained gravel RP 1 and a short southeast lateral. Motorists can proceed south to Camarones via scenic but desolate Cabo Raso. If you can get a group together, it may be worth renting a car in Trelew or Puerto Madryn to come here.

Camarones

☑0297 / POP 1300

In the stiff competition for Patagonia's sleepiest coastal village, Camarones takes home the gold. But don't diss its languorous state: if you've ever needed to run away, this is one good option. Its empty beaches are conducive to strolling and townsfolk are masters of the art of shooting the breeze. It is also the closest hub to the lesser-known Cabo Dos Bahías nature reserve, where you can visit 25,000 penguin couples and their fuzzy chicks.

Spanish explorer Don Simón de Alcazaba y Sotomayor anchored here in 1545, proclaiming it part of his attempted Provincia de Nueva León. When the wool industry took off, Camarones became the area's main port. The high quality of local wool didn't go unnoticed by justice of the peace Don Mario Tomás Perón, who operated the area's largest *estancia,* Porvenir, on which his son (and future president) Juanito would romp about. The port flourished, but after Comodoro Rivadavia finished its massive port, Camarones was all but deserted.

In 2009 the paving of RN 1 meant the start of direct bus services from Comodoro Rivadavia. To a moderate degree, tourism is increasing, so hurry to this coastal village now if you want to be able to say you knew Camarones way back when.

◉ Sights

Museo Perón   MUSEUM
(☑496-3014; JM Estrada s/n; admission AR$10, free Tue; ⊗9am-6pm Mon-Fri, noon-6pm Sat & Sun) This new multistory museum documents the life of ex-president Juan Domingo Perón.

⌲ Tours

Patagonia Austral Expediciones   TOUR
(☑0297-15-451-7660; patagoniaustralexpeditions @hotmail.com) Contact for fishing excursions and outings to see dolphins and nearby islands.

CABO RASO

Old Patagonia still lives, breathes and gusts on this rocky, arid coast replete with a reviving ghost town and near-secret surf spots.

Formerly a booming sheep-ranching settlement founded in the late 1800s, the cape was abandoned by the 1950s. Now a wonderful Argentine family is attempting a slow revival through sustainable tourism. They labored for eight years to restore the coast; once littered with decades of garbage, it now sparkles with the powerful, spare beauty nature intended. There's plenty of coastal walks, DIY bird-watching, kayaking and fishing. Surfing's at its best when the north wind blows in August.

At **El Cabo** (📞0280-15-467-3049, 0280-442-0354; www.caboraso.com.ar; RP 1, Km294; per person campsite US$12, dm US$18, per person hostería with half-board US$70, cabins for 2-6 US$60-180) 🏄 guests can stay at the guesthouse or rent simple stone cottages from the original settlement, artfully restored with recycled and repurposed materials. Budget travelers can stay in cool retro-style buses converted to bunkhouses, or camp alongside a former military bunker, now a *quincho*, with sheltered cooking facilities for campers. Be aware that reservations may take time as there is no on-site cell service or wi-fi.

Access is via private vehicles, though it's possible to arrange pickups from Punta Tombo with advance notice. It's 80km north of Camarones via gravel roads and 55km south of Punta Tombo.

🎊 Festivals

Fiesta Nacional del Salmón CULTURAL
A weekend of deep-sea-fishing competitions featuring a free Sunday seafood lunch and the crowning of Miss Salmoncito; celebrated in February.

🛏 Sleeping & Eating

Las Cabañas CABIN $
(📞15-422-2270, 15-400-0818; patagoniamara@hotmail.com; cnr Roca & Estrada; tr US$55-60) Located opposite the plaza, these pastel shoebox cabins are good value. Like new, they feature small, clean bedrooms with a bathroom and kitchenette. If no one is here, ask at Alma Patagonica (p421), which runs the cabins.

Camping Camarones CAMPGROUND $
(📞0297-15-494-7080; www.campingcamarones.com; San Martín; campsite per person/vehicle US$6/5, cabin s/d US$25/50; 🐾) At the waterfront port, this peaceful campground with hot showers and electricity is run by a friendly older couple. A basic store sells provisions and ice cream.

⭐ El Faro Casas de Mar APARTMENT $$
(📞0297-414-5510; www.elfaro-patagonia.com.ar; r US$90, house US$140) This brand-new option consists of two shiny corrugated tin houses trimmed with varnished wood and with sea views. Guests can rent a comfortable four-bedroom house or a room for two. There's no street address. It's in front of the historic Casa Rabal near the port.

Hotel Indalo Inn HOTEL $$
(📞496-3004; www.indaloinn.com.ar; cnr Sarmiento & Roca; d/cabin US$78/110; 🐾) A proper yet somewhat indifferent hotel. Remodeled rooms are a bit of a squeeze, but feature good bedding and strong showers. The cabins are more expensive but offer sea views.

Alma Patagonica CAFE $$
(cnr Sarmiento & Roca; mains AR$115-136; ⏰11:30am-3pm & 7:30pm-midnight Mon-Sat) This restored century-old frontier bar is run with an eye on preserving local tradition. Homemade fish empanadas (baked, savory turnovers) are excellent, washed back with a massive cold beer. They also run Las Cabañas (p421), located one block away.

ℹ Information

Tourist Office (📞496-3013; Acceso Ruta 30; ⏰8am-8pm Dec-May) Very helpful, with maps, good tips on scenic outings and lodging information.

ℹ Getting There & Away

At a gas-station junction 180km south of Trelew, RP 30 splits off from RN 3 and heads 72km east to Camarones. Buses leave from the **bus terminal** (cnr 9 de Julio & Rivadavia). El Ñandú buses go to Trelew (AR$125 to AR$220, four hours) at 4pm on Monday, Wednesday and Friday. Etap goes to Comodoro Rivadavia (AR$195, 3½ hours) on Tuesday and Thursday at 1pm.

Local taxis make the 30-minute ride to Cabo Dos Bahías.

Patagonian Wildlife

Thanks to deep ocean currents that bring nutrients and abundant food, the coast of southern Argentina plays host to bountiful marine life. To see them hunt, court, nest and raise their young renews one's sense of wonder along these lonely Atlantic shores.

Magellanic Penguins

Adorable and thoroughly modern, penguins co-parent after chicks hatch in mid-November. See the action at Punta Tombo (p420), Ría Deseado (p428) and Bahía Bustamante (p425).

Southern Sea Lions

Found year-round along the southern coast of Argentina, these burly swimmers feed on squid and the odd penguin.

Commerson's Dolphins

These small dolphins often join boaters in play. See them all year at Playa Unión (p418), in Ría Deseado (p428) and at Puerto San Julián (p429).

Southern Right Whales

In spring, the shallow waters of Península Valdés (p410) attract thousands of these creatures to breed and bear young.

Orcas

To witness raw nature at work, visitors flock to Punta Norte (p414) on Península Valdés, where these powerful creatures almost beach themselves in the hunt for sea lions, from mid-February to mid-April.

Southern Elephant Seals

Consummate divers, these monsters spend most of the year at sea. In austral spring, spy on their breeding colony at Punta Delgada (p413) on Península Valdés. Watch for beachmasters – dominant males controlling harems of up to 100 females.

Clockwise from top left
1. Magellanic penguins 2. Southern sea lions
3. Commerson's dolphins 4. Southern right whale

Cabo Dos Bahías

A rough 30km southeast of Camarones, the isolated **Cabo Dos Bahías** (admission AR$50; ⊘ year-round) rookery attracts far fewer visitors than Punta Tombo, making it an excellent alternative. You'll be rewarded with orcas, a huge colony of nesting penguins in spring and summer, whales in winter, and a large concentration of guanacos and rheas. Seabirds, sea lions, foxes and fur seals are year-round residents.

You can pitch a tent for free at Cabo Dos Bahías Club Náutico or on any of the beaches en route from Camarones.

Comodoro Rivadavia

✏ 0297 / POP 177,000

Comodoro (as it's commonly known) is surrounded by dry hills of drilling rigs, oil tanks and wind-energy farms. Tourism in this dusty port usually means little more than a bus transfer. What this modern, hardworking city does provide is a gateway to nearby attractions with decent services (cue the Walmart). It sits at the eastern end of the Corredor Bioceánico highway that leads to Coyhaique, Chile.

Founded in 1901, Comodoro was once a transport hub linking ranches in nearby Sarmiento. In 1907 the town struck it rich when workers drilling for water found oil instead. With the country's first major gusher, Comodoro became a state pet, gaining a large port, airport and paved roads. Today it is a powerhouse in the now-privatized oil industry with the dubious status of the largest consumer of plasma TVs in Argentina. Although the current downswing of the oil industry looks foreboding, there's still a flashy casino and hot rods on the streets.

Commerce centers on principal streets Avs San Martín and Rivadavia. Between Mitre and Belgrano, San Martín has upscale boutiques and shops unknown to most of Patagonia.

◉ Sights

Museo Nacional del Petróleo　MUSEUM
(✏ 455-9558; admission AR$10; ⊘ 9am-5pm Tue-Fri, 3-6pm Sat) Museo Nacional del Petróleo gives an insider look at the social and historical aspects of petroleum development. Don't expect balanced treatment of oil issues – the museum was built by the former state oil agency YPF (it is now managed

by the Universidad Nacional de Patagonia). While its historical photos are interesting, the detailed models of tankers, refineries and the entire zone of exploitation are best left to the diehard. Guided tours are available.

The museum is in the suburb of General Mosconi, 3km north of downtown. Take a *remise* from downtown or bus 7 'Laprida' or 8 'Palazzo'; get off at La Anónima supermarket.

Museo Regional Patagónico　MUSEUM
(✏ 477-7101; cnr Av Rivadavia & Chacabuco; ⊘ 9am-6pm Mon-Fri, 11am-6pm Sat & Sun) FREE Decaying natural-history specimens overshadow some small yet entertaining archaeological and historical items, including well-crafted pottery, spear points and materials on early South African Boer immigrants.

☞ Tours

Several agencies arrange trips to Bosque Petrificado Sarmiento and Cueva de las Manos.

Ruta 40　TOUR
(✏ 0294-452-3378; www.ruta-40.com) If you're really up for a road trip, contact Ruta 40. The small, multilingual outfitter is based in Bariloche but some tours start in Comodoro, like the eight-day Ruta 40 tour, with stops at Puerto Deseado, Cueva de las Manos and several lovely *estancias* before ending up in El Calafate. Contact them for current rates and departure dates.

Circuito Ferroportuario　TRAIN TOUR
FREE The urban train tour Circuito Ferroportuario takes visitors on a circuit from the tourism office to visit containers, warehouses, historical installations and workshops on the port.

🛏 Sleeping

Catering mainly to business travelers and long-term laborers, lodging here fits two categories: the ritzy and the run-down. Brisk business means lodgings are overpriced and often full – book ahead.

Hotel Victoria　HOTEL $$
(✏ 446-0725; www.hotelvictoriacrd.com.ar; Belgrano 585; d/tr US$96/116) The friendliest hotel on the block, with soothing, good-sized rooms with firm twin beds, desks and cable TV, but oddly without internet. If the aroma of baking pastries is any indication, it's worth taking breakfast.

BAHÍA BUSTAMANTE

A number of coastal reserves feature Patagonia's diverse marine life, but few illuminate the exuberance of this ecosystem like this historic 80-hectare **estancia** (☎0297-480-1000, in Buenos Aires 011-4778-0125; www.bahiabustamante.com; s/d/tr sea cottage incl full board & activities US$500/620/750, basic 3-person cottage US$145; ☎) located between Trelew and Comodoro Rivadavia. The sprawling steppe, rolling grass dunes and pebble beaches beg you to bask in the slow rhythms of life on this deserted coast. Excursions are thoughtfully guided by bilingual naturalists, and include sea kayaking, trekking the on-site 65-million-year-old petrified forest and boat trips to see Magellanic penguins, sea lions and marine birds.

Another quirky footnote in Patagonian history, Bahía Bustamante was founded by an entrepreneurial Andalucian immigrant who used the abundant algae in the bay to manufacture agar-agar, a natural food thickener. At one point hundreds of workers lived on the *estancia*, which became a kind of Wild West, complete with a police station and jail cell. In pre-settlement times, Tehuelches traveled the area, leaving behind their small tools and middens.

These days the much-reduced algae harvests also include comestible seaweed, which is mostly exported to Japan. An *estancia* tour explains the sheep-farming operation, which is transitioning to better ecological practices. Grazing rotation promotes soil and native plant recovery and recently introduced merino hybrids are better adapted to the ecosystem.

The *estancia* has the sleepy feel of a ghost village coming back to life. Its heart is the former general store, now converted to a rustic-chic living room and dining area where you might dine on local lamb or seaweed crepes. Lodgings are in comfortable seafront cabins with big red loungers recycled from shipping palettes. For a more economical approach, cabins facing the steppe offer an optional salad box with provisions from the on-site greenhouse and à la carte excursions.

Once you've come all this way, it's optimal to stay at least three days. The time to see fauna is between mid-September and early March, with January and February ideal for swimming. Bird-watching is best during November hatching but it's also cool to watch sea lions nurse new pups in January. Most visitors fly into Comodoro, but if you have a car, it's worthwhile taking the scenic coastal route from nearby Camarones.

Lucania Palazzo Hotel
HOTEL $$$

(☎449-9300; www.lucania-palazzo.com; Moreno 676; s/d US$166/201; @☎) Comodoro's answer to the Trump Towers, the sparkling Palazzo offers ocean views from every room and tasteful modern decor, although ventilation could be better. While its features only add up to those of a solid chain hotel, there's a decent restaurant and the eager staff offers helpful recommendations.

WAM
BOUTIQUE HOTEL $$$

(☎406-8020; www.wamhotel.com.ar; Av Hipólito Yrigoyen 2196; d US$203; ❄@☎☲) Think industrial boutique, with an unfortunate office-building-like exterior. Contemporary rooms have crisp white linens, neutral tones and glass-walled tubs. There's restaurant service and a gym. Guests have access to spa, Jacuzzi and pool. Located just off the *costanera*, south of downtown.

✖ Eating

The oil boom has bankrolled a taste for fine dining. Look for the free *Sabores del Sur* restaurant directory in hotels.

Puerto Mitre
PIZZA $

(☎446-1201; Ameghino 620; mains AR$90; ☉noon-3pm & 8-11pm) The place for pizza and classic Argentine empanadas – staple traveler fare.

Chocolates
ICE CREAM $

(Av San Martín 231; cones AR$40; ☉9am-6pm; ☝) Ice-cream junkies will appreciate this parlor's selection of velvety chocolate and rich *dulce de leche* flavors. If you're traveling with children, bring them here to ride the miniature carousel.

★ La Tradición
PARRILLA $$

(☎446-5800; Mitre 675; mains AR$120-180; ☉noon-3pm & 8:30pm-midnight Mon-Sat) A favorite of townsfolk, this elegant *parrilla* grills excellent beef, whole roast lamb and crisp shoestring fries in a setting of white linens and oil paintings (literally, since their subjects are oil rigs!).

🍸 Drinking & Nightlife

Molly Malone CAFE
(📞 447-8333; cnr 9 de Julio & Av San Martín 292; ⊙ 7:30am-midnight Mon-Thu, 7:30am-3am Fri & Sat, 4pm-midnight Sun) Run by the Golden Oldies rugby club, this funky little restopub is a pleasant stop for an evening Quilmes, though you could also get breakfast or a set lunch. The food's just average but the atmosphere is fun and inviting.

☆ Entertainment

Cine Teatro Español CINEMA
(📞 447-7700; www.cinecr.com.ar; Av San Martín 668) A stately, old-fashioned cinema showing the latest Hollywood flicks.

ℹ Information

ACA (Automóvil Club Argentino; 📞 446-0876; cnr Dorrego & Alvear) Maps and road info.

Banco de la Nación (cnr Av San Martín & Güemes) Most of Comodoro's banks and ATMs, including this one, are along Avs San Martín or Rivadavia.

Hospital Regional (📞 444-2287; Av Hipólito Yrigoyen 950)

Post Office (cnr Av San Martín & Moreno)

Tourist Office (📞 444-0664; www.comodoro turismo.gob.ar; Av Rivadavia 430; ⊙ 8am-8pm Mon-Fri, 9am-3pm Sat & Sun) Friendly, well stocked and well organized.

ℹ Getting There & Away

The Corredor Bioceánico – RN 26, RP 20 and RP 55 – is a straight highway link to Coyhaique, Chile, and its Pacific port, Puerto Chacabuco. Developers are promoting this commercial transport route as an alternative to the Panama Canal, since the pass is open year-round and it is the continent's shortest distance between ports on both oceans. Paved RN 26, RP 20 and RN 40 lead to Esquel and Bariloche.

AIR

Aeropuerto General Mosconi (CRD; 📞 454-8190) is 9km north of town.

Aerolíneas Argentinas (📞 444-0050; Av Rivadavia 156) and **LAN** (📞 454-8160; Airport) fly a couple of times daily to Buenos Aires (one way from AR$2410).

Comodoro is the hub for **LADE** (📞 447-0585; Av Rivadavia 360), which wings it at least once a week to El Calafate (AR$912), Río Gallegos (AR$970), Trelew (AR$927), Ushuaia (AR$1529), Buenos Aires (AR$2102) and points in between. Schedules and routes change as often as the winds.

BUS

The chaotic **bus terminal** (Pellegrini 730) receives all buses plying RN 3. Stop at the helpful tourist desk to inquire about maps and travel assistance.

Most bus schedules are divided into northbound and southbound departures. **Andesmar** (📞 446-8894) departs five times daily (between 1:15am and 3pm) for points north including Trelew, Rawson and Puerto Madryn.

TAC (📞 444-3376) follows the same route and continues to Buenos Aires. **Etap** (📞 447-4841) runs to Esquel and Río Mayo daily, to Sarmiento four times daily and to Coyhaique, Chile, at 8am on Wednesday and Saturday.

Sportman (📞 444-2988) services Los Antiguos and connections to Chile Chico, via the town of Perito Moreno. **Taqsa/Marga** (📞 447-0564) goes to Bariloche and El Calafate in the evening.

Schedules are in constant flux; upon arrival at the bus terminal, ask at each bus line's desk for information on departure times.

Buses from Comodoro Rivadavia

DESTINATION	COST (AR$)	TIME (HR)
Bariloche	750-860	12
Buenos Aires	1615-1825	24
Coyhaique, Chile	681	11
El Calafate	1210	14
Esquel	530-610	10
Los Antiguos	410	5
Puerto Deseado	300	4
Puerto Madryn	433-533	6
Río Gallegos	715-815	10-12
Río Mayo	226	3½
Sarmiento	150-180	2
Trelew	378-464	5

ℹ Getting Around

Bus 8 'Directo Palazzo' goes directly to the airport from outside Comodoro's bus terminal. A taxi to the airport costs AR$130 from downtown.

Expreso Rada Tilly links the bus terminal to the nearby beach resort (AR$6) every 20 minutes on weekdays and every 30 minutes on weekends.

Rental cars are available from **Avis** (📞 454-9471; Airport) and **Localiza** (📞 446-1400; Airport). **Dubrovnik** (📞 444-0073; www.rentacar dubrovnik.com; Moreno 941) rents 4WD vehicles.

Puerto Deseado

📞 0297 / POP 14,200

Some 125km southeast of the RN 3 junction, RN 281 weaves through valleys of rippling pink rock, past guanacos in tufted grassland, to end at the serene and attractive deep-sea-fishing town of Puerto Deseado. While the town is ripe for revitalization, change takes a glacial pace here: witness the vintage trucks rusting on the streets like beached cetaceans. But the draw of the historic center, plus the submerged estuary of Ría Deseado, brimming with seabirds and marine wildlife, make Puerto Deseado a worthy detour.

In 1520 the estuary provided shelter to Hernando de Magallanes after a crippling storm waylaid his fleet; he dubbed the area 'Río de los Trabajos' (River of Labors).

In 1586 English privateer Cavendish explored the estuary and named it after his ship *Desire*, its name today. The port attracted fleets from around the world for whaling and seal hunting, compelling the Spanish crown to send a squadron of colonists under the command of Antonio de Viedma. After a harsh winter, more than 30 of them died of scurvy. Those who survived moved inland to form the short-lived colony of Floridablanca. In 1834 Darwin surveyed the estuary, as did Perito Moreno in 1876.

Puerto Deseado is two hours southeast of the RN 3 junction at Fitz Roy via dead-end RN 281. The center of activity is the axis formed by main streets San Martín and Almirante Brown.

◎ Sights & Activities

Estación del Ferrocarril
Patagónico   HISTORIC SITE
(admission by donation; ⊙4-7pm Mon-Sat) Train fans can check out the imposing English-designed train station off Av Oneto, built by Yugoslav stonecutters in 1908. Puerto Deseado was once the coastal terminus for a cargo and passenger route that hauled wool and lead from Chilean mines from Pico Truncado and Las Heras, located 280km northwest.

Vagón Histórico   LANDMARK
(cnr San Martín & Almirante Brown; ⊙5-8pm) In the center of town, this restored 1898 wagon is famous as the car from which rebel leader Facón Grande prepared the 'Patagonia Rebellion.' In 1979 the car was almost sold for scrap, but townspeople blocked the roads to stop the sale. A few blocks west is the attractive **Sociedad Española** (San Martín 1176), c 1915.

Museo Municipal Mario Brozoski   MUSEUM
(📞487-1358; cnr Colón & Belgrano; admission AR$15; ⊙8am-5pm Mon-Fri, 3-6pm Sat) Displays relics of the English corvette *Swift*, sunk off the coast of Deseado in 1776. Divers continue to recover artifacts from this wreck, which was discovered in 1982.

City Tour   FISHING
A self-guided tour is a good start if you want to catch the vibes of Deseado. Pick up a *Guía Historica* map (in Spanish) from either tourist office (p428).

👉 Tours

Darwin Expediciones   ADVENTURE TOUR
(📞0297-15-624-7554; www.darwin-expeditions. com; Av España 2601; Isla Pingüinos excursion AR$1200) Offers sea-kayaking trips, wildlife observation, and multiday nature and archaeology tours with knowledgeable guides. Its best seller is the EcoSafari tour of Reserva Natural Ría Deseado (AR$600), the agency's prime wildlife-watching tour, with sightings of dolphins, sea lions, Magellanic penguins and marine birdlife.

Los Vikingos   ADVENTURE TOUR
(📞0297-15-624-5141, 0297-15-624-4283; www.los vikingos.com.ar; Moreno & Prefectura Naval) Trips on land and sea. Tours, some led by marine biologists, include Reserva Natural Ría Deseado and Monumento Natural Bosques Petrificados. Contact via the website or by phone.

🛏 Sleeping

Ask at the tourist office about (relatively) nearby *estancias*.

Residencial Los Olmos   HOTEL $
(📞487-0077; Gregores 849; s/d/tr US$40/60/80; 🖗) A solid budget option kept spotless, this brick house has 19 small rooms with TV, ample heat and private bathrooms.

Tower Rock   APARTMENT $$
(📞in Buenos Aires 011-3935-0150, 011-3935-0188; www.tower-rock.com; Pueyrredón 385 or Almirante Zar 305; apt US$85-165; ❄🖗) With studios and multiple-bedroom apartments, this comfortable option offers peace and privacy. Apartments come fully equipped with outfitted kitchen, flat-screen TV, lock box and daily maid service. Hosts Patricia and Jorge are happy to answer questions.

Hotel Los Acantilados   HOTEL $$
(📞487-2167; www.hotelosacantilados.com; cnr Pueyrredón & Av España; d superior US$91; @🖗)

PATAGONIA PUERTO DESEADO

More inspiring from outside than in, these cliff-top digs boast an extensive lounge with fireplace: the perfect chill spot. Mattresses are firm and comfortable. The dining room looks out on the waterfront; the few rooms with views go fast.

✕ Eating

Puerto Deseado has chicken rotisseries all over town, good for a quick bite.

Lo de Piola   CAFE $$
(☎487-2644; San Martín 1280; mains AR$80-167; ⊙11:30am-10pm Mon-Sat) Recommended by locals, this unassuming *confitería* serves satisfying meals and snacks, with grilled meats, beer and wine.

Puerto Cristal   SEAFOOD $$
(Av España 1698; mains AR$85-165; ⊙noon-3pm & 8pm-midnight Thu-Tue) Bridezilla decor aside, this popular seafood haunt satisfies with sturdy portions of grilled fish, fried calamari and an extensive wine selection.

❶ Information

Banks, ATMs, *locutorios* and internet options are all found along San Martín.

Banco de la Patagonia (San Martín & Almirante Brown)

CIS Tours (☎487-2864; www.cistours.com.ar; San Martín 916) Handles local tours and flight reservations.

Dirección Municipal de Turismo (☎487-0220; http://puertodeseado.tur.ar; San Martín 1525; ⊙8am-8pm) Helpful with maps; there's another English-speaking desk at the **bus terminal** (Sargento Cabral 1302), but its hours are limited. See their Facebook page for events.

Hospital Distrital (☎487-0200; España 991)

Post Office (San Martín 1075)

❶ Getting There & Around

The **bus terminal** (Sargento Cabral 1302) is on the northeast side of town, nine long blocks and slightly uphill from San Martín and Av Oneto. **Taxis** (☎487-2288, 487-0645) are metered.

There are five daily departures to Comodoro Rivadavia (AR$295, four hours) with **La Unión** (☎487-0188) and **Sportman** (☎487-0013). Sportman also goes to Río Gallegos (AR$700, 13 hours) twice daily. Schedules change frequently; inquire at the bus terminal about departures.

If you're thinking of getting off at godforsaken Fitz Roy (where locals claim the only thing to see is the wind!) to make progress toward Comodoro or Río Gallegos, think again: buses arrive at a demonic hour and the only place to crash is the campground behind Multirubro La Illusion.

Reserva Natural Ría Deseado & Parque Interjurisdiccional Marino Isla Pingüino

Flanked by sandy cliffs, the aquamarine waters here create sculpted seascapes you won't forget. Considered one of South America's most important marine preserves, Ría Deseado is the unique result of a river abandoning its bed, allowing the Atlantic to invade 40km inland and create a perfect shelter for marine life. The recent designation of Parque Interjurisdiccional Marino Isla Pingüino (a mouthful, but essentially a national park) will likely expand offerings for visitors.

The marine life is abundant. Several islands and other sites provide nesting habitats for seabirds, including Magellanic penguins, petrels, oystercatchers, herons, terns and five species of cormorant. Isla Chaffers is the main spot for the penguins, while Banco Cormorán offers protection to rock cormorants and the striking gray cormorant. Isla Pingüino has nesting rockhoppers (arriving mid-October) and elephant seals. Commerson's dolphins, sea lions, guanacos and ñandús (ostrich-like rheas) can also be seen while touring the estuary.

The best time to visit is December to April. Darwin Expediciones (p427) runs circuits that take in viewing of Commerson's dolphins, Isla Chaffers, Banco Cormorán as well as a walk to a penguin colony. The main attraction of the all-day Isla Pingüinos excursion (AR$1200) is the punked-out rockhopper penguins with spiky yellow and black head feathers, but the tour also includes wildlife-watching, sailing and hiking. Tours have a four-person minimum. Los Vikingos (p427) makes similar excursions with bilingual guides and organizes overland trips.

Monumento Natural Bosques Petrificados

During Jurassic times, 150 million years ago, this area enjoyed a humid, temperate climate with flourishing forests, but intense volcanic activity buried them in ash. Erosion later exposed the mineralized *Proaraucaria* trees (ancestors of the modern araucaria, unique to the southern hemisphere), up to 3m in diameter and 35m in length. Today the 150-sq-km **Monumento Natural Bosques Petrificados** (Petrified Forests Natural Monument; ⊙9am-9pm year-round) FREE has a small visitor center, English-language brochure and short interpretive trail, leading from park headquarters to the largest concentration of petrified trees. Until its legal protection in 1954, the area was plundered for some of its finest specimens; these days you're not allowed to take home souvenirs.

The park is 157km southwest of Caleta Olivia, accessed from the good gravel RP 49, leading 50km west from a turnoff at Km2074 on RN 3. There's no public transportation. Buses from Caleta Olivia leave visitors at the junction, but you may wait several hours for a lift into the park. Los Vikingos (p427) runs tours from Puerto Deseado.

There's basic camping and provisions at **La Paloma**, 20km before park headquarters. Camping in the park is prohibited.

Puerto San Julián

☑02962 / POP 7900

The perfect desolate-yet-charismatic locale for an art film, this small town bakes in bright light and dust, in stark contrast to the startling blue of the bay. Considered the cradle of Patagonian history, the port of San Julián was first landed in 1520 by Magellan, whose encounter with local Tehuelches provided the region's mythical moniker. Viedma, Drake and Darwin followed. While its human history is proudly put forth, the landscape speaks of geologic revolutions, with its exposed, striated layers, rolling hills and golden cliffs.

Puerto San Julián's first non-native settlers came from the Falkland Islands (Islas Malvinas) with the late-19th-century wool boom. Scots followed with the San Julián Sheep Farming Company, which became the region's primary economic force for nearly a century. Recent growth has the city developing like never before with mining and seafood-processing industries; there's also a local university. For travelers, it is a relaxed and welcoming stop, as well as a great place to see Commerson's dolphins.

◉ Sights & Activities

The most popular attractions are the museum and the penguin colony. Another option is trekking the coastline and checking out the abundant birdlife. For more information, consult the tourist information booth in the bus terminal, or the branch on the highway.

Museo Nao Victoria   MUSEUM
(admission AR$15; ⊙8am-9:30pm) Relive Magellan's landing at this museum and theme park with life-sized figures cloaked in armor and shown celebrating Mass and battling mutiny, at the port on a reproduction of the original ship.

Circuito Costero   DRIVING TOUR
Take a *remise* or your own poor, abused rental car on the incredibly scenic 30km drive following Bahía San Julián on a dirt road. A series of golden bluffs divides beautiful beaches with drastic tides. The area includes a sea-lion colony and the penitent attraction of Monte Cristo (with its stations of the cross).

☞ Tours

Banco Cormorán   WILDLIFE-WATCHING
(admission per person AR$150; ⊙Oct-Apr) The last census found 130,000 penguins inhabiting this stretch of Bahía San Julián, which you can visit by boat. When conditions permit, you'll be able to step off the boat and walk around an island where penguins swim, doze and guard their eggs. From December to March there's a good chance you'll see Commerson's dolphins, the world's smallest dolphins.

The tour also stops at Banco Justicia's cormorant rookeries.

Expediciones Pinocho   TOUR
(☑454600; www.pinochoexcursiones.com.ar; Costanera s/n; ⊙9am-9pm Jan & Feb) Two-hour excursions on Bahía San Julián are run by a marine-biologist-led team at Expediciones Pinocho. The office is in a small cabin on the waterfront.

🛏 Sleeping & Eating

Hotel Ocean   HOTEL $
(☑452350; San Martín 959; s/d/tr US$46/60/68; ☏) This remodeled brick building has attractive, well-scrubbed rooms with firm beds and a backdrop of tropical tones. Friendly staff are happy to assist travelers – when you're tired and hungry and the bus has dropped you off in town around midnight (as it probably will), they'll help you find an open restaurant.

Camping Municipal   CAMPGROUND $
(☑454506; Magallanes 650; tent US$5, RV US$7-10) On the waterfront at the north end of Vélez Sarsfield, this full-service campground has hot showers, laundry and windbreaks.

Hostería Miramar GUESTHOUSE $
(✆454626; hosteriamiramar@uvc.com.ar; San Martín 210; d US$68; @ 🛜) Natural light fills this cheerful waterfront option. The 11 rooms, including a family-sized apartment, are superclean with TV, decent beds and carpeted floors. Showers spray in powerful torrents.

Costanera Hotel HOTEL $
(✆452300; www.costanerahotel.com; 25 de Mayo 917; s/d/tr US$55/69/80; 🛜) After major renovations, this waterfront mainstay feels new again. Rooms are standard but tidy, and the restaurant, open evenings only, is passable.

Hotel Bahía HOTEL $$
(✆453144; www.hotelbahiasanjulian.com.ar; San Martín 1075; s/d/tr US$65/87/165; @🛜) This glass-front hotel feels decadent in a place like San Julián. Rooms are modern and beds firm, while TV and laundry service are perks. The cafe-bar is open to the public.

★ **Naos** SEAFOOD $$
(Costanera s/n; mains AR$85-145; ☺8-11pm) The best restaurant in town sits on the waterfront but without ocean views. Still, you will be entertained enough with the excellent wine recommendations, fresh fish and salads. Starters feature local Patagonian game like guanaco empanadas and *escabeche de vizcacha*, marinated game. Go early, as the tables fill up.

🛍 Shopping

Centro Artesenal Municipal ARTS, CRAFTS
(Costanera s/n; ☺9am-7pm Mon-Fri) A cool cooperative selling handmade ceramics, woven goods and an excellent but powerful homemade cherry liqueur.

ℹ Information

Banco Santa Cruz (cnr San Martín & Moreno) Has a Link ATM.

Dirección de Turismo (✆454396; www.san julian.gov.ar; San Martín 1552; ☺8am-midnight Mon-Fri, 9am-10pm Sat & Sun) The main office is located in the bus terminal, with friendly service. A new office at the **rotunda** (RN 3; open 7am to 6pm from December to February) is useful if you're traveling by car but not by bus, as the town is still a good distance away and transport is infrequent.

Post Office (cnr San Martín & Belgrano)

ℹ Getting There & Away

BUS

Most RN 3 buses visit Puerto San Julián's **bus terminal** (San Martín 1552) at insane hours. Before settling for a bus that will drop you off in the port at 4am, try **Don Otto** (✆452072), which delivers southbound travelers to San Julián at civilized evening hours. **Via Tac** (✆454049) goes to Puerto Madryn (AR$840, 12 hours). **Andesmar** (✆454403) goes to Comodoro Rivadavia (AR$385, six hours). **Taqsa/Marga** (✆454667) goes to Bariloche (AR$1170, 14 hours) and Río Gallegos (AR$370, 4½ hours) at 4am, where travelers can make connections south.

There are slightly more expensive door-to-door service options, all operating Monday to Saturday in the early morning hours. **Cerro San Lorenzo** (✆452403; Berutti 970) serves Gobernador Gregores at 8am (AR$300, four hours).

Bus schedules may change, so always confirm departures ahead of time.

Parque Nacional Monte León

Inaugurated in 2004, this fine coastal national park protects over 600 sq km of striking headlands and archetypal Patagonian steppe, and 40km of dramatic coastline with bays, beaches and tidal flats. Once a hunting ground for nomads, and later frequented by the Tehuelche, this former *estancia* is home to abundant Magellanic penguins, sea lions, guanacos and pumas. Bring binoculars: the wildlife-watching is prime.

Hiking along the coastline, with its unusual geographic features, is best when low tide exposes stretches of sandy and rocky beach. In October 2006 the park lost its signature landscape attraction, **La Olla** (a huge cave-like structure eroded by the ocean), when it collapsed from repeated tidal action. Accessible at low tide, **Isla Monte León** is a high offshore sea stack that was heavily mined for guano between 1933 and 1960. Now it has been recolonized by cormorants, Dominican gulls, skuas and other seabirds. Use caution and know the tide tables before setting out: the tidal range is great, exposed rocks are slippery and the water returns quickly.

Nature trails split off from the main road, leading to the coast. The **penguin trail** crosses the steppe, leading to an overlook of the rookery. It's forbidden to leave the trail, but seeing these 75,000 couples shouldn't be difficult. The roundtrip takes 1½ hours. Cars can reach the prominent cliff **Cabeza de León** (Lion's Head), where a 20-minute trail leads to the sea-lion colony.

Campers must stay in the designated camping area. The other lodging option is **Hostería Monte León** (✆in Buenos Aires 011-6155-1360; www.monteleon-patagonia.com; d incl half-board US$490; ☺Nov-Apr), a refurbished century-old *casco* (ranch house) of a charming 1895 *estancia*. The four-bedroom house retains the spartan yet elegant style of the Patagonian farmhouse, with rod-iron beds, fireplaces with handpainted tiles and tasteful original furnishings. There's also a wonderful collection of fossils, bones and photography books.

For boat excursions or fly-fishing for steelhead, consult with the **park office** (www.pnmonteleon.com.ar). The park entrance is 30km south of Comandante Luis Piedrabuena or 205km north of Río Gallegos, directly off RN 3. Watch for it carefully as signage is poor. Note that beach access is impossible after heavy rains, when the clay roads become impassible.

Río Gallegos

📞 02966 / POP 95,800

Hardly a tourist destination, this coal shipping, oil-refining and wool-raising hub is a busy port with a few merits for travelers. Since the reign of the Kirchners, the capital city of their home province has been spruced up and spit polished. Outside of town, visitors can find some of the continent's best fly-fishing, traditional *estancias* and amazingly low tides (retreating 14m). Traveler services are good here but most zip through en route to El Calafate, Puerto Natales or Ushuaia.

Gallegos' economy revolves around nearby oilfields, with coal deposits shipped to ocean-going vessels at Punta Loyola. Home to a large military base, the city played an active role during the Falklands War. The main street, formerly Roca, was renamed Kirchner in honor of the former president.

◉ Sights

Museo Provincial Padre Jesús Molina   MUSEUM
(📞426427; cnr Av San Martín & Ramón y Cajal; AR$5; ☺9am-7pm Mon-Fri, 11am-7pm Sat & Sun) FREE Satiate your appetite for dinosaur dioramas and modern art at this museum offering exhibits on anthropology, paleontology, geology and fine arts. The Tehuelche ethnology exhibit includes fascinating photographs and local history.

Museo de Arte Eduardo Minnicelli   MUSEUM
(📞436323; Maipú 13; ☺8:30am-7pm Tue-Fri, 2-6pm Sat & Sun) FREE Shows rotating exhibits from larger museums and paintings by Santa Cruz artists, with a mission to educate through art. Also a good spot to get news on local cultural gatherings.

Museo Malvinas Argentinas   MUSEUM
(📞437618; cnr Pasteur & Av San Martín; ☺11am-6pm Mon-Fri, 10am-5pm Sat & Sun) FREE Perhaps a must-see for Brits, this museum gets inside the Argentine claim to the Islas Malvinas. New exhibits include signs made by ex-combatants and a video on the subject in English.

Plaza San Martín   PLAZA
Pretty, with quiet benches in the shade of poplars and purple-blossom jacarandas.

Museo de los Pioneros   MUSEUM
(📞437763; cnr Elcano & Alberdi; ☺10am-5pm) FREE In a prefabricated 1890s metal-clad house shipped from England, this museum has good displays on early immigrant life.

Funda Cruz   CULTURAL CENTER
(G Lista 60; ☺4-8pm Fri-Sun) An attractive, imported, prefabricated wooden house. Once a customs office, it now hosts cultural activities as well as a *salón de té* (teahouse).

☞ Tours

The large penguin rookery at Cabo Vírgenes, 140km southeast of Río Gallegos, can be visited from October to March. Excursions can be booked through **Al Sur Turismo** (📞436743; www.alsurturismo.com.ar; Errazuriz 194); an eight-hour trip costs AR$700 per person, with a minimum of three travelers (plus AR$20 park admission). Prices go up for smaller groups.

🛏 Sleeping

Since hotels cater mainly to business travelers, good-value budget accommodations are scarce.

El Viejo Miramar   HOTEL $
(📞430401; hotelviejomiramar@yahoo.com.ar; Av Kirchner 1630; d US$58) Snug carpeted rooms and spotless bathrooms make this choice a good one. At the time of research it was changing ownership. Rates include breakfast.

Hotel Covadonga   HOTEL $
(📞420190; www.hotel-alonso.com.ar; Av Kirchner 1244; d/tr with bathroom US$55/70, without bathroom US$50/60; 🛜) Good value and grandmotherly, the tidy Covadonga has large rooms with creaky floors, and a sunny living room with worn leather sofas. Rooms with private bathrooms are worth the upgrade.

Río Gallegos

Hostel Elcira

HOSTEL $

(☑429856; Zuccarino 431; dm/d US$17/40; 🛜)
An impeccable yet kitschy family home with
friendly hosts. It's far from the town center
but just a 10-minute walk from the bus
terminal.

Hotel Sehuen

HOTEL $

(☑425683; www.hotelsehuen.com; Rawson 160; d
from US$48) In a town short of budget rooms,
this will do, but it seems overpriced. Rooms
are small, thin walled and bathrooms posi-
tively tiny. Local newspapers and a basic buffet are available in the ample breakfast area.

Hotel Aire de Patagonia

BOUTIQUE HOTEL $$

(☑444950; www.hotelairepatagonia.com.ar; Vélez
Sársfield 58; s/d US$79/89; 🛜) Modern but
showing a little wear and tear, this wel-
coming boutique hotel has rooms with soft
Egyptian cotton sheets, radiant floors and
flat-screen TVs. The cute *confitería* is a good
spot for a quiet espresso or board game.

🍴 Eating

Mostaza

FAST FOOD $

(Alberdi 9400; mains AR$53-106; ⊙9am-11:30pm
Mon-Sat, 10am-midnight Sun) Modern fast food
with extensive hours and decent versions of
the basics: sandwiches, salads and burgers.
Features neat and minimalist decor and a
playhouse to entertain children.

Pizza Express

PIZZA $

(☑434400; Av San Martín 650; pizzas AR$60-90;
⊙11am-late) Cheap and casual, with service
that's friendlier than you'll find elsewhere in
town, this is where students and families dine
on burgers, gnocchi and salads, and older
gents share big bottles of cold Quilmes beer.

★La Lechuza

ARGENTINE $$

(☑425421; Sarmiento 134; mains AR$115-168;
⊙11:30am-4pm & 8pm-midnight) Hands down
the most ambient eatery in Río Gallegos is
this chic pizzeria and restaurant that first
found success in El Calafate. The room is

Río Gallegos

◎ Sights
1	Funda Cruz	C1
2	Museo de Arte Eduardo Minnicelli	C3
3	Museo de los Pioneros	A2
4	Museo Malvinas Argentinas	C4
5	Museo Provincial Padre Jesús Molina	C4
6	Plaza San Martín	C3

◎ Activities, Courses & Tours
7	Al Sur Turismo	D3

◎ Sleeping
8	El Viejo Miramar	A3
9	Hotel Aire de Patagonia	B3
10	Hotel Covadonga	B3
11	Hotel Sehuen	B2

◎ Eating
12	Buffalo Grill	C1
13	La Lechuza	C2
14	Mostaza	C2
15	Pizza Express	C3

low-lit, with walls sheathed in old newspapers and wine crates. There's an encyclopedic list of pizzas, including spinach, caprese and Patagonian lamb and mushroom. Also offers wines and liquor.

Buffalo Grill AMERICAN $$$
(☑ 439511; G Lista 198; mains AR$180-298; ⊗ noon-2:30pm & 8:30pm-midnight) American Tex-Mex has arrived in Patagonia. Buffalo wings, potato skins and steak dishes are just some of the unlikely but well-executed offerings served alongside a tiny bottle of Tabasco. Fajitas come with abundant, sizzling toppings – we only hope the leaden tortillas find improvement.

❶ Information

Banks on Av Kirchner have ATMs. Internet is widely available in internet cafes and some restaurants.

ACA (Automóvil Club Argentino; ☑ 420477; Orkeke 10) Gas station, maps and traveler services.

Centro de Informes Turistico (Av San Martín s/n; ⊗ 9am-8pm Oct-Apr) Useful info kiosk on median strip.

Hospital Regional (☑ 420289; José Ingenieros 98)

Immigration Office (☑ 420205; Urquiza 144; ⊗ 9am-3pm Mon-Fri)

Municipal Tourist Office (☑ 436920; www.turismo.riogallegos.gov.ar; Av Beccar 126; ⊗ 8am-6pm Mon-Fri, 8am-8pm Sat & Sun) Helpful

tourist office outside the downtown area. A desk at the bus terminal keeps sporadic hours.

Post Office (cnr Avs Kirchner & San Martín)

Provincial Tourist Office (☑ 438725; Av Kirchner 863; ⊗ 9am-4pm Mon-Fri) Most helpful, with maps, bilingual staff and detailed info.

❶ Getting There & Away

AIR

Río Gallegos' airport is 7km northwest of town.

The following are one-way base rates. **Aerolíneas Argentinas** (☑ 0810-2228-6527; Av San Martín 545) flies daily to Buenos Aires (AR$3170) and frequently to Ushuaia (AR$645). **LADE** (☑ 422316; Fagnano 53) flies several times a week to Buenos Aires (AR$2102), Río Grande (AR$540), El Calafate (AR$594), Comodoro Rivadavia (AR$993) and Ushuaia (AR$882). **LAN** (☑ 02966-457189; www.lan.com) also has a ticket counter at the airport.

BUS

Río Gallegos' **bus terminal** (cnr RN 3 & Av Eva Perón) is about 3km southwest of the city center. Companies include **El Pingüino** (☑ 442169), **Don Otto** (☑ 442160), **Bus Sur** (☑ 442687), **Andesmar** (☑ 442195), **Sportman** (☑ 442595) and **TAC** (☑ 442042). Companies going to Chile include **Ghisoni** (☑ 457047), **Pacheco** (☑ 442765) and **Tecni-Austral** (☑ 442427). **Taqsa/Marga** (☑ 442003; www.taqsa.com.ar; Estrada 71) beelines straight from the airport to Puerto Natales and El Calafate.

Buses from Río Gallegos

DESTINATION	COST (AR$)	TIME (HR)
Buenos Aires	2680	36-40
Comodoro Rivadavia	715	9-11
El Calafate	360	4
El Chaltén	410	9
Esquel	1150	19
Puerto Madryn	1151	15-20
Puerto San Julián	370	4½
Punta Arenas (Chile)	300	5-6
Río Grande	488	8-10
Trelew	1091	14-17
Ushuaia	628	12

❶ Getting Around

It's easy to share metered taxis (AR$60) between the city center, the bus terminal and the airport. From Av Kirchner, buses marked 'B' or 'terminal' link the city center and the bus terminal (AR$8.50).

Car rental is expensive due to the poor conditions of the roads to most places of interest. Despite exchange rates, rental deals are often better in Punta Arenas, Chile. For local rentals, try **Riestra Rent A Car** (☑421321; www.riestra rentacar.com; Av San Martín 1508).

Around Río Gallegos

From September through March Magellanic penguins nest at **Reserva Provincial Cabo Vírgenes** (entry AR$20), Argentina's second-largest penguin rookery. There's also a lighthouse and snack bar that's open seasonally. It's 140km from Río Gallegos on slow gravel roads; the drive can take three hours one way.

Travel agencies in Río Gallegos offer day trips to both the *estancia* and reserve starting in mid-November.

INLAND PATAGONIA

Save for the travel hubs of El Calafate and El Chaltén, RN 40 and its offshoots are a bit of a backwater. The ultimate road trip, RN 40 parallels the backbone of the Andes, where ñandús doodle through sagebrush, trucks kick up whirling dust and gas stations rise on the horizon like oases.

Now that most of the 1228km stretch between Esquel and El Calafate is paved, travel is considerably easier, although rough parts remain. For now, public transport remains limited to a few summer-only buses and tourist shuttle services, and driving requires both preparation and patience.

RN 40 parallels the Andes from north of Bariloche to the border with Chile near Puerto Natales, then cuts east to the Atlantic Coast. Highlights include the Perito Moreno and Los Glaciares national parks, the rock art of Cueva de las Manos and remote *estancias*.

This section picks up RN 40 in Esquel, it continues south paved but with large potholes. At the time of research, the 100km between Gobernador Gregores and Tres Lagos were still unpaved.

Esquel

☑ 02945 / POP 32,400 / ELEV 570M

If you tire of the gnome-in-the-chocolate-shop ambience of Bariloche and other cutesy Lakes District destinations, regular old Esquel will feel like a breath of fresh air. Set in western Chubut's dramatic, hikeable foothills, Esquel is a hub for Parque Nacional Los Alerces and an easygoing, friendly base camp for abundant adventure activities – the perfect place to chill after hard travel on RN 40.

Founded at the turn of the 20th century, Esquel is the region's main livestock and commercial center. It's also the historical southern end of the line for *La Trochita*, the narrow-gauge steam train. The town takes its name from the Mapudungun, and means either 'bog' or 'place of the thistles.'

RN 259 zigzags through town to the junction with RN 40, which heads north to El Bolsón and south to Comodoro Rivadavia. South of town, RN 259 passes a junction for Parque Nacional Los Alerces en route to Trevelin.

LA TROCHITA: THE OLD PATAGONIAN EXPRESS

Clearly an anachronism in the jet age, Ferrocarril Roca's **La Trochita** (☑02945-451403; AR$400), Argentina's famous narrow-gauge steam train, averages less than 30km/h on its meandering journey between Esquel and El Maitén – at top speed. The train Paul Theroux facetiously called *The Old Patagonian Express* provides both a tourist attraction and a service for local citizens.

Like many state projects, its completion seemed an interminable process, beginning in 1906 and reaching completion in 1945. It has suffered some of the oddest mishaps in railroad history. In the late 1950s and early 1960s, the train was derailed three times by high winds, and ice has caused other derailments. In 1979 it collided with a cow.

La Trochita's original 402km route between Esquel and Ingeniero Jacobacci was probably the world's longest remaining steam-train line. Belgian Baldwin and German Henschel engines refilled their 4000L water tanks at strategically placed *parajes* (pumps) every 40km to 45km. Most of the passenger cars, heated by wood stoves, date from 1922, as do the freight cars.

During summer the **Tren Turístico** (tickets AR$250; ☺10am twice weekly, additional departures Jan-Feb) travels from Roca train station in Esquel to Nahuel Pan, 20km east. At Nahuel Pan, the train stops for photo ops and a small artisan market.

DON'T MISS

THRU TREKKING PATAGONIA

The US has the Appalachian Trail, New Zealand has the Te Araroa Trail, and now Argentina has **Huella Andina** (huellaandina.desarrolloturistico.gov.ar), the country's first long-distance trail. Huella, literally 'footprint,' is the local term for footpaths.

The project was the brainchild of Estefanía Chereguini and Walter Oszust, two young mountaineers in Esquel. It took them three years to mark 430km of trails through the Andes with 31 stages. Huella Andina crosses from Neuquén to Chubut, passing through five national parks, including Parque Nacional Los Alerces, and private lands. Scenery shifts from araucaria to alerce forest, from mountain heights to river valleys and pristine lakes. It's marked by a couple of blue and white parallel bands.

Now managed by the Ministerio Nacional de Turismo, the project is expected to eventually feature over 600km of linked trails. Visit the website for details on trail stages and a map.

Sights & Activities

Esquel's best attractions are of the outdoor variety, notably Parque Nacional Los Alerces and La Hoya. Esquel's nearby lakes and rivers offer excellent **fly fishing**, with the season running from November to April. You can purchase a license at the ACA (p437) inside the YPF gas station. **Mountain biking** is a good way to explore the surrounding hills and trails.

Museo de Culturas Originarias Patagónicas
MUSEUM

(451929; Nahuel Pan; donations accepted; 7am-1pm & 3-9pm Mon-Fri, 5-9pm Sat & Sun) **FREE** Displays a modest collection of Mapuche artifacts; *La Trochita* stops here, 20km east of Esquel.

Museo del Tren
MUSEUM

(451403; cnr Roggero & Urquiza; 9:30am-noon Mon, Wed & Fri) **FREE** Just outside town, this train museum is in the Roca train station where *La Trochita*, Argentina's famous narrow-gauge steam train, stops. In summer several tour agencies sell tickets for roundtrip rides on the antique train.

Cerro La Hoya
SNOW SPORTS

(453018; www.cerrolahoya.com; lift ticket adult/child AR$380/240; skiing Jun-Oct) Despite wide open bowls and some of Argentina's best powder skiing, this 1350m resort is just starting to become well known. While cheaper and less crowded than Bariloche, it is smaller and comparatively tame, ideal for families. Equipment can be rented on-site or at sport shops in Esquel. There are minibus transfers and taxi service. It's 13km north of Esquel.

Summer activities include hiking, chairlift rides and horseback riding.

Coyote Bikes
BICYCLE RENTAL

(455505; www.coyotebikes.com.ar; Rivadavia 887; all-day rental AR$120; 9am-1pm & 3:30-8pm Mon-Fri, 9am-1pm Sat) For mountain-bike rentals and trail details in summer.

Tours

Independent and nationally certified guides **Estefanía Chereguini** (02945-549357; echereguini@gmail.com) and **Walter Oszust** (02945-682915; walteroszust@gmail.com), the creators of Huella Andina, lead guided hikes in Parque Nacional Los Alerces and in off-the-beaten path Patagonia. English spoken.

Circuito Lacuestre
BOAT TOUR

Numerous travel agencies sell tickets for the Circuito Lacustre boat excursion in Parque Nacional Los Alerces; buying a ticket in Esquel assures a place on the often-crowded trip. Full-day excursions, including the lake cruise, cost AR$490 when sailing from Puerto Chucao or slightly more from Puerto Limonao, including transfers to and from the park.

EPA
ADVENTURE TOUR

(Expediciones Patagonia Aventura; 457015; www.epaexpediciones.com; Av Fontana 484) Offers rafting, canyoning, horseback riding and trekking. Those whitewater rafting (half-day AR$1550 with transport) on Río Corcovado (90km away) can overnight at the recommended riverside hostel. Canopy tours, horseback riding and trekking use the mountain center, an attractive wooden lodge in Parque Nacional Los Alerces. Guests have access to kayaks, and camping is also available.

✨ Festivals & Events

Semana de Esquel
CULTURAL

A week-long February event that celebrates the city's 1906 founding.

Fiesta Nacional de Esquí
SPORTS

(National Skiing Festival) Takes place in mid-September at La Hoya.

🛌 Sleeping

Esquel has many accommodations; check with the tourist office (p437) for listings too, which include cabins and apartments geared for ski vacations.

★ Sol Azul
HOSTEL $

(☑455193; www.hostelsolazul.com.ar; Rivadavia 2869; dm US$15; @🛜) With the good looks of a mountain lodge, this welcoming hostel ups the ante with a sauna and a fully decked-out kitchen with industrial stoves lined with spices. There are also dinners serving local products. Dorms are in a house at the back, with small but tidy bathrooms. It's a taxi ride to the center, on the northern edge of town. Breakfast is not included.

Hostería Angelina
INN $

(☑452763; www.hosteriaangelina.com.ar; Av Alvear 758; d US$65-85; @🛜) Hospitable and polished, with a courtyard fountain, Angelina follows international standards with professional service and a good breakfast buffet.

Planeta Hostel
HOSTEL $

(☑456846; www.planetahostel.com; Av Alvear 1021; dm/d US$25/70; 🛜) This old but boldly painted downtown house features friendly service but cramped rooms. Down comforters, a spotless communal kitchen and a TV lounge are a cut above the usual.

Hostería La Chacra
B&B $$

(☑452802; www.lachacrapatagonia.com; RN 259, Km5; d/tr US$90/120; @🛜⛵) If you want a shot of local culture, nothing is better than this country lodging in a 1970s home with ample bright rooms, generous gringo breakfasts and thick down bedding. The owner Rini is a consummate host and expert on local Welsh history. Get here via shuttle, taxi or Trevelin bus – they pass hourly.

Sur Sur
HOTEL $$

(www.hotelsursur.com; Av Fontana 282; d/tr US$75/90; 🛜) A popular option, this family enterprise delivers warmth and comfort. Small tiled rooms feature TV, fan and hairdryers, and the hallways are decked with regional photos taken by former guests. Breakfast is served buffet-style.

Plaza Esquel Hostería & Spa
HOTEL $$

(☑457002; www.plazaesquel.com.ar; Av Ameghino 713; d/superior incl spa US$80/96; @🛜) On the plaza, this attractive *hostería* has small rooms with modern decor but a little wear and tear. The spa features a sauna and Jacuzzi, but not much ambience.

★ Las Bayas Hotel
BOUTIQUE HOTEL $$$

(☑455800; www.lasbayashotel.com; Av Alvear 985; d/tr US$255/270; 🛜) Simply lovely, this elegant boutique lodging sits heads and tails above other hotels. Tasteful decor includes wood accents, warm woolen throws and modern touches. Spacious rooms feature LCD screens and DVD libraries, kitchenettes, and tubs with massage jets. There are also spa services available and deep discounts in low season.

BIG FEET, TALL TALES

Say 'Patagonia' and most think of fuzzy outdoor clothes, but the name that has come to symbolize the world's end still invites hot debate as to its origin.

One theory links the term 'Patagón' to a fictional monster in a best-selling 16th-century Spanish romance of the period, co-opted by Magellan's crew to describe the Tehuelche as they wintered in 1520 at Puerto San Julián. Crew member and Italian nobleman, Antonio Pigafetta, described one Tehuelche as 'so tall we reached only to his waist... He was dressed in the skins of animals skillfully sewn together... His feet were shod with the same kind of skins, which covered his feet in the manner of shoes... The captain-general [Magellan] called these people Patagoni.'

Another theory suggests that the name comes from the Spanish *pata*, meaning paw or foot. No evidence corroborates the claim that the Tehuelche boasted unusually big feet (it's possible that the skins they wore made their feet seem exceptionally large). But it's good fodder for the genre of travelers' tales, where first impressions loom larger than life.

Hostería Canela B&B
B&B $$$

(☑453890; www.canelaesquel.com; cnr Los Notros & Los Radales, Villa Ayelén; d/tr US$165/203, q apt US$280; ☎) Veronica and Jorge's refined B&B, tucked away in a pine forest 2km outside the town center, feels elegant and comfortable, an ideal match for mature guests. The English-speaking owners offer in-room tea service and the comfortable beds are topped with pristine white linens.

✖ Eating

Dimitri Coffeehouse
CAFE $

(Rivadavia 805; mains AR$45-80; ☺9am-8pm Mon-Sat) Overboard adorable, this pastel cafe serves big salads, baked goods and sandwiches on mismatched china. There's both beer and barista drinks in a cheerful, casual atmosphere.

La Abuela
ARGENTINE $

(☑451704; Rivadavia 1109; mains AR$90-130; ☺noon-3pm & 7:30-11pm Mon-Fri) Shoehorn yourself into this family nook decked out in lace tablecloths, and enjoy cheap gnocchi, homemade pasta and home-cooked classics like *puchero* (vegetable and meat stew) with a carafe of passable house wine.

María Castaña
CAFE $

(cnr 25 de Mayo & Rivadavia; snacks AR$50-110; ☺9am-late) A favorite at this frilly cafe is waffles with *dulce de leche;* it's also good for breakfast, sandwiches and ice-cream sundaes. Grab an overstuffed chair at the back. It also serves more substantial fare.

Quillen
VEGETARIAN $$

(☑400212; Av Fontana 769; mains AR$90-180; ☺9am-3pm Tue, 9am-3pm & 8pm-1am Thu-Sat; ☑) Serving organic pizza, pastas, fresh lemonade and artisan beer, Quillen might be more at home in Palermo, Buenos Aires than the Andean foothills, but here it is. The light vegan and vegetarian options are a godsend for those fresh from the Ruta 40.

★Don Chiquino
ITALIAN $$

(Av Ameghino 1641; mains AR$160; ☺noon-3:30pm & 8pm-midnight) Of course, pasta is no novelty in Argentina, but the owner-magician performing tricks while you wait for your meal is. The ambience is happy-cluttered and dishes such as *sorrentinos* with arugula prove satisfying.

Cheers
PUB FOOD $$

(☑457041; cnr Sarmiento & Av Alvear; mains AR$80-150; ☺noon-late) Don't let the Irish-pub atmosphere fool you into thinking this is just another stock-standard watering hole: the restaurant serves up good set lunches, too, and a range of hearty soups, salads and sandwiches, with Guinness, of course.

La Luna
ARGENTINE $$

(Av Fontana 656; mains AR$85-180; ☺noon-4pm & 7pm-1am) This chic rock 'n' roll restaurant-bar offers tasty spinach pizza, vegetable crepes, and heaped portions of steak and fries. The evening crowd spills out of wooden booths and brick nooks, drinking Patagonia's artisan beers.

🍷 Drinking & Nightlife

El Bodegón
BAR

(☑02945-15-428117; Rivadavia 905; ☺11am-3pm & 7pm-late) A comfortable brick restobar with sidewalk tables and big cold beers made for splitting. With live performances daily in summer and weekly off-season, ranging from Argentine rock to blues and alt music.

Hotel Argentino
BAR

(25 de Mayo 862; ☺4pm-5am) This lanky and lowbrow Wild West saloon is much better suited to drinking than sleeping, but by all means stop by: the owner is friendly, the 1916 construction is stuffed with relics and sculptures, and the place gets more than a little lively on weekends.

☆ Entertainment

Dirección Municipal de Cultura
LIVE PERFORMANCE, CINEMA

(☑451929; www.esquelsemueve.com.ar; Belgrano 330) Sponsors regular music, cinema, theater and dance.

ℹ Information

ACA (Automóvil Club Argentino; ☑452382; cnr 25 de Mayo & Av Ameghino; ☺daylight hours) Inside the YPF gas station; sells fishing licenses.

Banco de la Nación (cnr Av Alvear & General Roca) Has an ATM and changes traveler's checks.

Banco del Chubut (Av Alvear 1147) Has an ATM.

Hospital Regional (☑450009; 25 de Mayo 150)

Post Office (Av Alvear 1192) Next to the tourist office.

Tourist Office (☑451927; www.esquel.gov.ar; cnr Av Alvear & Sarmiento; ☺8am-8pm Mon-Fri, 9am-8pm Sat & Sun) Well organized, helpful and multilingual, with an impressive variety of detailed maps and brochures.

ℹ Getting There & Around

AIR

Esquel's airport is 20km east of town off RN 40. Taxis shuttle visitors to town.

Aerolíneas Argentinas (☑ 453614; Av Fontana 406) flies to Buenos Aires (one way from AR$2890) several times a week.

BUS

Esquel's full-service **bus terminal** (cnr Av Alvear & Brun) is close to the town center.

Transportes Jacobsen (☑ 454676) goes to Futaleufú, Chile (AR$84, 1½ hours) at 8am and 6pm Monday and Friday. Buses go hourly to Trevelin (AR$19, 30 minutes), stopping near the corner of Av Alvear and 25 de Mayo on the way out of town.

In summer **Transportes Esquel** (☑ 453529; www.transportesesquel.com.ar) goes through Parque Nacional Los Alerces (AR$50, 1¼ hours) to Lago Futalaufquen at 8am daily (and also at 2pm and 6pm in January). The first bus goes all the way to Lago Puelo (AR$125, six hours),

---

THE EPIC RUTA NACIONAL 40

Patagonia's RN 40 is the quintessential road trip. It's not for rushing – the weather can be wily, winds overpowering and it can seem to go on forever. But it is also magical when the interminable flat line of steppe bursts open with views of glacial peaks and gem-colored lakes. As it is now mostly paved, travel here is becoming easier, though if you explore the road's offshoots, expect loose gravel.

Be Prepared

There is no cell-phone coverage outside of towns, so drivers must be self-sufficient. Travel with necessary repair equipment. If renting a car, check that the headlights work and that the suspension, tires, spare tire and brakes are all in good shape. Gas stations are few, so have extra fuel on hand, as well as oil and generous supplies of food and water. Gas is subsidized in Patagonia, so fill up at each opportunity.

Road Rules

The law requires seatbelts and headlights during daylight hours. Respect speed limits: on gravel 65km/h to 80km/h is a safe maximum speed. Sheep *always* have the right of way. Guanacos and ñandús are other potential hazards. Slow down, give them space and watch out for unsigned *guardaganados* (cattle guards).

Take the Backseat

Several travel agencies coordinate two- to five-day minivan transport along RN 40 from El Calafate to Bariloche, via El Chaltén, Perito Moreno and Los Antiguos. Service follows fair weather, from mid-October/November to early April, depending on demand and road conditions. Pricier guided tours stretch the trip over four or five days.

If you're really up for a road trip, contact **Ruta 40** (p424). This small, multilingual outfitter takes travelers on 10-day journeys on RN 40 from Bariloche to El Calafate, with stops at Cueva de las Manos and *estancias* El Condor and La Oriental. Consult for rates and departure dates.

Quicker, more straightforward travel along RN 40 can be arranged through **Chaltén Travel** (☑ 011-4326-7282; www.chaltentravel.com; Sarmiento 559, piso 8, Buenos Aires), which runs northbound two-day shuttles, leaving at 8am from El Calafate, with accommodation in Perito Moreno. Southbound three-day shuttles leave Bariloche at 6:45am on odd-numbered days, with accommodations in Perito Moreno and El Chaltén. Buses stop in Los Antiguos as well. The trip is usually available from November to March. The one-way trip between El Calafate and Bariloche (AR$2190 per person) does not include accommodation or food. It's possible to hop on and off along the route, but space on the next shuttle cannot be reserved. Combinations to Puerto Madryn are also available for northbound travelers. Chaltén Travel has branches in **El Calafate** (p459), **El Chaltén** (p455), **Puerto Madryn** (p408) and **Bariloche** (☑ 0294-442-3809; www.chaltentravel.com; Quaglia 262).

Some travelers have had good experiences with bus line **Taqsa/Marga** (p445), which offers high-season service north and south between El Calafate and Bariloche (AR$2180, 28 hours, October to April), with stops in El Chaltén, Perito Moreno and Esquel.

stopping in Lago Verde (AR$75) at 10:30am and Cholila (AR$75) at noon. An open ticket allows passengers to make stops along the way between Esquel and Lago Puelo or vice versa. Note that the service is reduced in low season.

Buses from Esquel

DESTINATION	COST (AR$)	TIME (HR)
Bariloche	280	4¼
Buenos Aires	1998	25
Comodoro Rivadavia	530	8
El Bolsón	180	2½
Neuquén	600	10
Puerto Madryn	644	7-9
Río Gallegos	1300	18
Trelew	601	8-9

CAR

Compact rentals start at around AR$1000 per day, including 100km and insurance. Try **Patagonia Travel Rent A Car** (☑455811; Av Alvear 1041), which has a good range of vehicles.

TRAIN

The narrow-gauge steam train *La Trochita* departs from the diminutive **Roca train station** (www.latrochita.org.ar; cnr Roggero & Urquiza; ☻8am-2pm Mon-Sat). There's a frequent tourist-oriented service to Nahuel Pan. For the timeless *Old Patagonian Express* feeling, it's best to catch a bus to El Maitén for the less touristy excursion to Desvío Thomae, but this service is only available from time to time. Confirm schedules online or via the tourist office.

Trevelin

☑ 02945 / POP 7900 / ELEV 735M

Historic Trevelin (treh-*veh*-lehn), from the Welsh for town *(tre)* and mill *(velin),* is the only community in interior Chubut with a notable Welsh character. Easygoing and postcard pretty, this pastoral village makes a tranquil lodging alternative to the much busier Esquel (remember, everything is relative here), or an enjoyable day trip for tea. The surrounding countryside is ripe for exploration.

Just 22km south of Esquel via paved RN 259, Trevelin centers around the octagonal Plaza Coronel Fontana. Eight streets radiate from it, including the principal thoroughfare, Av San Martín (also the southward extension of RN 259). RN 259 forks west 50km to the Chilean border and to Futaleufú, 12km beyond.

◉ Sights

Museo Regional Andes   MUSEUM
(☑480461; cnr 25 de Mayo & Molino Viejo; adult/child under 12 AR$60/free; ☻10am-6pm Mon-Fri, 2-6:30pm Sat & Sun) Occupies the restored remains of a 1922 grain mill. At the time of research it was closed for renovation. It's a couple of blocks east of the plaza, at the end of 25 de Mayo.

★★ Festivals & Events

Aniversario de Trevelin   CULTURAL
Commemorates the founding of the city on March 19.

Eisteddfod   CULTURAL
The biggest Welsh celebration of the year, this multilingual festival where bards compete in song and poetry takes place at the end of October.

🛏 Sleeping

Círculo Policial   CAMPGROUND $
(☑480947; Costanera Río Percy & Holdich; campsite per person US$9) Fine, grassy campsites with shade. From Av San Martín 600, walk two blocks west on Coronel Holdich and turn left down the gravel road. Open January to February; sometimes extended depending on weather.

Hostería Casa de Piedra   LODGE $$
(☑480357; www.casadepiedratrevelin.com; Brown 244; d US$99; ❄☎) A haven for anglers and 4WD enthusiasts, this elegant stone lodge boasts a huge fireplace and rustic touches. Buffet breakfast includes yogurt, homemade bread, cakes and fruit.

Cabañas Wilson   CABIN $$
(☑480803; www.wilsonpatagonia.com.ar; RP 259 at RP 71; 4-/6-person cabin US$95/105; ☎) Savor the serenity surrounding these wood-and-brick cabins with log furniture on the edge of town. The cabins include daily cleaning service, extra covers and a barbecue deck. An abundant breakfast is optional.

Cabañas Oregon   CABIN $$
(☑480408; www.oregontrevelin.com.ar; cnr Av San Martín & JM Thomas; 4-person cabin US$100; ☎🖶) Scattered around an apple orchard on the south side of town, these appealing log cabins come with handmade wooden furniture. Features include kitchen and TV. Kid-friendly, there's also a swingset. The on-site grill restaurant (buffet grill AR$250 to AR$280, closed Tuesday) is reputed to be the best spot in town to eat meat, and has good service.

Eating & Drinking

Just as visitors to Trelew flock to Gaiman, so visitors to Esquel head to Trevelin for Welsh tea. Teahouses are typically open from 3pm to 8pm. Often the portions are big enough to share – ask first if it's OK to do so.

★Nikanor   ARGENTINE $$
(📞480400; Libertad 56; mains AR$90-210; ⊙12:30-2:30pm & 8:30-11pm) If you're not in the mood for tea, make this excellent home-style restaurant your first choice. A husband-and-wife team serve up ravioli stuffed with local lamb, a list of Argentine wines and flambé crepes for dessert. In a lovely, renovated early-20th-century home, with exposed brick and beams, and a window showing the original adobe and bamboo construction.

Nain Maggie   TEAHOUSE
(📞480232; www.casadetenainmaggie.com; Perito Moreno 179; ⊙3:30-8:30pm) Trevelin's oldest teahouse occupies a modern building but has high traditional standards. Along with a bottomless pot, there's cream pie, *torta negra* and scones (tea service AR$150).

La Mutisia   TEAHOUSE
(📞480165; Av San Martín 170; ⊙3:30-8:30pm) Everything is reliably homemade at this teahouse (tea service AR$110).

🛍 Shopping

Mercado de Artisanos   MARKET
(⊙9am-3pm) This artisans market fills Plaza Coronel Fontana on Sundays in summer and on alternate Sundays the rest of the year.

ℹ Information

Banco del Chubut (cnr Av San Martín & Brown) Just south of the plaza, with an ATM.
Gales al Sur (📞480427; www.galesalsur.com.ar; Patagonia 186) Arranges regional tours.
Post Office (Av San Martín) Just south of the plaza.
Tourist Office (📞480120; www.trevelin.gov.ar; ⊙8am-8pm) Helpful, with a free town map, information on local hikes and English-speaking staff.

ℹ Getting There & Away

The **bus terminal** (cnr Roca & RN 40) faces the main plaza. Most services originate in Esquel. Near **Gales al Sur** (📞480427; RN 259) there's a bus stop with hourly departures to Esquel (AR$19, 30 minutes). Buses cross the border to Chile's Futaleufú (AR$84, one hour) on Monday and Friday at 8:30am and 6pm, plus Wednesday in summer.

Parque Nacional Los Alerces

📞02945

This collection of spry creeks, verdant mountains and mirror lakes resonates as unadulterated Andes. The real attraction, however, is the alerce tree *(Fitzroya cupressoides)*, one of the longest-living species on the planet, with specimens that have survived up to 4000 years. Lured by the acclaim of well-known parks to the north and south, most hikers miss this gem, which makes your visit here all the more enjoyable.

Resembling California's giant sequoia, the alerce flourishes in middle Patagonia's temperate forests, growing only about 1cm every 20 years. Individual specimens of this beautiful tree can reach over 4m in diameter and exceed 60m in height. Like the giant sequoia, it has suffered overexploitation because of its valuable timber. West of Esquel, this 2630-sq-km park protects some of the largest alerce forests that still remain.

Because the Andes are relatively low here, westerly storms deposit nearly 3m of rain annually. The park's eastern sector, though, is much drier. Winter temperatures average 2°C, but it can be much colder. The summer average high reaches 24°C, but evenings are usually cool.

While its wild backcountry supports the seldom-seen huemul (Andean deer) and other wildlife, Los Alerces functions primarily as a trove of botanical riches that characterize the dense Valdivian forest.

🏃 Activities

As well as sailing and hiking, travel agencies in Esquel have fishing, canoeing, mountain biking, snorkeling and horseback riding.

Sailing

Traditionally, **Circuito Lacustre** is Los Alerces' most popular excursion. Low water makes it necessary to hike the short distance between Puerto Mermoud, at the north end of Lago Futalaufquen, and Puerto Chucao on Lago Menéndez. Launches from Puerto Chucao (1½ hours) go to the northern nature trail **El Alerzal**, the most accessible stand of alerces. Another option (recommended) is to arrive at Puerto Chucao via a very scenic 1500m trail that crosses the bridge over Río Arrayanes.

Parque Nacional Los Alerces

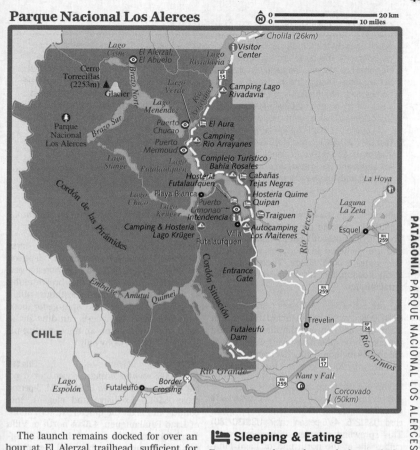

The launch remains docked for over an hour at El Alerzal trailhead, sufficient for an unhurried hike around the loop trail that passes **Lago Cisne** and an attractive waterfall to end up at **El Abuelo** (Grandfather), a 57m-tall, 2600-year-old alerce.

Excursions leave from Puerto Chucao (AR$560), departing at 11:30am and returning around 5pm. In summer, purchase tickets in Esquel to ensure a seat.

Hiking

Hikers must sign in at the one of the ranger stations before heading out.

Day hikes can be undertaken from several interpretive trails located near **Lago Futalaufquen**. There is also a 25km trail from **Puerto Limonao** along the south shore of Futalaufquen to **Hostería Lago Krüger**, which can be done in a long day, or broken up by camping at **Playa Blanca**.

For longer hikes, see Lonely Planet's *Trekking in the Patagonian Andes*.

🛏️ Sleeping & Eating

En route to the park, watch for roadside signs advertising ideal picnic goods: homemade bread, delicious Chubut cheese, fresh fruit and Welsh sweets. In Villa Futalaufquen there are a couple of basic grocery stores and a summer-only restaurant, but it's best to bring your own provisions.

Los Alerces has several full-service campgrounds, all of which have showers, grocery stores and restaurants on-site or nearby. Free (no services) and semi-organized campgrounds exist near most of these fee sites.

With a group, *cabañas* can be an affordable option.

Camping Río Arrayanes   CAMPGROUND **$**
(📞 454381; campsite per adult/child US$12/8) A new campground, with showers, bathrooms and grills, located in one of the most scenic areas of the park. Also has basic yurts (*domos*).

ON BUTCH CASSIDY'S TRAIL IN CHOLILA

Butch Cassidy, the Sundance Kid and Etta Place tried settling down and making an honest living near this quiet farming community outside the northeast entrance to Parque Nacional Los Alerces. The bandits' tale is recounted by Bruce Chatwin in the travel classic *In Patagonia*. Though the threesome's idyll only lasted a few years, their partially restored homestead still stands, just off RP 71 at Km21, 8km north of Cholila. Cholila's enthusiastic **Casa de Informes** (☏02945-498040, 02945-498208; www.turismocholila.gov.ar; RP 71 at RP 15; ⊗Dec-Mar) has a helpful regional map and will gladly point you in the right direction.

To overnight in this funky Patagonian outpost, check out the hospitable **Piuke Mapu Hostel** (☏02945-15-553545, 02945-15-685608; www.piukemapu.com; Av Soberanía Argentina 200; dm US$20, 6-person cabin US$100), located three blocks from the plaza. Young owners Laura and Dario also run a community garden and mountain refuge and guide local trekking and Alpine excursions. They also rent bikes.

Camping Lago Rivadavia CAMPGROUND $
(☏454381; campsite per adult/child US$13/8) These idyllic spots at Lago Rivadavia's south end are sheltered in the trees with picnic tables and a boat launch. There's an electricity hookup, too. It's 42km north of Villa Futalaufquen.

Autocamping Los Maitenes CAMPGROUND $
(☏471006; campsite per adult/child US$13/8) On a slip of grass between the main road and the lake, these spots have lovely water views. Campsites include shade, electricity hookup and fire pits, 200m from the Intendencia.

**Complejo Turístico
Bahía Rosales** CAMPGROUND $
(☏02945-15-403413, 471044; campsite per adult/child US$12/6, 4-/6-person cabin US$130/180) This sprawling complex with sporting facilities sits at the north end of Lago Futalaufquen, 1.5km from the main road via a dirt path. At the time of research, the campsites were closed for the season; check for changes.

Cabañas Tejas Negras CABIN $$
(☏471012, 471046; www.tejasnegras.com.ar; 4-/5-person cabin US$160/240; ⊗year-round) With a lawn like a golf course and a handful of prim A-frames, Nilda and Hector have hosted guests for 40 years. Think retreat: there are no *fútbol* matches on these greens where tranquillity is savored. Note to parents – they only take kids who are well-behaved! Requires a three-night minimum. Contact via phone since internet runs slow here.

Traiguen CABIN $$
(☏02945-15-68-3606; 4-person cabin US$80; ⊗year-round) You might need good clearance to make it up the dirt road, but these few, ample cabins have lovely lake views and their going rate is a steal. Run by the *simpatico* Graciela and her giant tomcats.

Hostería Quime Quipan INN $$
(☏471021; www.quimequipan.com.ar; 5-person apt/cabin US$250/270, d lake/forest view US$175/140; ⊗Nov-Apr; ☎) In a breathtaking setting, this old-fashioned guesthouse offers pleasant but dated rooms – splurge for those with lake views. Nonguests can dine at the cozy, sunlit restaurant, an après-fishing pit stop. Wi-fi in the lobby only.

★**Hostería Futalaufquen** INN $$$
(☏471008; www.hosteriafutalaufquen.com; d incl half-board lake/forest view US$244/194, 3-person cabin US$410) Exclusive and elegant, this country inn is on the quieter western shore of Lago Futalaufquen, 4.5km north of Villa Futalaufquen at the end of the road. It offers well-appointed doubles and log cabins (without kitchens). Activities ranging from kayaking to rappelling can be arranged from here. Afterwards, collapse by the fire with a plate of dessert. Cabins come in varying sizes for up to eight guests. Make reservations at Sarmiento 635 in Esquel.

El Aura CABIN $$$
(Lago Verde Lodge; ☏in Buenos Aires 011-4816-5348; www.hosteriaselaura.com; 2-/4-person cabin US$349/523, 2-person yurt US$120; ⊗Nov-Apr) Rustic yet ritzy, these raspy stone *cabañas* feature big cozy beds, panoramic forest views and earthy motifs. Yurts, aka *domos*, offer an economical option. Anglers can rent motorized rafts to cast from Lago Futalaufquen's every nook and cranny. Guided trekking, horseback riding and fly-fishing are also offered. A gourmet restaurant and teahouse cater to travelers and guests. It's 35km north of Villa Futalaufquen.

❶ Information

During the high season (Christmas to Semana Santa) foreigners pay AR$120 admission. In Villa Futalaufquen you'll find the **Intendencia** (Park Office; ✆471015; ☉8am-9pm summer, 9am-4pm rest of year), the park administration center where rangers have details about hiking, camping and guided excursions. Get your fishing permits here. The headquarters also houses the **Museo y Centro del Interpretación**, a natural-history museum. The visitor center at the northern end of the park is only open December through February.

Gobernador Costa

✆ 02945 / POP 2400

When you find a town where a child snaps the tourist's picture (and not the reverse), it's something of an anomaly. This rusted little cattle town abuts the yawning stretch of RN 40 between Esquel and Río Mayo, at the intersection of RP 20 for Sarmiento and Comodoro Rivadavia. Some 20km west of town, RP 19 leads to **Lago General Vintter** and several smaller blue-ribbon lakes near the Chilean border; camping is possible along the shores.

Traveler services are few but reasonable. **Banco del Chubut** (cnr Sarmiento & San Martín) has an ATM. Motel-style **Hotel Roca** (✆491126; Av Roca s/n; per person US$25; ☎) has tidy brick rooms and a restaurant. Meals can be taken from **Kaserita** (Aguado 128; mains AR$60-110; ☉10am-2pm & 6-10:30pm), essentially a fresh pasta kitchen with folding-chair seating.

From the **bus terminal** (Av Roca s/n), buses go to Esquel (AR$248, two hours) and continue to Bariloche at 3:45am every day but Saturday. For Comodoro Rivadavia, buses leave at 11:30pm every day except Sunday (AR$530, eight hours). Both routes are paved.

Río Mayo

✆ 02903 / POP HUMANS 2800, SHEEP 800,000

The national capital of sheep shearing is a surprisingly humdrum place, save for the petroleum workers and waylaid gauchos practicing their wolf whistles on female *turistas*. This barren pit stop is 200km south of Gobernador Costa and 135km north of Perito Moreno.

The **Casa de Cultura** (✆420400; Ejército Argentino s/n; ☉9am-noon & 3-6pm) houses a tourist office, with information on local mountain-biking options. **Banco del Chubut** (cnr Yrigoyen & Argentina) has an ATM.

January's **Festival Nacional de la Esquila** features merino-wool-quality competitions

and guanaco shearing in preparation for the main event: the much-anticipated crowning of the national sheep-shearing queen.

The picture of eccentricity, **El Viejo Covadonga** (✆420020; San Martín 573; s/d US$35/60; ☎) features rooms of varying quality but with good down covers. Its coveted feature is the orange vinyl bar. **Hotel Akatá** (✆420054; San Martín 640; s/d US$40/65; @☎) has meals and internet but little else; its wood-panel rooms are dark and airless. Otherwise the YPF is a good bet for a quick sandwich and coffee.

Located 2.5km west of Río Mayo, **Estancia Don José** (✆02903-420015; www.turismo guenguel.com.ar; per person US$200; ☉Oct-Apr; ☎) is a welcoming alternative to barren Río Mayo. The friendly *estancia* offers horseback riding, fishing and walks to cave paintings. There are guanacos and ñandú on-site to admire. Activities and home-cooked meals with organic meat are included. See the website for good directions.

There are daily morning services from the **bus terminal** (✆420174; cnr Fontana & Irigoyen) to Comodoro Rivadavia (AR$226, 4½ hours) and Sarmiento (AR$113, two hours). Services go twice weekly to Coyhaique, Chile (six hours), currently Wednesday and Saturday. Schedules change regularly so check at the bus terminal. Heading north, there's service to Esquel (AR$460, six hours). At the time of research there was 43km of unpaved road heading south to Perito Moreno. The only regularly scheduled services on this rugged stretch of RN 40 are summer-only backpacker shuttles.

Perito Moreno

✆ 02963 / POP 4620

Don't confuse this dull town with the jaw-dropping national park of the same name or the glacier near El Calafate – the only tourist attraction here is cruising the strip on Saturday night. A brief stopover en route to the more inviting Andean oasis of Los Antiguos, Perito Moreno does have a good range of services for a town on RN 40, though area mining means hotels are often booked. Attractions Cueva de las Manos and Parque Nacional Perito Moreno are not far off. A dedicated archaeological museum, Museo Gradin, exhibiting discoveries from the Río de las Pinturas, was in the works at the time of research and promises to be a useful companion stop.

The town's glory came in 1898, when explorer Perito Moreno challenged Chile's border definition of *'divortum aquarum continental'* (which claimed the headwaters of Pacific-flowing rivers as Chilean territory) by rerouting Río Fénix, which flows through town, to Atlantic-bound Río Deseado. The river and the area remained Argentine, and the town took his name. The main drag, San Martín, leads north to RP 43 and south to RN 40; it's 128km south to Bajo Caracoles and 135km north to Río Mayo.

☞ Tours

GuanaCondor Tours
TOUR
(☑ 432303; jarinauta@yahoo.com.ar; Perito Moreno 1087; ☺ 10am-noon & 4-8pm Mon-Wed & Sat, 5-8pm Sun) An experienced operator with summer trips to Cueva de las Manos, accessing the park via the former Estancia Los Toldos, with a challenging hike that adds considerably to the experience. Also ask about trips to Monte Zeballos, a high mesa with excellent views, and the overnight trip to Paso Tehuelche.

Hugo Campañoli
TOUR
(☑ 432336) Hugo Campañoli is a local guide who takes groups of three or more to Cueva de las Manos on day trips.

Zoyen
TOUR
(☑ 432207; www.zoyenturismo.com.ar; Perón 1008) Good local travel agency with trips to Cueva de las Manos in high season.

🛏 Sleeping & Eating

There are a couple of well-stocked *panaderías* (bakeries) and supermarkets along San Martín.

Hotel Americano
HOTEL $
(☑ 432074; www.hotelamericanoweb.com.ar; San Martín 1327; s/d US$34/51, d superior US$66; ☜) Thriving Americano also has a decent grill and cafe that's busy in the evenings. Rooms vary widely – some lack windows, others can be quite cozy – so ask to see a few before deciding.

Hotel Belgrano
HOTEL $
(☑ 432019; www.hotelbelgrano.guiapatagonia.net; San Martín 1001; dm/s/d/tr US$20/50/70/90) This big, boxy corner hotel has spacious concrete rooms with decent mattresses but not much ambience. Most folks shuffle in during the wee hours from Chaltén Travel shuttles. Breakfast is extra (AR$20).

Camping Municipal
CAMPGROUND $
(Laguna de los Cisnes, off Mariano Moreno; per tent US$2, plus per vehicle from US$3.50, 4-person

cabaña US$30) The cheapest option for backpackers is this campground with rustic cabins on the south side of town. It's shaded by breezy poplars and has hot showers. Renovations already under way at the time of research might bring prices up.

★ Chacra Kaiken Lodge
B&B $$
(☑ 0297-15-408-6996, 432079; www.chacrakaiken.com.ar; Yrigoyen 2012; s/d/tr from US$107/130/162; ☺ Oct-Mar; ☜) A solid new option, this four-room B&B is run by Petty and Coco, lifelong area residents who used to run a well-known *estancia*. So in addition to a snug sleep, they offer a lovely setting and a fresh taste of real Patagonia.

Salón Iturrioz
CAFE $
(cnr Rivadavia & San Martín; sandwiches AR$40-150; ☺ 8am-11pm; ☜) With cappuccino, snacks and wi-fi, this charming brick corner cafe is a godsend to RN 40. It's also a social hub, and the best place to get information on Museo Gradín across the street.

ℹ Information

Banco de Santa Cruz (cnr San Martín & Rivadavia) Has an ATM and changes traveler's checks.
Hospital Distrital (☑ 432040; Colón 1237)
Post Office (cnr JD Perón & Belgrano)
Tourist Office (☑ 432732; peritomoreno@santacruzpatagonia.gob.ar; San Martín; ☺ 7am-11:30pm Mon-Fri, 8am-3pm Sat & Sun) Helpful, with a surprising number of pamphlets and brochures, and information on homestay lodgings. There is also a desk at the bus terminal (access road to RN 43).

ℹ Getting There & Away

LADE (☑ 432055; San Martín 1065) flies to El Calafate, Río Gallegos, Río Grande and Ushuaia.

The **bus terminal** (access road to RN 43) sits behind the YPF rotunda at the northern entrance to town. Taxis (AR$25) provide the only transport between here and the town center; other than that it's a flat 15-minute walk. Buses leave a few times daily for Los Antiguos (AR$94, 40 minutes), though departure times aren't reliable as they're usually scheduled to connect with incoming buses from RN 40, which are often delayed. In the afternoon, starting at 3:50pm, multiple buses also head for Comodoro Rivadavia (AR$518, six hours) and Río Gallegos (AR$882, 16 hours) via RN 3.

Several shuttle services also offering excursions serve travelers on RN 40. From November to April, **Chaltén Travel** (☑ 02902-492212; www.chaltentravel.com) goes north to Bariloche (11 hours), departing from Hotel Belgrano in Perito

Moreno at 8pm on even-numbered days. Shuttles leave Hotel Belgrano at 8am to head south to El Chaltén (11 hours) on odd-numbered days.

The bus company **Taqsa/Marga** (☏432675) now runs the entire stretch of RN 40 between El Calafate and Bariloche (AR$2180) several times a week starting at the end of October, stopping at El Chaltén, Bajo Caracoles, Perito Moreno and Esquel (AR$600) along the way. The route between Perito Moreno and El Calafate costs AR$1300.

Los Antiguos

☏02963 / POP 3360

Situated on the windy shores of Lago Buenos Aires, the agricultural oasis of Los Antiguos is home to *chacras* (small independent farms) of cherries, strawberries, apples, apricots and peaches. Before Europeans arrived, it was known as I-Keu-khon (Place of the Elders) to Tehuelches. It makes an attractive crossing to Chile and the stretch of road between Perito Moreno and Los Antiguos affords spectacular lake views.

Volcán Hudson's 1991 eruption covered the town in ash, but farms have bounced back. In summer **Lago Buenos Aires**, South America's second-biggest lake, is warm enough for a brisk swim. The stunning **Río Jeinemeni** is a favored spot for trout and salmon fishing.

Most services in the town are on or near east–west Av 11 de Julio, which heads west to the Chilean frontier at Chile Chico, the region's most convenient border crossing. Perito Moreno and RN 40 are 60km east.

◎ Sights & Activities

Parque Nacional Patagonia NATURE RESERVE
(RN 41) Out on the steppe, this new 530-sq-km park was created in 2015 primarily to protect the *maca tobiano,* an endangered duck that has been brought to the brink of extinction by non-native mink. It's also a bird-watching destination. While most of the park infrastructure and trails are still under construction, visitors can stay at the El Sauco campground, which has wild camping on Río Blanco. It's located 190km from Los Antiguos via RN 40 and RN 41 (Paso Zeballos).

Maca Tobiano BICYCLE RENTAL
(☏0297-15-5014-4444; kayakmacatobiano@hotmail.com.ar; Costanera s/n) On the lakefront, this kayak- and bike-rental agency also offers adrenaline-stoked mountain-biking descents from Monte Zeballos. Has wet suits for lake activities. See their Facebook page for information.

☞ Tours

Chelenco Tours TOUR
(☏02963-491198; www.chelencotours.tur.ar; Av 11 de Julio Este 584; ◷10am-1pm & 4:30-9:30pm) In a log cabin office, this tour operator offers trekking to Cueva de Las Manos and trips to the scenic road to Monte Zeballos, in addition to longer excursions and transfers from Comodoro Rivadavia.

✿ Festivals

Fiesta de la Cereza CULTURAL
Rodeos, live music and the crowning of the national Cherry Queen during the second weekend of January. Artisan goods are sold and *peñas folklóricas* (Argentine folk-music concerts) at private farms go on all night long – see the tourist information office for more information.

⬛ Sleeping & Eating

Cabañas Rincon de los Poetas CABIN $
(☏491051; Patagonia Argentina 226; d/tr/q US$60/75/90; ☏) These snug and kitschy wooden cabins equipped with kitchenettes are nothing fancy, but they prove good value for groups and families. It's located two blocks from the town center.

Camping Municipal CAMPGROUND $
(☏491265; Av 11 de Julio s/n; campsite tent US$10 plus per person AR$20, dm/cabin US$40/50) Windbreaks help considerably at this lakeshore site 1.5km east of town. Dorms are in windowless cabins with hot showers available in the evening; whole cabins sleep up to four. Campsites are rented by tent and by person.

Hotel Los Antiguos Cerezos HOTEL $$
(☏491132; hotel_losantiguoscerezos@hotmail.com; Av 11 de Julio 850; s/d/tr US$50/78/90; ☏) A large cement building with modern but somewhat sterile rooms that come with single beds, TV and a good dose of heat when you need it.

Hostería Antigua Patagonia HOTEL $$
(☏491038; www.antiguapatagonia.com.ar; RP 43 Acceso Este; s/tw/d US$124/142/160; ☏❀) In a stunning setting, this lakefront complex is comfortably rustic, with wooden trunks, sturdy four-poster beds and a stone fireplace that begs you to curl up in front like a cat. Avoid the ground floor, with flimsy patio door locks. With good service, sauna, pool, and bikes and kayaks for guests. It's 2km east of town, by the police checkpoint.

Hotel Mora HOTEL $$
(☑0297-15-420-7472; www.hotelmorapatagonia.
com; Av Costanera 1064; s/d with lake view
US$96/122, s/d/tr without view US$72/102/128;
☎) With its corrugated-tin facade and lovely
outdoor deck, this lodging holds promise.
The best rooms are doubles with lake views.
Others run toward the basic end with fa-
tigued mattresses and showerheads without
stalls. Still, the deck overlooking a water-
front promenade is ideal for a sunset beer.

Viva El Viento CAFE $$
(☑491109; www.vivaelviento.com; Av 11 de Julio
447; mains AR$40-220; ☺9am-9pm Oct-Apr; ☎)
This stylish cafe and restaurant is the go-to
spot for strong coffee and warm service. The
menu offers fresh juices and salads, good
gnocchi and steak. Avoid the trout – it's a
little too fishy and very dry. The kitchen is
willing to make adaptations for vegetarians.

❶ Information

Banco de Santa Cruz (Av 11 de Julio 531) Has
a 24-hour ATM.

Parques Nacionales (☑29-6662-2852; www.
sib.gob.ar; Costanera s/n; ☺9am-4pm Mon-Fri)
The administrative office of National Parks that
handles the new Parque Nacional Patagonia.
Has information on camping and directions.

Post Office (Gregores 19)

Tourist Information Office (☑491261; info@
losantiguos.tur.ar; Av 11 de Julio 446; ☺8am-
8pm) Helpful, with a map of town and farms selling fresh produce. Check their Facebook page
Los Antiguos Santa Cruz Patagonia for news.

❶ Getting There & Around

The gradual paving of RN 40 may alter transportation options and times, so get current information.

Buses go several times daily to nearby Perito
Moreno (AR$94, 40 minutes). Those in a rush
to move on will find more transport links there
to other parts of Patagonia. For Chile, **La Unión**
(☑491078; cnr Perito Moreno & Patagonia
Argentina) crosses the border to Chile Chico
(AR$100) on weekdays at noon.

From mid-November to March, **Chaltén Travel**
(www.chaltentravel.com) goes to El Chaltén on
even-numbered days at 9am, stopping first in
Perito Moreno.

A Chilean ferry run by **Naviera Sotramin** (☑in
Chile 56-067-223-7958; Chile Chico; passenger/
car CH$2100/18,650) crosses Lago General
Carrera daily from Chile Chico to Puerto Ibañez
almost daily, a big shortcut to Coyhaique. If driving, make your reservation a week in advance
and arrive 30 minutes before departure time.
Alternatively, it's possible to continue overland

around the lake's southern shore to Carretera
Austral and Coyhaique.

Leiva Remise (☑491228) taxi service is useful
when it's pouring rain and you need a ride.

Cueva de las Manos

Unesco World Heritage site **Cueva de las
Manos** (Cave of the Hands; www.cuevadelas
manos.org; admission AR$120; ☺9am-7pm) fea-
tures incredible rock art, a must-see if you
pass through. Dating from about 7370 BC,
these polychrome paintings cover recesses
in the near-vertical walls with imprints of
human hands, drawings of guanacos and,
from a later period, abstract designs. Of
around 800 images, more than 90% are of
left hands; one has six fingers.

The approach is via rough but scenic
provincial roads off RN 40, abutting Río de
las Pinturas. Drive with caution: bounding
guanacos are abundant. There are three
points of access: a 28km unpaved road from
RN 40, direct but with loose gravel; a route
via Bajo Caracoles, with 46km of gravel
roads; and another from the north side and
Hostería Cueva de las Manos (closed in low
season), with 22km of gravel and 4km on
foot via a footbridge.

Guides in Perito Moreno organize day
trips (around AR$600 per person plus park
entrance fee). The trip from Perito Moreno is
about 3½ hours (one way) over rocky roads.
Once you arrive at the caves, free 45-min-
ute guided walks are given every hour by
knowledgeable staff. There's an information
center and a basic *confitería* at the reception house near the southern entrance, but
it's best to bring your own food.

On the doorstep of Argentina's best deposit of rock art, **Hostería Cueva de las
Manos** (☑02963-432207, in Buenos Aires 011-
5237-4043; www.cuevadelasmanos.net; dm/s/d/
tr US$14/52/62/72, 4-6 person cabin from US$96;
☺Nov-Apr), formerly Estancia Los Toldos, sits
a short distance off RN 40, 52km south of
Perito Moreno. Guests can stay in cabins, the
hostería or a 20-person dormitory. Rooms
are plain but well appointed. Guests and tour
groups can approach Cueva de las Manos via
a scenic but challenging hiking trail (summer
only) that starts from the *hostería,* descends
the canyon and crosses Río de las Pinturas.

Rustic but welcoming **Estancia Casa de
Piedra** (☑02963-432199; off RN 40; campsites
per person AR$60; ☺Jan & Feb), a basic ranch
76km south of Perito Moreno, has plain
rooms and allows camping. It's a good spot

BOSQUE PETRIFICADO SARMIENTO

Fallen giants scatter the pale sandstone landscape at this **petrified forest** (⊙10am-6pm) FREE, 30km southeast of Sarmiento. The forest, brought here by strong river currents from the mountainous regions about 65 million years ago, has logs 100m in length and 1m wide. For travelers, this area is much more accessible than the Monumento Natural Bosques Petrificados further south.

Go with your own rental car, or ask at the tourist office in Sarmiento for *remise* (taxi) rates for the 1½-hour roundtrip. Try to stay through sunset, when the striped bluffs of Cerro Abigarrado and the multihued hills turn brilliantly vivid.

Located 10km west of Sarmiento, working cherry farm **Chacra Labrador** (☎0297-489-3329; www.hosterialabrador.com; s/d/tr US$80/100/150; ⊙Oct–mid-Apr; ☏) is a charming 1930s homestead offering bed and breakfast. Rooms are few but luxuriant, with big cozy beds, antique furniture, pots of tea and crackling fires.

The eager staff at Sarmiento's **tourist office** (☎0297-489-2105; www.sarmientochubut. gob.ar; cnr Infanteria 25 & Pietrobelli; ⊙7am-7pm Mon-Fri, 9am-7pm Sat & Sun) can provide *remise* rates, maps and lodging information. Sarmiento is 148km west of Comodoro along RN 26 and RP 20. **Etap** (☎0297-489-3058) buses run daily to Comodoro Rivadavia (AR$115, two hours); its buses to Río Mayo (AR$113, 1½ hours) go at 9:30pm daily.

for trekkers to hunker down: there are nearby volcanoes and you can take a beautiful day-long hike to the Cueva de las Manos via Cañon de las Pinturas (nonguests pay AR$30 for access). From the *estancia,* it's 12km to the canyon, then another 6km to the cave – estimate about 10 hours roundtrip. Hikers should get an early start and bring their own food; guides can be contracted here but the trail is clear enough to go without one.

Bajo Caracoles

Blink and you'll miss this dusty gas stop. Little has changed since Bruce Chatwin dubbed it 'a crossroads of insignificant importance with roads leading all directions apparently to nowhere' in *In Patagonia* in 1975. If you're headed south, fill the tank, since it's the only reliable gas pump between Perito Moreno (128km north) and Tres Lagos (409km south). From here RP 39 heads west to Lago Posadas and the Paso Roballos to Chile.

Lodgers put on a brave face for **Hotel Bajo Caracoles** (☎02963-490100; RN 40 s/n; d US$60), with old gas heating units that require a watchful eye. It also stocks basic provisions, serves decent coffee and has the only private telephone in town.

Heading south, RN 40 is paved to Las Horquetas, a blip on the radar screen where RN 40, RP 27 and RP 37 intersect. From here it's another 128km southeast via RP 27 to Gobernador Gregores, which was almost completely paved at the time of research.

Parque Nacional Perito Moreno

Wild and windblown, **Parque Nacional Perito Moreno** (⊙visitor registration 9am-9pm, park open Oct-Apr) is an adventurer's dream. Approaching from the steppe, the massive snowcapped peaks of the Sierra Colorada rise like sentinels. Guanacos graze the tufted grasses, condors circle above, and wind blurs the surface of aquamarine and cobalt lakes. If you come here, you will be among 1200 yearly visitors – that is, mostly alone. Solitude reigns and, save for services offered by local *estancias,* you are entirely on your own.

Honoring the park system's founder, this remote but increasingly popular park encompasses 1150 sq km, 310km southwest of the town of Perito Moreno. Don't confuse this gem with Parque Nacional Los Glaciares (home to the Glaciar Perito Moreno) further south.

The sedimentary Sierra Colorada is a palette of rusty hues. Beyond the park boundary, glacier-topped summits such as 3706m **Cerro San Lorenzo** (the highest peak in the area) tower over the landscape. The highest peak within the park is Cerro Mié (2254m).

As precipitation increases toward the west, the Patagonian steppe grasslands along the park's eastern border become sub-Antarctic forests of southern beech, lenga and coihue. Because the base altitude exceeds 900m, weather can be severe.

Summer is usually comfortable, but warm clothing and proper gear are imperative in any season. The water is pure but you must bring all food and supplies.

◉ Sights & Activities

Behind the information center, a one-hour interpretive trail leads to **Pinturas Rupestres**, somewhat denigrated cave paintings with interpretive signs in English. Consult park rangers for backpacking options and guided walks to the pictographs at **Casa de Piedra** on Lago Burmeister, and to **Playa de los Amonites** on Lago Belgrano, where there are fossils.

Lago Burmeister is an eight-hour roundtrip walk. The peninsula of **Lago Belgrano** has two hikes: an all-day walk around the perimeter or a four-day roundtrip to an interior lake. When conditions are very windy, the above options, and El Rincón, are the best: stay off the peaks!

From Estancia La Oriental, it's a 3½-hour hike to the summit of 1434m **Cerro León** for a dazzling panorama. Immediately east of the summit, the volcanic outcrop of **Cerro de los Cóndores** is a nesting site, with numbers of condors circling a 300m cliff. Pumas have also been spotted here and guanacos down below.

🛏 Sleeping & Eating

There are free campgrounds at the information center (barren and exposed); on the steppe at Lago Burmeister, 16km north from the information center (more scenic and well sheltered among dense lenga forest); and at El Rincón, 15km south. Fires are not allowed. Campgrounds have pit toilets, picnic tables and potable water. Pack trash out.

Estancia La Oriental　　ESTANCIA $$$
(📮15-407197, in Buenos Aires 011-41526901; www.estanciasdesantacruz.com/LaOriental/laoriental.htm; 3-person tent US$30, 4-person dm US$70, s/d/tr/q US$140/175/230/260; ☺Nov-Mar) At the foot of Cerro León and the end of the road on Lago Belgrano's north shore, La Oriental is the ideal base camp for exploring the park's varied backcountry. The ranch mostly caters to groups, and does a good job with food, 4WD and horseback-riding trips. Two-night stays are required. Guests must register in the park before entering.

Gasoline at the *estancia* is for guests only. Transfers are available from RN 40 (US$200) and Gobernador Gregores.

❶ Information

Visitors must register at the park's information center on the eastern boundary upon arrival. It's stocked with informative maps and brochures. Information can also be obtained at the National Parks Administration Office in Gobernador Gregores.

❶ Getting There & Away

Access road RN 37 is not transitable in winter, and the park is closed then anyway. In shoulder seasons the road may be impassable – check with the National Parks Administration Office in Gobernador Gregores before heading out.

Public transportation only goes to the junction of RN 37 and RN 40, and hitchhiking is a poor option (trailheads are far from the information center). If you're driving, carry spare gas and tires.

Gobernador Gregores

📞 02962 / POP 4500

Sleepy Gobernador Gregores is one of the better stops on RN 40, with hotels and shops offering a cheerful demeanor.

Gregores is 60km east of RN 40 on RP 25. It's the nearest town to Parque Nacional Perito Moreno (still 200km west) and an ideal spot to get supplies and arrange transportation. There's a very enthusiastic **tourist office** (📮491259; www.turismoengregores.com; Paseo 9 de Julio 610; ☺8am-2pm Mon-Fri) with comprehensive information on lodgings. The **National Parks Administration Office** (📮491477; San Martín 882; ☺9am-4pm Mon-Fri) can be helpful if you have plans to go to Parque Nacional Perito Moreno.

Around 70km west of town via RP 29, the waters of **Lago Cardiel** are well loved by anglers for blue-ribbon salmon and rainbow-trout fishing. From the junction to the lake it's another 116km to **Tres Lagos**, where a jovial couple run a 24-hour YPF gas station, then another 123km west to El Chaltén.

Summer-only **Camping Nuestra Señora del Valle** (📮491398; gregoresturismo@yahoo.com.ar; campsites free) **FREE** has showers, hot water and stone grills. Get a hot meal (AR$100), including excellent homemade pasta, friendly conversation and firm beds, at **Cañadón León** (📮491082; Roca 397; s/d/tr US$45/65/75; 🛜), with 25 rooms that are ample and spotless. Reserve ahead. It also rents cars and provides regional transfers.

A new bus terminal is promised for the future. **Cerro San Lorenzo** (📮491340; cnr San Martín & Alberdi) buses leave for Puerto San Julián (AR$300, four hours) Monday to Saturday at 4pm or 6pm – ask at the office for exact departure times. **Taqsa/Marga** (🏢 in Río Gallegos 02966-442003; Paralello 956) goes to Río Gallegos (AR$435, seven hours) daily and Esquel (AR$990, 13½ hours) with varying frequency.

Heading south on RN 40, there are still 100km of unpaved road between Gobernador Gregores and the useful gas stop Tres Lagos, though paving is ongoing.

El Chaltén

🏢 02962 / POP 1630

This colorful village overlooks the stunning northern sector of Parque Nacional Los Glaciares. Every summer thousands of trekkers come to explore the world-class trails that start right here. Founded in 1985, in a rush to beat Chile to the land claim, El Chaltén is still a frontier town, albeit an offbeat one, featuring constant construction, hippie values and packs of roaming dogs. Every year more mainstream tourists come to see what the fuss is all about, but in winter (May to September) most hotels and services board up and transportation links are few.

El Chaltén is named for Cerro Fitz Roy's Tehuelche name, meaning 'peak of fire' or 'smoking mountain' – an apt description of the cloud-enshrouded summit. Perito Moreno and Carlos Moyano later named it after the *Beagle's* Captain FitzRoy, who navigated Darwin's expedition up the Río Santa Cruz in 1834, coming within 50km of the cordillera.

⊙ Sights & Activities

The streets of El Chaltén are empty at noon when travelers are out hiking, rock climbing and horseback riding in the surrounding mountains.

Capilla de los Escaladores
CHAPEL

A simple chapel of Austrian design memorializes the many climbers who have lost their lives to the precarious peaks since 1953.

Reserva Los Huemules
NATURE RESERVE

(🏢 satellite phone 011-4152-5300; www.loshuemules.com; admission AR$100) This private 56-sq-km reserve has 25km of marked trails, and offers a quiet alternative adjacent to Parque Nacional Los Glaciares. Stop by the visitor center first. It's 17km beyond El Chaltén, just after Río Eléctrico.

Spa Yaten
HEALTH & FITNESS

(🏢 493394; spayaten@gmail.com; San Martín 36; one-hour massage AR$650; ⊙10am-9pm) Spa

Yaten has showers, robes and slippers, so sore hikers can come straight here off the trail. There are various therapies, massage, Jacuzzi tubs in a communal room and dry sauna. Reserve massages ahead.

✯ Festivals & Events

Fiesta Nacional de Trekking
SPORTS

In the first week of March, this event brings a circus of outdoor freaks for rock climbing, bouldering and woodcutting competitions, as well as running and mountain-bike races.

Fiesta del Pueblo
CULTURAL

On October 12, on the wet heels of winter while streets are still mired in mud, El Chaltén celebrates the town anniversary, with dancing in the school gym, barbecues and live music.

🛏 Sleeping

Reservations should be made at least one month in advance for the January–February high season – demand here is that great. Plus it would be particularly depressing to arrive in the dark with the wind howling and no bed waiting. One solution is to bring a bombproof tent – there's always space in the campgrounds.

Dorm beds fill up fast in summer. Unless otherwise noted, thin walls, cramped dorms and insufficient shared facilities are the norm.

Albergue Patagonia
HOSTEL $

(🏢 493019; www.patagoniahostel.com.ar; Av San Martín 392; s/d/tr with bathroom US$65/77/88, dm/s/d without bathroom US$17/40/45; ⊙Sep-May; @ 🌐) A gorgeous and welcoming wooden farmhouse with helpful staff. Dorms in a separate building are spacious and modern, with good service and a humming atmosphere. The B&B features rooms with private bathrooms, kitchen use and a sumptuous buffet breakfast at Fuegia Bistro.

Also rents bikes and offers a unique bike tour to Lago del Desierto with shuttle options.

Lo de Trivi
HOSTEL $

(🏢 493255; www.lodetrivi.com; Av San Martín 675; dm US$22, d with/without bathroom US$84/62; 🌐) A good budget option, this converted house has added shipping containers and decks with antique beds as porch seating. It's a bit hodgepodge but works. There's various tidy shared spaces with and without TV; the best is the huge industrial kitchen

El Chaltén

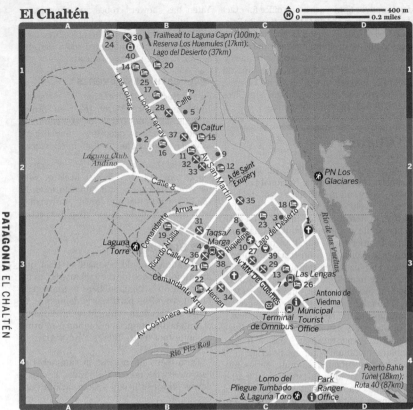

Trailhead to Laguna Capri (100m);
Reserva Los Huemules (17km);
Lago del Desierto (37km)

Caltur

A de Saint Exupery

PN Los Glaciares

Laguna Club Andino

Calle 8

Arrua

Taqsa/Marga

Laguna Torre

Lago del Desierto

Río de las Vueltas

Las Lengas

Antonio de Viedma

Municipal Tourist Office

Terminal de Omnibus

Río Fitz Roy

Lomo del Pliegue Tumbado & Laguna Toro

Park Ranger Office

Puerto Bahía Túnel (18km); Ruta 40 (87km)

for guests. Doubles in snug containers can barely fit a bed.

Condor de Los Andes　　HOSTEL $
(☎493101; www.condordelosandes.com; cnr Río de las Vueltas & Halvor Halvorsen; dm/d/tr US$18/66/79; @🛜) This homey hostel has the feel of a ski lodge, with worn bunks, warm rooms and a roaring fire. The guest kitchen is immaculate and there are comfortable lounge spaces.

Posada La Base　　GUESTHOUSE $
(☎493031; www.elchaltenpatagonia.com.ar; Calle 10, No 16; d/tr US$70/90) A smart, sprawling house with spacious rooms that all face outside and have access to an immaculate kitchen. Large groups should book rooms 5 and 6, which share an inside kitchen with dining area. The reception area has a popular video loft with a multilingual collection. The rates we have indicated don't include the discount for two or more nights.

Inlandsis　　GUESTHOUSE $
(☎493276; www.inlandsis.com.ar; Lago del Desierto 480; d US$63-75; ☺Oct-Apr) This small, relaxed brick house offers economical rooms with bunk beds (some are airless, check before booking) or larger, pricier doubles with two twin beds or a queen-sized bed. It also has bilevel cabins with bathtubs, kitchens and DVD players.

Rancho Grande Hostel　　HOSTEL $
(☎493092; www.ranchograndehostel.com; Av San Martín 724; dm/d/tr/q US$25/98/120/140; @🛜) Serving as Chaltén's Grand Central Station (Chaltén Travel buses stop here), this bustling backpacker factory has something for everyone, from bus reservations to internet (extra) and cafe service. Clean four-bed rooms are stacked with blankets, and bathrooms sport rows of shower stalls. Private rooms have their own bathroom and free breakfast.

El Chaltén

PATAGONIA EL CHALTÉN

Hostel Pioneros del Valle HOSTEL $
(☏491368; www.caltur.com.ar/pioneros/hostel.html;
Av San Martín 451; dm/d/tr US$15/70/85; ☎) This
behemoth has mixed six-bed dorms with in-
room bathrooms, lockers, free wi-fi, and a
plasma TV. Run by a transport company, there
are also travel and sleep packages.

Camping El Relincho CAMPGROUND $
(☏493007; www.elrelinchopatagonia.com.ar; Av San
Martín 545; campsite per person/vehicle US$10/5,
4-person cabin US$100) A private campground
with wind-whipped and exposed sites.

★Nothofagus B&B B&B $$
(☏493087; www.nothofagusbb.com.ar; cnr Hensen
& Riquelme; s/d/tr with bathroom US$84/92/110,
without bathroom US$68/76/95; ☼ Oct-Apr; @☎)
✐ Attentive and adorable, this chalet-style
inn offers a toasty retreat with hearty break-
fast options. Practices that earn them the
Sello Verde (green seal) include separating
organic waste and replacing towels only
when asked. Wooden-beam rooms have
carpet and some views. Those with hallway
bathrooms share with one other room.

Anita's House CABIN $$
(☏493288; www.anitashouse.com.ar; Av San
Martín 249; 4-/6-person cabin from US$140/240;
☎) When the wind howls, these few modern
cabins are a snug spot for groups, couples
or families, smack in the center of town.
Owner-run and impeccable service. Kitchens come fully equipped and there's room
service and cable TV. Two-story cabins, with
higher rates, are more spacious.

Posada Lunajuim INN $$
(☏493047; www.lunajuim.com; Trevisán 45; s/d/
tr US$95/115/140; ☎) ✐ Combining modern
comfort with a touch of the offbeat, this wel-
coming inn gets good reviews from guests.
The halls are lined with the owner's mono-
chrome sculptures and textured paintings,
and a stone fireplace and library provide a
rainy-day escape. Nice touches include DIY
box lunches and a buffet breakfast.

Pudu Lodge HOTEL $$
(☏493365; www.pudulodge.com; Calle Las Loicas
97; d US$140; @☎) This comfy lodging with
modern style has 20 spacious rooms and a
cathedral-ceilinged great room where buffet
breakfasts are served. Service is congenial.
The building itself has some construction
snafus and it would be considered overpriced
if rooms were not in such high demand.

Senderos Hostería B&B $$$
(☏493336; www.senderoshosteria.com.ar; Peri-
to Moreno 35; s/d/ste US$170/190/215) This

contemporary, corrugated-tin home offers wonderful amenities for trekkers seeking creature comforts. The on-site restaurant serves exquisite gourmet meals with excellent wines and attentive service – a real perk when you've spent a day outdoors. Smart rooms have soft white sheets, firm beds, lock boxes and occasional Fitz Roy views.

Kaulem BOUTIQUE HOTEL **$$$**
(☑ 493251; www.kaulem.com.ar; cnr Av Antonio Rojo & Comandante Arrua; s/d US$160/175, s/d cabin US$135/150; ☎) ✦ With a cozy lodge atmosphere, this boutique hotel is rustic and stylish, with just four rooms, all with Fitz Roy views, and an adjacent cabin. The buffet breakfast includes yogurt, homemade bread and fruit. Guests share a huge open dining and living area piped with good music and stocked with books and chess.

Hostería El Puma LODGE **$$$**
(☑ 493095; www.hosteriaelpuma.com.ar; Lionel Terray 212; s/d/tr US$148/185/221; ☎) This luxury lodge with 12 comfortable rooms offers intimacy without pretension, as well as huge buffet breakfasts. The rock-climbing and summit photographs and maps lining the hall may inspire your next expedition, but lounging by the fireplace is the most savory way to end the day.

Destino Sur HOTEL **$$$**
(☑ 493360; www.hoteldestinosur.com; Lionel Terray 370; d/tr US$234/295) Storm this castle via the oversized medieval doors and a perfectly acceptable high-end hotel awaits. Indeed, with 24 rooms and floors yet to finish, it is an impressive block of stone, rod iron and finished wood. Amenities include satellite TV, minibar and lock boxes in tasteful rooms with native accents,and there is a gym and spa with Jacuzzi and sauna.

Hotel Poincenot HOTEL **$$$**
(☑ 493252; www.hotelpoincenot.com; Av San Martín 668; d US$145-165; ☎) New and modern, this busy hotel has 20 rooms with flat-screen TVs, and comfortable beds decked in down bedding and colorful throws. Spacious rooms include a cathedral-ceiling living room, dining area and bar. Service is professional and attentive.

ESTANCIAS IN PATAGONIA

Most assume *estancias* (ranches) are all about livestock, but these offbeat offerings prove otherwise.

A Wealth of Wildlife

➡ Meet the neighbors – that would be the penguins, seabirds and elephant seals – around Península Valdés' Estancia Rincón Chico (p413).

➡ Spot dozens of the namesake species of Estancia El Cóndor (p459) at this rugged mountain ranch north of El Chaltén.

➡ View the diverse fauna of Magellanic penguins, sea lions, guanacos and pumas at Hostería Monte León (p430).

Breathtaking Beauty

➡ Luxuriate among glaciers, lakes and the ragged Cerro Fitz Roy in the exclusive Hostería Estancia Helsingfors (p470).

➡ Explore the wonders of a petrified forest and sea islands inhabited solely by birds, penguins and sea lions at the magical Bahía Bustamante (p425).

Just Like Indiana Jones

➡ Trek to Unesco World Heritage site Cueva de las Manos from Hostería Cueva de las Manos (p446), via the serpentine red-rock canyon of Río de las Pinturas.

The Bargain Bin

➡ Grab your zzzs in a bunk bed and save some bucks: Estancia El Cóndor (p459), Hostería Cueva de las Manos (p446) and Estancia Casa de Piedra (p446) all offer affordable *refugio* (rustic shelter) lodgings. Those with higher price tags can include all meals and excursions, delivering a lot for your money.

✖ Eating

Groceries, especially produce, are limited and expensive. Bring what you can from El Calafate.

La Lucinda
CAFE $

(☑ 493202; Av San Martín 175; mains AR$84-143; ☺ 7am-midnight; ✐) With hot sandwiches (including good vegetarian options) and a selection of coffee, tea and wine. This artsy, sky-blue cafe is friendly and almost always open – a godsend when the weather is howling. Breakfast is served too.

Domo Blanco
ICE CREAM $

(Av MM De Güemes s/n; snacks AR$40; ☺ 2pm-midnight) Homemade ice cream made with flavors like lemon ginger and blueberry marscapone. The fruit is harvested from a local *estancia* and calafate bushes in town.

Distrisur Supermercado
SUPERMARKET $

(☑ 02902-494784; San Martín 580; ☺ 9am-10pm) The grocery store with the widest selection in town. Cash only.

★ La Cervecería
PUB FOOD $$

(☑ 493109; Av San Martín 320; mains AR$80-160; ☺ noon-midnight) That après-hike pint usually evolves into a night out in this humming pub with *simpatico* staff and a feisty female beer master. Savor a stein of unfiltered blond pilsner or turbid bock with pasta or *locro* (a spicy stew of maize, beans, beef, pork and sausage).

Techado Negro
CAFE $$

(☑ 493268; Av Antonio Rojo; mains AR$60-145; ☺ noon-midnight; ✐) ✔ With local paintings on the wall, bright colors and a raucous, unkempt atmosphere in keeping with El Chaltén, this homespun cafe serves up abundant, good-value and sometimes healthy Argentine fare. Think homemade empanadas, squash stuffed with *humita* (sweet tamale), brown rice vegetarian dishes, soups and pastas. It also offers box lunches.

Patagonia Rebelde
ARGENTINE $$

(☑ 493208; San Martín 430; mains AR$130-240; ☺ 12:30-4pm & 6pm-midnight) With left-leaning murals and a rustic finish, this no-frills eatery serves huge, tasty portions *al disco,* cooked in enormous iron platters. One portion of orange chicken or lamb with mushrooms and bacon could easily serve two famished hikers, veggies and fries included. The fried *provoleta* cheese is nice too. Service is friendly but no one is rushing.

Ahonikenk
ARGENTINE $$

(Av MM De Güemes 23; mains AR$90-180; ☺ noon-3pm & 7-11pm) This pint-sized log restaurant is known for its good price-to-quality ratio. Bus drivers feed on oversized *milanesas* that could feed a family of four, particularly if you order yours with fried eggs on top. There's also good trout, pasta, pizza and salads.

El Muro
ARGENTINE $$

(☑ 493248; Av San Martín 912; mains AR$40-190; ☺ noon-3pm & 7-11pm) For ribsticking mountain food (think massive stir-fry, tenderloin stroganoff or trout with crisp grilled veggies), head to this tiny outpost at the end of the road.

Patagonicus
PIZZA $$

(☑ 493025; Av MM De Güemes 57; pizza AR$80-160; ☺ 11am-midnight Nov-Apr) The best pizza in town, with 20 kinds of pizza, salads and wine served at sturdy wood tables surrounded by huge picture windows. Cakes and coffee are also worth trying.

★ La Tapera
ARGENTINE $$$

(☑ 493195; Antonio Rojo 74; mains AR$142-275; ☺ noon-3pm & 6:30-11pm Oct-Apr) With tender steak in balsamic sauce, ultra-fresh trout from Lago del Desierto and red-wine glasses as big as your head, it is hard to go wrong at Chipo's place, reminiscent of a log cabin with open fireplace. Service is snappy, portions generous and there are wonderful wine options.

Estepa
ARGENTINE $$$

(☑ 493069; cnr Cerro Solo & Av Antonio Rojo; mains AR$90-270; ☺ 11:30am-2pm & 6-11pm) Local favorite Estepa cooks up consistent, flavorful dishes such as lamb with calafate sauce, trout ravioli or spinach crepes. Portions are small but artfully presented, with veggies that hail from the on-site greenhouse. For a shoestring dinner, consider their on-site rotisserie takeout service.

Fuegia Bistro
INTERNATIONAL $$$

(☑ 493243; Av San Martín 342; mains AR$120-240; ☺ 6-11pm Mon-Sat; ✐) This eatery boasts good veggie options, such as brown rice felafel and stuffed eggplant, though it's a little dependent on its long-standing presence and expensive for the quality.

☕ Drinking & Nightlife

La Vinería
WINE BAR

(☑ 493301; Av Lago del Desierto 265; ☺ 4pm-3am) Transplanted from Alaska, this tiny wine bar offers a long Argentine wine list accompanied by craft-beer options and standout appetizers.

OFF THE BEATEN TRACK

TREKKING INTO CHILE

Gonzo travelers can skirt the Southern Ice Field on foot to get from Argentina's Parque Nacional Los Glaciares and El Chaltén to Villa O'Higgins, the last stop on Chile's Carretera Austral. This one- to three-day trip can be completed between November and March. Bring all provisions, Chilean currency, plus your passport and rain gear. Boat delays are not unheard of, so be prepared to stay overnight and pack enough food. Here's the nuts and bolts:

Step 1 Grab the shuttle bus from El Chaltén to the south shore of Lago del Desierto, 37km away (AR$350, one hour).

Step 2 A ferry/tour boat travels to the north shore of Lago del Desierto (AR$480, one-hour ferry or 4½-hour tour). Another option is to hike the demanding mountain trail (15km, five hours) that follows the coast at a distance. Warning: cyclists will have to carry their bikes in many places. Pass through Argentine customs and immigration here. Camping is allowed at the border post only.

Step 3 From the north shore of Lago del Desierto, trek or ride to Laguna Larga (1½ hours). Camping is not allowed.

Step 4 Trek or ride to Laguna Redonda (1½ hours). Camping is not allowed.

Step 5 Trek or ride to Candelario Mansilla (two hours). Candelario Mansilla has lodging in a family farmhouse, guided treks and horse rental (riding or pack horse per day CH$30,000). Pass through Chilean customs and immigration here.

Step 6 Take the Hielo Sur catamaran (CH$44,000, four hours) from Candelario Mansilla, on the south edge of Lago O'Higgins, to Puerto Bahamondez. Trips go one to three times a week, usually on Saturday with some Monday or Wednesday departures. A bus goes from Puerto Bahamondez to Villa O'Higgins (CH$2500).

In Villa O'Higgins, **El Mosco** (☑067-243-1819; www.patagoniaelmosco.blogspot.com; Carretera Austral Km1240; campsites per person CH$5000, dm CH$9000, d CH$45,000, s/d without bathroom CH$18,000/30,000) has good lodging options. For Chilean ferry information, consult **Hielo Sur** (☑067-243-1821; www.villaohiggins.com) in O'Higgins.

La Chocolatería   CAFE
(☑493008; Lago del Desierto 105; chocolate & coffee drinks AR$60; ⊙11am-9pm Mon-Fri, 9am-9pm Sat & Sun Nov-Mar) This irresistible chocolate factory tells the story of local climbing legends on the walls. It makes for an intimate evening out, with options ranging from spirit-spiked hot cocoa to wine and fondue.

🛍 Shopping

Viento Oeste   BOOKS
(☑493200; Av San Martín 898; ⊙10am-9pm) Sells books, maps and souvenirs and rents a wide range of camping equipment, as do several other sundries shops around town.

ℹ Information

El Chaltén has been slow to catch up to modern times, but now boasts cell-phone service, slow internet and two ATMs. Those coming from El Calafate might want to bring extra cash in case the El Chaltén's ATMs are out of service. There's one gas station at the entrance to town. Euros and US dollars are widely accepted but credit cards are not, though some restaurants, high-end hotels and tour operators accept them. Visit www.elchalten.com for a good overview of the town.

Banco de Santa Cruz (Terminal de Omnibus) LINK-access ATM machine in the bus terminal.

Banco La Nacion (Av MM De Güemes 151) Has a LINK-access ATM.

Chaltén Travel (☑493092; www.chaltentravel.com; cnr Avs MM De Güemes & Lago del Desierto) Books airline tickets and bus travel on RN 40.

Municipal Tourist Office (☑493370; Terminal de Omnibus; ⊙9am-10pm) Friendly and extremely helpful, with lodging lists and good information on town and tours. English is spoken.

Park Ranger Office (☑493004, 493024; pnlgzonanorte@apn.gov.ar; donations welcome; ⊙9am-8pm Dec-Feb, 10am-5pm Mar-Nov) Many daytime buses stop for a short bilingual orientation at this visitor center, just before the bridge over the Río Fitz Roy. Park rangers distribute a map and town directory and do a good job of explaining Parque Nacional Los Glaciares' ecological issues.

Climbing documentaries are shown at 2pm daily – great for rainy days. Open 10am to 5pm in the low season.

Puesto Sanitario (☑ 493033; AM De Agostini 70) Provides basic health services.

❶ Getting There & Away

El Chaltén is 220km from El Calafate via newly paved roads. A bicycle path heads from town to Hostería El Pilar, in Parque Nacional Los Glaciares. Bike rentals (three hours for AR$150) are available in various locations.

All buses go to the new **Terminal de Omnibus**, located near the entrance to town. For El Calafate (AR$350, 3½ hours), **Chaltén Travel** (☑ 493092, 493005; Av San Martín 635) has daily departures at 7:30am, 1pm and 6pm in summer. **Caltur** (☑ 493079; Av San Martín 520) and **Taqsa/Marga** (☑ 493068; Av Antonio Rojo 88) also make the trip for slightly cheaper (AR$340). Service is less frequent in low season.

Las Lengas (☑ 493023; www.transportelaslengas.com.ar; Antonio de Viedma 95) has shuttle service directly to El Calafate's airport (AR$500) in high season. It also has minivans to Lago del Desierto (AR$250), Hostería El Pilar (AR$100) and Río Eléctrico (AR$150). There is also a taxi service to El Calafate's airport (AR$2000).

Chaltén Travel goes to Bariloche on odd days of the month in high season (AR$1100, two days), with an overnight stop in Perito Moreno (meals and accommodations extra).

Parque Nacional Los Glaciares (North)

In the northern part of the park, the Fitz Roy Range – with its rugged wilderness and shark-tooth summits – is the de facto trekking capital of Argentina. It also draws world-class climbers for whom **Cerro Torre** and **Cerro Fitz Roy** are milestone ascents notorious for brutal weather conditions. But you don't have to be extreme to enjoy the numerous well-marked trails for hiking and jaw-dropping scenery – that is, when the clouds clear.

Parque Nacional Los Glaciares is divided into geographically separate northern and southern sectors. El Chaltén is the gateway town for the northern part of the park. El Calafate is the gateway town for the southern section of the park, which features the Glaciar Perito Moreno.

🏃 Activities

Before heading out on hikes, stop by El Chaltén's Park Ranger Office (p454) for updated trail conditions. The most stable weather for hiking comes not in summer but in March and April, when there is less wind (and fewer people). From May to September hikers must register pre and post-hike at the office. During the winter months of June and July trails may be closed or high water may flood bridges – check first with the Park Ranger Office.

Experienced backpackers can register to hike in the remote areas, which require some route finding. A first-person ranger update is necessary for these hikes. For more information on hiking, read Lonely Planet's *Trekking in the Patagonian Andes*.

Laguna Torre   HIKING

Views of the stunning rock needle of Cerro Torre are the highlight here. If you have good weather – ie little wind – and clear skies, make this hike (9km, three hours one way) a priority, since the toothy Cerro Torre is the most difficult local peak to see on normal blustery days.

There are two trail options that later merge. One starts at the northwestern edge of El Chaltén. From a signpost on Av San Martín, head west on Eduardo Brenner and then right to find the signposted start of the track. The Laguna Torre track winds up westward around large boulders on slopes covered with typical Patagonian dry-land plants, then leads southwest past a wet meadow to a junction with a trail coming in from the left after 35 to 45 minutes.

Starting from the southern end of El Chaltén, follow Lago del Desierto west past the edge of town, then drop to the riverbed, passing a tiny hydroelectric installation. At a signpost the route climbs away from the river and leads on through scattered lenga and ñire woodland (a small, deciduous southern beech species), with the odd wire fence to step over, before merging with a more prominent (signposted) path coming in from the right.

Continue up past a rounded bluff to the **Mirador Laguna Torre**, a crest with the first clear view up the valley to the extraordinary 3128m rock spire of Cerro Torre, above a sprawling mass of intersecting glaciers.

The trail dips gently through stands of lenga, before cutting across open scrubby river flats and old revegetated moraines to reach a signposted junction with the Sendero Madre e Hija, a shortcut to Campamento Poincenot,

Parque Nacional Los Glaciares (North)

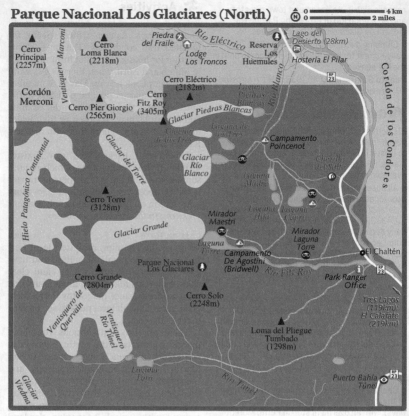

50 to 90 minutes on. Continuing upvalley, bear left at another signposted fork and climb over a forested embankment to cross a small alluvial plain, following the fast-flowing glacial waters of the Río Fitz Roy. You'll arrive at **Campamento De Agostini** (formerly Bridwell) after a further 30 to 40 minutes. This free campground (with pit toilet) gets busy; it serves as a base camp for Cerro Torre climbers. The only other nearby camping is in a pleasant grove of riverside lengas below Cerro Solo.

Follow the trail along the lake's north side for about an hour to **Mirador Maestri** (no camping).

Laguna de Los Tres   HIKING

This hike to a high alpine tarn is a bit more strenuous (10km and four hours one way) than the hike to Laguna Torre. It's also one of the most photogenic spots in the park. Exercise extra caution in foul weather as trails are very steep.

The trail starts from a yellow-roofed pack station. After about an hour there's a signed lateral to excellent free backcountry **campsites** at Laguna Capri. The main trail continues gently through windswept forests and past small lakes, meeting the Lagunas Madre and Hija trail. Carry on through wind-worn ñire forest and along boggy terrain to **Río Blanco** (three hours) and the woodsy, mice-plagued **Campamento Poincenot**. The trail splits before Río Blanco to Río Eléctrico. Stay left to reach a climbers' base camp. Here the trail zigzags steeply up the tarn to the eerily still, glacial **Laguna de los Tres**, in close view of 3405m Cerro Fitz Roy. Be prepared for high, potentially hazardous winds and allow extra time.

Piedra del Fraile   HIKING

This walk is approximately 8km (three hours) one way.

From **Hostería El Pilar** walk 1km northeast on the main road to hit the signposted trailhead for Piedra del Fraile, near a big iron bridge. The trail follows the Valle Eléctrico. There are some stream crossings with sturdy tree trunks to cross on and one bridge crossing; all are well-marked.

Pass through pastures and branches left up the valley along **Río Eléctrico**, enclosed by sheer cliffs, before reaching the private **Lodge Los Troncos** (campsites per person US$20, dm US$50). There's a restaurant but no guest kitchen. Dorm rates are cheapest with your own sleeping bag. Visitors must pay an entry fee (AR$500). Reservations are not possible since there are no phones – simply show up. The campground has a kiosk, restaurant and excellent services, and the owners can recommend trails.

Buses to Lago del Desierto drop hikers at the Río Eléctrico bridge (AR$100).

Lomo del Pliegue Tumbado & Laguna Toro
HIKING
Heading southwest from the Park Ranger Office, this trail (10km and four to five hours one way) skirts the eastern face of Loma del Pliegue Tumbado going toward Río Túnel, then cuts west and heads to Laguna Toro. It's less crowded than the main routes. The hike is gentle, but prepare for strong winds and carry extra water.

It's the only hike that allows views of both Cerros Torre and Fitz Roy at once.

⟲ Tours

Las Lengas
BUS TOUR
(☎02962-493023; Antonio de Viedma 95, El Chaltén) Minibus service to Lago del Desierto (AR$250, two hours), leaving El Chaltén at 8am, noon and 3pm daily. At the south end of the lake, travelers can dine in the inviting restaurant at **Hostería El Pilar** (☎02962-493002; www.hosteriaelpilar.com.ar; mains AR$110-300; ⊙with advance reservation only Nov-Mar).

Exploradores Lago del Desierto
BOAT TOUR
(☎02966-15-467103; www.exploradoreslagodeldesierto.com; tour with/without bus transfer AR$950/500) This new tour takes visitors boating on Lago del Desierto with a short trek to Glaciar Vespignani. Rates are discounted without the transfer from El Chaltén.

Hielo Sur
BOAT TOUR
(☎in Chile 56-0672-431821; www.villaohiggins.com) This Chilean catamaran takes border-crossers from Candelario Mansilla. Some trips go to Glaciar O'Higgins (CH$72,000) on the Southern Ice Shelf on the way, others go directly to Villa O'Higgins (CH$45,000) via Puerto Bahamondez. From Puerto Bahamondez, bus service to Villa O'Higgins is CH$2500.

Camino Abierto
TOUR
(☎493043; www.caminoabierto.com; off San Martín s/n, El Chaltén) Operator offering trekking throughout Patagonia and guided crossing to Villa O'Higgins.

Ice Climbing & Trekking
Many companies offer ice-climbing courses and ice treks, some including sleds pulled by Siberian huskies. Multiday guided hikes over the Hielo Patagónico Continental (Continental Ice Field) have the feel of polar expeditions. Catering to serious trekkers, this route involves technical climbing, including use of crampons and strenuous river crossings.

Fitzroy Expediciones
MOUNTAINEERING
(☎02962-436424; www.fitzroyexpediciones.com.ar; Av San Martín 56, El Chaltén) Runs glacier-trekking excursions on Viedma Glacier, a five-day itinerary that includes trekking in the Fitz Roy and Cerro Torre area, as well as other excursions. Note that Fitzroy Expediciones does accept credit cards, unlike most businesses in town.

Casa de Guias
MOUNTAINEERING
(☎02962-493118; www.casadeguias.com.ar; Lago del Desierto s/n, El Chaltén) Friendly and professional, with English-speaking guides certified by the Argentine Association of Mountain Guides (AAGM). It specializes in small groups. Offerings include mountain traverses, ascents for the very fit and rock-climbing classes.

Patagonia Aventura
ADVENTURE TOUR
(☎02962-493110; www.patagonia-aventura.com; Av San Martín 56, El Chaltén) Offers ice trekking (AR$1700, two hours) and ice climbing (AR$3000, all day) on Glaciar Viedma with cruise-ship access. Tours do not include transportation to Puerto Bahía Túnel (AR$170), where excursions depart.

El Chaltén Mountain Guides
MOUNTAINEERING
(☎02962-493251; www.chaltenmountainguides.com; cnr Av Antonio Rojo & Comandante Arrua, El Chaltén) Licensed guides do ice-field traversing, trekking and mountaineering. Rates decrease significantly with group size. The office is in the Kaulem hotel.

Fly-Fishing
Anglers should contact **Chaltén Fishing** (☎02962-493169; www.chaltenfishing.com.ar; Cabo García 267 , El Chaltén) for half-day trips to

Lago del Desierto or for full-day excursions that include a few hours at Laguna Larga. Equipment is provided; call for current rates and information on fishing licenses.

Horseback Riding

Horses can be used to trot round town and to carry equipment with a guide (prices negotiable), but are not allowed on national-park trails. Outfitter **El Relincho** (02692-493007, in El Calafate 02902-491961; www.elrelinchopatagonia.com.ar; Av San Martín 505, El Chaltén; 4hr ride AR$850) takes riders to the pretty valley of Río de las Vueltas and also offers more challenging rides combined with a ranch barbecue. Cabin-style accommodations are also available.

Kayak & Canoe Trips

As El Chaltén grows, so do the aquatic offerings. Fitzroy Expediciones (p457) has half-day guided kayaking trips on the Río de las Vueltas that stop for lunch at the company's adventure camp. (Overnight stays are also available in the timber lodge and eight cabins, 17km north of town – ask at the office in El Chaltén for more info.) You can also book two-day canoe and camping trips to Río La Leona.

Lake Cruises

Patagonia Aventura (p457) offers cruises (per person AR$650, plus AR$170 transfer) on Lago Viedma with impressive views of the 40m Glaciar Viedma, grinding from Cerro Fitz Roy. Boat trips leave from Puerto Bahía Túnel and last 2½ hours.

Rock Climbing

Outfitters around town rent equipment; **Patagonia Mágica** (02692-486261; www.patagoniamagica.com; Fonrouge s/n, El Chaltén) runs one-day rock-climbing workshops for beginners. Experienced climbers can go on the Glaciar Laguna Torre with certified guides.

🛏 Sleeping

Free backcountry campgrounds have one pit toilet. Some sites have dead wood for windbreaks but fires are prohibited. Water is pure as glacial melt; only wash downstream from the campground and pack out all trash.

❶ Getting There & Away

Parque Nacional Los Glaciares is just outside El Chaltén, which is convenient if you're driving your own car; otherwise, most excursions offer transfers (AR$100 one way) in and out of the park; taxis cost more (AR$300).

El Calafate

📞 02902 / POP 21,130

Named for the berry that, once eaten, guarantees your return to Patagonia, El Calafate hooks you with another irresistible attraction: Glaciar Perito Moreno, 80km away in Parque Nacional Los Glaciares. The glacier is a magnificent must-see, but its massive popularity has encouraged tumorous growth and rapid upscaling in once-quaint El Calafate. However, it's still a fun place to be, with a range of traveler services. The strategic location between El Chaltén and Torres del Paine (Chile) makes it an inevitable stop for those in transit.

Located 320km northwest of Río Gallegos, and 32km west of RP 11's junction with northbound RN 40, El Calafate flanks the southern shore of Lago Argentino. The main strip, Av del Libertador General San Martín (typically abbreviated to Libertador), is dotted with cutesy knotted-pine souvenir shops, chocolate shops, restaurants and tour offices. Beyond the main street, pretensions melt away quickly: muddy roads lead to ad-hoc developments and open pastures.

January and February are the most popular (and costly) months to visit, but as shoulder-season visits grow steadily, both availability and prices stay a challenge.

◎ Sights

★ Glaciarium   MUSEUM

(497912; www.glaciarium.com; adult/child AR$230/100; ⊙9am-8pm Sep-May, 11am-8pm Jun-Aug) Unique and exciting, this gorgeous museum illuminates the world of ice. Displays and bilingual films show how glaciers form, along with documentaries on continental ice expeditions and stark meditations on climate change. Adults suit up in furry capes for the *bar de hielo* (AR$140 including drink), a blue-lit below-zero club serving vodka or fernet and Coke in ice glasses.

The gift shop sells handmade and sustainable gifts crafted by Argentine artisans. It also hosts international cinema events. It's 6km from Calafate toward the national park. To get there, take the free hourly shuttle from 1 de Mayo between Av Libertador and Roca.

Reserva Natural
Laguna Nimez   WILDLIFE RESERVE

(admission AR$100; ⊙daylight hours) Prime avian habitat alongside the lakeshore north of town, with a self-guided trail and staffed Casa Verde information hut with binocular

ESTANCIA EL CÓNDOR

A burly slice of heaven, this remote **estancia** (✉ in Buenos Aires 011-4735-7704, satellite phone 011-4152-5400; www.cielospatagonicos.com; per person casco incl meals & excursions US$220; ☉ Oct-Mar) sits tucked into the shores of Lago San Martín. A private nature reserve, tawny steppe, mossy beech forest and frozen mountaintops comprise its 400 sq km.

Even for Patagonia this landscape seems oversized – from the massive turquoise lake (known as O'Higgins on its Chilean side), to the 13 kinds of orchids and craggy cliffs where condors wheel on the wind. Riding enthusiasts could do a week on horseback without running out of fresh terrain; in addition, the adjoining mountain refuge of La Nana provides a base camp even deeper in the wilderness. Trails are also apt for hiking, though river crossings should always be made with a guide. A day trip to the condorera (where condors nest) is a highlight.

The estancia occupies a curious footnote in Patagonian history. Its puesto (homestead) La Nana was home to an infamous Brit named Jimmy Radburn, who kidnapped a Tehuelche woman named Juana (with her consent – she had already been sold off by her father to pay a gambling debt) and came to this ultra-remote spot at the turn of the 20th century to raise a family. Currently La Nana is only accessible by a day-long hike or ride from the main casco (ranch house).

Rates include all meals and excursions. Lodgings are comfortable but not luxuriant. The casco has six rooms, each with a private bathroom, a large stone fireplace and a small collection of literature on the region. Meals include fresh vegetables from the greenhouse and meat from the ranch. Cheaper accommodations are at a more rustic bunkhouse; send an email for options.

Visitors can drive on their own or take a five-hour transfer from El Calafate (US$120), with set departures on Monday and Friday. El Cóndor is located three hours from Tres Lagos, 118km off RN 40, on the way to El Chaltén. There is no legal border crossing here.

rental. It's a great place to spot flamingos – but watching birds from El Calafate's shoreline on Lago Argentino can be just as good.

Centro de Interpretacíon Historico MUSEUM
(✉ 497799; www.museocalafate.com.ar; Av Brown & Bonarelli; admission AR$100; ☉ 10am-8pm Sep-May, 11am-5pm Jun-Aug) Small but informative, with a skeleton mold of *Austroraptor cabazai* (found nearby) and Patagonian history displays. The friendly host invites museum-goers for a post-tour *mate* (a bitter ritual tea).

☞ Tours

Some 40 travel agencies arrange excursions to Glaciar Perito Moreno and other local attractions, including fossil beds and stays at regional *estancias,* where you can hike, ride horses or relax. Tour prices for Glaciar Perito Moreno don't include the park entrance fee. Ask agents and other travelers about added benefits, such as extra stops, boat trips, binoculars or multilingual guides.

★ Glaciares Sur ADVENTURE TOUR
(✉ 02902-495050; www.glaciarsur.com; 9 de Julio 57; per person US$225-250) Get glacier stunned *and* skip the crowds with these day tours to the unexplored end of Parque Nacional Los Glaciares. Small groups drive to Lago Roca with an expert multilingual guide to view Glaciar Frias. The adventure option features a four-hour hike, the culture option includes a traditional *estancia asado* (barbecue grill) and off-hour visits to Glaciar Perito Moreno.

Caltur TOUR
(✉ 491368; www.caltur.com.ar; Libertador 1080) Specializes in El Chaltén tours and lodging packages.

Chaltén Travel TOUR
(✉ 492212; www.chaltentravel.com; Libertador 1174; ☉ 9am-9pm) Recommended tours to Glaciar Perito Moreno, stopping for wildlife viewing (binoculars provided); also specializes in RN 40 trips. Outsources some excursions to **Always Glaciers** (www.alwaysglaciers.com).

Overland Patagonia TOUR
(✉ 491243, 492243; www.glaciar.com; glacier tour AR$640) Operates out of both Hostel del Glaciar Libertador and Hostel del Glaciar Pioneros; organizes the alternative glacier trip to Glaciar Perito Moreno, which consists of an *estancia* visit, a one-hour hike in the park and optional lake navigation (AR$250 extra).

El Calafate

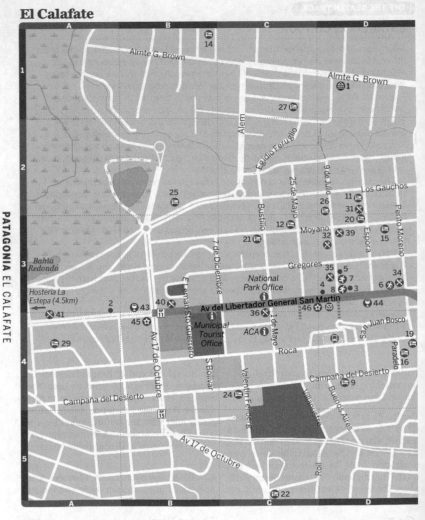

Enjoy! ADVENTURE TOUR

(📞497722; www.enjoycalafate.com; Via Ferrata AR$580) A popular outfitter specializing in adventure tours, with bilingual guides leading activities like climbing Cerro Roca and Via Ferrata (assisted ascent), rappelling and ziplining. There's no office – guests are picked up at their accommodations. Operations are based out of Estancia 25 de Mayo.

Calafate Fishing FISHING

(📞496545; www.calafatefishing.com; Libertador 1826; ☺10am-7pm Mon-Sat) Offers fun fly-fishing trips to Lago Roca (half-day AR$1700) and Lago Strobbel, where you can test ru-

mors that the biggest rainbow trout in the world lives here.

🛏 Sleeping

Though lodgings are abundant, popular offerings may book out well in advance. The core high season is January to February, although some places extend it from mid-October until April. Luxury hotels are being added at a quick clip, though not all offer the same standard. Look for deep discounts in low season.

The Municipal Tourist Office has a complete list of *cabañas* and apartment hotels,

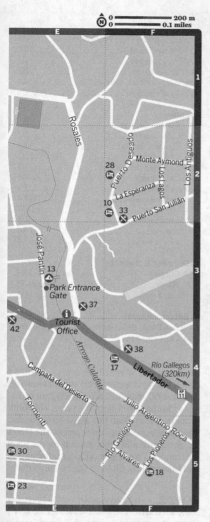

which are the best deals for groups and families. Most hostels offer pickup from the bus terminal.

Camping El Ovejero
CAMPGROUND **$**

(🖉 493422; www.campingelovejero.com.ar; José Pantín 64; campsite per person US$9; @ 🛜) Woodsy, well-kept (and slightly noisy) campsites with spotless showers that have 24-hour hot water. Locals boast that the on-site restaurant is one of the best deals in town for grill food. Extras include private tables, electricity and grills. It's located by the creek just north of the bridge into town.

Hostal Schilling
GUESTHOUSE **$**

(🖉 491453; http://hostalschilling.com; Paradelo 141; dm US$25, s/d/tr with bathroom US$63/75/95, d without bathroom US$60; 🛜) Good value and centrally located, this friendly guesthouse is a good choice for travelers. Much is due to the family owners, Cecilia, Marcelo and Raimiro, who look after guests with a cup of tea or help with logistical planning. It also has multiple living rooms and cafe service, with hearty lentil stew, if you don't feel like eating out.

They can also help with reservations for Estancia El Cóndor.

America del Sur
HOSTEL **$**

(🖉 493525; www.americahostel.com.ar; Puerto Deseado 151; dm US$35, d/q US$97/153; @ 🛜) This backpacker favorite has a stylish lodge setting with views and heated floors. Doubles are pleasant and uniform. There's a well-staffed and fun social scene, including nightly barbecues with salad buffet in high season.

I Keu Ken Hostel
HOSTEL **$**

(🖉 495175; www.patagoniaikeuken.com.ar; FM Pontoriero 171; dm AR$23, cabin per person US$80; @ 🛜) With helpful staff, artisan beer and a pet sheep, this quirky hostel has proven popular with travelers. Features include inviting common areas, a deck for lounging and first-rate barbecues (with amnesty for the pet sheep). Its location, near the top of a steep hill, offers views and a workout.

Las Cabañitas
CABIN **$**

(🖉 491118; www.lascabanitascalafate.com; Valentín Feilberg 218; 2-/3-person cabin US$84/105, dm/d without bathroom AR$25/65; ⊙ Aug-Jun; @ 🛜) A restful spot that has snug storybook A-frames with spiral staircases leading to loft beds and apartments. The energetic owner Gerardo also provides worthy meals, lunch boxes and helpful information. Touches include English lavender in the garden, a barbecue area and guest cooking facilities.

Bla! Guesthouse
HOSTEL **$**

(🖉 492220; www.blahostel.com; Espora 257; dm US$20-25, d/tr US$80/95; 🛜) If you're wondering where all the hipsters are, check out this tiny, mellow design hostel. While dorms are cramped, private rooms are comfortable, although walls are on the thin side.

Hostel del Glaciar Pioneros
HOSTEL **$**

(🖉 491243; www.glaciar.com; Los Pioneros 251; dm US$17, s US$48-67, d US$62-73; ⊙ Nov-Mar; @ 🛜) A 15-minute walk from town, this sprawling, renovated red house is one of the town's most long-standing hostels. Sociable, it includes

El Calafate

comfortable common areas, snug dorms and a small restaurant with homemade meals.

Calafate Hostel
HOSTEL $

(☏ 492450; www.calafatehostels.com; Moyano 1226; dm/s/d US$20/60/80/100; @ 🛜) Best suited to large groups, this mammoth log cabin ends up feeling blander than the competition. Double-bunk dorms are cozy, while the new annex features tidy brick doubles.

Hostel del Glaciar Libertador
HOSTEL $

(☏ 492492; www.glaciar.com; Libertador 587; dm/d/tr/q US$22/92/109/123; @ 🛜) The best deals here are dorm bunks with thick covers. Behind a Victorian facade, modern facilities include a top-floor kitchen, radiant floor heating, computers and a spacious common area with a plasma TV glued to sports channels. Breakfast is extra for dorm users (AR$84).

Hospedaje Jorgito
GUESTHOUSE $

(☏ 491323; Moyano 943; per person r with/without bathroom US$13/10) The lovely Señora Virginia has received generations of travelers in her modest home, decorated with vintage Barbies, doilies and synthetic flowers. Rooms vary in size but are bright and well kept. Guests can use the large kitchen.

Albergue Lago Argentino
HOSTEL $

(☏ 491423; lagoargentinohostel.com; Campaña del Desierto 1050; dm/s/d US$26/85/95) Run by Estela, who has been here for years, this pink property offers clean but squat basic dorms. The more appealing annex across the street has attractive and quiet garden rooms ideal for couples. Provides good local information and bike rentals. Close to the bus terminal.

Hosteria La Estepa
BOUTIQUE HOTEL $$

(☏ 493551; www.hosterialaestepa.com; Libertador 5310; s/d US$110/130, deluxe US$130/150; @ 🛜) Guests happily tuck into this snug, rustic lodging with panoramic lake views and farm antiquities. Of the 26 rooms, a handful have water views; the deluxe versions have small living areas. A sprawling 2nd-floor social area is strewn with regional maps and board games. The restaurant serves homemade meals. It's 5km west of the town center, toward the national park.

Cauquenes de Nimez
B&B $$

(☏ 492306; www.cauquenesdenimez.com.ar; Calle 303, No 79; d/tr US$98/120; ❄ 🛜) 🍃 Both modern and rustic, Gabriel's welcoming two-story lodge offers views of flamingos on the lake (from November through summer). Smart rooms decorated with corduroy duvets and nature photography also feature lock boxes and TVs. Personalized attention is a plus, as is the complimentary tea time with lavender muffins, and free bikes (donations support the nature reserve).

Posada Karut Josh
B&B $$

(☑496444; www.posadakarutjosh.com.ar; Calle 12, No 1882, Barrio Bahía Redonda; d US$75) Run by an Italian-Argentine couple, this peaceful aluminum-sided B&B features big, bright rooms and a lovely garden with lake views. Breakfast is abundant and satisfying meals (AR$85) are also available.

Miyazato Inn
B&B $$

(☑491953; www.miyazatoinn.com; Egidio Feruglio 150, Las Chacras; s/d US$120/150; @) Resembling a simple Japanese inn, this elegant B&B wins points for personalized service. Breakfast include sweets and *medialunas* (pastries), and excursionists get a hot thermos of coffee or tea to go. It's a five-minute walk away from the center of town.

Newenkelen
GUESTHOUSE $$

(☑493943; www.newenkelenposada.com.ar; Puerto Deseado 223; d/tr US$97/130; @☎) Perched on a hill above town, this intimate option features six immaculate brick rooms with tasteful bedding, tea in rooms and mountain views.

La Posada del Angel
GUESTHOUSE $$

(☑495025; posadadelangelcalafate.com; Madre Teresa de Calcutta 909; d/q US$90/120; ☎) Mature travelers or those who want a homey touch will appreciate this comfortable brick family home with just a few rooms for guests, as well as ample bathrooms, immaculate shared spaces and adorable pets. It's uphill from the town center.

Hotel La Loma
INN $$

(☑491016; www.lalomahotel.com; Roca 849; dm US$30, r US$91-137; ⊙Jul-May; ☎▨) Colonial furnishings and a lovely rock garden enhance this ranch-style retreat with chandeliers and antiques in creaky hallways. Superior rooms are spacious and bright, though dorms run toward monastic. Rates vary depending on views and room quality.

South B&B
B&B $$

(☑489555; www.southbb.com.ar; Av Juan Domingo Perón 1016; d/tr US$100/150; ⊙Oct-May; ☎) You would need a drone to get views of Lago Argentino to beat those of this enormous hillside hotel converted to a large B&B. Rooms are spacious and bright, though wi-fi reaches

only some. It's attentive and family run, with a trio of toy poodles standing guard.

Hotel Michelangelo
HOTEL $$

(☑491045; www.michelangelohotel.com.ar; Moyano 1020; d/tr US$128/156; ☎) Tour groups favor this Swiss-chalet-style lodging in the center of town. Recently renovated, it has a chic lobby and living area with stone fixtures and low lighting. Guest rooms have tasteful, muted colors, high ceilings and full amenities.

★ Madre Tierra
BOUTIQUE HOTEL $$$

(☑498880; www.madretierrapatagonia.com; 9 de Julio 239; d US$165) A beaut wrapped in Andean textiles and rustic simplicity. The biggest draw is the 2nd-floor living room, with comfy sofas and a blazing woodstove on chilly days. The house has just seven rooms, outfitted with oversized dressers and a clean, modern sensibility. It's run by longtime area guides Natacha and Mariano who also offer 4WD tours and transfers.

Los Sauces Casa Patagónica
HOTEL $$$

(☑495854; www.casalossauces.com; Los Gauchos 1352; d/ste from US$290/360; @☎) With an award-winning restaurant, full spa and spacious, immaculately manicured grounds where exotic birds roam and staff members zip by in golf carts, Los Sauces feels less hotel than luxury compound. The varied monochromatic interiors are gorgeous, with first-class beds, huge flat-screen TVs and stone bathrooms with Jacuzzis.

Hotel Posada Los Álamos
RESORT $$$

(☑491144; www.posadalosalamos.com; Moyano 1355; s/d US$241/264; @☎) Considering the amenities, prices are pretty reasonable at Calafate's original resort. There are lush rooms, overstuffed sofas, spectacular gardens, tennis courts, putting greens and a spa. It's enough to make you almost forget about seeing Glaciar Perito Moreno.

✖ Eating

For picnic provisions, small shops selling fresh bread, fine cheeses, sweets and wine are found on the side streets perpendicular to Libertador. Head to **La Anónima** (cnr Libertador & Perito Moreno; ⊙9am-10pm) for cheap takeout and groceries.

Esquina Varela
ARGENTINE $

(☑490666; Puerto Deseado 22; mains AR$85-110; ⊙7pm-late) Marrying good and cheap, this corrugated-tin eatery is a find in expensive Calafate. Start with some fried calamari

PATAGONIA EL CALAFATE

WORTH A TRIP

AGUAS ARRIBA

Set on the remote Lago del Desierto by the Chilean border, this exclusive **nature lodge** (☑ in Buenos Aires 11-15-6134-8452; www.aguasarribalodge.com; Lago del Desierto; per person per day incl meals & activities US$430) 🍃 provides a wonderous retreat into a silent lenga forest frequented by endangered huemul (Andean deer). The lodge itself has only five guest rooms and decks facing the massive Glacier Vespignani, with distant views of Cerro Fitz Roy on a clear day. There's guided fly-fishing and hiking on an extensive trail system with waterfalls, lookouts and secluded beaches. Green practices include composting, recycling and sustainable building, but it's made a true haven by the warm welcome from owners Pato and Ivor. Just getting there takes a while; guests arrive by private transfer and boat. A three-night stay is ideal. For ages 12 and up.

and beer. Filling lamb stew, steak and *locro* grace a short menu with vegetarian options. There's also live music.

La Fonda del Parillero   PARRILLA $
(9 de Julio 29; mains AR$45-180; ⊙ 10am-11pm) Skip the pretension and dine at this busy grill with a few sidewalk tables and takeout, a boon for late-night snacking. In addition to lamb steaks, it also offers homemade pastas, pies and a variety of empanadas.

Viva la Pepa   CAFE $
(☑ 491880; Amado 833; mains AR$60-120; ⊙ noon-9pm Mon-Sat) Decked out in children's drawings, this cheerful cafe specializes in crepes, but also offers great sandwiches with homemade bread (try the chicken with apple and blue cheese), fresh juice and gourds of *mate*.

María Brownies   DESSERTS $
(☑ 496817; Libertador 524; snacks AR$60; ⊙ 3:30-8:30pm Wed-Mon) This adorable teahouse is your go-to spot for homemade brownies, tart lemon pie and scones.

Panaderia Don Luis   BAKERY $
(Av Libertador 2421; snacks AR$10; ⊙ 7am-9pm) *Medialunas* and much more at this enormous bakery.

★**Buenos Cruces**   ARGENTINE $$
(☑ 492698; Espora 237; mains AR$130-220; ⊙ 7-11pm Mon-Sat) The new sensation in town is this tiny family-run enterprise bringing a twist to Argentine classics. Start with a warm beet salad with balsamic reduction. The nut-crusted trout is both enormous and satisfying, served on a bed of risotto, as are baked raviolis crisped at the edge and bubbling with Roquefort cheese. With good service.

Pura Vida   ARGENTINE $$
(☑ 493356; Libertador 1876; mains AR$90-185; ⊙ 7:30-11:30pm Thu-Tue; 🖉) Featuring the rare treat of Argentine home cooking, this offbeat, low-lit eatery is a must. Its longtime owners are found cooking up buttery spiced chicken pot pies and filling wine glasses. For vegetarians, brown rice and wok veggies or various salads are satisfying. Don't skip the decadent chocolate brownie with ice cream, steeped in warm berry sauce. Reserve ahead.

La Tablita   PARRILLA $$
(☑ 491065; www.la-tablita.com.ar; Rosales 24; mains AR$100-150; ⊙ noon-3:30pm & 7pm-midnight) Steak and spit-roasted lamb are the stars at this satisfying *parrilla*, popular beyond measure for good reason. For average appetites a half-steak will do, rounded out with a good malbec, fresh salad or garlic fries.

El Cucharón   ARGENTINE $$
(☑ 495315; 9 de Julio 145; mains AR$130-230; ⊙ noon-3pm & 8-11pm) This sophisticated eatery, tucked away in a small space a few blocks off the main street, is a relatively undiscovered gem and an excellent place to try the regional classic *cazuela de cordero* (lamb stew). The trout with lemon sauce and grilled vegetables is delicious, too.

La Lechuza   PIZZA $$
(Libertador 1301; mains AR$93-220; ⊙ noon-3pm & 6:30-11:30pm) Serves a classic selection of empanadas, salads and pizza on round wooden plates – try the sheep cheese and olive pizza with a local microbrew.

★**Mi Rancho**   ARGENTINE $$$
(☑ 490540; Moyano 1089; mains AR$160-230; ⊙ noon-3:30pm & 8pm-midnight) Inspired and intimate, with the owners themselves cooking and serving oversized osso buco, delicious braided pastas stuffed with king crab, divine salads and sweetbreads with wilted spinach on toast. For dessert, chocolat fondant or passion fruit semifreddo are

both worth the calorie hit, and more. In a tiny brick pioneer house with space for few. Reserve a few days ahead.

🍷 Drinking & Nightlife

Chopen   PUB
(Cervecería Artisanal; ☑249-6096; Libertador 1630; ☺8pm-2am) After a day in the wind and sun, this snug brewpub is a godsend. Beer is brewed on-site and the tiny kitchen churns out heaping trays of meats and cheeses and spicy beef empanadas.

Librobar   PUB
(Libertador 1015; ☺10am-3am; 🛜) Upstairs in the gnome village, this hip bookshop-bar serves coffee, bottled beers and pricey cocktails. Peruse the oversized photography books on Patagonian wildlife or bring your laptop and take advantage of the free wi-fi.

el ba'r   CAFE
(9 de Julio s/n; ☺9am-2pm) This trendy patio cafe is the hot spot for you and your sweater-clad puppy to order espresso, *submarinos* (hot milk with melted chocolate bar), green tea, gluten-free snacks or sandwiches (mains AR$80 to AR$115).

☆ Entertainment

La Tolderia   LIVE MUSIC
(☑491443; www.facebook.com/LaTolderia; Libertador 1177; ☺noon-4am Mon-Thu, to 6am Fri-Sun) This petite storefront opens its doors to dancing and live acts at night; it's probably the best spot to try if you're feeling boisterous.

Don Diego de la Noche   LIVE MUSIC
(Libertador 1603; ☺8pm-late) This perennial favorite serves dinner and features live music such as tango, guitar and *folklórica* (folk music).

🛈 Information

MEDICAL SERVICES
Hospital Municipal Dr José Formenti
(☑491001; Roca 1487)

MONEY
Withdraw your cash before the weekend rush – it isn't uncommon for ATMs to run out on Sundays. If you are headed to El Chaltén, consider getting extra cash here.
Banco Santa Cruz (Libertador 1285) Changes traveler's checks and has an ATM.

POST
Post Office (Libertador 1133)

TOURIST INFORMATION
ACA (Automóvil Club Argentino; ☑491004; cnr 1 de Mayo & Roca) Argentina's auto club; good source for provincial road maps.
Municipal Tourist Office (☑491090, 491466; www.elcalafate.tur.ar; Av Libertador 1411; ☺8am-8pm) Has town maps and general information. There's also a kiosk at the bus terminal (☑491090; www.elcalafate.gov.ar; cnr Libertador & Rosales; ☺8am-8pm); both have some English-speaking staff.
National Park Office (☑491545; Libertador 1302; ☺8am-8pm Dec-Apr, to 6pm May-Nov) Offers brochures and a decent map of Parque Nacional Los Glaciares. It's best to get information here before reaching the park.

TRAVEL AGENCIES
Most agents deal exclusively with nearby excursions and are unhelpful for other areas.
Tiempo Libre (☑491207; www.tiempolibre viajes.com.ar; Gregores 1294) Books flights.

🛈 Getting There & Away

AIR
The modern **Aeropuerto El Calafate** is 23km east of town off RP 11; the departure tax is US$38.

The following rates are one way. **Aerolíneas Argentinas** (☑492816, 492814; Libertador 1361) flies daily to Bariloche or Esquel (from AR$2491), Ushuaia (AR$1200), Trelew (AR$4224), and Aeroparque and Ezeiza in Buenos Aires (from AR$1930).
LADE (☑491262; Jean Mermoz 168) flies a few times a week to Río Gallegos (AR$665), Comodoro Rivadavia (AR$984), Ushuaia and Buenos Aires. **LAN** (☑495548; 9 de Julio 57) flies to Ushuaia weekly.

BUS
El Calafate's hilltop **bus terminal** (Roca s/n) is easily reached by a pedestrian staircase from the corner of Libertador and 9 de Julio. Book ahead in high season, as outbound seats can be in short supply.

For Río Gallegos, buses go four times daily; contact **Taqsa/Marga** (☑491843) or **Andesmar** (☑494250). Connections to Bariloche and Ushuaia may require leaving in the middle of the night and a change of buses in Río Gallegos.

For El Chaltén, buses leave daily at 8am, 2pm and 6pm. Both **Caltur** (☑491368; www.caltur.com.ar; Libertador 1080) and **Chaltén Travel** (p459) go to El Chaltén and drive the RN 40 to Bariloche (AR$2190, two days) in summer.

For Puerto Natales, Chile, **Cootra** (☑491444) and **Turismo Zahhj** (☑491631) depart at 8am and 8:30am daily (three times weekly in low season), crossing the border at Cerro Castillo, where it may be possible to connect to Torres del Paine.

Buses from El Calafate

DESTINATION	COST (AR$)	TIME (HR)
Bariloche	1740-2190	14/28 summer/winter
El Chaltén	350	3½
Puerto Natales (Chile)	475	5
Río Gallegos	360	4

❶ Getting Around

Airport shuttle **Ves Patagonia** (📞 494355; www.vespatagonia.com) offers door-to-door service (one way AR$120). There are several car-rental agencies at the airport. **Localiza** (📞 491398; www.localiza.com.ar; Libertador 687; ⊙ 9am-8pm) and **Servi Car** (📞 492541; www.servi4x4.com.ar; Libertador 695; ⊙ 9:30am-noon & 4-8pm Mon-Sat) offer car rentals from convenient downtown offices.

Renting a **bike** is an excellent way to get a feel for the area and cruise the dirt roads by the lake. **Albergue Lago Argentino** (p462) offers rentals.

Around El Calafate

From El Calafate, paved RN 40 cuts southeast across vast steppe for 95km, then jogs south at **El Cerrito** and turns to gravel. Staying on paved RP 5 means a slow-going, five-hour, 224km bore of a trip southeast to **Río Gallegos**. From there, paved RP 7 connects back to RN 40 for the Chilean border crossing at Cerro Castillo–Cancha Carrera, Parque Nacional Torres del Paine and Puerto Natales.

Parque Nacional Los Glaciares (South)

Among Earth's most dynamic and accessible ice fields, **Glaciar Perito Moreno** is the stunning centerpiece of the southern sector of **Parque Nacional Los Glaciares** (admission AR$260, collected after 8am). It's 30km long, 5km wide and 60m high, but what makes it exceptional in the world of ice is its constant advance – it creeps forward up to 2m per day, causing building-sized icebergs to calve from its face. Watching the glacier is a sedentary park experience that manages to be thrilling.

The glacier formed as a low gap in the Andes allowed moisture-laden Pacific storms to drop their loads east of the divide, where they accumulate as snow. Over millennia, under tremendous weight, this snow has recrystallized into ice and flowed slowly eastward. The 1600-sq-km trough of **Lago Argentino**, the country's largest body of water, is evidence that glaciers were once far more extensive than today.

While most of the world's glaciers are receding, Glaciar Perito Moreno is considered 'stable.' Regardless, 17 times between 1917 and 2006, as the glacier has advanced, it has dammed the Brazo Rico (Rico Arm) of Lago Argentino, causing the water to rise. Several times the melting ice below has been unable to support the weight of the water behind it and the dam has collapsed in an explosion of water and ice. To be present when this spectacular cataclysm occurs is unforgettable.

Glaciar Perito Moreno is as much an auditory as a visual experience when icebergs calve and collapse into the **Canal de los Témpanos** (Iceberg Channel). This natural-born tourist attraction at Península de Magallanes is close enough to guarantee great views, but far enough away to be safe. A series of steel catwalks (almost 4000m total) and vantage points allow visitors to see, hear and photograph the glacier. Sun hits its face in the morning and the glacier's appearance changes as the day progresses and shadows shift.

There is a free shuttle from the parking area to the catwalks. A closed *refugio* with glass walls allows for glacier viewing in bad weather; there's also a snack bar and two-story restaurant Nativos, serving cappuccinos and sandwiches to sightseers. If you bring a picnic, remember that it is difficult and costly to remove trash from the area – please pack yours out.

For student rates, visitors must have a student ID. The main gateway town to the park's southern sector, El Calafate, is 80km east of the glacier by road. It's where you'll find most operators for tours and activities.

🏃 Activities

🏃 Glaciar Perito Moreno

Beyond a short walk that parallels the shoreline at the boat dock and climbs to the lookout area, there are no trails in this sector of the park accessible without boat transportation. These nautical excursions allow you to sense the magnitude of Glaciar Perito Moreno, still from a safe distance. Tours do not include transfers to Parque Nacional Los Glaciares (AR$130 roundtrip) and park entry fee.

Around El Calafate & PN Los Glaciares (South)

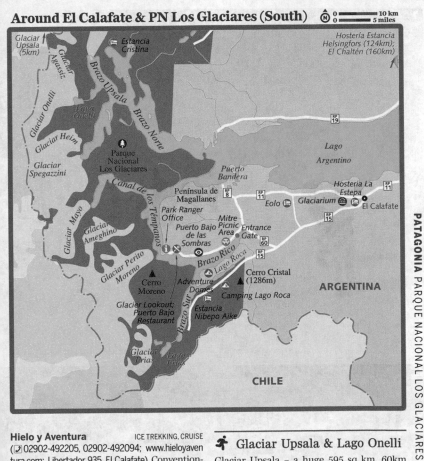

Hielo y Aventura
ICE TREKKING, CRUISE

(☎ 02902-492205, 02902-492094; www.hieloyaventura.com; Libertador 935, El Calafate) Conventional cruise Safari Nautico (AR$120, one hour) tours Brazo Rico, Lago Argentino and the south side of Canal de los Témpanos. Catamarans crammed with up to 130 passengers leave hourly between 10:30am and 4:30pm from Puerto Bajo de las Sombras. If it's busy, buy tickets in advance for afternoon departures.

To hike on the glacier, try minitrekking (AR$1200, under two hours on ice), or the longer and more demanding Big Ice (AR$2200, four hours on ice). Both involve a quick boat ride from Puerto Bajo de las Sombras, a walk through lenga forests, a chat on glaciology and then an ice walk using crampons. Children under eight are not allowed; reserve ahead and bring your own food. Don't forget rain gear: it's often snowing around the glacier and you might get wet and cold quickly on the boat deck. Transfers cost extra (AR$300).

🏃 Glaciar Upsala & Lago Onelli

Glaciar Upsala – a huge 595 sq km, 60km long and 4km wide in parts – can be admired for its monumental dimensions alongside the strange and graceful forms of the nearby icebergs. The downside is that it can only be enjoyed from the crowded deck of a massive catamaran: just nature, you and 300 of your closest friends.

On an extension of the Brazo Norte (North Arm) of Lago Argentino, it's accessible by launch from Puerto Punta Bandera, 45km west of El Calafate by RP 11 and RP 8. Not included in cruise prices is the bus transfer (approximately AR$50) from El Calafate.

Solo Patagonia S.A.
CRUISE

(☎ 02902-491115; www.solopatagonia.com; Libertador 867, El Calafate) Offers the Rios de Hielo Express (AR$1350) from Puerto Punta Bandera, visiting Glaciar Upsala, Glaciar

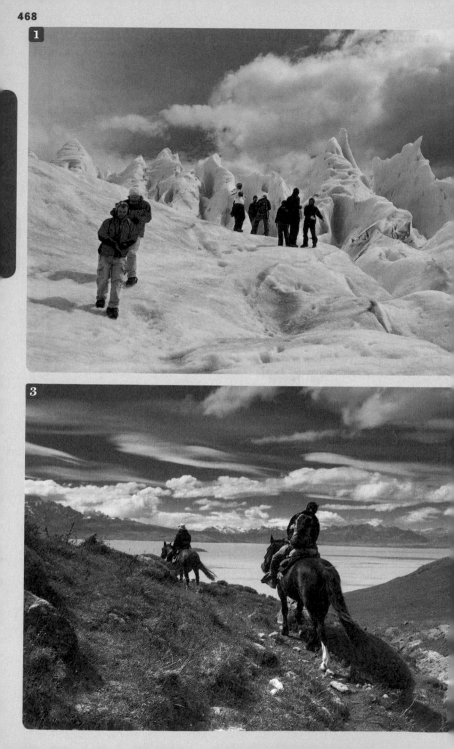

RACHEL LEWIS/GETTY IMAGES ©

Extreme Patagonia

More than 130 years ago, Lady Florence Dixie ditched high society to ride horses across the Patagonian steppe. Today, you can still fulfill a dream of scaling unnamed peaks, paddling alongside sea lions or tracing a glacier's edge.

Horseback Riding

Estancias (ranches; p131) remind us how good it is to ride without fences, to feel the heat of a campfire and to sleep under the stars.

Ice Climbing

Adrenaline, check. Near El Chaltén, ecocamps help you tackle the surreal frozen terrain in Parque Nacional Los Glaciares (p466), where good guiding services make it accessible even to amateurs.

2

MARTIN HARVEY/GETTY IMAGES ©

Glacier Trekking

More than a hike, it's a full-immersion aesthetic experience. Strap on crampons and explore these living sculptures in Torres del Paine (p483) or Parque Nacional Los Glaciares (p455 and p466).

Diving

Clear waters, nearby shipwrecks and cool marine life make Península Valdés (p410) the diving capital of Argentina, with the best visibility in August.

Sea Kayaking

Paddle with penguins and Commerson's dolphins in Ría Deseado (p428) and Bahía Bustamante (p425), or play alongside sea lions near Península Valdés (p410).

Driving Ruta Nacional 40

Watch herds of dusky guanaco, or the slow approach of shimmering peaks; the sky was never bluer or bigger than on this remote road (p438), an icon of slow travel that flanks the Andes.

Clockwise from top left
1. Glacier trekking, Glaciar Perito Moreno (p466)
2. Ice climbing
3. Horseback riding

Spegazzini and Glaciar Perito Moreno. Weather may alter the route. Transfers from El Calafate extra (AR$300). Meals are expensive, but you can bring your own.

Mar Patag CRUISE
(📞02902-492118; www.crucerosmarpatag.com; 9 de Julio 57, Office 4, El Calafate; day cruise US$315; ⏰7am-7pm Mon-Fri, 7-11am & 5-9pm Sat & Sun) Luxury cruises with a chef serving gourmet meals. The day trip leaves from the private port of La Soledad and visits Glaciar Upsala, with a four-course meal served on board. The three-day cruise (from US$1680 per person, double occupancy) leaves five times per month and also visits glaciers Mayo and Perito Moreno. Transfers from El Calafate not included (US$30).

🏃 Lago Roca

The serene south arm of Lago Argentino, with lakeshore forests and mountains, features good hikes and pleasant camping. *Estancia* accommodations occupy this section of Parque Nacional Los Glaciares, where most visitors rarely travel. No entrance fee is charged. For transportation, contact Caltur.

Cerro Cristal HIKING
A rugged but rewarding 3½-hour hike, with views of Glaciar Perito Moreno and the Torres del Paine on clear days. The trail begins at the education camp at La Jerónima, just before the Camping Lago Roca entrance, 55km southwest of El Calafate along RP 15.

Cabalgatas del Glaciar HORSEBACK RIDING
(📞495447; www.cabalgatasdelglaciar.com; full day AR$900) Day and multiday riding or trekking trips with glacier panoramas to Lago Roca and Paso Zamora on the Chilean border. Also available through Caltur.

🛏 Sleeping & Eating

★**Camping Lago Roca** CAMPGROUND $
(📞02902-499500;www.losglaciares.com/camping lagoroca; per person US$15, cabin dm per 2/4 people US$63/95) This full-service campground with restaurant-bar, located a few kilometers past the education camp, makes an excellent adventure base. The clean concrete-walled dorms provide a snug alternative to camping. Hiking trails abound, and the center rents fishing equipment and bikes and coordinates horseback riding at the nearby Estancia Nibepo Aike.

★**Estancia Cristina** ESTANCIA $$$
(📞02902-491133, in Buenos Aires 011-4803-7352; www.estanciacristina.com; d 2 nights incl full board & activities US$1145; ⏰Oct-Apr) Locals in the know say the most outstanding trekking in the region is right here. Lodging is in bright, modern cabins with expansive views. A visit includes guided activities and boating to Glaciar Upsala. Accessible by boat from Puerto Punta Bandera, off the northern arm of Lago Argentino.

Hostería Estancia Helsingfors ESTANCIA $$$
(📞satellite phone 011-5277-0195; www.helsingfors.com.ar; per person incl full board, transfer & activities

---

THE STORY OF GLACIERS

Ribbons of ice, stretched flat in sheets or sculpted by weather and fissured by pressure, glaciers have a raw magnificence that is mind-boggling to behold.

As snow falls on the accumulation area, it compacts to ice. The river of ice is slugged forward by gravity, which deforms its layers as it moves. When the glacier surges downhill, melted ice mixes with rock and soil on the bottom, grinding it into a lubricant that keeps pushing the glacier along. At the same time, debris from the crushed rock is forced to the sides of the glacier, creating features called moraines. Movement also causes cracks and deformities called crevasses.

The ablation area is where the glacier melts. When accumulation outpaces melting at the ablation area, the glacier advances; when there's more melting or evaporation, the glacier recedes. Since 1980 global warming has contributed greatly to widespread glacial retreat.

Another marvel of glaciers is their hue. What makes some blue? Wavelengths and air bubbles. The more compact the ice, the longer the path that light has to travel and the bluer the ice appears. Air bubbles in uncompacted areas absorb long wavelengths of white light so we see white. When glaciers calve into lakes, they dump a 'glacial flour' comprised of ground-up rock that gives the water a milky, grayish color. This same sediment remains unsettled in some lakes and diffracts the sun's light, creating a stunning palette of turquoise, pale mint and azure.

US\$385; ⊙Oct-Apr) The simply stunning location ogling Cerro Fitz Roy from Lago Viedma makes for lots of love-at-first-sight impressions. Intimate and welcoming, this former Finnish pioneer ranch is a highly regarded luxury destination, though it cultivates a relaxed, unpretentious ambience. Guests pass the time on scenic but demanding mountain treks, rides and visits to Glaciar Viedma.

Transfers are made on Tuesday, Thursday and Saturday, otherwise you can order a chartered van. It's on Lago Viedma's southern shore, 170km from El Chaltén and 180km from El Calafate.

Estancia Nibepo Aike ESTANCIA **\$\$\$**
(☑02902-492797, in Buenos Aires 011-5272-0341; www.nibepoaike.com.ar; RP 15, Km60; per person with d occupancy, full board & activities from US\$220; ⊙Oct-Apr; ☏) This Croatian pioneer ranch, still a working cattle ranch, offers the usual assortment of *estancia* highlights, including demonstrations and horseback riding with bilingual guides. Rooms are simply lovely and high-quality photos give a sense of the regional history. Guests can also explore the surroundings on two wheels from the bicycle stash. Transfers to and from El Calafate are included.

Eolo HOTEL **\$\$\$**
(☑in Buenos Aires 011-4700-0075; www.eolo.com. ar; RP 11; s/d incl full board from US\$770/950; ☒) Ringed by miles of Patagonian steppe, this luxury Relais & Chateaux property leaves the rustic life outside the double-glass windows. Guests first see an interior courtyard filled with lavender. There are 17 tasteful guest rooms, a sauna, small pool and spa services. Beautiful antique *estancia* furniture and a collection of old regional maps and publications set the mood. Transfer included.

Adventure Domes CAMPGROUND **\$\$\$**
(☑02962-493185; adventure-domes.com; per person US\$430) Reviews have been mixed for this all-inclusive nature camp, which features hikes and ice trekking on the glacier and overnights in domes with comfortable beds, hot-water showers and all meals (lunch boxes for day trips). Provides transfers.

❶ Getting There & Away

Glaciar Perito Moreno is 80km west of El Calafate via paved RP 11, passing through the breathtaking scenery around Lago Argentino. Bus tours (AR\$450 roundtrip) are frequent in summer. Buses leave El Calafate in the early morning and afternoon, returning around noon and 7pm.

CHILEAN PATAGONIA

Rugged seascapes rimmed with glacial peaks, the stunning massifs of Torres del Paine and howling steppe characterize the other side of the Andes. Once you come this far, it is well worth crossing the border. Chilean Patagonia consists of the isolated Aisén and Magallanes regions, separated by the southern continental ice field. This area covers Punta Arenas, Puerto Natales and Parque Nacional Torres del Paine. For in-depth coverage of Chile, pick up Lonely Planet's *Chile & Easter Island*.

Most nationals of countries that have diplomatic relations with Chile don't need a visa. Upon entering, customs officials issue a tourist card, valid for 90 days and renewable for another 90; authorities take it seriously, so guard your card closely to avoid the hassle of replacing it.

Temperature-sensitive travelers will soon notice a difference after leaving energy-rich Argentina: in public areas and budget accommodations central heating is rare; warmer clothing is the norm indoors.

US cash is not widely accepted. Prices here are given in Chilean pesos (CH\$), except where hotels and tours list their prices in US dollars.

Punta Arenas
☑061 / POP 130,136

A sprawling metropolis on the edge of the Strait of Magellan, Punta Arenas defies easy definition. Today's Punta Arenas is a confluence of the ruddy and the grand, witnessed in the elaborate wool-boom mansions, and port renovations contrasted with windblown litter and urban sprawl. Visitors will find it the most convenient base to travel around the remote Magallanes region, with good traveler services. Watch for more cruise-ship passengers and trekkers to replace the explorers, sealers and sailors of yesterday at the barstools – but save a spot for the old guard.

Founded in 1848 as a penal settlement and military garrison, Punta Arenas was conveniently situated for ships headed to Alta California during the gold rush. The economy took off in the late 19th century, after the territorial governor authorized the purchase of 300 pure-bred sheep from the Falkland Islands (Islas Malvinas). This experiment encouraged sheep farming and, by the turn of the century, nearly two million grazed the territory.

⊙ Sights & Activities

Museo Regional de Magallanes   MUSEUM
(Museo Regional Braun-Menéndez; ☎ 061-224-4216; www.museodemagallanes.cl; Magallanes 949; admission CH$1000; ☺ 10:30am-5pm Wed-Mon, to 2pm May-Dec) This opulent mansion testifies to the

wealth and power of pioneer sheep farmers in the late 19th century. The well-maintained interior houses a regional historical museum (ask for booklets in English) and original exquisite French-nouveau family furnishings, from intricate wooden inlaid floors to Chinese vases. In former servants' quarters,

Punta Arenas

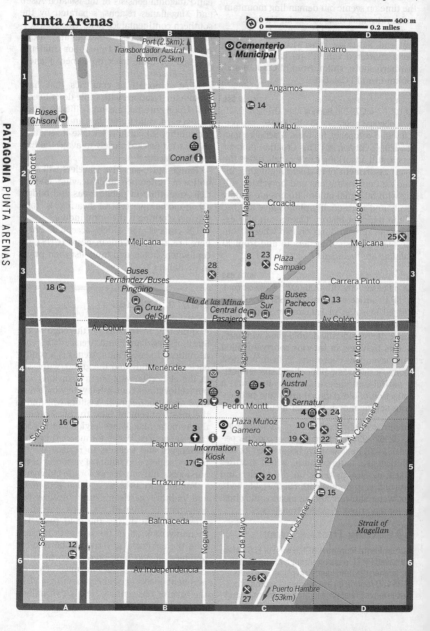

a downstairs cafe is perfect for a pisco sour while soaking up the grandeur.

Plaza Muñoz Gamero   PLAZA
A central plaza of magnificent conifers surrounded by opulent mansions. Facing the plaza's north side, **Casa Braun-Menéndez** ([✓]061-224-1489; admission CH$1000; [⊙]10:30am-1pm & 5-8:30pm Tue-Fri, 10:30am-1pm & 8-10pm Sat, 11am-2pm Sun) houses the private Club de la Unión, which also uses the tavern downstairs (open to the public). The nearby **monument** commemorating the 400th anniversary of Magellan's voyage was donated by wool baron José Menéndez in 1920. Just east is the former **Sociedad Menéndez Behety**, which now houses Turismo Comapa. The **cathedral** sits west.

★**Cementerio Municipal**   CEMETERY
(main entrance at Av Bulnes 949; [⊙]7:30am-8pm) [FREE] Among South America's most fascinating cemeteries, with both humble immigrant graves and flashy tombs, like that of wool baron José Menéndez, a scale replica of Rome's Vittorio Emanuele monument, according to Bruce Chatwin. See the map inside the main entrance gate.

It's an easy 15-minute stroll northeast of the plaza, or catch any taxi *colectivo* (shared taxi with specific route) in front of the Museo Regional Braun-Menéndez on Magallanes.

Museo Naval y Marítimo   MUSEUM
([✓]061-220-5479; www.museonaval.cl; Pedro Montt 981; adult/child CH$1200/600; [⊙]9:30am-12:30pm & 2-5pm Tue-Sat) A naval and maritime museum with historical exhibits that include a fine account of the Chilean mission that rescued Sir Ernest Shackleton's crew from Antarctica. The most imaginative display is a replica ship complete with bridge, maps, charts and radio room.

Museo Regional Salesiano   MUSEUM
([✓]061-222-1001; Av Bulnes 336; adult/12yr & under CH$2500/200; [⊙]10am-12:30pm & 3-6pm Tue-Sun) Especially influential in settling the region, the Salesian order collected outstanding ethnographic artifacts, but their museum touts their role as peacemakers between the Yahgan and Ona and settlers.

Reserva Forestal Magallanes   PARK
([⊙]daylight hours) [FREE] Great hiking and mountain biking through dense lenga and coihue, 8km from town.

☞ **Tours**
Torres del Paine tours are abundant from Punta Arenas, but the distance makes for a very long day; it's best to organize transport from Puerto Natales.

The town's first settlements at Fuerte Bulnes and Puerto Hambre comprise **Parque Historia Patagonia** (Parque del Estrecho de Magallanes; [✓]061-272-3195; www.phipa.cl; Km56 Sur; admission CH$12,000; [⊙]9:30am-6:30pm). Visit with a tour group or a rental car.

If you have the time, a more atmospheric alternative to Seno Otway is a visit to the thriving Magellanic penguin colonies of

Punta Arenas

Monumento Natural Los Pingüinos (p477) on Isla Magdalena.

Turismo Aonikenk
TOUR

(☑061-222-8616; www.aonikenk.com; Magallanes 570) Recommended English-, German- and French-speaking guides. Offers Cabo Froward treks, visits to the king penguin colony in Tierra del Fuego, and cheaper open expeditions geared at experienced participants.

Kayak Agua Fresca
KAYAKING

(☑cell 9655-5073; www.kayakaguafresca.com; half-day tour CH$50,000) On the rare day in Punta when winds are calm and the sea is glass, the sea kayaking can be spectacular. There's no office; see the website for information.

🛏 Sleeping

On the cruise-ship circuit, Punta Arenas has a plethora of hotels. Foreigners are not required to pay the additional 18% IVA charge if paying with US cash, traveler's checks or credit card. Prices drop low season (mid-April to mid-October).

Hospedaje Magallanes
B&B $

(☑061-222-8616; www.aonikenk.com; Magallanes 570; dm/d without bathroom CH$18,000/40,000; 🐾🖥) A great inexpensive option run by a German-Chilean couple who are also Torres del Paine guides with an on-site travel agency. With just a few quiet rooms, there are often communal dinners or backyard barbecues by the climbing wall. Breakfast includes brown bread and strong coffee.

Hostal La Estancia
GUESTHOUSE $

(☑061-224-9130; www.estancia.cl; O'Higgins 765; d with bathroom CH$48,000, dm/s/d without bathroom CH$12,500/20,000/38,000; 🐾🖥) An old downtown house with big rooms, vaulted ceilings and tidy shared bathrooms. Longtime owners Alex and Carmen are eager to help with travel plans. There's a book exchange, kitchen use, laundry and storage.

Hostal Independencia
GUESTHOUSE $

(☑061-222-7572; www.hostalindependencia.cl; Av Independencia 374; campsite per person/dm CH$2000/7000; 🐾🖥) One of the last diehard backpacker haunts with cheap prices and bonhomie to match. Despite the chaos, rooms are reasonably clean and there are kitchen privileges, camping and bike rentals.

Hostel Keoken
GUESTHOUSE $

(☑061-224-4086; www.hostelkeoken.cl; Magallanes 209; s/d with bathroom CH$30,000/38,000, without bathroom CH$20,000/28,000; 🐾) In-

creasingly popular with backpackers, Hostel Keoken features comfortable beds topped with fluffy white down comforters and homemade pastries for breakfast. The center of town is a few minutes away on foot.

Al Fin del Mundo
HOSTEL $

(☑061-271-0185; www.alfindelmundo.hostel.com; O'Higgins 1026; dm/s/d without bathroom CH$13,500/23,000/34,000; 🖥) On the 2nd and 3rd floors of a musty downtown building, these rooms are cheerful but due for updates. All share bathrooms with hot showers and a large kitchen, as well as a living area with a big TV, pool table and DVD library. Has bikes for rental (CH$1000 per hour).

Hotel Patagonia
HOTEL $$

(☑061-222-7243; www.patagoniabb.cl; Av España 1048; s/d/tw CH$30,000/40,000/50,000; 🖥) A solid midrange option offering no-nonsense rooms with crisp white linens and simple style. Service could be a few degrees warmer. It's accessed via a long driveway behind the main building.

★ Ilaia Hotel
BOUTIQUE HOTEL $$$

(☑061-272-3100; www.ilaia.cl; Carrera Pinto 351; s/d/tr from US$105/140/195; 🖥) Playful and modern, this high-concept boutique hotel is run with family warmth. Sly messages are written to be read in mirrors, rooms are simple and chic and an incredible glass study gazes out on the Strait. Offers a shuttle to yoga classes and healthy breakfasts with chapati bread, homemade jam, avocados, yogurt and more. But you won't find a TV.

Hotel Plaza
HOTEL $$$

(☑061-224-1300; www.hotelplaza.cl; Nogueira 1116; s/d CH$65,500/83,500; 🖥) This converted mansion boasts vaulted ceilings, plaza views and historical photos lining the hall. Inconsistent with such grandeur, the country decor is unfortunate. But service is genteel and the location unbeatable.

Hotel Dreams del Estrecho
HOTEL $$$

(☑toll-free 600-626-0000; www.mundodreams. com/detalle/dreams-punta-arenas; O'Higgins 1235; d/ste CH$76,000/134,000; 🐾🖥🌊) Parked at the water's edge, this glass oval high-rise brings a little Vegas to the end of the world. It's a glittery atmosphere, with spacious and luxuriant rooms, but the showstopper is the swimming pool that appears to merge with the ocean. There's also a spa, casino and swank restaurant on-site.

✗ Eating

Local seafood is an exquisite treat: go for *centolla* (king crab) between July and November or *erizos* (sea urchins) between November and July.

Café Almacen Tapiz   CAFE $
(☑cell 8730-3481; www.cafetapiz.cl; Roca 912; mains CH$5000; ⊗9am-9:30pm; ☎) Cloaked in alerce shingles, this lively cafe makes for an ambient coffee break. In addition to gorgeous layer cakes, there's salads and pita sandwiches with goat cheese, meats or roasted veggies.

Mercado Municipal   MARKET $
(21 de Mayo 1465; ⊗8am-3pm) Fish and vegetable market with cheap 2nd-floor *cocinerías* (eateries); a great place for inexpensive seafood dishes.

La Mesita Grande   PIZZA $
(☑061-224-4312; O'Higgins 1001; mains CH$3000-6000; ⊗noon-11:30pm) If you're homesick for Brooklyn, La Mesita Grande might do the trick. This mod exposed-brick pizzeria serves them up thin and crisp, with organic toppings and pints of local brew. Save room for their homemade ice cream. The original outlet is in Puerto Natales.

Kiosco Roca   SANDWICHES $
(Roca 875; snacks CH$500; ⊗7am-7pm Mon-Fri, 8am-1pm Sat) An irresistible stop, with locals patiently waiting for counter stools and U of Chile paraphernalia plastering the walls. They only turn out bite-sized sandwiches with chorizo or cheese or both, best paired with a banana milkshake.

Los Inmigrantes   CAFE $
(☑061-222-2205; www.inmigrante.cl; Quillota 559; mains AR$5000; ⊗noon-8pm) In the historic Croatian neighborhood, this cafe serves decadent cakes in a room full of interesting relics from Dalmatian immigrants.

Fuente Hamburg   CHILEAN $
(☑061-224-5375; Errázurriz 856; mains CH$2500-6000; ⊗10:30am-8:30pm Mon-Fri, 10:30am-3pm Sat) Shiny barstools flank a massive grill churning out quickie bites. Grab a *churrasco* (thin-sliced beef) topped with tomatoes and green beans, served with fresh mayo on a soft bun.

Unimarc   SUPERMARKET $
(Bories 647; ⊗9am-10pm Mon-Sat, 10am-9pm Sun) A large, well-stocked supermarket.

★ La Marmita   CHILEAN $$
(☑061-222-2056; www.marmitamaga.cl; Plaza Sampaio 678; mains CH$6000-12,000; ⊗12:30-3pm & 6:30-11:30pm Mon-Sat; ☑) This classic bistro enjoys wild popularity for its lovely, casual ambience and tasty fare. Besides fresh salads and hot bread, hearty dishes such as casseroles or seafood hark back to grandma's cooking, Chilean style. With good vegetarian options and takeout service.

La Cuisine   FRENCH $$
(☑061-222-8641; O'Higgins 1037; mains CH$8000-9000; ⊗11am-10pm Mon-Sat) If you're craving veggies beyond the trusted potato, this plain-Jane French restaurant is a good bet. Seafood dishes come with sautéed vegetables, green salad or ratatouille. There's also homemade pâté, and wine by the glass is cheap.

Remezón   CHILEAN $$
(☑061-224-1029; 21 de Mayo 1469; mains CH$5000-15,000; ⊗noon-3pm & 7-11:30pm) An innovative mainstay with homey atmosphere. Garlic soup made with fragrant beef broth is a good starter, even shared. Game dishes are the house specialty, but the delicate *merluza negra* (black hake) shouldn't be missed, served with *chupe de espinaca* (spinach casserole).

☖ Drinking & Nightlife

La Taberna   BAR
(Casa Braun-Menéndez, Plaza Muñoz Gamero; ⊗7pm-2am Mon-Fri, 7pm-3am Sat & Sun) This dark and elegant subterranean bar, with polished wood fixtures and cozy nooks reminiscent of an old-fashioned ship, is a classic old boys' club. The rooms fill with cigar smoke later in the evening, but the opportunity to sip pisco sours in this classy mansion shouldn't be missed.

Jekus   PUB
(O'Higgins 1021; ⊗6pm-3am) A restaurant that serves as a popular meeting spot for drinks, with happy hours, karaoke and soccer on the tube.

ⓘ Information

Travel agencies in the city center, along Roca and Navarro, change cash and traveler's checks. All are open weekdays and Saturday, with a few open on Sunday morning. Banks with ATMs dot the city center.

Conaf (☑061-223-0681; Bulnes 0309; ⊗9am-5pm Mon-Fri) Has details on the nearby parks.

Hospital Regional (☏061-220-5000; cnr Arauco & Angamos) Large regional hospital.

Information Kiosk (☏061-220-0610; Plaza Muñoz Gamero; ⊙8am-7pm Mon-Sat, 9am-7pm Sun Dec-Feb) South side of the plaza.

Post Office (Bories 911) Located one block north of Plaza Muñoz Gamero.

Sernatur (☏061-224-1330; www.sernatur.cl; Navarro 999; ⊙8:30am-8pm Mon-Fri, 10am-6pm Sat & Sun) With friendly, well-informed, multilingual staff and lists of accommodations and transportation. Reduced hours in low season.

Sur Cambios (Navarro 1001) Exchanges money.

❶ Getting There & Away

The tourist offices distribute a useful brochure that details all forms of transportation available.

AIR

Punta Arenas' airport is located 21km north of town.

Aerovías DAP (☏061-261-6100; www.aerovias dap.cl; O'Higgins 891) From November to March, flies to Porvenir (CH$55,000 roundtrip) Monday through Saturday several times daily, and to Puerto Williams (CH$143,000 roundtrip) Monday through Saturday at 10am. Luggage is limited to 10kg per person.

LanChile (☏061-224-1100; www.lan.com; Bories 884) Flies several times daily to Santiago (CH$162,000 roundtrip) with a stop in Puerto Montt (CH$153,000), and on Saturday to the Falkland Islands/Islas Malvinas (roundtrip CH$530,000).

Sky Airline (☏061-271-0645; www.skyairline. cl; Roca 935) Flies daily between Santiago and Punta Arenas, with a stop either in Puerto Montt or Concepción.

BOAT

Cruceros Australis (☏in Santiago 02-442-3110; www.australis.com; ⊙Sep-May) Runs luxurious four- and five-day sightseeing cruises to Ushuaia and back. Turismo Comapa (☏061-220-0200; www.comapa.com; Magallanes 990) handles local bookings.

Transbordador Austral Broom (☏061-258-0089; www.tabsa.cl) Operates three ferries to Tierra del Fuego from the Tres Puentes ferry launch. The car/passenger ferry to/from Porvenir (CH$6200/39,800 per person/vehicle, 2½ to four hours) usually leaves at 9am but has some afternoon departures; check the current online schedule.

From Punta Arenas, it's faster to do the Primera Angostura crossing (CH$1700/15,000 per person/vehicle, 20 minutes), northeast of Punta Arenas, which sails every 90 minutes between 8:30am and 11:45pm.

Broom sets sail for Isla Navarino's Puerto Williams (reclining seat/bunk CH$103,000/143,000

including meals, 30 hours) three or four times per month on Thursday only, returning Saturday.

BUS

Buses depart from company offices, most situated within a block or two of Av Colón. Buy tickets several hours (if not days) in advance. The **Central de Pasajeros** (☏061-224-5811; cnr Magallanes & Av Colón) is the closest thing to a central booking office.

Bus Sur (☏061-261-4224; www.bus-sur.cl; Av Colón 842) To El Calafate, Puerto Natales, Río Gallegos, Ushuaia and Puerto Montt.

Buses Fernández/Buses Pingüino (☏061-224-2313; www.busesfernandez.com; Sanhueza 745) To Puerto Natales, Torres del Paine and Río Gallegos.

Buses Ghisoni (☏061-224-0646; www.buses barria.cl; Av España 264) Comfortable buses to Río Gallegos, Río Grande and Ushuaia.

Buses Pacheco (☏061-224-2174; www. busespacheco.com; Av Colón 900) To Puerto Natales, Río Gallegos and Ushuaia.

Cruz del Sur (☏061-222-7970; www.buses cruzdelsur.cl; Sanhueza 745) Buses to Puerto Montt, Osorno and Chiloé.

Tecni-Austral (☏061-222-2078; Navarro 975) To Río Grande.

Buses from Punta Arenas

DESTINATION	COST (CH$)	TIME (HR)
Puerto Montt	45,000	32
Puerto Natales	6000	3
Río Gallegos	12,000	5-8
Río Grande	25,000	9
Ushuaia	30,000	10

❶ Getting Around

TO/FROM THE AIRPORT

Buses depart directly from the airport to Puerto Natales. **Transfer Austral** (☏061-272-3358; www.transferaustral.com) runs door-to-door shuttle services (CH$3000) to/from town to coincide with flights. Buses Fernández does regular airport transfers (CH$3000).

BUS & TAXI COLECTIVO

Taxi *colectivos*, with numbered routes, are only slightly more expensive than buses (about CH$800, or a bit more late at night and on Sundays); and far more comfortable and much quicker.

CAR

Cars are a good option for exploring Torres del Paine, but renting one in Chile to cross the border into Argentina can become prohibitively expensive due to international insurance requirements. If heading for El Calafate, it is best to rent your vehicle in Argentina. Purchasing a car to explore Patagonia has its drawbacks, as Chilean Patagonia has no through roads that link northern and southern Patagonia, so it is entirely dependent on the roads of Argentina or expensive ferry travel.

Punta Arenas has Chilean Patagonia's most economical rental rates, and locally owned agencies tend to provide better service. Recommended **Adel Rent a Car/Localiza** (☑ 061-222-4819; www.adelrentacar.cl; Pedro Montt 962) provides attentive service, competitive rates, airport pickup and good travel tips. Other choices include **Hertz** (☑ 061-224-8742; O'Higgins 987) and **Lubag** (☑ 061-271-0484; Magallanes 970).

Monumento Natural Los Pingüinos

If you have the time, a more atmospheric alternative to Seno Otway is to visit the thriving Magellanic penguin colonies of Monumento Natural Los Pingüinos on Isla Magdalena. Five-hour **ferry tours** (adult/child CH$35,000/17,500) land for an hour at the island and depart the port on Tuesday, Thursday and Saturday, December through February. Confirm times in advance. Book tickets through Turismo Comapa (p476) and bring a picnic.

Parque Nacional Pali Aike

Rugged volcanic steppe pocked with craters, caves and twisted formations, Pali Aike means 'devil's country' in Tehuelche. This desolate landscape is a 50-sq-km **park** (www.conaf.cl/parques/parque-nacional-pali-aike; adult/child under 12yr CH$1000/free) along the Argentine border. Mineral content made lava rocks red, yellow or green-gray. Fauna includes abundant guanaco, ñandú, gray fox and armadillo. In the 1930s Junius Bird's excavations at 17m-deep **Pali Aike Cave** yielded the first artifacts associated with extinct New World fauna, such as the *milodón* and the native horse *Onohippidium*.

The park has several trails, including a 1.7km path through the rugged lava beds of the **Escorial del Diablo** to the impressive **Crater Morada del Diablo**; wear sturdy shoes or your feet could be shredded. There are hundreds of craters, some four stories high. A 9km trail from Cueva Pali Aike to **Laguna Ana** links a shorter trail to a site on the main road, 5km from the park entrance.

Parque Nacional Pali Aike is 200km northeast of Punta Arenas via RN 9, Ch 255 and a graveled secondary road from Cooperativa Villa O'Higgins, 11km north of Estancia Kimiri Aike. There's also access from the Chilean border post at Monte Aymond. There is no public transport, but Punta Arenas travel agencies offer full-day tours.

Puerto Natales
☑ 061 / POP 18,000

On the windswept shores of Seno Última Esperanza (Last Hope Sound), this formerly modest fishing village is now the well-trodden hub of the continent's number-one national park, Torres del Paine. Though tourism has transformed its rusted tin shop fronts into gleaming facades, Natales maintains its weathered charm, especially in the shoulder seasons.

The Navimag ferry through Chile's fjords ends and begins its trips here. Located 250km northwest of Punta Arenas via RN 9, Puerto Natales also offers frequent transport to El Calafate, Argentina.

◎ Sights & Activites

Museo Histórico   MUSEUM
(☑ 061-241-1263; Bulnes 28; admission CH$1000; ⊙ 8am-7pm Mon-Fri, 10am-1pm & 3-7pm Sat & Sun) A crash course in local history, with archaeological artifacts, a Yahgan canoe, Tehuelche bolas and historical photos.

Mandala Andino   SPA
(☑ cell 9930-2997; mandalaandino@yahoo.com; Bulnes 301; massages from CH$18,000; ⊙ 10am-10pm Nov-Mar) A recommended full-service wellness center with spot-on massages, tub soaks and various pampering treatments. Also sells interesting gifts and local crafts.

⛟ Tours

Antares/Big Foot Patagonia ADVENTURE TOUR
(☑ 061-241-4611; www.antarespatagonia.com; Ave Pedro Montt/Costanera 161) Specializing in Torres del Paine, Antares can facilitate climbing permits and made-to-order trips. They also have the park concession for Lago Grey activities including Glaciar Grey ice trekking and kayak trips.

Baqueano Zamora   HORSE RIDING
(☑ 061-261-3530; www.baqueanozamora.cl; Baquedano 534) Runs recommended horseback-riding trips and wild horse viewing in Torres del Paine.

Puerto Natales

PATAGONIA PUERTO NATALES

Chile Nativo   ADVENTURE TOUR

(☎061-241-1835, cell 9078-9168; www.chilenativo.cl; Eberhard 230, 2nd fl) Links visitors with local gauchos, organizes photo safaris and can competently plan your tailor-made dream adventures.

Pingo Salvaje   HORSE RIDING

(☎cell 6236-0371; www.pingosalvaje.com; Estancia Laguna Sofia; 3hr horse ride CH$33,000; ⊘Oct-Apr) This lovely *estancia* getaway offers horseback riding and condor-spotting. You can stay over in a comfortable shared cabin (CH$15,000 per person; bring a sleeping bag) or campsite (CH$4000 per person) under a

stand of trees, outfitted with grills, tables and hot showers. It's 30km from Puerto Natales; transport costs CH$10,000 per person.

Turismo 21 de Mayo   TOUR

(☎614420; www.turismo21demayo.com; Eberhard 560) Organizes day-trip cruises and treks to the Balmaceda and Serrano glaciers.

🛏 Sleeping

Options abound, most with breakfast, laundry and cheaper rates in the low season. Reserve ahead if arriving on the ferry. Hostels often rent equipment and arrange park transport.

attentive hosts, spoiling guests with filling breakfasts, steady water pressure and travel tips. Among the town's most long-standing lodgings, the place is spotless.

Lili Patagonico's Hostal
HOSTEL $

(☎061-241-4063; www.lilipatagonicos.com; Arturo Prat 479; dm CH\$10,000, d with/without bathroom CH\$32,000/24,000; @⊛) A sprawling house with a climbing wall, a variety of dorms and colorful doubles with newer bathrooms and down comforters.

4Elementos
GUESTHOUSE $

(☎cell 9524-6956; www.4elementos.cl; Esmeralda 811; s/d with bathroom CH\$20,000/25,000, dm/d/q without bathroom CH\$15,000/20,000/40,000; ⊛) ✿ A pioneer of Patagonian recycling, the passionate mission of this spare guesthouse is educating people about proper waste disposal. The hostel itself produces zero waste. Guests enjoy Scandanavian breakfasts made with care. Guide service, park bookings and greenhouse tours are available. By reservation only, as it isn't always open.

Singing Lamb
HOSTEL $

(☎061-241-0958; www.thesinginglamb.com; Arauco 779; dm US\$22-30, d US\$80; @⊛) ✿ A clean and green hostel with compost, recycling, rainwater collection and linen shopping bags. Dorm rooms are priced by the number of beds (maximum nine) and shared spaces are ample. Nice touches include central heating and homemade breakfasts. To get here, follow Raimírez one block past Plaza O'Higgins.

Hostal Dos Lagunas
GUESTHOUSE $

(☎cell 8162-7755; hostaldoslagunas@gmail.com; cnr Barros Arana & Bories; dm/d CH\$12,000/\$30,000; ⊛) Natales natives Alejandro and Andrea are

Residencial Bernardita
GUESTHOUSE $

(☑ 061-241-1162; www.residencialbernardita.cl; O'Higgins 765; s/d without bathroom CH$17,000/ 28,000; 🖥) Guests highly recommend Bernardita's quiet rooms with central heating and mismatched granny decor. Choose between rooms in the main house or more private ones in the back annex. There's also kitchen use and breakfast.

★We Are Patagonia
B&B $$

(☑ cell 7389-4802; www.wearepatagonia.com; Galvarino 745; r with/without bathroom US$70/ 60; 🖥) A lovely art hotel with central heating and minimalist Nordic and homespun charm. Mantras stenciled on the walls provide some not-so-subliminal positive messaging. The breakfast of champions includes real coffee, fruit, oatmeal and whole wheat bread. It's located in a small house.

Kau
B&B $$

(☑ 061-41-4611; www.kaulodge.com; Ave Pedro Montt/Costanera 161; d CH$50,000-60,000; 🖥🖭) 🏄 With a mantra of simplicity, this aesthetic remake of a box hotel is cozy and cool. Thick woolen throws, picnic-table breakfast seating and well-worn, recycled wood lend casual intimacy. Rooms boast fjord views, central heating, bulk toiletries and safe boxes. The **Coffee Maker** espresso bar boasts killer lattes and staff have tons of adventure information on tap.

Amerindia
B&B $$

(☑ 061-241-1945; www.hostelamerindia.com; Barros Arana 135; d with/without bathroom CH$45,000/35,000, 6-person apt CH$80,000; ☺Aug-Jun; @🖥) An earthy, tranquil retreat with a wood stove, beautiful weavings and raw wood beams. Guests wake up to cake, eggs and oatmeal in a cozy cafe open to the public, also selling organic chocolate, teas and gluten-free options. Also rents cars.

★Singular Hotel
BOUTIQUE HOTEL $$$

(☑ 061-241-4040, bookings in Santiago 02-387-1500; www.thesingular.com; RN 9, Km1.5; d US$428, d incl full board & excursions US$1360; @🖥🖭) A regional landmark reimagined, the Singular is a former meatpacking and shipping facility on the sound. Heightened industrial design, like chairs fashioned from old radiators in the lobby, mixes with vintage photos and antiques. The snug glass-walled rooms have water views, and a well-respected bar/ restaurant (alongside the museum, open to the public) serves fresh local game.

Guests can use the spa with pool and explore the surroundings by bike or kayak. It's located in Puerto Bories, 6km from the center.

Indigo Patagonia
BOUTIQUE HOTEL $$$

(☑ 061-241-3609; www.indigopatagonia.com; Ladrilleros 105; d with spa from US$309; @🖥) Hikers will head first to Indigo's rooftop Jacuzzis and glass-walled spa. Materials like eucalyptus, slate and iron overlap the modern with the natural to interesting effect, though rooms tend to be small. The star here is the fjord in front of you, which even captures your gaze in the shower. The hotel is part of Chile's upscale Noi hotel chain.

Remota
LODGE $$$

(☑ 061-241-4040, bookings in Santiago 02-387-1500; www.remota.cl; RN 9, Km1.5; s/d US$300/350, all-inclusive from US$1950; @🖥🖭) Unlike most hotels, this one draws your awareness to what's outside: silence broadcasts gusty winds, windows echo old stock fences and a crooked passageway imitates *estancia* sheep corridors. Though rooms are cozy, there's a feeling of isolation here and service can be cool.

✖ Eating

Cafe Kaiken
CHILEAN $

(☑ cell 8295-2036; Baquedano 699; mains CH$5000-7000; ☺1-3:30pm & 6:30-11pm Mon-Sat) With just five tables, and one couple cooking, serving and chatting up customers, this is as intimate as it gets. The owners moved here to get out of the Santiago fast lane, so you'd best follow their lead. Dishes like slow-roasted lamb or homemade smoked-salmon-stuffed ravioli are well worth the wait. Arrive early to claim a spot.

La Mesita Grande
PIZZA $

(☑ cell 6141-1571; www.mesitagrande.cl; Arturo Prat 196; pizza CH$5000-7000; ☺12:30-3pm & 7-11:30pm Mon-Sat, 1-3pm & 7-11:30pm Sun) Happy diners share one long, worn table for outstanding thin-crust pizza, quality pasta and organic salads.

El Bote
CHILEAN $

(☑ 061-241-0045; Bulnes 380; set menu CH$3500; ☺noon-11:30pm Mon-Sat) A haven for Chilean comfort food, this unpretentious restaurant dishes out roast chicken, seafood casseroles and homemade soups in addition to more expensive game dishes featuring guanaco and venison. For dessert, go with the classic chestnuts in cream.

CUEVA DEL MILODÓN

In the 1890s Hermann Eberhard discovered the remains of an enormous ground sloth just 24km northwest of Puerto Natales. Nearly 4m tall, the herbivorous *milodón* survived on the succulent leaves of small trees and branches, but became extinct in the late Pleistocene. This 30m-high **cave** (cuevadelmilodon.cl; adult/child 12yr & under CH$4000/500; ⊙8am-7pm Oct-Apr, 8:30-6pm May-Sep) pays homage to its former inhabitant with a life-size plastic replica of the animal. It's not exactly tasteful, but still worth a stop, whether to appreciate the grand setting and ruminate over its wild past or to take an easy walk up to a lookout point.

Camping (no fires) and picnicking are possible. Torres del Paine buses pass the entrance, 8km from the cave proper. There are infrequent tours from Puerto Natales; alternatively, you can hitchhike or share a taxi (CH$20,000). Outside of high season bus services are infrequent.

El Living
CAFE $

(www.el-living.com; Arturo Prat 156; mains $4000-6000; ⊙11am-10pm Mon-Sat Nov–mid-Apr; 🖉) Indulge in the London-lounge feel of this chill cafe, one of Natales' first. There's fresh vegetarian fare (plus vegan, gluten-free), stacks of European glossies and a hidden backyard with outdoor tables.

Cangrejo Rojo
CAFE $$

(📞061-241-2436; Santiago Bueras 782; mains CH$6000-8500; ⊙1:30-3pm & 5:30-10pm Tue-Sun) Unfathomably friendly and reasonable, this cute corrugated-tin cafe serves pies, ice cream, sandwiches and hot clay pot dishes like seafood casserole or lamb chops. To get here, follow Baquedano four blocks south of Plaza O'Higgins to Bueras.

La Aldea
MEDITERRANEAN $$

(📞cell 6141-4027; www.aldearestaurant.cl; Barros Arana 132; mains CH$7000-10,000; ⊙7-11pm Wed-Mon) Chef Pato changes the offerings daily, but the focus is fresh and Mediterranean. Think grilled clams, lamb *tagine* and quinoa dishes.

Afrigonia
FUSION $$

(📞061-241-2877; Eberhard 343; mains CH$10,000-14,000; ⊙12:20-3pm & 6:30-11pm) Outstanding and wholly original, you won't find Afro-Chilean cuisine on any NYC menu. This romantic gem was dreamed up by a hard-working Zambian-Chilean couple. Fragrant rice, fresh ceviche and mint roasted lamb are prepared with succulent precision. Make reservations.

🍷 Drinking & Nightlife

Baguales
MICROBREWERY

(www.cervezabaguales.cl; Bories 430; ⊙6pm-2:30am; 🖥) Climber friends started this microbrewery as a noble quest for quality

suds and the beer (crafted on-site) does not disappoint. A 2nd-floor addition seeks to meet the heavy demand. The gringo-style bar food is just so-so.

Por Que no te Callas
BAR

(📞061-241-4942; Magallanes 247; ⊙7pm-1:30am Mon-Thu, to 2am Fri & Sat) For a local vibe, you can't go wrong with a bar called 'Why don't you shut up.' It's friendlier than the name implies and even a bit gentrified. Besides a pool table, there's live music ranging from bossa nova to rock on weekends. Drinks like the fernet-based *caballo negro* come sized to do damage.

ℹ Information

MEDICAL SERVICES

Hospital (📞061-241-1582; Pinto 537) Emergency services.

MONEY

Most banks in town have ATMs.

La Hermandad (Bulnes 692) Decent rates on cash and traveler's checks.

POST

Post Office (Eberhard 429)

TOURIST INFORMATION

Conaf (📞061-241-1438; Baquedano 847; ⊙8:30am-12:45pm & 2:30-5:30pm Mon-Fri) National parks service administrative office.

Municipal Tourist Office (📞061-261-4808; Plaza de Armas; ⊙8:30am-12:30pm & 2:30-6pm Tue-Sun) Can also be found in the Museo Histórico and the Rodoviario (bus station), with regionwide lodgings listings.

Sernatur (📞061-241-2125; infonatales@sernatur.cl; Ave Pedro Montt/Costanera 19; ⊙9am-7pm Mon-Fri, 9:30am-6pm Sat & Sun) With useful city and regional maps and a second plaza location in high season.

TRAVEL AGENCIES

Fantastico Sur (☑ 061-261-4184; www.fantas ticosur.com; Esmeralda 661; ⊙9am-1pm & 3-6pm Mon-Fri) Runs Refugios Las Torres, Chileno and Los Cuernos in Torres del Paine and offers park tours, guiding and trek planning services, including a popular self-guided option.

Turismo Comapa (☑ 061-241-4300; www. comapa.com; Bulnes 541; ⊙9am-1pm & 3-7pm Mon-Fri, 10am-2pm Sat) Navimag ferry and airline bookings; also runs *refugios* (mountain huts) in Torres del Paine.

Vertice Patagonia (☑ 061-241-2742; www. verticepatagonia.com; Bulnes 100) Runs Ref ugios Grey and Lago Dickson, Mountain Lodge Paine Grande and Camping Los Perros in Torres del Paine. Advance bookings essential.

USEFUL WEBSITES

The best bilingual portal for the region is www. torresdelpaine.cl.

ⓘ Getting There & Away

AIR

At the time of research Puerto Natales' small airport did not offer commercial flights but this situation may change.

BOAT

For many travelers, a journey through Chile's spectacular fjords aboard the **Navimag Ferry** (☑ 061-241-1421, Rodoviario 061-241-1642; www.navimag.com; Ave Pedro Montt/Costanera 308; 2nd office in the Rodoviario; ⊙9am-1pm & 2:30-6:30pm Mon-Fri) becomes a highlight of their trip. Departing every Tuesday from Puerto Natales, this four-day and three-night north-bound voyage has become so popular it should be booked well in advance. You can also try your luck. To confirm when the ferry is due, contact Turismo Comapa (p482) a couple of days before your estimated arrival date. The ferry transports cars and passengers. It leaves Puerto Natales and stops in Puerto Edén (or the advanc ing Glaciar Pía XI on southbound sailings) en route to Puerto Montt. Schedules vary according to weather conditions and tides. Disembarking passengers must stay on board while cargo is transported; those embarking have to spend the night on board.

Accommodations are in six-bunk cabins with private bathrooms. Fares include all meals (in cluding veggie options if requested while booking, but bring water, snacks and drinks anyway) and interpretive talks. Per-person fares start from US$450. Check online for current schedules.

BUS

Puerto Natales recently added a bus terminal, **Rodoviario** (Bus Terminal; Av España 1455), though companies continue to have offices in the center for ticket purchases.

A second road has been opened to Torres del Paine and, although gravel, it is much more direct and several tour operators use it. This al ternative entrance goes alongside Lago del Toro to the Administración (park headquarters).

Buses leave for Torres del Paine two to three times daily at around 7am, 8am and 2:30pm. If you are headed to Mountain Lodge Paine Grande in the low season take the morning bus to meet the catamaran. Tickets may also be used for transfers within the park, so save your stub. Schedules are in constant flux, so double-check them before heading out.

Bus Sur (☑ 061-261-4220; www.bus-sur.cl; Baquedano 668) To Punta Arenas, Torres del Paine, Puerto Montt, El Calafate, Río Gallegos and Ushuaia.

Buses Fernández/El Pingüino (☑ 061-241-1111; www.busesfernandez.com; cnr Esmeralda & Ramírez) To Torres del Paine and Punta Arenas. Also goes directly to Puerto Natales from the airport.

Buses Gomez (☑ 061-241-5700; www.buses gomez.com; Arturo Prat 234) To Torres del Paine.

Buses JBA (☑ 061-241-0242; Arturo Prat 258) To Torres del Paine.

Buses Pacheco (☑ 061-241-4800; www.buses pacheco.com; Ramírez 224) To Punta Arenas, Río Grande and Ushuaia.

Cootra (☑ 061-241-2785; Baquedano 244) To El Calafate daily at 8:30am.

Turismo Zaahj (☑ 061-241-2260; www.turismo zaahj.co.cl; Arturo Prat 236/270) To Torres del Paine and El Calafate.

Buses from Puerto Natales

DESTINATION	COST (CH$)	TIME (HR)
El Calafate	15,000	5
Punta Arenas	6000	3
Torres del Paine	8000	2
Ushuaia	36,000	13

ⓘ Getting Around

Car rental is expensive and availability is lim ited; you'll get better rates in Punta Arenas or Argentina. Try **Emsa/Avis** (☑ 061-261-4388; Eberhard 577).

Many hostels rent bikes.

Parque Nacional Bernardo O'Higgins

Virtually inaccessible, O'Higgins remains an elusive cache of glaciers. As it can only be en tered by boat, full-day excursions (CH$75,000 including lunch) to the base of Glaciar Serrano are run by Turismo 21 de Mayo (p478).

You can access Torres del Paine via boat to Glaciar Serrano. Passengers transfer to a Zodiac (a motorized raft), stop for lunch at Estancia Balmaceda and continue up Río Serrano, arriving at the southern border of the park by 5pm. The same tour can be done leaving the park, but may require camping near Río Serrano to catch the Zodiac at 9am. The trip, which includes park entry, costs CH\$100,000 with Turismo 21 de Mayo.

Parque Nacional Torres del Paine

🎵 061

Soaring almost vertically to nearly 3000m above the Patagonian steppe, the Torres del Paine (Towers of Paine) are spectacular granite pillars that dominate the landscape of what may be South America's finest **national park** (www.parquetorresdelpaine.cl; high/low season CH\$18,000/10,000).

Before its creation in 1959, the park was part of a large sheep *estancia*. Part of Unesco's Biosphere Reserve system since 1978, it shelters flocks of ostrich-like rheas (known locally as ñandús), Andean condors, flamingos and many other bird species. Conservation has been most successful with the guanaco *(Lama guanicoe)*, which grazes the open steppe where predatory pumas cannot approach undetected. Herds of guanacos don't even flinch when humans or vehicles approach.

Weather can be wildly changeable in this 1810-sq-km park. Expect four seasons in a day. Sudden rainstorms and knock-down gusts are part of the adventure. Bring high-quality wet-weather gear, a synthetic sleeping bag and, if you're camping, a good tent.

Guided day trips from Puerto Natales are possible, but permit only a glimpse of what the park has to offer. Nature lovers should plan to spend anywhere from three to seven days here.

At the end of 2011, a raging fire burned over 16,000 hectares. The fire took weeks to contain, destroyed old forest, killed animals and burned several park structures. An international visitor was charged with accidentally setting the fire while trying to start an illegal campfire. The hiker denied setting the fire but paid a US\$10,000 fine and agreed to help with reforestation efforts. Chile has since enacted a stricter 'Ley del Bosque' (forest law) to protect parks and Conaf has started to actively remove visitors found breaking park guidelines. The affected area, mostly between Pehoé and Refugio Grey, is essentially the western leg of the 'W' trek.

Be conscientious and tread lightly – you are among hundreds of thousands of yearly guests.

🏃 Activities

Torres del Paine's 2800m granite peaks inspire a mass pilgrimage of hikers from around the world. Most go for the Paine Circuit or the 'W' to soak in these classic panoramas, leaving other incredible routes deserted. The Paine Circuit (the 'W' plus the backside of the peaks) requires seven to nine days, while the 'W' (named for the rough approximation to the letter that it traces out on the map) takes four to five. Add another day or two for transportation connections.

Most trekkers start either route from **Laguna Amarga**. You can also hike from Administración or take the catamaran from Pudeto to Lago Pehoé and start from there; hiking roughly southwest to northeast along the 'W' presents more views of black sedimentary peaks known as Los Cuernos (2200m to 2600m). For more detailed information of the following hikes, see Lonely Planet's *Trekking in the Patagonian Andes*.

As more trekkers arrive in the shoulder season, they should be aware of early season and foul-weather route closures. Trekking alone, especially on the backside of the circuit, is unadvisable, and may soon be regulated by Conaf. Tour operators in Puerto Natales offer guided treks, which include all meals and accommodations at *refugios* or hotels. Per-person rates decrease significantly in groups.

In a move to emphasize safety in the park, Conaf requires all visitors to sign a contract upon entering. The document details park regulations and explains the penalties for breaking them.

Hiking the 'W'

Most people trek the 'W' from right to left (east to west), starting at Laguna Amarga – accessible via a twice-daily 2½-hour bus ride from Puerto Natales. But hiking west to east – especially between Lago Pehoé and Valle Francés – provides superior views of Los Cuernos. To start the 'W' from the west, catch the catamaran across Lago Pehoé, then head north along Lago Grey or Campamento Italiano, from which point excellent (and pack-free) day hikes are possible. Going this direction, the hike is roughly 71km in total.

Parque Nacional Torres del Paine

Parque Nacional Torres del Paine

The following segments are some of the most memorable; all distances are one way.

Refugio Las Torres to Mirador Las Torres (8km, four hours) A moderate hike up Río Ascencio to a treeless tarn beneath the eastern face of the Torres del Paine for the closest view of the towers. The last hour is a knee-popping scramble up boulders (covered with knee- and waist-high snow in winter). There are camping and *refugios* at Las Torres and Chileno, with basic camping at Campamento Torres. In summer stay at Campamento Torres and head up at sunrise to beat the crowds.

Refugio Las Torres to Los Cuernos (12km, seven hours) Hikers should keep to the lower trail as many get lost on the upper trail (unmarked on maps). There's camping and a *refugio*. Summer winds can be fierce.

Los Cuernos/Lago Pehoé to Valle Francés (10km, five hours) In clear weather, this hike is the most beautiful stretch between 3050m Cerro Paine Grande to the west and the lower but still spectacular Torres del Paine and Los Cuernos to the east, with glaciers hugging the trail. Camp at Italiano and at Británico, right in the heart of the valley, or at the valley entrance at Camping Francés.

Valle Francés to Mountain Lodge Paine Grande (13km, five hours) From Campamento Británico, the trail heads downhill out of Valle Francés, over a hanging bridge toward Mountain Lodge Paine Grande. The spectacular Cuernos loom overhead on the right, and Lago Skottsberg is passed on the left. The ferry dock is just before the *refugio* and campground.

Mountain Lodge Paine Grande to Refugio Grey (10km, four hours one way from Lago Pehoé) A relatively easy trail with a few challenging downhill scampers. The glacier lookout is another half-hour's hike away. It has camping and *refugios* at both ends. This is the primary area that burned in 2011, so expect ash, burned forest and areas in recovery.

Mountain Lodge Paine Grande to Administración (16km, five hours) Up and around the side of Lago Pehoé, then through extensive grassland along Río Grey. Not technically part of the 'W,' but after completion of the hike, cut out to the Administración to avoid backtracking to Laguna Amarga. Mountain Lodge Paine Grande can radio in and make sure that you can catch a bus from the Administración back to Puerto Natales. You can also enter the 'W' this way to hike it east to west.

Hiking the Paine Circuit

For solitude, stellar views and bragging rights doing the 'W,' this longer trek is the way to go. This loop takes in the 'W,' plus the backside between Refugio Grey and Refugio Las Torres; the total distance is roughly 112km. The landscape is desolate yet beautiful. **Paso John Gardner** (the most extreme part of the trek) sometimes has knee-deep mud and snow. There's one basic *refugio* at Los Perros; the other option is rustic camping.

Many hikers start the Paine Circuit by entering the park (by bus) at Laguna Amarga, then hike for a few hours to Refugio and Camping Chileno. From this point, the circuit continues counterclockwise, ending in Valle Francés and Los Cuernos. The Paine Circuit is closed during winter.

The following segments are some of the most memorable; all distances are one way.

Refugio Grey to Campamento Paso (10km, four hours heading north, two hours going south) Hikers might want to go left to right (west to east), which means ascending the pass rather than slipping downhill.

Campamento Paso to Campamento Los Perros (12 km, four hours) This route has plenty of mud and sometimes snow. Don't be confused by what appears to be a campsite right after crossing the pass; keep going until you see a shack.

Campamento Los Perros to Campamento Lago Dickson (9km, around 4½ hours) A relatively easy but windy stretch.

Campamento Lago Dickson to Campamento Serón (19km, six hours) As the trail wraps around Lago Paine, winds can get fierce and the trails vague; stay along the trail furthest away from the lake. On the way, Campamento Coiron has been closed since the 2005 fire.

Campamento Serón to Laguna Amarga (15km, four to five hours) You can end the trek with a chill-out night and a decent meal at Refugio Las Torres.

Day Hikes

Walk from Guardería Pudeto, on the main park highway, to **Salto Grande**, a powerful waterfall between Lago Nordenskjöld and Lago Pehoé. Another easy hour's walk leads to **Mirador Nordenskjöld**, an overlook with superb views of the lake and mountains.

For a more challenging day hike with tranquillity and gorgeous scenery, try the four-hour trek to **Lago Paine**; its northern shore is only accessible from Laguna Azul.

The 'W'

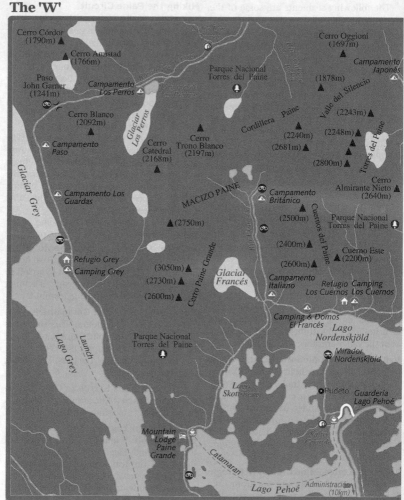

Kayaking

A great way to get up close to glaciers, Antares/Big Foot Patagonia (p477) leads 2½-hour tours (per person CH$55,000) of Lago Grey several times daily in summer.

Family-oriented floating trips that take rafts down the mild Río Serrano are run by Fantastico Sur (p482).

Horseback Riding

Due to property divisions within the park, horses cannot cross between the western sections (Lagos Grey and Pehoé, Río Serrano) and the eastern part managed by Fantastico Sur/Hotel Las Torres (Refugio Los Cuernos is the approximate cut off). Baqueano Zamora (p477) runs excursions to Laguna Azul, Valle Francés, Glaciar Dickson and more remote locations, with one-day (US$60) and multiday options.

Hotel Las Torres (p489) is part of an *estancia* that comprises the eastern area of the park; it offers full-day horseback-riding trips around Lago Nordenskjöld and beyond.

Ice Trekking

A fun walk through a sculpted landscape of ice, and you don't need experience to go. Antares/Big Foot Patagonia (p477) is the sole company with a park concession for ice

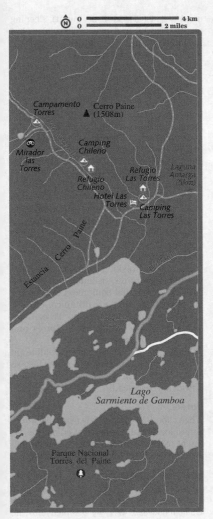

('domes,' also known as yurts) or campsites along the way. It is essential to reserve your spot and specify vegetarian meals in advance. Try to do this as soon as you book your trip.

Refugio rooms have four to eight bunk beds each, kitchen privileges (for lodgers and during specific hours only), hot showers and meals. If you don't bring a sleeping bag, a rental or bedding is extra (from US$11). Meals are also extra (US$14 to US$26). Should a *refugio* be overbooked, staff provide all necessary camping equipment. Most *refugios* close by the end of April. *Domos* are either cloth or plastic permanent camp structures with bunks or cots. Their operating season may be shorter.

Guests should use resources wisely and conserve water and electricity. There are no plugs in rooms, so bring a solar charger or extra batteries to charge electronics.

Accommodations may require photo ID (ie a passport) upon check-in. Photocopy your tourist card and passport for all lodgings in advance to expedite check-in. Staff can radio ahead to confirm your next reservation. Given the huge volume of trekkers, snags are inevitable, so practice your Zen composure.

Rates listed are basic – if you want bed linens (versus your own sleeping bag), it's extra.

Refugio Las Torres
LODGE **$**

(☎061-261-4184; www.fantasticosur.com; dm US$86, incl full board US$145; ☺Sep-Apr; @) An ample, attractive base camp with 60 beds and the added feature of a comfortable lounge, restaurant and bar. In high season, a nearby older building is put into use to handle the overflow, at discounted rates.

Refugio Chileno
CABIN **$**

(☎061-261-4184; www.fantasticosur.com; dm US$55, incl full board US$114; ☺Oct-Mar) Nearest to the fabled Torres del Paine, Chileno is one of the smallest *refugios*, with 32 beds and a small provisions kiosk. It's run on wind energy and toilets use composting biofilters.

Refugio Los Cuernos
CABIN **$**

(☎061-261-4184; www.fantasticosur.com; dm US$55, incl full board US$114, 2-person cabin US$187, incl full board US$305; ☺Sep-Apr) This mid-'W' location tends to bottleneck with hikers going in either direction. But with eight beds per room, this small lodge is more than cozy. New separate showers and bathrooms for campers relieve some of the stress. For a deluxe option, eight two-person cabins with shared bathroom offer privacy, with skylights and access to a piping-hot wooden hot tub.

hikes on Glaciar Grey (CH$90,000), using the Conaf house as a starting point. The five-hour excursion is available from October to May, in high season at 8:30am and 2:30pm.

🛏 Sleeping

Make reservations! Arriving without them, especially in high season, limits you to camping. Travel agencies offer reservations, but it's best to deal directly with the various management companies.

Refugios & Domos
If you are hiking the 'W' or the Paine Circuit, you will be staying in *refugios, domos*

Mountain Lodge Paine Grande
CABIN $

(☑ 061-241-2742; www.verticepatagonia.cl; dm from US$50, incl full board US$95; @) Though gangly, this park installation on the 'W' hiking circuit is nicer than most dorms, with sublime Los Cuernos views in all rooms. Its year-round presence is a godsend to cold, wet winter hikers, though meals are not available in winter (May to September). There's on-site camping, a kiosk with basic kitchen provisions and dome camping.

Between Lago Grey and Valle Francés, it's a day hike from either location and also accessible by ferry across Lago Pehoé.

Refugio Grey
HUT $

(☑ 061-241-2742; www.verticepatagonia.cl; dm from US$50, incl full board US$80; ☺ year-round) Inland from the lake, this deluxe trekkers' lodge features a decked-out living area with leather sofas and bar, a restaurant-grade kitchen and snug bunkrooms that house 60, with plenty of room for backpacks. There's also a general store, and covered cooking space for campers.

It runs in winter without meal service (May to September).

Refugio Lago Dickson
CABIN $

(☑ 061-241-2742; dm US$35, incl full board US$80; ☺ Nov-Mar) One of the oldest and smallest *refugios* in Parque Nacional Torres del Paine, with 30 beds, in a stunning setting on the Paine Circuit near Glaciar Dickson.

Domos Los Cuernos
DOME $

(☑ 061-261-4184; www.fantasticosur.com; dm US$66, incl full board US$125; ☺ Sep-Mar, varies) Next to Refugio Los Cuernos.

Domos El Serón
DOME $

(☑ 061-261-4184; www.fantasticosur.com; dm US$38, incl full board US$118) Located at Camping Serón.

Domos El Francés
DOME $

(☑ 061-261-4184; www.fantasticosur.com; dm US$73, incl full board US$132; ☺ Oct-Mar, varies) New domes with dining hall located at Camping Francés, a 40-minute walk from Los Cuernos. Each has four bunks, central heating and individual bathrooms with showers. More private 'cubos' (shelters) were under construction at the time of research.

Camping

The park has both fee camping and free camping. More services can be found at the former options.

Camping at the *refugios* costs CH$4000 to CH$8500 per campsite. *Refugios* rent equip-

ment – tent (CH$9500 per night), sleeping bag (CH$5500) and mat (CH$2000) – but potential shortages in high season make it prudent to pack your own gear.

Where there are *refugios*, meals are available to campers, with prices from CH$9000 for breakfast to CH$17,500 for dinner. Small kiosks sell expensive pasta, soup packets and butane gas, and cook shelters (at some campgrounds) prove useful in foul weather. Campgrounds generally operate from mid-October to mid-March, though those on the backside of the Paine Circuit may not open until November due to harsher weather. The decision is made by Conaf Centro de Visitantes.

For bookings, Vertice Patagonia (p482) looks after Camping Grey, Lago Dickson, Los Perros and camping at Mountain Lodge Paine Grande. Fantastico Sur (p482) owns Camping Las Torres, Francés, Chileno, Los Cuernos and Serón.

Sites on the trekking routes administered by Conaf Centro de Visitantes are free but basic, with no rental equipment or showers. These are Campamento Británico, Campamento Italiano, Campamento Paso, Campamento Serón, Campamento Torres and Camping Guardas.

Many campers have reported wildlife (in rodent form) lurking around campsites, so don't leave food in packs or in tents – hang it from a tree instead.

Hotels

When choosing lodgings, pay particular attention to location. Lodgings that adjoin the 'W' circuit offer more independence and flexibility for hikers. Most offer multiday packages.

★ Tierra Patagonia
LODGE $$$

(☑ in Santiago 02-207-8861; www.tierrapatagonia.com; d per person 3 nights incl full board & transfers from US$2390; @ 🛜 ☒) Sculpted into the sprawling steppe, this sleek luxury lodge is nothing if not inviting, with a lively living room and circular bar focused on a grand fire pit and a beautiful oversized artist's rendition of a park map. Large, understated rooms enjoy panoramas of the Paine Massif. All-inclusive rates will get you airport transfers, daily excursions, use of spa, meals and drinks.

Located on Cerro Guido *estancia*, the hotel's ranch-focused activities are a strong asset. It's on Lago Sarmiento, just outside the national park, 20km from Laguna Amarga.

Hotel Lago Grey
HOTEL $$$

(☑ 061-271-2100; www.lagogrey.cl; booking address Lautaro Navarro 1061, Punta Arenas; s/d

US$290/310; @⍟) Open year-round, this tasteful hotel has snug white cottages linked by raised boardwalks. The new deluxe rooms are lovely, featuring lake views and a sleek modern style. The cafe (open to the public) overlooks the grandeur. Boat tours visit the glacier, stopping at the Conaf office on the other side of Lago Grey to pick up and drop off passengers.

Awasi
LODGE $$$

(☑ in Santiago 022-233-9641; awasipatagonia.com; 3-night all-inclusive per person US$3250; ⍟) The appetite for upscale lodges in Paine does not abate. Awasi enters the mix with modern, understated style and a remote location that drinks in the wild surroundings. Its 12 villas with individual hot tubs surround a main lodge offering fine dining, lounge areas and wi-fi. Villas are connected by radio. It's sheepskin-chic and well attended, with quality, individually tailored tours included.

It's located outside the park, on the northeast side of Lago Sarmiento. Travel time might require a little patience: it's a good distance by gravel road from the main attractions, though transfers are provided.

Explora
HOTEL $$$

(☑ in Santiago 022-395-2800; www.explora.com; d 4 nights incl full board & transfers from US$6156; @⛉) These upscale digs sit perched above the Salto Chico waterfall at the outlet of Lago Pehoé. Views of the entire Paine massif pour forth from every inch of the hotel. The spa features a heated lap pool, sauna and open-air Jacuzzi. Rates include airport transfers, full gourmet meals and a wide variety of excursions led by young, affable, bilingual guides.

Hotel Las Torres
HOTEL $$$

(☑ 061-261-7450; www.lastorres.com; booking address Magallanes 960, Punta Arenas; d from US$304; ⊘ Jul-May; ⍟) ⌀ A hospitable and well-run hotel with international standards, spa with Jacuzzi and good guided excursions. Most noteworthy, the hotel donates a portion of fees to nonprofit park-based environmental group AMA. The buffet serves organic vegetables from the greenhouse and organic meat raised on nearby ranches.

Hostería Mirador del Payne
INN $$$

(☑ 061-222-8712; www.miradordelpayne.com; s/d/tr US$200/245/265) On the Estancia El Lazo in the seldom-seen Laguna Verde sector, this comfortable inn is known for its serenity, proximity to spectacular viewpoints and top-rate service – but not for easy access to the most popular trails. Activities include bird-watching, horseback riding and sport fishing. Call to arrange a ride from the road junction.

Hotel Cabañas del Paine
CABIN $$$

(☑ 061-273-0177; www.cabanasdelpaine.cl; Pueblito Río Serrano; s/d/tr US$264/275/308) On the banks of the Río Serrano, these cabin-style rooms stand apart; they're tasteful and well integrated into the landscape with great views.

Hostería Pehoé
HOTEL $$$

(☑ 061-272-2853; http://altopehoe.cl; s/d/tr from US$165/185/240) On the far side of Lago Pehoé, linked to the mainland by a long footbridge. Pehoé enjoys five-star panoramas of Los Cuernos and Paine Grande, but it's poor value, with dated rooms reminiscent of a roadside motel. The restaurant and bar are open to the public.

❶ Information

Parque Nacional Torres del Paine is open year-round, subject to your ability to get there. Unfortunately, Conaf's new National Parks Pass (CH$10,000) does not include entrance here.

Transportation connections are less frequent in the low season, lodging and services are more limited and winter weather adds additional challenges to hiking. However, the months of November and March are some of the best times for trekking, with fewer crowds and windy conditions usually abating in March. Check the opening dates of all the services you will require in advance (they change based on the weather in any given year). The Torres del Paine website (www.torresdelpaine.com) also has useful information.

The main entrance where fees are collected is **Portería Sarmiento** (⊘ daylight hours). **Conaf Centro de Visitantes** (⊘ 9am-8pm Dec-Feb), located 37km from Portería Sarmiento, has good information on park ecology and trail status. Administración is located also here. There is a small cafeteria at Pudeto and another in the works at the southern tip of Lago Grey.

Trekking maps are widely available in Puerto Natales. For detailed trekking suggestions and maps, consult Lonely Planet's *Trekking in the Patagonian Andes*.

❶ Getting There & Away

Going to El Calafate from Parque Nacional Torres del Paine on the same day requires joining a tour or careful advance planning, since there is no direct service. Your best bet is to return to Puerto Natales.

ⓘ Getting Around

Shuttles (CH$2800) drop off and pick up passengers at Laguna Amarga, at the catamaran launch at Pudeto and at Administración.

Catamaran **Hielos Patagónicos** (☑ 061-241-1380; info@hielospatagonicos.com; one way/roundtrip CH$15,000/24,000) leaves Pudeto for Mountain Lodge Paine Grande at 9:30am, noon and 6pm December to mid-March, at noon and 6pm in late March and November, and at noon only in September, October and April.

Another launch travels Lago Grey between Hotel Lago Grey and Refugio Grey (CH$45,000, 1½ to two hours) a couple of times daily; contact Hotel Lago Grey (p488) for current schedules.

FALKLAND ISLANDS/ ISLAS MALVINAS

☑ 500 / POP HUMANS 2932, SHEEP 500,000

Besides their status as an unusually polemical piece of property, what do the Falklands offer the intrepid traveler? Bays, inlets, estuaries and beaches create a tortuous, attractive coastline flanked by abundant wildlife. Located 500km to the east of Argentina in the South Atlantic Ocean, these sea islands attract striated and crested caracaras, cormorants, oystercatchers, snowy sheathbills, and a plethora of penguins – Magellanic, rockhopper, macaroni, gentoo and king – share top billing with elephant seals, sea lions, fur seals, five dolphin species and killer whales.

Stanley (population 2115), the islands' capital on East Falkland, is an assemblage of brightly painted metal-clad houses and a good place to throw down a few pints and listen to island lore. 'Camp' – as the rest of the islands are known – hosts settlements that began as company towns (hamlets where coastal shipping could collect wool) and now provide rustic backcountry lodging and a chance to experience pristine nature and wildlife. Though there are 400km of roads, the islands have no street lights.

Planning

The best time to visit is from October to March, when migratory birds (including penguins) and marine mammals return to the beaches and headlands. Cruise ships to South Georgia and Antarctica run from November through March. The annual sports meetings, with horse racing, bull riding and sheepdog trials, take place in Stanley between Christmas and New Year, and on East and West Falkland at the end of the shearing season in late February. Summer never gets truly hot (the maximum high is 24°C/75°F), but high winds bring chills. For more details, pick up Lonely Planet's *Antarctica* guide.

History

The sheep boom in Tierra del Fuego and Patagonia owes its origins to the cluster of islands known as Las Islas Malvinas to the Argentines or the Falkland Islands to the British. They had been explored, but never fully captured the interest of either country until Europe's mid-19th-century wool boom. After the Falkland Islands Company (FIC) became the islands' largest landholder, a population of stranded gauchos and mariners grew rapidly with the arrival of English and Scottish immigrants. In an unusual exchange, in 1853 the South American Missionary Society began transporting Yahgan Indians from Tierra del Fuego to Keppel Island to proselytize them.

Argentina's claim goes back to 1833, but it wasn't until 1982 that Argentine President Leopoldo Galtieri, then drowning in economic chaos and allegations of corruption, gambled that reclaiming the islands would unite his country. British Prime Minister Margaret Thatcher (also suffering in the polls) didn't hesitate in striking back, thoroughly humiliating Argentina in the Falklands War.

In 2010 Argentine President Cristina Fernández de Kirchner renewed Argentina's claim on the Falklands, diffusing the progress that had been made in the previous decade for increased cooperation between British, Falkland Islands and Argentine governments. To settle the lingering controversy, the Falklands held a referendum on its political status in March 2013, when 99% of voters supported continuing British rule. Relations with Argentina remain cool, with most South American trade going via Chile.

Visas & Documents

Visitors from Britain and Commonwealth countries, the EU, North America, Mercosur countries and Chile don't need visas. If coming from another country, check with the British consulate in that country. All nationalities must carry a valid passport, an onward ticket and proof of sufficient funds (credit cards are fine) and prearranged accommodations. In practice, arrivals who don't have prebooked accommodations are held in the arrivals area while rooms are found.

Falkland Islands/Islas Malvinas

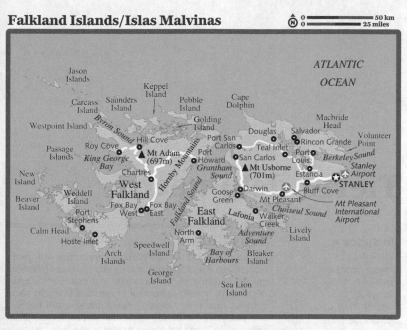

Money

There's no ATM on the Falklands and only one bank in Stanley, though credit and debit cards are widely accepted. Pounds sterling and US dollars in cash are readily accepted, but the exchange rate for US currency is poor. Don't bother changing to Falkland pounds (FK£). In peak season, expect to spend US$175 to US$350 per day, not including airfare; less if camping or staying in self-catering cottages.

ℹ️ Information

Visit Stanley's **Jetty Visitors Centre** (📞 22215; info@falklandislands.com; ⏰10am-5pm Mon-Fri, 9am-5pm Sat, 10am-4pm Sun), at the public jetty on Ross Rd. The Visitor Accommodation Guide lists lodgings and campgrounds. For trip planning, see the essential Falkland Islands Tourism website (www.falklandislands.com). In the UK, contact **Falkland House** (📞 020-7222-2542; www.falklands.gov.fk/self-governance/london-office; 14 Broadway, London SW1H 0BH).

ℹ️ Getting There & Away

From South America, **LanChile** (www.lan.com) flies to Mt Pleasant International Airport (MPA; near Stanley) every Saturday from Santiago, Chile, via Puerto Montt, Punta Arenas and – one Saturday each month – Río Gallegos, Argentina.

Roundtrip fares are US$788 from Punta Arenas with advance booking.

From **RAF Brize Norton** (www.raf.mod.uk/rafbrizenorton), in Oxfordshire, England, there are regular Royal Air Force flights to Mt Pleasant (18 hours, including a two-hour refueling stop on tiny Ascension Island in the South Atlantic). Travelers continuing on to Chile can purchase one-way tickets for half the fare from the UK. Bookings from the UK can be made through the **Falkland Islands Government Office** (📞 020-7222-2542; www.falklands.gov.fk; 14 Broadway, Falkland House, Westminster, London SW1H 0BH). Payment is by cash, or personal or bank check; credit cards are not accepted.

ℹ️ Getting Around

From Stanley, **Figas** (📞 27219; reservations@figas.gov.fk) serves outlying destinations in eight-seater aircraft.

Several Stanley operators run day trips to East Falkland settlements, including **Discovery Falklands** (📞21027, 51027; discovery@horizon.co.fk). **Adventure Falklands** (📞21383; pwatts@horizon.co.fk) specializes in wildlife (featuring king, gentoo and Magellanic penguins) and historical tours.

Trekking and camping are feasible; however, there are no designated trails and getting lost is not unheard of. Always seek permission before entering private land.

Tierra del Fuego

Best Places to Eat

➡ Kalma Resto (p506)

➡ Kaupé (p506)

➡ María Lola Restó (p506)

➡ Chiko (p506)

➡ Don Peppone (p513)

Best Places to Stay

➡ Galeazzi-Basily B&B (p501)

➡ Antarctica Hostel (p501)

➡ Estancia Las Hijas (p512)

➡ Hostería Yendegaia (p516)

➡ Los Cauquenes Resort & Spa (p503)

Why Go?

The southernmost extreme of the Americas, this windswept archipelago is as alluring as it is moody – at turns beautiful, ancient and strange. Travelers who first came for the ends-of-the-earth novelty discover a destination that's far more complex than these bragging rights. Intrigue still remains in a past storied with shipwrecks, native peoples and failed missions. In Tierra del Fuego, nature is writ bold and reckless, from the scoured plains, rusted peat bogs and mossy lenga forests to the snowy ranges above the Beagle Channel.

While distant and isolated, Tierra del Fuego is by no means cut off from the mainland, though the Argentine half is far more developed than its Chilean counterpart. Ports buzz with commerce and oil refineries prosper while adventure seekers descend in droves to fly-fish, hike and start Antarctic cruises. Shared with Chile, this archipelago features one large island, Isla Grande, Chile's Isla Navarino and many smaller uninhabited ones.

When to Go
Ushuaia

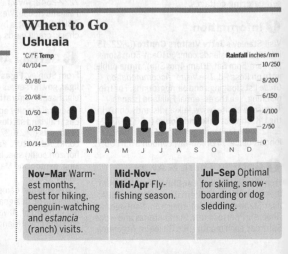

Nov–Mar Warmest months, best for hiking, penguin-watching and *estancia* (ranch) visits.

Mid-Nov–Mid-Apr Fly-fishing season.

Jul–Sep Optimal for skiing, snowboarding or dog sledding.

ℹ Getting There & Around

The most common overland route from Patagonia is via the ferry crossing at **Punta Delgada** (Primera Angostura; ✆ +(56) 61-2728100; www.tabsa.cl; per car/passenger CH$15,000/1700; ☉ daylight hours, 20min), Chile. Unlike the rest of Argentina, Tierra del Fuego doesn't have designated provincial highways but secondary roads known as *rutas complementarias*, modified by a lowercase letter. These roads are referred to as 'RC-a,' for example.

If renting a car in mainland Argentina, be aware that you must pass through Chile a couple of times to reach Tierra del Fuego. This requires special documents, special attention to banned items (mainly fruit, dairy products, meat and seeds) and additional international insurance coverage. Most car-rental agencies can arrange the paperwork with advance notice.

At the time of writing, Chile was building an alternate road to the southern end of the island. It currently links with Lago Fagnano, but a 4WD vehicle is required.

Visitors can fly into Río Grande or Ushuaia. Buses take the ferry from Chile's Punta Delgada; all pass through Río Grande before reaching Ushuaia.

Ushuaia

✆ 02901 / POP 57,000

A busy port and adventure hub, Ushuaia is a sliver of steep streets and jumbled buildings below the snowcapped Martial Range. Here the Andes meet the southern ocean in a sharp skid, making way for the city before reaching a sea of lapping currents.

It's a location matched by few, and chest-beating Ushuaia takes full advantage of its end-of-the-world status as an increasing number of Antarctica-bound vessels call in to port. Its endless mercantile hustle knows no irony: the souvenir shop named for Jimmy Button (a native kidnapped for show in England), the ski center named for a destructive invasive species... You get the idea. That said, with a pint of the world's southernmost microbrew in hand, you can happily plot the dazzling outdoor options: hiking, sailing, skiing, kayaking and even scuba diving are just minutes from town.

Tierra del Fuego's comparatively high wages draw Argentines from all over to resettle here, and some locals lament the loss of small-town culture. Meanwhile, expansion means haphazard development advancing in the few directions the mad geography allows.

History

In 1870 the British-based South American Missionary Society set its sights on the Yahgan (or Yámana), a nomadic tribe whose members faced brutal weather conditions almost entirely naked – they didn't have any permanent shelter to keep clothing dry, and believed that the natural oil of their skin was better protection than soaking wet animal fur. Charles Darwin branded them 'the lowest form of humanity on earth.' Missionary Thomas Bridges didn't agree. After years among them, he created a Yahgan-English dictionary in the late 19th century, deeming their language complex and subtle.

The mission made Ushuaia its first permanent Fuegian outpost, but the Yahgan, who had survived 6000 years without contact, were vulnerable to foreign-brought illnesses and faced increasing infringement by sealers, settlers and gold prospectors. Four Yámana, including a teenager dubbed 'Jimmy Button,' were kidnapped by the naval captain Robert Fitz Roy and shipped back to England to be educated and paraded around as examples of gentrified savages. One died of disease. After months of public criticism, Fitz Roy agreed to return the rest to their homeland.

The tribe's legacy is now reduced to shell mounds, Thomas Bridges' famous dictionary and Jimmy Button souvenirs. At the time of writing, one elderly Yámana woman was still alive on Isla Navarino, the only native speaker of the language.

Between 1884 and 1947 the city became a penal colony, incarcerating many notorious criminals and political prisoners, both here and on remote Isla de los Estados. Since 1950 the town has been an important naval base.

◉ Sights

Paralleling the Beagle Channel, Av Maipú becomes Malvinas Argentinas west of the cemetery, then turns into RN 3, continuing 12km to Parque Nacional Tierra del Fuego. To the east, public access ends at Yaganes, which heads north to meet RN 3 going north toward Lago Fagnano. Most visitor services are on or near Av San Martín, a block from the waterfront.

The tourist office distributes a free city-tour map with information on the historic houses around town. The 1894 **Legislatura Provincial** (Provincial Legislature; Av Maipú 465) was the governor's official residence. The

Tierra del Fuego Highlights

1 Exploring the ancient Fuegian forests of **Parque Nacional Tierra del Fuego** (p508).

2 Speeding through frozen valleys on a **dog sledding tour** (p498) near Ushuaia.

3 Landing the big one while fly-fishing at an **estancia** (p512) near Río Grande.

4 Reliving grim times in Ushuaia's infamous prison-turned-museum, **Museo Marítimo & Museo del Presidio** (p496).

5 Skiing and snowboarding with sublime views at the world's southernmost resort, **Cerro Castor** (p498).

6 Browsing back in time in the quiet seaside village of **Porvenir** (p515).

7 Trekking around the jagged peaks and sculpted landscapes on the five-day circuit of **Dientes de Navarino** (p514) near Puerto Williams.

century-old **Iglesia de la Merced** (cnr Av San Martín & Don Bosco) was built with convict labor. **Casa Beban** (cnr Av Maipú & Plúschow; ⏱11am-6pm) was built in 1911 using parts ordered from Sweden, and sometimes hosts local art exhibits.

★ Museo Marítimo & Museo del Presidio
MUSEUM

(☏02901-437481; www.museomaritimo.com; cnr Yaganes & Gobernador Paz; admission AR$200; ⏱9am-8pm) Convicts were transferred from Isla de los Estados (Staten Island) to Ushuaia in 1906 to build this national prison, finished in 1920. The cells, designed for 380 inmates, held up to 800 before closing in 1947. Famous prisoners include illustrious author Ricardo Rojasand and Russian anarchist Simón Radowitzky. The depiction of penal life is intriguing, but information is only in Spanish.

Maritime exhibits provide a unique glimpse into the region's history. Remains of the world's narrowest-gauge freight train, which transported prisoners between town and work stations, sit in the courtyard. From December to March, guided tours (also in English) are at 11:30am and 4:30pm. If you can, take your tour with Horacio.

Museo Yamaná
MUSEUM

(☏02901-422874; Rivadavia 56; admission AR$75; ⏱10am-7pm) Small but carefully tended, this museum has an excellent overview of the Yahgan (Yamaná) way of life. It delves into their survival in harsh weather without clothing, why only women swam and how campfires were kept in moving canoes. Expertly detailed dioramas (also in English) show the bays and inlets of Parque Nacional Tierra del Fuego; useful before a park visit.

Museo del Fin del Mundo
MUSEUM

(☏02901-421863; www.museodelfindelmundo. org.ar; cnr Av Maipú & Rivadavia; admission AR$130; ⏱10am-7pm) Built in 1903, this former bank contains exhibits on Fuegian natural history, stuffed birdlife, life of natives and early penal colonies, and replicas of moderate interest. Guided visits are at 11am and 3:30pm.

Parque Yatana Park
PARK

(Fundación Cultiva; ☏425212; cnr Magallanes & 25 de Mayo; ⏱9am-noon Mon-Fri) Part art project, part urban refuge, a city block of lenga forest is preserved from encroaching development by one determined family.

🏃 Activities

Hiking possibilities should not be limited to Parque Nacional Tierra del Fuego; the entire mountain range behind Ushuaia, with its lakes and rivers, is a hiker's high. However, many trails are poorly marked or not marked at all, and some hikers who have easily scurried uphill have gotten lost trying to find the trail back down. For their safety hikers going outside the national park are asked to register at the tourist office (p507) upon their departure and return. Club Andino Ushuaia (p507) has maps and good information. In an emergency, contact the **Civil Guard** (☏02901-22108, 103). Boating can be undertaken year-round.

Summer Activities

Cerro Martial & Glaciar Martial OUTDOORS (⏱10am-4pm) The fantastic panoramas of Ushuaia and the Beagle Channel are more impressive than the actual smallish glacier. Weather is changeable so take warm, dry clothing and sturdy footwear. You can hike or do a canopy tour. To get here, catch a taxi or minivan (AR$120) to Cerro Martial; the latter leave from the corner of Av Maipú and Juana Fadul every half-hour from 8:30am to 6:30pm.

Canopy Tours ADVENTURE TOUR (www.canopyushuaia.com.ar; Refugio de Montaña, Cerro Martial; adult/child incl transfer US$32/28; ⏱10am-5:15pm Oct-Jun) Evening canopy tours offer an hour's worth of Tarzan time, zipping through the forest with 11 zip-line cables and two hanging bridges. By reservation only.

Cruceros Australis CRUISE (☏in Santiago 022-442-3115; www.australis.com; 3 nights & 4 days per person from US$1190; ⏱late Sep-early Apr) Luxurious three- to four-night sightseeing cruises from Ushuaia to Punta Arenas, with the possibility to disembark at Cape Horn.

Aeroclub Ushuaia SCENIC FLIGHTS (☏421717, 421892; www.aeroclubushuaia.com; 5-passenger charter per person US$335) Offers scenic rides over the channel and may travel to Puerto Williams, Chile (10kg allowed). Leaves before 1pm; confirm three days in advance.

Winter Activities

With the surrounding peaks loaded with powder, winter visitors should jump at the chance to explore the local ski resorts. Accessed from RN 3, resorts offer both

ANTARCTICA: THE ICE

For many travelers, a journey to Antarctica represents a once-in-a-lifetime adventure. Despite its high price tag, it is much more than just a continent to tick off your list. You will witness both land and ice shelves piled with hundreds of meters of undulating, untouched snow. Glaciers drop from mountainsides and icebergs form sculptures as tall as buildings. The wildlife is thrilling, with thousands of curious penguins and an extraordinary variety of flying birds, seals and whales.

More than 90% of Antarctic-bound boats pass through Ushuaia; in the 2014–15 season, that meant almost 40,000 tourists – a stunning contrast to the continent's population of 5000 (summer) or 1200 (winter) scientists and staff. But travel here is not without its costs. On November 23, 2007, the hull of the MV *Explorer* was gashed by ice but evacuated successfully before sinking. The circumstances were highly unusual, although the incident provoked further safety measures.

So long as you've got two or three weeks to spare, hopping on board a cruise ship is not out of the question. Some voyages take in the Islas Malvinas (Falkland Islands) and South Georgia (human population 10 to 20, estimated penguin population two to three million); some go just to the Antarctic Peninsula; others focus on retracing historic expeditions. A small but growing handful of visitors reach Antarctica aboard private vessels. All are sailboats (equipped with auxiliary engines).

The season runs from mid-October to mid-March, depending on ice conditions. It used to be that peak-season voyages sold out; now most trips do. When shopping around, ask how many days you will actually spend in Antarctica, as crossing the Southern Ocean takes up to two days each way, and how many landings will be there. The smaller the ship, the more landings there are per passenger (always depending on the weather, of course). Tour companies charge anywhere from US$7000 to US$70,000, although some ships allow walk-ons, which can cost as little as US$5000 for 10 days. Required insurance costs extra (around US$800). Check to see if your ship provides outdoor clothing.

Due to Ushuaia's proximity to the Antarctic Peninsula, most cruises leave from here. If you are chasing the discounts, it is best to check in with agencies a few weeks in advance, once you are actually in South America. Last-minute bookings can be made through **Freestyle Adventure Travel** (☏2901-609792; www.freestyleadventuretravel.com; Gobernador Paz 866), a 1% for the Planet member that also offers discount Cape Horn trips, and Ushuaia Turismo (p500). Other travel agencies and tour operators offering packages include Rumbo Sur (p507), All Patagonia (p507) and Canal Fun (p499), though there are many more.

Check that your company is a member of **IAATO** (www.iaato.org), which mandates strict guidelines for responsible travel to Antarctica. The following are just a few companies that go to Antarctica:

Adventure Associates Cruise (www.adventureassociates.com) Australia's first tour company to Antarctica, with many ships and destinations.

National Geographic Expeditions (www.nationalgeographicexpeditions.com) Highly recommended, with quality naturalists and experts, aboard the 148-passenger *National Geographic Explorer*.

Peregrine Adventures (www.peregrineadventures.com) Offers unique trips that include visiting the Antarctic Circle, with kayaking and camping options.

WildWings Travel (www.wildwings.co.uk) UK-based company that focuses on bird-watching and wildlife in Antarctica.

For more information see Lonely Planet's *Antarctica* guidebook. Also check http://polarconservation.org for up-to-date information and articles. In Ushuaia consult the very helpful **Oficina Antártica** (☏02901-430015; www.tierradelfuego.org.ar/antartida; Av Maipú 505; ⊙9am-5pm with ship in port) at the pier.

Ushuaia

downhill and cross-country options. The ski season runs from June to September, with July (winter vacation) the busiest month.

Cerro Castor
SKIING
(☎02901-499301; www.cerrocastor.com; full-day lift ticket adult/child AR$730/500; ⊗mid-Jun–mid-Oct) Fun and incredibly scenic, the largest resort has 15 runs spanning 400 hectares, a number of lodges with cafes and even a hip sushi bar. Rentals are available for skis, boards and cross-country skis. Multiday and shoulder-season tickets are discounted. Clear windbreaks are added to lifts on cold days. It's 26km from Ushuaia via RN 3.

Tierra Mayor
SNOW SPORTS
(☎02901-430329; http://antartur.com.ar; RN 3, Km3018; guided dog sledding US$50) Offers competitively priced adventure tours and has its own mountain base. Snowshoe a beautiful alpine valley or dogsled with Siberian and Alaskan huskies bumping across Tierra Mayor. For a memorable night, combine either with an evening bonfire (US$130 to US$145). It also does guided snowcat rides and many travelers have enjoyed the 4WD day trip to Lago Fagnano with canoeing and a full barbecue. It's 19km from Ushuaia via RN 3.

Cerro Martial &
Glaciar Martial
SNOW SPORTS
(☎cell 1551-0307; http://www.escuelaushuaia.com; Nordic ski classes AR$520, all-day snowshoe rental AR$110; ⊗10am-4pm) Ideal for families or a few hours of fun, this winter sports center offers Nordic skiing and rents equipment and clothing; ask about snowshoes to take a winter walk.

👉 Tours

Many travel agencies sell tours around the region. You can go horseback riding, hiking,

canoeing, visit Lagos Escondido and Fagnano, stay at an *estancia* (ranch) or spy on birds and beavers.

Navigating the Beagle Channel's gunmetal-gray waters overlooking distant glaciers and rocky isles offers a fresh perspective and decent wildlife-watching. Harbor cruises (around AR$750) are usually four-hour morning or afternoon excursions to sea lion and cormorant colonies. The number of passengers, extent of snacks and hiking options varies between operators. A highlight is an island stop to hike and look at *conchales,* the middens or shell mounds left by the native Yahgan. Tour operators offering cruises line the entrance to Ushuaia's pier.

Canal Fun
ADVENTURE TOUR

(☏02901-435777; www.canalfun.com; Roca 136) Run by hip young guys, these popular all-day outings include hiking and kayaking in Parque Nacional Tierra del Fuego, the famous 4WD adventure around Lago Fagnano, and a multisport outing around Estancia Harberton that includes kayaking around Estancia Harberton and a visit to the penguin colony.

Che Turismo Alternativo
BOAT TOUR

(☏cell 02901-15-517967; www.facebook.com/elcheturismoalternativo; Tourist Wharf; half-day tour AR$850) This owner-run tour includes a trek on Bridges Island and local beer on tap served for the cruise back to the harbor – very popular with the hostel crowd.

★Compañía de Guías de Patagonia
ADVENTURE TOUR

(☏02901-437753; www.companiadeguias.com.ar; full-day hike US$105) A reputable outfitter organizing expeditions and multiday treks around Ushuaia and further afield in remote Tierra del Fuego. Also offers glacier trekking, mountain biking and Antarctica trips with sea kayaking.

Patagonia Adventure Explorer
BOAT TOUR

(☏02901-15-465842; www.patagoniaadvent.com.ar; Tourist Wharf) Comfortable boats with snacks and a short hike on Isla Bridges. For extra adventure, set sail in the 18ft sailboat. Full-day sail trips with wine and gourmet snacks or multiday trips are also available.

Piratour
BOAT TOUR

(☏02901-435557; www.piratour.net; Av San Martín 847; penguin colony tour US$150; ⏰9am-9pm) Runs 20-person tours to Isla Martillo for trekking around Magellanic and Papúa penguins, with a visit to Harberton. Also boats to Puerto Williams, Chile (December to March). There's a second office on the Tourist Wharf.

Rayen Aventura
ADVENTURE TOUR

(☏02901-437005; www.rayenaventura.com; Av San Martín 611) Known for their upbeat 4x4 tours to Lago Fagnano, with trekking or kayak options and *estancia* visits. Also has winter tours.

★Tierra
ADVENTURE TOUR

(☏02901-433800, 02901-15-486886; www.tierraturismo.com; Onas 235, office 4C) Doing active tours and unusual tailored trips with aplomb, this small agency was created by former guides going for a more personalized experience. Options include a 4WD trip to Lago Fagnano with boating and hiking (AR$1400), treks in Parque Nacional Tierra

Ushuaia

del Fuego (half-day AR$650) and Estancia Harberton visits.

Tres Marías Excursiones BOAT TOUR
(☑ 02901-436416; www.tresmariasweb.com; Tourist Wharf) The only outfitter with permission to land on Isla 'H' in the Isla Bridges natural reserve, which has shell mounds and a colony of rock cormorants. It takes only eight passengers.

Tolkar TOUR
(☑ 02901-431408, 02901-431412; www.tolkarturismo.com.ar; Roca 157) A helpful, popular, all-round agency, affiliated with Tecni-Austral buses.

Turismo Comapa TOUR
(☑ 430727; www.comapa.com; Av San Martín 409) Confirm Navimag and Cruceros Australis passages at this long-standing agency also selling conventional tours and boat transfer to Puerto Williams, Chile.

Turismo de Campo TOUR
(☑ 02901-437351; www.turismodecampo.com; Fuegia Basquet 414) Organizes light trekking, Beagle Channel sailing trips and visits to Estancia Rolito near Río Grande. Also sells nine- to 12-night Antarctica passages.

Ushuaia Turismo TOUR
(☑ 02901-436003; www.ushuaiaturismoevt.com.ar; Gobernador Paz 865) Offers last-minute Antarctica cruise bookings.

✪ Festivals & Events

Desafío Ushuaia SPORTS
(⊙ early Mar) A hugely popular international marathon on the southernmost course on the continent.

Festival Nacional de la Noche Más Larga FESTIVAL
(Longest Night; ⊙ mid-Jun) This festival features two weeks of shows and music recitals (ranging from tango to jazz and popular music), with free events at locations throughout

the city. For more information, contact the Municipal Tourist Office (p507).

Marcha Blanca SNOW SPORTS
(www.marchablanca.com; ⊘mid-Aug) Running for a quarter of a century, Ushuaia's biggest ski event is the annual cross-country event which re-creates San Martín's historic August 17, 1817 crossing of the Andes. There's also a master class for ski enthusiasts, snow sculptures and a Nordic ski marathon.

🛏 Sleeping

Reserve ahead from January to early March. Check when booking for free arrival transfers. Winter rates drop a bit, and some places close altogether, though winter visits are becoming popular. Most offer laundry service.

The Municipal Tourist Office (p507) has lists of B&Bs and *cabañas* (cabins), and also posts a list of available lodgings outside after closing time.

Hostels abound, all with kitchens and most with internet access. Rates typically drop 25% in low season (April to October).

★ Antarctica Hostel HOSTEL $
(☏02901-435774; www.antarcticahostel.com; Antártida Argentina 270; dm/d US$26/85; @ 🛜) This friendly backpacker hub delivers with a warm atmosphere and helpful staff. The open-floor plan and beer on tap are plainly conducive to making friends. Guests lounge and play cards in the common room and cook in a cool balcony kitchen. Cement rooms are clean and ample, with radiant floor heating.

Hostel Cruz del Sur HOSTEL $
(☏02901-434099; www.xdelsur.com.ar; Deloquí 242; dm US$25; @ 🛜) This easygoing, organized hostel comprises two renovated houses (1920 and 1926), painted tangerine and joined by a passageway. Dorm prices are based on room capacity, the only disadvantage being your bathroom might be on another floor. There's a fine backyard patio, though indoor shared spaces are scant.

Torre al Sur HOSTEL $
(☏02901-430745; www.torrealsur.com.ar; Gobernador Paz 855; dm/d US$20/35; 🛜) The sister hostel to Cruz del Sur may seem like not much on the outside but inside there's a welcoming, organized ambience with colorful rooms, renovated bathrooms and a well-stocked kitchen. Marisa is the warm host.

La Posta HOSTEL $
(☏444650; www.laposta-ush.com.ar; Perón Sur 864; dm/d US$27/80; @ 🛜) This cozy hostel and guesthouse on the outskirts of town is hugely popular with young travelers thanks to warm service, homey decor and spotless open kitchens. The downside is that the place is far from the town center, but public buses and taxis are plentiful.

Los Cormoranes HOSTEL $
(☏02901-423459; www.loscormoranes.com; Kamshen 788; dm US$31-40, d/tr/q US$107/132/155; @🛜) This friendly, mellow HI hostel is a 10-minute (uphill) walk north of downtown. Six-bed dorms with radiant floors face outdoor plank hallways, some with private bathrooms. Doubles have polished cement floors and down duvets – the best is room 10, with bay views. Linens could use an update and common spaces are so-so. Breakfast includes DIY eggs and fresh orange juice.

Yakush HOSTEL $
(☏435807; www.hostelyakush.com; Piedrabuena 118; dm US$28-30, d with/without bathroom US$105/95; ⊘mid-Oct–mid-Apr; @ 🛜) A colorful hostel that seems expensive for what you get, particularly for the dark doubles.

Camping Municipal CAMPGROUND $
(RN 3; campsites free) About 10km west of town, en route to Parque Nacional Tierra del Fuego, this free campground boasts a lovely setting but minimal facilities.

★ Galeazzi-Basily B&B B&B $$
(☏02901-423213; www.avesdelsur.com.ar; Valdéz 323; s/d without bathroom US$45/65, 2-/4-person cabin US$110/140; @🛜) The best feature of this elegant wooded residence is its warm and hospitable family who will make you feel right at home. Rooms are small but offer a personal touch. Since beds are twin-sized, couples may prefer a modern cabin out back. It's a peaceful spot, and where else can you practice your English, French, Italian and Portuguese?

Mysten Kepen GUESTHOUSE $$
(☏02901-430156, 02901-15-497391; http://mystenkepen.blogspot.com; Rivadavia 826; d/tr/q US$94/144/175; 🛜) If you want an authentic Argentine family experience, this is it. Hosts Roberto and Rosario still recount stories of favorite guests from years past, and their immaculate two-kid home feels busy and lived in – in a good way. Rooms have newish installations, bright corduroy duvets and

OFF THE BEATEN TRACK

ESTANCIA HARBERTON

Tierra del Fuego's first *estancia*, **Harberton** (✉ Skype estanciaharberton.turismo; www.estanciaharberton.com; entrance adult/child AR$180/free, s/d full board & activities US$325/580, dm US$50; ⊙10am-7pm Oct 15-Apr 15), was founded in 1886 by missionary Thomas Bridges and his family. The location earned fame from a stirring memoir written by Bridges' son Lucas, titled *Uttermost Part of the Earth,* about his coming of age among the now-extinct Selk'nam and Yahgan people. Available in English, the book is an excellent introduction to the history of the region and the ways of native peoples.

In a splendid location, the *estancia* is owned and run by Thomas Bridges' descendants. There's lodging and day visitors can attend guided tours (featuring the island's oldest house and a replica Yahgan dwelling), dine at the restaurant and visit the Reserva Yecapasela penguin colony. It's also a popular destination for bird-watchers.

On-site, the impressive **Museo Acatushún** (www.acatushun.com; entrance with estancia visit AR$180) houses a vast collection of mammal and bird specimens compiled by the late biologist Natalie Prosser Goodall. Emphasizing the region's marine mammals, the museum has inventoried thousands of mammal and bird specimens; among the rarest is a Hector's beaked whale. Much of this vast collection was found at Bahía San Sebastián, north of Río Grande, where a difference of up to 11km between high and low tide leaves animals stranded. Confirm the museum's opening hours with the *estancia*.

Reserve well in advance as there are no phones at the *estancia*, though Skyping may be possible. With advance permission, free primitive camping is allowed at Río Lasifashaj, Río Varela and Río Cambaceres. Harberton is 85km east of Ushuaia via RN 3 and rough RC-j, a 1½- to two-hour drive. In Ushuaia, shuttles leave from the base of 25 de Mayo at Av Maipú at 9am, returning around 3pm. Day-long catamaran tours are organized by local agencies.

handy shelving for nighttime reading. Airport transfers and winter discounts available.

La Casa de Tere B&B
B&B $$

(☎ 02901-422312; www.lacasadetere.com.ar; Rivadavia 620; d with/without US$120/85) Tere showers guests with attention, but also gives them the run of the place in this beautiful modern home with great views. Its three tidy rooms fill up fast. Guests can cook, and there's cable TV and a fireplace in the living room. It's a short but steep walk uphill from the town center.

Posada Fin del Mundo
B&B $$

(☎ 02901-437345; www.posadafindelmundo.com.ar; cnr Rivadavia & Valdéz; d US$140) This expansive home exudes good taste and character, from the snug living room with folk art and expansive water views to the doddling chocolate Lab. With nine distinct rooms, the best of which are upstairs. Some are small but beds are long. Breakfast is abundant and there's also afternoon tea and cakes. Sometimes booked by entire ski teams in winter.

Familia Piatti B&B
B&B $$

(☎ 437104; www.familiapiatti.com; Bahía Paraíso 812, Bosque del Faldeo; d US$90; @ 🛜) 🍴 If idling in the forest appeals, head for this friendly B&B with warm down duvets and native lenga-wood furniture. Hiking trails nearby lead up into the mountains. The friendly owners are multilingual (English, Italian, Spanish and Portuguese) and can arrange transportation and guided excursions. Check the website for location directions.

Cabañas del Beagle
CABIN $$$

(☎ 02901-432785; www.cabanasdelbeagle.com; Las Aljabas 375; 2-person cabin US$260, 4-night minimum) Couples in search of a romantic hideaway delight in these rustic chic cabins with heated stone floors, crackling fireplaces, and full kitchens stocked daily with fresh bread, coffee and other treats. The personable owner, Alejandro, wins high praise for his attentive service. It's 13 blocks uphill from the town center and accessed via Av Leandro Alem.

Cabañas Aldea Nevada
CABIN $$$

(☎ 02901-422851; www.aldeanevada.com.ar; Martial 1430; 2-/4-person cabins from US$140/190, 2-night minimum; @ 🛜) You expect the elves to arrive here any minute. This beautiful patch of lenga forest is discreetly dotted with 13 log cabins with outdoor grills and rough-hewn benches contemplatively placed by the ponds. Interiors are rustic but modern, with functional kitchens, wood stoves and hardwood details.

Cumbres del Martial
INN $$$

(☑02901-424779; www.cumbresdelmartial.com.ar; Martial 3560; d/cabin US$365/525; @🛜) This stylish place sits at the base of the Glaciar Martial. Standard rooms have a touch of the English cottage, while the two-story wooden cabins are simply stunners, with stone fireplaces, Jacuzzis and dazzling vaulted windows. Lush robes, optional massages (extra) and your country's newspaper delivered to your mailbox are some of the delicious details.

Los Cauquenes Resort & Spa
RESORT $$$

(☑441300; www.loscauquenes.com; d from US$365; @🛜🏊) Precious and exclusive, this sprawling wooden lodge sits directly on the Beagle Channel, in a private neighborhood with gravel-road access. Rooms are tasteful and well appointed; special features include a play room stocked with kids' games and outdoor terraces with glass windbreaks and stunning channel views. Free shuttles go downtown every few hours. It's 4km west of the airport.

There's also a spa, sauna and indoor-outdoor pool. Proof that Argentines will market anything, the spa features *yerba mate* scrubs and Andean peat masks.

Arakur
HOTEL $$$

(☑02901-442900; www.arakur.com; Cerro Alarken; d with valley/ocean view US$370/400; @🛜🏊) Towering over the city on a wooded promontory, Arakur is the latest luxury hotel, well known to locals for hosting an annual music festival. The look is sleek and woodsy, with neutral tones and snooty service that begs softening. Still, views are beyond comparison. Rooms feature a panel of electronic controls and glass-walled bathrooms. The infinity pool is indoor-outdoor.

Mil 810
HOTEL $$$

(☑437710; www.hotel1810.com; 25 de Mayo 245; d US$200; @) Billed as boutique, this is more like a small upscale hotel. The design is modern with elements of nature, such as a retention wall of river stones and a rock face trickling with water. Its 38 rooms feature brocade walls, rich tones, luxuriant textures and touches of abstract art. Rooms have flat-screen TVs and safes, and halls are monitored.

✖ Eating

Almacen Ramos Generales
CAFE $

(☑02901-4247317; Av Maipú 749; mains AR$73-175; ⊙9am-midnight) With its quirky memorabilia and postings of the local environmental issues you've never heard of, this former general store is a peek inside the real Ushuaia. Locals hold their powwows here. Croissants and crusty baguettes are baked by the French pastry chef. There's also local beer on tap, a wine list, and light fare such as sandwiches, soups and quiche.

Cafe Bar Banana
CAFE $

(☑02901-424021; Av San Martín 273; mains AR$60-130; ⊙8am-1am Mon-Fri, to 2am Sat, 9am-1am Sun) Serving homemade burgers and fries, sandwiches and steak and eggs, this is a local favorite for high-octane, low-cost dining with friends.

Freddo
ICE CREAM $

(Av San Martín 209; cones AR$50; ⊙9:30am-12:30am) One of Argentina's best gelato shops has opened its doors to snowbound Ushuaia – and suddenly it's summer.

El Turco
CAFE $

(☑02901-424711; Av San Martín 1410; mains AR$50-119; ⊙noon-3pm & 8pm-midnight) Nothing fancy, this classic, dated Argentine cafe nonetheless charms with reasonable prices and swift bow-tied waiters game to try out their French on tourists. Standards include *milanesa* (breaded meat), pizzas, crispy fries and roast chicken.

Lomitos Martinica
ARGENTINE $

(☑02901-432134; Av San Martín 68; mains AR$65-125; ⊙11:30am-3pm & 8:30pm-midnight Mon-Sat) Cheap and cheerful, this greasy spoon with grill-side seating serves enormous *milanesa* sandwiches and offers a cheap lunch special.

La Anónima
SUPERMARKET $

(cnr Gobernador Paz & Rivadavia; ⊙9am-10pm) A grocery store with cheap takeout.

Placeres Patagónicos
ARGENTINE $$

(☑02901-433798; www.patagonicosweb.com.ar; 289 Deloquí; snacks AR$65, tablas from AR$100; ⊙noon-midnight) This stylish cafe-deli serves wooden cutting boards piled with homemade bread and mouth-watering local specialties such as smoked trout and wild boar. It's a good place to sip *mate* with a plate of *tortas fritas* (frybread). Coffee arrives steaming in a bowl-sized mug.

504

MICHAEL TAYLOR/GETTY IMAGES ©

Ushuaia (p493)
wildlife-watching cruise on the Beagle
annel offers a fresh perspective on the
dscape.

Estancia Harberton (p502)
unded in 1886, this ranch now houses an
site museum with a vast collection of
mmal and bird specimens.

Cerro Castor (p498)
e largest ski resort here has runs
nning 400 hectares among incredible
tas.

El Tren del Fin de Mundo (p510)
ce used to transport prisoners, this train
w offers a slow but scenic way to get to
que Nacional Tierra del Fuego (p508).

MIKE TRUELOVE/GETTY IMAGES ©

Chiko
SEAFOOD $$

(☑ 02901-431736; 25 de Mayo 62; mains AR$110-260; ⊙ noon-3pm & 7:30-11:30pm Mon-Sat) A boon to seafood lovers. Crisp oversize calamari rings, *paila marina* (shellfish stew) and fish dishes like *abadejo a pil pil* (pollock in garlic sauce) are done so right that you might not mind the slow service. An odd assemblage of Chilean memorabilia spells homesickness for the owners from Chile.

María Lola Restó
ARGENTINE $$

(☑ 02901-421185; Deloquí 1048; mains AR$165-264; ⊙ noon-midnight Mon-Sat) 'Satisfying' defines the experience at this creative cafe-style restaurant overlooking the channel. Locals pack this silver house for homemade pasta with seafood or strip steak in rich mushroom sauce; the weekday set lunch (AR$104) is a steal. Service is good and portions tend toward humongous: desserts can easily be split. It's among few downtown restaurants with off-street parking.

Paso Garibaldi
ARGENTINE $$

(☑ 02901-432380; Deloquí 133; mains AR$150-250; ⊙ noon-3pm & 7-11:30pm Tue-Sat, 7-11:30pm Sun) Serving hearty local fare including black bean stew, flavorful salads and roasted hake, this new addition is refreshingly without pretension. The recycled decor looks a little too improvised, but service couldn't be more attentive and dishes are well priced.

Bodegón Fueguino
PATAGONIAN $$

(☑ 02901-431972; Av San Martín 859; mains AR$95-215; ⊙ noon-2:45pm & 8-11:45pm Tue-Sun) The spot to sample hearty home-style Patagonian fare or gather for wine and appetizers. Painted peach, this century-old Fuegian home is cozied up with sheepskin-clad benches, cedar barrels and ferns. A *picada* (shared appetizer plate) for two includes eggplant, lamb brochettes, crab and bacon-wrapped plums.

La Estancia
STEAK $$

(☑ 02901-431421; cnr Godoy & Av San Martín; mains AR$120-240; ⊙ noon-3pm & 8-11pm) For authentic Argentine *asado* (barbecue grill), it's hard to beat this reliable, well-priced grill. There are many others along the main drag, but this is the one that consistently delivers. Enthusiastic appetites should go for the *tenedor libre* (AR$330). Locals and travelers feast on whole roast lamb, juicy steaks, sizzling ribs and heaping salads.

Christopher
PARRILLA $$

(☑ 425079; www.christopherushuaia.com.ar; Av Maipú 828; mains AR$100-254; ⊙ noon-3pm & 8pm-midnight, to 1am Sat) This classic grill and brewpub is deservedly popular with the locals. Standouts include BBQ ribs, big salads and burgers. It's good value, with large portions that you might want to share and a talented bartender mixing cocktails. Grab a table by the window for great harbor views.

Küar Resto Bar
PUB FOOD $$

(☑ 437396; www.kuar.com.ar; Av Perito Moreno 2232; mains AR$115-300; ⊙ 6pm-late) This chic log-cabin-style hangout offers local beer, cheese boards and tapas, as well as complete dinners with ample fresh seafood. The interior is stylish but the highlight, especially at sunset, is the jaw-dropping views over the water. It's five minutes from downtown by cab (AR$50), or visit **Küar 1900** (☑ 02901-436807; Av San Martin 471, 2nd fl; mains AR$120-180; ⊙ noon-3:30pm & 6:30pm-midnight Mon-Sat), a smaller downtown venue focused on tapas.

Tante Sara
CAFE $$

(☑ 423912; www.tantesara.com; cnr Av San Martín & Juana Fadul; mains AR$154-265; ⊙ 8am-2am) This corner bistro serves the usual suspects in a bubbly atmosphere. For a late-night bite, this is your best bet – it's the only kitchen open until 2am. Its **sister branch** (☑ 433710; Rivadavia & Av San Martín; mains AR$60-130; ⊙ 8am-8:30pm Mon-Thu, to 9pm Fri & Sat) offers nice pastries and weekend brunch.

★ Kalma Resto
INTERNATIONAL $$$

(☑ 02901-425786; www.kalmaresto.com.ar; Antártida Argentina 57; mains AR$180-390; ⊙ 4-11pm Mon-Sat) This tiny chef-owned gem presents Fuegian staples like crab and octopus in a giddy new context. Black sea bass, a rich deep-sea dweller, wears a tart tomato sauce for contrast; there's stuffed lamb seasoned in pepper and rosemary; and the summer greens and edible flowers come fresh from the garden.

Service is stellar, with young chef Jorge making the rounds of the few black-linen tables. For dessert, splurge with a not-too-sweet deconstructed chocolate cake.

Kaupé
INTERNATIONAL $$$

(☑ 422704; www.kaupe.com.ar; Roca 470; mains AR$180-260) For an out-of-body seafood experience, head to this candlelit house overlooking the bay. Chef Ernesto Vivian employs the freshest of everything and service is impeccable. The tasting menu features two starters, a main dish and dessert, with standouts such as king crab and spinach chowder or black sea bass in blackened butter.

Chez Manu   INTERNATIONAL **$$$**
(☑432253; www.chezmanu.com; Martial 2135; mains AR$150-260) If you are headed to Glaciar Martial, don't miss this gem on the way, 2km from town. Chef Emmanuel puts a French touch on fresh local ingredients, such as Fuegian lamb or mixed plates of cold *fruits de mer,* and service stands out. The three-course set lunch is the best deal. Views are a welcome bonus.

🍷 Drinking & Nightlife

Geographically competitive drinkers should note that the southernmost bar in the world is not here but on a Ukrainian research station in Antarctica.

Dublin Irish Pub   PUB
(☑02901-430744; 9 de Julio 168; ⊙7pm-4am) Dublin doesn't feel so far away with the lively banter and free-flowing drinks at this dimly lit foreigners' favorite. Look for occasional live music and be sure to try at least one of its three local Beagle beers.

Viagro   BAR
(☑02901-421617; Roca 55; ⊙8pm-4am) If you can get past the unfortunate name, this cocktail nook is the perfect low-lit rendezvous spot, with exotic concoctions and appetizing tapas to fuel your night out. There's dancing on Saturday nights.

☆ Entertainment

Cine Pakawaia   CINEMA
(☑436500; cnr Yaganes & Gobernador Paz; tickets AR$70) First-run movies are shown at the Presidio's fully restored hangar-style theater.

**Casa de la Cultura
Performing Arts**   PERFORMING ARTS
(☑422417; cnr Malvinas Argentinas & 12 de Octubre) Hidden behind a gym, this center hosts occasional live-music shows. It's 6km north of the center via Av Maipú.

🛍 Shopping

Boutique del Libro   BOOKS
(☑02901-424750; Av San Martín 1120) Outstanding selection of Patagonia- and Antarctica-themed material, with literature, guidebooks and pictorials (also in English).

ℹ Information

IMMIGRATION
Immigration Office (☑02901-422334; Beauvoir 1536; ⊙9am-noon Mon-Fri) Argentine office for immigration issues.

MONEY
Several banks on Avs Maipú and San Martín have ATMs.

TOURIST INFORMATION
Automóvil Club Argentino (ACA; www.aca. org.ar; cnr Malvinas Argentinas & Onachaga) Argentina's auto club; good source for provincial road maps.

Club Andino Ushuaia (☑02901-422335; www. clubandinoushuaia.com.ar; Alem 2873, Refugio Walker; ⊙10am-1pm & 3-8pm Mon-Fri) Sells a map and bilingual trekking, mountaineering and mountain-biking guidebook. The club occasionally organizes hikes and can recommend guides. Located 5km west of Ushuaia.

Instituto Fueguino de Turismo (Infuetur; ☑02901-421423; www.tierradelfuego.org. ar; Av Maipú 505) Tourism office for Tierra del Fuego. Ask here about the development of island trekking routes called Huella del Fin del Mundo. It's on the ground floor of Hotel Albatros.

Municipal Tourist Office (☑02901-437666; Prefectura Naval 470; ⊙8am-9pm) Very helpful, with English- and French-speaking staff, a message board and multilingual brochures, as well as good lodging, activities and transport info. Also at the Airport (☑02901-423970; ⊙during flight arrivals).

National Parks Administration (☑02901-421315; Av San Martín 1395; ⊙9am-5pm Mon-Fri) Offers information on Parque Nacional Tierra del Fuego.

TRAVEL AGENCIES
All Patagonia (☑02901-433622; www.allpatagonia.com; Juana Fadul 48; ⊙10am-7pm Mon-Fri, to 1pm Sat) Amex rep offering conventional and luxurious trips.

Rumbo Sur (☑02901-421139; www.rumbosur.com.ar; Av San Martín 350; ⊙9am-7pm Mon-Fri) Ushuaia's longest-running agency specializes in conventional activities, plus a catamaran harbor cruise. It also handles bookings to Antarctica.

MEDICAL SERVICES
Hospital Regional (☑107, 02901-423200; cnr Fitz Roy & 12 de Octubre) Emergency services. It's southwest of the center via Av Maipú.

POST
Post Office (cnr Av San Martín & Godoy; ⊙9am-6pm Mon-Fri) For mail.

ⓘ Getting There & Away

AIR

LAN is the best bet for Buenos Aires; purchase tickets through local travel agencies. **Aerolíneas Argentinas** (☑ 0810-2228-6527; cnr Av Maipú & 9 de Julio) jets to Buenos Aires (one way from US$250, 3½ hours) several times daily, sometimes stopping in El Calafate (70 minutes).

LADE (☑ 02901-421123; Av San Martín 542) flies to Buenos Aires, El Calafate, Río Grande and may serve other destinations.

BOAT

A few private yachts charter trips around the Beagle Channel, to Cape Horn and Antarctica. These trips must be organized well in advance.

For Puerto Williams, **Ushuaia Boating** (☑ 02901-436193; www.ushuaiaboating.com. ar; Tourist Wharf s/n; one-way US$135 on Sat) goes daily in Zodiac boats. Tickets include a 40-minute crossing plus an overland transfer from Puerto Navarino. Note: inclement weather often means cancellations. Options include a 9:30am departure and sometimes a 6pm departure (with sufficient demand). Another option to Puerto Williams is offered by Piratour (p499).

A small departure tax *(tasa de embarque)* is paid at the pier.

BUS

Ushuaia has no bus terminal. Book outgoing bus tickets as much in advance as possible; many readers have complained about getting stuck here in high season. Depending on your luck, long waits at border crossings can be expected.

Bus Sur (☑ 02901-430727; Av San Martín 245) has buses to Punta Arenas and Puerto Natales, Chile, three times weekly at 5:30am, connecting with Montiel. The office is in Comapa, which also does tours and runs ferries in Chile.

Tecni-Austral (☑02901-431408; Roca 157) buses head to Río Grande at 5am via Tolhuin; to Punta Arenas three times weekly; and to Río Gallegos daily at 5am. Taqsa has buses to Río Grande at 5am via Tolhuin; to Punta Arenas and Puerto Natales, Chile, three-times weekly at 5am; and to Río Gallegos, El Calafate and Bariloche daily at 5am.

Lider (☑ 02901-442264; Gobernador Paz 921) runs door-to-door minivans to Tolhuin and Río Grande six to eight times daily, with fewer departures on Sunday. **Montiel** (☑ 02901-421366; Gobernador Paz 605) has similar services.

Buses from Ushuaia

DESTINATION	COST (AR$)	TIME (HR)
Calafate	1150	18
Punta Arenas, Chile	920	12
Río Gallegos	750	13
Río Grande	250	3½
Tolhuin	150	1½

ⓘ Getting Around

Taxis to/from the modern airport, 4km southwest of downtown, cost AR$120. Taxis can be chartered for around AR$1300 for three hours. There's a local bus service along Av Maipú.

Rental rates for compact cars, including insurance, start at around AR$800 per day; try **Localiza** (☑ 02901-430739; Av Maipú 778). Some agencies may not charge for drop-off in other parts of Argentine Tierra del Fuego.

Hourly ski shuttles (AR$250 roundtrip) leave from the corner of Juana Fadul and Av Maipú to resorts along RN 3, from 9am to 2pm daily. Each resort also provides its own transportation from downtown Ushuaia.

Parque Nacional Tierra del Fuego

Banked against the Beagle Channel, the hushed, fragrant southern forests of Tierra del Fuego are a stunning setting to explore. West of Ushuaia some 12km along RN 3, **Parque Nacional Tierra del Fuego** (admission AR$170, collected 8am-8pm) was Argentina's first coastal national park and extends 630 sq km from the Beagle Channel in the south to beyond Lago Fagnano in the north. For information, visit the **Centro de Visitantes Alakush** (☉ 9am-7pm, shorter hours Mar-Nov).

The public has access to only a couple of thousand hectares along the southern edge of the park, with short, easy trails designed more for day-tripping families than backpacking trekkers. The rest is protected as a *reserva natural estricta* (strictly off-limits zone). Despite this, a few scenic hikes along the bays and rivers, or through dense native forests of evergreen coihue, canelo and deciduous lenga, are worthwhile. For spectacular color, come in autumn when hillsides of ñire glow red.

Birdlife is prolific, especially along the coastal zone. Keep an eye out for condors, albatross, cormorants, gulls, terns, oystercatchers, grebes, kelp geese and the comical, flightless, orange-billed steamer ducks. Common invasive species include the European rabbit and the North American beaver, both wreaking ecological havoc despite their cuteness. Gray and red foxes, enjoying the abundance of rabbits, may also be seen.

🛏 Sleeping & Eating

There is one *refugio* and various, mostly free campgrounds. Most get crowded, which

Parque Nacional Tierra del Fuego – Lapataia Sector

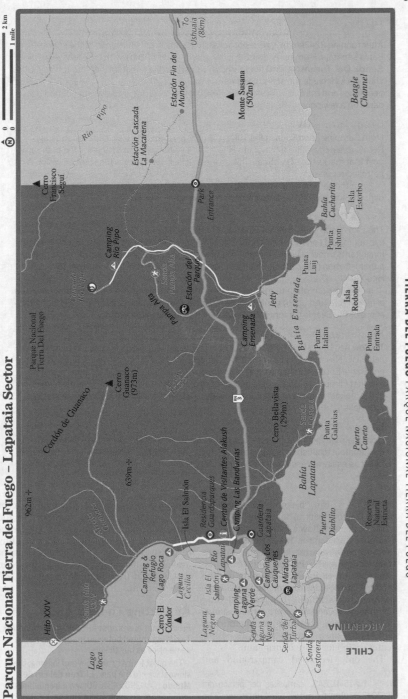

HIKING

After running 3242km from Buenos Aires, RN 3 reaches its terminus at the shores of Bahía Lapataia. From here, trails **Mirador Lapataia** (500m), with excellent views, and **Senda Del Turbal** (400m) lead through winding lenga forest further into the bay. Other short walks include the self-guided nature trail **Senda Laguna Negra** (950m), through peat bogs, and the **Senda Castorera** (400m), showcasing massive abandoned beaver dams on a few ponds.

Senda Hito XXIV

From Camping Lago Roca, a flat 10km (four-hour) roundtrip trek leads around Lago Roca's forested northeast shore to Hito XXIV – *veinticuatro* in Spanish – the boundary post that marks the Argentina–Chile frontier. It is illegal to cross the frontier, which is patrolled regularly.

From the same trailhead you can reach **Cerro Guanaco** (973m) via the steep and difficult 8km trail of the same name; it's a long uphill haul but the views are excellent.

Senda Costera

This 8km (four-hour) trek leads west from Bahía Ensenada along the coastline. Keep an eye out for old *conchales* (archaeologically important mounds of shells left by Yahgan inhabitants), now covered in grass. The trail meets RN 3 a short way east of the park administration (*guardería*) center at Lapataia. From here it is 1.2km further to Senda Hito XXIV.

It might be tempting to roll up the cuffs and go clamming, but be aware that occasional *marea roja* (red tides) contaminate mollusks (such as clams and mussels) along the shore of the Beagle Channel. This seasonal trail opens in December.

Senda Pampa Alta

The low heights of Pampa Alta (around 315m) grant long views across the Beagle Channel to Isla Navarino and Isla Hoste. RN 3 meets the trailhead 1.5km west of the Río Pipo and Bahía Ensenada road turnoffs (3km from the entrance gate). The 5km roundtrip trail first climbs a hill, passing a beaver dam along the way. Enjoy the impressive views at the lookout. A quick 300m further leads to a trail paralleling the Río Pipo and some waterfalls.

Laguna Negra

From the road 2km southwest of Lapataia, a trail leads north along the western side of Río Lapataia to a fishing spot opposite Isla El Salmón. Laguna Negra, a lovely lake in the forest, is easily accessible via a 1km circuit loop.

means sites can become unreasonably messy. Do your part to take your trash out of the park and follow a leave-no-trace ethic. Camping Ensenada is 16km from the park entrance and nearest the Senda Costera trail; Camping Río Pipo is 6km from the entrance and easily accessed by either the road to Cañadon del Toro or the Senda Pampa Alta trail. Camping Laguna Verde and Camping Los Cauquenes are on the islands in Río Lapataia. There are no amenities at any of the sites; contact the park visitor center (p508) for more information.

The only fee-based campground and *refugio* is **Camping & Refugio Lago Roca** (☑15-412649; campsites per person/dm US$10/22), 9km from the park entrance. The *refugio* dorm is available year-round except when weather prohibits transport to the park. Both offer hot showers, a good *confitería* (cafe offering light meals) and a tiny (expensive) grocery store. There is plenty of availability for camping at wild sites. Note that water at Lago Roca is not potable; boil it before using.

❶ Getting There & Away

Private tour buses cost AR$300 for a roundtrip. Taxi fares shared between groups can be the same price as bus tickets.

The most touristy and, beyond jogging, the slowest way to the park, **El Tren del Fin de Mundo** (☑02901-431600; www.trendelfinde mundo.com.ar; adult/child plus park entrance fee AR$500/100) originally carted prisoners to work camps. It departs (without the convicts) from the Estación del Fin de Mundo, 8km west of Ushuaia (taxis one way AR$120), three or four times daily in summer and once or twice daily in winter.

The one-hour, scenic narrow-gauge train ride comes with historical explanations in English and Spanish. Reserve in January and February, when cruise-ship tours take over. You can take it one way and return via minibus, though the train fee is the same one way or roundtrip.

Hitchhiking is feasible, but many cars may already be full.

Tolhuin & Lago Fagnano

☏ 02901

Named for the Selk'nam word meaning 'like a heart,' Tolhuin (population 2000) is a lake town nestled in the center of Tierra del Fuego, 132km south of Río Grande and 104km northeast of Ushuaia via smooth asphalt. Muddy streets and clear-cut forests mark this fast-growing frontier town that fronts the eastern shore of Lago Fagnano, also known as Lago Kami. Lago Fagnano, with low-key horseback riding, mountain biking, boating and fishing, is worth checking out as a tranquil lake spot.

Shared with Chile, the glacial-formed Lago Fagnano offers 117km of beaches, with most of its shoreline remote and roadless. Plans to create road access from Chile and put a catamaran here are developing.

◉ Sights

Museo Histórico Kami   MUSEUM
(tdf@gmail.com; Lago Fagnano s/n; ⊘3-7pm Tue-Sun) FREE If you make one stop in Tolhuin, check out this museum, especially worthwhile for Spanish speakers. A former 1920s police post, the little house is now dedicated to regional history, starting with the Selk'nam. One exhibit documents community members' stories of the still-recent pioneer times. It's next to Camping Hain, on Lago Fagnano. Don't be shy to ask for a tour.

Parque Hain   AMUSEMENT PARK
(Parque de Diversiones Reciclado; Lago Fagnano s/n; child/adult AR$50/20; ⊘9am-5pm) The product of a creative mind that never sleeps, this offbeat playground is styled entirely from recycled materials, namely 5000 wooden palettes, tires fashioned into playforms and bottles forming decorative motifs. Created by Roberto Barbel, who also owns the campground across the street with similar whimsy on display, it's a kick to take in.

🛏 Sleeping & Eating

Camping Hain   CAMPGROUND $
(☏02964-15-603606; Lago Fagnano; campsite per person US$6, 3-/6-person refugio US$50/100) Located on Lago Fagnano, with hot showers, grassy sites with wooden windbreaks, a huge barbecue pit and a *fogon* (sheltered fire pit and kitchen area). There's plenty of creative handiwork but no internet by design: unplug and enjoy. The owner can pick up guests from Panadería La Unión.

Hostería Ruta Al Sur   HOTEL $$
(☏492278; www.rutalsur.com.ar; RN 3, Km2954; d US$115; ⊘mid-Oct–Apr; @ 🛜 🏊) Considering that it's on the side of the main road, this lovely lodge surrounded by old beech trees is a bit of a surprise. So is the uneven service. Confirm rates in advance since you may be charged more as a foreigner (to be fair, it has rates for Tierra del Fuego residents and nonresidents). Rooms are sparkling and there's a sprawling living room as well as a restaurant that serves a basic breakfast.

Panadería La Unión   BAKERY $
(☏02901-492202; www.panaderialaunion.com.ar; Jeujepen 450, Tolhuin; snacks AR$20; ⊘24hr) First-rate *facturas* (pastries) and second-rate instant cappuccinos keep this roadside attraction hopping. You may or may not recognize the Argentine celebrities gracing the walls (hint: the men are aging rock stars). Buses break here to pick up passengers and hot water for *mate* (a bitter ritual tea).

ℹ Information

Tolhuin's **tourist office** (☏492380, 492125; www.tierradelfuego.org.ar/tolhuin; Av de los Shelknam 80; ⊘8am-10pm Mon-Fri), behind the gas station, has information on hiking, horseback riding tours and gear rentals. Those coming from Ushuaia might get more-complete info from Ushuaia's tourist office. **Banco de Tierra del Fuego** (Menkiol s/n) has an ATM.

ℹ Getting There & Away

Throughout the day, buses and minivans passing along RN 3 (often already full in high season) stop at Panadería La Unión en route to Ushuaia or Río Grande (AR$150).

Río Grande

02964 / POP 66,500

A monster trout sculpture at the entrance to town announces the de facto fly-fishing capital of Tierra del Fuego, with world-class blue-ribbon angling for colossal sea-run trout. But nonfishers will likely stay in windswept Río Grande for a few hours, before hopping on a bus to Ushuaia, 230km southwest.

As wool baron José Menéndez' sheep stations developed, Río Grande grew as a makeshift service town. In 1893 the Salesian order, under the guidance of Monseñor Fagnano, set up a mission in an unsuccessful attempt to shelter the Selk'nam from the growing infringement. As a petroleum service center, the town has an industrial feel: even the public art looks like giant, grim tinker toys. Geared at the business traveler, it's also pricey for visitors. Duty-free status, meant to foster local development, has brought in electronics manufacturing plants and wholesale appliance stores. During the Falklands War the military played an important role here; memorials pay tribute to fallen soldiers.

🏃 Activities

Hollywood stars, heads of state and former US presidents all flock to desolate stretches around Río Grande with dreams of the big one. Usually they are in luck. Rivers around Río Grande were stocked in the 1930s with brown, rainbow and brook trout. It's now one of the world's best sea-run trout-fishing areas, with some local specimens weighing in at 15kg. Rainbow trout can reach 9kg.

Fishing excursions are mostly organized through outside agents, many in the US. 'Public' fishing rivers, on which trips can be organized, include the Fuego, Menéndez, Candelaria, Ewan and MacLennan. Many of the more elite angling trips are lodged in *estancias* (ranches) with exclusive use of some of the best rivers.

There are two types of fishing licenses. License 1 is valid throughout the province, except in Parque Nacional Tierra del Fuego. Contact **Asociación Caza y Pesca** (02901-422423; www.cazaypescaushuaia.org; Av Maipú 822) in Ushuaia (its website also has tidal charts), or **Club de Pesca John Goodall** (02964-15-503074; http://clubdepescatdf.blogspot.com; Ricardo Rojas 606) in Río Grande. License 2 is valid for Parque Nacional Tierra

---

ESTANCIAS AROUND RÍO GRANDE

Much of Tierra del Fuego was once the sprawling backyard of wool baron José Menéndez. His first *estancia* – La Primera Argentina (1897), now known as **Estancia José Menéndez**, 20km southwest of Río Grande via RN 3 and RC-b – covered 1600 sq km, with more than 140,000 head of sheep. His second and most-treasured venture was La Segunda Argentina, totaling 1500 sq km. Later renamed **Estancia María Behety** (in Buenos Aires 011-4331-5061; www.maribety.com.ar; 1 week per person from US$4295; Dec-Apr) after his wife, it's still a working ranch, 17km west of Río Grande via RC-c. Besides boasting the world's largest shearing shed, it is a highly exclusive lodge, catering to elite anglers eager to fish some of the world's largest brown sea trout, which grow up to 16kg (35lb). Two lodges accommodate up to 18 fly-fishers, the full quota for the river.

Several *estancias* have opened to small-scale tourism, offering a unique chance to learn about the region's history and enjoy its magic. Reserve as far in advance as possible. The lauded **Estancia Las Hijas** (02901-15-554462, 02901-15-617022; www.estancialashijas.com.ar; RP16; per person overnight or day trip US$85, day trip incl transport $290) offers small-scale family visits for small groups (inquire ahead since different parties can combine). Indeed, they are known around these parts as *'locos divinos'* (crazy but fun). After horseback riding, rounding sheep and barbecues, guests stay in basic lodgings with shared bathrooms. It's located 33km north of Tolhuin, 7km in on the dirt road RP 16 (formerly 'G'). If you go with transportation included (from Ushuaia or Río Grande), there must be a minimum of two people. A stay includes dinner, breakfast and activities.

The rustic and charismatic **Estancia Rolito** (02901-437351, 02901-432419; www.tierradelfuego.org.ar/rolito; RC-a, Km 14; s/d full board US$330/550) is very Argentine and very inviting. Guests rave about the hikes through ñire and lenga forest. Day trips from Ushuaia with Turismo de Campo (p500) stop by for lunch or dinner and activities. Rates are based on double occupancy. Rolito is 100km from Río Grande and 150km from Ushuaia.

del Fuego and Patagonia. Contact the National Parks Administration office (p507) in Ushuaia or find more information on sport fishing in Argentina through the online portal **Pesca Argentina** (www.pescaargentina.com.ar). Other useful information:

Flies Rubber legs and wooly buggers.

License fees AR$270 per day or AR$1080 per season, depending on where you fish.

Limit One fish per person per day, catch and release.

Methods Spinning and fly casting; no night fishing.

Season November 1 to April 15, with catch-and-release restrictions from April 1 to April 15.

Sleeping & Eating

Posada de los Sauces　　　　HOTEL **$$**
(☑ 02964-432895; www.laposadadelossauces.com; Elcano 839; d US$110; ☺ 🖥) Catering to high-end anglers, Posada de los Sauces fosters a lodge atmosphere, with fresh scents and woodsy accents.

Hotel Villa　　　　　　　　HOTEL **$$**
(☑ 02964-424998; hotelvillarg@hotmail.com; Av San Martín 281; d/tr US$70/77; ☺ 🖥) Opposite Casino Status, Hotel Villa has a popular restaurant, and a dozen spacious and stylish rooms.

Don Peppone　　　　　　ITALIAN **$$**
(☑ 02964-432066; Perito Moreno 247; mains AR$100-135; ☺ noon-midnight Tue-Sun) On weekends there's a dose of madness at Don Peppone, a busy pizzeria with gooey brick-oven creations as well as a huge variety of pastas and meat dishes. Credit cards are accepted.

Tante Sara　　　　　　　　CAFE **$$**
(Belgrano 402; mains AR$80-160; ☺ 8am-1am Sun-Thu, to 2am Fri & Sat) Hosting both ladies having tea and cake and boys at the varnished bar downing beer and burgers, Tante Sara serves good cafe food, though service can be sluggish.

ℹ Information

Most visitor services are along Avs San Martín and Belgrano. For tourist information, visit **Instituto Fueguino de Turismo** (Infuetur; ☑ 02964-426805; www.tierradelfuego.org.ar; Av Belgrano 319; ☺ 9am-9pm) on the southern side of the plaza, or the **Municipal Tourist Kiosk** (☑ 02964-431324; turismo@riogrande.gob.ar; ☺ 9am-8pm), a helpful kiosk on the plaza, with maps, *estancia* brochures and fishing details.

Mariani Travel (☑ 02964-426010; mariani@marianitravel.com.ar; Rosales 281) books flights and represents nearby *estancias*.

ℹ Getting There & Away

The **airport** (☑ 02964-420699; off RN 3) is a short taxi ride from town. **Aerolíneas Argentinas** (☑ 02964-424467; Av San Martín 607) flies daily to Buenos Aires (one way from AR$2760).
LADE (☑ 02964-422968; Lasserre 429) flies a couple of times weekly to Río Gallegos, El Calafate and Buenos Aires.

The following bus companies depart from **Terminal Fueguina** (Finocchio 1194):

Buses Pacheco (☑ 02964-421554) Buses to Punta Arenas three times weekly at 10am.

Lider (☑ 02964-420003; www.lidertdf.com.ar; Av Belgrano 1122) Best option for Ushuaia and Tolhuin is this door-to-door minivan service, with several daily departures. Call to reserve.

Montiel (☑ 02964-420997; 25 de Mayo 712) Buses to Ushuaia and Tolhuin.

Taqsa/Marga (☑ 02964-434316) Buses to Ushuaia via Tolhuin.

Tecni-Austral (☑ 02964-430610; ticket office Moyano 516) Buses to Ushuaia via Tolhuin three times weekly at 8:30am; to Río Gallegos and Punta Arenas three times weekly.

Buses from Río Grande

DESTINATION	COST (AR$)	TIME (HR)
Punta Arenas, Chile	900	9
Río Gallegos	750	8
Tolhuin	150	2
Ushuaia	240	4

Puerto Williams (Chile)

☑ 061 / POP 2300

Forget Ushuaia: the end of the world starts where colts roam Main St and yachts rounding Cape Horn take refuge. Naval settlement Puerto Williams is the only town on Isla Navarino, the official port of entry for vessels en route to Cape Horn and Antarctica, and home to the last living Yahgan speaker.

Just outside Puerto Williams is some of the Southern Cone's most breathtaking scenery. With more than 150km of trails, Isla Navarino is a rugged, backpackers' paradise, with slate-colored lakes, mossy lenga forests and the ragged spires of the Dientes de Navarino. Trails lead past beaver dams, bunkers and army trenches as they climb steeply into the mountains and deeper into forests. The beaver plague, introduced from Canada in the 1940s, is diminishing due to an active eradication campaign.

Mid-19th-century missionaries, followed by fortune-seekers during the 1890s gold rush, established a permanent European presence here. The remaining mixed-race descendants of the Yahgan (Yámana) people are established in the small seaside village of Villa Ukika, a 15-minute walk east of town along the waterfront.

◉ Sights

Museo Martín Gusinde MUSEUM
(cnr Araguay & Gusinde; donation requested; ⊙ 9am-1pm & 3-6:30pm Tue-Fri, 3-6:30pm Sat & Sun, reduced hours off-season) An attractive museum honoring the German priest and ethnographer who worked among the Yahgans from 1918 to 1923. The focus is on ethnography and natural history. Public wi-fi is available in the library.

Club de Yates Micalvi LANDMARK
(⊙ late Sep-May) A grounded German cargo boat, the *Micalvi* was declared a regional naval museum in 1976 but found infinitely better use as a floating bar, frequented by navy men and yachties. Unfortunately, the bar isn't open to the general public.

Yelcho LANDMARK
Near the entrance to the military quarters is the original bow of the ship that rescued Ernest Shackleton's Antarctic expedition from Elephant Island in 1916.

✦ Activities

Winter hikes are only recommended for experienced mountaineers. For detailed trekking routes, refer to Lonely Planet's *Trekking in the Patagonian Andes*.

★ Dientes de Navarino HIKING
This trekking circuit offers impossibly raw and windswept vistas under Navarino's toothy spires. Beginning at the Virgin altar just outside town, the five-day, 53.5km route winds through a spectacular wilderness of exposed rock and secluded lakes. Fit hikers can knock it out in four days in the (relatively) dry summer months. Markings are minimal: GPS, used in conjunction with marked maps, is a handy navigational tool.

Cerro Bandera HIKING
With expansive views of the Beagle Channel, this four-hour roundtrip covers the first approach of the Navarino Circuit. The

trail ascends steeply through lenga to blustery stone-littered hillside planted with a Chilean flag.

Lago Windhond HIKING
This remote lake is a lesser-known but worthy alternative to hiking the Dientes de Navarino circuit, with sheltered hiking through forest and peat bogs. The four-day roundtrip is a better bet if there are high winds. For route details, ask at Turismo Shila (p515) or go with a guide.

☞ Tours

Fuegia & Co TOUR
(☏ cell 7876-6934; fuegia@usa.net; Ortiz 049) For guided trekking or logistical support, Denis Chevallay guides in French, German and English and has a wealth of botanical and historical knowledge. Guiding includes porter support and a satellite emergency phone. Day trips to archaeological sites are available.

🛏 Sleeping & Eating

Residencial Pusaki GUESTHOUSE $
(☏ cell 9833-3248; pattypusaki@yahoo.es; Piloto Pardo 222; s/d CH$12,500/27,000) With legendary warmth, Patty welcomes travelers into this cozy home with comfortable, carpeted rooms with private bathrooms. Patty also organizes group dinners, which are open to nonguests.

Refugio El Padrino HOSTEL $
(☏ 061-262-1136, cell 8438-0843; Costanera 276; camping per person CH$6000, dm CH$12,000) Friendly and conducive to meeting others, this clean, self-service hostel doubles as a social hub hosted by the effervescent Cecilia. The small dorm rooms are located right on the channel.

Lakutaia Lodge HOTEL $$$
(☏ 061-262-1733; www.lakutaia.cl; s/d/tr US$210/265/315) About 3km east of town toward the airport, this modern full-service lodge offers respite in a lovely, rural setting. There is a full-service restaurant and the library contains interesting history and nature references. Its only disadvantage is its isolation: you might leave without getting much of a feel for the quirky town.

Puerto Luisa Cafe CAFE $
(☏ cell 9934-0849; Costanera 317; snacks CH$3000; ⊙ 10am-8pm Mon-Fri, 7am-8pm Sat Nov-Mar) Next to the dock, this welcoming haven offers espressos, chocolates and pies in a cozy setting of oversized chairs with great sea views.

LAGO DESEADO & BEYOND

South of Camerón, access to Chilean Tierra del Fuego once petered out into stark, roadless wilderness and the rugged Cordillera Darwin. But the Ministry of Public Works is working hard to create access to these southern points and develop future tourism destinations.

Projects are under way to build a road to the new Parque Nacional Yendegaia, on the island's southern shore. It currently reaches Seno Almirantazgo in the Cordillera Darwin.

For now, there's at least one worthy destination on the road. **Lodge Deseado** (☑061-9165-2564; www.lodgedeseado.cl; 2-/3-person cabin US$310/370), on the lake of the same name, marks a cozy spot to reel in wild trout, kick back in cool modern cabins and swap stories with the engaging owner Ricardo. Transportation from Punta Arenas is available. Weeklong packages visit major nature sights throughout Tierra del Fuego (including the king penguin colony).

A 4WD is required for this remote region. A road now connects to the Argentine side, with an official border crossing at mountain pass Río Bellavista (open only mid-December through March).

El Alambique ITALIAN, PUB $
(☑cell 5714-2087; Piloto Pardo 217; set menu CH$5500; ☺noon-2:30pm Mon-Fri, 8pm-1am Tue-Sat) Covered in murals, this homespun pub delivers good homemade pastas (and pizzas on all-you-can-eat Fridays). It's the only venue with a pub atmosphere at night.

ⓘ Information

Near the main roundabout, the Centro Comercial contains the post office, internet access, Aerovías DAP and call centers. ATM, money exchange (US cash only, US$100 minimum) and Visa cash advances are possible at Banco de Chile.

Municipal Tourist Information (☑cell 8383-2080; www.ptowilliams.cl/Turismo.html; cnr Piloto Pardo & Arturo Prat; ☺8am-1pm & 2-5pm Mon-Fri) Offers city maps, day trek maps, as well as weather and route conditions for the Lago Windhond and Dientes de Navarino treks. Located in a small kiosk.

Turismo Shila (☑cell 7897-2005; www.turismoshila.cl; O'Higgins 220) Very helpful stop for trekkers. Offers local guides, camping rentals, bicycle rentals (CH$5000 per day), snowshoes, fishing gear and GPS maps. Also sells boat tickets and can arrange charter flights to Ushuaia.

ⓘ Getting There & Away

Puerto Williams is accessible by plane or boat, though the weather frequently causes delays.

Transbordador Austral Broom (☑061-272-8100; www.tabsa.cl) has a new ferry *Patagonia* that sails from the Tres Puentes sector of Punta Arenas to Puerto Williams three or four times a month on Wednesday, with departures from Puerto Williams back to Punta Arenas on Saturday (reclining seat/bunk CH$103,000/143,000 including meals, 38 hours). Travelers rave about the trip: if the weather holds there are good

views on deck and the possibility of spotting dolphins or whales.

Aerovías DAP (☑061-262-1051; www.aerovias dap.cl; Plaza de Ancla s/n; one-way CH$75,000) flies to Punta Arenas Monday to Saturday from November to March, with fewer winter options. Often passengers are wait-listed until the company has enough bookings to run a flight; the practice can be frustrating for visitors with little extra time to spare. Note luggage restrictions when you purchase your ticket. DAP flights to Antarctica may make a brief stopover here.

Ushuaia Boating (☑in Argentina 02901-436-193; www.ushuaiaboating.com; one-way US$130; ☺service Mon-Sat) offers a sporadic service which usually goes daily in high season with Zodiac boats. Tickets include a sometimes bumpy and exposed 40-minute crossing plus a 1½-hour overland transfer to/from Puerto Navarino. Note: inclement weather often means cancellations and indefinite postponement.

Porvenir (Chile)

☑061 / POP 5900

If you want a slice of home-baked Fuegian life, this is it. Most visitors come on a quick day trip from Punta Arenas tainted by seasickness. But spending a night in this rustic village of metal-clad Victorian houses affords you an opportunity to explore the nearby bays and countryside and absorb a little of the local life; bird-watchers can admire the nearby king penguins, and lively populations of cormorants, geese and seabirds. While known for inaccessibility (there's no bus route here), the government is investing in completing roads through the southern extension of Chilean Tierra del Fuego, which will open up a whole untouched wilderness to visitors.

Porvenir experienced waves of immigration, many from Croatia, when gold was discovered in 1879. Sheep *estancias* provided more reliable work, attracting droves of Chileans from the island of Chiloé, who also came for fishing work. Today's population is a unique combination of the two.

◎ Sights

Museo de Tierra del Fuego   MUSEUM
(☏061-258-1800; Jorge Schythe 71; admission CH\$1000; ◷8am-5pm Mon-Thu, to 4pm Fri, 10:30am-1:30pm & 3-5pm Sat & Sun) On the Plaza de Armas, this intriguing museum has some unexpected materials, including Selk'nam skulls and mummies, musical instruments used by the mission Indians on Isla Dawson and an exhibit on early Chilean cinematography.

☞ Tours

Though little-known as a wildlife-watching destination, Chilean Tierra del Fuego has abundant marine and birdlife, which includes Peale's dolphins around Bahía Chilota and king penguins, found seasonally in Bahía Inútil. This new king penguin colony has created quite a stir, though the fragile population has yet to have reproductive success. Make your visit with a reputable agency, give penguins out of the fenced area ample berth, and respect the nesting season.

Gold-panning, horseback riding and 4WD tours can be arranged through the tourist office.

Far South Expeditions   OUTDOORS
(www.fsexpeditions.com) Offers transport to the king penguin colony or guided naturalist-run tours, with packages from Punta Arenas available.

🛏 Sleeping & Eating

Hotel Rosas   GUESTHOUSE $
(☏061-258-0088; hotelrosas@chile.com; Philippi 296; s/d CH\$23,500/34,000; ☎) Eleven clean and pleasant rooms offer heating and cable TV; some have wonderful views. Alberto, the owner, knows heaps about the region and arranges tours to Circuito del Loro, a historical mining site. The restaurant (*plato del día* CH\$6200), serving fresh seafood and more, gets crowded for meals.

★Hostería Yendegaia   B&B $$
(☏061-258-1919; www.hosteriayendegaia.com; Croacia 702; s/d/tr CH\$25,000/40,000/55,000; ☎)

Everything a B&B should be, with naturalist books (some authored by the owner) to browse, abundant breakfast, views of the strait, and spacious rooms with thick down duvets. This historic Magellanic home (the first lodging in Porvenir) has been lovingly restored, and its family of hosts are helpful. Its tour agency, Far South Expeditions , runs naturalist-led trips.

The recently added cafe service features espresso drinks, sandwiches and pizza.

Club Croata   SEAFOOD $$
(☏061-258-0053; Señoret 542; mains CH\$5000-10,000; ◷11am-4pm & 7-10:30pm Tue-Sun) Formal by tradition, the town's most reliable restaurant serves good seafood at reasonable prices. There are also Croat specialties, such as pork chops with *chucrut* (sauerkraut). The pub is open to 3am.

❶ Information

Banco de Estado (cnr Philippi & Croacia) Has a 24-hour ATM.

Hospital (☏061-258-0034; Wood, btwn Señoret & Guerrero)

Post Office (Philippi 176) Faces Plaza de Armas.

Tourist Office (☏061-258-0098, 061-258-0094; www.muniporvenir.cl; Zavattaro 434; ◷9am-5pm Mon-Fri, 11am-5pm Sat & Sun) Information is also available at the handicrafts shop on the *costanera* (seaside road) between Philippi and Schythe.

❶ Getting There & Away

A good gravel road runs east along Bahía Inútil to the Argentine border at San Sebastián; allow about four hours. From San Sebastián (where there's gas and a motel), northbound motorists should avoid the heavily traveled and rutted truck route directly north and instead take the route from Onaisín to the petroleum company town of Cerro Sombrero, en route to the crossing of the Strait of Magellan at Punta Delgada–Puerto Espora.

Aerovías DAP (☏061-261-6100; www.aeroviasdap.cl; cnr Senoret & Philippi) flies to Punta Arenas (CH\$29,000, 15 minutes) Monday to Saturday from November to March, with fewer flights in low season. Also provides local transfer (CH\$2000).

Transbordador Austral Broom (☏061-258-0089; www.tabsa.cl; passenger/vehicle Porvenir-Punta Arenas CH\$6200/39,800) has a pedestrian and vehicle ferry service to Punta Arenas. Reserve vehicle spaces ahead in summer high-season.

Uruguay

📱 598 / POP 3.3 MILLION / AREA 176,215 SQ KM

Best Places to Eat

➡ Charco Bistró (p542)
➡ Café Picasso (p552)
➡ Bodega y Granja Narbona (p545)
➡ Parador La Huella (p560)

Best Places to Stay

➡ La Posadita de la Plaza (p541)
➡ El Galope Horse Farm & Hostel (p542)
➡ Estancia Panagea (p551)
➡ Posada Lunarejo (p566)

Why Go?

Wedged like a grape between Brazil's gargantuan thumb and Argentina's long forefinger, Uruguay has always been something of an underdog. Yet after two centuries living in the shadow of its neighbors, South America's smallest country is finally getting a little well-deserved recognition. Progressive, stable, safe and culturally sophisticated, Uruguay offers visitors opportunities to experience everyday 'not made for tourists' moments, whether caught in a cow-and-gaucho traffic jam on a dirt road to nowhere or strolling with *mate*-toting locals along Montevideo's beachfront.

Short-term visitors will find plenty to keep them busy in cosmopolitan Montevideo, picturesque Colonia and party-till-you-drop Punta del Este. But it pays to dig deeper. Go wildlife-watching along the Atlantic coast, hot-spring-hopping up the Río Uruguay, or horseback riding under the big sky of Uruguay's interior, where vast fields spread out like oceans.

When to Go
Montevideo

Feb Street theater and drumming consume Montevideo during Carnaval celebrations.

Mar Tacuarembó's gaucho festival, plus lower prices on the still-sunny Atlantic coast.

Oct Soak in Salto's hot springs, or channel Carlos Gardel at Montevideo's tango festival.

Uruguay Highlights

1 Dancing to a different drummer during Montevideo's month-long **Carnaval** (p534).

2 Catching a wave or a late-night beach party along the untamed shoreline at **Punta del Diablo** (p565).

3 Soaking your weary traveling muscles in the **thermal baths** (p549) near Salto.

4 Getting way off the beaten track in the rural nature preserves of **Quebrada de los Cuervos** and **Valle del Lunarejo** (p566).

5 Sunbathing on the 18th-century town wall, or wandering the leafy plazas and cobbled streets of picturesque **Colonia del Sacramento** (p537).

6 Losing yourself in the sand dunes and surveying the sea lions from atop the lighthouse at **Cabo Polonio** (p563).

7 Touring Uruguay's newest Unesco World Heritage site, the historic El Anglo meat-processing factory in **Fray Bentos** (p546).

8 Hitting the beaches by day and the clubs by night in glitzy **Punta del Este** (p553).

9 Herding cattle on horseback and discovering the simple joys of *estancia* living under the starry skies around **Tacuarembó** (p550).

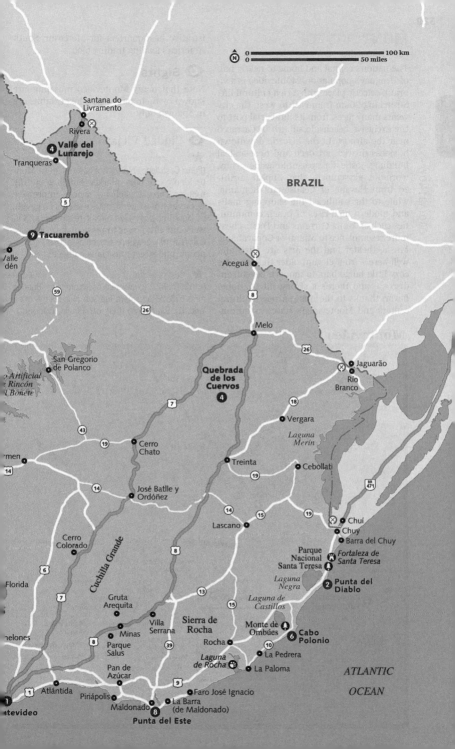

MONTEVIDEO

POP 1.3 MILLION

The nation's capital and home to nearly half of Uruguay's population, Montevideo is a vibrant, eclectic place with a rich cultural life. Stretching 20km from east to west, the city wears many faces, from its industrial port to the exclusive beachside suburb of Carrasco near the airport. In the historic downtown business district, art deco and neoclassical buildings jostle for space alongside grimy, worn-out skyscrapers that appear airlifted from Havana or Ceauşescu's Romania, while to the southeast the shopping malls and modern high-rises of beach communities such as Punta Carretas and Pocitos bear more resemblance to Miami or Copacabana. Music, theater and the arts are alive and well here – from elegant older theaters and cozy little tango bars to modern beachfront discos – and there's a strong international flavor, thanks to the many foreign cultural centers and Montevideo's status as administrative headquarters for Mercosur, South America's leading trading bloc.

◉ Sights

Note that many Montevideo museums are known by their acronyms. Most exhibits are in Spanish only.

◉ Ciudad Vieja

★ Mercado del Puerto   MARKET

(Pérez Castellano) No visitor should miss Montevideo's old port market building, at the foot of Pérez Castellano, whose impressive wrought-iron superstructure shelters a gaggle of bustling *parrillas* (steak restaurants). On weekend afternoons in particular, it's a lively, colorful place where the city's artists, craftspeople and street musicians hang out.

★ Teatro Solís   THEATER

(☑1950-3323; www.teatrosolis.org.uy; Buenos Aires 678; ⊙tours 4pm Tue-Sun, plus 11am & noon Wed, Fri, Sat & Sun) Just off Plaza Independ-

Montevideo

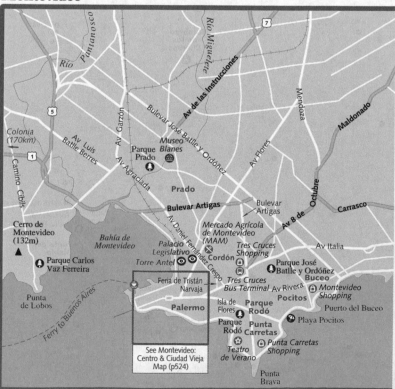

encia, elegant Teatro Solís is Montevideo's premier performance space. First opened in 1856, and completely renovated during the past decade or so, it has superb acoustics. Regularly scheduled tours provide an opportunity to see the actual performance space without attending a show. Spanish-language tours are free on Wednesdays, UR$20 other days; English- and Portuguese-language tours cost UR$50.

Plaza Matriz   PLAZA

Also known as Plaza Constitución, this leafy square was the heart of colonial Montevideo. On its west side stands the **Iglesia Matriz** (Plaza Matriz), Montevideo's oldest public building, begun in 1784 and completed in 1799. Opposite is the **Cabildo** (Map p524), a neoclassical stone structure finished in 1812. Benches under the trees and eateries along the adjacent sidewalk offer opportunities for a noon break.

Museo de los Andes   MUSEUM

(☑ 2916-9461; www.mandes.uy; 619 Rincón; admission UR$200; ⊘ 10am-5pm Mon-Fri, 10am-3pm Sat) Opened in 2013, this unique museum documents the 1972 Andean plane crash (made famous in the book *Alive!*) that cost 29 Uruguayans their lives and profoundly impacted Uruguay's national psyche. Using original objects and photos from the crash site, it tells the story of the 16 survivors, who battled harrowing conditions for 72 days before returning alive to a stunned nation. The museum is a labor of love for director Jörg Thomsen, a personal friend of many of the families affected.

Museo del Carnaval   MUSEUM

(☑ 2916-5493; www.museodelcarnaval.org; Rambla 25 de Agosto 218; admission UR$90; ⊘ 11am-5pm Wed-Sun Apr-Nov, daily Dec-Mar) This museum houses a wonderful collection of costumes, drums, masks, recordings and photos documenting the 100-plus-year history of Montevideo's Carnaval. Behind the museum is a cafe and a courtyard where spectators can view performances during the summer months. Touch-screen displays added in 2014 offer limited English-language commentary.

Casa Rivera   MUSEUM

(☑ 2915-1051; Rincón 437; ⊘ 11am-4:45pm Wed-Sun) FREE Former home of Fructuoso Rivera (Uruguay's first president and Colorado Party founder), this neoclassical 1802 building is the centerpiece of Montevideo's National Historical Museum, with a collection of paintings, documents, furniture and artifacts that trace the history of Uruguay's 19th-century path to independence. Several other historic Ciudad Vieja homes nearby, officially part of the museum, are rarely open to visitors.

Museo de Arte Precolombino e Indígena   MUSEUM

(MAPI; ☑ 2916-9360; www.mapi.org.uy; 25 de Mayo 279; admission UR$80; ⊘ 10:30am-6pm Mon-Sat) This museum displays a permanent collection of artifacts and information about Uruguay's earliest inhabitants, along with rotating exhibits focused on native peoples of the Americas.

Museo de Artes Decorativas   MUSEUM

(☑ 2915-1101; 25 de Mayo 376; ⊘ 12:30-5:30pm Mon-Fri) FREE The Palacio Taranco, a wealthy 1910 merchant's residence designed by famous French architects Charles Girault and

Jules Chifflot, is filled with ornate period furnishings and paintings by European artists including Ghirlandaio and Goya.

◉ Centro

Plaza Independencia   PLAZA
(Map p524) Montevideo's largest downtown plaza commemorates independence hero José Artigas with a 17m, 30-ton statue and the subterranean **Mausoleo de Artigas** (◷ 9am-5pm) where an honor guard keeps 24-hour vigil over Artigas' remains. Other notable structures surrounding the plaza include the stone gateway **Puerta de la Ciudadela** (Map p524) (a lonely remnant of the colonial citadel demolished in 1833); the 19th-century **Palacio Estévez** (Map p524); and the 26-story **Palacio Salvo** (Map p524), the continent's tallest building when it opened in 1927, and still a classic Montevideo landmark.

★ Museo del Gaucho   MUSEUM
(☏ 2900-8764; Av 18 de Julio 998; ◷ 10am-4pm Mon-Fri) **FREE** Housed in the ornate Palacio Heber, this museum eloquently conveys the deep attachments between the gauchos, their animals and the land. Its superb collection of historical artifacts includes horse gear, silver work, and *mates* and *bombillas* (metal straws with filters, used for drinking *mate*, a bitter ritual tea) in whimsical designs.

◉ North of Centro

Torre Antel   TOWER
(☏ 2928-8517; Guatemala 1075; ◷ tours half-hourly 3:30-5pm Mon, Wed & Fri, 10:30am-noon Tue & Thu) **FREE** For great views out across the city, take the elevator to the top of Montevideo's most dramatic modern skyscraper.

Palacio Legislativo   HISTORIC BUILDING
(☏ 2924-1783; www.parlamento.gub.uy; Av General Flores s/n; tours UR$70) Dating from 1908, and still playing host to Uruguay's Asamblea General (legislative branch), the three-story neoclassical Parliament building is also open for guided tours at 10:30am and 3pm Monday to Friday.

◉ East of Centro

Espacio de Arte Contemporáneo   GALLERY
(☏ 2929-2066; www.eac.gub.uy; Arenal Grande 1930; ◷ 2-8pm Wed-Sat, 11am-5pm Sun) **FREE** This gallery makes thought-provoking use of the cells of a 19th-century prison, creating an avant-garde exhibit space for revolving exhibitions of contemporary art.

Museo del Fútbol   MUSEUM
(☏ 2480-1259; www.estadiocentenario.com.uy/site/footballMuseum; Estadio Centenario, Av Ricaldoni s/n, Parque José Batlle y Ordóñez; admission UR$150; ◷ 10am-5pm Mon-Fri) A must-see for any *fútbol* (soccer) fan, this museum displays memorabilia from Uruguay's 1930 and 1950 World Cup wins. Visitors can also tour the stands.

◉ Parque Rodó, La Rambla & Eastern Beaches

La Rambla, Montevideo's multi-kilometer coastal promenade, is one of the city's defining elements, connecting downtown to the eastern beach communities of Punta Carretas, Pocitos, Buceo and Carrasco. This is Montevideo's social hub on Sunday afternoons, when the place is packed with locals cradling thermoses of *mate* and mingling with friends.

Museo Nacional de Artes Visuales MUSEUM
(MNAV; ☑2711-6124; www.mnav.gub.uy; Giribaldi 2283, Parque Rodó; ☺9am-4pm Tue, Wed & Fri, 2-4pm Thu) FREE Uruguay's largest collection of paintings is housed here in Parque Rodó. The spacious rooms are graced with works by Blanes, Cúneo, Figari, Gurvich, Torres García and other famous Uruguayans. For a closer look at some of these same artists, visit the **Museo Torres García** (☑2916-2663; www.torresgarcia.org.uy; Sarandí 683; admission UR$100; ☺10am-6pm Mon-Sat), **Museo Figari** (☑2915-7065; www.museofigari.gub.uy; Juan Carlos Gómez 1427; ☺1-6pm Tue-Fri, 10am-2pm Sat) FREE and **Museo Gurvich** (☑2915-7826; www.museogurvich.org; Sarandí 524; admission UR$100; ☺10am-6pm Mon-Fri, 11am-3pm Sat) in Ciudad Vieja, or the **Museo Blanes** (☑2336-2248; blanes.montevideo.gub.uy; Av Millán 4015; ☺1-7pm Tue-Sun) FREE in the Prado neighborhood north of Centro.

Castillo Pittamiglio HISTORIC BUILDING
(☑2710-1089; www.castillopittamiglio.com; Rambla Gandhi 633; guided tours UR$125) On the Rambla between Punta Carretas and Pocitos is this eccentric legacy of local alchemist and architect, Humberto Pittamiglio. Its quirky facade alone is worth a look. Guided Spanish-language tours of the interior are available; see the website for monthly schedules.

Museo Naval MUSEUM
(☑2622-1084; cnr Rambla Costanera & Av LA de Herrera; admission UR$60; ☺8am-noon & 2-6pm Fri-Wed) Along the eastern waterfront in Buceo, this museum traces the role of boats and ships in Uruguayan history, from the indigenous Charrúa's canoe culture to the dramatic sinking of the German *Graf Spee* off Montevideo in 1939.

🏃 Activities

One of Montevideo's great pleasures is cruising along the walking-jogging-cycling track that follows the riverfront Rambla. A few kilometers east of the center you'll reach Playa Pocitos, which is best for **swimming** and where you should be able to jump in on a game of **beach volleyball**. A couple of bays further along at Buceo's Yacht Harbor you can get **windsurfing lessons** at the yacht club. The entire Rambla is a picturesque spot for a stroll and a popular Sunday afternoon hangout.

Orange Bike BICYCLE RENTAL
(☑2908-8286; www.facebook.com/orange.bike.7; Pérez Castellano 1417bis; bike rental per 4/24hr US$15/20) This outfit just above Mercado del Puerto rents out quality bikes. Pick up at their office, or they'll deliver one to your doorstep.

🎓 Courses

Academia Uruguay LANGUAGE COURSE
(☑2915-2496; www.academiauruguay.com; Juan Carlos Gómez 1408; group classes per week US$245, individual classes per hr US$30) One-on-one and group Spanish classes with a strong cultural focus. Also arranges homestays, private apartments and volunteer work.

Joventango COURSE
(☑2901-5561; www.joventango.org; Aquiles Lanza 1290) Tango classes for all levels, from beginner to expert.

🎉 Festivals & Events

Much livelier than its Buenos Aires counterpart, Montevideo's late-summer **Carnaval** (p534) is the cultural highlight of the year.

At Parque Prado, north of downtown, Semana Criolla festivities during **Semana Santa** (Holy Week) include displays of gaucho skills, *asados* (barbecues) and other such events.

In the last weekend of September or first weekend of October, Montevideo's museums, churches and historic homes all open their doors free to the public during the **Días del Patrimonio** (National Heritage Days).

For 10 days in October, tango fills Montevideo's streets and performance halls during the **Festival del Tango**, organized by Joventango (p523).

🛏 Sleeping

Montevideo offers a smattering of boutique and luxury hotels, a thriving hostel scene, and a host of dependable midrange options in the Centro.

🛏 Ciudad Vieja

⭐ **Hotel Palacio** HOTEL $
(☑2916-3612; www.hotelpalacio.com.uy; Bartolomé Mitre 1364; r without/with balcony US$45/50, all without breakfast; ❄️🛜) If you can snag one of the two 6th-floor rooms at this ancient family-run hotel one block off Plaza Matriz, do it! Both feature air-conditioning and balconies with superb views of Ciudad

Montevideo: Centro & Ciudad Vieja

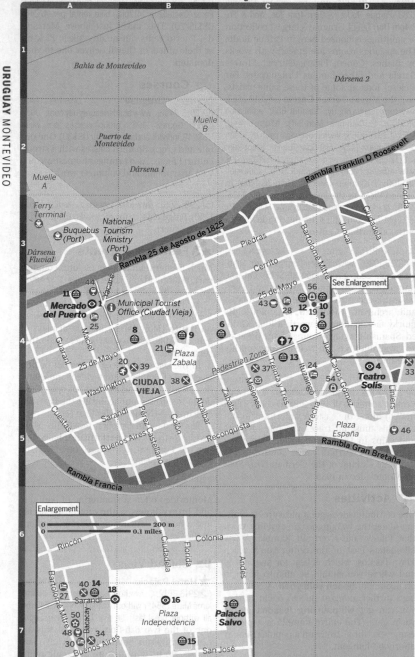

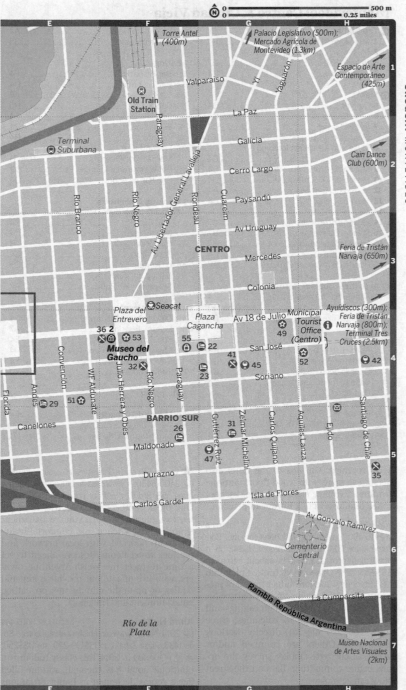

Montevideo: Centro & Ciudad Vieja

Vieja's rooftops. The rest of the hotel also offers great value, with wood floors, antique furniture, a vintage elevator and old-school service reminiscent of a European pensión.

Spléndido Hotel   HOTEL $
(☏2916-4900; www.splendidohotel.com.uy; Bartolomé Mitre 1314; d with bathroom US$48-55, d without bathroom US$38-45, s without bathroom US$32-38; @🛜) The faded, funky Spléndido offers decent value for budget travelers preferring privacy over a hostel-style party vibe. The better rooms have 5m-high ceilings and French doors opening to balconies; three rooms (106, 220 and 221) directly overlook Teatro Solís. Others are cramped and/or reeking of cigarette smoke; survey the options before committing. Bars on the street below can get noisy.

★**Casa Sarandi Guesthouse** GUESTHOUSE $$
(☏2400-6460; www.casasarandi.com; Buenos Aires 558, 3rd fl; r without breakfast US$75; 🛜) One block south of Plaza Matriz, three attractive guest rooms in a vintage apartment share a guest kitchen and comfortable living room adorned with local artwork and parquet wood floors. Reserve ahead to set a time to meet the Welsh-Argentine owners, who live off-site but provide a key and oodles of up-to-the-minute tips on eating, entertainment and transport.

Alma Histórica   BOUTIQUE HOTEL $$$
(☏2914-7450; www.almahistoricahotel.com; Solis 1433, Plaza Zabala; r US$199-220, ste US$250; ❄🛜) Opened in 2014, this classy Italian-run boutique hotel has themed, antique-filled guest rooms decorated in honor of famous

Uruguayans (artists, writers, sports stars etc). Amenities include fine Swiss mattresses, Egyptian cotton sheets, comfy pillows, natural beauty products, laptop-sized safes, and YouTube and Netflix streaming on large flat-screen TVs.

Other classy touches include an original 1900s marble staircase and an elegant library filled with art books and travel guides.

Don Hotel BOUTIQUE HOTEL **$$$**

(✆2915-9999; www.donhotel.com.uy; Piedras 234; d US$130-170, ste US$305; ✳@🛜🏊) Directly opposite Mercado del Puerto and the ferry docks, this modern boutique hotel is a study in refined black, white and silver, with Iberian wallpapers and tiles throughout, plus Jacuzzis and full-on views of the market's ornate rooftops from the superior rooms up front. A swimming pool, solarium and rooftop bar overlooking Montevideo's port enhance its comfortable, classy appeal.

🛏 Centro

⭐**Ukelele Hostel** HOSTEL **$**

(✆2902-7844; www.ukelelehostel.com; Maldonado 1183; dm US$16-22.50, tw US$48-52, d US$50-60; @🛜🏊) This attractive 1920s family home, lovingly renovated into a hostel, features high ceilings, beautiful wood floors, vintage architectural details, an on-site bar, a cozy music room and a grassy pool and patio area out back for lounging. Top it off with friendly staff and a good mix of dorms and private rooms and you've got the perfect midtown budget option.

Caballo Loco Hostel HOSTEL **$**

(✆2902-6494; www.caballolocohostel.com; Gutierrez Ruiz 1287; dm US$18-22; ✳🛜) This newer hostel in a remodeled historic building enjoys an unbeatable downtown location, only steps from leafy Plaza Cagancha and the bus stops for Montevideo's bus station and beaches. Six spic-and-span four- to 10-bed dorms surround a welcoming, high-ceilinged common area with guest kitchen, pool table and TV lounge. Other pluses include friendly owners and on-site bike rentals.

Hotel Iberia HOTEL **$**

(✆2901-3633; www.hoteliberia.com.uy; Maldonado 1097; d/tr/q from US$45/72/82; ✳🛜) Just south of Centro, Iberia offers solid midrange amenities at reasonable rates.

Smart Hotel HOTEL **$$**

(✆2903-3222; www.smarthotelmontevideo.com; Andes 1240; r US$75-120; ✳🛜) 'Smart' perfectly describes the modern lines, clean white furnishings and blond wood decor of this well-positioned newcomer near Plaza Independencia. All rooms come with fridges, couches and coffee tables; pricier units add sofa beds, microwaves and/or terraces, while corner lofts have writing desks and ample extra space. There's an attached restaurant and parking garage, and discounts apply for longer stays.

Balmoral Plaza Hotel HOTEL **$$**

(✆2902-2393; www.balmoral.com.uy; Plaza Cagancha 1126; s US$70-156, d US$85-166, ste US$150-181; ✳@🛜) Central downtown location and bird's-eye views of leafy Plaza Cagancha are the big draws here. All rooms have minibars, safes, big TVs and double-glazed, soundproof windows. There's also a garage, gym, sauna, business center and restaurant.

🛏 Parque Rodó, La Rambla & Eastern Beaches

Punto Berro Hostel HOSTEL **$**

(✆2707-7090; puntoberrohostel.com; Berro 1320, Pocitos; dm US$18-22, s US$32-45, d US$50-65, tw US$54-65; 🛜) Only two blocks from the beach in the upscale neighborhood of Pocitos, this hostel has clean, bright rooms and homey touches including comfy couches, a well-equipped guest kitchen and an affectionate geriatric cat. The same management offers a more urban experience at its sister hostel in the heart of **Ciudad Vieja** (✆2914-8600; puntoberrohostel.com; Ituzaingó 1436; dm US$16-22, d US$50-60; @🛜), a stone's throw from lively Plaza Matriz.

ℹ **HOTEL PRICING: DOLLARS VS PESOS**

Accommodations in Uruguay often quote prices in US dollars rather than Uruguayan pesos, especially in tourist destinations such as Montevideo, Colonia and the Atlantic coast. We have chosen to list prices in the currency quoted to us by each business during research. This means that some hotel and hostel prices will be listed in US dollars (US$), while others will be listed in Uruguayan pesos (UR$). So keep an attentive eye as you look through the listings!

Cala di Volpe
BOUTIQUE HOTEL $$

(2710-2000; www.hotelcaladivolpe.com.uy; cnr Rambla Gandhi & Parva Domus, Punta Carretas; r US$99-159, ste US$150-239; ❄@🔊🏊) This classy place across from the beach abounds in boutique hotel features: comfy couches, writing desks, gleaming tile-and-marble bathrooms, and floor-to-ceiling picture windows with sweeping river views. There's a small rooftop pool and a nice restaurant.

Sofitel Montevideo Casino Carrasco & Spa
CASINO HOTEL $$$

(2604-6060; www.sofitel.com; Rambla Republica de Mexico 6451, Carrasco; r US$244-363, ste from US$460; ❄@🔊🏊) Renovated top to bottom and reopened as a luxury hotel in 2013, Carrasco's historic casino is easily Montevideo's showiest lodging option. The monumental early-20th-century building, long a major waterfront landmark in this well-heeled neighborhood, sports 116 rooms, including 23 distinctive suites, complemented by a casino, a spa with indoor and outdoor swimming pools, and Uruguay's most sumptuous breakfast spread.

✖ Eating

For a break from the downtown restaurant scene, check out Montevideo's newest foodie attraction, the **Mercado Agrícola de Montevideo** (MAM; www.mam.com.uy; José Terra 2220; ◷9am-10pm), a renovated early-20th-century market building 2.5km north of the center housing more than 100 merchants, including fruit and veggie vendors, cafes, restaurants, specialty food shops and a microbrewery.

✖ Ciudad Vieja

For a relaxing break, join the crowds enjoying beer and snacks at the sidewalk eateries along Sarandí, facing Plaza Matriz.

★Estrecho
INTERNATIONAL $$

(Sarandí 460; mains UR$270-390; ◷noon-4pm Mon-Fri) Grab a seat at the long stove-side counter and watch the chefs whip up delicious daily specials at this cozy Ciudad Vieja lunch spot. French owner Bénédicte Buffard's international menu includes baguette sandwiches with steak or smoked salmon, a variety of salads, fresh fish of the day and divine desserts.

La Fonda
VEGAN, HEALTH FOOD $$

(097-300222; www.facebook.com/lafondamori; Pérez Castellano 1422; mains UR$300-370; ◷noon-4pm Tue-Sun, plus 8-11pm Thu-Sat) Grab a table on the pedestrianized street, or enter the high-ceilinged, brick-walled interior to watch the cheerfully bantering, wild-haired chefs at work: bopping to cool jazz as they roll out homemade pasta, carefully lay asparagus spears atop risotto or grab ingredients from the boxes of organic produce adorning their open kitchen. The ever-changing chalkboard menu always includes one vegan option.

Jacinto
INTERNATIONAL $$

(www.jacinto.com.uy; cnr Sarandí & Alzáibar; sandwiches UR$210-260, mains UR$480-540; ◷9am-6pm Mon, to midnight Tue-Sat) Fresh-baked bread, flavorful salads and soups, and savory tarts and sandwiches are served alongside more substantial main dishes at this high-ceilinged eatery with checkerboard marble floors. The homemade *aguas saborizadas* (UR$140), spring water flavored with fresh fruits and herbs, such as grapefruit-thyme, orange-rosemary or lemon-ginger-mint, make a refreshing accompaniment.

PV Restaurante Lounge
URUGUAYAN $$

(pvloungerestaurante.com; Peatonal Sarandí 675; mains UR$280-450; ◷10am-8pm Mon-Fri, 10am-6pm Sat) Occupying the elegant upper floor of Más Puro Verso bookstore, this art nouveau eatery with floor-to-ceiling bookshelves and grand windows overlooking Ciudad Vieja's pedestrian zone makes a pleasant hideaway at tea time, or at lunch for the UR$395 *menu del día* (appetizer, main dish and dessert, served noon to 3:30pm).

Café Bacacay
FUSION $$

(www.bacacay.com.uy; Bacacay 1306; dishes UR$310-490; ◷10am-1am Mon-Sat) This chic little cafe across from Teatro Solís serves a variety of goodies, including fish of the day with wasabi or *limoncello* (lemon liqueur) sauce, meal-sized salads and a wide-ranging drinks menu. Desserts include pear tart and *torta quarteto* (a cake made with ricotta, almonds and quince paste).

★Mercado del Puerto
PARRILLA $$$

(www.mercadodelpuerto.com; Pérez Castellano; mains UR$260-700; ◷noon-5pm daily year-round, to 11pm Tue-Fri Nov-Feb) This converted market on Ciudad Vieja's waterfront remains a Montevideo classic, even if the steady influx of cruise ships into the adjacent port has made it increasingly pricey. Take your pick of the densely packed *parrillas* and pull up a stool. Weekends are ideal for savoring the market's vibrant energy.

MONTEVIDEO WEEKEND HIGHLIGHTS

Weekends are the time to enjoy several of Montevideo's quintessential experiences. Note that Ciudad Vieja, outside of Mercado del Puerto, is a virtual ghost town on Sundays, when businesses are closed and the pulse of local life moves east to the long Rambla waterfront.

Saturday morning Browse the antiques market on Plaza Matriz.

Saturday afternoon Discover your inner carnivore over lunch at Mercado del Puerto.

Saturday night Attend a performance at Teatro Solís or Sala Zitarrosa, sip *uvitas* (sweet wine drinks) and listen to live music at Fun Fun, mingle with locals dancing tango at Mercado de la Abundancia or party all night at the city's clubs.

Sunday morning Explore the labyrinth of market stalls at Feria de Tristán Narvaja.

Sunday afternoon Join the parade of *mate*-toting locals strolling the 20km-long beachfront Rambla.

Sunday evening Catch a pre-Carnaval drumming rehearsal on the streets of Palermo or Parque Rodó.

✕ Centro

★ Candy Bar TAPAS, BURGERS $
(☎ 2904-3179; www.facebook.com/CandyBarPalermo; Durazno 1402; tapas UR$100, mains UR$240-260; ⊙ noon-3pm & 7pm-1am Tue-Fri, noon-4pm & 8pm-3am Sat, noon-6pm Sun) At this stellar street corner eatery, colorful folding chairs fill the sidewalk beneath a spreading sycamore tree, while the chefs inside mix drinks, whip up meals and juggle fresh-baked bread behind a countertop overhung with artsy lampshades. Reasonably priced tapas and burgers (carnivorous and vegetarian) rule the menu, complemented by artisan beers and mixed drinks. Sunday brunch is especially popular.

Shawarma Ashot MIDDLE EASTERN $
(www.facebook.com/ShawarmaAshot; Zelmar Michelini 1295; sandwiches UR$130-220; ⊙ 11am-5pm Mon-Fri, noon-4pm Sat) Superbly prepared Middle Eastern classics such as falafel and shawarma draw loyal lunchtime crowds at this unpretentious hole-in-the-wall. For a special treat, don't miss the Saturday special: Uruguayan lamb with rice pilaf!

Bar Tasende PIZZA $
(cnr Ciudadela & San José; pizza slices UR$90; ⊙ 10am-1am Sun-Thu, to 2am Fri & Sat) This classic high-ceilinged corner bar has been wooing patrons since 1931 with its trademark *muzzarella al tacho*, simple but tasty pizza slices laden with mozzarella, a perfect snack to accompany a beer any time of day.

Comi.K BRAZILIAN $$
(☎ 2902-4344; www.facebook.com/COMIKRestaurante; Av 18 de Julio 994, 2nd fl; specials incl drink & dessert UR$320; ⊙ 9am-9pm Mon-Fri, 9am-4pm Sat) Inside the Brazilian cultural center, reasonably priced meals – including *feijoada* (Brazil's classic meat-and-black-bean stew) – are served in an elegant 2nd-floor salon with high ceilings and stained glass. There's live Brazilian music most Friday evenings.

Bar Hispano URUGUAYAN $$
(San José 1050; meals UR$210-395; ⊙ 7am-1am) Old-school neighborhood *confiterías* (cafes offering light meals) like this are disappearing fast. The gruffly efficient waiters can take any order you throw at them – a stiff drink to start the day, a full meal at 5pm or a chocolate binge in the wee hours.

✕ Parque Rodó, La Rambla & Eastern Beaches

Casitanno URUGUAYAN $$
(☎ 2409-7236; Maldonado 2051, Parque Rodó; mains UR$205-350; ⊙ 9pm-3am Tue-Sat, to midnight Sun) With its colorful cocktail list, intimate bar area, and street-facing front deck, this lively corner place draws a youthful late-night crowd for designer comfort food and drinks. Gourmet *chivitos* (steak sandwiches) are the star attraction, served on ciabatta bread with tasty add-ons like arugula, caramelized onions and roasted peppers; vegetarians can sink their teeth into a meat-free version.

La Pulpería PARRILLA $$
(www.facebook.com/LaPulperiaMvdeo; cnr Lagunillas & Nuñez, Punta Carretas; mains UR$270-395; ⊙ 8pm-12:30am Tue-Sat, noon-4pm Sun) The epitome of an intimate neighborhood *parrilla*, this corner place doesn't advertise its

presence (drop by before 8pm and you won't even find a sign outside); instead, it focuses on grilling prime cuts of meat to perfection, and relies on word of mouth to do the rest. Grab a barstool by the blazing fire or a table on the sidewalk outside.

Foc
FUSION $$$

(☑2915-3006; www.facebook.com/restaurantefoc; Ramón Fernández 285, Punta Carretas; multicourse menus from UR$1000; ☺8pm-midnight Tue-Sat) After nine years honing his culinary technique at Michelin-starred restaurants in Catalonia, chef Martín Lavecchia returned to Montevideo to open this divine restaurant. Five- to seven-course menus feature seafood delights like mussel-squid risotto or shrimp in coconut milk with cilantro, lime and guindilla peppers, followed by flamboyant desserts such as lemon mousse with mandarin ice cream and Pop Rock crumble.

La Perdiz
PARRILLA $$$

(☑2711-8963; www.restaurantlaperdiz.com; Guipúzcoa 350, Punta Carretas; mains UR$315-550; ☺noon-3:30pm & 7:30pm-12:30am) Reserve ahead for this ever-popular *parrilla*, one block from the waterfront near Punta Carretas Shopping. Enjoy the best of Uruguay's carnivore culture at a fireside seat by the open grill, or spread out at one of the larger tables around the periphery. Save room for trademark desserts like *dulce de leche* mousse and *frutillas con nata* (strawberries with whipped cream).

🍷 Drinking & Nightlife

Montevideo offers an intriguing mix of venerable old cafes and trendy nightspots. Bars are concentrated on Bartolomé Mitre in Ciudad Vieja, south of Plaza Independencia in the Centro and along Juan Jackson in Parque Rodó.

🍷 Ciudad Vieja

★Café Brasilero
CAFE

(www.cafebrasilero.com.uy; Ituzaingó 1447; ☺9am-8pm Mon-Fri, 10am-6pm Sat) This vintage 1877 cafe with dark wood paneling and historic photos gracing the walls makes a delightful spot for morning coffee or afternoon tea. It's also an excellent lunch stop, with good-value *menus ejecutivos* (all-inclusive daily specials for UR$400).

Café Roldós
BAR

(roldos.com.uy; Mercado del Puerto; ☺9am-5pm) Since 1886, this venerable bar-cafe in Mercado del Puerto has been pouring its famous

medio y medio, a refreshing concoction made from half still, half sparkling wine (per bottle/glass UR$200/70). Throw in a couple of tasty sandwiches (UR$95 each), and you've got a meal! It's a perennial favorite with Montevideanos on weekends.

Shannon Irish Pub
PUB

(www.theshannon.com.uy; Bartolomé Mitre 1318; ☺7pm-late) Always hopping, the Shannon features seven Uruguayan microbrews plus a full complement of other beers from over a dozen countries. There's live music 365 days a year, from rock to traditional Irish bands.

🍷 Centro

La Ronda
BAR

(Ciudadela 1182; ☺noon-late Mon-Sat, 7pm-late Sun) At this often jam-packed bar, youthful patrons straddle the windowsills between the dark interior plastered with vintage album covers and the sidewalk tables cooled by breezes off the Rambla.

Barón: la Barbería que Esconde un Secreto
COCKTAIL BAR

(www.facebook.com/LaBarberiaQueEscondeUnSecreto; Santiago de Chile 1270; ☺6pm-2am Tue-Sat) Like a trip back to America's Prohibition days, 'the barbershop that hides a secret' is a cocktail bar tucked behind an unassuming-looking storefront. Walk past the vintage barber chairs and open the secret door into one of Montevideo's coolest new nightspots. (And yes, you can get your hair cut too!)

El Lobizón
BAR

(ellobizon.com.uy; Zelmar Michelini 1264; ☺7pm-2am) Lobizón's cellar-bar atmosphere, free-flowing pitchers of sangria and *clericó* (white wine mixed with rum and fruit), and tasty snacks such as its famous *gramajo* (potatoes, ham and eggs fried up with onions and parsley) make it a perennial local favorite.

Museo del Vino
WINE BAR

(☑2908-3430; www.museodelvino.com.uy; Maldonado 1150; ☺1-5pm Tue-Sat, 9pm-1am Wed-Sat) A wine shop by day, this downtown venue also hosts frequent live tango performances in the evenings, accompanied by an excellent selection of Uruguayan wines.

🍷 North of Centro

Chopería Mastra
MICROBREWERY

(mastra.com.uy; Mercado Agrícola de Montevideo, Local 17; ☺11am-11pm) This convivial pub in Montevideo's agricultural market is the flagship outlet for Uruguay's beloved Mastra microbrewery. Pints go for UR$130, but with a dozen varieties to choose from you may prefer to opt for the *tabla degustación* (a four-beer sampler for UR$260, available weekdays only). Mastra has recently opened several other pubs around town, including near the beach in **Pocitos** (mastra.com.uy; Benito Blanco 1017, Pocitos; ⊙8pm-3am Mon-Sat).

Cain Dance Club GAY
(www.facebook.com/caindanceuruguay; Cerro Largo 1833, Cordón; ⊙midnight-7am Fri & Sat) Montevideo's premier gay nightspot (but also hetero-friendly), Cain is a multilevel club with two dance floors playing everything from techno to Latin beats.

🍷 Parque Rodó, La Rambla & Eastern Beaches

Montevideo Brew House MICROBREWERY
(www.mbh.com.uy; Libertad 2592; ⊙7pm-late Mon-Sat) Serving six beers brewed on-site (including an excellent Guinness-like dry stout), along with half a dozen offerings from Montevideo's Davok microbrewery (don't miss the IPA), this corner pub is one of Pocitos' most popular drinking spots.

Philomène TEAHOUSE
(⌨2711-1770; www.philomenecafe.com; Solano García 2455, Punta Carretas; ⊙9am-8:30pm Mon-Fri, 11am-8:30pm Sat) This cozy spot in Punta Carretas specializes in big pots of tea served alongside cookies and light meals in a pair of gaily wallpapered parlor-sized rooms.

☆ Entertainment

Spanish-language websites with entertainment listings include www.cartelera.com.uy, www.vivomontevideo.com/cartelera, www.elpais.com.uy/divertite and www.socioespectacular.com.uy.

Live Music & Dance
Tango legend Carlos Gardel spent time in Montevideo, where the tango is no less popular than in Buenos Aires. Music and dance venues abound downtown.

★Fun Fun LIVE MUSIC
(⌨2904-4859; www.barfunfun.com; Soriano 922, Centro; ⊙8:30pm-late Tue-Sat) Since 1895 this intimate, informal venue has been serving its famous *uvita* (a sweet wine drink) while hosting tango and other live music on a tiny stage. Temporarily moved to Calle Soriano in 2014, it's due to return four blocks west to its tradi-tional location in Mercado Central once renovation work is finished (most likely in 2017).

★Teatro Solís PERFORMING ARTS
(⌨1950-3323; www.teatrosolis.org.uy; Buenos Aires 678, Ciudad Vieja; admission from UR$75) The city's top performing-arts venue is home to the Montevideo Philharmonic Orchestra and hosts formal concerts of classical, jazz, tango and other music, plus music festivals, theater, ballet and opera.

★Mercado de la Abundancia LIVE MUSIC
(cnr San José & Aquiles Lanza, Centro; admission free Sat, UR$150 Sun; ⊙10pm-late Sat, 8pm-late Sun) On Saturday evenings from 10pm, locals throng the upper floor of this historic market to dance to live tango music. Join in, or watch from the sidelines at one of the adjacent restaurants. On Sundays, Montevideo's leading tango organization, Joventango (also based in the market), sponsors regular tango shows at 8pm, then opens its floor for dancing from 9:30pm onwards.

Sala Zitarrosa PERFORMING ARTS
(⌨2901-7303; www.salazitarrosa.com.uy; Av 18 de Julio 1012, Centro) Montevideo's best informal auditorium venue for big-name music and dance performances, including tango, rock, flamenco, reggae and *zarzuela* (traditional Spanish musical theater).

El Pony Pisador LIVE MUSIC
(⌨2915-7470; www.facebook.com/pony.pisador.1; Bartolomé Mitre 1324; ⊙5pm-late Mon-Fri, 8pm-late Sat & Sun) This venerable Ciudad Vieja club stages live music nightly and opens early on weekdays for 'after-office' drinks. Depending on the evening, you may find yourself dancing to blues, Brazilian, cumbia, flamenco, reggaeton, soul, Latin or rock covers in English and Spanish.

Paullier y Guaná LIVE MUSIC
(www.paullieryguana.com; Paullier 1252; ⊙8pm-late Tue-Sat) Tucked beneath a beautifully restored early-20th-century grocer, this intimate stone-walled cellar bar hosts regular rock, jazz, blues and other live shows. Upstairs, there's a high-ceilinged resto-bar with tiled floors, original architectural details and tables individually painted by Uruguayan artists.

El Tartamudo Café LIVE MUSIC
(⌨2480-4332; www.eltartamudobar.com; cnr 8 de Octubre & Presidente Berro, Tres Cruces; ⊙8pm-2am Wed-Sat) Performances at this place just east of Tres Cruces bus terminal run the gamut from rock to tango to *candombe* to jazz.

OLAFSPEIER/GETTY IMAGES ©

RICHARD I ANSON/GETTY IMAGES ©

1. Colonia del Sacramento (p537)
The cobbled streets of this Unesco World Heritage Site invite hours of aimless wandering.

2. Punta del Diablo (p565)
A laid-back lifestyle makes this the epicenter of Uruguay's backpacker beach scene.

3. Plaza Matriz (p521)
A flea market (p535) is held once a week in Montevideo's leafy square.

4. Carnaval, Montevideo (p534)
In February, the Uruguayan capital holds a festival full of parades, music and dancing.

RICHARD I ANSON/GETTY IMAGES ©

DON'T MISS

CARNAVAL IN MONTEVIDEO

If you thought Brazil was South America's only Carnaval capital, think again! Montevideanos cut loose in a big way every February, with music and dance filling the air for a solid month.

Not to be missed is the early February **Desfile de las Llamadas**, a two-night parade of *comparsas* (neighborhood Carnaval societies) through the streets of Palermo and Barrio Sur districts, just southeast of the Centro. *Comparsas* are made up of *negros* (persons of African descent) and *lubolos* (whites who paint their faces black for Carnaval, a long-standing Uruguayan tradition). Neighborhood rivalries play themselves out as wave after wave of dancers whirl to the electrifying rhythms of traditional Afro-Uruguayan *candombe* drumming, beaten on drums of three different pitches: the *chico* (soprano), *repique* (contralto) and *piano* (tenor). The heart of the parade route is Isla de Flores, between Salto and Gaboto. Spectators can pay for a chair on the sidewalk or try to snag a spot on one of the balconies overlooking the street.

Another key element of Montevideo's Carnaval are the *murgas*, organized groups of 15 to 17 gaudily dressed performers, including three percussionists, who perform original pieces of musical theater, often satirical and based on political themes. During the dictatorship in Uruguay, *murgas* were famous for their subversive commentary. All *murgas* use the same three instruments: the *bombo* (bass drum), *redoblante* (snare drum) and *platillos* (cymbals). *Murgas* play all over the city, and also compete throughout February in Parque Rodó at the **Teatro de Verano** (admission from UR$70). The competition has three rounds, with judges determining who advances and who gets eliminated.

The fascinating history of Montevideo's Carnaval is well documented in the city's **Museo del Carnaval** (p521). Another great way to experience Carnaval out of season is by attending one of the informal *candombe* practice sessions that erupt in neighborhood streets throughout the year. Two good places to find these are at the corner of Isla de Flores and Gaboto in Palermo, and in Parque Rodó, where the all-female group **La Melaza** (www.lamelaza.com) gathers at the corner of Blanes and Gonzalo Ramírez and continues down San Salvador. Drumming at both locations usually starts around 7pm on Sunday nights.

Cinema

The three big shopping malls east of downtown (Punta Carretas, Montevideo and Portones) all have modern multiscreen cinemas.

Cinemateca Uruguaya CINEMA
(2900-9056; www.cinemateca.org.uy; Av 18 de Julio 1280, Centro; film tickets members/nonmembers free/UR$160) For art-house flicks, this film club charges a modest membership (UR$390 per month, plus UR$195 one-time sign-up fee), allowing unlimited viewing at its four cinemas; non-members pay a small entry fee (AR$160) per film. It hosts the two-week Festival Cinematográfico Internacional del Uruguay in March or April.

Spectator Sports

Estadio Centenario STADIUM
(Av Ricaldoni, Parque José Batlle y Ordóñez) *Fútbol*, a Uruguayan passion, inspires large and regular crowds. Montevideo's main stadium, the Estadio Centenario, opened in 1930 for the first World Cup, in which Uruguay defeated Argentina 4-2 in the final. Even when no game is on, you can tour the stadium in conjunction with a visit to Montevideo's Museo del Fútbol (p522).

Fanáticos Fútbol Tours SPECTATOR SPORT
(099-862325; www.futboltours.com.uy) This small company offers highly personalized *fútbol*-themed tours led by knowledgeable, multilingual aficionados; prices include tickets to a match of your choosing, plus hotel transport.

Shopping

Central Montevideo's traditional downtown shopping area is Av 18 de Julio. Locals also flock to several large shopping malls east of downtown, including Punta Carretas Shopping, Tres Cruces Shopping (above the bus terminal) and Montevideo Shopping in Pocitos/Buceo.

Feria de Tristán Narvaja MARKET
(Tristán Narvaja, Cordón; 9am-4pm Sun) This colorful Sunday-morning outdoor market is a decades-long tradition begun by Italian

immigrants. It sprawls from Av 18 de Julio northwards along Calle Tristán Narvaja, spilling over onto several side streets. You can find used books, music, clothing, jewelry, live animals, antiques and souvenirs in its many makeshift stalls.

Saturday Flea Market MARKET
(Plaza Matriz, Ciudad Vieja; ⊘8am-1pm Sat) Every Saturday, vendors take over Ciudad Vieja's central square, selling antique door knockers, saddles, household goods and just about anything else you can imagine.

Manos del Uruguay CLOTHING
(☑2900-4910; www.manos.com.uy; San José 1111, Centro; ⊘11am-7pm Mon-Fri, 10am-2pm Sat) This national cooperative, a member of the World Fair Trade Organization, is famous for its quality woolen goods. In addition to its downtown branch, it also has shops in Montevideo Shopping and Punta Carretas Shopping east of downtown.

Pecarí CLOTHING, ACCESSORIES
(www.pecari.com.uy; Juan Carlos Gómez 1412; ⊘10am-7pm Mon-Fri, 10:30am-1:30pm Sat) For quality Uruguayan leather goods, including jackets, handbags, shoes and accessories, check out this shop just off Plaza Matriz in Ciudad Vieja.

La Pasionaria HANDICRAFTS
(☑2915-6852; www.lapasionaria.com.uy; Reconquista 587, Ciudad Vieja; ⊘10am-6pm Mon-Fri, 11am-5pm Sat) This colorful Ciudad Vieja shop sells clothing in its upstairs boutique and Uruguayan handicrafts downstairs. The attached cafe serves tasty soups, salads, and daily specials (UR$280 to UR$410), including vegetarian and vegan options.

Hecho Acá HANDICRAFTS
(☑2622-6683; www.hechoaca.com.uy; Montevideo Shopping, 1st fl, Local 147; ⊘10am-10pm) Woolen goods and other handicrafts from around the country are nicely displayed here.

Ayuídiscos MUSIC
(☑2403-1526; www.tacuabe.com/ayui-discos; Av 18 de Julio 1618, Centro; ⊘10am-8pm Mon-Fri, 10am-1pm Sat) This little store is an excellent source for Uruguayan music of all kinds.

❶ Orientation

Montevideo lies almost directly across the Río de la Plata from Buenos Aires. For many visitors, the most intriguing area is the Ciudad Vieja, the formerly walled colonial grid straddling the western tip of a peninsula between the sheltered port and the wide-open river. Just east of the old-town gate, the Centro (downtown) begins at Plaza Independencia, surrounded by historic buildings of the republican era. Av 18 de Julio, downtown Montevideo's commercial thoroughfare, runs east past Plaza del Entrevero, Plaza Cagancha and the Intendencia (town hall) toward Tres Cruces bus terminal, where it changes name to Av Italia and continues east toward Carrasco International Airport and the Interbalnearia highway to Punta del Este.

Westward across the harbor, 132m Cerro de Montevideo was a landmark for early navigators and still offers outstanding views of the city. Eastward, the Rambla hugs Montevideo's scenic waterfront, snaking past attractive Parque Rodó and through a series of sprawling residential beach suburbs – Punta Carretas, Pocitos, Buceo and Carrasco – that are very popular with the capital's residents in summer and on evenings and weekends.

❶ Information

DANGERS & ANNOYANCES

Montevideo is pretty sedate by Latin American standards, although you should exercise caution as in any large city. The recent installation of security cameras throughout Ciudad Vieja and the Centro has led to a radical decrease in petty crime. Montevideo's *policia turística* (tourist police) patrol the streets and can help if you encounter any problems.

EMERGENCY
Ambulance (☑105)
Police (☑911)

INTERNET ACCESS

Most accommodations have a guest computer in the lobby, free in-room wi-fi, or both. Many restaurants and cafes also offer free wi-fi.

MEDIA

Montevideo's leading dailies are **El País** (www.elpais.com.uy), **El Observador** (www.elobservador.com.uy) and **Últimas Noticias** (www.unoticias.com.uy). The newsweekly **Búsqueda** (www.busqueda.com.uy) is also widely available at newsstands.

MEDICAL SERVICES
Hospital Británico (☑2487-1020; www.hospitalbritanico.com.uy; cnr Av Italia & Avelino Miranda) is a highly recommended private hospital with English-speaking doctors; 2.5km east of downtown.

MONEY

Banks, exchange houses and ATMs are everywhere, including the airport and bus terminal; downtown they're concentrated along Av 18 de Julio.

POST

Post Office Centro (Canelones 1358); Ciudad Vieja (Misiones 1328); Tres Cruces bus terminal (cnr Bulevar Artigas & Av Italia)

TELEPHONE

Antel Centro (San José 1101); Ciudad Vieja (Rincón 501); Tres Cruces bus terminal (cnr Bulevar Artigas & Av Italia)

TOURIST INFORMATION

Municipal Tourist Office (www.descubrimonte video.uy) Centro (⌨1950-1830; cnr Av 18 de Julio & Ejido; ⊙10am-4pm); Ciudad Vieja (⌨2916-8434; cnr Piedras & Pérez Castellanos; ⊙9am-5pm Mon-Fri) City maps and general Montevideo information. Downloadable visitor's guide to the city in English, Spanish and Portuguese.

National Tourism Ministry (⌨2188-5100; www.turismo.gub.uy) Carrasco Airport (⌨2604-0386; ⊙8am-8pm); Port (⌨2188-5111; Rambla 25 de Agosto & Yacaré; ⊙9am-5pm Mon-Fri); Tres Cruces Bus Terminal (⌨2409-7399; cnr Bulevar Artigas & Av Italia; ⊙8am-8pm) Info about Montevideo and destinations throughout Uruguay.

USEFUL WEBSITES

An excellent resource for English-speakers is the website guruguay.com. Developed by Karen Higgs, owner of **Casa Sarandi Guesthouse** (p526), it's jam-packed with useful insider information about Montevideo and Uruguay as a whole.

❶ Getting There & Away

AIR

Montevideo's stylishly modern **Carrasco International Airport** (⌨2604-0272; www.aero puertodecarrasco.com.uy) is served by fewer airlines than Ezeiza airport in Buenos Aires.

Direct flights are available from Madrid and Miami, and one-stop service is available from several other European and North American cities via Buenos Aires or São Paulo.

At the time of research there were no airlines offering domestic service within Uruguay.

BOAT

Buquebus (⌨130; www.buquebus.com.uy) runs daily ferries direct from Montevideo to Buenos Aires on the high-speed Francisco boat (2¼ hours), named after Pope Francis. Full *turista*-class fares run UR$3320. Buquebus also offers less expensive bus-boat combinations from Montevideo to Buenos Aires via Colonia (slow boat UR$1100, 6½ hours; fast boat UR$1930, 4½ hours). Better fares for all services above are available with online advance purchase; you can also buy direct from Buquebus counters at

Montevideo's **port** (Terminal Fluvio-Marítima, Montevideo Port) and **Tres Cruces bus terminal** (ticket counters 28 & 29; ⊙5:30am-1:30am Sun-Fri, to 11:30pm Sat).

Seacat (⌨2915-0202; www.seacatcolonia. com.uy; Río Negro 1400; ⊙9am-7pm Mon-Fri, 9am-noon Sat) offers more economical bus-boat connections from Montevideo to Buenos Aires via Colonia (4¼ hours). One-way fares cost between UR$960 and UR$1398.

Even more affordable, but less comfortable, are the bus-boat combinations offered by **Colonia Express** (⌨2401-6666; www.colonia express.com; Tres Cruces Bus Terminal, ticket counter 31A; ⊙5:30am-10:30pm). Full one-way fares for the 4¼-hour trip are UR$998 per person; online advance-purchase rates drop as low as UR$560.

Cacciola Viajes (⌨2407-9657; www.cacciola viajes.com; Tres Cruces Bus Terminal, ticket counter 25B; ⊙8:30am-11:30pm) runs a scenic twice- to thrice-daily bus-launch service from Montevideo to Buenos Aires via the riverside town of Carmelo and the Argentine Delta suburb of Tigre. The eight-hour trip costs UR$850 one way.

BUS

Montevideo's modern **Tres Cruces Bus Terminal** (⌨2401-8998; www.trescruces.com.uy; cnr Bulevar Artigas & Av Italia) is about 3km east of downtown. It has tourist information, clean toilets, luggage storage, ATMs and a shopping mall upstairs.

A taxi from the terminal to downtown costs between UR$150 and UR$180. To save your pesos, take city bus CA1, which leaves from directly in front of the terminal (on the eastern side), traveling to Ciudad Vieja via Av 18 de Julio (UR$19, 15 minutes).

For the beach neighborhoods of Punta Carretas and Pocitos, take city buses 174 and 183, respectively, from in front of the terminal (UR$26). A taxi to either neighborhood costs between UR$150 and UR$180.

All domestic destinations are served daily, and most several times a day. A small *tasa de embarque* (departure tax) is added to the ticket prices. Travel times are approximate.

EGA (⌨2402-5164; www.ega.com.uy) provides the widest range of service to neighboring countries. Destinations in Argentina include Paraná, Santa Fe and Mendoza (all once weekly, on Friday), plus Córdoba and Rosario (each four times weekly). EGA also runs buses once weekly to Santiago, Chile (Monday) and São Paulo, Brazil (Sunday), twice weekly to Asunción, Paraguay (Wednesday and Saturday), four times weekly to Florianópolis, Brazil, and daily except Saturday to Porto Alegre, Brazil.

Service to Buenos Aires is more frequent, with several competing companies offering multiple daily departures.

International Buses from Montevideo

DESTINATION	COST (UR$)	TIME (HR)
Asunción (Paraguay)	3730	21
Buenos Aires (Argentina)	1345	10
Córdoba (Argentina)	2535	15½
Florianópolis (Brazil)	3475	18
Porto Alegre (Brazil)	2285	12
Santiago (Chile)	4590	28
São Paulo (Brazil)	4895	28

Domestic Buses from Montevideo

DESTINATION	COST (UR$)	TIME (HR)
Carmelo	424	3¼
Colonia	318	2¾
La Paloma	424	3½
La Pedrera	442	4
Mercedes	494	4
Paysandú	671	4½
Piriápolis	177	1½
Punta del Diablo	530	5
Punta del Este	256	2¼
Salto	883	6½
Tacuarembó	689	4½

❶ Getting Around

TO/FROM THE AIRPORT

From **Terminal Suburbana** (☑ 1975; cnr Río Branco & Galicia), five blocks north of Plaza del Entrevero, local Copsa buses 700, 710 and 711 and Cutcsa buses C1 and C5 run to Carrasco airport (UR$51, 45 minutes). Alternatively take COT's direct service between the airport (UR$159, 30 minutes) and Tres Cruces bus terminal. Coming from the airport, board at the stop directly in front of the arrivals hall.

Fixed-rate taxis charge UR$1050 to UR$1420 (depending on neighborhood) for the 30- to 45-minute taxi ride from the airport into Montevideo; the return trip to the airport is cheaper (between UR$700 and UR$900). Shared shuttle vans (five-person minimum) also travel from the airport to the center (UR$350 per person); buy tickets from the taxisaeropuerto.com taxi counter in the airport arrivals hall.

BUS

Montevideo's city buses, operated by **Cutcsa** (☑ 19333; www.cutcsa.com.uy), go almost everywhere for UR$26 per ride. For bus connection info based on your point of origin and destination, see the useful Spanish-language website Como Ir (www.montevideo.gub.uy/aplicacion/como-ir).

CAR

Most international rental-car companies have counters at Carrasco airport. In downtown Montevideo, you can also try the following Uruguayan companies (with nationwide branches).

Multicar (☑ 2902-2555; www.redmulticar.com; Colonia 1227, Centro)

Punta Car (☑ 2900-2772; www.puntacar.com.uy; Cerro Largo 1383, Centro)

TAXI

Montevideo's black-and-yellow taxis are all metered. Cabbies carry two official price tables, one effective on weekdays, the other (20% higher) used at night between 10pm and 6am, and on Sundays and holidays. It costs UR$32 to drop the flag (UR$40 nights and Sundays) and roughly UR$2 per city block thereafter. Even for a long ride, you'll rarely pay more than UR$200, unless you're headed to Carrasco airport. Taxis can be hailed on any street corner by raising your hand – look for the illuminated red 'Libre' (Free) sign on the windshield.

WESTERN URUGUAY

From Colonia's tree-shaded cobblestone streets to the hot springs of Salto, the slow-paced river towns of western Uruguay have a universally relaxing appeal, with just enough urban attractions to keep things interesting. Here, the border with Argentina is defined by the Río de la Plata and the Río Uruguay, and the region is commonly referred to as *el litoral* (the shore).

Further inland you'll find the heart of what some consider the 'real' Uruguay – the gaucho country around Tacuarembó, with *estancias* sprinkled throughout the rural landscape and some beautiful, rarely visited nature preserves.

Colonia del Sacramento

POP 26,230

On the east bank of the Río de la Plata, 180km west of Montevideo, but only 50km from Buenos Aires by ferry, Colonia is an irresistibly picturesque town enshrined as a Unesco World Heritage site. Its Barrio

Colonia del Sacramento

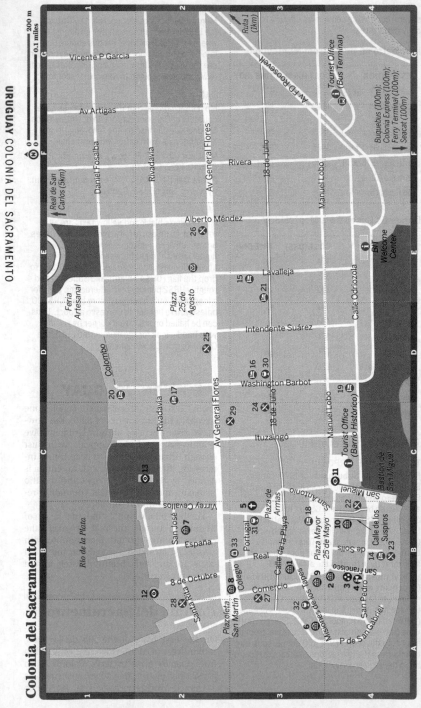

Río de la Plata

Real de San Carlos (5km)

Ruta 1 (1km)

Buquebus (100m); Colonia Express (100m); Ferry Terminal (100m); Seacat (100m)

Tourist Office (Bus Terminal)

BIT Welcome Center

Vicente P Garcia

Av Artigas

Av FD Roosevelt

Daniel Fosalba

Rivadavia

Av General Flores

Rivera

18 de Julio

Manuel Lobo

Alberto Méndez

26

Feria Artesanal

Plaza 25 de Agosto

Lavalleja

15 21

Calle Odriozola

Intendente Suárez

25

Colombo

20

Rivadavia

Av General Flores

16 30

Washington Barbot

29 24

18 de Julio

17

Ituzaingó

Manuel Lobo

19

Tourist Office (Barrio Histórico)

13

Virrey Cevallos

Plaza de Armas

San Antonio

11

San Miguel

Bastión de San Miguel

San José

7

España

Portugal

31

5

Calle de la Playa

18

Plaza Mayor 25 de Mayo

22

10

Calle de los Suspiros

23

12

8 de Octubre

Colegio

8

Real

33

Comercio

27

de Solís

San Francisco

14

28

Santa Ruta

Plazoleta San Martín

Mistones de los Tapes

32

6

9

Comercio

4

2

3

San Pedro

San Gabriel

P de San Gabriel

Colonia del Sacramento

URUGUAY COLONIA DEL SACRAMENTO

Histórico, an irregular colonial-era nucleus of narrow cobbled streets, occupies a small peninsula jutting into the river. Pretty rows of sycamores offer protection from the summer heat, and the riverfront provides a venue for spectacular sunsets. Colonia's charm and its proximity to Buenos Aires draw thousands of Argentine visitors; on weekends, especially in summer, prices rise and it can be difficult to find a room.

Colonia was founded in 1680 by Manuel Lobo, the Portuguese governor of Rio de Janeiro, and occupied a strategic position almost exactly opposite Buenos Aires across the Río de la Plata. The town grew in importance as a source of smuggled trade items, undercutting Spain's jealously defended mercantile monopoly and provoking repeated sieges and battles between Spain and Portugal.

Although the two powers agreed over the cession of Colonia to Spain around 1750, it wasn't until 1777 that Spain took final control of the city. From this time, the city's commercial importance declined as foreign goods proceeded directly to Buenos Aires.

⊙ Sights & Activities

⊙ Barrio Histórico

Colonia's Barrio Histórico is filled with visual delights. Picturesque spots for wandering include the roughly cobbled 18th-century **Calle de los Suspiros** (Street of Sighs), lined with tile-and-stucco colonial houses, the **Paseo de San Gabriel**, on the western riverfront, the **Puerto Viejo** (Old Port) and the historic center's two main squares: vast **Plaza Mayor 25 de Mayo** and shady **Plaza de Armas** (the latter also known as Plaza Manuel Lobo).

A single UR$50 ticket covers admission to Colonia's eight **historical museums** (☑ 4523-1237; www.museoscolonia.com.uy; ⊙ 11:15am-4:45pm). All keep the same hours, but closing day varies by museum.

Faro   LIGHTHOUSE
(admission UR$25; ⊙ 11am-sunset) One of the town's most prominent landmarks, Colonia's 19th-century lighthouse provides an excellent view of the old town and the Río de la Plata. It stands within the ruins of the 17th-century **Convento de San Francisco** (Plaza Mayor 25 de Mayo), just off the southwest corner of Plaza Mayor 25 de Mayo.

Portón de Campo   GATE
(Manuel Lobo) The most dramatic way to enter Barrio Histórico is via the reconstructed 1745 city gate. From here, a thick fortified wall runs south along the Paseo de San Miguel to the river, its grassy slopes popular with sunbathers.

Museo Portugués   MUSEUM
(Plaza Mayor 25 de Mayo 180; 8-museum admission UR$50; ⊙ 11:15am-4:45pm, closed Wed & Fri) In this beautiful old house, you'll find Portuguese relics including porcelain, furniture,

maps, Manuel Lobo's family tree and the old stone shield that once adorned the Portón de Campo.

Museo Municipal
MUSEUM

(📞 4522-7031; Plaza Mayor 25 de Mayo 77; 8-museum admission UR$50; ⊗ 11:15am-4:45pm Wed-Mon) Houses an eclectic collection of treasures including a whale skeleton, an enormous rudder from a shipwreck, historical timelines and a scale model of Colonia (c 1762).

Casa Nacarello
MUSEUM

(Plaza Mayor 25 de Mayo 67; 8-museum admission UR$50; ⊗ 11:15am-4:45pm Wed-Mon) One of the prettiest colonial homes in town, with period furniture, thick whitewashed walls, wavy glass and original lintels (duck if you're tall!).

Museo Indígena
MUSEUM

(Comercio s/n; 8-museum admission UR$50; ⊗ 11:15am-4:45pm, closed Mon & Thu) Houses Roberto Banchero's personal collection of Charrúa stone tools, exhibits on indigenous history, and an amusing map upstairs showing how many European countries could fit inside Uruguay's borders (it's at least six!).

Museo del Azulejo
MUSEUM

(cnr Misiones de los Tapes & Paseo de San Gabriel; 8-museum admission UR$50; ⊗ 11:15am-4:45pm, closed Wed & Fri) This dinky 17th-century stone house has a sampling of French, Catalan and Neapolitan tilework.

Archivo Regional
MUSEUM

(Misiones de los Tapes 115; 8-museum admission UR$50; ⊗ 11:15am-4:45pm Mon-Fri) On the northwest edge of the plaza, Archivo Regional contains historical documents along with pottery and glass excavated from the 18th-century Casa de los Gobernadores nearby.

Museo Español
MUSEUM

(San José 164; 8-museum admission UR$50; ⊗ 11:15am-4:45pm, closed Tue & Thu) Scheduled to reopen in 2016 after a long period of restoration, this museum has a varied collection of Spanish artifacts, including colonial pottery, engravings, clothing and maps.

Iglesia Matriz
CHURCH

(Plaza de Armas) Uruguay's oldest church – begun by the Portuguese in 1680, then completely rebuilt twice under Spanish rule – is the centerpiece of pretty Plaza de Armas. The plaza also holds the foundations of a house dating from Portuguese times.

Teatro Bastión del Carmen
THEATER, GALLERY

(Rivadavia 223; ⊗ noon-8pm) **FREE** Incorporating part of the city's ancient fortifications, this theater and gallery complex adjacent to Colonia's **Puerto Viejo** (Old Port) hosts rotating art exhibits and periodic concerts. The grassy riverside grounds out back, with outdoor sculptures and an industrial chimney dating to 1880, make a picturesque spot for a mid-afternoon break.

◉ Real de San Carlos

At the turn of the 20th century, Argentine entrepreneur Nicolás Mihanovich spent US$1.5 million building an immense tourist complex 5km north of Colonia at Real de San Carlos. The complex included a 10,000-seat bullring, a 3000-seat *frontón* (court) for the Basque sport of *jai alai*, a hotel-casino and a racecourse.

Only the racecourse functions today, but the ruins of the remaining buildings make an interesting excursion, and the adjacent beach is popular with locals on Sundays.

Museo Paleontológico
MUSEUM

(Real de San Carlos; 8-museum admission UR$50; ⊗ 11:15am-4:45pm Thu-Sun) This two-room museum displays glyptodon shells, bones and other locally excavated finds from the private collection of self-taught palaeontologist Armando Calcaterra.

☞ Tours

Walking Tours
WALKING TOUR

(📞 9937-9167; asociacionguiascolonia@gmail.com; tour per person in Spanish/other languages UR$150/200) The tourist office outside Colonia's old-town gate organizes good walking tours led by local guides. Spanish-language tours leave at 11am and 3pm daily year-round, with occasional sunset tours added at 7pm in January and February. Tours in other languages (English, French, Italian and Portuguese) take place on a rotating basis; ask the tourist office for the current week's schedule.

🛏 Sleeping

Many hotels charge higher rates Friday through Sunday. Summer weekends are best avoided or booked well in advance.

El Viajero Hostel
HOSTEL $

(📞 4522-2683; www.elviajerohostels.com/hostel-colonia; Washington Barbot 164; dm US$17-19, s/d US$40/65; ✳ @ 🛜) With bike rental, a bar for guests and air-con in all rooms, this hostel is brighter, fancier and somewhat cozier than the competition, and the location two blocks east of Plaza de Armas couldn't be better.

Hostel del Río
HOSTEL $

(☑ 4523-2870; www.hosteldelrio.com; Rivadavia 288; dm US$15-20, d US$61-108) Well-placed at the edge of the historic center, this new hostel offers squeaky-clean four- to six-bed dorms and private rooms, along with a guest kitchen and back patio. The atmosphere is rather sterile, but the bright white rooms come with thoughtful features like individual bedside reading lights on the bunk beds.

Remus-Art Hostel
B&B $

(☑ 9206-6985; www.facebook.com/remusarthostel; 18 de Julio 369; r UR$60-65) This new B&B in the home of German visual artist Christiane Brockmeier has three comfortable, colorful rooms with shared bath and a spacious roof terrace where you can sunbathe, reach out and touch the overhanging sycamore leaves, or enjoy home-cooked candlelight dinners (specialties include raclette and fondue from Switzerland, where Christiane lived for 20 years).

★ La Posadita de la Plaza
B&B $$

(☑ 4523-0502; www.posaditadelaplaza.com; Misiones de los Tapes 177; r UR$125-150) At this whimsical guesthouse on Colonia's most historic square, friendly Brazilian photographer Eduardo has poured his creative genius into building a magical space resembling a life-sized Joseph Cornell collage. Four guest rooms, an interior patio-deck with pretty old-town perspectives, and a cozy library-lounge are all decorated with found objects from Eduardo's world travels. Ample breakfasts feature fresh-squeezed orange juice.

Posada del Ángel
HOTEL $$

(☑ 4522-4602; www.posadadelangel.net; Washington Barbot 59; d US$85-125; ✴@🛜🌊) Conveniently located midway between the ferry port and Colonia's 18th-century town gate, this little hotel has down comforters and a sauna for chilly nights, plus a grassy back yard with swimming pool for the summer heat. Most of the high-ceilinged rooms face an interior courtyard, and the cheapest are rather dark; consider splurging on the lone garden-view superior (number 12).

★ Colonia Suite
B&B $$$

(☑ 9861-8966; www.coloniasuite.com; Lavalleja 169; d US$125-190; ✴🛜) Incorporating three spacious suites and a cozy 'garden house,'

this is one of Colonia's most unique lodging options, abounding in homey features such as armchairs, colorful carpets, flat-screen TVs with DVD players, well-equipped kitchenettes, local artwork and a woodstove in one unit. Enhancing the charm is **La Taza de Té** (afternoon tea for two UR$490; ⊙1:30-7pm), an on-site tearoom serving crepes, blinis, cakes and afternoon tea.

Charco Hotel
BOUTIQUE HOTEL $$$

(☑ 4523-5000; charcohotel.com; San Pedro 116; r UR$150-350 Mon-Wed, UR$200-400 Thu-Sun; ✴🛜) Colonia's newest hotel offers an incomparable old-town location, a chic waterfront resto-bar and beautifully landscaped grounds. Seven refined rooms in an elegantly remodeled historic building sport gleaming white decor and exposed stone and brickwork. Standouts include the suite with riverside terrace and the Rancho, an historic, kitchen-equipped Portuguese home sleeping up to six. Prepaid or multinight stays qualify for discounts.

Radisson Colonia Hotel
CASINO HOTEL $$$

(☑ 4523-0460; www.radissoncolonia.com; Washington Barbot 283; s/d from US$280/330 Fri-Sun, from US$170/180 Mon-Thu; ✴@🛜🌊) A stone's throw from Colonia's colonial center, this rather incongruous modern chain hotel features two pools and a fabulous deck directly overlooking the river, plus sauna, gym, solarium, children's play area and garage. Visit during the week for much better rates. Deluxe rooms with river-facing terraces cost about 25% more than standard rooms.

✖ Eating

★ Don Joaquín
PIZZA $

(☑ 4522-4388; www.facebook.com/donjoaquinartesanalpizza; 18 de Julio 267; pizzas UR$120-190; ⊙8pm-midnight Tue-Sun, noon-3pm Sat & Sun) After 13 years in Europe, Colonia natives Yancí and Pierina returned home with a genuine Neapolitan pizza oven in tow. The result is this cheerful, high-ceilinged eatery where diners can watch the *pizzaiolo* (pizza chef) creating thin-crusted beauties with superb homemade sauce. Don't miss the carbonara with cheese, egg and delicately crunchy bacon, or the *pescatore* with mussels and shrimp.

Los Farolitos
FAST FOOD $

(Av General Flores 272; sandwiches UR$40-200; ⊙12:30pm-1am) Renowned for its *chivitos*, this simple streetside stand also sells other

WORTH A TRIP

ESTANCIA LIVING ON A LIMITED BUDGET

What do you get when you cross a tourist *estancia* and a hostel? Find out at **El Galope Horse Farm & Hostel** (☎099-105985; www.elgalope.com.uy; Colonia Suiza; dm US$25, d with/without bathroom US$80/70; ▦), a unique country retreat 115km west of Montevideo and 60km east of Colonia. Experienced world travelers Mónica and Miguel offer guests a chance to 'get away from it all' and settle into the relaxing rhythms of rural life for a few days.

Horseback jaunts for riders of all levels (US$40 for beginners within the farm property, US$80 for experienced riders on longer rides) are expertly led by Miguel himself, and there's a sauna (US$8) and small swimming pool to soothe those aching muscles at the end of the day. Breakfast is included; other meals, from lunches to fondue to full-fledged *asados* (barbecues) are available for US$9 to US$15. Taxi pickup from the bus stop in nearby Colonia Valdense is available upon request (US$10).

low-cost, fast-food treats like hot dogs and *milanesas* (breaded cutlets).

Irene's VEGETARIAN $
(☎4522-4433; Av General Flores 441; mains UR$140-340; ⊗11am-6pm Mon-Sat; ☒) Vegetarian dishes and wholemeal pastas complement your standard pizza, pasta and *parrilla* offerings at this low-key eatery outside the historic center. The daily *menu vegetariano* (fixed-price vegetarian meal) goes for UR$190.

Buen Suspiro PICADAS $$
(☎4522-6160; www.buensuspiro.com; Calle de los Suspiros 90; picadas for 2 UR$255-830; ⊗11am-midnight) Duck under the wood beams into this cozy spot specializing in *picadas* (little snacks eaten with a toothpick). Sample local wines by the bottle or glass, accompanied by spinach and leek tarts, ricotta-and-walnut 'truffles,' local cheese, sausage, soups and salads. Reserve ahead for a fireside table in winter, or while away a summer afternoon on the intimate back patio.

La Bodeguita INTERNATIONAL $$
(www.labodeguita.net; Comercio 167; mini pizzas UR$140, dishes UR$270-440; ⊗8pm-midnight Tue-Sun, 12:30-4pm Sat & Sun) Nab a table out back on the sunny two-level deck and soak up the sweeping river views while drinking sangria (UR$260 per liter) or munching on La Bodeguita's trademark mini pizzas, served on a cutting board. The wide-ranging menu also includes pasta, salads, steaks and *chivitos*.

Lentas Maravillas INTERNATIONAL $$
(Santa Rita 61; sandwiches UR$300-320; ⊗2-8:30pm Thu-Tue) Cozy as a friend's home, this is an agreeable spot to kick back with tea and cookies, or savor a glass of wine accompanied by homemade soup, sandwiches or goulash. Flip through an art book from owner Maggie Molnar's personal library and enjoy the river views, either from the upstairs fireplace room or the chairs on the grassy lawn below.

El Portón PARRILLA $$
(☎4522-5318; Av General Flores 333; mains UR$190-450; ⊗noon-4pm & 8pm-midnight Tue-Sat, noon-4pm Sun) With cheery reddish-orange and yellow decor, this is a long-standing local favorite for good-value grilled meats.

★**Charco Bistró** INTERNATIONAL $$$
(☎4523-5000; charcohotel.com; San Pedro 116; mains UR$340-520; ⊗8am-11pm) Outstanding both for its location and its food, Colonia's hottest new eatery is tucked down a colonial side street, with a spacious deck overlooking the Río de la Plata's grassy shoreline. Tantalizing treats like grilled squid with caponata, steak with chimichurri, and homemade ravioli come complemented by minted ginger lemonade, superb mixed drinks and ample glasses of local tannat wine.

🍷 Drinking & Nightlife

Papá Ramón BAR
(Misiones de los Tapes 49; ⊗11am-1am Wed-Mon) Opened in 2015, this friendly retro corner bar has a compact tiled interior and sidewalk tables perfect for gazing down the cobbled street toward the river at sunset. It prides itself on reasonably priced (by Colonia standards), cold beer, sandwiches, empanadas and *platos del día* (daily specials under UR$300).

Barbot MICROBREWERY
(☎4522-7268; www.facebook.com/barbotcerveceria; Washington Barbot 160; ⊗6pm-2am Mon-Thu,

noon-4am Fri-Sun) This sleek brewpub (Colonia's first, opened in 2013) is well worth a visit for its ever-evolving collection of 15 home brews on tap, although the bar snacks (pizza, *picadas* and Mexican fare) are best avoided.

El Drugstore
COCKTAIL BAR

(Portugal 174; ⊙noon-midnight) Touristy but fun, this funky corner place has polka-dot tablecloths, a vividly colored interior, outdoor seating with perfect views of Plaza de Armas, and two vintage cars on the cobblestones doubling as romantic dining nooks. Half of the 24-page menu is devoted to drinks; the other half to so-so tapas and international fare (mains UR$180 to UR$500). There's frequent live guitar music.

🛍 Shopping

Malvón
CLOTHING

(✆4522-1793; Av General Flores 100; ⊙11am-7pm) Sells woolens from the national cooperative Manos del Uruguay, along with other Uruguayan handicrafts.

ℹ Information

Antel (cnr Lavalleja & Rivadavia)

BBVA (Av General Flores 299) One of several ATMs along Av General Flores.

BIT Welcome Center (✆4522-1072; www. bitcolonia.com; Odriozola 434; ⊙9am-6pm) In a sparkling glass-walled building opposite the port, this modern welcome center, operated by Uruguay's national tourism ministry, has tourist information, touch-screen displays, a handicrafts shop and an overpriced (UR$50) 'Welcome to Uruguay' video presentation.

Post Office (Lavalleja 226)

Tourist Office (✆4522-8506; www.colonia turismo.com) Barrio Histórico (Manuel Lobo 224; ⊙9am-6pm); Bus Terminal (cnr Manuel Lobo & Av FD Roosevelt; ⊙9am-6pm)

ℹ Getting There & Away

BOAT
From the ferry terminal at the foot of Rivera, **Buquebus** (✆130; www.buquebus.com.uy; ⊙9am-10pm) runs two slow boats (UR$750, 3¼ hours) plus three or more fast boats (UR$1580, 1¼ hours) daily to Buenos Aires.

Colonia Express (✆4522-9676; www.colonia express.com.uy; Ferry Terminal; ⊙9am-10pm) and **Seacat** (✆4522-2919; www.seacatcolonia. com.uy; Ferry Terminal; ⊙7:30am-7pm) run less frequent but more affordable high-speed ferry services. Each company offers two to three departures daily. Crossings take one

hour, with day-of-departure fares ranging from UR$798 to UR$1198.

All three companies offer child, senior and advance-purchase discounts.

Immigration for both countries is handled at the port before boarding.

BUS
Colonia's modern **bus terminal** (cnr Manuel Lobo & Av FD Roosevelt) is conveniently located near the port, within easy walking distance of the Barrio Histórico. It has tourist information and luggage-storage, money-changing and internet facilities.

Buses from Colonia del Sacramento
The following destinations are served at least twice daily.

DESTINATION	COST (UR$)	TIME (HR)
Carmelo	141	1¼
Mercedes	318	3½
Montevideo	318	2¾
Paysandú	583	6
Salto	795	8

ℹ Getting Around

Walking is enjoyable in compact Colonia, but motor scooters, bicycles and gas-powered buggies are popular alternatives. **Thrifty** (✆4522-2939; www.thrifty.com.uy; Av General Flores 172; bicycle/scooter/golf cart per hr US$6/12/17, per 24hr US$24/40/66) rents everything from high-quality bikes to scooters to golf carts. Several other agencies rent cars and motorbikes near the bus and ferry terminals, including **Multicar** (✆4522-4893; www.multicar. com.uy; Manuel Lobo 505), **Motorent** (✆4522-9665; www.motorent.com.uy; Manuel Lobo 505), **Punta Car** (✆4522-2353; www.puntacar. com.uy; cnr 18 de Julio & Rivera), **Avis** (✆4522-9842; www.avis.com.uy; Bus Station) and **Europcar** (✆4522-8454; www.europcar.com.uy; Av Artigas 152). The last two offer one-way car rentals between Colonia and Montevideo.

Local COTUC buses go to the beaches and bullring at Real de San Carlos (UR$19) from along Av General Flores.

Carmelo
POP 18.040

Carmelo, dating from 1816, is a laid-back town of cobblestone streets and low old houses, a center for yachting, fishing and exploring the Paraná Delta. It straddles the Arroyo de las Vacas, a stream that widens into a sheltered harbor just below the Río

ESTANCIA TOURISM IN URUGUAY

Estancias, the giant farms of Uruguay's interior, are a national cultural icon. The Uruguayan Ministry of Tourism has designated 'Estancia Turística' as a distinct lodging category, and dozens of such places have opened their doors to tourists, from traditional working farms to historic rural hotels. Typically, *estancias* organize daily activities with a heavy emphasis on horseback riding; many also provide overnight accommodations. Most are difficult to reach without a vehicle, although they'll sometimes pick guests up with advance notice.

One of Uruguay's most impressive *estancias* is **San Pedro de Timote** (☑4310-8086; www.sanpedrodetimote.com; Ruta 7, Km142, Cerro Colorado; s/d incl breakfast from US$80/150, incl full board & all activities from US$205/300; ✱ ✹), whose remarkable setting – 14km up a dirt road amid 253 hectares of rolling cattle country – is greatly enhanced by the complex of historic structures, some dating to the mid-19th century: a gracious white chapel, a courtyard with soaring palm trees, a library with gorgeous tilework and a circular stone corral. Common areas feature parquet wood floors, big fireplaces, comfy leather armchairs, two pools and a sauna. Full-board rates include three meals, afternoon tea and two daily horseback-riding excursions, plus occasional bonfires and full-moon walks. The turnoff is just outside the town of Cerro Colorado, 160km northeast of Montevideo on Ruta 7.

Other favorite tourist *estancias* include include **La Sirena** (p546), near Mercedes, **Guardia del Monte** (p564), near the northern Atlantic coast, **Panagea** (p551), northwest of Tacuarembó, and **Yvytu Itaty** (p551), southwest of Tacuarembó.

In Montevideo, **Cecilia Regules Viajes** (☑2916-3011; www.ceciliaregulesviajes.com; Bacacay 1334, Local C) and **Lares** (☑2901-9120; www.lares.com.uy; WF Aldunate 1341) are travel agencies specializing in *estancia* tourism.

Uruguay's confluence with the Río de la Plata. The town center, seven blocks north of the arroyo (creek), is Plaza Independencia. South of the arroyo across the bridge lies the pleasant beach of Playa Seré, backed by a large park with open space, camping, swimming and a huge casino. Daily launches connect Carmelo to the Buenos Aires suburb of Tigre.

◉ Sights & Activities

The arroyo, with large, rusty boats moored along it, makes for a great ramble, as does the 30-minute stroll to the beach. Local wines have an excellent reputation, and vineyard visits are a popular activity.

Bodega Irurtia   WINERY
(☑099-692545, 4542-2323; www.irurtia.com.uy; Av Paraguay, Km2.3) Just outside town (look for the gigantic wine bottle!), this winery produces award-winning tannats and pinot noirs. With advance notice, visitors can take a 90-minute tour of the cellars, followed by tastings of one to five wines (US$8 to US$32, depending on the number of wines sampled).

Almacen de la Capilla   WINERY
(☑4542-7316; almacendelacapilla.wix.com/almacendelacapilla; Camino Vecinal de Colonia Estrella; ⊙11am-6pm) Surrounded by vineyards, this historic general store sits at a country crossroads 5km north of Carmelo (look for signs along Hwy 21 at Km257). The fifth-generation Cordano family, originally from Genoa, Italy, has been making wine here since 1870. Tastings and picnic lunches are available. Ask to see the wine cellar, hidden beneath a trap door behind the counter.

🛏 Sleeping & Eating

★**Ah'Lo Hostel Boutique**   HOSTEL $
(☑4542-0757; ahlo.com.uy; Treinta y Tres 270; dm US$18-23, d US$61-87, d without bathroom US$46-55, ste US$59-99; ✱ 🛜) Hands down Carmelo's best downtown option, this brand-new hostel delivers on its 'boutique' moniker, offering super-comfortable dorms with plush duvets, immaculate shared bathrooms and well-priced private rooms, all in an attractively restored colonial building seven blocks from the ferry terminal and two blocks from the main square. Bike rentals (US$10 per day) and cycling tours to local wineries are available.

Camping Náutico Carmelo CAMPGROUND $
(☑4542-2058; dnhcarmelo@adinet.com.uy; Arroyo de las Vacas s/n; tent sites UR$322, shower per 7min UR$49) South of the arroyo, this pleasant tree-shaded campground, with hot showers, caters to yachties but accepts walk-ins too. Sites accommodate up to four people.

Piccolino URUGUAYAN $
(☑4542-4850; cnr 19 de Abril & Roosevelt; dishes UR$175-300; ⊙9am-midnight Wed-Mon) This corner place has decent *chivitos* and views of Carmelo's central square.

Fay Fay URUGUAYAN $$
(☑4542-4827; 18 de Julio 358; dishes UR$170-390; ⊙11am-4pm & 7:30pm-12:30am Tue-Sun) A fantastic little family-run restaurant on the plaza. The menu sticks closely to Uruguayan standards, but throws in a few surprises. Homemade desserts are wonderful.

⭐**Bodega y Granja Narbona** ITALIAN $$$
(☑4540-4778; www.narbona.com.uy; Hwy 21, Km268; dishes US$22-32; ⊙noon-midnight) Set amid vineyards and orchards 13km from Carmelo, this restaurant in a restored 1908 farmstead serves gourmet pasta, Uruguayan beef, organic vegetables and fabulous tannat and *grappamiel* (honey-infused grape brandy) from Narbona's award-winning cellars. Inside, browse shelves stacked floor-to-ceiling with local olive oil, peach preserves and *dulce de leche* (milk caramel). The adjacent **Narbona Wine Lodge** (☑4540-4778; www.narbona.com.uy/en/lodge; Hwy 21, Km268; ste US$185-310, with vineyard view US$215-360; 🖥) offers luxurious overnight accommodations.

ℹ Information

Casa de la Cultura (☑4542-2001; carmelo turismo.com.uy; 19 de Abril 246; ⊙9am-6pm Mar-Nov, to 7pm Dec-Feb) Three blocks south of the main square and eight blocks northeast of the launch docks.

Post Office (Uruguay 360)

Scotiabank (Uruguay 401) One of several ATMs opposite the main square.

ℹ Getting There & Away

BOAT

Cacciola (☑4542-4282; www.cacciolaviajes. com; Wilson Ferreyra s/n; Carmelo-Tigre one way UR$770; ⊙ticket office 3:30-4:30am & 8:30am-8pm) Runs twice-daily launches to the Buenos Aires suburb of Tigre, at 4:30am and 1:30pm Monday through Saturday and 12:30pm and 6:30pm on Sunday. Service is sometimes expanded to thrice-daily in summer. The 2½-hour trip through the Paraná Delta is the most scenic crossing between Uruguay and Argentina.

BUS

All bus companies are on or near Plaza Independencia. **Berrutti** (☑4542-2504; www. berruttiturismo.com/horarios.htm; Uruguay 337) has the most frequent service to Colonia; **Chadre** (☑4542-2987; www.agenciacentral. com.uy; 18 de Julio 411) is the best bet for all other destinations.

Buses from Carmelo

DESTINATION	COST (UR$)	TIME (HR)
Colonia	141	1½
Mercedes	177	2
Montevideo	424	3½
Paysandú	424	5
Salto	636	7

Mercedes
POP 42,000

Capital of the department of Soriano, Mercedes is a livestock center with cobblestone streets and a small pedestrian zone around an 18th-century cathedral on central Plaza Independencia. The town's most appealing feature is its leafy waterfront along the south bank of the Río Negro.

⊙ Sights & Activities

Activities along the riverfront include boating, fishing and swimming at the sandy beaches, or simply strolling along the Rambla (especially popular on Sunday afternoons).

Museo Paleontológico Alejandro Berro MUSEUM
(☑4532-3290; Parque Castillo Mauá; ⊙11am-5pm) FREE About 3km west of town, this museum displays a substantial fossil collection, including an impressively well-preserved glyptodon shell discovered in a nearby riverbank.

☞ Tours

Catamarán Soriano I BOAT TOUR
(☑4532-2201 ext 2503; tours per person UR$200-500) This cruise boat offers occasional excursions on the Río Negro and Río San Salvador. For schedules and tickets, inquire at Mercedes' downtown tourist office.

WORTH A TRIP

THE LITTLE BEEF CUBE THAT CIRCLED THE GLOBE

In 1865 the Liebig Extract of Meat Company located its pioneer South American plant near the river town of Fray Bentos, 35km west of Mercedes. It soon became Uruguay's most important industrial complex. British-run El Anglo took over operations in the 1920s and by WWII the factory employed 4000 people, slaughtering cattle at the astronomical rate of 2000 a day.

Looking at the abandoned factory today, you'd never guess that its signature product, the Oxo beef cube, once touched millions of lives on every continent. Oxo cubes sustained WWI soldiers in the trenches, Jules Verne sang their praises in his book *Around the Moon*, Stanley brought them on his search for Livingstone, Scott and Hillary took them to Antarctica and Everest. More than 25,000 people from more than 60 countries worked here, and at its peak the factory was exporting nearly 150 different products, using every part of the cow except its moo.

Enshrined as Uruguay's newest Unesco World Heritage site in July 2015, the former factory is now a museum – the **Museo de la Revolución Industrial** (museo.anglo@ rionegro.gub.uy; admission UR$40, incl guided tour UR$50-90, free on Tue; ⊘ 9:30am-5pm Tue-Sun). Dozens of colorful displays, ranging from the humorous to the poignant, bring the factory's history vividly to life: a giant cattle scale where school groups are invited to weigh themselves; or the old company office upstairs, left exactly as it was when the factory closed in 1979, with grooves rubbed into the floor by the foot of an accountant who sat at the same desk for decades. Note that most signs are in Spanish only.

One- to two-hour guided tours (schedule varies) grant access to the intricate maze of passageways, corrals and abandoned slaughterhouses behind the museum. At 11am on Thursdays, Saturdays and Sundays visitors can also tour the Casa Grande, a mansion that once housed the factory's manager.

The adjacent town of Fray Bentos, with its pretty riverfront promenade, is the southernmost overland crossing over the Río Uruguay from Argentina. It's 45 minutes by bus from Mercedes (UR$53), four hours from Colonia (UR$389) or Buenos Aires (UR$1010), and 4½ hours from Montevideo (UR$547).

🛏 Sleeping & Eating

Camping Isla del Puerto CAMPGROUND $
(☑ 9401-6049; Isla del Puerto; sites per person/tent UR$24/78) Mercedes' spacious campground, one of the region's best, occupies half the Isla del Puerto in the Río Negro. Connected to the mainland by a bridge, it has swimming, fishing and sanitary facilities.

★**Estancia La Sirena** ESTANCIA $$$
(☑ 9953-2698, 4530-2271; www.lasirena.com.uy/ hosteria.html; Ruta 14, Km4.5; r per person with half/full board US$110/135, all incl horseback rides & other activities) Surrounded by rolling open country 15km upriver from Mercedes, this *estancia* is one of Uruguay's oldest and most welcoming. The spacious 1830 ranch house, with its cozy parlor and fireplaces and end-of-the-road setting, makes a perfect base for relaxation, late-afternoon conversation under the eucalyptus trees, stargazing and horseback excursions to the nearby Río Negro. Homemade meals are delicious.

Martiniano Parrilla Gourmet PARRILLA $$
(☑ 4532-2649; Rambla Costanera s/n; dishes UR$190-390; ⊘ noon-3pm & 7:30pm-midnight Tue-Sun) Prime riverfront setting at the foot of 18 de Julio is complemented by a varied menu featuring homemade pasta, grilled meat and fish.

🛍 Shopping

★**Lanas de Soriano** CLOTHING
(☑ 4532-2158; www.lanasdesoriano.com; Colón 60; ⊘ 9am-noon Mon-Fri, 3-6:30pm Mon & Wed-Fri) A rainbow of beautiful handmade woolens is available in this shop, hidden away in a residential neighborhood near the waterfront.

ℹ Information

Municipal Tourist Office (☑ 4532-2201 ext 2501; turismo@soriano.gub.uy; Plaza El Rosedal, Av Asencio btwn Colón & Artigas; ⊘ 8am-6:30pm) In a crumbling white building opposite the bridge to the campground.

Post Office (cnr Rodó & 18 de Julio)
Scotiabank (Giménez 719) ATM on Plaza
Independencia.

ℹ️ Getting There & Away

Mercedes' modern, air-conditioned **bus termi-nal** (Plaza General Artigas) is about 10 blocks
from Plaza Independencia, in a shopping center
with ATMs, a post office, free public bathrooms,
luggage storage and an emergency medical
clinic. A local bus (UR$20) leaves hourly from
just in front of the terminal, making a circuit
around downtown.

Buses from Mercedes

The following destinations are served at least
once daily.

DESTINATION	COST (UR$)	TIME (HR)
Buenos Aires	1010	5
Carmelo	177	2
Colonia	318	3
Montevideo	494	3½-4½
Paysandú	217	2
Salto	491	4

Paysandú

POP 76,400

On the east bank of the Río Uruguay, con-nected to Colón, Argentina by the Puente
Internacional General Artigas, Uruguay's
third-largest city is just a stopover for most
travelers en route to or from Argentina. The
activity is on Plaza Constitución, six blocks
north of the bus terminal.

Founded as a mid-18th-century outpost
of cattle herders from the Jesuit mission
at Yapeyú (in present-day Argentina), Pay-sandú gradually rose to prominence as a
meat-processing center. Repeated sieges of
the city during the 19th century (the last in
1864–65) earned it the local nickname 'the
American Troy.'

Despite its turbulent history and ongoing
status as a major industrial center, mod-ern-day Paysandú is surprisingly sedate. To
see the city's wilder side, visit during **Carna-val** or the annual week-long **beer festival**
(held during Semana Santa).

◉ Sights & Activities

Museo Histórico   MUSEUM

(☑ 4722-6220 ext 247; Av Zorrilla de San Martín
874; ☺ 9am-2pm Tue-Sat, to 3pm Sun) **FREE** This
historical museum displays evocative imag-es from the multiple 19th-century sieges of
Paysandú, including of the bullet-riddled
shell of the cathedral and women in exile
watching the city's bombardment from an
island offshore.

Museo de la Tradición   MUSEUM

(☑ 4722-3125; Av de los Iracundos 5; ☺ 9am-2pm
Tue-Sat) **FREE** In parkland near the river-front, this museum features a small but
well-displayed selection of anthropological
artifacts and gaucho gear.

🛏️ Sleeping

Hotel Rafaela   HOTEL $

(☑ 4722-4216; 18 de Julio 1181; s/d with fan & with-out bathroom UR$650/850, with air-con & bath-room UR$900/1150; ❈ 🛜) A decent budget
option just west of the main square. Rafae-la's rooms are dark but large, and some have
their own small patios.

★ Hotel Casagrande   HOTEL $$

(☑ 4722-4994; www.hotelcasagrande.com.uy;
Florida 1221; s UR$1800, d UR$2782-3615; ❈
@🛜) Homey and conveniently located, Pay-sandú's nicest downtown hotel has comfy
armchairs, marble tabletops, big brass beds,
free parking and a gourmet restaurant
on-site.

Estancia La Paz   ESTANCIA $$

(☑ 4720-2272; www.estancialapaz.com.uy; Ruta
24, Km86.5; d/ste/4-person apt from US$100/
130/145; ❈@🛜🏊) The tennis courts,
swimming pool and Muzak-filled common
areas feel incongruous among the histor-ic buildings and pristine natural setting
at this tourist *estancia* 25km southeast of
Paysandú. Equestrians will appreciate the
horseback-riding excursions, lasting from
one day to a full week. Access is via a long
dirt road: turn off at Km86.5 on Ruta 24 or
Km336 on Ruta 3.

🍴 Eating & Drinking

Confitería Las Familias   SWEETS $

(www.postrechaja.com; 18 de Julio 1152; chajá
UR$65; ☺ 9am-7pm) If you've got a sweet
tooth (and we mean a *really* sweet tooth)
pull up a stool at this old confectioner's shop
and sample one of Uruguay's classic des-serts: *chajá*, a dentist-friendly concoction of
sugary meringue, fruit and cream invented
here in 1927.

Pan Z
URUGUAYAN $$

(☑4722-9551; cnr 18 de Julio & Setembrino Pereda; dishes UR$195-495; ⊙noon-3pm & 7pm-1am) Popular 'Panceta' serves steaks, pizza, *chivitos* stacked high with every ingredient imaginable, and tasty desserts such as strawberry cake and tiramisu.

El Bar
PIZZA, URUGUAYAN $$

(☑4723-7809; es-es.facebook.com/ElBarPaysandu; cnr 18 de Julio & Herrera; mains UR$140-420; ⊙6:30am-late) Smack in the heart of town (one block west of Plaza Constitución), this corner resto-bar is open all day long for pizza, burgers and standard Uruguayan fare. After dark it shifts smoothly into bar mode, getting especially packed on Fridays when there's live music.

☆ Entertainment

Along the waterfront, 4km northwest of the center, Paysandú's intimate, tree-encircled **Teatro de Verano** is just across the street from the larger **Anfiteatro del Río Uruguay**, which seats up to 20,000 people and hosts major concerts during Paysandú's annual beer festival. Check with the tourist office for details of upcoming events at both venues.

ℹ Information

Post Office (cnr 18 de Julio & Montevideo)

Scotiabank (18 de Julio 1026) One of several ATMs along Paysandú's main street.

Tourist Office Centro (☑4722-6220 ext 184; turismo@paysandu.gub.uy; 18 de Julio 1226; ⊙9am-7pm); Riverfront (☑4722-9235; plande lacosta@paysandu.gub.uy; Av de Los Iracundos; ⊙9am-5pm); Bus Terminal (cnr Artigas & Av Zorrilla de San Martin; ⊙7am-1pm Dec-Apr, noon-6pm May-Nov) The Centro office is on Plaza Constitución; the riverfront office is next to the Museo de la Tradición.

ℹ Getting There & Away

Paysandú's **bus terminal** (☑4722-3225; cnr Artigas & Av Zorrilla de San Martín), six blocks due south of Plaza Constitución, is a hub for travel to and from Argentina. **Flechabus** (www.flechabus.com.ar) and **COIT** (www.coitviajes.com) both go to Buenos Aires, while **EGA** (www.ega.com.uy) serves Córdoba (via Paraná and Santa Fe) and Asunción, Paraguay.

To get from the bus station to the main square, take any local Copay bus (UR$20) running down Av Zorrilla de San Martín.

Buses from Paysandú

DESTINATION	COST (UR$)	TIME (HR)
Asunción (Paraguay)	3720-4555	17
Buenos Aires (Argentina)	750	5½
Carmelo	424	5
Colón (Argentina)	109	¾
Colonia	543	6
Córdoba (Argentina)	1715	11
Mercedes	217	2½
Montevideo	679	4½
Paraná (Argentina)	905	5¼
Salto	217	2
Santa Fe (Argentina)	950	6
Tacuarembó	432	3½

Salto

POP 104,000

Built near the falls where the Río Uruguay makes its 'big jump' (Salto Grande in Spanish), Salto is Uruguay's second-largest city and the most northerly crossing point to Argentina. It's a relaxed place with some 19th-century architecture and a pretty riverfront. People come here for the nearby hot springs and the recreation area above the enormous Salto Grande hydroelectric dam.

⊙ Sights & Activities

Salto's museums all close during January.

Museo de Bellas Artes y Artes Decorativas
MUSEUM

(Uruguay 1067; ⊙1-7pm Tue-Sat, 4-7pm Sun Feb-Dec) **FREE** Displays a nice collection of Uruguayan painting and sculpture in an historic two-story mansion with a grand staircase, stained glass and back garden.

Museo del Hombre y la Tecnología
MUSEUM

(cnr Av Brasil & Zorrilla; ⊙1-7pm Mon-Fri, 2-7pm Sat Feb-Dec) **FREE** Housed in an historic market building, this museum features excellent displays on local cultural development and history upstairs, and a small archaeological section downstairs.

Represa Salto Grande
DAM

(☑4732-6131; www.saltogrande.org; ⊙7am-4pm) **FREE** A source of national pride, this massive hydroelectric dam 14km north of Salto

DON'T MISS

SALTO'S HOT SPRINGS

A whole slew of hot springs bubbles up around Salto.

Termas San Nicanor (☑4730-2209; www.sannicanor.com.uy; Ruta 3, Km475; campsites per person UR$200-250, dm US$25-40, d US$100-150, 4-person cabins US$180-230; ☎☒) Surrounded by a pastoral landscape of cows, fields and water vaguely reminiscent of a Flemish painting, this is the most tranquil of Salto's hot-springs resorts. It has two gigantic outdoor thermal pools, a restaurant, and accommodations for every budget, including campsites, no-frills dorms, four-person cabins and private rooms in a high-ceilinged *estancia* house with large fireplaces and peacocks strolling the grounds.

Day use of the springs (8am to 10pm, available Friday to Sunday only) costs UR$150 (UR$100 in low season).

The 12km unpaved access road leaves Ruta 3 10km south of Salto. Occasional **shuttles** (☑driver Martín Lombardo 099-732368; one way UR$400) to San Nicanor depart from Salto (corner of Larrañaga and Artigas) and Termas de Daymán. Schedules vary; phone ahead to confirm schedules.

Termas de Daymán (☑4736-9711; www.termasdedayman.com; admission UR$100; ☺9am-9pm) About 8km south of Salto, Daymán is a heavily developed theme pa of thermal baths complete with kids' water park. It's popular with Uruguayan and Argentine tourists who roam the town's block-long main street in bathrobes. For comfortable accommodations adjacent to the springs, try **La Posta del Daymán** (☑camping 4736-9094, hotel 4736-9801; www.lapostadeldayman.com; campsites per person UR$150, r per person incl breakfast UR$1100-1550; ☎☒)

Empresa Cossa runs hourly buses between Salto and the baths (UR$25), leaving Salto's port via Av Brasil at 30 minutes past every hour (7:30am to 10:30pm), returning hourly from 7am to 11pm.

Termas de Arapey (☑4768-2101; www.termasarapey.com; admission UR$100; ☺7am-11pm) About 90km northeast of Salto, Uruguay's oldest hot-springs resort offers multiple pools surrounded by gardens, fountains and paths to the Río Arapey Grande. **Hotel Municipal** (☑4768-2441; www.hoteltermasdelarapey.com; s/d UR$1670/2290, optional breakfast per person UR$125; ☒☎☒), down near the river, offers the area's best-value accommodations. **Argentur** (☑4732-9931; minibusesargentur.blogspot.com) runs one or two buses daily from Salto (UR$170, 1½ hours).

provides more than 50% of Uruguay's electricity. Free 90-minute guided tours (half-hourly) visit both the Uruguayan and Argentine sides. A taxi from Salto costs about UR$1000 roundtrip. En route, check out the stands selling homemade empanadas and freshly squeezed local orange juice (two liters for UR$45!).

🛏 Sleeping

Nearby hot springs offer some of the region's best-value accommodations.

Hostal del Jardín   HOTEL $
(☑4732-4274; www.hostaldeljardin.com.uy; Colón 47; s/d UR$800/1000; ☒☎) Convenient to the port, this place has simple, clean rooms (the cheapest in town) lined up motel-style along a small, grassy side yard.

Gran Hotel Concordia   HOTEL $
(☑4733-2735; www.facebook.com/granhotelconcordia; Uruguay 749; s/d UR$800/1500; ☒☎) This faded 1860s relic, a national historical monument, remains Salto's most atmospheric downtown budget option. A life-size cutout of Carlos Gardel, who once stayed in room 32, beckons you down a marble corridor into a leafy courtyard filled with murals and sculptures, surrounded by tired and musty rooms with tall French-shuttered windows.

★Art Hotel Deco   BOUTIQUE HOTEL $$
(☑4732-8585; www.arthoteldeco.com; Sarandí 145; s/d/ste US$90/120/150; ☒☎) Just paces from the city center, this classy newcomer (opened in 2013) easily outshines Salto's other downtown sleeping options. The lovingly renovated historic building abounds in period details, including high ceilings,

polished wood floors, art deco door and window frames, an elegant sitting room and a lush back garden. Amenities include Egyptian cotton sheets, cable TV, sauna and gym.

✗ Eating

La Caldera
PARRILLA $
(Uruguay 221; dishes UR$130-300; ⊘11am-3pm & 8pm-midnight Tue-Sun) With fresh breezes blowing in off the river and sunny outdoor seating, this *parrilla* makes a great lunch stop; at dinnertime, the cozy interior dining room, with its view of the blazing fire, is equally atmospheric.

Casa de Lamas
URUGUAYAN $$
(☑4732-9376; Chiazzaro 20; dishes UR$190-445; ⊘8pm-midnight Wed, noon-2:30pm & 8pm-midnight Thu-Mon) Down near the riverfront, Salto's swankiest eatery is housed in a 19th-century building with pretty vaulted brick and stonework. The *menú de la casa* (set menu including appetizer, main dish, dessert and drink) goes for UR$430.

La Trattoria
URUGUAYAN $$
(Uruguay 754; dishes UR$180-415; ⊘noon-2am) Locals flock to this high-ceilinged downtown eatery for fish, meat and pasta. Sit in the wood-paneled dining room or people-watch from a sidewalk table on busy Calle Uruguay.

ⓘ Information

BBVA (cnr Uruguay & Lavalleja) One of several banks at this intersection.
Post Office (cnr Artigas & Sarandí)
Tourist Office (☑4733-4096; turismo@salto.gub.uy) Bus Terminal (Salto Shopping Center, cnr Ruta 3 & Av Bastille; ⊘8am-10pm); Centro (Uruguay 1052; ⊘8am-7pm Mon-Sat)

ⓘ Getting There & Away

BOAT
Transporte Fluvial San Cristóbal (☑4733-2461; cnr Av Brasil & Costanera Norte) runs launches across the river to Concordia, Argentina (adult/child UR$160/70, 15 minutes) three to four times daily between 8:45am and 6pm Monday through Saturday (no service on Sunday).

BUS
Salto's **bus terminal** (Salto Shopping Center, cnr Ruta 3 & Av Batlle), in a spiffy modern shopping center 2km east of downtown, has a tourist info kiosk, ATMs, internet facilities, free public restrooms and a supermarket.

Buses from Salto

DESTINATION	COST (UR$)	TIME (HR)
Buenos Aires (Argentina)	1005	7
Colonia	809	8
Concordia (Argentina)	121	1
Montevideo	883	6½
Paysandú	217	2
Tacuarembó	526	4

Connect in Concordia for additional Argentine destinations, including Puerto Iguazú and Córdoba.

Tacuarembó

POP 54.800

In the rolling hills along the Cuchilla de Haedo, Tacuarembó is gaucho country. Not your 'we pose for pesos' types, but your real-deal 'we tuck our baggy pants into our boots and slap on a beret just to go to the local store' crew. It's also the alleged birthplace of tango legend Carlos Gardel.

Capital of its department, Tacuarembó has pleasant sycamore-lined streets and attractive plazas. The town center is Plaza 19 de Abril, linked by the main thoroughfares 25 de Mayo and 18 de Julio.

◉ Sights

Museo del Indio y del Gaucho
MUSEUM
(cnr Flores & Artigas; ⊘10am-5pm Tue-Sat) FREE
Paying romantic tribute to Uruguay's gauchos and indigenous peoples, this museum's collection includes stools made from leather and cow bones, elegantly worked silver spurs and other accessories of rural life.

✪ Festivals & Events

Fiesta de la Patria Gaucha
CULTURAL
(www.patriagaucha.com.uy) This colorful, authentically home-grown five-day festival in early March attracts visitors from around the country to exhibitions of traditional gaucho skills, music and other activities. It takes place in Parque 25 de Agosto, north of town.

⨇ Sleeping & Eating

To experience Tacuarembó's traditional culture up close and personal, stay at a nearby *estancia*.

Hospedaje Márfer
HOTEL $

(☑4632-3324; Ituzaingó 211; s/d with bathroom UR$650/1150, without bathroom from UR$390/780) New owners at this downtown guesthouse have added several air-conditioned en-suite units with brand-new mattresses and bedspreads, but peso-pinchers can still opt for the fan-cooled cheapies out back. The optional breakfast is overpriced at UR$150.

★Estancia Panagea
ESTANCIA $$

(☑4630-2670, 9983-6149; panagea-uruguay.blog spot.com.uy; Ruta 31, Km189; dm per person incl full board, farm activities, horseback riding & transport US$60) For a spectacular introduction to life on the Uruguayan land, head to this 2400-acre working *estancia* 40km northwest of Tacuarembó. Juan Manuel, who was born and raised here, his Swiss wife Susana and gaucho Bilingue invite guests to get fully immersed in farm activities from the mundane (tagging and vaccinating animals) to the classic (herding cattle on horseback).

Guests sleep dorm-style in simple rooms, eat three home-cooked meals a day (including self-serve bacon and eggs cooked on the woodstove), hit the basketball and volleyball courts at sunset and congregate around the fireplace at night. Call ahead to coordinate dates and arrange transportation from Tacuarembó's bus station.

★Yvytu Itaty
ESTANCIA $$

(☑099-837555, 4630-8421; www.viviturismorural. com.uy; s incl full board, farm activities & horseback riding UR$2200, per person, minimum of 2 people UR$2000) ✿ Pedro and Nahir Clariget's unpretentious ranch-style home, 50km southwest of Tacuarembó, offers a first-hand look at real gaucho life. Guests are invited to accompany Pedro and his friendly cattle dogs around the 636-hectare working *estancia* on horseback, participate in daily *estancia* routines and sip *mate* on the patio at sunset in anticipation of Nahir's tasty home cooking.

Call in advance for driving directions or to arrange pickup at Tacuarembó's bus station (UR$1500 roundtrip for a group of any size).

La Rueda
PARRILLA $

(W Beltrán 251; dishes UR$140-300; ☺noon-3pm & 7pm-midnight Mon-Sat, noon-4pm Sun) With its thatched roof and walls covered with gaucho paraphernalia, this neighborhood *parrilla* is a perennial local favorite.

Cabesas Bier
PUB FOOD $

(cabesasbier.uy/#brewpub; Sarandí 349; pub food from UR$200; ☺8pm-late Thu-Sat) One of Tacuarembó's unexpected pleasures is this great little microbrewery, serving eight varieties of craft beer on tap, accompanied by pizza, *picadas* and other pub food.

ⓘ Information

Banco Santander (18 de Julio 258) One of several ATMs near Plaza Colón.

Post Office (Ituzaingó 262)

Tourist Office (☑4632-7144; tacuarembo.gub. uy; ☺8am-7pm Mon-Fri, 8am-noon Sat & Sun) Just outside the bus terminal.

ⓘ Getting There & Around

The **bus terminal** (☑4632-4441; cnr Ruta 5 & Av Victorino Pereira) is 1km northeast of the center. A taxi into town costs about UR$70.

Buses from Tacuarembó

DESTINATION	COST (UR$)	TIME (HR)
Montevideo	689	4½
Paysandú	436	3½
Salto	512	4

Valle Edén

Valle Edén, a lush valley 24km southwest of Tacuarembó, is home to the **Museo Carlos Gardel** (☑099-107303; admission UR$25; ☺9:30am-5:30pm Tue-Sun). Reached via a drive-through creek spanned by a wooden suspension footbridge, and housed in a former *pulpería* (the general store and bar that used to operate on many *estancias*), the museum documents Tacuarembó's claim as birthplace of the revered tango singer – a claim vigorously contested by Argentina and France!

Accommodations in Valle Edén are available at **Camping El Mago** (☑4632-7144; campsites per tent/person UR$100/40) or at **Posada Valle Edén** (☑098-800100, 4630-2345; www.posadavalleeden.com.uy; d UR$1480-2160; ☒), where you can eat and stay in the lovely historic mud-and-stone main inn, or sleep in one of the modern *cabañas* across the street.

Empresa Calebus runs two buses daily from Tacuarembó to Valle Edén (UR$60, 20 minutes).

EASTERN URUGUAY

The gorgeous 340km sweep of beaches, dunes, forests and lagoons stretching northeast from Montevideo to the Brazilian border is one of Uruguay's national treasures. Still largely unknown except to Uruguayans and their immediate neighbors, this region lies nearly dormant for 10 months of each year, then explodes with summer activity from Christmas to Carnaval, when it seems like every bus out of Montevideo is headed somewhere up the coast. For sheer fun-in-the-sun energy, there's nothing like the peak season, but if you can make it here slightly off-season (in March or the first three weeks of December), you'll experience all the same beauty for literally half the price.

Near the Brazilian border, amid the wide-open landscapes and untrammeled beaches of Rocha department, abandoned hilltop fortresses and shipwrecks offer mute testimony to the era when Spain and Portugal struggled for control of the new continent. Where lookouts once scanned the wide horizon for invading forces, a new wave of invaders has taken hold, from binocular-wielding whale watchers in Cabo Polonio to camera-toting celebrity watchers in Punta del Este.

Piriápolis

POP 8800

With its grand old hotel and beachfront promenade backed by small mountains, Piriápolis is vaguely reminiscent of a Mediterranean beach town and exudes a certain old-school coastal resort charm. It was developed for tourism in the early 20th century by Argentine entrepreneur Francisco Piria, who built the imposing landmark Argentino Hotel and an eccentric hillside residence known as Castillo de Piria (Piria's Castle).

Almost all the action happens in the 10-block stretch of beachfront between Av Artigas (the access road from Ruta 9) and Av Piria (where the coastline makes a broad curve southwards). Streets back from the beach quickly become residential.

The surrounding countryside holds many interesting features, including two of Uruguay's highest summits.

◉ Sights & Activities

Swimming and **sunbathing** are the most popular activities, and there's good **fishing** off the rocks at the end of the beach, where

Rambla de los Argentinos becomes Rambla de los Ingleses.

For a great view of Piriápolis, take the **chairlift** (Aerosilla; adult/child UR$160/140; ⊙10am-sunset) to the summit of **Cerro San Antonio** at the east end of town.

🛏 Sleeping & Eating

Accommodation prices drop dramatically outside of peak summer season. For a good selection of seafood restaurants and *parrillas*, stroll along the beachfront Rambla.

Bungalows Margariteñas   BUNGALOW $
(☑4432-2245, 099-890038; www.margaritenias. com; cnr Zufriategui & Piedras; d/tr/q US$60/ 65/70; 🅿️🛜) Near the bus terminal, this place has well-equipped, individually decorated bungalows that sleep two to four. Affable owner Corina speaks English and meets guests at the bus station upon request.

Hostel de los Colores   HOSTEL $
(☑4432-6188; www.hosteldeloscolores.com.uy; Simón del Pino, btwn Barrios & Reconquista; dm US$15-27, d from US$47; 🅿️🛜) Directly opposite Piriápolis' more institutional 240-bed HI hostel, this newcomer two blocks from the beach offers clean, colorful four- and six-bed dorms, plus a lone double. Bikes (UR$400 per day) and a kayak (per day UR$500) are available for rent.

Argentino Hotel   HISTORIC HOTEL $$$
(☑4432-2791; www.argentinohotel.com; Rambla de los Argentinos s/n; r per person incl breakfast US$89-159, incl half board US$108-180; 🅿️🅿️🛜🅿️) Even if you don't stay here, you should visit this elegant 350-room European-style spa hotel with two heated river-water pools, a casino, an ice-skating rink and other luxuries.

★**Café Picasso**   SEAFOOD $$
(☑4432-2597; cnr Rojas & Caseros; dishes UR$240-480; ⊙noon-3:30pm & 8-11:30pm daily Dec-Apr, noon-3:30pm daily & 8-11:30pm Fri & Sat May-Nov) Hidden down a residential backstreet several blocks from the beach, septuagenarian chef-owner Carlos has converted his carport and front room into an informal, colorfully decorated restaurant with open-air grill. Locals chat astride plastic chairs and listen to tango recordings while Carlos cooks up some of the best fish anywhere on Uruguay's Atlantic coast, along with paella (UR$560) on Sundays.

ⓘ Information

Banco de la República (Rambla de los Argentinos, btwn Sierra & Sanabria) Convenient ATM.

Post Office (Av Piria s/n) Two blocks in from the beachfront.

Tourist Office (☑4432-5055; www.destino piriapolis.com; Rambla de los Argentinos; ⊙10am-6pm Apr-Nov, 9am-8pm Dec & Mar, to midnight Jan & Feb) Helpful staff and public toilets, on the waterfront near Argentino Hotel.

ⓘ Getting There & Away

The **bus terminal** (☑4432-4526; cnr Misiones & Niza) is a few blocks back from the beach. COT and COPSA run frequent buses to Montevideo (UR$177, 1½ hours) and Punta del Este (UR$116, 50 minutes).

Around Piriápolis

In the hills north of town, **Castillo de Piria** (☑4432-3268; Ruta 37, Km4; ⊙8am-3:30pm Tue-Sun Apr-Nov, to 6pm Dec-Mar) **FREE**, Francisco Piria's opulent, castle-like former residence, has Spanish-language displays on the history of Piriápolis. About 1km further inland, hikers can climb Uruguay's fourth-highest 'peak,' **Cerro Pan de Azúcar** (389m). The trail (2½ hours roundtrip) starts from the parking lot of the **Reserva de Fauna Autóctona** (Ruta 37, Km5; ⊙7am-8:30pm) **FREE**, narrowing from a gradual dirt road into a steep path marked with red arrows.

The private nature reserve **Sierra de las Ánimas** (☑SMS only 094-419891; www.sierradelasanimas.com; Ruta 9, Km86; admission UR$80; ⊙9am-sunset Sat & Sun, plus Carnaval & Easter weeks) 🅿 is just off the Interbalnearia (coastal highway), 25km toward Montevideo from Piriápolis. There are two good hiking trails, each three to four hours roundtrip: one leads to the 501m summit (Uruguay's second-highest), the other to the **Cañadón de los Espejos**, a series of waterfalls and natural swimming holes that are especially impressive after good rainfall. Other activities include rustic camping (UR$50 per person, by prior arrangement only) and mountain biking. Coming from Montevideo by bus, get off at Parador Los Cardos restaurant and cross the highway. In cold or rainy weather, send an SMS in advance to verify it's open.

Punta del Este

POP 9300

OK, here's the plan: tan it, wax it, buff it at the gym, then plonk it on the beach at 'Punta.' Once you're done there, go out and shake it at one of the town's famous clubs.

Punta del Este – with its many beaches, elegant seaside homes, yacht harbor, high-rise apartment buildings, pricey hotels and glitzy restaurants – is one of South America's most glamorous resorts, extremely popular with Argentines and Brazilians, and easily the most expensive place in Uruguay.

Celebrity watchers have a full-time job here. Punta is teeming with big names, and local gossip-mongers keep regular tabs on who's been sighted where. Surrounding towns caught up in the whole Punta mystique include the famed club zone of La Barra to the east and Punta Ballena to the west.

◎ Sights

Town Beaches   BEACH
Beaches are the big daytime draw in sunny Punta. On the peninsula's western (Río de la Plata) side, Rambla Gral Artigas snakes past calm **Playa Mansa**, then passes the busy **yacht harbor**, overflowing with boats, restaurants and nightclubs, before circling east to meet the open Atlantic Ocean. On the peninsula's eastern side, waves and currents are rougher, as reflected in the name **Playa Brava** (Fierce Beach) and in the surfers flocking to **Playa de los Ingleses** and **Playa El Emir**.

Outlying Beaches   BEACH
(W along Rambla Williman) From Playa Mansa, west along Rambla Williman, the main beach areas are La Pastora, Marconi, Cantegril, Las Delicias, Pinares, La Gruta at Punta Ballena, and Portezuelo. Eastward, along Rambla Lorenzo Batlle Pacheco, the prime beaches are La Chiverta, San Rafael, La Draga and Punta de la Barra. In summer, all have *paradores* (small restaurants) with beach service.

Isla de Lobos   ISLAND
About 10km offshore, this small island is home to the world's second-largest southern sea-lion colony (200,000 at last count), along with colonies of southern fur seals and South America's tallest lighthouse. The island is protected and can only be visited on an organized tour.

Uruguay's Beaches

Stretching from Montevideo to Brazil, 300km of beaches hug the Río de la Plata and the Atlantic Ocean. Choose the style that suits: from Punta del Este's glitz to Cabo Polonio's rusticity.

Cabo Polonio

Its lighthouse beckoning from a lonely point dotted with lounging sealions and makeshift houses, Cabo Polonio (p563) is a nature-lover's dream. Getting here, on a pitching truck ride through the dunes, is half the fun.

La Paloma

Grab an ice cream and head for the waves. Family-friendly La Paloma (p561), tucked behind a wall of sand dunes, is the very picture of unadorned beachside fun.

Punta del Este

The dividing line between the Atlantic and the Río de la Plata, Punta del Este's (p553) tidy peninsula full of high-rises and perfect beaches morphs annually from sleepy beach town to summer playground for South America's 'see and be seen' party set.

Punta del Diablo

Punta del Diablo (p565) is the end of the line. A few steps down the beach and you're in Brazil, but most folks stay put, seduced by waves, seafood shacks, beach bonfires and the national park.

Piriápolis

A throwback to the 1930s, Piriápolis (p552) is about strolling the beachfront promenade past the grand hotel, or surveying the calm waters from the top of the chairlift.

La Pedrera

No view on Uruguay's entire Atlantic coast matches the wide-angle perspective from La Pedrera's (p562) cliffs. Join the surfers up top and contemplate your beach options for the day.

Clockwise from top left
1. La Pedrera 2. Punta del Este 3. Piriápolis 4. Cabo Polonio

DON'T MISS

WATCH OUT! IT'LL REACH OUT & GRAB YOU!

Punta's most famous landmark is **La Mano en la Arena** (The Hand in the Sand; Playa Brava), a monster-sized sculpted hand protruding from the sands of Playa Brava. Constructed in iron and cement by Chilean artist Mario Irarrázabal, it won first prize in a monumental art contest in 1982 and has been a Punta fixture ever since. The hand exerts a magnetic attraction over thousands of visitors every year, who climb and jump off its digits and pose for photos with it. Look for it just southeast of the bus station.

Isla Gorriti   ISLAND
Boats leave every half-hour or so (daily in season, weekends in off-season) from Punta del Este's yacht harbor for the 15-minute trip to this nearby island, which has excellent sandy beaches, a couple of restaurants and the ruins of Baterías de Santa Ana, an 18th-century fortification.

★ Casapueblo   GALLERY
(☑ 4257-8041; carlospaezvilaro.com.uy/nuevo/museo-taller; admission UR$220; ☺ 10am–sunset) Gleaming white in the sun and cascading nine stories down a cliffside, Uruguayan artist Carlos Páez Vilaró's exuberantly whimsical villa and art gallery sits atop Punta Ballena, a jutting headland 15km west of Punta del Este. Visitors can tour five rooms, view a film on the artist's life and travels, and eat up the spectacular views at the upstairs cafeteria-bar. There's a hotel and restaurant, too. It's a 2km walk from the junction where Codesa's Línea 8 bus drops you.

🏃 Activities

In summer, **parasailing**, **waterskiing** and **jet skiing** are possible on Playa Mansa. Operators set up on the beach along Rambla Claudio Williman between Paradas 2 and 20.

Sunvalleysurf   SURFING
(☑ 4248-1388; www.sunvalleysurf.com; Parada 3, Playa Brava; ☺ 11am-7pm) Wet suits, surfboards, bodyboards and lessons are available from the original shop on Playa Brava, plus branches on **Playa El Emir** (☑ 4244-8622; Calle 28, btwn Calles 24 & 26) and in **La Barra** (Ruta 10, Km160).

👉 Tours

Dimar Tours   BOAT TOUR
(☑ 4244-4750; www.isladelobos.com.uy; Puerto; adult/child to Isla Gorriti UR$300/200, to Isla de Lobos US$50/30) Offers tours from Punta's port to Isla de Lobos and Isla Gorriti, daily in high season, weekends only in low season. A highlight of the Isla de Lobos tour is the chance to swim with sea lions. Other operators, including **Crucero Samoa** (☑ 094-954660; crucerosamoa.com; Puerto), have offices along the same boardwalk; take a wander to compare your options. Reserve ahead during peak season.

🛏 Sleeping

In summer Punta is jammed with people, and prices are astronomical; even hostels double their prices in January. In winter it's a ghost town, and places that stay open lower their prices considerably. During peak season, even places classified as midrange tend to charge top-end rates. Off-season visitors will find prices more in keeping with standard ranges.

★ Tas D'Viaje Hostel   HOSTEL $
(☑ 4244-8789; www.tasdviaje.com; Calle 24 btwn 28 & 29; dm US$15-35, d US$50-100; ❄ @ 🛜) Just one block from Playa El Emir, Punta's best-located hostel offers everything from low-cost fan-cooled dorms to brand-new air-conditioned suites with private bathrooms, nice wood floors and flat-screen cable TV. There's a sea-facing breakfast deck, an inviting living room with fireplace, an attractive guest kitchen and a hammock-strung back patio. On-site bike and surfboard rentals cost US$10 each per day.

Trip Hostel   HOSTEL $
(☑ 4248-8181; www.thetriphostel.com; Sader btwn Artigas & Francia; dm US$12-30, d US$50-80; @ 🛜) Founded by three Uruguayan friends, this small hostel has plenty of *onda* (good vibes), with its cozy lounge, on-site bar selling local microbrews, and rooftop terrace sporting six homegrown cannabis plants (Uruguay's new legal maximum). It's on a residential street within a five-minute walk of the bus station and beaches. Avoid the lone private room, which is windowless and claustrophobic.

Hostel del Puerto   HOSTEL $
(☑ 4244-4949; www.hosteldelpuerto.com; cnr Calles 11 & 12; dm US$15-40, d without bathroom US$60-100; ☺ mid-Nov–Feb; ❄ 🛜) Perfect location

compensates for the rather sterile atmosphere at Punta's newest hostel, one block up from the yacht harbor and its lively nightlife scene. Dorms sleep from four to 13 people, and there's a big kitchen and yard with barbecue facilities.

Camping San Rafael CAMPGROUND $
(☎4248-6715; www.campingsanrafael.com.uy; Saravia s/n; campsites per person US$11, plus US$2 per vehicle; ⏲Nov-Easter) This campground, near the bridge to La Barra, has well-kept facilities on woodsy grounds, complete with store, restaurant, laundry, 24-hour hot water and other amenities.

La Lomita del Chingolo GUESTHOUSE $
(☎099-758897, 4248-6980; www.lalomitadelchingolo.com; Las Acacias btwn Los Eucaliptus & Le Mans; dm/d US$20/40 Dec & Mar, US$50/100 Jan & Feb, US$17/30 Apr-Nov; @📶) With one six-person dorm and five private rooms, this relaxed place is in a residential neighborhood about 4km north of the center. Hospitable owners Rodrigo and Alejandra welcome guests with kitchen facilities, tasty breakfasts, impromptu backyard barbecues and plenty of information about the local area.

Bonne Étoile HOTEL $$
(☎4244-0301; www.hotelbonneetoile.com; Calle 20, btwn Calles 23 & 25; low season s/d US$55/65, high season US$135/145; ❄@📶) In a 1940s beach house adjoining a more modern six-story tower, Bonne Étoile offers clean, spacious rooms, some with river views. Off-season rates are among the best in town, and the location between Gorlero and the port is hard to beat.

Hotel Bravamar HOTEL $$
(☎4248-0559; hotelbravamar.com.uy; Rambla Costanera, Playa Brava; r low season US$50-80, high season US$100-140; ❄📶) Friendly and family run, this humble hotel is one of the best deals on Playa Brava, although the intervening highway doesn't do much to enhance the view!

★**Las Cumbres** BOUTIQUE HOTEL $$$
(☎4257-8689; www.cumbres.com.uy; Ruta 12, Km3.5, Laguna del Sauce; d US$155-375, ste US$315-675; ❄@📶🏊) Near Punta Ballena, this understatedly luxurious hilltop paradise is eclectically decorated with treasures from the owners' world travels. The spacious rooms abound with special features, such as writing desks, fireplaces and outdoor whirlpool tubs. Guests have access to spa treatments, beach chairs and umbrellas, and free mountain bikes, and the tearoom terrace (open to the public) has magnificent sunset views.

★**Casa Zinc** BOUTIQUE HOTEL $$$
(☎4277-3003, 9962-0066; www.casazinc.com; Calle 9, La Barra; r US$140-470; @📶) Replete with vintage furniture, claw-foot bathtubs and checkerboard marble floors, this magical La Barra getaway features six luxurious high-ceilinged theme rooms, including the Library, the luminous Architect's Studio and Back To School, with its twin beds and old-fashioned blackboards. Guests can enjoy breakfast till 4pm, prepare dinners in the beautifully appointed kitchen, or pore through the hotel's collection of art books.

Atlántico Boutique Hotel BOUTIQUE HOTEL $$$
(☎4244-0229; hotelatlanticopuntadeleste.com; cnr Calles 7 & 10; r US$92-292, ste US$138-384; ❄📶🏊) With gleaming white decor and a backyard swimming pool and bar area, this boutique hotel between the port and the tip of the peninsula is one of Punta's newest, classiest and best located accommodations. Amenities include 32-inch TVs in every room, an on-site pizzeria, an extensive video library and ample buffet breakfasts.

Conrad Resort & Casino CASINO HOTEL $$$
(☎4249-1111; www.conrad.com.uy; Parada 4, Playa Mansa; d US$350-761, ste from US$578; ❄@📶🏊) A longtime downtown fixture, this high-rise five-star remains one of the focal points of Punta's summertime 'see and be seen' social life. Better rooms have terraces with sea views, the pool and spa complex is fabulous, and the casino offers entertainment extravaganzas.

Eating

Rustic INTERNATIONAL $
(☎092-007457; www.facebook.com/Rusticbarpuntadeleste; Calle 29, btwn Gorlero & Calle 24; mains UR$150-350; ⏲11am-4pm Wed-Mon, plus 8pm-3am Fri & Sat) Rustic wood tables, exposed brick walls, retro decor, and tasty food at affordable prices make this one of the peninsula's most attractive lunch spots. Friendly young owners Luciana and Sebastian offer service with a smile, bustling from table to table with *chivitos*, *milanesas*, quesadillas, salads and fish of the day. There's a UR$150 lunch special daily (UR$130 for takeaway).

Punta del Este

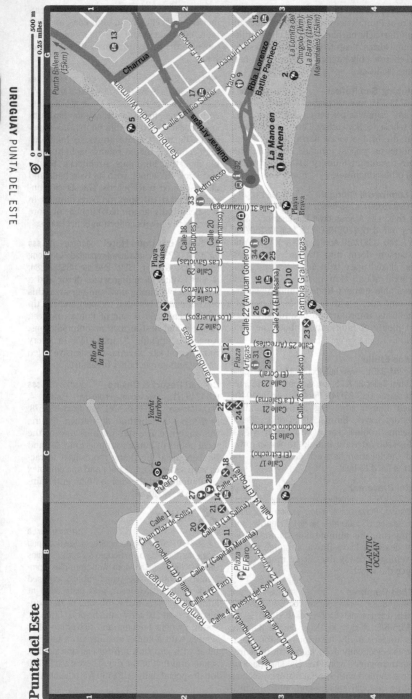

ATLANTIC
OCEAN

Río de
la Plata

Yacht
Harbor

Puerto

Plaza
Artigas

Plaza
El Faro

Playa
Mansa

Playa
Brava

1 La Mano en
la Arena

Punta Ballena
(15km)

La Lomita del
Chingolo (1km);
La Barra (1km);
Manantiales (15km)

Charrua

Rambla Claudio Williman

Bulevar Artigas

Rambla Artigas

Rambla Gral Artigas

Rambla Gral Artigas

Av Francia

Joaquín Lenzina

Rbla. Lorenzo
Batlle Pacheco

Yaro

Calle Emilio Sader

Pedro Risso

Calle 18
(Baupres)

Calle 20
(El Remanso)

Calle 29
(Las Gaviotas)

Calle 28
(Los Meros)

Calle 27
(Los Muergos)

Calle 22 (Av Juan Gorlero)

Calle 24 (El Mesana)

Calle 25 (Arrecifes)

Calle 23

Calle 26 (Resalsero)

Calle 23
(El Coral)

Calle 21
(La Galerna)

Calle 19
(Comodoro Gorlero)

Calle 17
(El Estrecho)

Calle 14 (El Foque)

Calle 13

Calle 11
(Juan Díaz de Solís)

Calle 9 (La Salina)

Calle 7 (Capitán Miranda)

Calle 5 (El Faro)

Calle 4 (Puesta del Sol)

Rambla Gral Artigas

Calle 31 (Inzaurraga)

Calle 30 (El Resalsero)

Punta del Este

Punta del Este

◎ Top Sights
1 La Mano en la Arena F3

◎ Sights
2 Playa Brava G3
3 Playa de los Ingleses C3
4 Playa El Emir D3
5 Playa Mansa F1
6 Yacht Harbor C2

✪ Activities, Courses & Tours
7 Crucero Samoa C2
8 Dimar Tours C2
9 Sunvalleysurf G3
10 Sunvalleysurf (Playa El Emir) E3

⬣ Sleeping
11 Atlántico Boutique Hotel B2
12 Bonne Étoile D2
13 Conrad Resort & Casino G1
14 Hostel del Puerto C2
15 Hotel Bravamar G3
16 Tas D'Viaje Hostel E3
17 Trip Hostel G2

✴ Eating
18 Chivitería Marcos C2
19 Guappa D2
20 Il Baretto B2
21 Lo de Charlie B2
22 Lo de Tere C2
23 Miró D3
24 Olivia C3
25 Rustic E3

◉ Drinking & Nightlife
26 Capi Bar D3
27 Moby Dick C2
28 Soho C2

◉ Shopping
29 Feria de los Artesanos D3
30 Manos del Uruguay E3

ℹ Information
31 Municipal Tourist Office D3
32 Municipal Tourist Office (Bus Station) F3
33 Municipal Tourist Office (Playa Mansa) F2
34 National Tourism Ministry E3

Chivitería Marcos　　　SANDWICHES $$

(☑ 4243-7609; Rambla Artigas, btwn Calles 12 & 14; chivitos UR$335; ⊙ 11am-4am Dec-Mar, noon-midnight Fri & Sat, noon-5pm Sun Apr-Nov) Montevideo-based Marcos earned its fame building *chivitos* (Uruguay's famous steak sandwich) to order. Choose from the 11 toppings and seven sauces, then try to balance the thing back to your table

Olivia　　　INTERNATIONAL $$

(☑ 4244-5121; Calle 21, btwn Rambla Artigas & Gorlero; mains UR$320-490; ⊙ noon-midnight) Popular for its varied menu and moderate (by Punta standards) prices, Olivia serves tacos, pizza, salads, sandwiches and more substantial fish and meat dishes, along with caipirinhas, mojitos, sangria or fresh ginger-mint lemonade. In good weather sit on the scenic rooftop terrace overlooking the port.

Lo de Tere　　　INTERNATIONAL $$$

(☑ 4244-0492; www.lodetere.com; Rambla Artigas & Calle 21; mains UR$580-980; ⊙ noon-3pm & 8pm-midnight) Even with early-bird discounts (20% to 40% depending on time of arrival) Lo de Tere is hard on the wallet, but you won't find finer food anywhere in Punta. The wide-ranging menu includes black crab ravioli, orange-scented shrimp risotto, Uru-

guayan steak with rock salt and homemade chimichurri, and the famous rack of lamb, all accompanied by fine harbor views.

Lo de Charlie　　　SEAFOOD, MEDITERRANEAN $$$

(☑ 4244-4183; www.lodecharlle.com.uy; Calle 12, No 819; dishes UR$520-840; ⊙ 8pm-late Dec-Mar, 8pm-midnight Thu-Sat & 11am-4pm Fri-Sun Apr-Nov) Owned by a fishing buddy of local artist Carlos Páez Vilaró and decorated with some of his work, this is one of Punta's premier restaurants. The culinary delights include gazpacho, paella, risotto, homemade pasta, fish and shellfish.

Guappa　　　URUGUAYAN $$$

(☑ 4244-0951; guappa.com.uy; Rambla Artigas btwn Calles 27 & 28; mains UR$350-790; ⊙ 10am-midnight) For seafood, salads, pasta, panini or *chivitos* in one of Punta's prettiest waterfront settings, grab a spot on the beachside deck here, then enjoy watching the waiters try to look dignified as they cross the street with loaded trays. A popular spot to watch the sun go down.

Miró　　　SUSHI, SEAFOOD $$$

(www.facebook.com/miro.restomusicbar; cnr Calles 26 & 27; mains UR$390-680; ⊙ 10am-midnight Fri-Sun Mar-Nov, daily Dec-Feb) Sushi, grilled fish, fried squid and *mejillones a la provenzal* (mussels simmered in white wine, garlic,

WORTH A TRIP

FARO JOSÉ IGNACIO

The rich and famous flock to this highly fashionable beachside town with its pretty lighthouse and long expanses of powdery sand, 30km east of Punta.

For a classic taste of José Ignacio's rarefied atmosphere, day-trippers should drop in at the chic beachside eatery **Parador La Huella** (☑4486-2279; www.paradorlahuella.com; Playa Brava, José Ignacio; mains UR$450-700; ☺noon-5:30pm & 8pm-1am daily Dec-Mar, noon-3pm Fri-Sun & 8pm-midnight Fri & Sat Apr-Nov), which specializes in sushi, grilled fish and clay-oven-fired pizza, all served up with dreamy ocean views.

Staying overnight here is not for the faint of wallet; US$1000-a-night accommodations are the norm, such as the oceanfront **Playa Vik** (☑093-704866; playavik.com; cnr Los Cisnes & Los Horneros; ste US$900-1200, houses US$1300-2300), one of three luxury hotels in the José Ignacio area launched by billionaire Scandinavian businessman and art patron Alex Vik. To experience this beautiful stretch of coast without breaking the bank, try digging around on sites like joseignaciouruguay.com, where you'll find cool, less expensive alternatives such as the shipping-container-turned-bohemian-beach-house **El Farolito** (☑098-345323; Republica Argentina btwn Las Toninas and Av Soria; up to 5 people per night/week US$150/1000).

COT (☑4248-3558; www.cot.com.uy) runs two buses daily from Punta to José Ignacio (UR$98, 40 minutes).

---

parsley and olive oil) are the specialties at this beachfront eatery. The outdoor terrace, directly overlooking Playa El Emir, is one of the peninsula's best spots for a scenic sundowner or a snack between stints at the beach.

Il Baretto　　　　　ITALIAN $$$
(☑4244-5565; www.ilbarettopunta.com; cnr Calles 9 & 10; pizza UR$270-395; dishes UR$495-750; ☺11am-4pm & 8pm-midnight daily mid-Dec–Carnaval, 11am-4pm Sat & Sun & 8pm-midnight Fri & Sat rest of year) Candlelit garden seating on plush chairs and couches provides a romantic setting for 'after-beach' drinks, along with homemade pasta, pizza and desserts.

🍸 Drinking & Nightlife

A cluster of clubs in Punta's port area stays open all year (weekends only in low season). During the super-peak season from Christmas through January, an additional slew of beach clubs with ever-changing names open along Playa Brava, on the beach road to La Barra.

Bear in mind that it's social suicide to turn up at a nightclub before 2am here. In general, Punta's bars stay open as long as there's a crowd and sometimes have live music on weekends.

Capi Bar　　　　　BAR
(www.facebook.com/capipde; Calle 27, btwn Gorlero & Calle 24; ☺noon-late) Launched in 2015, Punta del Este's first artisanal brewpub

serves up its own Capitán home brew along with craft beers from all over Uruguay. The classy, low-lit interior also makes a nice place to linger over reasonably priced fish and chips, *rabas* (fried squid) and other bar snacks.

Moby Dick　　　　　PUB
(www.mobydick.com.uy; Calle 13, btwn Calles 10 & 12; ☺6pm-5am Mon-Thu, noon-5am Fri-Sun) This classic pub near the yacht harbor is where Punta's dynamic social scene kicks off every evening. It's open year-round, with a mix of DJs and live music.

Soho　　　　　CLUB
(www.facebook.com/SohoPuntaUy; Calle 13, btwn Calles 10 & 12; ☺midnight-6am) Another dependable year-round dance spot featuring live bands and international DJs.

Ocean Club　　　　　CLUB
(www.facebook.com/OceanClubPunta; Rambla Batllé Parada 12; ☺1-7am) One of Punta's best and most reliable beach clubs, in the dunes between Punta and La Barra.

☆ Entertainment

Medio y Medio　　　　　JAZZ
(☑4257-8791; www.medioymedio.com; Camino Lussich s/n, Punta Ballena; ☺10:30pm-late) This jazz club and restaurant near the beach in Punta Ballena brings in top-name performers from Uruguay, Argentina and Brazil.

🛍 Shopping

Manos del Uruguay   CLOTHING
(www.manos.com.uy; Gorlero btwn Calles 30 & 31;
⊗ 11am-7pm Mar-Nov, 10am-8pm Dec, to midnight
Jan & Feb) The local branch of Uruguay's national cooperative, selling fine woolens.

Feria de los Artesanos   HANDICRAFTS
(Plaza Artigas; ⊗ 11am-7pm Apr-Nov, longer hours
Dec-Mar) Artisan fair on Punta's central square.

ℹ Orientation

Punta itself is relatively small, confined to a narrow peninsula that officially divides the Río de la Plata from the Atlantic Ocean. The town has two separate grids: north of a constricted isthmus, just east of the yacht harbor, is the high-rise hotel zone; the southern area is largely residential. Street signs bear both names and numbers, though locals refer to most streets only by their number. An exception is Av Juan Gorlero (Calle 22), the main commercial street, universally referred to as just 'Gorlero' (not to be confused with Calle 19, Comodoro Gorlero).

Rambla Claudio Williman and Rambla Lorenzo Batlle Pacheco are coastal thoroughfares that converge at the top of the isthmus from northwest and northeast, respectively. Locations along the Ramblas are usually identified by numbered *paradas* (bus stops, marked with signs along the waterfront).

ℹ Information

Most hotels and restaurants offer free wi-fi, and there's free municipal wi-fi on Plaza Artigas. Punta's many banks, ATMs and exchange offices are concentrated along Gorlero.

Antel (cnr Calles 24 & 25; ⊗ 9am-5pm Mon-Fri; 🛜) Phone services.

Municipal Tourist Office (📞 4244-6510; www.maldonado.gub.uy; Plaza Artigas; ⊗ 8am-11pm mid-Dec–Feb, 11am-5pm rest of year) Full-service office with hotel-booking desk attached. Additional branches at the port, the bus terminal (📞 4249-4042; ⊗ 8am-10pm mid-Dec–Feb, 11am-5pm rest of year) and Playa Mansa (📞 4244-6519; cnr Calles 18 & 31; ⊗ 9am-10pm mid-Dec–Mar, 11am-5pm rest of year).

National Tourism Ministry (📞 4244-1218; puntadeleste@mintur.gub.uy; Gorlero 942; ⊗ 10am-5pm Mon-Sat)

Post Office (Calle 30, btwn Gorlero & Calle 24)

ℹ Getting There & Away

AIR

Punta del Este International Airport (p574) is at Laguna del Sauce, 20km west of Punta del Este. Direct international flights include Aerolíneas Argentinas to Buenos Aires' Aeroparque and TAM to São Paulo.

BUS

From Punta's **bus terminal** (📞 4249-4042; cnr Calle 32 & Bulevar Artigas), dozens of daily buses ply the coastal route to Montevideo. COT also runs two daily buses northeast up the coast to the Brazilian border, with intermediate stops at Rocha (transfer point for La Paloma, La Pedrera and Cabo Polonio) and Punta del Diablo.

Buses from Punta del Este

DESTINATION	COST (UR$)	TIME (HR)
Carrasco Airport	266	1¾
Montevideo	266	2¼
Piriápolis	116	1
Punta del Diablo	363	3
Rocha	187	1½

ℹ Getting Around

TO/FROM THE AIRPORT

Door-to-door **minivan transfers** (📞 099-903433, 4223-0011; transfer btwn airport & bus terminal or port UR$220, btwn airport & hotel UR$320) are the most convenient way to reach Punta del Este's airport. Alternatively, any Montevideo-bound bus can drop you at the airport entrance on the main highway (UR$81), about 250m from the terminal building.

BUS

Bus 14, operated by **Codesa** (📞 4266-9129; www.codesa.com.uy), runs from Punta's bus terminal via the eastern beaches to La Barra (UR$49, 10 minutes) and José Ignacio (UR$60, 50 minutes); other Codesa buses run year-round to points west, including Punta Ballena.

CAR

Major international car-rental companies, along with Uruguayan rental agencies such as **Punta Car** (📞 4248-2112; www.puntacar.com.uy; Bulevar Artigas 101) and **Multicar** (📞 4244-3143; www.redmulticar.com; Gorlero 860), have counters at Punta del Este's airport. Downtown offices for all companies are concentrated along Gorlero and Calle 31.

La Paloma

POP 3500

La Paloma sits on a small peninsula 225km east of Montevideo, in the pretty rural department of Rocha. The town itself is rather bland and sprawling, but the surrounding beaches offer some of Uruguay's best surfing. On summer weekends the town often hosts free concerts on the beach, making accommodations bookings essential.

◎ Sights & Activities

El Faro del Cabo Santa María LIGHTHOUSE
(admission UR$25; ⊙3pm–sunset) The 1874 completion of this local lighthouse marked La Paloma's genesis as a summer beach resort. The unfinished first attempt collapsed in a violent storm, killing 17 French and Italian workers, who are buried nearby. Outside is a solar clock using shadows cast by the lighthouse.

Laguna de Rocha NATURE RESERVE
An ecological reserve protected under Uruguay's SNAP program (p566), this vast and beautiful wetland 10km west of La Paloma has populations of black-necked swans, storks, spoonbills and other waterfowl.

Peteco Surf Shop SURFING
(www.facebook.com/peteco.surf; Av Nicolás Solari, btwn Av El Sirio & Av del Navío; ⊙10am–8pm Thu-Mon, to 6pm Tue & Wed) This friendly surf shop rents all the necessary equipment (shortboards, longboards, bodyboards, sandboards, wet suits and kayaks) and can hook you up with good local instructors. The best surfing beaches are Los Botes, Solari and Anaconda southwest of town, and La Aguada and La Pedrera to the north.

🛏 Sleeping & Eating

La Balconada Hostel HOSTEL $
(☑4479-6273; www.labalconadahostel.com.uy; Centauro s/n; dm US$18-35, d with bathroom US$60-80, d without bathroom US$50-60; 🛜) This surfer-friendly hostel has an enviable location near La Balconada beach, about 1km southwest of the center. Take a taxi from the bus station and the hostel will pick up the tab.

Hotel Bahía HOTEL $$
(☑4479-6029; www.elbahia.com.uy; cnr Av del Navío & del Sol; d US$55-115; ❄🛜) For its central location and overall comfort, Bahía is hard to beat. Rooms are clean and bright, with firm mattresses and bedside reading lights. The seafood restaurant downstairs (mains UR$295 to UR$525, closed Tuesday) has been in business since 1936 and regularly gets recommended by locals as La Paloma's best.

Lo de Edinson PARRILLA, PIZZA $$
(☑4479-8178; www.facebook.com/LoDeEdinson; Av Nicolás Solari, btwn Antares & de la Virgen; mains UR$155-310; ⊙8am-11:30pm Wed-Mon) Best known for its grilled meats, this popular eatery in the heart of town also does decent pizzas and has a well-stocked bakery selling takeaway treats.

Punto Sur SEAFOOD $$
(☑099-624630, 4479-9462; Centauro s/n; dishes UR$280-450; ⊙noon-1am Christmas–Carnaval) For casual dining with an ocean view, this summer-only place on Playa La Balconada is the obvious choice, featuring tapas, paella, grilled fish and homemade pasta.

❶ Information

Banks, post and telephone offices are all on the main street, Av Nicolás Solari.

Tourist Office (☑4479-6088; Av Nicolás Solari; ⊙10am-10pm daily mid-Dec–Easter, 10:30am-4:30pm Mon-Sat rest of year) On the traffic circle at the heart of town. A second office in the bus terminal opens seasonally.

❶ Getting There & Around

From La Paloma's bus terminal, 500m northwest of the center, COT, Cynsa and Rutas del Sol all run frequently to Montevideo (UR$424, four hours). There's also frequent local service to La Pedrera (UR$53, 15 minutes). Rutas del Sol runs twice daily to the Cabo Polonio turnoff (UR$106, 45 minutes) and once daily to Punta del Diablo (UR$212, two hours). For other destinations, take a bus to the departmental capital of Rocha (UR$57, 30 minutes, frequent), where hourly buses ply the coastal route in both directions.

La Pedrera

POP 230

Long a mecca for surfers, laid-back La Pedrera sits atop a bluff with magnificent sweeping views of the beaches stretching north toward Cabo Polonio and south toward La Paloma. In recent years, the town has also become famous for its Carnaval, which has grown increasingly raucous with the influx of out-of-town visitors. Even so, La Pedrera remains downright sleepy outside the summer months, with most hotels and tourist services closing between April and November.

🛏 Sleeping & Eating

As with elsewhere along the coast, rates drop dramatically in the off-season.

El Viajero La Pedrera Hostel HOSTEL $
(☑4479-2252; www.elviajerolapedrera.com; Venteveo, btwn Pirincho & Zorzal; dm US$18-38, d US$60-120; ⊙mid-Dec–early Mar; @🛜) Part of Uru-

guay's largest hostel chain, this well-located seasonal hostel is tucked down a side street, a five-minute walk from the bus stop and only 500m from the beach.

Brisas de la Pedrera BOUTIQUE HOTEL **$$$**
(☑099-804656; brisasdelapedrera.com; d US$130–280; ❄☎) La Pedrera's oldest lodging – completely remodeled in boutique style and reopened in 2009 by Argentine-American owner Laura Jauregui – woos guests with sunny, spacious rooms, high-end amenities (but no TVs), and spectacular ocean views from the upstairs units with private terraces.

La Pe SEAFOOD, ITALIAN **$$**
(☑094-408955; www.facebook.com/Restaurant LaPe; Calle Principal; mains UR$300-450; ☺1-4pm & 8:30pm-12:30am Dec-Mar) 'P' is for pasta, paella and – in Spanish – *pescado* (fish). This popular place, smack in the heart of La Pedrera's main street, serves all three, with outdoor seating under the trees and a nice play area for kids. Look for the red, vine-covered building with the fish logo.

Costa Brava SEAFOOD **$$**
(dishes UR$260-450; ☺noon-3pm & 8pm-midnight daily Dec-Mar, 8pm-midnight Fri & Sat, noon-3pm Sat & Sun Apr-Nov) Perched atop the bluffs overlooking the Atlantic, Costa Brava is all about seafood accompanied by an unbeatable view.

Lajau MEDITERRANEAN, SEAFOOD **$$$**
(☑099-922091; mains UR$320-590; ☺1-4pm & 9pm-1am) Presided over by a Santa Claus–bearded Basque chef, this cozy family-run spot one block from the waterfront has a short, sweet menu of pasta and seafood. Locally caught crab, rays, shark and shrimp make their way into house specialties like *fidegua* (a paella-like dish made with fish, shellfish and noodles instead of rice).

❶ Information

La Pedrera's seasonally operating **tourist office** (☑4472-3100; turismorocha.gub.uy; Principal s/n; ☺10am-6pm Dec-Easter, to 10pm during Jan-Carnaval period) is a few blocks in from the beach, in a tiny wooden kiosk next to the OSE water towers (the town's tallest landmark). The closest ATMs are in La Paloma.

❶ Getting There & Away

Buses southbound to Montevideo (UR$442) and northbound to the Cabo Polonio turnoff (UR$65) stop near the tourist office on La Pedrera's main street. Schedules vary seasonally; a list

OFF THE BEATEN TRACK

HORSING AROUND IN THE HILLS

At **Caballos de Luz** (☑099-400446; www.caballosdeluz.com; horseback rides from US$45, s/d US$40/50, s/d incl full board US$95/170), high in the Sierra de Rocha – a lovely landscape of gray rocky crags interspersed with rolling rangeland – multilingual Austrian-Uruguayan couple Lucie and Santiago offer memorable hill-country horse treks lasting from two hours to a week, complete with delicious vegetarian meals and overnight accommodation in a pair of comfortable thatched guest-houses.

Call for pickup at the bus station in Rocha (US$20), take a taxi (US$25) or drive there yourself (30 minutes from Rocha, or an hour from La Pedrera).

is posted at the tourist office, opposite the bus stop. There are also frequent buses to Rocha (UR$88), where you can make connections north and south.

Cabo Polonio

POP 100

Northeast of La Paloma at Km264.5 on Ruta 10 lies the turnoff to Cabo Polonio, one of Uruguay's wildest areas and home to its second-biggest sea-lion colony, near a tiny fishing village nestled in sand dunes on a windswept point crowned by a lonely lighthouse. In 2009 the region was declared a national park, under the protective jurisdiction of Uruguay's SNAP program (p566). Despite a growing influx of tourists (and an incongruously spiffy entrance portal erected in 2012), Cabo Polonio remains one of Uruguay's most rustic coastal villages. There are no banking services, and the town's limited electricity is derived from generators, and solar and wind power.

◉ Sights

Faro Cabo Polonio LIGHTHOUSE
(admission UR$25; ☺10am-1pm & 3-6:30pm) Cabo Polonio's striking lighthouse provides a fabulous perspective on the point, the sea-lion colony and the surrounding dunes and islands.

WORTH A TRIP

LAGUNA DE CASTILLOS

Northwest of Cabo Polonio is the Laguna de Castillos, a vast coastal lagoon that shelters Uruguay's largest concentration of *ombúes*, graceful treelike plants whose anarchic growth pattern results in some rather fantastic shapes. In other parts of Uruguay the *ombú* is a solitary plant, but specimens here – some of them centuries old – grow in clusters, insulated by the lagoon from the bovine trampling that has spelled their doom elsewhere.

Monte de Ombúes (☑ 099-295177; tours per person UR$450-500, 5-person minimum) On Laguna de Castillos' western shore (near Km267 on Ruta 10), brothers Marcos and Juan Carlos Olivera, whose family received this land from the Portuguese crown in 1793, lead two- to three-hour nature excursions. Tours begin with a 20-minute boat ride through a wetland teeming with cormorants, ibis, cranes and black swans, followed by a hike through the *ombú* forest.

Departures are frequent in summer (anytime five people show up); other times of year, reserve ahead. With advance notice, longer bird-watching tours of the lagoon can be arranged in the off-season.

Guardia del Monte (☑ 099-872588, 4470-5180; www.guardiadelmonte.com; Ruta 9, Km261.5; r per person incl breakfast/half-board/full board US$110/150/180) Overlooking Laguna de Castillos' northern shore is this tranquil hideaway, originally established in the 18th century as a Spanish guard post to protect the Camino Real and the coastal frontier from pirates and Portuguese marauders. The lovely *estancia* house oozes history, from the parlor displaying 18th-century maps and bird drawings to the kitchen's Danish woodstove salvaged from an 1884 shipwreck.

Overnight rates include afternoon tea and meals served on the old brick patio or by the fireplace in the cozy dining room. Activities include horseback excursions (US$30) and walks along the lakeshore or into the surrounding *ombú* forest. It's at the end of a 10km dead-end road, off Ruta 9, 4km south of the town of Castillos.

🏃 Activities

In high season, Cabo Polonio's surf school, operated by local residents Mario and Ruben, offers **surfing** classes and board rentals.

★Cabalgatas Valiceras   HORSEBACK RIDING
(☑ 099-574685; cabalgatasvaliceras.com.uy; Barra de Valizas) Based in nearby Barra de Valizas, this excellent operator offers horseback excursions into the national park, through the dunes and along the beaches north of Cabo Polonio, including monthly full-moon rides.

Wildlife-Watching   WILDLIFE-WATCHING
Wildlife viewing in Cabo Polonio is excellent year-round. Below the lighthouse, southern sea lions (*Otaria flavescens*) and South American fur seals (*Arctocephalus australis*) frolic on the rocks. You can also spot southern right whales from August to October, penguins on the beach between May and August, and the odd southern elephant seal (*Mirounga leonina*) between January and March on nearby Isla de la Raza.

🛏 Sleeping & Eating

Many locals rent rooms and houses. The hardest time to find accommodation is during the first two weeks of January. Off-season, prices drop dramatically (40% to 70%).

Viejo Lobo Hostel   HOSTEL **$**
(☑ 091-413013; www.viejolobohostel.com; dm/d Dec-Feb US$25/60, Mar-Nov US$12.50/34; ☎) On the sandy plaza where buses turn around, this newer hostel has three dorms sleeping four to seven people, plus a couple of basic doubles. Electricity is generated with solar panels and a windmill, and wi-fi is available one hour per night (to quote friendly English-speaking manager Vicky: enough to stay connected, but not enough to turn people into zombies!).

Cabo Polonio Hostel   HOSTEL **$**
(☑ 099-445943; www.cabopoloniohostel.com; dm/d US$33/100 mid-Dec–Feb, US$16/50 other times; ☉ Oct-Apr) 🌿 Recently expanded to include a larger, brighter kitchen and a brand-new ocean-view dorm, this rustic beachfront hostel is a Polonio classic, with a hammock-strewn patio and a woodstove for stormy nights. The abandoned TV in the

dunes out front and the custom-designed NoFi logo epitomize owner Alfredo's low-tech philosophy: if you're in Polonio, it's time to slow down and unplug!

Pancho Hostal del Cabo HOSTEL $
(📞095-412633; dm Jan & Feb US$30, Mar-Dec US$11) Providing bare-bones dorms on two levels, Pancho's popular hostel is impossible to miss; look for the yellow corrugated roof, labeled with giant red letters, toward the beach from the bus stop. Nice features include a spacious new kitchen, a beachfront lounging area and the 2nd-floor dorm under the A-frame roof, with its small terrace looking straight out at the ocean.

Mariemar HOTEL $$
(📞4470-5164, 099-875260; posadamariemar@hotmail.com; d Dec-Feb US$150, Mar-Nov US$55-65) Tucked below the lighthouse, with beach access right outside the back door, this hotel-restaurant is one of Polonio's oldest year-round businesses. The simple rooms all have ocean views, with downstairs units costing slightly less than those upstairs. The attached restaurant (mains UR$290 to UR$425) serves everything from afternoon snacks (seaweed fritters and cold beer) to full seafood meals.

La Majuga EMPANADAS $
(snacks from UR$45; ⊙7:30am-11pm Nov-Apr) At this teal-green shack half a block from the bus stop, Señora Neli cooks up delicious empanadas (UR$45) filled with *siri* (crab) and *pescado* (fish), along with *chivitos, milanesas*, fries and other reasonably priced Uruguayan snacks.

El Club PARRILLA, INTERNATIONAL $$
(mains UR$200-400; ⊙11am-late mid-Dec–Easter) Decked out in mosaics and colorfully painted furniture, Cabo Polonio's newest eatery combines the creative efforts of Colombian artist Camila, her Uruguayan partner Fernando and revered local chef Martín. Specialties include grilled fish, artisanal beer, wood-fired pizza and fondue cooked atop recycled tin cans. It doubles as a social club where people gather to play chess and enjoy live music.

🍷 Drinking & Nightlife

Lo de Joselo BAR
(⊙6pm-late) For an unforgettable Polonio experience, head to this captivatingly ramshackle bar, overgrown with dense shrubbery and flowering vines. Blind bartender Joselo presides over the funky candlelit interior, serving up *licor de butia* (alcohol made from

local palm fruit), *grappamiel* and stiff shots of *caña* (sugarcane alcohol). It's a few paces from the bus stop toward the lighthouse.

❶ Getting There & Away

Rutas del Sol runs two to five buses daily from Montevideo to the Cabo Polonio entrance portal on Ruta 10 (UR$530, 4½ hours). Here you'll pile onto a 4WD truck for the lurching, bumpy ride across the dunes into town (UR$170 roundtrip, 30 minutes each way).

Punta del Diablo
POP 820

Once a sleepy fishing village, Punta del Diablo has long since become a prime summer getaway for Uruguayans and Argentines, and the epicenter of Uruguay's backpacker beach scene. Waves of uncontrolled development have pushed further inland and along the coast in recent years, but the stunning shoreline and laid-back lifestyle still exert their age-old appeal. To avoid the crowds, come outside the Christmas-to-February peak season; in particular, avoid the first half of January, when as many as 30,000 visitors inundate the town.

From the town's traditional center, a sandy 'plaza' 200m inland from the ocean, small dirt streets fan out in all directions.

◉ Sights & Activities

During the day you can rent surfboards or horses along the town's main beach, or trek an hour north to Parque Nacional Santa Teresa. In the evening there are sunsets to watch, spontaneous bonfires and drum sessions to drop in on...you get the idea.

🛏 Sleeping

The town's hostel scene has taken off dramatically in recent years. *Cabañas* are the other accommodations of choice; this term applies to everything from rustic-to-a-fault shacks to designer condos with all modern conveniences. Most *cabañas* have kitchens; some require you to bring your own bedding. For help finding something, ask at Supermercado El Vasco in the heart of town, or check online at www.portaldeldiablo.com.uy. Rates skyrocket between Christmas and February.

★El Diablo Tranquilo HOSTEL $
(📞4477-2519; www.eldiablotranquilo.com; Av Central; dm US$12-25, d with bathroom US$50-90, d without bathroom US$38-70; @🛜) Follow the

URUGUAY'S OFF-THE-BEATEN-TRACK NATURE PRESERVES

Uruguay's vast open spaces are a naturalist's dream. The Uruguayan government has designated several natural areas for protection under its **SNAP program** (Sistema Nacional de Áreas Protegidas; mvotma.gub.uy). Funding remains minimal, and tourist infrastructure rudimentary, but intrepid travelers will be richly rewarded for seeking out these little-visited spots. Valle del Lunarejo and Quebrada de los Cuervos are two preserves that best capture the spirit of Uruguay's wild gaucho country. Other SNAP preserves include Cabo Polonio (p563), Cerro Verde (p567) and Laguna de Rocha (p562).

Valle del Lunarejo

This gorgeous valley, 95km north of Tacuarembó, is a place of marvelous peace and isolation, with birds and rushing water providing the only soundtrack.

Visitors can spend the night at enchanting **Posada Lunarejo** (☑ 4650-6400; www.posadalunarejo.com; Ruta 30, Km238; r per person incl full board UR$1700 Mon-Thu, UR$2000 Fri-Sun), a restored 1880 building 2km off the main road, 3km from the river and a few steps from a bird colony teeming with *garzas* (cranes) and *espátulas rosadas* (roseate spoonbills). The *posada* organizes nearby hikes (UR$200, three hours) and horseback rides (UR$200, one hour).

CUT (www.cutcorporacion.com.uy) offers the most convenient bus schedule to Valle del Lunarejo on its daily Montevideo–Tacuarembó–Artigas bus (leaving Montevideo at noon (UR$830, six hours), and leaving Tacuarembó at 4:50pm (UR$141, 1½ hours). Posada Lunarejo can meet your bus if you call ahead.

Quebrada de los Cuervos

This hidden little canyon cuts through the rolling hill country 40km northwest of Treinta y Tres (325km northeast of Montevideo), providing an unexpectedly moist and cool habitat for a variety of plants and birds. There are two self-guided hiking trails: a 2½-hour loop through the canyon (UR$50 park admission fee required), and a privately owned trail to the Cascada de Olivera waterfall just outside the park (30 minutes each way, UR$30).

A perfect base for exploring this region is **Cañada del Brujo** (☑ 4452-2837, 099-297448; www.pleka.com/delbrujo; per person incl breakfast/half-board/full board UR$720/1210/1650), a rustic hostel in an old schoolhouse 8km from the park and 14km from Ruta 8. Hostel owner Pablo Rado leads hikes (UR$250) and horseback rides (UR$480) to the nearby Salto del Brujo waterfall and enjoys introducing guests to the joys of gaucho life: drinking *mate,* eating simple meals cooked on the wood stove and watching spectacular sunsets under the big sky. With advance notice, he can provide transportation to the hostel from Treinta y Tres (UR$300 per person) or from the highway turnoff at Km306.7 on Ruta 8 (UR$150 per person).

Nuñez (nunez.com.uy) and **EGA** (www.ega.com.uy) run frequent buses from Montevideo to Treinta y Tres (UR$512, 4¼ hours).

---

devilish red glow into one of South America's most seductive hostels, whose endless perks include inviting chill-out areas, bike and surfboard rentals, yoga and language classes, horseback excursions and PayPal cash advances. At the beachside Playa Suites annex, upstairs rooms have full-on ocean views, while the raucous bar-restaurant offers meals, beach service and a late-night party scene.

La Casa de las Boyas HOSTEL $
(☑ 4477-2074; www.lacasadelasboyas.com.uy; Playa del Rivero; Christmas-Feb dm US$18-55, d US$100-150, rest of year dm/d/tr/q from US$15/50/60/70;

@ 🤶 🏊) A stone's throw from the beach and a 10-minute walk north of the bus stop, this hostel offers a pool, a guest kitchen and 13 dorms of varying sizes. Outside of peak season, the better rooms – equipped with ensuite bathrooms, kitchenettes and satellite TV – are rented out as private apartments.

Hostel de la Viuda HOSTEL $
(☑ 4477-2690; www.hosteldelaviuda.com; cnr San Luis & Nueva Granada; dm US$18-29, d US$54-58; @ 🤶 🏊) Friendly, family-run La Viuda sits on a forlorn, remote back street 2km southwest of the town center, but compen-

sates with super-clean dorms and doubles, free bus-station pickup, a backyard pool, a spacious kitchen and a lounge that's perfect for movie-watching by the fireplace on chilly nights. It's five long blocks inland from Playa La Viuda, Punta del Diablo's southern beach.

Posada Nativos BOUTIQUE HOTEL **$$**
(☑099-641394; www.nativos.com.uy; cnr Santa Teresa & General San Martín; r US$80-160; ☜) Artist Eduardo Vigliola's labor of love, this boutique hotel incorporates gorgeous local stone and wood details, surrounded by landscaped grounds dotted with water lilies, papyrus, edible and medicinal plants, a small stream and a Japanese-style pond. The four-bedroom Casa Nativos out back, complete with living room and kitchen, doubles as part of the hotel and as a stand-alone vacation rental.

✖ Eating

In high season, simply stroll the beachfront for your pick of snack shacks by the dozen. Eateries listed below are among the few that remain open in winter. Another dependable year-round choice is the bar-restaurant at El Diablo Tranquilo hostel.

★ Resto-Pub 70 ITALIAN **$**
(mains UR$200-280; ☺12:30-4pm & 7:30-11pm Nov-Easter) Run by an Italian family from the Veneto, this portside eatery serves divine, reasonably priced homemade pasta such as *lasagne alle cipolle* (veggie lasagna with walnuts and caramelized onions), accompanied by UR$50 glasses of house wine. Afterwards, don't miss the *cantucci con vino dolce* (almond biscotti dipped in sweet wine) and *limoncino* (an artisanal liqueur made with fragrant Uruguayan lemons).

Empanada Stands EMPANADAS **$**
(Feria Artesanal, de los Pescadores s/n; empanadas UR$60; ☺10am-4pm daily Jan & Feb, Sat & Sun only Mar-Dec) Tucked in among the artisan's stalls down by the port, sisters Alba, Mónica and Noelia Acosta operate three no-frills stands that serve up Punta del Diablo's tastiest low-cost snack: hot-from-the-fryer empanadas filled with fish, mussels, meat, cheese, olives and other savory goodies.

Cero Stress INTERNATIONAL **$$**
(Av de los Pescadores; mains UR$290-450; ☺noon-5pm & 7:30pm-midnight; ☜☝) By far the greatest asset at this laid-back eatery is its outdoor deck, which offers amazing ocean views. It's the perfect place to sip a *caipirinha* (Brazilian cocktail with sugarcane alcohol) at sunset while contemplating your evening plans. There's also occasional live music.

Il Tano INTERNATIONAL **$$$**
(☑4477-2538, 096-589389; www.iltanocucina.com; cnr Calles 5 & 20; mains UR$340-550; ☺noon-3pm & 7-11pm) Punta del Diablo's classiest restaurant is this cozy house with wraparound porch, overlooking a pretty garden whose veggies and herbs complement the Italian-influenced menu of pasta, meat and seafood. Specialties include homemade shrimp-and-zucchini ravioli, ham-and-cheese agnolotti with a creamy wild mushroom sauce and pork shoulder with a sweet-and-sour sauce featuring fruit from local butiá palms.

❶ Information

Punta del Diablo has no ATMs except for the temporary ones set up briefly each summer. Bring cash with you; only some businesses accept credit cards, and the nearest banks are an hour away in Castillos (40km southwest) or Chuy (45km north).

❶ Getting There & Away

Rutas del Sol, COT and Cynsa all offer service to Punta del Diablo's dreary new bus terminal, 2.5km west of town. Between Christmas and Carnaval, all buses terminate here, leaving you with a five- to 10-minute shuttle (UR$25) or taxi (UR$100) ride into town. During the rest of the year, buses continue from the terminal to the town plaza near the waterfront.

Several direct buses run daily to Montevideo and Chuy on the Brazilian border; for other coastal destinations, you'll usually need to change buses in Castillos or Rocha.

Buses from Punta del Diablo

DESTINATION	COST (UR$)	TIME (HR)
Castillos	70	1
Chuy	88	1
Montevideo	530	5
Punta del Este	363	3
Rocha	177	1½

Parque Nacional Santa Teresa

This **national park** (☑4477-2101; sepae.web node.es; Ruta 9, Km302; ☺8am-8pm Dec-Mar, to 6pm Apr-Nov) **FREE**, 35km south of the Brazilian border, is administered by the army and attracts many Uruguayan and Brazilian visitors to its relatively uncrowded beaches.

It offers 2000 dispersed campsites (UR$170 to UR$220 per person) in eucalyptus and pine groves, a very small zoo and a plant conservatory. There's also a variety of four- to 10-person *cabañas* for rent; in January, prices range from UR$1400 for a basic four-person tent cabin with shared bathroom to UR$4800 for a fancier six-person oceanfront unit; between March and December these rates get slashed by 30% to 35%.

Buses from Punta del Diablo (UR$47, 15 minutes) will drop you off at Km302 on Ruta 9; from here, it's à flat 1km walk to the **Capatacía** (park headquarters), where there's a phone, post office, market, bakery and **restaurant** (dishes UR$130-390; ☺10am-10pm). Alternatively, walk north along the beach a couple of kilometers from Punta del Diablo to reach the park's southern edge at **Playa Grande**.

The park's star attraction, 4km north of park headquarters on Ruta 9, is the impressive hilltop fortress, **Fortaleza de Santa Teresa** (admission UR$30; ☺10am-7pm daily Dec-Mar, 10am-5pm Wed-Sun Apr-Nov), begun by the Portuguese in 1762 and finished by the Spaniards after they captured the site in 1793. At the park's northeastern corner is **Cerro Verde**, a coastal bluff providing important sea-turtle habitat, protected under Uruguay's SNAP program (p566).

Directly opposite the park entrance, on the west side of Ruta 9, a 5km dead-end dirt road leads to **Laguna Negra**, a vast lagoon where flamingos, capybaras and other wildlife can be spotted.

UNDERSTAND URUGUAY

Uruguay Today

The past decade has seen remarkable developments in Uruguayan culture and politics. After nearly two centuries of back-and-forth rule between the two traditional parties, Blancos and Colorados, Uruguayans elected the leftist Frente Amplio (Broad Front) to power in 2004 and again in 2009 and 2014. Over that span, the Frente Amplio government has presided over numerous social changes, including the legalization of marijuana, abortion and same-sex marriage.

Many of these changes occurred during the five-year term of José Mujica (2010–15), a former guerrilla who famously survived 13 years of imprisonment and torture during Uruguay's period of military rule. As president, Mujica (affectionately nicknamed 'Pepe') was best known for his grandfatherly style and humility, famously donating the majority of his salary to charities and refusing to live in the presidential palace. Mujica's tenure saw substantial decreases in poverty and income inequality and increases in per-capita income, and he left office with a 65% approval rating.

Uruguay's October 2014 elections returned the Frente Amplio to power, with former president Tabaré Vázquez reassuming the position he had held from 2005 to 2010. Under Vázquez' leadership, Uruguay has continued to buck the status quo, opting out of the massive TISA international trade agreement in late 2015 and making bold strides in the development of renewable energy; Uruguay already expects to have the world's highest percentage of wind power by the end of 2016 and aims to achieve total carbon neutrality by 2030.

History

Uruguay's aboriginal inhabitants were the Charrúa along the coast and the Guaraní north of the Río Negro. The hunting-and-gathering Charrúa discouraged European settlement for more than a century by killing Spanish explorer Juan de Solís and most of his party in 1516. In any event there was little to attract the Spanish, who valued these lowlands along the Río de la Plata only as an access route to gold and other quick riches further inland.

The first Europeans to settle on the Banda Oriental (Eastern Shore) were Jesuit missionaries near present-day Soriano, on the Río Uruguay. Next came the Portuguese, who established present-day Colonia in 1680 as a beachhead for smuggling goods into Buenos Aires. Spain responded by building its own citadel at Montevideo in 1726. The following century saw an ongoing struggle between Spain and Portugal for control of these lands along the eastern bank of the Río de la Plata.

Napoleon's invasion of the Iberian peninsula in the early 19th century precipitated a weakening of Spanish and Portuguese power and the emergence of strong independence movements throughout the region. Uruguay's homegrown national hero, José Gervasio Artigas, originally sought to form an alliance with several states in present-day Argentina and southern Brazil against the European powers, but he was ultimately forced to flee to Paraguay. There he regrouped and organized the famous '33 Orientales,' a feisty band of Uruguayan patriots under General Juan Lavalleja who, with Argentine support, crossed the Río Uruguay on April 19, 1825, and launched a campaign to liberate modern-day Uruguay from Brazilian control. In 1828, after three years' struggle, a British-mediated treaty established Uruguay as a small independent buffer between the emerging continental powers.

For several decades, Uruguay's independence remained fragile. There was civil war between Uruguay's two nascent political parties, the Colorados and the Blancos (named, respectively, for the red and white bands they wore); Argentina besieged Montevideo from 1838 to 1851; and Brazil was an ever-present threat. Things finally settled down in the second half of the 19th century, with region-wide recognition of Uruguay's independence and the emergence of a strong national economy based on beef and wool production.

In the early 20th century, visionary president José Batlle y Ordóñez introduced such innovations as pensions, farm credits, unemployment compensation and the eight-hour work day. State intervention led to the nationalization of many industries, the creation of others, and a new era of general prosperity. However, Batlle's reforms were largely financed through taxing the livestock sector, and when exports faltered mid-century, the welfare state crumbled. A period of military dictatorship began in the early 1970s, during which torture became routine, and more than 60,000 citizens were arbitrarily detained, before the 1980s brought a return to democratic traditions.

Culture

The one thing Uruguayans will tell you that they're *not* is anything like their *porteño* cousins across the water. Where Argentines can be brassy and sometimes arrogant, Uruguayans tend to be more humble and relaxed. Where the former have always been a regional superpower, the latter have always lived in the shadow of one. Those jokes about Punta del Este being a suburb of Buenos Aires don't go down so well on this side of the border. There are plenty of

FESTIVALS & EVENTS

Uruguay's Carnaval lasts for more than a month and is livelier than Argentina's. Semana Santa (Holy Week) has become known as Semana Turismo – many Uruguayans travel out of town, and finding accommodations is tricky during this time. Other noteworthy events include Tacuarembó's Fiesta de la Patria Gaucha and the nationwide Días del Patrimonio in early October, during which visitors are invited to tour Uruguay's most important historical and cultural monuments free of charge.

similarities, though: the near-universal appreciation for the arts, the Italian influence and the gaucho heritage.

Uruguayans like to take it easy and pride themselves on being the opposite of the hot-headed Latino type. Sunday's the day for family and friends, to throw half a cow on the *parrilla*, sit back and sip some *mate*. The population is well educated, and the gap between rich and poor is much less pronounced than in most other Latin American countries.

Population

With 3.3 million people, Uruguay is South America's smallest Spanish-speaking country. The population is predominately white (88%) with 8% mestizo (people with mixed Spanish and indigenous blood) and 4% black. Indigenous peoples are practically nonexistent. The average life expectancy (77 years) is one of Latin America's highest. The literacy rate is also high, at 98.5%, while population growth is a slow 0.27%. Population density is roughly 19 people per sq km.

Religion

Uruguay has more self-professed atheists per capita than any other Latin American country. According to a 2008 American Religious Identification Survey, only slightly more than half of Uruguayans consider themselves religious. Some 47% identify themselves as Roman Catholic, with 11% claiming affiliation with other Christian denominations. There's a small Jewish minority, numbering around 18,000.

Sports

Uruguayans, like just about all Latin Americans, are crazy about *fútbol* (soccer). Uruguay has won the World Cup twice, including the first tournament, played in Montevideo in 1930. The national team (known commonly as La Celeste) has continued to excel periodically at the international level, winning the 2011 Copa America and appearing in the 2014 World Cup in Brazil.

The most notable teams are Montevideo-based Nacional and Peñarol. If you go to a match between these two, sit on the sidelines, not behind the goal, unless you're up for some serious rowdiness.

Asociación Uruguayo de Fútbol (☑2400-7101; www.auf.org.uy; Guayabos 1531), in Montevideo, can provide information on matches and venues.

Arts

Despite its small population, Uruguay has an impressive literary and artistic tradition. The country's most famous philosopher and essayist is José Enrique Rodó, whose 1900 essay *Ariel,* contrasting North American and Latin American civilizations, is a classic of the country's literature. Major contemporary writers include Juan Carlos Onetti, Mario Benedetti and Eduardo Galeano. Theater is also popular and playwrights like Mauricio Rosencof are prominent.

Uruguay's most renowned painters are Juan Manuel Blanes, Pedro Figari and Joaquín Torres García, each of whom has a museum dedicated to their works in Montevideo. Sculptors include José Belloni, whose life-size bronzes can be seen in Montevideo's parks.

Tango is big in Montevideo – Uruguayans claim tango legend Carlos Gardel as a native son, and one of the best-known tangos, 'La Cumparsita,' was composed by Uruguayan Gerardo Matos Rodríguez. During Carnaval, Montevideo's streets reverberate to the energetic drumbeats of *candombe,* an African-derived rhythm brought to Uruguay by slaves from 1750 onwards, and to the sounds of *murgas,* satirical musical theater groups who perform throughout the city. On the contemporary scene, several Uruguayan rock bands have won a following on both sides of the Río de la Plata, including Buitres, La Vela Puerca and No Te Va Gustar.

Food & Drink

Uruguayan cuisine revolves around grilled meat. *Parrillas* (restaurants with big racks of meat roasting over a wood fire) are everywhere, and weekend *asados* (barbecues) are a national tradition. *Chivitos* (steak sandwiches piled high with toppings) are hugely popular, as are *chivitos al plato* (served with fried potatoes instead of bread). Vegetarians often have to content themselves with the ubiquitous pizza and pasta, although there are a few veggie restaurants lurking about. Seafood is excellent on the coast. Desserts are heavy on meringue, *dulce de leche* (milk caramel), burnt sugar and custard.

Tap water is OK to drink in most places. Uruguayan wines (especially tannats) are excellent, and local beers (Patricia, Pilsen and Zillertal) are reasonably good.

Uruguayans consume even more *mate* (a bitter tea-like beverage indigenous to South America) than Argentines. If you get the chance, try to acquire the taste – there's nothing like whiling away an afternoon with new-found friends passing around the *mate.*

In major tourist destinations such as Punta del Este and Colonia, restaurants charge *cubiertos* – small 'cover' charges that theoretically pay for the basket of bread offered before your meal.

ESSENTIAL FOOD & DRINK

Asado Uruguay's national gastronomic obsession, a mixed grill cooked over a wood fire, featuring various cuts of beef and pork, chorizo, *morcilla* (blood sausage) and more.

Chivito A cholesterol bomb of a steak sandwich piled high with bacon, ham, fried or boiled egg, cheese, lettuce, tomato, olives, pickles, peppers and mayonnaise.

Ñoquis The same potato dumplings the Italians call *gnocchi,* traditionally served on the 29th of the month.

Buñuelos de algas Savory seaweed fritters, a specialty along the coast of Rocha.

Tannat Uruguay's beloved, internationally acclaimed red wine.

Grappamiel Strong Italian-style grappa (grape brandy), sweetened and mellowed with honey.

Environment

Though one of South America's smallest countries, Uruguay is not so small by European standards. Its area of 176,215 sq km is greater than England and Wales combined, or slightly bigger than the US state of Florida.

Uruguay's two main ranges of interior hills are the Cuchilla de Haedo, west of Tacuarembó, and the Cuchilla Grande, south of Melo; neither exceeds 500m in height. West of Montevideo the terrain is more level. The Río Negro flowing through the center of the country forms a natural dividing line between north and south. The Atlantic coast has impressive beaches, dunes, headlands and lagoons. Uruguay's grasslands and forests resemble those of Argentina's pampas or southern Brazil, and patches of palm savanna persist in the east, along the Brazilian border.

The country is rich in birdlife, especially in the coastal lagoons of Rocha department. Most large land animals have disappeared, but the occasional ñandú (rhea) still races across northwestern Uruguay's grasslands. Whales, fur seals and sea lions are common along the coast.

SURVIVAL GUIDE

❶ Directory A-Z

ACCOMMODATIONS

Uruguay has an excellent network of hostels and campgrounds, especially along the Atlantic coast. Other low-end options include *hospedajes* (family homes) and *residenciales* (budget hotels).

Posadas (inns) are available in all price ranges and tend to be homier than hotels. Hotels are ranked from one to five stars, according to amenities.

Country *estancias turísticas* (marked with blue National Tourism Ministry signs) provide lodging on farms.

SLEEPING PRICE RANGES

The following price ranges refer to a double room with bathroom in high season. Breakfast is usually included in the price.

$ less than US$75

$$ US$75–150

$$$ more than US$150

EATING PRICE RANGES

The following price ranges are for a standard main course.

$ less than UR$300

$$ UR$300–450

$$$ more than UR$450

ACTIVITIES

Punta del Diablo, La Paloma, La Pedrera and Punta del Este all get excellent surfing waves, while Cabo Polonio and the coastal lagoons of Rocha department are great for whale and bird-watching, respectively. Punta del Este's beach scene is more upmarket, with activities such as parasailing, windsurfing and jet skiing.

Horseback riding is very popular in the interior and can be arranged on most tourist *estancias*.

ELECTRICITY

Uruguay uses the same plugs as Argentina.

EMERGENCIES

Dial ☑ 911 for emergency police and fire services.

EMBASSIES & CONSULATES

All of the below listings are in Montevideo:

Argentine Embassy Embassy (☑ 2902-8166; eurug.cancilleria.gov.ar; Cuareim 1470); Consulate (☑ 2902-8623; cmdeo.mrecic.gov.ar; WF Aldunate 1281)

Australian Consulate (☑ 2901-0743; www.dfat.gov.au/missions/countries/uy.html; Cerro Largo 1000)

Brazilian Embassy Embassy (☑ 2707-2119; montevideu.itamaraty.gov.br; Artigas 1394); Consulate (☑ 2901-2024; cgmontevideu.itamaraty.gov.br; Convención 1343, 6th fl)

Canadian Embassy (☑ 2902-2030; uruguay.gc.ca; Plaza Independencia 749, Oficina 102)

French Embassy (☑ 1705-0000; www.amba franceuruguay.org; Av Uruguay 853)

German Embassy (☑ 2902-5222; www.monte video.diplo.de; La Cumparsita 1435)

UK Embassy (☑ 2622-3630; ukinuruguay.fco.gov.uk; Marco Bruto 1073)

US Embassy (☑ 1770-2000; uruguay.usem bassy.gov; Lauro Muller 1776)

GAY & LESBIAN TRAVELERS

Uruguay is generally LGBTIQ-friendly. In 2008 Uruguay became the first Latin American country to recognize same-sex civil unions, and in 2013 same-sex marriage was legalized. In Montevideo, look for the pocket-sized **Friendly Map** (www.friendlymap.com.uy) listing GLBT-friendly businesses throughout the country.

HEALTH

No vaccinations are required for Uruguayan travel. Uruguay has a good public-health system, and tap water is generally safe to drink.

INSURANCE

Worldwide travel insurance is available at www.lonelyplanet.com/travel-insurance. You can buy, extend and claim online anytime – even if you're already on the road.

INTERNET ACCESS

Wi-fi zones and internet cafes are commonplace in cities and larger towns. Antel (state telephone company) offices sell SIM cards with reasonably priced data plans for unlocked phones, and also provide free wi-fi in many cases.

LEGAL MATTERS

Uruguay has some of Latin America's most lenient drug laws. Possession of small amounts of marijuana or other drugs for personal use has been decriminalized, but their sale remains illegal.

MONEY

Prices are in *pesos uruguayos* (UR$), the official Uruguayan currency. Banknote values are 20, 50, 100, 200, 500, 1000 and 2000. There are coins of one, two, five, 10 and 50 pesos.

US dollars are commonly accepted in major tourist hubs, where many accommodations quote US$ prices. However, beware of poor exchange rates at hotel desks. In many cases, you'll come out ahead paying in pesos. Away from the touristed areas, dollars are of limited use.

Unlike Argentina, Uruguay has no black or 'blue' market offering higher exchange rates for US and European banknotes.

ATMs

ATMs are widespread and in all but the smallest interior towns, getting cash with your ATM card is easy. Machines marked with the green Banred or blue Redbrou logo serve all major international banking networks. ATMs dispense bills in multiples of 100 pesos. Many also dispense US dollars, designated as US$, but only in multiples of US$100.

SET YOUR BUDGET

Budget hotel room UR$1200-1800

Chivito (Uruguayan steak sandwich) UR$155-330

Montevideo bus ride UR$26

1L bottle of local beer UR$150

Coffee UR$70

Credit Cards

Credit cards are widely accepted: most up-market hotels, restaurants and shops accept credit cards.

Money Changers

There are *casas de cambio* in Montevideo, Colonia, the Atlantic beach resorts and border towns such as Chuy. They typically keep longer hours than banks but may offer lower rates.

EXCHANGE RATES		
Argentina	AR$1	UR$2.13
Australia	A$1	UR$23.67
Canada	C$1	UR$24.17
Chile	CH$100	UR$4.60
Euro zone	€1	UR$35.10
Japan	¥100	UR$28.42
New Zealand	NZ$1	UR$21.37
UK	UK£1	UR$43.99
USA	US$1	UR$30.93

Tipping

➡ In restaurants, leave 10% of the bill.

➡ In taxis, round up the fare a few pesos.

OPENING HOURS

Banks 1-6pm Monday to Friday.

Bars, pubs & clubs 6pm-late. Things don't get seriously shaking until after midnight.

Restaurants noon-3pm & 8pm-midnight or later. If serving breakfast, open around 8am.

Shops 9am-1pm & 3-7pm Monday to Saturday. In larger cities, many stay open at lunchtime and/or Sundays.

POST

Correo Uruguayo (www.correo.com.uy), the national postal service, has offices throughout Uruguay.

PUBLIC HOLIDAYS

Año Nuevo (New Year's Day) January 1

Día de los Reyes (Epiphany) January 6

Viernes Santo/Pascua (Good Friday/Easter) March/April (dates vary)

Desembarco de los 33 (Return of the 33 Exiles) April 19; honors the exiles who returned to Uruguay in 1825 to liberate the country from Brazil with Argentine support

Día del Trabajador (Labor Day) May 1

Batalla de Las Piedras (Battle of Las Piedras) May 18; commemorates a major battle of the fight for independence

Natalicio de Artigas (Artigas' Birthday) June 19

Jura de la Constitución (Constitution Day) July 18

Día de la Independencia (Independence Day)
August 25
Día de la Raza (Columbus Day) October 12
Día de los Muertos (All Souls' Day)
November 2
Navidad (Christmas Day) December 25

TELEPHONE

Uruguay's country code is 📞 598. **Antel** (www.
antel.com.uy) is the state telephone company,
with offices in every town.

All Uruguayan landline numbers are eight
digits long, beginning with 2 for Montevideo
or 4 for elsewhere in the country. Cell (mobile)
phone numbers consist of a three-digit prefix
(most commonly 📞 099) followed by a six-digit
number. If dialing internationally, drop the leading zero.

Cell Phones

Three companies – **Antel** (www.antel.com.uy),
Claro (www.claro.com.uy) and **Movistar** (www.
movistar.com.uy) – provide cell-phone service
in Uruguay. Rather than use expensive roaming
plans, many travelers bring an unlocked cell
phone (or buy a cheap one here) and insert a
local pay-as-you-go SIM card. SIMs can readily
be purchased at Antel offices and recharged at
service stations, shopping malls and streetside
kiosks throughout Uruguay.

TIME

Uruguay Standard Time is three hours behind
GMT, same as in Argentina. Daylight-saving time
was abolished in 2015.

TOURIST INFORMATION

The **National Tourism Ministry** (Ministerio de
Turismo y Deporte; www.turismo.gub.uy) operates 10 offices around the country. It distributes
excellent free maps for each of Uruguay's 19
departments, along with specialized information
on *estancia* tourism, Carnaval, surfing and other
subjects of interest to travelers. Most towns also
have a muncipal tourist office on the plaza or at
the bus terminal.

TRAVELERS WITH DISABILITIES

Uruguay is slowly beginning to plan for travelers
with special needs. In Montevideo, for example,
you'll find newly constructed ramps and dedicated bathrooms in high-profile destinations
such as Plaza Independencia and Teatro Solís,
disabled access on some bus lines and a growing number of ATM machines for the visually
impaired. However, there's still a long way to
go. Spanish-language websites providing useful
resources for the disabled include pronadis.
mides.gub.uy, www.accesibilidad.gub.uy and
www.discapacidaduruguay.org.

VISAS

Nationals of Western Europe, Australia, the USA,
Canada and New Zealand automatically receive
a 90-day tourist card, renewable for another 90
days. Other nationals may require visas. For an
official list of current visa requirements by nationality, see migracion.minterior.gub.uy.

WOMEN TRAVELERS

Women are generally treated with respect, and
traveling alone is safer here than in many other
Latin American countries.

ℹ Getting There & Away

Most visitors cross by ferry from Buenos Aires,
arriving in Colonia, Montevideo or Carmelo. A few
airlines, including American, Iberia and Air Eu-
ropa, offer direct international flights to Montevideo; several others connect through Buenos Aires
or São Paulo. Land links include three international bridges across the Río Uruguay to Argentina,
and six main border crossings into Brazil.

Flights, cars and tours can be booked online at
lonelyplanet.com/bookings.

Border Crossings from Argentina

FROM	TO	ROUTE
Buenos Aires	Montevideo	Boat (Buquebus)
Buenos Aires	Carmelo	Boat (Cacciola)
Tigre	Colonia	Boat (Buquebus, Colonia Express, Seacat)
Gualeguaychú	Fray Bentos	Puente General San Martín (bridge)
Colón	Paysandú	Puente General Artigas (bridge)
Concordia	Salto	Represa Salto Grande (dam)
Concordia	Salto	Boat (Transporte Fluvial San Cristóbal)

Border Crossings from Brazil

FROM	TO	ROUTE
Aceguá	Aceguá	Hwy BR-153/UR-8
Barra do Quaraí	Bella Unión	Hwy BR-472/UR-3
Chuí	Chuy	Hwy BR-471/UR-9
Jaguarão	Río Branco	Hwy BR-116/UR-26
Quaraí	Artigas	Hwy BR-377/UR-30
Santana do Livramento	Rivera	Hwy BR-293/UR-5

ENTERING THE COUNTRY

Uruguay requires passports of all foreigners, except those from neighboring countries (who need only national identification cards).

AIR

Montevideo's **Carrasco International Airport** (p536) is the main port of entry. A few direct flights from Argentina and Brazil also serve **Punta del Este International Airport** (Aeropuerto de Punta del Este; ☑ 4255-9777; www.puntadeleste.aero).

Uruguay's new national airline **Alas Uruguay** (☑ 2710-4149; www.alasuruguay.com.uy) initiated service in December 2015, taking the place of former national carrier Pluna, which declared bankruptcy and ceased operations in July 2012.

LAND & SEA

Uruguay shares borders with the Argentine province of Entre Ríos and the southern Brazilian state of Rio Grande do Sul. Major highways and bus services are generally good, although buses from Montevideo to Buenos Aires are slower and less convenient than the ferries across the Río de la Plata. For Iguazú Falls, traveling via Argentina is faster, cheaper and more straightforward than traveling through Brazil.

❶ Getting Around

BUS

Buses are comfortable, the government-regulated fares are reasonable and distances are short. Many companies offer free wi-fi on board. In the few cities that lack terminals, all companies are within easy walking distance of each other, usually around the main plaza.

Reservations are unnecessary except during holiday periods. On peak travel dates a single company may run multiple departures at the same hour, in which case they'll mark a bus number on your ticket; check with the driver to make sure you're boarding the right bus, or you may find yourself in the 'right' seat on the wrong bus!

Most towns with central bus terminals have a reasonably priced left-luggage facility.

CAR & MOTORCYCLE

Visitors to Uruguay who are staying less than 90 days need only bring a valid driver's license from their home country. Uruguayan drivers are extremely considerate, and even bustling Montevideo is quite sedate compared with Buenos Aires.

Due to government regulation, all service stations, including the ubiquitous state-owned Ancap, charge the same price for fuel. Unleaded gasoline cost UR$42.50 a liter at the time of research.

Car Hire

Economy cars rent locally for upwards of UR$1500 a day in the high season, with tax and insurance included. Advance online bookings are often cheaper than in-country rentals. Most credit-card companies' automatic LDW (loss-damage-waiver) insurance covers rentals in Uruguay.

Road Rules & Hazards

Drivers are required to turn on their headlights during the daytime on all highways. In most towns, alternating one-way streets are the rule, with an arrow marking the allowed direction of travel.

Outside Montevideo, most intersections have neither a stop sign nor a traffic light; right of way is determined by who reaches the corner first. This can be nerve-racking to the uninitiated!

Main highways fanning out from Montevideo are generally in excellent condition, especially Ruta 1 to Colonia del Sacramento and Ruta 9 (the Interbalnearia) to Punta del Este. Outside the capital and coastal tourist areas, traffic is minimal and poses few problems, though some interior roads can be rough. Keep an eye out for livestock and wildlife.

Speed limits are clearly posted but rarely enforced. Arbitrary police stops are rare.

LOCAL TRANSPORTATION

Taxis, *remises* (radio-dispatched taxis) and local buses are similar to those in Argentina. Taxis are metered; between 10pm and 6am, and on Sundays and holidays, fares are 20% higher. There's a small additional charge for luggage, and passengers generally tip the driver by rounding fares up to the next multiple of five or 10 pesos. City bus service is excellent in Montevideo and other urban areas, while *micros* (minibuses) form the backbone of the local transit network in smaller coastal towns such as La Paloma.

Understand Argentina

Argentina Today

Argentina has two faces: it's a country that has harbored both prosperity and decline. Today inflation remains rampant and the economy continues to stumble, yet an economic comeback is always around the corner. A new president was sworn in after more than a decade of Kirchner presidential rule, bringing optimism and welcome change to the country. Meanwhile, Pope Francis continues to shake up the Catholic Church and status quo wherever he goes, but remains beloved by millions.

Best in Print

Kiss of the Spider Woman (Manuel Puig, 1976) Two prisoners and their developing relationship in a Buenos Aires prison; made into the Oscar-winning 1985 film.

In Patagonia (Bruce Chatwin, 1977) Evocative writing on Patagonia's history and mystique.

The Motorcycle Diaries (Ernesto Che Guevara et al, 1993) Based on the travel diary of the Argentine-born revolutionist.

And the Money Kept Rolling In (and Out) (Paul Blustein, 2005) How the IMF helped bankrupt Argentina.

Best on Film

La historia oficial (The Official Story, 1985) Oscar-winning film on the Dirty War.

Nueve reinas (Nine Queens, 2000) Two con men chasing the big score.

El secreto de sus ojos (The Secret in Their Eyes, 2009) Thriller that won the 2010 Oscar for Best Foreign Language Film.

Relatos salvajes (Wild Tales, 2014) Black comedy showcasing six short, entertaining stories.

A New Beginning

In December 2015 Mauricio Macri took over Argentina's presidential reins. He had been Buenos Aires' mayor since 2007 and was a former president of the Boca Juniors *fútbol* team. In a surprising run-off election he narrowly beat Cristina Kirchner's preferred candidate, Daniel Scioli, ending 12 years of Peronist-run government. Macri promised drastic economic changes, and he immediately started implementing them: controls over foreign currencies were abolished (essentially ending the 'blue' – ie black – market for US dollars), export taxes were lowered to boost agricultural trade, and thousands of redundant public-sector jobs were eliminated.

His idea is to encourage economic growth and foreign investment (once again) while reducing Argentina's immense deficit and, eventually, its unsustainable inflation rate. It's quite a difference from Cristina Kirchner's practices, which implemented heavy state intervention and spending, and used the country's central bank reserves to artificially prop up the peso. Macri also plans to strengthen ties with economic powers like Brazil and the USA, while cooling off relations with Iran and Venezuela, which Cristina had forged. His pro-business, free-market reform stances set him apart from his leftist, pro-government predecessor. Argentines asked for a radically different president – and they got one.

Economic Woes

Argentina's currency devaluation in 2002 caused surging demand for its suddenly cheap agricultural products. Helped along by skyrocketing government spending and strong growth in Brazil and China, this economic boom lasted through 2007 and revved up again in 2010. But high inflation, a stronger peso and lower commodity prices reined in the economy.

From October 2011, in an effort to curb capital heading overseas, the government required Argentines to substantiate their purchases of US dollars. This is what had created the black market for US dollars, which are highly sought after as a stable currency. And the real-estate market stalled, since purchases were pretty much always transacted in US dollars.

Economists believe that Macri's new government needs to reduce spending and control inflation, and that government policies must become more transparent to encourage both domestic and foreign investment. But only time will tell if Argentina's new president can kick-start the sluggish economy, which could very well continue to sputter or even worsen. However, there is a new optimism in the air – after all, many people believe that after hitting rock bottom, things can only go up. And considering the country has been through these cycles many times before, they have no choice but to take a ride on Argentina's economic roller-coaster once again.

Everyone Loves the Pope

After Cardinal Jorge Mario Bergoglio, the archbishop of Buenos Aires, was named pope in March 2013 he took the name Francis I. Not only was he the first pontiff to bear that moniker, he was also the first to hail from the Americas and the first to belong to the Jesuit order. It's a fair bet that he's also the first pope to have grown up drinking *mate,* tangoing at *milongas* and ardently supporting the San Lorenzo *fútbol* club.

Bergoglio was a humble man who had eschewed the archbishop's palace in Olivos, remaining in his modest apartment and getting around Buenos Aires by bus and the Subte. As pope he has continued these habits, emulating his namesake and personal hero, the saint from Assisi who once renounced all worldly possessions. This humility, coupled with the very personable humanity Francis displays, has made him an extremely popular pontiff.

Over the past few years, however, some of Francis' declarations have been controversial with the religious establishment and certain political parties. He has criticized capitalism, practically supported evolution and highlighted the need to protect the natural environment. He's also noted the importance of women's roles in the church, and while he opposes same-sex marriage, he does believe that homosexuals should be treated with love and respect.

Many Catholics speak of feeling 'understood' by Francis, and his popularity extends beyond the faithful. After decades of suspected corruption, sex-abuse scandals and widening parishioner dissatisfaction, the Catholic Church here has finally gained back its goodly reputation.

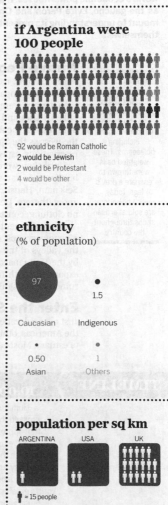

AREA: 2.8 MILLION SQ KM

POPULATION: 43 MILLION

GDP: US$540 BILLION

INFLATION: 26% (UNOFFICIAL)

UNEMPLOYMENT RATE: 7.5%

if Argentina were 100 people

92 would be Roman Catholic
2 would be Jewish
2 would be Protestant
4 would be other

ethnicity
(% of population)

97 Caucasian

1.5 Indigenous

0.50 Asian

1 Others

population per sq km

ARGENTINA   USA   UK

= 15 people

History

Like all Latin American countries, Argentina has a tumultuous history, one tainted by periods of despotic rule, corruption and hard times. But its history is also illustrious, the story of a country that fought off Spanish colonial rule and was once among the world's economic powerhouses. It's a country that gave birth to international icons such as the gaucho, Evita Perón and Che Guevara. Understanding Argentina's past is paramount to understanding its present and, most importantly, to understanding Argentines themselves.

Argentina's native peoples hunted guanaco and ñandú (a large bird resembling an emu) with various weapons, including *boleadoras*. These weighted balls were thrown to ensnare a prey's legs. Today, replica *boleadoras* are sold at artisan shops throughout the country.

Native Peoples

Many different native peoples ranged throughout what became Argentina. On the pampas lived the hunter-gatherer Querandí, and in the north the Guaraní were semisedentary agriculturalists and fishermen. In the Lake District and Patagonia, the Pehuenches and Puelches gathered the pine nuts of the araucaria, while the Mapuche entered the region from the west as the Spanish pushed south. Today there are several Mapuche reservations, especially in the area around Junín de los Andes.

Until they were wiped out by Europeans, there were indigenous inhabitants as far south as Tierra del Fuego (Land of Fire), where the Selk'nam, Haush, Yahgan and Alacaluf peoples lived as mobile hunters and gatherers. Despite frequently inclement weather, they wore little or no clothing; constant fires kept them warm and gave the region its name.

Of all of Argentina, the northwest was the most developed. Several indigenous groups, notably the Diaguita, practiced irrigated agriculture in the valleys of the eastern Andean foothills. Inhabitants were influenced by the Tiahuanaco empire of Bolivia and by the great Inca empire, which expanded south from Peru from the early 1480s. In Salta province the ruined city of Quilmes is one of the best-preserved pre-Incan sites.

Enter the Spanish

Just over a decade after Christopher Columbus accidentally encountered the Americas, other European explorers began probing the Río de la Plata estuary. Most early explorations of the area were motivated by rumors

TIMELINE	10,000 BC	7370 BC	4000 BC
	Humans, having crossed the Bering Strait approximately 20,000 years earlier, finally reach the area of modern-day Argentina. The close of one of the world's greatest human migrations nears.	Toldense culture makes its first paintings of hands inside Patagonia's famous Cueva de las Manos. The paintings prove humans inhabited the region this far back.	The indigenous Yahgan, later referred to as Fuegians by the English-speaking world, begin populating the southernmost islands of Tierra del Fuego. Humans could migrate no further south.

of vast quantities of silver. Spaniard Sebastian Cabot optimistically named the river Río de la Plata (River of Silver), and to drive the rumors home, part of the new territory was even given the Latin name for silver (*argentum*). But the mineral riches that the Spanish found in the Inca empire of Peru never panned out in this misnamed land.

The first real attempt at establishing a permanent settlement on the estuary was made in 1536, by Spanish aristocrat Pedro de Mendoza. He landed at present-day Buenos Aires, but after the colonists tried pilfering food from the indigenous Querandí, the natives turned on them violently. Within four years Mendoza fled back to Spain without a lick of silver, and the detachment of troops he left behind headed upriver to the gentler environs of Asunción, present-day capital of Paraguay.

Northwest Supremacy

Although Spanish forces re-established Buenos Aires by 1580, it remained a backwater in comparison to Andean settlements founded by a separate and more successful Spanish contingency moving south from Alto Perú (now Bolivia). With ties to the colonial stronghold of Lima and financed by the bonanza silver mine at Potosí, the Spanish founded some two dozen cities as far south as Mendoza (1561) during the latter half of the 16th century.

The two most important centers were Tucumán (founded in 1565) and Córdoba (1573). Tucumán lay in the heart of a rich agricultural region and supplied Alto Perú with grains, cotton and livestock. Córdoba became an important educational center, and Jesuit missionaries established *estancias* (ranches) in the sierras to supply Alto Perú with mules, foodstuffs and wine. Córdoba's Manzana Jesuítica (Jesuit Block) is now the finest preserved group of colonial buildings in the country, and several Jesuit *estancias* in the Central Sierras are also preserved. These sites, along with the central plazas of Salta (founded in 1582), boast the finest colonial architecture.

Buenos Aires: Bootlegger to Boomtown

As the northwest prospered, Buenos Aires suffered the Crown's harsh restrictions on trade for nearly 200 years. But because the port was ideal for trade, frustrated merchants turned to smuggling, and contraband trade with Portuguese Brazil and nonpeninsular European powers flourished. The wealth passing through the city fueled its initial growth.

With the decline of silver mining at Potosí in the late 18th century, the Spanish Crown was forced to recognize Buenos Aires' importance for direct transatlantic trade. Relaxing its restrictions, Spain made Buenos Aires the capital of the new viceroyalty of the Río de la Plata – which included Paraguay, Uruguay and the mines at Potosí – in 1776.

The Mission (1986), starring Robert De Niro and Jeremy Irons, is an epic film about the Jesuit missions and missionaries in 18th-century South America. It's the perfect kickoff for a trip to northern Argentina's missions.

AD 1480s	1536	1553	1561
The Inca empire expands into present-day Argentina's Andean northwest. At the time, the region was inhabited by Argentina's most advanced indigenous cultures, including the Diaguita and Tafí.	Pedro de Mendoza establishes Puerto Nuestra Señora Santa María del Buen Aire on the Río de la Plata. But the Spaniards anger the indigenous Querandí, who soon drive the settlers out.	Francisco de Aguirre establishes Santiago del Estero, furthering Spain's expansion into present-day Argentina from Alto Perú. Today the city is the country's oldest permanent settlement.	The city of Mendoza is founded by Spaniards during their push to establish access to the Río de la Plata, where Spanish ships could deliver more troops and supplies.

The new viceroyalty had internal squabbles over trade and control issues, but when the British raided the city in 1806 and again in 1807 (in an attempt to seize control of Spanish colonies during the Napoleonic Wars), the response was unified. Locals rallied against the invaders without Spanish help and chased them out of town.

The late 18th century also saw the emergence of the gauchos of the pampas. The South American counterpart to North America's cowboys, they hunted wild cattle and broke in wild horses whose numbers had multiplied after being left behind by expeditions on the Río de la Plata.

One of the best-known contemporary accounts of post-independence Argentina is Domingo Faustino Sarmiento's *Life in the Argentine Republic in the Days of the Tyrants* (1868). Also superb is his seminal classic, *Facundo, or Civilization and Barbarism* (1845).

Independence & Infighting

Toward the end of the 18th century, criollos (Argentine-born colonists) became increasingly dissatisfied and impatient with Spanish authority. The expulsion of British troops from Buenos Aires gave the people of the Río de la Plata new confidence in their ability to stand alone. After Napoleon invaded Spain in 1808, Buenos Aires finally declared its independence on May 25, 1810.

Independence movements throughout South America soon united to expel Spain from the continent by the 1820s. Under the leadership of General José de San Martín and others, the United Provinces of the Río de la Plata (the direct forerunner of the Argentine Republic) declared formal independence at Tucumán on July 9, 1816.

Despite achieving independence, the provinces were united in name only. With a lack of any effective central authority, regional disparities within Argentina – formerly obscured by Spanish rule – became more obvious. This resulted in the rise of the *caudillos* (local strongmen), who resisted Buenos Aires as strongly as Buenos Aires had resisted Spain.

Argentine politics was divided between the Federalists of the interior, who advocated provincial autonomy, and the Unitarists of Buenos Aires, who upheld the city's central authority. For almost 20 years bloody conflicts between the two factions left the country nearly exhausted.

The Reign of Rosas

In the first half of the 19th century Juan Manuel de Rosas came to prominence as a *caudillo* in Buenos Aires province, representing the interests of rural elites and landowners. He became governor of the province in 1829 and, while he championed the Federalist cause, he also helped centralize political power in Buenos Aires and proclaimed that all international trade be funneled through the capital. His reign lasted more than 20 years (to 1852), and he set ominous precedents in Argentine political life, creating the infamous mazorca (his ruthless political police force) and institutionalizing torture.

1573	1580	1609	1767
The city of Córdoba is founded by Tucumán Governor Jerónimo Luis de Cabrera, establishing an important link on the trade routes between Chile and Alto Perú.	Buenos Aires is re-established by Spanish forces, but the city remains a backwater for years, in comparison with the growing strongholds of Mendoza, Tucumán and Santiago del Estero.	Jesuits begin building missions in northeast Argentina, including San Ignacio Miní (1610), Loreto (1632) and Santa Ana (1633), concentrating the indigenous Guaraní into settlements known as *reducciones*.	The Spanish Crown expels the Jesuits from all of New Spain, and the mission communities decline rapidly.

Under Rosas, Buenos Aires continued to dominate the new country, but his extremism turned many against him, including some of his strongest allies. Finally, in 1852 a rival *caudillo* named Justo José de Urquiza (once a staunch supporter of Rosas) organized a powerful army and forced Rosas from power. Urquiza's first task was to draw up a constitution, which was formalized by a convention in Santa Fe on May 1, 1853.

The Fleeting Golden Age

Elected the Republic of Argentina's first official president in 1862, Bartolomé Mitre was concerned with building the nation and establishing infrastructure. His goals, however, were subsumed by the War of the Triple Alliance (or Paraguayan War), which lasted from 1864 to 1870. Not until Domingo Faustino Sarmiento, an educator and journalist from San Juan, became president did progress in Argentina really kick in.

Buenos Aires' economy boomed and immigrants poured in from Spain, Italy, Germany and Eastern Europe. The new residents worked in the port area, lived tightly in the tenement buildings and developed Buenos Aires' famous dance – the tango – in the brothels and smoky nightclubs of the port. Elsewhere in the country, Basque and Irish refugees became the first shepherds, as both sheep numbers and wool exports increased nearly tenfold between 1850 and 1880.

Still, much of the southern pampas and Patagonia were inaccessible for settlers because of resistance from indigenous Mapuche and Tehueche. In 1878 General Julio Argentino Roca carried out an extermination campaign against the indigenous people, in what is known as the Conquista del Desierto (Conquest of the Desert). The campaign doubled the area under state control and opened Patagonia to settlement and sheep.

By the turn of the 20th century Argentina had a highly developed rail network (financed largely by British capital), fanning out from Buenos Aires in all directions. Still, the dark cloud of a vulnerable economy loomed. Industry could not absorb all the immigration, labor unrest grew and imports surpassed exports. Finally, with the onset of the worldwide Great Depression, the military took power under conditions of considerable social unrest. An obscure but oddly visionary colonel, Juan Domingo Perón, was the first leader to try to come to grips with the country's economic crisis.

Tomás Eloy Martínez' The Perón Novel (1998) is a fascinating, fictionalized version of the life of ex-president Juan Perón, culminating in his return to Buenos Aires in 1973.

1776	1806–07	May 25, 1810	July 9, 1816
Spain names Buenos Aires the capital of the new viceroyalty of the Río de la Plata. The territory includes the areas of present-day Paraguay, Uruguay and the mines at Potosí (Bolivia).	Attempting to seize control of Spanish colonies, British forces raid Buenos Aires in 1806 and in 1807. Buenos Aires militias defeat British troops without Spain's help, which kindles ideas of independence.	Buenos Aires declares its independence from Spain, although actual independence is still several years off. The city names the Plaza de Mayo in honor of the event.	After successful independence movements throughout South America, the United Provinces of the Río de la Plata (Argentina's forerunner) declares formal independence from Spain at Tucumán.

Juan Perón

Juan Perón emerged in the 1940s to become Argentina's most revered, as well as most despised, political figure. He first came to national prominence as head of the National Department of Labor, after a 1943 military coup toppled civilian rule. With the help of his second wife Eva Duarte (Evita), he ran for and won the presidency in 1946.

During previous sojourns in fascist Italy and Nazi Germany, Perón had grasped the importance of spectacle in public life and also developed his own brand of watered-down Mussolini-style fascism. He held massive rallies from the balcony of the Casa Rosada, with the equally charismatic

EVITA, LADY OF HOPE

'I will come again, and I will be millions.'
Eva Perón, 1952

From her humble origins in the pampas, to her rise to power beside President Juan Perón, María Eva Duarte de Perón is one of the most revered political figures on the planet. Known affectionately to all as Evita, she is Argentina's beloved First Lady, in some ways even eclipsing the legacy of her husband, who governed Argentina from 1946 to 1955.

At the age of 15 Eva Duarte left her hometown of Junín for Buenos Aires. She was looking for work as an actor, but eventually landed a job in radio. Her big chance came in 1944, when she attended a benefit at Buenos Aires' Luna Park. Here Duarte met Colonel Juan Perón, who fell in love with her; they were married in 1945.

Shortly after Perón won the presidency in 1946, Evita went to work in the office of the Department of Labor and Welfare. During Perón's two terms, Evita empowered her husband both through her charisma and by reaching out to the nation's poor, who came to love her dearly. She built housing for the poor, created programs for children, and distributed clothing and food items to needy families. She campaigned for the aged, offered health services to the poor and advocated for a law extending suffrage to women.

Perón won his second term in 1952, but that same year Evita – at age 33 and at the height of her popularity – died of cancer. It was a blow to Argentina and her husband's presidency.

Although remembered for extending social justice to those she called the country's *descamisados* (shirtless ones), Evita and her husband ruled with an iron fist. They jailed opposition leaders and newspapers, and banned *Time* magazine when it referred to her as an 'illegitimate child.' However, there is no denying the extent to which she empowered women at all levels of Argentine society and helped the country's poor.

Today Evita enjoys near-saint status. Get to know her at Museo Evita, or visit her tomb in the Recoleta cemetery; both are in Buenos Aires. You can also read her ghostwritten autobiography *La razón de mi vida* (My Mission in Life, 1951).

1829	1852	1862	1864–70
Federalist *caudillo* Juan Manuel de Rosas becomes governor of Buenos Aires province and de facto ruler of the Argentine Confederation. He rules with an iron fist for more than 20 years.	Federalist and former Rosas ally Justo José de Urquiza defeats Rosas at the Battle of Caseros and, in 1853, draws up Argentina's first constitution.	Bartolomé Mitre is elected president of the newly titled Republic of Argentina and strives to modernize the country by expanding the railway network, creating a national army and postal system, and more.	The War of the Triple Alliance is fought between Paraguay and the allied countries of Argentina, Brazil and Uruguay. Paraguay is defeated and loses territory.

Evita at his side. Although they ruled by decree rather than consent, the Peróns legitimized the trade-union movement, extended political rights to working-class people, secured voting rights for women and made university education available to any capable individual. Of course, many of these social policies made him disliked by conservatives and the rich classes.

Economic hardship and inflation undermined Juan Perón's second presidency in 1952, and Evita's death the same year dealt a blow to both the country and the president's popularity. In 1955 a military coup sent him into exile in Spain. Thirty years of catastrophic military rule would follow.

During his exile, Perón plotted his return to Argentina. In the late 1960s increasing economic problems, strikes, political kidnappings and guerrilla warfare marked Argentine political life. In the midst of these events, Perón returned to Argentina and was voted president again in 1973; however, after an 18-year exile, there was no substance to his rule. Chronically ill, Perón died in mid-1974, leaving a fragmented country to his ill-qualified third wife, Isabel.

The Dirty War & the Disappeared

In the late 1960s and early '70s, antigovernment feeling was rife and street protests often exploded into all-out riots. Armed guerrilla organizations emerged as radical opponents of the military, the oligarchies and US influence in Latin America. With increasing official corruption exacerbating Isabel Perón's incompetence, Argentina found itself plunged into chaos.

On March 24, 1976, a military coup led by army general Jorge Rafael Videla took control of the Argentine state apparatus and ushered in a period of terror and brutality. Videla's sworn aim was to crush the guerrilla movements and restore social order. During what the regime euphemistically labeled the Process of National Reorganization (known as 'El Proceso'), security forces went about the country arresting, torturing and killing anyone on their hit list of suspected leftists.

During the period between 1976 and 1983, often referred to as the Guerra Sucia (Dirty War) human-rights groups estimate that 10,000 to 30,000 people 'disappeared.' Ironically, the Dirty War ended only when the Argentine military attempted a real military operation: liberating the Falkland Islands (Islas Malvinas) from British rule.

The Falklands War

In late 1981 General Leopoldo Galtieri assumed the role of president. To stay in power amid a faltering economy and mass social unrest, Galtieri played the nationalist card and launched an invasion in April 1982 to dislodge the British from the Falkland Islands, which had been claimed by Argentina as its own Islas Malvinas for nearly 150 years.

Nunca más (Never Again, 1984), the official report of the National Commission on the Disappeared, systematically details military abuses from 1976 to 1983 during Argentina's Dirty War.

The Falklands War is still a somewhat touchy subject in Argentina. If the subject comes up, try to call them the 'Malvinas' instead of the 'Falklands,' as many Argentines have been taught from a young age that these islands have always belonged to Argentina.

1865	1868	1869–95	1926
More than 150 Welsh immigrants traveling aboard the clipper *Mimosa* land in Patagonia and establish Argentina's first Welsh colony in the province of Chubut.	Domingo Faustino Sarmiento, an educator and journalist from San Juan, is elected president. He encourages immigration to Argentina, ramps up public education and pushes to Europeanize the country.	The Argentine economy booms, immigration skyrockets as Italian and Spanish immigrants flood in, and Buenos Aires' population grows from 90,000 to 670,000. The tango emerges in Buenos Aires.	Novelist and poet Ricardo Güiraldes publishes *Don Segundo Sombra*, a classic work of gaucho literature evoking the spirit of the gaucho and its impact on Argentine society.

LAS MADRES DE LA PLAZA DE MAYO

In 1977 after a year of brutal human-rights violations under the leadership of General Jorge Rafael Videla, 14 mothers marched into the Plaza de Mayo in Buenos Aires. They did this despite the military government's ban on public gatherings and despite its reputation for torturing and killing anyone it considered dissident. The mothers, wearing their now-iconic white head scarves, demanded information about their missing children, who had 'disappeared' as part of the government's efforts to quash political opposition.

The group, which took on the name Las Madres de la Plaza de Mayo (The Mothers of Plaza de Mayo), developed into a powerful social movement and was the only political organization that overtly challenged the military government. Las Madres were particularly effective as they carried out their struggle under the banner of motherhood, which made them relatively unassailable in Argentine culture. Their movement showed the power of women – at least in a traditional role – in Argentine culture, and they are generally credited with helping to kick-start the re-establishment of the country's civil society.

After Argentina's return to civilian rule in 1983, thousands of Argentines were still unaccounted for, and Las Madres continued their marches and their demands for information and retribution. In 1986 Las Madres split into two factions. One group, known as the Línea Fundadora (Founding Line), dedicated itself to recovering the remains of the disappeared and to bringing military perpetrators to justice. The other, known as the Asociación Madres de Plaza de Mayo, held its last yearly protest in January 2006, saying it no longer had an enemy in the presidential seat. Línea Fundadora, however, still holds a silent vigil every Thursday afternoon in remembrance of the disappeared – and to protest other social causes.

And there is hope: in 2014, one of the most famous and respected grandmothers, Estela Carlotta, finally found her grandson after 36 years of searching. Argentina cried with her in joy – and perhaps in the hope of more future reunions.

However, Galtieri underestimated the determined response of British Prime Minister Margaret Thatcher. After only 74 days Argentina's ill-trained, poorly motivated and mostly teenaged forces surrendered ignominiously. The military regime collapsed, and in 1983 Argentines elected civilian Raúl Alfonsín to the presidency.

Aftermath of the Dirty War

In his successful 1983 presidential campaign, Alfonsín pledged to prosecute military officers responsible for human-rights violations during the Dirty War. He convicted high-ranking junta officials for kidnapping, torture and homicide, but when the government attempted to try junior officers, these officers responded with uprisings in several different parts of the country. The timid administration succumbed to military

1946	1952	1955	1976–83
Juan Perón is elected president and makes changes to the Argentine political structure. Evita embarks on her social-assistance programs to help lower-class women and children.	Eva Perón dies of cancer on July 26 at age 33, one year into her husband's second term as president. Her death would severely weaken the political might of her husband.	After the economy slides into recession President Perón loses further political clout and is finally thrown from the presidency and exiled to Spain after another military coup.	Under the leadership of General Jorge Videla, a military junta takes control of Argentina, launching the country into the Dirty War. In eight years an estimated 30,000 people 'disappear.'

demands and produced the Ley de la Obediencia Debida (Law of Due Obedience), allowing lower-ranking officers to use the defense that they were following orders, as well as the Ley de Punto Final (Full Stop Law), declaring dates beyond which no criminal or civil prosecutions could take place. At the time these measures eliminated prosecutions of notorious individuals; in 2003, however, they were repealed. Dirty War crime cases have since been reopened, and in recent years several officers have been convicted for Dirty War crimes. Despite these arrests, many of the leaders of El Proceso remain free, both in Argentina and abroad.

The Menem Years

Carlos Saúl Menem was elected president in 1989, and quickly embarked on a period of radical free-market reform. In pegging the peso to the US dollar, he effectively created a period of false economic stability, one that would create a great deal of upward mobility among Argentina's middle class. However, his policies – which included privatization of state-owned companies – are widely blamed for Argentina's economic collapse in 2002, when the overvalued peso was considerably devalued.

Menem's presidency ran until 1999, and in 2003 he made another presidential bid – only to withdraw after the first round. He then became a senator for his home province of La Rioja in 2005 (but two years later failed to win the governorship). All the while, Menem's post-presidential career has been characterized by scandals. In 2001 he was charged with illegally dealing arms to Croatia and Ecuador; after five months of judicial investigation, the charges were dropped (in 2008 the charges were reinstated, though he was later acquitted). In 2009 he was indicted for bribery and obstruction of justice in the 1994 bombing of AMIA, a Jewish community center in Buenos Aires. That trial is still pending, though in December 2015 he was sentenced to 4½ years in prison for embezzling public funds back in the '90s. It appears Menem's golden political years are over.

'La Crisis'

Fernando de la Rua succeeded Menem in the 1999 elections, inheriting an unstable economy and US$114 billion in foreign debt. With the Argentine peso pegged to the US dollar, Argentina was unable to compete on the international market and exports slumped. A further decline in international prices of agricultural products pummeled the Argentine economy, which depended heavily on farm-product exports.

By 2001 the Argentine economy teetered on the brink of collapse, and the administration, with Minister of Economy Domingo Cavallo at the wheel, took measures to end deficit spending and slash state spending. After attempted debt swaps and talk of devaluing the peso, middle-class

Hectór Olivera's 1983 film *Funny Dirty Little War* is an unsettling but excellent black comedy set in a fictitious town just before the 1976 military coup.

Carlos Menem's Syrian ancestry earned him the nickname 'El Turco' (The Turk). And in 2001 he married Cecilia Bolocco, a former Miss Universe who was 35 years his junior; they're now divorced.

1982	1983	1989	1999–2000
With the economy on the brink of collapse once again, General Leopoldo Galtieri invades the Falkland Islands/Islas Malvinas, unleashing a wave of nationalism and distracting the country from its problems.	After the failure of the Falklands War and with an economy on the skids, Raúl Alfonsín is elected the first civilian leader of the country since 1976.	Peronist Carlos Menem succeeds Alfonsín as president and overcomes the hyperinflation that reached nearly 200% per month by instituting free-market reforms.	Fernando de la Rua succeeds Menem as president, inheriting a failing economy. Agricultural exports slump and strikes begin throughout the country. The IMF grants Argentina US$40 million in aid.

Argentines began emptying their bank accounts. Cavallo responded by placing a cap of US$250 per week on withdrawals, but it was the beginning of the end.

By mid-December unemployment hit 18.3% and unions began a nationwide strike. Things came to a head on December 20 when middle-class Argentines took to the streets in protest of de la Rua's handling of the economic situation. Rioting spread throughout the country and President de la Rua resigned. Three interim presidents had resigned by the time Eduardo Duhalde took office in January 2002, becoming the fifth president in two weeks. Duhalde devalued the peso and announced that Argentina would default on US$140 billion in foreign debt, the biggest default in world history.

Enter Néstor Kirchner

Duhalde's Minister of Economy, Roberto Lavagna, negotiated a deal with the IMF in which Argentina would pay only the interest on its debts. Simultaneously, devaluation of the peso meant that Argentina's products were suddenly affordable on the world market, and by 2003 exports were booming. The surge was great for the country's GNP, but prices at home skyrocketed, plunging more of Argentina's already shaken middle class into poverty.

A presidential election was finally held in April 2003, and Santa Cruz Governor Néstor Kirchner emerged victoriously after his opponent, former president Carlos Menem, bowed out of the election.

By the end of his term in 2007, Kirchner had become one of Argentina's most popular presidents. He reversed amnesty laws that protected members of the 1976–83 junta against being charged for atrocities committed during the Dirty War. He took a heavy stance against government corruption and steered the economy away from strict alignment with the US (realigning it with that of Argentina's South American neighbors). And in 2005 he paid off Argentina's entire debt to the IMF in a single payment. By the end of Kirchner's presidency in 2007, unemployment had fallen to just under 9% – from a high of nearly 25% in 2002.

But not everything was bread and roses. The fact that Argentina had repaid its debt was fantastic news indeed, but economic stability didn't necessarily follow. In fact, a series of problems ensued during Kirchner's presidency: high inflation rates caused by a growing energy shortage, unequal distribution of wealth, and a rising breach between rich and poor that was slowly obliterating the middle class.

However, things were going well enough for Kirchner. When the presidential seat was up for grabs in 2007, Argentines expressed their satisfaction with Kirchner's policies by electing his wife, well-known Senator

2002	2003	2007	2010
Interim president Eduardo Duhalde devalues the peso, and Argentina defaults on a US$140 billion international debt (US$800 million owed to the World Bank), the largest default in history.	Néstor Kirchner is elected president of Argentina after Carlos Menem bows out of the presidential race, despite winning more votes in the first round of elections.	Former First Lady Cristina Fernández de Kirchner is elected president.	Néstor Kirchner dies suddenly, dealing a serious blow to the Kirchner dynasty. Many thought he would run for president in 2011, and very likely win.

Cristina Fernández de Kirchner, as president. Cristina won the presidency with a whopping 22% margin over her nearest challenger and became Argentina's first elected female president.

The Trials & Tribulations of Cristina

When Néstor Kirchner stepped aside in favor of his wife's candidacy for the presidential race, many started wondering: would 'Queen Cristina' (as she was often called due to her regal comportment) be just a puppet for her husband, who intended to rule behind the scenes?

Weak opposition and her husband's enduring clout were some of the reasons for Cristina's clear-cut victory, despite the lack of straightforward policies during her campaign. While this was not the first time Argentina had had a female head of state (Isabel Perón held a brief presidency by inheriting her husband's term), Cristina was the first woman to be elected president by popular vote in Argentina. As a lawyer and senator she was often compared to Hillary Clinton; as a fashion-conscious political figure with a penchant for chic dresses and designer bags, she also evoked memories of Evita.

Cristina's tumultuous presidency was laced with scandals, unpopular decisions and roller-coaster approval ratings, along with inflation unofficially estimated at up to 30%. Yet her presidency also saw some positive sides, including a stronger economy during the first part of her tenure, the strengthening of certain social programs and the legalization of same-sex marriage in July 2010.

On October 27, 2010, Cristina's presidency was dealt a serious blow when Néstor Kirchner died suddenly of a heart attack. As Néstor was expected to run for the presidency in 2011, this was widely seen as a disaster for the Kirchner dynasty. But the country rallied around Cristina's sorrow, and her popularity in early 2011 remained high enough that she ran for office again and was easily re-elected. She had run on a platform that appealed to the populist vote, promising to raise incomes, restore industry and maintain Argentina's economic boom. Her approach worked like a charm, but her acclaim wasn't to last.

At least two terms came about due to Argentina's economic crisis: *el corralito* (a small enclosure) refers to the cap placed on cash withdrawals from bank accounts during 'La Crisis,' while *cacerolazo* (from the word *cacerola*, meaning pan) is the street protest where angry people bang pots and pans.

HISTORY THE TRIALS & TRIBULATIONS OF CRISTINA

2011	2012	January 2015	November 2015
Cristina Kirchner wins the presidential re-election race; a few months later she undergoes successful surgery after a cancer scare.	Inflation is running at about 25%, though the government's official figures say that it's less than 10%. Kirchner passes a law restricting the sale of US dollars, creating huge black-market demand.	State prosecutor Alberto Nisman is found shot dead in his apartment. He had accused Cristina Kirchner of covering up 1994's AMIA (Jewish community center) bombing investigation.	Buenos Aires mayor Mauricio Macri wins the presidential election against Daniel Scioli, in Argentina's first-ever presidential run-off vote.

Life in Argentina

Throughout Latin America, Argentines endure a reputation for being cocky. 'How does an Argentine commit suicide?' goes the old joke. 'By jumping off his ego.' And while you might find a nugget of truth in this stereotype – which applies mainly to *porteños* (Buenos Aires' residents) – you'll also realize that a warm and gregarious social nature more accurately defines the Argentine psyche.

Regional Identity

Opinionated, brash and passionate, Argentines are quick to engage in conversation and will talk after dinner or over coffee until the wee hours of the morning. But they also hold a subtle broodiness to their nature. This stems from a pessimism they've acquired watching their country, one of the world's economic powerhouses during the late 19th and early 20th centuries, descend into a morass of international debt. They've endured military coups and severe government repression, while witnessing their beloved Argentina plundered by corrupt politicians. But melancholy is just a part of the picture. Add everything together and you get a people who are fun, fiery and proud. And you'll come to love them for it.

> Argentines almost always exchange a kiss on the cheek in greeting – even between men. In formal and business situations, though, it is better to go with a handshake.

Lifestyle

Although Buenos Aires holds more than one-third of the country's population, it's surprisingly unlike the rest of Argentina or, for that matter, much of Latin America. As is the case throughout the country, one's lifestyle in the capital depends mostly on money. A modern flat rented by a young advertising creative in Buenos Aires' Las Cañitas neighborhood differs greatly from a family home in one of the city's impoverished *villas* (shantytowns), where electricity and clean water are luxuries.

Geography and ethnicity also play important roles. Both of these Buenos Aires homes have little in common with that of an indigenous family living in an adobe house in a desolate valley of the Andean Northwest, where life is eked out through subsistence agriculture and earth goddess Pachamama outshines Evita as a cultural icon. In regions such as the pampas, Mendoza province and Patagonia, a provincial friendliness surrounds a robust, outdoor lifestyle.

> Argentina's workforce is more than 40% female, and women currently occupy over a third of Argentina's congressional seats.

Argentina has a reasonably sized middle class, though it's been shrinking significantly in recent years, and poverty has grown. At the other end of the spectrum, wealthy city dwellers have moved into *countries* (gated communities) in surprising numbers.

One thing that all Argentines have in common is their devotion to family. The Buenos Aires advertising exec joins family for weekend dinners, and the cafe owner in San Juan meets friends out at the family *estancia* (ranch) for a Sunday *asado* (barbecue). Children commonly live with their parents until they're married, especially within poorer households.

SOCIAL DOS & DON'TS

When it comes to social etiquette in Argentina, knowing a few intricacies will keep you on the right track.

Dos

➡ Greet people you encounter with *buenos días* (good morning), *buenas tardes* (good afternoon) or *buenas noches* (good evening).

➡ In small villages, greet people on the street and when walking into a shop.

➡ Accept and give *besos* (kisses) on the cheek.

➡ Use *usted* (the formal term for 'you') when addressing elders and in formal situations.

➡ Dress for the occasion; only tourists and athletes wear shorts in Buenos Aires.

Don'ts

➡ Don't refer to the Islas Malvinas as the Falkland Islands, and don't talk to strangers about the Dirty War.

➡ Don't suggest that Brazil is better than Argentina at *fútbol,* or that Pelé is better than Maradona. And don't refer to *fútbol* as soccer.

➡ Don't show up at bars before midnight, or nightclubs before 3am, or dinner parties right on time (be fashionably late).

➡ Don't refer to people from the United States as Americans or *americanos;* use the term *estadounidenses* (or even *norteamericanos*) instead. Most Latin Americans consider themselves 'American' (literally from America, whether it be North, Central or South).

The Sporting Life

Fútbol (soccer) is an integral part of Argentines' lives, and on game day you'll know it by the cheers and yells emanating from shops and cafes. The national team has reached the World Cup final five times and has triumphed twice, in 1978 and 1986. The Argentine team also won Olympic gold twice, at the 2004 and 2008 games. The most popular teams are Boca Juniors and River Plate (there are around two dozen professional teams in Buenos Aires alone) and the fanatical behavior of the country's *barra brava* (hooligans) rivals that of their European counterparts. Among the best-known *fútbol* players are Diego Maradona, Gabriel Batistuta, and of course Lionel Messi, who has been voted FIFA's best player of the year five times.

Rugby's popularity has increased in Argentina ever since Los Pumas, their national team, beat France in the first game of the 2007 Rugby World Cup and again in the play-off for third place. The Pumas also made it to the semifinals of the 2015 World Cup, another huge accomplishment given their company in the semifinals – the long-established best teams in the world of South Africa, Australia and New Zealand.

Horse racing, tennis, basketball, golf and boxing are also popular. Argentina has the top polo horses and players in the world, and the Dakar Rally has been taking place partly or mostly in Argentina since 2009.

Pato is Argentina's traditional sport, played on horseback and mixing elements from both polo and basketball. It was originally played with a duck (a 'pato'), but now, thankfully, uses a ball encased in leather handles. Despite its long history and tradition, however, relatively few people follow it.

Jimmy Burns' *Hand of God* (1997) is the definitive book about football legend Diego Maradona and makes a great read – even if you're not a soccer fanatic.

The Sounds of Argentina

A variety of music genres are well represented in Argentina, especially when it comes to the country's most famous export, the tango. But the country also grooves to different sounds, be it *chamamé* in Corrientes, *cuarteto* in Córdoba or *cumbia villera* in the poor neighborhoods of Buenos Aires.

Cumbia villera is a relatively recent musical phenomenon: a fusion of *cumbia* and gangsta posturing with a punk edge and reggae overtones. Born of Buenos Aires' shantytowns, its aggressive lyrics deal with marginalization, poverty, drugs, sex and the Argentine economic crisis.

Tango

There's no better place to dive into tango than through the music of the genre's most legendary performer, singer Carlos Gardel (1887–1935). Violinist Juan D'Arienzo's orchestra reigned over tango throughout the 1930s and into the 1940s. Osvaldo Pugliese and Héctor Varela are important bandleaders from the 1940s, but the real giant of the era was *bandoneón* (small type of accordion) player Aníbal Troilo.

Modern tango is largely dominated by the work of Astor Piazzolla, who moved the *tango nuevo* (traditional tango music infused with modern elements) genre from the dance halls into the concert halls. Piazzolla paved the way for the tango fusion, which emerged in the 1970s and is popularized by neo tango groups such as Gotan Project, Bajofondo Tango Club and Tanghetto.

While in Buenos Aires, keep an eye out for Orquesta Típica Fernández Fierro, who put a new twist on traditional tango songs but also perform original creations (check out their award-winning documentary, *Orquesta Típica,* by Nicolas Entel). Other orchestras to watch out for are Orquesta Típica Imperial and El Afronte.

Contemporary influential tango singers include Susana Rinaldi, Daniel Melingo, Adriana Varela and the late Eladia Blásquez.

GARDEL & THE TANGO

In June 1935 a Cuban woman committed suicide in Havana; meanwhile, in New York and Puerto Rico two other women tried to poison themselves. It was all over the same man – tango singer Carlos Gardel, who had just died in a plane crash in Colombia.

Gardel was born in France (a claim contested by both Argentina and Uruguay), and when he was three his destitute single mother brought him to Buenos Aires. In his youth he entertained neighbors with his rapturous singing, then went on to establish a successful performing career.

Gardel played an enormous role in creating the tango *canción* (song) and almost single-handedly took the style out of Buenos Aires' tenements and brought it to Paris and New York. His crooning voice, suaveness and overall charisma made him an immediate success in Latin American countries – a rising star during tango's golden years of the 1920s and 1930s. Unfortunately, Gardel's later film career was tragically cut short by that fatal plane crash.

His devoted followers cannot pass a day without listening to him; as the saying goes, 'Gardel sings better every day.'

Folk Music

The folk (*folklore* or *folklórico*) music of Argentina takes much of its inspiration from the northwestern Andean region and countries to the north, especially Bolivia and Peru. It spans a variety of styles, including *chacarera*, *chamamé* and zamba.

The late Atahualpa Yupanqui (1908–92) was Argentina's most important *folklórico* musician of the 20th century. Yupanqui's music emerged with the *nueva canción* ('new song') movement that swept Latin America in the 1960s. *Nueva canción* was rooted in folk music and its lyrics often dealt with social and political themes. The genre's grande dame was Argentina's Mercedes Sosa (1935–2009) of Tucumán, winner of several Latin Grammy awards. Another contemporary *folklórico* musician is accordionist Chango Spasiuk, a virtuoso of Corrientes' *chamamé* music. Singer-songwriter-guitarist Horacio Guarany's 2004 album *Cantor de Cantores* was nominated for a Latin Grammy in the Best Folk Album category.

Mariana Baraj is a singer and percussionist who experiments with Latin America's traditional folk music as well as elements of jazz, classical music and improvisation. Soledad Pastorutti's first two albums have been Sony's top sellers in Argentina – ever!

Other big names in *folklórica* are Eduardo Falú; Víctor Heredia; Los Chalchaleros and León Gieco (aka 'The Argentine Bob Dylan').

Murga is a form of athletic musical theater composed of actors and percussionists. Primarily performed in Uruguay, *murga* in Argentina is more heavily focused on dancing than singing. You're most likely to see this exciting musical art form at Carnaval celebrations.

Rock & Pop

Musicians such as Charly García, Fito Páez and Luis Alberto Spinetta are *rock nacional* (Argentine rock) icons. Soda Stereo, Sumo, Los Pericos and Grammy winners Los Fabulosos Cadillacs rocked Argentina throughout the 1980s. Bersuit Vergarabat endures as one of Argentina's best rock bands, with a musical complexity that is arguably without peer. R&B-influenced Ratones Paranoicos opened for the Rolling Stones in 1995, while La Portuaria fuse Latin beats with jazz and R&B.

Other big-name groups are offbeat Babasónicos, punk rockers Attaque 77, fusion rockers Los Piojos, plus Los Redonditos de Ricota, Los Divididos, Catupecu Machu and Gazpacho. Illya Kuryaki and the Valderramas are metal-meets-hip-hop, while catchy Miranda! has an electro-pop style. Finally, eclectic Kevin Johansen sings in both English and Spanish.

Born in Córdoba in the early 1940s, *cuarteto* is Argentina's original pop music: despised by the middle and upper classes for its arresting rhythm and offbeat musical pattern, as well as its working-class lyrics, it is definitely music from the margins. Although definitively *cordobés* (from Córdoba), it's played in working-class bars, dance halls and stadiums throughout the country.

Electrónica & More

Electrónica exploded in Argentina in the 1990s and has taken on various forms in popular music. Heavyweights in DJ-based club and dance music include Aldo Haydar (progressive house), Bad Boy Orange (drum 'n' bass), Diego Ro-K ('the Maradona of Argentine DJs') and Gustavo Lamas (blending ambient pop and electro house). Award-winning Hernán Cattáneo has played with Paul Oakenfold and at Burning Man.

Música tropical – a lively, Afro-Latin sound of salsa, *merengue* and especially *cumbia* – has swept Argentina in recent years. Originating in Colombia, *cumbia* combines an infectious dance rhythm with lively melodies, often carried by brass.

Argentine music has experienced the hybrid phenomenon of blending electronic music with more traditional sounds. Onda Vaga's smooth harmonies add a jazzy feel to traditional *folklore*, while Juana Molina's ambient-electronic music has been compared to Björk's. Finally, there's Chancha Via Circuito, who fuses electronic music with *cumbia*.

Literature & Cinema

Perhaps because of its history of authoritarian rule, Argentina has developed a strong literary heritage, with many contemporary writers using the country's darkest moments as inspiration for their complex and sometimes disturbing novels. Argentina also has a vibrant, evolving film industry. The country has won two Oscars for Best Foreign Language Film (in 1985 and 2009) – the only Latin American country ever to have won the award – and continues to produce excellent directors and movies.

Victoria Ocampo (1890–1979) was a famous writer, publisher and intellectual who founded *Sur*, a renowned cultural magazine of the 1930s. You can also visit her mansion near Buenos Aires.

Literature

Journalist, poet and politician José Hernández (1831–86) gave rise to the *gauchesco* literary tradition with his epic poem *Martín Fierro* (1872), which acknowledged the role of the gauchos in Argentina's development. Argentine writing only reached an international audience during the 1960s and 1970s, when the stories of Jorge Luis Borges, Julio Cortázar, Ernesto Sabato, Adolfo Bioy Casares and Silvina Ocampo, among many others, were widely translated for the first time.

Jorge Luis Borges (1899–1986), the brightest light of Argentine literature, is best known for the complex labyrinthine worlds and sophisticated mind teasers constructing his stories. His early stories, such as *Death and the Compass* and *Streetcorner Man,* offer a metaphysical twist on Argentine themes, while his later works – including *The Lottery in Babylon, The Circular Ruins* and *Garden of the Forking Paths* – are works of fantasy. *Collected Fictions* (1999) is a complete set of his stories.

Despite being discovered and influenced by Borges in the 1940s, the writing of Julio Cortázar (1914–84) was considerably different. His short stories and novels are more anthropological and concern people living seemingly normal lives in a world where the surreal becomes commonplace. Cortázar's most famous book is *Hopscotch.*

Another great writer is Ernesto Sabato (1911–2011), whose complex and uncompromising novels have been extremely influential on later Argentine literature. *The Tunnel* (1948) is Sabato's engrossing existentialist novella about an obsessed painter and his distorted personal take on reality.

Adolfo Bioy Casares' (1914–99) sci-fi novella *The Invention of Morel* (1940) not only gave Alain Resnais the plot for his classic film *Last Year at Marienbad,* but also introduced the idea of the holodeck decades before *Star Trek* existed.

The contemporary, post-boom generation of Argentine writers is more reality-based, often reflecting the influence of popular culture and directly confronting the political angles of 1970s authoritarian Argentina. One of the most famous post-boom Argentine writers is Manuel Puig (1932–90; author of *Kiss of the Spider Woman*). In the Argentine tradition, Puig did much of his writing in exile, fleeing Argentina during the Perón years and ultimately settling in Mexico.

Osvaldo Soriano (1943–97), perhaps Argentina's most popular contemporary novelist, wrote *A Funny Dirty Little War* (1986) and *Winter Quarters* (1989). Juan José Saer (1937–2005) penned short stories and complex crime novels, while Rodrigo Fresán (1963–), the youngster of the post-boom generation, wrote the international bestseller *The History of Argentina* (1991).

Other notable contemporary writers include Ricardo Piglia, Tomás Eloy Martínez, Andrés Neuman, César Aira, Oliverio Coelho, Pedro Mairal, Iosi Havilio and Samanta Schweblin.

Cinema

One of Argentina's major contributions to cinema is Luis Puenzo's *The Official Story* (1985), which deals with the Dirty War. Another well-known international movie is Héctor Babenco's *Kiss of the Spider Woman* (1985), based on the novel by Argentine-born Manuel Puig. Both movies won Oscars.

New Argentine Cinema developed in the 1990s, brought about by economic and political unrest. Films that spearheaded this movement include Martín Rejtman's *Rapado* (1992) and *Pizza, birra, faso* (Pizza, Beer, Cigarettes, 1998) by Adrián Caetano and Bruno Stagnaro.

Pablo Trapero is one of Argentina's foremost filmmakers. Among his works are award-winning *Mundo grúa* (Crane World, 1999), the ensemble road movie *Familia rodante* (Rolling Family, 2004) and *Nacido y criado* (Born and Bred, 2006), a stark story about a Patagonian man's fall from grace. His 2010 film noir *Carancho* played at the Cannes Film Festival, and in 2015 *The Clan* won the Silver Lion award at the Venice international Film Festival.

Daniel Burman's films include *Esperando al mesías* (Waiting for the Messiah, 2000), *El abrazo partido* (Lost Embrace, 2004) and *Derecho de familia* (Family Law, 2006). His most recent effort, *El misterio de la felicidad* (The Mystery of Happiness, 2015), is a warm comedy about love, friendship and happiness. Burman's other claim to fame is his co-production of Walter Salles' Che Guevara–inspired *The Motorcycle Diaries*.

Another director to have made a mark on Argentine cinema is the late Fabián Bielinsky. He left behind a small but powerful body of work that includes his award-winning feature *Nueve reinas* (Nine Queens, 2000). His last film, the 2005 neo-noir flick *El aura,* screened at Sundance and was the official Argentine entry for the 2006 Oscars.

Lucrecia Martel's 2001 debut *La ciénaga* (The Swamp) and *La niña santa* (The Holy Girl, 2004) deal with the themes of social decay, Argentine bourgeois and sexuality in the face of Catholic guilt. Her powerful *La mujer sin cabeza* (The Headless Woman, 2008) was showcased at Cannes. Another acclaimed director, Carlos Sorin, bases his dramas – which include *Historias mínimas* (Minimal Stories, 2002), *Bombón el perro* (Bombón the Dog, 2004), *La Ventana* (The Window, 2008) and *Días de pesca* (Gone Fishing, 2012) – in Patagonia.

Juan José Campanella's *El hijo de la novia* (Son of the Bride) received an Oscar nomination for Best Foreign Language Film in 2001, while *Luna de avellaneda* (Moon of Avellaneda, 2004) is a clever story about a social club and those who try to save it. In 2009 he won the Oscar for best Foreign Language Film with *El secreto de sus ojos* (The Secret in Their Eyes). That same year, Mariano Cohn and Gastón Duprat's *El hombre de al lado* (The Man Next Door, 2009) won a cinematography award at the 2010 Sundance Film Festival.

Other noteworthy films include Lucía Puenzo's *XXY* (2007), the tale of a 15-year-old hermaphrodite, and Juan Diego Solanas' *Nordeste* (Northeast, 2005), which tackles difficult social issues such as child trafficking; both were screened at Cannes. In 2013 Puenzo directed *Wakolda* (The German Doctor), the true story of the family who unknowingly lived with Josef Mengele during his exile in South America. Finally, Damián Szifron's black comedy *Relatos salvajes* (Wild Tales, 2014) was Oscar-nominated for Best Foreign Language Film.

Metegol (Underdogs; 2013) is a 3D film directed by Juan José Campanella; it cost US$22 million, making it the most expensive Argentine movie ever produced.

LITERATURE & CINEMA CINEMA

Argentina's biggest film event is the Buenos Aires International Festival of Independent Film, held in April. Check out www.bafici.gov.ar for more information.

The Natural World

Argentina. For anyone raised on *National Geographic* and adventure stories, the name is loaded with images: the Magellanic penguins of the Atlantic coast, the windswept mysteries of Patagonia and Tierra del Fuego, the vast grasslands of the pampas, the towering Andes and raging Iguazú Falls. Spanning from the subtropics to the edge of Antarctica, the country is simply unmatched in natural wonders.

The Land

With a total land area of about 2.8 million sq km, Argentina is the world's eighth-largest country. It stretches from La Quiaca on the Bolivian border, where summers can be brutally hot, to Ushuaia in Tierra del Fuego, where winters are experienced only by seasoned locals and the nuttiest of travelers. It's a distance of nearly 3500km, an expanse that encompasses a vast array of environments and terrain.

Above Iguazú Falls
(p196)

The Central & Northern Andes

In the extreme north, the Andes are basically the southern extension of the Bolivian *altiplano*, a thinly populated high plain between 3000m and 4000m in altitude, punctuated by even higher volcanic peaks. Although days can be surprisingly hot, frosts occur almost nightly. The Andean Northwest is also known as the *puna*.

Further south, in the arid provinces of San Juan and Mendoza, the Andes climb to their highest altitudes, with 6962m Cerro Aconcagua topping out as the highest point in the western hemisphere. Here, the highest peaks lie covered in snow through the winter. Although rainfall on the eastern slopes is inadequate for crops, perennial streams descend from the Andes and provide irrigation water, which has brought prosperity to the wine-producing provinces of Mendoza, San Juan and San Luis. Winter in San Juan province is the season of the *zonda*, a hot, dry wind descending from the Andes that causes dramatic temperature increases.

The Chaco

East of the Andes and the Andean foothills, much of northern Argentina consists of subtropical lowlands. This arid area, known as the Argentine Chaco, is part of the much larger Gran Chaco, an extremely rugged, largely uninhabited region that extends into Bolivia, Paraguay and Brazil. The Argentine Chaco encompasses the provinces of Chaco, Formosa and Santiago del Estero, the easternmost reaches of Jujuy, Catamarca and Salta provinces, and the northernmost parts of Santa Fe and Córdoba.

The Chaco has a well-defined winter dry season, and summer everywhere in the Chaco is brutally hot. Rainfall decreases as you move east to west. The wet Chaco, which encompasses the eastern parts of Chaco and Formosa provinces, and northwestern part of Santa Fe, receives more rain than the dry Chaco, which covers central and western Chaco and Formosa provinces, most of Santiago del Estero and parts of Salta.

Mesopotamia

Also referred to as the Litoral (as in littoral), Mesopotamia is the name for the region of northeast Argentina between the Río Paraná and Río Uruguay. Here the climate is mild and rainfall is heavy in the provinces of Entre Ríos and Corrientes, which make up most of Mesopotamia. Hot and humid Misiones province, a politically important province surrounded on three sides by Brazil and Paraguay, contains part of Iguazú Falls, whose waters descend from southern Brazil's Paraná Plateau. Shallow summer flooding is common throughout Mesopotamia and into the eastern Chaco, but only the immediate river floodplains become inundated in the west.

The Pampas & Atlantic Coast

Bordered by the Atlantic Ocean and Patagonia and stretching nearly to Córdoba and the Central Sierras, the pampas are Argentina's agricultural heartland. Geographically, this region covers the provinces of Buenos Aires and La Pampa, as well as southern chunks of Santa Fe and Córdoba.

This area can be subdivided into the humid pampas, along the Litoral, and the arid pampas of the western interior and the south. More than a third of the country's population lives in and around Buenos Aires. Annual rainfall exceeds 900mm, but several hundred kilometers westward it's less than half that.

The absence of nearly any rises in the land makes some parts of this area vulnerable to flooding from the relatively few, small rivers that cross it. Only the granitic Sierra de Tandil (484m) and the Sierra de la Ventana (1273m), in southwestern Buenos Aires province, and the Sierra de Lihué Calel disrupt the otherwise monotonous terrain.

At its mouth, the Río de la Plata is an amazing 200km wide, making it the widest river in the world – though some consider it more like a river estuary.

Iguazú Falls consists of more than 275 individual falls that tumble from heights as great as 80m. They stretch for nearly 3km and are arguably the most amazing waterfalls on earth.

Parque Nacional Tierra del Fuego (p508)

Along the Atlantic coast, the province of Buenos Aires features the sandy, often dune-backed beaches that attracted the development of seaside resorts. South of Viedma, cliffs begin to appear but the landscape remains otherwise desolate for its entire stretch south through Patagonia.

Patagonia & the Lake District

Ever-alluring Patagonia is the region of Argentina south of the Río Colorado, which flows southeast from the Andes and passes just north of the city of Neuquén. The Lake District is a subregion of Patagonia. Provincewise, Patagonia consists of Neuquén, Río Negro, Chubut and Santa Cruz. It's separated from Chilean Patagonia by the Andes.

The Andean cordillera is high enough that Pacific storms drop most of their rain and snow on the Chilean side. In the extreme southern reaches of Patagonia, however, enough snow and ice still accumulate to form the largest southern hemisphere glaciers outside of Antarctica.

East of the Andean foothills, the cool, arid Patagonian steppes support huge flocks of sheep. For such a southerly location, temperatures are relatively mild, even in winter, when more uniform atmospheric pressure moderates the strong gales that blow most of the year.

Except for urban centers such as Comodoro Rivadavia and Río Gallegos, Patagonia is thinly populated. Tidal ranges along the Atlantic coast are too great for major port facilities. In the valley of the Río Negro and at the outlet of the Río Chubut (near the town of Trelew), people farm and cultivate fruit orchards.

Tierra del Fuego

The world's southernmost permanently inhabited territory, Tierra del Fuego ('Land of Fire') consists of one large island (Isla Grande), unequally divided between Chile and Argentina, and many smaller ones. When

The largest dinosaur ever discovered (so far!) is *Argentinosaurus huinculensis*, uncovered in Neuquén province; the herbivore measured a massive 40m long and 18m high, and weighed 70 tons.

Llamas

Europeans first passed through the Strait of Magellan (which separates Isla Grande from the Patagonian mainland), the fires that gave this land its name stemmed from the activities of the now endangered Yahgan people.

The northern half of Isla Grande, resembling the Patagonian steppes, is devoted to sheep grazing, while its southern half is mountainous and partly covered by forests and glaciers. As in Patagonia, winter conditions are rarely extreme.

Wildlife

With such variances in terrain and such great distances, it's no wonder Argentina boasts a wide range of flora and fauna. Subtropical rainforests, palm savannas, high-altitude deserts and steppes, humid-temperate grasslands, alpine and sub-Antarctic forests and rich coastal areas all support their own special life forms.

Animals

Northeast Argentina boasts the country's most diverse animal life. One of the best areas on the continent to enjoy wildlife is the swampy Esteros del Iberá, in Corrientes province, where animals such as swamp deer, capybara and caiman, along with many large migratory birds, are common. It's comparable – arguably even better – than Brazil's more famous Pantanal.

In the drier northwest the most conspicuous animal is the domestic llama, but its wild cousins, the guanaco and vicuña, can also be seen. Your odds of seeing them are excellent if you travel by road through Parque Nacional Los Cardones to Salta. Their yellow fur is often an extraordinary puff of color against the cactus-studded backdrop. Many

Península Valdés is one of the few places on earth where killer whales (orcas) have been seen hunting sea lions by beaching themselves. You'd be *very* lucky to witness this phenomenon, however.

CAPYBARAS

Treading, with its webbed feet, a very fine line between cute and ugly, the capybara is a sizable semiaquatic beast that you're bound to encounter in the Esteros del Iberá area. Weighing in at up to 75kg, the *carpincho*, as it's known in Spanish, is the world's largest rodent.

Very much at home both on land and in the water, the gentle and vaguely comical creature eats aquatic plants and grasses in great quantity. They form small herds, with a dominant male living it up with four to six females. The male can be recognized by a protrusion on its forehead that emits a territory-marking scent. The lovably roly-poly babies are born in spring.

Though protected in the Iberá area, the capybara is farmed and hunted elsewhere for its skin, which makes a soft, flexible leather. The meat is also considered a delicacy in traditional communities.

migratory birds, including flamingos, inhabit the high saline lakes of the Andean Northwest.

In less densely settled areas, including the arid pampas of La Pampa province, guanacos and foxes are not unusual sights. Many bodies of water, both permanent and seasonal, provide migratory bird habitats.

Most notable in Patagonia and Tierra del Fuego is the wealth of coastal wildlife, ranging from Magellanic penguins, cormorants and gulls to sea lions, fur seals, elephant seals, orcas and whales. Several coastal reserves, from Río Negro province south to Tierra del Fuego, are home to enormous concentrations of wildlife that are one of the region's greatest visitor attractions. Inland on the Patagonian steppe, as in the northwest, the guanaco is the most conspicuous mammal, but the flightless rhea, resembling the ostrich, runs in flocks across the plains.

Plants

When it comes to plant life, the country's most diverse regions are in northeast Argentina, the Lake District, the Patagonian Andes and the subtropical forests of northwest Argentina.

The high northern Andes are dry and often barren, and vegetation is limited to sparse bunch grasses and low, widely spaced shrubs. In Jujuy and La Rioja provinces, however, huge, vertically branched cardón cacti add a rugged beauty to an otherwise empty landscape. In the Andean *precordillera,* between the Chaco and the Andes proper, lies a strip of dense, subtropical montane cloud forest known as the Yungas. This area sees heavy summertime rains and is one of the most biologically diverse regions in the country.

The wet Chaco is home to grasslands and gallery forests with numerous tree species, including the quebracho colorado and caranday palm. The dry Chaco, although extremely parched, is still thick with vegetation. It hosts taller trees and a dense understory of low-growing spiny trees and shrubs.

In Mesopotamia rainfall is sufficient to support swampy lowland forests and upland savanna. Misiones' native vegetation is dense subtropical forest, though its upper elevations are studded with araucaria pines.

The once lush native grasses of the Argentine pampas have suffered under grazing pressure and the proliferation of grain farms that produce cash crops such as soy beans. Today very little native vegetation remains, except along watercourses like the Río Paraná.

Most of Patagonia lies in the rain shadow of the Chilean Andes, so the vast steppes of southeastern Argentina resemble the sparse grasslands of the arid Andean highlands. Closer to the border there are pockets of

Above Sea lion and cormorants, Ushuaia (p493)
Right Purmamarca (p251)

ESTIVILLML / GETTY IMAGES ©

Glaciar Perito Moreno (p466)

dense *Nothofagus* (southern beech), *Araucaria araucana* (aka monkey puzzle trees) and coniferous woodlands that owe their existence to the winter storms that sneak over the cordillera. Northern Tierra del Fuego is a grassy extension of the Patagonian steppe, but the heavy rainfall of the mountainous southern half supports verdant southern beech forests.

Argentina's National Parks

Argentina's national and provincial parks offer a huge variety of environments, from the sweltering tropics of Parque Nacional Iguazú to the crashing glaciers of Parque Nacional Los Glaciares to the animal-rich coastal waters of Reserva Faunística Península Valdés.

One of Latin America's first national park systems, Argentina's dates from the turn of the 20th century, when explorer and surveyor Francisco P Moreno donated 75 sq km near Bariloche to the state in return for guarantees that the parcel would be preserved for the enjoyment of all Argentines. In 1934 this area became part of Parque Nacional Nahuel Huapi, Argentina's first national park.

Since then the country has established many other parks and reserves, mostly but not exclusively in the Andean region. There are also important provincial parks and reserves, such as Reserva Faunística Península Valdés, which do not fall within the national park system but deserve attention. Some national parks are more visitor-oriented than the provincial parks, but there are exceptions.

Visitors in Buenos Aires can stop at the national parks administration (www.parquesnacionales.gob.ar) for maps and brochures, which are sometimes in short supply in the parks.

Survival Guide

Directory A–Z

Accommodations

➡ Accommodations in Argentina range from campgrounds to five-star luxury hotels. At the tourist-oriented hotels staff members will speak some English, though at more provincial accommodations you'll be practicing your *castellano* (what Argentina calls its Spanish).

➡ All but the cheapest hotels have private bathrooms, and most accommodations include breakfast – usually *medialunas* (croissants) and weak coffee or tea. Note that many hotels offer discounted rates for extended stays, usually a week or more; negotiate this *before* you begin your stay.

➡ Inflation in Argentina is rampant, running (unofficially) at around 26%. To avoid getting price shock, check current prices.

➡ Prices in this guidebook are listed in US dollars rather than in pesos; many accommodations will also quote their rates in US dollars to combat inflation.

➡ Budget and midrange hotels almost always include taxes when quoting their prices, but top-end hotels usually do not – and it's 21%.

➡ Payment in cash (usually at midrange to top-end hotels) sometimes results in a 10% discount. Likewise, you can be charged a 'fee' for using credit cards. Paying with a foreign debit card is sometimes – but not always – possible at no extra charge.

➡ High season is generally January and February (when Argentines take their summer breaks), Semana Santa (Easter week) and July and August (except in Patagonia). Reserve ahead during these times. Outside these times, prices can drop anywhere from 20% to 50%.

➡ For online bookings try www.despegar.com, though you can usually get a cheaper rate by contacting the hotel directly.

Cabañas

➡ Some tourist destinations, especially at the beach or in the country, have *cabañas* (cabins) for rent. These are usually stand-alone cabin-type accommodations, and nearly always have a stocked kitchen. They are a great deal for groups or families (as they often have several rooms), though sometimes their off-the-beaten-track location means you'll need a vehicle to reach them. A destination's tourist office is a good place to find a list of local *cabañas*.

Camping & Refugios

➡ Camping can be a splendid way to experience Argentina, particularly the Lake District and Patagonia, where there are many good campgrounds.

➡ Many Argentine cities or towns have a fairly central municipal campground, but these are hit-and-miss – sometimes delightfully woodsy, sometimes crowded and ugly.

➡ Private campgrounds usually have good facilities: hot showers, toilets, laundry, barbecue for grilling, restaurant or *confitería* (cafe) and small grocery store. Free campgrounds are often excellent, especially in the Lake District, although they lack facilities. Municipal campgrounds are cheap, but can become party central on weekends.

➡ Argentine camping equipment is often more expensive and inferior than you may be used to.

➡ Camp stoves take locally available butane cartridges

(which should *not* be taken on airplanes).

➡ There are definitely mosquitoes in Argentina, but mosquito repellent is widely available.

➡ Backpacking and backcountry camping opportunities abound in and around the national parks, especially those in the Lakes District and the south. Some parks have free or cheap *refugios* (basic shelters), which have cooking facilities and rustic bunks.

Estancias

➡ Few experiences feel more typically Argentine than staying at an *estancia* (a traditional ranch, often called *fincas* in the northwest). *Estancias* are a wonderful way to spend time in remote areas of the country – and wine, horses and *asados* (traditional barbecues) are almost always involved.

➡ *Estancias* are especially common in the area around Buenos Aires, near Esteros del Iberá, and throughout the Lake District and Patagonia, where they're often geared toward anglers. They're not cheap, but rates generally include room, board and some activities.

Hospedajes, Pensiones & Residenciales

➡ Aside from hostels, these are Argentina's cheapest accommodations, and the differences among them are sometimes ambiguous.

➡ A *hospedaje* is usually a large family home with a few extra bedrooms (and, generally, a shared bathroom).

➡ Similarly, a *pensión* offers short-term accommodations in a family home, but may also have permanent lodgers.

➡ *Residenciales* generally occupy buildings designed for short-stay accommodations, although some (known euphemistically as *albergues transitorios*) cater to clientele

who intend only *very* short stays – of two hours maximum. These are mostly used by young Argentine couples.

➡ Rooms and furnishings at these accommodations are modest, often basic and usually clean, and rooms with shared bathrooms are the cheapest.

Hostels

➡ Hostels are common in Argentina, and range from basic no-frills deals to beautiful, multi-perk offerings more luxurious than your basic hotel. Most fall in between, but all have common kitchens, living areas, shared bathrooms and dorm rooms. Most have a few private rooms with or without bathroom.

➡ Hostels are a great way to meet other travelers, both Argentines and foreigners, especially if you're by yourself. Social events such as *asados* often take place, and local tours can be offered. However, remember that Argentines are night owls and hostelers tend to follow suit, so earplugs can be handy indeed.

➡ Hostel organizations, which offer discounts with membership, include **Hostelling International** (HI; www.hihostels.com) and **HoLa** (www.holahostels.com).

Hotels

➡ Argentine hotels vary from depressing, utilitarian

one-star places to luxurious five-star hotels with all the usual top-tier services. Oddly enough, many one- and two-star hotels can prove better value than three- and four-star lodgings.

➡ In general, hotels provide a room with private bathroom, often a telephone and usually a TV with cable; some have microwaves and/or kitchenettes. Sometimes they have a *confitería* or restaurant and almost always include breakfast, whether it be a few *medialunas* with coffee or a full American-style buffet.

Rentals & Homestays

➡ House and apartment rentals often save you money if you're staying in one place for an extended period. This can be an especially good deal during high season at resort locations, such as Bariloche or beach cities along the Atlantic coast (just book way ahead) – especially for groups. Tourist offices can be good sources for listings, and there are always organizations like www.airbnb.com.

➡ During the tourist season, mostly in the interior, families rent rooms to visitors. Often these are excellent bargains, permitting access to cooking and laundry facilities while encouraging contact with Argentines. Tourist offices in many smaller towns or cities sometimes maintain lists of such accommodations.

Courses

➡ Argentina is a hot destination in which to learn Spanish. Most opportunities for Spanish-language instruction are based in Buenos Aires, though larger cities such as Mendoza and Córdoba are also excellent.

➡ Tango classes are hugely popular in Buenos Aires, where cooking classes – both for Argentine and international cuisine – are also available.

➡ Asking fellow travelers for recommendations is the best way to pick a good institute, or tango and cooking classes that cater to your needs.

Customs Regulations

➡ Argentine officials are generally courteous and reasonable toward tourists. Electronic items, including laptops, cameras and cell (mobile) phones, can be brought into the country duty free, provided they are not intended for resale. If you have a lot of electronic equipment, however, it may be useful to have a typed list of the items you are carrying (including serial numbers) or a pile of purchase receipts.

➡ If you're entering Argentina from a neighboring country, officials focus on different things. Travelers southbound from the central Andean countries may be searched for drugs, while those from bordering countries will have fruits and vegetables confiscated. Carrying illegal drugs will pretty much get you into trouble no matter which country you're coming from.

Discount Cards

➡ The International Student Identity Card (ISIC) is available through www.isic.org. It can help travelers obtain discounts on public transportation and admissions to museums. Any official-looking university identification may (or may not) be accepted as a substitute.

➡ An HI card, available at any **HI hostel** (www.hihostels.com), will get you discounts on your stay at any HI facility. The **HoLa** (www.holahostels.com) card works in a similar way for a different network of hostels.

➡ Travelers over the age of 60 can sometimes obtain senior-citizen discounts on museum admissions and the like. Usually a passport with date of birth is sufficient evidence of age.

Electricity

➡ Argentina's electric current operates on 220V, 50 Hertz. Adapters are readily available from almost any *ferretería* (hardware store).

➡ Most electronic equipment (such as cameras, telephones and computers) are dual/multi-voltage, but if you're bringing something that's not (such as a hairdryer), use a voltage converter or you might short out your device.

220V/50Hz

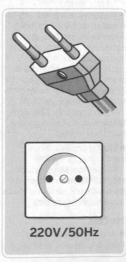

220V/50Hz

Embassies & Consulates

Embassies and consulates are found in Buenos Aires. Some other cities around Argentina (especially near the borders) also have consulates to certain countries.

Australian Embassy (☏011-4779-3500; www.argentina.embassy.gov.au; Villanueva 1400)

Bolivian Embassy (☏011-4394-1463; www.embajadadebolivia.com.ar; Av Corrientes 545)

Brazilian Embassy & Consulate (☏011-4515-6500; www.conbrasil.org.ar; Carlos Pellegrini 1363, 5th fl)

Canadian Embassy (☏011-4808-1000; www.embassy-canada.com; Tagle 2828)

Chilean Embassy (☏011-4808-8601; www.chile.gob.cl/argentina; Tagle 2762)

Dutch Embassy (☏011-4338-0050; http://argentina.nlembajada.org; Olga Cossettini 831, 3rd fl)

French Embassy (☏011-4515-7030; www.embafrancia-argentina.org; Cerrito 1399)

German Embassy (☎011-4778-2500; www.buenosaires.diplo.de; Villanueva 1055)

Italian Consulate (☎011-4114-4800; www.consbuenosaires.esteri.it; Reconquista 572)

New Zealand Embassy (☎011-5070-0700; www.nzembassy.com/argentina; Carlos Pellegrini 1427, 5th fl)

Spanish Embassy (☎011-4809-4900; www.exteriores.gob.es/Embajadas/buenos aires; J Figueroa Alcorta 3102)

UK Embassy (☎011-4808-2200; www.ukinargentina.fco.gov.uk; Dr Luis Agote 2412)

Uruguayan Embassy (☎011-4807-3040; www.embajadadeluruguay.com.ar; Av General Las Heras 1907)

US Embassy (☎011-5777-4533; http://argentina.usembassy.gov; Colombia 4300)

Food

See Eat & Drink Like a Local (p39) for information on Argentine cuisine.

The following price ranges refer to a standard main course.

$ less than AR$110

$$ AR$110–180

$$$ more than AR$180

Gay & Lesbian Travelers

➡ Argentina has become increasingly gay-friendly over recent years. Buenos Aires is one of the world's top gay destinations – with dedicated hotels and B&Bs; bars and nightclubs. The capital is home to South America's largest annual gay pride parade and in 2002 became the first Latin American city to legalize same-sex civil unions; in July 2010 Argentina became the first Latin American country to legalize same-sex marriage.

➡ Although Buenos Aires (and, to a lesser extent, Argentina's other large cities) is becoming increasingly tolerant, most of the rest of Argentina still feels uncomfortable with homosexuality. Homophobia rarely takes the form of physical violence, however, and gay people regularly travel throughout the country to return home with nothing but praise.

➡ When it comes to public affection, Argentine men are more physically demonstrative than their North American and European counterparts. Behaviors such as kissing on the cheek in greeting or a vigorous embrace are innocuous even to those who express unease with homosexuality. Lesbians walking hand in hand should attract little attention, since heterosexual Argentine women frequently do so, but this would be very conspicuous behavior for men. When in doubt, it's best to be discreet.

Health

➡ Argentina is a modern country with good health and dental services. Sanitation and hygiene at restaurants is relatively high, and tap water is generally safe to drink throughout the country. If you want to make sure, ask *¿Se puede tomar el agua de la canilla?* (Is the tap water drinkable?).

➡ Public health care in Argentina is reasonably good and free, even if you're a foreigner. Waits can be long, however, and quality inconsistent. Those who can afford it usually opt for the superior private-care system, and here most doctors and hospitals will expect payment in cash. Many medical personnel speak English.

➡ If you develop a life-threatening medical problem you may want to be evacuated to your home country. Since this may cost thousands of dollars, be sure to have the appropriate insurance before you depart. Your embassy can also recommend medical services.

➡ A signed and dated note from your doctor, describing your medical conditions and medications (with their generic or scientific names) is a good idea. It's also a good idea to bring medications in their clearly labeled, original containers. Most pharmacies in Argentina are well supplied.

➡ For more specific information on vaccinations to get before traveling to Argentina, see wwwnc.cdc.gov/travel/destinations/argentina.htm.

Dengue Fever

➡ Dengue fever is a viral infection found throughout South America. It is transmitted by Aedes mosquitoes, which prefer to bite during the daytime and breed primarily in artificial water containers, such as cans, cisterns, plastic containers and discarded tires. As a result, dengue is especially common in densely populated, urban environments.

➡ In 2009, several thousand cases of dengue were reported in the northern provinces of Argentina, but since then the numbers have dropped dramatically.

➡ Dengue usually causes flu-like symptoms, including fever, muscle aches, joint pains, headaches, nausea and vomiting, often followed by a rash. The body aches may be quite uncomfortable, but most cases resolve uneventfully in a few days.

PRACTICALITIES

Addresses In Argentine addresses, the word *local* refers to a suite or office. If an address has 's/n' – short for *sin numero* (without number) – the address has no street number.

Laundry Affordable *lavanderías* are widely available in Argentina.

Newspapers Argentina's biggest papers are centrist *Clarín* (www.clarin.com), conservative *La Nación* (www.lanacion.com.ar) and lefty *Página 12* (www.pagina12.com.ar). The English-language daily is the *Buenos Aires Herald* (www.buenosairesherald.com). The *Argentina Independent* (www.argentinaindependent.com) is an excellent English-language online newspaper.

Photography Many photo stores can affordably transfer images from your digital camera to CD; you can also get them printed out. Old-fashioned print and slide film are available, as is developing.

Smoking Smoking bans differ by province. In Buenos Aires, smoking is banned in most enclosed public spaces, including the majority of bars, restaurants and public transportation.

Weights & Measures Metric.

Insurance

➧ A travel insurance policy to cover theft, loss, medical problems and trip cancellation or delays is a good idea. Some policies specifically exclude dangerous activities such as scuba diving, skiing, rock climbing and even trekking; read the fine print. Check that the policy covers ambulances or an emergency flight home.

➧ Keep all your paperwork in case you have to file a claim later. Paying for your flight with a credit card often provides limited travel insurance – ask your credit card company what it is prepared to cover.

➧ Worldwide travel insurance is available at www.lonelyplanet.com/travel-insurance. You can buy, extend and claim online anytime – even if you're already on the road.

Internet Access

➧ Wi-fi is available at many (if not most) hotels and cafes, restaurants and airports, and it's generally good and free.

➧ Internet cafes and *locutorios* (telephone centers) with very affordable internet access can be found in practically all Argentine towns and cities.

➧ To find the @ *(arroba)* symbol on keyboards, try holding down the Alt key and typing 64, or typing AltGr-2. You can also ask the attendant '*¿Cómo se hace la arroba?*' ('How do you make the@sign?').

Legal Matters

➧ Police can demand identification at any moment and for whatever reason, though it's unlikely to happen. Always carry a photo ID or a copy of your passport, and – most importantly – *always* be courteous and cooperative.

➧ Drugs and most other substances that are illegal in the USA and many European countries are also illegal here, though marijuana has been somewhat decriminalized in Argentina (and is legal in Uruguay).

➧ If arrested, you have the constitutional right to a lawyer, a telephone call and to remain silent (beyond giving your name, nationality, age and passport number). Don't sign anything until you speak to a lawyer. If you don't speak Spanish, a translator should be provided for you.

Maps

➧ Tourist offices throughout the country provide free city maps that are good enough for tooling around town.

➧ With offices in nearly every Argentine city, the **Automóvil Club Argentino** (ACA; Map p84; www.aca.org.ar) publishes excellent maps of provinces and cities that are particularly useful for driving. Card-carrying members of foreign automobile clubs can get discounts.

➧ Geography nerds will adore the topographic maps available from the **Instituto Geográfico Nacional** (☑011-4576-5576; www.ign.gob.ar; Av Cabildo 381) in Buenos Aires.

Money

➧ The Argentine unit of currency is the peso (AR$).

➧ Carrying cash and an ATM card is the way to go in Argentina.

ATMs

➧ *Cajeros automáticos* (ATMs) are found in nearly every city and town in Argentina and can also be used for cash advances on major credit cards. They're the best way to get money, and nearly all have instructions in English. Depending on your home bank there are varying upper limits per withdrawal, and a small fee is charged on ATM transactions by the local bank (not including charges by your home bank). You can withdraw several times per day, but beware these charges – which are per transaction. Banelco ATMs tend to allow larger withdrawals.

Cash

➡ Notes come in denominations of two, five, 10, 20, 50 and 100 pesos (though new 200- and 500-peso notes are due to be printed in 2016, with a possible 1000-peso note to be introduced in 2017).

➡ One peso equals 100 *centavos*; coins come in denominations of five, 10, 25 and 50 *centavos*, as well as one and two pesos.

➡ At present, US dollars are accepted by many tourist-oriented businesses, but you should always carry some pesos.

➡ Don't be dismayed if you receive dirty and hopelessly tattered banknotes; they'll be accepted everywhere. Some places refuse torn or marked foreign banknotes, however, so make sure you arrive in Argentina with pristine bills.

➡ Counterfeiting, of both local and US bills, has become a problem in recent years, and merchants are very careful when accepting large denominations. You should be too; look for a clear watermark or running thread on the largest bills, and get familiar with the local currency *before* you arrive in Argentina. See www. landingpadba.com/ba -basics-counterfeit-money. Being aware of fake bills is especially important in dark places like nightclubs or taxis.

➡ Getting change from large denominations can be a problem for small purchases. Large supermarkets and restaurants are your best bet. Always keep a stash of change with you, in both small bills and coins.

Credit Cards

➡ Many (but not all!) tourist services, larger stores, hotels and restaurants – especially in the bigger cities – take credit cards such as Visa and MasterCard.

➡ The most widely accepted credit cards are Visa and MasterCard, though American Express and a few others are valid in some establishments. Before you leave home, warn your credit-card company that you'll be using it abroad.

➡ Some businesses add a *recargo* (surcharge) of 5% to 10% toward credit-card purchases. Also, the actual amount you'll eventually pay depends upon the official exchange rate not at the time of sale, but when the purchase is posted to an overseas account, sometimes weeks later.

➡ If you use a credit card to pay for restaurant bills, be aware that tips can't usually be added to the bill. Many lower-end hotels and private tour companies will not accept credit cards. Many places will give you a small discount if you pay in cash, rather than use a credit card.

Money Changers

➡ US dollars are by far the preferred foreign currency, although Chilean and Uruguayan pesos can be readily exchanged at the borders.

➡ Cash dollars and euros can be changed at banks and *cambios* (exchange houses) in most larger cities, but other currencies can be difficult to change outside Buenos Aires.

➡ You'll need your passport to change money; it might be best to avoid any sort of street-tout money changer.

Taxes & Refunds

➡ One of Argentina's primary state revenue-earners is the 21% value-added tax known as the Impuesto de Valor Agregado (IVA). Under limited circumstances, foreign visitors may obtain IVA refunds on purchases of Argentine products upon departing the country. A 'Tax Free' window decal (in English) identifies participants in this program, but always check that the shop is part of the tax-free program before making your purchase.

➡ You can obtain tax refunds on purchases of AR$70 or more made at one of these participating stores. To do so, present your passport to the merchant, who will

TWO-TIER PRICING

Over the last decade, Argentina's popularity as a tourism destination has birthed an annoying two-tier pricing system: some businesses in certain areas (mostly in Buenos Aires, but also in Patagonia and parts of the Lake District) charge Argentines one price and 'nonresidents' a higher price. While you won't find this everywhere, you will encounter it at some tango shows, museums, tours, *estancias* (ranches), national parks, airlines and upmarket hotels throughout the country.

Many accommodations also quote prices in US dollars rather than pesos. This doesn't necessarily mean you're getting charged more than Argentines; the peso is just so unstable that places prefer to use a currency that isn't always fluctuating.

make out an invoice for you. On leaving the country keep the purchased items in your carry-on baggage. A customs official will check them and stamp your paperwork, then tell you where to obtain your refund. Be sure to leave yourself a bit of extra time at the airport to get this done.

Tipping & Bargaining

In restaurants and cafes it's customary to tip about 10% of the bill for decent service. An interesting note: when your server is taking your bill with payment away, saying 'gracias' usually implies that the server should keep the change as a tip. If you want change back, don't say 'gracias' – say 'cambio, por favor' instead.

Note that tips can't be added to credit-card bills, so carry cash for this purpose. Also note that the cubierto that some restaurants charge is not a tip; it's a sort of 'cover charge' for the use of utensils and bread.

Bartenders They don't expect a tip, but it's OK to give a few pesos for a drink or good cocktail.

Bus porters A few pesos.

Delivery persons A few pesos.

Hotel cleaning staff A few small bills per day (only at fine, upscale hotels).

Hotel porters A few pesos.

Restaurant servers 10%; 15% for fine restaurants with great service.

Spas 15%.

Taxi drivers No tip unless they help with luggage; many people round up to the nearest peso.

Tour guides 10% to 15%.

Traveler's Checks

➡ Very high commissions are levied on traveler's checks, which are difficult to cash anywhere and specifically not recommended for travel in Argentina. Stores will not accept traveler's checks, and outside Buenos Aires it's even harder to change them.

Opening Hours

There are always exceptions, but the following are general opening hours:

Banks 8am to 3pm or 4pm Monday to Friday; some open till 1pm Saturday.

Bars 8pm or 9pm to between 4am and 6am nightly (downtown, some open and close earlier).

Cafes 6am to midnight or much later; open daily.

Clubs 1am to 2am to between 6am and 8am Friday and Saturday.

Office business hours 8am to 5pm.

Post offices 8am to 6pm Monday to Friday, 9am to 1pm Saturday.

Restaurants Noon to 3:30pm and 8pm to midnight or 1am (later on weekends).

Shops 9am or 10am to 8pm or 9pm Monday to Saturday.

Post

➡ The often unreliable **Correo Argentino** (www.correoargentino.com.ar) is the government postal service.

➡ Essential overseas mail should be sent certificado (registered).

➡ You can send packages less than 2kg from any post office, but anything heavier needs to go through aduana (a customs office). In Buenos Aires, this office is near Retiro bus terminal and is called Correo Internacional. Take your passport and keep the package open as you'll have to show its contents to a customs official.

➡ Domestic couriers, such as **Andreani** (www.andreani.com.ar) and **OCA** (Map p58; ☎4311-5305; www.oca.com.ar; Viamonte 526, Microcentro), and international couriers like DHL and FedEx are far more dependable than the post office. But they're also far more expensive. The last two have offices only in the largest cities, while the first two usually serve as their connections to the interior of the country.

➡ If a package is being sent to you, expect to wait awhile before receiving notification of its arrival. Nearly all parcels sent to Buenos Aires go to the international Retiro office, near the Buquebus terminal. To collect the package you'll have to wait (sometimes hours), first to get it and then to have it checked by customs. There's also a processing fee. Don't expect any valuables to make it through.

Public Holidays

Government offices and businesses are closed on Argentina's numerous public holidays. If the holiday falls on a midweek day or weekend day, it's often bumped to the nearest Monday; if it falls on a Tuesday or Thursday, then the in-between days of Monday and Friday are taken as holidays.

Public-transportation options are more limited on holidays, when you should reserve tickets far in advance. Hotel booking should also be done ahead of time.

The following list does not include provincial holidays, which may vary considerably.

January 1 Año Nuevo, New Year's Day.

February/March Carnaval. Dates vary; a Monday and Tuesday become holidays.

March 24 Día de la Memoria; Memorial Day. Anniversary of the day that started the 1976 dictatorship and subsequent Dirty War.

March/April Semana Santa; Easter week. Dates vary; most businesses close on 'Good Thursday' and Good Friday; major travel week.

April 2 Día de las Malvinas; honors the fallen Argentine soldiers from the Islas Malvinas (Falkland Islands) war in 1982.

May 1 Día del Trabajador; Labor Day.

May 25 Día de la Revolución de Mayo; commemorates the 1810 revolution against Spain.

June 20 Día de la Bandera; Flag Day. Anniversary of death of Manuel Belgrano, creator of Argentina's flag and military leader.

July 9 Día de la Independencia; Independence Day.

August (third Monday in August) Día del Libertador San Martín; marks the anniversary of José de San Martín's death (1778–1850).

October 12 (second Monday in October) Día del Respeto a la Diversidad Cultural; a day to respect cultural diversity.

November 20 (fourth Monday in November) Día de la Soberanía Nacional; Day of National Sovereignty.

December 8 Día de la Concepción Inmaculada; celebrates the immaculate conception of the Virgin Mary.

December 25 Navidad; Christmas Day.

Note that Christmas Eve and New Year's Day are treated as semi-holidays, and you will find some businesses closed for the latter half of those days.

Safe Travel

➔ For tourists, Argentina is one of the safest countries in Latin America. This isn't to say you should skip down the street drunk with your money belt strapped to your head, but with a little common sense you can visit Argentina's big cities as safely as you could London, Paris or New York. That said, crime has been on the rise.

Petty Crime

➔ The economic crisis of 1999–2001 plunged a lot of people into poverty, and street crime (pickpocketing, bag-snatching and armed robbery) has subsequently risen, especially in Buenos Aires. Here, be especially watchful for pickpockets on crowded buses, on the Subte and at busy *ferias* (street markets). Still, most people feel perfectly safe in the big cities. In the small towns of the provinces you'd have to *search* for a crook to rob you.

➔ Bus terminals are common places where tourists become separated from their possessions. For the most part bus terminals are safe, as they're usually full of families traveling and saying goodbyes, but they can also be prime grounds for bag-snatchers. Always keep an eagle eye on your goods. This is especially true in Buenos Aires' Retiro station.

➔ At sidewalk cafe or restaurant tables, always have your bag close to you, preferably touching your body. You can also place the strap around your leg or tie it around the furniture. Be careful showing off expensive electronics like laptops, iPods or iPads. Other places to be wary are tourist destinations and on crowded public transportation.

➔ In Buenos Aires the **Tourist Police** (☎011-4346-5748, 0800-999-5000) provide interpreters and help victims of robberies and rip-offs.

Pickets & Protests

➔ Street protests have become part of daily life in Argentina, especially in Buenos Aires' Plaza de Mayo area. Generally these have little effect on tourists other than blocking traffic or making it difficult to see Buenos Aires' Plaza de Mayo and the Casa Rosada.

➔ The country has many *gremios* or *sindicatos* (trade unions), and it seems that one of them is always on strike. Transportation unions sometimes go on strike, which can affect travelers directly by delaying domestic flights and bus services. It's always a good idea to keep your eye on the news before traveling.

Drivers

➔ Being a pedestrian in Argentina is perhaps one of the country's more difficult ventures. Many Argentine drivers jump the gun when the traffic signal is about to change to green, drive extremely fast and change lanes unpredictably. Even though pedestrians at corners and crosswalks have legal right of way, very few drivers respect this and will hardly slow down when you are crossing. Be especially careful of buses, which can be reckless and, because of their large size, particularly dangerous.

Police & Military

➔ The police and military have a reputation for being corrupt or irresponsible, but both are generally helpful and courteous to tourists. If you feel you're being patted down for a bribe (most often if you're driving), you can respond by tactfully paying up or asking the officer to accompany you to the police station to take care of it. The latter will likely cause the officer to drop it – though it could also lead you in to the labyrinthine bureaucracy of the Argentine police system. Pretending you don't understand Spanish may also frustrate a potential bribe.

Telephone

➡ To use street phones, you'll pay with regular coins or *tarjetas telefónicas* (magnetic phone cards available at many kiosks). You'll only be able to speak for a limited time before you get cut off, so carry enough credit.

➡ Toll-free numbers begin with ☏0800; these calls can only be made within Argentina. Numbers that start with ☏0810 are charged at a local rate only, no matter where (in Argentina) you are calling from.

➡ The cheapest way to make an international call is to use an online service (such as Skype or Google Voice) or use a phone card. International calls can be made at *locutorios* but they're more expensive this way. When dialing abroad, dial ☏00, followed by the code of the country you're calling, then the area code and number.

Directory Assistance (☏110)

Fire (☏100)

Medical Emergency (☏107)

Police (☏101, in some larger cities 911)

Tourist Police (☏011-4346-5748, 0800-999-5000) In Buenos Aires.

Cell Phones

➡ It's best to bring your own unlocked tri- or quad-band GSM cell phone to Argentina, then buy an inexpensive SIM chip (you'll get a local number) and credits (or *carga virtual*) as needed. Both SIM chips and credits can be bought at many kiosks or *locutorios*; look for '*recarga facil*' or '*saldo virtual*' signs. Many Argentines use this system with their cell phones, and you can buy SIM chips with data as well for wi-fi access. Phone unlocking services are available; ask around.

➡ You can also buy cell phones that use SIM chips; these usually include some credits for your first batch of calls. Be careful renting phones as they're not usually a better deal than outright buying a cell phone.

➡ If you plan to travel with an iPhone or other G3 smart phone, prepare yourself – you may need to purchase an international plan to avoid being hit with a huge bill for roaming costs. On the other hand, it's possible to call internationally for free or very cheap using a VoIP (Voice over Internet Protocol) system such as Skype. This is a constantly changing field, so do some research before you travel.

➡ Cell phone numbers in Argentina are always preceded by '15.' If you're calling a cell phone number from a landline, you'll have to dial '15' first (add the area code before the '15' as necessary). However, if you're calling a cell phone

from another cell phone, you don't need to dial '15.'

➡ You don't need to dial '15' to send text messages. Whatsapp is a popular way of sending free texts in Argentina, providing both parties have it installed.

Phone Cards

➡ Telephone calling cards are sold at many kiosks and make domestic and international calls far cheaper than calling direct. However, they must be used from a fixed line such as a home or hotel telephone (provided you can dial outside the hotel). They cannot be used at most pay phones.

➡ Some *locutorios* allow you to use them, and although they levy a surcharge, the call is still cheaper than dialing direct. When purchasing one, tell the clerk the country you will call so they give you the right card.

Locutorios & Internet Cafes

➡ The easiest way to make a local phone call is to find a *locutorio*, a small telephone office that has private cabins where you make calls and then pay at the register.

➡ *Locutorios* are fairly common everywhere. They cost about the same as street phones, are much quieter and you won't run out of coins. Most *locutorios* are supplied with phone books.

➡ When making international calls from *locutorios* ask about off-peak discount hours, which generally apply after 10pm and on weekends. Making international calls over the internet using Skype is a cheap option; many internet cafes have this system in place.

➡ Faxes are cheap and widely available at most *locutorios* and internet cafes.

ELECTRONICS WARNING

Note that buying a smart phone, and especially an iPhone, is extremely expensive in Argentina due to import restrictions – and they are not widely available. If you do bring your smart phone, don't flash it around unnecessarily or leave it unprotected somewhere. This goes for tablet computers and laptop computers, too.

CALLING ARGENTINA

To call a number in Argentina from another country, dial your international exit code, then the country code for Argentina, then the area code (without the zero) and number. For example, if you're calling a Buenos Aires landline number from the United States, you'd dial:

➜ 📱011-54-11-xxxx-xxxx

➜ 📱011 is the United States' international exit code

➜ 📱54 is Argentina's country code

➜ 📱11 is Buenos Aires' city code without the beginning zero

➜ xxxx-xxxx is your local Buenos Aires phone number, usually eight digits

When dialing an Argentine cell phone from another country, dial your international exit code, then 54, then 9, then the area code without the 0, then the number – leaving out the 15 (which most Argentine cell phone numbers start with). For example, if you're calling a Buenos Aires cell phone number from the United States, you'd dial:

➜ 📱011-54-9-11-xxxx-xxxx

Time

➜ Argentina is three hours behind GMT and generally does not observe daylight saving time (though this situation can easily change). When it's noon in Argentina, it's 7am in San Francisco, 10am in New York, 3pm in London and 1am the next day in Sydney (add one hour to these destinations during their daylight saving times).

➜ Argentina uses the 24-hour clock in written communications, but both the 12- and 24-hour clocks can be used conversationally.

Toilets

➜ Public toilets in Argentina are better than in most of South America, but there are certainly exceptions. For the truly squeamish, the better restaurants and cafes are good alternatives. Large shopping malls often have public bathrooms, as do international fast-food chains.

➜ Always carry your own toilet paper, since it often runs out in public restrooms, and don't expect luxuries such as soap, hot water and paper towels either.

➜ In smaller towns, some public toilets charge a small fee for entry. Changing facilities for babies are not always available.

➜ Some may find bidets a novelty; they are those strange shallow, ceramic bowls with knobs and a drain, often accompanying toilets in hotel bathrooms. They are meant for between-shower cleanings of nether regions. Turn knobs slowly, or you may end up spraying yourself or the ceiling.

Tourist Information

➜ Argentina's national tourist board is the **Ministerio de Turismo** (www.turismo. gov.ar); its main office is in Buenos Aires.

➜ Almost every destination city or town has a tourist office, usually on or near the main plaza or at the bus terminal. Each Argentine province also has its own representation in Buenos Aires. Most of these are well organized, often offering a computerized database of tourist information, and can be worth a visit before heading for the provinces.

Travelers with Disabilities

➜ Negotiating Argentina as a disabled traveler is not the easiest of tasks. Those in wheelchairs in particular will quickly realize that many cities' narrow, busy and uneven sidewalks are difficult to negotiate. Crossing streets is also a problem, since not every corner has ramps (which are often in need of repair) and traffic can be ruthless when it comes to pedestrians and wheelchair-users.

➜ A few buses do have *piso bajo* – they 'kneel' and have extra-large spaces – but the Subte (subway) in Buenos Aires does not cater to the mobility-impaired.

➜ International hotel chains often have wheelchair-accessible rooms, as do other less fancy hotels. Some restaurants, tourist sights and public buildings have ramps, but bathrooms are not always wheelchair-accessible (in bigger cities, shopping malls are a good bet for these).

➜ In Buenos Aires, **QRV Transportes Especiales** (📱011-4306-6635, 011-15-6863-9555; www. qrvtransportes.com.ar) offers private transportation and city tours in vans fully equipped for wheelchair users.

➜ Other than the use of Braille on ATMs, little effort has been dedicated to bettering accessibility for the vision impaired. Stoplights are rarely equipped with sound alerts.

➡ The **Biblioteca Argentina Para Ciegos** (Argentine Library for the Blind; BAC; ☐011-4981-0137; www. bac.org.ar; Lezica 3909) in Buenos Aires maintains a Braille collection of books in Spanish, as well as other resources.

Also check out the following international organizations:

Flying Wheels Travel (www. flyingwheelstravel.com)

Mobility International USA (www.miusa.org)

Society for Accessible Travel & Hospitality (www.sath.org)

Visas

➡ Nationals of the USA, Canada, most Western European countries, Australia and New Zealand do not need a visa to visit Argentina. Upon arrival, most visitors get a 90-day stamp in their passport. Those from the USA, Canada and Australia, however, must pay a significant 'reciprocity fee' before arriving.

➡ Dependent children traveling without *both* parents theoretically need a notarized document certifying that both parents agree to the child's travel. Parents may also wish to bring a copy of the custody form; however, there's a good

chance they won't be asked for either document.

➡ Depending on your nationality, very short visits to neighboring countries sometimes do not require visas. For instance, you *might* not be asked for a Brazilian visa to cross from the Argentine town of Puerto Iguazú to Foz do Iguaçu, as long as you return the same day – but doing so is at your own risk.

➡ The same is true at the Bolivian border town of Villazón, near La Quiaca. Officials at Paraguayan crossings can give day-stamps, however. Check current regulations for the latest situation.

Visa Extensions

➡ For a 90-day extension on your tourist visa, get ready for bureaucracy and visit Buenos Aires' immigration office **Dirección Nacional de Migraciones** (☐4317-0234; www.migraciones.gov. ar/accesibleingles/?categorias; Antártida Argentina 1355; ⊗8am-2pm Mon-Fri). The fee is currently AR$600 for non-Mercosur nationals. Interestingly enough, the fee for overstaying your visa is also AR$600 (but this can change).

➡ Another option if you're staying more than three months is to cross into Colonia or Montevideo (both in Uruguay; Colonia can be an easy day trip) or into Chile

for a day or two before your visa expires, then return with a new 90-day visa. However, this only works if you don't need a visa to enter the other country.

Volunteering

➡ There are many opportunities for volunteering in Argentina, from food banks to *villas miserias* (shantytowns) to organic farms. Some ask for just your time, or a modest fee – and some charge hundreds of dollars (with likely a low percentage of money going directly to those in need). Before choosing an organization, it's good to talk to other volunteers about their experiences.

Aldea Luna (www.aldealuna. com.ar) Work on a farm in a nature reserve.

Anda Responsible Travel (www.andatravel.com.ar/en/ volunteering) Buenos Aires travel agency supporting local communities.

Centro Conviven (http:// centroconviven.blogspot.com) Helps kids in Buenos Aires' *villas* (shantytowns).

Conservación Patagonica (www.conservacionpatagonica. org/) Help to create a national park.

Eco Yoga Park (www.eco yogavillages.org/volunteer-programs) Work on an organic farm, construct ecobuildings and teach local communities.

Fundación Banco de Alimentos (www.bancode alimentos.org.ar) Short-term work at a food bank.

Habitat for Humanity Argentina (www.hpha.org.ar) Building communities.

Patagonia Volunteer (www. patagoniavolunteer.org) Opportunities in Patagonia.

Volunteer South America (www.volunteersouthamerica. net) List of NGOs offering volunteer opportunities in South America.

ARGENTINA'S RECIPROCITY FEE

Citizens from some countries have to pay a reciprocity fee *(tasa de reciprocidad)* before arriving in Argentina; ideally you'll be reminded of this when you buy your airplane ticket. This fee is equal to what Argentines are charged for visas to visit those countries. You'll need to pay this fee online via credit card; see www.migraciones. gov.ar/accesibleingles and click on 'Reciprocity Fee.'

These fees are US$100 for Australians (good for one year), US$160 for Americans (good for 10 years) and US$92 for Canadians (good until a month before your passport expires). Check current regulations as rules can change quickly.

WWOOF Argentina (www.wwoofargentina.com) Organic farming in Argentina.

Women Travelers

➡ Being a woman traveling in Argentina can sometimes be a challenge, especially if you are young, alone and/or maintaining an inflexible liberal attitude. In some ways Argentina is a safer place for a woman than Europe, the USA and most other Latin American countries, but dealing with its machismo culture can be a real pain in the ass.

➡ Some males brimming with testosterone feel the need to comment on a woman's attractiveness. This often happens when the woman is alone and walking by on the street; it occasionally happens to two or more women walking together, but never to a heterosexual couple. Verbal comments include crude language, hisses, whistles and *piropos* (flirtatious comments), which are often vulgar – although some can be eloquent.

➡ The best thing to do is completely ignore the comments. After all, many Argentine women enjoy getting these 'compliments' and most men don't necessarily mean to be insulting; they're just doing what males in their culture are brought up to do.

➡ On the plus side of machismo, expect men to hold a door open for you and let you enter first, including getting on buses; this gives you a better chance at grabbing an empty seat, so get in there quick.

Work

➡ Unless you have a special skill, business and/or speak Spanish, it's hard to find paid work in Argentina other than teaching English – or perhaps putting time in at a hostel or expat bar. And it's good to realize that you're not likely to get rich doing these things.

➡ Native English speakers usually work out of language institutes. Twenty hours a week of actual teaching is about enough for most people (note you aren't paid for prep time or travel time, which can add another hour or two for each hour of teaching). Frustrations include dealing with unpleasant institutes, time spent cashing checks at the bank, classes being spread throughout the day and cancelled classes. Institute turnover is high and most people don't teach for more than a year.

➡ A TEFL certification can certainly help but isn't mandatory for all jobs (check out www.teflbuenosaires.com). You'll make more money teaching private students, but it takes time to gain a client base. And you should take into account slow periods, such as December through February, when many locals leave town on summer vacation.

➡ To find a job, call up the institutes or visit expat bars and start networking. March is when institutes are ramping up their courses, so it's the best time to find work. Many teachers work on tourist visas (which is not a big deal), heading over to Uruguay every three months for a new visa or visiting the immigration office for a visa extension.

➡ For job tips, check out www.landingpadba.com/jobs-and-working-in-argentina. There are job postings at http://buenosaires.en.craigslist.org, and you can try posting on expat website forums such as www.baexpats.org.

Transportation

GETTING THERE & AWAY

➡ Flights, tours and rail tickets can be booked online at lonelyplanet.com/bookings.

Entering Argentina

➡ Entering Argentina is straightforward; immigration officials at airports are generally quick and to the point, while those at border crossings may take more time scrutinizing your documents and belongings.

➡ Citizens from the United States, Canada and Australia have to pay a reciprocity fee (p612) before entering Argentina.

Passports

➡ Anyone entering Argentina should have a passport valid for at least six months from date of entry, and ideally past the date the passport holder leaves the country.

➡ Once you're in Argentina, police can still demand identification at any moment (but rarely do without reason), so carry at least a photocopy of your passport around at all times (when it will also come in handy for entering government buildings, getting tax-free purchases, changing money at a bank etc).

Onward Ticket

➡ When entering by air, you officially must have a return ticket, though this is rarely asked for by officials once you're in Argentina. However, it is commonly asked for by the airline in the country of origin. Most airlines prohibit the boarding of any passengers without proof of onward travel, regardless of whether the person was sold a one-way ticket or not. They do this becase they'd be responsible for flying you back home should you be denied entrance once you're in Argentina. Check with your airline for details.

Air

➡ Argentina has direct flights between North America, the UK, Europe, Australia and South Africa, and from nearly all South American countries. You can also fly to a neighboring country, such as Brazil or Chile, and continue overland to Argentina.

Airports & Airlines

➡ Most international flights arrive at Buenos Aires' **Aeropuerto Internacional Ministro Pistarini** (Ezeiza; ☎011-5480-6111; www.aa2000.com.ar), which is a 40- to 60-minute shuttle bus or taxi ride out of town (35km).

➡ Close to downtown Buenos Aires is **Aeroparque Internacional Jorge Newbery** (Aeroparque; ☎011-5480-6111; www.aa2000.com.ar), which handles mostly

---

CLIMATE CHANGE & TRAVEL

Every form of transport that relies on carbon-based fuel generates CO_2, the main cause of human-induced climate change. Modern travel is dependent on airplanes, which might use less fuel per kilometer per person than most cars but travel much greater distances. The altitude at which aircraft emit gases (including CO_2) and particles also contributes to their climate change impact. Many websites offer 'carbon calculators' that allow people to estimate the carbon emissions generated by their journey and, for those who wish to do so, to offset the impact of the greenhouse gases emitted with contributions to portfolios of climate-friendly initiatives throughout the world. Lonely Planet offsets the carbon footprint of all staff and author travel.

ARRIVAL TIPS: AEROPUERTO INTERNACIONAL MINISTRO PISTARINI (EZEIZA)

➡ If you want to change money at Ezeiza, note that the *cambios* (exchange houses) there generally offer bad rates. Better rates are found at the local bank branch; after exiting customs into the reception hall, make a U-turn to the right to find Banco de la Nación's small office. Its also has an ATM and is open 24 hours, though long lines are common. There are other ATMs at Ezeiza, too, all of which offer the official exchange rate.

➡ There's a tourist information booth just beyond the city's 'Taxi Ezeiza' stand.

➡ Shuttle buses and taxis frequently run from Ezeiza to the center.

➡ When flying out of Ezeiza, get there at least two to three hours before your international flight. Security and immigration lines can be long, and be aware that traffic is often bad getting to Ezeiza – it can take an hour or more to go the 35km from downtown BA.

---

domestic flights but also a few international ones from neighboring countries.

➡ There are several other international airports around Argentina. Basic information on most Argentine airports can be found online at **Aeropuertos Argentina 2000** (www.aa2000.com.ar).

➡ **Aerolíneas Argentinas** (www.aerolineas.com.ar) is the national carrier and has a decent international reputation.

Land

Border Crossings

➡ There are numerous border crossings from neighboring Bolivia, Brazil, Chile, Paraguay and Uruguay; the following lists are only the principal crossings. Border formalities are generally straightforward as long as all your documents are in order.

BOLIVIA

La Quiaca to Villazón Many buses go from Jujuy and Salta to La Quiaca, where you walk across a bridge to the Bolivian border.

Aguas Blancas to Bermejo From Orán, reached by bus from Salta or Jujuy, take a bus to Aguas Blancas and then Bermejo, where you can catch a bus to Tarija.

Salvador Mazza (Pocitos) to Yacuiba Buses from Jujuy or Salta go to Salvador Mazza at the Bolivian border, where you cross and grab a shared taxi to Yacuiba.

BRAZIL

➡ The most common crossing is from Puerto Iguazú to Foz do Iguaçu. Check both cities for more information on the peculiarities of this border crossing, especially if you're crossing the border into Brazil only to see the other side of Iguazú Falls. There is also a border crossing from Paso de los Libres to Uruguaiana (Brazil).

CHILE

There are numerous crossings between Argentina and Chile. Except in far southern Patagonia, every land crossing involves crossing the Andes. Due to weather, some high-altitude passes close in winter; even the busy Mendoza–Santiago route over RN 7 can close for several days (sometimes longer) during a severe storm. Always check road conditions, especially if you have a flight scheduled on the other side of the mountains. The following are the most commonly used crossings:

➡ **Bariloche to Puerto Montt** This border crossing over the Andes to Chile is usually no fuss; an optional 'tour' is the famous, scenic 12-hour bus-boat combination. It takes two days in winter.

➡ **El Calafate to Puerto Natales and Parque Nacional Torres del Paine** Probably the most beaten route down here, heading from the Glaciar Perito Moreno (near El Calafate) to Parque Nacional Torres del Paine (near Puerto Natales). Several buses per day in summer; one to two daily in the off-season.

➡ **Los Antiguos to Chile Chico** Those entering Argentina from Chile can access the rugged RN 40 from here and head down to El Chaltén and El Calafate. Best in summer, when there's actually public transportation available.

➡ **Mendoza to Santiago** The most popular crossing between the two countries, passing 6962m Aconcagua en route.

➡ **Salta to San Pedro de Atacama (via Jujuy, Purmamarca and Susques)** A 10-hour bus ride through the altiplano with stunningly beautiful scenery.

➡ **Ushuaia to Punta Arenas** Daily buses in summer, fewer in winter, on this 10- to 12-hour trip (depending on weather conditions), which includes a ferry crossing at either Porvenir or Punta Delgada/Primera Angostura.

PARAGUAY & URUGUAY

➜ There are two direct border crossings between Argentina and Paraguay: Clorinda to Asunción, and Posadas to Encarnación. From Puerto Iguazú, Argentina, you can also cross through Brazil into Ciudad del Este, Paraguay.

➜ Border crossings from Argentine cities to Uruguayan cities include Gualeguaychú to Fray Bentos; Colón to Paysandú; and Concordia to Salto. All involve crossing bridges. Buses from Buenos Aires to Montevideo and other waterfront cities, however, are slower and less convenient than the ferries (or ferry-bus combinations) across the Río de la Plata.

Bus

➜ Travelers can bus to Argentina from most bordering countries. Buses are usually comfortable, modern and fairly clean. Crossing over does not involve too many hassles; just make sure that you have any proper visas beforehand.

River

There are several river crossings between Uruguay and Buenos Aires that involve ferry or hydrofoil, and often require combinations with buses.

➜ **Buenos Aires to Colonia** Daily ferries (one to three hours) head to Colonia, with bus connections to Montevideo (an additional three hours).

➜ **Buenos Aires to Montevideo** High-speed ferries carry passengers from downtown Buenos Aires to the Uruguayan capital in only 2¼ hours.

➜ **Tigre to Carmelo** Regular passenger launches speed from the Buenos Aires suburb of Tigre to Carmelo in 2½ hours (services also go to Montevideo from Tigre).

GETTING AROUND

Air

Airlines in Argentina

➜ The national carrier, **Aerolíneas Argentinas** (www.aerolineas.com.ar), offers the most domestic flights, but it's not necessarily better than its competitors. Other airlines with domestic flights include **LAN** (www.lan.com) and **Líneas Aéreas del Estado** (LADE; www.lade.com.ar), the air force's passenger service. The latter has some of the least expensive air tickets and specializes in Patagonia, but it has very few flights and most are short hops.

➜ Demand for flights around the country can be heavy, especially during some holidays (such as Christmas or Easter) and the vacation months of January, February and July. Seats are often booked out well in advance so reserve as far ahead as possible.

➜ Nearly all domestic flights land at **Aeroparque Internacional Jorge Newbery** (Aeroparque; ☎011-5480-6111; www.aa2000.com.ar), a short distance north of downtown Buenos Aires. It's worth noting that Argentina's domestic flight system can be very unreliable – flights are often cancelled or delayed, and there can be frequent labor strikes. It might be a good idea to avoid tight itineraries; for example, leave a day's cushion in between your domestic and international flights.

Bicycle

➜ If you dig cycling your way around a country, Argentina has potential. You'll see the landscape in greater detail, have far more freedom than you would if beholden to public transportation, and likely meet more locals.

➜ Road bikes are suitable for many paved roads, but byways are often narrow and surfaces can be rough. A *todo terreno* (mountain bike) is often safer and more convenient, allowing you to use the unpaved shoulder and the very extensive network of gravel roads throughout the country. Argentine bicycles are improving in quality, but are still far from equal to their counterparts in Europe or the USA.

➜ There are two major drawbacks to long-distance bicycling in Argentina. One is the wind, which in Patagonia can slow your progress to a crawl. The other is Argentine motorists: on many of the country's straight, narrow, two-lane highways, they can be a serious hazard to cyclists. Make yourself as visible as possible, and wear a helmet.

➜ Bring an adequate repair kit and extra parts and stock up on good maps, which is usually easier to do once you're in Argentina. Always confirm directions and inquire about conditions locally. In Patagonia, a windbreaker and warm clothing are essential. Don't expect much traffic on some back roads.

Rental

➜ Bicycle rentals (mostly mountain bikes) are available in many popular tourist destinations, such as along the Atlantic coast, Mendoza, Bariloche and other towns throughout the Lake District and Córdoba's Central Sierras. Prices are by the hour or day, and are affordable.

Purchase

➜ Many towns have bike shops, but high-quality bikes are expensive, and repair parts can be hard to come by. If you do decide to buy while you're here, you're best off doing so in Buenos Aires – selection in other major cities can be pretty slim.

Boat

➡ Opportunities for boat or river travel in and around Argentina are limited, though there are regular international services to/ from Uruguay and to/from Chile via the Lake District. Further south, from Ushuaia, operators offer boat trips on the Beagle Channel in Tierra del Fuego.

➡ Otherwise, if you must be on the water, head to the Buenos Aires suburb of Tigre, where there are numerous boat excursions around the delta of the Río de la Plata.

Bus

➡ If you're doing any serious traveling around Argentina, you'll become very familiar with the country's excellent bus network. Long-distance buses (known as *micros*) are fast, surprisingly comfortable and can be a rather luxurious experience. It's the way most Argentines get around. Larger luggage is stowed in the hold below, security is generally good (especially on the 1st-class buses) and attendants tag your bags. If you have a long trip – say, Buenos Aires to Mendoza – overnight buses are the way to go, saving you a night's accommodations.

➡ Most cities and towns have a central bus terminal where each company has its own ticket window. Some companies post schedules prominently, and the ticket price and departure time is always on the ticket you buy. Expect restrooms, left luggage, fast-food stalls, kiosks and newspaper vendors inside or near almost every large terminal. In tourist destination cities they'll often have a tourist information office. There are generally few if any hotel touts or other traveler-hassling types at terminals;

El Calafate is one notable exception.

➡ Two websites that sell long-distance bus tickets online (and without commission) are www.plataforma10.com and www.omnilineas.com.

Classes & Costs

➡ Most bus lines have modern coaches with spacious, comfortable seats, large windows, air-conditioning, TVs, toilets (bring toilet paper) and sometimes an attendant serving coffee and snacks.

➡ On overnight trips it's well worth the extra pesos to go *coche cama* (sleeper class); seats are wide, recline almost flat and are very comfortable. For even more luxury there's *ejecutivo* (executive), which is available on a few popular runs. For less luxury, *semi-cama* (semisleeper) seats are manageable. If pinching pesos, *común* (common) is the cheapest class. For trips less than about five hours, there's usually no choice and buses are *común* or *semi-cama*, which are both usually just fine.

➡ Bus fares vary widely depending on the season, class and company. Patagonia runs tend to be the most expensive. Many companies accept credit cards.

Reservations

➡ Often you don't need to buy bus tickets beforehand unless you're traveling on a Friday between major cities, when overnight *coche cama* services sell out fast. During holiday stretches, such as late December through February, July and August, tickets sell quickly. As soon as you arrive somewhere, especially if it's a town with limited services, find out which companies go to your next destination and when, and plan your trip.

➡ When the bus terminal is on the outskirts of a big

town or city, there are often downtown agencies selling tickets without commission.

Seasonal Services

➡ In the Lake District and northern Patagonia, bus services are good during summer (November through March), when there are many microbus routes to campgrounds, along lake circuits, to trailheads and to other destinations popular with tourists. Outside summer, however, these services slow way down.

➡ In Patagonia the famed stretch of RN 40, or Ruta Nacional Cuarenta (Route 40), was once infrequently traveled and rough – though most of it is now paved (it's still good to have a 4WD for side roads, however). But there's still little public transportation despite the road improvements, and it's mostly via expensive, summertime microbus 'tours.'

Car & Motorcycle

➡ Because Argentina is so large, many parts are accessible only by private vehicle, despite the country's extensive public transportation system. This is especially true in Patagonia, where distances are great and buses can be infrequent.

Automobile Associations

➡ Whenever driving in Argentina, it's worth being a member of the **Automóvil Club Argentino** (ACA; Map p84; www.aca.org.ar), which has offices, gas stations and garages throughout the country and offers road service and towing in and around major destinations. ACA recognizes members of most overseas auto clubs and grants them privileges including road service and discounts on maps and accommodations. Bring your card.

Bringing Your Own Vehicle

➡ Chile is probably the best country on the continent for shipping a vehicle from overseas, though Argentina is feasible. Getting the vehicle out of customs typically involves routine but time-consuming paperwork.

Driver's License & Documents

➡ An International Driving Permit can supplement your national or state driver's license, though car-rental agencies are unlikely to ask you for one. If you are stopped, police will inspect your automobile registration and insurance and tax documents, all of which must be up to date.

➡ Drivers of Argentine vehicles must carry their title document (*tarjeta verde* or 'green card'); if it's a rental, make sure it's in the glove box. For foreign vehicles, customs permission is the acceptable substitute.

➡ Liability insurance is obligatory, and police often ask to see proof of insurance at checkpoints.

Fuel

➡ *Nafta* (gas) prices are more expensive than the US. Avoid *común* (regular) as it's usually low quality. Super and premium are better choices. In Patagonia gas prices are about a third less than elsewhere.

➡ *Estaciones de servicio* (gas stations) are fairly common, but outside the cities keep an eye on your gas gauge. In Patagonia it's a good idea to carry extra fuel.

Rental

➡ To rent a car, you must be at least 21 years of age and have a credit card and valid driver's license from your country. Agencies rarely ask for an International Driving Permit.

➡ When you rent a vehicle find out how many kilometers are included. Unlimited-kilometer deals exist but are usually much more expensive, depending on the destination.

➡ Reserving a car with one of the major international agencies in your home country often gets you lower rates; you can also try online sites such as www. despegar.com.

➡ One of the cheapest places to rent a car is Bariloche; if you're heading to Patagonia for example, this is a good place to rent. Taking a rental car into Chile might be allowed for an extra fee.

➡ For motorcycle rentals, you must be at least 25 years of age; head to **Motocare** (☎4761-2696; www.motocare. com.ar/rental; Echeverria 738, Vicente Lopez, Buenos Aires) located in Buenos Aires (or Neuquén). Honda Transalp 700s are available; bring your own helmet and riding gear. For driving outside big cities only.

Purchase

➡ Purchasing a vehicle in Argentina can be complicated for foreigners. This usually involves having a permanent local address, obtaining a CDI (a tax ID number) and paying for the vehicle in cash. To buy a used vehicle, you must transfer the title at a title transfer office, with the current owner and all their proper papers present. Make sure all licenses, unpaid tickets and taxes have been paid.

➡ Speaking Spanish helps. Getting insurance without a DNI (national document) can be difficult but not impossible. As a foreigner without a DNI you may own a vehicle in Argentina; however, you theoretically cannot take it out of the country without a notarized authorization, which can be difficult to obtain.

➡ It's wise to supplement this information with your own current research.

Insurance

➡ Liability insurance is obligatory in Argentina, and police ask to see proof of insurance at checkpoints.

➡ If you plan on taking the car to neighboring countries, make sure it will remain covered (you'll have to pay extra).

➡ Among reputable insurers in Argentina are **Mapfre** (www.mapfre.com.ar) and **ACA** (www.aca.org.ar).

Road Rules & Hazards

➡ Anyone considering driving in Argentina should know that Argentine drivers are aggressive and commonly ignore speed limits, road signs and even traffic signals.

➡ Night driving is not recommended; in many regions animals hang out on the road for warmth.

➡ Have on hand some emergency reflectors (*balizas*) and a fire extinguisher (*matafuego*).

➡ Headrests are required for the driver and passengers, and seatbelts are obligatory (though few wear them).

A HANDY WEBSITE FOR DRIVERS

A very handy website for those driving around Argentina is www.ruta0.com. Among other things, you can punch in two destinations and get the recommended routes (and whether they're paved or not), distances in kilometers, driving times and even how much it will cost in gas consumption. Now if it could only warn you where to avoid those crazy Argentine drivers.

➡ Motorcycle helmets are also obligatory, although this law is rarely enforced.

➡ You won't often see police patrolling the highways, but might meet them at major intersections and roadside checkpoints where they conduct meticulous document and equipment checks. Sometimes these checks are pretexts for graft. If you are uncertain about your rights, politely state your intention to contact your embassy or consulate. If you *do* want to pay a bribe for the sake of expediency, ask *¿Puedo pagar la multa ahora?* ('Can I pay the fine now?').

Hitchhiking

➡ Along with Chile, Argentina is probably the best country for hitchhiking *(hacer dedo)* in all of South America. The major drawback is that Argentine vehicles are often stuffed full with families and children, but truckers will sometimes pick up backpackers. A good place to ask is at *estaciones de servicio* on the outskirts of large Argentine cities, where truckers gas up their vehicles.

➡ In Patagonia, where distances are great and vehicles few, hitchers should expect long waits and carry warm, windproof clothing and refreshments.

➡ Having a sign will improve your chances for a pickup, especially if it says something like *visitando Argentina de Canada* ('visiting Argentina from Canada'), rather than just a destination. Argentines are fascinated by foreigners.

➡ Be aware that hitchhiking is never entirely safe in any country in the world, and we don't recommend it. Travelers who decide to hitch should understand that they are taking a small but potentially serious risk. People who who choose to hitch will be safer if they travel in pairs and let someone know where they are planning to go.

Local Transportation
Bus

➡ Local Argentine buses, called *colectivos*, are notorious for charging down the street and spewing clouds of black smoke while traveling at breakneck speeds. Riding on them is a good way to see the cities and get around, providing you can sort out the often complex bus systems. Buses are clearly numbered and usually carry a placard indicating their final destination. Sometimes, identically numbered buses serve slightly different routes (especially in big cities), so pay attention to the placards. To ask 'Does this bus go (to the town center)?' say *¿Va este colectivo (al centro)?*

➡ Most city buses operate on coins; you pay as you board. In some cities, such as Buenos Aires, Mendoza or Mar del Plata, you must buy transportation cards, purchased at many kiosks.

Subway

➡ Buenos Aires is the only Argentine city with a subway system (known as the Subte), and it's the quickest and cheapest way of getting around the city center.

Taxi & Remise

➡ The people of Buenos Aires make frequent use of taxis, which are digitally metered and cheap by US and European standards. Outside the capital, meters are common but not universal, and you'll need to agree on a fare in advance.

➡ Remises are unmarked radio taxis, usually without meters, that have fixed fares (comparable to taxis) within a given zone. Any business will phone one for you if you ask.

➡ Where public transportation is scarce it's possible to hire a taxi or *remise* with a driver for the day. This can be especially convenient and economical for a group, especially for taking an area tour. Always negotiate the fee in advance.

Train

➡ For many years there were major reductions in long-distance train services in Argentina, but recent years have seen some rail lines being progressively reopened.

➡ Good sources for information are www.seat61.com/southamerica.htm and www.sofse.gob.ar.

➡ Trains serve most of Buenos Aires and some surrounding provinces. During the holiday periods, such as Christmas or national holidays, buy tickets in advance.

➡ Train fares tend to be lower than comparable bus fares, but trains are slower and there are fewer departure times and destinations.

➡ Long-distance trains have sleepers.

➡ Train buffs will want to take the narrow-gauge *La Trochita*, which runs 20km between Esquel and Nahuel Pan. Another legendary ride is Salta's touristy but spectacular *Tren a las Nubes* (Train to the Clouds), which at one point spans a desert canyon at an altitude of 4220m – though it's famously unreliable. And finally, the scenic *Tren Patagónico* connects Bariloche to Viedma.

Language

Latin American Spanish pronunciation is easy, as most sounds have equivalents in English. Read our colored pronunciation guides as if they were English, and you'll be understood. Note that kh is a throaty sound (like the 'ch' in the Scottish *loch*), v and b are like a soft English 'v' (between a 'v' and a 'b'), and r is strongly rolled. Also note that the letters *ll* (pronounced ly or simplified to y in most parts of Latin America) and *y* are pronounced like the 's' in 'measure' or the 'sh' in 'shut' in Argentina, which gives the language its very own local flavor. In this chapter, we've used the symbol sh to represent this sound. You'll get used to this very quickly listening to and taking your cues from the locals.

The stressed syllables are indicated with an acute accent in written Spanish (eg *días*) and with italics in our pronunciation guides.

The polite form is used in this chapter; where both polite and informal options are given, they are indicated by the abbreviations 'pol' and 'inf'. Where necessary, both masculine and feminine forms of words are included, separated by a slash and with the masculine form first, eg *perdido/a* (m/f).

BASICS

Hello.	*Hola.*	o·la
Goodbye.	*Adiós./Chau.*	a·dyos/chow
How are you?	*¿Qué tal?*	ke tal
Fine, thanks.	*Bien, gracias.*	byen gra·syas

WANT MORE?

For in-depth language information and handy phrases, check out Lonely Planet's *Latin American Spanish Phrasebook*. You'll find it at **shop.lonelyplanet.com**, or you can buy Lonely Planet's iPhone phrasebooks at the Apple App Store.

Excuse me.	*Perdón.*	per·*don*
Sorry.	*Lo siento.*	lo syen·to
Please.	*Por favor.*	por fa·*vor*
Thank you.	*Gracias.*	gra·syas
You're welcome.	*De nada.*	de na·da
Yes./No.	*Sí./No.*	see/no

My name is ...
Me llamo ...　　　　me sha·mo ...

What's your name?
¿Cómo se llama usted?	ko·mo se sha·ma oo·*ste* (pol)
¿Cómo te llamas?	ko·mo te sha·mas (inf)

Do you speak English?
¿Habla inglés?	a·bla een·*gles* (pol)
¿Hablas inglés?	a·blas een·*gles* (inf)

I don't understand.
Yo no entiendo.　　　yo no en·*tyen*·do

ACCOMMODATIONS

I'd like a ... room.	*Quisiera una habitación ...*	kee·sye·ra oo·na a·bee·ta·syon ...
single	*individual*	een·dee·vee·*dwal*
double	*doble*	do·ble

How much is it per night/person?
¿Cuánto cuesta por noche/persona?	kwan·to kwes·ta por no·che/per·so·na

Does it include breakfast?
¿Incluye el desayuno?	een·*kloo*·she el de·sa·*shoo*·no

campsite	*terreno de cámping*	te·*re*·no de kam·peeng
hotel	*hotel*	o·*tel*
guesthouse	*hostería*	os·te·*ree*·a
youth hostel	*albergue juvenil*	al·*ber*·ge khoo·ve·*neel*

air-con	aire acondi-cionado	ai·re a·kon·dee·syo·na·do
bathroom	baño	ba·nyo
bed	cama	ka·ma
window	ventana	ven·ta·na

DIRECTIONS

Where's ...?
¿Dónde está ...? don·de es·ta ...

What's the address?
¿Cuál es la dirección? kwal es la dee·rek·syon

Could you please write it down?
¿Puede escribirlo, por favor? pwe·de es·kree·beer·lo por fa·vor

Can you show me (on the map)?
¿Me lo puede indicar (en el mapa)? me lo pwe·de een·dee·kar (en el ma·pa)

at the corner	en la esquina	en la es·kee·na
at the traffic lights	en el semáforo	en el se·ma·fo·ro
behind ...	detrás de ...	de·tras de ...
in front of ...	enfrente de ...	en·fren·te de ...
left	izquierda	ees·kyer·da
next to ...	al lado de ...	al la·do de ...
opposite ...	frente a ...	fren·te a ...
right	derecha	de·re·cha
straight ahead	todo recto	to·do rek·to

EATING & DRINKING

Can I see the menu, please?
¿Puedo ver el menú, por favor? pwe·do ver el me·noo por fa·vor

What would you recommend?
¿Qué me recomienda? ke me re·ko·myen·da

Do you have vegetarian food?
¿Tienen comida vegetariana? tye·nen ko·mee·da ve·khe·ta·rya·na

I don't eat (red meat).
No como (carne roja). no ko·mo (kar·ne ro·kha)

That was delicious!
¡Estaba buenísimo! es·ta·ba bwe·nee·see·mo

Cheers!
¡Salud! sa·loo

The bill, please.
La cuenta, por favor. la kwen·ta por fa·vor

I'd like a table for ...	Quisiera una mesa para ...	kee·sye·ra oo·na me·sa pa·ra ...
(eight) o'clock	las (ocho)	las (o·cho)
(two) people	(dos) personas	(dos) per·so·nas

LUNFARDO

Below are some of the spicier *lunfardo* (slang) terms you may hear on your travels in Argentina.

boliche – disco or nightclub

boludo – jerk, asshole, idiot; often used in a friendly fashion, but a deep insult to a stranger

bondi – bus

buena onda – good vibes

carajo – asshole, prick; bloody hell

chabón/chabona – kid, guy/girl (term of endearment)

che – hey

diez puntos – OK, cool, fine (literally '10 points')

fiaca – laziness

guita – money

laburo – job

macanudo – great, fabulous

mango – one peso

masa – a great, cool thing

mina – woman

morfar – eat

pendejo – idiot

piba/pibe – cool young guy/girl

piola – cool, clever

pucho – cigarette

re – very, eg *re interestante* (very interesting)

trucho – fake, imitation, bad quality

¡Ponete las pilas! – Get on with it! (literally 'Put in the batteries!')

Me mataste. – I don't know; I have no idea. (literally 'You've killed me')

Le faltan un par de jugadores. – He's not playing with a full deck (literally 'He's a couple of players short')

che boludo – The most *porteño* phrase on earth. Ask a friendly local youth to explain.

Key Words

appetisers	aperitivos	a·pe·ree·tee·vos
bottle	botella	bo·te·sha
bowl	bol	bol
breakfast	desayuno	de·sa·shoo·no
children's menu	menú infantil	me·noo een·fan·teel
(too) cold	(muy) frío	(mooy) free·o
dinner	cena	se·na
food	comida	ko·mee·da

fork	*tenedor*	te·ne·dor
glass	*vaso*	va·so
hot (warm)	*caliente*	ka·lyen·te
knife	*cuchillo*	koo·chee·yo
lunch	*almuerzo*	al·mwer·so
main course	*plato principal*	pla·to preen·see·pal
plate	*plato*	pla·to
restaurant	*restaurante*	res·tow·ran·te
spoon	*cuchara*	koo·cha·ra
with/without	*con/sin*	kon/seen

Meat & Fish

beef	*carne de vaca*	kar·ne de va·ka
chicken	*pollo*	po·sho
duck	*pato*	pa·to
fish	*pescado*	pes·ka·do
lamb	*cordero*	kor·de·ro
pork	*cerdo*	ser·do
turkey	*pavo*	pa·vo
veal	*ternera*	ter·ne·ra

Fruit & Vegetables

apple	*manzana*	man·sa·na
apricot	*damasco*	da·mas·ko
artichoke	*alcaucil*	al·kow·seel
asparagus	*espárragos*	es·pa·ra·gos
banana	*banana*	ba·na·na
beans	*chauchas*	chow·chas
beetroot	*remolacha*	re·mo·la·cha
cabbage	*repollo*	re·po·sho

carrot	*zanahoria*	sa·na·o·rya
celery	*apio*	a·pyo
cherry	*cereza*	se·re·sa
corn	*choclo*	cho·klo
cucumber	*pepino*	pe·pee·no
fruit	*fruta*	froo·ta
grape	*uvas*	oo·vas
lemon	*limón*	lee·mon
lentils	*lentejas*	len·te·khas
lettuce	*lechuga*	le·choo·ga
mushroom	*champiñón*	cham·pee·nyon
nuts	*nueces*	nwe·ses
onion	*cebolla*	se·bo·sha
orange	*naranja*	na·ran·kha
peach	*durazno*	doo·ras·no
peas	*arvejas*	ar·ve·khas
(red/green) pepper	*pimiento (rojo/verde)*	pee·myen·to (ro·kho/ver·de)
pineapple	*ananá*	a·na·na
plum	*ciruela*	seer·we·la
potato	*papa*	pa·pa
pumpkin	*zapallo*	sa·pa·sho
spinach	*espinacas*	es·pee·na·kas
strawberry	*frutilla*	froo·tee·sha
tomato	*tomate*	to·ma·te
vegetable	*verdura*	ver·doo·ra
watermelon	*sandía*	san·dee·a

Other Foods

bread	*pan*	pan
butter	*manteca*	man·te·ka
cheese	*queso*	ke·so

egg	huevo	we·vo
honey	miel	myel
jam	mermelada	mer·me·la·da
oil	aceite	a·sey·te
pasta	pasta	pas·ta
pepper	pimienta	pee·myen·ta
rice	arroz	a·ros
salt	sal	sal
sugar	azúcar	a·soo·kar
vinegar	vinagre	vee·na·gre

Drinks

beer	cerveza	ser·ve·sa
coffee	café	ka·fe
(orange) juice	jugo (de naranja)	khoo·go (de na·ran·kha)
milk	leche	le·che
tea	té	te
(mineral) water	agua (mineral)	a·gwa (mee·ne·ral)
(red/white) wine	vino (tinto/ blanco)	vee·no (teen·to/ blan·ko)

EMERGENCIES

| Help! | ¡Socorro! | so·ko·ro |
| Go away! | ¡Vete! | ve·te |

Call ...!	¡Llame a ...!	sha·me a ...
a doctor	un médico	oon me·dee·ko
the police	la policía	la po·lee·see·a

I'm lost.
Estoy perdido/a.   es·toy per·dee·do/a (m/f)

I'm ill.
Estoy enfermo/a.   es·toy en·fer·mo/a (m/f)

I'm allergic to (antibiotics).
Soy alérgico/a a   soy a·ler·khee·ko/a a
(los antibióticos).   (los an·tee·byo·tee·kos) (m/f)

Where are the toilets?
¿Dónde están los   don·de es·tan los
baños?   ba·nyos

Question Words		
How?	¿Cómo?	ko·mo
What?	¿Qué?	ke
When?	¿Cuándo?	kwan·do
Where?	¿Dónde?	don·de
Who?	¿Quién?	kyen
Why?	¿Por qué?	por ke

Signs	
Abierto	Open
Cerrado	Closed
Entrada	Entrance
Hombres/Varones	Men
Mujeres/Damas	Women
Prohibido	Prohibited
Salida	Exit
Servicios/Baños	Toilets

SHOPPING & SERVICES

I'd like to buy ...
Quisiera comprar ...   kee·sye·ra kom·prar ...

I'm just looking.
Sólo estoy mirando.   so·lo es·toy mee·ran·do

Can I look at it?
¿Puedo verlo?   pwe·do ver·lo

How much is it?
¿Cuánto cuesta?   kwan·to kwes·ta

That's too expensive.
Es muy caro.   es mooy ka·ro

Can you lower the price?
¿Podría bajar un   po·dree·a ba·khar oon
poco el precio?   po·ko el pre·syo

There's a mistake in the bill.
Hay un error   ai oon e·ror
en la cuenta.   en la kwen·ta

ATM	cajero automático	ka·khe·ro ow·to·ma·tee·ko
credit card	tarjeta de crédito	tar·khe·ta de kre·dee·to
internet cafe	cibercafé	see·ber·ka·fe
market	mercado	mer·ka·do
post office	correos	ko·re·os
tourist office	oficina de turismo	o·fee·see·na de too·rees·mo

TIME & DATES

What time is it?	¿Qué hora es?	ke o·ra es
It's (10) o'clock.	Son (las diez).	son (las dyes)
It's half past (one).	Es (la una) y media.	es (la oo·na) ee me·dya

morning	mañana	ma·nya·na
afternoon	tarde	tar·de
evening	noche	no·che
yesterday	ayer	a·sher
today	hoy	oy
tomorrow	mañana	ma·nya·na

Monday	*lunes*	loo·nes
Tuesday	*martes*	mar·tes
Wednesday	*miércoles*	myer·ko·les
Thursday	*jueves*	khwe·ves
Friday	*viernes*	vyer·nes
Saturday	*sábado*	sa·ba·do
Sunday	*domingo*	do·meen·go

TRANSPORTATION

boat	*barco*	bar·ko
bus	*colectivo/ micro*	ko·lek·tee·vo/ mee·kro
plane	*avión*	a·vyon
train	*tren*	tren
first	*primero*	pree·me·ro
last	*último*	ool·tee·mo
next	*próximo*	prok·see·mo
A ... ticket, please.	*Un boleto de ..., por favor.*	oon bo·lee·to de ... por fa·vor
1st-class	*primera clase*	pree·me·ra kla·se
2nd-class	*segunda clase*	se·goon·da kla·se
one-way	*ida*	ee·da
return	*ida y vuelta*	ee·da ee vwel·ta

I want to go to ...
Quisiera ir a ... kee·sye·ra eer a ...

Does it stop at ...?
¿Para en ...? pa·ra en ...

What stop is this?
¿Cuál es esta parada? kwal es es·ta pa·ra·da

What time does it arrive/leave?
¿A qué hora llega/sale? a ke o·ra she·ga/sa·le

Please tell me when we get to ...
¿Puede avisarme cuando lleguemos a ...? pwe·de a·vee·sar·me kwan·do she·ge·mos a ...

I want to get off here.
Quiero bajarme aquí. kye·ro ba·khar·me a·kee

airport	*aeropuerto*	a·e·ro·pwer·to
bus stop	*parada de colectivo*	pa·ra·da de ko·lek·tee·vo
platform	*plataforma*	pla·ta·for·ma
ticket office	*taquilla*	ta·kee·sha
timetable	*horario*	o·ra·ryo
train station	*estación de trenes*	es·ta·syon de tre·nes

Numbers

1	*uno*	oo·no
2	*dos*	dos
3	*tres*	tres
4	*cuatro*	kwa·tro
5	*cinco*	seen·ko
6	*seis*	seys
7	*siete*	sye·te
8	*ocho*	o·cho
9	*nueve*	nwe·ve
10	*diez*	dyes
20	*veinte*	veyn·te
30	*treinta*	treyn·ta
40	*cuarenta*	kwa·ren·ta
50	*cincuenta*	seen·kwen·ta
60	*sesenta*	se·sen·ta
70	*setenta*	se·ten·ta
80	*ochenta*	o·chen·ta
90	*noventa*	no·ven·ta
100	*cien*	syen
1000	*mil*	meel

I'd like to hire a ...	*Quisiera alquilar ...*	kee·sye·ra al·kee·lar ...
4WD	*un todo-terreno*	oon to·do·te·re·no
bicycle	*una bicicleta*	oo·na bee·see·kle·ta
car	*un coche/ auto*	oon ko·che/ aw·to
motorcycle	*una moto*	oo·na mo·to
helmet	*casco*	kas·ko
hitchhike	*hacer dedo*	a·ser de·do
mechanic	*mecánico*	me·ka·nee·ko
petrol/gas	*nafta*	naf·ta
service station	*estación de servicio*	es·ta·syon de ser·vee·syo

Is this the road to ...?
¿Se va a ... por esta carretera? se va a ... por es·ta ka·re·te·ra

Can I park here?
¿Puedo estacionar acá? pwe·do e·sta·syo·nar a·ka

The car has broken down.
El coche se ha averiado. el ko·che se a a·ve·rya·do

I've run out of petrol.
Me he quedado sin nafta. me e ke·da·do seen naf·ta

I have a flat tyre.
Tengo una goma pinchada. ten·go oo·na ·go·ma peen·cha·da

GLOSSARY

aerosilla – chairlift

alcalde – mayor

alerce – large coniferous tree, resembling a California redwood, from which Argentina's Parque Nacional Los Alerces takes its name

arbolito – literally 'little tree'; a street moneychanger and to be avoided

arroyo – creek, stream

autopista – freeway or motorway

baliza – emergency reflector

balneario – any swimming or bathing area, including beach resorts

bandoneón – an accordion-like instrument used in tango music

barrio – neighborhood or borough of the city

cabildo – colonial town council; also, the building that housed the council

cajero automático – ATM

cambio – money-exchange office; also *casa de cambio*

campo – the countryside; alternately, a field or paddock

cartelera – an office selling discount tickets

casa de cambio – money-exchange office, often shortened to *cambio*

casa de familia – family accommodations

casa de gobierno – a government building

castellano – the term used for the Spanish language spoken throughout Latin America

catarata – waterfall

cerro – hill, mountain

certificado – certified mail

chacra – small, independent farm

coche cama – sleeper class on a train

coima – a bribe; one who solicits a bribe is a *coimero*

colectivo – local bus

combi – long-distance bus

común – common class on a train

correo – post office

costanera – seaside, riverside or lakeside road or walkway

criollo – a term used for any Latin American of European descent

cruce – crossroads

dique – a dam; the resultant reservoir is often used for recreational purposes; can also refer to a drydock

edificio – a building

ejecutivo – executive class on a train

esquina – street corner

estacion de servicio – gas station

estancia – extensive ranch for cattle or sheep; some are now open to tourists

este – east

feria – a street fair or street market

fútbol – soccer

horario – schedule

locutorio – private long-distance telephone office, often with fax and internet

manzana – literally 'apple'; also used to define one square block of a city

mercado artesanal – handicraft market

mestizo – a person of mixed Indian and Spanish descent

mirador – scenic viewpoint, usually on a hill but often in a building

municipalidad – city hall

nafta – gasoline or petrol

neumático – spare tire

norte – north

oeste – west

parada – a bus stop

paseo – an outing, such as a walk in the park or downtown

peatonal – pedestrian mall, usually in the downtown area of major Argentine cities

peña – club that hosts informal folk-music gatherings

piropo – a flirtatious remark

piso – floor

primera – 1st class on a train

propina – a tip, for example, in a restaurant or theater

pulpería – a country store or tavern

quebrada – a canyon

rambla – boardwalk

rancho – a rural house, generally of adobe, with a thatched roof

recargo – additional charge, usually 10%, that many Argentine businesses add to credit-card transactions

refugio – a usually rustic shelter in a national park or remote area

remise – taxi

ripio – gravel

rotisería – takeout shop

rotonda – traffic circle, roundabout

RN – Ruta Nacional; a national highway

RP – Ruta Provincial; a provincial highway

s/n – sin número, indicating a street address without a number

semi-cama – semisleeper class on a train or long-distance bus

sendero – a trail in the woods

sur – south

tarjeta magnética – magnetic bus card, such as a SUBE card

tarjeta telefónica – telephone card

turista – 2nd class on a train, usually not very comfortable

zona franca – duty-free zone

zonda – a hot, dry wind descending from the Andes

FOOD GLOSSARY

a punto – cooked medium well (referring to steak)

agua de la canilla – tap water

agua mineral – mineral water, usually available con/sin gas (sparkling/still)

ajo – garlic

alfajor – two flat, soft cookies filled with dulce de leche and covered in chocolate or meringue

almuerzo – lunch

amargo – bitter

asado – Argentine barbecue (both the food and the event), often a family event on Sunday

bien cocido – well done (referring to steak)

bife (de chorizo/costilla/lomo) – (sirloin strip/T-bone/tenderloin) steak

bombilla – metal straw with filter for drinking mate

bondiola – cured pork shoulder

budín de pan – bread pudding

café – coffee

casero – homemade

carne – meat (usually beef)

cerdo – pork

cena – dinner

cerveza – beer

chimichurri – a spicy marinade for meat, usually made of parsley, garlic, spices and olive oil

chinchulines – intestines

choclo – corn

chopp – draft beer

choripán – a spicy sausage served in a bread roll

chorizo – sausage (note the difference from bife de chorizo)

comedor – basic cafeteria

confitería – a shop that serves quick meals

cortado – espresso with steamed milk added

costillas – short ribs

crudo – raw

cubierto – in restaurants, the cover charge you pay for utensil use and bread

desayuno – breakfast

dulce – sweet

dulce de leche – Argentina's national sweet, found in many desserts; a type of thick, milky caramel

empanada – meat or vegetable hand pie; popular Argentine snack

entrada – appetizer

entraña – skirt steak

facturas – pastries; also receipts

frito/a – fried

fruta – fruit

frutos secos – nuts (nuts are also called nueces)

helado – ice cream

heladería – an ice-cream shop

hielo – ice

hígado – liver

hongo – mushroom (also called champignon)

huevos – eggs

jamón – ham

jarra – pitcher

jengibre – ginger

jugo (exprimido) – juice (freshly squeezed)

jugoso – medium rare (referring to steak); also general term for juicy

lengua – tongue

lenguado – flounder (fish)

licuado – fruit shake

locro – a traditional meat and corn stew from northern Argentina

lomito – a steak sandwich

lomo – tenderloin

manteca – butter

mariscos – seafood

matambre – a thin cut of beef, sometimes made into a stuffed roll (matambre relleno)

mate – a gourd used for drinking yerba mate or the tea itself

medialuna (de manteca/de grasa) – croissant (sweet/savory)

merienda – afternoon tea

merluza – hake (fish)

mermelada – jam or jelly

miel – honey

milanesa – breaded cutlet (usually beef)

minuta – in a restaurant or confitería, a short order such as spaghetti or milanesa

mollejas – sweetbreads

morcilla – blood sausage

ñoquis – gnocchi

ojo de bife – rib-eye steak

pancho – hot dog

papas frita – french fries

parrillada – a mixed grill of steak and other beef cuts

parrilla – a restaurant specializing in steak dishes

pescado – fish

picada – a cheese and cured meat sample plate

pollo – chicken

postre – dessert

propina – tip (gratuity)

puchero – soup combining vegetables and meats, often served with rice

recargo – an additional charge (such as for use of a credit card, usually about 10%)

rotisería – takeout shop

sandwiches de miga – thin sandwiches made from crustless white bread

sorrentino – a stuffed pasta, like ravioli but large and round

submarino – hot milk served with a bar of dark chocolate

tallarines – noodles

tenedor libre – literally 'free fork'; an all-you-can-eat restaurant

tira de asada – grilled beef ribs

vacio – flank steak

verduras – vegetables

vegetariano/a – (m/f) vegetarian

vinoteca – wine bar

vino (blanco/tinto) – (red/white) wine

yerba mate – 'Paraguayan tea' (Ilex paraguariensis), which Argentines and Uruguayans consume in very large amounts

Behind the Scenes

SEND US YOUR FEEDBACK

We love to hear from travelers – your comments keep us on our toes and help make our books better. Our well-traveled team reads every word on what you loved or loathed about this book. Although we cannot reply individually to your submissions, we always guarantee that your feedback goes straight to the appropriate authors, in time for the next edition. Each person who sends us information is thanked in the next edition – the most useful submissions are rewarded with a selection of digital PDF chapters.

Visit **lonelyplanet.com/contact** to submit your updates and suggestions or to ask for help. Our award-winning website also features inspirational travel stories, news and discussions.

Note: We may edit, reproduce and incorporate your comments in Lonely Planet products such as guidebooks, websites and digital products, so let us know if you don't want your comments reproduced or your name acknowledged. For a copy of our privacy policy visit lonelyplanet.com/privacy.

OUR READERS

Many thanks to the travellers who used the last edition and wrote to us with helpful hints, useful advice and interesting anecdotes: Badong Abesamis, Nicole Binkert, Segimon Castañer, Andrew Chang, Sebastian Dawid, Ian Dicks, Annemieke Drenth, Jessica Edmonds, Jonathan Freeman, Marta Garicano, Juliette Giannesini, Tim Laslavic, Guadalupe Lazzaroni, Felipe Leder, Carolina Lozano, Oleg Margulis, Caroline Monja, Malena Motta, Dennis Oman, Toine van Riel, Christoph Ris, Annett Schlenker, Linda Thomson, Daniëlle Wolbers, Jeroen Zomerdijk

AUTHOR THANKS

Sandra Bao

This was the first time I've returned to Buenos Aires without seeing my godmother, Elsa Mallarini, who had passed earlier in the year. I'll miss her welcoming arms and smiles.

My co-authors were stellar and patient with all my demands, as usual. Also many thanks to Graciela and Silvia Guzmán, Lucas Markowiecki, Lisa Power, Sylvia Zapiola, Madi Lang, Jed Rothenburg and Ivan Carrasco. *Cariños* to my parents Fung and David Bao, and brother Daniel. Finally, lots of love to my husband, Ben Greensfelder.

Gregor Clark

Muchísimas gracias to the many Uruguayans and resident expatriates who shared their love of country and local knowledge with me, especially Gloria, Tino, Miguel, Monica, Karen, Pasca, Alain, Youri, Cecilia, Juan Manuel, Susana, Bilingue, Lucia and Rodney. Back home, *abrazos* to Gaen, Meigan and Chloe, who always make coming home the best part of the trip.

Bridget Gleeson

Thank you to my friends in Buenos Aires for making personal connections for me in La Pampa and in the province of Buenos Aires. Thanks to Sebastián, my personal guide in Santa Rosa, and to my sister Elizabeth for enduring the crowded train ride to La Plata with me, and to Rodolfo, for introducing me to so many of these places — San Antonio de Areco, the beaches, Tandil, Luján— in the first place.

Carolyn McCarthy

I'm grateful to the many locals whose expertise enriches this book. Heartfelt thanks to Ben and Wendy for their fine company and driving. Thanks to Cecilia, RAMIRO and Marcelo, gracious hosts Pato and Ivor, the crew at Cabo Raso, amigo Gaston, Tinio and Silvina for returning my hat and more, Jaime for his original guiding, Anita for her help and Sandra for her leadership. Finally, no penguins were harmed in the making of this book.

Andy Symington

I owe thanks to many people for information and conversation along the way. Particular thanks for various things go to Ernesto Aguirre, Fernanda Rubio, Lisandro Trini, Carolina Morgado, the late Douglas Tompkins, Ignacio Jiménez Pérez, China Sánchez, Laura Hoogen, Ezequiel Bermejo, Juan Antonio Lauro, Verónica Iwasita, F.Ocampo, Ceferino the truckie and more. In León Eduardo Cuadrado Diago, José Eliseo Vázquez González, Conchi Martínez Velasco, Mark Hayward and Manuel Sánchez Villalba keep things ticking for me. Thanks also to my family for their support, to MaSovaida Morgan, Sandra Bao and my co-authors and the rest of the LP team.

Lucas Vidgen

Thanks once again to the Argentines for making a country where it's such a joy to travel and work. On the road, to Guillermo Santos for driving way out of his way just to make sure I got there and "Peluca" Dominguez for the serious schooling on San Marcos history. To América for an amazing year on top of an amazing decade and to Sofía and Teresa for being there, and being there when I got back.

ACKNOWLEDGMENTS

Climate map data adapted from Peel MC, Finlayson BL & McMahon TA (2007) 'Updated World Map of the Köppen-Geiger Climate Classification', *Hydrology and Earth System Sciences*, 11, pp1633–44.

Cover photograph: Cerro Torre, Galyna Andrushko/Shuttershock ©

THIS BOOK

This 10th edition of Lonely Planet's *Argentina* guidebook was researched and written by Sandra Bao, Gregor Clark, Bridget Gleeson, Carolyn McCarthy, Andy Symington and Lucas Vidgen. Sandra, Gregor, Carolyn, Andy and Lucas also wrote and researched the previous edition. This guidebook was produced by the following:

Destination Editor MaSovaida Morgan
Product Editors Kate Chapman, Saralinda Turner
Senior Cartographer Mark Griffiths
Book Designer Virginia Moreno
Senior Editors Andi Jones, Karyn Noble
Coordinating Editor Nigel Chin

Assisting Editors Bruce Evans, Carly Hall, Victoria Harrison, Gabrielle Innes, Bella Li, Anne Mulvaney, Susan Paterson, Monique Perrin, Fionnuala Twomey
Cartographers Michael Garrett, Anthony Phelan
Cover Researcher Naomi Parker
Thanks to Carolyn Boicos, Anita Banh, Victoria Smith, Luna Soo, Tony Wheeler

Index

Map Pages **000**
Photo Pages **000**

Map Pages **000**
Photo Pages **000**

Map Legend

Sights

- Beach
- Bird Sanctuary
- Buddhist
- Castle/Palace
- Christian
- Confucian
- Hindu
- Islamic
- Jain
- Jewish
- Monument
- Museum/Gallery/Historic Building
- Ruin
- Shinto
- Sikh
- Taoist
- Winery/Vineyard
- Zoo/Wildlife Sanctuary
- Other Sight

Activities, Courses & Tours

- Bodysurfing
- Diving
- Canoeing/Kayaking
- Course/Tour
- Sento Hot Baths/Onsen
- Skiing
- Snorkeling
- Surfing
- Swimming/Pool
- Walking
- Windsurfing
- Other Activity

Sleeping

- Sleeping
- Camping

Eating

- Eating

Drinking & Nightlife

- Drinking & Nightlife
- Cafe

Entertainment

- Entertainment

Shopping

- Shopping

Information

- Bank
- Embassy/Consulate
- Hospital/Medical
- Internet
- Police
- Post Office
- Telephone
- Toilet
- Tourist Information
- Other Information

Geographic

- Beach
- Gate
- Hut/Shelter
- Lighthouse
- Lookout
- Mountain/Volcano
- Oasis
- Park
- Pass
- Picnic Area
- Waterfall

Population

- Capital (National)
- Capital (State/Province)
- City/Large Town
- Town/Village

Transport

- Airport
- Border crossing
- Bus
- Cable car/Funicular
- Cycling
- Ferry
- Metro station
- Monorail
- Parking
- Petrol station
- Subway/Subte station
- Taxi
- Train station/Railway
- Tram
- Underground station
- Other Transport

Note: Not all symbols displayed above appear on the maps in this book

Routes

- Tollway
- Freeway
- Primary
- Secondary
- Tertiary
- Lane
- Unsealed road
- Road under construction
- Plaza/Mall
- Steps
- Tunnel
- Pedestrian overpass
- Walking Tour
- Walking Tour detour
- Path/Walking Trail

Boundaries

- International
- State/Province
- Disputed
- Regional/Suburb
- Marine Park
- Cliff
- Wall

Hydrography

- River, Creek
- Intermittent River
- Canal
- Water
- Dry/Salt/Intermittent Lake
- Reef

Areas

- Airport/Runway
- Beach/Desert
- Cemetery (Christian)
- Cemetery (Other)
- Glacier
- Mudflat
- Park/Forest
- Sight (Building)
- Sportsground
- Swamp/Mangrove

Carolyn McCarthy

Patagonia, Tierra del Fuego Carolyn first fell for Argentina while teaching English in Buenos Aires when the peso floated on par with the US dollar. She is a frequent visitor to Patagonia. For this trip, she traveled over 7500km overland, exploring parks, *estancias* and wine lists. Carolyn has contributed to over twenty Lonely Planet titles, including *Trekking in the Patagonian Andes*, and has written for *National Geographic*, *Outside*, *Boston Globe* and other publications.

Andy Symington

Iguazú Falls & the Northeast, Salta & the Andean Northwest Andy's relationship with Argentina is a story of four generations: his grandmother lived here in the '20s, and her father ran a *mate* plantation in the northeast. Andy first visited the country with his own father, the start of a long love affair with the country that has involved many trips all around the nation, a spell living and working in Buenos Aires, and a deep-rooted respect for provincial Argentina. Andy hails from Australia, lives in northern Spain, and has contributed to many Lonely Planet products.

Lucas Vidgen

Córdoba & the Central Sierras, Mendoza & the Central Andes, Bariloche & the Lake District Lucas first visited Argentina in 2001 and was captivated by the country's wide open spaces and cosmopolitan cities. The huge amount of quality beef and wine didn't go unnoticed, either. Lucas has contributed to a variety of Latin American Lonely Planet titles, including various editions of the *Argentina* and South America books. He currently divides his time between his hometown in Melbourne, Australia and his adopted mountain home in Quetzaltenango, Guatemala.

OUR STORY

A beat-up old car, a few dollars in the pocket and a sense of adventure. In 1972 that's all Tony and Maureen Wheeler needed for the trip of a lifetime – across Europe and Asia overland to Australia. It took several months, and at the end – broke but inspired – they sat at their kitchen table writing and stapling together their first travel guide, *Across Asia on the Cheap*. Within a week they'd sold 1500 copies. Lonely Planet was born. Today, Lonely Planet has offices in Franklin, London, Melbourne, Oakland, Beijing and Delhi, with more than 600 staff and writers. We share Tony's belief that 'a great guidebook should do three things: inform, educate and amuse'.

OUR WRITERS

Sandra Bao

Coordinating Writer, Buenos Aires Sandra's mom and her family escaped China's communist regime in the years following WWII, eventually boarding a freighter bound for Argentina in 1952. After her parents met and married in Montevideo, Uruguay, the Baos lived the carefree *porteño* life (with *asados* every Sunday) until 1974, when things in Argentina got politically dicey. Once again the family emigrated to greener pastures, this time the USA.

Sandra is proud to be a *porteña* and has regularly returned to her homeland as an adult, watching the peso fluctuate wildly through the decades. Highlights from this trip to Buenos Aires included investigating new steak eateries, wine bars and local sights. Over the last 15 years she's contributed to dozens of Lonely Planet guidebooks. Sandra also updated the Plan Your Trip, Understand and Survival Guide sections.

Gregor Clark

Uruguay Over the past 25 years, Gregor has travelled South America from tip to tail, developing a special fondness for Uruguay while researching the last five editions of this book. Favorite memories from this trip include herding cattle on horseback at Estancia Panagea, eating buñuelos de algas in Cabo Polonio and watching roseate spoonbills in Valle del Lunarejo. He has contributed to two dozen other Lonely Planet titles, including *Brazil* and *South America on a Shoestring*. He lives in Vermont (USA).

> Read more about Gregor at:
> http://auth.lonelyplanet.com/profiles/gregorclark

Bridget Gleeson

The Pampas & the Atlantic Coast Based in Buenos Aires, Bridget is a travel writer and occasional photographer. Though she's been to nearly every far-flung corner of the country for work and for pleasure, she'd never set foot in La Pampa until now — and her travels for this title proved to be an interesting window into Argentine character and culture.

 OVER PAGE MORE WRITERS

Published by Lonely Planet Publications Pty Ltd
ABN 36 005 607 983
10th edition – August 2016
ISBN 978 1 74360 118 1
© Lonely Planet 2016   Photographs © as indicated 2016
10 9 8 7 6 5 4 3 2 1
Printed in China